Towards Freedom

ICHR: Towards Freedom

General Editor Sabyasachi Bhattacharya

Volume Editors Amit K. Gupta and Arjun Dev

Towards Freedom

Documents on the Movement for Independence in India
1941

PART 1

Edited by

Amit K. Gupta
and
Arjun Dev

With a Preface by the General Editor

Sabyasachi Bhattacharya

Indian Council of Historical Research

OXFORD
UNIVERSITY PRESS

OXFORD
UNIVERSITY PRESS

YMCA Library Building, Jai Singh Road, New Delhi 110 001

Oxford University Press is a department of the University of Oxford. It furthers the University's objective of excellence in research, scholarship, and education by publishing worldwide in

Oxford New York

Auckland Cape Town Dar es Salaam Hong Kong Karachi Kuala Lumpur Madrid Melbourne Mexico City Nairobi New Delhi Shanghai Taipei Toronto

With offices in

Argentina Austria Brazil Chile Czech Republic France Greece Guatemala Hungary Italy Japan Poland Portugal Singapore South Korea Switzerland Thailand Turkey Ukraine Vietnam

Oxford is a registered trademark of Oxford University Press in the UK and in certain other countries

Published in India
by Oxford University Press, New Delhi

First published 2010

ISBN-13: 978-0-19-806537-1
ISBN-10: 0-19-806537-X

Typeset in Baskerville BE Regular 11.5/14 at Le Studio Graphique, Gurgaon 122 001
Printed in India by Repro India Pvt. Ltd
Published by Oxford University Press
YMCA Library Building, Jai Singh Road, New Delhi 110 001

Contents

General Editor's Preface

The agenda of an endeavour such as this series of volumes defines itself in part through editorial practice and partly through attempts towards a statement of objectives. The historical context in which this project developed initially is generally known. While it will be excessively deterministic to overestimate the influence of that historical conjuncture on the academic inputs which went into the making of the project's agenda, one has to take that into account as one of the formative factors. After the vertiginous years leading to 1947, there came a time when historians turned their attention to those years and archives began to acquire and provide access to source materials. The last years of 'British India' began to be addressed by professional historians and indeed the theme attracted national attention both in India and in Britain. In June 1967, the British Prime Minister Harold Wilson made an important statement in this regard in the House of Commons: 'in view of the great interest now being shown in historical circles in the last days of British rule in India', there would be published 'documents from the India Office records on the Transfer of Power and the events leading up to it.'[1] The announcement included the assurance that 'the editors will be independent historians who will be given unrestrained access to the records, and freedom to select and edit the documents for publication.' The outcome of the project thus framed at the highest level in England was the series known as *The Transfer of Power* edited by Nicholas Mansergh, Smuts Professor of the History of the British Commonwealth at Cambridge. In addition to the announcement made in Parliament, Mansergh, as 'the Editor-in-Chief', stated that the 'purpose of the series' was 'to make available to scholars in convenient printed form the more important British historical records relating to the transfer of power in India'.[2]

Arguably, there is an obvious inadequacy in the notion that all that happened in 1947 was a 'transfer of power'. In Indian perception the attainment of Independence was a significant moment in the history of the struggle against British rule in the subcontinent. The representation of the emergence of independent India and Pakistan as transfer of power, solely an alteration of constitutional relations, tended towards the occlusion of that history. The focus on the legalistic notion of power transfer and the discourse of modalities of transfer, marginalized the more significant part of the historical processes at work. Likewise, the self-imposed limitations of the British documentation enterprise left many issues unaddressed: the project was to select documents from British state papers relating to the constitutional arrangements from the Cripps Mission of 1942 to 15 August 1947. In that discourse, in the official archives and the Viceroys' papers, the Indian voice was recorded only in so far as a few important spokesmen of political parties were among those present in negotiations with the British Indian government. The Indian institutions, personalities, and events were included in the documentation only to the extent the official papers took cognizance of them.

---

[1] *Parliamentary Debates*, 5th Series, House of Commons, vol. 749, 30 June 1967, cols 147–8.

[2] Nicholas Mansergh, ed., 'Foreword', *The Transfer of Power*, London, 1976, vol. VI, p. viii.

That is not to say that the task of documentation in the twelve volumes produced between 1970 and 1983 by the HMSO was not competently handled by Professor Mansergh and his editorial assistants. These volumes were products of the best of British scholarship. But the initial conception of the project was delimited to certain issues and historical sources. I recall that in 1971 when I invited Sir Penderel Moon, a brilliant officer of the Indian Civil Service and later a member of Mansergh's editorial team, to a seminar at St Antony's College, Oxford, a number of us questioned him about this and he pointed out that perhaps we had not paid attention to the subtitle of the Mansergh volumes, 'Constitutional Relations between Britain and India'. Clearly the agenda for any Indian endeavour towards the documentation of the years leading to Independence in 1947 would be different. How it would be different was suggested by Professor Sarvepalli Gopal in a luminous General Editor's Preface to the first volume produced under the present project. He said that the projected volumes aimed to 'present, within limits set by the sources, documents relating to the activities, attitudes and ideas of the diverse classes and sections of Indian society, all of which contributed to the attainment of Indian independence with partition.'[3]

It is significant that the title chosen for this series was 'Towards Freedom'. While the subtitle emphasizes the focus upon the 'movement for independence', the title evokes discourses in other domains as well—the struggle for social justice, for economic empowerment against exploitation, and for cultural autonomy. These were also prominent discourses within the overarching framework of the Indian people's struggle for freedom. One is reminded of the words of Mahatma Gandhi in an essay he wrote in the *Harijan* a few days before his death, on 27 January 1948: 'the Congress has won political freedom but it has yet to win economic freedom, social and moral freedom.'[4] This awareness of different categories of freedom allows space for a conception of the freedom struggle far wider in amplitude than the textbook approach to the struggle for independence from British rule. It makes a struggle for freedoms of many kinds thinkable. And it broadens the idea of a history of freedom struggle. This is how I understand the choice of the title for this series: *Towards Freedom.*

To sum it up, the present series of volumes focuses upon not just the legal processes of the transfer of power and the overtly political activities which brought that about, but also the struggle for freedom in different domains—economic, social, and cultural. The agenda of the series, therefore, is open to the entry of themes relating to the struggle of the peasantry, the working classes, and different sections of people as well as to a broad spectrum of political organizations who in their own light worked towards attainment of freedom.

To anyone interested in the craft of history a pertinent question will be how the documentation will reflect this agenda. The selection of appropriate documents is not an easy task. We are here looking at long term historical processes such as the slowly evolving ideas about nationhood or class solidarity, the dynamics of popular participation in political movements, the links being forged between movements of the peasantry, the industrial labour and the freedom struggle, the youth and student movements vis-à-vis the political parties, the changing social hierarchy in caste terms in relation to electoral and agitational politics, the

---

[3] S. Gopal, 'General Editor's Preface', in Partha Sarathi Gupta, ed., *Towards Freedom 1943–44*, Delhi, 1997, p. vii.

[4] M.K. Gandhi, 'Congress Position', *Harijan*, 1.2.48, *Collected Works of Mahatma Gandhi*, vol. 90, p. 497. Also see 'His Last will and Testament', *Harijan*, 15.2.48 where he spoke of economic, social and moral dimensions of independence, beyond the political independence which had been attained, ibid., p. 526. This document was written c. 29 January 1948, shortly before Gandhi's death, and it was also referred to in the AICC papers as 'Draft Constitution of the Congress'.

gender relationships evolving from the traditional patriarchal structure towards developments that had liberating potentials, the anti-feudal and anti-British movement in the princely states, and the interface between all these trends in the ideational and cultural domains. The instantiation of these long-term processes through events as reflected in the documents is the task at hand. The documents reflect fragments of the events which constitute links in the chain of certain historical processes of long duration.

It was decided years ago at an early stage of this project to distribute the work among editors on a purely chronological basis, that is to say each of the volumes in this series would relate to a particular year assigned to an editor. This opened the project to the possibility that the long-term processes would be lost sight of in the depiction of the particularities of the year each editor is taking care of. I incurred unpopularity in the Indian Council of Historical Research (ICHR) when I suggested many years ago that a thematic division of labour between the various editors, rather than a chronological one assigning one year to each, would have been a better organizing principle.[5] I will not elaborate that point again. Whatever the drawbacks or merits of the chronological frame for assigning editorial responsibility might have been, it has been in operation for twenty years and hopefully it will enable us to complete the task before us. For the volume editors the limitation of chronological framework has been probably an irksome constraint. On the whole, the volume editors, each a distinguished historian, bore with fortitude the limits set on their temporal range, and they situate the particular historical conjuncture of a given year in the broader perspective of the long-term processes as they see them in the Introduction to the volume. The Editor's Introduction is thus a bridge between the narrative of events and the narrative of the freedom struggle as he or she sees it. The editor's introductory observations also provide a space for the presentation of his or her approach to the themes and issues the volume addresses and the explication of that approach.

As regards the sources from which the documents are collected for the volumes in this series, Professor Sarvepalli Gopal, in his General Editor's Preface, remarked in 1997: 'Although some of the volumes contain documents drawn from regional language sources, a fully comprehensive selection from these sources merit a separate project.'[6] This was an accurate prediction of the future output, that is the volumes now coming out. In deciding on what non-English and regional language sources will be collected, the volume editors have exercised their judgement in deploying the research assistance they were provided. Judging by volumes produced till now and the manuscripts now being received from editors and being processed in the editorial office at the ICHR, the editors possibly felt that on most of the themes addressed there exist sufficient source material in the English language and in translation. A more systematic search for and selection of non-English sources would have made this collection more complete, but it was evidently not found to be feasible. We are committed to a schedule which requires us to complete as early as possible the project undertaken in 1988–9 rather than to expand the scope of the editors' search to new sources.

One more point needs to be made about the sources. Probably, in the last decade of the Raj, specially during the Second World War, perspicacious observers began to sense a debilitation of the imperial powers and the impending decolonization process on a global scale, and the consequent shift in the power relationships—this altered their perception of the

[5] S. Bhattacharya, 'The Empire on Borrowed Time: Towards Freedom 1943–44', *The Book Review*, vol. XXII, January–February 1998, pp. 24–5.

[6] Gopal, 'General Editor's Preface', in Gupta ed., *Towards Freedom 1943–44*, p. vii.

politics of independence struggle radically. This was happening globally in old empires, among the people and leaders in the imperial metropolises as well as their colonial peripheries. On the latter process we do have some documentation in the present series, but not much on the shift in the imperial metropolis. This is because *ab initio* the project was meant to be mainly for the collection of sources in India. This was probably because it was clear from the beginning that we have our hands full if we look at the Indian archival sources alone. The mass and density of archival sources generated by the Government in India will be evident to even a layman who glances at the following pages. Moreover, as I mentioned earlier, unlike similar enterprises in England, Pakistan, and Sri Lanka to collect sources throwing light on the last days of the British Raj, this series includes a great many activities and events which are not overtly political or constitutional.

A few words on the editorial apparatus in these volumes may be in order. The chapters are thematically organized while the sequence of placement of documents in each chapter is strictly chronological. There are two guides for the reader, first the Calendar of Documents indicating the subject of each document and the source, and second, the Index at the end of the volume. An effort has been made to make the volumes as 'reader-friendly' as possible. In some collections of this nature the editorial practice has been to provide a synoptic account of the contents of each document. This has not been the pattern in this series chiefly because it would increase the size of the volumes. As it is the present volume is very bulky and the editors are to be applauded for trying to trim them down.

I would like to put on record the annoying delays this project was subjected to on account of political interference to the detriment of academic autonomy. One result of such interference was that the ICHR authorities appointed no successor to the General Editor, Professor Sarvepalli Gopal when he passed away in April 2002; in fact all work on the project was suspended for about five years. I was asked in March 2005 to take up the task initiated by Professor Gopal, my senior colleague at Jawaharlal Nehru University. Upon accepting this position, an honorary one, my first task was to assemble an editorial team at ICHR and to request the editors of the different volumes to resume the work.

The disruption in the production of the volumes in the series for several years up to 2005 was tantamount to political censorship of academic work. It is interesting to note here that the British developed a system which prevented political parties' interference in such matters. The British project for the documentation of the Transfer of Power was processed through a mechanism which ensured inter-party consensus in parliament.[7] For this purpose a standing inter-party group of Privy Counsellors was appointed and it included a minister of the ruling party and representatives of the opposition parties, the Conservative and Liberal Parties; thus, once the project was passed by that committee, the task was left to experts duly appointed and no political interference occurred. In the light of what happened in our country on account of governmental changes, one might say that there was much that was commendable in the mechanism devised in Britain.

It is hoped that the agenda outlined above makes it amply clear what have been and remain the principles of documentation in the Towards Freedom series. The editors of the volumes have had the freedom to exercise their choice within certain parameters and they focus upon the themes which emerge from the selected documents. An editor of a volume in

---

[7] *Parliamentary Debates*, 5th series, House of Commons, vol. 733, col. 1706.

this series stated what most other editors would endorse: this is not 'an attempt to provide materials for an "official" or "definitive" statement on the history of the freedom movement.'[8] I accepted the responsibility of being the General Editor of this series since I believe that although the Government of India has funded this enterprise, like many other research projects and institutions in this country, the output of the project is the work of autonomous minds of scholars guided by standards of the discipline of historiography. As I have said in the beginning, not only agenda statements like the one I have attempted now, but practice has defined principles as well, and that is how an academic community works.

* * *

It is possible to look upon the year 1941 as no more than a prelude to the tumultuous year 1942 when India's freedom struggle entered a new phase. It is equally possible to think of 1941 as a sequel, just a predictable denouement following the developments of 1939–40, ending in a deadlock. The documents in this volume show how this betwixt-and-between year 1941 witnessed the slow unravelling of the complex lineaments of the deadlock originating in 1940. The documents also record the somewhat tame beginnings of the movement which assumed massive proportions in 1942. Compared to the years immediately before or after, 1941 was not a very eventful year. However, it witnessed the slow formation of a firm commitment to an uncompromising position on the part of the nationalist leadership and also the consolidation of internal and external forces against the nationalist agenda. This was also the year when new ideas about the future of the subcontinent were taking shape, as if both the rulers and the ruled saw the path before them in a new light in the sulphurous glare of the Second World War.

The War forced the hand of the British authorities and thus actions were taken which under other circumstances might have been left in the limbo of indefinite deferral. Further, these actions as well as the course of the War, read at that time differently from different perspectives, led to the formation and hardening of positions taken by the chief protagonists in the theatre of politics.

Since the documentation in this series of volumes focuses on India, documents or references pertaining to the global scene impacted by the Second World War are not to be found here. Thus, for instance, the Japanese attack on Pearl Harbour on 7 December 1941, leading to declaration of war by United States of America, finds no mention. The beginning of Japan's Burma and Singapore campaigns on 7–9 December 1941 also have not been discussed although the consequences for the Indian political scene are reflected in the documents reproduced. Here we need to examine such global developments in order to understand the significance of what happened in India both in terms of the British stance and the Indian protagonists' response. I shall try and provide a sketchy outline.

In the European theatre of war, the remarkable events, after the fall of Paris in the previous year, were the defeat of the Italian forces in March 1941 at Tepeleni by the Greeks, and the advance of the Germans into Yogoslavia and later Crete. On one hand, the defeat of the Italians in Tepelini, under the eyes of Mussolini himself, signalled the inability of the Italian forces to overcome the Greeks fighting for their freedom. On the other hand, the advance of the Germans in the Balkans meant a grave threat to the Allied Powers. On the whole, from fall of France to the entry of USA into the war, Britain was in perilous isolation. She was fighting in 1941 a war of which the outcome was as yet quite uncertain and this situation affected Britain's attitude to the world including India. One ray of hope for Britain was that increasingly USA took a pro-Allied stance; hence the Lend-Lease agreements were signed, Britain was assured of support in terms of resources, and USA held out to Britain the prospect of 'all aid short of War'.

Closer to India, on the North African front Britain did not fare so badly. From January 1941 in a series of battles Wavell managed to protect Alexandria and the Suez Canal, vitally important to British India, from the designs of the Italian forces. He took about 150,000 enemy soldiers as prisoners while he lost no more than 1,700. However, from March 1941 the Germans, advancing into North Africa in support of their demoralized Italian allies, struck with a speed which made Rommell a legend. In August 1941 Auchinleck took over from Wavell in the North African front while battle-worn Wavell was given the Indian command. In East Africa the struggle between German and British forces was in a stalemate almost throughout 1941, a state described in contemporary records as 'a strategic equilibrium'; ultimately this stalemate ended in British victory at El Alamein in October 1942, a turning point in the African sector war.

On 22 June 1941 German invasion of the USSR began, setting aside the agreement which had been negotiated with USSR in August 1939. Historians have speculated about the motives of Hitler. In 1939, perhaps with a view to neutralizing Russia during his campaigns on the western front, he had negotiated with Russia, and now in 1941 Hitler possibly wanted to utilize Russian resources for war purposes and also to make up for the loss of face after German failure in the 'Battle for Britain' in 1940–41. Be that as it may, both the agreement of 1939 and the invasion of 1941 undoubtedly affected Indian politics, particularly the attitude of the Left in India to the War. In Russia the main German thrust was towards Moscow through Smolensk. But German advance was retarded by guerrilla warfare behind the battle front. Nevertheless, Kiev fell on 20 September 1941 and only forty miles separated the German frontline from Moscow. But supply line problems and the Russian winter campaign in December 1941 halted the German thrust towards the Russian capital.

In December 1941 another crucial development was the bombing of Pearl Harbour (7 December 1941) by the Japanese, thus precipitating the entry of USA in the war against Axis Powers. From the Indian perspective, of immediate consequence were the parallel events in South-east Asia. On 7 December 1941 Japan began a campaign in Burma from Tenaserrim. On 9 December Japanese forces moved towards Singapore. Some observers thought that the Japanese threat to poorly defended British positions in South-east Asia appeared to foretell a similar fate for British India. This crisis for Britain was the climax of the year 1941. Thus was prepared the ground for a higher level of struggle for freedom which the year 1942 witnessed.

It is possible to construct a blow by blow narrative of the political developments in India from the documents in the following pages. It is not necessary to do so in this brief Preface. The broad trends are in two directions, as we have noted earlier: first, a drift towards a constitutional impasse or a deadlock, and secondly, the slow transition to a higher level of conflict which eventually culminated in the movement of August 1942.

These two trends may be said to be at the core of the story which unfolds in the documents which follow. The able editors of this volume, Dr Amit K. Gupta and Professor Arjun Dev, have put together in this book, Part I of the volume of 1941, documents relating to the deadlock in constitutional politics, and the governments measures designed to handle the deadlock and to respond to the War situation (Chapter 1). This is followed by documents under the title 'National Struggle and Government Repression', covering not only the Congress party but also the Left parties and other political organizations, excepting the Communalist ones (Chapter 2). An important theme in the social history of the freedom struggle is addressed in the following chapter on 'Students' and Women's Movements' (Chapter 3). This is appropriate because the youth and women took a prominent part in the movement that began in India next year in the month of August. In Part II of this volume, forthcoming in 2010, documentation relates to the communal question (Chapter 4), the Praja Mandal movement in the princely states (Chapter 5) and finally the peasant movements in different parts of India (Chapter 6) as well as the movements of industrial workers, mainly in the metropolitan cities (Chapter 7).

In conclusion, I would like to thank Dr Amit K. Gupta and Professor Arjun Dev and acknowledge my indebtedness to the editorial team at the ICHR. In the latter half of 2005 as I was casting around for colleagues to work with me in the Towards Freedom project, I was fortunate to obtain as colleagues the editors of the present volume; later Dr Rajesh Kumar, Dusi Srinivas, V.I. Benaseer, and Satheesh P. joined us. Needless to say, the Editorial Committee which has met from time to time was of great help. As the General Editor I would like to put on record my indebtedness to my distinguished fellow-editors in charge of different volumes, other than those mentioned above: Professors Partha Sarathi Gupta, Bimal Prasad, Bipan Chandra, K.N. Panikkar, Sumit Sarkar, Mushirul Hasan, Basudev Chatterjee, and Dr Sucheta Mahajan. I would also like to thank the Oxford University Press, New Delhi, for their cooperation.

SABYASACHI BHATTACHARYA
General Editor

Editor's Introduction

The documents in Part 1 of this volume[1] covers developments that took place, almost exclusively, in and in relation to 'British India'. It is further limited by the almost total exclusion of communal politics, movements in the Princely States, and peasant and labour movements. These will be subsequently covered in Part 2 of this volume. Insofar as the British policies vis-à-vis the nationalist demands are concerned, there was little departure in 1941 from what the British government had pursued in 1940 except that the repression resorted to was much more widespread and more blatantly intense than before. The Civil Disobedience launched by the Congress in October 1940, following the decision of the All India Congress Committee (AICC) at its Bombay meeting on 15–16 September 1940, in the form of Individual Satyagraha on the limited issue of Freedom of Speech, remained its sole political campaign throughout 1941. While it led to the participation of thousands of strictly disciplined Congress cadres throughout the country and serve varying terms of imprisonment—thousands of *Satyagrahis* were not arrested and thus deprived of undergoing a prison term—it did not, nor was it designed to, pose a threat to the British rule. The parties and groups that had campaigned in favour of a *mass* civil disobedience movement to challenge the British rule at a time they thought was most opportune, felt frustrated but except for blaming Mahatma Gandhi's leadership for 'surrender to imperialism', were in no position to give a call for a mass campaign. The Congress, while sticking to Individual Satyagraha as the sole mode of struggle, did not enter into any negotiations with the British government or make any compromise on its basic objectives.

The constitutional deadlock remained undiminished throughout 1941 with the British refusing to go beyond the 'August Offer' of 1940. Amery, Secretary of State for India, made this clear in his interview on 23 January 1941. The offer of 'an enlarged Executive Council which in the present circumstances can only be responsible to His Majesty's Government' was, according to him, 'a generous and far-reaching one'.[2] The Non-party Leaders' Conference which was welcomed by *The Hindu* 'as a conscientious attempt to find a way out of the present deadlock' met on 14 March in Bombay and through a resolution stated that 'As a first step towards the removal of the present deadlock', 'the whole Executive Council should consist of non-official Indians', to be 'treated on the same footing as the Dominion Governments' and the government making a declaration 'that within a specified time limit after the conclusion of the war India will enjoy the same measure of freedom as will be enjoyed by Britain and the Dominions'.[3] Mahatma Gandhi showed no interest in commenting on the Bombay Resolution.

---

[1] We have retained the spellings of the names of persons as we found them in the original documents included in the volume. Similarly we have generally refrained from making any corrections in the language used in documents.

[2] See Chapter 1, 'Constitutional Politics and War Measures' in this volume, Document No. 1, 'Mr. Amery on Indian Deadlock', *Tribune*, 24 January 1941.

[3] Ibid., Document No. 7, 'Text of the Resolution Approved by Non-Party Leaders' Conference, Bombay', *Indian Annual Register*, 1941, Vol. I, pp. 307–8.

The Viceroy rejected it. In his telegram to the Secretary of State, he stated that it 'does not present a basis on which we can wisely or properly do business' and that 'we must stick to the offer of last August'.[4] Amery moved a resolution in the House of Commons 'to extend for another year the proclamation under which the Governors of the Indian Provinces can assume the powers of Provincial Legislature'—to continue the authoritarian rule of Governors in provinces which had been ruled by Congress Ministries. In his speech, he referred back to the 'August Offer' and rejected the proposal of the Bombay conference for reconstruction of the Executive Council as 'going beyond what we think practicable'.[5] Mahatma Gandhi issued a statement on Amery's speech which V.S. Srinivasa Sastri described as 'Every line and every word of it breathes indignation—of a type somewhat unusual with the Mahatma'.[6] On 21 July, the government issued a communique announcing the expansion of the Executive Council and the constitution of a National Defence Council. The expanded Executive Council had five new members and the National Defence Council had about 30 members which included 'representatives of Indian States as well as of Provinces and of other elements in the national life of British India in its relation to the war effort'.[7] Mahatma Gandhi told *The Hindu* that he had no statement to make on the communiqué and that 'I would rather observe silence'. However, he answered some of the questions that were put to him in writing. To the question whether the Government of India's announcement affected the stand taken by the Congress and whether it met the Congress demand to any extent, he replied, 'The announcement does not affect the stand taken by the Congress; nor does it meet the Congress demand to any extent'.[8] The Liberal Non-party leaders were unhappy particularly over Defence, Home and Finance not being given to Indians. Ambedkar had been included in the National Defence Council. He described the non-inclusion of a Depressed Classes Member in the Viceroy's newly reconstituted Council as 'an outrage and breach of faith'. The Muslim League asked the Premiers of Bengal, Punjab and Assam who were members of the Muslim League to resign from the National Defence Council or face expulsion, and two newly inducted members of the Executive Council who were members of the Muslim League to do likewise.[9] There was little further serious discussion on constitutional issues. A few days after his release, Jawaharlal Nehru told a press conference, 'I am not very much interested in the repeated performances of Mr. Amery on the public stage for he repeats the same *ad nauseam.* My only answer to him and to the British Government in the words of Oliver Cromwell quoted by Mr. Amery in the House of Commons, is "We have had enough of you: get out".'[10] In his response to the British daily *News Chronicle* which had sent him a message on his release, Jawaharlal Nehru said,

---

[4] Ibid., Document No. 9, 'Viceroy's Telegram to Secretary of State on Bombay Resolution', Linlithgow Papers, Acc. No. 2163, National Archives of India (NAI).

[5] Ibid., Document No. 14, 'Amery's Statement in House of Commons', *Bombay Chronicle,* 23 April 1941.

[6] Ibid., Document No. 16, 'Mahatma Gandhi's Statement on Amery's Speech', *Indian Annual Register,* 1941, Vol. I, pp. 326–7.

[7] Ibid., Document No. 22, 'Non-Party Leaders' Conference at Poona: Large Number of Men Accepted Invitation', *Amrita Bazar Patrika,* 15 July 1941.

[8] Ibid., Document No. 21, 'No Statement by Mahatma Gandhi on the Communiqué', *CWMG,* Vol. LXXIV, pp. 180–2.

[9] Ibid., Document No. 27 (i), 'Muslim League's Stand on Expansion of the Executive Council and the Setting up of the National Defence Council', 'Resolution Adopted by Muslim League Working Committee, Bombay, 24–26 August 1941', A.M. Zaidi (Chief Editor), *Evolution of Muslim Political Thought, Vol. Five, The Demand for Pakistan,* Delhi, 1978, pp. 312–13, 315–19.

[10] Ibid., Document No. 37, ' "We have had Enough of You, Get Out!" Jawaharlal's Reply to Amery', *Bombay Chronicle,* 18 December 1941.

> India will never accept any position in an Empire by whatever name it is called.... Therefore, the first essential is the recognition of Indian Independence and the consignment to the dustbin of the infamous August Declaration and all other similar declarations of the British Government. Then only can we get over the dismal and crushing heritage of our past relations and join hands in friendship.[11]

An issue which aroused much concern in India and was in a way also related to the constitutional question was the declaration of British Prime Minister Churchill on 9 September that the Atlantic Charter 'does not qualify in any way the various statements on policy which have been made from time to time about the development of constitutional government in India'. On 14 August 1941, the US President Franklin D. Roosevelt and British Prime Minister Winston Churchill had issued a joint declaration, popularly known as Atlantic Charter, which stated, among others, that 'they respect the right of all peoples to choose the form of government under which they will live; and they wish to see sovereign rights and self government restored to those who have been forcibly deprived of them'. The interpretation which the British authorities gave to this provision was that it was applicable only to countries which had been occupied by Germany and her allies during the Second World War. The India League in Britain organized a meeting on 28 October which was attended by, besides Indians, many British friends of India, including Members of British Parliament. The meeting decided to campaign for including India in the scope of the Atlantic Charter.[12] The demand to make it applicable to India was also made in the Central Legislative Assembly and the Council of State and both these bodies passed resolutions in this regard.[13]

On 22 June 1941 took place an event which was to determine the future course of the war and had implications for the understanding of the nationalist movement regarding the character of the war and the reconsideration of its policy and activities that it may need to make. Jawaharlal Nehru, then in prison, wrote his immediate reaction on 23 June in his Prison Diary: 'What will happen, it is rash to guess—Probably early German victories, even big victories—but this seems to sound the death knell of the Nazi regime some time or other.'[14] M.N.Roy, who had been advocating participation in the war from the beginning for its anti-fascist nature, was of the view that 'the fighters of India's freedom can no longer remain indifferent to the outcome of this struggle much less oppose India's participation in it, holding that this is an imperialist war'.[15] The Communist Party of India (CPI), which had been an illegal party for many years and had been functioning through underground activities with most of its leaders in detention, advocated aid for Soviet Union but its basic political position may be summed as 'How else can we aid it (Soviet Union) except by intensifying our own struggle for freedom?'[16] This remained the basic political position of CPI until December 1941 when a different line was adopted. The attitude of the Congress Socialist Party (CSP) was expressed by Jayaprakash

---

[11] Ibid., Document No. 39, 'Jawahar's Plain Talk to British People', *Bombay Chronicle*, 22 December 1941.

[12] Ibid., Document No. 28 (v), 'Atlantic Charter and India', 'India League (UK) on the Atlantic Charter', Intelligence Bureau Report, 28 October 1941, File No. 1/5/41–Poll (I), NAI.

[13] Ibid., Document No. 28 (vii; viii), How Far the Fundamental Principles Apply to India, Sir Tej Bahadur's Statement, *Amrita Bazar Patrika*, 3 November 1941; 'Central Legislative Assembly Approves Resolution Recommending Application of Atlantic Charter to India', 12 November 1941, *Indian Annual Register*, 1941, Vol. II, p. 125.

[14] Ibid., Document No. 87, Jawaharlal Nehru's Reaction to German Invasion of USSR, Note dated 23 June, in his Prison Diary', *SWJN*, Vol. 11, pp. 636–8.

[15] Ibid., Document No. 88, 'War Policy of Congress: Mr. M. N. Roy's Criticism', *Amrita Bazar Patrika*, 1 July 1941.

[16] Ibid., Document No. 89 (i), 'Communist Party's View: Aid Soviet Union by Intensifying Our own Struggle', *Communist*, July 1941.

Narayan who was at the time in Deoli Detention Camp in what came to be known as Deoli Papers. He wrote: 'Our attitude should be that we sympathise fully with Russia but are helpless to do anything about it. At the same time our opposition to Britain's war and our national struggle continues....'[17] Many Congress leaders were associated with the campaigns of support and aid to the Soviet Union but the political question of support to participation in the war was articulated only in December when most Congress leaders were released from prison. The basic position, which the Congress adopted, was articulated by Jawaharlal Nehru. In a speech at Lucknow on 8 December, soon after his release, he said,

> I shall be sorry if Russia loses, though I do not entertain that fear; if I were asked with whom my sympathies lay in this war, I would unhesitatingly say with Russia, China, America and England. [America had entered the war when Japan attacked Pearl Harbour on 7 December 1941.] But, in spite of my sympathy for the group, there is no question of my giving help to Britain. How can I fight for a thing, freedom, which is denied to me?"[18]

Addressing students a few days later, he said, 'The phase of war beginning with the attack on Russia has changed the complexion of war no doubt, but not the outlook and attitude of the British ruling class.'[19] By December 1941, the attitude of the CPI had changed to one of unconditional support to the war, 'independent of imperialism'.[20] In the meantime, the support for the Soviet Union and calls for providing aid to the Soviet people had grown in many parts of the country and brought in its fold intellectuals, students and peasant and workers' organizations. However, except for the Communists and the groups and mass organizations under their influence, participation in the war did not become a national alternative despite the upsurge in the support that the cause of defending the Soviet Union evoked in the country.

The Individual Satyagraha launched by Congress, and confined to Congress cadres with Mahatma Gandhi deciding on the names of those found eligible to offer it, continued to be the main political form of nationalist movement throughout the greater part of 1941. Almost all through the year, the official reports submitted by the provincial governments on political developments at regular intervals gave primacy to the state of satyagraha, providing details of arrests made and the decline or rise in their number in a particular fortnight, and the overall assessment of the interest it aroused. The press strictly observing the censorship rules imposed by the authorities, regularly published reports covering events connected with it from all parts of the country. Mahatma Gandhi continued to issue detailed instructions to those selected for offering satyagraha and those awaiting decision on their applications. The AICC also issued circulars from time to time to the Congress Committees in different parts of the country conveying detailed instructions; it also monitored the implementation of the instructions issued. The organizational details that the Congress leadership, and Mahatma Gandhi himself, went into reflect features that generally characterize a cadre-based party than a mass party like Congress. The documentation presented in this regard seeks to adequately bring out all these features.

---

[17] Ibid., Document No. 91, 'Jayaprakash Narayan on the New War Situation', Bimal Prasad (ed), *Jayaprakash Narayan Selected Works*, Vol. 3 (1939–46), pp. 97–9.

[18] Ibid., Document No. 102, 'Jawaharlal Nehru on his Sympathies in the War', *SWJN*, Vol. 12, p. 2.

[19] Ibid., Document No. 105, 'Jawaharlal Nehru's Address to Students, Allahabad', 15 December 1941, *SWJN*, Vol. 12, pp. 30–2.

[20] Ibid., Document No. 108, 'Communist Party's Attitude Towards War Effort', *Communist*, December 1941–January 1942.

Maulana Azad, Congress President, was arrested on 3 January 1941. The arrest was made not for offering satyagraha which he was to do a few days later but under the Defence of India Rules for a speech he had made about three weeks earlier. Violet Alva described it as the government's new year offering.[21] There were protests and rallies against the arrest in different parts of the country. The press reported country-wide arrests that took place soon after.[22] On 10 January, Mahatma Gandhi issued Instructions to satyagrahis on Payment of Fines. According to these Instructions, it was 'the essence of civil disobedience that the resister becomes indifferent whether the authorities take away all his property or not'. If the satyagrahis were only fined and not jailed, they were required to offer satyagraha again and again until they were jailed.[23] Mahatma Gandhi clarified more than once that 'Whatever may be the expansion, the present struggle launched by the Congress will never develop into a mass movement; and, so far as I can see, it will remain individual civil disobedience and may be confined only to those who believe in and fulfil my conditions'.[24] Critical voices were raised sometimes on the limited nature of the movement as well as over the insistence on non-violence. K.F.Nariman, for example, in a press statement said,

> Gandhiji has, by progressive steps, driven his followers and the Congress to the only logical and inevitable choice—political and economic independence or non-violence. Obviously under present conditions, political independence cannot be achieved or maintained, without the use of violence in external and even internal affairs. The result is, that Gandhiji would rather not strive for that independence at the cost and sacrifice of his cherished creed of non-violence.[25]

In spite of the critical voices, and there were many, Mahatma Gandhi did not depart from his position. When Subhas Bose wrote to him a few days before he escaped from India, about Forward Bloc joining the Civil Disobedience movement, Mahatma Gandhi wrote back that 'As for your Bloc joining Civil Disobedience I think with the fundamental differences between you and me, it is not possible'.[26] The British government were pleased to learn from an Intelligence Bureau report that there had been a sharp decline in Congress membership between 1939 and 1941. It is stated to have reduced from about 29 lakhs in 1939–40 to less than 15 lakhs in 1940–41. The Home Member was immensely pleased and wrote that 'the figures of membership for 1940–41 once more demonstrate the hollowness of the Congress claim to represent the whole country'.[27] According to the Home Department's statistical data on persons detained and imprisoned, the number was 14, 419 on 1 May as against 8, 825 on 1 April. On 1 August, it was 9, 829.[28] It may be remembered that satyagrahis generally were not sentenced

---

[21] See Chapter 2, 'National Struggle and Government Repression', Document No. 3, 'Bombay Deplores Azad's Arrest', *Bombay Chronicle*, 4 January 1941.

[22] Ibid., Document No. 8, 'Satyagraha Arrests and Convictions', *Bombay Chronicle*, 8 January 1941.

[23] Ibid., Document No. 9, 'Mahatma Gandhi's Instructions to Satyagrahis on Payment of Fines', *Bombay Chronicle*, 10 January 1941.

[24] Ibid., Document No. 10, 'Independence through Freedom of Speech: Gandhi on Scope of Present Struggle', *Bombay Chronicle*, 10 January 1941.

[25] Ibid., Document No. 25, '"Deterioration of Congress" Nariman on "Impossibility of Achieving Independence"', *Bombay Chronicle*, 22 February 1941.

[26] Ibid., Document No. 28, 'Gandhi-Bose Correspondence', *Tribune* (Editorial), 25 February 1941.

[27] Ibid., Document No. 41, Intelligence Bureau's Note on Primary Membership of Congress', Intelligence Bureau File No. 4/7/41-Poll (I), NAI.

[28] Ibid., Document No. 54, 'Extracts from Fortnightly Reports on Satyagraha and other Political Developments in Madras Province', Fortnightly Reports from Government of Madras to Conran Smith, Secretary to Government of India from July to December 1941, Home Department, Government of India, Tamil Nadu State Archives.

to long terms of imprisonment and they were often released before they completed their full term in jail. That there was no sharp decline in the number of persons wanting to offer satyagraha till the middle of 1941 is clear from instructions issued by the AICC General Secretary in consultation with Mahatma Gandhi laying down thirteenfold items of the Constructive Programme from which the prospective satyagrahis should choose one or more items while awaiting the sanction for offering satyagraha.[29] Mahatma Gandhi himself, in a statement to the press issued on 28 October, critically reviewed the one year experience of Individual Satyagraha, including the question of waning Satyagraha. He decided against withdrawal of the movement.[30] In a little over a month after, most Congress leaders and satyagrahis began to be released and the process was nearly complete by the end of December. This followed the debate in the Central Legislative Assembly on a resolution moved by N.M.Joshi for the immediate and unconditional release of political prisoners.[31] The government had decided that those prisoners who had committed an offence symbolic in character would be set free. This was not a matter of rejoicing. Soon it would be time for the Congress to decide on its future policy. As the year 1941 neared its end, the Civil Disobedience Movement in the form of Individual Satyagraha which was launched over 14 months ago was over. On 4 December 1941, Mahatma Gandhi issued a press statement. He said, 'And now that the Congress President is expected to be out, it will be for him to consider whether & when to call the Congress Working Committee and the AICC. These two bodies will determine the future policy of the Congress. I am but a humble instrument of service in conducting civil resistance.'[32] On the release of political prisoners, he said, 'I would say, however, one word about the detenus and other prisoners. It sounds strange that those who have sought imprisonment are to be discharged and not those who are either detained without trial or imprisoned because they hold the freedom of their country dearer than their personal liberty. There is surely something wrong somewhere. I, therefore, cannot rejoice over the Government of India's decision.'[33] Three days later, he issued another statement in which he said that until the decision regarding it is reversed, 'civil disobedience has to go on' though he admitted that 'the conduct of the campaign has been rendered difficult by the Government action in discharging civil disobedience prisoners'.[34] The Congress Working Committee in a confidential note dated 28 December reviewed the progress of the Satyagraha and stated,

> The satyagraha has now proceeded for over 14 months and about 25,000 Congressmen have suffered imprisonment, when many thousands of others who had offered satyagraha in the Frontier Provinces and elsewhere were not arrested. The Committee desire to express their respectful appreciation of Gandhiji's leadership and of the response of the nation to it, and are of opinion

---

[29] Ibid., Document No. 44, 'Instructions to Satyagrahis Issued by Congress General Secretary in Consultation with Mahatma Gandhi', *CWMG*, Vol. LXXIV, pp. 398–9.

[30] Ibid., Document No. 59, '"Our Struggle": Mahatma Gandhi's Statement to the Press', AICC Papers, File No. G-18 (P-II), 1941, NMML.

[31] See Chapter 2, "National Struggle and Government Repression", Document No. 61, 'Debate in the Central Legislative Assembly on N.M.Joshi's Resolution Recommending Release of Political Prisoners', *Indian Annual Register*, 1941, Vol. II, pp. 133–5.

[32] Ibid., Document No. 63, 'Mahatma Gandhi's Press Statement on Release of Satyagrahis', Rajkumari Amrit Kaur Papers, File No. Miscellaneous VII/4; *CWMG*, Vol. LXXV, pp. 131–2.

[33] Ibid.

[34] Ibid., Document No. 65, 'Congress President Advised to Convene Meetings of Working Committee and AICC', *CWMG*, Vol. LXXV, pp. 136–8.

> that this has strengthened the people.... The recent release of a number of political prisoners has no significance or importance and the circumstances attending it and official pronouncements made, make it clear that it is not connected with any change of policy.[35]

On 30 December, the Congress Working Committee passed a resolution relieving Mahatma Gandhi of the responsibility laid upon him by the Bombay resolution of AICC. It also passed a resolution on 'Political Situation' to be placed before the AICC meeting which was scheduled to be held at Wardha. The Working Committee also took note of the latest developments in the war and the possible threat of invasion of India. In the Instructions it issued on 30 December, it stated, 'The Committee do not contemplate any invasion of India in the near future, but in the event of any such attempt Congressmen can on no account submit to it or cooperate with it even if the consequences of such noncooperation be death'.[36] The broad contours of the attitude of other non-communal parties to the national struggle and to developments in the war have been indicated in Chapter 1. The details of their attitude and the policies pursued by them have been documented in Chapter 2. This chapter also provides detailed documentation of the repressive measures adopted by the British rulers and the condition of political prisoners and detenus in different parts of the country, and more particularly in what came to be known as Deoli-Hell. The debates in the Central Legislative Assembly on a resolution moved by N.M.Joshi bring out the near-fascist like policy of repression pursued by the government.[37]

The documentation provided in Chapter 3 reflects the significant role which students and women played in the national struggle and in dealing with their specific problems. The radicalization of the student community in 1941 throughout the country and its massive participation in various protest movements against repressive policies and in support of the national struggle, particularly of its more radical expressions, was unprecedented in its spread and intensity. The period also saw the further widening of the unfortunate split that had taken place in the student movement in December 1940. This was largely a reflection of the serious differences between different political formations broadly belonging to the Left that had become accentuated in 1941.[38]

The preparation of this volume owes much to the work done by my colleague and co-editor Dr. Amit Kumar Gupta. With his vast knowledge of Indian history in the twentieth century and particularly of the freedom struggle, and extensive knowledge of the variety of source materials and their repositories, he guided the research team in the process of collection of documents and selection. The research team comprising young and bright scholars—Dr Rajesh Kumar, D. Srinivas (in the initial stages), Satheesh P., and Benaseer V.I.—worked with exemplary dedication in fulfilling every task that was assigned to them. Each one of them provided valuable assistance and support in giving the volume its final shape. Benaseer was particularly helpful during the last stages of the work in checking and rechecking various

---

[35] Ibid., Document No. 68, 'Individual Satyagraha, from August 1940 to December 1941: Confidential Note of the Congress Working Committee', AICC Papers, File No. 1/1941-42, NMML.

[36] Ibid., Document No. 73, 'Instructions Issued by the Congress Working Committee', *SWJN,* Vol. 12, pp. 56–7.

[37] Ibid., Document No. 143, N.M. Joshi's Resolution on Conditions of Detenus', *The Legislative Assembly Debates,* Official Report, Vol. I, Government of India, New Delhi, 1941, pp. 107–43.

[38] See Chapter 3, 'Students' and Women's Movements', Document Nos—12, 'Farooqui-Gandhi Correspondence on Split in the Student Movement', *The Student,* May 1941; 35, 'Jawaharlal Nehru's Reply to Mian Iftikhar-ud-Din Regarding Schism in Student Federation', *SWJN,* Vol. 12, pp. 599–600; 38, 'Students Assert India is One and Indivisible', *Bombay Chronicle,* 30 December 1941; and 40, 'Annual Session of All India Students Federation', *Amrita Bazar Patrika,* 1–3 January 1942.

elements of the manuscript. Devinder Singh Bisht and Sanjeev Singh typed the manuscript with meticulous care and much competence. I am grateful to each one of them for their contribution in the preparation of this volume and giving it its final shape. I would like to put on record our special thanks to Professor Sabyasachi Bhattacharya, Chairman of Indian Council of Historical Research (ICHR), who is also General Editor of the Towards Freedom series, and to Dr Ishrat Alam, Member Secretary of ICHR, for giving their approval to every demand made by us.

ARJUN DEV

Abbreviations

AIARC	All-India Anti-Repression Campaign
AICC	All India Congress Committee
AIHMS	All India Hindu Mahasabha
AIKS	All India Kisan Sabha
AILRC	All-India League of Radical Congressmen
AIML	All India Muslim League
AIMSF	All India Muslim Students Federation
AISF	All India Students' Federation
AITUC	All-India Trade Union Congress
AIVIA	All-India Village Industries Association
AIWC	All India Women's Conference
AP	Associated Press
APCC	Andhra Provincial Congress Committee
API	Associated Press of India
APSF	Andhra Provincial Students' Federation
ARP	Air Raid Protection
ASP	Assistant Superintendent of Police
AUSF	All-Utkal Students' Federation
BPCC	Bombay/Bengal/Bihar Provincial Congress Committee
BPSF	Bengal Provincial Students' Federation
BPTUC	Bombay/Bengal Provincial Trade Union Congress
CA	Constituent Assembly
CD	Civil Disobedience
CDM	Civil Disobedience Movement
CI	Communist International
CID	Criminal Investigation Department
CKC	Central Kisan Council
Comintern	Communist International
CP	Central Provinces
CPGB	Communist Party of Great Britain
CPI	Communist Party of India
CrPC	Criminal Procedure Code
CRR	Crown Representative Records
CSP	Congress Socialist Party
CWC	Congress Working Committee
CWMG	*Collected Works of Mahatma Gandhi*
DC	Deputy Commissioner
DCC	District Congress Committee
DIO	Defence of India Ordinance

DIR	Defence of India Rules
DM	District Magistrate
DPCC	Delhi Provincial Congress Committee
DPSF	Delhi Provincial Students' Federation
DSP	Deputy Superintendent of Police
GKU	Girni Kamgar Union
GPCC	Gujarat Provincial Congress Committee
HE	His Excellency
IAR	Indian Annual Register
ICS	Indian Civil Service
INC	Indian National Congress
IPC	Indian Penal Code
JNU	Jawaharlal Nehru University
KPCC	Karnataka Provincial Congress Committee
MLA	Member Legislative Assembly
MLC	Member Legislative Council
MP	Member of Parliament
MPCC	Mahakoshal Provincial Congress Committee
MSO	Madura Students' Organisation
NAI	National Archives of India
NMML	Nehru Memorial Museum and Library
NWFP	North-West Frontier Province
PAD	Preparation for Air-Defence
PCC	Provincial Congress Committee
PLA	Punjab Legislative Assembly
PPCC	Punjab Provincial Congress Committee
PPSF	Punjab Provincial Students' Federation
PWD	Public Works Department
RAF	Royal Air Force
RSP	Republican Socialist Party
SDO	Sub-Divisional Officer
SGPC	Shiromani Gurdwara Parbandhak Committee
SP	Superintendent of Police
SSP	Senior Superintendent of Police
SWJN	*Selected Works of Jawaharlal Nehru*
TNPCC	Tamil Nad Provincial Congress Committee
TUC	Trade Union Congress
UK	United Kingdom
UP	United Provinces/United Press/Unionist Party
UPCC	United Provinces Congress Committee
UPPCC	United Provinces Provincial Congress Committee
UPSF	United Provinces Students' Federation
VPCC	Vidarbha Provincial Congress Committee
WC	Working Committee

Calendar of Documents

Chapter 1: Constitutional Politics and War Measures

D. Provincial Ministries

I. Sind

Chapter 2: National Struggle and Government Repression

A. Congress

S. No.	Date	Document	Subject	Source	Pg No.
90.		Conspiracy Cases Against Communists in Madras Province			483
	5.1.42	(i) Madras Conspiracy Case [Extracts]		GOMs. No. 41, Public (General) Department, Dated 5.1.1942, Tamil Nadu State Archives	483
	6.1.42	(ii) Communist Conspiracy Case, Tirunelvelly, 1941 [Extracts]		GOMs. No. 63, Public (General) Department, Dated 6.1.1942, Tamil Nadu State Archives	487
91.	January–December 41	Monthly Surveys Outlining Activities of the Communist Party of India	Secret File	File No. 7/1/41, Home (Political) Department, NAI	489
	January 41	(i) Summary of Information Relating to Communist Party Activity			489
	February 41	(ii) Summary of Information Relating to Communist Party Activities			493
	March–April 41	(iii) Summary of Information Relating to Communist Party Activities			498
	May 41	(iv) Summary of Information Relating to Communist Party Activities			503
	June 41	(v) Summary of Information Relating to Communist Party Activities			511
	July 41	(vi) Summary of Communist Activities in India			514
	August 41	(vii) Summary of Communist Party Activities in India			516
	September–October 41	(viii) Summary of Communist Activities			521
	November–December 41	(ix) Summary of Communist Activities in India			524

S. No.	*Date*	*Document*	*Subject*	*Source*	*Pg No.*
144.	8.3.41	Bengal Politicals: Proposal for Placing them in One Class Voted Down, Demand for Revision of Jail Rules		*Amrita Bazar Patrika*	647
145.	March 41 [Presumably end of March 1941]	Jawaharlal Nehru's Description of Conditions in Camp Jail, Lucknow from Jawaharlal Nehru's 'Prison Diary with Letters'		*SWJN*, Vol. 12, pp. 568–70	649
146.	April and July 1941	Deoli Camp Detenus Not to be Permitted to Sit for University Examinations			651
	18.4.41	(i) Letter from Government of Madras to the Additional Secretary, Government of India		Letter Ms. No. 768, Dated 18 April 1941, Public (General) Department, Tamil Nadu State Archives	651
	9.7.41	(ii) Reply from the Under Secretary of Government of India to the Chief Secretary, Government of Madras		Confidential letter No. 43/19/41-Political (I), dated 9 July 1941, Tamil Nadu State Archives	651
147.	April–May 41	'Comrade Ajoy!'	Demand for Transfer of Ajoy Ghosh from Deoli	*Communist*, Vol. III, No. 3, April–May 1941, P.C. Joshi Archives on Contemporary History, JNU	651
148.	16.1.41, 17.4.41 and 24.4.41	Hunger Strike in Vellore and Alipuram		*Bombay Chronicle*	652
149.	April–May 41	Behind the Bars!	Editorial	*Communist*, Vol. III, No. 3, April–May 1941, P.C. Joshi Archives on Contemporary History, JNU	653
150.	9.5.41	Madras Government's Order on Conditions of Detention of Security Prisoners		GO No. 962, Public (General) Department, Government of Madras, 9 May 1941, Tamil Nadu State Archives	656

S. No.	*Date*	*Document*	*Subject*	*Source*	*Pg No.*
49.	21.3.41	'The Woman's Role'	Editorial	*The Hindu*	805
50.	9.4.41	Better Status for Indian Women	Suggestions to Hindu Law Reform Committee	*The Hindu*	806
51.	17.5.41	Women Satyagrahis Jailed in Nainital		*National Herald*	806
52.	26.5.41	Hansa Mehta on Hardships of Women Prisoners in Yeravada	Women Prisoners	*Bombay Chronicle*	806
53.	1.6.41	Complete Overhaul of Hindu Law	Women's Conference Executive's Demand	*The Hindu*	808
54.	2.6.41	Women's Conference	Editorial	*Bombay Chronicle*	809
55.	24.6.41	Insanitary Conditions in Yeravada Prison Must Go	AI Women's Conference Executive Urges Jail Reforms for Women Prisoners	*Bombay Chronicle*	810
56.	7.8.41	'This 'Mahatma' is a Woman'	An Article by Freda Bedi, 'From My Village Window'	*Bombay Chronicle*	810
57.	7.8.41	Baby Princess to Occupy Kolhapur Gadi?	Maharashtra Mahila Mandal's Memorial to Viceroy Supports Women's Conference Resolution	*Bombay Chronicle*	812
58.	15.10.41	Maharashtra Mahila Mandal	Resolutions Passed at the Constituent Conference, Malsiras	File No. 37, AIWC Papers, NMML	813
59.	7.11.41	Mrs Rameshwari Nehru's Call to Women of India		*The Tribune*	813
60.	15.12.41	All-India Women's Conference: Madras Constituency Resolutions		File No. 37, AIWC Papers, NMML	814
61.	24.12.41	All-India Women's Conference: Mrs Pandit's Appeal to Delegates		*Bombay Chronicle*	814
62.	31.12.41	All-India Women's Conference, Cocanada Session		*Amrita Bazar Patrika*	815
63.	30.12.41	Vijayalakshmi Pandit's Presidential Address at 16th Session of All-India Women's Conference, Cocanada	Indian Women and New World Order: Call to Britain to Abandon Dual Role of Democrat at Home and Autocrat in India	*Bombay Chronicle*	816

Chapter 1. Constitutional Politics and War Measures

A. Constitutional Politics

1. Mr Amery on Indian Deadlock

The Tribune, 24 January 1941.

Solution Lies in Hands of Indians, he Says

London, 23 January. Mr L.S. Amery, Secretary of State for India, in an interview with Sir Alfred Watson, editor of *Great Britain and the East* said that the real problem today is one that only Indians can solve for themselves. When asked if the possibility of a quick solution of the Indian problem rested with India, Mr Amery suggested that it was worthwhile clearly to understand how far the Government of India policy had really gone, 'As regards the future,' he said, 'it has met the widely expressed Indian demand for a constitution framed in accordance with Indian ideas and not dictated by the British Parliament in accordance with British views or British interests.'

Limitations

Subject to certain limitations, due in the main to the actual facts of the present defence situation and the obligations incurred to Indian States or the present personnel of the Services, 'there is nothing to prevent the new constitution for India giving Indians maximum control after the war.' As regards the near future a great deal must depend on whether leaders of Indian opinion are prepared to take the opportunities now offered of facing the inherent difficulties of the problem and working out a solution which will both maintain the essential unity of India without which India can never enjoy internal peace or external security and at the same time give to the main elements in Indian life an assurance that they can develop their culture and institutions in their own way.

Real Problem

'That is the real problem and a far more difficult one than that of transferring authority from British to Indian hands. The latter process is one about which there is no difference in principle and regarding which problems of application present no insurmountable obstacle. On the other hand, it is clear that the first condition of a transfer of authority to Indian Government that can take over without risk of disintegration and confusion. The British Government has after all the responsibility for the peace and welfare of India inherited from the past and cannot devolve that responsibility upon any system of government that would be violently contested by important and formidable elements in Indian national life.'

From Indian Side

'The problem is one that only Indians could solve for themselves', said Mr Amery and continued:

> It is for them not only to get together with common goodwill for India and with a common desire to reconcile the collective interest of India with the safeguarding of their own interest but also to face the intellectual problem of finding a constitution by which that reconciliation can be effected. It is from the Indian side, from Indians to Indians that the only effective new approach can be made so far as the general constitutional position is concerned.

Dealing with the question as to whether the Indian Government has not already gone a long way to secure participation of all Indian parties, Mr Amery said,

> The Indian Government offered not only to give Indian political leaders an important share in the prosecution of the war but also the opportunity for the creation of an atmosphere in which the solution of the constitutional problem could be more hopefully approached. Considering the fact that we are engaged in a life and death struggle concerning the whole future of the world it is surely going a long way for the British Government to be prepared so to enlarge the Executive Council as to make it predominantly Indian. It would hardly have been a practical proposition to change the whole basis of the Indian Government in the middle of a war and substitute an entirely new administration for that which is conducting the war at present.

Generous and Far-reaching

Referring to the suggestion of an enlarged Executive Council which in the present circumstances can only be responsible to His Majesty's Government, Mr Amery said:

> On the other hand it is a mistake to assert, as have some Indian critics and some British critics, that an enlarged Executive Council would not continue to have the same collective responsibility as the present Executive Council or that its members would not have important administrative duties. It is in any case obvious apart from any question of constitutional theory, that in actual operation, such an executive would have carried great weight with His Majesty's Government and that an enlarged executive would have been a feature that once embarked upon would have been permanent. I still maintain that the offer is a generous and far-reaching one. It still remains open as the Viceroy has made plain in his recent statement to the Bengal Chamber of Commerce. The approach can come at any time now from the Indian side.

First Things First

Emphasizing the importance at this moment of keeping constitutional and political issues in their proper perspective and asserting that all Indian political leaders are well aware of the fact that every hope they cherish would be crushed if Nazism and Fascism dominated the world and that they should remember the adage 'first things first', Mr Amery concluded: 'All these things are effective expression of India's rightful claim to a fuller national life. There can be no wrangling between Indians and the British over these practical steps taken towards the attainment, after the war, of that political goal. Upon essentials there is no disagreement.'

2. The Deadlock in India: Question of Fresh Approach

The Hindu, 26 January 1941.

New Delhi, 25 January. Decision on important questions await the arrival of the Viceroy in Delhi tomorrow morning. His Excellency's first duty will be to receive the new Commander-in-Chief[1] into the Executive Council.

Sir R. Cassels, it is believed, will spend a brief holiday somewhere in India, possibly Kashmir, before making his plans for the future. Then there is the question of the appointment of a new Reforms Commissioner in succession to Sir Lewis Hawthorne,[2] who is leaving Delhi on the 31st instant for Ootacamund, before going to Orissa. The Reforms Office being now part of the Governor-General's Secretariat, no one knows whether the Viceroy will appoint a new Reforms Commissioner or allow the Reforms Section to be absorbed into the Governor-General's Secretariat (Public) under Mr Thorne's general direction.

Finally, there is the all important question whether the Viceroy will make another positive effort to reach a settlement. That question has practically been answered by Mr Amery in the course of his latest statement. It is significant that within the last twelve months, but particularly since the Churchill Government came into office on every important occasion that the Viceroy could conceivably have taken the initiative, the lines of policy have been outlined by the Secretary of State in advance so that the Viceroy could merely cross the *t*'s and dot the *i*'s. The plain fact of the present situation is that neither the Viceroy nor the members of the Executive Council can take any step in regard to the political situation without the sanction of Whitehall.

British Labour's Attitude

The myth of Labour members of the Cabinet feeling uncomfortable over the British Government's India policy has been finally exploded by the recent episode concerning Mr V.K. Krishna Menon. Since the general elections of 1931, there has been a definite revulsion of feeling in the Labour Party against the non-working class elements in the Party as a result of what many regarded as Mr Macdonald's betrayal of the movement in forming the national Government. Socialist principles, which Messrs Macdonald and Henderson espoused until that year, have little hold on the working classes so far as Labour's imperial policy is concerned. Mr Lansbury's personality exercised a certain amount of fascination for the underdog from East End, but Mr Lansbury went out of leadership a couple of years before his death. Today it is Messrs Bevin and Morrison who speak for the Party, more than the Socialists—in other words, trade unionists who do not believe much in self-government for India until Indian workers achieve the same position as they have for themselves in Britain. For divergent reasons, the diehards among the Labourites seem to think that the Indian problem is incapable of immediate solution except on the basis of the Viceroy's August offer.

---

[1] General Sir Claude Auchinleck took over as the Commander-in-Chief on 26 January 1941.

[2] Lewis Hawthorne became Governor of Orissa on 1 April 1941.

3. What Dominion Status Means

Editorial, *The Tribune*, 31 January 1941.

Mr Srinivasa Iyengar, Ex-President of the Congress, says that he does not understand the significance of the persistent cry that is being raised in this country that the British Government should promise to give India Dominion status immediately after the war. Dominion status, he contends, is not something static, 'it is a fluctuating phenomenon'; and nobody is sure what the term will connote when the present conflagration subsides. 'In a swiftly changing world,' he declares, 'there will be no finality even if any formal Dominion Status were promised to us.' He believes that 'with the example of Eire staring her in the face, England cannot afford to grant India Dominion Status of the older type.' In other words it means that Britain will evolve another variety of Dominion Status for India—a status which will not confer the same powers on her as are enjoyed by the Dominions. The possibility of such a thing happening cannot be entirely ruled out. But if the British Government, even after promising to make India a full-fledged Dominion after the termination of the war, try to circumvent their promise by putting a novel interpretation on Dominion Status and evolve a constitution that does not transfer real power to India, they will be going back on their plighted word. If such a situation arises, India will know how to wrest power from unwilling hands.

But one thing should not be forgotten. When India demands Dominion Status, she means something definite, something that is already enjoyed by certain members of the British Commonwealth. It is true that Dominion Status is an organic growth; it does not mean now what it used to mean before 1926. Before that year the status of the Dominions was in several respects inferior to that of Britain. But the Statute of Westminster put them on the same level with Britain; and today they are as free in internal as well as external matters as any other independent country of the world is. Today they are members of the British Commonwealth not by compulsion, but of their own free will and choice. So when India asks for Dominion Status, it means that like other Dominions she wants to be the mistress of her own house, to have full control over her own destiny. It is true, as Mr Srinivasa Iyengar says, that none can foretell what changes will occur in the relations between the Dominions and the mother country after the war and what their future constitution will be. But whatever those changes may be and whatever the constitution they may have in future the Dominions will continue to function as independent sovereign units. So far as India is concerned, she is fighting for substance, and not for shadow. She is not enamoured of any particular status. She wants Dominion Status because she knows that that status will satisfy her political aspirations. As a Liberal leader stated the other day, 'what we want is the reality of power, full control over our destiny, the control that the United Kingdom, Canada, Australia and South Africa have.' Therefore, whatever constitution Britain offers to India will have to be judged finally by the test whether it gives full power to Indians to shape their own destiny in any manner they like. The mere mention of the term Dominion Status will not make an otherwise unacceptable constitution acceptable to political India.

Mr Srinivasa Iyengar feels convinced that the British Government will not willingly part with power. Even if the Congress, the League and the Princes, arrive at a settlement, India will not get freedom, 'for the defence of India and military exigencies and the needs of essential services require Englishmen to remain in India to operate some measure of British control.' As regards an interim settlement, he rightly declares that Mr Amery has given a quietus to all hopes of such a settlement on the basis of a popular government at the centre. Under such circumstances the only question to be considered, according to him, is what Indians can or should do, and not what the British Government will or can do. 'My view has always been,' observes Mr Iyengar,

> that there should be only two parties in the country, formed of the Congress and the members of other parties and groups. One party consisting of Congressmen, wholly independent of the Congress High Command, members of the Muslim League and Hindu Sabha, Liberals and Sikhs, Indian Christians and Harijans should form a non-party national administration in the provinces and at the centre. All that such a party should be anxious about is not to commit the country to the acceptance of Dominion Status or any other status but to work the constitution, whatever it is at the time, and to strive to wrest from the British hands all the power it can.

The other party of Congressmen, vowed to complete independence, he thinks, should carry on the struggle outside. Mr Iyengar does not want these two parties to work in opposition to each other but says that each party should 'use the other as its lever for the attainment of their common objective.' The idea behind this suggestion is to bring the maximum pressure to bear on the British Government so that it may be compelled to grant independence to India. But the acceptance of this suggestion presupposes two things—first, that the constitution is such as can be utilized for achieving the objective that political India has in view; and secondly, that there should be an agreement not only between the two major parties, but also between the members of the non-Congress parties. As regards the first, it may be stated at once that the Government of India is still a subordinate branch of the British Government. The Central Assembly does not enjoy any real power. Nor can it exercise effective control over the Viceroy's Executive Council whose members owe no allegiance to it and who have to carry out the policy laid down by an authority outside India. How can then the machinery of the Government of India be utilized for furthering the cause of Indian freedom? It was its realization of this fact that made the Congress ask for the establishment of a national government at the centre. As regards the second, it is absurd to expect a political party to function under a self-denying ordinance like the one under which Mr Iyengar wants the Congress to function. Such a party has to vary its programme according to the exigencies or the situation that may develop from time to time. And suppose the Congress gives the guarantee that Mr Iyengar wants it to give, will the component parts of the non-Congress party agree to a common line of programme and policy? Will the members of the Hindu Mahasabha and the Muslim League be able to pull on together and utilize the opportunity, afforded to them by the constitution, to further the cause of India? These are pertinent questions to which we do not find any reply in Mr Srinivasa Iyengar's statement. He will have to elucidate his position further and explain how he wants the two political parties to work as a lever to each other to attain the common objective of *Swaraj*.

4. Menzies,[1] Nehru and Dominion Status

File No. 32/3/41-Poll (I), Home (Political) Department, Government of India, National Archives of India (NAI), New Delhi.

Confidential

No. S.D/W-664
Home (Political) Department—War
Bombay Castle, 6 March 1941.

From
N.P.A. Smith, Esquire, OBE, IP,
Joint Secretary to the Government of Bombay
Home Department.

To
The Secretary to the Government of India
Home Department.

Sir,

I am directed to forward herewith, for the information of the Government of India, a copy of a message, dated the 1st March 1941, from Kabadi [code] London, to Press Chronicle [code], Bombay, which has been withheld.

I have the honour to be,
Sir,
Your most obedient servant,
Joint Secretary to the Government of Bombay
Home Department

Copy of a cable message dated 1st March 1941.

From ... Kabadi, London.
To ... Press Chronicle, Bombay.

Seriously suggested here Menzies Australian premier, should Indiawards preAustraliawarding emphasize circles which distrustful British Governments intention as represented Amery's several speeches Indoconstitutional evolution and August offer Australian circles support this suggestion well as influential trade unionists one whom said me at lunch on Wednesday quote if our premier could only persuade Menzies visit your leaders talk matters over Australian Dominion rendering great noble service present crisis Indo-British relations unquote Australian circles very hopeful Menzies would serve as great via media intra British Government and Indo people I understand todays issue Truth of Newzealand allied newspapers Australia carry frontpage story extheir London Correspondent course thereof it stated quote Menzies is young he can serve India Empire parhaving heart heart talk cum Nehru who represents young India which deadly opponent venomous creeds Nazism Fascism Menzies will able convince Nehru other Indoleaders British Government darent repudiate its solemn pledges word because Dominions never tolerate such thing Dominions especially Australia insist transfer power Indohands confer Dominion Status Indiawards earliest possible date postwar unquote questions asked London whether Menzies can undertake such mission whether Australian can afford absent her premier prolonger period whether above all British Cabinet think prudent ask Menzies intervene.

---

[1] Sir Robert Gordon Menzies (1894–1978) was Prime Minister of Australia from 26 April 1939 to 26 August 1941 and, later, from 19 December 1949 to 26 January 1966.

5. Mahatma Gandhi on Congress Stand

The Hindu, 7 March 1941.

'Bombay Resolution Holds the Field'
Mahatma Gandhi's Statement
Allahabad Talks have 'No Political Bearing'
(Associated Press of India)

Wardhaganj, 6 March.

Mahatma Gandhi has issued the following statement to the press:

'I must warn the public against journalistic flights of imagination. No importance need be attached to my visits to Sir Tej Bahadur Sapru and there meeting, quite accidentally, Kunwar Sir Jagdish Prasad, then Pandit Malaviyaji and the morning following, Smt Vijaya Lakshmi Pandit and finally Maulana Saheb Abul Kalam Azad. They were all of them friendly visits, wholly unarranged when I left Sevagram for Allahabad.

'I had gone for one mission and that alone. What little other work I did was purely accidental. I refer to my meeting some students and Garhwali workers. Sir Tej Bahadur, I went to see because he was ailing. We are old friends. He was to have come to see me, but, when I heard that he was ill, I insisted on going to him. No doubt, we talked about the political situation and even more about the Hindu–Muslim problem. Sir Jagdish, who dropped in and who was to dine at Sir Tej Bahadur's joined the conversation. But not the slightest political importance attaches to these conversations. We talked as individuals and not with regard to any mission.

Friendly Inter-change of Views

'Sir Tej Bahadur is anxious (who is not?) to end the present deadlock. He would give anything to bring about Hindu–Muslim unity. He ascribes to me overmuch capacity for bringing about unity. Sir Jagdish is no less anxious. But the talks were no more than a friendly interchange of views.

'As to the visit to Malaviyaji Maharaj, the same thing happened. He is aged. He ought not to talk about current events. He is too weak. But the country's affairs are his daily food. He will cease to think about them when he ceases to read and think of the Bhagwat Gita. These things are the breath of his life and they will stop with the stoppage of his last breath. Who knows but that he will take them where the disembodied spirit goes? It was a privilege to meet these friends, but our talks have no bearing on the political situation in the country. And there could be none in the purely prison visits to the Maulana and Smt Vijaya Lakshmi Pandit.

Common Action Needed for Fulfilment of Aim

'I know that the imaginary descriptions of such visits and the eagerness with which the public devour them show their desire for communal unity and a solution of the political deadlock. But mere desire will take us no nearer its fulfilment. For, fulfilment can only come through common action on the part of those who share the desire. All are searching for common action. Speculation interferes with the search. So far as the Congress is concerned, its policy and the action based thereon are well known. It is a gross misrepresentation to suggest that the Congress is out for securing terms for itself. Freedom of speech is for all even as Independence will be for all. The content of the latter will be decided not by the Congress but by the vote of all. And if it is to be achieved non-violently, it follows that the mere vote of the majority will have little play. The Charter of Independence must be the product of the willing consent of the minorities and other relevant interests which are not in conflict with the interests of the vast mass of Indian humanity.

'Be this as it may, in order that all the units may have full freedom of expression even against the war itself, the Congress has embarked upon Civil Disobedience. That is the contribution of the Congress to the fulfilment of the common desire. As an effort in direct action, it must hold the field till a better is found.

The Bombay Resolution[1]

'Strong objection has been raised against my interpretation of the Bombay Resolution. I regard it as a true interpretation. But it is that of an individual. I have no authority from Congress to interpret or vary the Congress Resolutions. That is essentially the function of the President of the Working Committee and finally of the AICC. The only authority I have is to conduct the campaign of Civil Disobedience. But when the time for a settlement comes, it will be for the Working Committee to decide what the terms shall be. My contribution will be confined to advising the Committee. The Working Committee may reject the interpretation I have given it; or the AICC may even alter the resolutions they have passed. Meanwhile, let everyone, whether Congressmen or others, be guided by the Bombay Resolution, and not by my interpretation. I have, therefore, failed to understand the consternation created by my statement that there can be no settlement short of Independence during the pendency of the war.'

[1] The reference is to the Resolution on Satyagraha adopted by the AICC at its meeting held in Bombay on 15–16 September 1940.

6. The Non-party Leaders' Conference

Editorial, *The Hindu*, 11 March 1941.

The Leaders' Conference that is scheduled to meet in Bombay in the course of this week is to be welcomed as a conscientious attempt to find a way out of the present deadlock. Without being unduly optimistic, we may hope that it will reveal the true nature of the obstacles the country is up against and help to focus public attention on their removal. Though a few of those who will be meeting at Bombay happen to belong to the Liberal Party, the Conference as a whole has no particular political affiliations, and this is a distinct advantage for the purpose in view, which is to lay the foundations of a national front. Again, the Conference as a body is non-communal in outlook and is composed of men who believe in constitutional methods of promoting political advance. Many of them have occupied high offices of state and all of them have great experience of public life and are used to the exercise of power and responsibility. While they may be expected to approach the questions at issue without that *parti pris* of which the Congress and the Muslim League may be suspected, the conclusions they come to and the proposals they make are bound to receive the respectful attention of all parties. His Majesty's Government, who have affirmed their belief in the wisdom of representative men, will, in particular, be hard put to it to persist, in their negative policy in the face of such suggestions for action as the Conference may make, since it would be hardly possible to get together a gathering of public men more widely representative, than that which Bombay will witness.

The aim of the Conference, as we understand it, will be limited and strictly practical. It will seek to remedy the fatal weakness of the Government of India to-day that, at a time when popular sanction and support is all important, that Government has neither and is virtually a one-man dictatorship. If that Government is to become truly responsive, radical changes are necessary both in personnel and in the modes of its functioning, though it might not be necessary or practicable in the midst of the war to make corresponding changes in the constitutional structure. As an essential preliminary to such changes, it should be made clear by His Majesty's Government that there would be forthwith a substantial transfer of power, and that Britain would within a year after the termination of the war arrange that India shall have the same amplitude of freedom and power as the Dominions now self-governing will then have and shall frame her own constitution with the willing consent of her minorities. On this basis no important party in the country should have any objection to co-operating in the common task of preparing the ground for the constitutional advance; so that the change-over, when it comes, may take place without a hitch, and coordinating administrative and defence policies in such a manner that the dangers threatened by the war developments should operate as a stimulus to India becoming strong and self-reliant enough to defend her freedom against all comers.

The interim arrangements that must be made with these objects in view, for the duration of the war, should obviously include, first and foremost, the transformation of the character of the Viceroy's Executive Council. While it will continue to be, legally speaking, responsible to the Viceroy and not to the legislature, it should be so composed and function in such a manner as to enjoy the confidence and support of the public. It is therefore necessary that the Council should consist entirely of non-officials, one of whom should be in charge of Defence. The statutory difficulties in the way of giving effect to this change in full forthwith can be got over by simple constitutional amendments. Equally important is the transformation, in the shortest possible time, of the administrative, military and economic framework to suit the requirements of a self governing country. The principle of widening the basis of recruitment to the defence forces has already been accepted. But it is necessary, not only to devise measures to give effect to this principle with the least possible delay, but also to quicken enormously the pace of Indianization of the officer ranks in all arms. On the civil side, while there is far less excuse for delay, it is an undoubted fact that there has been not only delay but a serious setback in many respects, the war having proved a handy excuse for appointing Europeans to many posts filled by Indians with distinction in the past and for creating any number of new posts for which Europeans have been imported. This wrong trend must be vigorously reversed. Side by side with these reforms, the financial and industrial policy of the Government should be given a new orientation which would make it impossible that India's resources should be exploited except for her sole benefit and which would ensure the rapid growth on firm and sound foundations of those industries which are indispensable for the maintenance of national integrity and prosperity. Put briefly, what is needed is that the Government of India should forthwith become truly Indian—in personnel, in outlook, and in its aims. If the Bombay Conference takes its stand on this basic demand, it may attract to itself such a large volume of support in the country that Britain might yet see the wisdom of abandoning her do-nothing policy.

7. Text of the Resolution Approved by Non-party Leaders' Conference, Bombay, 14 March 1941

Indian Annual Register, 1941, Vol. I, pp. 307–8.

Sir N.N. Sircar then moved the following resolution:

'While India should not take advantage of Britain's difficulties in her heroic struggle, the Conference is equally desirous that India's domestic problems should not be pressed to her disadvantage. As a first step towards the removal of the present deadlock and until a permanent constitution is brought into force, the Conference desires to emphasize the immediate need for the reconstruction of the Governor-General's Executive Council.

'The Conference considers that the present Council, which consists of three European members for the Indian Civil Service, and three Indians of whom two are non-officials and one is a member of the Indian Civil Service, in addition to His Excellency the Viceroy and His Excellency the Commander-in-Chief, is neither adequate nor sufficiently representative to organize and direct India's war efforts at this moment of grave peril. This Conference is anxious that India's defences should be put on a firm basis and that resources of this great country in men and material should be used to the fullest advantage not only for defending her own frontiers but for helping the British people to the fullest extent possible consistently with the best interests of India.

'For the reasons mentioned above, this Conference is of the opinion that the whole Executive Council should consist of non-official Indians drawn from important elements in the public life of the country. This would naturally involve the transfer of all portfolios, including the vital ones of Finance and Defence, to Indians.

'The Conference would be content during the period of the war that the reconstructed centre remains responsible to the Crown: and so far as Defence is concerned, the position of the Commander-in-Chief as the Executive head of the defence forces of the country should not be in any way prejudiced. At the same time the Conference is strongly of the view that the reconstructed Government should not merely be a collection of departmental heads, but should deal with all important matters of policy on a basis of joint and collective responsibility. In regard to all inter-imperial and international matters, the reconstructed Government should be treated on the same footing as the Dominion Governments.

'The Conference is further of the opinion that with a view to create a favourable atmosphere for the working of the reconstructed Central Government, it is necessary to remove the doubts and misgivings of the people of this country as regards the genuineness of the intentions of His Majesty's Government by making a declaration simultaneously with the reconstruction of the Government that within a specified time limit after the conclusion of the war India will enjoy the same measure of freedom as will be enjoyed by Britain and the Dominions.

'The Conference authorizes its President, the Rt Hon Sir *Tej Bahadur Sapru,* to communicate the terms of the resolution to His Excellency the Viceroy and the Secretary of State for India and to take such other steps as may be necessary to achieve its objects.'

8. Mahatma Gandhi on Bombay Resolution

Collected Works of Mahatma Gandhi (*CWMG*), Vol. LXXIII, p. 393.

Cable to Agatha Harrison[1]

Wardhaganj
[On or before 23 March 1941]

Agatha Harrison
Brabourne Court
Albert Bridge Road, London

Bombay suggestions not likely receive Congress countenance. Am remaining silent.

[1] Agatha Harrison (1883–1954) was a supporter of India's freedom struggle and a close friend of Mahatma Gandhi and Jawaharlal Nehru. She was Secretary, India Conciliation Group and had sought Mahatma Gandhi's views on the Resolution adopted by the Non-Party Leaders' Conference at Bombay on 14 March 1941.

9. Viceroy's Telegram to Secretary of State on Bombay Resolution

Viceroy to Secretary of State, Telegram R, 2 April 1941, Telegraphic Correspondence between Viceroy and Secretary of State, Vol. VI, Linlithgow Papers, Acc. No. 2163, NAI.

Immediate. No. 684-S. I have now had Sapru's promised memorandum on the Bombay Resolution and despite its length I am telegraphing it separately so that you may have authoritative text in case it comes up in Debate. It has not so far been published here. I am asking him to come and see me. [...]

2. The memorandum is a carefully drafted and plausible document I have examined with great care. But I remain of opinion that for the reasons I have already given in my telegram of 30th March, No. 652-S. (which may be read with my telegram of 19th March, No. 561-S.) it does not represent a basis on which we can wisely or properly do business. I would add in that connection to the points taken in paragraph 2 of my telegram of 30th March, No. 652-S., the following:

(a) Further reflection confirms and emphasizes my view of importance of the surrender of the safeguards and indeed of all the protective arrangements embodied in Part I of the Act which would be involved. Were we to give way now and to accept the proposal put forward we should have lost all hope of maintaining those protective arrangements in such degree as may be necessary in any post-war constitutional scheme. Their importance calls for no emphasis from me nor (their British Indian aspect apart) the reaction of their existence on the Princes.

(b) There are increasing signs that Gandhi is considerably interested in the fate of the Bombay Resolution. He is in my judgment in an extremely tight position. I have little doubt that he would welcome acceptance by us of the Resolution, and that his calculation would be that, the Resolution once accepted, the Congress would be able to climb back into authority through the indifferent material which my expanded Executive Council would contain; that the probability of embroiling us with the Muslim League in the event of our accepting an expanded Council which would unquestionably be strongly Hindu in composition is a further consideration while, at the worst, if we decline to accept the resolution Congress would be able to urge that even moderate opinion is now united with the Congress against Government, ignoring of course the fact that the reasons for which our offer of last August has not met with general acceptance are mutually destructive. Birla has indicated that he regards the Bombay resolution as a useful bridge, but clearly did not contemplate the possibility of any Government based on the personnel of the conference either giving any permanent satisfaction or lasting long. I think it would be a very great mistake at such large cost to ourselves to reduce pressure on Gandhi or to give the Congress a gateway.

(c) Not only, as I have already pointed out in my telegram of 30th March, are we asked to make these very substantial concessions to a body which has no real backing and cannot claim to have the support of the major parties. It is increasingly clear that if taken into power they would endeavour to negotiate with Congress and the Muslim League. In any such discussions they would of course *ex-hypothesi* start from a position in which we had surrendered to them, as the condition of their accepting office, defence, finance, control of International and inter-Imperial relations and the non-official character of the new Cabinet. We might expect in other words to be pressed, and without delay, for still more far-reaching concessions designed to make it worth the while of Congress (or possibly the League) to lend support. Equally, if their position as Ministers became impossible, and they threw their hands in, we should have abandoned all those vital points beyond recovery for we could not hope that any alternative government could be formed on terms less favourable than the Bombay Conference had secured.

3. I am anxious to treat the Bombay Conference and in particular Sapru with all possible care and respect. One does not want to sour men of high standing more than one can help, little as their active support may be worthy to us. But I am quite clear that we must stick to the offer of last August; and I would advise that in debate you should again emphasize that it remains open, and that we are as anxious as ever to see Indians get together among themselves and produce the degree of support necessary for the practical working of the scheme. I should be very strongly opposed to taking the burden of getting together and reaching agreement off Indian shoulders.

4. My line with Sapru, subject to any comment from you, would be that I have communicated the text of his memorandum to His Majesty's Government that I was anxious to see if he wished to amplify it in any way; that His Majesty's Government and I welcome any initiative which will put an end to the present deadlock, though we feel our consciences are clear; that he and his friends (though I observe that there has not been complete unanimity) are in a position to give great assistance by bringing the major parties together and that they have our good-will in trying to do so; that we cannot conceal from ourselves that little as we like them there are internal differences in this country which have got to be overcome if we are to go ahead and that they are best overcome by Indians rather than by outsiders. I had examined the impressive list of those present at the Conference, though it struck me that the Muslims who were so important were not represented by anyone of much substance; that I had observed Chimanlal Setalvad's attack on the resolution after the meeting had broken up and the criticisms voiced by Cowasjee Jehangir; that I had been informed that Ambedkar had not been present at the final meeting at which the resolution was approved and that might be true of others; that in a matter such as this inevitably one must check the degree of real support behind the resolution; and that fully accepting his sincerity and *bona fides* of his friends, we must apply the test of the degree of support which any solution put forward by them would command not merely from intellectual quarters or administrators of proved merit but from the great political

parties. I would develop the damaging effect on a government formed on the basis of the Bombay Resolution of repeated defeats or consistent hostility in the Legislature particularly as that government would unquestionably have a political flavour and could not hope to get away with it on the ground that it was frankly a bureaucratic and irresponsible government.

5. I would proceed to draw his attention to the very far-reaching character of his proposals; the extent to which they would compromise the post-war discussions to which we were committed; the very wide general support in the press, in Parliament, and abroad, given to our proposals of last year; and the unlikelihood that even the Conference proposals would prove to be the last word once negotiations started. I would repeat that while His Majesty's Government would, I was certain, consider what he had said with every sympathy, the practical difficulties which had prevented us from going beyond the declaration of last August and which in my judgment still existed were very great; though we remained as anxious as ever to see a solution and to encourage men of standing and experience such as Sapru to work upon their friends to try to bring that about.

10. Viceroy's Telegram to Secretary of State on his Interviews with Tej Bahadur Sapru

Viceroy to Secretary to State, Telegram R, 10 April 1941, Telegraphic Correspondence between Viceroy and Secretary of State, Vol. VI, Linlithgow Papers, Acc. No. 2163, NAI.

Important. No. 737.S. I had two lengthy interviews with Sapru on the 7th gist of which is as follows:

(a) He described his recent correspondence with Gandhi and Jinnah, general result of which was that neither was prepared to make the first move and that Gandhi was apprehensive that Jinnah would deal with him only as a Hindu. Asked by Sapru whether Gandhi would come to a settlement with us, Gandhi had replied that he would be very glad if Sapru got a settlement, but could not himself participate or make himself responsible for one. He would advise Congress not to oppose, but also not to take office. Asked whether he would come to a conference with Government if one could be arranged, he had replied, 'yes but the time has not yet come for a settlement', which Sapru interpreted as meaning that Jinnah would not yet come to terms. Mr Gandhi had added that the Working Committee alone could omit Congress and if there was to be any move, they must be released from prison and given the opportunity of discussion.

(b) At the Bombay Conference Sapru had insisted first on an entirely non-communal approach the question of how many Muslims or Hindus should be in the Council must be left to the Viceroy; secondly that responsibility was to the Crown and not to the Legislature. For the duration of war he did not want a removable Executive at the centre and had made that clear. He admitted that Muslim representation at Bombay was open to the charge of not being representative, but felt that resolution represented the feelings of a large number of Muslims who were disgusted with Jinnah's handling of affairs and anxious to break away. He admitted, however, that none of these people would be prepared to get up to say so in public. In the country generally, leaving out the extreme element, there was a genuine desire found help in the war. The constitutional statement was telling on the younger men and their impatience was affecting the average man. He therefore urged most earnestly an early settlement.

(c) Developing certain points in his Memorandum he explained that 'Non-official Indians' who were to form the reconstructed Council could include non-official Europeans or even European members of the Services who had retired before taking up appointment or business. Question of who should hold what portfolio must be left to the unfettered decision of the Viceroy. I put gently to him the difficulty which the expanded Council were likely to have in the absence of any majority in the Legislature. He showed some reluctance to come to grips with this and hoped that serious trouble would not arise. If however, the new Government were beaten and certification was necessary, it would go down much more easily with the existing Executive Council. I hinted that I doubted if he was correct on this, Developing the point, he took the line that he would not pretend that his expanded Council would in any sense be a popular Council. It would be an irremovable body and able and entitled to ignore defeat. Members would hold on their portfolios and see the Viceroy through. I reminded him that his Bombay speech made it clear that in the event of repeated defeats the new Government would have to resign. He admitted that if the Government were repeatedly defeated, other men would have to come in, but added that on the assumption that Council was to be composed of reasonable men, he had every reason to hope that such a state of things could be avoided. I suggested to him that he had repeatedly commended the workability of his scheme on the ground that members of the new Council would be reasonable men. Could one feel so sure that his successors would be all so reasonable.

(d) Tested on his intentions in regard to the Governor-General's discretions and discretionary control of Provincial Governments or Governors by the Governor-General whether in or out of a Section 93 position, he made it clear at once that he contemplated that the new Executive Council ought to enter this field and added that on the assumption that we were dealing with reasonable men, we could avoid a difference of view between council and the Governor General in 8 cases out of 10. In any event, if the Viceroy did in any such matter disagree, the Viceroy's view must prevail. The Bombay Conference had not raised the position of the Section 93 provinces, but his own view was that for the period of the war we should revert to the old fashioned Council's in the provinces. He would be prepared himself to accept an irremovable Executive for both the Centre and the Provinces after the war, though he recognized the difficulties. He thought it essential that all the communal issues should be left to the Governor-General, he should be given powers in excess even of those which he exercised at present and he would be prepared to say so publicly.

(e) Reminded of the Indian States and of the reaction on them of proposals such as those put forward at Bombay, he said that the Conference had deliberately not touched on the States and did not want to. I put it to him that issues of great moment from time to time arose between Governments in British India and the States. But here again he took the line to leave it to the Crown Representative if any question of Paramountcy or any question affecting the interest of the States arose. Any ruler or representative of rulers whom I might wish to put into my Council, I can.

(f) I said that I had noted that he admitted that if he was defeated or if Congress were willing to come in, he and his friends would go out. He would appreciate that while the Princes were not represented at Bombay and the Muslims only very lightly the future might well be prejudiced in view of the undertaking that we had given to throw the whole position open to review after the war by acceptance of the Bombay proposals. He replied that it must be clearly understood that nothing done by the interim reconstructed Council could be binding for the future. We ought to go forward in the clear future with the reconstruction of the Council and to show moderate men that we mean business. For that reason also he wished to press me for an announcement as to a time-limit for the implementing of the new constitution post-war, and the granting of the Dominion Status.

I explained the difficulties, but he held to his point and urged that if the worst came to the worst, the period could always be extended to proclamation or some such device. I said that I did not think His Majesty's Government would be prepared to make promises which they might not be in a position to implement when the time comes.

(g) He then endeavoured to set me to commit myself in regard to Pakistan and urged that we should publicly state that His Majesty's Government did not stand for it, I said we might have our own views as to the arguments for and against Pakistan, but that as a possible solution it must in terms of the offer we had already made, remain an open question, for post war discussion and I could not commit myself in any way.

11. On Bombay Conference Proposals

Editorial, *The Hindu*, 10 April 1941.

The Minimum Demand

Now that the implications of the Bombay Conference proposals have been authoritatively explained to him by Sir Tej Bahadur Sapru, HE the Viceroy should be able fully to realize the reasonableness of the proposals as well as the country-wide support they enjoy. We trust that in communicating to His Majesty's Government the gist of the conversations Lord Linlithgow will impress upon them these basic facts as well as the need for making an early and sincere effort to secure India's co-operation on the lines indicated at Bombay. We regret to have to say it, but there is no denying that there are forces at work both in Delhi and at Whitehall which are averse to any constitutional change and have been sedulous in finding excuses for inaction and imaginary difficulties that are supposed to stand in the way of the Bombay proposals being accepted, at any rate, without considerable emasculation. From such sources, we imagine, must have emanated the canard that certain leaders associated with the Bombay Conference had privately expressed the view that they were prepared to accept the August offer or something very much less than what the Bombay Conference demanded. Sir Tej Bahadur Sapru has effectively disposed of this by stating in the press interview he gave yesterday that in his conversations with the Viceroy he stood by the Bombay resolution. When it is recalled that the precise value of the Bombay resolution lies in its representing the maximum amount of agreement in the country and in its offering a close approximation to the Congress demand, it will be seen that any whittling down of the proposals would be simply defeating the purpose for which they were made.

The Bombay Conference concentrated on so readjusting the Central Government, in the words of Sir T.B. Sapru's memorandum, 'as to produce the necessary psychological effect on the people and evoke their whole-hearted co-operation in the war effort.' Anything that falls short of producing this intended effect will obviously be futile. It is, therefore, pointless to suggest, as Delhi official circles seem to do, that 'Mr Amery's statements can legitimately be interpreted as having introduced new elements into His Excellency's August offer.' So far as the Central Government is concerned, India insists that it should be completely Indian in personnel and outlook, and enjoy the confidence of the country, and that it should have the substance of authority and not the mere shadow of it. Even if a slight change in the Constitution

Act is found to be necessary in order that the composition of the Viceroy's Council may be transformed, why should it be supposed that the necessary alterations are impracticable or would be dangerous, seeing that after the war began the Constitution Act has been changed in vital respects because it suited the British Government to do so? As to the powers and functions of the Council, the transfer of Defence and Finance to Indian hands and the recognition of India's equal status in international affairs are crucial tests of the sincerity of Britain's intentions in regard to India's future. She is, it must be remembered, committed to the pledge that as soon as possible after the war ends India shall have the same freedom, powers and status as the other Dominions. If she at all means this how can she possibly argue that the appointment of an Indian as Member for Defence should be dependent on the consent of the Princes, for instance—the Princes can have no right to veto or delay India's political progress any more than any minority community or special interest can claim to do so—or that the Defence Member in India should be content with the same status and powers as the Defence Councillor who has been appointed in Burma? To argue that even after the inauguration of Federation Defence would have been a reserved subject under a Councillor and that the Governor-General would have had a Financial Adviser to assist him and to suggest that it is therefore unreasonable for India to demand that the interim arrangements at the Centre now contemplated should mark a greater advance in these respects than what would have been the position under Federation—to take up such an attitude is not only to ignore the entire political history of India of recent times but also to betray a complete failure to understand the realities of the situation and the inflexible resolve of the people not to be put off with gaudy trifles. Delhi seems dismayed by the suggestion that India should be independently represented in international and inter-imperial conferences. But its horrified response—'Why, it is Dominion Status in action! It goes beyond the implications of the existing Constitution'—can only be regarded as extremely diverting, as indicating a pathetic faith in the miracle of making omelettes without breaking eggs. India does not exist for the Constitution; the Constitution exists for India, and since it is proving a straight waistcoat it must be changed to the extent necessary in order to make India breathe freely and release her energies for worthwhile purposes. It is to be hoped that the British Government will see that the one chance of doing this is by declaring forthwith that they will accept the Bombay Proposals in the spirit in which they were made. If they do this, we feel that the Congress will not fail to respond in the same spirit.

12. Jinnah and Savarkar on Bombay Proposals

Viceroy to Secretary of State, Telegram R, Letter No. 156, 16 April 1941, Telegraphic Correspondence between Viceroy and Secretary of State, Vol. VI, Linlithgow Papers Acc. No. 2163, NAI.

... My telegram of 15th April No. 768-C contains summary of Jinnah's speech at Madras. This is directly relevant to debate. As you will see it is quite uncompromising on the Pakistan issue, and he was at pains to emphasize that any suggestions or statements meant for postponement of Pakistan only represented wishful thinking and in terms remarked that Sapru is entirely on the 'wrong line'. He also was frankly contemptuous of the Bombay Conference. Given great importance of securing reasonable degree of Muslim support for any compromise, this is material.

As regards Mahasabha, Jinnah in his Madras speech says—I read in the Press this morning—that Savarkar and the Working Committee of the Mahasabha had repudiated the Bombay

Conference. It was mentioned in the memorandum of Sapru that the Conference included the leaders of the Hindu Mahasabha, but Savarkar had disowned that. Reference appears to be to Press message from Nagpur where the working committee of the Mahasabha met on the 13th and 'the view was expressed at the meeting that the Hindu Mahasabha is not officially connected with the Bombay Conference and that the Mahasabha will be free to take its own decision on any settlement that may arise out of these negotiations'. I have heard nothing further on the point directly from Savarkar. Naidu, General Secretary of Mahasabha has however stated to the press that the Mahasabha will not co-operate in any scheme for the expansion of the Central Government unless the communal proportion of the Indian population is reflected in the communal proportion of the Council.

In general I think that Jinnah has got pretty near the mark in his suggestion both that Bombay Conference has insufficient substance behind it and that Congress have been leading Sapru up the garden path. His emphasis on declared anti-war policy of Congress is a good point and may be developing ....

13. Dr Rajendra Prasad's Rejoinder to Jinnah

The Tribune, 20 April 1941.

India is One and Indivisible—'Congress Could Not Commit Suicide'

Patna, 19 April. Dr Rajendra Prasad has issued the following statement:

I have seen Mr Jinnah's statement, issued from Madras on the 17th April, in which he has sought to make two points and charged me with turning and twisting things. The first point is that the Congress need not wait for the details of the scheme of Pakistan but should accept the principle forthwith and then the details may be worked out. The second is that the Congress is responsible for the failure of the negotiations to arrive at a settlement and that the Congress position was most arrogant and dictatorial.

I propose to deal with these points. I will take the second first.

I take it that Mr Jinnah's that in the conversations which have taken place during the last three or four years between him and the representatives of the Congress the two parties could never progress beyond the preliminary stage of settling their respective status and no concrete proposals for a settlement of the communal question had arisen.

As public memory is proverbially short. I may be excused for quoting from the published correspondence which passed between Mr Subhas Chandra Bose, the then Congress President, and Mr Jinnah in 1938. Mr Jinnah's first proposal was that the conversations should proceed on the following lines—'The All-India Muslim League as the authoritative and representative organization of the solid body of the Muslim opinion, have hereby agreed to the following terms by way of a pact between the two major communities and as a settlement of the Hindu–Muslim question.'

After a further consideration, a somewhat different wording was suggested by him as follows:

'The Congress and the All-India Muslim League as the authoritative and representative organization of the Musalmans of India, have hereby agreed to the following terms of a Hindu–Muslim settlement by way of a pact.'

As was pointed out by the Congress President, the second statement though shorter apparently embodies the same ideas as the first, namely that the Congress should represent the Hindus and the League the Musalmans of India.

Congress Could Not Commit Suicide

It is obvious that the Congress could not commit suicide with one stroke of the pen dubbing itself as a communal organization of the Hindus alone, obliterating its history of more than fifty years in which non-Hindus, like Christians, Parsis and Muslims, including Mr Jinnah himself had played a most conspicuous part, and dealing a death blow to the ideals for which it had laboured, suffered and sacrificed. All this was pointed out by Mr Subhas Chandra Bose in his note dated 14th May 1938 which was considered by the Executive Council of the All-India Muslim League whose decisions were embodied in three resolutions which were communicated to the General President by Mr Jinnah with his letter dated 6th June 1938.

The Executive Council of the All-India Muslim League has considered the note handed by the President, Mr Subhas Chandra Bose on behalf of the Congress to Mr Jinnah, the President of the All-India Muslim League, on the 14th May and his letter of the 15th May 1938 and find that it is not possible for the All-India Muslim League to treat or negotiate with the Congress the question of Hindu–Muslim settlement except on the basis that the Muslim League is the authoritative and representative organization of the Musalmans of India.

The Council have also considered the letter of Mr Gandhi dated the 22nd May 1938 and are of the opinion that it is not desirable to include any Muslim in the personnel of the proposed committee, that may be appointed by the Congress.

The Executive Council wish to make it clear that it is the declared policy of the All-India Muslim League that all other minorities should have their rights and interests safeguarded so as to create a sense of security amongst them and win their confidence and the All-India Muslim League will consult the representatives of such minorities and any other interests as may be involved when necessary.

In his letter dated 25th July 1938 the Congress President pointed out that the Working Committee of the Congress had received warnings against recognizing the exclusive status of the League that there were other Muslim organizations functioning independently of the League, so that some of them were staunch supporters of the Congress and that there were individual Musalmans, who were Congressmen and exercised no inconsiderable influence in the country. It was in the face of these known facts, not only impossible but improper for the Congress to make an admission which the first resolution of the League apparently commanded of the Congress. The Congress Working Committee found it impossible also to conform to the desire expressed in the second resolution, which sought to dictate who the Congress representative should or would not be in case such representatives have to be appointed for carrying on negotiations on behalf of the Congress. Regarding the third resolution it was pointed out that the Congress would be ready to deal with the grievances of other minorities, but that it was unable to understand, in this regards the positions of Muslim League which was a purely Muslim organization where membership was open only to Muslims. The Congress President expressed the hope that it would be possible to take up the next stage in the negotiations.

Mr Jinnah replied in his letter dated 2nd August 1938, re-emphasizing the position taken up by the League in their resolutions.

As the Congress Working Committee was keen on proceeding with the negotiations, mentioned in the President's letter, he wrote that the Working Committee would confer with the League representatives, if the League did not insist on an admission or acknowledgment by the Congress of the exclusively representative character of the League.

It is from this letter of the 2nd October 1938, that Mr Jinnah has noted in his statement of the 17 April 1941.

Mr Jinnah's reply was dated 9 October 1938 and ended with the sentence: 'The Muslim League is still ready to proceed with the negotiation for a settlement of the Hindu–Muslim question on the basis defined in my letter referred to above and would appoint its representatives to meet a committee that may be appointed by the Congress on the footing indicated by us in our three resolutions on 5 June already communicated to you.' This practically brought the negotiations to a close as the Congress was not prepared to accept the basis insisted upon by the League.

'I have quoted the three resolutions of the Executive Council of the League at length. The first resolution insists upon the Congress recognizing and acknowledging the Muslim League as the authoritative representative Muslim organization and ignoring the existence of all other organizations. The second insists on the League's right to dictate to the Congress as to who its representatives for carrying on negotiations shall not be.

The third claims the right of the League to safeguard the interests of all other minorities although the League itself was an organization of a minority community.

In our talk at Mr Jinnah's place in New Delhi in November 1939 the very first question Mr Jinnah put to Mahatma Gandhi was whether we accepted our status as representative of the Hindus and he clinched the whole thing in his own characteristic way: 'If you do not accept that position, why should I talk to you.'

This resume of the conversations will show who has been arrogant and dictatorial.

Coming to the second question of Pakistan. I do not know why and how Mr Jinnah has gathered that I am not opposed to the basic principles of the scheme of partition of India. I want the details of the second partition of India, as embodied in the resolution of the Muslim League—to enable me to judge its implications and to understand what I am expected to accept. The analogy of the joint Hindu family with which I am undoubtedly familiar does not apply in this case at all. For one thing, does Mr Jinnah admit what the Hindus and the Muslims of India have so far constituted one joint family and that a partition has now become necessary? As I understand it the *raison-de-etre* of the proposal is that Hindus and Muslims have always been, are to-day and ever shall in future be two irreconcilable 'groups, whose safety and salvation lies in a complete cutting off of all relations and setting up as two independent States'. But that is only by the way, it will cite, by way of an illustration, one or two points which will show why it is necessary to know the details before forming a final opinion on the proposal for Pakistan.

The Lahore resolution of the League lays down the following basic principles, namely that, geographically continuous units are demarcated into regions which should be so constituted with such territorial adjustments as may be necessary that the areas in which the Muslims are numerically in a majority—as in the north-western and southern zone of India—should be grouped to constitute—'Independent State'—in which the constituent units shall be autonomous and sovereign; that adequate effective and mandatory safeguards be specifically provided in the constitution for minorities in the units and in the regions for the protection of the religious, cultural, economic, political administrative units with them and in other parts of India where Musalmans are in a minority, for whom similar safeguards are to be provided. These 'basic principles' have now been embodied in the creed of the League at its session at Madras, which has just concluded.

The first question which, naturally, arises: What are the territories to be included in the two zones? Several schemes have been put forward, one of which, adumbrated by a Punjabee in his book 'Confederacy of India', contemplates the splitting up of the continent of India into various countries and reassembled in a confederacy of India: two of the zones, contemplated in the League resolution will be (1) the Indus region federation with the Punjab (minus its eastern Hindu tracts, comprising the Ambala division of the Kangra district: Una and Gahshanker), Sind, the NWFP, Kashmir, Baluchistan, Bahawalpur and Swat, Chitral, Khanpur, Kalat, Lasbela, Kapurthala and Malerkotla. This will have a population in which 82 per cent will be Musalmans, 6 per cent will be Sikhs and 8 per cent will be Hindus.

After analysing the various schemes regarding the partition of India Dr Rajendra Prasad says:

> In this statement I have not touched upon the general question of the unity of India. If Mr Jinnah wanted, a general answer to a general question, without going into details himself and without expecting us to go into details, he has got it more than once, when the Congress has declared, that India is one and indivisible.
>
> One could have thought that Pakistan suggested a solution of the communal problem. It does not touch that question at all, as it leaves the Muslim minorities in the so-called Hindu India and Hindu minorities in the so-called Pakistan, as they are to-day. The problem will not cease to exist because Pakistan has been created any more than it has ceased to exist because there are in existence today the independent Muslim States of Afghanistan, Persia, Turkey and the Arab states and the independent Hindu state of Nepal. One would like to know from Mr Jinnah how and what respects will Pakistan differ from these existing independent Muslim states and, if it will not differ, how it will be able to give protection to the Muslim minorities in the rest of India and more than those existing Independent Muslim states have been able to give.

14. Amery's Statement in House of Commons, 22 April 1941

Bombay Chronicle, 23 April 1941.

Non-party Leaders' Demand: Amery's Posers for Sapru
Organize Centre Party and Work for Unity
India Secretary Harps on Old Tune
Dig at Congress: Reply to Jinnah: Condition for Transfer of Responsibility

Mr L.S. Amery, Secretary of State for India, moved a resolution in the House of Commons this afternoon to extend for another year the proclamation under which the Governors of the Indian Provinces can assume the powers of Provincial Legislature.

Amery's Statement

'The purpose of resolution which I am submitting to the House', Mr Amery said, 'is to extend for another twelve months proclamations issued under provisions of Section 93 of the Government of India Act. Under terms of that Section, the Governor of a province, if he is satisfied that a situation has arisen wherein Parliamentary Government cannot be carried on in accordance with the Act can by proclamation assume all or any of powers vested in provincial bodies and authorities. This situation arose in October 1939 in consequence of the action of Congress Party's so called High Command in ordering Congress Ministries to resign. Proclamations under Section 93 were accordingly issued in seven provinces and their continuance in force for a further twelve months was duly approved by the House on 19 April last year. There has been no change in the situation since than and I regret we have no alternative to further extension of these emergency provisions. These resolutions, however, are only concerned with seven out of eleven provinces of British India.

Self Government at Work

'In the four provinces of Bengal, Assam, Sind and the Punjab with a population something like 100,000,000 people—one third of the whole population of British India—provincial self-Government has continued to work uninterruptedly under composite Governments including Muslim and Hindu Ministries. On all questions which most nearly affect ordinary life of the citizen—all questions in fact which occupy most of the attention of this House in times of peace—these hundred millions of Indians have now for four years been enjoying advantages of democratic self-Government ministers and legislators have continued to gain experience and are making their contribution not only to the welfare of their constituents within the wide sphere of their direct authority but also to India's general war effort. We ought not to underestimate the significance of this remarkable advance in self-Government over so large a field. Nor can we afford to ignore the importance of the voice which these provinces through their Governments are bound to exercise in any deliberations affecting the future constitution of India.'

In Congress Provinces

From this point of view it is a matter of deep regret that the 200,000,000 inhabitants of other seven provinces were by an ukase of the Congress High Command forbidden to continue to build up the practice and tradition of self-Government. Their Governments too had made satisfactory beginning and if they made mistakes—as even we have been known to do—the remedy lay with their electors.

So far indeed as provincial electorates are concerned, it must be admitted that they have nowhere showed any signs of distress at the suspension of Parliamentary Government—in this respect, no doubt, differing greatly from what would be the attitude of our own electors if deprived of the services of this front bench.

Change to Direct Personal Government by Governors and Permanent Officials Met with General Acquiescence and Indeed Goodwill

Whatever political unrest there may be in India today has certainly not arisen in any way from the suspension of provincial self-Government. There has been no discontinuity or abrupt reversal in either administrative or legislative policy. In few instances indeed, notably in connection with prohibition legislation has had to be modified in consequence of legal decision. But generally speaking work of beneficent social progress continues in full swing and with broad public approval....

Danger to Democratic Government

I can only say, whatever may have been the motives which inspired the conduct both of the Congress High Command and the Provincial Ministries, that there is no greater danger to democratic Government in India as elsewhere than party totalitarianism. What has been even more immediately serious in its effect has been the demonstrations of Congress methods upon other important elements in India—non-Congress Provinces, Muslim community generally, and the Princes. It has confirmed to the point of a fixed determination of their already growing reluctance to take part in or come under any Central Government in India which is likely to be subject to the control on a majority in the Legislature which in its turn would simply obey orders of the Congress Central Executive.

Dangers of Pakistan

The Congress repudiated the federal provisions of Act of 1935 largely because they had weighted representation to some extent in the Legislature in favour of the minority element, in what Congress regarded as an undemocratic sense. The Congress is, I fear, blind to the risk that no alternative Constitution is now likely to emerge which could secure for it as great a measure of influence and control over India as a whole as it would have exercised under the present Act. The most significant symposium of the changed situation is the growing strength of the demand voiced by Mr Jinnah, Leader of Muslim League for complete severance from the rest of India of north-western and north-eastern zones, wherein Muslims constitute a majority and their establishment as completely Independent States controlling their own foreign policy, defence, customs and finance....

That August Offer

It is enough for my purpose if I can impress upon the House on the one hand the underlying determination of Muslim India not to accept any Constitution which does not give a reasonably free play to the individual life of the pre-dominantly Muslim units, and on the other the growing danger of preaching on both sides, Hindu and Muslim, of extreme and incompatible policies (hear hear). It was the recognition of this danger as well as the hope that the gravity of the war situation might bring the parties together in a spirit of co-operation and responsibility that led His Majesty's Government to make a new statement of policy which was made public by Lord Linlithgow in August last. What was the essence of that statement?

It was that the framework of India's future constitution should be devised by Indians for themselves and not by this House. That was a far-reaching and indeed revolutionary announcement the full importance of which has not, I think, even yet been fully appreciated either in this country or in India. It was in fact the recognition in advance of India's status as a Dominion.

That recognition was coupled with two conditions. One was that provision would have to be made for the due fulfilment of whose obligations which Great Britain's long connection with India has imposed on her.

India's Future Constitution

Some of these, as for instance obligations towards existing member of the Services, are by their very nature terminable. But others like those arising from India's present dependence upon this country for defence will naturally be subject to modification with the growth of India's own capacity to defend herself unaided. Others such as Treaty Obligations of the Crown towards the Princes are of more enduring character. In any case none of them stand in the way of shaping the structure of India's future Constitution which is to be essentially an Indian Constitution framed in accordance with Indian conceptions of Indian conditions and Indian needs.

Even more important in this connection is the stipulation that the Constitution itself and also the body which is to frame. It must be the outcome of agreement between the principal elements in India's national life. That is an essential prerequisite to the success of the future constitution. For, if Indians cannot agree upon the kind of constitution they are prepared to work, how are they likely to agree upon the actual working of it?

Our Constitution here works because there is behind it an unwritten agreement based upon centuries of tradition as to the limits within which a majority can exercise its position of advantage. In all Federal Constitutions previous free agreement upon the nature of the constitution and of the limits within which majority rule can be exercised has been the condition upon which the various elements of the Federation have been prepared to come together.

Choice for Indian Statesmen

Anxious as we are to see the responsibility of Indian Government resting upon Indian shoulders, we can only transfer the responsibility to some body which can assume it without immediately breaking down or breaking up subject to the requisite of agreement which is inherent in the circumstances of the Indian situation and not arbitrarily imposed by ourselves, the whole constitutional field is open for modification or fundamental reconstruction of the existing Act. Indian statesmen need not be bound by the system of Government at the Centre contemplated in that Act or by relations between that Centre and Provinces and States. If they agree regarding redistribution of powers or electoral system, that is a field open to them for settlement. If they come to the conclusion that our type of Democracy with an Executive dependent upon a parliamentary majority stands in the way of agreement and that India's needs would be better met by an Executive deriving its authority more directly from Federated Units like the American Executive, independent of Legislature, that again is their responsibility. We who in this House wrestled for months with the intricacies of the existing Act—which I still look upon as a very remarkable piece of constructive legislation—should be the last to underrate the difficulty of the task which lies before Indian statesmanship....

No Change Over

There could, of course, be no question of changing over the whole basis of administrative and legislative power or placing India's war effort in the hands of an entirely new Executive. Nor could that have been done without at once raising those very issues of the division of power between the conflicting elements in India which are still unresolved. What we could do was to invite Indian leaders representing main political factors to join the Viceroy's Executive Council.

The invitation to them was not only individually to take charge of important Departments of State, but also to partake fully in the collective responsibility of the Council. Their inclusion would have brought Indian membership of the Council official and unofficial up to a substantial majority of the whole. But it would not have so altered the essential character of the Council as to deprive the Governor-General of his existing trusted advisers or as to commit Indian leaders who joined it to any course which would have deprived them of a free hand in dealing with the major problems of constitutional future. We believed and still believe that it would give real power and valuable experience to men who have hitherto been in political opposition. We still believe that the creation of such a Coalition of Executive would have afforded opportunity for Indian leaders in an atmosphere of common effort for India's security to forget for a while their differences and begin to envisage their problems in the light of wider Indian patriotism.

Amery on Congress Position

So far, our hopes have been disappointed. The Congress rejected out of hand both our major and interim proposals. Its attitude is 'all or nothing at all'. It means immediate independence of an India governed by a constitution which would ensure Congress control. It refused even to discuss the matter and proceeded to launch a curious campaign of Mr Gandhi's devising. In pursuance of that campaign Congress leaders including ex-Premiers and ex-Ministers as well as select members of the rank and file have made speeches intended and calculated to interfere with war effort. They have deliberately challenged fine or imprisonment with the same unquestioning obedience to party whip as when they resigned office in the provinces and in many cases, I believe, with the same misgiving and reluctance. The situation thus created is naturally embarrassing as it was meant to be. But clearly Government cannot punish ordinary offenders and overlook the same offences when committed by men whose position and course of action deliberately enhances their significance and their political effect. This campaign of civil disobedience by installments has now been in progress for nearly six months....

On the whole, the movement has proceeded languidly and without evoking much popular interest except in the United Provinces which have in recent months contributed more than half the offences. By middle of March some 7,000 offenders had been convicted and some 5,000 are still in prison. The whole business is as regrettable as it is irrational, but Government had and has no alternative to enforcing law....

Viceroy's Council

As regards the more immediate policy of the extension of Viceroy's Council, acceptance in principle unfortunately did not lead to actual agreement in detail. The Muslim League in particular ask for a measure of representation as against Hindu elements and made stipulations as to the future which the Viceroy could not see his way to accepting. It was of course always open to the Viceroy to add to his Council individual Indians of high character and ability. But such a course would not have achieved the desired object which was to associate representative Hindu and Muslim political leaders with the conduct of the war and so bring them closer together for the future. Very reluctantly, therefore, Lord Linlithgow decided in November to discontinue for the time being his unwearied efforts carried on ever since war began to bring the parties together, leaving the door open to further reconsideration by those directly concerned. No one can look upon the present deadlock with satisfaction. Least of all patriotic Indians who looking beyond narrower aims of sectional leaders, are deeply concerned with India's progress towards equal partnership in our family of five nations which is alike their goal as well as ours.

They, better than anyone else, can help to find a solution. But they can do so only if they direct their efforts to the real source of difficulty.

The Sapru Conference

In the last few weeks that distinguished veteran statesman, Sir Tej Bahadur Sapru, whose breadth of outlook and courageous initiative played no small part in the deliberations which led up to the existing Federal Scheme brought together in Bombay a number of eminent Indian public men outside the two main contending political organizations to consider the situation. In the end a resolution was passed. But I am not quite clear as to how many of those who attended one or more meetings of this conference actually concurred in the resolution. That resolution has since been discussed by Sir Tej with the Viceroy and submitted to His Majesty's Government and has been published. It asked for complete reconstruction of the Executive Council converting it into one consisting entirely of unofficial Indians drawn from important elements of public life. This new Council would be responsible, while war is still in progress, to the Crown and not to the Legislature, but it should in substance be treated in regard to all inter-Imperial and international matters on the same footing as a Dominion Government.

Demand Goes Beyond Viceroy's Offer

The resolution also asked that this reconstruction should be accompanied by the announcement of a definite time-limit within which India is to attain to the same measure of freedom as is enjoyed by the Dominions. I should be the last to approach in a critical or unsympathetic spirit the proposals brought forward by men of such eminent public service as those who have associated themselves with this resolution or animated by such genuine desire both to promote India's constitutional progress and her active participation in war effort. I will, therefore, only touch very briefly on some of the more obvious difficulties which such a scheme, if it were carried into effect, would present in practice.

The scheme proposed by the resolution would amount not to modification of the present form of Government, but to its supersession by an entirely different type of Government. That is certainly something going beyond what we think practicable in the midst of the ever-increasing strain and urgency of the war situation.

It would also create internal constitutional problems of no little difficulty both in relation to Provinces, whether those now enjoying self-government or those administrated under Section 93 and to the Princes, and in that and other ways it would raise still unresolved issues of the constitutional future....

Appeal to Sapru

My appeal to Sri Tej and his friends would, therefore, be not to cease from their efforts but to concentrate first and foremost on bringing contending elements in India together. Whether they can best do that by exercise of their persuasion upon existing party leaders or by building up a strong central party of men who are prepared to put India first their effort may well be decisive in shaping whole future of their country ....

15. Yet Another 'No'

Editorial, *The Hindu*, 24 April 1941.

Mr Amery like the Bourbons learns nothing and forgets nothing. With an ostrich-like complacency that is truly appalling he assures the House of Commons that 'whatever political unrest there may be in India to-day, has certainly not arisen in any way from the suspension of provincial self-government', and that the House could safely agree to the extension of the Adviser regimes for another twelve month. Mr Amery cannot help contrasting what he regards as 'the absence of any signs of distress' in the Indian provincial electorates over the eclipse of popular government with 'what would be the attitude of our own electors if deprived of the services of this Front Bench'. No doubt he was conscious of a pleasant sense of national superiority in instituting the comparison. But if he really believed that 'the change to direct personal government by the Governors and permanent officials met with general acquiescence and indeed with good-will', the logical conclusion would be that the Indian people positively hugged their slavery, being unique in this respect. How comes it, then, that Mr Amery, nevertheless, interlarded his speech with references to democracy and self-government and worked in a peroration about 'our further contribution towards the completion of our own task in India, the task of joining with them (Indians) in crowning the peace and unity already achieved with freedom'? Poor Mr Amery has not the eyes to see that, if there is no trouble in India to-day for him and his subordinates to worry over, it is not because the people of the

Congress Provinces delight in their chains but because they are intelligent enough and disciplined enough to follow the leadership of the Congress and to respect Gandhiji's resolve that Britain shall in no way be embarrassed in her time of trial. Mr Amery cannot apparently understand such chivalry and considerateness.

His little lecture on the implications of responsible government and the menace of party totalitarianism similarly suffer in impressiveness from his inability to see beyond his nose. Could anything be more comic than his solemn effort to discover in the non-Congress Provinces patterns of democratic self-government? He assures them that they shall have their due reward—an important voice 'in any deliberations affecting the future constitution of India'. It is in the fitness of things that Mr Amery should proclaim in advance his resolve to be guided by those communalists who in Sind and Bengal have abdicated the elementary function of governments—to maintain peace and security—and have encouraged communal ill-feeling so blatantly that men like Prof. H.C. Mookerji, who are no Congressmen and who belong to minority communities themselves, declare that what is happening in these non-Congress Provinces to-day is a tragic foretaste of Pakistan. Mr Amery, we quite realize, will not be much impressed by such disinterested testimony. All his fulminations are reserved for the Congress High Command; towards Mr Jinnah and the Muslim League he takes care to use language, which if it is not quite like the cooing of the dove is hardly more terrible than the squeak of the mouse. The terms of his reference to Pakistan reveal, not a stern resolve to turn down once for all Mr Jinnah's plan for destroying that unity of India to which Britain still pays lip-service, but a painful anxiety to placate the League by suggesting that what worries Mr Amery is not the idea of vivisection itself but the practical difficulties it involves and that none would be happier than he if the League could assure him that these difficulties could be overcome. But if he is so impressed—as to impress it, in his turn, on the House of Commons—by 'the underlying determination of Muslim India not to accept any constitution which does not give reasonable free play to the individual life of predominantly Muslim units', is it not idle to suppose that the legitimate aspirations of a great nation could be checked and thwarted indefinitely by Britain, even though her will may be backed by big battalions? Mr Amery makes the mistake, common enough to those in his position, of supposing that the Congress is a back number; this will be obvious from his jocose references to the Satyagraha movement and from the pitying tone in which he tells it that it is 'blind to the risk that no alternative constitution is now likely to emerge which could secure for it as great a measure of influence and control over India as a whole as it would have exercised under the present Act'. 'Praise in departing' is, in Prospero's language, the friendly caution we would give Mr Amery, who is a little premature in proclaiming the demise of the Congress. And, though he may not understand it, we would assure him that the Congress, having never planned to dominate India, will not be sorry to hear that the chance has passed. Its aim is something very different—that neither Britain nor the communalists and vested interests who dance to her tune, deluding themselves all the while that it was they who called the tune, shall keep the people of India out of their lawful heritage.

Regarded from this point of view, the Congress's refusal to accept the Viceroy's August offer should not at all be difficult to understand, Mr Amery glibly recounted once again all the reasons why India should see in his farmyard goose a royal swan. In reply we need only cite the testimony of one of his most ardent admirers. Sir George Schuster, in the course of the debate yesterday, said: 'Let Indians come in as members of the Viceroy's Council in the same positions in which other Indians had gone into the Council in the past .... That was what the Secretary of State offered, but all Indian political leaders, not only the Congress, would not have it.' So much for Mr Amery's elaborate pretence, on the one hand that the Viceroy's offer meant real transfer of power, on the other that it had found 'acceptance in principle' among all parties other than the Congress. He had equally little warrant for the complacent remark that, 'apart from the Congress, the Government's major policy for the constitutional future'—to distinguish it, from the interim proposals—'may be said to have relieved the anxieties of the various elements which compose India's national structure.' Apart from the Muslim League, which pace Mr Jinnah and his new admirer, the Secretary for India, is neither India, nor even Muslim India by a long chalk, no party in India—nor all Englishmen, as will be seen from the note of dissent struck by more than one speaker in the course of the Commons debate, though Mr Amery likes to think otherwise—feels reassured by the British Government's policy or shares its ridiculous optimism. Mr Amery violently disagrees with the view that his policy is one of drift. But what other description could possibly apply to the British Government's attitude that, in the absence of agreement between the major political parties, nothing can be done and that, even as regards exploring the avenues of agreement, 'the main responsibility for both the initiation and the completion of this high inquiry rests with Indians themselves?' That the absence of agreement among Indians is but a mere pretext will be seen from the casual manner, bordering on levity, with which Mr Amery has dismissed the Bombay Conference proposals. Their plan for reconstitution of the Viceroy's Council, he says, 'is certainly something going beyond what we think practicable'; then, why pretend that it is India's united demand and not Britain's high pleasure that really matters? Having taken up the stand that it is for Britain to decide what is the quantum of power that the reconstituted Centre shall have and having made it clear that that power will be practically nil, what is the sense in urging, as an objection against the Bombay proposals, that 'there is obviously no such agreement here (that is, between the Muslim League and the Hindu Mahasabha over the Bombay proposals) as would afford the reconstructed Council political support, or even acquiescence in the Legislature'? And why should Mr Amery regard the possible lack of the Legislature's backing as a fatal defect in the Bombay Scheme when, with regard to his pet scheme of August last, he insisted that irresponsibility of the new Councillors to the Legislature would be regarded as a positive merit? And when he advises Sir Tej Bahadur Sapru and his friends to build up a Centre Party on which, he suggests, they could climb to power, can he have forgotten that he began by positing that the Indian electorate was a cypher—an assumption which, if true, would make a Centre Party based on such an electorate equally a cypher?

Mr Amery declared that he could not contemplate without 'a certain sense of frustration or depression' the difficulty, 'not so much in the devolution of authority, as in making sure that there is an authority in India which can take over and will not break down or break up in the process'. But if, as he says, 'there is no essential difficulty so far as this country's (Britain's) intentions are concerned' and if she is really anxious and united in wishing to confer on India Dominion Status immediately after the war, how can she justifiably delay implementing her pledges solely because a break-down or a break-up is a remote possibility? It is humanly impossible to make sure, before handing over power, that such a thing shall not happen at all; and in fact Britain made no such stipulation with regard to other Dominions. And very sensibly too; in the improbable event of a break-up or a break-down it is the Dominion's own business to find a way out as best it can. It must 'dree its own weird', as the Scots say. Britain simply cannot expect India any longer to believe that she is afraid to part with power in India's own interests. If chaos must come as a result of self-government, it will come some day and India alone will have to deal with it. That is a prospect which, to her, is far less grim than the desperate frustration she feels, confronted with Britain's policy or dealing with her as cavalierly as if she were a conquered country under military occupation. It cannot be good for Britain, either, to inspire in India that feeling of futility.

16. Mahatma Gandhi's Statement on Amery's Speech, 25 April 1941

Indian Annual Register, 1941, Vol. I, pp. 326–7.

In this connection Mahatma Gandhi issued the following statement on Mr Amery's speech which is charged with such emotion as he rarely puts into his public utterance. 'Every line and every word of it breathes indignation—of a type somewhat unusual with the Mahatma', said the Rt Hon'ble V.S. Srinivasa Sastri referring to it in his Ranade Hall speech at Madras on the 27th April. The explanation must be sought in the fact that nothing repels Gandhiji so much as insincerity and Mr Amery in his speech was so obviously concerned with making debating points that he had no use for sincerity. The following is the text of the statement:

'I have read painfully the long report of the debate in the House of Commons on India. Distress has been known to have softened people's hearts and made them mindful of facts. But Britain's distress has evidently left Mr Amery absolutely cool and untouched. This callousness makes me more than ever confirmed in my opinion that the Congress must abide by its policy of non-violence in spite of the heavy odds facing it.

'Mr Amery has rendered no service to Great Britain by his contemptuous disregard of the situation as it exists in India and the facts that stare one in the face. He talks glibly of British rule having given peace to India. Did he not know what was happening in Dacca and Ahmedabad? Who was responsible for keeping the peace in these two places? I hope he will not throw in my face the fact that Bengal, at any rate, has self-government. He knows what a mockery that self-government is. He knows what little power for such emergencies toy Ministers have, whether they wear the Congress label, the League label or any other.

'I ask the very pertinent question: Why has this long spell of British rule left the people so emasculated as to disable them from standing up against a few hundred goondas? It is a humiliating spectacle, more for the British than for us, to see thousands of people running away from their homes through sheer fight, because a few goondas have found a favourable atmosphere for resorting to arson, murder and loot. The first act of any Government worth the name would be to teach its people the art of self-defence, but the foreign British Government had no concern about this fundamental welfare of India's citizens and so it deprived the people of the use of arms.

'All the handsome tribute that Mr Amery pays to Indian troops falls flat on Indian soil, because, leaving aside Congress non-violence for the time being, if India had been equipped and trained for self-defence and if India had become a voluntary ally of Great Britain, I hold that all European Powers combined for destruction would not have touched Great Britain.

'Mr Amery has insulted Indian intelligence by reiterating *ad nauseam* that Indian political parties have but to agree among themselves and Great Britain will register the will of a united India. I have repeatedly shown that it has been the traditional policy of Great Britain to prevent parties from uniting. "Divide and rule" has been Great Britain's proud and ill-conceived motto. It is the British statesmen who are responsible for the divisions in India's ranks and the divisions will continue so long as the British sword holds India under bondage.

'I admit that there is unfortunately an unbridgeable gulf between the Congress and the Muslim League. Why do not British statesmen admit that it is after all a domestic quarrel? Let them withdraw from India and I promise that the Congress and the League and all other parties will find it to their interest to come together and devise a home-made solution for the Government of India. It may not be scientific; it may not be after any western pattern; but it will be durable. It may be that before we come to that happy state of affairs, we may have to fight amongst ourselves. But if we agree not to invite the assistance of any outside Power, the trouble will last perhaps a fortnight and it will not mean even one day's destruction of human heads such as goes on in Europe today, for the simple reason that thanks to the British rule we are wholly unarmed.

'Mr Amery in utter disregard of truth, misleads his ignorant audience that the Congress wants "all or nothing". Let me remind him that in order to placate British sentiment, the Congress descended to the Poona Resolution and when at Bombay it undid the Poona Resolution, I authoritatively stated that the British Government could not at the present moment grant or declare India's independence and that, therefore, for the time being, we should be satisfied with complete freedom of speech and pen. Was that "All or nothing"? With Mr Amery's state of mind, I suppose it is too much to expect him to have the elementary grace to acknowledge the studied moderation of the Congress in its desire not to embarrass the British Government whilst it is fighting for its very existence. Not having that grace, he turns the Congress moderation against it and claims that the Congress civil disobedience has fallen flat.

'It took my breath away when I read his statement about India's prosperity. I say from experience that it is a legendary thing. India's millions are becoming progressively pauperized. They are miserably clothed and underfed. Because there is one man's rule, he is able to produce a budget of millions. But I make bold to say that it is not only no proof of the prosperity of the famishing millions, but it is proof positive that India is being ground down under the British heel. It is the duty of every Indian, who knows anything about the distress of the peasantry, to rise in rebellion against this autocratic rule. Fortunately for humanity, India's rebellion is a peaceful revolt and I hope it will be through exclusively peaceful effort that India will realise her natural destiny.

'But I must not carry any further the painful dissection of Mr Amery's performance. It hurts me to have to undertake even this very brief analysis of his speech. But it is so amazingly misleading that I felt I would be falling in my duty if I did not point out at least some of the most glaring discrepancies in that unfortunate utterance. Surely he could have rested content with the undisputed sway that he exercises over the destinies of over four hundred million people.'

17. Statement Issued by Standing Committee of the Bombay Conference on Amery's Speech

The Tribune, 29 April 1941.

'It is Difficult to Understand Working of Mr Amery's Mind'

He Assumes that People Like Governor's Rule

He Thinks that Mr Jinnah Represents All Muslims

[House of] Commons is Not Told That Provinces Like Sind and Frontier are Against Him [Jinnah]

His Majesty's Govt Won't Do Anything Until Mr Jinnah Approves of a Scheme

Liberal Leaders' Statement

Allahabad, 28 April. The following statement has been issued by the Standing Committee of the Bombay Conference after its deliberations yesterday:

'The Standing Committee of the Bombay Conference have read Mr Amery's speeches in the House of Commons with the care which they deserve. The Committee very much regret that the speeches should have betrayed such an amazing misunderstanding of the real political situation in India and displayed such an unsympathetic and unbending attitude towards the aspirations of India. The Committee feel that Mr Amery has missed the opportunity of winning public confidence which was offered to the British Government with the best intentions by those who have a vivid appreciation of the dangers of the international situation. They have, however, reason to apprehend that one certain effect of these speeches would be to strengthen the forces of disruption in the country and to create the impression that in point of fact the British Government have no desire to part with real power at this juncture. The Committee regret very much that Mr Amery should have adopted an attitude of self-complacency with regard to the position in India which was bound to create a wrong impression in Parliament and probably on a large audience in America that the present system of Government in India commands not only the acquiescence of the people of this country but also their goodwill. The Committee have no hesitation in saying that this is a complete travesty of the situation in India.

2. They, however, note with satisfaction that there were men in Parliament belonging to different parties, some with considerable knowledge of India, such as Sir Stanley Reed, and Sir George Schuster, who controverted Mr Amery's assumptions then and there and warned him against the unwisdom and unfairness of his policy of drift at a time of such a grave peril. The Committee feel, however, that it would be unfair to Mr Amery to hold him wholly responsible for creating this impression as the original responsibility for giving a true estimate of the situation in India rests with the Government of India.

Congress and Muslim League

3. No one in this country and no one particularly connected with the Bombay Conference has ever minimized the desirability of reconciliation between the two important political bodies of India—the Congress and the Muslim League.

4. The President of the Bombay Conference (who will issue a separate statement) was not unmindful of the desirability of removing misunderstanding at an early date, and he made endeavours before the Conference met at Bombay to explore the possibilities of bringing the contending parties together. The organizers of the Conference were, however, satisfied that in view of the fundamental differences between the Congress and the Muslim League, there was no prospect within a reasonable distance of time of those contending parties coming together. The Conference felt, at the same time, that it was intolerable that the progress of the country should be held up by His Majesty's Government merely because the two contending parties would not or could not compose their differences. In this connection the committee would refer to the statement made by His Excellency the Viceroy on the 8th August last.

'It is clear,' said His Excellency, 'that the earlier difference, which had prevented the achievement of national unity, remain unbridged. Deeply as His Majesty's Government regret this they do not feel that they should any longer, because of these differences, postpone the expansion of the Governor General's Council'. For Mr Amery now to insist upon agreement as a condition precedent to any change at the centre is really to go back on the declared policy of his Majesty's Government.

5. The Committee would like the Secretary of State to consider whether the repetition of the advice that Indians should first settle their differences among themselves before expecting any constitutional change could absolve him from the reproach, so pointedly made by Sir Chimanlal Setalvad in his recent statement on Mr Amery's speech: 'However profuse the assurances of the British Government may be as regards their intentions to make India self-governing Dominion, no political party is convinced because of past experience of the British Government's sincerity as regards parting with power.'

Growing Dangers to India

6. In view of the growing dangers to India from the war, those who assembled at Bombay put forward certain proposals which they were satisfied were practicable, and which, if accepted, would have had an excellent psychological effect on the country and stimulated genuine voluntary war effort to a much greater extent. The present policy of the Secretary of State is bound to have a deleterious effect on the minds of the people and on the situation in India for which the entire responsibility must be his and of his advisers in India.

7. Practically the present position of the Secretary of State is that, until it pleases Mr Jinnah to approve of any scheme, His Majesty's Government can do nothing to give effect even to their own intentions as announced in August last. Mr Amery has referred to an unworthy insinuation made by Mr Jinnah in his speech at Madras to the effect that the Bombay Conference was held in consultation with or at the instigation of some Congress leaders in the interests of the Congress. The Committee repudiate this categorically. The Committee would not have noticed such an aspersion but for the fact that the Secretary of State referred to it in his speech in the House of Commons to the prejudice of the Conference and its organizers.

8. It is not difficult to understand the working of the mind of the Secretary of State. He assumed that in the seven provinces where the constitutional machinery of Government had been replaced by the personal rule of Governors, people were contented with the system of administration—an assumption which, if true must bear out all proposals of advance even after the war. He apparently thought that the attitude of the Hindus did not require to be taken seriously into account whereas he assumed that the Muslim League in its present state of intransigence represented the attitude of all the Muslims of India or of an overwhelming majority of them, even though provinces like Sind and the North-West Frontier Province and considerable sections of Muslims in other provinces repudiate the authority and policy of the Muslim League and the leadership of Mr Jinnah. These facts should in fairness have been brought to the notice of the House of Commons.

9. The Secretary of State has advised the Conference as to what it should do in future. Its members are according to him to devote their energies to bringing about a settlement between the Congress and the League and failing that to attempt to form a Centre Party. Meanwhile they are to remain satisfied with his promise of Dominion Status at an indefinite date with an unrepresentative and un-influential centre and personal rule in seven provinces. The Standing Committee are compelled, in view of their knowledge of the country to reject this advice for reasons of which Mr Amery and his advisers in India cannot surely be ignorant. The Conference at Bombay was concerned with the immediate future during the war and not with long-range policies which must bide their time. Even if a Centre Party were to emerge after a number of years, what guarantee is there that its proposals would receive any better treatment than have

the united demands of Indian politicians in the past? The burden of the Secretary of State's speech is that before he can be prepared to consider any proposal, there must be the prior approval of Mr Jinnah—a preposition which no self-respecting political party can accept it or tolerate.

10. The Committee desire to meet some of Mr Amery's objections and raise some questions with regard to them. One of his objections is that the Conference proposal would mean not a modification of the present form of Government but its supersession by entirely different form of Government. The present Government consists of four official and two non-official Indians in addition to His Excellency the Commander-in-Chief. All the members of the Government at present are appointed by the Crown and are responsible to it. The Committee understand that under the proposals made last August by the British Government the number of official members was to be reduced to two and the total strength of the Executive Council increased to eleven. In respect of the appointing authority or in their responsibility of the members of the Government to the Crown, all that it has suggested is that not only two but all the four official members should be replaced to non-officials. Does such a proposal amount to a supersession of the present system of Government?

11. The Secretary of State has chosen not to show his hand. The Committee are entitled to ask the British Government what their concrete proposals are. Does the Secretary of State object to the transfer of the important portfolios of Finance and Defence, and if so why? Sir George Schuster, himself the Finance Member of the Government of India from 1928 until 1934, expressed his belief in the House of Commons that competent Indian could be found for the Finance portfolio. The Committee have equally little doubt that a competent Indian can be found for the Defence portfolio. The Conference did not, as will appear from the resolution, want to affect the position and responsibility of the Commander of Chief and as both he and the Defence Member would be appointed by the Crown, it should not be difficult to adjust their mutual relations. The only construction that the Committee can put on the position taken by Mr Amery is that key portfolios would not be transferred to Indian hands. It is quite clear from this that even if there had been a previous agreement between the main political parties, these portfolios would not have been entrusted to Indian members....

18. Tej Bahadur Sapru's Statement on Amery's Speech

Bombay Chronicle, 30 April 1941.

Sapru's Rejoinder to Secretary of State
Centre Party will Not Fare Better with Present Government Policy
Says Amery has Contributed Nothing to Solution of Communal Problems

Allahabad, 29 April.

Sir Tej Behadur Sapru, Chairman of the Bombay Moderate Leaders' Conference has the following statement:

The Standing Committee of the Bombay Conference has already issued a statement on Mr Amery's speech in the House of Commons. There are however certain matters to which I should like to refer in my personal statement.

I was most reluctant hitherto to say publicly that for nearly two months before the Conference met at Bombay I did all I could in my individual capacity to bring Mahatma Gandhi and

Mr Jinnah together. Even now I should not like to disclose without their permission anything of the correspondence that passed between them and me.

Amery's Ignorance

All that I can say is that I have not been unmindful of the need for a communal settlement. Indeed since December last when I issued my first statement and again in January when I wrote an article in the 'Twentieth Century' I have been emphasizing the need of these two leaders meeting each other. I gave this suggestion of mine the first place among the several suggestions that I made.

I am surprised to note that Mr Amery's speech shows that he is unaware of it as I presumed that he would know something of it after conversations with the Viceroy.

This is not the time for me to apportion blame between the leaders. I regret to say that my efforts bore no fruit. As matters stand now I am more than doubtful if the chances of a settlement between the two parties can be looked upon as at all bright.

Mr Jinnah's speech at Madras and Mr Gandhi's recent pronouncement show that if anything the gulf is wider than ever before.

It was just when I was carrying on this correspondence that a European member of the Legislature who has since been criticizing the Bombay Conference wrote to me as follows:

Government Must Take Initiative

'I have been feeling for sometime that HM's Government ought to take the initiative in the matter of a communal agreement. It is no use merely saying that such an agreement is a pre-requisite to any further constitutional discussions and then leaving it at that. That was and still is my view.

Those who talk of an agreement being a pre-requisite of further constitutional changes should not in my opinion content themselves with making repeated references to them but should also take a hand in promoting such settlement.

I have seen no evidence of that either in England or in India. Long range discussions and criticisms of the internal situation cannot help the people and do not redound to the credit of the Government'.

Mr Amery says in his speech that we have not been able to secure before hand for our scheme any kind of agreement if not between the Congress and the Muslim League at any rate between the latter and other representatives of the Hindu majority.

Surely this new condition which is now so solemnly put forward by Government could not have been absent from the minds of those who were responsible for making the declaration on 8 August, and if it was present to their minds then why did they not say that time that no kind of change in the constitution would be brought about except with agreement between the major contending parties.

During the Round Table Conference discussions when Mr Ramsay MacDonald consulted me about the Communal Award I told him point blank that if I were a British Prime Minister I should not undertake that responsibility and yet notwithstanding the fact that there was no agreement between the Hindus and the Muslims Mr MacDonald's Government which consisted also of Conservatives went on with their scheme, gave first the communal award and then introduced the India Bill.

Mortgaging India's Interests

Bluntly put, Mr Amery is mortgaging our future to certain intractable decaders.

Expediencies of the hour are not always consistent with lasting polices seeking to achieve the permanent good of a vast country like India.

HAS MR AMERY SUCH PERMANENT POLICY? IF SO WHAT STEPS IS HE TAKING TO IMPLEMENT THAT POLICY? WHAT IS HIS REAL CONTRIBUTION TO THE SOLUTION OF THE COMMUNAL TANGLE? IS HE NOT BY HIS SPEECHES MAKING THE TASK OF THOSE WHO WANT A REAL SETTLEMENT MORE AND MORE DIFFICULT? IS HE STRENGTHENING THE FAITH OF INDIANS IN BRITISH INTENTIONS?

New Manners in Controversy

In ordinary circumstances, I should not have taken notice of what Mr Jinnah said about me or the Conference over which I presided at Bombay and I should certainly not have followed his example by lowering the level of public controversy by indulging in personalities.

Let me, however, say that I am not aware of any kind of wire-pullers Congress or non-Congress and during my long public life I have never known anybody laying any kind of trap for me.

These are clap-trap methods of controversy intended to create a prejudice against those from whom you differ and I am surprised that Mr Amery, a seasoned politician and one accustomed to dealing with public controversies should have even referred to what Mr Jinnah said about the wire-pullers having laid a trap for me.

Not a Word

I can only assume that like several Europeans in India who have been publicly in their speeches saying that the Bombay Conferences was really inspired by Congress, Mr Amery is obsessed with the same idea.

I can only say that not a word passed between Mr Gandhi or any other Congress leader and myself at any time either in correspondence or in personal conversation with regard to the idea of holding the Bombay Conference or to the charter of the resolution it should adopt.

I may however, say that when the presidentship of the Conference was offered to me, I made it a condition precedent to my accepting it that at the Conference no kind of communal issue should be raised.

I was more than gratified that men like Mr Savarkar and Dr Moonje who were present at the Conference played the game and accepted the resolution.

They are men with strong party convictions and yet for the sake of a settlement they subordinated their party feelings to the common goal we had in view I should have expected in fairness that Mr Amery would have drawn the attention of the house to this fact.

Let me say once again that I take the fullest responsibility for my judgment—it may be right or it may be wrong—but I have never in my life felt that anybody had laid a trap for me—neither a Secretary of State nor a Political leader in India.

Mr Amery has appealed to me and my friends not to crease from our efforts to concentrate first and foremost on bringing the contending elements together or on building up a strong Centre Party of men who are prepared to put India first. I shall be absolutely frank.

I BELIEVE MR AMERY'S INDISCREET AND UNFORTUNATE SPEECHES ON THE SUBJECT HAVE DONE THE WORST SERVICE TO US AND HE HAS NO BUSINESS TO MAKE THAT PIOUS

APPEAL TO US WHEN HE HIMSELF HAS DONE NOTHING TO PROMOTE UNITY AMONG THE CONTENDING ELEMENTS IN INDIA.

As regards our continuing these efforts, I shall be very glad if those in India who parrot like repeat Mr Amery's pious sentiments will do something to show that they are in earnest about it.

So far as I am concerned, I do not want any encouragement from any quarter nor shall I feel discouraged in carrying out my convictions merely because the Secretary of State who is credited with having good intentions has the unfortunate knack of expressing those good intentions in such language.

Central Party Trap

As regards the formation of a Centre Party all that I wish to say is that I do not see any prospect of such a party coming into existence of functioning effectively so long as the present policy of Mr Amery and of the Government of India is maintained.

At the same time I should not like to stand in the way of those of my friends in Bombay and elsewhere who have a faith in the formation of such a party. I would wish them every success but let them take steps and not merely repeat what Mr Amery has been saying from a distance of 6000 miles.

I am very doubtful if a Centre Party was brought into existence it would fare better at the hands of Mr Amery of the Government of India.

They could dispose of it easily by saying that it did not contain an adequate number of Muslims or the Depressed Classes, that it had not yet developed a sufficient backing in the country and that it was bound to meet with opposition on the part of the Congress or the Muslim League—a fear which seems to have un-nerved and indeed paralysed both Mr Amery and the Government of India.—AP

19. Viceroy's Letter to UP Governor Regarding Proposed National Defence Council, 19 June 1941

Correspondence with Governor of UP and his Secretary, Linlithgow Papers, 1941, Acc. No. 2237, NAI.

[Secret and Personal]

My Dear Hallett,[1]

You will have gathered from my circular telegram of 19th May the general line of the proposals which I then contemplated putting to the Cabinet in connection with the expansion of my Council and the association of non-official opinion in this country in a greater degree than at present with the prosecution of the war. I would like to take the opportunity to say again how very grateful I am to you for your most helpful comment which at the time I let Amery have so that he and the Cabinet should know your view. I am glad to say that I have now heard that the Cabinet have given general approval. The effect is a small expansion of my Council plus the establishment of a War Advisory Committee of the type which I had in view last autumn but which I will now rename 'National Defence Council'.

2. I need not trouble you with the details of what I contemplate in regard to my Council, for there are various points still to be settled. But broadly speaking I have it in mind to create

three new portfolios of Supply, Information, and Civil Defence and Man-Power, into the last of which I shall put ARP and connected questions. For your very personal information I am proposing to ask Sir Akbar Hydari to accept one of these portfolios—I am, for obvious reasons, keeping this entirely secret: and while he is getting on and is probably not quite the man he was, if I can get him to serve, I think that he will represent a valuable reinforcement and one too not so closely associated with the Muslim League as to make various trouble with Jinnah likely. For a further vacancy which may occur (this again is most secret) I have it in mind to approach Kunzru. I do not know whether Kunzru would be willing to serve, and I recognize that he might well be rather tiresome as a colleague. But he again, if I took him into my Council, would, I am sure, be a reassurance to many moderate Hindus that the progressive moderate point of view was strongly represented.

3. But what will of course be of greater interest to you is the National Defence Council. I am anxious, I need not say, that this body should be as generally representative as possible not only of Provinces and of functions but of the minor political parties and the like. There is of course no hope of getting Congress to serve. The Muslim League attitude and Jinnah's general non-co-operation present one with a further problem. On that, for your personal information, I have it in mind to take the change of trouble with Jinnah, invite the four Muslim Premiers to serve and, if possible, secure their acceptance before I give any hint to Jinnah of my intentions. It is very difficult to judge: but on the whole I am inclined to doubt whether he would want to quarrel with the four Premiers (assuming them to be willing to serve) as well as with Government: and since the Premiers are after all the heads of governments functioning normally under the Act, there is no reason why they should not accept an invitation. Personal jealousies may of course complicate the matter. Sikander, Huq, Saadulla or the Prime Minister of Sind may all of them feel that they ought to be in my Executive Council rather than in the National Defence Council. But I hope that relatively petty consideration will not stand in the way.

4. I contemplate a Council of about 30. Of these about 9 will be Princes. The remainder, say, 20 will be designed to represent, firstly, Provinces: secondly, Functions (the Cabinet have laid particular emphasis on the importance of securing functional representation of labour, etc.). I must, too, try in making up my team to get in representatives of minor minorities and of the Political parties—the Mahasabha, the Liberals, the Sikhs, and others. The Council would meet about every two months, probably for two or three days (possibly four days): the Governor-General would preside (or in his absence the vice-President of the Executive Council). The proceedings would be *in camera*: there will be an oath of secrecy: and we contemplate on each occasion a review, first, of the war position since the last meeting of the Defence Council; secondly, a review of the position in relation to Supply; thirdly, possibly a review of the position as regards ARP and other aspects of Civil Defence. Those attending would be at liberty to ask questions and to send up in advance points which they wanted dealt with (I have no doubt that in practice we ought to be able to cover the great majority of those points in the general statements as regards the war position, the supply position, the propaganda position, and other things, for it is of course important, unless the whole machine of government here is to be badly clogged, that questions and points, for discussion should be confined to matters of real importance and should not deal with petty details). Members would receive no pay, would be placed in Article 17 of the Warrant of Procedure (unless they were already in a higher number), and would receive Ist class travelling and subsistence allowances for their journeys to and fro and for the period of the meeting of the Defence council.

5. A very important aspect of this matter is the relation of the members of the Council to war work in the Province and to the Provincial Government. The Governors of the Section 93 Provinces have, speaking as a whole, been opposed to the appointment of non-official advisers, and I personally accept the arguments in that matter as entirely cogent, as have also His Majesty's Government. Had non-official advisers existed, they might of course very usefully have been nominated as provincial delegates to the War Council. But as that is not the case the choice of individuals from a Province assumes an importance even greater than before. It is essential if the Council is to pull its weight that those of its members who represent a Province should be in close touch with the provincial war effort and should be able to come up to Delhi or Simla forearmed with the questions they wish to ask or to investigate on behalf of their Province: and equally that they should be able to return after the meeting of the Council fully primed as to the position on these and on other questions of general interest.

6. It may be assumed that the persons chosen from a Province will normally be persons who enjoy the confidence and the respect of the Governor (and his advisers). The suggestion which I should like to put to you and which I am putting also to other Governors is that it should be laid down that the representatives appointed or drawn from each Province shall, prior to attending a meeting of the Defence Council, formally run over the ground with the Governor and his advisers as well perhaps as with the Governor personally; and that on their return to the Province after the conclusion of the meeting they should again be invited to discuss with the Governor and with his advisers what has passed in the War Advisory Council. It ought, I should think, to be possible for them also with the background they will have secured, to be of valuable help to the Provincial War Committees or War Councils as well as in making speeches in their Province. I am inclined to suggest further that it should be laid down that just as they must discuss with the Governor and with his advisers before and after attending a meeting of the Central National Defence Council, so before and after those meetings they should have confidential discussions with the Provincial Defence Committee or War Council, or whatever organization of that type there may be. If we could get such an arrangement generally accepted, it would, I think, be well calculated to blunt the edge of the criticism that public opinion, and even Defence Committees and the like in Provinces are much out of touch with what is being done to further the prosecution of the war, and on the other side that the highest authorities in the Government of India, are not alive to, or in touch with, provincial criticisms? I should greatly welcome your comment on these suggestions.

7. Now for the matter of personnel. It will be obvious that, given the relatively small size of the representation available for the whole of British India, the number of individuals who come from any Province cannot be large. I am only too conscious, too of the difficulty which Governors are likely to experience in suggesting names, more particularly since Congress is non-cooperating and since there is at least a possibility that the Muslim League equally may be reluctant to cooperate or to allow the members of their organization to accept appointment. I should be most grateful if you can let me have by telegraph a short list of possible names which I could consider above circumstances make it possible for me to invite Kunzru to serve in my Executive Council, that will give substantial representation in the expanded government to the United Provinces. Other names which I have had in mind from the United Provinces are Maharaj Singh (who, if selected, would incidentally represent the Indian Christians better I think than anyone who comes to mind, and who has the further advantage of being in touch with Congress elements and of representing indirectly the smaller landowners); and Srivastava who not only been a Minister in the United Provinces under the old dispensation but could

reasonably be regarded as a substantial representative of Indian Commerce and incidentally a representative of the Mahasabha who included him in one of the lists which they sent me last year. It is difficult to make any suggestions about the Muslims until one knows better where one stands with Jinnah. Let me only say on that point that I see no reason why we should not approach individual Muslim Leaguers whom we may regard as well qualified for appointment. We may take it for granted that the moment such approaches are made whether in the United Provinces or elsewhere, there will be an appeal to Jinnah for a ruling as to whether those invited to serve may accept the invitation. If Jinnah (as previously in the case of the War Committees) climbs down and raises no objection to their serving, so much the better. If, on the other hand, he is adamant and refuses to allow them to serve and they accept his mandate, it will at any rate be clear that the under-representation of Muslims (or rather of the Muslim League) in the National Defence Council is not any fault of ours. As to the total number of places to be filled from the United Provinces it is, as you will understand, very difficult for me to say—I shall have to try to strike a balance when I have the suggestions of all the Provinces before me and am in a position to make up my list: but I would hope that you would be safe for two at any rate, and on the list so far as I can envisage it today I should have thought that both Maharaj Singh and Srivastava had an excellent chance of being included. From my point of view they have the additional advantage of counting against functional representation in addition to representing the Province.

8. I would only add that while these changes are well within the four walls of the declaration of that August, I do not propose to suggest for a moment that they represent a solution even a temporary solution of the political problem. The wise line, I am certain to take is that with the intensification of the war and the greater burden now falling upon the Central Government, some expansion of that Government is unavoidable, and that in making that expansion our anxiety to give ever-increasing representation and weight to non-official elements and to see that these elements are represented, since we cannot look for the active help of the parties, by public men of high standing and reputation, is manifested by the choice we are making (it is my intention, quite apart from the actual expansion to adopt exactly the same principle in filling any other vacancies that may occur in my council whether in the immediate or in the remoter future, subject to the maintenance of the necessary statutory service minimum).

9. I have set out the general positions very fully and frankly for your personal information only at this stage. If there are any comments that you care to let me have or any enquiries you would like to make you have only to telegraph and I will do my best to answer. I should greatly welcome an early reply since I am anxious if I can to make some announcement by the end of the month and though I shall not necessarily publish the names of the gentlemen to serve in the National Defence Council simultaneously with my announcement of the expansion of the Executive Council. I should like to be able to do so very shortly afterwards. I should be most grateful if you would let me have a reply by telegram on the various points taken in this letter. I need not say how anxious I am that this delicate matter should be kept wholly secret for the present even though that may mean some delay in our actually approaching individuals.

Yours sincerely,
Linlithgow

---

[1] Sir Maurice Garnier Hallett, Governor of United Provinces.

20. Expansion of the Viceroy's Council: Government Communiqué, New Delhi, 21 July 1941

Indian Annual Register, 1941, Vol. II, pp. 300–1.

The expansion of the Viceroy's Council and the constitution of a National Defence Council were announced in a communiqué issued from New Delhi on the 21st July 1941.

'As a result of the increased pressure of work in connection with the war,' says the communiqué, 'it has been decided to enlarge the Executive Council of the Governor-General of India in order to permit the separation of the portfolios of Law and Supply and Commerce and Labour; the division of the present portfolio of Education, Health and Lands into separate portfolios of Education, Health and Lands and Indians Overseas; and the creation of the portfolios of Information and Civil Defence.'

His Majesty the King has approved the following appointments to the five new seats on the Council:

Member of the Supply—Sir Hormusji P. Mody, KBE, MLA (Central)
Member for Information—The Rt Hon Sir Akbar Hydari, PC
Member for Civil Defence—Dr E. Raghavendra Rao
Member for Labour—Malik Sir Firoz Khan Noon, KCIE
Member for Indians Overseas—Mr M.S. Aney, MLA (Central)

For the vacancies which will occur when Sir Muhammad Zafrulla Khan and Sir Girija Sankar Bajpai take up the posts to which they have recently been appointed, His Majesty has approved the appointment of:

Member of Law—Sir Sultan Ahmed
Member of Education, Health and Lands—Mr Nalini Ranjan Sarkar, MLA

Members of the present Viceroy's Council who will continue to be members of the new Council are:

HE the Commander-in-Chief, Sir Reginald Maxwell, Sir Andrew Clow, Sir Jeremy Raisman and Sir A. Ramaswami Mudaliar.

The National Defence Council

In pursuance of the desire of His Majesty's Government to associate Indian non-official opinion as fully as possible with the prosecution of the war, approval, on the recommendation of the Viceroy, has also been given to the establishment of a National Defence Council, the first meeting of which will take place next month.

The Council, the strength of which will be about 30 members, will include representatives of Indian States as well as of Provinces and of other elements in the national life of British India in its relation to the war effort. The following will be the members from British India:

Dr B.R. Ambedkar, MLA
The Hon Maulavi Saiyid Sir Muhammad Saadulla, MLA, Chief Minister of Assam
The Hon Mr A.K. Fazlul Huq, MLA, Chief Minister of Bengal
Sir Muhammad Ahmad Said Khan, Nawab of Chhatari, KCSI, ECIE, MBE
Kumararajah Sir Muthiah Chettiyar of Chettinad, MLA
The Hon Mr Maharajadhiraja of Darbhanga, KCIE

Mr Ramrao Madhavrao Deshmukh, MLA
Lieut Col Sir Henry Gidney, MLA
Sir Cowasjee Jehangir, Bart, KCIE, OBE, MLA
Raja Bahadur of Kallikote, MLA
The Hon Malik Khuda Baksh Khan, MLA
Mr Jamnadas M. Mehta, MLA
Mr G.B. Morton, OBE
Mr Biren Mukherjee
Lieutenant Sardar Naunihal Singh Man, MBE, MLA
Begum Shah Nawaz, MLA
The Hon Khan Bahadur Major Sirdar Sir Sikandar Hyat Khan, KBE, MLA, Premier of the Punjab
Rao Bahadur M.C. Rajah
Professor E. Ahmad Shah
The Hon Khan Bahadur Allah Baksh Muhammad Umar Soomro, OBE, MLA, Chief Minister of Sind
Sir Jwala Prasad Srivastava, MLA
Khan Bahadur Sir Muhammad Usman, KCIE

Object Underlying Expansion

Described as 'non-political and non-communal', the expansion now announced will result in a council with three officials and eight non-officials, as against the existing Council of four officials and three non-officials excluding the Commander-in-Chief.

It is claimed that the announcement implements the offer of last August substantially, so far as the present attitude of the major political parties permits. It is emphasized that there has been no change of policy since the August offer was made: that the object of the present expansion is efficient government of a country at war; and that the changes made are within the framework of the constitution and without prejudice to the future constitutional settlement by agreement among the political parties.

By way of explanation of the policy underlying the expansion as well as the constitution of the national Defence Council, it is pointed out that they should be regarded purely as a war measure and not as intended to satisfy any political demand. No political demand is excluded or prejudged by what is being done. All the promises made in the August offer still stand. The individuals to be appointed, it is pointed out, are persons whose status as representative Indians is beyond question. They will hold office at His Majesty's pleasure.

21. No Statement by Mahatma Gandhi on the Communiqué

CWMG, Vol. LXXIV, pp. 180–2.

Interview to *The Hindu*

22 July 1941

When I asked Gandhiji, who was at work on his charkha when I called on him, whether he had read the communiqué, he said he had not and asked me to read it. With his hands busy operating his charkha, stopping only now and then to wind the thread, Gandhiji listened as I read the communiqué including the personnel of the National Defence Council. When

I concluded reading, Gandhiji looked up and, laughing loudly, asked whether I had finished. I said I had, and asked him whether he wished to say anything. Gandhiji said that he had no statement to make and added:

I would rather observe silence, Monday silence, whatever it may mean and you can say so in the papers.

When I asked him whether it could be taken that he was not interested in the announcement, he said:

I can't say so. That will be pedantic.

Then I handed him a sheet of paper containing a few questions drafted by me earlier. Gandhiji read the questions and remarked:

I can answer some of these questions. But I don't know what purpose it will serve.

Pressed further to say whatever he wished, Gandhiji replied to my first question, whether the Government of India's announcement affected the stand taken by the Congress and whether it met the Congress demand to any extent.

The announcement does not affect the stand taken by the Congress; nor does it meet the Congress demand to any extent.

To my next question whether the members of the AICC, if released from jail, will be permitted to consider the present situation in the light of recent developments in the country, Gandhiji replied:

I understand you to mean whether I shall permit AICC members, if they are released, to consider the present situation. If that is the meaning of your question, I can at once say that I have no authority to prevent members of the AICC from doing anything they wish. The authority given to me by the AICC does not permit my interference with the fullest freedom of its members. And in any case the body that gave me the authority can at any time refuse it or withdraw it.

I certainly consider the demand made by the Mysore Legislative Council[1] as not only modest but any day opportune.

When I asked him whether the present situation in the country was an opportune one for embarking on the programme, Gandhiji added:

As a matter of fact it should have been made long ago. The present situation in the country cannot be allowed to interfere with elementary justice being done to Harijans.

When I asked him whether non-arrest of satyagrahis shouting anti-war slogans can be construed, as some people seemed to, as amounting to grant of liberty to preach against war, Gandhiji said:

There is no warrant for the belief implied in the opinion. Some Provincial Governments have clearly stated that they do not want to arrest unimportant members. But they are arresting those whom they consider important enough if they recite anti-war slogans.

The Hindu, 24 July 1941

---

[1] The reference is to the demand relating to the issue of Harijans' right to temple entry.

22. Non-party Leaders' Conference at Poona: Large Number of Men Accepted Invitation

Amrita Bazar Patrika, 15 July 1941.

A very large number of prominent leaders from all parts of the country have accepted the letters of invitation addressed by Kunwar Sir Jagdish Prasad to attend the next non-party leaders' conference at Poona on July 26 and 27 under the Presidentship of the Rt Hon Sir Tej Bahadur Sapru.

Among those who are likely to attend the conference are:

Sir Mirza Ismail[1], Sir M. Visweswarayya, Sir Ardeshir Dalal, Mr Chunilal B. Mehta, Hon Mr Shantidas Askuran, Sir Purshottam Das Thakurdas, Mr M.S. Aney, Mr V.D. Savarkar, Mr Srinivasan, Editor of *The Hindu*, Sir N.N. Sarcar, Dr B.S. Moonje, Dr Shyama Prasad Mookerjee, Mr H.C. Mukherjee, Dr Sachidananda Sinha, Hon Mr V.V. Kalikar, Mr K.C. Neogi, Sir P. Srivastava, Rani Phool Kumari of Sherkot, Hon Pandit Hirdayanath Kunzru, Hon Mr P.S. Sapru, Raj Sahib of Ajodhya, Raja Sahib of Oel, Raja Saheb of Tirwa, Raja Maheswar Dayal Seth of Kotra, Rai Bahadur Lala Ram Saran Das, Sardar Sant Singh, MLA (Central), Sardar Ujjal Singh, MLA, Raj Bahadur Sohanlal, MLA, Dr Paranjpye, Hon Mr Srinarain Mehta, Mr Venkatram Sastry, Sir Gokul Chand Narang, Mr Jadhav, ex-Minister Bombay, Sir Jogendra Singh, Hon Sardar Boota Singh, Mr Mehr Chand Khanna of the NWFP, Mr Jagannath Agarwal, Mr J.N. Basu, MLA, Mr P.D. Das, Sardar Mohan Singh, Sardar Beldeo Singh, MLA, Sardar Santokh Singh, MLA, Dewan Bahadur Haribilas Sarda, Mr B. Shivarao, Rai Bahadur Mukund Lal Puri, Babu Sham Nandan Sahai of Bihar, Sardar Jogindar Singh Mann, MLA, Sardar Ajit Singh, MLA, Mr A.S.N. Moorthy, President of the National Liberal Federation, Orissa, Kunwar Guru Narain, Lala Hari Ram Seth, Raja Sri Ram and others.

Acceptances are being received every day, and it is expected that the conference this time will be more comprehensive comprising larger number of leaders than those who participated in the last Bombay conference.

---

[1] Sir Mirza Ismail (1883–1959) was Dewan of Mysore from 1926 to 1941.

23. Sapru's Speech at the Non-party Leaders' Conference, Poona, 26 July 1941 (Extracts)

Indian Annual Register, 1941, Vol. II, pp. 260–3.

The Non-Party Political Leaders' Conference commenced at Poona on the 26th July 1941. Sir Tej Bahadur Sapru, in his presidential address, gave a lead to the Conference as to the attitude it should adopt on the problems facing the country.

Sir Tej Bahadur spoke for sixty minutes and severely criticized the Secretary of State and the British Government in regard to their attitude towards India's demands and particularly, the announcement of the expansion of the Viceroy's Executive Council 'to meet the pressure of work created by the war.' Dealing with the allocation of portfolios to the new Indian members, Sir Tej Bahadur Sapru said: 'The meaning of it is obvious. The three portfolios, Defence, Home and Finance, are portfolios with which power and initiation of policy are associated. We resent very strongly, and I think there is hardly any Indian who will not resent it, that in regard to the distribution of portfolios, Indians should have been dealt with so unfairly. We were particularly anxious that the Defence Portfolio should be transferred to us.' Sir Tej maintained that anyone of the eight Indian members was competent enough to hold any of the three portfolios now withheld from Indian hands.

The President welcomed the inclusion of these eight Indians in the Executive Council of the Viceroy and deprecated any idea of rejection. He said: 'I am not a believer in the ascetic idea that we should give up everything. We should seize as much power as comes into our hands and ask for more.'

Task before the New Members

Discussing the task ahead of the new Executive Councillors, the President said:

> Their primary task will be to render every assistance in the prosecution of the war, but while doing so, they cannot forget the internal situation in the country. They will have to bring pressure to bear upon the holders of those portfolios of power which have been withheld from them, as peaceful conditions have got to be restored inside the country and the time and energy of the people which, at the present moment, are being wasted in fruitless slogans and cries must be harnessed towards constructive work. They will have to advocate and press for a policy of conciliation. It can be no pleasure to anyone of us that many thousands of our countrymen should be in jail. It is true that they have gone to jail because they wanted to go to jail, they were obliging enough to go to jail, but I still maintain that in the existing conditions no Government can afford for a long time to defy or ignore the pressure of public opinion in this matter, and whatever may be my views with regard to the Satyagraha Movement—I am a confirmed sinner in that respect—I do hold very strongly that so long as thousands of men are in jail, so long will the Indian mind be diverted from constructive channels to fruitless channels. It will be up to the members of the new Executive Council to discuss this question with their colleagues and do their best to restore normal peaceful condition. I have no doubt that they are men strong enough to do it. A mere expression of hope by them will not do. What is necessary is that those who are now going to the Executive Council should interest themselves in this matter.

The President referred to the appointment of a separate Minister in the United Kingdom to deal with matters connected with reconstruction of society after the war and said that similarly the work of reconstruction in India should be taken in hand; reconstruction of our political life, particularly our economic life.

Sir Tej Bahadur Sapru also emphasized the need for the Indian members of the expanded Executive Council to interest themselves in bringing about communal harmony in the country and said:

> I think the greatest service which men who have been appointed to the Executive Council can render to the country is to take some steps, with the authority belonging to their office, with the resources at their disposal to bring about harmony and goodwill between the warring communities of India. It should be made to appear to the people of this country that the Government are really anxious that the communities, which have been warring so far, should bury the hatchet and should approach each other with a view to establishing harmonious relations and an atmosphere of peace. Unfortunately, the history of our country has been full of despair in regard to this matter. I do not think we can allow the communal situation as it has developed in certain parts of the country to deteriorate still further. I have always maintained that in a matter of this character it is not only our duty to render every service that we can, but also it is the duty of the duly constituted Government to place itself at the head of the movement so that the people will understand that the Government is genuinely anxious that there should be peace and harmony in this country.

The Bombay Conference

Earlier in his speech, Sir Tej Bahadur Sapru exhaustively reviewed the events that occurred since the Bombay meeting of the Conference in March last. He recalled the Bombay Resolution and said:

> According to the Resolution passed by the Conference, I submitted a copy of the Resolution, together with a memorandum to the Viceroy and subsequently interviewed him and had a long and friendly talk on the various subjects covered by the Resolution. Events have moved very fast since then on the international side. As you all know the war has been approaching nearer India and there is not one amongst us who does not realize the danger to which India is exposed. If for no other reason at least for the reason that it is up to us that we should make the best of our opportunities and contribute the utmost we can towards the war effort. We had a vivid realization of the dangers at that time when we met in Bombay, and it was because of that feeling that we ventured to tell the British Government and the Government of India that the policy they had hitherto followed was a very narrow and short-sighted one which circumstances in the country did not justify and which would not tend to arouse enthusiasm for war effort. We said so in plain and unvarnished language and that is our conviction even now.

Sir Tej Bahadur Sapru, proceeding, said, that the Bombay Conference was exposed to criticism on certain sides, but it also met with a substantial measure of support from all sides. He had carefully followed the trend of opinion as expressed in the Press throughout India, 'I do not think' he said, 'I am putting the case too high when I say that the vast majority of Indian newspapers took a very fair view of the Conference at Bombay and gave it a substantial measure of support even though some papers might have thought that we did not go far enough.'

Sir Tej recalled the debate in the House of Commons in April last and said that the stand taken by the Bombay Conference had found supporters in the British Parliament, in persons like Sir George Schuster and Sir Stanley Reed. The British Press also, generally speaking, was sympathetic. There was a growing feeling in England that in the midst of many preoccupations, His Majesty's Government had got to tackle the Indian problem and tackle it in a generous and bold, statesman-like spirit.

Repudiating the suggestion made in certain quarters that the Conference was sailing under false colours, that it was a pale shadow of the Congress or the Hindu Mahasabha, Sir Tej said:

> There is no iota of truth in the statement that this Conference was called in the interests of any particular political party. It was a Conference of independent men, who thought that, in the circumstances that had arisen in the country, it was clearly their duty to give a warning to the Government. The Conference had also been assailed on the ground that it was a gathering of old, estimable people, who occupied no representative character. We never claimed a representative character. We do not say that we have been elected by any class of men. As citizens and taxpayers of this country, we had a right to say what should be done and what should not be done. Speaking for myself, I say I represent myself, which is saying a great deal more than what many people can say of themselves. A leader is yet to be born in India who can lead me by the nose. (Cheers)...

Progress Should Not be Hindered

Replying to the argument by certain officials and politicians that it was absurd for anyone to demand or to expect during the war that anything big could be hoped for or achieved, unless the two major political Parties came to an agreement, the President said:

> The position we took up then was that nothing would please us more if the two Parties could come to a settlement at once. Nothing would please us more if the two Parties could come to a settlement with the British Government. We said it then and we say it now that everyone of us will

> step aside. (Cheers) We are not working in a spirit of rivalry. But we maintained at that time, and we maintain now, that events should not be allowed to wait upon the pleasure of any particular Party, howsoever strong it may be, or leader, howsoever distinguished he may be. The rest of the country should not be penalized, because certain individuals do not come to a settlement between themselves. It was in this spirit the Bombay Resolution was passed.

Sir Tej Bahadur Sapru referred to Mr Amery's speech in the House of Commons in April last and said:

> When I read the speech for the first time, I was disappointed, but when I read it for the second time I found that Mr Amery was emphatic that nothing was to be expected in India until the two major communities settled their differences, and when I further read it I found Mr Amery's anxiety in advising us that the best thing for us to do was not to go on with the Conference, but to bring about a Central Party and a rival party. I saw he was on the way to surrender. I do not think he has surrendered. It would be giving a false impression if I suggested that Mr Amery has surrendered. British politicians do not easily surrender, and particularly Conservatives, and Mr Amery is a very distinguished member of the Conservative Party. But they have got to yield to the pressure of public opinion, both in England and India and that they must yield sooner or later. I have no doubt in my mind. I am clear, that if we go on pressing our demand, the time is not very distant, even for Mr Amery, to find a suitable formula and say that for these reasons he is taking another step.

Sir Tej Bahadur Sapru recalled the background of the Bombay meeting and also referred to the background of the present meeting and said that when they met in Bombay there was a general feeling of depression and frustration all over the country. People did not know what to do. People felt that there was no reasonable likelihood of the two major parties coming to an early settlement, or the British Government or the Government of India showing any signs of mobility. But in the month of July 1941 His Majesty's Government in England and the Government of India had shown some signs of mobility.

Indianization of Executive Council

The President recalled the Bombay Resolution and referred to the criticism in certain quarters that it had suggested certain impracticable or revolutionary proposals and said:

> There was not a single section in the Government of India Act which required that a certain number of persons to the Executive Council should be Indians and certain others Europeans. The statutory qualification laid down was that there should be three members who had put in ten years' service under the Crown in India. This did not lay down that they should be Europeans only or Indians only. Therefore if to-day His Majesty's Government decided to appoint all eleven members to the Executive Council from among Indians it would no more be irregular or constitutional than it would be if they decided to appoint eleven Europeans. I, therefore, do not see how exception can be taken to our proposal for appointment of all members from among Indians. I can understand the criticism if it is argued that it is impolitic to do so (cheers). The policy of the British Government at the present moment is that there must be a certain element of British Services in the Executive council which, in its turn, implies that the British Government is not prepared to trust you. We frankly resent this. We say if the British Government has not been wise so far, although it should have been wise long ago, it is time that during the present war, when the greatest challenge has been thrown at its supremacy, it should prove wise. There is nothing unconstitutional in appointing an Indian National Government, particularly when this Government is going to be responsible to the Crown during the duration of the war, just as the present members are....

Transfer of Powers

Sir Tej Bahadur Sapru, proceeding, dealt with the recent expansion of the Viceroy's Executive Council. He said that the changes had been effected on the ground that it was an administrative need. They were being introduced to relieve pressure of work in certain Departments. 'It has been frankly admitted,' Sir Tej said, 'by the Secretary of State and others that no merit can be claimed for these changes on the constitutional side. Indeed, the Secretary of State has been over-anxious to state publicly that the policy of His Majesty's Government on the constitutional side remains unaffected. Not taking that statement at its face value, one is tempted to ask whether it is only in these Departments which were hitherto held by Indians that there is congestion of work and whether the Departments which were held by English members of the Civil Service, namely, Defence. Home and Finance, had not had additional work. If the departmental work is examined, I should be surprised if it did not turn out to be the case that the work in the Defence, Finance and Communications Departments has increased. I should be reluctant to believe that the work in Public Health and Education Departments has so much increased that it has necessitated a splitting of that portfolio into several portfolios. Finance, Home and Defence Portfolios should have been divided and sub-divided. This process of division should not have been confined to the Departments, which were held by Indians. The meaning of it is obvious. The three Portfolios of Finance, Defence and Home are portfolios with which initiation of policy is associated. The Thomas Committee on Indian Defence had reported that it was the policy of His majesty's Government that the defence of India should be, in an increasing measure, the concern of India. How is it going to be the concern of India when Indians are deprived of the chance of studying the problems?'

Acknowledging the ability of the eight Indian members who had been appointed the Executive Council, Sir Tej Bahadur Sapru referred to the Portfolio of Information given to Sir Akbar Hydari and said that Sir Akbar was hitherto in-charge of Finance and Communications in Hyderabad State. Why should he not have been given the Portfolio of Defence or Communication, he asked. Similarly, Mr N.R. Sarkar, who was well-known in business circles and who was in-charge of the finances of Bengal, could have been given the Finance Portfolio of the Government of India. Dr E. Raghavendra Rao was a Minister in the Central Provinces, was the Home Member of the Province and then acted as the Governor of the Province. The machinery of Law and Order did not break down under his administration. Sir Tej added, 'I for myself am not willing to believe that the genius of Sir Reginald Maxwell is so indispensable for the Government of India that he should not be replaced by Dr Raghavendra Rao. When I look at this aspect of the question, I am tempted to say that mere multiplication of the number of Indian members will not produce that psychological change in the Indian mind.'

In conclusion, Sir Tej Bahadur declared that until the objective of the Conference was achieved they would have to hold repeated conference of this kind from to time to time. The Conference then adjourned....

24. 'Want of Good Faith' Charge Against Amery: Adding One Depressed Classes Member to Viceroy's Council 'Cannot Hurt', Says Ambedkar

Bombay Chronicle, 1 August 1941.

'Depressed classes regard that exclusion from the Viceroy's Reconstituted Council as an outrage and breach of faith,' says Dr B.R. Ambedkar, Leader of the Depressed Classes, in a cable addressed to the Secretary of State for India, Mr L.S. Amery.

Want of Good Faith

The cable adds: 'Your flouting 60 millions Depressed Classes altogether and giving 43 per cent representation to Muslims, which is nearly equal to that of Hindus, is astounding. Government appears mortgaged to some communities only. After solemnly recognizing Depressed Classes as important distinct element in Indian national life after insisting on their consent to constitutional changes essential, after exploiting their cooperation in war, their exclusion from the Council bespeaks want of good faith on your post.

'Protesting in the interest and name of Depressed Classes, personally I have never asked, depended or had support from British. I can do without it in future. You are absolutely free in your choice. I want justice to Depressed Classes. I warn you Depressed Classes are not prepared to surrender their right to representation in Council. I strongly urge you to recognize the same. Adding one cannot hurt.'—AP

25. Newspaper Report on Immediate Issues

Bombay Chronicle, 27 August 1941.

Future of Indian Defence Council
Lively Speculations in Official and Non-official Circles in Simla
All-India Radio Gives One-sided View of India's Reactions to Churchill–Roosevelt Broadcast

Simla, 24 August.

Simla has been buzzing with intense activity during the last few days, the imbroglio in Punjab Ministerialist politics, the Indo-Burma talks behind closed doors, the dissection of the Government of India's financial policy at the Public Accounts Committee and various other conferences. As the Viceroy is also back from his long, though uneventful, tour it has given added interest to the political and other activities in the capital. An important visitor to Simla last week was the Nawab of Chhattari, the Prime Minister designate of Hyderabad, who met both the Viceroy and the Governor of the Punjab. His talks are said largely to have related to the recent sensational developments in Muslim League politics. Sir Sikandar had an interview with the Viceroy before he left for Bombay with his two Muslim colleagues in the Punjab Cabinet. At the moment political circles in the Punjab are anxiously awaiting the outcome of the Bombay meeting for upon it depends the course of politics in the provinces in the next few months. Important developments are expected at the coming meeting of the Punjab Assembly, partly because of the Sikh opposition which is gathering strength and partly because of the new turn in Muslim League politics which is bound to reflect itself in the party alignments in the Legislature.

Uncertain Future

Indications of what may be expected during the coming autumn session of the Central Legislature are already available in the talks here among members now in Simla for various meetings. The Muslim League party is awaiting Mr Jinnah's instructions whether they should boycott the Legislature as a protest against the Council expansion or whether they should stay and show their resentment in other ways. Even if they decide to stay, their role is expected to be one of increased opposition to the Government in a manner more pronounced than ever before. As they are the largest single party left in the House, it would be interesting to watch their activities. The Nationalist party, formerly led by Mr Aney, is in a peculiarly difficult position. One section of it, particularly the Bengal group, which is strongly nationalist, does not seem to be happy over Mr Aney's decision. There are members like Sirdar Sant Singh in it who are strongly opposed to the 'expansion' proposals and cannot be expected to change their attitude merely because of the presence of their ex-leader on the Treasury Bench. While efforts are being made to reorganize the party so as to include Muslim and other members, there are also proposals to make it a limb of the All-India Hindu League. Its future is now in the balance. So also is that of the newly formed party of Independents led by Sir Henry Gidney, as there are already reports of defections. There is reason to think that though the number of elected members attending the session may be comparatively small, it will have a fairly exciting time—all the more so if the Government decides to introduce a supplementary Finance bill for additional taxation.

Churchill Declaration

The Eight-point Roosevelt–Churchill declaration—particularly the commentary of Mr Attlee which accompanied it—came as a pleasant surprise to Simla. It is not unlikely that the British Government anticipated fully the reactions in this country. In any case official circles in Simla are reported to have paid more than ordinary attention to the comments in his country on the declaration. The Secretary of State must by now be fully aware of the universal feeling in India that Mr Winston Churchill should follow up this declaration by an unequivocal statement assuming the people of India that the declaration applies in every respect to their future also. A broadcast by the Viceroy on the subject would be helpful also if he can take an early opportunity to do it on behalf of His Majesty's Government. It is not known however, if anything in this direction can be expected in the near future to satisfy Indian demands.

In this connection, there is a good deal of criticism of the policy pursued by the All-India Radio. In giving Indian press comments on the Roosevelt–Churchill declaration the All-India Radio took a one-sided view and made no mention whatever of the demand made in every Indian paper that if, as was stated in the declaration, the principle of self-determination was accepted by the British Government. It should be made clear that it would apply equally to India. It is only fair to ask that if the All-India Radio wishes to give a summary of Indian Press comments; it should be impartial and fully representative and not one-sided.

New Cabinet

Only one new member of the Viceroy's Council has so far taken charge—Sir H.P. Mody. He has already settled down to his new duties as the head of the Supply organization. The general anticipation in political circles is that though from the political point of view Sir Homi may not be able to influence the Government policy, his drive and energy may be helpful to the cause of industrialization. Sir Homi, even as a non-official, was one of the chief advisers of Sir Ramaswami Mudalliar who, as Commerce Member, has been trying to do something for promoting industrial research and helping the establishment of new industries. The two together have now the opportunity to show a more forward policy for the rapid development of Indian industries than has been evident so far. The next two to join the Viceroy's Council are Sir Akbar Hydari and Sir Sultan Ahmed. There have been rumours that Sir Akbar may serve in the Government of India only for six months or so. It is true that owing to his age he may like to retire from active official life, but it is difficult to believe that he would have accepted the appointment only for six months. If he is not able to continue longer, he would rather have declined the appointment altogether. The general impression is that the Viceroy has selected Sir Akbar Hydari owing to his unique standing in the country as an elder statesman so that he may virtually come to occupy the position of leader for the Indian non-official members and aid the working of the Cabinet in the arduous and difficult days to come. Nothing is yet known definitely about the date of arrival of Sir Firoze Khan Noon and Dr Raghavendra Rao nor of the assumption of office of the other two. It does not appear that the first meeting of the expanded Cabinet in its full strength will be possible before October. Sir Girja leaves this week for Ceylon and will probably not be able to return before the middle of September. After completing the work in connection with the Indo-Burma agreement and the Indo-Ceylon talks, he expects to hand over charge to his successors and leave for America before the end of the month....

26. The National Defence Council: Secretary of State's Statement, 27 August 1941

Indian Annual Register, 1941, Vol. II, pp. 316–19.

Mr Amery, Secretary of State for India, made the following statement dated London, the 19th August 1941, regarding the recent invitation to the Indian Provincial Premiers to join India's newly constituted National Defence Council:

> The Prime Ministers of all the Provinces in which working of the constitution has been uninterrupted were invited by the Viceroy to join the National Defence Council in their capacity as Prime Ministers and regardless of their personal, party or communal affiliations. Not only were they invited in their capacity as Prime Ministers, but they accepted the invitations in that capacity and in the light of their constitutional responsibility and obligations to the peoples and the provinces as a whole.

The Government of India Communiqué

Attention has been drawn to the recent proceedings of the Working Committee of the Muslim League and to the statement which has been issued by the Premier of the Punjab consequent on his resignation from the National Defence Council, stated a communiqué issued from Simla on the 27th August 1941.

In view of the statements which have been made on the important matter, it adds, it seems desirable to make it clear in the first place that the Premiers of Assam, Bengal, Punjab and Sind were invited to serve on the National Defence Council in terms of their capacity as Premiers of their provinces and on no other basis. It was on that basis that they accepted the invitation which was extended to them. As a corollary, should they cease to be Premiers of their provinces, they would cease capacity and automatically to be members of the National Defence Council, and their successor as Premier, irrespective of his party or his community, would be invited to replace them.

In framing the Defence Council, His Majesty's Government and the Viceroy were concerned to bring about as complete a representation of the face of India as was practicable and to ensure that the Council should be as representative as circumstances made it possible of all areas, communities and interests in this country. The allocation of the seats assigned to British India was primarily by provinces. The Premiers of all those provinces in which the constitution was functioning normally were accordingly invited in every case to join the Council. That was the primary and essential basis of the composition of the Council. It goes without saying that in the conditions of India, it is not possible to separate in estimating the character or the composition of any public body, the community or an individual from his general representative capacity. It was clearly desirable, too, that in a body designed to be as generally representative as was practicable, care should be taken to ensure adequate representation of the great Muslim community. The fact that certain individual members including the recent Premiers of Assam, Bengal, the Punjab and Sind themselves professed the Muslim faith was an advantage from this point of view. That consideration was however, and must be entirely a secondary one and the basis on which the Premiers were invited and agreed to serve was essentially that they were Premiers of the Provinces.

There can be no justification for any misunderstanding of this position. It was made quite clear to the Premiers concerned when invitations were extended to and accepted by them that they were being invited to serve as Premiers. It was brought out by the Secretary of State in his speech in the House of Commons on 1 August. The position was further made clear by the Governor General to Mr Jinnah and the Secretary of State was at pains to issue a statement designed to remove any possible misunderstanding regarding it. The Governor-General's conversation with Mr Jinnah and the Secretary of State's Statement both took place some days before the meeting of the Working Committee of the Muslim League.

27. Muslim League's Stand on Expansion of the Executive Council and Setting up of the National Defence Council

(i) Resolution Adopted by Muslim League Working Committee, Bombay, 24–26 August 1941

A.M. Zaidi (Chief Editor), *Evolution of Muslim Political Thought*, Vol. Five, *The Demand for Pakistan*, Delhi, 1978, pp. 312–13, 315–19.

League Premiers Called to Resign

After full discussion and consideration, the Working Committee are unanimously of the opinion that the Hon Sir Sikander Hyat Khan, the Hon Mr Fazlul Huq and the Hon Sir Mohamed Saadulla, should resign from the National Defence Council. In view of all the facts placed before the Committee by the President, including the message of His Excellency the Viceroy sent to him through the Governor of Bombay on 21 July 1941, the Hon Sir Sikander Hyat Khan, the Committee is glad to note, has decided to tender his resignation from the National Defence Council and the Committee have been informed telephonically that the

Hon Sir Mohamed Saadulla has also decided to resign from the National Defence Council. The question, therefore, of disciplinary action against Sir Sikander Hyat Khan and Sir Mohamed Saadulla does not arise.

The Hon Mr Fazlul Huq has communicated that he would like to have time to consider the matter. If he also resigns from the National Defence council within ten days and informs the President accordingly, no further action will be necessary. Failing the receipt of a satisfactory reply from Mr Fazlul Huq by the President within the time aforesaid, the Committee hereby authorize the President taking such action as he may deem proper and necessary.

Canvassing by Viceroy

The Working Committee of the All-India Muslim League deplore that His Excellency the Viceroy should have gone out of his way to canvass the members of the Muslim League for securing their association with the scheme of expansion of the Executive Council and the Constitution of the so-called National Defence Council within the terms of the offer of the 8th of August 1940, behind the back of the leader of the organization, knowing full well the express decision of the Council of the League rejecting a scheme on similar lines by its resolution dated the 28th of September 1940, which was duly communicated to him by the President.

Further, the Committee condemn the observations of Mr Amery, the Secretary of State for India, made in the House of Commons, in his speech on the 1st of August 1941, to the effect that he was glad to think that regardless of party leaders and in defiance of party discipline, patriotic Indians have come forward to work for India's defence, thereby casting a serious reflection on the patriotism of those who do not approve of the scheme, and lauding the conduct of those who have been deliberately and by various manoeuvers weaned to commit a breach of party discipline.

The Working Committee are of the considered opinion that the recent decision to resuscitate and impose upon India, the scheme of expansion of the Viceroy's Executive Council and the setting up of a National Defence Council was undertaken as a concession to the demands of the Hindus in utter disregard of the wishes of the Muslims of India and the solemn promises made to them and is intended to mislead public opinion in Great Britain and aboard.

Objection to Mr Amery's Statement

The Working Committee of the All-India Muslim League are amazed and alarmed that Mr Amery, the Secretary of State for India and a responsible Minister of the Crown, should be permitted to make pronouncements which amount to a breach of faith with Muslim India and to resile from the declared policy of the British Government, namely that the constitutional issue will, in no way, be prejudged by His Majesty's Government and that the solution of the constitutional issue will be dependent upon an agreement between the principal parties, as the following extracts from his speeches and the announcement of the Viceroy dated the 8th of August 1940, clearly disclose:

1. Viceroy's announcement dated the 8th August 1940:

There are two main points which have emerged. On these two points His Majesty's Government now desire me to make their position clear.

The first is as to the position of minorities, in relation to any future constitutional scheme. It has already been made clear that my declaration of 1st October does not exclude the examination of any part, either of the Act of 1935 or of the policy and plans on which it is based.

His Majesty's Government's concern that full weight should be given to the views of the minorities in any revision, has also been brought out. That remains the position of His Majesty's Government. It goes without saying that they could not contemplate the transfer of their present responsibilities, for the peace and welfare of India to any system of Government whose authority is directly denied by large and powerful elements in India's national life.

Nor could they be parties to the coercion of such elements into submission to such a Government.

The second point of general interest is the machinery for building within the British Commonwealth of Nations, a new constitutional scheme, when the time comes. There has been very strong insistence that the framing of that scheme should be primarily the responsibility of Indians themselves, and should originate from Indian conceptions of the social, economic and political structure of Indian life.

His Majesty's Government are in sympathy with that desire, and wish to see it given the fullest practical expression, subject to the due fulfilment of the obligation, which Great Britain's long connection with India has imposed upon her, and for which His Majesty's Government cannot divest themselves of the responsibility.

Meanwhile they will welcome and promote, in any way possible every sincere and practical step that may be taken by representative Indians themselves, to reach a basis of friendly agreement, firstly, on the form which the post-war representative body should take, and secondly, upon the principles and outlines of the constitution itself.

2. Mr Amery's statement dated the 14th August 1940:

Agreement, or consent, is indeed the foundation of all free Governments, of all true democracy. Decision by majority is not so much of the essence of democracy as a practical convenience which presupposes, for its proper working, an antecedent general consent to the constitution itself. It has indeed in most federal constitutions been limited in various ways in order to safeguard the separate interests of the federating elements. To describe the need for such agreement as a veto on constitutional progress is, I think, to do an injustice to the patriotism and sense of responsibility of those concerned. Agreement means not veto by any element but compromise, and willingness to compromise, in India as elsewhere, is an essential test of the sense of responsibility on which free Government must be based.

3. Mr Amery's statement dated 22nd of April 1941:

It was decided that the framework of India's future constitutions should be devised by Indians themselves and not by this House. That was a far-reaching and indeed, revolutionary announcement, the full importance of which has not, I think, even yet been fully appreciated either in this country or in India.

Even more important in this connection is the stipulation that the constitution itself, and also the body which is to frame it, must be the outcome of agreement between the principal elements in India's national life. That is an essential prerequisite to the success of the future constitution. For, if Indians cannot agree upon the kind of constitution they are prepared to work out, how are they likely to agree upon the actual working of it?

I have dwelt deliberately upon Indian responsibility in the matter, for unless Indians are prepared to face that responsibility now, they will fail to fact it hereafter. Any agreement imposed by us from without cannot survive the withdrawal of our power to enforce it. Only a real agreement, freely reached, can stand that test.

The Working Committee strongly condemn the adverse criticism and remarks of Mr Amery in his recent speech in the House of Commons with regard to the Lahore resolution of the All-India Muslim League, popularly known as Pakistan resolution, without examining the scheme embodied therein and the circumstances which have driven the Muslims to demand partition of India into zones predominantly Muslim.

Demand for Assurance from British Government

The Working Committee calls upon His Majesty's Government to reassure the Muslims of India that His Majesty's Government will stand by their declarations and pledges, solemnly given by the Viceroy and the Secretary of State for India on behalf of His Majesty's Government.

If this assurance reaffirming the declaration, which has been shaken by the recent ill advised utterances of the Secretary of State for India, practically prejudging and condemning the Muslim League scheme of partitioning India, is not forthcoming within a reasonable time, the Muslim League will be compelled to revise, out of necessity, its policy and adopt such measures as it may deem necessary to resist any departure from the solemn pledges and assurances, and the responsibility for the consequences that may accrue on account of this gross breach of faith will entirely rest on the British Government.

Sir Sultan Ahmad

The Working Committee have considered the explanation of Sir Sultan Ahmad. It seems that he has not realized the gravity of the complaint, namely that while he was a member of the Council of the All-India Muslim League he has associated himself with the scheme of the expansion and reconstruction of the personnel of the Viceroy's Executive Council, as notified in the communiqué dated 21 July 1941, and the constitution of the National Defence Council which is a part and parcel of the scheme as has been explained by the highest authority, the Secretary of State for India, in his statement in the House of Commons on 22 July, and further amplified by his speech and his reply to the debate in the House of Commons on 1 August 1941 in which he makes it quite clear that the appointment of Sir Sultan Ahmad to the Executive Council was a part of the scheme.

In view of these facts, Sir Sultan Ahmad, having associated himself with the scheme against the express decision of the Muslim League and its general policy, the Committee are of opinion that Sir Sultan Ahmad should resign his appointment to the Viceroy's Executive Council within ten day's failing which the Committee hereby give full authority to the President to take such action as he may deem necessary and proper.

Nawab of Chhatari's Case

The Working Committee, after considering the explanation of the Nawab of Chhatari, are of opinion that he, while still a member of the Council of the All-India Muslim League, by accepting the membership of the National Defence Council has acted against the express decision of the Muslim League and its general policy, and call upon him to resign his membership of the National Defence Council.

If the Nawab of Chhatari resigns the membership of the National Defence Council before he takes charge as the President of His Exalted Highness the Nizam's Council of Ministers and communicates the fact to the President, no action will be necessary. In case the Nawab of Chhatari fails to submit his resignation from the National Defence Council within the time prescribed, the president is hereby given full authority to take such action as he deems necessary and proper.

Begum Shah Nawaz's Case

The Working Committee, after considering the explanation of Begum Shah Nawaz, are of opinion that she, while still a member of the Council of the All-India Muslim League, by accepting the membership of the National Defence Council, has acted against the express decision of the Muslim League and its general policy, and calls upon her to resign her membership of the National Defence Council.

If Begum Shah Nawaz resigns the membership of National Defence Council within ten days and communicates the fact to the President, no action will be necessary. In case Begum Shah Nawaz fails to submit her resignation from the National Defence Council within the time prescribed, the President is hereby given full authority to take such action as he deems necessary and proper.

(ii) Jinnah's Statement on the Communiqué, 28 August 1941

Indian Annual Register, 1941, Vol. II, pp. 317–19.

Mr M.A. Jinnah issued the following statement to the press from Bombay on the 28th August 1941:

'The explanation that has been given, presumably, on behalf of Lord Linlithgow, in the communiqué dated 27 August 1941, Simla, regarding the recent decision of the Working Committee of the All-India Muslim League and the statement which has been issued by Sir Sikandar Hyat Khan consequent on his resignation from the National Defence Council, is a lengthy and wordy explanation of points other than the real and vital one, which forms the basis of the resignation of Sir Sikandar Hyat Khan namely, that according to the text of the message of His Excellency the Viceroy, Sir Sikandar Hyat Khan was appointed as a representative of the great Muslim Community. This message I received through the Governor of Bombay on the morning of 21 July and replied to it on the same day. It is surprising that no reference whatever has been made to it in the whole of the communiqué.

'The statement of Sir Sikandar Hyat Khan runs as follows: "I was surprised however to find that in the letter dated 20 July last from the Governor of Bombay to Mr Jinnah, communicating to him a message from His Excellency the Viceroy, an entirely different complexion had been put on the basis of appointment of the Muslim Premiers on this Council, and *inter alia* it was stated that we were being appointed to the Defence Council as representatives of the great Muslim community ... I could not, in fairness to my province or the Muslim League, continue to serve on this Council."

'According to Sir Sikandar Hyat Khan, the Viceroy was double-crossing him. That point is not met in the whole of the communiqué. Had he asked Sir Sikandar Hyat Khan to join the Council in his personal capacity, the probability is so obvious that he would have refused, or at any rate, asked for time to consult the Leader and the Executive of the Muslim League organization. This evidently did not suit the Viceroy to put it to him in that way, and he was sworn to strict secrecy.

'It is somewhat difficult to understand why the Working Committee has been dragged in the communiqué. The position of the Working Committee has been made quite clear by its resolution that the gentlemen concerned had clearly associated themselves with the scheme and had thereby gone against the express decision of the mandate of the League, and had acted without any reference to the Leader or the Executive of the organization. The decision of the Working Committee therefore was that they should resign from the National Defence Council. It is quite immaterial whether they accepted the invitation in their official capacity or otherwise.

'The various stages of the development of this plea that these gentlemen were appointed in their official capacity as Premiers, ending with the statement of the Secretary of State for India which he was at pains to make on 19 August 1941, were merely intended to create confusion before the Muslim public and in the deliberations of the Working Committee which was called upon to decide as to what action should be taken in the matter.

'Lastly, there is a reference of His Excellency the Viceroy in the communiqué to the conversation that he had with me on 16 August 1941. It is quite correct that he informed me that these gentlemen were invited in their official capacity, but in fairness to me it also ought to have been stated as to what was my reply. Here I give the substance of it. I said, 'It was quite immaterial to the real issue; nevertheless, it is the first time I hear, on your authority, that they were invited in their official capacity; and even after my reply to your message which you must have received on the 21st, or the 22nd, you did not suggest, that they were appointed in their official capacity, till today'. I pointed out to him that this was quite contrary to the message that he was good enough to send to me through the Governor of Bombay. The text of the message did not leave the slightest doubt that they were appointed essentially as representatives of the great Muslim community, because they were Muslims of the highest eminence and capacity. I asked him to send for the copy of his message that he had sent to me and verify what I was saying in which he replied that he would look it up.

'I think in fairness to all parties concerned I should release to the press the full text of his message and my reply to it.'

Lumley–Jinnah Correspondence

Bombay Governor's Letter

Government House
Ganeshkhind, 20th July 1941.

Dear Mr Jinnah,

'His Excellency the Viceroy has asked me to let you know his intentions on the matters, which follow. I had hoped that I would be able to see you myself in order that I might convey this message to you personally, as was his desire: but unfortunately, now that I am in a position to give you the message, I am not entirely fit, and I am, therefore, writing to convey it to you by this letter, which I am sending down to Bombay by special messenger.

'The Viceroy has continued to have very much in mind the whole situation in regard to the war effort and the association of non-official opinion with the prosecution of the war. The obstacles, however, to any settlement on the basis of the complete offer of August last, which emerged so clearly during the discussions last autumn, still exist, to his very great regret, as the last few months, and the reactions to the Secretary of State's statement in the House of Commons on April the 22nd, have made clear. In these circumstances, it is equally clear that he cannot look for that degree of support from the major parties, for the proposals embodied in the August Offer, which he desires. Nevertheless, the burden of the conduct of the war on the

Central Government has greatly increased, and for administrative reasons it is essential to proceed with some increase in the membership of the Viceroy's Council within the terms of the August Offer. The Viceroy, accordingly, is anxious that you should know that he is now, with the approval of His Majesty's Government, creating five new portfolios. These new portfolios, and the names of the gentlemen by whom they have been accepted, are as follows: Supply: Sir Homi Mody. Information: Sir Akbar Hydari. Civil Defence: Mr Raghavendra Rao. Indians Overseas: Mr Aney. Labour: Sir Firoze Khan Noon.

'The Viceroy would also like you to know that he proposes to fill the vacancies arising in the portfolio of Law, when Sir Zafrullah Khan goes to the Federal Court, and in the portfolio of Education, when Sir Girija Sankar Bajpai takes up a mission overseas, by the appointment of Sir Sultan Ahmed and Mr Sarkar.

'In addition, the Viceroy does not feel that, because of the difficulty in securing the support of the major political parties, it is possible to delay further the more active association of non-official Indian opinion with the prosecution of the war. He is accordingly establishing with the approval of His Majesty's Government, a National Defence Council. This Council will consist of some thirty members, nine of whom will be drawn from the Indian States. The Viceroy regards it as essential that the great Muslim community should be represented on that Council by persons of the highest prominence and capacity. He has accordingly invited the Premiers of Assam, Bengal, the Punjab and Sind to serve as members of it, and he has extended invitations also to certain other prominent Muslims, such as Sir Mahomed Usman. He has considered whether he should invite you to let him have any suggestions as to the possible personnel for this Council, but being aware, as he is, of your general attitude, he has concluded that it would be preferable not to embarrass you by inviting you to make suggestions.

'It is intended that an announcement about these changes will be made on the morning of Tuesday, July the 22nd, and the Viceroy is anxious that you should have, through me, this advance information of what is proposed. I would have much preferred to have given you this message orally, but this letter contains the substance of it.

'I hope that you have now fully recovered from your recent illness'.

Mr Jinnah's Reply

Copy of the letter sent by Mr M.A. Jinnah, Mount Pleasant Road, Malabar Hill, 21st July 1941.

Dear Sir Roger,

'I am in receipt of your letter of the 20th July 1941 which embodies the message of His Excellency the Viceroy. I deeply regret the decision taken by him with the approval of His Majesty's Government. I appreciate him when he says that he does not wish to embarrass me by inviting me to make suggestions, knowing, as he does, not only my general attitude but that of the All-India Muslim League. Further, I cannot approve of his having invited the Muslim League Premiers or any other Muslim Leaguer under the scheme of the expansion of the Viceroy's Council as well as what is now called the National Defence Council, because it is obvious that it would embarrass the Muslim League organization, and I do hope and trust that His Excellency will avoid such a contingency. Besides, it is hardly fair or proper that they should be approached by His Excellency over the head of the President and the Executive of the All-India Muslim League, knowing full well the position and the attitude that the All-India Muslim League has adopted.

It is stated in his message that the Viceroy regards it as essential that the Great Muslim community should be represented by persons of the highest prominence and capacity. Would it be creditable for any individual prominent or capable Mussalman belonging to an organization to accept the invitation contrary to the position and the attitude taken up by that organization, and would it do any credit to the Government, if they succeed in alluring him and create a breach in the organization, in the hope that he may throw up his allegiance to the party to which he belongs in order to accept the invitation of His Excellency? I maintain that the great Muslim community is represented authoritatively only by the All-India Muslim League organization. Persistence in this course will not improve matters but, on the contrary, it will lead to bitterness on the part of the Muslim League, which up to the present moment fortunately does not exist, however emphatically we have disapproved of the policy which has been pursued by His Majesty's Government and the Viceroy'.

(iii) Resolutions on Viceroy's Executive Council and Mr Fazlul Huq's Case Adopted by Muslim League Council, New Delhi, October 1941

Indian Annual Register, 1941, Vol. II, pp. 218–19.

a. Viceroy's Executive Council

This meeting of the Council of the All-India Muslim League while endorsing the decision of the Working Committee and the steps taken by the President of All-India Muslim League in connection with expansion of the Executive Council of HE the Viceroy and the so-called National Defence Council congratulates the Working Committee and the President of their decision and proper steps taken in the matter, and severely condemns the action of Hon Dr Sir Syed Sultan Ahmad and Begum Shah Nawaz, in refusing to accept the mandate of the Working Committee and in insisting to remain on the said Council in flagrant disregard of the wishes of the Muslims.

The Council further declares that the Muslims taken in the Expanded Council of HE the Viceroy and the so-called National Defence Council are in no way representative of and cannot in any way represent the interests of Muslims.

This Council further condemns the attitude of the Government in this connection which is only to create a rift in the ranks of Muslims.

b. Mr Fazlul Huq's Case

The Working Committee of the All-India Muslim League considered the letter dated 8 September addressed to the Secretary of the All-India Muslim League by Mr Fazlul Huq tendering his resignation from the Working Committee and the Council of the All-India Muslim League and also the letter of Mr Fazlul Huq dated 26 October received today in which he says:

'I feel that the matter relating to my letter addressed to you (Secretary of the All-India Muslim League) should be disposed of in my absence. My presence in the discussion may put some members of the League in an awkward position if I were to be present at the time the criticisms are made when this letter comes up for discussion. I shall be grateful if you convey my regrets to the President that I shall not be able to attend the meeting.'

The Working Committee consider that the following allegations contained in Mr Fazlul Huq's letter are untrue, offensive and cast serious aspersions on the President, the Working Committee and the council of the League and Muslim Leaguers of the Provinces where Muslims are in a minority:

1. I maintain that this action of the President was unconstitutional in the highest degree.
2. The Working Committee endorsed this action of the President because they had no alternative before them. If they had refused to ratify the President's action it would have amounted to a vote of no-confidence in the President and this contingency, the Working Committee were not prepared to face. It is for this reason that the Working Committee passed the resolution, a copy of which you have forwarded to me calling upon me to resign unconditionally from the National Defence Council.
3. But before I conclude, I wish to record a most emphatic protest against the manner in which Muslim interests of Bengal and the Punjab are being imperilled by Muslim Leaguers in the Muslim Minority Provinces.
4. As a mark of protest against the arbitrary use of powers vested in its president, I beg to tender my resignation from the membership of the Working Committee and the Council of the All-India Muslim League. Much as I deplore this course I feel that I cannot usefully continue to be a member of a body which shows scant courtesy to Provincial leaders and which arrogates to itself the functions which ought to be exercised by provincial executives.
5. The President of the All-India Muslim League has singularly failed to discharge the heavy responsibility of his office in a constitutional and reasonable manner.
6. Recent events have forcibly brought home to me that the interests of Muslim India are being subordinated to the wishes of a single individual who seeks rule as omnipotent over the destiny of thirty-three millions of Muslims in the Province of Bengal, who occupy the key position in Muslim India.

The Working Committee, therefore, calls upon Mr Fazlul Huq to withdraw these allegations and express his regret within ten days of the receipt of this resolution by him. On the expiry of this specified time, the Working Committee will decide what action is called for after considering any explanation that Mr Fazlul Huq may offer either in writing or in person and for this purpose and for any other business, the Working Committee will meet at its Central Office at 11 a.m. on 16 November.

(iv) Central Legislative Assembly: Muslim League Walk-out, 28 October 1941

Indian Annual Register, 1941, Vol. II, pp. 108–9.

Muslim League Walk-out

28 October: The Muslim League party walked out of the Assembly, this morning, after a statement was made by Mr M.A. Jinnah declaring that they were doing so in order to register their protest against the way in which the Muslims' offer of cooperation in the war effort had been completely ignored by the Government. 'We have said from the beginning', he declared, 'that the major issues will be considered later, and within the framework of the present existing constitution you must, if you want our cooperation, associate with us now with a real genuine

share in the authority of the Government not only at the Centre but in the provinces. Ignoring that and ignoring everything else that had gone before, Government had come to its decision about the expansion of the Executive Council. 'We have come to this conclusion now', said Mr Jinnah 'in the hope that the protest that we are registering today will open the eyes of the blind and the ears of the deaf (cheers) and that you will have the wisdom and the statesmanship to revise this scheme of yours, for I assure you, this will not help you by a little in the intensification of the war effort. On the contrary it is going to harm you. I am interested in it as much as any body else. I advise you to think over it.'

'Finally, I say to the Government, the hon Members the press and the public outside, 'please do not misrepresent us. It is the Government and Government alone that is responsible. One cannot come to any other conclusion but that they do not want our assistance and cooperation. When they talk of cooperation they mean it on such terms that no self-respecting man could accept it' (cheers).

Mr Jinnah, earlier in his statement said: 'So far as the Muslim League was concerned, we have made it clear that, apart from major issues, from the beginning we were ready and willing to render every possible assistance in the prosecution of the war. Without prejudice to the adjustment of larger issues later on, we were willing, as far back as November 1939, to consider the proposal of the Viceroy to bring about an honourable and workable arrangement in the provincial field and at the centre.

'When the announcement of 8 August 1940 came, the spirit and even the letter of it was almost exactly what the Muslim League had urged. The League welcomed it: but they were not told what the total number of the expanded Executive Council would be, what would be the portfolios and what would be their powers. Nothing was told them except that their representatives would be two. "Was that," he asked, "the spirit in which to treat those who were to be co-sharers in the authority of Government and in the danger which we were willing to face?" (cheers). No self-respecting man could have accepted that offer.'

'Government thereafter went to sleep, all the time telling us "you are not cooperating". I have always admitted that there is not the slightest doubt that there is great danger and menace to India. We have repeatedly said, as far back as June 1940, that the efforts you were making and the schemes suggested by the Government of India and the Commander-in-Chief were not sufficient. And that you must increase and intensify your war effort. But all we were told was "you are in danger." Think what will happen to you. Why can't you say: "Think what will happen to us all, to you, and to us both?" I want you to enter into that spirit.' Then came the decision announced on 22 July, and the manner in which it was undertaken and carried through ignoring everybody. 'Why ignore us?' he asked.

(v) Resolution on Expansion of Executive Council Adopted by Muslim League Working Committee, New Delhi, 16 November 1941

Indian Annual Register, 1941, Vol. II, pp. 220–1.

The Working Committee of the All-India Muslim League regrets that the British Government has not only failed to accept the offer of cooperation made by the Muslim League by its resolution dated June 17 June 1940 but in utter disregard of it, has expanded the Governor-General's Executive Council by associated with it persons representing nobody except themselves. This ill-advised and unfair action on the part of the Government, in the opinion of the committee, was due to the fact that the British Government was not prepared to concede the just demands of the Muslim League even when the Congress Party was engaged in obstructionist tactics and civil disobedience and refused to even consider any agreement within the framework of the present constitution. The Working Committee therefore urge upon the Government that no further steps be taken or adjustments be made in the future even within the framework of the present constitution and law without the approval and consent of the All-India Muslim League and once more warn the Government that any action in this connection without the approval of the Muslim League will be deeply resented.

The responsibility for the consequences that may ensure will be entirely that of the Government.

28. Atlantic Charter and India

(i) No Statement by Mahatma Gandhi on Churchill's Speech

Interview to *The Hindu*
CWMG, Vol. LXXIV, pp. 314–15.

Wardhaganj
11 September 1941

I interviewed Gandhiji today and asked him a few questions on Mr Churchill's reference to India in his latest speech in the Commons. Gandhiji declined to answer any question. Then I asked him, 'I see you are disinclined to answer the most important and relevant questions that I put to you. Do you think that this silence of yours is helpful for the cause of Indian independence for which the Congress is fighting?' Gandhiji replied:

If I did not believe so I would have come out with a statement without any prompting from you. But I sincerely believe that my silence is much more eloquent than any words that I may utter. After all it is not words that matter. Action is all in all. My action is before all India and, if you like, the whole world.

The Hindu, 12 September 1941

(ii) Mr Churchill's 'No'

Editorial, *The Tribune*, 12 September 1941.

Mr Churchill's explicit declaration in his latest review of the war that what has been described as the Atlantic Charter[1] 'does not qualify in any way the various statements on policy which have been made from time to time about the development of constitutional government in India' will not break the heart of India. It is after all neither more nor less than the last of a long series of utterances of British statesmen, betraying in an equal measure the spirit of imperialistic arrogance and a complete lack of that imagination and that understanding sympathy which are of the essence of statesmanship. The first of these utterances in recent years was the famous speech in which Lord, then Mr Morley said that he could not foresee a time when India would have parliamentary government and that for as long a time as his imagination could pierce through, for so long would India remain under despotic and personal rule. Then came the speech of a Secretary of State, who has already been forgotten both in India and in his own country, in which India was told that she could never aspire to the position of a Dominion.

Lord Morley lived to see the day when one of his own political disciples laid the foundation of parliamentary government in India, which necessarily connoted the ultimate death of despotic and personal rule; and the attainment of Dominion status by India is not merely the immediate goal of political India but the declared objective of the British Government themselves.

* * * *

Oddly enough the very person who as Prime Minister sanctioned what is known as the August announcement, in which the gradual development of self-governing in strengths with a view to the progressive realization of responsible government in India was declared to be the policy of the British Government made the famous Steel Frame speech in which the people of India were told that whatever changes might take place in their country, the status, the functions and the responsibility of the British services would remain unimpeded. The same authority declared a short time ago that the only solution of the Indian problem that he could think of was the application of the same method that he had himself followed in the case of Ireland, namely to make a treaty with free India as Britain had made a treaty with free Ireland. He knew fully well while making that statement that there was and could possibly has no such thing as a British Frame in the services of the Irish Free State. Who can have forgotten the previous speeches of the Secretary of State who sent out to India an all-British Commission with the authority of all parties in the British Parliament? Yet that Commission was boycotted by political India and its elaborately written report was consumed by the British Government themselves to the limbo of oblivion. A new organization had to be given to British policy in India. The method of Inquiry by Royal Commission had to be discarded in favour of the method of Round Table Conferences in which Indians participated on avowedly equal terms with Britishers, and it was declared by His Majesty's Government through the mouth of the Viceroy, in complete disregard of all that Lord Birkenhead had said to the contrary, that Dominion status was the natural issue of the Constitution that had already been introduced in India and that in future India was to have provincial autonomy and a responsible federal Government at the Centre which would exercise the rights of self-government subject only to safeguards conceived in the interest of India herself. Repeated efforts were made during the passage of the present Government of India Act through Parliament, to go behind the pledged word of His Majesty's Government, but the then Secretary of State was forced to declare that the Government adhered to all the pledges that ever were given to India. And these pledges have now been consolidated into one compendious pledge which whatever its other defects, and they are serious enough, has made the complete freedom and equality of India as a member of the British Commonwealth the declared goal of Britain's policy.

* * * *

To-day what is in dispute is not the goal, but the method of reaching it and the date when it is to be reached. British reactionaries and diehards having been defeated on the main issue are now making desperate attempts to regain by a flank attack the ground they have been forced to abandon by the failure of their frontal attack. This flank attack, which consists in the insertion of the so-called minorities safeguard and the clause about the obligations imposed by history on the British Government in the declaration of August 1940, was hitherto believed to have been led by Mr Amery, Mr Churchill's speech shows that the real leader of this attack is Mr Churchill himself. Mr Churchill is the very last man to repeat parrot-like someone else's phraseology. The fact that in his speech he used the exact argument and almost the exact words of the August Declaration in defining the safeguards to which India's free and equal partnership is to be subject can leave no room for doubt in one's mind that in spite of his preoccupation with the war Mr Churchill did find time to inspire, if not actually to draw up, that declaration. The knowledge that this is so is a great advantage, for it will effectively prevent any section of Indian opinion from reposing its child-like faith in the Premier and appealing to him from the Secretary of State.

* * * *

The whole of India knows to-day that it is not Mr Amery but Mr Churchill who has offered to India what Sir N.N. Sircar aptly described as 'hot ice'. As per with even a hundredth part of Mr Churchill understanding could have no difficulty in realizing that democratic self-government subject to the right of a minority to impose its will on the majority and to the fulfilment of Britain's so-called historical obligations would be neither self-government nor democracy, but a complete negation of both. There were minorities in many of the countries to which Britain has before now either voluntarily or under the compelling pressure of circumstance conceded the full rights of self-government. To cite the latest case in point there were minorities in the Irish Free State. In that country as in India, it was open to Britain to make the concession of Freedom subject to its own work obligations and its so-called responsibility to various creeds, faces and interests. For long it was on the very ground of these obligations and responsibilities that it had resisted the just demand of the Irish people for complete national freedom. Where were Mr Churchill, Mr Amery and the rest of them when in the Anglo-Irish Treaty not a word was said about these obligations and their responsibilities? And where would have been the much wanted freedom and democracy of Britain itself if the Stuarts had missed and with success on the fulfilment of their historic obligations and their responsibilities to the diverse creeds, regions and interests in the country as a condition precedent to the establishment of parliamentary sovereignty, as so many British statesmen are done in relation to India to-day?

* * * *

We repeat that there is nothing in what Mr Churchill has said to dishearten the party of self-government in India. Mr Churchill with all his splendid and manifold gifts has for more than twenty years been the accredited leader and spokesman of British reactionaries and die-hards in Indian affairs. His ways and methods are the ways and methods by which reactionaries and die-hards have always sought to obstruct the progress of light and freedom all through history. India will survive these ways and methods as certainly and as completely as she has survived such attempts in the past and as other countries have survived similar attempts in their cases. The only possible effect of such attempts is to make the party of freedom redouble their efforts. That will be the precise effect of Mr Churchill's attempt. He has unconsciously rendered a service of great value to India. Our only regret is that in the process of rendering this service he has done a grave disservice both to his own country and to the cause of freedom and democracy in the name and on behalf of which he is so magnificently and vacantly fighting the scourge of Nazism.

(iii) Amery's Commentary on Churchill's Statement: No Change in British Policy Towards India

Bombay Chronicle, 10 October 1941.

London, 9 October: Mr Churchill's statement of 9 September in connection with the Atlantic Charter and India was reaffirmed by Mr Amery in the House of Commons.

He said that the statement expressly made it clear that the Government's previous declaration regarding the goal of India's attainment of free and equal partnership in the British Commonwealth and with regard to the British desire to see the goal attained with the least possible delay after the war under a constitution framed by agreement among Indians themselves, held good and was in no way qualified.

Sorensen's Question

Mr Sorensen (Labour) asked Mr Amery whether he was aware that Sir Sikander Hyat Khan, the Punjab Premier, had publicly expressed his concern and embarrassment at the recent Government statement, respecting the relationship of the Atlantic Charter to the future Government of India whether the Punjab Premier had communicated with him on the matter and whether he had any statement to make regarding it.

Mr Amery replied, 'I have seen the reports. I can only repeat in order to remove any possible grounds for misunderstanding that the Prime Minister's Statement of 9 September with reference to the Atlantic Charter expressly made it clear that the Government's previous declaration with regard to the goal of India's attainment of free and equal partnership in the British Commonwealth and with regard to our desire to see the goal attained with the least possible delay after the war under a constitution framed by agreement among the Indians themselves held good, and is in no way qualified.

The answer to the remainder of the question is in the negative.'

India Policy under Fire

Mr Sorensen: 'Do you appreciate the fact that a gentleman of this eminence who can in no way be classified as an extremist would not take this attitude, unless he had very grave doubts as to the real intention of the Government, *and does that not mean that it is necessary to reconsider the whole question of Indian policy to satisfy the people of this country and in India*?'

No answer was given.

'The manufacture of internal combustion engines in India is not a practicable proposition so far as the present war is concerned,' said Mr Amery, replying to Col Wedgwood who asked whether this would be done, in view of the need for supplying Russia as well as the Near East from India.

Mr Amery added that India's capacity to assist Russia as well as the Near East would be made available to the fullest extent.

Col Wedgwood said: 'Isn't it about time with 400 million people to start making something which is vital to war?'

(iv) India and Atlantic Charter

Editorial, *The Tribune*, 11 October 1941.

The question of the applicability of the Atlantic Charter to India was again raised in the British House of Commons on Thursday last, this time with particular reference to Sir Sikander Hyat Khan's recent statement on the subject. Mr Churchill and Mr Amery whether it was aware that Sir Sikander Hyat Khan had publicly expressed his concern and embarrassment at the recent Government statement in respect of the relationship of the Atlantic Charter to the future government of India. Mr Amery's reply was a masterpiece of evasion. 'I have,' he said, 'seen the reports, I can only repeat, in order to remove any possible grounds for misunderstanding that the Prime Minister's statement of 9 September with reference to the Atlantic Charter expressly made it clear that the Government's previous declaration with regard to the goal of India's attainment of free and equal partnership in the British Commonwealth and with regard to our desire to see the goal attained with the least possible delay after the war under a constitution framed by agreement among the Indians themselves held good and was in no way qualified.' In reply to the further question whether he appreciated the fact that a gentleman of the eminence of the Punjab Premier who could in no way be classified as an extremist would not take up the attitude he had taken up unless he had very grave doubts as to the real intention of the Government, and whether that did not mean that it was necessary to reconsider the whole question of Indian policy to satisfy with India and Britain. Mr Amery preferred to maintain discreet silence.

As constitutional situation would indeed have been far better with regard to the original question itself than the evasion occupied by the Secretary of State for India. The statement made by him will certainly create more misunderstanding than it can possibly remove. Mr Sorensen had in effect asked Mr Amery what reactions, if any, had been produced in the attitude and policy of the British Government by the concern and embarrassment expressed by the Punjab Premier at the recent Government statement respecting the relationship of the Atlantic Charter to the future government of India. That straight question, called for an equally straight answer. Instead of giving that answer Mr Amery only repeated what Mr Churchill himself had said, namely, that the Atlantic Charter did not in any way qualify the previous declaration of policy made by the British Government. There would have been something to be said for this repetition if the previous declaration had satisfied Indian opinion and if the complaint of India had been that the Atlantic Charter had so altered the declaration as to make it unacceptable to India. No one knew better than Mr Amery that the exact reverse of this was the case. The very fact that the Government had been forced, in the matter of the expansion of the Viceroy's Executive Council to do without the co-operation of the most important and influential political parties in India, showed beyond the possibility of doubt that the previous declaration had not satisfied India. What political India had asked for on the morrow of the promulgation of the Atlantic Charter was not an assurance that the Charter did not alter or qualify the previous declaration, but that it did qualify it in such a manner as to bring it into harmony with itself. This assurance is as conspicuous by its absence in Mr Amery's latest statement as in Mr Churchill's statement of 9 September.

* * * *

But this is not our only complaint with regard to Mr Amery's statement. He did not give mature picture of the Government's previous declaration itself, familiarly known as the August announcement. That declaration was not that India should attain the goal of free and equal partnership in the British Commonwealth under a constitution framed by agreement among the Indians themselves, but that she should do so subject to the fulfilment by Britain of the obligations imposed upon her by her long association with India and subject also to the proviso that the authority of the government established by that constitution was not denied by any large and powerful element in India's political life even though that element might not believe in India's constitutional life but all and might actually stand for the satisfaction at India. Individually and collectively the two provisions reduce the commitment of the British Government in the goal of free and equal partnership in the British Commonwealth to perfect nullity. The historic obligations of Britain mean and can mean nothing else except her so-called obligations in the matter of the State's Defence and of British vested interest, including the British Services. The man must be completely devoid of political understanding who imagines that India can ever be a 'free and equal partner in the British Commonwealth' on the basis of the fulfilment of these obligations by Britain.... We have it to any fair-minded and dispassionate person to say if this is not taking away with one hand what is given with the other, if Sir N.N. Sircar was not perfectly justified in describing the declaration as an offer of 'hot-ice' to India. And may we inquire what possible objection the British Government can have to stating explicitly that the Atlantic Charter shall apply to India, if, as Mr Churchill said the principles underlying that Charter are also the principles that underlie the British Government's Indian policy? Does it not occur to them that in the very act of denying the applicability of the Atlantic Charter to India they are emphasizing the difference between their Indian policy and the principles laid down in the Atlantic Charter?

* * * *

Now that Mr Amery has given as categorically negative a reply to Sir Sikander Hyat Khan's demand for a new declaration of policy as Mr Churchill himself gave to political India's demand for a declaration admitting the applicability of the Atlantic Charter to India, it is for Sir Sikander Hyat Khan to say what steps he proposes to take to bring about a 'united front' in this country. He said that he would wait for two or three weeks for the British Government's answer. He has not had to wait for even a week. The Secretary of State made it clear in his statement of 9 October that the British Government did not consider any new declaration necessary and had no intention of making it. What is Sir Sikander now going to do? The country generally and the Punjab in particular has the same right to expect a clear and unambiguous declaration of policy from the Punjab Premier as he himself had to expect a clear and unambiguous declaration of policy from the British Government. Our suggestion is that before he makes such a declaration he should consult at least his fellow Premiers in the other three provinces in which the constitution is functioning as well as the ex-Premiers in the Congress provinces who are now out of prison. It was an old idea of Sir Sikander Hyat Khan that the Premiers of the eleven provinces should put their heads together and arrive at a settlement on the main lines of India's future constitution. The conference we suggest would be the nearest approach to that idea that is possible in the existing conditions. It is a very fortunate circumstance that by far the wishes and most powerful of the ex-Congress Premiers. Mr Rajagopalachariar is now out of prison. His advice, if available is bound to be of immense value to Sir Sikander and others who may be thinking in terms of a united front. We are quite sure that the benefit of this advice will not be denial to them if, they meant business and want to bring the maximum pressure of

India's united and organized opinion to bear upon the British Government to secure the satisfaction of her national demand.

(v) India League (UK) on the Atlantic Charter

File No. 1/5/41-Poll (I), Home (Political) Department, Government of India, Intelligence Bureau Report, 28 October 1941, NAI.

The meeting organized by Mrs Rebecca SIEFF 'to discuss the problems of India' was duly held in a private room at the Savoy Hotel at 5 p.m. on Thursday, 23.10.41. Mrs Sieff herself was unable to be present owing to a cold. In her absence the guests were received by Miss BATLIVALA. Thirty-four people were present, including H.G. WELLS, Professor HALDANE, Professor LEVY, KINGSLEY MARTIN, SILVERMAN, MP, COVE, MP, MELLOR (Daily Herald), Commander CADBURY, Sir Francis YOUNG HUSBAND, SORENSEN, Dame Elizabeth the Rev. HICKMAN JOHNSON, Edward THOMPSON, Michael FOOT, Dr P.C. BHANDARI, and V.K. Krishna MENON.

There were no set speeches and the party was in the nature of a discussion. On their arrival the guests took tea, and for the first quarter of an hour stood about talking in small groups. The Chairman, Michael FOOT, then announced that it was intended to discuss the following suggestions:

(1) To send a deputation of about four or five influential persons to Mr Amery urging him to persuade the government to include India within the scope of the Atlantic Charter.
(2) To organize meetings to enlist public support for the inclusion of India in the Atlantic Charter.

Following a general discussion, a resolution was passed to the effect that the meeting agreed in principle to the terms of the Atlantic Charter.

The meeting then proceeded to discuss the sending of a deputation to Mr Amery. The general view was that more could be achieved by approaching the Prime Minister himself. A speaker suggested that the Prime Minister was already an over-worked man, much pre-occupied with the Anglo-Soviet Alliance, and the speaker did not think the Indian question was of such urgency that it demanded the personal attention of the Premier. Another speaker, however, maintained that the question was of sufficient importance to deserve the personal attention of the Prime Minister. He (the last speaker) added that the public was astonished at Mr Churchill's announcement excluding India from the scope of the Atlantic Charter and was of the opinion that the inclusion of India would greatly enhance the prestige of this country. Vague promises of independence to India in the distant future served no useful purpose; an immediate declaration was wanted. The meeting eventually resolved that a deputation of prominent persons should approach the Prime Minister on the question of including India in the scope of the Atlantic Charter.

Further discussion on the deputation then followed. The composition of the deputation was raised and it was suggested that one or two persons from outside the meeting should be included so as 'to give it more weight'. It was also pointed out that since the Labour members of the Government were believed to be more favourably disposed to dominion status for India than were the Conservative members, and as Mr Churchill relied to a great extent on the Labour members, he should be approached through the latter.

A third resolution was then put by Kingsley MARTIN (Editor of *The New Statesman* and *Nation*) that a committee should be set up to organize a press campaign for the release of

Nehru and the political prisoners. H.G. WELLS made the point that he was not concerned with political issues, but felt that the people of India should have the same civil liberty as the people of this country and so long as that was not so, English civilization stood condemned.

At this stage some one from the Fabian Society caused a diversion by asking what was the meeting about. Was it suggested that this country was an autocracy? Now that a third resolution was being moved, he would like to know what the other resolution had been about. An explanation was given him, presumably by FOOT, but he was not satisfied and protested that he still understood nothing. He was eventually silenced by FOOT and MARTIN, who pointed out that as he was in the minority (of one), he should give in to the majority view of the meeting. A resolution was then passed to appoint a committee for the purpose of electing a deputation and to decide whether the deputation should wait on the Prime Minister or the Secretary of State for India. The committee would also undertake to arrange meetings and a press campaign (as originally proposed by Kingsley Martin) either before or after the deputation had served its purpose, as the committee thought fit. A subsidiary proposal was adopted that the committee should consist of the convenors of this meeting (Michael FOOT, Julian HUXLEY, Storm JAMESON, R. SORENSEN, MP, Mrs Rebecca SIEFF, Miss Bhicoo BATLIVALA, and V.K.K. MENON) and have power to co-opt other members and call further meetings.

The final topic of discussion was the question of getting in touch with Indian leaders. It was pointed out that many of them were free and could be communicated with but it was not easy, and at times impossible, to get in touch with those in prison (the name of Jawaharlal Nehru was quoted as example), and the view of the meeting was that the Government should be pressed to grant facilities for messages to reach political prisoners. The meeting agreed that Nehru should be urged to make a statement which might help to resolve the present deadlock and a final resolution, that there should be free communication with all the Indian leaders, whether in or out of jail, was then carried ....

(vi) Central Legislative Assembly Discusses Resolution on India and the Atlantic Charter, 29 October 1941

Indian Annual Register, 1941, Vol. II, pp. 111–13.

29th October: The Assembly took up for discussion *Maulvi Abdur Rasheed Chaudhury's* resolution recommending immediate steps to give effect in the case of India also, to the joint decision of the British Premier and the President of the United States of America, commonly known as the Atlantic Charter, for creating a new world order. The mover said that when President Roosevelt announced his eight points of peace and war aims of the Democracies, Indians thought that they would be equally applicable to India. They have had experience with President Wilson's Fourteen Points which were trampled upon when the war ended, but the people in this country considered that America had a certain partnership in the British Empire and the words of the President of the United States would not be taken lightly by the British authorities. He asserted that unless a declaration was made applying the Charter to India, the Government could not get as much co-operation and help from Indians as they wanted.

Sardar Sant Singh was glad that Mr Churchill had been frank and blunt in saying that the Charter did not apply to India. Referring to that portion of the Charter which stated that the Democracies did not seek any territorial or other aggrandizement, Sardar Sant Singh said that under the name of acquiring naval bases, America was really splitting up the British Empire and depriving them of portions of the Empire. Sardar Sant Singh declared that India did not look to any outsider for giving her freedom but would stand on her own legs.

Mr *G.V. Deshmukh* declared that it was the instinct of self-preservation that induced the British Government to make the Atlantic Declaration and said that, after having declared that the Charter would not be applicable to Indians, the British Government should be ashamed to appeal to them to give help in the war and send their men into the battlefields.

Mr *Kazmi* said that Mr Churchill was not really frank in many matter but he was quite frank about India because he knew that India was too weak to make any effective protest against his remarks.

In response to a request from members that the Government's attitude should be indicated before the debate proceeded further, Mr *M.S. Aney,* Leader of the House, intervened at this stage. The question raised in the resolution, he said, was no doubt one of great interest to India and he was, therefore, anxious that the House should be given an opportunity of discussing the matter. He believed that for experienced members of the House it would not have been difficult, particularly after the replies given to interpolations on the question to know what the Government's attitude could be. They left it to the members of the House to draw their own inferences from the pronouncement of Mr Churchill constituted as they were in this House. It was not for them to comment upon these pronouncements or criticize them. The Government of India were no party to the Charter. Those who signed it were the proper persons to say what was in their mind when they framed it; and we had the authoritative statement of one of them on one of the clauses, namely Clause 3 extending the right to all people to choose the form of government under which they wanted to live and declaring readiness to restore freedom and independence to those who had been forcibly deprived of them. Evidently the latter clause indicated that the framers had before them those countries which had lost their independence and freedom during the present war.

As regards India, Mr Churchill had made it clear that the declaration of self-determination contained in the Atlantic Charter did not have the effect of abrogating or qualifying the pledges already given about her political goal. Assuming that a declaration was made that the Atlantic Charter was applicable to India, would that satisfy India? Even before the Atlantic Charter was there, the Declaration of August 1940, defective though it was, had conceded the principle of self-determination to India. By merely stating that the Atlantic Charter would apply to India, India's cause, in his opinion, would not progress to any extent at all. (Mr Joshi: It would be some progress). Even me like the Premier of the Punjab, Mr Aney went on, did not share the view that a mere pronouncement applying the Atlantic Charter to India would satisfy India or help them towards their goal. The point of view had been expressed that India should not bother about getting any more promises from the British Government and that Indians should rely on something else than mere promises coming from any outside authority. Why, then, he suggested, ask for any declaration at all? Either we believed that promises coming from statesmen of eminence had some meaning or we did not believe it.

Mr Aney also reminded the House that Clause 3 of the Atlantic Charter would only be applied at the end of the war. In a matter of this kind, he went on, it was impossible to expect that the Government of India could form conclusions independently. All that the Government of India could be interested in was to find out the views of the public and it was the duty of the Government of India to keep His Majesty's Government duly informed of the feelings and sentiments expressed in the House. The attitude of the Government of India would therefore be to leave it free for the House to decide its attitude.

Mr *L.K. Maitra,* speaking on the resolution, asserted that the wording of the Atlantic Charter was quite clear and was equally applicable to all countries and races of the world including India. However Mr Churchill might now try to wriggle out of a position created by the force of circumstances, he did not agree with Mr Aney that even if the Charter was declared applicable to India it would make no vital difference; such a declaration would make a good deal of difference from the point of view of international law.

Mr *Jamnadas Mehta,* while feeling that there was an air of unreality about the whole debate, strongly criticized Mr Churchill's statement which he said threw them back to the declaration of August 1940. This declaration, he asserted, was not a declaration of freedom—it was a declaration of bondage—to perpetuate vested interests, and the British hold over this country, giving the minorities power to veto the progress of India. He held that Article 3 of the Atlantic Charter was an unequivocal declaration that all races and countries had the right of self-determination and that after the war, this country too would have the right to frame its own constitution, chosen by its representatives, and be free to live under that constitution. This had been borne out by Mr Attlee's statement.

Sir Cowasji Jehangir contended that the real grievance against Mr Churchill's explanation of the Atlantic Charter was that part of it which contained the reservation that the pledges to India were subject to Britain's responsibilities to India's many creeds, races and interests. If those words were omitted, would the Mussalmans accept that statement, asked Sir Cowasji. He urged Indians to face the realities and not to drug their conscience. Without those words, he declared, no statement made by the British Government would be acceptable to millions and millions of the people of India. 'Unless you get these minorities to feel contented, you are not going to have the Government of this country.' (Mr *Jamnadas Mehta* at this stage kept up a running fire of interruption by exclaiming: 'You are talking like Mr Amery. You are Mr Amery.')

Discussion on the resolution had not concluded, when it was time to take up Mr *N.M. Joshi's* adjournment motion on the Deoli jail hunger-strike.

(vii) How Far the Fundamental Principles Apply to India, Sir Tej Bahadur's Statement

Amrita Bazar Patrika, 3 November 1941.

Allahabad, 2 November. The meeting of the Standing Committee of the Bombay Non-Party Leaders conference concluded to-day. Kunwar Sir Jagdish Prasad attended to-day's discussions and the Hon P.N. Sapru was also present for sometime.

The Committee has issued a statement on the present political situation.

Plea for Ending Satyagraha

The following statement has been issued by the Right Hon'ble Sir Tej Bahadur Sapru in pursuance of a resolution of the Standing Committee of the Non-Party Conference which met in Allahabad on the 1st and the 2nd of November 1941. The Standing Committee of the Non-Party Conference have considered the joint Anglo-United States declaration setting out the objectives for which the Allies are fighting, and indicating the fundamental principles on which plans for a permanent world peace must be based. In particular they have noticed with satisfaction that of the fundamental principles to which expression was given authoritatively by President Roosevelt and Mr Churchill at their meeting in the Atlantic Ocean in August last, the third laid down that 'They respect the right of all peoples to choose the form of Government under which they will live; and they wish to see sovereign rights and self-Government restored to those who have been forcibly deprived of them'. Their opinion while the latter part of the third principle just quoted, obviously applied to those sovereign countries in Europe which lost their independence or territory owing to the totally unjustifiable and immoral action of Hitlerite Germany, the first part of the third fundamental principle using as it does, the expression 'all people' is sufficiently wide to include the case of India. It is difficult to believe that it could have been the intention of President Roosevelt to exclude India from the operation of the first part of that Mr Churchill could have ignored at that time India's claim to self-Government when it is a matter of common knowledge that American opinion for some time past had been definitely critical of British policy towards India. As regards President Roosevelt, the committee cannot believe that he could have been a party to the exclusion of India from the benefits of this principle, particularly when they remember that, on his return to America, the President is reported to have observed that 'Not a single section of a single continent went undiscussed during the meetings'.

The August Declaration

The Committee also note that Mr Cordell Hull, the United States Secretary of State, described the Churchill–Roosevelt declaration as a statement of basic principles and fundamental ideas that are universal in their practical application. The Committee would further point out that Mr Attlee, the Deputy Prime Minister, is reported to have said that the declaration of peace principles applied to all countries including Asiatics. The Committee however, have noted with profound disappointment that in his first and unfortunately only reference to India since he became Prime Minister, Mr Churchill used language which has made many people to doubt whether he and his Government do really mean to part with power and whether India will ever attain real self-government. 'The joint declaration' said Mr Churchill, 'does not qualify in any way the various statements of policy which have been made from time to time about the development of constitutional government in India, Burma or other parts in the declaration of August 1940 to help India to obtain free and equal partnership in the British Commonwealth of Races, subject of course to the fulfilment of the obligations arising from our long connection with India and our responsibilities to its many creeds, races and interests.' It seems to the Committee that so far as Mr Churchill is concerned, the fundamental principles to be applied to India are those contained in the declaration of August 1940—a declaration which has afforded no satisfaction to any section of Indian opinion, and which far from easing the tension in India or winning over those sections which had withheld their support from British Government and strengthening the position of those which have been friendly to the British Government and which would like to remain so, has given rise to grave misgivings and has caused a great deal of resentment. In the opinion of the Committee, the declaration of August 1940 is not wholly consistent with the noble and generous sentiments contained in fundamental principles on three of the joint declaration quoted above. His Majesty's declaration of August 1940 is hedged in by too many conditions, is so incomplete in the enunciation of the aim and so non-committal in regard to its being implemented within any reasonable distance of time, that it can afford no satisfaction whatever to the people of this country.

Future of India

The Committee think that the whole position in regard to the future of India should have been made clear long ago by using definite, certain and unambiguous language, so that India may feel sure that after the war, in the vent of victory, her position shall be the same as that of Britain and the Dominions. In short the Committee are strongly of the opinion that after victory the position of India in regard to her status and powers shall not be that of a dependency but shall be one of perfect equality. In the opinion of the Committee the question of the internal Constitution of India with proper provisions for one safeguarding of different interests, should not be allowed to stand in the way of making such a declaration of policy regarding the political and constitutional relations of England and India. For this reason the Committee hold that immediate steps should be taken to secure that India's representatives at the peace conference or any other international conference shall be selected by the Government in India and be answerable to it and shall on no account be in the leading strikes of the Secretary of State. A change like this can be effected without amending the Statute by the adoption of a suitable convention.

Essential Steps

.... In regard to international matters, India should be treated to all intents and purposes on terms of perfect equality and that her internal constitution should during the interim period be so worked in practice as to approximate as far as possible under the existing conditions to the working of the self-governing Dominions. For this reason the Bombay and Poona conferences and this Committee at its previous sittings have emphasized that all the portfolios including Defence, Finance, Home and Communication should be put in the hands of Indian Members of the Executive Council who would in the interim period be responsible to the Crown.

Change in Policy Needed

In the opinion of this Committee these steps are essential for a successful prosecution of the war and therefore necessary changes should be introduced without delay so as to hearten the people and make them feel sure of their destiny. The Committee while they realize that in times like these war preparations must have the foremost place; they nevertheless strongly feel that the fullest measure of help from the public cannot be hoped for without making the people of this country relies that they shall be, in the full sense of the word participators in the fruits of victory. In the opinion of the Committee to make the cry of 'Win the war first' as the only cry would be very poor statesmanship, indeed and far from easing the situation; it would widen the estrangement between the people and the Government—a result which must be avoided at all costs.

For this reason they are pressing the view set forth above and they trust that the expanded Executive Council of the Viceroy which has now eight Indian members will use their influence and their moral pressure for bringing about a desirable change in the policy of the Government. The primary responsibility for a satisfactory change in policy must rest with the Government and the Committee have no hesitation in saying, that in the recent past those who have been responsible for the conduct of affairs in India or at Whitehall have shown neither a correct appreciation of the situation nor done anything striking to appeal to the imagination of the people or to strengthen constructive forces. They trust that in matters of high policy the principle of collective responsibility will be observed scrupulously and that Indian members of the

Executive Council will claim it as a matter of Constitutional right. While the Committee recognize that there are eight Indian members of the Executive Council they also note with regret that the important portfolios of Defence, Finance, Home and Communications have been withheld from Indians. Until and unless such a transfer takes places, it cannot be said that more power has been made over to Indians. The Committee, therefore, urge that as a preparation for full responsible government in future, the entire Viceroy's Executive Council should consist of non-official public men. Similarly they hold very strongly that in the provinces the rule of the Governors with the aid of that advisers under Section 93, should be brought to a speedy end, and, therefore, they appeal both to the people and to the Government to change their outlook. They are also strongly of the view that parliamentary institutions such as they are should be utilized as instruments for the advancement of the freedom of the country and its effective defence. We are convinced that to stimulate war effort a big scale change of policy is necessary.

The Committee would also particularly emphasize the need for a more rapid and thorough industrialization of the country with special reference to war needs.

The Committee are also strongly of the opinion that the policy which the Government have hitherto followed in regard to political prisoners should undergo a change and that those who are in detention and those who have been imprisoned for acts not involving violence should be released. Such a gesture is necessary in order to create an atmosphere in which political questions can be discussed without passion or prejudice and in a spirit of hopefulness. For similar reasons the Committee would also earnestly urge that the Satyagraha movement and the boycott of parliamentary institutions should be ended.—AP

(viii) Central Legislative Assembly Approves Resolution Recommending Application of Atlantic Charter to India, 12 November 1941

Indian Annual Register, 1941, Vol. II, p. 125.

12 November: The House continued the debate on Mr *Abdur Rashid Choudhury's* resolution recommending the application of the Atlantic Charter to India and passed it without a division. Government members not opposing.

In the course of the debate, Dr *R.D. Dalal,* opposing the resolution, reminded the House that although Mr *Churchill* had said that the declaration would not apply to India, he had not stated that the pledges given to India had disappeared or no longer stood. Dominion Status, declared Dr *Dalal,* would exist automatically if certain required conditions were present. When the various political elements were agreed on the kind of constitution under which they were prepared to live and if the minorities were satisfied with the conditions under which they were expected to live, then the country would have secured Dominion Status, for the simple reason that the British Government would have neither the power nor the desire to reject or resist that demand.

Mr *N.M. Dumosia,* also speaking against the resolution, declared that it was the Congress and the Muslim League which stood in the way of Dominion Status. He asserted that if India were given independence at this stage, there would be civil war. If India wanted self-government in the near future, the Congress must actively help the Government in the present war.

Mr *A.C. Datta* supporting the resolution, pointed out that there was no ground for controversy over the resolution as worded. It merely made a recommendation to the Governor-General to take steps to give effect in the case of India also to the Atlantic Charter. Controversies on the question whether the Charter was applicable to India or not, whether the Viceroy's declaration of August, 1940, was or was not similar to the Atlantic Charter were irrelevant.

Rao Saheb Sivaraj recalled the saying that when a promise made which we knew was not likely to be kept, we said: 'write it in water.' Remembering this, it was unfortunate, he said, that the Charter was entered into in mid-ocean (laughter). He could not, however, imagine that persons placed as Mr *Churchill* and Mr *Roosevelt* were, in constant danger from enemy forces, were in a fit state of mind, unless they were supermen, to give a declaration of any real practical consequence. Such promises as they made were like those which a Banya caught in the hands of dacoits might make to those who tried to rescue him. It was futile to expect any good from the Charter and he asked the mover to withdraw his resolution. After Mr *A.R. Chaudhury* had replied, the resolution was passed without a division.

(ix) Resolution on Atlantic Charter Passed by the Council of State, 18 November 1941

Indian Annual Register, 1941, Vol. II, pp. 98–9.

Mr V.V. Kalikar next moved the resolution relating to the non-applicability of Atlantic Charter to India which 'in the opinion of this House is likely to prejudice the war effort of this country at this critical juncture'. Mr Kalikar said that the Congress party were never under the illusion that the Charter would be applicable to India. But many others were and they felt that after all commonsense had dawned on British rulers of India. They were fortified in their belief by the declaration of Mr Attlee that the Charter would be applicable to all races and people inhabiting the world.

Chair: Members of Parliament are liable to make mistake.

Mr Kalikar: Mr Attlee is not an ordinary member of Parliament. He is a member of the British Cabinet and deputy Prime Minister.

Chair: The correct interpretation of the Charter can only be given by the persons who were a party to it. Mr Churchill has declared that the Charter would apply to only those countries which were under the Nazi yoke.

Pandit Kunzru: Sir, it would be difficult for non-official members to carry on discussion with the Chair.

Chair: No. I do not wish to carry on discussion but only wanted to correct a mis-statement of fact. Mr Kalikar, please proceed.

Mr Kalikar: referred to Mr Churchill's statement and said that the Prime Minister had maintained a studied silence over the question of India ever since he became the Prime Minister. He, however, promptly corrected the impression that the Charter could be applicable to India. In doing so, the Prime Minister had greatly prejudiced the war effort of this country and had weakened the stand taken by the protagonists of war effort. Mr Roosevelt had not spoken so far and in the face of different interpretations placed on the Charter it would be best to obtain the judicial interpretation of its applicability. As for the demand of the British Government for cent per cent agreement in India as a condition for any constitutional advance, Mr Kalikar asked whether there was any country where 100 per cent agreement existed and was there cent per cent agreement in the dominions before self-government was granted to them.

Mr M.N. Dalal, supporting the resolution, argued that it was clear from Mr Churchill's words that India was also discussed at the meeting between Mr Churchill and President Roosevelt. By saying that the Atlantic Charter was meant primarily for those countries which had lost their freedom in this war, Mr Churchill implied that other countries including India were also discussed in connection with the general declaration. If it had been an original idea to exclude India and other countries from the scope of the declaration, then they would have made a specific exception in such cases in its clauses. He went on to say that the August declaration of the Viceroy could not really satisfy India because it was made subject to arriving at an agreed solution of their differences, and no specific period for India's attaining Dominion Status had been mentioned.

Mr P.N. Sapru vehemently condemned Mr Churchill's statement and declared that if Britain was really fighting a battle of freedom for all countries in which they wanted India's support, they could not deny the same freedom to countries over which they dominate. He felt that President Roosevelt had really meant to include India also in the scope of the declaration and had made this point clear in his address at the International Labour Conference. If he did not come out with any special statement questioning Mr Churchill's interpretation, it was because he did not want to give the Isolationists in America a handle.

Sir A.P. Patro, opposing the resolution, said that to his mind the declaration of August 1940 was fully comprehensive and conceded the right of Indians to frame their own constitution, subject only to the existing obligations of the British Government to various interests like the minorities, the Indian States, and others. He deplored the existence of communal differences and expressed the opinion that they were the real barriers to the progress of India.

Sir Mohd Yakub, opposing the resolution, declared that it was the 'height of hypocrisy' to say that Mr Churchill's statement would adversely affect India's war efforts because none of the political parties or statesmen was really doing anything to help the war, even before the Atlantic declaration was made. He went on to argue that the type of western democracy envisaged in the Atlantic Charter was unsuitable to India. His own opinion was that democracy was not suitable to any part of the world.

Mr Sapru: Do you want Nazi rule? (Laughter)

Sir Mohd Yakub: There is only one Hitler in Germany; but there are a number of Hitlers in this country. I hate all Hitlers. (More laughter.)

Sir Mohammed then proceeded to say that there was no use blaming the third party for perpetuating their communal differences; they must do away with their politicians and statesmen who were really responsible for the present disharmony.

Sir Akbar Hydari, Leader of the House, intervening at this stage, announced that so far as the resolution was concerned, the Government would remain neutral. He added that the report of the debate would in any case be forwarded to his Majesty's Government. Turning to the subject of the resolution, Sir Akbar said that he did not think that Mr Churchill in his statement had denied India any benefit which India would have derived if the declaration had been applicable to her also. Mr Churchill himself had declared that the principles of the Atlantic Charter were embodied in the declaration which the Viceroy had made in India on behalf of his Majesty's Government. Mr Churchill had not in any way disassociated India from the principles laid down in the Atlantic Declaration; on the contrary, he had specially associated India with them. Sir Akbar declared that it was for all of them to put their heads and their hearts together and bring out an agreed constitution—agreed to the extent that it was possible to agree in any constitutional matter. He assured them that he and others who were with him on the Government side, even though they did not have a backing in the country in the sense that they had no organized party in the country would give them all the help they could in arriving at a solution.

Pandit Kunzru, speaking after Sir Akbar, welcomed the gesture of goodwill made by him, and said that the presence of such members as Sir Akbar Hydari, Sir Feroz Khan Noon and Dr Raghvendra Rao in the Executive Council was in his opinion an indication of the advance they could make if they all worked single-minded for the upliftment of the country. He did not agree with Sir Akbar that Mr Churchill's statement had not made any difference. It would make a vital difference to the moral effect of the charter on the world.

Referring to India, Pandit Kunzru said that he was humiliated, intensely humiliated, by the existence of such differences in the country; but they should look at them from the proper perspective. They should not be allowed to become a bar to the progress of the country. The best way to solve those differences was not to say that until they composed their differences, they would not be given freedom. On the contrary, with a definite promise and hope of freedom before them, the people would be made to forget their smaller issues.

After a brief reply by Mr Kalikar, the resolution was pressed to a division and was passed by 10 votes to 6.

---

[1] Franklin D. Roosevelt, President of USA, and Winston Churchill, Prime Minister of Britain, held secret meetings aboard the US ship *USS Augusta* and the British ship *HMS Prince of Wales* from 12 August 1941 to 14 August 1941. The text of the joint declaration, known as the Atlantic Charter, adopted by them on 14 August 1941, is reproduced below.

> The President of the United States of America and the Prime Minister, Mr Churchill, representing His Majesty's Government in the United Kingdom, being met together, deem it right to make known certain common principles in the national policies of their respective countries on which they base their hopes for a better future for the world.
> First, their countries seek no aggrandizement, territorial or other;
> Second, they desire to see no territorial changes that do not accord with the freely expressed wishes of the peoples concerned;
> Third, they respect the right of all peoples to choose the form of government under which they will live; and they wish to see sovereign rights and self government restored to those who have been forcibly deprived of them;
> Fourth, they will endeavor, with due respect for their existing obligations, to further the enjoyment by all States, great or small, victor or vanquished, of access, on equal terms, to the trade and to the raw materials of the world which are needed for their economic prosperity;
> Fifth, they desire to bring about the fullest collaboration between all nations in the economic field with the object of securing, for all, improved labor standards, economic advancement and social security;
> Sixth, after the final destruction of the Nazi tyranny, they hope to see established a peace which will afford to all nations the means of dwelling in safety within their own boundaries, and which will afford assurance that all the men in all the lands may live out their lives in freedom from fear and want;
> Seventh, such a peace should enable all men to traverse the high seas and oceans without hindrance; Eighth, they believe that all of the nations of the world, for realistic as well as spiritual reasons must come to the abandonment of the use of force. Since no future peace can be maintained if land, sea or air armaments continue to be employed by nations which threaten, or may threaten, aggression outside of their frontiers, they believe, pending the establishment of a wider and permanent system of general security, that the disarmament of such nations is essential. They will likewise aid and encourage all other practicable measures which will lighten for peace-loving peoples the crushing burden of armaments.
>
> Signed by: Franklin D. Roosevelt and Winston S. Churchill

29. Preserving Unity of India: Jayakar's Appeal to Prevent Vivisection War and India's Support

Amrita Bazar Patrika, 2 October 1941.

The importance of preserving the unity of India was stressed by the Right Hon'ble M.R. Jayakar speaking at a dinner of the Madras Rotary Club. The speaker emphasized that the design of nature as well as of Hindu and Muslim rulers and British administrators had always been to keep India as a single entity. Taking a bird's eye view of India they would always find that nature always intended India to be a self-contained unit.

Most Vicious System

Proceeding he pointed out how the British had brought a single set of laws for application to the whole of the country. But in 1892 by some curious process the origins of which they had not been able to find out the British threw an apple of discord into India. This gave rise to the political feeling that religion could create political compartments. He characterized it as a most vicious system introduced in the country and added that its fruits were obvious now.

Rotarians' Duty Towards Unity

Mr Jayakar concluding said that the question was whether the British and the Indians should not combine to preserve the British made unity of India. This unity had been the dream of British administrators for centuries. Macaulay had said that it would be the proudest day of his life when he found the several communities of India combining for purposes of asking that the British models of administration and Government on democratic models established on the basis of a democratic system must be granted to India. That day had come. His appeal was that the British or Indians must put their hands together to prevent the vivisection of India, and exhorted the members of the Rotary Club to render what service they could towards preserving the unity of India.

Congress and Government Drift

Referring in general to the present political situation in our country, Dr Jayakar summed it up by saying that war was coming nearer and nearer India and the frontiers of India were extending as far as Iran, Iraq and perhaps Russia; but strange as it may seem the discontent, apathy and sense of frustration of the Indian people are simultaneously increasing (cheers).

When the war broke out, the very instinct of self-defence which they possessed would have actuated them to give their unstinted support to Britain, for, Dr Jayakar said, the instinct of self-preservation or self-defence was the first impulse of humanity. But unfortunately owing to various causes a conflict was set up between the instinct of self-defence and the instinct of self-respect.

In this connection he referred to the comments of the *London Times* that war was nearing India and that India should present a solid rock not only of physical resistance, but spiritual resistance.

Unfortunately, Dr Jayakar observed, the Indian authorities took a contrary view and the conditions in India, instead of becoming more and more of a solid rock of spiritual resistance grew more and more disintegrated. The spiritual or moral resistance to the war of the entire people of India should have been regarded as far more valuable than assistance with men, money and munitions. The moral resistance of an entire country which for centuries has been pledged to a deep rooted aversion to bloodshed and violence was a far greater asset to a country fighting for the assertion of moral principles than merely tons of munitions (loud cheers). That being the true principle, men like the speaker were making attempts to tell the Government on the one hand and the dominant Indian political party to take stock of the circumstances and rearrange affairs in such a way that this conflict between self-defence and self-respect might be removed at an early date to the benefit of both, but they had not yet succeeded in their efforts.

The Four Parties

Dr Jayakar proceeding pointed out that there were four parties in the present deadlock or impasses. The first was the Government, both Central and Provincial, the second was the Indian National Congress, 'the predominant political party, the best knit and best organized one in this country' (loud applause). The third important party was the Muslim League. The fourth perhaps equally important was the group of men like the speaker and the audience who belonged to none of these groups, but who continued to maintain that India being their parent country, had a stake in the quarrel. But this group although very large in number did not count at present because it was not well organized.

Which is Responsible

Dr Jayakar next proceeded to analyse as to which of these four parties were responsible for the present state of things. For the moment he wanted to leave out the Muslim League not because he failed to recognize its importance, but because he felt that it was hopeless and futile to make any suggestion to that party. Under its present leadership it was impossible to hope that it would agree to any negotiations. Its attitude in short was one of 'touch-me-not' (laughter). The leadership of that organization had been saying that 'no talk at all' except with the leader of the Congress and that too on the condition that the Muslim League was recognized as the only organization representative of the Muslim community and that the negotiation to proceed only on the basis of an acceptance of Pakistan. Perhaps the first condition might not have been difficult to accede if it stood by itself but the second made all negotiations impossible. Even for the interim agreement proposed by the Government of India during the period of war, the League demanded fifty per cent representation at the Centre if the Congress came in and more if the Congress did not come in. Apparently they thought that India was the Congress plus the Muslim League and when the Congress had reduced itself to a zero by its own action it meant that India was equal to the Muslim League (loud laughter). 'It is an entirely irrational demand and no compromise with the League is possible on these terms. The best way under the circumstances is to leave it alone'. He however wished to distinguish the Muslim League from Muslim India, among which were to be found many friendly factors opposed to such an intransigent attitude which were unfortunately not sufficient vocal or assertive in the present circumstances....

Congress and Government Drift

Dr Jayakar proceeding explained the circumstances under which the Congress and the British Government drifted away. The Congress had at a critical occasion offered to give their moral support to the war. But it was not accepted. More attention was paid to obtaining India's men and material, as if they were of greater consequence than the spiritual support of India, as the

London Times called it. The situation thus drifted woefully. The Congress went its own way and the Government went another way.

Coming to details, Mr Jayakar proceeded to say that the position taken by the Government was thus: 'Nothing doing until minorities agree'.

The speaker in this connection referred to the speech of Mr Amery who at a later stage brought other interests into the question such as geographical and regional. What is exactly meant by these is not clear, and Mr Jayakar added that the seeds of disunion planted in this country as early as 1892 when separate political representation was allowed on the ground of religion, and with the working of this principle for half a century, leading to greater divisions and antagonism, it was unfair to expect an agreement on the question at issue in the present crisis.

Satyagraha: A Moral Protest

Referring to the satyagraha campaign started by Mahatma Gandhi, Dr Jayakar said that this movement was a moral protest against the action of the British Government in having declared India a belligerent country without her consent. Its author regards himself as a God-appointed apostle of the principle of non-violence. If he succeeded in this doctrine the world might gain. But if he failed it would cause the ruination of India. So far it had not succeeded in winning India her freedom or bringing her any the nearer to freedom, which would be a layman's test of its success.

Dr Jayakar said that the differences in this country, caused as explained above, could hardly be a reason for refusing to concede India's demand. Such difference existed among people in other countries like Canada and Egypt. Yet they were given freedom without any such conditions.

The speaker incidentally referred to the latest statement of Mr Amery in reply to American critics and said that it was full of half-truths. Mr Amery wanted the people in India to come together and frame a constitution. How can it be possible with the sham created by the half a century working of a fissiparous principle of political voting seeking to divide the people more and more into compartments having no friendly contact with each other. 'It is a Frankenstein's monster issued by the British people and it is their responsibility to lay it.'

Non-party Conference

It was under these circumstances, Dr Jayakar went on that some of his friends took it upon themselves to convene a non-party conference. It succeeded but only partially. 'The firm and immobile citadel of the Government of India has been shaken a bit, and there has been a little change in the Executive Council of the Viceroy.' The speaker regarded it as an important experiment but felt at the same time that the persons selected might have been entrusted with the more important portfolios. 'I value the experiment of eight Indians being selected. This is an important experiment in the sense that the Viceroy will be surrounded by eight Indians and will take counsel with them on the principle of joint and collective responsibility. Our great difficulty in those days while we were in the Central Legislature was that the Viceroy was not surrounded by sufficient Indian sentiment. Now we have got eight Indians, be they Hindus or Muslims. I am not disposed to make this distinction or to suppose that these eight men will be communal to their outlook'. It was also a fortunate circumstance that the Indians, Hindus and Muslims, were *prima facie* worthy of their selection.

Stressing the urgent need for entrusting the more important portfolios like defence, finance and communication to the Indian members of the Council, Dr Jayakar referred to the statement made by Mr Amery that they had got together the 'best team' that could be found anywhere in the world. If so, Dr Jayakar asked 'why don't you give your best portfolios to these best men?'

He agreed with Mr Amery in his hope that the bringing together of these Indians would lead to an increasing understanding and sympathy so as to facilitate the removal of obstacles which the British regarded as standing in the way of India's obtaining her place as a free and equal partner in the British Commonwealth of Nations.

How to Resolve Deadlock

Continuing the speaker said that the only way to resolve the deadlock was to bring it into 'larger air and ampler light' so that the difficulties could be more clearly seen. We must proceed to adjust our own affairs on the basis of practical politics, uninfluenced by suggestions of 'vision and inner voices'. 'As a member of a conservative religious family', said Dr Jayakar, 'I am accustomed to the doctrine of vision and inner voice, which my domestic priests often used to proclaim. But I am not disposed to accept these illusory guides as infallible portents of political truths or accuracy'.

The speaker emphasizing the necessity for reconsidering the stand taken by the Congress said that staunch Congressmen had stated publicly that the time had come for the Congress to reconsider its programme. The Orissa Congressmen and Messrs Satyamurti, Rajan, Gidwani and C.R. Srinivasan had boldly suggested this. None could question their loyalty to the Congress and its dictator, and it was perfectly true that to one man who boldly expressed his view, there were scores who kept silent.

Congress and Legislature

He appealed to the non-party men who formed the bulk of the population to create strong public opinion, so that Government might be forced to bend before it. Appealing to the Congress to change its present policy of Satyagraha, Dr Jayakar said that 'these pin-pricks were not going to succeed'. He would suggest to the Congress either to stiffen the present movement if they really wanted to embarrass the Government, or if not, to go back to Parliamentary activities. 'You (Congress) have neglected the Parliamentary activities. People sent you there not to run away from your places, but to stand in your places and fight.' (applause). As one who knew something of the Government of India Act, he could assure them that if by some miracle the Congress was persuaded to resume parliamentary activities, no one could prevent them from doing so. The present rule of Governor and his civilian advisers in the provinces look back to 80 or 90 years ago. He regretted to learn during his stay here that the Congress Ministry in the course of twenty-four months had created extreme distrust and suspicion in the mind of non-Congressmen.

If there was in consequence any difficulty in reinstalling an 'unadulterated' Congress Ministry, the alternative might be the formation of a coalition Ministry which would be better than no Ministry at all if the Congress was not willing to go back to power, it should make room for others who would be willing to fill up the place. In such a case it would be best to leave the Congress and its dictator alone.

Concluding he said: 'We all who are outside the Congress must carry on agitation to compete the Congress and the government to yield' (cheers).—AP

30. Jinnah's Move to Isolate Congress: Letter to MP's Offering to Make Combination of Princes, British and League

Bombay Chronicle, 6 November 1941.

Declares League does not Want Severance of Connection with Commonwealth

The New Delhi Correspondent of *The Hindu* writes:

Interesting details are available of a letter which Mr M.A. Jinnah addressed to a certain Member of Parliament regarding the situation in this country.

After pointing out that democratic institutions cannot thrive in this country inhabited by two communities with no common interests or affinities—whether political, religious or cultural—he makes a bid for British support on the ground that British, the Princes and his own party could, provided his demand are granted, combine and isolate the Congress thus substantially easing British anxiety about co-operation.

Claiming to speak on behalf of at least ninety per cent of his community, Mr Jinnah observes he does not contemplate severance from the British Commonwealth of Nations, but recognizes the necessary transition period during which suitable arrangements would be made for defence, external affairs communications and customs.

'Please don't' he appeals 'fall a victim to the intensive propaganda of the Congress'.

Throwing the blame for the British Cabinet's incorrect appreciation of the Indian situation on the Viceroy, Mr Jinnah most emphatically demanded termination of Lord Linlithgow period of office next April without another extension. As for Mr Wedgwood Benn's claims in the post Mr Jinnah is not satisfied with his attitude as disclosed in the Commons debate on India. Mr Jinnah however hopes there might be others in the Labour Party who sympathizes with his demand for the division of India.

Question in Commons

It will be recalled in this connection that in the House of Commons on 27 February 1941, Mr Sorensen asked the Secretary of State whether he was aware that communications with Indian political leaders have not reached their addresses in this country although cabled references to these conversations have been received whether he can give the reason for these communications being held up by authorities in India; what political proposals Mr Jinnah has propounded within the last three months to HM's Government and why information respecting Indian political life and movement is being withheld or suspended from publication in this country.

Mr Amery replied: I am not aware on what grounds the Hon Member makes the assumptions involved in the first and last part of his question. It is of course the fact that under present conditions letters take much longer time to arrive from India than normally. Members of the Government have recently received from Mr Jinnah documents setting out the claims of the Muslim League and urging HM's Government to reject the demands of the Indian National Congress.

31. India's Future After War: Congress Demand for Constituent Assembly an Impossible One! Says Amery

Amrita Bazar Patrika, 21 November 1941.

Stress on League's and States' Objection to Majority Rule at Centre

London, November 19. The following is the full text of Mr Amery's speech at Manchester:

Few problems have ever confronted human statesmanship more important, more complex and more difficult than that of India's future after the war. The task with which its solution confronts alike British and Indian statesmanship is tremendous. Those of us who have to play any part, however, small in dealing with it can only approach it with certain awe at the thought of their responsibility and not without a deep sense of humility. In saying that I am not suggesting that we of this country should address ourselves to our share of the task in any spirit of apology for our own past record; far from it. We can well be proud of Britain's contribution to India. We have given her unity and peace within her borders, an all pervading reign of impartial law. These are indispensable foundations for the fulfilment of those ideals of political freedom which we have implanted in Indian minds.

Effective Central Government

What the Norman conquest gave us of an effective Central Government, what the Magna Carta won for us in the rights of the individual under the law, that we have given to India. That achievement itself was something of a miracle. We have now set ourselves to achieve, in co-operation with Indian statesmanship, the far greater miracle of building up in India, within the space of a few years, that superstructure of responsible freedom, which we here took centuries after the Magna Carta to complete, if indeed it can ever be said to be completed. It is indeed essential, if we are to have the hope of success, that we should have faith in ourselves, faith in our capacity and our courage, faith in the principles by which we have grown great, by which we live and for which we are fighting today. But faith and hope are not enough. We need also charity, goodwill, understanding, and sympathy. We need goodwill towards Indian aspirations; I would say, indeed there is nothing more remarkable than the growth of that goodwill and understanding in Parliament and outside in recent years.

Understanding from Indians

We need no less goodwill and understanding from Indians for our own endeavours. In spite of much criticism and suspicion we still, I believe, retain a real fund of underlying goodwill and confidence in India as well as much personal goodwill among Indians and their British associates in administration or in business. Above all there is the need for goodwill among Indians themselves. There perhaps lies the greatest difficulty and danger before India and one which our particular form of democracy with its rivalry for power between organized parties, has almost inevitably tended to accentuate. It is only by mutual goodwill and by wider patriotism, which puts India first that it will be possible to find those compromises and adjustments without which no solution is possible....

Facing Facts

But no less essential than goodwill is the intellectual honesty of facing facts as they are. Goodwill need not mean loose thinking or easy sentimentality. The problem of India is not solved by catch phrases. 'We are fighting for democracy, therefore, why not give India what she wants?' That sounds plausible and generous. But where is the boy in existence or yet to be constituted which can in that sense speak for India or express an agreed demand? What form of democracy can be found under which the peoples of India are prepared to live together?

Atlantic Charter

The question brings us not a step nearer the solution of the problem. There could not be a more typical instance of loose thinking than the clamour for what is called the application of the Atlantic Charter to India and the protest against the Prime Minister's perfectly clear explanation that Article 111 of the Charter, primarily referred to the restoration of national life in Europe and in any case did not qualify in any way our own declaration as to India's future with which it is in entire harmony. After all what does that Article say?

Dominion Status

It says that among the principles on which the Prime Minister and President Roosevelt base their hopes for a better future for the world is respect for the right of all peoples to choose the form of Government under which they will live. How far does that carry us with regard to India? It gives no indication as to whether India is to be regarded as one people or several; it does not say by what method the form of Government is to be decided; it lays down no procedure, no timetable. On all these points it naturally does not attempt either to give guidance or impose precise obligation. I can well imagine, if in answer to the demand for a statement of our Indian policy we had answered merely in terms of the Atlantic Charter, the derision and indignation which would have met so vague and unsatisfying a reply. The answer we did give in August last year was no less far reaching in its scope and far more definite in the procedure envisaged and in the pledge involved. It defined as our proclaimed and accepted goal that free and equal partnership in the British Commonwealth which is usually referred to as Dominion Status.

Indian Constitution

That status, combining as it does all the advantages of unfettered freedom with those of an association of calculable value both in peace and war, is, I venture to assert the highest in the world. It is the status of this country, and we at any rate are not insensible either of the practical advantages or of the honour of our position. It went on in the very spirit of the Atlantic Charter to make it clear that we wished India to enjoy that position under a constitution framed primarily by Indians or Indians in accordance with Indian conceptions.

Unity Among Indians

We added that while the completion of that undertaking obviously could not take place in the middle of a life and death struggle. We were ready to welcome and promote any steps representative Indians might take now to come together and prepare the ground, and that we agreed to the setting up, with the least possible delay after the war, of a body representative of the principal elements of India's national life, and pledged ourselves to lend every aid in our power to hasten decision on all relevant matter. So far as we are concerned, we have offered the utmost expedition in bringing about a constitutional settlement after the war.

Problem of States

The actual timetable is in the main in the hands of the Indians themselves. All but I shall be told that all this is limited and circumscribed by saying that it is 'subject to due fulfilment of obligations which Great Britain's long connection with India has imposed on her'. But would anyone suggest that the framing of any new form of Government in pursuance of the Atlantic Charter could take place anywhere without provision for the fulfilment of pre-existing obligations? What, after all, are those obligations? They fall into certain main categories, I am not of course giving an exhaustive list. There are for instance actual contractual obligations to the existing members of the services, which will naturally expire in due course. Is it suggested that the fulfilment of these is an impairment of freedom? There are obligations of the Crown towards Indian States, except in so far as and to the extent to which, they may have joined the Indian federation. Here again the continuance of similar obligations has been no detraction from self-Government whether in Canada, Australia, or in South Africa.

Control of Army

Of somewhat different character is continuing the responsibility of His Majesty's Government for the defence of India until India is in a position to take over the burden unaided. So long as the defence of India requires the permanent presence as distinguished from help in a great emergency of British forces, it is obvious that a Government which provides those forces is entitled to retain a measure of control on their employment in peace as well as on the external policy which may call for their employment in war. That is not derogation of status but a concession to the facts of a particular situation. That situation will be modified on the one hand by the growth of India's own military resources and they are growing day by day. It may be modified also by changes in the nature of possible dangers which may confront India after the war. The precise adjustment of these matters is clearly one that must depend on circumstances of the immediate post-war situation and on its subsequent development. It needs in no way prejudice or delay the establishment in India of a system of Government framed by Indian for themselves or the recognition of equality of that Government with other free Governments of the Commonwealth.

Constitution by Agreement

How then are the Indians to frame a system of Government for India? How I might ask, has it been found possible elsewhere to frame a scheme of free self-Government, not for a comparatively small and homogeneous people but for a complex of races, interests and political units which have nevertheless recognized the need for a wider constitutional framework as essential for their security or their economic welfare, or to the expression of the underlying national sentiment?

The answer is that it has never been possible except on the basis of free negotiation, compromise and eventual agreement among the main elements concerned. It has been so in the case of every British dominion. In Canada and South Africa the elements to be reconciled were racial as well as local. No American, I imagine, who thinks of the way American Union came about would imagine that in the application of the Atlantic Charter for India any other method could solve the problem.

That at any rate has been the view of His Majesty's Government who have made it clear that the future constitution of India must be framed by agreement among representatives

of the principal elements of her national life and have refused to contemplate the transfer of their present responsibilities for the peace and welfare of India in any system of Government whose authority is directly denied by large and powerful elements of that national life.

Political Units

What are these political elements of India's national life? They are firstly the political units into which India is already divided. There are eleven provinces in British India. Bengal with a population larger than that of the United Kingdom and Madras with an area as large as Italy, enjoying already or at any rate in a position to enjoy a wide extent of self-Government. There are the States equally excluded from the control of India's general, foreign, defence and economic policy but with no similarly precise demarcation between their powers and those of the Crown. There are secondly great religious and cultural communities above all two main ones, Hinduism and Islam, with a third, that of the so-called scheduled castes, numbering perhaps forty millions or more, but unorganized and only gradually acquiring collective consciousness. Fortunately from the viewpoint of the solution of the problem of the central constitution, Muslims though less than one third of the population in British India are not in minority everywhere. They are actually in majority in four out of eleven provinces. It should, therefore, be possible for them in a large measure to safeguard their interests by provisions already defining the rights of units.

Meaning of Agreement

Their outlook is likely to that extent at any rate to coincide with that of the States. You may ask what is meant by agreement. Does it mean that the attainment of full Indian self-Government can be indefinitely held up by the veto of some extreme section over some issue of detail? Obviously not. It means a substantial agreement by the main elements on the main principles of the constitution. I do not believe that if an agreement on those main principles is once reached, the details will present an insuperable difficulty in India any more than elsewhere. Nor can I bring myself to believe that there is among Indian statesmen, so little constitutional capacity, so little genuine patriotism or for that matter, so little real desire to see India governed by Indians that they would prefer to disagree indefinitely rather than work out some solution reasonably acceptable all-round. It would be inconsistent with the assumption on which the whole of our policy is based, the assumption of India's fitness for Dominion Status to accept the view that Indians are incapable of agreeing at any rate on the basis of the constitution. For, if they are incapable of that moral and intellectual efforts, how are they likely to be capable of no less a great effort of working any constitution that might be imposed on them?

Congress Demand

This insistence on the necessity of agreement rules out naturally any constitution decided by a mere majority vote. Nor has the principle of majority vote, applicable as it is to the decision of day-by-day issues under an accepted constitution has ever been regarded as applicable either to the framing of a constitution embracing varied elements or even to its modification. It is this issue more than any other which underlies the vehement opposition of the Congress party to the policy laid down by His Majesty's Government and acceptable in general principle to other elements which make up India's national life.

What the Congress has demanded is that India's future constitution should be settled by a Constituent Assembly elected by universal adult suffrage over the whole of India. It is an impossible demand and yet a natural and intelligible one. It is not merely that the Congress as by far the best organized political machine, would hope to sweep most of the Hindu constituencies. It is more than that. The Congress originated and grew up as the first vigorous expression of Indian national ideals in a unified bureaucratic India. It has tended throughout to think of itself as representatives of India in opposition to an alien rule and as natural heir and successor to that rule. In so doing it is apt to forget that conditions under which it has grown, under which it secured its majorities and under which those majorities exercised power will no longer be present if British control and support of the British armed forces are removed.

Party System of Government

It has yet to learn that conditions under which it can exercise its influence and fulfil its ideals in a self-governing India have yet to be agreed upon with other elements which are not prepared to consider Congress majorities as having a moral authority over them or any other material sanction than that of the existing British authorities. The difficulty extends not only to the method of finding a constitution, but to the character of the constitution itself. Here again Congress leaders have quite naturally imbibed not only British democratic ideals, but British ideals as to the best type of a democratic constitution. Nor have we for our part ever encouraged India to think in any other terms than those familiar to us of a constitution under which the executive is directly responsible to the party majority in the legislature. What we and most Indian politicians in the past have overlooked is that our type of constitution, in which parties are the machinery for the expression of differences of views on specific public issues, is a nucleus round which the main fluctuating mass of the electorate forms and reforms itself, but embody no permanent differences either of the way of life or underlying loyalties. Unfortunately these conditions do not exist in India, at any rate in the India of today. That is why the All-India Federal Constitution of 1935 was devised with such infinite care and forethought but failed to command support.

Imposing a Constitution

Rightly or wrongly the experience of provincial self-Government on British Parliamentary lines has convinced Moslems and the States that they cannot submit to any Central Government for India in which the executive is directly dependent on a Parliamentary majority which, if provincial experience is any guide, would be an obedient mouthpiece of the Congress high command. Inherent difficulties in the way of a federation on British Parliamentary lines are not of course in themselves obstacles either to federalism or to democracy. A free Government has many forms and we should be the last to proclaim a sealed pattern for liberty. I am not going to suggest to you any particular direction in which an alternative solution can best be sought. That is precisely the task which we have invited Indians to undertake for themselves in accordance with their own conceptions and their own conditions and for which they are clearly the best fitted. Moreover it is in the process of coming to an agreement on their future constitution that Indian statesmen will be in the best position and in the best mood to work it satisfactorily. No constitution is likely to work when imposed on those who don't believe in it....

32. Basis for Negotiations

Editorial, *Bombay Chronicle*, 5 December 1941.

The release of many Congress leaders, including the President and Pandit Jawaharlal Nehru and the prospect of the amnesty being completed in the next few days have caused no jubilation among Congressmen. That is partly because they resent the discrimination against other political prisoners, many of whom as Mr N.M. Joshi rightly points out, have committed no offence whatever. A more important cause of the lack of enthusiasm is the uncertainty as to whether Government will take further steps essential for a settlement and whether, if they do so, Congress will adequately respond to their efforts. An encouraging feature is the report from Madras that the authorities are not likely to arrest Satyagrahis, if any, for some time. In all probability the same policy will be followed in all other provinces. Whatever may be Government's motives, the amnesty and the temporary non-arrest of Satyagrahis deserve at least this response from Gandhiji that he should suspend Satyagraha till the Working Committee and the AICC get a chance of reviewing the developments during a whole year. Nothing is lost thereby, not even prestige. Whether there will ultimately be a settlement depends upon many things which today are uncertain. If there is one per cent chance of a settlement let it not be marred by lesser issues.

Gandhiji's Statement

Gandhiji's statement on the amnesty may not be regarded as encouraging by many. But he makes it clear that the statement is not made in a representative capacity but 'so far as I am concerned'. From his own point of view he says: 'The Government of India's decision can not evoke a single responsive or appreciative chord in me'. The main reason for this, he states, vividly in the following vivid terms: 'British representatives hold India as a bond slave. All freedom that India enjoys is the freedom of a slave and not the freedom of an equal, which is otherwise known as complete independence. Mr Amery's pronouncements do not soothe the festering sore, but they are like sprinkling chillies on it. It is in that setting that I am called upon to examine this release'. Gandhiji will doubtless make this position clearer at the meeting of the Working Committee and the AICC which, he says, it is for the President to decide whether and when to call. As we have pointed out before, even in ordinary times these meetings are obligatory constitutionally and morally. In the present circumstances they are essential and urgent. There is no option in the matter except in fixing the dates. What the meetings will decide will, of course, depend on various circumstances but the meetings have got to be held. The public are entitled to know from their representatives what are their considered views on the grave developments in the country during all these many months when the meetings could not be held. Now they can be held and should be held.

Revive Poona Offer

Hinting at some of the issues raised by the amnesty, Gandhiji says: 'The only meaning I can attach to the release is that the Government of India expects the prisoners to have changed their opinion regarding their self-invited solitude. I am hoping that the Government of India will soon be disillusioned'. We agree that few, if any, are afraid of repeating their self-invited solitude if there should be need for it. But whether there is need for it or not will depend on Government's terms for a settlement. Last year Satyagraha was started because the Poona offer of the Congress was flouted. If today Government are prepared to concede the substance of the demand, there is no reason why those who supported the Poona Offer and whose views thereon are unchanged should still persist in 'inviting solitude'. If, on the other hand, Government still flout those demand and offer terms not worth looking at, there will then be disillusionment on either side. The question is asked whether at this stage it is desirable for the Congress to revive the Poona offer. If the offer was wise then it is wise now and there is not the least harm in agreeing to, negotiations on that basis, details being left, in the first instance, to a few leaders who believe in the offer. Whether Government will agree to negotiations on that basis is a question which they must decide at once if they expect the present truce to lead to a settlement. It is difficult to imagine a settlement except on this basis. Even the demands of the Non-Party Conference are a fair approximation to the Poona offer. The British Press, while welcoming the amnesty and appealing for a compromise, does not yet suggest a definite basis for it. But if Congress revive the Poona Offer, opinion here, in Britain and America may so rally in its support as to be irresistible.

33. Will Poona Offer be Revived? Completely Indianized and Independent Council Can Satisfy National Demand and End Political Deadlock

Bombay Chronicle, 5 December 1941.

New Delhi, 1 December. So far as political talks are concerned the week has been unusually quite. Mr Jinnah has been confined to bed owing to indisposition. An important visitor was Mr Mahadev Desai from Wardha but though he casually visited one or two members of Government, his visit was really in connection with the Deoli hunger strike, which has not happily ended. As a result of the Wardha talks, in which Mr C. Rajagopalachari and Mr Bhulabhai Desai participated after the party consultations in New Delhi, the only conclusion that can safely be drawn is that if all the Congress prisoners are released, Mahatma Gandhi will agree to a meeting of the Congress Working Committee and also of the AICC to review the situation. As to what the AICC will decide or what Mahatma Gandhi may himself suggest as a result of its discussions it is difficult at this stage to say, but one hears anxious talk everywhere of a reorientation of policy.

From all accounts it is clear that the only chance for ending the political deadlock lies in reviving the Poona offer—a completely Indianized Council with complete power and responsible to the Legislature within the framework of the present constitution. So far as the communal proportion in the Central Cabinet is concerned it is not considered difficult to, bring about some understanding between the Congress and the Muslim League.

CR's Sporting Offer

Referring to talks here, Mr C. Rajagopalachari is reported to have said that 'the sporting offer' which he made, namely, that Mr Jinnah may be the Premier and constitute the Cabinet as he likes, still stands. So far as Mr Jinnah is concerned, his demand is only for parity with the Congress in its representation in the Cabinet. But as the principle of a National Government has first to be accepted by the British Government before the Congress is prepared to consider any offer, it is at the moment premature to talk of future possibilities.

In New Delhi the next stage in political development which official circles appear to be contemplating is the reduction of the ICS element gradually. It may be recalled that when

Sir T.B. Sapru met the Viceroy last year His Excellency, according to report here, was not prepared to agree to the transfer of Finance and Defence to non-officials during war time. A compromise appears to have been suggested by Sir Tej Bahadur that the present Finance Member can become Financial Adviser to the Viceroy as provided in the Government of India Act itself and that an Indian Defence Member can be associated with the Commander-in-Chief without in any way interfering with the latter's existing responsibilities. The mind of the new Indian Members of Government appears to be moving in this way also for reconstructing the Government on more popular lines for ending the deadlock....

34. Freedom the Only Basis of Action
Report of Jawaharlal Nehru's Interview to the Press, 9 December 1941

Reproduced from *National Herald,* 10 December 1941, in *Selected Works of Jawaharlal Nehru* (*SWJN*), Vol. 12, pp. 3–7.

Every sensitive person must feel to a greater or less degree the agony of the world today. No individual or nation can or should think in terms of narrow self-interest in the face of this great catastrophe. We have to take the wider outlook ultimately even in terms of self-interest for there can be no doubt that national isolation is dead and the future is hardly likely to consist of a large number of separate national entities. Whatever attitude we take up in India we must keep the wider aspects in view. This war is something much bigger than a war, and out of its womb all manner of changes will arise.

I should like India to use its strength and resources in favour of possible good changes. In the grouping of powers struggling for mastery, on both sides there seem to be dreams entertained by governments of world domination. Undoubtedly this is so on the part of Hitler. It is not proclaimed as such by the other side. I have no doubt that any attempt at world domination by any group of powers will be harmful and must be resisted. Still I think that in the grouping that exists there is also no doubt that progressive forces of the world are aligned with the group represented by Russia, Britain, America and China. In addition to these progressive forces this group has also got strongly entrenched reactionary forces as evidenced by the treatment accorded to India. This treatment inevitably governs our own policy. Yet at the same time we must sympathize and wish well to the group which contains the progressive forces, more specially those of China and Soviet Russia.

In regard to India we have amongst us many differences of opinion, some of which are vital. Yet I think so far as Indians are concerned, to whatever group they might belong, one thing should be common and that is the freedom of India. It should be possible for all of us to accept this common basis for the present, and cooperate together to that end, keeping, if necessary, all our differences for future consideration and settlement. Possibly even this period of working together, in spite of our differences, will help in resolving those very differences. We are up against very big things in the world. None of us can forget this without becoming petty and little-minded. We have seen how some countries of Asia have in the course of this war lost their independence—Iraq, Iran and now practically Thailand. We must, therefore, take this larger view and if we cannot make up our differences now, at least keep them for a future occasion, and meanwhile work together for the independence of India within the framework of larger world freedom.

Question: In the given conditions today, would you comment on Mahatma Gandhi's leadership?

Jawaharlal Nehru: Mahatma Gandhi's leadership has been brilliant; he has stood firm as a rock on certain fundamental principles and has not allowed himself to be diverted by various smaller happenings. It is very very easy for me or anyone else to criticize here or there certain minor developments with which we may not wholly agree but, looking at the scene as a whole, I think that Gandhi's leadership has not only been straight and sound but brilliant.

Q: What are your views in regard to non-violence?

JN: I have been unable in the past to accept all the implications of the doctrine in so far as its practical application is concerned. But I have held that this is an ideal worth striving for, with all our might, and even this World War has demonstrated the utter folly of continued application of violence to the settlement of any problem. In fact, violence today can be effectively used only by three or four big powers; the others may be hangers-on. By themselves, they are completely incapable of thinking in terms of violence.

Q: How do you reconcile yourself to non-violence in international affairs?

JN: I am convinced that the only way out for the world is complete disarmament or else more or less complete destruction. I can conceive, however, of general disarmament being accompanied by an international air force which might be used for police purposes. But it is essential that this should not be under the control of a few great powers who can thus impose their will upon others. National freedom for each nation is essential before any such step can be taken.

Q: What is the position of the Congress vis-à-vis the war?

JN: The Congress position was first fully stated in the declaration of September 1939 and subsequently added to by the All India Congress Committee resolutions. It remains till it is modified. Its application must necessarily depend on many factors. For instance, if it were made clear by the British Government that they accept that position completely, not just for the Congress, but for India, and give effect to it, this in itself would be a major international event, changing the whole character of the war. Inevitably the many drawbacks and obstacles towards giving support to the Allied cause would then be removed.

How India would give practical effect to its undoubted moral support to that cause then would be a matter for full consideration; it will have to be decided by the representatives of the people of India. The immediate object before India would necessarily be to defend itself.

Q: Will you advise Congressmen to cooperate with the Government in ARP measures?

JN: I am not fully in touch with the situation. Congressmen obviously will always give help in the protection of life, whenever such danger arises. Ordinarily, cooperation with the authorities means submission to the authorities. To my mind there are few people in this wide world who are so incompetent as the authorities in India in any matter. It is very difficult for intelligent people to submit to the decisions of unintelligent people.

Q: What do you think about the Indianization of the Viceroy's Executive Council?

JN: I have never been able to understand the significance of Indianization in anything, whether it is the Government or the army. One does not talk of the Anglicization of the British army or the British Government. One talks about nationalization of the country's government or army, one talks of power being transferred. The question, therefore, is not one of Indianization but of transfer of power and the authority controlling that power. If the Executive Council of the Viceroy consisted of Indians of his choice, under the present circumstances, it would make no difference to the seat of power; but if representatives who are responsible to others are chosen, that means an independent, responsible government and the Viceroy fades out.

Parliamentary activity means nothing unless there is a responsible parliament functioning. Mere going to the Central Assembly, delivering speeches or asking questions are not functioning in parliament at all, but whether it is desirable or not is another question. We must not delude ourselves by such vague phrases. But to me this kind of activity is entirely ineffective and unjustified and not in accordance with the general policy of the Congress at the present moment.

Q: What is the present policy of the Congress?

JN: The present policy of the Congress is not hundred per cent but largely one of non-cooperation. But if you have followed the various movements conducted by the Congress during the last twenty years or so, you will have some picture of what that means. When we were not doing anything effective or taking any action we allowed the opposition to function, but it does not now fit in.

Q: What are your views about the Muslim League's demand for minority protection in the Constituent Assembly?

JN: I cannot conceive of any valid opposition to that suggestion. I can conceive of an organization or a minority saying that in certain matters which it considers important the will of the majority should not prevail against its own wishes. In such cases either there is agreement between the so-called majority and the so-called minority in the Constituent Assembly or there is disagreement. The question then arises how to meet that disagreement. To say that an attempt should not be made by the representatives of the country even to find a basis for agreement seems entirely unjustified. As for the British Government they have succeeded in creating by their own misguided policy so many knots and tangles in India that they have themselves tied up in all of them. It is not for me to suggest how they should untie themselves.

Q: Do you think that the minorities should be given separate electorates or joint electorates in the Constituent Assembly?

JN: Every minority which has a separate electorate at present and desires to have it should have it.

Q: How far has the country gained from the satyagraha movement?

JN: It is very difficult to weigh moral issues. The fundamental thing behind the satyagraha movement during these twenty-two years has been the strengthening of the Indian people. I think it has succeeded in an ample measure not only in so far as Congressmen are concerned, but even those who may not be within the Congress. In a sense India has gained tremendously by it. Further, it has put forward before the world a method of peaceful struggle which, though it may fall into errors owing to human frailty, is undoubtedly a great evolution in the world of thought as well as action. In the present instance, I feel that the satyagraha movement has enabled us to maintain the self-respect and dignity of India, to prevent the demoralization which a passive submission to foreign authority brings in, and to impress the world not only with the Indian demand for freedom but also with the value of the peaceful technique of struggle while inhuman war goes on in a great part of the world.

35. Poona Offer Again

Editorial, *Bombay Chronicle*, 15 December 1941.

For weeks after his release Mr C. Rajagopalachari imposed upon himself strict silence on political matters. But now that the entire Congress policy is to be reviewed at the next meetings of the Working Committee and the AICC he has found it necessary to discuss some of its general principles. That he should have done so in the convocation address of the Lucknow University, rather than at a political meeting or in a press interview, shows perhaps his desire to emphasize the point that University students, the citizens and leaders of tomorrow ought to study the general principles of current politics. The gist of his speech is, like that of the recent statements of Pandit Jawaharlal, that sublime as is the principle of non-violence, it has its limitations in the present day political affairs and that, in spite of it, Congress can help in war effort for national defence provided Government concede its minimum constitutional demands. Putting the position in a general way Mr Rajagopalachari says: 'The just and reasonable demand of the Indian people is that the Government of India should be fully transferred now, during this war, and, indeed, more especially on account of this war, to a provisionally formed National Coalition Government. Even from the point of view of mere efficiency, the present unconstitutional and wholly undemocratic arrangement of the Centre and in most of the provinces is a fatally weak arrangement, and will crumble at the onslaught of real danger.' Transfer of real power to the people is the sovereign need of the hour and Mr Rajagopalachari does well to warn Britain that 'on anything but this basis' Britain 'cannot get the free and willing co-operation of India, the India either of the National Congress or of the Muslim League.' On any other basis Britain 'can only coerce and exploit, it cannot get co-operation'. There is little doubt that this view will be unequivocally endorsed by the AICC Mr Rajagopalachari is painfully aware of his difference with Gandhiji in this matter of conditional co-operation in war effort as the latter will discountenance such co-operation in any circumstances. But he says: 'Many are the ties that bind me to him and it is not a pleasure to discover a difference and recognize it, as leading to a parting of ways. But prayerfully and in all humility, must we face such a recognition, if it must come.' One need not be too sure of Gandhiji's attitude in the event of Government conceding Congress demands. There is every possibility of his being consent, for the time being with the right of preaching, pacifism even during the war.

Basis of Negotiation

The main question now is what precisely will be the minimum demands of the Congress and whether Government will accept them. Mr Rajagopalachari seems determined to hark back to the Poona offer. But Pandit Jawaharlal seems disposed to put the demand higher. The *National Herald* which usually expresses his views, says: 'It is amazing that there are some who are still thinking in terms of the Poona offer, which is now an exploded myth.' The offer was exploded because Government rejected it. But those who made it have not so far changed their views as to regard it as irrevocable. The best way out of the difficulty is for the AICC to revive the offer to the extent of making it a basis for negotiations and agree to negotiations only on that basis. Pandit Jawaharlal will necessarily be among those who will carry on the negotiations or give the final decision thereon. As regards Government, one can only hope that before it is too late they will abandon the impossible attitude indicated by Mr Amery's latest dictum that 'no change is involved in the declared policy of Government regarding the future Constitutional advance'.

Need for Communal Unity

The Country can certainly achieve more than the terms of the Poona offer if the Congress arrives at a complete settlement with the Muslim League. And without a substantial measure of communal unity even the Poona offer may not be irresistible. In his final appeal to the Lucknow University students Mr Rajagopalachari rightly observed: 'Lucknow is one of the pre-eminently historic cities of India. It has long been the fostering centre of great culture. But Lucknow's best luck is perhaps its association with Indian national unity in our own times. May it contribute once again to the further consolidation of Indian unity. I appeal to you specially at this convocation, young men and women of Lucknow, that you should make Indian unity your special mission.' We earnestly hope all patriotic men, old and young, will strive their utmost to ensure national unity. But leaders like Mr Rajagopalachari can do great things in this direction if they abjure the policy of drift and waiting indefinitely for a more favourable opportunity to bring about communal unity and set the right example to the people by concerting necessary measures to hasten the attainment of that unity.

36. Full Independence Wanted: Pandit Nehru's Assertion Talk of Time Limit has No Meaning

Amrita Bazar Patrika, 17 December 1941.

Allahabad, 15 December. In relation to the question of India's independence it is impossible for me to think of Dominion Status even with a time limit. What we contemplate is complete independence, said Pandit Jawaharlal Nehru addressing the students this evening under the auspices of the Allahabad University Union. Those who talk of Dominion Status, said Pandit Nehru, however high-placed and sincere, are doing a dis-service to the country. We are not an offshoot of Britain and England is not our mother country. Nor are we to accept the position of cultural off-spring of Britain, who have to wait to come of age and to be given responsibility and powers gradually. We have a cultural heritage and history of our own.

Besides in a fast changing world with the pace of things altering with each turn-off events the talk even of a time limit has no meaning. What we want is independence, continued Pandit Nehru. That means severance of connection with Britain. Of course, he said, that does not mean a position of isolation for us. What it does mean is that we should form part of the new order in our own light. On this question of independence of India, emphasized Pandit Nehru, there could be no compromise either with the British Government or with any group in India.

Epic Fight

Characterizing Russian fight as epic in courage and as an outstanding landmark in the history of this war and especially commending the scorched earth policy which entailed immense sacrifice in order to serve a larger cause, Pandit Nehru said that it has been proved beyond a shadow of doubt that the Soviet political economic structure had proved to be stable and strong enough to withstand the onslaught.

In conclusion Pandit Nehru exhorted the students not to waste away their energies in dissension, indiscipline and electioneering. He said it would be meaningless to reiterate slogans and catch phrases mechanically with a closed mind.

37. 'We have had Enough of You; Get Out': Jawaharlal's Reply to Amery

Bombay Chronicle, 18 December 1941.

Mass Civil Disobedience Unwise, ARP and the Congress

'I am not very much interested in the repeated performances of Mr Amery for he repeats the same *ad nauseam*', declared Pandit Jawaharlal Nehru at a press conference in Bombay on Wednesday, referring to the latest statement of the Secretary of State for India.

With regard to the talk about the revival of the Poona offer, he said that he was not a believer in revivalism either in religion or politics. The question of violence and non-violence had also cropped up recently like King Charles' head. For him and for the Congress said Pandit Jawaharlal, this issue in the form that it had been raised, did not arise at present, though events might bring it into greater promises at a later time.

Mass Civil disobedience was unwise both politically and from an international point of view.

Pandit Jawaharlal said that he could not translate into practice his sympathy for Russia because there were no avenues open to Indians to do so.

Referring to ARP, he said it was obvious that persons, whether Congressmen, or not, must help in the protection of life and property. But the organization of their protection in cities bombed or likely to be bombed must await further considerations.

'I have been quite clear and decisive on the question of India's relations with Britain. Watching events that is to my British Government's policy and the activities of officials in India, my old conclusion has been confirmed a thousand-fold that under the prevailing conditions, an Indian can only be rebel against the British Government which has audacity and the insolence to speak to us so often through their officials in patronizing terms, telling us about the moral values spiritual values and political values. But then they demonstrate to the world that they themselves posses none of these nor efficiency either in war or in peace. I am not very much interested in the repeated performances of Mr Amery on the public stage for he repeats the same *ad nauseam.* My only answer to him and to the British Government in the words of Oliver Cromwell quoted by Mr Amery in the House of Commons, is "We have had enough of you: get out".

Poona Offer

'Some people thought of the revival of the Poona offer or of some other thing that is dead and over. I am not a believer in revivalism either in religion or politics. Naturally a politician must take into consideration changing circumstances in a changing world. But for anyone to think in terms of eighteen months ago after at that has happened is to exhibit singular rigidity of the mind. And that is fatal in this period of war and revolution.

'During the last few days that I have been out of prison, I have tried to avoid dealing with specific issues for authoritative pronouncement on these can only come from the Working Committee, the Congress President or Mahatma Gandhi. I have dealt with general questions of principles and broad policy. Recently the question of violence and non-violence has suddenly cropped up like King Charles' head. This is a matter which has been frequently discussed in India for years past and everyone knows Gandhiji's views on it as well as general reactions of the Congress.

'The Congress view was framed concisely at the last meeting of the AICC in Bombay when a resolution was passed with which Gandhiji agreed in so far as it went for Congress purposes. No doubt, he personally goes further. But as the leader of the Congress he accepted it and adapted himself to it. On my part I accepted it completely. I should like to say that during the past year of war and worldwide disaster, I have been drawn even nearer to the ideal of political non-violence and complete disarmament.

'I cannot say that this can be applied "in toto" regardless of circumstances and always as the AICC said external factors and internal conditions will have to be considered.

Try Our Utmost

'But I do think that we should try our utmost in that direction. For me and I think for Congress this issue in the form that it has now been raised does not arise at present, though events may bring it into greater prominence at any time. Other issues precede it and result be considered first or else there will be confusion of thought and issues.

'When people talk of any kind of co-operation between India and British Government, they seem to forget two factors, one is the enormous bitterness of people today greater than ever, against British Policy. Any one who takes the trouble of finding out what people's feeling is has merely to speak to the man in the street from Peshawar to Cape Comorin.

'During my past 25 years or so of my political experience, I have never known feelings so strained and bitter. No politician, whatever his individual views may be, can ignore this background.'

Panditji then proceeded to give an instance though far from being parallel but nevertheless interesting. The British Labour Party, he said, in spite of being completely in line with war efforts in England refused to co-operate with the Government in England till the Chamberlain Government was pushed out. They were faced with the immediate danger of invasion. They maintained that attitude and Chamberlain had to go. Our case is infinitely stronger from every point of view.

'It is absurd for anyone to imagine', he continued to say, 'that we can cooperate with this Government that rules over us. It is, however, true that looking at the international situation all manner of considerations arise which induce us to give our sympathy to the group of Powers fighting Germany. If I have been in favour of giving help to China all these years I cannot change my attitude now. If I am in favour as I am of giving assistance to the Soviet, I cannot change my line on that subject, because of Soviet's association with Britain. Undoubtedly, all this creates difficulties. There is no problem in the world today which is free from difficulties. But I cannot in any circumstances function as a camp follower and a recruiting sergeant for the British Government and thus support their policy in India and their general policy towards their subject countries.

Concerned with Present

'Some people and some organizations talk about what might happen after the war is over or a year or two later. I have been totally unable to understand this. And I am concerned with the present here and now. It will not be Mr Amery or British Government that will shape things for the future. But vast elements forced that are already rising in the world.'

In this connection he referred to the fact that the British Government had to face not only its 150 years of past in India and such a past would always be with us. But even the recent past during which it had sown seeds of trouble which would bear evil fruit. Whether they were carrying this war efficiently or not might be a matter for expert opinion. But it was amazing how much bad blood they had created not only in India but also in Iraq and Iran. Only by an entirely different policy based on the ending of their Empire and their Imperialist policy could they have avoided this and gained mass sympathy of the Eastern peoples.

In reply to questions regarding the feasibility of mass Civil disobedience in view of the reaction in the country, Panditji said that mass Civil disobedience was unwise politically and from an international point of view. Whether the Individual Civil disobedience was effective or not depended upon the view one took in this matter. It was true that it did not obstruct the British Government in its war efforts. But it certainly had the effect of rousing the feelings of people in the country.

Conserve Vitality

Gandhiji had clearly stated that this movement was bound to go on for a long time as no immediate results could be expected. It was necessary to conserve people's vitality and national energy. Our purpose was to conserve that energy and strengthen the morale of the people and thereby serve India's cause and the larger cause by exposing the dual face of Imperialism.

With regard to the question as to how his sympathy towards Russia could be given a practical shape, he stated that there were no avenue open for Indians to do so. The only avenue open was to be a camp follower. But he believed what Russia wanted today was not men but machines, tanks and aeroplanes. He could not naturally supply these things to Russia, although he could create the necessary atmosphere for the manufacture of these equipment. But even there the Government was not prepared to help them.

To a question seeking clarification on his statement regarding the Congress co-operation for the ARP work, he said that it might be divided into several parts. It was obvious that persons, Congressmen or not, must help in the protection of life and property. But the organization of their protection in cities bombed or likely to be bombed must await further consideration. He was opposed to the ARP work two years ago because it appeared to him to be a political stunt.

38. India's Demand for Freedom: Maulana on Congress Policy Towards War

Amrita Bazar Patrika, 20 December 1941.

Bombay, 19 December. 'The issue before the Congress today is not one of violence versus non-violence. The main obstacle is the British Government's attitude towards India; unless that attitude is changed there can be no change in our attitude,' said Maulana Abul Kalam Azad, addressing a mass meeting at Choupathi this evening. Mr Bhulabhai Desai, President of the Bombay Provincial Congress Committee presided.

The Maulana continued, 'No self-respecting Indian can think of changing his attitude in the face of the intransigent attitude of the British Government.'

'During the last 15 months the world has seen vast changes which had not taken place in the history of the world for centuries. But our position has not changed. We are where we were 15 months ago. When we were arrested we were not sorry about it and now that we have been released. We are not happy about it either. When we decided on the course of courting jail we did not do so for the purpose of getting the jail gates open but we did so with a view to getting the greater jail gate that is India to be opened, namely, freedom of the country.

Congress Position

'The Congress position has been and is absolutely clear. We are meeting at Bardoli on 23 December. This meeting will afford us an opportunity of meeting our great leader Mahatma Gandhi and discussing with him the situation in all its aspects. Meanwhile I cannot be expected to say anything definite or categorical as to what our next step should be. Nevertheless I want to remind you of the position the Congress has taken up 15 months ago. The question of violence and non-violence has been discussed so often that it does not require any further clarification.

'We all know what Mahatma Gandhi's position in this respect is. The Working Committee defined its attitude on this question in what is called the Wardha statement. That position has not changed and it remains.

Congress and War

'I would like to make it clear that it is not the issue of violence or non-violence that has prevented the Congress from participating in the war. What has really prevented the Congress from co-operation is the attitude of the British Government towards India's demand for freedom. You will remember that in September 1939, the Congress demanded from the British Government a declaration of their war aims. The Government failed to meet our demand but still the Congress made yet another offer by our Poona resolution which definitely declared that the Congress would cooperate in the war provided the British Government climbed down from their insolent attitude towards India. It is well-known what the British Government's reply was. It was the August offer made by the Viceroy which left us with two alternatives either to slavishly obey the behests of the British Government or to resist the British Government's effort to drag India into the war. Consistent with honour, self-respect and policy of the Congress, the Congress decided to resist and at Bombay passed a resolution requesting Mahatma Gandhi to give the correct lead.

Real Stumbling Block

'The position as stated above clearly shows that the real stumbling block in the way of any settlement between the Congress and the British Government is the intransigent attitude of the British Government. It is up to the British Government to change this attitude if they want the cooperation of the Congress.'

The Congress President deplored panic and scare among the people of India following Japan's entry into the war and appealed to the people of India especially of Calcutta to maintain complete calm and self-confidence. He said even though British rule over India for hundred and fifty years had emasculated the people there was no reason why they should not muster courage and self-possession even in the midst of extraneous difficulties. There was no reason for them to be scared.

39. Jawahar's Plain Talk to British People

Bombay Chronicle, 22 December 1941.

Consign August Declaration to Dustbin and Recognize Indian Independence

'Recent developments in the war situation are of intense interest to India and the political and psychological background is ever-changing. Resolution of this, however, cannot reach the masses unless the basic fact of the Indo-British relationship is converted into recognition of Indian Independence and Co-operation between the nations,' says Pandit Jawaharlal Nehru responding to a friendly message from the '*News Chronicle*', London, on his release from prison.

The First Essential

Pandit Nehru declares: 'The release from prison of some people means nothing at all. By itself it is a challenge which has to be accepted' and says that 'the first essential for Indo-British Co-operation in friendship is the recognition of Indian Independence and consignment to the dustbin of the infamous August Declaration and all other similar Declarations of the British Government.'

Objectives of War

Pandit Nehru declares: 'It is not enough to say that the war has to be won; we must win the objectives of the war and for this purpose the objectives must be clearly stated and acted upon in the present in so far as possible. That has been the Congress position throughout and it remains so today'.

Text of Statement

Lucknow, 20 December. In a statement to the *News Chronicle*, London, reproduced by the *National Herald*, Pandit Jawaharlal Nehru says:

'I am grateful for the friendly message of the *News Chronicle* and I appreciate the warm sympathy for India's cause of many friends in England in these difficult days when passions are aroused obscuring the mind and when the relations between the Indian people and the British Government are strained to the utmost, the companionship of even some minds in different countries is of importance and helps to prevent narrow mindedness. But it must be remembered that this is of little avail if the whole background is one of hostility.

Nothing is more obvious in India today than the deep and widespread hostility among all sections of the people to the system that the British Government has represented here. That hostility was an inevitable consequence of past and present history, but the policy and utterances of the British Government during the last two years of war have intensified it. For the people generally that is the governing factor and wider considerations which may move individuals, become secondary.

Disruptive Factor

It is true that we in India have great differences amongst us, but have all a great deal in common which is basically more important, and wise statesmanship should have emphasized and encouraged those common bonds. Instead of this the British Government has become the greatest disruptive factor in India in addition to being completely authoritarian, alien and oppressive. The only possible response to that is non-cooperation with that Government, for nationalism is far the strongest urge of the Indian people. Even if individual for wider reasons desire a variation of that policy, they cannot overcome the people's deep-rooted hostility and distrust of the British Government and the governmental structure in India which can only lessen by a complete change of scene and a pleasant psychological shock accompanied by the conviction that the old order has completely gone never to come back again.

More Belief Left in Words

Not even in the most far reaching promises of what will happen when the war ends, will bring this conviction, for there is no belief left in words. It is the present that counts. The Atlantic Charter, if applied to India, would have made no difference. But the deliberate non-application of it to India was significant and made it clear as the midday sun what British policy stands for. Only the independence of India has any real meaning for us though we believe that the day of a large number of separate national entities is past and there must be world co-operation among free nations based on certain fundamental principles. For my part I would welcome these principles as outlined in H.G. Wells Declaration of the Rights of Man with certain additions.

No Position in Empire

India will never accept any position in an Empire by whatever name it is called. India is a great nation and a mother country which has influenced in the past vast sections of the human race in Asia; she is not a colony off-shoot of another nation growing to nationhood. She wants to live in peace and friendship with all nations in the world, but she is inevitably drawn to her neighbours with whom she has had thousands of years of cultural contact more especially to China and Burma in the East and Iran and other countries of Western Asia.

First Essential

Therefore, the first essential is the recognition of Indian Independence and the consignment to the dustbin of the infamous August Declaration and all other similar declarations of the British Government. Then only can we get over the dismal and crushing heritage of our past relations and join hands in friendship.

I realized that in the past elemental conflicts that are raging national issues must not absorb our attention and we must view the picture as a whole. Out of this war all manner of things arise whether we like them or not and all we can do is to try our utmost to further the things we want to have. It is not enough to say that the war has to be won; we must win the objectives of the war and for this purpose the objectives must be clearly stated and acted upon in the present in so far as possible. That has been the Congress position throughout and it remains so today.

Releases Mean Nothing

Some of us as individuals may wish to go further in alighting ourselves with the larger causes, but our efforts will remain ineffective unless the whole background changes in India and popular hostility is removed by vital changes. It must be realized that the release from prison of some people means nothing at all. By itself it is a challenge which is to be accepted.

This war has convinced me of the utter folly and criminality of armed conflict and the methods of violence in international affairs. I am no pacifist, but I believe that complete disarmament of all nations must be one of the declared objectives of the war. I realize that the war must go on whether we like it or not and it is not possible for any one to take up a negative attitude to it.

Sympathy with Soviet and China

Given the background I have indicated above it follows that all possible support has to be given. Without that background and those steps effective help is not possible. More particularly, I should like to express our solidarity with the people of China and the Soviet Union who represent many ideals that we value and who have given magnificent demonstrations of their invincible courage and spirit of sacrifice. For my part I should like help to flow to them.

Recent developments in the war situation are of intense interest to India and the political and psychological background is ever changing. Realization of this cannot however, reach the masses unless the basic fact of the Indo-British relationship is converted into recognition of Indian Independence and co-operation between the nations'.

B. War Measures

40. How War Industries Could Not Develop on Account of Lack of Support by Government?

Amrita Bazar Patrika, 3 January 1941.

Banares, 2 January. 'When the titanic conflict now being waged ends as end it must in the triumph of the democracies and the cause of human freedom, I pray that India may emerge from it with the foundations of its industrial as well as political freedom well and truly laid, so that she may be properly equipped to play her rightful part in peace and in war as a worthy member of this great Commonwealth of Nations.'

This hope was expressed by Sir Ardeshir Dalal, ICS (retired) in the course of his address as General President of the twenty eight session of the Indian Science Congress which commenced at Benaras on Thursday morning...

Sir A. Dalal's Address

Sir Ardeshir Dalal in his speech stressed the value of research in industry and observed: 'A substantial part of the export trade of India has been lost since the war. Science can help in the utilization within the country itself of some of the raw materials which used to be exported. Researches are being conducted for instance on use in India for lubrication purposes of some of the oil seeds of which the export has dwindled down and the surplus of which is likely to create serious economic trouble for the cultivators. Even a more acute problem is the stoppage of the import of many commodities essential for the economic life of the country, such as machinery, chemicals, and other things. It is imperative that India should make herself self-sufficient with regard to such materials as are vital to the maintenance of her economic and industrial life so that the situation which has arisen once again never recur'.

Referring to the Board of Scientific and Industries Research recently established, the speaker observed: 'No institution however well conceived and assigned won't flourish except in suitable political atmosphere and conditions. It was the unfortunate experience of the last war that industries create under the stress of the war period for want of encouragement and protector from Government. The activities of the Board will not lead to the creation of new industries unless industrialists are assured of reasonable protection from Government in the post-war period when foreign competition will be keen.

The progress hitherto made by the Board is not as rapid as we would have wished in war time. This is partly due to the constitution of the Board under which executive authority is concentrated in a central department of Government and partly to the inadequate staff provided for the very urgent and important work that has to be done. There is one other aspect on which I desire to touch and that is the financial. Even for a beginning, a grant of rupees five lakhs is inadequate of the task involved. Associated with the Department of Scientific and Industrial Research in Great Britain are the great National Physical Laboratory at Teddington and important Boards, such as Fuel Research Board, the Food Investigation Board, the Forest Products and Building Research Institutes and a number of similar bodies as well as Research Associations. While we must necessarily make modest beginning the development of the Alipore Test House into a National Physical and Chemical Laboratory seems to be obviously and urgently required'.

Steel Industry

Dwelling upon the steel industry in India the speaker said: 'The last decade has been a great expansion of the steel industry accompanied by improvement in the various processes and the application of scientific methods of control. In terms of tonnage, the progress can be measured by the fact that while the Tata Iron and Steel Company produced 422,000 tons of finished steel in 1929–30, the corresponding production in 1939–40 was 777,000 tons. Ten years ago only thirty per cent of the demand of the country for Steel was met by the indigenous industry, whereas in 1939–40 about eighty four per cent of the demand was so met and the day is not distant when India will be able to supply not only the whole demand of the country except in a few very specialized directions but also to spare some steel for export.

The last ten years have also been important developments in steel-making practice and a considerable increase in production. The installation of electric furnaces has been of the greatest assistance in the making of superior quality ally steel required by the Defence Department. The most important advance made during the last decade from the point of view of scientific research, in the practical development of the rapid dephosphorizing process'.

Manufacture of Rails

'In the manufacture of rails, advance has been made as a result of metallurgical research during the last ten years. An interesting advance has been the installation of Sandberg controlled cooling process for rails. All over the world the controlled cooling rails has come to be locked upon as a definite and desirable advance on the old practice of cooling rails on pen hot-beds. The Tata Iron and Steel Company have obtained exclusive rights in India for the working of the Sandberg process. In the Plate Mill, the most interesting development in the last decades is the installation of a modern normalizing furnace for plates. The furnace was first installed to normalize some of the high tensile steel plates for the new Howrah Bridge. By the aid of this furnace it is now possible to produce in India normalized plates which had formerly to be imported'.

Continuing the speaker said: 'To facilitate research work, a modern well-equipped laboratory was erected in 1937 at a cost of over rupees ten lakhs. May I express the hope that with the facilities for metallurgical research provided by this laboratory and its workers, Jamshedpur may in the near future become the centre of National Metallurgical Laboratory and the Research

Institute and thus be enabled to play a greater and worthier part in the development of the metallurgical industry in India.'

41. War Industry in India: Government Policy Mr Walchand Hirachand's Severe Criticism

Amrita Bazar Patrika, 6 January 1941.

In the course of a statement issued in connection with the recent communiqué of the Government of India dealing with the schemes for the manufacture of aircraft and automobile as well as for ship-building, Mr Walchand Hirachand, who has been connected with all the three projects observed that he wished the Government took as much pains to assist and encourage schemes for establishing vital industries in India as they have recently being taking in order to justify their policy of inaction and their measures of control and restriction of Indian shipping while offering financial assistance to the extent of Rs 4.12 lakhs to a non-Indian shipping concern for carriage of Haj pilgrims. What Indian industry and Indian public want is positive and vigorous action on the part of the Government of the country and not defence and apologia for inability or unwillingness to adopt such a policy. Press communiqués, however well-argued and whatever their total number, cannot build up industries. In the present conditions of emergency, Government should give up their usual policy of hesitation about promoting and safeguarding Indian industries and they must cease to examine zealously the claims of various key industries for assistance or protection more with a view to find out loopholes in such schemes than to further them. The public cannot help feeling that the whole outlook of the authorities is fundamentally wrong because instead of trying to overcome difficulties, there is undue dilatoriness and a policy which can only be characterized as one of obstruction.

I shall take in order the three industries mentioned in the Government communiqué of 16th December. As regards the aircraft industry, a proposal for setting up an aircraft factory in India without any Government loan or subsidy was placed before the Government at the very commencement of the war, provided the Government were very prepared to purchase a small number of aircraft from this factory. Nothing happened to this concrete proposal while Australia and Canada were fast developing their aircraft industries and expanding them. Even after the project was revived in June last, it has taken the Government over four months before deciding to place an order with this factory. Altogether, therefore, fifteen precious months of the war have been wasted before the Government of India could decide to have one small aircraft factory in this country while Canada would soon be building 360 aero-planes a month and Australia is producing 2 aero-planes daily. I do not know if this can be called an attitude of either 'sympathy' or 'assurance on active assistance'. If the Government had only responded when the project was first mooted India would by now have been building her own military aircraft.

Ship Building

The same story holds true of ship-building. It was over sixteen years ago that the Indian Mercantile Marine Committee, appointed by the Government themselves and comprising British technical men, favoured the establishment of a ship-building industry in India and recommended certain specific forms of Government aid. The report remains a dead-letter till today and its other central proposal of reservation of Indian coastal trade for Indian shipping has also been completely ignored and statutorily provided against in the Constitution of the country. For five years, the Scindia Company has been endeavouring to obtain a suitable site in Calcutta but without success and at last when a site was brought to the notice of the Port Commissioners by the Company's own representatives, the rent quoted was so exorbitant as to render such a project impossible. The Port Trust are under the general control and supervision of the Central Government who however, seem to be helpless when confronted by British opposition or British vested interests. It is true that the Company has been able to obtain at last 3 site in Vizagapatnam but I do not know what credit is due to the Government for this because the Government have offered no concessions nor provided any special facilities, let alone any financial assistance or subsidy. Besides, the port of Vizagapatnam has been unremunerative to the Government and the land was lying as a burden on the hands of the Government for a long time. In fact, the attitude of the Board of Trade and the British Admiralty to the whole project of a shipyard in India has been entirely unsympathetic and unfavourable.

Transfer of Shipyard

A proposal made at the instance of the Government of India themselves to transfer bodily a shipyard from the United Kingdom was rejected despite the assurance that the steamers built in this shipyard would be placed at the disposal of His Majesty's Government for maintaining essential services during the war. While Britain requires every available ship and is purchasing and building ships not only from the Dominions but also from the United States, the British authorities were not prepared to recognize the promotion of ship-building in India as a war effort. In fact, the Government of India themselves through their Commerce Secretary, Sir Allan Lloyd, stated in the Council of State only a month ago that the Government do not propose to encourage actively the merchant ship-building industry in India as part of their war effort. This was an astounding statement after all their profession of sympathy for key industries and their zeal for mobilizing industrial resources in India for the prosecution of the war. In this respect also even the Government communiqué stresses difficulties about obtaining steel and machinery. But it is for the authorities to try and remove such obstacles, if any do exist, in respect of priorities and dollar exchange if they really mean to help a national industry which is as essential in peace as in war. Those who are promoting this ship-building industry have not yet asked for financial assistance from the Government, but a test of Government's sincerity would be provided when such a demand would be made and it would be interesting to see what fresh excuses and plausible arguments are then adopted by the authorities to avoid any direct help. While on this subject, I cannot also help observing that despite their undertaking eleven years ago that it would be government's responsibility to assist the development of Indian shipping in the coastal and overseas trade of the country, they have taken no action at all to implement this pledge nor have they followed a national shipping policy. The only time the Government seem to recognize the existence of Indian shipping is when they want to obtain some ships for His Majesty's Government or to impose obligations, burden and restrictions upon Indian shipping while reserving their patronage and preference for British shipping.

The most unsatisfactory part of the Government communiqué is, of course that relating to the automobile industry. In trying to raise difficulties about developing this industry, the Government have really side-tracked the broad issue of establishment of this industry which is of considerable potential value to the country. As Sir Visvesvaraya has pointed out in a recent statement on the subject, the Government have consistently denied any help to this project previously on the ground that they were bound by the conditions laid down in the Fiscal Commission Report and could not help an industry until it was started and found itself in difficulties and now on the ground that it cannot be considered a part of war effort. Yet it was in August last that the Government placed orders on motor cars with non-Indian firms while expressing unwillingness to save an indigenous industry built up on the basis of their own purchases.

Government Programme

The programme outlined by the Finance Member of the Government of India recently of the purchases of 60,000 vehicles, worth about Rs 24 crores would, on the basis of replacement alone, provide an adequate starting point for the establishment of a motor industry in India. It must add in this connection that the Government assumption that the scheme is one of mere assembling plant is not at all correct as the whole objective of the sponsors of the scheme from the outset has been the establishment of a complete manufacturing plant in the shortest possible time. In any event, the unhelpful attitude of the Government towards this industry is unjustified and is one further proof of bureaucratic obduracy and dilatoriness.

I must emphasize in conclusion that there is a real danger of the intrusion of foreign capital as a result of recent conferences and enquiries in regard to India's war efforts and of the establishment of non-Indian concern behind the tariff wall and under Government patronage and on the basis of Government purchases and orders. Indian commercial and public opinion has emphatically urged and demanded that industries which are established or encouraged in India today should be under Indian ownership, control and management and I trust that the authorities concerned will not compromise the principle of sacrifice the vital interests of India in any scheme of industrialization.

42. Let us Keep Enemy Away from India's Doors

The Tribune, 14 January 1941.

Giving the impressions of his visit to the Middle East front, Sir Sikandar Hyat Khan referred to the marked discrimination between the Italian and Libyan Soldiers. While the Italians were well-clothed and well-equipped, the Libyan soldiers were ill-clothed and badly equipped. They had been told by the Italians that Indians gave no quarter to anyone and shot everyone who came their way. This had been deliberately done in order to overawe the Libyans so that they should not surrender. But when the Libyan prisoners were differently treated at Cairo they were greatly surprised. They were served with tea, cigarettes and chocolates and British nurses washed their wounds and dressed them. Since they saw this treatment they expressed their wish to fight for the British.

The Achievement

Continuing, the Premier said that the great achievement in the Western Desert was largely to three reasons; firstly, all members of the great family of the British Commonwealth of Nations had got common ideal and common cause. In this war they had closely identified themselves that there was complete harmony among them; secondly there was the fullest cooperation between the three fighting services, and that was the main reason why causalities were so few and the achievement so great. The third reason was that the plans had been carefully laid out in a manner so as to cause the minimum loss on our side. There was complete cooperation and friendship between all fighting services among whom the prestige of Indian troops was very high.

Indian Soldiers' Popularity

Giving an instance of the popularity of Indian soldiers; he mentioned a party held on the Christmas day in which Egyptian officers, Australians, New Zealanders, South Africans, British and Indians participated. When the Indian wounded arrived at the party, they were given such an ovation that Egypt had not seen before. The Egyptians and Sudanese, he added, were treating them very cordially and Australians and New Zealanders vied with each other to do them honour.

The victory, he said, was due to comradeship, co-operation among fighting services and above all, brilliant staff work. When the history of this war would be written, General Wavell's name would go down as one of the greatest generals. He was a great and unassuming person.

Sir Sikander's impression of the situation was that Indians had done remarkably well. They had not only lived upto the highest traditions of the Indian army, but had shown to the world that Indians could fight as well as any other soldier in any part of the world. A British officer told him that he had yet to see braver soldiers than Indians. Even when some of them were raw and new to their job, they acted like veterans.

'Future Political Stunts'

'Our soldiers were doing their duty bravely, away from their homes, and he had seen them on their posts of duty. They said they were very happy and would continue to be happy until they redeemed the honour by capturing Abyssinia, Eritrea and other parts of Africa.

In this total war, he said that we in India must also do our bit. Unfortunately, we were not realistic enough and some of us were frittering away our energy in futile political stunts. If those engaged in these activities saw what was happening in Egypt, they would scorn politics and would join him in saying 'God save the King and God save India.'

'Do Not Side-track Our Countrymen'

Sir Sikander hoped that even now they would see the wisdom of retracing their steps and realize their duty to the country. India had not tasted the miseries which had befallen other countries and that was because of the gallantry of those who were keeping the enemy away from India's doors. It was not fair, he asserted, to thwart the good work of those who were trying to save our country from misery. He fervently hoped and prayed that they would desist from side-tracking our countrymen. He maintained they had not been able to achieve anything by their methods and he, therefore, asked them to follow his method and work with him to see the results. He was sure that they would then achieve their goal much earlier.

Referring to the additional amenities required by Indian troops, who were bearing all hardships cheerfully, the Premier said that they were in need of gramophone records, indoor games, a few buses and cars. He was sure that his countrymen, particularly the Punjabis, who had already done their duty, would help to meet those requirements. So far as the Punjab was concerned, they had done their duty and it was due to the inspiration and guidance of His Excellency Sir Henry Craik that the Punjab was leading the rest of India. They had not only secured foremost place in the supply of manpower but had also contributed generously towards the war fund. He knew it personally how His Excellency had been working hard to organize the war effort and inspired those engaged in it by visiting them in almost all districts of the province. He said that he was voicing the feelings of not only his colleagues but also the whole of the Punjab that the recent title conferred on His Excellency was well deserved. In conclusion, he hoped that Punjabis would contribute liberally in response to his appeal. He hoped they would rise to the occasion.

Sir Henry Craik's Speech

His Excellency the Governor, while thanking Sir Sikander for the absorbingly interesting talk, said that he had indeed been through wonderfully exciting and interesting experiences. He envied his good fortune. It was a happy idea that suggested itself to someone that the Punjab Premier should go to Egypt. His visit had been of infinite value not only to Indian troops there but to us in India.

It seemed to His Excellency that they had not made much of our victories in Egypt. That deficiency, he hoped, would be largely met by the vivid account and details given by Sir Sikander Hyat Khan. He did not know which to admire most perfect co-operation between the services, the plan of the staff or the dashing courage of troops. He had heard with the greatest satisfaction that none of the troops had higher morale and greater determination than the Indians. His Excellency, however, felt that in his characteristic modesty, Sir Sikander Hyat had omitted to mention the incident relating to the capture of his son. The details would take too long for His Excellency to relate but he felt that they reflected the greatest credit on Lieutenant Shaukat Hyat Khan. It was with the greatest satisfaction that His Excellency had learnt that Shaukat Hyat's wounds had healed and that he was in good health.

A Great Deal Remains to be Done

Endorsing the appeal made by Sir Sikander Hyat Khan for amenities for troops in the Middle East, His Excellency felt that a great deal remained to be done. Sir Sikander was going to Delhi to place his proposals before the Commander-in-Chief. They in the Punjab had special obligation to do what they could. They had already contributed Rs 37 lakhs to the War Purposes Fund. He said that he would like to see before he laid down the reins of office, the total raised to Rs 50 lakhs.

43. India's Defence Preparations: Governor's Speech at Dacca Race Course

Amrita Bazar Patrika, 22 January 1941.

'You must not imagine that defensive preparations are the business of a few officials or experts in Delhi or Calcutta. They are a vital matter in which everyone must take a hand' said His Excellency the Governor of Bengal addressing a large crowd on the Dacca Race course this afternoon. His Excellency reminded his listeners of the speech recently made in Dacca by the Hon'ble Home Minister, Sir K. Nazimuddin[1], in which he compared the present war to a fire which might spread in any direction without warning.

'We have seen how war has developed since I was last here in Dacca,' continued His Excellency. 'The first phase' His Excellency said, 'was that frightful series of air attacks on the people of Britain. We saw also the preparations made in autumn by German for invasion of Great Britain. When this attempt seemed unlikely to succeed the fire broke out in a new direction against Greece.' The heroic endurance of British people, the strength of Royal Air Force and the resistance of Greek Army had checked the fire and even carried it into the enemies' midst.'

India's Danger Not Over

His Excellency paid a tribute to the spirit of cooperation of the Dominions, Indian and British troops in north Africa. The Italians had intended to cut a vital line of communication between Europe and the East and their frustration counted as a major victory in the defence of India in which the Indian forces had played an important part.

His Excellency continued, 'Let no one think that because the Italians have suffered a reverse India is no longer in danger.' The war was a vital concern to all who were resolved to maintain their rights and its problems affected all sections of the population. 'For this reason', said His Excellency, 'I have made a point of travelling widely throughout Bengal and of returning to Dacca for a second time in six months.' His Excellency further observed that Bengal had already contributed much and would contribute more.'

Defence of Calcutta

The Governor did not want to give any details of munitions which were being supplied from Bengal because the enemy, no less than his listeners would like that information. But he could assure them that an ever increasing volume of munitions was being supplied from this province. There was no other province which had supplied as many men to the air force as had Bengal from the Dum Dum Training School. The province had also raised a coastal defence battery for immediate defence of Calcutta and the 16th Bengal Battalion which, His Excellency said, he had twice inspected and which he could assure them was worthy of the highest military traditions of India.

In conclusion His Excellency deplored the waste of energy caused by internal dissensions and appealed for communal unity and a combined effort to achieve the common purpose of peace.

His Excellency was welcomed in a short speech by the Hon'ble the Nawab of Dacca who spoke of the deplorable fate which had overtaken the conquered countries of Europe. He referred to the part which America was taking and to the dismay which the American policy was causing to Axis powers. 'I should be failing in my duty,' said the Nawab Bahadur, 'if I did not call the attention of my fellow countrymen to dangers which confront them'. The democratic ideals of Britain and America had become India's ideals. India's battle was now being fought in north Africa and for its support the Nawab called for maximum contribution to men, materials and money.

Purse Presented

A purse of Rs 45,000 to be spent on war purposes was presented on behalf of the district by Mr J. George, District Magistrate, and was accepted by His Excellency the Governor of Bengal. Thanking the people of the Dacca district His Excellency assured them that he would respect the wishes expressed by their collector that if possible a fighter plane would be named after the district.

Among other speakers Prof. Haridas Bhattacharji urged the audience the necessity of giving all possible help to Britain. Every contribution however small was of assistance. He referred to the attitude adopted by the Congress party and the Muslim League and said that although neither party was actually opposed to war effort yet they were not supporting it whole-heartedly even though their own very existence is at stake. The danger threatened Hindus and Muslims alike and it was therefore essential that they should unite. He reminded the audience that if they wanted freedom they may pay for it and added that having obtained freedom they would have to maintain it. But they could not do so unless the war was won.

---

[1] Khawaja Sir Nazimuddin, Minister for Home, Constitution and Election, Government of Bengal.

44. Curbs on the Press

(i) Letter from Sir J.G. Laithwaite[1] to Mahatma Gandhi

CWMG, Vol. LXXIII, pp. 459–60.

The Viceroy's House, New Delhi
28 January 1941

Dear Mr Gandhi,

Thank you very much for your letter of the 16th January which I have laid before His Excellency. He is very glad to note your decision, and he asks me to say that he much appreciates the emphasis you have laid in your letter on your attitude towards the embarrassing of authority.

I see that you are under some misapprehension as to the manner in which the statements enclosed with your letter failed to appear in the Press. There is no such thing as the censorship of matter intended for publication in the Indian Press nor has any prohibition been issued in respect of your two statements. In view, however, of the provisions of the Defence of India Rules regarding the publication of prejudicial reports, Press agencies and editors have the option of voluntarily submitting for advice messages in regard to which they feel any doubt. In giving advice on such references the Press Advisers have regard only to the question whether the matter submitted contains any prejudicial report, the publication of which would render the person concerned liable to prosecution under the Defence of India Rules. You will see, for instance, that both the Congress Pledge and your own statement about Independence Day, although similarly referred for Press advice, were passed for publication, because they had no direct connection with movement intended to interfere with the prosecution of the war. On the other hand, both the statements[2] enclosed with your letter were, I regret to say, of this nature. Although considerable portions of them could have been published without objection, at least from the point of view of the war, each of them contained numerous passages which were clearly intended or likely to encourage and instruct persons engaged in your civil disobedience movement. This movement in its present form consists of the uttering in public of slogans purporting to dissuade the public from participation in the war effort and thus in the words of the Defence of India Rules 'to influence the conduct or attitude of the public or any section of the public in a manner likely to be prejudicial to the defence of British India or to the efficient prosecution of the war'. In so far as they contained such passages, the statements in question could not have been published without exposing the editor or Press agency concerned to the risk of prosecution and the Press Advisers were only performing their clear duty in advising the Press against their publication. The Press were of course not obliged to take this advice, but you would not expect them, I think, to take a risk of which they were warned and you will see the dilemma in which they are placed when they receive such statements from you for publication. His Excellency feels sure that you will appreciate that the liberty of the Press does not and cannot in any country mean the right to publish anything without prosecution, more especially at a time of grave emergency such as this, and that without any interference with such liberty the Press Advisers were fully justified in giving the advice they did and the Press in accepting it.

Yours sincerely,
J.G. Laithwaite

[1] Private Secretary to the Viceroy.
[2] The statements referred to were *Instructions to Satyagrahis* dated 10 January 1941 and *Instructions to Satyagrahis* dated 12 January 1941. For the text of these statements, see Chapter 2, Document Nos 9 and 12.

(ii) Mahatma Gandhi's 'Letter to Newspaper Editors'

CWMG, Vol. LXXIII, pp. 304–6.

Sevagram
28 January 1941

Dear Editor,

We have become so used to the Press gag that we hardly know that there is a partial paralysis of the Press. In the name of 'war effort' all honest expression of opinion, if it is opposed to war effort as conceived by the official world, is effectively suppressed, unless an enterprising editor or publisher risks the loss of his Press. Thus my own effort, if my honesty be not questioned, is the true effort to end all war and therefore in no way anti-British or pro-German. If public opinion desired suppression, the Press would on its own initiative exclude news and opinions disliked by the public. But in India the majority of Indian Editors would gladly publish all the news about satyagraha if there was no gag.

I wish to use my case by way of illustration. For the conduct of the campaign and for the sake even of keeping it within restraint, I have to issue statements from time to time. During four days two out of three such statements were suppressed. The reason assigned was as follows:

1. 16 January 1941. I am writing this to inform you that Mahatma Gandhi's statement of 12 January regarding continuance of the Civil Disobedience Movement was submitted for Press advice by two of the Press agencies but was not passed for publication. I am accordingly bringing the above fact to your notice.
2. 28 January 1941. I am writing this to inform you that Mahatma Gandhi's statement of 10 January regarding payment of fines by satyagrahis, which was submitted for Press advice by two of the Press agencies, was not passed for publication, as being a prejudicial report containing incitement to carry, on anti-war civil disobedience. I am accordingly bringing the above fact to your notice.

I used to send my statements through the usual news agencies. But when I found that they were censored, I had to send my statements to selected newspapers and so they found place in some of them. You can judge for yourself whether they were objectionable news. This method of sending statements on chance publication is precarious. As I had no intention of extending civil disobedience to the special Press laws and ordinances, I stopped the three *Harijan* weeklies whose chief aim was to propagate non-violence and what is known as the constructive programme. I do not want so far as possible to extend the scope of civil disobedience beyond the present limit. But I do not know that I can exercise that restraint if the Press abdicates its function of publishing relevant news. I therefore appeal to the Press not to succumb to the gag but to assert its independence by publishing all the satyagraha news in its fullness. Of course it is open to the Editors to criticize and condemn the movement or the statements that may be issued. Editors can signify their disapproval of the gag by either publishing the offending statements and risking prosecution or even confiscation of the Press or by stopping publication of their papers altogether by way of protest. These are only two out of many ways for signifying your disapproval.

I observe that the Standing Committee of Editors is meeting on the 1st proximo.[1] The Committee is expected fearlessly to vindicate the liberty of the Press. It must cease to be the power it should be, if it submits to suppression of free public opinion.

I need hardly draw attention to the fact that in a subject country like India, the liberty of the Press is doubly precious. And your responsibility, if you represent British-owned Press, is very great at the present critical moment in the history of this country.

I need hardly also draw attention to the fact that I represent unadulterated non-violence whose spread can do nobody any harm. It is false and cruel to suggest that I could have anything in common with Nazism or Fascism because I happen to oppose imperialism.

Yours sincerely,
M.K. Gandhi

[1] The reference is to the Standing Committee of the All-India Newspaper Editors' Conference which met on 1 February 1941.

(iii) Government's Reply to Editors' Conference Resolutions

The Hindu, 28 February 1941.

'Anxious to Maintain Delhi Agreement'

(Associated Press of India)

New Delhi, 27 February. The Government of India recognize the duty of newspapers to give legitimate publicity to news in which their readers are interested, and so long as newspapers will refrain, in accordance with their own declared intention of doing nothing to impede the war effort, from publishing news or views which will incite persons to take part in the anti-war movement and which are, therefore, 'prejudicial reports' within the meaning of the law, the Government see no difficulty in maintaining the Delhi Agreement and the good relations between the Government and the Press, which it is its purpose to preserve.

This declaration is made in a letter received by the President of the All India Newspaper Editors' Conference from Sir Richard Tottenham, Additional Secretary, Government of India, in reply to the resolutions passed by the Standing Committee of the Conference held in February in New Delhi.

The letter, which is dated 25 February, says:

'I am directed to communicate the following decisions of the Government of India on the resolutions passed at the meeting of the Standing Committee of the All India Newspaper Editors' Conference held in New Delhi on 1, 2, and 3 February.

Resolution 1: 'That in order to ensure the satisfactory working of the Delhi Agreement, this Committee is of the opinion that (a) it is desirable for the Chief Press Adviser, as far as practicable to consult the Central Press Advisory Committee in matters in which he is inclined in advise non-publication and (b) report to the Central Advisory Committee at its next meeting all those cases on which he deemed it necessary to advise non-publication.'

The Government of India do not consider that it would be practicable for the Chief Press Adviser to Consult the Central Press Advisory Committee about all messages referred to him for advice, since many of these are of a purely routine nature and there is no room for any difference of opinion about them. For example, it would be a waste of time to refer to the Central Press Advisory Committee a message giving the location of a new aerodrome, since the publication of such a message is specifically prohibited under the Defence of India Rules, or to report that such a message had been stopped.

The Government of India agree, however, to refer to the committee important messages in regard to which there is legitimate room for doubt as to the nature of the press advice to be given provided that the Press themselves are willing to accept the delay involved and not to publish doubtful messages before receiving such advice.

Similarly, the Government of India are prepared to accept part (b) of the resolution with the addition of the word 'important' before the word 'cases'.

Uniformity in Interpreting Rules

Resolution II: 'The Committee having considered the correspondence between the Provincial Press Adviser to the Government of Bengal and the Convener of the Bengal Provincial Press Advisory Committee regarding publication of a report concerning a camp, strongly deprecate the different interpretation of the Defence of India Rules by official provincial interpreters as placing editors in an impossible position. If, as the Bengal Press Adviser states, the passing for publication of a message by a Press Adviser does not constitute a release permit, the normal working of newspaper offices will be rendered more difficult.'

There may be special circumstances which render the publication of a particular message in a particular province undesirable, even though there may be no objection to its publication in other provinces. Subject to this qualification the Government will endeavour to secure uniformity of treatment and agree that messages concerning Central subjects such as Defence, Foreign Affairs and others, if they have been passed for publication by the Chief Press Adviser, should be accepted as passed for publication in all provinces. The matter has already engaged the attention of the Press Adviser's Conference.

Action Re: *Sainik* and *National Herald*

Resolution III: 'This Committee regrets that the United Provinces Government have taken no action with regard to the *Sainik* newspaper of Agra as suggested in the resolutions of the Newspaper Editors' Conference in Delhi in November and of the United Province's Provincial Advisory Committee. The Committee also notes with regret the demand of security of Rs 6,000 from *The National Herald* of Lucknow, and requests the United Provinces Government to withdraw the orders now in force against the *Sainik* newspaper and *The National Herald* and to return the press to the keeper.'

The Government of India will consult the Government of the United Provinces regarding this resolution and obtain their views.

Gandhiji's Statements

Resolution IV: 'The Standing Committee is glad to note that the authorities appreciate the importance of Mahatma Gandhi's position in the public life of this country and the interest which attaches to his utterances and statements. It, therefore, requests the Government ordinarily not to ban publication of statements issued by Mahatma Gandhi, and in cases where they are inclined to take such a step, they should consult the Central Press Advisory Committee before passing any orders thereon.'

The Government of India are prepared to accept this resolution provided that newspapers for their part are prepared to accept the delay which must be involved in following the procedure suggested. They must, however, point out that it can only be followed in the case of formal statements by Mr Gandhi issued through the news agencies and not sent to editors direct and that only by this means can equal treatment for all newspapers be ensured.

Press Advisory Committees

Resolution V: 'While noting with satisfaction the working of the Advisory Committees in some of the provinces, this Standing Committee appeals to other Provincial Governments and to the Central Government to see that the consultative machinery suggested in the Government Communiqué of 11 November 1940, is fully utilized both at the Centre and in the provinces and that the Convention set up in Madras and Bombay that ordinarily no action will be taken against a press or newspaper without prior consultations with the Committee is extended to all the provinces.'

The Government of India accept this resolution so far as they themselves are concerned and will ask those Provincial Governments which have not already done so to establish the convention that ordinarily no action will be taken against a newspaper without prior consultation with the local Press Advisory Committee.

Resolution VI: 'In view of the fact that the Government have withdrawn the notification of October, 1940, and that the Government have indicated that they have no desire to suppress Gandhiji's statements and are not disinclined to give them special consideration, the Committee desires to assure Mahatma Gandhi it will welcome the re-appearance of the *Harijan* weeklies whenever Mahatma Gandhi in his judgment, thinks it fit to restart them. In the opinion of the Committee the temporary disappearance of the weeklies has left a void in Indian journalism.'

This resolution is addressed to Mr Gandhi and not to the Government of India.

Fair Trail for Delhi Agreement

Resolution VII: 'The Standing Committee reaffirms the determination of the Press of India to strive for the freedom of the country without fear or favour and consequently to give legitimate publicity to news about the political movement in the country. The Committee further records its opinion that the Indian Press is wholly opposed to the totalitarian doctrines of Nazism and Fascism and has no intention of hindering Britain's war effort against her enemies. It, therefore, urges the Government to continue to give a fair trial to the Delhi Agreement.'

The Government of India are themselves anxious to maintain the Delhi Agreement and to improve its working. They recognize the duty of newspapers to give legitimate publicity to news in which their readers are interested. They also appreciate the clear declaration of the attitude of the Press towards the war which is contained in the above resolution. So long as newspapers will refrain, in accordance with their own declared intention of doing nothing to impede the war effort, from publishing news and views which will incite persons to take part in the anti-war movement and which are, therefore, 'prejudicial reports' within the meaning of the law, they see no difficulty in maintaining the agreement and the good relations between the Government and the Press which is its purpose to preserve.

45. War Effort in Bengal

From Sir John Herbert, Governor of Bengal to Viceroy, 6 February 1941, Confidential Correspondence with the Governor of Bengal and his Secretary, 1941, Linlithgow Papers, Acc. No. 2183, NAI.

Dear Linlithgow,

... 4. War Effort. District contribution to the war effort have varied considerably, but on the whole donations are now coming in steadily. I have been considering, however, whether there should be a limit to the amount asked for in donations, and whether it would not ultimately be to the benefit of the war effort as well as to the future security of the country if we concentrate more upon contributions to defence loans and defence savings certificates, rather than upon donations. I am preparing plans for savings groups throughout the districts down to union boards, so that a district which has contributed a certain amount in donations, will be in a position to divert its income to defence bonds and defence savings certificates. I am impressed by the idea of encouraging thrift among the poorer classes, and feel that if we can make them into minor 'capitalists' this will have a steadying influence in the future. This system would also meet 'nationalist' complaints that money subscribed for the purchase of aero-planes is being spent outside this country.

I believe that Bengal has put more money than any other Province into the purchase of 3 per cent defence bonds and savings certificates. But so far, the money has come mainly from firms and well-to-do individuals in Calcutta who have purchased bonds as an ordinary investment. A much wider campaign will have to be undertaken in order to increase the scale of investments throughout the Province.

I gained the impression from Puckle that you are thinking on the same lines. In spite of occasional complaints, I do not believe that any coercion has been exercised in collecting donations, but I feel that if we continue to put the whole emphasis on donations, inter-district competition may result in over-zealousness and may spoil the good-will which we are now obtaining through the propaganda of our war committees. I look forward to having an opportunity of discussing the general question of propaganda with you and the officers concerned when I visit Delhi. ...

46. Defence of India

Editorial, *The Tribune*, 11 February 1941.

His Excellency the Commander-in-Chief's broadcast was concerned more with a description of British achievement in the existing and potential theatres of war than with an enunciation of official policy about the defence of this country. While his account of defence preparations in Britain and of the various operations in Africa, in which Indian troops have played a conspicuously gallant parts, would be read throughout the country with satisfaction and with pride, the attention of politically-minded Indians would be directed towards one observation this speech. 'Today', said the Commander-in-Chief, 'Indian troops in North Africa are fighting side by side with British, Australian, New Zealanders, South African and Free French Forces to destroy once and for all the threat to bring war to the shores of India from North Africa. Our duty to them is three-fold. We must ensure that their efforts are not rendered in vain by any failures on our part to make this country secure against direct attack from any direction. We must place ourselves in a position to give our men actually facing the enemy in the field the greatest possible assistance and support of which we are capable in the form of trained reinforcements and supplies. We must also provide our men overseas with all the comforts and amenities we can to lighten the hardships they are enduring so cheerfully....'

From the Head of the army in India who had been appointed newly to his office we would have liked to receive some information about the precise steps which he intends to take to make this country secure against direct attack from any direction, and to make it self-sufficient in the matter of the supply of war equipment. Under the old command, which general Sir Claude Auchinleck has replaced, even the Liberal Party in this country was not satisfied with the speed with which the army in India was being Indianized, and preparations for the supply of war equipment were being made. Particularly, as regards the latter, even the *Statesman* condemned in unequivocal terms the obduracy of British vested interests, which stood in the way of the manufacture of ships, war planes, tanks and other vital instruments of defence in this country. From reports which now and again emanate from Government sources, it appears that munitions are being manufactured with expedition but it is more than sixteen months since the war broke out, and not a single plane or a ship has been manufactured in this country.

It is no doubt an old adage that Rome was not built in a day. But the Commander-in-Chief himself expressed amazement in his speech at the speed with which the defence of British since last June have been organized. Given vision and imagination could the same not have been done in this country? Rome was not built in a day, but its completion came within sight once the work on its building was begun. Unless the Government of India is particularly modest about its achievements, it does not seem that we have even made a beginning towards the manufacture of the most vital instruments of defence and warfare in the country.

Indeed, the 'three-fold' task of which His Excellency spoke can not be divorced from the political situation in the country. There is no lack of men here, nor of material. Nor, indeed, in spite of the *satyagraha* campaign of the Congress can it be said that the Indian people are not both willing and anxious to see Hitlerism destroyed and to organize the defences of this country to the highest possible extent. But while some effort is being made the actual achievement in this direction, must remain a fraction of what it can be until the responsibility for these tasks is thrown on the shoulders of the Indian people themselves. This the British Government does not seem willing to do. Motives are difficult to discern. British perhaps still distrust India; perhaps there is the persistent desire to hold on to privilege and position to ideas inconsistent with the splendour of the adventure to rid this world of the pest of Nazism that Britain has embarked upon. Or what is still worse, Britain is perhaps satisfied with what is being done. If that is so, it shows complacency of a suicidal order, suicidal both for Britain and for this country. A bureaucratic and irresponsible Government with the best of motives in the world will continue in this country to suffer from serious limitations.

47. India's Second War Budget

Editorial, *The Tribune*, 3 March 1941.

As we have said already, the budget introduced by the Finance Member in the Central Legislative Assembly on Friday was primarily and principally a war budget. This is indubitably established by even a casual comparison of the figures of revenue and expenditure during the last three years. In the financial year 1939–40 the Government of India had an actual surplus of revenue over expenditure of Rs 7,77 lakhs as compared with the surplus of 91 lakhs provided for in the revised estimates for the year. In the current year 1940–1, while the revised estimates for revenue, excluding the additional Rs 6,86 lakhs which had been transferred to the Revenue Reserve Fund in the preceding year, showed a net improvement of Rs 4,21 lakhs compared with the budget estimates, the revised estimates for expenditure showed a net increase of no less than Rs 19,54 lakhs, of which Rs 18½ crores were on account of the defence services and Rs 1,04 lakhs were for expenditure borne by the civil estimates mainly on account of schemes connected with the war.

The result of this increase in expenditure, which was due wholly to the war, was to convert the budgeted surplus of Rs 5 lakhs into an estimated deficit of Rs 13 crores, which has been brought down to Rs 8,42 lakhs, partly by the proceeds of new taxation imposed last November and partly by increased revenue from the Railways to the tune of Rs 2,81 lakhs. But for the war, therefore, not only would there have been no fresh taxation, but the year would have ended with a substantial surplus instead of a substantial deficit. In the ensuing year the budgeted deficit amounts to no less than Rs 20,46 lakhs, which is more than accounted for by the increased expenditure on defence due to war, which is estimated at the enormous figure of Rs 35,40 lakhs as against Rs 24,31 lakhs provided for in the revised estimates in the current year. But for this increased expenditure, due directly to the war, not only would no additional burdens have been imposed on the people in the shape of new taxes, whatever now or in the November last, but there would, again, have been a substantial surplus. Add to this the fact that one third of the total estimated revenue for the year will be consumed by the direct expenditure on the war and a little less than one half by direct and indirect expenditure on the war taken together, and the essential character of the budget as a war budget is estimated beyond dispute.

This is not said by way of complaint either against the Government of India generally or against the Finance Member in particular. We have never agreed with those who consider that the Government of India could have avoided being involved in the war or forced to incur additional expenditure on defence simply by remaining neutral. The mere fact that India was a part of the British Empire would at one stage or another have made her a target of attack by the Nazis, even if the Government of India had taken no part in the war. Nor could India have avoided strengthening her defence forces materially even if she had not been a part of the British Empire. One has only to remember how many countries, that are not even remotely connected with the British Empire, have been invaded and overrun by the Nazis during the last eighteen months, and that even America, which is divided from Europe by the wide expanse of the Atlantic ocean, has been forced to spend enormous sums of money on strengthening her defence, to see the fallacy of this argument. And the strengthening of a country's defence is essentially a matter of money. One has only to remember the huge amounts which the belligerents have to spend daily to form some idea of the difference between the conditions today and the conditions even during the last war. From this point of view we can both understand and appreciate the view expressed by the Finance Member in the part of his speech in which he confessed that he was 'more sensitive to the criticism of that smaller and less vocal body who may feel that the contemporary contribution by taxation to the cost of the war is too little than of the doubtless large multitude who would say that it is too great'. There can be no comparison between the sacrifices which Britain, for instance, has made and is making to win the war and the sacrifices that India has so far been called upon to make for the same purpose, even without forgetting the tremendous difference between the resources and the tax bearing capacity of the two countries.

But to say this is to forget the two most vital aspects of the matter. Whatever contribution is being made by the average Britisher to his Government's war effort is being made by him voluntarily and, therefore, ungrudgingly. The Government is his own Government and the war is being carried on with his full consent and approval. He has effective control both over the general policy of the Government, including its policy with regard to the war itself, and over the expenditure of the money he contributes to the public exchequer, whether for the carrying on the normal administration or for the conduct of the war. Not one of these things can be said with regard to the Indian. His sympathies may be and certainly are with Britain but he was made a party to the war without his consent, and the most important and best organized political party in India had actually to relinquish the task of government in seven provinces because they failed to obtain from the British Government the necessary assurance that India's war effort and war expenditure would be under the control of her own chosen representatives. This one fact rules out all analogy between the Indian and British tax payer and both explains and justifies the substantial differences between their respective attitude towards their Government's war measures and war expenditures. 'No taxation without representation' has from the first been the corner-stone of the British constitution and no British statesman or official can justifiably find fault with the Indian critic who takes up the position that no Government has a moral right to impose taxes on India or add to India's already heavy burdens in the matter of taxation even for so laudable a purpose as that of strengthening her defence without the consent of India's chosen representatives.

The second important thing to be borne in mind in this connection, which is closely connected with the first, is that while the British tax-payer as the ultimate controller of the policy of his Government has it in his power, while making all the contribution he can to the country's war effort, to see that full advantage is taken by the Government of his country of the opportunity afforded by the war so to develop the country's material resources as to enable her successfully to bear the burden that would otherwise crush it, the Indian tax-payer has no such power. Here, as elsewhere, it is for him only to pay the piper and to leave it to some one else to call the tune. More than once in his speech the Finance Member refers to the advantages that India is deriving from the War. 'These tremendous developments in the supply field,' he says at one place, 'must necessarily give great stimulus to Indian industries. One of the most important results has been the investigation of the possibilities of establishing new industries in India for the production of stores that have hitherto been imported.' Elsewhere he reminds us that while the number of workmen of all classes and trades employed in the Government Dockyard was 1168 before the war, today it has risen to 5000. But it is no disparagement of the efforts of the Government in these directions to say that they are wholly inadequate. The present Government in its very nature and by its very constitution and composition is incapable of doing all that a national Government, representative of and responsible to India could have done. The Finance Member therefore has only himself and his Government to thank for the strong opposition which his financial proposals are bound to evoke in the country even though they are inspired by a purpose with which India is in full sympathy.

48. Communist Party's View of the War Measures

Communist, Vol. III, No. 2, March 1941, P.C. Joshi Archives on Contemporary History, Jawaharlal Nehru University (JNU), New Delhi.

Whither?

> If you look at the map of the world you will see a chain of territories belonging to the British Empire or politically associated or allied with it, extending from the Cape to Cairo, from Jerusalem to Basra and Bombay, from Calcutta to Singapore and Sydney to Wellington, in a vast semi-circle or arch round the Indian Ocean. The keystone of that arch both in position and in human material resources is India.

Amery's broadcast, 24 February 1941.

This is the British Empire and India's place in it and its importance is further enhanced by the fact that there are only two gateways through the arch—the Suez and Singapore, and India lies centrally between these vital points—vital above all to her own defence—able to send to either point reinforcements whether of troops or aeroplanes, of munitions or supplies, in far less time and with far less danger of enemy interference than they can be sent from England.

This determines that India would never be free as long as Amery and Co. can help it but must slave hard, harder, its hardest, producing war materials, and to see this done is the job of Amery and his gang here. India is worth not only itself but as means of saving the rest of the Empire. This is more so today than ever before.

No 'Threat to India'

War has now entered the phase when positions are being taken up and fortified, in the three centres of world imperialist conflict. Battle for sea power—in the Atlantic. Battle for Africa—covering Suez and stretching to the Balkans and Near East. Battle for Singapore—Pacific.

Britain is hard pressed in the West, but in the East she has cleaned up Africa and is biding time to turn to offensive in the Balkans, and in the Far East, with American co-operation, she is fully prepared to meet any Jap threat.

Where is the 'threat to India'? It is an imperialist scare. War-weeks, Parades, and Posters propaganda, are needed to create the necessary background to befool the enslaved and whip up more and ever more war-effort so that the British rulers may get the wherewithals to go over to the offensive.

Gigantic quantities of war-materials—arms, munitions, planes are required. They are being manufactured in the countries of the Eastern Group—really only in Australia, where an industrial building up on a huge scale is taking place. The Eastern Group Council is the imperialist device to keep India as a source of cash, and half-finished raw materials, cotton, etc., and to prevent any large-scale industrial development.

War Policy

The Central Budget was based on this very policy, and was attacked by all bourgeois parties and above all the bourgeois organization, the Merchants' Chamber. The Defence expenditure is 84 instead of 50 crores. The deficit is met by new taxation and not through borrowing in

India as the Indian capitalists demanded. Sir Cowasji figured it out that the Indian tax-payer is taxed 44 per cent more than the British to meet the deficit. Extra taxation is by raising Excess Profit-Tax, excise on matches, kerosene and petrol, duty on rayon and on motor tyre, against each of these the bourgeoisie has protested through its Chambers.

But imperialism cares a fig for these protests. What are the sanctions? None whatsoever. Imperialism carries on leaving the imbeciles to bleat and pray. Mr Kazmi's cut motion in the Assembly to 'discuss repression', was replied to by the Home Member with an air of 'what is all the other about' and he went on regaling 'good stories' about the satyagrahis, with Sir F.E. James demanding, 'give us one more', and general laughter all round.

The atmosphere was such that it was not even found worth-while by the 'Nationalists' and others to raise a discussion on the Deadlock.

In the Council of State, Kunzru made the servile gesture of withdrawing his resolution on 'Indianization of the Army' when the Commander-in-Chief graciously promised that as soon as possible recruitment would be thrown open to all classes.

The Viceroy read a sermon to the Princes: You have been doing your duty all right but...., pay more for the war, remember 'changed times' and be a wee bit more careful as regards administration in your States, think of amalgamating small states to save more money and hand it over to us.

John Bull, in India, is not gone crazy with our Inquilab at his throat, but feels quite merry as he cracks the whip to keep the war-effort going strong and unhindered, sometimes stooping to pat the slaves on the back or being gracious and modern enough to tell a good yarn, at the cost of our national movement.

49. India's Economic Conditions: Means of Improvement Dr Meghnad Saha on National Planning

Amrita Bazar Patrika, 8 March 1941.

'Back to the village is a cry of despair. India's problem of poverty and unemployment will not be solved by sending people from urban areas to the villages. But the solution lies other way about by attracting more people from villages to the towns and cities and creating work for them by utilizing power which modern science places at the hands of any one who can use it,' said Dr Meghnad Saha, FRS, in the course of a lecture on 'National Planning' which he delivered at the Ashutosh Hall on Friday afternoon. The lecture was organized by the Bengal Students' Economic Society. Sir Sarvepalli Radhakrishnan presided.

Quoting the words of the famous British scientist, Dr Rutherford, Dr Saha said that when a problem was known three-fourths of it was solved. So they had first to know what their problems were. The national Planning Committee was set up by the Indian National Congress with the co-operation of several provincial Governments for the purpose of determining and finding out the means of improving the economic conditions of the country. Dr Saha expressed surprise at the ignorance which even Ministers displayed about the problems which confronted the country. One of the Ministers of the province, he said, after opening a soap factory, declared on the next day that they had started large scale industry in their province. On account of the ignorance of the problems what had been attempted by provincial governments had been in most cases haphazard, irrelevant and useless. In fact he made bold to say, that these national governments had not been able to increase the national income by a single pice.

Economic Condition

Referring to the economic condition of India, Dr Saha said that average national income was Rs 65 per capita per year and in the case of rural population it was even less, being about Rs 35 per capita per year, while the corresponding figure for England was about Rs 2,000, for Sweden Rs 1,300 and for Japan which had emerged out of medievalism only about 80 or 90 years ago the figure was four or five times of the Indian figure.

Why was India so backward? Wealth of a country was not a gift from heaven, but had got to be worked out by the people. In order a country could advance it was necessary that it must have natural resources, good agricultural lands, resources of power, minerals, mines, and other things and the people must have the genius to develop the country. From the point of view of natural resources India was an ideal country. As a matter of fact there were few countries so richly endowed as India in this respect. Even the United States of America suffered from comparison with India. India, Soviet Russia and USA were the three political units which were the richest countries in the world so far as natural resources were concerned. Japan and England were not so rich from this standpoint.

Causes of Poverty in India

Why India so rich in natural resources, her people should be so abnormally poor? Modern science had placed in the hands of the people such discoveries and inventions that there was no need that anybody should suffer from poverty or disease. India was in this plight because her resources had not been developed. Then, there was the genius of the people United States of America was being peoples by Europeans for about 200 years. During this period they had harnessed the forces of nature and developed the country in such a way that they had made her the richest country in the world and were in the forefront of civilization.

So far as India was concerned, the Government so long concerned itself only with the maintenance of peace and order. But this idea of the function of government had been given up elsewhere long ago. Now a progressive government must find out the solutions for poverty, unemployment and create wealth for the nation. Figures of India were the greatest accusers of the past administration of the country. There was a certain section of people, said Dr Saha, who held that the problem of poverty could be solved if a large part of the population went back to the villages. That was a remedy which the speaker thought was worse than the disease. People who were directly connected with agriculture formed 70 per cent of India's population while the urban population were 11 per cent. If more peoples were sent back to village the problem would not be solved but would rather be accentuated. For already there was too great pressure on the land and villagers lacked many amenities of the life. Their problem, said Dr Saha, would not be solved by sending people from towns to villages but would rather be solved by attracting more people to urban areas and creating work for them. This was the only solution. If they took the figures of the civilized countries of the world it would be found that large proportion of people were town dwellers. In England 23 per cent of the population lived in villages while 77 per cent lived in cities. There was no cry that there was no proper balance between agriculture and industry. In France, 52 per cent of the population lived in cities and 48 per cent in villages. In India, China and Abyssinia which stood at the bottom so far as standard of life was concerned, the cry was heard 'Go back to the villages'. 'Our problem', said Dr Saha, 'will not be solved that way. It is a cry of despair.'

Solution of Problem

Their problem was to how to start more industries and how to create more national wealth. There was the wildest confusion as to how this problem would be approached. There was a school of thought which held that industrialization would spoil the soul of the nation. This was wrong. They had to accept industrialization.

Proceeding Dr Saha said that formerly work was done by human hands but since the invention of steam power things had been revolutionized. The average unit of work per worker in England was 20 times greater than in India. This was because India's resources had not been developed for the purpose of creating wealth. So far only 2 per cent of river power had been developed; the rest was going untapped.

Referring to heavy and light industries, Dr Saha said that unless heavy industries were developed in the country there were great difficulties in the way of developing light industries. He cited for instance the soap industry of which there were a large number in the country, but they were not doing well. This was because they had to purchase two principal ingredients, soda and palm oil, from two huge foreign combines, who had beaten off all competitors from the field and sold those commodities at prices fixed at their sweet will. Here was the need for Government protection if infant industries were to have a chance of survival.

Power Resources

Proceeding Dr Saha emphasized the need for Government developing power resources of the country and distributing them at the cheapest rate. Referring to the Calcutta Electric Supply Corporation, Dr Saha said that the cost of production per unit was only one pice while the Company charged 10 pice per unit. Dr Saha called the report of the Electricity Committee appointed by the Bengal Government as the stupidest one came across. It was because there was no representative of the people on the Committee. The Bengal Government without understanding the report of the Committee renewed the license of the Calcutta Electric Supply Corporation for 10 years.

In conclusion Dr Saha said that national planning required national mind.

50. Forcible Collection of War Funds

The Tribune, 21 March 1941.

New Delhi, 20 March. Maulana Zafar Ali attempted to get admission for an adjournment motion in the Central Assembly this morning to discuss the unwarranted interference of the local police with the lawful activities of Khaksars near Juma Masjid yesterday.

In answer to the President's questions, Maulana Zafar Ali explained that the Khaksars under an agreement between them and the Government of India had been allowed to move in a single file and carry their *belchas*, but the local police yesterday interfered with a group of Khaksars who were marching. The Police, he said, refused to listen to the Khaksars' plea that they were acting in accordance with the agreement. Eventually the Khaksars dispersed under protest.

The Leader of the House, in the absence of the Home Member, said that the Chief Commissioner, Delhi, to whom a reference was made, said that he had no information and was making enquiries and would let the Government know.

The Chair ruled that the motion would in these circumstances stand over till tomorrow.

Mr Kazmi had an adjournment motion in his name to discuss the forcible collection of war funds as reported in the *Hindustan Times.* Mr Kazmi alleged that such collection was going on everywhere but the particular instance reported in the newspaper was in Gorakhpur (United Provinces).

The President observed that the Government of India had no power of supervision or control over a local Government even though it was not a Government responsible to the local legislature. He, therefore, disallowed the motion.

Questions and Answers

'I Understand that the total number of the injured was 85 of whom 65 were treated in the hospital', said Sri Andrew Clow[1] in reply to Mr A.N. Chattopadhyaya's question in the Assembly today about the number of persons injured in the Railway accident which occurred on the 5th August last near Jairampur station, E.B.R. Sir Andrew added that the information received in January showed that 57 had been discharged. Eleven persons died in the hospital. About 50 claims for compensation had been received by the Railway. No compassion had been paid by the Railway administration which, he stated, was in no way responsible for the accident.

Sir Frederick James asked what improvements has been made in the timings, accommodation and service on the Grand Trunk Express since the cut motion on the subject was carried against the Government by the Assembly on the 24th January 1940.

Sir Andrew Clow replied: 'The running time between Madras and Delhi has been reduced by 40 minutes, and an earlier arrival at Delhi has permitted a more punctual and early delivery of mails from the south in Delhi. A more frequent examination of stock is made and the period between overhauls of stock is made and the period between overhauls of stock is reduced by one-third. Return tickets at reduced fares have been introduced.'

Sir Frederick complained that the arrangements for the supply of food to passengers still continued to be unsatisfactory for the greater part of the journey. Sir Andrew informed him that the arrangements for the supply of food for lower class passengers were generally satisfactory. There were not sufficient through upper class passengers to justify the running of a dining car, but arrangements had been made for the supply of meals to upper class passengers from the Indian refreshment car.

Maulana Zafar Ali Khan: 'Is the Honourable the Railway Member aware that there are no facilities for providing good food for Muslims?'

Mr Andrew Clow replied that there was an Indian refreshment car which supplied food.

---

[1] Member (Communications), Executive Council.

51. Bengal's War Effort: Governor's Appreciation Contribution Total Nearly Rs 70 Lakhs

Amrita Bazar Patrika, 6 April 1941.

At a meeting of the Advisory Committee of the Bengal War Purposes Fund held at Government House on 2nd April 1941, His Excellency the Governor presiding expressed deep appreciation of the manner in which Bengal had responded to appeals to assist the war effort which had resulted in contributions totaling nearly Rs 70 lakhs. This sum includes more than half a crore of rupees credited to the East India Fund which has already paid in full for two complete squadrons of fighter aircraft.

It was decided at this meeting to allocate over Rs 5 lakhs for purchase of fighter aircraft for the East India Squadrons. It was further decided by arrangement with the East India Fund to offer to districts in Bengal the same privilege as has been given by Lord Beaverbrook, Minister for Aircraft Production, to donors of £5,000 in the United Kingdom, so that a fighter plane of one of the East India squadrons will be given the name of any district subscribing total of Rs 66,000 for purchase of fighter aircraft.

Districts which have so far qualified to benefit from this offer are:

Burdwan for three fighter planes (one of which will be named Asansol), Dacca for two fighter planes (one of which will be named Narayanganj), and the districts of 24 Parganas, Howrah, Midnapur, Chittagong, Tippera, Mymensingh, Darjeeling, Jalpaiguri and Bakerganj for one fighter plane each.

In addition to purchase of aircraft, the Bengal War Purpose Fund provides for relief of suffering among wounded and blinded troops, as well as civilian victims, and for amenities for the fighting services. The fund has already paid Rs 1,35,000 to the Red Cross, Rs 35,000 to St Dunstan's, Rs 1,67,000 for the relief of air raid victims and Rs 90,000 to provide amenities for the fighting services.

At a meeting of the Committee on the 4th April, the following allocations were made for these purposes:

For the Indian Red Cross and St John Ambulance, rupees one lakh, for St Dunstan's, Rs 50,000, amenities for Indian troops in Africa, Rs 50,000, amenities for Indian and British seamen, Rs 25,000.

52. India's Military Value: Way to Exploit

Amrita Bazar Patrika, 28 April 1941.

Mr M.N. Roy on Commons Debate

Dehra Dun, 26 April. 'The most remarkable feature of the Secretary of State's speech is belief in the fullest development of India's military potentiality, not conditional upon democratization of her political life'. Thus observed Mr M.N. Roy in a statement on Mr Amery's speech in the India debate in the Commons. He added: 'Hostile popular feeling might be disregarded if war remained a distant affair. From the selfish British view point, if not for the sake of destroying international Fascism, the prevailing sentiment of the Indian people should not be disregarded. India's present war efforts may be creditable to Government machinery but it is an illusion to interpret them as evidence of popular co-operation yet Mr Amery seems to labour under that illusion and believes that India's military value can be fully exploited irrespective of the general dissatisfaction prevailing at the state of political affairs. Only Indians fully conscious of the grave issues involved in this war can strengthen the home front against potential dangers. From the very beginning they have offered the fullest co-operation and have recommended measures which would enable them to educate public opinion so that India might become a reliable military asset in this grim struggle against Fascism. Their recommendations of ending the constitutional deadlock are neither impractical for imply fundamental changes immediately. Therefore, the objections raised by Mr Amery are not valid against them. Why was he silent in that respect? Those recommendations of the conference of independent public men which met several months before the Bombay conference were not formally submitted to Government.

Mr Amery's Mistake

But I am glad to find they are not quite unknown to the Secretary of State, who suggested that a way out of the Indian political impasse was in that direction. It is to be hoped that Indian leaders not obsessed with dreamy political idealism, nor concerned with group or personal prestige, will have boldness to take up Mr Amery's challenge by endorsing the recommendations of the Calcutta conference namely, inclusion in the Viceroy's Executive Council of independent public men with popular appeal and the formation of emergency Ministries to resolve the deadlock in the Provinces with such men as are ready to face the electorate as soon as possible. Another grave mistake of the Secretary of State is regarding India's value as a strategic point in the matter of supply. His idea that the army raised in India must depend for supplies from England and America is simply fantastic. The development of India's striking power is entirely conditional on her industrialization. The entire popular energy should be mobilized to expedite the process. Even to-day India is almost behind the front lines where decisive battles of war will be fought. Unless the organization of her resources and manpower is entrusted to those Indians, who are anxious that the war must be won, one cannot be very optimistic about the future.'—AP

53. War and Textile Industry: Injustice to Bengal Mills by Supply Department Deplored

Amrita Bazar Patrika, 28 April 1941.

Presiding at the quarterly general meeting of the Bengal Millowners' Association yesterday Rai Sahib S.C. Ghose said:

> You will all agree that what is uppermost in our minds today is the War in Europe and Africa, which has been progressing with a frightful rapidity, and it is only a question of time when it may develop into a world conflagration. Although we have not yet had a taste of the horrors of modern warfare, my predecessors in office have had occasions to describe the repercussions of the War on the Cotton Textile Industry of Bengal with which we are immediately concerned. To put it in a nutshell once again, the increase in the cost of production of textile goods due to various factors, directly or indirectly, attributable to the War, has been out of all proportions to the increase in the prices of such goods that has taken place so far. A buoyant feeling in the market, which is so very necessary for a smooth and unhampered progress of Trade and Industry, is conspicuous by its absence owing to uncertainties of the future, the crushing poverty of the people in general and heavy taxation by Central and Provincial Governments, in addition to the economic dislocation caused by War conditions, especially in the sphere of International trade.
>
> It is argued that the cotton mill industry of the country has derived immense benefit from the war efforts owing to the huge orders for cotton textiles placed with them by the Department of Supply. But, as you are well aware Gentlemen, the Bengal mills have not so far received any share worth mentioning in these War orders and for this glaring default the mills themselves are as much to blame as the Department of Supply, which do not seem to have taken any steps for an equitable distribution of the orders among the different centres of the Cotton Mill Industry in India. The mills also apparently lack the initiative and enthusiasm expected of them owing partly to inadequacy of equipment and partly to the inscrutable policy followed by the Supply Department. It is of some consolation to note that the Director General of Supply has convened a meeting of the representatives of different millowners' associations to be held in the offices of the Millowners' Association, Bombay, where he will explain a new policy which his Department propose to adopt for securing their requirements for war supplies of cotton textiles. We shall await with interest the outcome of the proposed meeting.

I would also refer to the doubling of the premium rate for War Risk Insurance, which has added considerably to the already onerous burdens imposed on the Cotton Mill Industry since the outbreak of War. Apart from the fact that the commercial community were not consulted before effecting the increase, the justification for the enhancement was also not satisfactorily made out.

Government's decision to disallow increments in wages, salaries or bonuses to the staff or workers as an 'expenditure' for purposes of Excess Profits Tax, Income-tax and Super-tax assessments is also highly regrettable and most ill-advised. This would naturally tend the stoppage of all increments or bonuses which employees could legitimately expect, if profits were higher, and thus would create dissatisfaction among them. I would earnestly appeal to Government to modify what I must call an unwise decision, which would hamper the development of Trade and Industry in India.

54. Inside Calcutta: An Under-ground [Communist] Reporter's Note Book

Communist, Vol. III, No. 3, April 1941, P.C. Joshi Archives on Contemporary History, JNU.

Gamble Your Way to Victory!

GAMBLING is considered to be the chief attraction at the War Fund Carnivals. Severely condemned by the citizens. Heard in a tram. Two old gentlemen, rearing 50, most probably Anglo-Indian, discuss the Spitfire Carnival. One says: 'It is all bosh'. He had been to it the day before. It can only interest the young things. The whole thing is taken in a spirit of fun.

The 'Spitfire Carnival' can be visited at reduced prices of admission, says an Attorney's apprentice, but the buses to the Carnival ply empty. Do they think they can continue the war with this state of affairs here?

'Forced Savings' at Martin's

An officer at Martin's says that the boss offered to advance three months' salaries to the officers if they bought war bonds. He gave an emphatic NO for an answer.

Grumbling and Rumbling

Wayside grumbling by impoverished petty-bourgeois house holders:

'These rascals and their war. They fight for their own skins and we poor fish here have to pay for their mischiefs. The prices of foodstuffs are rocketing, like blazes. How long do you think we are going to put up with it?'

'Just think of the cheek of these shalas! They are losing every battle. The Germans are giving them hell, yet here they bully us. They take away our food for their war. They squeeze money out of us and throw us into prison.'

'This stalemate is sickening. Italy is a washout. These shalas might win in the end, damn them!'

The Carrion Men

The police won't listen to their masters. Mrs Colson (wife of the Calcutta Police Chief) has asked for worn-out clothes for bandages. The carrion men working at the SPECIAL BRANCH, Calcutta, refuse to give anything. One of them suggested: Go to Kalighat, pay two *annas* and you will get nice, clean, well-laundered pieces of cloth. No one will make out that they belong to the DEAD. Why come to us, poor fellows?

Wanted a Policemen's Trade Union!

While travelling by bus, I overheard an interesting conversation between the bus driver and a Hindustani Policeman (in ordinary dress). I got into the bus just in time to hear the concluding remarks. This is how it went:

The driver: 'But your job is better than ours. You get a pension at the end of your period of service'.

The policeman (in a contemptuous and angry tone) denied the advantage: 'Sala lok bara julum karta hai abhi. They don't even give us our full pay, now. They chisel a bit off our pay every month. Sala lok pension bhi band kar dia. They say, after the war is won, we shall get our pension. Not before then. All new pensions have been stopped'.

The policeman spat angrily and got down from the bus.

The Police are Touchy!

At a Calcutta restaurant frequented by students from a near by college, the wits nick-named the two waiters 'Chamberlain' and 'Churchill'. The whole college picked up the nick-names. The waiters enjoyed themselves.

But one fine day, a sub-inspector swaggered up to the proprietor: 'Look here, stop this nonsense about your waiters. Chamberlain and Churchill are not to be slighted!' He threatened to cancel the restaurant licence.

Meanwhile, the students not only insist on keeping the nick-names, they have threatened to boycott the place if the owner's son (or may be his nephew) does not resign from the Civic Guards.

The poor proprietor is in a fix.

Civic Guards into Red Guards?

'Civic Guards are treated with contempt and jeered at on all occasions.

'One black-out night six of us went on an excursion through the streets. We started deriding the Civic Guards. One of them got offended because we called him a Civic Guard! We noted that the Civic Guards, thinly disguised by their uniforms and Sarkar's hats, were some Muslim shop-keepers, bullock-cart drivers, one or two Hindustani coolies and some middle-class youth.

'I have just found out that during the second corporation workers' strike, a sympathizer of ours with Rs 200 in his pocket was moving up and down Calcutta to get a link and hand over the sum to the Communist Party. It was a contribution from a group of Civic Guards.'

M.N. Roy: A Rai Bahadur?

'Some of us paid a visit to a Rai Bahadur. A number of other tight-fisted Rai Bahadurs were also there. They were chattering away, suspicious of everybody and everything, desperately proud of their titles. One of them said: 'Who is this M.N. Roy? What's his game?' The reply came (in a very anxious tone) 'Bodh hoi fank tale Rai Bahadur hote chai?' (perhaps he wants to bluff the Government and become a Rai Bahadur?)'

Recruiting Sergeant gets a Kick

B.N. Roy Chaudhuri (the Maharaja of Santosh's son) who has been working as a recruiting sergeant for Imperialism has been telling his friends: 'They really don't want us you know. We have sent quite a few. But not one has a chance of being accepted'.

Our Dens Can become Fortresses

'One day, our underground den was raided. Two comrades lived there. One was out, but the other one fell into the clutches of the Police. AFTER the raid when the people round about found out that our comrades were 'swadeshi lok', they wrung their hands and said: 'God, why didn't you tell us? We could have saved them from the Police blood-hounds. They were working for us—it's a shame we could not save them'. True. When I returned to the den, a man living in an adjoining room hurried up to me and said: 'Fly for your life! All arrested. The Police are lying in wait to catch you! That is how I was saved.'

Our dens can become our fortresses—with the love of the people.

When You are Out in the Black-out

The black-out was the chief topic of conversation in buses, trams, everywhere. Opinion is definitely hostile. The shop-keepers take it very seriously because it affects their trade.

A Muslim was impressed with the Communist poster on the black-out: 'This is what everyone is feeling to-day'.

By the end of February a real black-out scheme is being put into operation. This time the middle-class people are taking it very seriously. It is connected with the Japanese threat. The shopkeepers are indignant, particularly because the order is so sudden.

55. Press and Defence of India Rules in Bengal, April to July 1941

Confidential File No. F.W. 141/41, Home (Political) Department, Government of Bengal, West Bengal State Archives.

Twelve Warnings (4 formal and 8 informal) were issued to newspapers under the Defence of India Rules during the period under review.

The printer and publisher of the *Hindu Ranjika* of Rajshahi has been ordered to furnish a cash security deposit of Rs 100 under Section 7(1) of the Indian Press (Emergency Powers) Act, 1931.

A printed pamphlet entitled 'Leaguer Bani' in Bengali has been declared by the District Magistrate, Noakhali to be an unauthorized news-sheet under the Indian Press (Emergency Powers) Act. The author and printer of the pamphlet have been arrested and prosecuted. The case is sub-judice.

The editor of the weekly Bengali paper *Damru* of Malda had been asked by the District Magistrate to show cause why action should not be taken against him for publishing false news in respect of the Civil Guards. The office of the Bina Printing Press of Jalpaiguri, was searched on 8.6.1941 and the Manager of the Press was prosecuted on 3.7.41. under Defence of India Rules 38(5) and 39(6) for publishing a prejudicial pamphlet entitled 'Brother Agriculturalists, why are you poor'.

In general the relations between the authorities and the editors and representatives of the muffasil press are satisfactory. They continue to co-operate with the authorities in the matter of publishing articles based on the pamphlets issued by the Public Relations Committee of Calcutta.

Register of War Activities—Press

Date	Narrative
29.4.41	In connection with a request made by the American Consul General for copies of regulations, leaflets, posters, and other things issued in India relating to War for transmission to the Congress Library at Washington (USA), a reference was made to the Central Government and on their advice the Publicity Department of this Government was informed that there was no objection to compliance with the Consul General's request
5.5.41	As instructed by the Government of India, copies of the proscribed publications seized in Bengal have been forwarded to the Keeper of Records of the Government of India, the India office and the British Museum.
6.5.41	The attention of the Assam Government was drawn to certain objectionable speeches delivered by some leaders of the Bengal Mahasabha in the conference held at Habiganj, Assam on the 11th and 12th April 1941 and they were requested to examine the speeches with a view to prosecution in those cases in which they were advised that action would lie and would be likely to result in conviction. That Government were not in favour of any prosecution as it would aggravate the Hindu–Muslim tension in that province and thereupon the proposal was dropped.
7.5.41	At the instance of the Military authorities and the Chief Press Adviser, Government of India, this Government order No. 7024 P, dated the 24th November 1940 requiring the submission before publication of all news relating to military matters within the Presidency and Assam District to the Commander, Presidency and Assam District, for scrutiny has been rescinded.
7.5.41	Copies of Correspondence between the Government of India and the Government of the United Provinces regarding the action to be taken against the pamphlet entitled *The Parting of the Ways* by Jawaharlal Nehru have been forward to DIC, IB and DC, SB, Calcutta.
10.5.41	The editor of the Gurumukhi newspaper *Desh Darpan* was prosecuted under rule 38(5), 38(2) and 38(1)(c) of the Defence of India Rules by the Commissioner of Police, Calcutta in respect of an objectionable article published in the paper in its issue of the 30th April 1941. The case ended in acquittal of the accused.
27.5.41	In respect of the publication in the *Dainik Basumati*, *Ananda Bazar Patrika* and *Bharat* newspapers of some objectionable articles contravening orders under Defence of India Rules 41(1)(a) the editors, printers and publishers of the said newspapers have been prosecuted under rule 38(5) of the Defence of India Rules and the case is pending in the Chief Presidency Magistrate's Court, Calcutta.
30.5.41	Issue of an order under rule 40(1)(b) and (c) of the Defence of India Rules prohibiting further publication, sale or distribution and declaring to be forfeited to His Majesty all copies of the booklet in Bengali entitled *Forward—Peoples' Government.*

(*Contd*) ...

... (*Contd*)

Date	Narrative
31.5.41	Instructions were issued to all local officers regarding the procedure to be followed with regard to conditional release of repentant *Satyagrahi* prisoners convicted under the Defence of India Act and Rules.
31.5.41	The order dated the 10th April 1941 authorizing the District Magistrate of Dacca to exercise power under Section 5(1)(b) of the Indian Telegraph Act, 1885 during the communal disturbances at Dacca, having expired on the 30th May 1941, was extended upto the 31st July 1941.
31.5.41	The order issued under rule 41(1)(a) of the Defence of India Rules requiring the submission before publication of all matter relating to communal disturbances in Bengal to the Special Press Adviser for scrutiny, was rescinded.
24.6.41	Instructions were issued to local officers regarding the use of powers under rules 124 and 126 of the Defence of India Rules so far as the seizure of presses is concerned.
25.6.41	Issue of an order under rule 40(1)(c) of the Defence of India Rules proscribing the leaflet in Bengali entitled *Hindu Ke Hindu-i-raksha Karibe.*
28.6.41	Instructions were issued to local officers with regard to the procedure to be followed in respect of prosecution for possession of pre-judicial documents prescribed before the Defence of India Rules came into force.
5.7.41	Government of India's instructions regarding the prohibition of inclusion of information regarding military road projects in any official publication without consulting the Defence Department of the Government of India have been forwarded to all Departments of this Government.
22.7.41	The Chief Press Adviser's instructions regarding the attitude to be adopted towards Russia's entry into the war were forwarded to all District Press Advisers.
22.7.41	As instructed by the Government of India, copies of printed publications seized in Bengal were forwarded to the Keeper of Records of the Government of India, the India Office and the British Museum.

56. Defending India

Editorial, *Amrita Bazar Patrika*, 25 May 1941.

Those who are sincerely anxious for an effective and satisfactory solution of the political deadlock in the country will whole-heartedly welcome the efforts initiated in this behalf by Mr A.K. Fazlul Huq and Sir Sikandar Hyat Khan. Besides being Premiers of two important Muslim majority provinces they hold high positions in the supreme executive of the Muslim League. The utterances each of them has made recently are in essence repugnant to Mr Jinnah's stand which, both as regards the interim arrangements and the future constitution of the country, insists on the acceptance of a scheme deliberately directed against India's territorial integrity and the traditions that have been established by the labours of far-sighted Hindu and Moslem leaders working in co-operation. We had occasion to make our observations on the scheme propounded by Mr Fazlul Huq and no further reference to that scheme is necessary at this stage, speaking practically in the same strain in an interview to a news agency, the Punjab

Premier has pleaded for what may be described as a political moratorium, a sort of 'war contract' as he himself puts it under which all sections of Indian community should devote their entire attention and energy to the prosecution of the war and securing effective defence of the country. This, he argues, may be done without prejudice to the future constitution and the claims of various parties in that connection. The idea is that all parties for the time being and in the face of the war crisis should put politics aside and get together for effective defence of India. His concrete scheme to give effect to his proposals is the summoning of a Round Table Conference of Premiers of the Provinces and readers of various parties in the legislatures, whether in jail or outside. While endorsing in broad principles the sentiments expressed by Sir Sikandar Hyat Khan, we must point out that we have not been able to appreciate the implications in their entirety of his approach to the issues which confront the nation.

The summoning of a Round Table Conference or a Constituent Assembly implies British acquiescence or, alternatively, seizure of political power by the Indians themselves; and so far as Sir Sikandar Hyat Khan or Mr Fazlul Huq is concerned they count on British acquiescence. The practical side of the question apart, the public is entitled to know what authority Sir Sikandar or Mr Fazlul Huq has got to assure their countrymen of Britain's readiness to summon a Round Table Conference or a Constituent Assembly in the present circumstances. Mr Amery's attitude has been throughout unhelpful. Mr Churchill is engaged in fighting in land and sea and air with all his might and the strength providence has given him against the ruthless Nazi menace in defence of the Empire and its obligations and interests. His Excellency Lord Linlithgow has nothing more to offer than expansion of his Executive Council and appointment of an Advisory War Council, an offer which has been rejected practically by all sections of public opinion. In his speech to the Bevin boys, Mr Amery has once again returned to his old slogan 'India First' while all the time inciting, if indirectly, the reactionaries and communalists not only to veto India's constitutional advance but also to indulge in activities that may, unless brought under control, lead to the disruption of India. That there is a strong feeling of bitterness and hatred against the Nazi cult and the Fascist philosophy of social frustration in India there is absolutely no doubt. But is the Nazi cult or the fascist philosophy confined to the borders of Germany or Italy? Are there no Fascists, pro-Fascists, pseudo-Fascists and Fascists in the making in different parts of the world today including Britain and India?

Much has been said in recent weeks of the elevation of Lord Beaverbrook to the position of Minister of State, an office created for the first in Britain and reserved for this Press Lord. We have more than once pointed out that that appointment is a dangerous symptom of a growing evil. Lord Beaverbrook has never been known for democratic sympathies on the contrary his lordship has been known for several years now as a 'peace monger' at all costs. In a book recently published entitled *The Case against Pacifism*, we find that the 'Peace Pledge Union found itself in close alliance with Lord Beaverbrook, the National Government and the British Union of Fascists, all of whom were strong for peace at almost any price and who accused socialists and supporters of the League of Nations of being war-mongers'. Their motives, the author adds, were exactly opposite to those of the pacifists. It was war in, defence of smaller nations of democracy, of genuine self-government to which Lord Beaverbrook, the National Government and the British Union of Fascists were opposed, not war itself. Are British men and women aware of his Lordship's antecedents and political sympathies? Are Sir Sikandar Hyat Khan and Mr Fazlul Huq aware of them? Has Mr Churchill given his Lordship his present high position in the War Cabinet upon these considerations or in spite of them? Take Mr Bevin, the gentleman who is supposed to have released the forces of democracy in the Supreme

Counsels of the British Cabinet. During the negotiations for the abortive Anglo-Russian pact prior to the declaration of war, Germany was being given the Czech gold from London and the royalties on the stolen patents of the Bren gun. Negotiations were reopened between the Federation of British industries and the Nazi industrialists. Mr Hudson proposed a gigantic loan to Germany and Mr Bevin suggested sharing economic spheres of interest. It looked, as the author of *The Case against Pacifism* puts it, increasingly like 'peace' in the West and 'war' in the East to the humiliation and dismemberment of Russia. That is the story of Mr Bevin.

There are grounds for suspicion that if those who happen to rule and control the destiny of Britain today are not made under the pressure of public opinion to abdicate in favour of the 'war-mongers' who would not hesitate to give Hitler's philosophy the mortal blow it so richly deserves for the emancipation of mankind, there may be an attempt to make Britain a gift to the Nazi overlord in the manner of Marshal Petain and his co-adjutors in the conspiracy of dark betrayal and shameful surrender. That danger is there and this talk of defending India against the Fascist menace now and then indulged in by Sir Sikandar Hyat Khan seems to have no relation to the objective situation with which we are confronted. Nor is there sense in Sir Sikandar Hyat's call for a political moratorium. The war itself is political issue. The war technique is not less so. Unless the war objectives and the peace aims are fully explained to the people, there is no possibility of mobilizing the country's resources on a wide scale. Men must know what they are fighting for and for whom. They cannot be left in the dark as to the possibilities and implications of social reconstruction. Political aims cannot in any circumstances be isolated from a war programme and men and women must know whether they are being asked to fight for the emancipation of the humanity. On this fundamental issue Mr Churchill unfortunately has thrown no light and evidently neither Sir Sikandar Hyat Khan nor Mr Fazlul Huq is in a position to 'deliver the goods' in this respect. The situation on the whole is intriguing. There is awful confusion which leads one to darkness.

57. War and Indian Industries: Should British and Indian Interests Conflict?

Amrita Bazar Patrika, 25 May 1941.

Since the summer of 1940, there has been published a spate-full of editorials, special contributions, memoranda from Chambers of Commerce, inter-leaved with exhortations from political and business leaders—all vaguely hinting at the coming industrial renaissance in India. With the military collapse of the Lowlands, followed by the surrender of France and increasing hostilities in the Mediterranean, the life lines of the Empire became almost overnight taut, thrice in length and more and more exposed to threat from under the sea and from above in the air. The importance of supplies to the army of the Nile was brought home to the Empire countries east of Suez and we have witnessed the heartening spectacle of an Eastern Group Supply Conference and the roving Commission of Sir Alexander Roger and his colleagues. The winter of 1940 provided for the press and the public in India appropriate opportunity for expositions on the tremendous possibilities opening up for Indian industrial expansion on a scale which would be commensurate with the vast potentialities of this land. An elaborate publicity campaign was being built up and India as the base for Empire armies in the Middle East, promised to reach a high industrial stature within an incredibly short time. There were no bottlenecks in the country—neither in aspirations nor in cooperative efforts. The Government of India's publicity departments heroically paraded all over the country the fast growing multiplicity or work demanded by the needs of the moment. Commerce and Supply Departments, inundated with requests for more explicit expositions on industrial advance, regaled the legislature and the public with visions and prospects which, though vague and dimly defined, were magnificent in structure and promise. From time to time the aggregate value of orders placed by the Supply Department on firms, in India was given—it was announced the other day that these orders have reached the imposing figure of Rs 84 crores since the beginning of 1940 as against Rs 9–12 crore in 1939. We have not, however, been told how far and to what extent Government agencies have simply displaced private business in the 84 crores volume of orders; nor are we vouchsafed any information about the categories to which these orders relate. While the recommendations of the Roger Mission remain confidential the purpose for which the Eastern Supply Council was set up has never been clearly defined. Only the other day the Indian member of the Council, Mr Hydari, in a broadcast made the first positive statement that it was not the objective of the Council to consider the setting up of new industries in any country; that their function was one of correlation of existing supplies available in each Empire unit east of Suez; that the availability of production circumscribed their control which was mainly on distribution. So far as the Supply Council is concerned, the advancement of new industries and new production lines is outside their domain. Remain the supply Department, with its tiny sub-section on industrial research confined mostly to chemistry problems. The Commerce Department has not announced any vital departure from the pre-war policies of the Government; nor has the Supply Department undertaken any such onerous functions outside the routine of purchase and distribution. Control over imports and exports the diversion of production from civil consumption to military purposes; the counting of existing supply of machine tools in India or an inventory of workshop capacity and a wider distribution of munitions orders—these do not connote any advancement of new industries nor do they imply any guarantee for setting up additional plant units for expansion. The press campaigns about aircraft production, ship-building yards and the automobile industry—mostly inaccurate in statement of fact, nevertheless indicate a lack of 'ability' on the part of the Government to sponsor such schemes. This lack is defined by the limits under which this Government of India works—and apparently there has been no relaxation of control since the war started.

Control from Whitehall

The rigidity of Treasury control over expenditure is maintained in the pre-war sense, and the policies, which present day needs demand, do not fit in with the pre-war finance and audit regulations. In a way the Government of India is helpless and unless Whitehall relinquishes its grip over these controls, there can be no change in the industrial outlook of the country. From another angle Mr Arthur Moore's novel proposal of 'Home Rule for the Viceroy' finds support in the detailed scrutiny which Whitehall usually exercises over the expenditure of the Government of India and from recent experience it is becoming evident that the controls have become tighter and more stringent since the war commenced.

It appears that the 'laissez-faire' or rather the 'let-alone' policy of the Government of India in pre-war days has suffered no change or modification under the stress of war conditions, as far as one can conclude from the impact of Government action on the industrial activity of the country. We have known the financial and audit rigidities in the past; and we know that such rigidities still continue without modification. Vision may have broadened, but day dreams will receive no concrete incarnation unless power is there to enforce the new policy. Pious aspirations will not reach achievement unless a radical change in methods of control is established. We have named Whitehall to be the culprit; in other words pointed attention needs to be drawn to the absolutely subsidiary role of the Government of India in such matters.

Does Whitehall desire that under the impress of war demands India should be allowed to grow up in her industrial stature? There is no denying the vast potential of this country; the needs of the army in the middle east demand an all-sufficient supply base east of Aden. We look at South Africa and Australia and are amazed at the magnificent progress made in these two countries in respect of war industries. India remains where it was—despite unanimous and repeatedly expressed desire on the part of the industrial section of the public in India, both British and Indian. Where is the obstacle? The one irresistible conclusion is that the Government of Britain does not wish it to be so. It was for no idle purpose that to a body of technical experts like the Roger Mission there was attached a layman Director of Federation of British industries. It is no idle speculation either that the objectives of the Eastern Group Supply Council have been purposely made extremely restrictive and routed to ordinary co-ordination of purchases. Does it mean that Britain does not require India's assistance to any great extent in the matter of war supplies? Or is it that Britain's overlords are obsessed by post-war considerations about the future of British vested interests in India?

Financial Settlement between UK and India

These questions need a straight and direct reply which, we hope, will be forthcoming. That these are not idle disturbances of a prejudiced mind will be clear from a perusal of the so-called Financial Settlement between India and the United Kingdom in respect of the Defence Services of India and future expenditure on war account. The Settlement was very lucidly explained by the Finance Member to the Government of India in his Budget speech last year. We make the following excerpts from the speech:

'It will be recalled that the capital outlay on modernizing the army in India, estimated at Rs 45.77 lakhs, was to have been provided by His Majesty's Government, three-fourths as a free gift to India and the balance of one-fourth as an advance to be repaid on easy terms. It was anticipated that the average net recurring cost of the Defence Services during the five-year period allotted for carrying out the proposals would not exceed the level of Defence expenditure obtaining immediately prior to modernization because there would be substantial savings during the first two years which could be devoted to meeting exercise in the later years....

'It will also be recalled that the Chatfield proposals postulated the acceptance by the Government of India of joint responsibility with His Majesty's Government for the external defence of India and in accordance with this principle provided for the earmarking of certain portions of the Defence Forces in India for purposes of external defence and a consequential increase of £300,000 in the amount of the annual grant made by His Majesty's Government towards the cost of maintaining the Defence Services in India in peace. It was stipulated that whenever circumstances should make it necessary to employ the whole or any portion of India's External Defence Forces outside Indian limits in the discharge of India's joint responsibility for the external defence, India should accept some share of the costs of doing so....

'An agreement on the subject has now been reached under which the whole of the defence expenditure incurred by India will be apportioned between the two Governments on the following basis. India is to bear:

(1) a fixed annual sum representing the normal net effective costs of the Army in India under peace conditions, plus

(2) an addition to allow for rises in prices, plus
(3) the cost of such war measures as can be regarded as purely Indian liabilities by reason of their having been undertaken by India in her own interests, and
(4) a lump sum payment of one crore of rupees towards the extra cost of maintaining India's External Defence Troops overseas.

'The total amount by which the net annual defence expenditure incurred in India during the war years will exceed the aggregate of items (1) to (3) will be recovered from His Majesty's Government.

'This settlement has been devised with two objects in view. The first object was to limit India's financial liability in connection with the war to such measures as are within her financial capacity and have clearly been or will be taken for the local defence of India itself, reckoning, of course, as such a measure the continued maintenance of the Army in India although only on its peace-time scale. The second object was simplicity, resulting in the avoidance of expense and dispute in the day-to-day application of the terms of the settlement in practice. Item (I) of the Settlement has been evaluated at 36.77 lakhs, being the net budget estimate for our Defence Services in the year1939–40, namely 45.18 lakhs after excluding from it non-effective charges of 8.41 lakhs which have been excluded from the settlement. I would emphasize that this item of 36.77 lakhs in the settlement is not an estimate of any specific expenditure on our Defence Services such as was the budget estimate of 45.15 lakhs for the year 1939–40 from which it is derived, but has now become a mere lump sum financial adjustment between the Government of India and His Majesty Government fixed for the duration of the war. ...

'The third item, namely, those measures which we must pay for ourselves, will as far as possible be determined by direct accounting but where this presents serious difficulty the amounts debitable to India will be assessed on the basis of estimates....

'The payment represented by item (4) was included in the settlement in pursuance of the principle of India's joint responsibility for her external defence on which the Chatfield settlement was based.

'The revised estimates of Defence expenditure for 1939–40 framed on the basis of this settlement work up to Rs 49.29 lakhs made up as follows:

	Rs (in lakhs)
(1) Normal Peace budget	36.77
(2) Effect of prices on (1)	.25
(3) Indian War measures	3.86
(4) Non-effective charges	8.41
	49.29

This picture of so-called Financial Settlement, as painted by the Finance Member, no doubt pleased the zealous economizers of the Assembly: they were given a firm assurance that none of the impending war expenditure would be debited to India.

Two Cardinal Facts

Two cardinal facts emerge from this settlement, which failed to attract the notice of the legislators and the public at large at that time. One is that the annual estimates of expenditure on Defence Services have become a fixed lump sum for the duration of the war and as a corollary if any additional expenditure is to be incurred on war-supplies or on production—plants, for war-supplies, this must necessarily obtain the previous sanction of His Majesty's Government. The elasticity of control over estimates is therefore, taken out of the hands of the Government of India. The second factor is that, although India is permitted to spend on such war measures as can be regarded to have been undertaken by India in her own interests, such measures must be 'within her financial capacity' and should be 'clearly for the local defence of India'. While imposing in this manner a rigid Treasury and Secretariat control, there has also been indicated what these measures can be, as for instance, censorship, port and coastal defence, internment of aliens recruitment and training (part share), and other things. A sum of 3 crores and 86 lakhs appears under the caption 'Indian war measures' in the estimates for 1940–1. So much for the prevision and foresight of our authorities. In actual fact, instead of Rs 3.86 crores, a total expenditure of Rs 24.31 crores was incurred and the Finance Member's Budget speech in February of this year is fully explanatory of the reasons for this increase. It will be instructive to tabulate the various items on which additional money was spent. There is first and foremost the expansion of the personnel of the Army: New armoured and mechanized cavalry regiments, new field artillery regiments, regular infantry battalions, engineer units, more MT Sections; expansion of Fighting Vehicles School, new cadet wing of the Artillery School, expansion of the RIASC Technical School, Signal Training centres, and others. In the matter of equipment, however, the Finance Member's statement speaks for itself:

His Majesty's Government have now agreed with regard to equipment generally to extending arrangements under which India will receive a substantial fix proportion of the output of the United Kingdom. In the matter of India preparing herself for the production of war material for the use of her own Defence forces, the following extract from the Budget speech are illuminating:

'His Majesty's Government have now agreed to a forward programme of supply covering the estimated requirements over a period of about two years ahead. The Department of Supply is thus able to enter into forward commitments within the limits of this programme and so maintain an even flow of production. A further improvement in the supply position has been rendered possible by the receipt of authority from His Majesty's government to purchase vehicles, machine tools and other essential war requirements in the United States and Canada, to the extent necessary to meet our needs for a considerable period, ahead.'

'With a view to stimulating private enterprises and coordinating the resources of the country to the fullest extent possible—a thorough re-organization of the Supply Department has been carried out during the last few months and this is already resulting in an increasingly cost liaison and co-operation between that Department, other Departments of Government and Indian Industry.'

The programme of ship-building in India has been further expanded and the recruiting and training of officers and men to man the new construction is proceeding apace. All instructional establishments have been greatly increased in capacity; a new Signal School is being built and a start has been made with a large new Gunnery school. Other new Naval establishments are in process of development.

'The scheme for establishing aero-plane manufacture in India has reached a new stage and there is now little doubt that the year 1941 will witness the appearance of the first aero-planes to be produced in India. This achievement, memorable in itself, should prove of great value in speeding up the expansion of India's air force—a development to which we attach supreme importance'.

'Steps have recently been taken to supplement the output of Ordinance and clothing factories by taking over railway and private workshops and utilizing their resources for the production of munitions of war. The Roger Mission, which has been investigating the possibilities of expanding India's output of war supplies has now submitted its reports to His Majesty's government who are giving them their urgent consideration. We hope that the result will be that India will before long be able substantially to increase her output of munitions.'

'Of the total expenditure of Rs 24.34 crores, approximately Rs 15 crores represents the initial cost of such measures: the balance consists of recurring expenditure. For 1941–2, Rs 35.40 crores is provided in the estimates; approximately half of this sum for initial costs. The entire plan envisages a total outlay of Rs 52 crores on initial cost and of Rs 19 crores as recurring expenditure per annum. Fifty two crores over a period of 3–4–5 years as against a provision of £180 millions by Australia (a country with a population of 8 millions) in 1941 and 1942 on war industries alone!

References to new industries and planning of increased production in the extracts quoted above are fully eloquent of the limitations of the Indian programme. It is no secret that the United Kingdom effectively bars the way to the establishment of a ship-building yard and the automobile industry; it is also no secret that for months His Majesty's Minister for Aircraft Production said No to the proposals for the establishment of an aircraft factory in India, despite repeated recommendations from the Indian Government. We are giving away no secrets either when we state that every proposal involving capital outlay of even so small a sum as Rs 10 lakhs has to be referred to His Majesty's Government for approval and sanction even when the entire charge is to be borne by the Indian Exchequer.

In this war, India as a subsidiary, must wait for Britain's orders. She possesses no rights of independent action. 'India is a great base and arsenal for ordered freedom in Asia'—forsooth!

58. Defence Advisory Committee: To be set up Immediately by Government of India

Amrita Bazar Patrika, 7 June 1941.

Commander-in-Chief to Preside: Maintaining Contact with Non-official Public Opinion

Simla, 6 June. The decision is announced to set up a departmental committee to advise on Defence matters. It is learned that Sir Mohammed Zafrullah Khan, Leader of the Central Legislative Assembly and Sir Girija Shankar Bajpai[1], Leader of the Council of State, have been requested to get into touch with the leaders of the parties in both the houses of the Central Legislature to secure nominations of party representatives on the committee.

The Committee will consist of ten members of whom six shall be from the Legislative Assembly and four from the Council of State. His Excellency the Commander-in-Chief shall be the Chairman of the committee, which will consist of non-officials only.

The committee shall meet whenever it is called by His Excellency the Commander-in-Chief, but it is laid down that ordinarily it shall meet at intervals of not less than every three months. The proceedings of the committee shall be formal and strictly confidential. The agenda for the meetings shall be circulated to the members beforehand and meetings on each occasion shall be opened by His Excellency the Commander-in-Chief by a statement on war situation. The members of the committee will be elected by both the Houses of Indian Central Legislature.

But pending the meetings of the Legislature, steps are being taken to constitute the committee as early as possible. In order that no time may be lost His Excellency Commander-in-Chief has desired that the committee, pending the meeting of the Central Legislature, may be set up by nominations. With this end in view the leaders of the parties have been approached to nominate their representatives on the committee.

It is also learned that the seats on the committee, other than those reserved for the representatives of various parties, shall be filled by nomination to secure representation of all interests. Similarly if any party refuses to nominate or return its representative on the committee, its quota shall be filled by nomination from unattached members. It is expected that by means of this committee the Defence Department and the Commander-in-Chief would be able to keep in close touch with the non-official opinion of the country in Defence matters. The Commander-in-Chief is confident that he will receive valuable advice on matters affecting Defence from non-official representatives in the Central Legislature and in his turn he will be able to give them regular appreciation of the situation and keep them confidentially informed in a way to enable them to discharge their duties.

It may be pointed out that the committee is being set up in pursuance of a promise the Commander-in-Chief made in the Council of State last session.

---

[1] Sir Zafrullah Khan and Sir Girija Shankar Bajpai were members of Viceroy's Executive Council at the time.

59. India's Major Share in War Supplies: How Eastern Group Council Functions

The Tribune, 10 June 1941.

Simla, 9 June. With the biggest signboard in Simla of the season, the Eastern Group Supply Council, constituted as a result of the Eastern Group Conference, is conducting its activities from a group of buildings which formerly housed the Indian Stores Department. The Council is an august body with its members placed high above most of Simla's hierarchy.

Hardly four months since its establishment, the Council is said to have already complied with the requirements of the Army in the several theatres of war to the tune of Rs 90 crores. This means that the capacity of the organization to pool the resources of the countries east and south of Suez is being tested almost daily. Naturally, therefore, the Indian industrialists, in particular have been following the activities of the Council rather closely, especially with a view to ascertain how India is being treated in the allotment of orders for war supplies. Their suspicions in this subject were aroused when they found the Australian Representative, Sir Bertram Stevens, convey the impression that Australia is dominating the Council by reason of the much advertised fact that his country is the most developed manufacturing country in the Eastern Group.

The demand for information as to the working of the Council became insistent both as regards the number of orders handed and the proportion and the value of the orders placed in India. But the greater the demand of the industrialists, the more shy became the Council on the easily explained ground that any such publicity would be indirectly to hand over valuable information to the enemy. Some attempts were made though in a general way, to allay the apprehensions of the industrial community by Mr M.S.A. Hydari, India's representative on the Council and Sir Guthrie Russell, the Director-General of Munitions Productions through their recent broadcasts from Simla and Calcutta respectively. And I learn that more direct contacts with industrialists to acquaint them with a few more permissible facts may be availed of next month by Mr M.S.A. Hydari during his tour to Calcutta, Cawnpore and other centres.

India Secures Bulk of Orders

Meanwhile as a result of my enquiries in several quarters, I shall try to lift the veil that surrounds the work of the Council to the limited extent possible. I do not pretend to know the exact figures as to the number of orders placed in India or what the percentage they bear to the total of the orders disposed of by the Council. But I am able to state with some confidence that the bulk of the orders have been secured for India. The total number of articles coming under the term 'Requirements of the Forces' now amounts to 50,000 and India can be said to have benefited considerably by the orders given by the Council for such of the so many items as she has been in a position to supply within the required time.

The supplies have ranged from products of major industries like steel and textiles to small manufactures like those of buttons and pins. And it is claimed that there is no industry in India which is capable of supplying war materials which is not being drawn upon to its utmost capacity, as stated by Mr Hydari in his recent broadcast and reflected by Sir Bertram Stevens in Calcutta few days ago. Of course, there is the long-standing complaint that in regard to major industries like ship building and automobile industry so essential for the successful prosecution of the war, no step has been taken even to make a beginning in India. But so far as the Eastern Group is concerned it has the explanation that its function is to utilize and coordinate the industries that exist.

The fact that the Government of India is a subordinate branch of the British Government has been adduced as a ground for the feeling that India's interests might have been relegated to the background and that the voice of India might have been hushed in order to humour the Dominions. Here again, I am in the happy position to state that two factors have prevailed to prevent any such thing happening. Firstly, there is the incontestable fact that India occupies the most central position in the earlier group and therefore, within the easiest reach of the several theatres of war. Secondly, the fact that India's representative has been able to exercise autonomous powers on the Council especially as regards the capacity of India to produce the required articles.

Supply Department to be Re-organized

Competent observers are able to mention with some confidence another factor viz., that the Supply Department in India has been found to be the most efficient of all the organizations that set up in countries constituting the Eastern Group and this has been largely responsible for the case with which the Council has been able to get most of the articles required for the Army from India. But the Indian industrialists who are not yet reconciled to the composition of the Supply Department have made no secret of their views and so according to one report there is every likelihood of some additions being made shortly to bring the organization into more effective touch with the industrial community of India.

Central Provision Office to be Formed

Side by side with the Eastern Group Council there will be set up in India sometime in August what is to be called the Central Provision Office, the magnitude of which may be imagined when it is known that its officers (who will all be military) will number over 80. The demands from all military authorities within the Eastern Group Council stores for the forces for which they are responsible but which they cannot obtain locally and which can be provided from other countries of the Group will be co-ordinated and submitted to the Eastern Group Supply Council by the Central Provision Office. Major General W.C. Holden, Military Member of the Council and Controller-General, Army Provision (Eastern Group) is engaged in organizing this office, an important function of which will be to secure the priority of allocation of the available supplies at the military commands should a shortage arise in any particular store or commodity.

One is assured that whatever be the manner in which the Central Provision Office might work the geographical position of India is able to tilt the balance in her favour in respect of the many orders for war supplies that this country is capable of. Broadly speaking the industries and trades that have proposed as a result of the Council's orders are textiles of various kinds down to mosquito nets, steel manufactures of several varieties, boots, drugs, oils, including groundnut and linseed oil, paper, blankets, forks, knives, and motor parts like armour plates. And these advantages are not confined to British India as at least three big Indian states have received several orders, namely Mysore, Hyderabad and Baroda. The former two have supplied steel and steel articles while the last has been able to make a considerable advance in the manufacture and supply of chemicals....

60. India's Big War Effort

Bombay Chronicle, 13 July 1941.

Calcutta, 12 July. The view that the Eastern Group Supply Council was being recognized as a composite instrument for the common good of the Group and eyes were already being lifted to the future, when collaboration, which was initiated for war, might be continued in peace, was expressed by Mr M.S.A. Hydari, representative of India on the Eastern Group Supply Council, speaking at a luncheon given in his honour by Sir Abdul Halim Ghuznavi, MLA (Centre), at the Calcutta Club this afternoon.

Mr Hydari said that the Supply Council was enabling India to plan her war production by means of demands spread over a reasonably long period of time. It was giving her opportunities of new production which she could take up if she considered them worthwhile. India was not the only beneficiary and the other countries in the group were obtaining the same advantage from the Council's operations.

India's Big Share

Speaking of India's war effort, Mr Hydari said that of the thousands of articles included in the terms 'requirements of the forces', India was producing three-fourths that is 75 per cent, and not only textile but engineering stores from bridges to bolts, guns, ammunitions, armour plates, medical stores, chemicals, and tyres. In addition to this, she was building ships, small no doubt, but definitely highly useful for the war effort, such as mine sweepers and submarine chasers and carrying on repairs to merchant fleet and to vessels of the line.

He mentioned that the Council thought that Indian supply effort was massive and that in its range and variety it was not surpassed by any country of the Eastern Group. The Council remembered that India had filled a breach, before the calling of the conference and the establishment of the Council, in so far as supplies to Middle East were concerned, which no other country in the group was in a position then to do. The Council remembered this with gratefulness.

'Equal Status'

Referring to the position of India on the Council, Mr Hydari stated that she took her place as an equal in status with others on this inter-Imperial body, and not as an inferior in achievement. And he took pride in himself being India's representative on the Council and did not feel any sense of inferiority in being so. During the four or five months of the existence of the Council, and since he had been on it, he has seen the achievements of India on the war efforts.

He explained why there was a lack of information regarding the Eastern Group Conference and of the Council, and stated that it would be obvious to them that valuable information could not be allowed to pass into the hands of the enemy.

He, however, stated that the Council was not entirely silent. It held a Press Conference at Delhi sometime ago and took the Press into confidence with what the Council was doing.

Job Getting Done

Referring to the Indian Supply Organization, Mr Hydari said that complacency was bad and, after a point, self-deprecation was almost equally bad. By the Indian Supply Organization was meant not only the Indian Supply Department but also the business community, which was helping in the war effort. He described all these as one household. 'We might fight and criticize, but the job is getting done.' He added.

Hydari's Hope

Taking a long view of things, he said that this war effort to which so much toll, so much enthusiasm, so much sacrifice of convenience was being given was not ephemeral.

Their one concern at this moment, said Mr Hydari, should be not what they were getting out of the war, but whether they were doing all they could to help to finish 'this nightmare soon and successfully.' At the same time, they had got to think of the peace. And all this war effort was going to be very useful to them when the war was over. Modern warfare required articles of the highest craftsmanship. It was not only high-scale production, but highly skilled production. The Indian workman would come out of this war probably a higher skilled technician than he had been before the war broke out. He asked his audience to imagine what this would mean to Indian industry. Machine tools, which they used to import, they were now making. Invention was going hand-in-hand with production. It was surprising he added, what a range of products their chemicals, their engineers and their mechanics had brought into being.

He pointed out that one thing that stood out more was that in India's war effort, the Indian and the European were as one. There was very good reason for it. 'We are in the same boat and if Hitler torpedoes it we are both sunk'. Whatever lugubrious economists may foretell of the post-war depression—and it was quite possible that there would be depression after the war—he could not believe that the great industrial surge forward, which was taking place in India, at the present moment, would not result in substantial benefits to the country even if as a result of increased industrial activity. Reflected in increased wages, the standard of living in India, rose by three *annas* per month per head of the population, there would be openings for Indian industries to supply the need so created.

Ghuznavi Wants Light

'No Indian is worth the name if he is not prepared to sacrifice and assist His Majesty's Government and their Allies to crush the Nazis and Fascists one and for all,' observed Sir Abdul Halim Ghuznavi, MLA (Central), in proposing the toast of Mr Hydari.

Referring to the work of the Eastern Group Supply Council, Sir Abdul Halim said that there has been some misunderstanding among the public and even amongst the commercial community in the country as to whether the opportunities afforded to India at the present time to put forward its maximum effort, were being fully utilized. He pointed out that no chance was missed and no opportunity lost to enable India to put its maximum effort in this direction.

61. The Defence of India

Editorial, *Amrita Bazar Patrika*, 19 July 1941.

The one department of Indian administration that has hitherto defied Indian control or equal collaboration is the Army Department. This is in sharp contrast to other departments of the administration. The Army had been the close preserve of European 'experts'. The present war however has elicited declarations from responsible British statesmen that India's defence should be more and more the concern of Indians. Indeed the Congress has, from its very inception, pressed the demand that Indians should be associated more and more with the control and management of the Army so that in due course, India, may have a national army. The British Government have yielded to other demands of political India more or less, but they have set their faces against any 'intrusion' into the military preserve, which for reasons best known to themselves, they have thought Indians should have little concern except carrying out orders.

One could, therefore, welcome what seems to be the first signs of the recognition that Indians should be actively associated with the Army not merely as soldiers but in more responsible capacities. The unfortunate fact is that the announcements made now are only half a century behind the time. Had they been made even twenty-five years earlier there might have been some enthusiasm. Today they are more likely to fall flat on the country.

Belated as the measures taken or proposed to be taken by the Government are, the constitution of the Defence Advisory Committee might have been more liberal than what it is. Why have the members been nominated? Could not the Assemblies and the Councils of State be trusted to elect them? We do not propose to criticize the personnel. The gentlemen selected may exercise their responsibilities, about which we have no knowledge, as real representatives of the people. But it goes without saying that they will feel handicapped almost at every important step in the knowledge that they have not been elected by the bodies whom they have been called upon to represent, and they will not be able to claim that they represent the Indian point of view. In fact they will represent none but themselves. The only improvement on the existing position is that they are Indians. But if it is expected that political India should be grateful for that fact, the authorities are bound to be disappointed.

In the next place, even if we assume that the gentlemen selected for the Defence Advisory Committee would behave as true representatives of their countrymen, we do not know what particular functions they will be called upon to exercise, and how far they will be trusted with military secrets. The Commander-in-Chief, whose speech we admire, regretted that the two principal organized political parties elected to stand aside. He could not help it, for the aloofness of the Congress and the League has been brought on by policies over which His Excellency had no control. Mr Amery has again stated in the House of Commons that the policy of His Majesty's Government had not undergone any change. That the Secretary of State did not mention at all the impending constitution of the Defence Advisory Committee shows that he recognized that no change of policy was implied in the action. We hope therefore that nobody in this country will dare claim greater importance for the announcements than the Secretary of State.

The Defence Committee, it is stated, will be followed by the constitution by the Viceroy of the Defence Advisory Council, to which the name 'national' will be given, consisting of thirty members among whom will be the Princes, the four Premiers of the provinces and other persons. The observations in regard to the Defence Committee apply *mutatis mutandis* to the Council, about whose functions the public do not know. The Council will be all Indian (not simply British Indian) in constitution, and the Committee is only British Indian, save and except that we do not know what exactly will be the relationship between the Council and the Committee.

The Council and the Committee will be advisory bodies. But for the first time an Indian has been appointed in the inner-Council of the Army Department. Sir Gurunath Bewoor, the present Director-General of Posts and Telegraphs, a popular official, has been appointed Additional Defence Secretary. We do not question Sir Gurunath's competence for the high office created or his patriotism. For we know he will do what he can as an Indian. What influence he will be able to exercise on such questions as the rapid nationalization of the army remains to be seen. But his position, more because of its uniqueness, will be one of great difficulty. In the first place, he is not elected by the legislature, but nominated. And he is not even a non-official but an ICS officer who has risen high in the service. He has had no connection with public life, and in his new role as spokesman of the Defence Department, he will have no alternative but to support any and every policy in the formulation of which he may have little or no share. An Indian defending military policy, which Indian public opinion disapproves, will not be a strange thing, and will not serve to impress even foreign opinion.

We know it will be said that having regard to the traditions of the Army Department, we should be thankful for the little mercies. This is, we will be told, the beginning and greater things are bound to come. We do not deny that all beginnings are difficult and the Army Department is by far the most impervious of all departments. But this is war time. In times of peace we could hold our souls in patience in the expectation of big things at some distant future. But the Commander-in-Chief who has just come from the Middle East, and also knows the real nature of the threat to India, more than any other man, said to the Press that 'a great threat to India is possible.' These are words the significance of which could not possibly be lost sight of. Indians are naturally interested to defend their hearths and homes, even more interested than the Britishers who only run the risk of losing an empire. The Commander-in-Chief indeed gave the assurance that he would follow his predecessor in the latter's initiation of policies and series of reforms which will be of immense value to the army in India and defence of India, but the pace has got to be rapid, not the kind of which we have evidence. The defence of India is not simply a question of military strategy. It is, if we may say so, politically psychological or psychologically political. The responsibility for initiating policies in these broad directions rests on His Majesty's Government. Along with the release of political prisoners, if their release comes, a bold and generous gesture will have to be made.

62. Rationing of Petrol: Coupons to be Issued to Consumers

Amrita Bazar Patrika, 1 August 1941.

Measure for Conservation of Stocks of Motor Spirit in India

THE rationing of motor spirit will come into force in Bengal on 15 August. It will not at present cover diesel oils used in motor vehicles, but only petrol, benzol and the lighter types of kerosene and the admixture of petrol and kerosene or of petrol and power alcohol.

The object of rationing is the conservation of stocks of motor spirit in India and the scheme is intended to effect reduction in civil consumption to the minimum essential requirements.

From the date the order comes into operation, motor spirit will only be available against the surrender of prescribed coupon and receipts. The coupons will represent a given number of unit, the value of which at present is one gallon.

For private cars the basic rations will be as follows:

For vehicles not exceeding 3 HP—2 units per month.
For vehicles exceeding 3 HP and not exceeding 4 HP—3 units per month.
For vehicles exceeding 4 HP and not exceeding 7 HP—5 units per month.
For vehicles exceeding 7 HP and not exceeding 9 HP—6 units per month.
For vehicles exceeding 9 HP and not exceeding 12 HP—8 units per month.
For vehicles exceeding 12 HP and not exceeding 15 HP—9 units per month.
For vehicles exceeding 15 HP and not exceeding 19 HP—10 units per month.
For vehicles exceeding 19 HP—12 units per month.

For the first quarter consumers of this class of vehicles will be entitled to the full quota without any proportionate reduction for the unexpired portion of the quarter, as will be made in the case of other vehicles.

In respect of other vehicles such as motor-buses, taxi-cabs, lorries and vehicles of local bodies the allotment of rations will be made on the basis of essential requirements to be assessed by the rationing authorities.

Supplementary grants of rations will be available according to individual needs to be determined by the Area Rationing Authorities.

The ordinary coupons will be issued on a quarterly basis and will be valid for three months, while supplementary coupons will be issued for a period of one month only at a time.

Application for Rations

Application for rations will have to be made in the appropriate form to the rationing authority. The application forms for coupons may be obtained in respect of Calcutta and suburbs at the

(a) office of the Area Rationing Authority.
(b) petrol filling stations.
(c) head-quarters of the automobile association, Bengal; and in respect of other areas at the office of the Area Rationing Authority and such other places as may be specified by that authority.

Applications should be accompanied by registration certificate and the tax token of the vehicle in respect of which rations are required.

The personal appearance of the applicant is not necessary. It will suffice if the application is presented to the Area Rationing Authority through an agent.

The Area Rationing Authority for Calcutta and suburbs is the Deputy Commissioner of Police, Public Vehicles Department, and for other areas the District Magistrate of the district concerned. The office of the Calcutta Area Rationing Authority is located at 77-B, Park Street.

Coupon System

Coupons will be issued at the offices of the Rationing Authorities. The Area Rationing Authority for Calcutta is issuing a press note detailing the arrangements made for the presentation of applications. Different dates have been fixed in respect of different categories of vehicles.

It is hoped that the general body of consumers will co-operate with the authorities in adhering to the arrangements made for the issue of coupons and thus ensure the smooth and easy working of the scheme.

63. India and the War

Editorial, *Bombay Chronicle*, 5 September 1941.

The second anniversary of the war presented Government with an excellent opportunity to inaugurate the day with a gesture that could grip the imagination of the people of India and stimulate war effort tenfold. But they have miserably failed to make the right use of opportunity. When for two long years the people have made heavy sacrifices and are called upon to make heavier sacrifices still, it was necessary to explain to them what precisely are the aims of the war and what they signify to India in particular. Till but a few weeks ago this explanation was either deliberately withheld or given in a casual, uncertain and equivocal manner, one representative of Government saying nothing more than that their main war aim was to win the war, as if any other belligerent country could not say the same thing. Only when more American help was urgently necessary and some of their critics had to be satisfied, President Roosevelt and Mr Churchill found it necessary to publish a joint statement setting forth the principal war aims. But this was done in an extremely vague manner which could be interpreted by different people in different ways. It was necessary that India, called upon to do a great deal more than sell goods to Britain for good consideration, should be told what precisely the Anglo-American Agreement meant to her. But it is most significant that in his broadcast the Viceroy did not make the slightest reference to the Agreement. Government are either not serious about it or are unwilling to emphasize it in its application to India.

Petty-minded

Even apart from this inexcusable omission, the Viceroy's broadcast was marred by petty-minded, if not spiteful, references to those who have seen through and refused to join his manoeuvres. 'There are those amongst us,' he said, 'who would like to reap the harvest of victory without having put their hands to the plough.' Now, as a matter of fact, Indians had little choice in applying the hands to the plough. But the more representative among them have rightly insisted that they would put their hands to the plough only if they themselves are to drive it. In plain language they state that they can accept responsibility for a truly national war effort only if there is in the country a truly national Government. Those who object to this reasonable demand lay themselves open to the charge that they want to reap the harvest of other men's labours.

A Boomerang

The Viceroy's reference to dividing the people is a nastier boomerang. With more spite than restraint he said: 'Others there are who for one reason or other are not ashamed, though the nation stands in grave peril, to seek to divide the people, to weaken war effort.' Tactics calculated to divide the people are certainly something to be ashamed of. But they are far older than the war, though it must be owned they are more virulent now than ever before. The suggestion is more persistent now than before that the various elements in India are all heterogeneous that they do not form one nation and that, therefore, democracy is unsuited to the country. It is not surprising, therefore, that several of the elements are even now at cross purposes in spite of the Viceroy's Herculean efforts to make them love each other. It is not surprising they have so far failed to agree to a democratic scheme, acceptable to Britain and other elements in India, though Britain has graciously offered to accept such a scheme, of course, with due safeguards, as the basis of a future constitution to be inaugurated as early after the war as she deems possible. However a sufficient number of Indians have seen tough the dividing tactics and will soon enough confound them. Already the tactics have begun to recoil on the very persons who have adopted them. And to those Indians who have determined to win national unity and freedom we heartily commend the Viceroy's words: 'Do not—this insidious fifth column eat like dry rot into the fabric of your determination.' We can also commend to nationalist Indians his following words: 'India is awake: she is mighty and formidable and she shall, if you so determine, be infighter yet.' Mighty and free, though through an oversight the Viceroy made no reference to India's freedom.

64. War at India's Door-steps: M.R. Jayakar on What Government Should do

Bombay Chronicle, 5 September 1941.

The increasing need for a livelier appreciation in India of the issues involved in the success or failure of the Allied cause in the war is stressed by the Hon'ble Mr M.R. Jayakar in the course of a foreword he has written to a new book entitled 'Will War Come to India?' written by Mr N.G. Jog of the *Bombay Chronicle*. The book is being published on the occasion of the second anniversary of the war.

'It was with a feeling of distant and comfortable safety,' says Mr Jayakar, that 'Indians looked on the war and read or heard war news. But now war is at their door-steps, with danger threatening from two ends. India's strategic frontiers are now around the Persian Gulf in the north-west and on the Gulf of Siam in the south-east and it is now officially announced that the defence of Egypt, Palestine and the whole position in the Middle East is the defence of India.'

'Whatever view one might take,' continues Mr Jayakar, 'of the wisdom of drawing a poor country like India into the war without its consent, the fact is now undeniable that a stage has been reached when, the war being next door, a wise Government would correct its past errors, and make special efforts to enlist the willing co-operation of Indians in consolidating India's capacity and willingness to defend herself by the powerful arm of her patriotic youth. This can be done only if Government follow the statesman-like view. Accepted at the Indian Round Table Conference, the defence of India should in future be increasingly the concern of the Indian people. Though this sound principle has been practically ignored since the outbreak of the war, it is not yet too late for His Majesty's Government implicitly to accept it as the guiding rule of their future war activities in India. Simultaneously with such an effort on the part of the Government, it will be necessary for Indians to acquire, in increasing measure, a correct and accurate knowledge of the events of the war, past, present and future, leading to a livelier sense of the issues involved in the success or failure of the cause of the Allies.'

65. War and Textile Industry

(i) War Demands on Textiles: India's Problem

Amrita Bazar Patrika, 10 September 1941.

Representative Conference Opens in Bombay

Bombay, 8 September. The Textile Conference convened by the Government of India commenced session this afternoon in the Bombay Millowners Association Premises, with Sir Homi Mody, Supply Member, in the Chair. Over sixty persons representing the Government of India, the Government of Bombay and the various Mill-owners' Associations and textile interests in the country were present.

The Government of India was represented by Sir A. Ramaswami Mudaliar, Commerce Member; Sir Allian Lloyd, Commerce Secretary; Mr Ghulam Mohammed, Additional Secretary; Brigadier Wood, Mr D.M. Passmore, Col Addison and Mr K.G. Morshed of the Supply Department and Dr Gregory, Economic Adviser to the Government of India.

Three representatives of the Government of Bombay, Mr H.V.R. Ayengar, Mr Advani, Director of Industries and Mr Punjabi also attended the conference.

The Bombay Millowners' Association was represented by sixteen members including the President of the Association Sir V.N. Chandavarkar, the Ahmedabad Millowners' Association by six members including Seth Kasturbhai Lalubhai, South India by six, Bengal by four, Upper India Chamber by four, United Provinces by three and the Federation of Baroda State Mills and Industries by five.

Among the seven others invited to participate in the conference was Sir Victor Sassoon.

The conference is expected to continue its deliberations until tomorrow.

The main object of the conference, it is understood, is to consider the question of adjusting supplies to increasing war demands and also to see that there is no artificial inflation of prices in view of increased war demands and cessation of Japanese imports of textiles.

Another purpose of the conference is to consider ways and means of the Indian textile industry meeting the increasing war demands and to regulate inflated prices for cotton textiles since the stoppage of textile imports from Japan towards the end of July.

One of the most important problems confronting the textile industry and the Government is the growing diversity between the prices of cotton manufactures purchased by the Supply Department and the prices of manufactures intended for civilian consumption; and examine the question in detail. When the substantial swelling of war orders placed with the textile mills by the Government and also with the very recent shrinkage in Japanese imports into India, prices of cotton textile have shot up and it is urged that Government should lay down a procedure for fixing equitable price for purchase by the Supply Department. Control of prices of textile manufactures for civilian consumption is also expected to be considered by the conference.

The conference is said to be of special interest to Bombay province and it is expected that the Government will urge upon manufactures in the province to play a more important role than hitherto as suppliers of textiles to the Supply Department especially in view of the mounting war demands. In this connection, Bombay delegates are expected to suggest to the Government the setting up of an organization for purchasing textile in the province.

It will be recalled that the last conference held in Bombay some time in May, envisaged the formation of a committee to advise the Supply Department on the distribution of war orders among the various mills....

(ii) War and Indian Textiles: Question of Supply

Amrita Bazar Patrika, 10 September 1941.

Agreement Reached at Bombay Conference

Bombay, 9 September. The Textile Conference concluded its deliberation this afternoon at 4.30 and the following was issued to the press:

The Hon'ble Sir Homi Mody and the Hon'ble Sir Ramaswami Mudaliar, Members respectively for Supply and Commerce, continued their deliberations today with the representative of the Indian cotton textile industry. The morning session was devoted to concluding the consideration concerning war supplies. The general agreement that has been reached for the purpose of meeting the full requirements of Government is based on certain agreed steps for co-operation on both sides. Government on their part have agreed to transfer that portion of the Supply Department concerned with the cotton textile to Bombay and it is expected that this will be in operation in Bombay in about one month's time.

In the afternoon session the matters more particularly taken into consideration concerned supplies and prices of cotton textiles goods, including yarn to the civil market. The discussion was on the basis of broad lines of policy and the general methods by which the requirements should be met were freely discussed. There was general unanimity of agreement on these points.

Textile Mills Production

The productive capacity of textile mills in this country is expected to attain concert pitch as a result of the general agreement reached between representatives of the Government and textile interests during the conference today.

India today occupies a predominant position as a source of supply of cotton textile to the eastern group countries, both for civil and military requirements. The needs of those countries and India have grown rapidly during the past twelve months and supply position has recently become somewhat acute. The main purpose of the conference was to evolve an agreed policy to meet these requirements at reasonable price.

The measure of agreement evolved during the morning session of the conference, it is pointed out, is based on certain agreed steps for cooperation on both sides. The Government have agreed to transfer the textiles section of the Supply Department to Bombay. Mr D.M. Passmore, Director of Textile will be in charge of the section, which will begin to function in Bombay very shortly.

Measure of Agreement

It is learnt that a measure of agreement has been reached in respect of prices the Supply Department would pay. It is stated that this will be based mainly on the prices the department had been paying at the beginning of May. But subsequent increase in cost of production will be taken into consideration.

No question of direct price control arose as that would properly come within the purpose of the price control conference which will be held in Simla in the middle of October.

66. The National Defence Council: First Session, Simla, 6 October 1941

Indian Annual Register, 1941, Vol. II, pp. 319–21.

The Viceroy's Opening Speech

The first session of the National Defence Council opened at the Viceregal Lodge, Simla on the 6th October 1941. There were meetings in the morning and in the afternoon, at both of which HE the Viceroy presided.

Those present were: Their Highnesses the Jam Sahib of Nawanagar, the Maharaja of Bikaner, the Maharaja of Jodhpur, the Maharaja of Patiala, the Maharaja of Gwalior, the Nawab of Bhopal, the Nawab of Rampur and the Maharaja of Cooch-Behar, Nawab Sir Muhammad Ahmad Said Khan of Chhatari, representing. HEH the Nizam of Hyderabad and Berar, Dr B.R. Ambedkar, Kumaraja Sir Muthia Chettiar of Chettinad, the Hon Maharajadhiraja of Darbhanga, Mr Ramrao Madhavrao Deshmukh, Lieut Col Sir Henry Gidney, Sir Cowasjee Jehangir, Raja Bahadur of Khallikote, the Hon Malik Khuda Baksh Khan, Mr Jamunadas M. Mehta, Mr G.B. Morton, Mr Biren Mukherjee, Captain Sardar Naunihal Singh, Begum Shah Nawaz, Rao Bahadur M.C. Raja, Professor E. Ahmad Shah, The Premier of Sind (the Hon Khan Bahadur Allah Bux), Mr Mohd Umar Soomro, Sir Jwala Prasad Srivastava and Sir Mahomed Usman.

Before the opening of the secret session, HE the Viceroy welcomed the National Defence Council in a short speech. HH the Chancellor of the Chamber among the British Indian representatives, responded. At the beginning of the secret session, Begum Shah Nawaz expressed, on behalf of the women of India, gratitude at the appointment of a woman representative to the Defence Council.

In the morning meeting a statement was made by HE the Commander-in-Chief in the course of which Sir Archibald Wavell read a message of greeting to the Council from Mr Winston Churchill. A number of matters of special interest in the defence field, which had been raised by various members of the Council, were explained by the Commander-in-Chief and a discussion followed. In the afternoon, the meeting heard and discussed a statement by General A.B. Haig, Adjutant-General in India, on recruiting and cognate issues. The Hon Sir Homi Mody, Supply Member, began his statement on the question of war supply.

His Excellency the Viceroy spoke as follows:

'This is a business gathering, and I am not going to make a long speech to you today. But I would like in the first place to extend to you the warmest possible welcome to this the first meeting of the National Defence Council, and to say how deeply I appreciate your public spirit in attending in many cases, I know at very great personal inconvenience. I would like too to say a word about the significance of this occasion before we go into secret session and to touch very briefly on the recent development in the great part which India is playing in this war.

This occasion is one of great significance. For the first time, the representatives of the Indian States and British India are met together to consider and discuss the war position and

India's war effort; to receive from myself and from my advisers information on important aspects of these matters; to give my advisers and myself the benefit the value of which I cannot over-estimate, of your own suggestions and advice. It is my hope and belief that this meeting will be the first of many and that the contribution which these meeting will make to the removal of misunderstanding to the furtherance of our common cause and to stimulating still further the efforts already so generously and widely made throughout India will be great indeed.

In the National Defence Council composed as it is of representatives of the Princely Order and of the provinces of British India, there has been established a body truly representative of all elements in the national life of India, whose sole object is the intensification of the war effort and the prosecution of war. My object and that of my Government will be, during our secret deliberations to acquaint the National Defence Council to the fullest degree, and in the fullest confidence with the position in relation to all important aspect of the war effort; to obtain the benefit of their advise; to improve and develop liaison; and so to secure that, in a war that is as much India's war as the war of Great Britain or of any other part of the Empire, the Princely Order and the provinces of British India are seized, through their representatives on the Defence Council of the problems that confront us from time to time in the conduct of the war, of the greatness of India's contribution, and of the background to and the justification for, the magnificent effort which India is putting forth.

There could be no more appropriate occasion than this to refer to the superb contribution so far made by India to the achievement of the ideals for which we are fighting. She has, without stint, poured out men, money and supplies. Her fighting men, whether by land, by sea, or in the air covered themselves, and the land of their birth with glory. In the face of every device of modern warfare, in conditions often most difficult, in unfamiliar surroundings, India's fighting men, whether they come from the Indian States or from the provinces of British India, have shown outstanding valour and endurance and have added still farther honour to the martial traditions of this country. The Empire and India owe them a debt of gratitude, a debt that will never be forgotten.

In paying the tribute that I have to the gallant fighting men of India, I would associate with it a word of gratitude for the immense assistance given us by our neighbour, the warrior kingdom of Nepal, to the sympathetic and enthusiastic support and cooperation of whose Prime Minister we owe so much, and whose troops have played their part with the distinction which we have come to expect of them in the various theatres of war in which they have been engaged.

In the field of supply India has again made a contribution of immense significance and value, a contribution recognized throughout the Empire—a contribution that has in no small degree helped to bring home to many distant lands not only the great natural resources of India, but the high intelligence and skill of her draftsmen and her workers and the readiness of all to play their part at times like these. My Supply Member will be able to give you some idea of what has been done in this field. Let me say now only that the location in India of the Eastern Group Supply Council is in itself a tribute both to the importance of her strategic and geographical position and to the magnitude of the assistance which she has given to the common effort.

The generous stream of contributions in gifts and loans, in money and in kind, for the purchase of munitions and equipments, of plants, of tanks, of ambulances and the like for the alleviation of suffering and the relief of distress, which has flowed from India since the war began, is undiminished today. I pay my deep and sincere tribute to the magnificent generosity of the gifts that have been made by your Highnesses of the Princely Order, the provinces of British India and by that great multitude of individuals throughout the country whose desire is to hasten by their personal sacrifices, the day of victory for our cause.

As the war goes on, every day reveals more clearly the place which India has won for herself in the world. She is today the base of operations for great campaigns and great strategic movements. The Commander-in-Chief, whom we are glad to welcome back today from his consultations with the Cabinet with His Majesty's representatives, civil and military, in the Middle East, and with our Russian Allies at Teheran, bears a responsibility which few, if any, of his predecessors in that great office can have held and in the discharge of that responsibility from India he links India still more closely with those mighty movements that are taking place around us. India, as I have said, is the centre of the great supply organization which serves the vital military needs of countries ranging from Australia to South Africa. Her contribution in fighting men has been on the grandest scale, and will be greater yet. She is ready, as we know, to make sacrifices greater still in every way than those which she has so far been called upon to make. We may be proud of the achievement of India. We may be certain that that achievement will not fade from the memory of the nations....

67. Air Defence

(i) Air Threat to India, Not Imaginary

Amrita Bazar Patrika, 8 October 1941.

Military Spokesman's Statement

The purpose of the North-West India Air Defence Exercise, which is scheduled to commence today, was fully explained this morning to a party of military officers and officers representing various civil services drawn from all parts of India and the press by a military spokesman.

He said that the principal object of the defence manoeuvres which were being staged in the Punjab and the Frontier Provinces was to test the defences of India which had been greatly strengthened since the outbreak of war, in the event of an aerial attack by enemy parachutists and troop-carrying aircraft. Efforts were being made to make the exercise as realistic as possible and to ensure the closest co-operation and understanding between the military and various civil services which were indispensable in successfully meeting any eventuality that might arise in case of an aerial invasion of India.

Threat to India

The threat to India, continued the spokesman, was not imaginary as some people in India thought but a real one. While admitting that India enjoyed a natural gift in gigantic closing defiles of mountains along its North-East Frontier, which would present innumerable obstacles to enemy, if he attacked through infantry the spokesman observed that in face or air bombing from high level and the modern method of attack by means of airborne troops and parachutists, elaborate arrangements to defend India's borders were of paramount importance.

Discussing the problem of the defence of North-West India in terms of German aggression and facing the facts as they were the spokesman said that this war had been full of surprises and possible occupation by enemy of Northern Iraq and Iran would constitute a direct threat to this country. Fast moving land forces, supported by aircraft, added the spokesman, could be dealt with successfully if there was the closest liaison between the defending troops and various civil services, namely Railway, Police, PWD, Posts and Telegraphs and others, and the civil population in maintaining the lines of communication.

A Gigantic Problem

The problem of the Defence of India, he added, was a gigantic one and one object of the exercise was to make the man in the street conscious of the fact that a threat to India did exist. In order to fight the most powerful enemy which was ruthlessly determined to become the master of the whole world it was of utmost importance to organize themselves in every way and take account of every possibility.

The spokesman then described the nature of the North-West India defence exercise which, he said, would consist of bombing aerodromes, strategic military points and dropping parachutists.

Concluding he referred to an organization of their own fifth columnists which had been formed in the light of lessons learnt in Belgium and Holland and said that they were applying various methods to test the efficacy of their defence arrangements and to allay panic noticeable in any quarter.—AP

(ii) Air Defence Exercise in Punjab and NWFP

Amrita Bazar Patrika, 9 October 1941.

Preparation for Meeting Enemy Attack

The North-West India Air Defence Exercise which is being staged in the Punjab and Frontier Provinces for a week in order to demonstrate India's preparedness to meet with an invasion of any description commenced today amidst feverish activities by the military and the RAF, writes the 'Associated Press' special correspondent from somewhere in Northern India on 7 October.

Columns of motorized vehicles were seen moving at a terrific speed in all directions to participate in the demonstration. An aircraft loomed overhead carrying out reconnaissance flights and spotting out enemy planes. The most thrilling show of the first day was when enemy bombers 'attacked' the arsenal showering high explosive and incendiary bombs on the area. The building received a direct hit from a delayed-action bomb necessitating evacuation. Two more buildings were hit by heavy caliber and incendiary bombs causing certain amount of damage. This was followed by enemy aircraft on 'military area' when high explosive and incendiary bombs were dropped across the workshops. The fire which were started were quickly dealt with.

The casualties among the staff were 10 'killed' and 20 injured. The hostile aircraft also attacked the oil company installations causing a few casualties among the staff.

The defence arrangements in all these cases were most impressive and efficient and the enemy attacks were met with the greatest confidence and effectiveness.

The casualties which occurred from bombs were quickly attended to and necessary facilities were provided.

Attacks on Various Targets

To-day the North-West India Air Defence Exercise entered its second phase during which aircraft representing the enemy air forces, commenced attack on various local targets. There was reconnaissance by a hostile aircraft flying at a great height over Peshawar City and Cantonment area. An air alarm was sounded and full defence precautions were taken by the civil and military authorities. Actually no bombs were dropped and presumably the enemy's object was merely to spy out land in view of future eventualities.

Later in the day a short sharp attack by enemy dive-bombers was made on a post in the Khyber Pass but this was repulsed without serious damage or any casualties.

Soon after dark some bombs fell unexpectedly in Nowshera area, evidently dropped by enemy aircraft operating at a very great height from sub-stratosphere. The umpires of the directing staff ruled that these bombs, if real, would have caused certain amount of damage on the main road and the railway in the vicinity. Arrangements were made to effect necessary repairs. In the meanwhile all civil, military, ARP (Air Raid Protection) and PAD (Preparation for Air-Defence) services are in constant state of readiness. The obscuration of lights and other necessary defensive measures have been enforced and everyone is waiting with great interest for further developments in this interesting and instructive exercise.—AP

68. Unwarranted Rise in Prices

Amrita Bazar Patrika, 12 October 1941.

Check Urged, Bengal National Chamber's Communication

Bengal National Chamber of Commerce in a communication to the Government of India regarding the issues before the Price Control Conference says that the Committee of the Chamber view with considerable sympathy the suggestion that the Government of India should maintain a very strict watch on the movement of prices and take steps for preventing any unwarranted rise in prices. At the same time they are definitely of opinion that before deciding on any particular line of action both the Government of India and the various Provincial Governments should carefully examine the position and analyse the causes which have led to the recent increase in prices.

The factors which have caused the recent rise in prices, according to the Chamber, are firstly the unsatisfactory supply position vis-à-vis demand, secondly rise in prices of practically all finished goods due to factors over which manufacturers have no control, thirdly phenomenal rise in retail prices due to activities of speculators and middlemen, and other things. The Committee urge Government should recognize that manufacturers should be allowed to make some extra profit within reasonable limits at present time.

The most important measure which Government can adopt for restoring prices to a more normal level is to take steps for correcting the present maladjustment between demand and supply. In so far as rice is concerned, the Committee stress the necessity of increasing production by inducing cultivators to bring larger and larger areas under rice. The present emergency can be met if Government of India can find it possible to negotiate with the Government of Burma for the supply of an adequate quantity of rice at a reasonable price. In regard to cotton piece-goods and yarns also the best solution is increase in production. The Indian mill industry can meet the extra demand in course of the next year if certain facilities are granted by Government. The Committee finally urge that any move for control of prices should be taken on an all-India basis and commercial interests must be adequately represented on any machinery that may be set up for controlling prices.

69. Price Control Conference

(i) Price Control Conference: Third Session to be Opened at New Delhi

Amrita Bazar Patrika, 15 October 1941.

New Delhi, 14 October. The third price control conference will be opened by the Hon'ble the Commerce Member on the 16th October in the Committee room of the Council House. Besides delegates from the provinces, the conference will be attended by officers of the Supply, Communication and Finance departments of the Government of India. The provincial representatives will be Hon'ble Mr S. Suhrawardy, Minister in charge, Commerce and Labour, and Mr M.K. Kripalani, Joint Secretary, Commerce and Labour and Chief Controller of Prices (Bengal); Mr A.V. Askwith, Chief Commissioner (Delhi); Hon Khan Bahadur Allabuksh, Premier and Mr I.H. Taunton, Secretary, Revenue Department (Sind); Mr Y.A. Godbole, Chief Secretary and Mr R.A.E. Williams, Chief Controller of Prices and Supplies (Bihar); Mr P.W. Marsh, Adviser to His Excellency the Governor, Mr M.W. Abbasi, Deputy Secretary, Price Control Department and Mr A.N. Sapru, Director of Industries (United Provinces) ....

(ii) Price Control Conference: Standard Cloth, to be Manufactured and Sold at Controlled Prices

Amrita Bazar Patrika, 17 October 1941.

New Delhi, 16 October.

The possibility of putting in the market one or two varieties of 'Standard Cloth' to be sold at controlled prices to the poorer classes was mentioned by Sir A. Ramaswami Mudaliar, Commerce Member, opening the Third Price Control Conference this morning. The suggestion, he said, had been made as a way out of the almost impossibly complicated task of regulating and controlling prices of about 500 different varieties of cloth produced by the Indian mills.

The problem of controlling prices of manufactured goods as well as primary products, he indicated, had assumed importance now because in June, July and the following months, particularly after the freezing order with reference to Japan, prices had shown ascendancy to rise steeply. He strongly refuted the suggestions that the Central Government were trying to prevent a rise in the price of agricultural commodities, because they wanted to avoid having to pay dearness allowance to their employees and because they wanted to export these products cheaply to the Dominions and the Middle East.

Agricultural Prices

The Commerce Member first recalled that the last two conferences had unanimously held the view that agricultural prices before the war had been low and it was only fair that the agriculturist should get some benefit from the improvement in the price position and sell his commodities on a more normal basis, and that as far as possible the interests of the agriculturist should be taken into consideration when any question of price control was discussed. The conferences had also agreed that where prices advanced so steeply as to be unfair to the consumer, both Central and Provincial Governments were justified and compelled to use what powers they had in order to see that the Consumer was not exploited.

Touching on the reasons for the increase, Sir Ramaswami Mudaliar pointed out that the expanding export markets open to this country, particularly after the freezing order with reference to Japan, had certainly been a factor. In the case of manufactured articles, prices had advanced because exports had to be made to countries in the Middle East.

The Government of India, went on the Commerce Member, had received various representations from Provincial Governments pointing out that the course of prices was causing them anxiety and that the time had come to consider the question of control. He had also seen newspaper articles and letters—none had appeared at the time of the earlier conferences—strongly criticizing Central, Provincial and State Governments for not adopting rigorous measures to prevent exploitation of the consumer.

Agriculturist and Consumer

He was emphasizing these facts in order to make clear that in the recommendations that the conference might make, the sole concern was to see on the one hand the agriculturist got a fair deal and on the other the consumer was not unduly exploited. He also strongly refuted two suggestions made against the Government of India.

Firstly, it had been said that the main anxiety of Central and Provincial Governments was to see that dearness allowance was not given to their employees and these Governments were, therefore, trying to stop legitimate rise in prices of agricultural commodities. In emphatically controversies this suggestion, he asked, after all, how many people could be comforted by a dearness allowance given by the Governments? This number was certainly not very large; and there were millions of others such as those in private employment and agriculturists, who felt the burden of the rise and for whom there could be no question of a dearness allowance.

The second suggestion was that attempts were being made by the Central Government to keep down prices because they wanted to export cheaply to the Dominions or Middle East markets. There was not an atom of truth in this suggestion. It was perfectly true, said the Commerce Member, that with reference to certain Inter-Governmental transactions there was a duty cost on this Government as on other Governments to supply each other commodities or manufactured articles at reasonable prices but apart from that there was no truth in the suggestion that for normal export to civilians abroad, this Government was interested in levelling down prices of commodities in this country. Far from it.

Rice and Wheat

There could, further, be no question of leveling down prices in the case of certain commodities such as rice or wheat. Out of ten million tons of wheat produced in India only a small quantity, about one lakh, was exported, and to suggest that in the interest of this small quantity, the Government wanted to keep down the price of 9,900,000 tons was to use the language of freakish extravagance.

Passing on to deal with cotton textiles, he explained that in their case also, prices in June and July, and since the freezing order with reference to Japan was issued, had gone up considerable. An explanation was that imports from Japan were virtually ceasing that India had to become self-dependent, and that the demands of the armies in the Middle East and the position of India as a country with a monopoly in these supplies to the Dominions and the Middle East forces were creating a position in which supplies were not keeping pace with the demand. Iran, Iraq, Syria, Egypt, Palestine and the African countries on the one side and

Singapore, Malaya and New Zealand on the other hand to depend more and more on Indian supplies of textiles to meet their civilian as well as military requirements.

Manufactured Goods

But the problem of control or regulation of manufactured goods like textiles was very different from the problem in relation to primary products. To attempt to regulate the price of even one of the 500 varieties of cloth produced in India by various mills was a task which we felt was beyond the realm of possibility. That did not mean that something could not be done in order to ensure that the poorest among us could get clothing at reasonable prices.

One remedy considered during the last war was the production of a 'Standard Cloth' made out of yarn below 20 and to be sold at a fixed price. Could that remedy be applied at the present moment? Or had we advanced so far in 'civilization' that Standard Cloth would be anathema to the poorer classes? In any case, the suggestion had been made that standard cloth or a few verities of standard cloth might be put in the market. If the suggestion was approved by the conference, questions such as Provincial and State Governments buying the cloth at fixed prices and disposing of them to the poorer classes would have to be considered at the conference.

A Complicated Question

The control of prices of yarn, said the Commerce Member, was an equally complicated question. In order to assist the conference in discussing the questions relating to textile goods, he had asked presidents of a number of Millowners' Associations to attend the conference as a special case tomorrow and put forward their proposals for a solution of the problem. After the conference had got out of them all the information needed, they would withdraw and the conference would proceed to discuss what remedies might be adopted. Today, the first day of the conference, they would confine themselves to the other items.—AP

70. Empire Casualties on all Fronts: Lord Croft's Statement

Amrita Bazar Patrika, 19 October 1941.

British 100,000, Indian 7,000 and Dominion 20,000

In a speech to-day Lord Croft, Under Secretary of State for War stated that Indian casualties on all fronts numbered 7,000.

Lord Croft in a speech on the war situation at Hornsey today (Saturday) said, 'Our real test of strength and endurance is only now about to commence. The German armies, fighting in Russia, have advanced over a 1,400 miles front to an average depth of 400 miles. The Germans will almost certainly come to Batoum and Baku across the Caucasus in the spring. If this is so the Iran Frontier becomes vital to us—the first in supporting the Russian defence of Baku if they will let us, and secondly to deny the road to Egypt and the East.'

Lord Croft criticized those who said that there was no need of an army and that victory could be left to bombers. 'What right have they to keep on asserting that an invasion can be ignored against the advice of those best qualified to judge? I believe that with the great army raised in India together with our own forces based on Egypt we can hold the line to the East. I believe that if the brave Russian people stick it like their forbears we may yet see two or three million Germans held. But even so your army is still faced with a mobile army of far greater strength in the hand of German Generals.'

After deprecating pressure to release thousands of men from the army for agriculture and industry and emphasizing the strength of the German army, Lord Croft declared, 'It is not only your coast-line you have to defend but every city, aerodrome and vital building in the interior may be an objective like Crete. Is an enemy who will squander two million men in Russia going to hesitate to throw great numbers say at Bristol or Coventry Hull or Tyneside and attempt to destroy a dozen of our most vital centres for what he would consider paltry losses?'

Lord Croft continued, 'When I see that the German army, in defiance of sea and air, has flung itself right across Europe in two years I must remind you that while nothing but an army or starvation can make us hold up our hands nothing but an army can meet and defeat the German army in battle.'

British Generals

Referring to the criticism in some newspapers that the army was commanded by 'aged blimps' who never took risk Lord Croft said, 'Our aged blimps happen to be young and brilliant leaders, all proved in war—five to fifteen years younger than the principal German Generals.'

As to risk, never had risks been so freely taken as in the conquest of the Italian East African Empire. Lord Croft said that the total British troops engaged in all operations overseas since the start of the war was five times the combined total of Australian, New Zealanders and South Africans, substantial though the Dominions total has been.

The total casualties of the British army including prisoners on all front has been about 100,000, those of the Dominion troops 20,000, 13,000 Australians, 6,000 New Zealanders and 600 South Africans. Casualties among African native troops were less than 500.—Reuter.

71. ARP Shelters and Trenches: Bengal Gives Lead 105,000 Workers to be Trained

Amrita Bazar Patrika, 31 October 1941.

New Delhi, 30 October. In response to the Government of India's Circular to the Provincial Governments urging them to make provisions for air raid shelters and split trenches in vulnerable towns, the province of Bengal is reported to have given the lead by undertaking construction of such shelters and trenches forthwith. The Central Government's Circular urges provision of safety of at least 25 per cent of the population in affected areas.

It is further learnt that the Government of India have convened an ARP Conference to be held in Delhi in the third week of November which will be attended by representatives of the various Provincial Governments.

On the conclusion of this conference Mr Ibbotson, Secretary of the newly created Civil Defence Department and Lieutenant Colonel Reeve, ARP expert of the Government of India will undertake a six weeks tour of Eastern India to inspect and strengthen the ARP organization in that part of the country.

According to the revised ARP scheme it is thought that India should at least have 105,000 trained ARP workers with a view to insuring the efficient maintenance of the services.

72. 'Famine' of Wheat and Flour in Lahore: Shopkeepers Refuse to Sell their Stocks; They are being Removed to 'Safer Places'

The Tribune, 11 December 1941.

Lahore, 10 December. On enquiries made from individual purchasers and sellers of wheat and wheat flour in different parts of the city, *The Tribune* representative found to-day that the Government's control of the prices of wheat and wheat flour was not being effectively maintained.

The retail sellers are practically refusing to sell on the plea that they have not got any stock. Those who have, only give one-third of what is demanded.

The educated class through threats or persuasion, get their demand fulfilled because the shopkeeper thinks that they would requisition the services of policemen but the illiterate buyers find it quite a difficult job to make purchases of wheat or flour in the city.

The retail sellers, when approached, complained of the exhaustion of the stock and the tight control maintained by the mill-owners and the big shopkeepers who are keeping away the stocks from them and the market. Whatever stock they have, these retail sellers pleaded they bought at a higher rate which prevailed before the control was introduced and that could not be disposed of at a cheaper rate as desired by the Government.

It is understood that some of the big shopkeepers in the city are deliberately removing their stocks of wheat and flour to 'safer places' so as to avoid the vigilance of the police. Cartloads of these commodities were [carried] away in the presence of the policemen on the plea that contracts made before the control was introduced, were being fulfilled: the dispatch of the goods, *The Tribune* representative was told was either to the mill-owners or big shopkeepers.

The mill-owners big or small, have totally stopped giving flour to the petty shopkeepers or to individual buyers. The already existing stocks, they say, have been disposed of and since the prices at which the Governments sell the stock to them is high, they cannot make new purchases of wheat and sell flour as the sale does not pay them in the long run. Some of the mill-owners revealed the fact that the tendency not to sell was actuated because of the little margin of profit they would have if the sale was effected at the prevailing price.

In Akbari Mandi, Chune Mandi and inside Shahalmi Gate, though the police constables were seen compelling the shopkeepers to sell flour and wheat, the buyers were feeling it difficult to make the purchases. Inside Shahalmi Gate it is a hard task to buy a bag of wheat or flour. In Akbari Mandi Hafiz Mohd Shafi's (Inspector of Police In-charge) efforts have succeeded in persuading the big shopkeepers to sell the commodities in as much quantity as is desired by the buyers, but the moment he or the police constables posted by him, move away, the shopkeepers begin to adopt their tactics. *The Tribune* representative actually saw poor women being refused wheat and flour even for eight annas.

Adulteration

The buyers in the city to-day also complained of adulteration. Maize flour is being freely mixed with wheat flour so as to increase the weight and to have a good margin of profit. It is held by the purchasers that unless the Government open their own depots, the situation will grow from bad to worse. In Mishri Shah and Bhagwanpura and the suburbs of Lahore, many of the poverty stricken people are practically living on 'bajra'.

In the Satta...[not legible], *The Tribune* representative found to-day that the prevailing rate of wheat was Rs 5–1–0. For the last three days it was Rs 4–15–0 Rs 4–14–0, Rs 4–14–6, though Rs 4–12–0 as officially recorded. The transactions were seen being made at the high rates.

It appears that a deadlock is being created in the markets in the city by keeping away the supply from petty shopkeepers as well as individual buyers. It is understood that the stock which the sellers or the buyers can use in the city is only sufficient for nine or ten days, the major portion having been drained of by the big stockists.

73. Suspend Working of Markets and Sales Tax Acts Unnecessary Severity of Price Control Should be Avoided

The Tribune, 11 December 1941.

Lahore, 10 December. The Punjab Markets Act Protest Standing Committee met this evening at the Haveli of Rai Bahadur L. Lachman Das. S. Santokh Singh presided. Forty members out of 59 were present.

Among the demands put forth by the Committee were that the Government should issue necessary instructions to their officers concerned to take into confidence the trading classes in order that the unnecessary severity of price control may not add to the already prevalent discontent, that the working of the Sales Tax Act and the Markets Act be suspended for the duration of the war; that all genuine trade members who have not yet resigned their seats on the Marketing Committees should do so by the 14th December, when a final decision in regard to the general suspension of business in agricultural commodities will be taken.

Among the resolutions passed by the Committee were the following:

1. The Markets Act Protest Standing Committee looks with sympathy and approval upon the spontaneous and voluntary suspension of business in the matter of purchase and sale of agricultural commodities, which has been brought about in most of the markets in the province from the date of enforcement of the Markets Act, and reiterates its view that it is not possible to carry on trade under this Act and the Rules and the Bye-laws made thereunder.

2. The Committee further resolves that a representative meeting of the Punjab traders be called at Lahore on 14th December 1941, at 2 p.m. in Bhopindra Hall, to take a final decision in regard to the general suspension of business in agricultural commodities in the whole province, and hereby urges upon all the markets where business has already been suspended to continue the same till the final decision on the 14th December.

3. This Committee is of opinion that the aggressive policy of Japan has brought the war very much nearer the doors of India. In order to show a united front it is most necessary to cease all controversies and bring about a better atmosphere in the province. The Committee, therefore, demands of the Government that the operation of this most contentious measure, namely, the Markets Act, be suspended for the duration of the war; all the more, so when it is admitted on all hands that it is not a fiscal measure.

This Committee is further of opinion that the operation of the Sales Tax Act should likewise be suspended for the duration of the war.

The suspension of these two measures can alone bring about the required change which is so very necessary for the prosecution of the war efforts.

4. This Committee calls upon all the genuine trade members who have not yet resigned their seats on Marketing Committees to do so by the 14th December on which date the final decision will be taken in respect of those who still refused to resign.

74. The Withholding of Wheat from Sale Forbidden Punjab Governor's Order

The Tribune, 11 December 1941.

Lahore, 10 December. His Excellency the Governor of the Punjab has prohibited the withholding from sale to the public of wheat and flour at the rate fixed by the District Magistrates and has prescribed imprisonment up to three years and fine for contravention of the order. The following is the text of the order:

'Whereas it appears necessary to the Governor of the Punjab, in order to maintain supplies and services essential to the life of the community, to ensure that wheat and flour are available to the public, it is hereby ordered, under the provisions of Rule 81 of the Defence of India Rules, that no person, firm or company ordinarily dealing in grain or flour, whether wholesale or retail, shall withhold from general sale any grain or flour kept by him as stock in trade. Such stock in trade shall be sold at the rate prescribed by the District Magistrate of the district in which the sale takes place in accordance with the powers delegated to him under this Rule.

'Any person contravening this order shall be deemed guilty of an offence under Rule 81 and shall be punishable with imprisonment for a term which may extend to three years and shall also be liable to fine.'

75. Viceroy's Appeal for Unity Against War Menace to India

Amrita Bazar Patrika, 16 December 1941.

'We stand to-day at a crucial moment in the history of mankind. Throughout the world mighty forces are engaged in a titanic struggle, the outcome of which will affect the destinies of the human race for centuries. In the Far East the clouds that we have watched gathering for so long have burst in a storm that brings the menace of war even more closely to this land. India is no mere spectator of these tremendous events.

'They affect here vitally and she is playing an outstanding part in them. Let us in such circumstances forget our domestic differences and work together as a whole for that common object—the attainment of which is so vitally necessary to India and so anxiously desired by all her people'.

This appeal to the people of India was made by His Excellency the Viceroy on Monday morning, addressing the annual meeting of the Associated Chambers of Commerce at the Royal Exchange, Calcutta.

Distinguished among the guests was His Excellency Sir John Herbert Governor of Bengal....

... A Year's Survey

'When I addressed you last year the Empire was but recovering from the blow inflicted on it by the defeat of our French allies, and the collapse of France. We were through the worst. We had stood up to the heaviest battering that any nation could have had to face. We had survived with success many months of acute peril and immense strain; and we were in a position to look forward with confidence to 1941.

'1941 has not belied the hopes that we entertained a year ago. It does not see the end of the war. There are before us many critical months, months in which we shall pass through grave anxiety in which we shall suffer heavy losses, in which we shall have to bear the strain of critical situations, before the desired outcome is achieved. But we are a year further on the way. The year which has just passed has been marked by many events of the utmost significance. The enemy's endeavours to strangle us by sea have failed. The Battle of the Atlantic still goes on and will go on. But the threat it constitutes, and the burden it represents are less great by far those a year ago.

Successes in Middle East

'By land, we have liquidated the Italian Empire in Africa. In that great task, with which the name of our present Commander-in-Chief, His Excellency General Sir Archibald Wavell, will forever imperishably be associated, the part played by India and Indian troops was of the first significance and of the highest value. I have the Commander-in-Chief's personal authority for the outstanding quality of their effort and of the contribution that they have made.

Help from USA

'From the United States of America, to which our sympathy goes out with such sincerity and depth in the shocking aggression of which they have been the victims, the Empire has had, and continues to have, help of inestimable value. Let me say in that connection how great a happiness it has been to me to see during my own term of office, and at a juncture so critical as the present the bonds between the United States of America and India more closely knit by the appointment as United States Commissioner to India of Mr Thomas Murray Wilson, so well known to many of us here; and by the appointment of sir Girija Shankar Bajpai as Agent-General of India in America.

Russo-German War

'When last I addressed you, few of us anticipated that a still more blatant exhibition of cynicism was to be given by a breach of relations between Germany and Russia, and by the wholly unprovoked, and wholly unjustified onslaught made without a moments notice, or a word of warning, by the Nazis on a nation to which they were bound by every form of engagement. Russia has had to meet and to carry the shock of a devastating and an unprovoked attack. But her response has been magnificent and I know gentlemen that I speak for you all to-day when I say that the deep and sincere good wishes of everyone of us go out to Russia and to her people in the battle they are waging; and that there is no one of us who does not feel admiration, real and profound for the supreme example which she and her people have given to the world of courage, resolution, and tenacity.

India's Contribution

'India's contribution to the war and to its successful outcome was great indeed even a year ago. In the twelve months that have passed since we met its growth has been immense. His Majesty's Government have shown themselves most anxious to take advantage of the men, the munitions and the supplies of various kinds which India is so well qualified to give, and which India has always been so anxious to give. The number of our fighting men who are defending India overseas is three times what it was a year ago and ten times what it was two years ago. The organization of our supply system has been—I will not say—perfected, for there is always room for imprisonment in any system but it has been brought to a height of performance which commands admiration and the results of which are striking in the highest degree. Let us pay due acknowledgment to the part which your help and your constructive, criticism have played in that achievement.

'In every form of war-like display we are playing our part, indeed more than our part. In every form of financial contribution—for weapons, for equipments, for amenities for the fighting forces, for the relief of distress arising from the war—India, the States and British India alike, remains most generous and open-hearted. And the spirit of this country since it first recognized what was involved in the struggle in which we are engaged has remained and remains calm, firm, convinced of the necessity of victory, ready to do and to give all in its power to bring victory about. But there is always more for us to do. There are always ways in which as a country and as individuals we can make a still greater contribution: I am ready to ask for the impossible and I know that if I do I shall get a ready response not only from you gentlemen and the great commercial community which you represent but from all classes and from every part of India.

Supplies from India

'I would like in the first place to say a word about supply. You can imagine how deep a satisfaction it has been to me to hear the encouraging and the friendly words which you were good enough to use to-day of the work of my Supply Department. I can bear personal witness to the intensity of the efforts made by the officers of that department since the beginning of the war, and to the anxiety both of Sir Zafrulla Khan and of his distinguished successor, Sir Homi Mody, to see that the very beat results possible are achieved whatever the difficulties that may confront us.

Steel and Shipyard

'I think that you will wish we to give you as briefly as I can a few outstanding facts which speak for themselves. The production of steel is being rapidly stepped up by the efforts, to which I should like to pay a warm tribute to the Tata Iron and Steel Company and the Steel Corporation of Bengal. Before the middle of 1942 production should touch a rate of 125 million tons per annum ....

'India's shipyards are employed to capacity in the construction of mine-sweeping trawlers and other small naval crafts as well as in repairs to ships of the line and merchant vessels.

Machine Tools

'Progress has been made I am glad to say in stimulating and developing the Indian machine tool industry and simple machine tools are now being manufactured in India in fairly large quantities. Engineering stores are being manufactured in very large quantities indeed and though there are still hold-ups owing to the uneven flow of material, the fabricating workshops are fully occupied. The demand for woolen textiles still absorbs India's capacity to the full. Cotton textile demands are increasing very rapidly and the great cotton textile industry, whose capacity we would all of us at one time have thought to be almost inexhaustible, is now beginning to feel the strain of the demands placed upon it both for direct war purpose and for various purposes arising out of war conditions.... The Government clothing factories are now turning out over 8 million garments a month. Leather manufactures are being organized on the same lines as clothing and the value of the monthly output already exceeds Rs 1.25 crores. The output of motor vehicles assembled in India has been much increased and so far as armoured vehicles are concerned, India will be able to produce all the armour plates required. India will shortly be producing her own refined sulphur and valuable progress has been made in the production of vital chemicals such as bichromates and of medical stores including both drugs and equipment.

'1941 saw something like a four-fold increase over the greater part of the Supply field, and the demands of 1942 may be literally gigantic.

Civil Defence

'In the circumstances of to-day the problem of civil defence assumes an importance greater than ever. I know what energy and zeal has been devoted in Calcutta to the handling of that problem, and to the development of passive air defence—an energy and zeal on which I warmly congratulate the Presidency and which will carry its own reward. I am glad to think that the whole of this very vital issue is now being handled in consultation with the provinces by a single Civil Defence Department at the headquarters of my Government and that in dealing with it, I have the assistance in Mr Raghavendra Rao—an adviser who has himself had much practical experience at home and who has had the advantage also of a very close contact with the Ministry of Home Security.

Transport Problem

'My Government has been encouraging the establishment of Boards at the leading cities to co-ordinate transport over large areas and I recognize that as the war goes on it may be necessary to impose further control than is operative at present. But compulsion always involves a certain sacrifice of elasticity and we are anxious to leave as much liberty to private enterprise as is compatible with the fullest war effort.

Inflation of Currency

'I listened with close attention to the observation which you Sir [President, Associate Chamber of Commerce], made your speech on the problem of inflation. My Government have been and are giving the matter their constant and most anxious consideration. But the ramifications of the problem are complex, possible counter-measures are beset with administrative difficulties and in our efforts to deal with it we need—and will I assure you most gratefully welcome—all the advice and all the active assistance whish we can get from the commercial and the non-official world.

Price Advances

'I do not propose to detain you with the special factors which have contributed to the substantial price advances of particular commodities or on the measures which have been taken or are in contemplation by my Government to ease the position in those cases. I can at once assure you that my Government are quite prepared to resort to methods of direct price control where they are satisfied that such action can with advantage be taken and they will not hesitate where need be to follow up this preliminary measure with such control over supply as may prove to be necessary and practicable.

The August Offer

'When we last met I spoke to you of the proposals in the constitutional field, which, with the full approval of His Majesty's Government, I made on the 8th August 1940. I was at pains to analyse those proposals in detail. I tried to bring out their far-reaching character; their great potentialities; their real significance both immediate and for the future. I repeated that they reaffirmed as the proclaimed and accepted goal of the Imperial Crown, and of the British Parliament, the attainment by India of free and equal partnership in the British Commonwealth. I emphasized the concern of His Majesty's Government that full weight should be given to the views of the minorities in framing the future constitutional scheme; the far-reaching significance of their decision that responsibility for the framing of that future constitutional scheme should be subject to the due fulfilment of the obligations which Great Britain's long connection with India has imposed upon her be primarily for Indians themselves. I referred to the readiness of His Majesty's Government to see the setting up after the conclusion of the war with the least possible delay a body representative of the principal elements in India's national life, to devise the framework of that scheme. I repeated that pending the conclusion of the war, His Majesty's Government were only too anxious to welcome and promote any sincere and practical step taken by Indians themselves to prepare the way for agreement about the form and procedure of this post-war body, and about the principles and basis of the constitution. I spoke of the anxiety of His Majesty's Government to see that sufficient degree of general agreement in this country behind any constitutional changes which is so essential if there is to be harmonious working. I made an appeal to all parties to sink their differences in times such as these when the fate of everything that we—all of us—hold most dear is in the balance and to co-operate in the defence of those common ideals.

'My appeal did not secure the response for which I had hoped. I was determined however to wait in the hope that the passing of time would make a difference, for I wanted to give every possible chance to the major parties to come together on the basis of these proposals. I hoped too that the increasing pressure of the war and its swift approach to India, would influence the decision. I was anxious finally as I always have been to secure for the expansion of my Government and for the other arrangements which I had in view for associating opinion in India more closely with the conduct of the war—the support of the great political parties.

Expansion of Executive

'As you know gentlemen, I was disappointed in those hopes. But though I was prevented from going ahead on the lines which I proposed in August of 1940, I would repeat that the guarantees, the undertaking, the pledges, the intentions and the attitude of His Majesty's Government as explained in my statement towards future constitutions development and the machinery by which it is to be brought about, are as valid to-day as when they were first spoken. But given the increasing pressure of the war I could not in justice to India itself longer postpone, because of the absence of support from the great political parties, the creation of additional departments in my Council, the reorganization of the work of that body and the taking of steps for the association of non-official opinion with what was going on.

'It was in those circumstances that with the full approval of His Majesty's Government, the reorganization announced in last July took place. That reorganization did not have any basis other than administrative convenience. But in making it though I could not look for help from the political parties, I was anxious, that I should get the best men I could, the most representative men, men of real standing and importance in this country. In that I can claim to have succeeded....

'The [expanded] Council in its present form is a body of great authority and great distinction. It represents wide experience political and administrative. On it are members of different communities from different parts of India, service and non-service Europeans and Indians. I would like to express to this important audience my own judgment of its entire competence in the administrative field and my own appreciation of the value of the assistance which it has been able to give me on wider political issues. It is a strong effective and distinguished body; and India may be well content; that in the direction of affairs she is so well served to-day.

National Defence Council

'The second limb of the new arrangements which were announced in July was the establishment of the National Defence Council and I would like to pay a tribute to the patriotism and public spirit of those gentlemen who have accepted my invitation to join that body. As you know my intention was and is that Prime Ministers of Provinces shall be ex-officio members. In these last few days we have welcomed to it the Maharaja of Parlakimedi, who on the happy occasion of the restoration of normal parliamentary government in Orissa, which we all so much welcome, has become the Prime Minister of that Province; while with the formation of a new Ministry in Bengal the Chief Minister of Bengal becomes a member of the Council.

Deadlock in Provinces

'But, while the two steps which I have just mentioned are of great significance and of great hope for the future our main problem still remains unsolved.

'While in five provinces the constitution is functioning normally with the assistance of the legislature, in six others its normal operation remains suspended. There could be no better advertisement of the practicability and the advantage of normal parliamentary government than the success with which it has been worked in great provinces such as Bengal and the Punjab, and in areas presenting problems so different as do Bengal and the Punjab, Assam and Sind. And it remains to me a bitter disappointment that those in other provinces who had asked for and had accepted the burden of government should have thrown it down so lightheartedly at a moment of such crisis in the fortunes of the world and of India and with so little consideration of what was involved. That that decision has provoked many regrets I am well aware....

Party Strifes

'And if the provincial position is as I have described it, there still remains unabridged the gulf between the parties as regards the future Government of India. That that problem remains unsolved is due to no lack of goodwill, no lack of earnest effort on the part of His Majesty's Government, the Secretary of State and myself. We have left nothing undone to bring the parties together, to try to provide the materials for an amicable agreement between them, to try to smooth India's path to the realization of her goal. At the critical point which matters have now reached in the international situation. I would ask again whether it is not possible for the divisions that unhappily exist to be bridged; and for India, which has made and is making so immense a contribution to the war, which stands for so much in the history of the world to go forward as one in support of ideals in which we know that she believes and for which there is such overwhelming and general support throughout the country. And it is my earnest prayer that the common detestation of the wickedness against which we are fighting today may reflect itself in that agreement in the internal political field which it has always been our hope and desire to see—always been our hope and desire to see achieved....

Appeal for Unity

'We stand to-day at a crucial moment in the history of mankind. Throughout the world mighty forces are engaged in a titanic struggle, the outcome of which will affect the destinies of the human race for centuries. In the Far East the clouds that we have watched gathering for so long have burst in a storm that brings the menace of war even more closely to this land—India is no mere spectator of these tremendous events. They affect her vitally and she is playing an outstanding part in them. Let us in such circumstances forget our domestic differences and work together as a whole for that common object, the attainment of which is so vitally necessary to India and so anxiously desired by all her people.

'When I addressed you a year ago I thought that if you did me the honour to ask me to speak to you at your meeting this year it would be for the last time. A seventh year in this great office would in any circumstances, even the most peaceful, be a heavy burden to carry. A seventh year in circumstances such as those of to-day, when so much has been crowded into one, Viceroyalty, and so many issues of most critical importance have fallen to my lot, is no light matter. For the best part of six years, you have given me, in full measure, the powerful aid of your comfort and support. I trust that you may find me deserving of these for yet another year, in which I shall strive, if strength is given me, to fulfill to the utmost of my powers the great charge which His Majesty has once again been pleased to place in my hands'.

76. Emergency in Calcutta: Facilities for Evacuation of Families of Government Employees

Bombay Chronicle, 18 December 1941.

Calcutta, 17 December. It is understood that in view of the possibility that Calcutta may be declared an emergency area, the Government of Bengal has directed that those of their employees who want to take their families out of Calcutta may draw one month's salary in advance. This amount will be realized by instalments later.

The rush of outgoing passengers at both Sealdah and Howrah stations is causing considerable strain on the traffic police in the city. Almost all the approaches to Howrah station were strongly guarded and admission had to be regulated by the police today. All vehicular traffic over the Howrah bridge was suspended towards the afternoon, in view of the stream of pedestrians proceeding towards the station.

77. Shortage of Vegetables, Coal and Other Articles: K.B. Allahbux Outlines Government Proposals to Relieve Situation

The Tribune, 19 December 1941.

Karachi, 17 December. The Sind Government's proposals to relieve the situation created by rise in the prices of articles were outlined by the Premier Khan Bahadur Allahbux, in the course of his reply to the debate on an adjournment motion of Mr N.A. Bechar which was talked out in the Sind Legislative Assembly this evening.

The Premier said that his Government had a Bill under consideration to compel merchants and those engages domestic labour to give compensation allowance to their employees.

He further said that the Government was considering a scheme which would be ready in a day or two to meet the shortage of vegetables in the city. According to the scheme extra acreage say about 500 acres or so would be brought about under vegetable cultivation solely for military use, thus leaving the present supply for civil consumption.

The Premier, referring to the control of price of wheat, said: 'As recommended by the Advisory Committee the wheat price found its level and it was now available in the market at Rupees 5.5 and Rupees 5.8 per maund in wholesale and retail respectively'.

As regards shortage of coal he assured the House that even if no wagons were available he had a scheme under preparation to bring coal by boats from the mofussil to the city.

The Premier added that if any time it was found that the present stock of food articles was not sufficient for consumption by the civil population, he would request the Central Government not to make further purchases from Sind, and also to control the export.

Earlier the House adjourned by 37 votes to 10 a Government Bill to increase tobacco licence fee from 4 annas to 10 annas as a measure of taxation. The Bill was opposed by the Congress Party.

78. War and Indian Newspapers: Their Duty Sir A. Hydari's Speech at Editors' Conference

Amrita Bazar Patrika, 19 December 1941.

The Rt Hon Sir Akbar Hydari, Member-in-Charge of the Information and Broadcasting Department met the Standing Committee of the Newspaper Editors' Conference in the Statesman House on Thursday morning. Mr Srinivasan, President of the Newspaper Editors' Conference, welcoming Sir Akbar expressed the gratitude of the Conference for a accepting their invitation and coming to Calcutta and meeting them. He hoped that the precedent which Sir Akbar had established yesterday would be continued for all time to come. It was most essential, said Mr Srinivasan, that personal contact and good relations should exist between the press in India and the head of the Information Department.

Sir Akbar, in thanking the Conference, said:

'As I rise to speak to you to-day, my gratification at the privilege of being the first Information Member of the Government of India to address a gathering of the leading editors of India, is tempered with the realization of the heavy responsibility which lies upon you and me alike at this crisis in human affairs. At such a time, you will expect from me, not a detailed discourse on domestic press matters, but rather a statement of my attitude towards some of those general questions with regard to which you gentlemen have to guide the public mind. I need not, therefore apologize further for putting before you certain convictions which are part of my very being.

Effect of Japan's War

'Japan's entry into the war—an act which was the natural culmination of a long period of Japanese filibustering and saber-rattling—must have put an end to any doubts which may have lingered in some minds as to India's vital interest in the result of the present war. Up to the 8th December there may have been some who felt that the war was remote and that India could remain a detached spectator of a grim contest between two rival systems of world polity. I did not share this view then, nor do I now believe that it was ever well-founded, but we all know that it was held by some Indians of undoubted patriotism and integrity.

'To-day, however, the last lingering reasonable doubt must have been swept away, India, which for nearly 200 years has been able to view international commotion with unconcern, is now a potential target for the forces of Japan. Every Indian to-day knows that whether he likes it or not, this is India's as well as America's or China's or anybody else's war; he knows too, that India dare not lose, and that in the parcelling out of the world which would result from an Axis victory, India would be allotted to the ruthless and aggressive Japanese.

'It is perhaps worth remembering that by the capitulation of Thailand, Japan has been brought to the threshold of Burma and that but for the separation of Burma from India—a separation which in no way affects India's strategic position—we should to-day have had to announce that enemy forces had reached the boundaries of India. This does not mean that there is undue cause for alarm, but it does mean that the war has now become, beyond all dispute, a serious practical business for each one of us.

Duty of the Press

'At such a time it is to you, as the leaders of public opinion, that India will look for guidance. Your influence, great in peace time, will now be magnified many times and the steadiness and soundness of Indian opinion will largely depend on your success in avoiding optimism and overconfidence on the one hand, and pessimism and defeatism on the other. This will not be an easy task in the days ahead, when accurate news of momentous events may sometime be slow in coming and when it may often be difficult to assess the importance of either successes or defeats. It is one of the main functions of a free press to keep up the public morale in times of trouble. This means that the press must tell the truth whether it be good or bad; but it also means that we must not put such emphasis on temporary reverses as to obscure the solid reasons for believing in the certainty of ultimate victory.

'It is true, for example, that Japan has scored some initial successes; but it is also true that for oil, scrap iron, steel, bauxite and all the main essentials of modern warfare Japan is dependent upon an outside world from which she can no longer get supplies. It is also true that the Axis Powers have against them four-fifths of the inhabitants of the globe and a very large proportion of the world's material resources. It rests with you gentlemen to see that these facts are presented in due proportion so that the public is assisted to preserve a balanced judgment in the midst of the confusing events around us. On me too, as Member for Information, rests a heavy responsibility. Much of the news which you, as editors have to interpret to the public comes to you through my Department. I can assure you that we shall in the future as in past be scrupulous purveyors of truth you expect from us, and we shall not fall you. This responsibility lies particularly heavily on me as a member of the Viceroy's first expanded Executive Council....

Defence Problem

'As for defence, should it not be in war time directly in charge of the Commander-in-Chief, so as to reduce circumlocution to the minimum and make for the utmost amount of directness and expedition? The more so when Sir Archibald Wavell in whose hands it is at present, is trusted by us all and is enjoying the confidence of the people. In this connection, let us not overtook one important fact that the portfolio of Civil Defence is held by a distinguished Indian who works in the closest collaboration with the Commander-in-Chief and has, so far as I have been able to ascertain, full access to the inner secrets of the Defence Department. As for the members for Finance and Communications these posts have been held by Indians in the past for short or long periods and the fact that they now happened to be held by Europeans is, I have little doubt, accidental, and it arises simply from the fact that the present Council is an expansion and adaptation of what was already in existence. And again (and of course without prejudice to the statutory responsibilities of the Governor-General) you will, I think be very wide off the mark if you undervalue the influence of the majority in the Council in regard to any important decision, which of course including questions within the portfolio of any member of Council, whether European or Indian.

'Let us then accept the fact that, whatever the theory may be, the expansion of the Viceroy's Council does mean a real advance towards the goal of complete self-government which we are all determined to attain in the not distant future.

Sense of Values

'It we are to help the public to see all these matters aright, perhaps our main task is to keep our own sense of values. This is not an easy task in the modern world, for it is indeed the widespread loss of this sense of values that is mainly responsible for the war, particularly for the aggression of the Japanese.

'I need not remind you of the great respect which was entertained for the Japanese in this city not many years ago—a respect based partly on a cultural and historical link between India and Japan through that great religion whose founder we are commemorating this week in the city where he attained Buddhahood, and partly on a sense of profound satisfaction that an Eastern people was taking its place amongst the great powers of the world. The Japanese had a great opportunity of bringing a new vitality to the ancient civilization of the East and our respect for them was at that time well-founded; but unfortunately for us they have been false to the spirit of the East and have dedicated themselves to the service of materialism and chauvinism. They have allowed a materialistic philosophy to dominate them and like all who fall a prey to that philosophy, they will have to learn its falseness in sorrow and suffering. Is there not here a lesson for us? Let us take heed lest we become so absorbed in bargaining and counting gains and losses that we lose our souls in the process.

Differences in India

'I speak of bargaining and counting gains and losses. Perhaps I am not probing deep enough; perhaps I should rather say that much of our trouble in India to-day arises from dwelling too much on our disagreements, Indians or Europeans, Hindus, Moslems, Sikhs, Parsis or Christians, we are perhaps all to much concerned to see how our other communities and how, therefore, we need special protection. Life is not entirely made up of disagreements and differences. We are faced at the moment with an enemy who would end all our differences by reducing us in a common level of slavery. Need we wait for defeat to find what we have in common? We are fully conscious of our point of difference. May I appeal to you the editors of India, to concentrate for the next six months on finding the points of agreement rather than disagreement between the different communities of the country? It is not difficult to suggest some of the points of agreement.

'First there is a common belief in reasonable freedom. Freedom in the abstract is perhaps not sufficiently definite, so let me say that there is amongst us a common belief in freedom to worship as we choose, freedom to speak our own language, freedom to buy and sell as we please and within limitations which are very wide even in time of war, freedom to speak as we please. We have a common belief in that 'rational liberty' the faith in which is so deeply implanted in the mind of every student of Burke—the 'manly moral regulated liberty' stated to the words of that great philosopher—consists in 'tempering together these opposite extremes of liberty and restraint in one consistent work'.

'Every single community in India to-day believes in this rational liberty. How long would it last under Axis rule?'

79. Approaching Danger of War: Calcutta's Position

Amrita Bazar Patrika, 23 December 1941.

The Question of Calcutta's Defence

Principal J.K. Choudhuri of Vidyasagar College, President of the Calcutta Civil Defence Committee (3, Chandney Chowk) has issued the following:

With the approaching danger of war the duties of the citizens of Calcutta are becoming quite clear. They must organize themselves for an effective defence of their town. Although ultimately military offensive will be responsible for the protection of Calcutta and other cities open to danger, the part to be played by civil population should not be underestimated. The immediate duties which the citizens should be called upon to perform in connection with the Civil Defence of Calcutta may be classified under the following heads:

1. Evacuation of citizens to Moffusil areas—This involves a number of considerations:
   (a) The place or places where the evacuees should go. During the last few days panic stricken people of Calcutta have left for places where there is no room for excess population, resulting in overcrowding, increase of prices of essential commodities and involving danger to public health.
   (b) Calcutta with its suburbs contains about 24 lakhs of people of which during the last few days, according to the testimony of a friend of mine—Mr K.B. Sen Gupta—only 3 to 4 lakhs have left Calcutta. The following table supplied by Mr Sen Gupta is instructive

   Classification of the people evacuated may be made:

   Eastern Bengal cum North Bengal Hawkers, Canvassers.

Menials	70 pc
Gentlemen having their own homes	20 pc
Miscellaneous	10 pc

Total about 1 lakh 25 thousand West Bengal and Diff Provinces—

Coolies, Servants, Cooks, and others	80 pc
Gentlemen	10 pc
Miscellaneous	10 pc

Total about 1 lakh 80 thousand.

Within a radius of 200 miles there is no town where more people can take shelter—Midnapur, Contai, Kalna, Katwa, Faridpur being excepted.

Out of the 20 lakhs of people, more than 10 lakhs are Bengalees whose evacuation elsewhere is in doubt, because:

(a) Though moneyed—no place to live in.
(b) Less solvent—no place to live in.
(c) No money and out—there is place to live in.

(d) No money and no place.

(c) Protecting the evacuees from the Gundas, Thieves and Dacoits.

(d) Overcrowding in Howrah and Sealdah Stations and congestion at Steamer Stations it is essential that proper arrangements should be made at these Stations and Junctions in order to lesson the extreme difficulties and inconveniencies to which the passengers are put.

2. Panic—

It is imperative at a critical time like the present that panic should be allayed and the citizens heartened to face the danger manfully.

3. Strict Regulations of Prices and Stoppage of Profiteering—

If the Railway authorities maintain adequate goods service to prevent shortage of foodstuffs and other essential commodities in areas, where there has been a sudden influx of people, it will go a great way to hearten the people and strengthen their morale.

It will be eminently helpful if the local authorities of the places where there has all ready been influx of people will kindly communicate to the public whether or not more accommodation is still available and any other relevant information.

The task is a huge one and it calls for service from everyone capable of rendering service. I call upon the authorities and heads of various educational institutions, engineering and commercial firms—merchants and traders to render the amount of service which Bengal in general and Calcutta in particular expect of them at this supreme hour.

I expect that in response to my appeal thousands of civil population will enlist as members, co-operators and workers and with the help and co-operation of the Central and Provincial Government and particularly the ARP, the Civil Guards and the Police Authorities will do their duties by their country.

80. Civil Defence Problems: Schemes Framed

Amrita Bazar Patrika, 26 December 1941.

The Public Health, Medical and Local Self-Government Department of the Government of Bengal is charged with the duty of dealing with subjects relating to Civil Defence. These subjects fall under the following main heads:

1. Maintenance of Communications;
2. Maintenance of essential services such as conservancy, public health, lighting, water supply, water works and mains and sewers;
3. Hospital arrangements for air-raid casualties;
4. Prevention of diseases;
5. Salvage operations;
6. Fire-fighting; and
7. Sanitary arrangements at the two railway stations.

The Local Self-governing Bodies have initially framed schemes with the help of Government experts, having regard to special needs of the areas concerned. The initial cost is being borne by Government for practically all the items, and what share of the cost, if any, will have to be borne eventually by the Local Self-governing Bodies will be settled in consultation with them later.

The Calcutta Corporation has taken a very big part in framing schemes for Calcutta and will have a very large hand in executing them. Stocks of materials necessary for executing the different schemes have already been secured and kept in readiness. Protective measures have been adopted in respect of institutions necessary for carrying on the essential services.

Hospital arrangements for air-raid casualties are being pushed on and the co-operation and assistance of medical men and nurses is being sought for. There is need for a good number of doctors and nurses, and it is hoped by Government that they will be forthcoming without delay.

Prevention of Diseases

With regard to the question of prevention of diseases, vaccination and anti-cholera inoculation will be resolved to on a mass scale. Provision has also been made for infectious diseases hospital in and near Calcutta.

A special Officer has been appointed in connection with the scheme for salvage operations and to take charge of the organization as Chief Salvage Officer.

Fire-fighting

Fire-fighting through the Calcutta Fire Brigade forms an important part of the scheme of Civil Defence. Extra fire pumps and the appointment of trained men for operating them have been sanctioned. A fire brigade training school is being set up in the City, which will be capable of training 250 recruits at a time. New fire stations are being built and steel fire barges have been constructed to deal with fires on shipping or areas on the river bank and partly to pump water into the city in case of necessity. Adequate arrangements have been made for storing of water in reservoirs which may be available for use for extinguishing fire.

Schemes for efficient sanitation and medical attention in Railway Stations have been put in hand.

For areas outside Calcutta arrangements for triller pumps are being made and sanction obtained for a large number. Triller pump squads have been raised and training given to them at the Calcutta Fire Brigade headquarters.

81. Congress on Effects of War: Working Committee Meeting, Wardha, 28 December 1941

File No. 1/1941–2, AICC Papers, Nehru Memorial Museum and Library (NMML), New Delhi.

Instructions Issued by the Working Committee

Recent developments in the world situation have brought war near to India's frontiers. This may lead to internal dislocation in certain parts of the country and there is a possibility of some cities being subjected to aerial attack. Whatever dangers and difficulties might arise, the real antidotes to them is to remain cool and collected and on no account to give way to nervousness and excitement. All Congressmen must remain at their posts and continue their service of the people; wherever necessity arises they should yield places of safety to those in greater need and be ready to render aid to those who may require it.

The Congress can help and serve the people in the difficult times ahead only if its organization is strong and disciplined and Congressmen individually and Congress Committees are able to command confidence in their respective localities. Congress Committees and Congressmen should therefore address themselves immediately to the task of strengthening the organization and reviving and maintaining contacts with the people in the villages and towns. Every village should, as far as possible, receive the message of the Congress and be prepared to face such difficulties as might arise.

The constructive programme adopted by the Congress, and explained from time to time by Gandhiji, is of particular importance at this juncture. It is meant not only to bring about unity among various groups to remove disabilities which keep sections of the community backward and depressed. To promote self-reliance and the cooperative spirit among the people, to increase production and have fairer distribution, but it also furnishes the best opportunity and means of contacts with the people and service to them which are necessary for winning their confidence. The Working Committee, therefore, call upon Congress Committees and workers to further this programme intensively it and thus exercise a steadying and strengthening influence in times of dislocation and one uneasiness.

During such times there is always a possibility of trouble being created by unsocial elements in the country. To avoid the emergence of such a situation and to meet it when it arises. Such organizations should be formed on the basis of strict non-violence and it should always be remembered that the Congress adheres to this principle. These volunteers may cooperate with other organizations working for similar ends. This volunteer organization is meant for rendering service to the people both normally and in the event of possible internal commotion. It should therefore avoid conflict with the authorities.

Prices of commodities have already risen and are causing distress among the people and no adequate steps have so far been taken by the authorities to meet this situation. These tendencies are likely to get accentuated in the future, and dislocation of trade and transport, due to stress of war, may lead to scarcity of the necessaries of life as well as of many other things which are of everyday use. Big scale industries in other countries have suffered heavily on account of the war and transport of goods has become difficult on account of military requirements, China has largely overcome these difficulties by a wide-spread development of village industries. India may have to face similar problems, and village and cottage industries afford a solution, desirable in itself, and more particularly suited to the needs of the moment. Such industries can escape to a larger extent the effects of dislocation of trade and transport. It is therefore necessary that this item of the constructive programme should be widely taken up and worked with vigour and earnestness so that the countryside may be rendered, as far as possible, self-sufficient in regard to the necessaries of life. The Committee would especially recommend to the villager the growing of food crops at least to cover the needs of the village and appeal to the grain dealer not to hold up stores for profit but to release them for consumption at fair prices.

In cases of emergency, when instructions are issued to the public by the authorities for the preservation of life and property and the maintenance of public order, Congressmen should avoid conflict with the authorities. They should carry out such instructions, unless they are contrary to Congress directions.

82. War Conditions and the Congress: Report of War Conditions Sub-committee Submitted to the President, INC by Asaf Ali, 28 December 1941

File No. 1/1941–2, AICC Papers, NMML.

The President,
Indian National Congress,
Camp Bardoli.

Sir,

I have the honour to submit the report of the War Condition's Sub-Committee, which met this morning. The Sub-Committee considered the following draft resolution and discussed the extent and practicability of the outline of the tasks mentioned therein. They generally approved it; but there was (i) a feeling that owing to the existing strength and limited capacity of the Congress organization, the tasks enumerated in the draft resolution appeared to be too ambitious; and the organization should not hope to carry them out in their entirety. Further, while Dr P. Ghosh was of the opinion that in the event of actual air raids, the population of affected areas should strictly obey the instructions of the authorities, Sjt B.G. Desai was clearly of the opinion that dissociation from ARP measures accepted by the authorities would be extremely inadvisable.

It was recognized by the Sub-Committee that the outline of the task mentioned in the draft resolution was fairly comprehensive, and subject to amplification of the outline and issuing detailed instructions under each head later on, it should be the concern of a wall-knit, popular organization. But there was a general feeling that at almost every stage of the performance of these tasks, the question of cooperating with the authorities, local bodies, and even the police would arise. The Sub-Committee was divided about cooperation with the ARP and the police.

The draft resolution was intended (i) to point out the inefficiency and inadequacy of the measures adopted by Government (ii) to refer very briefly to the sense of helplessness, engendered by the Government among the people (iii) to emphasize the importance of banishing exaggerated fears and panic, and of doing courageously in a spirit of self-confidence, endurance, sincere effort and mutual cooperation between the people themselves and finally (iv) to enumerate some of the main tasks to which People's committees in rural and urban areas should address themselves, in times of emergency. The draft resolution runs as follows:

The outbreak of war in Malaya and the news of air raids in Burma appear to have intensified fears of air attacks on India and caused a wave of panic among the people of the country. The ARP and some other measures of Civil Defence taken by the Government instead of allaying seem to be aggravating them in certain places. In a country where an alien Government has commanded only submission and unquestioning obedience from the people and has sedulously cultivated among them for long years a sense of helpless dependence, suppressing their initiative and self-confidence, it is not surprising that the civil population should entertain exaggerated fears of impending disasters and dangers and yield to unwarranted nervousness. It is also natural that in cities which are threatened by air, sea or land attacks they should be seriously apprehensive of the inadequacy of measures of civil defence. The population of other towns, too, appear to regard the hurried and ill-conceived schemes of internal security, which lack popular support, wholly insufficient, and inefficient for the difficult times that lie ahead. It is also conceivable that in the event of an actual invasion by sea, air or land, essential municipal services such as water supply, street lighting, medical aid, conservancy and firefighting arrangements may break down, the supply of necessary commodities may be seriously dislocated, and the activities of anti-social elements may go beyond the control of the police authorities. It is also conceivable that in such and even other areas local disorders may supervene, or large scale evacuations, voluntary or compulsory, may lend themselves to the congestion of roads and railways and serious problem of means of transport and communication may aggravate confusion. Only independent popular Governments, and local bodies fully alive to their responsibilities could devise measures to meet all the requirements of such a situation; but under the existing circumstances the main burden of responsibility must inevitably rest almost entirely on the people themselves. The Congress, as the people's organization, therefore, regard it as its imperative duty to do all that lies in its power to offer its services to the people in the hours of their need. It is obvious that whatever the Congress can do under existing circumstances will be to assist the population of both the rural and urban areas, wherever it is possible, to organize themselves in a spirit of fortitude, self-confidence and self-help, without in any way coming into conflict with the Government. Congress Committees will collaborate with any other Peoples' organizations in the execution of this. In order to meet the situation people's Committees will have to be set up to undertake among others the following duties:

(i) Non-violently assisting all persons in need of protection against anti-social elements, through voluntary Peace and Order Organizations, which should enlist the active support of influential men of the localities concerned; (ii) Concerting measures with local bodies, wherever possible to make alternative arrangements for the continuance of essential services, as pointed out above, (iii) Concerting measures with local bodies wherever possible, or with the aid of influential persons of the localities concerned for rendering such assistance as may be required, by voluntary evacuees and in any case by children and women, infirm persons, and persons rendered destitute. The range of such assistance may cover anything from the supply of food, clothes and shelter to medical aid.

All this may appear a rather ambitious undertaking, but its fulfilment will depend entirely on the measure of support and cooperation by the people themselves.

Above all fear and lack of self-confidence should be regarded as the worst enemies in times of emergency and confusion. People instead of running away from danger and meeting it in exile, or thinking of individual safety and losing it for want of a common and concerted effort, should find it in self-organization and in courageously facing and overcoming dangers in a spirit of manly endurance in common with others. Needless to say that the Congress cannot associate itself actively with the measures organized by Government under existing circumstances, but instructions issued by the authorities should be obeyed.

I have the honour to be
Sir,

Your most obedient servant,
Asaf Ali

83. War Threat to India: Liberals on Defence

Amrita Bazar Patrika, 29 December 1941.

Madras, 28 December.

...The National Liberal Federation resumed sitting for the third day this afternoon Sir Bijoy Prasad Singh Roy, presiding.

Sir Chimanlal Setalvad moved the first resolution relating to the war which runs:

'The National Liberal Federation of India feels that the war of aggression started by Nazi Germany supported by Fascist Italy and Imperial Japan, has proved to be a great menace to freedom peace and tranquility in the world. The Federation is of the opinion that the forces of progress and justice in this conflict are represented by the Allied powers such as Great Britain, America, Soviet Russia and China.

The Federation feels that the present Far East war situation has brought India into the front line of the conflict and therefore appeals both to the Government and the people to view the situation realistically and mobiles the resources of the country in men and material to protect the lives of India's teeming millions from the imminent danger which threatens the country. At the same time it feels that the unity between the Government and the people required for the necessary effort will not be possible unless a new psychological atmosphere is created by a change in the policy of His Majesty's Government towards India, which is urgently called for'.

After the resolution moved by Sir Chimanlal Setalvad was seconded by Pandit Kunzru and supported by others it was unanimously carried.

Sir Chimanlal said that the country was passing through very anxious times. With the entry of Japan into the way, the danger had come to the very door of India. One never knew when any of our towns might be attacked or bombed by see or air. It seemed to him that the people had not yet awakened to the danger or to the seriousness of the situation. 'We are still quarreling amongst ourselves, debating this question and that Pakistan separate electorates and Indian in Burma, when Burmese are running away from Burma'. He felt that these equations should be put in cold storage for the time being and realizing the real danger and gravity of the situation India should take immediate measures such as they could to defend the country.

Sir Chimanlal proceeding referred to Mahatma Gandhi's attitude to the war and said: 'The virtual dictator of the great political party is preaching non-violence under any circumstances and has asked his countrymen to allow themselves to be slaughtered by the enemy if he should come to India and offer him no resistance'.

The speaker proceeding stated that he was not unmindful that Britain had behaved very badly towards India to the past. If Britain had fitted us for defence India would have to-day raised forces that would defend not only the commonwealth but Britain herself. He regretted that that had not been done.

In doing so we would not be obliging Britain not defending our own country since the war is at our doors. In order that war effort in India might be intensified and the people might get enthusiastic it was necessary for the Government to make a proper gesture and ensure to India by definite promises and acts that at the end of the war the position of India in the commonwealth would be that of perfect equality with every other dominions and Britain herself.

Pandit Kunzru seconding the war resolution referred to the developments in the Far-East the utter helplessness of Malaya from the point of view of defence the bombing of Rangoon and said the question was now being asked in this country as to what would be the fate of India in the near future in the circumstances he thought they must do the utmost for the maintenance of the security of their country and protection of the lives of their people.

Mr K. Balasubramania Aiyer supported the resolution. He said that 'Great Britain had not succeeded in creating the proper atmosphere in India. The August offer still remained August'. Indians wanted to realize their manhood and fight for their country at the same time. They must be made to feel that to fighting in this war they were fighting to demand their own homes.

Mr P.N. Sapru said that while they abhorred Nazism, loathed Fascism and looked upon Imperial Japan as no better, in some respects even worse than the other two, it was necessary for them to make it clear that this ideological support and sympathy which India was prepared to offer to Britain wholeheartedly, and fully without any mental reservation, would not fructify unless Britain did the right thing by India.

Britain had not made an unequivocal declaration about the future and was not prepared to take steps immediately to nationalize the Government as an interim measure. How could people feel enthused about preserving the status quo?

...On resumption after tea, Pandit H.N. Kunzru moved the following resolution on defence:

'The National Liberal Federation reiterating its demand for a radical change in the defence policy of the Government feels that the war has shown that for making adequate preparations for the security of India, it is essential that (1) the defence portfolio should be entrusted to an Indian who commands the confidence of the people and (2) the defence forces of India should be organized on a national basis. It recognizes that it has been made with regard to the manufacture of war materials but is thoroughly dissatisfied with the policy in other respects. It urges in particular (a) that the policy of Indianization in all grades of the army, navy and air force should be implemented: (b) that the classification of people as martial and non-martial should be given up and people must be recruited from all classes to a greater extent than now'.

Dr R.P. Paranjape seconded the resolution. He said that in England there were civilian war ministers. A civilian could bring into the administration a wider outlook. This was why in this resolution they emphasized they need for the appointment of a member in charge of defence, who could voice public opinion.

The resolution was then put to vote and declared carried.

C. Responses to Changes in War Situation

84. Mahatma Gandhi's Letter to Carl Heath[1] [Extract]

CWMG, Vol. LXXIII, pp. 296–7.

Sevagram, Wardha
25 January 1941

...The Congress is as much anti-Nazism as anti-imperialism. If the Government had not thoughtlessly forbidden the anti-war activity of the Congress and had not proclaimed it as pro-Nazi, they could easily have claimed the whole of India as anti-Nazi—both that part which followed the Congress non-violence and the other which believed in the use of violence. Had it not done so, much bitterness would have been avoided and the world would have profited by the lesson of tolerance and its moral opinion would have been on the side of Britain. It is never too late to mend one's error....

Yours sincerely,
M.K. Gandhi

Friend Carl Heath
White Wings Manor Way
Guildford, Surrey

---

[1] Carl Heath, a Quaker, was Chairman of the Indian Conciliation Group.

85. Shadow of War Spreading Towards India: Country Must get Ready to Defend Herself, M.N. Roy

Bombay Chronicle, 9 May 1941.

Dehradun, 7 May. 'Engrossed in the discussion of Mr Amery's speech, Indian political leaders have taken no notice of the positively alarming pronouncement about the war situation, made by the Prime Minister' observes Mr M.N. Roy in the course of a statement to the Press.

Continuing Mr Roy says that assuming that Hitler will not be able to win the battle of the Atlantic, the mastery of Europe and of a large part of Asia and possibly of Africa, as anticipated by the Prime Minister, will increase his strength so tremendously that fascist world domination will be a reality.

There is nothing unexpected in the present military situation. Having established their domination practically on the whole of Europe and failed to subdue Britain, the Nazis were bound to strike eastwards through the Balkans, in order to avoid the risk of an indefinitely prolonged war.

'The east', Mr Roy proceeds, 'will not be easily thrown to the Wolves. Bits of news trickling through recently show that the Russians are at least getting ready for the day of reckoning.

The strategy of the Nazi drive eastwards implies in eventual attack upon the Soviet Union.

Mr Churchill has himself referred to that possibility more than once.

Knowing fully well that the Soviet Union alone can check their advance eastwards, if not on the Bosphorus, then in Iraq or Iran, the Nazis will certainly try to head that off by attacking the Soviet Union from the west.

The Soviet Government seems to anticipate that it signed the neutrality Pact with Japan in order to relieve some of the troops in Siberia for action on the Western front. There have been considerable troop movements from the east to the west since the pact was signed.

Get Ready to Defend India

'Finally, there remains India irrespective of the short sightedness of the British Government, she must get ready to defend herself. Her future now depends upon those who would neither sit idle by throwing the responsibility on the British rulers, nor welcome the fascist invaders, if only to spite the old masters.

And what about the Englishmen in India? Are they any more prepared to be thrown to the wolves? It is time for them to realize that India can supply millions of soldiers, not only to defend herself, but also to face the fascist invaders in the Middle East.

The problem of equipping and supplying a large Indian army can be solved by promoting the industrialization of the country.

The reluctance to draw upon India's manpower and develop the Indian source of supply has made the eastern front so vulnerable and laid the peoples of Asia open to fascist attack.

Now Englishmen in India should consider themselves as belonging to this country and throw of the reluctance which has prevented the full development of the defensive and striking power of India.'

86. All-India Women's Conference's Reply to British Women's Appeal,[1] 21 June 1941

CWMG, Vol. LXXIV, pp. 114–16.

Sevagram
15 June 1941

Dear Sisters,

We have very carefully studied your message addressed to India's women. We write this in our individual capacity, as also that of representative members of the AIWC which, as you know, is an organization of fifteen years' standing. We mention this to show that what we state here is not only our deep personal conviction, but also, as far as we can judge, the conviction of a large body of India's women.

It is scarcely necessary to tell you that we appreciate the sincerity of your appeal. But we are amazed at the ignorance betrayed in it of the realities. Indeed your Prime Minister by contrast shows a grasp of realities which is refreshing, however painful it may be. He has no misgivings about the status that India occupies in the British mind. It is a dependency which can and is being utilized at the British will. He knows that he does not need the consent or co-operation of India's thinking sons and daughters in anything that Britain wants for fighting her war. He takes care to pay tribute to the valour of the Indian soldiers who are part of the army of occupation in India. These soldiers you should know are wholly unconnected with the national life and activities. They may not freely see any nationalist without incurring heavy penalties, nor has your Prime Minister any difficulty in raising either by taxation or so-called voluntary contributions the money he wants. We cannot complain of this helplessness but we must not be blind to the facts. How can there be the association, in such a situation, of the India that is impatient of the foreign yoke with the forcible aid we have adverted to?

The fact is that you are wholly wrong in your estimate of things. We are surprised at your quoting the untruth contained in President Roosevelt's pronouncement. You quote: 'Today the whole world is divided between human slavery and human freedom.' The fact is that there is no such thing as human freedom for Asiatic races, certainly not for India, nor is there for the virile Africans. The result, whatever it may be, of the war will not alter their condition for the better, save through their own efforts. As we see the reality, it is this. It is a war between the British Empire and Nazis and Fascists for world domination, meaning in effect exploitation of the non-European races.

We cannot be in love with Nazism and Fascism. But we may not be expected to be in love with British Imperialism.

Now perhaps you will understand why we as women are against all war. Women's part is just now to stand up for truth and non-violence as against the untruth and violence which surround us. We admire the self-sacrifice of the British women of which you write with just pride. Here we wish you could have taken a braver and prouder part by telling your men to wash their hands clean of human blood. You might not have succeeded all at once. But you would have led the way to the establishment of permanent peace. We take leave to doubt the wisdom of women aping men in the black art of human slaughter on a scale hitherto unknown.

Lastly, let us point out the anomaly of British women asking India, though a slave nation, to help the slave-owner in distress instead of asking the slave-owner to undo the wrong and cure himself of the initial sin and thus ensure the moral justness of his position.

This presentation of the picture may appear unpleasant to you but it is none the less sincere. And we could not answer your sincerity except by being equally sincere.

---

[1] The statement was signed by Sarojini Naidu, Rameshwari Nehru, Vijayalakshmi Pandit, Amrit Kaur, Rani Lakshmibai Rajwade, Ammu Swaminathan and Radha Subbarayan. It had been drafted by Mahatma Gandhi.

87. Jawaharlal Nehru's Reaction to German Invasion of USSR,[1] Note Dated '23 June, Monday' in his Prison Diary [Extract]

SWJN, Vol. 11, pp. 636–8.

...So Germany and Russia are at war! In spite of some previous preparation for this development, it came as a thundering surprise. Somehow I expected war between the two some time or other—but much later. For Hitler to attack Russia at this stage and without any real or ostensible reason is extraordinary—What will happen, it is rash to guess—Probably early German victories, even big victories—But this seems to sound the death knell of the Nazi regime some time or other.

News of this invasion came last evening when I was busy copying out my letter to Miss Rathbone[2]. Suddenly I felt how futile that letter was after this development. Yet I decided to leave it as it was and rush it off before anything else happened which made it completely out of date.

---

[1] Germany invaded USSR on 22 June 1941.

[2] Eleanor Rathbone was a Member of British Parliament. Jawaharlal Nehru had written a long reply to her letter.

88. War Policy of Congress: Mr M.N. Roy's Criticism

Amrita Bazar Patrika, 1 July 1941.

Dehra Dun, 30 June. 'Is it not more honourable to be in company of a Churchill, who is fighting Fascism, in alliance with the Soviet Union, than to follow the pseudo-anti-Imperialists, who would still continue the policy of extending moral support to Fascism, even though condemning it verbally?', enquires Mr M.N. Roy of the rank and file Congressmen in an appeal issued to the latter.

Referring to the invasion of Russia by Germany, Mr Roy says that the fighters for Indian freedom can no longer remain indifferent to the outcome of this struggle, much less oppose India's participation in it, holding that this is an Imperialist war. It was a wrong view, now the march of events has proved that it was wrong.

Mr Roy criticizes the Congress policy with regard to the war and remarks that it is based on a wrong view and it has generally failed to achieve anything. He warns the masses not to support this policy nor share the attitude of the Congress as to the organization of war efforts, even when the Fascist war machine is fiercely hurling itself against the workers' and peasants' republics. It is not only the Soviet Union which is in danger, he continues, if the fascist hordes succeed, even partially, in their latest adventure, the danger of India coming within the range of their greedy tentacles will be greater than ever. 'If they can establish themselves even on the northern shores of the Black Sea and reach the Caucasus from there they will surely sweep through Persia and appear at the gates of India.'

'Now that the British Government is standing shoulder to shoulder by Soviet Government in the fierce fight against the common enemy, you can not refuse to co-operate with the former and yet be seriously concerned with the defence of the latter. The British Government has pledged all support to the Soviet Government. How can you still non-co-operate with the war efforts of the British Government if you wish to help the defence of the workers' and peasants' republic and thereby creating the guarantee against the eventful Fascist invasion of India?'

After pointing to the failure of the satyagraha movement in developing into a mass struggle, Mr Roy observes that however condemnable may be the attitude of the Government, and however justifiable the Congress demand, the fact remains that practically all classes of the Indian people have been all along co-operating with the war efforts of the Government, not because all of them want to do so, but they were being benefited therefrom, more or less, directly or indirectly. That being the case, he maintains, the masses cannot be mobilized in a movement for resisting India's participation in the war, even if such a movement was desirable.

Mr Roy urges the rank and file Congressmen to dissociate themselves with the policy of the Congress regarding the war and join the Radical Democratic Party whose war policy is only a logical consequence of its programme which is more comprehensive and far-reaching.

89. Communist Party's View: Aid Soviet Union by Intensifying Our Own Struggle

Communist, Vol. III, No. 5, July 1941, P.C. Joshi Archives on Contemporary History, JNU.

(i) A National War

The war which the Soviet Union and the Soviet people are waging today is a national war—a just war, a war against enslavement by fascist armies, a war to defend what the Soviets have built during the last 24 years with their blood and sweat. The National War of the Soviet people must be supported by our National movement just as we support China's war against Japanese aggression. Not new negotiations for compromise, but a nationwide mass campaign for the support of the Soviet Union run as a part of our own struggle for freedom is what the hour demands. The aid that Soviet people want from us is not tanks and aeroplanes, not even medical missions, which we cannot give in our present state. What they need is the moral support of our great national movement for freedom. That we must and can give in the form of launching mass campaign for the demonstration of our support to the Soviet. It will only add to the stature and the striking power of our own struggle for freedom. In order to aid the Soviet Union, we have to line up in the 'united front of peoples standing for freedom against enslavement'. How else can we aid it except by intensifying our own struggle for freedom?

(ii) Help the Soviet! By Fighting Harder!

MAD HITLER by attacking the mighty Soviet has signed his own doom. It is the last desperate gamble of a crazy criminal, drunk with his successes, terrorized by his own future. Country after country, weakened by the treachery and cowardice of its own capitalist rulers, fell to him as easy prey. Whole Europe was at his feet yet the mastery of the world had not been snatched from the Anglo-American rival, while the Soviet giant was growing stronger in the rear. Whether he won or lost the final battle for the suzerainty of the world he saw that the last word would be Stalin's and not his, for the post-war world meant not only defeat for one and victory for another but post-war revolutions in which the people, disillusioned and bitter, plunge headlong to take their fate in their own hands. If the Soviet remained at peace it grew stronger, ready to step in and help the peoples to win their revolutions. It is to scotch this nightmare of world revolution that the fascist leader struck treacherously at Red Revolutionary Soviet Raj. In only two weeks of war, the Red Army has made Hitler lose more than what he lost in 22 months of war with his capitalist rivals. This is how a free people fight, that was how the oppressive capitalists fought.

FOR us the situation grows grimmer. The Soviet–German War has meant a respite for our British masters and they are busy perfecting their plans to hold India in eternal bondage. They have despatched their best General Wavell to be the Commander-in-Chief here, to ensure that India remains British even if Hitler bursts into Caucasus or if the Reds after all win India is kept off the revolutionary wave. It is not the military measures alone that are being taken. The imperialist barrage is primarily political. It seeks to sow confusion in the national ranks and aims at capitalizing the undoubted sympathy of the Indian people towards the Soviet by trying to palm off Britain's own war also being anti-fascist! *London Times* sanctimoniously preaches that the spread of war to Russia 'has given an air of unreality to the political controversy....the freedom that the Indians have to demand more freedom in the best proof that exists of the fundamental difference between the British and Nazi way of life'. When the chief organ of a ruling class is capable of no more intelligence than this, and expects a great and civilized people to believe a yarn like this even after 200 years of slavery it is the most damning evidence of its own of wits.

THIS insolent imperialist policy would have acted the traditional spark to fan our peoples' flaming urge for freedom if the situation within the national front had been worthy of a fighting front with a leadership alive to every new opportunity, ranks always alert and all stood united together. Two weeks are gone by, the holy Mahatma has not a word to say for the Soviet and against Hitler. It took him far less time to rush to Linlithgow and shed tears for the Westminster Abbey. Such is his horror of peoples' revolution, which the Soviet Union undoubtedly embodies, and he is our national leader!

THE acting General Secretary of the Congress Socialist Party thinks that what the occasion demands is not the condemnation of fascist aggression nor the expression of solidarity with the First Socialist State, but above all a venomous attack against the Communists. This gentleman's 'Socialism' knows no shame. It is hardly necessary to criticize the Royists—the professional unlevied (so far) drum beaters of imperialism. They are knocking their heads off for joining ministries at the Centre and the provinces.

THE bourgeois leadership and their lackeys, faithful or renegade, remain blind to the course of events in the most fateful period of the war, they long to catch Churchill's eye and remain vicious towards their own people. They cut a contemplate figure but no serious Indian can afford a laugh for they are dragging the name of our nation through the mire.

THE whole world is now engulfed in the Second World War, every great power has been drawn into it. Comrade Stalin in his historic broadcast has vividly defined the character of the Soviet–German war and its relation to the world war. It has two sectors, apart and yet one, Soviet–German war is a just war, a peoples' war, for the defence of the Socialist Fatherland and for the freedom of the peoples, whose forces are rising within every belligerent country and who will have the final say when the war ends if not before it. British–German war is an unjust war, an imperialist war for the domination of the world by one of the rival oppressive capitalist gangs. Soviet-land is in danger, the whole world is in the melting pot. Never before in history was so much at stake. Never before was the fate of entire humanity so hung together.

THE national war of the Indian people would immediately tip the balance in favour of the peoples' movement the world over and be the biggest aid we can give the Soviet Union, we would be doing our share in pasting the noose round Hitler's neck, we would be helping the British people and colonial slaves of all the continents to blow up British Imperialism, we would be aiding the Soviet by ourselves struggling to realize what the Soviet peoples have already won and are defending to-day with such super-human heroism. The Chinese are already fighting their anti-imperialist battle, India's war against British Imperialism would mean a whole continent, Asia—ancient, vast and civilized—going out of the imperialist strangle-hold!

IF Hitler wins, the world goes back to medieval barbarity made unimaginably more gruesome by being embedded on the worst features of capitalist exploitation Hitler-ridden Europe has witnessed only the birth of this 'new order'.

IF the British win it is not difficult for us Indians to imagine what will happen to the world—every country would be reduced to the same plight as ourselves.

INSTINCTIVELY the peoples of the world realize what is at stake. Dimly they are figuring out the future. The sympathies of all go to the Soviet as the hope of humanity, for they know here is a real Peoples' State with a Socialist society, and the mightiest army which swears allegiance to the interests of the toiling masses of the whole world. Every thinking man in every country realize that the victory of the Soviet alone will be a peoples' victory, it alone will ensure a peoples' peace and establish a real new world order, which will be worth singing about by a liberated humanity.

SOVIET-LAND is the workers' Fatherland. Indian workers have stuck the first blows against the Second Imperialist War, that sent a thrill round the working class of the world. British imperialist terror has looked up their leaders, but the Indian workers' own Party, the Communist Party, holds the banner aloft. It is the only Party in our land to-day which has a truly national policy, which stands four-square against imperialism while all others seek to enter the imperialist parlour looking for Swaraj. Our Party is the only International Party in our country, part of the Communist International, whole units exist in every land and are heroically fighting their imperialist rulers against all odds, despite calumny, despite terror, and whose chief unit the Communist Party of the Soviet Union leads one-sixth of the Socialist world and whose Red Army has mauled Hitler as his capitalist peers could not, and which is engaged in mortal combat supremely confident of victory. Communists of the world, led by the great Stalin, are enacting an epic with their own arms, at a period in world history when capitalism is dying, Socialism is coming, destroying the decayed, old, ushering in a living new society. Immense responsibility rests on the Indian workers and their Party, we have to see that our nation plays its destined role worthily. We alone can do it, no one else will.

WE must reach out to every national fighter and the people as a whole.

Organize meetings and demonstrations to denounce fascist aggression against the Soviet Union throughout the country.

Get every meeting, every popular organization to send messages of solidarity to the Soviet people, to Soviet Trade Unions through the Soviet Ambassador in London.

Intensify agitation and propaganda about the achievements of the Soviet Union in every walk of life.

Raise a peoples' Soviet Aid Fund, one pice per contributor, as a concrete expression of our sympathy and solidarity. Let Trade Unions and Kisan Sabhas take the initiative in launching the Fund. Send the proceeds to the Soviet Ambassador in London with a message of solidarity.

SUCH a wide-spread country-wide campaign would be the beginning of realization by us that we have entered a new historic period and are strong and determined enough to unleash a mass movement that will CONVERT THIS IMPERIALIST WAR INTO A REVOLUTIONARY WAR.

90. Subhas Bose's Views on the Russia–German War

(i) Report of a German Foreign Office Official to the German Government on his Conversation with Subhas Bose, 17 July 1941

Sisir Kumar Bose and Sugata Bose (eds), *Netaji Collected Works, Vol. II: Azad Hind, Writings and Speeches, 1941–3,* Calcutta, 2002, pp. 60–2.

Mr Bose[1] came to meet me today after his return.

I first informed him about the tasks assigned to the Secretary of State Keppler. After his visit with me, Mr Bose called on Mr Keppler.

Bose at first spoke at length about the reactions of the Russo–German War on public opinion in India. The Soviet Union had been popular in India, especially among the intellectuals from whom the leaders are drawn. It is believed in India that the Soviet Union is an anti-imperialist power and would therefore be India's ally against England. The Russo–German Pact of 1939 was an event of the highest significance for India. It made it possible for the intellectuals, who anyway were drawn to National Socialism, to look upon Germany and Italy as forces which would bring about the end of British rule in India in friendship with the Soviet Union, although British propaganda had succeeded in keeping alive sentiments of enmity towards the Axis powers in most parts of India. In the German–Russian War, the sympathies of the Indian people were very clearly with Russia because the Indian people felt definitely that Germany was the aggressor and was for India, and without complete German victory over Russia, it would be difficult to change public opinion in India in this respect.

At the same time Bose expects—as is confirmed by reports received from London—that England is now going to introduce reforms in India, which will encourage that section of the Indian public that is always in favour of compromise, to continue to stake their cards on the English; simultaneously the threat of a German attack on India will be presented to the public not as one intended to liberate the Indian people but to substitute British rule by German rule.

Bose expects that India will become, more than before, a centre of British military expansion. He considers it very probable that England will proceed, not across Afghanistan, but via Iran in order, first, to take possession of the oilfields and then, to get close to the Soviet Union in the region of the Caucasus.

It was clear from his statements that Bose is, being far from Berlin, strongly influenced by the Soviet thesis on the question of the origin of the German–Russian conflict; it will therefore be one of our first tasks to put him right in this respect.

I told Bose that we remain firm in our intention regarding a proclamation for a free India; we have of course to choose a suitable time for it.

Here Mr Bose became very emphatic and asked that the Reich Foreign Minister be requested to issue this proclamation as speedily as possible. Each day that passed meant an advantage to England because of the reforms that the intended to introduce in India. On the other hand, he saw no reason to postpone this proclamation. He however agreed that the date had to be fixed with due consideration of the entire situation.

During this short interview I went thoroughly into the other current questions, especially the proposed Free India Centre. It was however obvious that these questions were of minor interest to Bose as long as he was not sure about the declaration on a Free India.

I request attention to the report of the German Embassy in Rome dated 13th July and the reports of the Italian Foreign Office concerning Bose's discussions in Rome. I consider the proposal No. 4 where it is suggested that Bose be kept in a neutral country in reserve until a more convenient time in future, to be inadvisable.

Submitted to the Reich Foreign Minister.

Suggestions for further discussion regarding relevant questions are being prepared by the Secretary of State Keppler and me.

Woermann

---

[1] Subhas Bose was in Rome when Germany invaded USSR. This conversation took place on his return to Berlin.

(ii) Subhas Bose's Letter to von Ribbentrop, German Foreign Minister, 15 August 1941

Sisir Kumar Bose and Sugata Bose (eds), *Netaji Collected Works, Vol. II: Azad Hind, Writings and Speeches, 1941–3,* Calcutta, 2002, pp. 63–5.

Your Excellency,

I feel constrained to take the liberty of addressing Your Excellency because the situation in India today is extremely serious.

I have been here since the beginning of April and my proposals were placed before Your Excellency soon after arrival.

The situation in my country was then exceedingly favourable for the success of my proposals. Unfortunately, no decision was arrived at by the German Government and since then, the situation in India has worsened considerably.

The outbreak of the war with Soviet Russia has been made to appear to India as an act of aggression and Soviet–British–American propaganda has made the fullest use of it. Day after day, the Soviet–British–American propaganda machine has been telling the Indian people that Germany is out for world-domination and, in particular, for the domination of the Orient. I am alarmed to see how effective this propaganda is gradually proving to be.

Even prominent people who have spent their whole life in fighting England and have been in prison for long years, are being increasingly influenced by this propaganda and are thinking that if there is no hope of obtaining India's freedom through the help of the Axis, it is better to make peace with Britain on the best terms available. If this process is not arrested the time will soon come when the majority of the Indian people will definitely take their stand on the Soviet–Britian–American side. We cannot hope to bring India over to the side of the Axis, if the Axis Powers do not first declare their policy regarding India.

India is being prepared as the central military base of the British Empire. An army of one million men is being raised in India which will be fully equipped by modern war industries newly established there. If this plan succeeds, we have no doubt that even after the German occupation of England, the British Empire will carry on the war, using India as the base.

America is now playing an increasing role in the internal politics of Oriental countries for example, of China, where she has brought about an agreement between Chiang-Kai-Shek and the Chinese Communist Party. With a new American Minister and an American Military Attaché in India, America will also have a role in the internal politics of India. And if America succeed in bringing about a similar compromise between Gandhi and the British Government, the position of the party standing for Independence and Revolution will be greatly weakened.

There is still time to save the situation in India, but if there is further delay in issuing the declaration regarding Indian Independence, I am afraid it will become extremely difficult for us to win over the Indian people to the side of the Axis. Once the majority of the Indian people go over definitely to the Soviet–British–American side, the declaration will no longer have any value for India.

Further, if there is no declaration regarding Indian Independence, the nearer the German armies move towards India, the more hostile will the Indian people become towards Germany. *The march of the German troops towards the East will be regarded as the approach not of a friend, but of an enemy.*

If, therefore, the declaration is to come at all, it should come before the German armies are moving further eastwards.

The new Anglo–Soviet guarantee to Turkey indicates that the British attack on Iran is imminent. The road to Afghanistan which has been open all these months will be out after the British occupy Iran and it will then be difficult for us to work out our plans regarding India. With Iran under British occupation, there will be one solid bloc under British control, stretching from the Mediterranean to Burma. The work in the Tribal Territory and in India will then be much more difficult than before.

The joint announcement made by President Roosevelt and Prime Minister Churchill regarding their programme of post-war reconstruction has been interpreted by the London radio to mean that India will get her freedom after the war. America has also decided to negotiate directly with the Dominions on outstanding problems of common interest, independently of Britain. All these facts further confirm the view that America will in future, intervene in the internal affairs of the British Empire and in consequence thereof a compromise between Gandhi and the British Government appears highly probable in the near future.

I fully realize the complexity of your problem and I certainly cannot expect your Excellency to do anything for India which may be considered prejudicial to your national interest. But India stands today at one of the crossroads of her history and the situation there is deteriorating day to day. If therefore we are to be effective in our work for India, we must act at once. I would, therefore, beg your Excellency not to leave us in suspense any longer but to come to an early decision, whatever that decision may be.

Thanking your Excellency,

Yours respectfully,
Subhas Chandra Bose

91. Jayaprakash Narayan on the New War Situation, Before 31 July 1941

Bimal Prasad (ed.), *Jayaprakash Narayan Selected Works,* Vol. 3 (1939–46), 2003, pp. 97–9.

[The notes reproduced below were part of what are known as Deoli Papers which were seized from Jayaprakash Narayan's wife Prabhavati during her meeting with her husband in Deoli Camp on 31 July 1941. These papers had been handed over by Jayaprakash Narayan to his wife to be smuggled out of the Camp.]

Regarding our Policy Concerning the War (Old Report)

The invasion of Russia by Nazi Germany has introduced a very complicating factor into the present war. Now, both Britain and Russia will be fighting against Germany, their common enemy. Does this mean that our attitude towards this war should be changed? Let us examine this question a little closely.

Till the invasion of Russia, we had looked upon the war as an imperialist war. Among other things, we knew that Britain was fighting in order that it might continue to rule over and exploit India. Clearly, it was none of our duty to help in any manner in the perpetuation of our slavery. We were, therefore, opposed to the war and were endeavouring to utilize it to attain our own freedom.

The recent action of Germany against Russia has in no way modified this position. The interests of Britain in fighting this war are still the same imperialist interests. If Russia and Britain are facing a common enemy it does not mean that their interests are the same. Britain cannot in the very nature of things cooperate with Russia in prosecuting the war to identical ends. It cannot be foretold when Britain, in order to protect its interests, would retire from the fight, leaving Russia alone to continue it. It is quite likely that Russia, in order to gain time and save what it can, agrees to settle with Germany. In any case, if Russia desires to destroy Nazism, it must in the end depend upon its own resources and strength.

It should follow from the foregoing that to help Britain in the war is not the same as to help Russia. Help to Britain would only strengthen British imperialism, which would doubtless use this strength to further its own interests. In fact, this added strength might become a factor in enabling Britain in reaching an independent settlement with Germany, and betraying Russia.

Therefore, the invasion of Russia cannot, in the least, affect our attitude towards Britain's war. Our opposition to it must continue, and likewise also our strength against British Imperialism.

The danger which Russia faces, however, is a question which as socialists it is our duty to seriously consider. With all its faults Soviet Russia is a giant fortress of world socialism and of the world proletariat. We cannot sit quiet when this fortress is under assault. But we shall not bring succour to it if we rushed to the aid of British imperialist forces. On the contrary, it would be a mistake to relax our attack on imperialism. To continue this attack as relentlessly as possible would itself be a service to Soviet Russia. But, the question remains, can we do anything to render direct aid to the Soviets, without helping in any manner British war efforts. The British Government have already announced that they are united with Russia in their common aim of destroying Hitlerism, and have offered all help to the Soviets. This opens up an opportunity for us to offer direct help to Russia, and, also incidentally, of putting British professions to test. Let us, accordingly, put it to the British Government that we are anxious to help Russia with men, money and materials, and that we desire to be given the opportunity to organize this help. We should further put it to them that if they are sincere about aid to Russia, our offer gives them an excellent opportunity to vindicate it. In making our offer, it should be made clear to them that our opposition to their own war would continue unabated, as would our struggle against their domination over India. The men that we would recruit and the resources that we would collect must be sent directly to the Russian front, to be used and commanded by the Russian forces.

If the British Government were to reject this offer, they would further expose their selfish imperial interests in this war and their insincerity towards Russia. This would help workers in Britain and the USA, and other countries to determine their attitude towards the present British Government, and exert pressure on it to adjust its war policies to the interests of the people of Britain and other peoples threatened by Nazism.

New Report, Note

The above was written when Prabhavati came here last time. Since then the situation outside has become clarified. Purushottam's statement was on correct lines, though a difference should have been drawn between the Anglo–German war and the Russo–German war. As far as Britain is concerned, the character of the war has not changed; but Russia is not fighting an imperialist war (That is why sympathy with Russia was expressed in your statement).

I suggest strongly that you should call a meeting of the Executive which should issue a statement on the war. The only purpose in this would be to associate all the provincial parties with the statement. It appears that we are not following the same policy everywhere.

I do not think that it is advisable now to talk of sending volunteers, and others, to Russia. At least, we should not appeal to the British Government in that behalf.

Our attitude should be that we sympathize fully with Russia but are helpless to do anything about it. At the same time our opposition to Britain's war and our national struggle continues and all our class movements.

I have written above somewhere that the present is a good time to carry on an ideological war against the CPI and the CI[1] I suggest that two small pamphlets should immediately be brought out, entitled the CPI and the War and the CI and the War in which the twists and turns of communist policy should be fully exposed. The CPI pamphlet should not be restricted to CPI policy regarding the war, but should also deal with their general political policy in India. Both should be effectively written. All the past documents of the CPI and the CI should be collected for this purpose. [I understand there was a special issue of the Communist, 4th issue (1940) most probably, which published the CI's policies regarding war. It was a special International issue. This might be of some use. Molotov's and Stalin's speeches also may be of use].

We are anxious to know what the policy of the CPI today is. The fellows here continue to talk of intensifying the national struggle, though at the same time they maintain that the character of the war now is anti-Fascist! From your statement it appeared that the CPGB[2] had changed its policy and the CPI, if there is one, [is deliberating] on their new war policy. Send us other news about them. It would help us in our work here.

What about the Cawnpore strike? Was it our show? What has been its result? Good or bad for us?

Send us all such material that may help me in recruitment here. Send illegal matter in the manner I have suggested. Send a copy of 'Betrayal of the Left'.

---

[1] Communist International.

[2] Communist Party of Great Britain.

92. 'Soviet Day' in Bengal, 28 July 1941

Communist, Vol. III, No. 6, August 1941, P.C. Joshi Archives on Contemporary History, JNU.

THE incredible degree of popularity which the Soviet Union enjoys among all classes of the people of Bengal was an unknown fact till the 'Soviet Day' which was observed on 21st July last in response to the call of the Central Kisan Council followed by the Students' Federation and other political organizations and parties. When in accordance with a recent decision of the Council an appeal was issued through the Press to the kisans and all other people interested in the Soviet Union and her victory against the Nazi aggressor, one scarcely expected that in the face of the prevailing restrictions the 'Day' would be observed with any appreciable amount of success.

But the announcement was quickly welcomed from all quarters, even by people who would never before stand the name of the Soviet being uttered in their presence. Eminent non-political intellectuals openly supported the Soviet because of its wonderful cultural achievements.

An incomparably greater appreciation of the Soviet was evinced by other people. Theirs was not merely a cultural appreciation; it was far more vital. They were stirred by the name of the Soviet and all that it implies, by the expectation for themselves of the new life that has been brought to each and every citizen of the Socialist fatherland, and hence by their irresistible desire to save the Soviet from the barbarous attack of the Fascist hordes.

The Kisan Committees and the Students' federation mainly organized the meetings and processions of the day in which thousands of kisans and students participated. The response made by workers and other people was equally encouraging. The fervour and enthusiasm which was noticed in Calcutta was no less visible in the remote village where the pessimistic and lukewarm middle class made it a common cause with the zealous youth and the famished and illiterate peasant. For to them all the only sources of ray of hope to-day is the Soviet.

In Calcutta a huge public meeting, called by a number of representative individuals, was held in the Town Hall. All classes of the people including thousands of workers and students, forming into processions and shouting revolutionary slogans, joined the meeting. There were three big festoons, three cartoons of Hitler, portraits of Stalin and Budenny, and about three hundred demonstrative posters bearing suitable slogans in one big procession of workers.

It is true that in Calcutta as well as everywhere else the Communist Party Comrades took the initiative but every thing had a non-Party look; nowhere a party-brand was the cause of any discrimination while all parties participated. It was purely a popular demonstration of sympathy and support for the Soviet. According to a decision of the Calcutta Town Hall meeting a non-Party organization called the 'Friends of Soviet Union' has already been brought into existence whose purpose will be to popularize the principles and activities of the Soviet.

Apart from this big meeting innumerable smaller meetings were held in colleges, schools, factories, and elsewhere, both Calcutta and outside—in towns and villages. Processions consisting of hundreds of peasants, workers, students and others; walking to meetings with the Red Flag and impressive festoons and shouting slogans of 'Soviet Union Zindabad', 'Inqilab Zindabad', 'Legalize the Communist Party', 'Release the Political Prisoners' and others, almost invariably constituted a feature of the day's demonstration. If the 'Day' gave us a clear indication of the immense popularity of the Soviet in this country, it served to increase that popularity also by a large measure—an unmistakable achievement in the cause of the Soviet.

Another important achievement of the 'Day' is the realization by many of our comrades of the revolutionary attitude of our downtrodden people. Oppressed, illiterate and superstitious, they have often been considered as having lost all sensitiveness to an outlook on better life. The 'Soviet Day' has belied such a notion. They are quite responsive to any appeal which they can believe is genuinely in their interest and points to an improved lot for them. It is not our people who are lacking in revolutionary potentiality. It is for our Party, in which the people are increasingly putting their faith, to prepare them for the coming revolution. The situation and the task can no more be mistaken after 21st July.

A cable message assuring support and goodwill to Soviet was sent to Maisky[1] by AIKS Secretary.

---

[1] Soviet Ambassador to Britain.

93. Intellectuals for the Soviet!

Communist, Vol. III, No. 6, August 1941, P.C. Joshi Archives on Contemporary History, JNU.

The following manifesto, signed by a large number of intellectuals of Bengal, headed by Acharya Prafulla Chandra Ray, has been issued calling for India's sympathy with Soviet Russia at this critical juncture.

The Nazi attack on the Soviet Union has opened a new and momentous phase in world history. The war of machines and of men rages to-day on a colossal front on a scale unheard-of before.

At this hour of trial we feel it is urgent that attention is drawn to the massive moral and material achievement which the Soviets have to their credit. Some of us have been critical of aspects of the Soviet regime; some, again, do not support the theory of Marxism which the Soviets have attempted to put into practice. But when one remembers the dark legacy of Czarist misrule, which was followed for years by a disastrous Civil War and the intervention against the infant Soviets by nearly all the Powers on earth, the Soviet achievement can only be described as magnificent.

Rabindranath Tagore has testified to it in glowing terms, and since the two leading sociological investigators in the world to-day—Sidney and Beatrice Webb—brought out their book on 'Soviet Communism—a new civilization,' information in regard to the USSR has been both reliable and abundant.

Complete Equality

In the Soviet Union, all factories, mines, railways and shipping, land and trading organizations are the property of the people as a whole. The economic and social life of the country is planned for the welfare of all and not for the profit of the few. The drama of Soviet planning cannot fail to grip even those who do not hold with socialist hypotheses. Complete equality of all citizens, irrespective of race or sex or nationality, enables them to participate in the business of the community.

Equal opportunity for education is provided universally, the school-leaving age is raised to seventeen, and payment is made to students at universities. Work is provided for all unemployment does not exist; economic crises, recurrent everywhere else, have ceased. The maximum working day is eight hours, the average less than seven. Free medical attention is provided for all; workers receive wages while sick, as though they are at work, and are besides entitled to paid holidays every year. Nowhere in the world, as impartial observers testify, are women and children so well cared for as in the Soviet Union.

MAJESTIC IN CONCEPTION, PRACTICAL IN DETAIL, SCIENTIFIC IN FORM, THE SOVIET PLANS ESSAY TASKS NEVER YET ATTEMPTED BY ANY STATE, ANCIENT OR MODERN.

Scientific Spirit

'There is no country, we imagine, in which so large and so varied an amount of scientific research is being carried on at the public expense, alike in the realm of abstract theory and in that of technology. There is certainly none in which there is so little chance of that frustration of science by the profit-making instinct of which the British and American scientists are now complaining.' (Soviet Communism).

WE IN INDIA CANNOT FORGET HOW IN ONE GRAND GESTURE AFTER THE REVOLUTION THE SOVIETS RENOUNCED ALL 'PRIORITIES' AND 'CAPITULATIONS' AND 'CONCESSIONS' AND 'PRIVILEGES' WHICH THE CZARIST GOVERNMENT HAD ENJOYED IN ASIATIC COUNTRIES ALONG WITH THE OTHER GREAT POWERS.

Scores of races and millions of people were condemned by the Czars to 'planned backwardness,' while the Soviet freedom for national and linguistic minorities has produced a high flower of culture, and a new intellectual life is astir on sites where superstition and dark ecclesiastical reaction once reigned supreme. For in the USSR, with its 185 peoples and 147 languages, there is no imposed privilege for a race or for a language.

Emancipation of Women

The first Mohammedan State to adopt legislation for women's emancipation was not Kemal's Turkey, but Soviet Azerbaijan. How different is Soviet Uzbekistan from the Bhukhara Khanate, where there were 8,000 witch-doctors and just one doctor for the Emir, his harem and his Court.

AS THE WEBBS POINT OUT, 'THE SOVIET UNION HAS SET ITSELF, DILIGENTLY, NOT MERELY TO TREAT THE "LESSER BREEDS WITHOUT THE LAW" WITH EQUALITY, BUT RECOGNIZING THAT THEIR BACKWARDNESS WAS DUE TO CENTURIES OF POVERTY, REPRESSION AND ENSLAVEMENT, HAS MADE IT A LEADING FEATURE OF ITS POLICY TO SPEND OUT OF COMMON FUNDS CONSIDERABLY MORE PER HEAD ON ITS BACKWARD RACES THEN ON THE SUPERIOR ONES, IN EDUCATION AND SOCIAL IMPROVEMENTS, IN INDUSTRIAL INVESTMENTS AND AGRICULTURAL REFORMS'.

Love of Knowledge

The figures for book-production in the USSR are astronomical. At the end of the first Five Year Plan, Soviet book-production was greater than that of England, Germany and Japan taken together.

Einstein, banished by the Nazis, sells more perhaps in the USSR, than anywhere else; between 1927 and 1936, 55,000 copies of his work were sold in the Union.

IN THE LAND OF HIS BIRTH, THE 375TH ANNIVERSARY OF SHAKESPEARE'S BIRTH PASSED UNNOTICED, WHILE THE EVENT WAS CELEBRATED BY WORKERS AND PEASANTS EVERYWHERE IN THE USSR SOME 200,000 PEOPLE SAW IN MOSCOW THE PERFORMANCE OF 'KING LEAR' IN THE SPRING OF 1939. IN THE SMALL REPUBLIC OF ARMENIA, 32,000 COPIES OF SHAKESPEARE SOLD IN THE LAST FIVE YEARS.

The Soviet people have no 'cultured classes' in our sense of the term and want none. They seek a wholly cultured people and try to offer leisure, security and opportunity to all.

New Civilization

In a little over twenty years and in face of the most stupendous odds, the common people of the Soviet Union have created what we believe is a new civilization. And even we in India, borne down by generations of inanity and degradation, cannot remain undisturbed when that civilization is in peril. Helpless and unfree, we can at least send our good wishes to the Soviets and wait anxiously for the day when they will come out victorious over the forces arrayed against them.

The Signatories to the appeal are:

P.C. Ray; Satyendra Nath Majumdar; Rabindranarayan Ghosh (Principal, Ripon College); Hem Chandra Nag (Editor, 'Hindusthan Standard'); Mrinal Kanti Bose ('Amrita Bazar Patrika'); Dhirendra Nath Sen ('Amrita Bazar Patrika'); Vivekananda Mukerjee (Editor, 'Yugantar'); Bankim Chandra Sen (Editor, 'Desh'); Jyotish Bhowmick (Editor, 'Forward'); A.R. Malihabadi (Editor, 'Rozana Hind'); Amal Home (Editor, 'Calcutta Municipal Gazette'); P.K. Bose (Principal, Bangabasi College); Bhupendra Nath Dutta.

Calcutta University
Biresh Chandra Guha (Ghosh Professor of Applied Chemistry, Calcutta University); Kalidas Nag; Amiya Kumar Sen; Narayan Chandra Banerjee; Jitendranath Banerjee; Tripurari Chakravarti; N.K. Sinha; Humayun Kabir; Niharranjan Ray; Batakrishna Ghosh; Surendranath Goswami; Hirendranath Mukerjee; R.P. Das Gupta; L.P. Sukul; A.B.M. Habibullah; P.C. Gupta; Haricharan Ghosh; Renu Roy; Nikil Chakravarti; Sarasi Kumar Sarswati.

Bar Library, High Court.
Arun Sen; Abany C. Banerjee; Sukumar Mitra; M.S. Salhjee; S.K. Acharya; Jyoti Basu; Pramatha Chaudhuri; Naresh Chandra Sen Gupta; Jamini Roy; Atul Chandra Gupta; Manik Banerjee; Tarashankar Banerjee; Amiya Chakravarti; Premendra Mitra; Budhadev Bose; Sajani Kanta Das; Bishnu Dey; Biren Kumar Sanyal; Niren Roy; Gopal Haldar; Abdul Kadir; Sriprasad Upadhyay; Samar Sen; Am Saiyid Ayyub; Benoy Ghosh; Subhas Mukerjee; Ajit Chakravarti; Bimala Prasad Mukerjee; Chanchal Chatterjee; Jyotirindra Maitra; Kamakshi Chatterjee; Jyotirmoy Roy.

Scottish Church College
N.C. Bhattacharyya; Sushil C. Dutt.

Ripon College
Ananda Krishna Sinha; Bejoy Kumar Roy; Satish Chandra Sengupta; Bhabatosh Datta; Nandalal Ghosh.

Bangabasi College
N.N. Sen Gupta; Karunamoy Mukherjee.

Vidyasagar College
Provash Chandra Ghosh.

Victoria Institution
Amarendra Prasad Mitra.

94. Mahatma Gandhi: Calling Off of Satyagraha Not Warranted

(On or before 10 August 1941)
CWMG, Vol. LXXIV, pp. 225–6.

Interview to *The Hindu*

I am surprised that such things appear in the papers when there is no foundation whatever. I have not received any communication either from the Maulana Sahib or any other prisoner; nor has any messenger come to me with such representations.

Asked what the position was of Congressmen in jail, who felt that the policy of the Congress should be revised in view of the altered situation at home and abroad, Gandhiji said:

If they have changed their views and want a change of colour, of course, they can do so at any time. They have only to declare this and the Government will be glad to oblige them.

When I asked him whether nothing that had happened in the country or outside recently warranted the calling off of satyagraha, Gandhiji said:

So far as I am concerned nothing has happened.

95. Harold J. Laski: 'I Speak to You as a Socialist'

Amrita Bazar Patrika, 22 August 1941.

I speak to you as a Socialist completely convinced that the whole future of our movement depends upon the defeat of the Axis powers in this war. I do not doubt that the ultimate causes of this war lie in a social and economic system against which socialism is essentially a magisterial protest. But the business of a socialist at a great crisis of history is not to turn his back on the crisis. His duty is to see what outcome will be to the maximum advantage of the workers, and to do all he can to secure that outcome. Since it is clear that Hitler and Mussolini are nothing so much as outlaws in the service of privilege; since, wherever they conquer, all the historic institutions for the defence of the working class rights are destroyed; since their avowed object is the foundation of a new imperialism far more brutal and ugly than anything in our own record; since they are careless of, even hostile to, all those principles for the attainment of which socialists have fought since the Labour movement began; since they replace the method of free discussion by the concentration-camp: I conclude that the socialist who desires a just and equal society must regard the overthrow of these outlaws as the necessary prelude to the viceroy of his faith ....

Reform an Essential Weapon

There are evils in our social system. Our Government has made and no doubt will still make, grave mistakes. There are inequalities in Britain that seem to me indefensible inequalities. Yet none of them is grave compared to what we should have to endure if the fate of France or Poland were to be ours. Our rulers know that they cannot win this war save as they convince the common people that their good is involved in the victory. Even in these hard months while we have been struggling for survival itself, important reforms have been set on foot; I believe that the dynamic of this conflict will call for even profounder changes before it is over. Indeed, I take the view that the great strategic lesson the Government is learning is that you can only win an international civil war, like that in which we are engaged, by retaining and making even more profound the confidence of the people and that you can only gain their confidence by giving them hope and exhilaration. These, in their turn, are the outcome of a diet of great reforms; and I think that, as the grim months of the battle go by, it will be found that a diet of great reforms is an essential weapon in the armoury of victory.

I may be asked whether I seriously expect a ruling class voluntarily to abdicate from its privileges; whether I believe that a Conservative Prime Minister like Mr Churchill will cooperate in measures which look to a socialist solution of our problems. My answer is that the general question is the wrong question. All I know is that the depth of our danger has made men's minds more responsive to the need for fundamental change than at any time in our history; and that, Conservative as he is, the test of measures that Mr Churchill will apply is not whether they are socialist or not, but whether they can be shown directly to contribute to the victory he so passionately desires. I think that we are nearer than ever before to that possibility Marx once spoke of when he said that Britain might achieve socialism without revolution. I do not say it is certain: I say only that great leadership now can, during war itself, find a new plane of political relations which will make possible a peaceful transition to a better social order. I do not say this will happen, I say only that the minds of men recognize as never before that the mere conflict of private interests is incompatible with a well-ordered commonwealth and that they are ready to see social experiments upon a scale undreamed of a decade ago. And not a little of this mood is the outcome of a universal sense that the victory is being won by the masses hardly less in field and factory and workshops than on land and sea and in the air....

96. Jawaharlal Nehru's Letter to Wenzel Jaksch and Reitzner, 21 September 1941

SWJN, Vol. 11, pp. 698–700.

Dear Friends,

Your letter[1] of 13th August 1941 has reached me here together with the two pamphlets you were good enough to send. It was a great pleasure to me to have news of you and I am grateful to you for having written. I have read the pamphlets and they have brought back to me the very painful memories of three years ago when I had the privilege of visiting the Sudetenland and seeing with my own eyes the tragedy that was being enacted there. I have never forgotten that visit and I shall always remember the courage and dignity with which you and your party faced a situation which was full of peril for you all. I cannot believe that so much courage and faith can ever be wasted, and so I console myself that your sufferings and sacrifices will bear fruit one day. Many thousands, as you point out, have been living a life of terrible persecution in Dachau; many have perished. But I am very glad that, at the last moment, 3,000 of your comrades managed to escape, and though they live as exiles in far countries, they keep the old flag flying and, with faith and courage, bide their time.

I appreciate the spirit in which you have written, and I want to assure you that during these last three years or more I have held fast to my old beliefs. At the time of the Sudeten crisis, before and after the Munich decision, I wrote a good deal on the trend of events, and it is no satisfaction to me now that what I wrote then has largely come true. I had no doubt then, and I have no doubt now, that Hitler and his subordinate colleagues, Mussolini and Franco, represent a system that is evil and fundamentally bad for Europe as well as the rest of the world. A victory for him would be a tragedy for all who believe in a free life for individuals as well as nations. You know well that Hitler was powerfully helped by the so-called policy of appeasement. That appeasement represented not just a foolish and short-sighted wish to escape trouble in the present; it represented even more sympathy and agreement with the general outlook of Hitler. It is true that there was no such feeling among the people generally in England or France. But powerful elements in the Governments of the two countries certainly felt that way and acted accordingly. Perhaps it may help you to understand, when I tell you that it is this outlook, and its translation into action and government, that we have to face in India. A change has come over that outlook in regard to the domestic situation in England because of perilous developments; but that does not apply to India. We are where we were.

All my sympathies are with those who are resisting Hitler because I feel that Hitler's triumph would be disastrous for the world's freedom. As I write to you, vast and terrible battles are taking place in Russia and we are naturally following these with the most anxious interest. I have not been enamoured of everything that Russia has done and I criticized her attack on Finland last year. But I am convinced that it would be a very great tragedy if Russia's great experiment in a socialistic order was crushed in war.

During the past few years, as I saw war approaching, I had hoped that all our resources, the resources of a free India, would be thrown in on the side of freedom and democracy. It was a world conflict for me from which no one could or should keep away. But always I realized that only a free India could do so effectively, a slave country cannot fight for other people's freedom. Perhaps you will remember that this was the answer I gave you to the question you put to me in that fateful summer of 1938. That was what I wrote on my return from Czechoslovakia before Munich had occurred, as well as afterwards. There is a book of mine, recently published in London, which gives some of these writings. It is called *The Unity of India* (Lindsay Drummond).

But all our hopes were destined to be crushed. This has nothing to do with the Hindu–Muslim problem. Difficult as that is, it is different from, and perhaps basically much easier than, the Sudeten problem, for it is not a racial problem: we have to deal with more or less the same racial and linguistic background. But anyhow, that problem stands apart from the main problem; that of England and India.

I cannot discuss all these intricate matters in this letter. But I want to tell you that, in spite of every desire to do so, we were not put in a position to render effective national assistance in this war. Even so, and in spite of our conflict with the British Government, we have deliberately refrained from coming in the way of the war effort. It is obvious that we could have injured and lessened this greatly if we had attempted to do so. But in the larger context, and whatever our own reactions to England's policy to India, we did not wish Hitler to win.

India happens to be a very big country with a population approaching 400 millions. It is obvious that no world settlement can be durable which ignores this great country or seeks to treat it as somebody's possession, regardless of the wishes of her people. I quite agree with you that Europe needs the partnership of a free India, and that India needs the partnership of a free Europe. But the partnership, in order to be fruitful, must be based on freedom.

I hope one day to have the privilege of being your guest in Prague and at Badenhock when I visit again the green hills and blue forests of your beautiful mountain country.

With all good wishes to you and the cause you represent.

Yours sincerely,
Jawaharlal Nehru

---

[1] According to a note dated '20 Sept., Saturday' in Jawaharlal Nehru's 'Prison Diary', the letter from 'Jaksch, the old Sudetan German S.D. leader, who is now a refugee in London' came with two pamphlets, 'reviving memories of the Sudetenland struggle three years ago and my visit there'. The letter was 'very friendly but with a hint that we in India should throw in our lot with the British in this 'war of liberation'. 'This letter and the pamphlets took me back three years and old scenes came before my eyes'. [*SWJN*, Vol. XI, p. 698.]

97. *The Times* on Solution of Present Deadlock

Amrita Bazar Patrika, 21 September 1941.

London, 19 September. The 'Times' in an editorial states, 'As the German armies thrust to the Caucasus, as Syria, Mesopotamia and Iran are swept by revolution, as stresses in the Pacific move to a crisis, forces of world war converge steadily to Asia. India, with a storm gathering on both sides of her, faces an insistent challenge to attend as a rock of material and still more of spiritual resistance to the moral Nihilism of Nazi attacks but the manifest unity of the country upon the supreme issue of the age still falls to transcend the political schism.

The Congress still stands rigidly for the dogma of majority rights which seems to its opposite to have no possible consummation but the establishment of a party state. The Muslim League have now officially espoused Mr Jinnah's project of Pakistan which means a partition of India and setting up of small sovereignties such as have lately shown themselves in Europe lamentably ill-fated to survive in the ruthless international climate of today. The resignation under Mr Jinnah's orders of three League Premiers who had joined the new National Defence Council has just given anchor regrettable example of the tendency to give a narrow cause precedence over broader.

Solution of Deadlock

So long as that precedence is allowed, it is all but impossible for the best of British friends of India to give effective help; for the dispute is between Indians and Indians. But they may still appeal to Indian statesmanship to remember that constitutional forms profound as may be the principles from which they derive, do not express the whole of the nation's life; and that the deadlock between rival schools of political philosophy may have a chance of resolution if it is brought out into larger air and view in more ample light. The people's welfare, not the interest of the British Raj, imposes on Indian statesmen the duty of seeking a solution with their utmost resources.

Future Constitution

It is certain that neither the Government of India nor the Imperial Parliament would wish to withhold any power that the Indians, engaged in the work of self-government have all agreed to be necessary. That also is a more hopeful line of approach to the burning question of the future constitution of India as a whole. If its lines could be permitted to draw themselves according to the empirically ascertained needs of the provinces that it will exist to co-ordinate, there is a far better chance of reaching an agreement among Indians than by the present process of declamation of party shibboleths.

Distrust of British Motives

What precludes any such rational approach to the solution of the constitutional problem is the Indian politician's distrust of British motives in proposing it. The disposition is always to assume that any reason advanced from England against immediate concession is no more than an excuse for clinging to power. There is a general desire in England to see India free and self-governing, though it is coupled with the sense that it remains the duty of the British Government to ensure that the new self-governing institutions shall be based on justice for all Indians. For what is beyond the reluctance to sever all connection between self-governing India and the British commonwealth is not based on selfish considerations, but on the belief that only by continued association can India play her full part in the modern world.

Cannot Stand Alone

India as has generally been agreed long since cannot stand alone—a lesson taught to us all by the present war is that no nation can stand alone. The extreme doctrine of the right of a nation to be law to itself is a doctrine against which we are fighting and we know Indian opinion is with us in the fight. What we have to build up as the foundation of a new world economy is the doctrine of duties of nations in cooperative independence. To transform the bond of force into a bond of consent is always progress to that goal; to dissolve the bond altogether is retrogression.

98. American Interest in India: Mrs Kamaladevi Impression About America, China and Japan

Amrita Bazar Patrika, 2 October 1941.

Bombay, 29 September. Some of her impressions of her tour in America were narrated today to city journalists by Mrs Kamaladevi who has just returned after an extensive tour of America, the Continent and the Far East.

Mrs Kamaladevi observed that the politically minded American public took some sort of interest in India and her problems, but no party was willing to make that an issue in any political programme. The average American had got the idea that India was a country torn into religious groups and the question was often put to her at many a meeting she addressed whether this was true. The American confused Indian politics with the personality of Mahatma Gandhi and the Congress satyagraha had not been understood quite in that country. But if explained, they gave a very sympathetic hearing. America's contact with India had been very remote.

The visit of Rabindranath Tagore some years ago and later of Uday Sankar had been cultural demonstrations of great value. Mrs Kamaladevi stressed the need for sending more cultural messengers to America. There was the need for telling America of the problems of India, because the Indian problem was an integral part of the world problem. The Friends of India Society, which had gone dormant after the last satyagraha campaign, was now being revived.

As an illustration of the American idea of India, Mrs Kamaladevi pointed out how during her stay there innumerable persons had come up to her desiring her to read their fortune. She said that she found in America many more astrological bureaus than any where else in the world, there was more superstition among them than among Indians. When the candidature of Wendell Willkie was announced for the presidential election some papers published how the candidate's stars had indicated his success.

As she appeared wearing 'chappals' press photographers were more interested in photographing her feet than her face.

Asked about the growth of labour organization in that country, Mrs Kamaladevi said that the Government was much younger than in Europe and their political sense had not developed to the same extent as their brethren in Europe. Nor did their sympathies extend beyond South America at the most.

But, added Mrs Kamaladevi, America was making a new wonderful experiment in prison reform. She visited the latest women's prison on the Californian Coast. She found that the institution had been designed much like a college. Each group lived in a different house and each prisoner had a separate room of her own which she could furnish as she liked. The prison atmosphere was entirely absent and the inmates were trained for different jobs. The prisoners were treated with courtesy and respect. They were allowed to read, write letters without any sort of censorship. Keeping radio sets, notebooks and interviews with outsiders were not subject censor. As Mrs Kamaladevi's visit had been arranged by the Government a note on the life of the visitor had already been circulated to the inmates before the visit. The inmates had known that she had herself been prisoner in India and wanted to know lots of things about the jail life in this country.

Mrs Kamaladevi returned to India via the Far East and on her way visited Japan and China, where she met Madame Chiang Kai Shek.

Speaking of her impressions about Japan, she said that Japan had put herself on a terrific war basis. At the same time she had received a setback in China. The war time economy had involved some sacrifice on the part of the Japanese and the Government was now confronted with the problems of showing them some achievement, although it would be difficult to say what her intentions were. Whatever that would be, one thing was certain that America had now a very definite positive policy in the Pacific. Mrs Kamaladevi in conclusion paid a tribute to the magnificent way the Chinese resisted the Japanese aggression.—AP

99. India's Political Demands: US Press Interest Criticism of British Policy

Amrita Bazar Patrika, 5 October 1941.

New York, 4 October. The American Press has devoted more space in recent months to India and India's increasingly important role in the present gigantic war. While the American Press is generally critical of Britain's attitude towards India's political demands. American newspapers also devote large space to Britain's difficulties in solving the Indian problem, the enlargement of the Viceroy's Executive Council with Indian majority on the Council and the establishment of a separate Indian Purchasing Commission in America are among the things which have received special attention.

Axis Pressure

Joint pressure of Germany and Japan, both menacing India's outer frontiers in the Middle East and the Far East, led part of the American Press to characterize General Wavell's transfer to India as Commander-in-Chief, as a significant anticipatory move on Britain's part. One result of this appreciation was a number of articles on India and her part in fighting Hitler. These presented favourable pictures of India's contribution to the general war effort laying special emphasis on her industrial development and the valuable contribution which India's armed forces had made in Eritrea and Libya.

British Policy in India

The Chicago Times published an article on India's war effort arguing that India was loath to co-operate with the British Government because of British Government's policy in India.

The New York *World Telegram* published an interview with an Indian businessman who arrived in New York recently. This interview was published under the headline 'British show down coming in India, says an Indian auto magnate.'

The Time published a news item on India under the caption 'Nation Grids', reporting dissatisfaction with the new members appointed to the newly expanded Executive Council of the Viceroy but also emphasizing that India was increasing her war effort to help Britain.

The New York *Daily Mirror* in a leading article under the caption 'India will win the war', argued India's industrial development was sure to be followed by her political independence.

Referring to Sir Girija Shankar Bajpai's appointment, the New York *Sun* said: 'So far as relations with the United States are concerned, India is henceforth substantially on a plane with the self-governing dominions of Canada, Australia and South Africa'.

India's War Role

The New York *Herald Tribune* published the news of the appointment under the heading 'Britain scraps tradition in recognition of India's war role,' and commenting editorially characterized it as a milestone in the constitutional development of India, pointing out that Mahatma Gandhi and his followers should henceforth co-operate with Britain.

Gandhiji's Article

A number of articles on India have also appeared in magazines. The *Look* carried an illustrated article by Mahatma Gandhi entitled 'What India wants from England.' The article contained a reiteration of Mahatma Gandhi's position, particularly emphasizing that India had no desire to score off Britain while the latter was 'suffering from the fury of the Nazi onslaught.'

Harper's carried an article entitled 'Britain's last chance in India', by a Sikh author. The article pleaded the cause of India's independence, emphasizing the prevalent dissatisfaction in India. 'Mr Churchill,' said the writer 'apparently does not realize that if he took the lead in winning India, not only would new forces immediately be released, vastly swelling India's war contributions, but a new basis would be laid for India's future co-operation with Britain.'

The Chicago *Tribune* balanced Mr Amery's speech by printing an interview with an American resident in India who has recently returned criticizing the British Government's policy in India resulting in the imprisonment of hundreds of Mahatma Gandhi's followers.—Reuter.

100. India and America

Editorial, *Amrita Bazar Patrika*, 6 October 1941.

A little more than a decade ago the American Press sent a number of representatives to this country to report on the Civil Disobedience Movement. Some of them stayed in India for months, witnessed the salt satyagraha at various places, interviewed prominent Indian nationalist leaders and left a record of their impressions about India in books and periodicals. There is no doubt that it is because of these American journalists that Mahatma Gandhi's great and unique non-violent movement got a good press in the United States and evoked considerable public interest in that country. That a similar interest is being evinced by the American Press and the public in Indian affairs, particularly in the political situation obtaining in this country, seems undeniable. Srimati Kamaladevi, who has returned from a tour of America, Europe and the Far East, stated in course of an interesting lecture at Bombay that there was a 'considerable amount of interest in India among Americans, but the average American thought that India was a land of snakes and fortune-tellers.' *Reuter* does not try to conceal the fact that the American newspapers 'are generally critical of Britain's attitude towards India's political demands', although, we are told, they 'devote large space to Britain's difficulties,' Srimati Kamaladevi related that Mr Phillip Duff Cooper had a very unpleasant experience in USA during his recent visit and that wherever he spoke he was asked about India. At last he became exasperated and blurted out: 'What has England's war with Germany to do with India?' An English author, she said, had a similar experience of having been heckled.

It is idle to deny that Britain has for some time past been carefully watching the barometer of public opinion in USA so far as India is concerned. Sometime ago, it will be recalled, Sir Feroze Khan Noon, the then High Commissioner for India in London, an Indian journalist in London and probably a few others were sent to lecture to the American public on the Indian political situation. That the Americans were not quite impressed by these propaganda lectures will be evident from the fact that their critical attitude still persists. Shall we be far wrong if we say that Mr Churchill's reference to India in relation to the Atlantic Charter—and that after a protracted alliance—was made primarily to satisfy the American public? Only the other day *Reuter* cabled the text of some of the searching questions from America about India and Mr Amery's vague and evasive replies thereto. *Reuter* mentions a number of American newspapers and periodicals, for instance, the *Chicago Times,* the *New York World Telegram, Time, New York Daily Mirror, New York Sun,* New York *Herald–Tribune, Chicago Tribune* and so on. The magazine *Look* published an illustrated article by Mahatma Gandhi entitled 'What India want from England', while *Harper's Magazine* carried an article entitled 'Britain's Last Chance in India' by a Sikh author. The article pleaded the cause of India's independence, emphasizing the prevalent dissatisfaction in this country. But the American Press, it seems, does not rest contest by merely publishing articles and interviews on India. It is taking a little more active interest. During the last week of last month Calcutta journalists had in their midst an American journalist said to be the Staff Correspondent of the *United Press of America.* It is understood Mr Pinkley, for that is the journalist's name, will be touring India for some time. We further learn that a party of American journalists representing *Time, Life, Chicago Tribune, Liberty, News*

Chronicle and *Toronto Star* has just arrived at Karachi. One may take it that the purpose of their visit is to study the situation in India at first hand instead of depending for their information on second and third hand reports.

We cordially welcome these American journalists to this ancient and historic land—this huge subcontinent where 400 million people constituting one-fifth of the human race just want to manage the affairs of their country in their own way without any interference from anybody. We hope more such journalists will come to India, study the situation carefully and impartially, probe the causes of the rift between India and Britain and educate their fellow countrymen on their return. India wants nothing more. India does not believe in propaganda because the stand Congress has taken is perfectly justified and because Mahatma Gandhi's movement is based on truth and non-violence. It is there for everybody to see and evaluate and judge. India does not and can never want Americans to fight her battle for freedom. She will stand on her own legs and fight her own battle despite a thousand obstacles at home and abroad. She only trusts that being an intelligent and freedom loving people they would take active and lively interest in the political destinies of the vast masses of people in this country. India does not stand in need of any help from Americans; she only expects to receive their sympathy and goodwill if, of course, they feel convinced that the Indian cause is just and righteous.

While we welcome the American publicists, we hope their visit to this country will be reciprocated by representatives of the Indian nationalist Press and by Indian cultural and political leaders of eminence, for it is by such reciprocation alone that a healthy and helpful contact between India and America can be established. India has of course sent some of her great national ambassadors to USA and other countries from time to time. But that is not enough. Steps should be taken by Congress—indeed, these should have been taken long ago—to send at regular intervals some of our ablest and most cultured men not to propagandize in America but to tell the American people the barest truth about India in the simplest possible language. Such contacts will contribute towards dispelling the profound ignorance of Americans about India, exposing the lies and half-truths sedulously spread about this country by interested propagandists and establishing a bond of cultural unity between two great peoples.

101. Slave-owner's Arguments Won't Satisfy India: Definite Declaration of Dominion Status for India is the Only Way Britain Can Get India's Full Support, M.R. Jayakar

Bombay Chronicle, 9 October 1941.

Dharwar, 7 October. 'War is daily drawing closer to India. It would be difficult to say what might happen to us if Russia were completely defeated. It is unfortunate that India should not still realize the seriousness of the war situation and that the war is as much India's as it is Britain's though for different reasons. British Government is mainly responsible for this state of affairs. They have done nothing to make us feel that this war is ours too. It is high time that the various political parties in India, including the Indian National Congress put their heads together and resolved the present deadlock', thus observed the Rt Hon M.R. Jayakar addressing a largely attended public meeting here.

His Mission

Mr Jayakar said that he was now touring the country with a view to meet the leaders of different schools of political thought on a mission of peace and goodwill. He regretted that Indians were not associated with the conduct of the war. The British Government cared more for India's men, money and material than for her moral and spiritual support in the war. It was necessary to associate Indian sentiment with the war effort.

Congress and Britain

Referring to the policy of the Congress Mr Jayakar observed that the first reaction of the Congress to the war as expressed in the earliest speeches of Gandhiji when he said of what avail is India's freedom if Westminster Abbey were to fall was admirable and was in keeping with the best traditions of India's goodwill and friendship towards Britain. But the later change of front was unfortunate. It was a mistake on the part of Britain to have turned down the Poona offer of the Congress.

England should have done far better if she had appealed to India's love of freedom and democracy than to fear and dreadful consequences of the Nazi victory.

It was the slave-owners' argument and India was naturally indifferent to the outcome of the war as long as she did not stand to gain anything as the result of the war.

Trust Indians

Referring to the wonderful unity that prevailed in England among various parties and the vigour with which the war was being prosecuted, Mr Jayakar said that the same thing could be repeated in India, provided defence was entrusted to Indians. Indians alone could appeal to Indian sentiment.

While welcoming the recent expansion of the Viceroy's Council as a step in the right direction, the speaker regretted that the key portfolios were exclusively reserved to Englishmen. Mr Jayakar however welcomed Mr Amery's declaration that the responsibilities of the Council would be joint or collective. He envisaged the possibility of the new Council with eight Indians on it making a fresh attempt to resolve the political impasse by calling the leaders of different parties for a conference. He thought a compromise formula was possible on the basis of Britain making a definite promise of full Dominion Status within a fixed period after the termination of war and establishing a national Government at the centre with non-officials who enjoy public esteem and confidence selected by the Viceroy. He urged the Congress to come out and revise its present 'futile' policy and co-operate in arriving at a compromise.

Concluding the speaker appealed to the English Government to create an atmosphere of reality by making definite promise of Dominion Status in order to enable the different parties in India to arrive at an understanding.—AP

102. Jawaharlal Nehru on his Sympathies in the War

SWJN, Vol. 12, p. 2.

Speech at Lucknow University, 8 December 1941
On War

I shall be sorry if Russia loses, though I do not entertain that fear; if I were asked with whom my sympathies lay in this war, I would unhesitatingly say with Russia, China, America and England. But, in spite of my sympathy for the group, there is no question of my giving help to Britain. How can I fight for a thing, freedom, which is denied to me? British policy in India appears to be to terrify the people, so that in anxiety we may seek British protection.

The release of political prisoners has not changed the situation; so far as Britain's policy towards India is concerned, it remains the same. While I cannot off-hand say what course the Congress will pursue, it has been demonstrably proved that the Congress stand is very correct. I admire the way Mahatma Gandhi has conducted the satyagraha movement and affirm my confidence in the Mahatma's leadership.

You are aware of the latest developments in the Far East where a new curtain has been rung down and no one knows what will follow. The war might even spread to India.

You should think for yourselves and should not be carried away by slogans. I am against disruption amongst students, which is a sign of weakness. You should work together, for you will have to shoulder responsibility in the future.

103. Jawaharlal Nehru's Telegram to V.K. Krishna Menon, 11 December 1941

SWJN, Vol. 12, pp. 10–11.

Allahabad
11 December 1941

Your cable. I have sent a message to *Daily Herald*, sending another long message to *News Chronicle* via Bombay. Reynolds requests message, but no press authority. Only the Working Committee is entitled to give an authoritative exposition of policy. Prisoners' release makes no difference to Indo–British relations, but desire express solidarity with peoples of China and Soviet Union in their magnificent struggle for freedom. Please convey my greetings and good wishes to Winant[1], Maisky[2], Wellington Koo[3].

Jawaharlal Nehru

---

[1] John Gilbert Winant, US Ambassador to Britain.
[2] I.M. Maisky, Soviet Ambassador to Britain.
[3] China's Ambassador to Britain.

104. Jawaharlal Nehru: India's Unchanged Attitude to War

SWJN, Vol. 12, pp. 7–10.

National Herald* [12 December 1941] Version of Statement to *Daily Herald

After over thirteen months spent in the solitude and isolation of prison it is not easy to adjust oneself to the activities of the changing world. Individual opinions may be expressed, but they will lack the reality which contact with people and a living situation gives them. I am seeking to regain these contacts and the Congress Working Committee will no doubt give expression to its views very soon.

My first impression is of the hardening in the situation in India. The repeated declarations on behalf of the British Government in regard to India and the policy that has been pursued have antagonized almost every section of Indian opinion and made people here believe that nothing can be expected from this Government. The attempts to play off different groups against each other and to promote every disruptionist activity, the support of reactionary elements, the reversion to conditions of fifty years ago and the openly offensive and authoritarian attitude of the permanent officials of the Indian Civil Service have made conditions far worse than they have ever been within my knowledge. Bitterness has been added by the ill-treatment of political prisoner and by the detention in concentration camps of large numbers without charge or trial.

This is the national background, and the release from prison of a number of Congressmen does not make any essential difference. Even now there are thousands in prisons and concentration camps. But even if all these were released the real problem will remain, made much harder of amicable solution by the events of the past two years. There was a time, soon after the war began, when a possibility arose of solving the problem. But that tide in the affairs of men was allowed to pass and everything was said and done to anger and humiliate the proud nationalism of India, which is by far the strongest force which moves our people. That nationalism is not the aggressive nationalism of Europe but the peaceful nationalism of a people demanding their own independence within a larger world order of free nations.

At the same time, the people of India had long sympathized and expressed their solidarity with the progressive forces in the world, in China, Europe, America and elsewhere. That sympathy continued and they viewed with anxiety the prospect of these forces being crushed by the fascist nations. On the British side, they saw a combination of imperialist and democratic forces, with the former completely controlling Indian policy. In spite of their evident sympathy with the anti-fascist forces and nations, they could not submit to conditions which meant national humiliation and an acceptance of their subject condition. Indeed, their very anti-fascist outlook made them rebel against the fascist and authoritarian nature of the Government of India. The spread of the war to the Soviet Union widened and intensified their sympathy for the progressive forces, but did not affect their reaction to the British Government's policy in India, for that was based on other causes. No self-respecting people or nation could tolerate a surrender on this issue, whatever the consequences.

Many of us were distressed that at this supreme moment in the world's history India was not playing a more active and effective part. We shared the agony of the world. Yet we felt that even so we were playing a not unworthy part by drawing attention to certain essential aspects of freedom without which a military victory would be valueless and would lead to even greater tragedies. It was essential to recognise that the entire world must be based on freedom and the cooperation of free peoples in a world order, that the economic order must be changed to prevent exploitation and to promote the fullest use of the world's resources for human betterment, that there must be full disarmament of all nations and an end of armed warfare between them. Hitler's victory would be a greater disaster, but it would also be a disaster if others who were victors established a hegemony over the world, supported armed might, which would develop into another type of fascist authoritarianism. The only alternatives were freedom and disarmament all round, and continuing warfare and destruction.

Mahatma Gandhi is a full believer in nonviolence. Most of us are not pacifists, but this war itself has convinced us of the futility of armed states trying to destroy each other as well as civilization periodically by war. The system which gives rise to this must go. This war will run its appointed course, but it must be made clear that this system must be ended. Personally I agree with Mr H.G. Wells' proposal that there should be an international air force and no national armies. But this must be really international, and not controlled by a few great powers. We want no great power, greater in armed might, but free nations.

The entry of Japan into the war has now made it world-wide, and it approaches India's borders. That is of vast interest to us, but it will not make us panicky. Our sympathies must inevitably be with the non-fascist nations. And such help as we can give them, consistently with our own principles, would flow to them, if we functioned as a free people. Only freedom can tone down the enormous antagonism that British policy in India has created.

Whether it is India or the world or the war, no petty hesitant half-measures are of any avail. This was so in September 1939, when the Congress issued its declaration on the war, by which it has stood throughout. This is much more so now, and the history of the past two years bears witness to it. People who think in terms of preserving the old order, or presuming to tell us in India that they are the best judges of what we should have, are not going to solve anything. They are dangerous relics of a past, which must be swept away if the ground is to be cleared for real victory and freedom. And of that the greatest test is India now, in the present, and not after the war.

105. Jawaharlal Nehru's Address to Students, Allahabad, 15 December 1941

SWJN, Vol. 12, pp. 30–2.

Simla and Vichy

You must be reading in the newspapers about the deaths of thousands of people every day in the present war. If it had happened only on one day then there would have been a feeling of grief at such a huge loss. But when it becomes a matter of daily event nobody ever thinks about it or feels about it. In Spain, Manchuria, China and Czechoslovakia greater tragedies have taken place but none cares to visualize whither the world is going.

As I was an eye-witness in Barcelona, Hungary and Prague, my sensibility to European events was sharpened. The picture of Europe that floated before my vision was a Europe stricken with panic and fear and many other weaknesses.

My hope about India became brighter when I compared European conditions with those obtaining in India. I found, to my relief, that we were free from some weaknesses which characterized the Europeans.

The present war can be divided into three well-defined periods—the period before Russia entered the war; the period after Russia's participation; and the period after Japan's attack in the Far East.

Many persons have asserted that due to the entry of the Soviet Union the war has changed its imperialistic character. Slogans and catchwords like the imperialistic war are impediments to real thinking. Let us not use them indiscriminately. There is no doubt that Britain is fighting for its freedom and its Empire. But even when faced with a life and death struggle its imperialistic ways have not changed. Russia's entry into the war has not changed the character of the British Government which is an enemy of Indian freedom.

The phase of war beginning with the attack on Russia has changed the complexion of the war no doubt, but not the outlook and attitude of the British ruling class. It does not see the revolutionary changes going on behind the war. The ruling class in England and France is played out, but the people in Russia have stood the test with courage and strength. The fact that the Soviet stood the German blitz, which called forth the admiration of all, was due to the structure of its state and economic system. In spite of war conditions, England has not been able to mobilize her war efforts like Russia. So far as the Government of India is concerned, its structure is not only out of date, but what is more surprising, it is living in the nineteenth century.

The Government of India invites comparison with the Vichy Government. It is also afraid of Indians. Vichy prostrated, lying low, always talks of maintaining the French Empire; and Simla, Delhi and London also talk of preserving the British Empire. The mental make-up of Britain's leaders is fascist. There is not much difference between fascism and imperialism.

One of the most remarkable features of the present war is the brave resistance put up by the Reds. The epic defence of the Soviet Union arouses our admiration. The destruction by Russians of the Dneproges dam, which was a product of twenty years labour, is symbolic of the spirit that animates the USSR. To serve a larger cause they destroyed one of their greatest achievements. In spite of reverses, the morale of the Soviet state is high.

I cannot understand the mentality of those who plead that India should have Dominion Status after the war; it might be two years or five years. The term Dominion Status applies only to those people who regard England as their mother country. Though India has been under British rule for the last 150 years or more she is not an offshoot or outgrowth of England. On the other hand, India is a mother country. Indian culture, Indian philosophy, Indian art have spread in Asia and elsewhere. There has been cultural contact between India and China and India and Greece. That cultural tie has not been broken. It is idle to talk of Dominion Status and the so-called British Commonwealth of Nations. Who knows what would be the state of affairs after the war? There might be a federal union between England and America. England might become a state of America. This idea of Dominion Status is implanted in the minds of those who believe in the permanence of British rule. It is a sheer waste of time to talk of the grant of Dominion Status two years after the war. Those who engage themselves in such discussions are doing a disservice to their country. What we want at the present moment is independence and nothing else. Who knows what will be the fate of Britain or the British Empire two years after the war. It matters little whether Mr Churchill talks of Atlantic Charter or Indian Ocean charter.

Besides, in a fast changing world with the fate of things altering with each turn of events, the talk even of a time-limit has no meaning. What we want is independence. That means severance of connection with Britain. Of course, that does not mean a position of isolation for us. What it does mean is that we should form a part of the new order in our own right. On this question of independence of India there can be no compromise either with the British Government or with any group in India.

At this moment there is a need for discipline among students. You should not fritter away your energies over small things such as elections. The time has come when you should all stand united because the map of the world is changing every day. If you keep your eyes shut and only continue shouting slogans you cannot reach your goal.

106. Jawaharlal Nehru's Telegram to V.K. Krishna Menon, 16 December 1941

SWJN, Vol. 12, p. 32.

Allahabad
16 December 1941

Your cable. I am just going to Bombay thence Bardoli. Your information about developments here misleading. Extreme bitterness here against British policy in India and attitude obscurantist and reactionary of officials. While fully realizing its implications recent international events consider recognition of independence with real transfer of power as essential prerequisites for effective step. Undesirable your interviewing British officials.

Nehru

107. Jawaharlal Nehru's Letter to Mian Iftikharuddin Regarding an All India Committee of Friends of Soviet Union

SWJN, Vol. 12, pp. 599–601.

Bombay
18 December 1941

My dear Ifti,

I have your letter of the 16th December. I have just returned after addressing two enormous mass meetings totalling an audience of a lakh and a quarter, and I am a little tired. But I am sending you this reply. For if I do not do so now I may have less time in future.

1. I am aware of the Friends of the Soviet Union in Calcutta. After my release from prison an effort was made in Allahabad to start such an organization and a similar effort is being made in Benares, Lucknow, and other places, chiefly University centres in the UP. The idea was to issue a manifesto from each of these places and then to develop an organization out of the signatories. It seemed to me and to most others that the whole object of these manifestoes and organizations would be frustrated if they were largely confined to those who may be considered as confirmed and well-known friends of the Soviet Union. The point was to get the average intellectual, professional, professor, and otheres. When the Allahabad manifesto appears, my name will of course be in it. But such importance as that manifesto will have will consist of other names, and it seems to me far better for these other people to be in the forefront of these organizations.

Personally I rather doubt if it is desirable at present to have any all India organization. The All India Committee you refer to is so in name only and any attempt to impose itself on people elsewhere is not likely to meet with success. I think it is far better to encourage the formation of local groups and then connect them rather loosely. Later these groups may elect an All India Committee. To start from the top is a wrong way and an artificial way and will come in the way of a natural growth. In this view the question does not arise of my being the chairman of an All India Committee. In any event I do feel that the chairman should be one who is not an aggressive politician. We can of course associate ourselves with the committee....

Yours sincerely,
Jawaharlal Nehru

108. Communist Party's Attitude Towards War Effort, December 1941

Communist, Vol. III, No. 9, December 1941–January 1942, P.C. Joshi Archives on Contemporary History, JNU.

Our Attitude Towards War Effort

Letter to Party Comrades

Our attitude towards the war is one of unconditional support, independent of imperialism. This is our war. It is a war of liberation for the people of the world. It is the war for our liberation also. We have to win it in the interest of our own people as much as in the interest of the peoples of the world who are our allies. That is why we want to build National peoples' war effort. THE EXISTING WAR EFFORT IS IMPERIALIST, COERCIVE AND INADEQUATE. We have to transform this enforced and coercive war effort into a free and voluntary one. For this purpose we seek to unite the nation and mobilize the people for creating conditions which alone will make this possible. We fight for a National Government commanding the confidence of the people. We fight for democratic liberties which will enable the people to move and act freely.

But while we fight for these key demands what is our attitude towards the war effort as it exists to-day? Do we say that we shall not touch the present war effort till National Government is achieved? No, that will be an attitude of negation and inaction. In order to develop the struggle for National Government we have to intervene in the present war effort. WE CO-OPERATE WHERE WE CAN. WE RESIST WHERE WE MUST. This sums up our attitude. This part is explained correctly in the following letter.

EDITOR

What should be our attitude to the various items of war effort in the immediate future? In general, our attitude towards war-effort even as it exists just now cannot be one of neutrality but one of positive intervention and co-operation where that ensures the mobilization of the people, their protection, and enables us to rally the people round the political demands.

Recruitment

In the case of recruitment we CANNOT, for instance, say: we cannot ask the people to join the army, though we do not oppose or do propaganda against joining. We cannot say we won't touch the issue of recruitment till the National Government is achieved. This is an attitude of NEUTRALITY which has nothing in common with our line. We want the recruitment to be increased a thousand fold in all the forces. Imperialism does not want it nor can it do it. Because it cannot enthuse the people to join the Army. Our propaganda for supporting and winning this war, for making this war our own, if it is sound, must enthuse people and create in them right consciousness to participate in this war. And our job is to see that recruits infected by our propaganda and those who have caught the peoples' war spirit do go in for the various forces. We must encourage the right type of people among our contacts, among students, workers, kisans, and others to join the various forces. We must get to know the conditions of recruitment in the different forces, expose the difficulties and disabilities. We expose the reality that people are willing to join the different forces to defend the country and to fight the war for freedom but it is the present government which is the main hindrance in the path of creating a real army which the country needs. That is why we need a National Government. We expose the conditions of soldiers, their pay, the discrimination and demand better conditions for Indian soldiers. All this you cannot do by continuing your 'touch not the war effort' attitude. 'THE WAR IS OURS BUT WE WON'T TOUCH THE WAR EFFORT TILL NATIONAL GOVERNMENT IS WON' IS A REMNANT OF THE BOURGEOIS ATTITUDE OF CONDITIONAL CO-OPERATION WHICH HAS NOTHING IN COMMON WITH OUR LINE.'

ARP

The attitude taken by the Congress is again a 'sit on the fence' attitude typical of its bargaining policy. Yes, the present ARP is a farce but the sooner we realize that it is a farce at the expense of our people the better. With the continued bombing of Rangoon it has become a real issue for the coastal towns like Calcutta, Madras and even for Bombay. We cannot merely say: hand over the ARP to the municipalities and sit quiet. We cannot support the policy of benevolent neutrally proposed by the Congress and imposed by it on the municipalities. We must stand for a positive and practical policy of people's co-operation and vigorous exposure. We must take initiative in forming people's ARP Committee in blocks of houses who will, through their representative, co-operate with the Government organization, carry out all the ARP instructions and take initiative in getting volunteer squads trained in fire-watching in extinguishing incendiary bombs, rendering aid and all that. Take the initiative in demanding from the house-owners and from the Government proper shelters for the locality. Co-operation enables you to mobilize the people and to make effective exposures and to hammer the point home how the present ARP is a farce. It enables you to rouse the Congress to take a positive attitude, to take initiative, to win power.

The Students' Federation of Bengal deserves to be congratulated for having boldly and correctly implemented the line. The students of Bengal are girding their lions, to co-operate in the ARP, to train volunteer squads in first aid. They are determined to play an active part in pacifying the panic-stricken people and in helping the sufferers from the horrors of war. Taking this attitude of co-operation with the ARP enables them at once to come out in a fighting opposition to the Government policy of closing down the educational institutions in Calcutta which has created such a terrific discontent among the students and their parents. Our Students' Federation gives a fighting lead to the dispirited people who are the victims of the vagaries of the Government orders. Why evacuate schools and colleges? We students are prepared to stick on and fight back the terrors of bombing, give us shelters, give us training in ARP and first aid. Let Calcutta have a fighting squadron. If Moscow, London and Chungking could carry on 'business as usual' in spite of terrific bombing, why can't Calcutta? That is the spirit we want. That's the spirit of the new line. Not the whining neutrality which the Congress leaders are preaching. Those who shirk co-operation do so because they do not want to mobilize the people, because they do not want to expose the vagaries of the Government measures, because they do not want to concretely intensify the people's struggle for the basic political demands.

Civic Guards

Civic Guards are a scandal. They are more auxiliaries of the police and used to do spying work against the people. For the present, for the most part loyalists only have joined it. What we want and must demand are popular guards—a sort of citizen army organized for the defence of cities and district towns. It should consist of citizens, workmen, professionals who follow their profession but get trained in their off time and do drill and patrol duty and get defence training in rotation. In the meanwhile, we send contacts in the Civic Guards too and form groups in it for the purpose of getting full information about it and to expose the swindle to reinforce the demand for popular guards and the military training of citizens for home defence. We demand arms for the Home Guard.

War Fund Contributions

We must strengthen our fight against the system of getting enforced contributions from the poor, from the workers and the peasants. We say certainly raise money but by taxing the rich and not by coercing the poor. We say raise money by creating new industries. You cannot fight the war by this parasitic sponging upon the workers and peasants. In the villages and taluk towns the collector comes and holds his durbar to get cash for war. In such meetings where well-to-do peasants and others have gathered, we should send contacts to make speeches, showing how this is a great war of liberation, how Indian people ought to fight it, how we are prepared to fight it that way, but what the Government is actually doing. Then comes a scathing exposure of the bankrupt policy of the Government. Are you fighting the war for freedom or fighting down the people?

Close with the demand for National Government. It is by such scoops and exposures that we would be able to create a new mentality and approach among the people. The essence of the new approach is confidence in their own power, will to fight our own battle, for the protection of the country and for the defence of the people. Let our cadres cast off the fear from their minds that if they do this then they will become the recruiting sergeants and agents of the imperialist government. They can never become that if they get the new line soaked into them properly. THEY ARE CALLED UPON TO BECOME THE WAR PROPAGANDISTS AND RECRUITING SERGEANTS IN A WAR FOR PEOPLES FREEDOM, WHICH IS ALSO THE WAR FOR THEIR OWN FREEDOM, FOR A WORLD ARMY OF LIBERATION AT THE HEAD OF WHICH STANDS COMRADE STALIN, THE BELOVED AND TRUSTED LEADER OF THE WORLD PROLETARIAT. YOU ARE CALLED UPON TO MARCH FORWARD AS THE SOLDIERS IN THE ARMY OF STALIN. THAT IS THE SPIRIT OF THE NEW LINE.

109. Resolution Adopted by Muslim League Working Committee, Nagpur, 26 December 1941

Indian Annual Register, 1941, Vol. II, pp. 222–3.

League's Attitude to War Effort

The second resolution begins with the words 'in view of the fact that the entry of Japan in the war on the side of the Axis powers has brought danger much closer to India and has forced into greater prominence the question of the defence of India, the Working Committee consider it necessary to reiterate that the Muslim League, from the very beginning, has expressed their willingness to share the responsibility of the defence of the country'. The resolution quotes the various resolutions passed by the Committee to that effect and mentions the attitude taken by the Congress in this matter. The resolution mentions the attitude taken by the Congress in this matter. The resolution then says that the League on 17 June 1940 passed a resolution which clearly showed that the League all along adhered to the policy enunciated by its President in

November 1939. The resolution concludes: 'The Working Committee once more declare that they are ready and willing as before to shoulder the burden of the defence of the country singly or in cooperation with other parties on the basis that real share and responsibility is given in the authority of Government at the Centre and in the provinces within the framework of the present constitution, but without prejudice to the major political issues involved in the framing of the future constitution'.

D. Provincial Ministries

[Following the resignation of the Congress ministries, October–November 1939, the seven Congress-ruled provinces were placed under the Governors' rule (Section 93, Provincial Autonomy, The Government of India Act, 1935). The rest of the non-Congress elected ministries continued to function rather unsteadily in Sind, Bengal and Assam, and slightly more steadily in Punjab. In their urgency for popularizing the war-efforts, the British authorities did manage during 1941 to foist an elected ministry on Orissa, but failed to safeguard the existing one in Assam.]

I. Sind

110. Sind Cabinet Reshuffle Mr Allah Bux's Statement

The Hindu, 22 January 1941.

Karachi, 21 January.

According to the Azad Agreement, the Premier, Mir Bundeh Ali Khan Talpur is to resign by the middle of February. Sir Ghulam Hussein Hidayatullah is to come into the Cabinet and the new Premier is not to be appointed from among the Ministers belonging to the League group, stated Khan Bahadur Allah Bux, Finance Minister, in an interview to the Associated Press.

Asked for a clarification of his position, Khan Bahadur Allah Bux said that it was quite simple. The entrance of his group into the Cabinet was not of its seeking but was secured because both the Muslim League Group and the Hindu Independent Party had insisted on it in their talks with Maulana Azad. If, therefore, Maulana Azad's agreement continued in force, this would be the case, but otherwise either his party or the Muslim League party would not be in the Cabinet and the Congress Party, he thought, would be free to pursue its own course of action. Even in that case, his group would do nothing to embarrass the Government.

Khan Bahadur Allah Bux revealed that during Christmas Week before he met Maulana Azad at Lahore, he had discussed the situation with the Muslim League Ministers, Shaikh Abdul Majid and Khan Bahadur Khuro, also Mr G.M. Syed, ex-League Minister, and on their assuring him that the Azad Agreement regarding reshuffling of the Ministry in the middle of February stood, he informed the Congress President accordingly.

111. Jinnah's Statement on Sind Affairs Sind Ministry Reshuffle

The Hindu, 8 February 1941.

League Not Behind Coalition, Mr M.A. Jinnah on 'Azad Agreement'

Bombay, 7 February.

Mr M.A. Jinnah, President of the All-India Muslim League, has issued the following statement in regard to Sind affairs:

'The Hindu and the Congress Press are misrepresenting the situation in Sind day in and day out. The correct facts as I have been able to ascertain are as follows:

The Congress Party and the Hindu Independent Party concluded an agreement with a few individual members of the Assembly who belong to the Muslim League on the basis of a so-called 21 points on the understanding that they will maintain the Mir Ministry for the remaining period of the Assembly. Prior to this agreement the Muslim League Party in the Assembly was disbanded as a condition precedent to the agreement forming the so-called League Ministry consisting of Mir Bundeh Ali Khan, Shaik Abdul Majid, K.B. Khurro, Syed and two other Hindu Ministers. Thereafter the Congress Party commenced its treacherous manoeuvres towards the Mir Ministry soon after this agreement was arrived at. Up to the present moment there has been no change in their attitude. And the Hindu Independent Party adopted the same attitude after some time under the cover of murders in Rohri division. They having succeeded in getting the Muslim League Party being disbanded, the result was that only two Hindu parties functioned, namely the Congress and the Hindu Independent Party which gave them a strength of about twenty-one together in a House of sixty; and with the help of Khan Bahadur Allah Bux and Sir Ghulam Hussein Hidayatullah and their individual following were in a dominant position in the Assembly; and the Ministry consisting of Mir Bundeh Ali Khan, Shaik Abdul Majid and Messrs Syed and Khurro who were individual members of the League and without any League Party behind them were at the mercy of the dominant power of the Hindus.

'A Secret Agreement'

Thereafter the machinations went on and with the help of the President of the Congress, who arrived in Karachi they got rid of, by a fresh arrangement, Mr Syed, who was a member of the Muslim League and brought in Khan Bahadur Allah Bux in his place. It is alleged there was some sort of this agreement which was to be carried out on 15th February. According to this agreement Bundeh Ali Khan was to resign and Ghulam Hussein Hidayatullah was to be installed in the Ministry and Allah Bux was to be the Premier. This agreement is a secret agreement. Between whom this agreement was arrived at is a mystery yet. But one thing is clear from the facts that I have ascertained, that Shaik Abdul Majid knew nothing about it, was no party to it, that there was no Muslim League Party in the Assembly, that the Working Committee or the Council of the Provincial Muslim League knew nothing about it and was not consulted by anybody. And the party most concerned namely Mir Bundeh Ali Khan, who is supposed to have agreed to resign on the 15th of February, informs me that he was not a party to any such agreement and that he is under no obligation to resign. The so-called "Azad Agreement" is obviously intended to get rid of Mir Bundeh Ali and put Khan Bahadur Allah Bux as the Premier and Sir Ghulam Hussein as a Minister, these being deadly opponents of the League with the two Hindu Ministers, and thereby leaving only two members of the Muslim League in the Ministry, namely, Khan Bahadur Khurro and Shaik Abdul Majid in their individual capacity, and passing this show as a Coalition Ministry with the Muslim League.

The two individual Ministers have no Muslim League Party behind them in the Assembly and have no sanction of the Muslim League in the province behind. In these circumstances, it is impossible for the Muslim League to allow its name to be exploited and assume the responsibility of a Ministry simply because the two who happen to be members of the Muslim League are allowed to be in such a Ministry. In these circumstances, if the Muslim League Ministers cannot carry on the Government, the only honourable course for them would be to resign from the Ministry and sit on the Opposition benches. I am sure they would resign from such a Ministry rather than resign from the League. But as individuals if they decide to continue then the Muslim League cannot accept the responsibility of their passing off as League Ministers in the circumstances I have described above. And Provincial Muslim League, who is the final authority to approve of the Coalition in the Assembly will have to consider whether it will not be a farce to call such a thing as Coalition and consider what action they should take in the matter against any individual member of the Muslim League sharing the responsibility of such a Ministry.

Joint Electorates Question

As regard the introduction of joint electorates, I am glad that in deference to the universal Muslim opinion in the province of Sind and outside, the Government have decided not to press on with these Bills. I hope that even in borough municipalities where the Joint Electorates Act has been already passed will be suspended *sine die* and finally withdrawn as requested by the Working Committee of the Sind Provincial Muslim League recently. I also hope that better counsels will prevail and the present personnel of the Ministry will not be disturbed, and that Mr Allah Bux will not insist upon becoming the Premier, nor would friends of Sir Ghulam Hussein insist upon his being brought in under the threat that otherwise the present Ministry will be broken. If such a thing happens the responsibility will rest with those who are bent upon causing disruption among the Muslims and those who are bent upon preventing the Muslim League Party being formed and functioning when the other two Hindu parties are left intact and free to function and working together hand in hand'.

112. Mr Jinnah on Sind Ministry

Editorial, *The Hindu*, 10 February 1941.

The statement on the Sind Ministry that Mr Jinnah has issued is characteristic alike of his peculiar logic and his inveterate desire to play the dictator. When he speaks of the treacherous 'manoeuvres' and the 'machinations' of the Congress Party, we may console ourselves that he has not fallen appreciably below the rather primitive standards of courtesy he has set for himself in political controversy. But when we proceed to examine the grounds of his complaint against the Congress, he appears even more perverse than usual. He charges the Congress and the Hindu Independent with a conspiracy 'to prevent the Muslim League Party being formed and functioning when the other two Hindu parties are left intact and free to function and working together hand in hand'. Now, that is a sufficiently remarkable complaint to make. If a Muslim League Party cannot be formed in the Legislature one would suppose that is because the principles and policies of the Muslim League do not appeal to a sufficiently large number of members of that body. Mr Jinnah does not disprove this assumption by referring to the disbandment of the League Party in the Assembly some time ago, which, he avers, had been insisted upon (by the 'Hindu parties' presumably) as a condition precedent to the Bundeh Ali Khan Ministry coming into existence. If the Provincial Muslim League was, as Mr Jinnah would like us to believe, a political factor of importance in the Province, how did it come to allow 'this disintegration of the League Party in the Legislature'. The reply—though Mr Jinnah may not choose to give it—is that the League has little or no following in the electorate. In Sind, as elsewhere, it was not able to capture more than a minute fraction of the Muslim seats at the elections. There, as in other Provinces, it tried after the elections to secure a foothold in the Legislature by inducing the Muslim members to enlist themselves under the League banner; but, though it succeeded in thus bringing into existence a League Party in the Legislature, it could not manage to keep it intact for the obvious reason that the League's influence was not derived from the electorate and its party in the Legislature was too small to attempt the task of governing the Province by itself, nor could it hope to secure the co-operation of other groups on the basis of the principles and policies favoured by the League.

Mr Jinnah maintains that the 'so-called League Ministry' headed by Mir Bundeh Ali Khan was never a real League Ministry, only the four (and later three) Muslim members in it were 'individual members of the League and without any League Party behind them'. If that was the case, why did the League acquiesce all these months in the anomalous position which it now vigorously condemns? Are we to understand that what galls Mr Jinnah is not the fact that the Coalition Ministry has no League Party to support it—according to him it never had that—but the prospect of Mr Allah Bux replacing Mir Bundeh Ali Khan as Premier and Sir Ghulam Hussain Hidayatullah coming in as Minister, since in his view these two men are 'deadly opponents of the League'? On a par with this extremely personalized politics which commends itself to the League under Mr Jinnah's inspiration is his notion of what would be a proper Coalition. His grievance against the Congress Ministries in the various Provinces was that though there were Muslim Ministers in them they contained no proper representative of the Muslim community, because by Mr Jinnah's definition only League Muslims could claim such representative status. Now he goes a step further. A man may be a member of the Muslim League in his individual capacity, but he will not on that account be accepted by the League as its representative. Apparently he must be labelled so by Mr Jinnah before he can qualify for that distinction. And yet Mr Jinnah and his colleagues have relied endlessly at what they have been pleased to describe as the autocracy of the Congress High Command. The latter, if it has insisted on a unified direction of the Congress forces in all the Provinces, has done so entirely on behalf of the public of these Provinces which has given it its fullest confidence and which expects the Congress Parties in the Legislature to conform to the general discipline of the Congress. But, by Mr Jinnah's own confession, neither the All-India Muslim League nor its Sind branch is able to command in that Province the allegiance of such a body of Muslim opinion as would give it authority with the Muslim members in the Legislature. Overlooking this basic fact, Mr Jinnah darkly warns the Muslim Ministers of the impending wrath of the Provincial Muslim League.

But, curiously enough, he is not averse to appealing to the Sind Government to scrap the legislation already passed introducing general electorates in borough municipalities, and he condescendingly pats them on the back for having decided 'in deference to the universal

Muslim opinion in the Province of Sind and outside', not to press on with the other pending Bills for the introduction of general electorates. Neither Mr Jinnah's threat nor his cajolery is likely to prove more successful than in the past in inducing any large section of the members to place themselves under the control of the League. What Sind needs above all else is a Government that will resolutely enforces law and order and restore peace and confidence in the countryside. Such a Government cannot be furnished by the Muslim League, whose President has nothing more to say about the lawlessness that prevailed in the Province for months on end than that the Hindus 'under the cover of murders in the Rohri division' withdrew their support to the Bundeh Ali Khan Ministry.

113. Jinnah's Advice to League Ministers

The Hindu, 20 February 1941.

The Azad Pact: Mr Jinnah's Criticism

(Associated Press of India)

New Delhi, 19 February.

Mr Mahomed Ali Jinnah, President of the All-India Muslim League, has issued the following statement:

'Khan Bahadur Khuhro was good enough to come all the way from Karachi to see me and he has placed the whole matter fully before me and in consultation with Sir Abdullah Haroon, President of the Provincial Muslim League, Sind, I have come to the conclusion that the so-called Pact of Agreement is a pure myth'.

'I am further strengthened in my opinion as I have been able to get a copy of the so-called secret document which is a letter dated 20th November 1940 addressed to Mr Nichaldas, signed only by Mr Sayed and Mr Khuhro, which was handed over to Mr Nichaldas to remain as a secret document Sheikh Abdul Majid, as soon as he was informed about it, repudiated it, and the very first proposal in the document, namely, that Sheikh Abdul Majid was to resign, was not carried out as he declined to do so. Mir Bundeh Ali says he was no party to it. The Provincial Muslim League, Sind, was not even consulted at any stage of the talks that were going on between certain individuals. To call this an agreement between the various groups and parties is, on the face of it, absurd.

'This document is now made the pivot upon which Khan Bahadur Allah Baksh, backed up by others, is threatening to create a crisis unless he is installed as the Premier and Sir Ghulam Hussain is included in the Ministry and one of the Muslim League members, who are in the Ministry, must go out of it.

'I think, if this threat is carried out, the entire responsibility will rest upon those who are bent upon creating a crisis in Sind. There is no obligation on the part of the League to comply with this demand. My advice, therefore to Mir Bundeh Ali, the Premier and the two other League Ministers is, not to surrender but to face any crisis that may be threatened, and continue the present Ministry so long as they have a majority in the Assembly, and if they are defeated, they should sit in the Opposition to any other Government that may be formed'.

114. Sind Cabinet Tangle

The Hindu, 22 February 1941.

Mr Allah Bux Replies to Mr Jinnah

(Associated Press of India)

Karachi, 21 February.

Two 'no-confidence' motions, one against the Ministry and another against the Premier, Mr Bundeh Ali Khan are understood to have been given notice of to-day by Pir Elahi Bux, a former Minister.

'Agreement Violated'

'We are determined to overthrow the Ministry. The three Muslim League Ministers by violating the Gentleman's Agreement have shown that they cannot be depended upon' declared Khan Bahadur Allah Bux, Finance Minister, who returned to Karachi this morning from Shikarpur, in an interview with the United Press. He added: 'One of my partymen is giving notice of a no-confidence motion to-day'.

Referring to Mr Jinnah's statement that the Azad Pact is a myth, Mr Allah Bux observed: 'Pact or no pact, the crux of the matter is, the Muslim League Ministers have violated the Gentleman's Agreement and made a meal of their own word of honour'.

As regards the party strength, the Minister stated: 'My party is composed of 15 Muslims, while the Muslim League cannot command more than 10 Muslims. I am confident, with the co-operation of the Congress and the Hindu Parties, I will be able to dislodge the Muslim League Ministers and form an alternative National Ministry'.

Premier Interviewed

Karachi, 20 February.

Mr M.A. Jinnah's firman from Delhi, issued with a view to sabotaging the Azad Pact, has been received in Karachi with mixed feelings. While the Muslim League circles welcome it, the Congress, the Allah Bux Group and the Hindu Parties characterize as unfortunate, as it foreshadows fresh trouble in the province.

Interviewed Mir Bundeh Ali Khan Talpur, the Premier said: 'I do not want to say anything till I have seen Khan Bahadur Khurro and obtained first-hand information from him. On his return from Delhi, we, the three Muslim League Ministers, will meet and decide the future course'.

Interviewed by the United Press, Sheikh Abdul Majid, Muslim League Minister, said: 'Mr Jinnah has voiced my feelings and those of the other Muslim Leaguers in Sind. The so-called Azad Pact has been repudiated by me from the beginning, and it bears no signatures of the parties concerned. It was an arrangement between individuals for which the parties should not be held responsible'.

Rai Sahib Gokuldas, Hindu Minister, in an interview, said: 'The Hindus stand by the Pact. We are bound by the solemn undertaking to implement its provisions. As the three Muslim League Ministers have been advised to back out, our duty, along with the Allah Buksh Group and the Congress, is clear. We may resign our seats from the Cabinet and support a no-confidence motion against the Muslim League Ministers. The final decision, however, rests with the Party, which is meeting on 21 February'.

Mr Khuro on League's Attitude

Mr Jinnah is anxious that the Muslim League should have a reasonable voice in shaping the Government's policy and fully safeguarding Muslim interests and holds that this cannot be achieved unless the League has an effective representation in the Cabinet, said Khan Bahadur Khuro, who returned to Karachi this morning from Delhi at a press conference at Premier Mir Bundeh Ali's residence this evening.

Khan Bahadur Khurro added that Mr Jinnah was anxious to maintain at least the present proportion of the Leaguers in the Government, namely, the strength of three out of the four Muslims in the Cabinet of six.

Proceeding, Khan Bahadur Khuro opined that although it was advantageous for the League to go into the Opposition for the purposes of making an effective appeal to the electorate in the forthcoming general elections, the Leaguers elected to remain in office purely in the larger interests of the province. Explaining the position, Mr Khuro asserted that he had made proper representation to Mr Jinnah to whom he had shown the Azad Pact and all its clauses. He added that merely 33⅓ per cent representation in the Cabinet was likely to leave Muslim interests divided and this question did not arise if Hindu Ministers joined hands with the Allah Buksh Party when crucial questions were brought before the Cabinet.

115. The Azad Pact: Details of Mr Nichaldas's Letter to Mr Jinnah

The Hindu, 24 February 1941.

(Associated Press of India)

...The following are the relevant portions of Minister Nichaldas's letter to Mr Jinnah dated 4 February:

'I have received your letter to Mr Abdul Majid, I find therefrom that you are not in possession of correct facts. I am therefore acquainting you with the full facts which I know personally with regard to the arrangement arrived at during the presence of Maulana Azad in Karachi. Long before Maulana Azad arrived in Karachi Mr G.M. Syed, Mr Abdul Majid and Mr Khuro, all three of them were most anxious to bring Khan Bahadur Allah Bux in the Cabinet. They had been requesting him for some months to come in the Cabinet but Mr Allah Bux was not prepared to do so. Again and again efforts were made to bring him in; again and again both Mr Abdul Majid and Mr G.M. Syed volunteered to resign in his favour. In fact, about twenty days or so before Maulana Azad's arrival, Mr Abdul Majid had actually written his resignation and handed it over to the Premier, Mr Abdul Majid had even gone and told the Governor of this move on his part. Mir Bundeh Ali also was anxious that Mr Allah Bux should come in the Cabinet and he went to the length of requesting the Governor to induce Mr Allah Bux to accept the offer but His Excellency's attempts failed. Maulana Azad at the time of arrival in Karachi was of the opinion that the then existing Cabinet should be overthrown and that Mr Allah Bux should form the Government, but I acquainted Maulana Azad with the conditions in the province and gave him my very considered opinion that it will be inadvisable to resort to that method. I further put forward my strong opinion that Muslim representatives in the

Cabinet should represent all Muslim parties in the Assembly. I believe that my arguments convinced him completely and I must say thereafter Maulana Azad's entire endeavour was to bring both the Muslim parties together. I convinced Maulana Azad that, even the good of Hindus lay in both the Muslim parties coming together as otherwise, if only one Muslim party is in the Government, the other in the Opposition would appeal to the fanatic sentiment of Muslim masses and carry on a virulent propaganda through party papers and hold up the Muslim party in Government as pro-Hindu....

'The Premier, Mr Bundeh Ali was to continue as Premier until 15 February and then resign and if Mr Syed and Mr Abdul Majid felt that by 15 February Mr Allah Bux was working harmoniously he should be made Premier, otherwise Sir Ghulam Hussain would be Premier.

'At this stage, Maulana Azad wanted things to be reduced to writing. I do not mind telling you Mr Jinnah I did not like the idea that a gentleman's word was more sacred than his writing, but I find now that Maulana Azad was wiser than myself. It was briefly to the following effect: that in order to bring about unity between the Muslim members of the Assembly, it was decided that one of the three Muslim League Ministers should resign immediately, that Mr Allah Bux should come in and that on 15 February Mr Bundeh Ali should resign the Premiership and in case he elected to remain as a junior Minister, one of the signatories, namely, Mr Syed or Mr Khuro would resign and Sir Ghulam Hussain would come in and Mr Allah Bux or Sir Ghulam Hussain would be eligible for the Premier's post'.

Mr Syed's Resignation

'Again thereafter, some complications arose. Sir Abdullah Haroon returned to Karachi and he issued a mandate to Mr Abdul Majid not to resign. Mr Majid told Maulana Azad his difficulty that he could not resign without clearing the matter further, and at the meeting Mir Bundeh Ali, Mr Syed, Mr Abdul Majid and Mr Khuro were present. My colleague, Rao Saheb Gokuldas and I were also present. It was there that Mr Syed said that if Shaikh Abdul Majid was not resigning, he was doing so and then and there wrote out resignation and we went to the Governor with him and Mr Allah Bux.

'All along, my Muslim League colleagues were fully alive to the risk of the Muslim League organization taking offence at their conduct. Therefore they felt that, if they gave anything in writing to Maulana Azad directly, that might in itself be taken as a breach of discipline and they might be expelled from the League. We however got over the difficulty. An undertaking was addressed to me and I passed it on to Maulana Azad with my endorsement. Mir Bundeh Ali did not agree to give anything in writing. He said that he belonged to a noble family and his word must be accepted. He assured me privately and also Maulana Azad that he would stand by his word and would resign on 15 February. He also undertook to acquaint the Governor of his promise, so that our doubts may be set at rest, and he actually did so. However thereafter, there was some sort of talk between Mr Khuro, Mr Syed and Mir Bundeh Ali. So, by the time the agreement was drawn up they had modified the arrangement slightly. The slight modification was to the effect that Mir Bundeh Ali might continue to be junior Minister if he so wished after 15 February, that, in that event, one of them, namely, Mr Khuro or Mr Syed would resign. The draft was dictated by Mr Khuro himself and then both Mr Syed and Mr Khuro signed the document with open eyes....'

116. Mahatma Gandhi's Advice to Sind Assembly Congress Party

CWMG, Vol. LXXIII, p. 351.

[Before 27 February 1941]

The Azad Arrangement should be adhered to, failing which the Congress members of the Assembly should help in dethroning the present Ministry and support Khan Bahadur Allah Baksh, in forming a new Ministry.

It is understood that Mahatma Gandhi had earlier expressed the opinion that in case the Azad pact was broken, the Congress members should resign and come out of the Assembly, but on a reference being made to him whether he was still of the same opinion, Mahatma Gandhi expressed the above view, having learned in the meanwhile Maulana Azad's mind in the matter.

117. (i) Sind Cabinet Resigns
Khan Bahadur Allah Baksh to Form New Ministry
Dramatic Turn of Events

Amrita Bazar Patrika, 7 March 1941.

The Premier Mir Bundeh Ali Khan Talpur, Khan Bahadur Khurro, and Shaikh Abdul Majid, the three League Ministers, tendered their resignations to the Governor at 4 p.m.

Khan Bahadur Allah Baksh, the Opposition leader, was summoned by HE the Governor this evening and he has agreed to form a new Ministry. It is almost certain that the following five namely, Khan Bahadur Allah Baksh (Premier), Sir Ghulam Hussain Hidayatullah, Pir Elahi Bux, Mr Nichaldas Vazirani and Rao Sahib Gokuldas will be sworn in while the choice of the sixth Minister (Muslim) is believed to be kept pending for the time being.

Mr Nichaldas Vazirani, Rai Saheb Gokuldas and Khan Bahadur Allah Baksh, Ministers, had resigned their seats in the Cabinet this morning.

The dramatic announcement was preceded by a tame debate on a revenue demand for Rs 22,44,000. All cuts tabled in the demand were either withdrawn or not moved.

Dramatic Announcement

The announcement of the resignation of the three ministers Khan Bahadur Allah Baksh, Mr Nichaldas Vazirani and Rao Saheb Gokuldas took their three colleagues by surprise. The ministerial benches were practically deserted except for the presence of half a dozen Muslim supporters of the League ministers and two European members. The public, expecting a battle royal tomorrow when the no confidence motion against the Premier which was due to be discussed, was totally unprepared for the dramatic turn of events and this was evidenced by the sparse attendance in the gallery. An inkling of the coming storm was provided by the good attendance on the opposition benches, thirty-four being present comprising sixteen Muslim supporters of Khan Bahadur Allah Baksh, eleven Hindus and seven Congressites.

In accordance with a pre-arranged plan the Opposition members withdrew all the one rupee cut motions. Mr M.H. Gazdar (Muslim League) also withdrew his one rupee cut motion under the head of land revenue. General discussion of the entire demand did not take more than one hour. Towards the end of the discussion Mr Nichaldas Vazirani, Minister in charge, replying said: 'I am quite convinced that the whole House is fully satisfied with my policy and my department'. He then suddenly announced the resignation of himself and his two other colleagues in the following words. 'Now, Sir the position is this. You know very well that the Premier made a statement here that some of his colleagues were not seeing eye to eye with him and he has been desiring my resignation. I therefore have submitted my resignation to the Governor. With your permission I may be allowed to cross over'.

Rao Saheb Gokuldas, Minister for Local Self-Government, then announced 'I also have resigned and submitted my resignation to the Governor'.

Khan Bahadur Allah Baksh next addressed the House.

He said that he would have liked to continue till the time of moving of the no-confidence motion against the Premier fixed for to-morrow but unfortunately he had received a leaflet in which the Muslim League had threatened members not remaining in their fold and expressed its intention of staging a demonstration at the secretariat. 'It was not possible for us', he said, 'to submit to that coercion. Coercion being there we decided that there should be no further talks and we therefore tendered our resignation'. Immediately after his statement Mr Allah Baksh walked over to the Opposition benches.

'We Have No Majority'

After the three ministers had crossed the floor, the Premier, Mir Bundeh Ali addressing the House and said: 'We have no majority. My three colleagues who ought to have resigned long ago say that they have resigned to-day. Therefore, I have no other alternative but to go out and I am handing my resignation as well as the Cabinet's resignation to HE the Governor this evening'.

Voices: 'Take votes.

The Speaker: 'I will put the demand to voice.

Khan Bahadur Khurro: 'The Premier has clearly stated that he has no majority for the Government and that he is tendering the Cabinet's resignation this evening'. Therefore he requests that the business of the House be suspended.

Several voice: 'No no.

Khan Bahadur Khurro: 'What is the objection?

Sir Ghulam Hussein: 'The demand has been moved and as the House is in possession of the demand, it should be put to vote and whether it is rejected or accepted depends upon the House.

Constitutional Issue

Mr M.H. Gazdar (Muslim League): 'This is a first class constitutional issue. Now that the Revenue Minister Mr Nichaldas says that he has resigned and the Premier says that he is resigning, no body takes the responsibility for the demand and the House should be adjourned.

Sir Ghulam: 'How can we trust the Premier when he says he is resigning this evening.

The Speaker Miran Mohamed Shah: 'The Premier is the head of the Government and if, he cannot maintain the sanctity of his promise made on the floor of the House, how can he occupy office?

Khan Bahadur Allah Baksh: 'I do not think that the Premier can get out of his announcement made in the House because the Chair will inform the Government that he had suspended the business of the House on the clear understanding that the Premier is tendering resignation. I personally feel that this ought to satisfy the Opposition.

The Speaker concurred with Mr Allah Baksh and adjourned the House till tomorrow 11 a.m.'—AP

(ii) New Cabinet for Sind
Mr Alla Bux Announces his Colleagues

Amrita Bazar Patrika, 9 March 1941.

Karachi, 8 March.

It is officially announced that Khan Bahadur Allah Baksh, the Premier, presented to His Excellency the Governor this morning his colleagues in the new Cabinet, Sir Ghulam Hussain Hidayatullah, Pir Elahi Bux, Mr Nichaldas Vazirani and Rao Saheb Gokuldas, who were then sworn in as Ministers.

The following will be the portfolios in the new Government: Khan Bahadur Allah Baksh, Premier Finance and Excise and PWD until a sixth Minister is appointed. Sir Ghulam Hussain Hidayatullah—Law and Order. Mr Nichaldas Vazirani—Revenue, Rao Saheb Gokuldas—Agriculture and Local Self-Government, Pir Elahi Bux—Education, Public Health Prisons and Labour.

The desire of the present Government is to continue the Azad arrangement with regard to the All Party Committee of the Assembly consisting of representatives of all sections of the House was expressed by the Premier Khan Bahadur Allah Baksh in an interview with the Associated Press. He added that the Committee's function will be in the nature of a High Command for the purpose of direction of the Government's policy.

'The present Ministry wishes it to be known that their first care will be the preservation of inter-communal harmony in Sind and the maintenance of law and order', said Sir Ghulam Hussein Hidayatullah, Minister for Law and Order, in a statement to the Associated Press. He added that any attempt whatsoever to provoke ill-feeling between the various communities either by making provocative speeches or by the organization of public demonstrations, which are likely to cause a breach of the peace will be promptly dealt with and all possible measures will be taken to ensure peace in the province.

Khan Bahadur Gabole has been appointed Parliamentary Secretary to Sir Gulam Hussein Hidayatullah, Minister for Law and Order.

An open invitation to Sheikh Abdul Majid the former League minister to join the Cabinet was extended in the Sind Assembly this morning by the Premier, Khan Bahadur Allah Baksh while replying to the debate on a Rs 100 cut motion sponsored by Doctor Popatlal (Congress) under the head excise. The invitation followed the Sheikh's offer of responsive cooperation in case the ministry adopted his five-year plan for achieving prohibition in the province.

The ministerial benches were well attended, the entire Hindu block of twelve members and seventeen Muslim supporters of the ministry occupying them. With the support of the Congressites (seven) and the Europeans (three) the ministry appears to command a strength of about forty. The new ministers were cheered as they took their seats on the Treasury benches.

118. Sind Governor's Letter to Viceroy on Divisive Politics in Sind

From Sir Hugh Dow, Governor of Sind to Viceroy, 23 July 1941
Correspondence with the Governor of Sind and his Secretary, 1941, Linlithgow Papers, Acc. No. 2231, NAI.

Government House, Karachi,
23 July 1941

No. 258 F.R.

Dear Lord Linlithgow,

This is my usual fortnightly letter, to which is appended the official Fortnightly Report for the first half of July. [...]

2. I had a talk with my Premier on his return from his discussions with Sir Sikander Hyat Khan at Lahore on the 6th instant. From him I gathered that Sikander, through his own membership of the Muslim League and his personal influence with many of its leading members in the Punjab, is confident that communal relations in the Punjab districts have improved to such an extent that communal outbreaks need not be feared if the war situation should develop into a real crisis. Sikander has managed to get members of the Muslim League and Congress working together on his 'unity' committees, and according to Allah Baksh, the intransigence of the Muslim League in Sind came as a surprise to Sikander who was inclined to take a serious view of it.

3. Undoubtedly Allah Baksh is handicapped in this matter by the fact that he is outside the League, with which his differences are probably irreconcilable as long as Jinnah remains in control. So long as the Muslim Leaguers here are outside the Ministry, and particularly while the question of the postponement of provincial elections remains undecided, they are likely to take advantage of accentuating their differences from the ministerial party, and will not willingly agree to any cessation of political propaganda in the name of Hindu–Muslim unity. In the Muslim League propaganda in Sind, Pakistan is very much to the fore: perhaps nobody takes Pakistan very seriously, but the arguments by which it is supported—that Hindus and Muslims are like oil and water and can never mix, and that Muslims should not abate any of their pretensions where they are in the majority—are ones from which ignorant rustics are apt to draw very practical conclusions, and the League's activities undoubtedly result in accentuating the state of apprehension in which many Hindus live in the villages of Sind.

4. I think Allah Baksh has come back with the feeling that he may have to take strong measures against individual members of the League if they persist in their highly communal propaganda, and if they continue to pour scorn on the 'unity' movement, which has now, with the passing of a grant by the Legislative Assembly for the purpose, been definitely adopted as a Government policy. I see no reason why I should attempt to dissuade him from this conclusion, and in view of the possibility of this having to be translated into action, you might like to have my estimate of the character and position of the leading Muslim Leaguers in Sind. There are only half a dozen of them who are prominent enough for action against them to make even a ripple outside the Province: they are Sir Haji Abdulla Haroon, MLA, G.M. Syed; K.B. Khurro and Abdul Majid, all of whom are ex-Ministers; M.H. Gazdar, Mayor of Karachi; and Mir Bundeh Ali Khan, ex-Premier.

5. Of these I regard only G.M. Syed as a potentially dangerous man. He is at the same time fanatical and shrewd and has courage. He is the only one whom I apprehend it might become

necessary to place under restraint: he is the real leader of the movement in Sind. The nominal leader is Haroon, who is also a fanatic, and he is influential because of his wealth and position. But he is an errant coward and would come to heel the moment he realized that Government meant business and were prepared to take repressive action. Abdul Majid (whose father's name is Lilaram) is capable of the usual excesses of the convert, but is not likely to give way to them in those purely political manoeuvres. Khurro is a dishonest, careerist, but I can't imagine him making sacrifices for any cause: when the Manzilgah agitation which he had fomented reached danger point, he was only too willing to accept the advice to withdraw himself. Gazdar would, for perhaps the first time in his dingy career, think it advisable to honour one of his own undertakings, and would refrain from undesirable political activities on the score of his mayoralty. There remains the ex-Premier, Mir Bundeh Ali Khan, whose connection with the League may be regarded as purely temporary: he has so far let down everyone of his political associates who was ill-advised enough to accept his word as a 'gentleman', and the only thing for which he can now be trusted is to do it again....

119. Sind Premier on his Grave Responsibility, 'Accepted Seat on Defence Council in Interest of Province'

Bombay Chronicle, 28 August 1941.

Karachi, 26 August.

'In view of the grave responsibility and also in view of the international situation and the vulnerable position of Sind in general and Karachi in particular, I felt in the interest of the province that I should accept a seat on the National Defence Council', declared the Premier, Khan Bahadur Allabaksh, in an interview to the Associated Press who asked what steps he proposed to take in view of the Muslim League resolution.

The Premier pointed out that the decision of those Muslim Premiers who belong to the Muslim League and are committed to follow its mandate to resign from the Council, cannot be a determining factor in his case. The governing factor so far as he was concerned, he added, was the duty he owed to his supporters in the Sind Legislature to whose suffering including the Congress Party in the Assembly, he owed his return to the Premiership of the Province.

No Sectional Considerations

Proceeding he said: 'The fact that I have returned to that office as a result of my having received the support of all communities and all political parties represented in the Sind Legislature with the exception of the Muslim League Party imposes upon me the distinct obligation that in all public matters, I should be solely guided by the interests of the province as a whole, and not by any partisan communal of sectional considerations whatsoever'.

He added, 'When I came back to my present office, it was with the general desire of the province that I should bring about peace and goodwill and a feeling of security among the various creeds and communities in the province. Having regard to that grave responsibility and also in view of the international situation and the vulnerable position of Sind in general and Karachi in particular, I felt that it was in the interest of the province that I should accept a seat on the National Defence Council.

In Premier's Capacity

'Before I accepted the appointment it was made perfectly clear between me and His Excellency the Governor of Sind that my going on the Defence Council was purely in my capacity as the Premier of the Province and there was no doubt or question in either of our minds that I was being asked in this capacity and in no other. Whether I am the Premier or whether any other member of the Sind Legislature holds that office, the Premier must fully protect the vital interests of the province. Since my duty as the Premier, as already stated, makes it incumbent upon me to represent the interests of my province in all matters vitally affecting its well-being, the question of my resignation from the Defence Council does not arise'.

Concluding, he said, the only parties whose views I should have to regard in coming to a decision on this matter are my supporters in the Sind Legislature whether belonging to my own party or to the Congress.—AP

120. Mahatma Gandhi's Letter to Vallabhbhai Patel on Congress Leaving the Ministry

CWMG, Vol. LXXIV, p. 335.

Sevagram
19 September 1941

Bhai Vallabhbhai,

I had long and frank talks with Khan Bahadur (Alla Bux). He is now going to Karachi. From there he will go to see Maulana. I am firmly of the view that the Congress should leave the Assembly. Khan Bahadur also, if he is on the Congress side, should do the same. The Congress in Sind helping the war effort while not doing so elsewhere would produce—is producing—a bad impression. Keeping up this arrangement will not benefit the country in any way, neither Sind nor the Hindus nor the Muslims. Can a wrong step benefit anybody? Even if there were no war, I would be in favour of the Congress leaving the Assembly in Sind. But that is a side issue just now. I will discuss it with you if you wish. Here, I have explained how my mind is working, so that you may be able to understand Khan Bahadur correctly. He says he is convinced by my reasoning.

Blessings from
Bapu

121. Sind Congress Party to Support K.B. Allah Baksh

Amrita Bazar Patrika, 22 September 1941.

Bombay, 20 September.

Khan Bahadur Allah Baksh interviewed on his mission to Wardha said that the Congress party in Sind would continue to lend support to the present Sind Ministry in accordance with instructions issued by Maulana Abul Kalam Azad. Mahatma Gandhi had now made it clear that the Congress party in the Sind legislature would follow those instructions as there was nothing to warrant a review of the present policy.

The Sind Premier said that he went to Wardha accompanied by Mr R.K. Sidhwa, leader of the Congress party in the Sind legislature, with a view to preventing any controversy arising out of his appointment on the National Defence Council.

Khan Bahadur Allah Baksh revealed that recently the Congress President had addressed from the Naini Jail a telegram to the President of the Sind Provincial Congress Committee stating that he considered it inadvisable for Congressmen in Sind to demand Khan Bahadur Allah Baksh's resignation from the National Defence Council. Maulana Azad had pointed out that the Sind Premier was not a member of the Congress. The Congress party had decided to support him because of the exceptional circumstances in Sind and those circumstances had not since altered. It would be deplorable for Sind Congressmen to change the course of conduct laid down by the Congress President, the Maulana had added.

Khan Bahadur Allah Baksh emphasized that he would always place the interest of his province in the forefront when in the National Defence Council. He added that now all parties in Sind were working very harmoniously. The Ministry at the moment was concerned with two important problems: the distribution of the Indus water between Sind and the Punjab and the repayment of the Lloyd Barage debt which would begin next year. The Sind Government hoped to tackle the problem as best they could.—AP

122. Allah Baksh Meets Azad: Will Meet Gandhiji Shortly

Bombay Chronicle, 4 October 1941.

Allahabad, 3 October.

Khan Bahadur Allah Baksh, Premier of Sind, left for Simla via Delhi this morning by the Calcutta–Delhi Mail.

The Premier had an interview with Maulana Abul Kalam Azad in the Naini Central Jail this morning for about two hours from 7.30 to 9.30 a.m. He returned to Anand Bhawan and immediately left for Simla.

Approached by pressmen Khan Bahadur Allah Baksh declined to say anything about the nature of his talks with the Maulana.

Asked if there was any question at this time of his resigning from the National Defence Council, he replied in the negative. Again asked if the unity scheme of the Sind Government came up for discussion, Khan Bahadur Allah Baksh reiterated that he was not in a position to say anything about the talks.

He said that he and the Maulana had a full discussion and they had decided not to say anything about the interview.

It is confirmed that Mr Allah Baksh will see Mahatma Gandhi shortly after the meeting of the National Defence Council...—AP

123. Sind Governor's Letter to the Viceroy on the Sind Ministry

From Sir Hugh Dow, Governor of Sind to Viceroy, 21 December 1941. Correspondence with the Governor of Sind and his Secretary, 1941, Linlithgow Papers, Acc. No. 2231, NAI.

Camp Bano
21 December 1941

Dear Lord Linlithgow,

In continuation of my letter of yesterday, I now enclose a printed copy of the statement which was made by the Premier in the Assembly on the 19th instant.

It may be of interest to you to know that the corrections in the Council Reporter's copy of the Premier's statement as actually taken down, and which I have seen, are some of them in the handwriting not of the Premier, but of Nichaldas, who is responsible for the interpolation which I have underlined on page 2 of the printed statement.

The Chief Secretary informs me that the whole business seems to have been staged by the Premier and HMs, and that copies of the statement were distributed to the press.

Yours sincerely,
H. Dow

[Enclosure]

Statement made by the Hon'ble Khan Bahadur Allah Bakhsh on the floor of the Sind legislative Assembly on 19th December 1941 regarding the appointment of Mr Harford as Revenue Officer Lloyd Barrage.

The Hon'ble Khan Bahadur Allah Bakhsh: Before I come to the question of the exercise of his individual judgment by His Excellency the Governor I think it will be necessary to provide a background which I think will take me a short time and therefore I would request the House to bear with me for a short while.

Now the House is fully aware that when the Government of India Act of 1935 was passed. It was held in political quarters that the responsibility of self-government which was transferred to the people of this country was to be retarded by various provisions in the Act and those provisions dealt with the individual judgment, the special responsibility and discretion of the Governor. After that an understanding was arrived at between the Congress on one side and His Excellency the Viceroy on the other which had the full approval of the British Government with regard to the exercise of those powers and in that it was suggested that there would be no interference from the Governor in the day to-day administration.

Mr Dialmal Daulatram: Which is within the four corners of the constitution.

The Hon'ble the Deputy Speaker: No interruption.

The Hon'ble Khan Bahadur Allah Bakhsh: Before the arrival of the present Governor and when I last resumed the reins of office as Premier the attitude of his predecessor with regard to the exercise of these powers was—and he made the position clear to me—that as far as possible he had no desire whatsoever to interfere with the administration of the Province.

Mr M.A. Khuhro: And that resulted in Sukkur riots.

The Hon'ble Khan Bahadur Allah Bakhsh: His attitude had been to avoid interference as far as possible. The present Governor has interpreted the exercise of these powers in a different way. What he feels is this. In all matters where under the Act he has to exercise his individual judgment and in all matters in which he has his special responsibility, he must exercise his own judgment in all matters where he holds an opinion different to those of his Ministers, whether the matter is so important and the Ministers advice so perverse that being guided by his Ministers' advice will be inconsistent with the exercise of his special responsibility, or whether it is a matter of mere difference of opinion regarding certain day to-day administration items. His Excellency does not seem to appreciate that even in matters in which His Excellency has special responsibility, the primary responsibility is of the Ministers. He has gone even so far as to say that in the provinces where Governors have abstained from exercising those powers it has been done not in accordance either with the instructions or the policy of the British Government as such. Therefore Hon'ble Members need not be anxious to know all those instances where such differences have arisen. If the present policy of His Excellency the Governor is approved by the Viceroy and the British Cabinet then it raises a constitutional issue. The House will agree with me that so far as we Ministers are concerned, we are responsible to the Legislature and we owe no responsibility to anyone else, and so far as the Governor is concerned, his position is that he owes responsibility to the Secretary of State for India. In view of the stand taken up by His Excellency, there can be no question of give and take, His Excellency has pointed out to me that the Government of India Act imposes a responsibility upon the Ministers that while tendering their advice they have to suggest whether his special responsibility or individual judgment is involved or not, and he has clearly indicated that he intends to act in future also according to his views quoted above. And he being responsible to the Secretary of State for India and we being responsible to the Legislature, there is bound to be a clash every day on the files. If the attitude which the present Governor has taken—namely, that irrespective of the issue, whether it is major or minor, he must exercise his individual judgment—then I think there will be a regular list to be prepared of all the instances in which the interests would clash.

Now, personally I do not know how the Act can work, nor do I feel that in other provinces where there were Congress Ministers....

(At this stage the Hon'ble Speaker came and occupied the Chair).

The Hon'ble the Speaker: Order, order. Yes, the Hon'ble the Leader of the House.

The Hon'ble Khan Bahadur Allah Bakhsh: It means that it is a question of measuring the strength between the Governor representing the British Government on the one side and the people on the other. It would be impossible to assume for a moment that in the Congress Provinces with the advice on various matters in which the individual responsibility of His Excellency was involved there should have arisen no occasion or instance where the Governor had not differed from his Ministers, but it seems that there they had to surrender and surrender not on the merits but because of the power of the political party in those provinces. Now it clearly proves that the British Government is not prepared to part with the powers. They wish to retain them as far as possible. Only when there is sufficient strength, then they would surrender. Now it is not a question of one, two or three instances. Questions have arisen during recent months where this power has been exercised where according to us it should not have been, and several such questions are bound to arise in future with the attitude that has been taken.

Mr R.K. Sidhwa: By this Governor?

The Hon'ble Khan Bahadur Allah Baksh: Yes, and the House will legitimately ask why the Ministers are continuing to be in office under these humiliating conditions.

Khan Bahadur M.A. Khuhro: Exactly.

The Hon'ble Khan Bahadur Allah Bakhsh: That will be a proper question which I think can rightly be put to Ministers.

As I said, so far as the first issue of the general attitude in the exercise of these powers is concerned, it raises an all-India issue. The second question would be with regard to the merits of the case.

When I went to Delhi last time, I took up this question with His Excellency the Viceroy complaining against the exercise of these powers, and I told him that I would send the instances and everything to His Excellency the Viceroy. Under the Public Declaration of the Viceroy it was made clear that where the Ministers and the Governor disagreed, the Ministers were free to disclose correspondence which was carried on between the Governor and the Ministers. So when I came back I had a desire to bring all these instances before the House, but it has been suggested to me by His Excellency the Governor that in the first instance it would be desirable that the cases over which we have disagreed may be sent to the Secretary of State for India and we should await his decision.

Khan Bahadur M.A. Khuhro: Or the Viceroy first!

The Hon'ble Khan Bahadur Allah Bakhsh: Through the Viceroy to the Secretary of State for India.

Now this raises two constitutional issues.

As I said, the whole issue can be divided into two parts—whether the Governor, as a matter of policy as he has said, irrespective of the fact whether the issue is major or minor, if he differs from the advice given by the Ministers, he is bound to exercise his individual judgment and no option is left to him. The second question would be with regard to the merits.

Now, so far as His Excellency the Governor is concerned, he has to satisfy the Secretary of State that he has exercised those powers in the fairest way, and we have to satisfy the House that the advice tendered by us to His Excellency the Governor was in the interests of the Province. Therefore on one side the advice which we have tendered will have to be judged by the House and no one else, and similarly on the other side so far as the overruling is concerned, the Governor has to satisfy the Secretary of State. So there will again come a clash between the people of the Province on one side and the British Government on the other. What we have to see is whether His Excellency the Governor exercised his power of individual judgment or special responsibility in the interests of the administration of this country or in the interests of the British Imperialism; and there the clash is bound to come. Although if has been suggested to me, I personally feel that it is no use our resigning in a huff. Let us wait, and since this offer has been made by His Excellency the Viceroy, let us get some more information and have a clear-cut answer from the British Government as such, to find out what their attitude is going to be. Then the House will have to be taken into confidence and will have to be apprised of all those instances which have taken place so far and which are likely to take place hereafter, and then we should decide on the merits whether the advice tendered by the Ministers was a right one or whether the decision which has been arrived at by His Excellency the Governor was in the interests of this country or not.

II. Punjab

124. Newspaper Report on Discussion in Punjab Legislative Assembly on Communal Situation

The Tribune, 12 March 1941.

Sir Sikander Stands for Zonal Division of India

'If Pakistan means Muslim Raj, I will have nothing to do with it', says he.

'I drafted the Lahore resolution of the Muslim League but now it cannot be called my resolution because the last part which related to a co-ordinating central authority was deleted.'

'India should be divided into zones. The units must be fully autonomous. A Central authority should act as their agent.'

'The apprehensions of the Muslims about the Centre must be removed.'

'I want raj of Punjabees here.'

'We are not a Muslim League Government; we are Punjabee Government.'

'The body controlling the Gurdwaras is acting beyond its scope and is actually taking sides in politics.'

'In the matter of services no injustice has been done to any community.'

—Sir Sikander.

Lahore, 11 March. Discussion was continued in the Punjab Assembly today on Mian Nurullah's cut motion to censure the Punjab Government for its failure to bring about communal harmony, on the demand for General Administration.

Lala Sita Ram resuming his incomplete speech of yesterday pleaded that joint electorates should be made the basis for elections. He suggested that all communal demonstrations like the holding of Pakistan conference should be banned.

Begum Rashida Latif Baji suggested that out of Rs One lakh, Rs 25,000 should be placed at the disposal of women who, she said, could help in establishing communal harmony. She was one of those who believed that God was not of the Muslims alone but of the whole of humanity. She, therefore, stood for complete unity among all sections of the populace.

R.B. Sohan Lal (Ministerial) said that communal harmony could not be established by providing one lakh of rupees. To achieve that object the Government should take a bold stand and introduce joint electorates and discourage denominational institutions.

Syed Amjad Ali maintained that communal harmony could not be established by replacing communal electorates by joint electorates or by giving services on merit alone. The problem was far deeper than it appeared to be. In his opinion the best method to achieve communal harmony was to demolish social barriers and encourage inter-dinning and inter-marriages. Joint electorates, he thought, would encourage more communalism.

At this stage, Sardar Santosh Singh, Leader of the Independent Party, asked that the 'question be put.' The motion when put to the House was declared lost.

Dr Narang pointed out that the party in power seemed to be manipulating in order to deprive the Opposition of a fair chance of having all their cut motions discussed.

The Speaker held that the Opposition was in a hopeless minority.

If all the members of the House would like to speak that would mean that no time would be left for important matters to be discussed.

It was, however, agreed that the Premier would be the last speaker on the subject.

Zonal Division of India

The Premier on rising explained his position with regard to Pakistan and availed of an opportunity to point out that he stood for the freedom of India under the British Commonwealth to cut away from which would be criminal in his opinion. He stood for the zonal division of India as stated by him in his scheme, each zone being fully autonomous with an elastic central authority not with the object of domineering the units but acting as their agent.

The Premier began by saying that the provision of a lakh of rupees for establishing communal harmony was not a joke and that they had no sinister motives. 'We want to make yet another attempt to achieve that object,' said the Premier, 'because we on this side of the house firmly believe that without communal harmony there could be no economic, political or commercial progress'.

Referring to the resolution of the unity conference on 'Jhatka', the Premier said that he would undertake to have the resolution sponsored for unanimous ratification if his friends opposite agreed to it. He pointed out that it would not mean that every person would have a licence to slaughter any animal, wherever he liked. But if the resolution could be ratified, he would be prepared to add a rider that due regard shall always be paid to the religious sentiments of all the communities concerned.

Regarding the question of languages, the Premier reiterated his position of sticking to status quo.

It had been stated, said the Premier, that the question of legislation in matters relating to religion should be left to the members of the community concerned. He wanted to remind the Sikhs, that the Gurdwara Act was passed only with the help of the Unionist Party and it was opposed by other sections of the House.

If the old Council had a right to legislate on a religious matter, why could not this assembly have the same right to legislate on the same matter?

Is Taking Sides in Politics

The Gurdwara Act, he said, was passed with a view to give a full and effective control to Sikhs of their Gurdwaras. But could any one deny that the body controlling the Gurdwaras was acting beyond its scope and was actually taking sides in politics. The Premier suggested it to the Sikh members opposite that, if they could get him an assurance that the controlling body of the Gurdwaras would refrain from participating in any non-secular activities, which was strictly speaking not their domain, he would be ready to make his friends agree to establishing a convention that in matters relating to religion the final decision shall be left to the vote of the members of the community concerned. In that case, any Amending Bill to the Gurdwara Act would be left to the vote of the Sikh members only.

Referring to the question of services, the Premier maintained that no injustice had been done to any community. The Government was acting upon the formula of 50 per cent for Muslims, 80 per cent for Sikhs and 30 per cent for Hindus and others and that formula was very just.

Replying to a query, the Premier said: 'We are not a Muslim League Government; we are Punjabi Government.'

The Premier appealed to everybody not to harp on that question or give any provocation to those sitting with him. The Punjab Government at present, he said, consisted of the Unionist Party cum the Khalsa Nationalist Party and the Independent Hindu Members.

Sir Sikander and Pakistan Scheme

Replying to the criticism regarding his attitude towards Pakistan, the Premier asked to which Pakistan scheme they referred. There was, for instance, the Jamal-ud-Din Afghani's Pakistan scheme, there was a scheme of Pakistan associated with the name of the late Sir Mohd Iqbal; a Pakistan scheme of Ch. Rehmat Ali and then there was a Pakistan scheme by an Englishman.

S. Lal Singh: We want to know your position regarding the Pakistan scheme as contained in the Lahore resolution of the League.

The Premier replied that the scheme set forth in the Lahore resolution of the Muslim League had been wrongly dubbed as a Pakistan scheme. The Premier admitted having drafted Lahore resolution but he pointed out that the resolution could not be called his resolution now as the last part of the resolution which related to co-ordinating central authority had been deleted.

To give that resolution of the League the name of Pakistan was in his view, the biggest mistake which his Hindu and Sikh friends had committed.

In fact, the Muslims themselves were not quite clear which Pakistan scheme they were supporting. Nor was Mr Jinnah in favour of the extra-territorial scheme. There prevailed a confusion, he said. The word 'Pakistan' had fascinated the Muslim masses, while the other communities were opposed to it. The fact remained that the label of Pakistan was being exploited and the scheme was not examined on its merits.

Criminal Folly

The future destiny of India, said the Premier, lay in accepting a position of freedom within the British Commonwealth. It would be criminal to cut ourselves away from the British Commonwealth. To talk of the independence outside the British Commonwealth was useless. 'Let us visualize what would be our fate without the British Navy at Singapore to protect us', he added. 'We shall not enjoy the privilege of British protection unless we remain within the British Commonwealth. Having helped Britain we would ask British help and protection to defend our country.' The Premier felt that it would be criminal folly to think of cutting away from the British Commonwealth.

Explaining what sort of constitution he would like for India, the Premier had no hesitation in saying that in spite of various developments he still maintained that his zonal scheme was most suitable.

The units, he said, would be fully autonomous and enjoy full freedom in matters economic, religious and cultural with a central authority. Fortunately, he said, India was divided in such a manner that every community had an opportunity to rule with the help of the minority. The Hindus could rule in seven provinces and the Muslims could do so in the remaining four provinces without grudging each other.

Referring to the apprehension of the Muslims, the Premier said that they thought that, if the provinces were to be under the Central Government they would always have to remain under Hindu majority. The Premier stressed the necessity of removing that apprehension whether that was well-founded or not. They had to be realistic and concede that the Hindus might rule in the 7 provinces and the Muslims in 4 with the help of minorities in their respective provinces. They ought to be more realistic and they should learn not to grudge each other or to look through communal glasses but look at that matter from the point of India as a whole. If they did it, he had no doubt that difficulties would vanish and that they would have bright sunshine in their land, which was marred by communalism today. He maintained that the provinces should not have a domineering Centre but a Centre with a Government or a Consolidation Committee acting as an Agent of all and every one of the units. India with autonomous units and a Centre representative of all the units would be far stronger than as India with a superimposed Government.

Elastic Centre

The Premier had no doubt that if the apprehensions of the Muslims regarding the Centre were set to rest, they would not insist upon cutting away from India. If any people did it, they should be considered mad and the only place for them would be lunatic asylums. 'Let the Centre be made elastic.' The details could be settled by experts.

Such a Government at the Centre would help in allaying Muslim apprehensions. He asked the Muslims to accept that and if they found after 10 years that they were not treated well, they would then be justified in asking for a complete separation. But they were not justified in asking for separation at the present time. A unifying centre, said the Premier, was necessary to remove disparities of various kinds. If they had no Central authority who would settle customs problems. If there was no Centre, Maulvi Fazlul Haq coming from Calcutta to Lahore to consult the Nawab of Mamdot on the Pakistan issue would have to face the customs authorities at Asansol and then at Patna and again at Saharanpur.

Defence

The question of defence, continued the Premier, was ever important and it could be dealt with by a Central authority only. The Punjab undoubtedly provided 62 per cent of the recruits of the army but 64 crores were spent by the Centre Government. Without a strong defence their independence would not be longer lived than a day.

Then there was the question of a currency which could be settled by a Central Government only. Freedom, said the Premier, could not be had by raising slogans and by shouting catch-phrases. If they want freedom that freedom must be not for one community alone but for all.

The Premier, added, amidst cheers: 'We don't want freedom for Muslim domination in the Punjab. If Pakistan means unalloyed Muslim *raj*, I will have nothing to do with it; I want the *raj* of the Panjabees here, a *raj* in which every community will have a share as an equal partner.

The Premier, proceeding further, claimed the right of self-determination for the Punjab. The Premier said that he, like any other man, would welcome any advice given by any outsider, but he wanted to make it clear that he would like to be left to himself to accept or reject that advice. He wanted outsiders not to exploit the situation here for, if any bloodshed occurred in the Punjab, the blood of the poor would be on the heads of those who exploited slogans. He pleaded once again that they should look at things not from the angle of one community but from the angle of the good of the whole of India.

Cat's Paw Sikhs

The Premier, referring to the declarations made by the Sikhs, said that he had no quarrel with them if they said that they would not let Pakistan be established. But he asked them not to allow themselves to be used as a cat's paw by the majority community in preventing the division of India. They would not be able to have more than 2 per cent at the Centre, while they were getting 20 per cent in the Punjab though their share on the issue of population was much less. If they merge themselves in the majority community, their independent existence would vanish.

Concluding the Premier made an appeal to the various communities in the Punjab to stand together like a bundle of sticks, which while together, could not be broken. 'Let us learn to live together and stand together so that no one will be able to attack us', he said.

125. The Demands of Sikhs

Amrita Bazar Patrika, 29 March 1941.

Punjab Govt's Attitude
Premier's Warning Against Direct Action

Lahore, 27 March.

The attitude of the Punjab Government towards certain demands of the Sikhs who are threatening to start 'Morcha' (direct action) at Sargodha from 4 April was defined by Sir Sikandar Hyat Khan, the Premier, replying to a short-notice question in the Punjab Assembly this afternoon.

The Premier said that the Sikh demands which were formulated at the Rurka Kalan Conference and subsequently repeated in a representation made to His Excellency the Governor by Master Tara Singh, were (1) that restriction on Jhatka should be removed at least in Government institutions; (2) that the Compulsory Primary Education Act would effect the teaching of Punjabi; (3) that the private member's Bill introduced by Tikka Jagjit Singh Bedi should not be passed unless supported by a majority of the Sikh members in the Assembly, and that a similar convention should apply to all legislative measures affecting the religious rights of any one community; (4) that the persons arrested at Sargodha for defying the orders of the District Magistrate should be released.

Sir Sikandar Hyat Khan pointed out that at the request of Master Tara Singh the Governor granted him an interview on Sunday, the 16th March at which he (Premier) was also present. Explaining the position of Government with regard to these demands, Sir Sikandar Hyat Khan said that so far as the question of Jhatka was concerned Government had introduced no changes whatsoever in the position which they found when they took office and were, in fact, bound by their declaration which they had made on assuming office that in such religious and quasi-religious matters the 'status quo' would be adhered to, in the absence of any agreement between the communities concerned.

The Premier recalled that soon after they took office, a Unity Conference was convened to deal with and compose the differences on this and other similar matters. A resolution was unanimously passed to which Master Tara Singh was a signatory and which was endorsed by the leading representatives of all communities. Sir Sikandar Hyat Khan said that if the Sikh and Hindu members of the House moved for a ratification of that resolution in the Assembly, Government would be prepared to provide every facility and he would himself be prepared to allot a Government day for the purpose, and he understood that the members of other communities would be prepared to support them.

As for the demand for the release of the Sargodha prisoners, Sir Sikandar Hyat Khan pointed out that the matter was still 'sub judice' and said that if either the accused or representatives of the local Sikh community on their behalf expressed their regret that there had been a defiance of law and gave an assurance that they would endeavour to prevent its repetition in future, then Government would be quite prepared to direct that the cases now pending in court would be withdrawn.

The Premier, continuing, said that leaders who deliberately urged their followers to adopt such a course at such a time were incurring a grave responsibility and it was his duty to warn them to think again, before they embarked on a course of action which could only lead to disorder and suffering and which must gravely imperil the safety of India at a time of supreme crisis. He earnestly hoped that the reports in the newspapers about the starting of 'Morcha' were not correct because if they were, the unreasonable attitude of persons who wished to take the law in their own hands, if they persisted in it, would lead to a disturbance of the peace and tranquility of the province and seriously interfere with the war effort of the Punjab, which his Government, whose duty was clear, could never allow.—AP

126. Punjab Governor's Letter to the Viceroy on Agricultural Produce Markets Act and General Sales Tax Act, 28 April 1941

Correspondence with Governor of Punjab and his Secretary, 1941, Linlithgow Papers, Acc. No. 2225, NAI.

Govt House, Lahore,
28 April 1941

[Private and Personal.]
D.O. No. 343-F.L.

Dear Lord Linlithgow,

The outstanding item of local interest during the last few weeks has been the organization by the trading classes of a widespread movement designed to defeat certain economic enactments passed, but not yet brought into effect, by the Punjab Government—in particular the Agricultural Produce Markets Act and the General Sales Tax Act. The Punjab Government have, as you are well aware, lost few opportunities of late to proclaim and give practical illustration to their policy of improving the lot of agricultural classes and distributing the burden of taxation more evenly between the rural and urban communities. A series of legislative reforms intended to secure these purposes has led the trading classes to express the belief that their interests were being consistently sacrificed and that the time had come for them to mobilize their forces. They proceeded accordingly to advertise and prepare for a general cessation of business designed to coincide with the time when the producer must bring his harvest to the market. The announcement by Government that the enforcement of the Markets Act was to be postponed until next September did not suffice to allay the traders' agitation. To what extent they could be successful in organizing a general business 'hartal' of any duration throughout the Province may be open to doubt: still it was obvious that a grave situation was threatened, since even a partial and temporary closing down of grain markets would have been a calamitous affair, leading almost inevitably to extensive outbreaks of disorder. Suggestions have been made that Government should themselves or through their agents arrange to purchase the bulk of the harvest, but the practical value of this idea appears to be very doubtful, since there is no adequate machinery available for so adventurous a programme.

Realizing the danger of the position, the Premier and his colleagues have very wisely decided to adopt a conciliatory attitude. They have agreed to modify in various respects the Markets Act as originally passed and the rules framed thereunder, and they have given out both in the Assembly and elsewhere that all interests concerned will be given a fair hearing and fair treatment. The amendments to be made in regard to the Markets Act go a very long way to meet reasonable objections. In the matter of the General Sales Tax Act also action has been taken to reassure the commercial community. The tension has now to some extent declined, though it cannot be said as yet that the forces arrayed for battle have been demobilized; there are, however, grounds for hoping that wiser counsels will prevail.

Many responsible people express the view that the Punjab Government have been showing a tendency to rush their moves in the matter of agrarian and economic legislation. However laudable their intentions, they would have been well advised to space out their programme of reforms instead of delivering a series of blows at short intervals to the trading classes, the cumulative effect of which has brought the victims to the verge of revolt. Also they would have done well to have made a more thorough preliminary examination of the measures on which they felt it necessary to embark. There can be no denying that the Markets Act and Rules as originally framed contained a number of serious defects, at least one of which would have reacted very unfavourably on the producers, whom the enactment was designed to protect. Considerable difficulty may be anticipated in bringing the General Sales Tax Act into practical operation....

127. Prospects of Settlement in Punjab Deadlock

Bombay Chronicle, 30 April 1941.

Premier's Assurance to Leader of Opposition in Assembly

Lahore, 29 April.

Fresh attempts are being made to bring about a compromise between the traders and the Punjab Government, with a view to resolve the deadlock created by the suspension of business in the grain markets throughout the Punjab since 15th April.

A reference to these efforts was made in the Punjab Assembly by Sardar Santokh Singh, Leader of the Opposition and President of the Punjab Traders Conference, Lyallpur, who said that certain talks had been going on since yesterday, as a result of which he was in a position to announce that there was not only a possibility but a likelihood of a compromise being effected in the dispute between the traders and the Punjab Government over the Agricultural Produce Markets Act. He therefore appealed to the Premier not to insist on the retention of clause 3 of the Markets Amendment Bill which proposed to penalize dealers who would not take out their licenses by first September 1941.

Appeal to Premier

Sardar Santokh Singh assured the Premier that if he agreed to his request, ways and means were likely to be found of bringing about a settlement. He hoped that the Premier's response would be satisfactory, and a situation which was serious for all might be ended. Sardar Santokh

Singh further assured that the traders were not doing any overacting; their leaders had been careful to impress on them in all meetings that the hartals proposed to be observed must be absolutely peaceful, unattended by processions or slogans of any kind.

As regards the General Sales Tax Act, Sardar Santokh Singh urged on the Government to postpone its application till 1st October 1941, so that within this period, both sides might put their heads together and find ways and means of achieving a settlement.

Sikandar's Assurance

Sir Sikandar Hyat Khan in his reply reiterated that it was the duty of the Government to redress the genuine grievances of the traders and any representation submitted to him would receive careful and sympathetic consideration. He, however regretted that it was not possible for him to change the principle of the Act or accept the traders' demand for majority representation in the market committees. The Premier reminded the House that every one of the traders' demands embodied in their original representation had been conceded, while operation of clause three (penal clause) had been suspended by incorporating an official amendment. The clause was intended to afford protection to those traders who were prepared to help the Government. If Sardar Santokh Singh, added the Premier, could persuade the traders to end the deadlock, he would be prepared to give an assurance that the clause would never come into operation. The Premier however uttered a stern warning to mischief-mongers, who were out to exploit the situation.

The third reading of the Bill was then passed without a division, and the Assembly adjourned 'sine die', the session having lasted nearly six months.

Plea for Postponement

A strong plea for the postponement of the enforcement of the Punjab Agricultural Produce Markets Act and the General Sales Tax, for the duration of the war, was made by Dr Sir Gokul Chand Narang, a former Minister of the Punjab Government, while speaking on the third reading of the Punjab Agricultural Produce Markets (amendment) Bill.

He said that the Marketing Act, which had caused great uneasiness in the province, was not yet in force and the Government would lose nothing if the enforcement was postponed. In case the Government was not prepared to postpone the Acts, added Sir Gokul, it should at least make some concessions in order to ease the situation which, if allowed to continue, would bring the trade of the province to a standstill.

Referring to the traders' demand for a majority on the market committees, Sir Gokul Chand suggested that equal representation should be given to growers and traders and that an official Chairman be appointed to hold the balance. There was, however, no justification for giving a statutory majority to growers, simply because there were a few black sheep among the traders.—AP

128. Punjab Government Announces Concessions Sales Act Controversy

The Tribune, 2 May 1941.

Lahore, 1 May.

A Press communiqué issued by the Punjab Government says:

There seems to be a certain amount of misunderstanding among the business community regarding various points connected with the provisions of the Punjab General Sales Tax Act and the way in which they will be carried out. It is desirable, therefore, to make the following points clear:

It has already been announced that as far as the present financial year is concerned, the Sales Tax will be leviable only during the second half of the year. This means that in effect the Act will not start to operate till 1 October 1941.

In order to avoid any unnecessary inconvenience to the prospective assessees it is contemplated to provide in the rules that the assessment will be made of the following basis. During the present year the dealers concerned will be assessed at their option on (a) the actuals of the previous year up to March 1941 or (b) the actual of any three consecutive months between 1 April and 31 December 1941 selected by the dealer concerned. It would be necessary to fix the final date somewhat earlier in the case of hill-stations.

No Harassment of Businessmen

An apprehension seem to exist regarding the powers vested in Inspectors under the Act. Actually, the rules are being so framed as to prevent any harassment of businessmen by the Inspectors. A provision is under consideration to ensure that an inspection will be held only when the Chief Taxation Authority of the district considers it necessary.

As regards the maintenance of accounts by businessmen, every attempt is being made in the rules to save them from unnecessary expenditure or inconvenience. What is really needed for the purposes of the Act is only that a shopkeeper should be able to give a correct return of his annual turnover. The rules will not require shopkeepers to keep a detailed record of their daily sales.

In order further to simplify the procedure of assessment in the case of those dealers whose annual turnover does not exceed Rs 25,000, Government are considering a rule by which the tax should be realized from them in the form of fixed license fees. The fees will be on the basis of the scale of taxation laid down in the Act, but it will mean that the assessment will become practically automatic and periodical examination of accounts in their cases will not be necessary.

Certain Classes of Dealers Exempted

It has also been decided to exempt from the operation of the Act certain classes of dealers such as fruit sellers, vegetable sellers, milk sellers, 'pan' (betel) sellers, 'nanbais', 'halwais', all hawkers, booksellers, and dealers in newspapers and periodicals.

The Honourable Premier explained on the floor of the Punjab Legislative Assembly and later to deputations of representatives of businessmen from Lahore, Amritsar and other places, who waited on him and the Honourable Ministers for Finance and Development, that Government were always prepared to give sympathetic consideration to any legitimate grievance which might be brought to their notice. Since the Act will not begin to operate in actual practice before 1 October 1941, there would be ample opportunity for any body of tradesmen or even individuals to make whatever representations they like to Government between now and 1st September.

Mr Chanana will Hear Various Points of View

Lala Behari Lal Channana, President of the Punjab Beopar Mandal, who has now decided to stay in Lahore for sometime in the Bhupendra Hall (office of the Sanaten Dharam Pratinidhi Sabha Punjab), when approached by the Pressmen regarding the Punjab Government's communiqué issued to-day about the Sales Tax Act, chose to keep silent. To the many questions that were put to him he gave no replies. He explained that he would hear the various points of view, which might be represented to him. Having heard the different views he would then decide about the next step.

It is however, understood, that there is a possibility of the meeting of the general body of the Punjab Beopar Mandal being convened to consider the situation arising out of the Government's communiqué.

Exemptions Welcomed

While satisfaction has been expressed over the further exemptions to book sellers, fruit sellers, vegetable sellers, nanbais, halvais, milk sellers, pan sellers, and hawkers, and some other important concessions which have been promised, it is generally felt that if this position which the Government has taken up today, had been taken up yesterday, there might have been no hartal at all to-day. The exemptions have been welcomed, especially because this would give a good deal of relief to these class of shopkeepers. But the situation created by the cessation of business can be changed only if the general body of Beoparies also expresses satisfaction. For this purpose meetings of the local Beoparies are called. These being held tomorrow (Friday) to consider the new situation. One of these meetings will be held in Jawahar Market at 9 a.m. on Friday.

But their final decision will depend on the decision of the Punjab Beopar Mandal.

It is further understood that the events leading to yesterday's breakdown in negotiations were discussed between Mr Henderson, Deputy Commissioner, Lahore and Mr Behari Lal Chanana to-day. The gist of this talk was communicated to the higher authorities.

The situation was also considered at a meeting of the Ministers. It is learnt the Government to communiqué was issued at the conclusion of this meeting.

129. General Hartal Called Off
Punjab Govt's Communiqué Changes Situation

The Tribune, 6 May 1941.

Lahore, 5 May.

Normal business, which had remained suspended during the last five days as a protest against the General Sales Tax Act will be resumed all over the province from Tuesday morning. This is being done under instructions issued by Lala Behari Lal Channana, President, Punjab Beopar Mandal, who had been authorized by the meeting of the General Body of the Punjab Beopar Mandal held at Lahore, in the Bhupendra Hall on 3 May, to call off the hartal and enter into negotiations with the Government if and when any occasion arises, provided the Government agrees:

(a) that they will frame the rules under this Act after consultation with the representatives of the Mandal;
(b) that in framing the rules they would agree to reduce the rigours of the Act as far as possible; and
(c) that in the matter of charging the tax under the Act at various stages, the Government will in consultation with the representatives of the Mandal try to levy the tax as far as possible only at one stage, in order not to ruin the trade and industry of the province.

Lala Behari Lal Channana was, in accordance with the powers vested in him, able to take a decision to call off the 'hartal' in response to the communiqué which was issued by the Punjab Government at 2.30 p.m. to-day. The communiqué after referring to the demands made by the meeting of the Beopar Mandal explained the Government's position and made it clear that not only after the draft rules are published, but before the rules are drafted, the Government would be prepared to take into consideration any representations made by any association including the Beopar Mandal.

With regard to the second demand, the communiqué said the rules would not be framed with any undue or avoidable rigour.

With regard to the question of attempting to confine the levy of the tax on any one article to one stage only, Government will be glad to consider in the light of representations to what extent this is practicable.

The position taken up in the communiqué became a possibility only to-day. Till day before yesterday and even yesterday, the Government was not prepared to take notice of the Beopar Mandal in any way. Even yesterday when an attempt was made by some common friends to have some sort of a communiqué issued on the subjects, it failed. It seemed yesterday that the situation would grow worse and the Beopar Mandal would be obliged to take even a stronger attitude....

130. Trade Deadlock in the Punjab An Article by Prof. Gulshan Rai

The Tribune, 11 May 1941.

The trade deadlock in the Punjab is on its way to settlement. For five days there was complete cessation of business in the province. All shops everywhere remained closed. This joint action of all the different communities, who are supposed to have conflicting interests, has vindicated one important truth—that economic ties are the strongest to bind different communities. If the Church divides the people, business combines them. If we want to build a common national edifice in India, it is evident it has to be built upon the strong foundation of common economic interests.

The recent hartal has demonstrated one other important truth, that organized effort, led by disinterested and sincere people, must always be crowned with success. The cause of the traders and the merchants was just. It had the active sympathy of the mass of the people. The consumers, who suffered by the hartal had no grievance against the merchants or the traders. The traders also tried to relieve distress by opening cheap provision shops and they agreed to forego their profit in opening the shops and the landlords agreed to remit the shops' rent for the *hartal* period. This shows that the shopkeepers had the goodwill of the people with them.

The Government also showed sound commonsense. No false prestige stood in their way in trying to meet the demands of the traders and the merchants. Both the measures, the Punjab Marketing Act and the Punjab General Sales Tax Act have, for the present been put off, and their enforcement postponed for six months. The Government have agreed that when they make rules under the General Sales Tax Act, they will consult the traders or the Beopar Mandal; they have also agreed to soften the rigours of the law, and that they will also consider favourably the idea that the tax on sales is levied as far as possible only once, and not at different stages. They have also promised suitable changes in the Marketing Law.

Compromise Vital Breath of Politics

Sir Sikander Hyat Khan's Government has given evidence of their desire to remove the legitimate grievances of minority communities and interests. They have shown a real democratic spirit in trying to meet the traders' reasonable demands. True democracy does not mean the arbitrary rule of the majority over the minorities. There can be such a thing as the tyranny of the majority. Under a democratic system of government, the feelings and sentiments of all the sections of the population, whether a majority or a minority, have to be respected.

Walpole was one of the earliest Prime Ministers of Great Britain. He held office as Head of the British Government for more than 20 years continuously. He once pushed forward a measure in the British House of Commons, which was economically sound but which was opposed vehemently by the traders of London. Walpole was very popular and with the help of the majority he commanded in the Parliament he could carry the measure through. But when he realized the strength of opposition among the traders, he withdrew the measure, and, thus, brought about peace and contentment in the metropolis. That showed good statesmanship of Walpole. His decision to withdraw the hated measure brought him strength, not weakness. Compromise is the vital breath of politics. A man who does not know how to compromise at the right moment is not a good politician. He cannot claim to be a statesman.

How to Bring about Lasting Peace

Now that the tension is, to some extent, gone and both the parties, the Government and the traders, are in a mood to discuss matters in a calmer atmosphere, it is time to discuss how a lasting peace could be brought about. Let us take the General Sales Tax Act first. It was originally proposed to levy a tax of two annas per hundred on sales between 5,000 per annum. It comes to an average daily sale of Rs 13–11–3. What can be the margin of profit on this? If we allow ten per cent which is ample, the daily profit comes to a little less than Rs 1–6. Out of this 22 annas the shopkeeper has to pay the shop rent, and meet other incidental expenses on light and hot and cold weather charges, and bazaar dues. A shopkeeper with a yearly sale of Rs 5,000 cannot thus have a daily net income of more than a rupee or 18 annas at the utmost. Within this amount he has to maintain a family of five or more members. Even if his yearly sales amount up to Rs 10,000 he cannot have for the subsistence of his family more than Rs 2 or Rs 2–4 per day. To impose a tax on a man like him is nothing short of cruelty. That is one aspect of the question.

Another Point of View

Look at the problem from another point of view. In order to enable the Government to make a proper estimate of the sales during the year, the shopkeepers must keep regular daily accounts of the sales. An overwhelmingly large majority of these petty shopkeepers have very small and petty transactions. Many a time a shopkeeper has to give four different articles in one piece. An average daily sale of 13–7 rupees may possibly mean 200 or more daily transactions. To expect this shopkeeper to record all these 200 and odd transactions daily, is to expect him to perform an impossible feat, especially when we consider that most of these petty shopkeepers are illiterate, not knowing even the Lunda script. The Government have in their recent communiqué, conceded that shopkeepers having annual sales of less than 25,000 rupees shall not be required to pay any 'ad valorem' tax, and shall be required instead to pay a fixed license fee, irrespective of the amount of the sales. A moment's reflection will show, that in actual practice this concession will prove valueless. How are the assessing officers of the Government to know that the annual sales of a shopkeeper do not exceed 25,000 rupees? In order to satisfy the assessing officers, the shopkeepers will be compelled to keep accounts of their daily transactions, which I have shown is in the case of the majority an impossibility. A measure which requires the petty shopkeepers to keep record of hundreds and thousands of petty transactions is nothing short of a heavy restraint on trade and commerce. Such a measure is bound to kill all trade and commerce in the province and land the general mass of the people in serious difficulties.

It is obvious this taxation proposal of Government, which applies to the sale of all commodities, luxuries as well as necessities of life, is quite impracticable. If the Government wants to insist upon the imposition of a sales tax, then it must select a few articles of luxury, and impose a tax on their sale. Such a tax will not affect the general mass of the people and in this case the tax will come from the pockets of the richer classes. This is what has been done in some of the other provinces. The Government has already given exemptions in the case of the sale of certain articles. But that is not the right way of doing things. What is required is to prepare a small fixed list of articles on the sale of which a tax might be imposed. It will not do only to prepare a small fixed list of articles the sale of which is to be exempted from tax. The Government must remember one thing. The surest way to make a Government unpopular in the country, is to have too much state interference with the activities of the people. People want to be left alone. If the Unionist Government wants the continued support of the masses, it must not put unnecessary restraints on their daily activities.

The Only Way

From what I have stated above it follows that an 'ad Valorem' tax on the sales of all commodities, or on a very large number of commodities, is out of the question. If Government wants to impose tax on the traders and merchants in addition to what they are required to pay in Income Tax, then the only way is to levy an occupation or profession tax or a tax on the sale of a very limited number of articles, which are not of daily use to the mass of the people. They may impose a license tax on those who sell certain specified articles. The General Sales Tax in its present shape must be scrapped. It is an ill-advised measure, and the sooner it is withdrawn the better it is for all concerned. No sense of prestige should stand in the way of the Government in doing the right thing.

Let us next take up what is popularly called the Marketing Act. We find that here the deadlock has not yet ended. The grain markets in the province still continue to be closed. The farmers have not so far been able to sell their agricultural produce in the *mandies*. Here again, as I pointed out in my last article on the subject, published in the 'Tribune' dated the 27th of April, I must repeat that it is wrong to have a majority of agriculturists on the Mandi Committees. If the Government wants that undue advantage should not be taken of the illiterate farmers, then the right way is to re-organize the co-operative societies. So far the only activity of the co-operative societies is to give loans to the farmers. Why cannot these co-operative credit societies do also the work of arranging the sale of agricultural produce of their ilaqas in the neighbouring *mandies*? The farmers, well organized in their village co-operative societies, are likely to get better terms from the traders in the *mandies*. The *mandies* as I pointed out in my last article are really local rural Chambers of Commerce. The internal discipline among traders within the *mandi* is the concern of the traders themselves. The agriculturists have no business to be on the Mandi Committees. These Mandi Committees should consist entirely of traders. What I visualize is that agriculturists, organized separately in their village co-operative societies, should deal with traders separately organized in the Mandi Committees. The Government should intervene only when there is a dispute between a *mandi* and a co-operative society. The special machinery for the settlement of disputes may either be the ordinary courts invested with the power of taking cognizance of these matters, or it may be suitable arbitrators appointed by Government. But the question of devising this special machinery for the settlement of disputes between the traders and the farmers arises only when the Government agrees to organize the agriculturists through their already existing co-operative societies and across to constitute Mandi Committees consisting entirely of traders and merchants.

131. Punjab Governor's Telegram to Viceroy on Sikandar's Unionist Party, 7 August 1941

Telegram R, Correspondence with Governor of Punjab and his Secretary, 1941, Linlithgow Papers, Acc. No. 2225, NAI.

(i) Telegram Dated 7 August 1941

(a) No. 7-G. His Excellency has asked me to let you know for His Excellency the Viceroy's information that Sikander is holding a party meeting in Lahore on 9th and 10th with a view to rallying his supporters and preparing them for a special session of the Assembly to be held from 17th to 24th. At this session a resolution would be moved expressing confidence in the Ministry and urging them to redouble their efforts for the successful prosecution of the war. This is of course with a view to strengthening Sikander's position against any possible move by Jinnah.

(ii) Telegram Dated 14 August 1941

(b) No. 9-G. Thank you for your two telegrams about reactions to Muslim League criticisms.

Sikander had a most successful meeting at Lahore of Muslim Members of Unionist Party. Over 60, including Nawab of Mamdot, President of Provincial Muslim League, have handed him their resignations from Muslim League to use if necessary. Remaining members (about 12) who were absent from Lahore have been asked by letter whether they wish to follow this lead, and a favourable response is expected. Sikander's present intention is to attend in person the meeting of Working Committee at Bombay, on 24th.

In view of success of Lahore meeting the idea of holding a special session of Assembly has been abandoned.

132. Punjab Governor's Letter to Viceroy on Sikhs and Akali Faction in Punjab, 22 November 1941

Correspondence with Governor of Punjab and his Secretary, 1941, Linlithgow Papers, Acc. No. 2225, NAI.

Govt House, Lahore,
22 November 1941

[Private and Personal.]
D.O. No. 372-F.L.

Dear Lord Linlithgow,

The Sikh community, especially the Akali faction, has of late been rather more clamorous than usual. Their spokesmen have been loud in denouncing the Unionist Government, which they accuse of being determined to abase the Sikhs at every opportunity. Wild allegations are made that Sikhs are never given their fair share in the public services and the old thorny problem of *Jhatka* meat is dragged into the forefront. The non-inclusion of a Sikh member in the enlarged Executive Council is ascribed to the machinations of Sikander and his friends, and Akalis and others are never tired of parading this grievance. The appointment of Sardar Dasaundha Singh as a member of the Punjab Cabinet has also become the subject of increasing indignation. This last complaint, I am afraid, is by no means entirely unjustified. The truth is that Dasaundha Singh has certainly not been a success. He has little, if any, influence with his community, his brain movements are glacial in their rate of progress, he finds it very difficult to get through his work and is a sore trial to those with whom it is his business to deal. He is well-meaning enough no doubt, but I sincerely wish that a more effective successor to the late Sir Sundar Singh Majithia had been put forward. The cry of the Sikhs is that in the face of all these affronts any member of the community who adheres to the Unionists can only be regarded as a traitor to the cause, and there is talk of liquidating the Khalsa Nationalist Party, forming a strong opposition with the aid of certain Hindus and a few disgruntled Muslims and turning the present Government out of power. Though the Unionist party machine creaks rather ominously at times, there are no signs of this programme succeeding in the near future. Some of the more prominent Akalis are fond of saying in the course of conversation that they now realize the folly of their having strayed from the right path a few years ago and made common cause with Congress and come to logger-heads with British high authorities by such indiscretions as discouraging recruitment to the Indian Army: they suggest that they no longer regard 'Khalistan' as a practical idea, that the thought of 'Pakistan' is of course quite intolerable and that they dislike still more the prospect of a closer union with the Congress Party, since this would eventually mean the submergence of their political identity; consequently they would like to make a virtue of necessity and be good friends with the British and so retain an impartial umpire in their differences with rival factions. Many of them, in particular Giani Kartar Singh, have been actively helpful, as far as they deem it expedient, in promoting Sikh recruitment. They confess that this policy is essential for the preservation of the Sikhs as a separate entity, but they maintain that they should be given some recognition for this manifestation of grace and repentance and should be rewarded with high appointments in the Central Government.

Another avenue which some of them have been exploring is the possibility of weaning Sikander and his adherents from the Muslim League; various tentative approaches have been or suggested in this respect, and there has been a certain amount of speculation about the reasons for Sikander's recent visits to Hyderabad and Bhopal. It is suggested that if Sikander would openly abandon the Pakistan theory, and if a Sikh Minister who is truly representative of the Khalsa could be appointed to the Cabinet, then all distrust would happily disappear. It seems very doubtful, however, whether Sikander, whatever his inclinations may be, will be afforded in the near future as good an opportunity of breaking with the Muslim League as he rejected a few months ago. The upshot of all this is that the Sikh community is growing more and more uneasy and there is a feeling that it must move in some direction or other to ensure its survival. But there is much jealousy and dissension in the ranks; the tendency to pass the time by heaping abuse on the Punjab Ministry does not help towards a general reconciliation.

I have been touring of late in several districts of the Province, mainly with the object of holding War Darbars, rewarding those who have done good service and trying to encourage others to follow their example. The results have, I think, been good. Certainly there has been a great demonstration of willingness to assist. As far as Jat Sikhs are concerned, recruitment has flagged again after its recent improvement, but one reason for this, though it is sometimes overstated, is that, as the Recruiting Officers point out, enlistment always tends to decline when agricultural operations are in progress. Opinion still varies widely as to the effects produced by the Khalsa Defence League, but I think there is no doubt that at least in certain districts it has been of considerable value. It might perhaps be well to give the League some open encouragement on a suitable opportunity, but the Ministers still regard it with a good deal of suspicion. Patiala is here now and I propose to have a talk with him on things in general; he made, as you know, a very helpful speech about Sikh recruiting the other day.

III. Assam

133. Congress Leaders Consider Congress Policy on Attending Assembly Session

Amrita Bazar Patrika, 20 November 1941.

Leaders Meet: Concerted Action for Bengal, Assam and Punjab

Wardhaganj, 18 November.

Mr Gopinath Bardoloi, former Premier of Assam, discussed with Dr Rajendra Prasad the advisability or otherwise of attending the Assam Assembly session commencing next month for which Dr Rajendra Prasad had already permitted Congress MLA's to send in questions, notices of resolutions and other things in case permission for attending was granted so that they could be ready if necessary. Mr Bardoloi also discussed the subject with Sardar Vallabhbhai Patel, President of the Congress Parliamentary Sub-committee. He also saw Mahatma Gandhi this afternoon.

It is understood that the cases of Bengal, Assam and the Punjab are being considered together with a view to evolving a uniform policy in the subject.—AP

134 (i) Assam Cabinet to Resign
Sequel to Resignation of Mr R.K. Chowdhury
New Party in Assam Formed

Amrita Bazar Patrika, 10 December 1941.

Shillong, 9 December.

The Hon Mr Rohini Kumar Chowdhury, Minister for Education, has, this morning, submitted his resignation from the Cabinet to the Premier, Sir Md Saadullah. It is learnt that the resignation has not yet been accepted.

Mr Chowdhury interviewed by the 'Associated Press representative, declined to make any statement at this stage as to why he was resigning, but disclosed the fact that a new party of eight MLA's had already been formed with himself as the leader'.

Cabinet Decides to Resign

In view of the resignation of the Hon Mr Rohini Kumar Chowdhury, Education Minister, the Cabinet will resign on 12 December when the Governor is expected to return to Shillong. This statement was made by the Premier Sir Md Saadullah in the Assembly this morning.

The Governor is Now Touring the Assam Frontier

In the Assam Assembly to-day Mr Munawar Ali, Agriculture Minister, sought the approval of the House to the policy of the Government to introduce Regulation and Control of areas for Jute Cultivation in Assam and the proposal for taking a loan of Rs 400,000 without interest from the Government of Bengal for the purpose.

Discussion on the motion is continuing.

Earlier the House voted a supplementary demand, totalling 146,130 without a division.

Notices of five no-confidence motions against the present Ministry were submitted by members of various groups before the commencement of the Assembly session this morning.

When the House met, the Premier, being called upon by the Speaker to make a statement on the extraordinary situation created by the resignation of Mr Rohini Kumar Chowdhury, announced his decision to tender the resignation of his Cabinet on 12 December.

Mr Chowdhury did not attend the session to-day.

The House granted leave to three of the no-confidence motions against the Ministry being moved. These motions, which stand in the names of Mr N.K. Dutta (Indian Tea Planting), Mr Bepin Behari Das (Scheduled Caste), and Mr Lalit Mohan Kar (Independent Hindu), will be taken up at 3 p.m., on 13 December. The other motions will not be moved.

The House adjourned till 13 December.

Immediately after the House adjourned this morning, the Ministerialist Party met in the committee room of the Assembly House and discussed the situation created by the decision of Sir Muhammad Saadullah to tender the resignation of his Cabinet.

Sir Muhammad is expected to make a statement shortly.

His Excellency the Governor, who is now touring the Sadiya Frontier Tract, has cancelled the remaining part of his programme, which was to have continued till 31 December, His Excellency is expected to arrive here on 12 December. As soon as the Governor arrives, the Premier Sir Muhammad Saadullah, according to a statement made in the Assembly to-day, will formally submit the resignation of his Cabinet.

Mr G.N. Bardoloi, former Premier, is now in telephonic communication with the Congress President, Maulana Abul Kalam Azad on the latest developments in Assam Parliamentary politics.—AP

(ii) Assam Cabinet Crisis New Nationalist Coalition Party Formed

Amrita Bazar Patrika, 12 December 1941.

Shillong, 11 December.

There have been further developments in parliamentary politics in Assam. A new party named Assam Nationalist Coalition Party with 25 members consisting of Muslims, Hindus, Tribals, both Surma and Assam Valley, has been formed under the leadership of Mr Rohini Kumar Chowdhury this evening. The formation of the new party has been notified to the Speaker Mr Rohini Kumar Chowdhury had a prolonged discussion with the Leader of the European Group in the Assembly to-day. The nature of the talk was not disclosed.

The Assam United Party has expressed determination to hold together under the leadership of Sir Md Saadullah at any cost.

Mr Rohini Kumar Chowdhury on behalf of the Nationalist Party has wired congratulating to Mr A.K. Fazlul Huq, Chief Minister of Bengal on the formation of a new Ministry.

A meeting of the provincial Muslim League Working Committee is likely to be held next week.—AP

135. Assam Governor's Telegram to Viceroy on Ministry-making in Assam

Correspondence with the Governor of Assam and his Secretary, 1941, Linlithgow Papers, Acc. No. 2176, NAI.

(i) Governor of Assam to Viceroy

Telegram R, 20 December 1941.

Important. No. 870-C. Saw Rohini Chowdhury today; says he has 26 supporters and relies on Congress for the rest. He has no written undertaking from latter but says airily there will be 'no practical difficulty' about the war; divides the administration into halves, ordinary and war, and if he has to promote a war measure in legislature and Congress remain neutral he says he can rely on European and other groups to support him in other words relies on his group *plus* Congress to maintain him over normal affairs and opposition over war: can produce no written guarantee from European or any other group, and I do not believe for a moment that any of them would support him on these terms.

His statements about strength of his supporters were vague and he did not even produce a list. So I said I was afraid I was not satisfied he could form a stable Ministry and terminated interview.

2. I then sent for Saadullah. He sticks to previous view that no stable Ministry is possible in the present circumstances but it might be possible after a period under Section 93. Is himself therefore still in favour of 93 no? Is going to consult colleagues and will give me answer on

Monday? Agrees with my view, about Gauhati culprits and would not hold any enquiry. Agrees Rohini has no chance of retaining power.

If he does agree to take office, I am afraid we shall be back at old precarious game of buying and selling support, incidental to which is his decided view that it would be impossible to face Assembly at once as I suggested he should. He would do so in February. On long view I have no doubt 93 best for war and for Province, but will see what he reports on Monday.

(ii) Governor of Assam to Viceroy

Telegram R, 22 December 1941.

No. 868-C. Have had final interview with Saadullah. He and present colleagues have come to the following conclusions over the week-end. They can find no majority now, but are hopeful that one would be forthcoming by the time the House meets again. They cannot contemplate meeting the House earlier than the last part of February. They would have to take in a Hindu *vice* Rohini. This would be Kamini Sen of Surma Valley and to counter-balance him would require an Assam Valley Hindu, as yet unspecified, that is, 11 Ministers instead of the present 10. I said, especially in the circumstances under which they resigned, I could not be party to two months interval before Assembly (meets?): and when I asked Saadullah, supposing I called the Assembly for January would he have a majority, he said no. I am quite clear after no-confidence motion carried by 56 *nil* any delay in meeting of Legislature by the same Ministry resuming office in un-defensible. That being the case, Saadullah agreed with me that Section 93 is the only resort. In fact that has been his view from the start, and this result coincides with his own wishes.

2. Have considered the possibility of all party Ministry and discussed it with Saadullah. He says, and I agree with him, it is impossible. Only three parties, (a) Congress which will not co-operate, (b) Saadullah's, (c) Rohini's 26. Any such all-party Ministry would have to include Rohini and neither Saadullah nor his colleagues will have anything to do with him after his recent behaviour. There is no other alternative, and I shall be grateful for very early orders to put in force Section 93. Saadullah wishes to be relieved at once and I should like to accept his resignation not later than tomorrow.

(iii) Governor of Assam to Viceroy

Govt House, Shillong,
22 December 1941.

Dear Lord Linlithgow,

This is in continuation of the correspondence on the subject of the Ministerial crisis in Assam. I think my telegram of the 20th December was sufficiently clear as to why it was impossible to accept Rohini's assurances and allow him to take office. I have telegraphed today giving the result of my final interview with Saadullah, after had thought over it during the week end, and also had thought over it during the same period. I may add that I had on Sunday a most informative chat with the Leader of the European Group (Mr Whittaker) in an informal way. He, of course, said at once that his Group would on no account support Rohini in the way which he expected them to and in which I indicated in my Saturday's telegram. He also informed me that in the course of his interview with the European Group, which was of his own seeking, Rohini told them that in attempting to form a Ministry he would merely be keeping the place warm for Congress whom he expected to come in within three months. Whittaker was clearly of opinion that it was much better to have Section 93 now and let Saadullah come back after a period, to be able to, as he said, 'craik the whip'. He has never been in that position and has always had to cajole, persuade and induce, a procedure for which he relied almost entirely on Rohini's assistance. He was also emphatic as to the undesirability of giving any interval of time for the present Ministry to try and win back supporters to their side.

2. My conversation with Saadullah this morning entirely confirms the information given me by Whittaker as well as the results of my own meditations. Leaving aside for the moment the war, it is quite clear—and I believe a great deal of decent public opinion agrees with this view—that we have had enough of this so-called system of Government by Ministries which depend for their support on a rabble of utterly unreliable followers. At every session one has had the system of MLAs' being dragged from this side to that, some being held under duress by the managers of this Party or the other, together with a perpetual state of uncertainty as to whose inducements are going to prevail in the end. It ought to be a lesson to the greedy and to the self-seeking to be deprived of their emoluments and the chances of making money for a period, and it certainly ought to have a good effect in general. I have very good hopes too that it will eventuate in something like a stable Ministry being thrown up under the leadership of Saadullah. On the other hand, if we have persuaded Saadullah to try and drag together a ramshackle Ministry under present conditions it would only have made things a great deal worse and further discredited constitutional institutions in Assam.

136. Ministry Making in Assam, Bardoloi's Statement

Amrita Bazar Patrika, 23 December 1941.

Gauhati, 22 December.

Mr G.N. Bardoloi, ex-Premier and leader of the opposition in the Assam Assembly has issued the following statement:

'During the past three weeks the political situation in Assam and the attitude of the Congress Party in the Legislature in particular has been the subject of so much confusion, speculation and misunderstanding that I consider it necessary to issue the following statements:

'The many acts of commission and omission by the last Ministry of Sir Mohammad Saadullah, particularly in reference to the Land Development scheme, University Bill, Agricultural Income tax Bill, the Census and other matters have stirred the public mind of Assam to such depths that the Congress MLAs who had abstained from attending the Assembly during the last 12 months had to face hostile criticisms for their failure to do their duty as Assembly members. Many of the Congress members in the Assembly, for reasons of health or other difficulties, were either prevented from offering Satyagraha or would not re-offer Satyagraha. The question that confronted us was whether these MLAs should continue their inactivity or should be allowed to resume their parliamentary activity. The offer of Satyagraha being purely one of individual choice based on personal conviction the Congress Party, and the President of the Provincial Congress after consultation with the District Committees came to the conclusion that such members as did not offer Satyagraha for one reason or the other and would be outside the jails, should be allowed to attend the Assembly and participate in the discussions in the subjects mentioned above. The Parliamentary Sub-Committee was accordingly moved and the permission was accorded to attend the whole session.

Congress Success in Assembly

'The Congress MLAs accordingly attended the Assembly and the record of work that they put up during the session must be considered very flattering to the party and deserving the confidence of the public. In reference to Census, the Premier assured that if there is no insurmountable opposition from the Government of India he would have the figures resorted according to religions. Although the land development resolution did not go to the stage of voting, sufficient indication was obtained of the attitude of the Government to the effect that all they did in the meantime was not the right thing. The Agricultural Income tax Amendment Bill which provided for relief to the companies floated in England could not even go to the stage of the select Committee and the University Bill did not come up before the House of account of the sudden resignation of the Ministry.

Chowdhury's Letter to Bardoloi

'From a long time we were hearing that all was not well in the Cabinet of Sir Saadullah. In the House however we were completely disillusioned; we found that they presented a united front to our sallies and attacks just as any composite group would do. We were therefore surprised to find on the 9th December at about 10 a.m. that Srijut Rohini Kumar Chowdhury, the Education Minister had resigned. On the 6th instant a great incident in the nature, of indiscriminate assault on the students at Gauhati had taken place and it felt us thinking whether this incident had something to do with the sudden resignation. But in the House the Premier stated that Sj. R.K. Chowdhury did not assign any reason for his resignations. Sir Saadullah also assured that he would tender resignation of his Cabinet on the 12th when the Governor was to come back to Shillong. He would, therefore not take any part in the proceedings of the House. On the same day at noon time Sj. Chowdhury wrote to me to say 'as many as 22 members of the Assembly including most of the non-Congress members of the Congress Coalition Party have accepted my leadership to form a Ministry and I expect that more members—Hindus and Muslims will join us soon. We agree to follow the Congress policy and programme in the Legislative Assembly excepting the war measures just like in Sind'. And he requested me 'to kindly obtain necessary formal permission from the Congress High Command', and added: 'I assure that should the Congress decide to accept office, I shall be too pleased to make room for them'.

'I should state in this connection that the non-Congress Coalition Group of our Party had formed a separate party of their own following our resignation in 1941.

'The impending resignation of the Ministry announced by Sir Md Saadullah, and the letter of Mr R.K. Chowdhury was considered by me to be of far important a nature to be decided by an ordinary party meeting. I accordingly decided on securing the advice of the President of the APCC and of Sj. H.O. Baruah, the outgoing APCC President as well as of Dr Bhubaneswar Barooah, the President of the Gauhati DCC before we take any decision on this important matter. I should also point out that the General Secretary of the Provincial Congress Sj S.R. Dutta and Sj. S.N. Sarmah were both present in the meeting as Assembly members. After prolonged discussions, the overwhelming majority decided that if Sj. Rohini Kumar Chowdhury formed a ministry the party would lend support in carrying out measures consistent with the Congress policy and programme excepting war measure; and that the freedom of offering Satyagraha as directed by Mahatma Gandhi should remain. The meeting wanted me to secure permission from the Parliamentary Sub-Committee for the above decision. I accordingly met Maulana Abul Kalam Azad the Congress President, at Calcutta and also informed by wire other members of the Sub-Committee. According to his advice we discussed the matter in a meeting of the Provincial Congress Committee on 14 and 15 December. Subsequently I received further instruction from the Sub-Committee as result of which, I am now in a position to announce that if a new ministry is formed, the Congress Party would not oppose it so long as Government would be carried on the basis of the Congress Policy and programme excepting war measures. It is also open to such members of our Party to offer Satyagraha as would like to do so.

Congress Standpoint

'For better elucidation of the Congress standpoint I desire to mention that (1) our party will function as an independent group and would not sit behind the Treasury Benches (2) will not take part in the actual forming of the ministry and (3) and after the ministry is formed our party would not oppose it as the party of Sj. R.K. Chowdhury has given undertaking to carry on the Congress policy and programme except the war measures.

'I further state for the information of the public that the Progressive Nationalist Party of which Sj. Rohini Kumar Chowdhury is the Leader has given us the further assurance of the manner in which it would carry on the Congress programme to my satisfaction.

'In my interview with the Governor on 17 December, I clearly explained the attitude of our Party on the whole situation as explained above.

'I understand that the Governor gave an interview to Sj. Chowdhury, Leader of the Progressive Nationalist Party. It is not of much interest to me what the Governor may be doing regarding the formation of a ministry but it seems clear that the Governor cannot retain the Ministry of Sir Saadullah who have resigned and against whom a no-confidence motion has been carried by 56 members in a House of 107. I also note that if the Governor acts with regard for the India Government Act and democratic principles he cannot disallow a ministry to come into existence simply because it has to exist on the suffrage of the Congress Party, which is not prepared to give support to war efforts'.—AP

137. Constitution, No Cabinet Available to Prosecute War: Tale of Futile Search for a Stable Ministry in Province, Governor's Proclamation

Bombay Chronicle, 26 December 1941.

Shillong, 25 December.

A 'communiqué' issued from the Government House this evening announces that the Governor has issued a proclamation under Section 93 of the Government of India Act taking upon himself the administration of the province of Assam.

No Stable Ministry

The 'communiqué' adds that a Ministry formed by Mr Rohini Kumar Chowdhury with the conditional support of the Congress Party would not be stable and that its instability would be most prominent in any matter affecting the war.

Sir Muhammad Saadullah also, the 'communiqué' continues, would not command a majority with which he could immediately face the legislature.

Futile Search

The Governor also considered the possibility of forming an all-party Cabinet. No such Cabinet could be formed in the present positions of the parties.

Text of 'Communiqué'

The following is the text of the 'communiqué' issued from Government House this afternoon:

The Honourable Maulvi Saiyid Sir Muhammad Saadullah, Prime Minister of Assam, having received on the 9th December the resignation of one of his colleagues, Mr Rohini Chowdhury, tendered his own resignation and that of his whole Cabinet to His Excellency the Governor on the 12th December last. On the 13th December a no-confidence motion was carried in the Assembly against the Ministry by 56 vote to all. Those who voted in favour of the motion included Mr Rohini Kumar Chowdhury and two Parliamentary Secretaries. On return from tour on the 15th December His Excellency saw Sir Muhammad and requested him and his colleagues excepting Mr Rohini Kumar Chowdhury to carry on with their duties until he could make other arrangements. He accepted the resignation of Mr Rohini Kumar Chowdhury.

Search for Ministry

The Governor at once sought to find a Ministry which could command a stable majority in the Legislature. In doing so he kept before him the paramount necessity of ensuring that any Ministry which he selected should be in a position to prosecute to the full all measures necessitated by the war situation His Excellency invited Mr Gopinath Bardoloi, Leader of the Congress Party to assist him in the formation of an alternative Ministry. Mr Bardoloi informed the Governor that, he was unable to take office, but stated that he was prepared to support Mr Rohini Kumar Chowdhury and his group should they take office. He made it clear however, that his support so far as the war was concerned would be severely limited.

No Stability

His Excellency then sent for Mr Rohini Kumar Chowdhury who had informed him that he had become the leader of a party of 26 members of the Assembly. A discussion with Mr Chowdhury made it indisputably clear that a Ministry formed by him with the conditional support of the Congress Party above referred to could not be a stable one and that instability would be most prominent in any matters which affected the war. His Excellency had to inform Mr Chowdhury that he was not satisfied with his prospects of commanding a stable majority and would, therefore, be unable to ask him to take office. The only other party with a substantial following in the House was that of Sir Muhammad Saadullah who had just been defeated on a no-confidence motion....

138. Suspension of Constitution in Assam

(i) Assam Tangle, Nationalist Coalition Party's Disapproval

Amrita Bazar Patrika, 28 December 1941.

Shillong, 26 December.

Disapproval of the suspension of the constitution of the province was voiced by the Nationalist Coalition Party in the Assam Assembly at its emergent meeting to-night, Mr J.J.M. Nicholsroy, ex-Minister, presiding. The party decided to create public opinion in favour of restoring constitutional form of Government of the province.

So far as war measures are concerned, in the event of a state of emergency prevailing, it is learnt that the Nationalist Coalitionists hope to receive support from the Congress Party in matters relating to protection of life and property of the civil population.—AP

(ii) A Strange Action: Mr R.K. Chowdhury's Criticism of Governor's Decision

Amrita Bazar Patrika, 28 December 1941.

Friday, 26 December.

The constitution in Assam has been suspended and the Governor has taken upon himself the administration of the province though the Nationalist Coalition Party under the leadership of Sj. Rohini Kumar Chowdhury, with the support of the Congress Party, were willing to work the constitution. In doing so, the Governor, according to the communiqué, explored all alternative possibilities and with the utmost reluctance His Excellency enforced Section 93 of the Government of India Act to end this deadlock. The public consider the concluding portion of the communiqué that 'whenever he is satisfied that a Ministry is prepared to take its full part in the prosecution of war, he will not hesitate to revoke the proclamation' is a direct challenge to the Congress and an indirect coercion to the legislature to veer round Sir Md Saadullah, the hero of the no-confidence motion. However, this is the blackest day for Assam and the name of Sir Robert Nell Reid will be long remembered in the parliamentary history of Assam.

On his attention being drawn to certain statements made in to-day's communiqué announcing the assumption by Governor of the administration of the Province, Mr Rohini Kumar Chowdhury, Leader of the Nationalist Coalition Party, stated to the special representative of the 'Amrita Bazar Patrika' that he was surprised to find that His Excellency could come to such a conclusion that a Ministry formed by him could not be a stable one. He had during his discussions with His Excellency made it abundantly clear that he could count upon the solid support of as many as 59 members of the Assembly in a House of 107, thus giving him a clear majority for carrying on the normal provincial administration. In measures, however, which did not directly come within the purview of provincial administration, described generally as war measures, Mr Chowdhury gave this distinct understanding that the Congress Party would be prepared to lend support to such measures which would be initiated by the Provincial Government in spheres connected with the defence of civil population, maintenance of internal peace and order and other things but in such other rare occasions in which the Assembly might be called upon to vote certain measures other than those of the nature described above the Congress Party would probably sit neutral, in which case he would get over in the Assembly with the expected support of the European members together with the members of his own Party. The apprehension of instability for Mr Chowdhury's cabinet was, therefore, out of place and without any reference to actual narration of facts, as emerged out of his discussions with His Excellency.

Furthermore, Mr Chowdhury complained that he was not definitely told during his interview with the Governor as was now stated in the communiqué, that the Governor could not ask him to take office.

Mr Chowdhury also expressed surprise that the Governor had ever in his contemplation the formation of an all party Cabinet because he was not aware of any Party leader having been consulted on such a possibility.

In conclusion, Mr Chowdhury referred to the three conditions mentioned in the communiqué as being precedent to the Governor's revoking the proclamation and stated that already his party fulfilled all of them, namely, (1) that a Ministry formed by him would command the confidence of the legislature, (2) was willing to assume the responsibilities of office and (3) was prepared to take its full part in the prosecution of the war. His Party, he added, was prepared to go a step further in that it could face that legislature immediately, which according to the admission made in the communiqué itself, the only other party in the House, namely, that of Sir Muhammad Saadullah admittedly could not undertake.

IV. Bengal

139. A Death-blow to Culture Scathing Condemnation of Secondary Education Bill

Amrita Bazar Patrika, 6 January 1941.

'UNITE at the critical juncture; chalk out your line of action after careful deliberations in this meeting. Sink all your differences and with one mind carry out into practice whatever line of action you may collectively decide upon in this meeting.

'It is my appeal to you that you should proceed forward with this firm determination that you will not fall back or retreat whatever obstacles or impediments may present themselves.'

With these stirring words Acharya Sir Prafulla Chandra Ray concluded the address he delivered on Sunday afternoon at a crowded meeting of the citizens of North Calcutta and suburbs held at Tallah Park, Belgachia.

Mr J.N. Basu who was to have presided could not attend on account of a sudden attack of pleurisy. 'The struggle that would have to be waged to prevent depreciation of education in this province will be strenuous,' observed Mr J.N. Basu in course of a letter regretting his inability to attend the meeting.

'But in the interests of our country it must be waged. I am confident that we shall emerge from the struggle a stronger and better-equipped people.'

Mr Santosh Kumar Basu occupied the chair.

Bengal's Grave Crisis

'In this hour of Bengal's grave crisis' observed Acharya Sir P.C. Ray, 'none has a right to remain idle and inactive. We are to-day destitute in wealth, broken in health and degraded in politics. But our object of glory and hope has been Bengal's culture and education. It is essential to resist by all means the evil attempts that are being made to strike at the foundations of such culture and education too. This Secondary Education Bill is an instance of such an attempt. Bengal can never accept such a Bill. We can never allow this temple of Education which Bengal has built up by her own efforts to serve as a tool for selfish ends, and to fan the flame of communal passion....

'This Bill is injurious to the Hindus and Muhammadans alike. By reason of separatist tendencies born of communal differences. Bengali language and literature too are in jeopardy.

Each of us has got to carry from village to village, from town to town, an appeal for good sense, demand for a perfect educational system and the message of national unity. We shall not tolerate any injustice and shall resist it if it comes. Else, the curse of God and country shall visit us. May our endeavours be fruitful.

Assault on Education

'As a result of the experience which I have gained being intimately connected throughout my life with the educational system of this province, I have become very much apprehensive to think of the ultimate result which this assault on the very foundations of education and culture will bring in its trail. Whatever I have got to say in the matter I have already tried to express in greater detail at the Conference held at Hazra Park. Your future lies in your hands.

'To each and every one of you—not to an individual, belongs the right and ability to repel the onslaughts that are yet to come. Unite at this critical juncture. Chalk out your line of action after careful deliberations in this meeting. Sink all your differences and with one mind carry out into practice whatever line of action you may collectively decide upon in this meeting. It is my appeal to you that you should proceed forward with this firm determination that you will not fall back or retreat whatever obstacles or impediment may present themselves.'

Death-blow to Culture

'That the whole of Bengal was determined to oppose the enactment of the Secondary Education Bill had been amply borne out by the proceedings of the recent conference at Hazra Park, observed Mr Santosh Kumar Basu. "This protest", Mr Basu hoped, "would echo and re-echo throughout the length and breadth of the province".

'The measure, if passed into law would indubitably deal a death blow to Bengal's age-old culture and tradition. Every patriotic Bengalee should therefore, be prepared to check its progress and save the institutions that had sprung up through the service and sacrifice of thousands.

'It might be', Mr Basu admitted, 'that the existing system of Secondary Education needed reform so that the youth of India might be fitted to shoulder the heavier responsibilities that the changed conditions were sure to bring in. But such a reform could alone be carried out by men possessing breadth of vision, patriotism and an earnest desire to serve their fellowmen. Men, inspired by communal motives, were the least fitted to undertake a task of such a magnitude. But Bengal's Chief Minister had chosen to imbibe an outlook narrow and sordid. The abuse he was making of his little power would however, awaken in the nation a new consciousness infusing them with new strength and determination to stand determinedly against the evil measure. Kumar Bimal Chandra Sinha thought that although the citizens had registered their protest against the Bill at the conference held at Hazra Park that by itself, was not enough. The agitation against it must be wider till it reached every hamlet in Bengal.'

Anti-national Measure

Rai Harendra Nath Chowdhury moved the following resolution which the meeting unanimously accepted:

'This meeting of the school authorities, teachers, guardians and general public of North Calcutta, Paikpara, Dum Dum, Cossipore, Chitpur, Belgachia and Baranagore condemns Secondary Education Bill as anti-national, political, non-academic in character and reiterates the demand made by the All Bengal Secondary Education Bill Protest Conference for the withdrawal of the said bill'.

The object with which the Bill had been introduced was, according to Rai Harendra Nath Chowdhury, to cripple the education of the province. Whatever the Chief Minister might have said in his statement it was made clear in the statement of objects and reasons that the purpose of the measure was to control secondary education in Bengal. It made the entire province apprehensive of the future of her education. They must put forth a strenuous opposition, for nothing would be effective once the Bill was placed on the statute book.

Dr Harendra Coomar Mookerjee opined that the bill violated every principle advocated by the Saddler Commission. The Board, proposed to be set up, would by no means command confidence of different sections and communities. No educational reform was possible in the absence of co-operation on the part of the people. The contemplated re-organization of education would not have the goodwill of the majority. The Moslems might have a slight majority in point of population but the number of non-Muslim students reading in schools and their guardians were by far the greater. Moreover, people could not have confidence in the impartiality and sound judgment of the board the Government would appoint. The formation of such a Board of Secondary Education would create a schism in the country and deal a death blow to the cause of education from which it was not likely to recover.

140. To-day's Requisition Meeting

Editorial, *Amrita Bazar Patrika*, 17 June 1941.

THE Corporation of Calcutta under the Bose–League Pact had been run during the year that it lasted not so much in the interest of the ratepayers as in the interest of the two groups or cliques that had joined hands. The correspondence that had passed between Mr Ispahani and Mr Sarat C. Bose on the eve of the last election of the Standing Committees has made that absolutely clear. Mr Ispahani made the definite statement which was uncontradicted by Mr Bose, that the arrangement was that 'Moslem matters' would be left entirely to the Moslem League group. This was nothing but division of spoils on the approved Tammany Hall methods. The citizens of Calcutta, at least the vast majority, boiled with indignation, but they were helpless. It is they who were really responsible for the situation, though it is possible that many of them had not the faintest suspicion that the distribution of their vote equally between the pseudo-Congress of the Boses and the Hindu Mahasabha would lead to the mischievous Bose–League Pact. There was every prospect that till another election the ratepayers would continue to 'stew in their own juice' as the saying goes. Fortunately, however, as it often happens in such cases the associates quarrelled and the Pact came to an end, and the last moment efforts to repair the breach failed.

The citizens of Calcutta have every reason to rejoice that the Pact, two years before the next election, has come to an end. Not that we entirely support what has happened since then. The constitution of the Standing Committees, in some cases, is capable of improvement, and there are clear indications that the Hindu Mahasabha had to agree to certain selections by Mr Bose for the Standing Committees, against their better judgment. The Mahasabha Councillors, we feel, took a broader view. The end of the Pact being the supreme objective, the desirability of which was insistent, they agreed to swallow a few bitter morsels. The larger interests of the ratepayers moved them. If they and the Moslem group that has left Mr Ispahani's clique, and the European group will only assert themselves there will be time and opportunity to rectify some of the patently bad selections for certain of the Committees. All that we want is that the affairs of the Corporation should be conducted, not in the interest of this or that group, this person or that, but in the interest of the ratepayers. There must not be exclusive 'Hindu', 'Moslem' or 'European' interests to be in charge of the Councillors of the communities, but the interests of the city as a whole must be the sole and the supreme concern of all.

Four of the elected Hindu Councillors have joined with the Moslem League for to-day's requisition meeting. Mr K.C. Chakravarty, one of these Councillors, has sought to make a fine distinction between Requisition A and Requisition B. He says that in Requisition A, it is the Moslem League that has joined them that is, these four Hindu Councillors, and that in the other Requisition, which he asserts is the Moslem League requisition, he and the three other Hindu Councillors have not put their signatures. This argument does not deserve to be called 'ingenious'. It is disingenuous, and a transparent bluff, for we find that the requisitions are, except in phraseology, exactly the same. While Requisition A seeks to 'rescind' and 'reconsider' the resolutions forming the Standing Committees, Requisition B seeks to 'dissolve' the Committees, and 'revive' and 'reconsider' the constitution and powers of the Committees. Both the Requisitions, we find, are headed by Mr A.R. Siddiqui. Mr Chakravarty's contention that in Requisition A, the 19 Moslem Leaguers followed the four Hindu Councillors, including Mr Chakravarty, is absolutely groundless and unworthy of him.

Mr Chakravarty's statement that six Hindu Councillors have altogether been omitted from the Committees is not correct. We find that all the four requisitionists, including Mr Chakravarty, are on the Committees. Mr Chakravarty is on more than one committee, namely, the Finance Committee and the Roads and Bustees Committee. Last year he was Chairman of one of the Buildings Committees. We trust the change made is not his grievance. Mr Jogesh Ghosh, Mr N. Dalal and Mr P.K. Dutta are all on the Committees. They are the Hindu elected Councillors among the requisitionists. We fail to understand what grievances they have except that they do not like the Committees on which they have been placed and would have preferred certain other Committees. That cannot however be any justification of their conduct in joining hands with Mr Ispahani, whose object is to restore the dominance of the Moslem League group. Mr Ispahani knows that he cannot achieve his end without the aid of other groups, and he must be congratulating himself that some of the disgruntled of the Bose group, the jetsam and flotsam of that group, have, for reasons of their own, agreed to further his plan.

We have seen how the legitimate interests of Bengalee Moslems have suffered because of the Bose–League Pact. They have taken this opportunity to assert themselves, and joined hands with other groups to frustrate the plan of Mr Ispahani. They will be sought, we doubt not, to be victimized by some of their co-religionists. They have, however, decided to do what they feel to be right. In view of their courageous stand, the attitude of Mr K.C. Chakravarty and three or four other elected Hindu Councillors, cannot but be highly disapproved by the Hindus. We hope that even now they will reconsider their position, and not betray the interests of the ratepayers who have elected them. We hope the Hindu Mahasabha Councillors, in their turn, will take the initiative in redressing genuine grievances, if any, in the matter of the composition of some of the Committees. Certain men of the Bose group who had made themselves prominent by their extreme partisanship, not to speak of other things, have been placed in Committees where their presence cannot but lead to suspicion.

We need hardly repeat that we ourselves do not approve all the selections made for the Standing Committees. But this is a matter of minor importance and the mistakes made may yet be rectified. The matter of supreme importance is the defeat of Mr Ispahani and his plan, and to repair, as far as possible, the mischief done by the Bose–League Pact. We trust the sinister influence of some of the adherents of the Bose Party that has done much to discredit the Corporation will be a thing of the past by the exertions of the Councillors who are sincerely desirous of placing the interests of the rate-payers above petty personal ends.

141. Coalition Government for Bengal

Amrita Bazar Patrika, 12 July 1941.

Failures of Efforts: Reasons Explained by Sj. Kiran Sankar Roy

Mr Kiran Sankar Roy, Leader of the Bengal Congress Parliamentary Party, has issued the following statement:

One of the stock in trade of those who have been for the last few years carrying on a lying propaganda against the Congress is to state that though the interest of Bengal required the formation of a Coalition Ministry, the Congress High Command, with characteristic disregard for the interest of Bengal, prevented its formation by withholding permission to do so. This propaganda was carried on with so much persistence and subtlety that a large section of the public which is not familiar with facts have come to believe it. Of course, it is not made quite clear when such permission was sought for and when it was refused. Nor is it clear with which party or parties the proposed coalition was to have been formed. It is also not apparent which Mahomedan leader offered to form a Coalition Ministry with the Congress and to whom the proposal was made.

Strength of Congress Party

It is not my purpose here to discuss whether it would have been honourable or wise for the Congress to form a coalition with parties which were opposed to it or fundamentally differed from it—specially when the Congress would only have been a minor partner in such a coalition. It should be borne in mind that the total strength of the Congress in the Assembly immediately after the general election was only 56 or 57 in a house of 250. And it should also be remembered that the Krishak Proja Party, which was the only party with which the Congress could have honourably combined, had not more than 45 members. To command a majority in the House it would have been necessary to bring in other groups, each demanding and getting its own price. At best a coalition of this nature would have been a strange mosaic, uncemented by any principle or policy and only held together by self-interest and self-preservation. It would have been a replica of the notorious Bose–League Pact in the Corporation. It should be clear to everybody that a coalition without an agreement on ideal, policy and programme would only have been a combination to share the portfolios and incidentally the salary. But as I have stated before, I have no desire for the present to enter into a discussion regarding the pros and cons of a Coalition Ministry. My only purpose is to point out that the charge that the Congress Working Committee prevented the formation of a Coalition Ministry in Bengal is untrue and is nothing but a part of the general propaganda against the Indian National Congress. I can also definitely state that the Bengal Congress Parliamentary Party never even discussed the possibility of the Congress joining a Coalition Ministry, much less seek permission of the Congress Working Committee for this purpose.

Points of Difference

I have already indicated that the only coalition possible for the Congress Party was a coalition with the Krishak Proja Party. Soon after the general election Mr A.K. Fazlul Huq, the then leader of the Krishak Proja Party, and some other leaders of the party met prominent members of the Congress Party and had several talks regarding the formation of a coalition. But these talks were inconclusive and no agreement as to policy and programme was actually arrived at. One of the main points of difference was what the parties should do if the political prisoners—of which there was a large number at the time—were not released forthwith. The Krishak Proja Party, while willing to put pressure for the release of political prisoners, did not agree that the Cabinet should resign if the political prisoners were not released immediately.

It should also be remembered that at the time the Indian National Congress had not yet decided to accept ministership even in the provinces where it commanded a majority in the Legislature. The Congress had demanded an assurance from the Government that the Governors of the provinces should act as constitutional Governors and should not act independently of the Ministers. The Congress did not agree to form Cabinets until this assurance was given by the Government. More than three months time elapsed before the above assurance was given and in the mean time the government had appointed Interim Ministries to carry on the administration. There was therefore, no occasion for the Congress Working Committee to give permission to the Bengal Congress Party to form a Coalition before the main constitutional issue between the Government and the nation was settled to the satisfaction of the Congress. It is well-known that so far as Bengal is concerned the Government had not to appoint an Interim Ministry. By the time the constitutional issue was settled Mr Fazlul Huq had already formed a ministry on the 1st April 1937, in alliance with the Moslem League, the Nationalist Party and the European Bloc, although a section of the Krishak Proja Party broke away as soon as the ministry was formed.

Public Opposition

Let us not also forget that the public feeling in Bengal at that time was very much against the idea of Congressmen entering the ministry. The entire Bengal press was against such a proposal, which was then considered preposterous.

That section of the press which today finds fault with the Congress for not entering into a coalition was at that time hurling its choicest vulgarities at those unfortunate persons whom it suspected of having any intention of entering the Cabinet. It became evident from the vigour of their language that to those papers patriotic duty became a positive pleasure. A reference to their old files will conclusively prove this.

Ever since Mr Huq formed his Cabinet and specially after the defeat of the censure resolution, we have never known Mr Huq to make any proposal to form a coalition with the Congress. On the contrary he has joined the League, accepted the leadership of Mr M.A. Jinnah and had become a protagonist of Pakistan. If he has raised hopes in the minds of this or that member of the opposition by vague talks, it can only be for his own purpose.

142. Reactionary and Retrograde Calcutta Municipal Second Amendment Bill, Citizens' Emphatic Protest

Amrita Bazar Patrika, 14 July 1941.

ASSEMBLED in large numbers on Sunday evening at the hall of the Calcutta University Institute, Muslim citizens of Calcutta, along with their Hindu brethren, registered an emphatic protest against the proposed Calcutta Municipal Second Amendment Bill.

Syed Jalaluddin Hashemy, MLA, who presided, characterized the provisions of the measure as highly undesirable inasmuch as they constituted a definitely retrograde measure totally destructive of the civic autonomy and freedom which the Corporation had been enjoying as a result of the Act of 1923.

A committee of Hindus and Muslims was formed at the meeting with a view to carrying on agitation against the Calcutta Municipal Amendment Act and the Calcutta Municipal Second Amendment Bill for the creation of a common political platform for the two communities and the furtherance of the Bengal National movement.

'The three main steps proposed by this bill' observed Mr Hashemy 'are: I. The appointment of the Chief Executive Officer by the Provincial Government, II. The setting up of a Service Commission to select appointments to higher posts under the Corporation and, III. The assumption of greater powers of control by the Provincial Government in cases of default or abuse of powers by the Corporation.

'The Bill was circulated for eliciting public opinion thereon and I am in possession of views expressed by more or less 44 different organizations of repute. A large majority of these organizations excepting a few conducted by Europeans is opposed to the principle of the Bill. Among the organizations who expressed views, the Corporation of Calcutta, Bengal National Chamber of Commerce, Indian Chamber of Commerce, Calcutta Traders Association, Marwari Chamber of Commerce, Howrah Municipality, Bengal Land Holders' Association, British Indian Association, Marwari Association are worth mentioning.

A Retrograde Measure

'They have uniformly characterized the provisions of the Bill as highly undesirable inasmuch as they constitute a definitely retrograde measure totally destructive of the civic autonomy and freedom which the Corporation has been enjoying as a result of the Act of 1923.

'They maintain and very rightly that the provisions, if enacted, are bound to lead to serious misuse or abuse of powers by the officers of the Government to whom such powers are proposed to be transferred and are wholly uncalled for, having regard to the fact that under the law, as it now stands, there is ample scope for the Government control over the activities of the Corporation, if and when such control is needed.

'The reasoning given in the statement of objects and reasons for the amendment proposed by the said clauses is vague and most unconvincing, and there is no occasion for any such interference by the Government with the Civic administration of the city, as is suggested by the said clauses.'

'In the Assembly' Mr Hashemy mentioned, 'I recorded my emphatic protest against the Bill which is calculated to take away the rights and powers of the Corporation even in internal management and appointment of officers.

'The proposed amendment empowering the Provincial Government to suspend any resolution of the Corporation or of any Standing Committee, or of Sub-Committee, or of Special Committee, is highly reactionary. Still more reactionary and vague is the reason of such suspension. It will be entirely left to the whim or party-spirit of the particular Minister-in-Charge of the portfolio.

Proposed Amendment

'Still more retrograde is the amendment proposed which authorizes the Provincial Government to supersede "any department" of the Corporation for incompetence and the most dangerous portion is the proposal for making the Provincial Government, sole judge of such incompetence and its decision being final.

'Another amendment proposed (Sec 19B) to supersede the Corporation is highly reactionary as it places the Corporation completely at the feet of the Minister-in-Charge and the position of the elected Councillors would be no better than the menial servants to be dismissed at the sweet will of his Master.

'The proposed Section 51A, is equally reactionary. It deprives the Corporation of all power to appoint its own servants and leaves such power to a small body of persons. This reduces the premier self-governing institution of Bengal to a mere force.

'The proposed proviso to Section 66A, empowering the Provincial Government to sanction or reject any estimate over two and a half lakhs of rupees cripples the power of the Corporation to an inordinate extent.'

Mayor's View

Mr Phanindra Nath Brahma, Mayor of Calcutta, regarded the Calcutta Municipal Second Amendment Bill as an absolutely uncalled for measure. One of the principal clauses of the bill provided for the appointment of the Chief Executive Officer of the Corporation by the Provincial Government. The Government could by no means argue that the administration of the city's affairs under the present Chief Executive Officer had deteriorated. Well-informed citizens knew what improvements had been made since the Corporation came into the hands of the people. In every sphere—in the field of free primary education, water supply, drainage, condition of roads, grants to hospitals and charitable institutions the improvement had been manifest and the difference between the two administrations, the present and its predecessor, had been marked.

For the last 17 years the same gentleman was being appointed the Chief Executive Officer and the Government had been sanctioning their approval to the appointment. What reason now led them to take into their hands the power of appointing the CEO?

If the Corporation had committed mistakes, and no human organization was above error, let the Government point it out to the city father. But instead of doing that they were bringing out a bill which, if enacted, would destroy the little civic right which the citizens enjoyed. In these circumstances people could be scarcely blamed if they suspected the motive of the Government in introducing such a reactionary measure.

Bengal Muslims' Position

The Bengalee Musalmans, said Syed Habibur Rahman, were nowhere in the Calcutta Corporation although the city of Calcutta was their own metropolis in their own province of Bengal. Under the system of joint electorate Bengalee Muslim Councillors were so long being elected in the majority of Muslim seats on the Corporation, as they secured vote not only from Bengalee Muslims and Hindus but also from non-Bengalee Hindus and Muslims. But under the present system of separate electorate, introduced by the Bengal Ministry, Bengalee Muslims did not get any votes from the Bengalee and non-Bengalee Hindus as before. Non-Bengalee Musalmans too did not vote for Bengalee Muslims.

Non-Bengalee-ridden Muslim League selected their fellow non-Bengalee Muslims to all Muslim Corporation Constituencies rejecting nominations of Bengalee Muslims set up by the district Muslim League at Calcutta. The Bengalee Muslims had no place in the Calcutta Corporation. Mr Huq, his Cabinet and his Coalition party members, although being themselves Bengalee Muslims, had enacted the Calcutta Municipal Amendment Act sacrificing the Bengalee Muslims at the altar of the up-country Musalmans and making a drive against the Bengalee Muslim not merely from all Muslim seats on the Calcutta Corporation but from its services. This Act had been passed not by the demand of the Bengalee Muslims of Calcutta or this province but by a coterie of non-Bengalee Mussalmans. The interests of the Bengalee Mussalmans had not only been betrayed but also trampled by Mr Huq, his Cabinet and the members of the Legislature, who supported him.

Separate Electorate

Separate electorate, therefore, meant exclusion of Bengalee Muslims from the Corporation altogether. Over and above this, the Second Calcutta Municipal Amendment Bill, offspring of its predecessor, if enacted into law, would ensure a mutual arrangement for distribution of 33 per cent of Corporation Muslim services among non-Bengalee Mussalmans. That was a challenge thrown out to Bengalee Mussalmans. Would the Bengalee Muslims, Mr Rahman enquired, surrender or accept the challenge? The proper reply to the challenge according to the speaker, would be the intensification of the Bengalee National movement and Bengalee National consolidation. Mr Rahman on behalf of the Mussalmans of Bengal called upon the Ministry to abandon the Second Calcutta Municipal Amendment Bill and restore without delay the system of joint electorate.

Maulvi Shamsul Huq, Councillor, Calcutta Corporation, expressed the view that in case the bill were passed it would in no way help the poor rate-payers. He reiterated his opposition to the provisions of the bill.

Supporting the idea of carrying on the Bengalee National movement Mr J.C. Gupta held that the movement would produce a feeling of amity between the two communities, Mr Gupta had every sympathy with the movement and he promised it his assistance in every possible way.

Maulavi Abdul Jalil Ahmed, Mr B.C. Bhattacharya and Sj. Dulal Chandra Mitra also addressed the gathering.

The committee which was formed at the meeting to carry on agitation against the Calcutta Municipal Amendment Act and the Calcutta Municipal Second Amendment Bill consist of the following members with power to co-opt. Syed Jelaluddin Hashemy, Mr J.C. Gupta, Maulvi Shamsul Huq, Syed Habibur Rahman, Mr Suresh Chandra Majumdar, Mr B.C. Bhattacharya and Sj. Dulal Chandra Mitra.

143. Congress and Bengal Ministry to Enter into a Coalition Would be Suicidal

Amrita Bazar Patrika, 17 July 1941.

Sj. Kiran Sankar Roy, Leader of the Bengal Congress Parliamentary Party, has issued the following statement:

I have to revert once again to the controversy regarding the formation of a Congress Coalition Ministry in Bengal in 1937 because of the editorial comments of the *Amrita Bazar Patrika* and the *Hindusthan Standard* on my statement published on the 12th instant.

Let me deal with the *Hindusthan Standard* first. This paper, following its well-known principle of not giving publicity to those who do not echo its master's voice, did not publish my statement—though it considered the statement important enough to devote its principal editorial to it. I do not know if it is journalistic etiquette to comment on a statement without publishing it. The *Standard* after admitting the facts cited in my statement has accused me of suppressing the truth. I have read and re-read its editorial to find out which are the varieties I have suppressed to my advantage. I found the *Standard* discovering and proclaiming the following great truths: First—that I am a clever politician. To this my humble submission is if one is a politician it is no offence to be clever. At least it is no great credit to be stupid in any sphere of life. Second—the *Hindusthan Standard* has never known me feel strongly about the release of the political prisoners, because I am associated with politicians who in their turn are associated with Mr Tushar Kanti Ghosh who again .... I do not think this profound nonsense really calls for any reply. I only regret that the Editor of the *Standard* has Mr Tushar Kanti Ghosh in his head all the time and also that he has nothing else in it. But according to the *Standard* the third and the most priceless truth I have cleverly suppressed is that the Bengal Congress leaders—whoever they may be, were really not against acceptance of ministry. They only pretended to be so because they expected that the Congress would not accept ministry in any province. These not very clever politicians were misled into thinking so because of the speeches of the All-India leaders—especially of Pandit Jawaharlal Nehru and also because the question of office acceptance was not made clear, according to the *Standard*, in the Congress Election Manifesto. If they had the slightest suspicion that the Congress was going to accept ministry in provinces where it had majority, these leaders would have tried utmost to form a ministry in Bengal even though the Congress was in a hopeless minority in this province. This of course is a fact I did not know. I thought their opposition to ministry was not conditional. Being opposed to acceptance of office in provinces where Congress was in a majority it is difficult to believe that they were in favour of its acceptance where Congress was in a hopeless minority. I am sure that the *Standard* has ill-served its masters by ascribing, perhaps without reason, such stupidity and insincerity to them.

A Sinister Suggestion

The *Standard* has also made a dishonest suggestion. It says that the Congress–Krishak Proja Coalition might not have a majority by themselves but that 'Power Counts, and it is not impossible that such a Coalition would have attracted to it members from other groups'. By power, I suppose the *Standard* means patronage. I consider this to be a sinister and mischievous suggestion. This belief that 'Power Counts' has been the bane of politics in Bengal. Leaders who pinned their faith on this motto, have sought 'power' by any means whatsoever and have only succeeded in disintegrating the Congress organization and destroying the idealism which inspired the Congress workers. Secondly, who does not know that men who join a party because of the powers and patronage it commands are sources of danger and not sources of strength as the *Standard* seems to think.

The Congress Position

It is also wrong to suggest that there was ground for misunderstanding the Congress position regarding the acceptance of office. The very fact that the Congress Election Manifesto did not mention anything about it clearly meant that the question of office acceptance was kept open and was to be decided upon later on according to the result of the election and other circumstances. Let me recapitulate briefly the sequences of events leading to the acceptance of office by the Congress. The General Election was held in January–February in 1937. In March 1937 the Congress demanded an assurance from the Government that Governors should function as Constitutional Governors. This assurance was not given till July. In the meantime Interim Ministers were appointed by the Governors in the provinces where Congress was in a majority. The assurance asked for being given in July, the Congress accepted office in seven provinces where it had a majority. But on the 1st of April that is, three months before this Mr Fazlul Huq had already formed his Cabinet in Bengal. This, according to the *Standard*, was a nasty trick of the Congress High Command which deprived the Bengal Congress leaders of the pleasure of being in a Coalition Cabinet and enjoying the powers of office.

Incorrect Analogy

Regarding the *Amrita Bazar Patrika*, it seems that the *Patrika* does not agree with me in thinking that the Congress could not have formed a Coalition Ministry in Bengal without sacrificing its principle and ideals and that further it was not also a practical proposition. In support of its contention that there was a possibility of forming a Congress Coalition Ministry in 1937 *Patrika* mentions the Bardoloi Ministry in Assam and the Alla Bux Ministry in Sind. I submit that the analogy is not correct. The Alla Bux Ministry is not a Congress Ministry. It is not a Congress Coalition Ministry either. The Congress has merely agreed not to oppose it on certain conditions. Further, being an Independent, it is open to Mr Alla Bux to form a Cabinet with other groups by making compromises, but it is not open to the Congress to have the same freedom of combination and compromise.

As regards the Bardoloi Ministry let us not forget that the Ministry that was formed in Assam after the General Election was the Saadulla Ministry and that the Bardoloi Ministry came into existence later. It was after the Saadulla Ministry was defeated time and again on most important issues and the Congress opposition obtained a majority in the House that the Bardoloi Ministry was formed. Secondly it was primarily a Congress Ministry. The Independents who joined the Assam Congress Parliamentary Party formed only a small section of the entire party and they agreed to accept the decisions and discipline of the Congress on all Parliamentary matters. Thus in Assam the Congress was predominant in the Cabinet, in the Party and also in the House.

Position in Bengal

Now look at the picture in Bengal. In a House of 250 the Congress having only 57 members, it would have been necessary to secure 69 other members in order to have a bare majority of one. Most of these 69 members had other affiliations and had different and sometimes contradictory ideologies. Some would have been careerists demanding a price. What would have been the position of the Congress in this conglomeration? Surely it is obvious that the Congress would have been a minority even in the proposed Coalition party itself—which was not the case in Assam. It is also well-known that the members of the Krishak Proja Party and most of the unattached members who might have joined the party, would not have agreed to accept the decision and discipline of the Congress even in Parliamentary matters. The Congress would have been completely swamped in such a Coalition. In the Cabinet also the Premier would have been a non-Congress Mahomedan. That was as far as I know the basis of all negotiations of Mr Huq. Considering all circumstances, it goes without saying that apart from the Chief Minister, half the seats in the Cabinet would have gone to the Mahomedans, not one of them belonging to the Congress. Of the remaining half some would have to be given to members belonging to the Scheduled Castes who would not necessarily have been Congressmen. So far I can see, it would have been impossible for the Congress to get more than three seats in the Cabinet. Having only 57 members in a Coalition Party of 126 and three Ministers in a Cabinet of 11, Congress would have been quite ineffective and futile in the Cabinet, in the party and in the House. In these circumstances I still maintain it would have been suicidal for the Congress to enter into a Coalition with other parties....

144. Bengal Governor's Reports to Viceroy on Fazlul Huq Ministry in Bengal and the Muslim League

Correspondence with the Governor of Bengal and his Secretary, 1941, Linlithgow Papers, Acc. No. 2183, NAI.

(i) Governor of Bengal to Viceroy

6 August 1941

[Confidential.]

Report No. 14.

Dear Linlithgow,

This is my report for the second half of July. I enclose the Home Department's report for that period. [...]

2. *Political.*—Opinion regarding the war situation remains very much the same and I need say nothing to supplement my last report. What is of more immediate concern is the situation that is developing over the Chief Minister's membership of the National Defence Council. I have reported these developments by telegram but it may be of interest to you to have a rather fuller account of the position.

3. Although there was a good deal of criticism in the Muslim press, and he had to face the opposition of the upcountry Muslims, the Chief Minister would have had an easier task, had it not been for the unfortunate impression that has been produced by the recent Commons debate. There can be no doubt that Muslim League opinion, as a whole, is strongly influenced by the belief that certain statements made in the course of this debate indicate a feeling of jubilation that prominent Muslims should have joined the National Defence Council in defiance of the authority of the League. The Secretary of State was reported on August the 3rd to have stated when winding up the debate: 'The Prime Ministers of Provinces enjoying democratic self-government have joined, with the consent of their colleagues, and presumably with the

consent of their elected majorities'. This statement, if correctly reported, is not accurate, since all members who were invited to join, were asked not to divulge the fact before the Press announcement was made. The Secretary of State is also reported to have said at the close of the same speech: 'I am glad to think that regardless of party leaders and in defiance of party discipline, patriotic Indians have come forward to work for India's defence'. This is regarded as being clearly a reference to the League. As I have already reported, the Chief Minister considers that these statements have made his position more difficult. I have suggested that it might help him if it could be clearly stated in any letter of appointment, or confirmation of his appointment, which may be issued (as presumably it will be) that he was invited as Chief Minister of the Province. It is also for your consideration whether any pronouncement, either by yourself or the Secretary of State, would help at this stage to remove the impression that a deliberate attempt has been made to undermine the authority of the League.

4. Nazimuddin supports the Chief Minister's action privately, but it is very doubtful whether he could stand against Jinnah openly. He informs me that a meeting of the Working Committee of the All-India Muslim League will take place on August the 24th, and he believes that the result will be unfavourable to Huq and Sir Sikander, both of whom are in Jinnah's bad books owing to earlier 'indiscipline'.

5. The position has not been made any the easier by the Hindu press, which has continued to taunt Jinnah with this encroachment upon his authority; and I have no doubt that every opportunity will be taken, unless the Muslims can close up their ranks, or bringing about a wider cleavage between the Bengali and non-Bengali Muslims....

(ii) Governor of Bengal to Viceroy

Telegram R, Calcutta, 7 August 1941.

No. 68. Muslim Ministers today discussed before me Chief Minister's position vis-à-vis forthcoming meeting of the All-India League Working Committee on August 24th. They took exception to Secretary of State's speech reported at page 10 of last Sunday's *Statesman,* column 3, 'the Prime Ministers of Provinces enjoying democratic self-government have joined with the consent of their colleagues, and presumably with the consent of their elected majorities'. After my confidentially explaining background there was general support for Chief Minister's decision to accept membership of National Defence Council. Nazimuddin and Suhrawardy desire to support his action as far as possible, though they are unwilling to go to the extent of causing a complete split in the All-India Muslim League. They consider however that the case is greatly weakened by Secretary of State's speech in Commons debate, particularly the sentence reported at foot of column 5 of same edition: 'I am glad to think that regardless of party leaders and in defiance of party discipline patriotic Indians have come forward to work for India's defence'. This statement is widely believed to have direct reference to Muslim League and Ministers agree that unless this impression can be removed before Working Committee meets, Huq will find it difficult to persuade Committee members that he was invited as Chief Minister. It would greatly strengthen his case if it could be made clear publicly that the Secretary of State's sentence quoted does not bear the interpretation implied.

145. Newspaper Report on Discussion in Bengal Legislative Assembly on Secondary Education Bill

Amrita Bazar Patrika, 5 September 1941.

A Blow to Calcutta University
Humiliating Measure
Communal Features of the Secondary Education Bill

In the Bengal Assembly on Thursday the motion for the recommittal of Bengal Secondary Education Bill to the Select Committee, moved by Rai Harendra Nath Chaudhury, was defeated by 124 to 56 votes after the motion had been debated for full three days.

Excepting the handful of Scheduled Caste members, who belong to the Coalition Party, all the Hindu members voted for the motion for recommittal, while the Krishak Proja members supporting the Government, the entire Moslem votes were cast against it. The European Party also supporting the Government, the majority for the Government was further swelled....

Dr N. Sanyal

Supporting the motion for recommittal Dr Nalinaksha Sanyal said that ever since the present measure was brought forward, it had been greeted with a chorus of condemnation in the press and on the platform and it had been subjected to scathing criticism both inside and outside the House. Even men like Dr Rabindranath, Acharya Profulla Chandra and Sir Sarvepalli Radhakrishnan deprecated the introduction of communal principle in the sacred field of education.

Dr Sanyal said that among their demands were: that the Board of Secondary Education in Bengal should be entrusted with the development and guidance of secular education only; the Board should deal with and develop vocational education such as agricultural, commercial and military education; the Board should be fully autonomous and free from any interference by Government or by politicians; the President should be a person of unimpeachable strength of character commanding public confidence; the inspectorate staff should be entirely under the control of the Board from the very date of its inception; the regulations of the Board are to be framed by the Board itself; the budget of the Board should not be interfered with except under some special circumstances; adequate protection should be provided to ensure the continued recognition of existing High schools at present enjoying recognition of the Calcutta University; conditions of recognition of high schools and for the payment of grants-in-aid should be statutorily provided and not left to the Board or the Government; syllabus and curricula for the matriculation examination of Universities should have the approval of the University; examinations should be conducted by an independent statutory committee purely on academic basis; there should be an adequate financial provision made to enable the Board to function properly; the Calcutta University should be fully compensated for to cover all the loss it might suffer from the institution of the Board and the Government schools should be deprovincialized....

Dr S.P. Mookerjee

'In the history of this province there had been occasions in the past,' said Dr Syama Prasad Mookerjee, 'when official masures called forth strenuous opposition from the public at large.

But within recent years no measure has aroused such bitter and widespread controversy as the Secondary Education Bill.

'To-day more than ever we stand in urgent need for devising a system of education which will not be governed by a rigid regimentation of rules and regulations drawing inspiration from the political views of a particular group or party. We must permit our educational institutions full freedom and scope to develop their activities according to their best light and judgment. This freedom will not be lost but will create the greater freedom on which our country's future will be based. If party politics or an aggressive totalitarian State policy be allowed to influence education, it will produce most baneful effects on the development of a true national life. We in this province have very special reasons to entertain deep distrust of wide powers being given to the Government constituted under the present law. So long as Communal Award and separate electorates continue, we see no chance of the establishment of a really representative Government which may command the confidence of the different sections of the people. In particular the administration of this province for the last four years under the control of the present Ministry has left us with bitter experiences. It has filled the minds of a very large section of the people with grave misgivings and uncertainty about the future protection of the legitimate rights and interests of nearly one half of the population of this province....

'Without funds no reform is possible. In fact want of resources has been our chief stumbling block in the past. The Bill, as revised, provides for an additional grant of 25 lakhs in five years. This amount is ridiculously low. A sum equal to at least 50 per cent of existing expenditure on secondary education should be the State grant. This should give us about 35 lakhs of rupees in place of the proposed 50 lakhs. Will Government make this provision before it claims to exercise control and supervision through the Board'?

The Proposed Board

The Board as contemplated will be a part and parcel of the Bengal Secretariat. The powers given to it do not endow the Board with that autonomy which it must possess, if it is going to serve the cause of education whether of Hindus or Moslems or of any other community.

The Bill as revised has a peculiar way of approach in respect of matters vitally affecting the University of Calcutta. The report of the Select Committee to crown the humiliation of the University of Calcutta, which is one of the objects of the pernicious Bill, suggests that the University Act should be amended and it should be laid down that the University will not be entitled to hold its own admission test but shall be bound to accept the examination of the Board for the purpose.

While the report of the Select Committee indicates the anxiety of the Government and its supporters to take away the University's right to hold its Matriculation Examination, there is no mention anywhere of the plans of the Government to compensate the University for the loss of its income. The activities of the University depend on its income from fees, endowments and State-grants. The State-grant covers only about 15 per cent of the total expenditure of the University.

The failure of the Government to provide by Statute for compensation of the loss of University revenue, will only be interpreted as its desire to see its activities crippled by giving the University a blow from which it can hardly recover.

Features of the Measure

'Let me now refer to the features of the Bill which are connected with communal considerations. It is one thing for Government to provide in the Bill that the Board should represent different interests both from the academic standpoint and also from the point of view of education of different communities. But one has only to glance at the detailed provisions of the Bill—the composition of the Board, the Executive Council and the various committees—to discover how deep has the canker of communalism entered into the body of the Bill. It is officialization and communalism of the Bengal brand that gives us a bitter mixture of gas and poison which even the special castor oil of Mesrs Worsworth and Co, will not be able to counteract. Not satisfied with providing for distribution of seats amongst elected and nominated non-officials on a communal basis, even the officials are divided into separate communal zones. If official X is a Hindu, official V must be a Moslem. If official A is a Hindu male official B must be a Moslem female. Let me ask if both communities are not prepared to call upon the officials to act as true servants of the people as a whole and not of a community in particular, will it be possible for any Government to run the administration of the province in a manner that will inspire the confidence of the public at large? We have taken strong objection to the appointment of the President being made by the Government directly. Particularly in view of the very wide executive powers that are vested in him, we do not want that the President of the Board should be appointed on any consideration other than interests of educational expansion and efficiency. Our alternative suggestions in this respect include first, the election of the President by Board itself, secondly, appointment by Government out of a Panel of names to be proposed by the Board and thirdly, appointment by Government on the recommendation of a specially composed committee which may include persons such as Minister of Education, the Chairman of the Public Service Commission, two Vice-Chancellors of Calcutta and Dacca Universities and any impartial expert adviser such as the Educational Commissioner with the Government of India.

... 'The House cannot possibly consider this Bill in its present form and be asked too to accept important amendments piecemeal which we have ourselves not seen yet. The entire structure of the Bill must be re-framed and only then can the House and the public determine how far it goes to meet the viewpoints of its critics. On this ground alone the Bill must be referred back to the Select Committee. Let there be no misgiving on one fundamental point. The Bill as it stands is utterly unacceptable to us.

'It is not aimed to serve education and it specially injures the interests of the Hindus who have been responsible for building up hundreds and thousands of schools in this province where all communities have received their education. By one stroke of the pen it is proposed to withdraw recognition automatically from all high schools after two years and the onus will be thrown on them to satisfy the Board in respect of their claim for continued existence. These schools have all been granted recognition under law and mostly on reports of Government Inspectors themselves. This alone shows the spirit of callousness which has characterized Government policy....'

Mr Sarat Bose

Mr Sarat Chandra Bose said that last year when the Assembly assembled they recorded their protest against the Secondary Education Bill. Few months had elapsed since and what had happened during these few months entitled him to say that with their protest they had carried the sympathy, the support and the convictions of the entire Hindu community and an overwhelming body of educationists in this province. They offered uncompromising opposition to the bill because they felt that the bill as presented last year was communal both in inspiration and in intention. Had the position changed since then? If they looked into the provisions of the bill as it had emerged out of the select committee, they would find that the provisions had become even more retrograde and reactionary, even more harmful to the cause of secondary education in Bengal.

A member of the coalition party had said that during the last 12 months the Opposition had offered no constructive proposal. Mr Bose was afraid that member had either not followed the speeches delivered in this House and outside or the constructive proposals which were given both by the press and from the platform. If he could remind him that the Opposition said that the bill showed no comprehension of the nature and function of the secondary education, it showed that its authors had not realized that the secondary education really was equivalent to technical education. Constructive proposals were put forward from the Opposition regarding the nature and scope of secondary education but not one of these constructive proposals had found place or formed part of the provisions of the bill as it had emerged out of the select committee. With respect to the vital question of finances, no serious attempt had been made to tackle the problem. The other constructive proposal the Opposition submitted in the course of the last 12 months was that provision must be made to administrative direction of secondary education but they found that policy had been discarded. The Opposition also said that provisions should also be made for improvement of the standard of schooling and also with respect to the improving the status and training of teachers. But the bill as it had emerged out of the select committee was silent on that point. Lastly the Opposition pointed out various omissions in the bill but no step was taken to rectify them.

Continuing Mr Bose said that during the last three years it had been the luck of the Opposition to offer opposition in the legislature to many reactionary measures but none of them were fraught with so much potentiality of mischief as the proposed secondary education bill, no other measure—though many of them had dealt grievous blow to the cause of democracy and nationalism in this country—had done greater injustice to certain community who had built up the system of education in this province. Before the special committee commenced sitting, Mr Bose told the members that let them be clear on one point. Was it their idea and ideal to train up their sons and daughters as good Bengalees and good Indians or whether their ideas and ideals were to train up their sons and daughters as mere Hindus or mere Mussalman. The response Mr Bose got was encouraging but unfortunately he found that on certain important matters, Government—at any rate those who represented Government for the moment—had been there with their minds made up and not with the minds open to response to the new idea.

Proceeding Mr Bose said that he had expected that the Minister for Education would draw the attention of the members of his own select committee to the fundamental which he initiated in the course of his speech—the fundamental was that on the Board adequate representations of the various communities must be guaranteed. But this fundamental had been ignored. The claim of the community which had sacrificed their sons and daughters and lakhs and tons of money for the development and expansion of the education in the province had been disregarded. Then again the bill did not provide for an autonomous board. The Opposition strongly objected a Board which would be completely officialized, as the bill as it stood now provided a body acting under the dictates of the Bengal Secretariat.

On all these grounds Mr Bose would submit that their case for recommittal of the bill to the select committee had been amply made out. He would like to address an appeal to the Chief Minister of Bengal who was also the Education Minister that he should give a lead to Bengal in the matter of improvement and expansion of the secondary education. He hoped that Mr Huq would come forward with an open mind and would approach the problem dispassionately, fairly and with due regard to the demands that had been put forward on behalf of the Opposition, demands which he must agree were just and reasonable. The special committee reached agreement on many points. But that agreement had been given a setback. They found that certain members of the Coalition party had come with their minds made up and they were putting communal demands to even higher points than what were provided in the bill. But even at this late stage Mr Bose believed that if Mr Huq came forward with an open mind and examined the questions all would not be lost. There was time yet to come to a satisfactory solution. He would appeal to the Government: 'Do not do what will destroy the synthesis of cultures that has grown during the last few centuries. Do not do anything which will make our children and our children's children to consider that they were Hindus and not Mussalmans and Mussalmans and not Hindus. Do not forget Bengal is our common land for common purposes.'

Hon Mr A.K. Fazlul Huq

The Hon Mr A.K. Fazlul Huq, Education Minister, thought that no useful purpose would be served if he went into details with a view to reply to the various criticisms that had been offered against the bill.

...Continuing he referred to the criticisms made by the Opposition and said that he meant no offence when he said that many of the remarks made by them were utterly irrelevant to the points at issue. The manner in which facts had been distorted and exaggerated and drawn upon imagination to make out a case showed to Mr Huq that the Opposition was convinced of the weakness of their case. Mr Sarat Bose had characterized the bill as not merely communal in conception but also communal in the manner in which its provisions had been drafted. He had referred to certain remark of Mr Huq which he made last year that the Muslims would be untrue to Islam if they did not place this Bill on the Statute Book. Mr Huq was ready to justify that remark. 'So long as' Mr Huq declared, 'the Opposition is un-Islamic, so long as the Opposition is communal, is unjust and unfair, our reply will be un-Islamic, communal and from our point of view just and fair; if the Opposition is Islamic our retort from this side will be Islamic, if you bring communalism you will have communalism in retort. If you be fair and honest, you will have fairness and honesty and justice'.

Proceeding Mr Huq referred to the Special Committee which sat for about a fortnight to bring about an agreed bill and said that every one knew as a result of their endeavours it was found possible to bring about an agreed bill if only they could agree on a certain point; namely the representation of the various communities on the Board. That was the crux of the matter and if they could satisfactorily settle that point the solution of other differences would easily follow. What is it that it was so difficult to get over that point? The members of the Opposition demanded a majority of the Hindus on it and the Muslims representatives demanded that no unfair majority should be given to any community. The Muslims did not want a majority on the Board but equality with other communities. So long as this was assured they would not press for anything else.

Continuing Mr Huq said that what was it that the Hindus had got to be afraid of if the Muslims were in majority on the Board? For 150 years the Hindus had controlled the primary, secondary and the University education. Why not give the Muslim community a chance of showing what they could do with secondary and primary education? If it was found that they were really mismanaging it, then and then only would be the time to condemn a Board of which the majority was Muslim. What right had the Hindus to assume that if the Muslims were in majority the secondary education would be something very disastrous that would happen to the educational system of the province? Mr Huq however was not pleading that the Muslims must be given a majority on the Board. He was merely submitting that the Hindus had nothing to be afraid of even if on the Board there was a majority of the Muslim members. He maintained that in reality the composition would show that the majority on the Board was not composed of Muslims but was a majority composed of all sections of various representatives of various communities, and it might be that for sometime the Hindus would be preponderately in majority. The bogey of Muslim majority like the proverbial devil on the tamarind tree, was merely a figment of imagination and in reality did not exist. There was nothing, Mr Huq asserted, that the Hindus needed be afraid of. On analysing the bill they would find that while some facilities were given to the Muslims, it did not take away everything from the Hindus.

146. In Bengal Political Tangle Mr Huq's Correspondence with Colleagues

Amrita Bazar Patrika, 18 October 1941.

Darjeeling, 17 October.

The trouble that had arisen in Muslim Parliamentary politics in Bengal about the end of the last session of the Assembly, leading to the tabling of several no-confidence motions, seems to have come to an end.

This is indicated by the correspondence between Sir Nazimuddin, Home Minister; Mr H.S. Suhrawardy, Finance Minister; and Mr Tamizuddin Khan, Minister for Agriculture on the one hand; and the Chief Minister, Mr A.K. Fazlul Huq on the other, which was released to the press to-night.

The letter from Sir Nazimuddin, Mr Suhrawardy and Mr Tamizuddin Khan to the Chief Minister *inter alia* says 'we regret to find that you feel aggrieved at the fact that we were parties to a resolution adopted at a meeting of the Working Committee of the Bengal Provincial Muslim League held on 13 September which was represented to you as being tantamount to a vote of no-confidence in you. We can assure you that we never entertained any such intention. On the other hand we definitely opposed a specific resolution of that nature and it was summarily rejected'.

The Chief Minister in the course of his reply *inter alia* says: 'In view however of the expression of regret contained in your letter and personally conveyed to me and in view of the assurance that none of you intended those resolutions to carry in any sense lack of confidence in me, I am prepared to allow the incident to be closed. So far as my letter to the Secretary of the All India Muslim League is concerned, I am taking suitable steps to disabuse the minds of such of my Muslim brethren as have interpreted the letter in a manner contrary to my intention. In fact, I have already written upon this subject to Nawabzada Liaqat Ali Khan with whom I intend to correspond further if necessary.

'I do not feel any special clarification of the position is called for, because nothing could be furthest from my thought than driving a wedge between Muslim Bengal and the rest of India for the very simple reason that I always desired no less than any one else the solidarity of Indian Muslims, working as one united people under one Organization, for the attainment of their political, social, cultural and economic progress. Nor does it seem necessary for me to refute the charge that I have defied the authority of the All India Muslim League, because nowhere in my letter to the Secretary of the All India Muslim League have I questioned the authority of that body to take a decision on important all-India issues, involving Muslims of India, including those of Bengal'.—AP

147. Congress in Bengal Legislature Participation Problem A General Policy in Bengal, Punjab and Assam Likely

Amrita Bazar Patrika, 24 October 1941.

Wardhaganj, 23 October.

Mr Kiranshankar Roy, Leader of the Bengal Congress Assembly Party, Mr A.K. Ghosh and Dr Nalinaksha Sanyal interviewed Mahatma Gandhi in the presence of Dr Rajendra Prasad, Sardar Vallabhbhai Patel, Mr Rajagopalachariar and Acharya Kripalani again this afternoon regarding the resumption of normal parliamentary activities in Bengal. Dr Rajendra Prasad after consulting Mahatma Gandhi and others, it is learnt, informed the Bengal delegation that the views represented by them would receive active consideration during the next few days and the Parliamentary Sub-committee's decision will be communicated to Mr Kiranshankar Roy at an early date. The Bengal Congress Leaders are leaving tomorrow reaching Calcutta on Saturday morning.

It is understood that the Parliamentary Sub-committee is receiving representation from the provinces where Congress legislators are in a minority. So their question, it is learnt, is being examined along with Bengal where also the legislature functions like that in the Punjab and Assam and it is not unlikely that a general policy may be adopted in these provinces. A decision is expected at an early date.—AP

148. Muslim League Working Committee Resolution Accepting Fazlul Huq's Explanation, New Delhi, 16 November 1941

Indian Annual Register, 1941, Vol. II, p. 220.

The Working Committee considered the following letter of explanation of the Hon'ble Mr Fazlul Huq, dated 14 November received by the Hon Secretary of the All-India Muslim League:

> I beg to acknowledge the receipt of your letter of 29 October forwarding for my information a copy of resolution No. 2 adopted by the Working Committee of the Muslim League and confirmed by the Council of the Muslim League at meeting of both the bodies held on 27 October at Delhi.
>
> I regret the delay in sending you my reply. It has been due entirely to the poor state of my health and I did not feel justified in replying to a communication of such serious importance without giving the matter most anxious consideration.
>
> No one knows better than the President himself that I have always been a loyal member of the League, have never hesitated to carry out its mandate and once decision was constitutionally

adopted by it, has never hesitated to obey it, even though that decision might not personally commend itself to me. If there were any doubts in regard to this point my resignation from the National Defence Council amply proves it.

It is an irony of fate that of all those who have given of their best to build up the only national organization of the Muslim India, I should have been the object of so much misunderstanding and so much uniformed criticism. It appears that portions of my letter have hurt the feelings of the President and some or my other friends. I convey to them, through you, my assurance that nothing was further from my intention than to hurt the feelings of or to cast aspersions on any one and I hope that my assurance in this respect will be accepted and the matter considered as closed.

Fazlul Huq

The Working Committee excuses the delay in not sending the reply within ten days on the ground of his ill health as the matter was of such serious importance that it required his anxious consideration. The Working Committee notes Mr Fazlul Huq's earnest re-affirmation of his loyalty to the Muslim League and his statement that he has never hesitated to carry out the mandates of the League, the latest instance in proof thereof is his resignation from the National Defence Council in obedience to the decision of the Working Committee. The Working Committee further notes his assurance that nothing was further from his intention than to hurt the feelings of or to cast aspersions on the President or the Executive of the League and others concerned; and as Mr Fazlul Huq requests the Working Committee, his assurance should be accepted, it is resolved that no further action should be taken in the matter.

149. Ministerial Crisis in Bengal

Amrita Bazar Patrika, 26 November 1941.

The Bengal Assembly meets to-morrow, Thursday, 27 November, in an atmosphere still thick with all sorts of speculations regarding the Ministerial crisis.

The fissures in the ranks of the coalitionists which were in evidence during the closing stage of the last Assembly session, which came to an abrupt end in circumstances of moving drama, yet show no sign of closing.

The section of the Coalition Party who are eager for the reshuffling of the Ministry and who have now formed into a separate bloc, 'Progressive Assembly Party', held a meeting of their group at the house of Hon'ble Mr A.K. Fazlul Huq on Tuesday afternoon to decide their attitude on the issue. After some discussion the meeting was adjourned till to-day when the final decision is expected to be reached.

What transpired at the meeting was kept a secret. But it is gathered that the group are still determined to force the issue and, according to a spokesman of the Party, the crisis still persists.

The other group of the Coalition Party following the leadership of Sir Nazimuddin, Nawab Bahadur of Dacca and Mr H.S. Suhrawardy also held a meeting of their own at the palace of the Nawab Bahadur of Dacca yesterday to decide their attitude on the issue. It is not denied even by them that the crisis is there, but they hope, rather very sanguinely, that the crisis will be averted.

A meeting of the Coalition Party—the Progressive Party have not yet broken away from it—has been called by the Chief Whip of the party, Mr Sahabuddin, at the palace of Nawab Musharuff Hossain to-day. A great importance attaches to this meeting when it is expected that the issues will be fully crystalized....

Mr Syed Badruddoza, Secretary of the Progressive Party in the Bengal Assembly, issued the following statement contradicting the Press statements that the Cabinet crisis had been averted.

'The attention of the Progressive Party has been drawn to a paragraph under the caption 'Bengal Cabinet Crisis Averted' in the issues of two local dailies of Tuesday, the 25th November. The statements appearing in these papers are a tissue of lies and maliciously false from beginning to end. In the first place, the Progressive Party is not a party of the Bengal Premier. It is a party composed of members of the legislature who stand for the programme which was published in the press some time ago. It is an absolute lie that the Hindu opposition MLA's have lost their faith in the Progressivities. It is also a lie that the application of Mr Syed Badrodduza for a separate bloc in the Assembly has not received the general approval of his party. In fact, the application has been made in pursuance of a unanimous resolution of the party. There is no basis for the misleading statement that the cabinet crisis has now been averted. The Cabinet crisis still persists. The rest of the paragraph is full of so many lies that it is not possible to give a definite contradiction of such a statement. I am writing to draw the attention of the public to the kind of stuff that generally appears in these section of the press.'

150. Resolution of Muslim League Working Committee Approving Action Against Mr Huq, Nagpur, 26 December 1941

Indian Annual Register, 1941, Vol. II, p. 223.

By another resolution, the Committee note with satisfaction the action taken by the President in expelling Mr Fazlul Huq from the league 'for the betrayal of the League organization and the Musalmans generally'. The resolution calls on every Leaguer 'not to rest content until the present Ministry which is composed of various elements antagonistic to the cause of Muslims in Bengal and of which Mr Huq is a mere titular head is overthrown'.

151. Ministerial Crisis
Mr Huq and New Party

Amrita Bazar Patrika, 30 November 1941.

Following the publication of the news of the formation of the Progressive Coalition Party with Hon'ble Mr A.K. Fazlul Huq, Chief Minister, as leader there was a great commotion in the political circles in Calcutta yesterday (Saturday).

The Chief Minister, it is understood, was summoned from Government House in the morning and saw His Excellency the Governor at 10.15 a.m. A hurried cabinet meeting was then arranged over which His Excellency presided. The cabinet meeting which was held at 12 noon, it is understood, was attended by all the ten members of the cabinet. It is also understood that at the meeting the Ministers asked for an explanation of Mr Huq about the formation of the new party in coalition with the groups now in Opposition in the Assembly and one of the Ministers, it is reported, used very strong language. The Chief Minister is stated to have told His Excellency that Mr Huq had always worked for the maintenance of the solidarity of Moslems and the Coalition Party. He therefore issued a statement in the press contradicting the report of his active participation in the formation of the party.

Removal of Undesirables

The Progressive Party was acquainted with this development in the afternoon. They got agitated over this and decided to press forward no-confidence motions against six of the members of the cabinet. It is reported that the Chief Minister also expressed that it is impossible for him to work with some of his colleagues in the cabinet and he would be only too glad to see them removed. But he is stated to have added that he had not yet been able to decide upon the procedure that he would adopt to get his undesirable colleagues removed from the cabinet.

The Chief Minister, it is expected, will be able to come to a definite conclusion by Monday or at the latest Tuesday next when there will be further clarification of the issues.

It is learnt that the Progressive Party will meet the Chief Minister on Sunday morning at 9 and the Coalition Party as a whole meets in the evening to discuss the present political situation. An emergency meeting will be held on Monday....

His Excellency the Governor of Bengal presided at a Cabinet meeting on Saturday morning.

After His Excellency had left the meeting, the Hon Chief Minister issued the following statement:

'Statements have appeared in the Press which indicates that as the outcome of disunity in the Cabinet I have accepted the leadership of a new party to be called the Progressive Coalition Party. I desire it to be known that there is no truth whatever in these reports. It is hardly necessary for me to point out that as Chief Minister and leader of the Coalition Party in the Assembly it would be unconstitutional for me to enter into negotiations with parties now in opposition with the object of forming a new party. It is my desire to maintain the solidarity of the Coalition Party no less than that of the Ministry and to ensure that the decision of the Coalition Party is accepted by every member of the party.'—AP

152. Bengal Ministerial Crisis Fazlul Huq May be Asked to Form Cabinet Again

Bombay Chronicle, 2 December 1941.

Calcutta, 1 December.

A Government House communiqué issued at 2.30 p.m. states: 'It is announced that ministers have to-day tendered to His Excellency the Governor their resignations as members of the Council of Ministers.

They will continue to remain in charge of their respective portfolios until His Excellency the Governor has decided whether or not to accept their resignations.'

Outgoing Ministers

The Huq Cabinet which resigned this morning consisted of the following:

1. The Hon Mr A.K. Fazlul Huq, Chief Minister and Minister in Charge of Education.
2. The Hon Sir Nazimuddin, Home Minister.
3. The Hon Sir B.P. Singh Roy, Revenue Minister.
4. The Hon Mr H.S. Suhrawardy, Minister in Charge of Finance, Labour and Commerce.
5. The Hon Nawab Bahadur of Dacca, Minister in Charge of Public Health and Local Self Government.

6. The Hon Maharaja Srish Chandra Nandy of Cossimbazar, Minister in Charge of Works and Communication.
7. The Hon Mr Tamizuddin Khan, Minister in Charge of Agriculture and Industries.
8. The Hon Nawab Mushareff Hosain, Judicial Minister.
9. The Hon Mr P.D. Raikut, Minister in Charge of Excise and Forests.
10. The Hon Mr M.B. Mullick, Minister in Charge of Cooperative and Rural Indebtedness.

Meetings and Consultation

The official announcement of the resignation of the Huq Cabinet was followed by a series of meetings and consultations by various groups and parties in the Assembly, all discussing the latest development.

The Progressive Party, which met in the afternoon at the residence of its Chief Whip, Prince Yusuf Mirza, adjourned to meet again to-morrow at the same place. Prince Yusuf informed the Press that at to-day's meeting about half a dozen more coalition members had joined and signed the pledge of the party.

The Hindu Nationalist Party, who also discussed the situation at a meeting, are expected to announce their attitude towards the newly formed Progressive Coalition Party in the Assembly tomorrow.

A meeting of the members of the Ministerialist Coalition Party has been called for December 4th in the Committee room of the Assembly, while the Working Committee of the Provincial Muslim League will meet to-morrow at 4 p.m. in the office of the League in order to discuss, among other matters, a requisition sent in by M.A.H. Ispahani, MLA.

The requisition was to call a meeting of the Working Committee to consider, *inter alia* the question of members of the Muslim League associating themselves or co-operating with a political party calling itself Progressive, 'which seek to strike at the root of Moslem solidarity and is hostile to the fundamental principles of the Muslim League', and to decide what action is called for and should be taken against members of the League 'whose activities in the Province recently have been directed towards the splitting up of Moslem solidarity and driving a wedge in the ranks of the Muslim League members of the Assembly.'

Huq May be Asked to Form Another Cabinet

If His Excellency the Governor accepts the resignations tendered by the ten ministers and calls upon anybody to form a new ministers, it will then be the second change in the ministry of the Province since the inauguration of provincial autonomy. About a year after its formation in April 1937 by Mr A.K. Fazlul Huq, following the general elections, the ministry resigned in June 1938, due to certain differences of opinion with Mr Nausher Ali, the then Minister for Local Self Government.

Following this, the late Lord Brabourne called upon Mr Huq again to form a cabinet which the latter did with all the previous ministers—except Mr Nausher Ali—and with two additions, namely, Mr Tamizuddin Khan and Mr Shamsuddin Ahmed, both of the Krishak Proja Party. Some months later, Mr Shamsuddin Ahmed resigned and this was followed by the resignation of Mr Nalini Ranjan Sarker, who was the Finance Minister—the latter over the issue of the war resolution in the assembly.

Political circles suggest that Mr Sarat Chandra Bose as Opposition leader, may in the first instance, be asked to form a new ministry, while the Nawab Bahadur of Dacca and Sir Nazimuddin are also mentioned as possibilities. It is however pointed out that the chances of Mr Fazlul Huq being asked to form another cabinet and resuming his position as Chief Minister cannot be entirely discounted.—AP

153. Huq Elected Leader Again First Formal Meeting of Progressive Coalition Party

Bombay Chronicle, 5 December 1941.

Calcutta, 4 December.

The first formal meeting of the Progressive Coalition Party was held this afternoon at the residence of the Chief Minister, Mr A.K. Fazlul Huq, who was unanimously elected Leader of the Party.

102 members, belonging to the various groups in the Assembly, forming the new Coalition, attended the meeting besides several members of the Upper House.

The name of Mr Huq was proposed by Mr Sarat Chandra Bose, Leader of the Bengal Congress Parliamentary Party and was seconded by Mr Shamsuddin Ahmed, Leader of the Krishak Proja Party.

The proposal was supported by Dr Shyamaprasad Mookerjee, Leader of the Nationalist Party, Nawab Musharruf Hussain, Judicial and Legislative Minister, Khan Bahadur Hashemali Khan, Deputy Leader of the Progressive Assembly Party, Mr Hem Chandra Nasker, Leader of the Independent Scheduled Caste Party and Mr W. Chippendale (Anglo-Indian).

Mr Huq, in the course of a short speech, said that he expected great things in Bengal as a result of the formation of this party, which represented the different parties and interests in the Legislature.

154. Governor Accepts Resignation

Bombay Chronicle, 8 December 1941.

Calcutta, 7 December.

The 'Associated Press' understands that the resignations submitted by all the ten members of the Huq Cabinet on 1 December have been accepted by HE Sir John Herbert, Governor of Bengal.

Party Chiefs Invited

It is believed in well-informed political circles that the leaders of the various groups and parties in the Legislature will be called in at Government House to-morrow for discussion with His Excellency in connection with the formation of a new Ministry....

Govt Communiqué

The following communiqué was issued from Government House to-night:

'It is announced that HE the Governor has this day been pleased to accept the resignations tendered on 1 December 1941, by the Honourable Ministers of their offices as members of the Council of Ministers.

'His Excellency proposes to consult to-morrow the leaders of various parties and groups in the Assembly.'

V. Orissa

155. Coalition Ministry in Orissa

The Statesman, 29 January 1941.

Cuttack Talks: Mr M.N. Roy Meets the Leaders

Cuttack, 28 January.

The possibilities of a Coalition Ministry in Orissa was discussed yesterday by Mr M.N. Roy with Pandit Nilakantha Das, MLA (Central), formerly President Orissa Congress Committee, Pandit Godavaris Misra, MLA, Mr S.B. Rath, Mr Divakar Patnaik, MLA and others.

Mr Roy told Press representatives that there was no reason why a Coalition Ministry should not be formed immediately in Orissa because it was sure to command a majority. He hopped that the Governor would act according to constitutional convention and help the termination of the deadlock without further delay.

Asked about the programme of the Coalition Ministry Mr Roy said that it should exclude all controversial matters and concentrate upon the democratization of war efforts as outlined in the declaration of the inaugural conference of the National Democratic Union in Calcutta.

Following further tasks this morning between Mr Roy and the Raja Bahadur of Khalikote, Pandit Godavaris Misra and others, the idea of seeing His Excellency the Governor with regard to the formation of a Coalition Ministry, has been abandoned for the time being.

Democratic Union

At a conference of non-Congress members of the Orissa Assembly last evening, it was resolved to form an Orissa Provincial Democratic Union and a provisional committee with Pandit Nilakantha Das, MLA (Central), Messrs Godavaris Misra, Brajosundar Das, Khan Bahadur Ahmed Bux, the Raja of Khallikote and Mr Sashibhusan Rath as members was appointed to convene a fully representative provincial committee. Mr S.B. Rath was appointed convener.

Addressing a public meeting in the Town Hall yesterday, Mr Roy said:

'Freedom Not a Gift'

'Freedom can never come as a gift. Therefore it is senseless to complain that the British Government do not want to give India freedom. Nobody can prevent India from being free if Indians are determined to attain freedom and know how to do it. Whatever may be the present attitude of the British Government, one thing is certain—this war is not going to end very soon. The Fascist Powers will not be defeated very easily. Even to-day they are as powerful as ever, and all the resources of the freedom-loving world will have to be mobilized before they can be defeated.

'India is bound to play her part in that struggle, which will determine the future of the world. Without the fullest support of the Indian people, this war cannot be won. If the British Government has not realized that yet, it will do so sooner or later.

'In anticipation of that inevitable change in the attitude of the British Government, Indians themselves must take the necessary initiative, instead of doing that the major political parties of the country have been sulking. Consequently, the popular forces are precluded from asserting themselves effectively on the situation and influencing the administration of the country. This position must change; otherwise, India will not be able to take advantage of the present situation.

'It is almost predetermined that India will come out of this war a first class military and industrial country. The decisive battles of this war are going to be fought in the Near East. The base of the major military operation on that important front will be India. If the British Government wants to win the war, it cannot continue the suicidal policy of preventing the rapid militarization and industrialization of India.

'Therefore, before long Indians must take up positions from which they will be able to hasten and shape that protest. By doing so, they will take India nearer to the goal of freedom because, having made the most decisive contribution to the defeat of Fascism India herself cannot be kept in her present position. This perspective grows out of the present political situation and should inspire confidence and determination in all Indian patriots who are not carried away by empty slogans or concerned with group of personal prestige'.—Associated Press.

156. Sarala Devi's Statement on Effort to Form Ministry in Orissa

File No. 1/41, Dr Rajendra Prasad Papers, NAI.

Translation of Srimati Sarala Devi's statement published in the Oriya Daily *Janata* of Cuttack dated the 18 May 1941:

'The consideration of, and arrangement for the formation of a Ministry in Orissa has gone on for nearly a year. At the time the Congress withdrew its Ministry from the Legislature, there was real necessity for the step. There is no reason to deny this when one considers it from the point of view of national aspiration, and of the principle of an independent India. Thereafter, when several members of the Assembly under the leadership of Pandit Godavari Misra tried to form a coalition ministry, we felt that the necessity for such a step had not arrived. We held this opinion, being promoted not only by the Congress pledge signed by us, but from individual principle, and we considered it against the interests of the country and therefore condemnable. I had written at the time a long statement in this connection in the "Samaj". It is foolish to pluck a fruit before it is ripe. At that time people thought similarly of the effort on the part of some Congress MLAs, and I was also of the same opinion. But, with the sharp and rapid change of situations and times my thought currents and political viewpoints are also changing in consonance with realities. Sometime after that effort, the initiation of training in Satyagraha camps, Satyagraha fight, interviews between Mahatma and the Viceroy, the resolution of the Congress Working Committee, and other events took place. Satyagraha was limited to individuals and specially to MLAs. Gradually it took into its fold the Congress members of Local Bodies, and ordinarily Congressmen belonging to Provincial, District and Primary Committees. Mahatmaji took up the leadership of this Satyagraha launched with the object of establishing the fundamental right of Civil liberty, that is, the freedom of expression of one's own opinion. The Government has also gone to the extreme limit of reactionarism and applied against the violators of the law their repressive measures according to their own will. At last the arrest or non-arrest of a Satyagrahi depends on their own choice. Instead of directions of Mahatmaji being carried out wholesale, only lists began to be approved. Lastly he laid down very rigourous terms and gave a higher place to quality and a lower one to numbers. However, the executives in the Provinces persisted in giving a higher place to numbers and recruitment of Satyagrahis became the order of the day. As a result of this, there is evident throughout the country a strong reaction and discontent. The general public have been unable to accept the high moral view and the high ideal of manhood set by Mahatmaji, and now even if they try to be inspired by these high ideals, their efforts will not bear fruit. This weakness of the general public is evident in various places. Those returning from jail are presenting their reasons for not offering Satyagraha a second time. Most of those, who are Satyagrahis, are doing so in the hope of having a claim on the future political spoils. The MLAs and the ministers everywhere have gone to jail in obedience to the orders of the leader. I am one of these. The order of the leader, and my gratefulness to the leader and to the organization which has conferred the high honour on me as a representative of the people, were the only reasons for my Satyagraha. On the one hand the Government have been trying all means with the objects of frustrating the Congress aim and Mahatmaji's noble ideal and individuality, on the other hand communal disturbances, and the consequent reaction and repression from the side of the Government, are not only holding a dagger against Satyagraha, but applying it. Under these circumstances those whose principle is to create disunity and to govern the country according to their own whims, have found a good opportunity and are ordering around the poor, starving, ignorant and diseased people of India. Orissa having newly attained provincial status, people here have had to suffer many perils. The situation in our province now is that God alone will listen to the wails of the people and redress the wrongs. Flood, fire, famine, Cholera, Fever and Small pox are constant occurrences. The unrestrained behaviour of the Zamindars has rendered lakhs of people half-dead. The Government have repealed some of the beneficial measures enacted by the Congress Ministry. The appropriations made by the Congress Ministry for education, village industries etc. have also been cancelled. Now, who is responsible for this state of affairs? The Government or Gandhiji? War contributions are being collected from everybody by means either direct or indirect. Those unwilling to pay are doing so through import and excise duties and through the railways. Men also, in order to save themselves from starvation, are taking up war services to die. Retrenchment in Government departments, no initiation of new schemes, rejection of schemes of the former ministry, collection of war subscriptions (compulsorily done by the officers) from all Government servants of high and low salaries, caste against caste, communal feeling and other things—these are some of the problems at work. The political principle of the English is always to show up black as white and white as black. Therefore there is nothing to be surprised at all this. In this situation, although we (even myself) had in the past condemned the efforts to form a ministry, today I do not see any reason for the condemnation of the same effort.

It is generally taken that this effort is being made in a spirit of revenge because of the disciplinary action taken by the Congress. I felt that way myself. But when I consider the feudal politics now at work in our country, and the blind injustices that are taking place, I do not think that those, who are trying to take control of the administration, are thus motivated. If their object is only a desire for revenge, and if that is their principle and their objective in forming the ministry, such a ministry will be short-lived. All classes of people are thinking in their own ways regarding independence and the good of their country. Therefore, it is against civilized behaviour to abuse one's opponent or group. It cannot be believed that the nation can indefinitely leave the future in the hands of God and to faith. This point of view, whether they succeed in their effort or not, I am unwilling to agree that those, who are trying to form a ministry without abusing and condemning Congress principle and present leadership and without calling the Congress leaders traitors, but are doing so out of their own conviction or belief, are wishing ill of the country. If I may state the contrary case, I must certainly state other things. Those, who have given up their individual power and their self-interest, and in order to render service to others, are honestly earning their bread by their service to the Government are also not condemnable. Viewed in this way, the object of those trying to form a ministry is noble; and it is wrong to wave black flag at them. Congress is observing its own principle and is carrying on throughout the country by entrusting the leadership to the Mahatma. Those, who, as faithful workers, are sincerely and selflessly treading the path of the Mahatma, are entitled to praise and respect from the nation. Similarly, I think it is a sign of natural and healthy state of mind not to hate and to level strong criticism too quickly against the principle and objective of those who desire to serve the nation and achieve its independence without having any rancour against the Congress organization and its principle, but who are, on the other hand, actuated by individual taste and ideal and are guided by a political objective. The political wheel is ever turning round, and its function takes place through its constant changes. The learned are few in our country and the number of half-educated and ignorant people is legion. We should therefore look at everything from all points of view, consider what is good and what is bad for the country, and learn things from this wider outlook. It is appropriate to scrutinize and consider, in the present political situation, whether the Congress is right or wrong, whether the programme and principle of the Liberal party is right or wrong, or whether the programme of the terrorists is right or wrong. Mere party squabbles, individual self-interest and recrimination of one another cannot be accepted as worthy of consideration by high class statesmen having political foresight'....

Extract from the Statement of Smt Sarala Devi, MLA (Orissa) published in the Samaj *dated 23.5.41 in reply to certain question of Sri Lokanath Misra, MLA:*

'I am giving a clear reply to your clear question. I consider that in this critical time for the country it is desirable that a ministry should administer. Because, in my opinion, the goal of the country's independence cannot be secured by symbolic protests, nor by Individual Civil Disobedience. This is the opinion of the majority of the people of the country. I have particularly heard such opinion from some Congress workers and Satyagrahis, and it has become my opinion also. I am thinking that the effect of the former mass Civil Disobedience movements on the Government has lost its sharpness in the present one.

I am not forming a ministry, nor have I taken that burden on myself, because, during the war the Government has not the intention, nor does it dare, to entrust the administration of the country to a ministry. This is my firm belief, and I say it to my friends.

Hence, if Orissa Congress, or the Dictator of the Satyagraha movement or Mahatmaji consider that the freedom to express my opinion is harmful to the cause of the country or to the movement launched by the Congress, and if the Provincial Executive or Mahatmaji requests me, I will certainly and humbly write out my resignation and send it to the Congress office. We have been benefitted by the Congress organization, and it will not be an exaggeration to say that the Congress has also derived benefit from the workers' ideal and service. There is no ambiguity in my thoughts anywhere. They have been clear everywhere'.

157. Formation of Ministry in Orissa
Attempts to Win Over Congress Members Fail

Amrita Bazar Patrika, 25 May 1941.

Cuttack, 23 May.

Mrs Sarala Devi, MLA, the first Satyagrahi of Orissa, who courted imprisonment on December 1 last by reciting anti-war slogans, published a few days ago a statement in a local paper in course of which she stated that time, circumstances and events were fast changing and along with that her way of thinking and political vision were changing. She did not see why the efforts of those who were trying to form a Ministry in this province should be condemned. Rumours were afloat that Mrs Sarala Devi had joined the Coalition group.

After the publication of the statement Mr Prankrishna Padhiary, President, Utkal Provincial Congress Committee addressed the following letter to Mrs Sarala Devi, MLA:

'My attention has been drawn to a statement issued in your name in *Janata* of the 18th instant under caption of "Attempt for formation of Ministry in Orissa". From this statement I understand that you have moral support for such an attempt of forming a ministry in this province at the present moment.

'I am of opinion that such a statement is positively harmful to the present movement and is against the official policy of the Congress. So I request you to let me know definitely by tomorrow what is your intention of issuing such a statement and whether you have decided to join the ministry, if formed, in the province'.

Mrs Sarala Devi, MLA, replied to the above as follows:

'I have your letter of to-day. I have given vent to what I have sincerely felt in the present circumstances. I am of opinion that such free expression of views is not harmful to the present movement which had been started by the Mahatmaji on the issue of freedom of speech.

'The question of my joining any ministry does not arise as no ministry as such is formed or is in existence.

'I do not intend to go back upon the pledge I had submitted to the Congress organization at the time of my election'.

It is stated Pandit Godavaris Misra is trying to enlist the support of some members of the Congress Party to the Coalition move. The name of Mr Sadhu Charan Das, MLA was being freely talked as being won over. Mr Das, however, in course of a letter to the President of the Utkal Provincial Congress Committee says:

'I express it very clearly that in the present circumstances I will never join any other ministry except the one controlled by the Congress and that I being a Congress member do always abide by and remain faithful to the Congress policy'.

It is learnt the President of the UPCC has asked for explanation from a Congress member who is reported to have lent support to the Coalition move.—UP

158. Orissa Governor's Letter to Viceroy Regarding the Formation of a Coalition Ministry in Orissa

Correspondence with the Governor of Orissa and his Secretary, 1941, Linlithgow Papers, Acc. No. 2218, NAI.

FROM HE SIR HAWTHORNE LEWIS, Governor of Orissa

Government House, Puri,
8 June 1941

[Secrete and Urgent]
D.O. No. 858-G.O.

My Dear Lord Linlithgow,

I enclose a copy of a letter I have just received from Pandit Godavaris Misra asking formally for an interview for the purpose of discussing the formation of a Coalition Ministry. An interim reply has been given by my Secretary to say that I am considering his request and that my reply will be given at my early convenience.

2. The General position so far as I am aware is still as stated in my fortnightly reports except that Khallikote whom I saw recently has since told me that he was being hard pressed by Godavaris to agree to proceed. Khallikote, as already reported, has reasons of his own for wishing to avoid an open breach with Godavaris. But while he has stated to me in private that he does not desire to be drawn into an alliance with the group represented by Godavaris, the line he has taken in his own conversations with Godavaris has (so he tells me) been that Godavaris should first be able to command a group of reliable supporters for a Coalition Ministry numbering not less than 10 before Khallikote would agree that it is worth while going forward. Khallikote hoped by putting the figure at 10 to place a coalition out of reach.

3. In his letter to me Godavaris seems to claim that Khallikote would now be satisfied with 8 in place of 10.

4. I have had no equivalent formal statement from Khallikote of his views, *qua* party leader, of the position and no request for an interview. I have no grounds to think that there is any sure foundation yet available for the formation of a Coalition Ministry likely to command a stable majority in the Orissa Assembly.

5. While the *ad interim* acknowledgment was sent by my Secretary, my reply to Godavaris Misra should presumably be a reply directly from myself to him. I enclose a draft which I have prepared for the purpose and shall very greatly welcome an expression by telegram of Your Excellency's approval to the terms of the draft reply subject to any modification or changes which may be thought desirable. I think it proper in my reply to correct any misleading impressions which might be drawn from the first two paragraphs of Godavaris Misra's letter to me which in one sense endevaour to make out that when we previously met I gave Godavaris encouragement or backing which, consistently with my own position as Governor, I had in fact declined.

Yours sincerely,
W.H. Lewis.

[Enclosure 1]

Durgha Basar, Cuttack,
7 June 1941

Dear Sir Hawthorne Lewis,

In the second week of last April I interviewed Your Excellency with the object of discussing the political situation. The formation of a Ministry also formed the subject-matter of the talks. I represented that I was expecting to get a majority in the legislature including 22 members of the Party which formed the Opposition when the Congress Ministry was there. From the Congress folds as many as 8 members were expected to support the new Ministry.

At present there are 59 members in the Assembly, one of whom is the Speaker. A Coalition of 80 members would thus give the Ministry the support of a majority of two. In my last interview I placed before Your Excellency the prospects of such a Ministry. Your Excellency was pleased to tell me to go with definite proposals, when these were ready.

In the meanwhile I have discussed the matter with the Raja Bahadur of Khallikote, who is the Leader of the Party of 22 members referred to above. He and I are of the opinion that a definite step should now be taken. I therefore propose to seek an interview with Your Excellency.

I think Your Excellency will permit me to take the liberty of suggesting a date for the interview. The Raja Bahadur of Khallikote will be at Puri from the 13th to the 15th instant. If Your Excellency is pleased to grant me an interview while he is there at Puri there will be the facility for referring any matter to him if necessary. If, however, these dates, namely, the three days from the 13th to the 15th instant, are not found suitable, any other date may kindly be fixed for the purpose.

A line of kind reply at the address given at the top of the letter will oblige me very much.

Your Excellency's sincerely,
Godavaris Misra

[Enclosure 2]

DRAFT REPLY

Dear Pandit Godavaris Misra,

An *ad interim* acknowledgment of your letter of the 7th June was sent to you by my Secretary in his letter of the 8th June in which he intimated that I was considering your request for an interview and that a reply would be given to you at my early convenience.

2. I now write to say that I have taken note of the statement of the position as given by you in your letter of your views in respect of the prospects of forming a Ministry based on a coalition between parties and groups in the Legislature. I have not received any similar statement of his views from the Raja Bahadur of Khallikote, nor have I had any request from the Raja Bahadur for an interview for this purpose. While your letter mentions discussions between yourself and the Raja Bahadur and claims agreement between you both that (in your words) a definite step should be taken, your letter does not claim that any coalition commanding a majority in the Legislature has in fact yet been made between different parties or groups for the purpose of forming a Ministry, nor, so far as I am aware, has there been any joint public statement or open manifesto to that effect put out by party leaders or their individual supporters indicating agreement between themselves on a plan of that description. In the circumstances a stage does not seem to have been reached in party negotiations to which I could with propriety

grant the request you now make to me for an early interview to discuss the formation of a Coalition Ministry.

3. In the first two paragraphs of your letter you refer to our earlier meeting. That was not an interview previously arranged for discussing a Ministry. You had asked to meet me shortly after I assumed charge in Orissa, and when we met you took the opportunity in a general way to inform me of your reading of the political position and the view you took of the prospects of forming a Coalition Ministry, which you gave me to understand was a plan which you yourself favoured. In your letter you now write to me (I am quoting your words) that I was pleased to tell you to go with definite proposals when these were ready. You will, I think, remember that while I thanked you for your interesting account of the political position, I very specifically refrained on my part consistently with my own position as Governor from giving you any advice whatever as to the manner in which you as a party leader should proceed in matters arising between yourself and your own supporters, and between yourself and other groups. I mention this to avoid any misunderstanding which might otherwise arise from the statement of the position as put in the first two paragraphs of your letter.

Yours sincerely,
W.H. Lewis

159. Ministry-making in Orissa Secret Parleys

Amrita Bazar Patrika, 22 September 1941.

Cuttack, 21 September.

Although political atmosphere in Orissa is thick with rumours for the last few weeks about formation of an alternative Ministry in the province, efforts for Ministry making which began in July 1940 have not yet taken any definite shape. It is very likely that like several other previous efforts another effort of these modern Robert Bruces will be nipped in the bud.

The Raja Bahadur of Khallikote who arrived here early this morning had an interview with the Governor to-day when the question of possibility of formation of an alternative Ministry in this province, was probably discussed. But those who are in the know are of the opinion that neither official circles nor the Raja Bahadur are sanguine about a stable majority for the Ministerial party in the Assembly, and are not therefore very keen about it.

Party Strength

It is learnt that some prominent members of the Opposition group in the Assembly feel that when their total strength is 22, premiership should go to the Raja Bahadur of Khallikote instead of to Mr Godavaris Misra who has only eight men under his leadership. Further it is gathered that they want that the seceders from the Congress should declare openly their views about the Hindu Religious Endowments Act and its orders and various other tenancy legislations and should also merge themselves into the Zamindars (Opposition) party instead of forming a new independent party of their own under the leadership of Mr Godavaris Misra.

It is now definitely believed in political circles that the Maharaja of Parlakimedi, Raja Bahadur of Parikud and Rai Bahadur M.G. Patnaik are indifferent to these efforts of formation of a ministry unless and until these questions are finally settled.

The seceders from the Congress Party met leaders of the non-Congress group last week and discussed these questions but the results of these discussions have been kept a close secret. Messrs Sadhucharan Das, Nidhi Das and Biswanath Behera who recently left the Congress bloc are now holding secret parleys at Chikiti with Mr Dibakar Patnaik, Mr Pyarisankar Roy, who was in Calcutta, reached Chikiti to-day to join these parleys.

What seems strange is that the Raja Bahadur of Khallikote went to see the Governor alone to-day leaving behind Pandit Godavaris Misra. Of course politics makes strange bed fellows and facts are always stranger than fiction. So none is surprised now to see Mr Pyarisankar Roy joining hands with Mr Godavaris Misra.

160. New Orissa Ministry: Governor Issues Proclamation

Bombay Chronicle, 24 November 1941.

Cuttack, 23 November.

The proclamation issued by the Governor of Orissa under Sub-Section Two of Section 93 of the Government of India Act 1935 on 6 November 1939, was revoked by His Excellency Sir Hawthorne Lewis, Governor of Orissa by a proclamation made to-day in concurrence with His Excellency the Viceroy.

This announcement was notified in an Extraordinary issue of the Orissa Gazette following further talks at Government House this morning between His Excellency and the Maharaja of Parlakimedi, Pandit Godavaris Misra and Mr A.S. Sobhan Khan in connection with the proposal for the formation of a ministry in Orissa.

The following press communiqué was issued by the Secretary to the Governor:

'On being invited by the Governor to form a ministry the Maharaja of Parlakimedi has named as his colleagues Pandit Godavaris Misra and Moulvi Abdus Sobhan Khan. His Excellency has summoned these three gentlemen to be sworn in as Ministers tomorrow morning'.—AP

161. Orissa Deadlock Ends: Ministry Formed by Maharaja of Parlakimedi

Amrita Bazar Patrika, 24 November 1941.

Cuttack, 23 November.

On being invited by the Governor to form a Ministry the Maharaja of Parlakimedi has named as his colleagues Pandit Godavaris Misra and Moulavi Abdus Sobhan Khan.

His Excellency has summoned these three gentlemen to be sworn in as Ministers this (Monday) morning.

The Maharaja of Parlakimedi arrived from Calcutta this morning. The Maharaja Saheb, along with Pandit Godavaris Misra and Mr Sobhan Khan left for Circuit House to see the Governor. This is the fourth interview with His Excellency in connection with the formation of the Ministry.

The Governor has summoned formally the Maharaja Saheb to form the Ministry. The oath of office will be administered tomorrow at 11 a.m.

Meanwhile Srimati Sarala Devi informed this morning Pandit Godavaris Misra by a letter that her support to the ministry was for her being against the pure and simple bureaucratic rule. Beyond that she had nothing to do either with the formation of the ministry or functioning of it.

Pandit Godavaris Misra it is understood replied to the effect that he had indeed counted on her support. He regretted that he could not explain his attitude and stand for Ministry-making to her.

Governor's Proclamation

Cuttack, 23 November.

The proclamation issued by the Governor of Orissa under Sub-Section 2 of Section 93 of the Government of India Act, 1935, on 6 November 1939 was revoked by His Excellency Sir Hawthorne Lewis, Governor of Orissa, by a proclamation made to-day in concurrence with His Excellency the Viceroy.

The Proclamation

The following is the text of the proclamation issued by His Excellency the Governor published in an extraordinary issue of the Orissa Gazette:

'In exercise of the powers conferred upon him by sub-section 2 Section 93 of the Government of India Act, 1935, the Governor of Orissa by this proclamation made with the concurrence of the Governor-General, is pleased to revoke the proclamation dated 6 November 1939, and subsequently yarled (?) by the proclamation dated 2 December 1939'.

Ministry Formed

The following press communiqué was issued by the Secretary of His Excellency the Governor:

'With the concurrence of His Excellency the Governor-General, His Excellency the Governor of Orissa has this morning, by a proclamation under Section 93 of the Government of India Act, 1935, revoked the proclamation under that section hitherto enforced in Orissa.

'On being invited by the Governor to form a Ministry the Maharaja of Parlakimedi has named as his colleagues Pandit Godavaris Misra and Moulavi Abdus Sobhan Khan. His Excellency has summoned these three gentlemen to be sworn in as Ministers tomorrow morning'.

The Governor has postponed his departure from Cuttack till 26 November.

Allocations of Portfolios

It is learnt that the Maharaja of Parlakimedi who will be the Chief Minister, will hold the Home, PWD, and LSG Portfolios, while Pandit Godavaris Misra will be given Finance, Education and Development and Mr A.S. Khan, Revenue, Law, Commerce, Labour and Health.

Adviser's Post Abolished

'With the proclamation by the Governor of Orissa revoking the proclamation under Section 93 of the Government of India Act, which was previously in force, the office of the Adviser to the Governor, hitherto held by Mr E.C. Ansorge, CIE, ICS, has been terminated', states a communiqué issued this afternoon by the Secretary to the Governor of Orissa.

The communiqué adds: 'His Excellency Sir Hawthorne Lewis takes this opportunity to express his great appreciation of the valuable services rendered by Mr Ansorge in that capacity, both to himself and to his predecessor, Sir John Hubback'.

Mr Ansorge is now on leave, pending resumption by himself, early next year, of the post of the Chief Commissioner of the Andaman and Nicobar Islands.

His Excellency the Governor will leave for Balasore on 26 November and after visiting Kanikara; will return to Cuttack on 1 December. He will proceed to Puri next day.—AP

162. Orissa Deadlock Ends: Ministry Formed by Maharaja of Parlakimedi The First Province to Revoke Suspension of the Constitution

Amrita Bazar Patrika, 25 November 1941.

Cuttack, 24 November.

Exactly after two years and 17 days, the constitution began to function in Orissa when the Maharaja of Parlakamedi, Pandit Godavaris Misra and Moulvi Abdus Sobhan Khan were sworn in as Ministers to-day at Cuttack Government House in presence of high officials....

Thus Orissa is the first among the 7 provinces where constitutions were suspended following the resignation of the Congress Ministries to end political stalemate.

Orissa was also the first province which declared a majority for the Congress Party in the general election to the Provincial Assembly.

Programme of New Ministry

A Gazette Extraordinary issued today states:

'His Excellency the Governor of Orissa has been pleased to appoint the following gentlemen to be members of his Council of Ministers:

'Capt. Maharaja Sree Sree Sree Krishna Chandra Gajapati Narayan Deo of Parlakamedi, Pandit Godavaris Misra and Moulvi Sobhan Khan and these gentlemen have in this forenoon taken the oaths of office'.

After the oath-taking ceremony which lasted for about 20 minutes the Governor met Hon'ble the Maharaja of Parlakamedi for informal talks and after sometime two other Ministers were called in. Informal were talks held with Ministers, because no Cabinet meeting is likely to take place now.

The Ministers left the Government House after they were photographed with His Excellency and other officers.

Allocation of Portfolios

A new portfolio of Publicity has been created which will be held by Pandit Godavaris Misra in the new ministry.

A Gazette Extraordinary notification says that the Maharaja of Parlakimedi will hold the portfolios of Home Affairs (excluding publicity), Local Self Government and PWD, Pandit Misra will hold the portfolios of Finance, Home Affairs (Publicity), Development and Education and Mr Sobhan Khan those of Law, Commerce, Revenue and Health.

Chief Minister's Observations

'We assumed charge to-day with a first and foremost point in our minds and that is to give a stimulus to war effort. The present situation is serious and my colleagues and myself are alive to the fact'.

Thus observed the Maharaja of Parlakamedi in course of an interview to the press after assumption of office.

Detailing the programme of the new Ministry the Maharaja said: 'In view of the peculiar situation in the province which has been curved of several provinces, different systems of administration and different laws and rules still prevail in several districts and it is necessary that they should be suitably unified so that the manifold difficulties experienced day to day in the working of the administration may be removed.

'Again the prosecution of war effort will receive a stimulus only if the members of the legislatures are enabled to discharge their duties as representatives of the people. This will be possible when the Ministry functions'.

Asked as to when the Assembly will meet, the Maharaja Saheb said: 'We will endeavour to face the Assembly as soon as possible, but we require a little time and at this stage I may say that it will not be later than the 3rd week of January'.

Concluding the Maharaja Saheb said: 'When our ideal is mainly to do good to the country and serve the King-Emperor, we expect whole-hearted support and co-operation from the public of Orissa and the different constituencies from which we were returned, and I hope our move to end the political impasse will be appreciated and receive popular support throughout India'.

Viceroy's Telegram

His Excellency the Viceroy has sent the following telegram to His Excellency the Governor of Orissa: 'I send my warm congratulation to you and to your Prime Ministry on the restoration of Parliamentary Government of Orissa and my best good wishes for the future'.

His Excellency the Governor has replied: 'The Maharaja of Parlakamedi joins me in thanking Your Excellency for your most gracious message on the restoration of Parliamentary Government in Orissa. Your good wishes for the future are deeply appreciated'.

The Maharaja of Parlakamedi has also received several other congratulatory message including those from the Kumararaja of Chettinad, the Raja Bahadur of Kanika, the Raja Bahadur of Khallikote and the Ruler of Narasingpur.

Mr Ramaswami Naicker, leader of the Justice Party, Madras, says: 'My heartiest congratulations on your successful demolition of Congress Fascist domination'.

Dr Sachchidananda Sinha says: 'Please accept heartiest felicitations on your having reintroduced constitutional Government in Orissa. I wish your effort success.'

Pandit Misra's View

After assumption of office, the Hon Pandit Godavaris Misra, interviewed by the 'Associated Press' said: 'Now that a Ministry has been formed in this province, its responsibility is greater than that of the previous Ministry. The previous Ministry had the support of an all-India organization. The present Ministry is wanting it. It is a combination of two groups of people whose views used to be very divergent. But they thought it necessary in the interests of the province to combine and co-operate.

'I am not a believer in the plea that one must learn to swim before one actually gets into the water. But the present policy of the Congress is to ask for independence without the people doing anything worth mentioning to wrest it from unwilling hands, and without preparations to defend that independence when achieved.

'Like that of all patriotic sons of India my goal is the achievement of independence within the quickest possible time, but there must be a logical way to have it. I believe that in the present situation, when the whole world is steeped in hostility and when the little privilege which India won from the British is being threatened. It is not in the country's interests to keep aloof from preparations in war. It is for this that I thought that a Ministry under the present circumstances would be useful. So I have joined hands.

'I am thankful to those of my colleagues who have chosen to think like myself, particularly to my esteemed friend and brother Pandit Nilkantha Das, MLA (Central) but for whose efforts a departure from the beaten track would not have been possible. I do not know how much we shall be able to contribute to war efforts and through those efforts to bring about a solution of the country's immediate and most important problem, but it is worth trying it and so I have deemed it necessary to give it a trial. I shall be glad if my past colleagues, with whom it was a pleasure for me to work, think differently from the manner they are now thinking and join hands to make the efforts of the present Ministry in preparing the province for independence as successful as they possibly can.

'Then, there are serious provincial problems which have for long not been properly attended. I hope the present Ministry can do something in that direction so that the new province of Orissa can aspire to march abreast times, subject of course to the limitations which are peculiar to it'.

After a very short interview with the Governor the Maharaja Saheb returned in a car to Madhupur Kothi and broke the news with a smile. Pt Godavaris Misra and Moulavi Abdus Sobhan Khan followed in another car.

As at present arranged these three gentlemen will be sworn in as Ministers tomorrow. Thus deadlock in Orissa ends from tomorrow. The Governor has issued the following proclamation in an extraordinary issue of the 'Orissa Gazette':

Sreemati Sarala Devi was not in correspondence with Dr Rajendra Prasad regarding the question of resignation from the Assembly and was awaiting his decision.

Chapter 2. National Struggle and Government Repression

A. Congress

1. United Front for Freedom, Ahrars' Reasons for Joining Congress 'One Platform: One Organization'

National Herald, 1 January 1941.

'We were always of the opinion that in the final struggle for freedom we must all get together on one platform and stand under one political organization.'

This is the reason given by the general secretary of the All-India Majlis-e-Ahrar in a statement announcing the leaders' decision to join the Congress.

The Secretary recalls the efforts of the Ahrar Party during the past ten years to create a living faith in the Independence of the country among the Muslims and holds, that it is that policy that induced them to join the final movement started by the Congress.

Ahrars in the UP have decided to join the satyagraha movement. Mr Wasi Ahmed, their dictator, has called upon his followers who believe in non-violence and in the constructive programme, to send their names to the Lucknow office of the Majlis-e-Ahrar....

2. Maulana Azad Arrested: Action Under Defence Act

The Hindu, 4 January 1941.

Allahabad, 3 January.

Maulana Abul Kalam Azad, Congress President, was arrested at the Allahabad Junction Railway Station this morning at about 5.15 a.m. while he was on the way from Delhi to Calcutta.

The arrest was made by Mr S.N. Aga, the City Deputy Superintendent of Police, Allahabad, on a warrant issued from Allahabad under Section 38 of the Defence of India Rules. He has been taken to the Naini Central Jail.

The arrest, it is believed, has been made in connection with a speech delivered by Maulana Azad in Purshotham Das Park on 13 December. The warrant, it is learnt, was issued on 29 December.

The charge sheet against Maulana Azad will be sent up by the police some time today and it is likely that he will be tried in the Naini Jail shortly.

Maulana Azad had intimated to the AICC Office yesterday that he would be coming to Allahabad on his way to Calcutta from Delhi, probably in connection with some office work here. He was due at 5.15 a.m., by the 8-Down Toofan Express. Mr Sadiq Ali, the Office Secretary of the AICC and Mr S.D. Upadhyaya, Private Secretary to Pandit Jawaharlal Nehru, were present at the Railway Station to receive Maulana Azad who was to stay in Anand Bhawan.

Maulana Azad was accompanied by his Secretary, Mr Ajmal Hussain, when he arrived here at about 5.10 a.m.

Mr S.N. Aga, City Deputy Superintendent of Police, accompanied by a Sub-Inspector, had been waiting at the railway station for some time. Maulana Azad was on the platform when he was presented the warrant of arrest. Maulana Azad cordially greeted Mr Aga and said with a smile, 'Thank you very much. You have made it very easy for me. I did not even have to offer Satyagraha.'

On a suggestion from Mr S.D. Upadhyaya, Mr Aga took Maulana Azad to the refreshment room at the railway station where the Maulana had a wash, change, and tea. He was then driven off to the Naini Jail.

The AICC Office has telephoned Mahatma Gandhi of Maulana Azad's Arrest.

Maulana Azad came to Allahabad last time from Calcutta on 10 December and stayed here for five days before returning to Calcutta. During his stay here, he addressed local Congress workers in Anand Bhawan in addition to seeing to the AICC Office work, and addressed a public meeting in the Purshotham Das Park on 13 December.

(The API report of the speech contained Maulana Azad's view on the issue in connection with which Satyagraha was started, Gandhiji's preconditions before offering Satyagraha, indications of who all would be allowed to court arrest in future and Maulana Azad's emphasis on discipline and tolerance.)

3. Bombay Deplores Azad's Arrest

Bombay Chronicle, 4 January 1941.

The fact that the Congress President was arrested during the truce declared by Mahatma Gandhi was deplored by several speakers at a huge public meeting, held under the auspices of the Bombay Provincial Congress Committee at Chowpatty on Friday evening. Dr D.T. Anklesaria presided.

India's Chosen Path

Dr Anklesaria said that they were in no way sorry for the arrest.

The Maulana was anyhow due to offer Satyagraha in a few days and Government had only anticipated that day. Just as the Government were carrying out its programme, the Congress too would carry on its programme.

Gandhi had put before the country the great programme of non-violence. In a world where nations were engaged in mutual destruction. India had chosen the path of non-violence and self-sacrifice, which was the best way to world peace.

Government Respects No Truce

Mr S.A. Brelvi said that it was a matter of surprise that the Congress President should have been arrested during the period of truce which Gandhiji had declared. It was hoped that the Government would respect the truce, but the Government of Sir Maurice Hallet,[1] which had allowed the sentence of four years imprisonment passed on Pandit Jawaharlal Nehru to remain, had also arrested the Congress President during the period of truce.

Gandhiji had not declared this truce with a view to carry on any negotiations but simply because he wanted the conduct of the campaign to be maintained on a high moral plane. However, had the Government any genuine desire for peace they would have gladly utilized the opportunity to bring about a settlement.

Government's Mistake

Maulana Azad had recently said that the Congress would be prepared to consider any proposal similar in import to the Poona offer. By that famous offer, Congress had suggested how India could help Britain as a free, equal, and self-respecting nation. Maulana Azad had said that the Government had committed a great mistake in turning down the offer. This mistake, the speaker thought, would bring no good either to Britain or to India.

Now that Gandhiji had launched the campaign, he was determined to keep it going till freedom was achieved. Not all were expected to offer Satyagraha, but it was the duty of all patriotic Indians to strengthen the Congress by taking to *Khaddar*, promoting Hindu–Muslim unity and by carrying on the other items of the constructive programme.

Mr Asok Mehta explained the object of the Satyagraha movement. All that the Congress had asked was the right to carry on anti-war propaganda.

Azad's Achievements

Mr Abidally Jafferbhoy said that Maulana Azad, through his influence, had achieved in his mission in Sind. He had also succeeded in bringing the Ahrars within the Congress fold. This had perhaps upset the Government who arrested him even before he offered Satyagraha.

Mr S.L. Silam exhorted the audience not to be angered or excited but steadily to carry on the constructive programme.

Call to Women

Mrs Violet Alva said that the Government had made a new year's offering, in the arrest of the Congress President. It meant that their protest had been felt. She appealed to the women in particular to make all necessary sacrifices in the cause of India's freedom.

---

[1] Governor of UP

4. 'Congress Bound to Succeed': Protest Against M. Azad's Arrest

The Tribune, 5 January 1941.

Lahore, 4 January.

'The unwise act of the Government' in arresting the Congress President Maulana Abul Kalam Azad, at the present juncture, was condemned at a huge public meeting held this evening, in the maidan of the Bradlaugh Hall. The meeting, which was held under the auspices of the Lahore District Congress Committee, was presided over by Lala Duni Chand, President of the PPCC. A very large number of Mussalmans were also present.

Eloquent tributes were paid to the Congress President, Maulana Azad, for the services he has rendered to the cause of the country before and during the time he had been at the helm of affairs of the Congress.

The President, Maulana Daud Ghaznavi (who has recently come back to the Congress fold), Malik Jeewan Lal Kapur, Bar-at-Law, L. Bhim Sen Sachar, MLA, Maulana Nasarullah Khan Aziz, Seth Kalifa Fazal, Lala Kidar Nath Saighal, and Mr Jai Gopal referred to the great qualities of head and heart of Maulana Azad. They opined that the arrest of the Congress President would not in any way deter the nation from following Gandhiji's lead.

Maulana Daud Ghaznavi moved the only resolution of the meeting, which was seconded and supported by the other speakers. The resolution recorded with deep appreciation the services, which Maulana Azad had rendered to the country as the President of the Indian National Congress. It further stated that the arrest of the Congress Chief would not in any way help the Government and would hardly further the object which the Government might have in view in arresting Maulana Azad.

The mover in the course of his speech said that Maulana Azad occupied a unique position in the country in the religious, intellectual, and political spheres. Not only the liberty loving Musalmans but else the entire country was proud of him. The speaker said that the Government had not acted wisely in arresting a person of the position of Maulana Azad.

Malik Jeewan Lal thought that the action of the Government in imprisoning the Congress leaders was not in keeping with the assertion of the Britishers that they are fighting for freedom and democracy.

Lala Bhim Sen Sachar held that with the arrest of the Congress President, the responsibility of the individual Congressmen had become greater. The Congress movement was based on truth and righteousness and was bound to succeed.

5. Ahrars Offer Satyagraha

The Hindu, 5 January 1941.

Lahore, 3 January.

Mr Ahmad Hassan, third 'Ahrar' dictator, who offered Satyagraha this afternoon by raising anti-war slogans at the main gate of the Badshahi Mosque after Jumma prayers, was arrested under the Defence of India Rules. He was removed to the Central Jail.

Frontier
Civil Disobedience Initiated

Mr Wahabdin, a Frontier 'Ahrar' leader, initiated civil disobedience on behalf of the Ahrars in Peshawar by shouting anti-war slogans in the Mahabakthan Mosque after Jumma prayers. A section of the gathering objected to a political meeting being held in the mosque. This was a signal for disturbance, which was, however, soon quelled. Some persons are said to have sustained minor bruises. The meeting was adjourned soon afterwards.

The Associated Press is informed that those who objected to the Ahrars holding a meeting in the mosque were Mohmand Afridi Tribesmen. This afternoon, they waited in a deputation on the Deputy Commissioner, and complained that 'they were violently attacked by Ahrars in the mosque'. They also stated that they had received numerous injuries. The Deputy Commissioner gave them a patient hearing.

6. Ahrars to have Separate Identity: Punjab Majlis-i-Ahrar's Decision

The Tribune, 6 January 1941.

A meeting of the Provincial Majlis-i-Ahrar was held this evening to give final verdict regarding the recent statement of Maulana Daud Ghaznavi declaring his severence from the Majlis-i-Ahrar and joining the Congress. The representatives of most of the districts of Punjab participated in the meeting.

After a long discussion it was decided that Maulana Daud Ghaznavi had joined the Congress in his individual capacity and his statement to this effect was quite clear. The statements of Ch. Afzal Huq and Sahibzada Pir Faiz-ul-Hassan were also quite clear that the Majlis-i-Ahrar as a body had not joined the Congress and it would carry on its programme and policy with the same intensity as had been doing in the past. It was resolved that the separate identity of the All-India Majlis-i-Ahrar was as essential now as it was in 1930–2.

7. Congress Attitude in Regard to War: Jamiat-ul-Ulema-i-Hind's Support

The Tribune, 7 January 1941.

The working committee of the Jamiat-ul-Ulema-i-Hind met here today under the presidentship of Moulana Hussain Ahmed Madni and discussed the political situation in the country for over twelve hours. Ten members attended the meeting.

The committee passed resolutions supporting the Congress attitude in regard to the war and criticized the policy of the Government in this respect. The committee also supported Mahatma Gandhi's non-violent satyagraha movement.

Another resolution stressed the need of discipline among members of the organization and of imbibing living faith in non-violence.—API

8. Satyagraha Arrests and Convictions

Bombay Chronicle, 8 January 1941.

In Bombay Suburbs

Dr Dinkarrao Galwankar of Arnala was tried in jail and sentenced to nine months' simple imprisonment and Rs 100 fine, under the Defence of India Rules. He was recommended 'B' Class.

In Maharashtra

Nasik: A sentence of two years' rigorous imprisonment was awarded to Mr P.S. Sane Guruji, well-known Congress leader from Amalner and a prominent litterateur of Maharashtra, on Saturday afternoon in the Nasik Road Central Prison, under the Defence of India Rules.

Poona Protest

Poona: The Poona City Municipality and the District Local Board adjourned its meetings today without transacting any business, presumably due to the arrest of Maulana Abul Kalam Azad, the Congress President.

At Sholapur

Sholapur: Mr V.B. Sathe, former Municipal President, and Mr Keshavial Shah, President of the City Congress Committee, who were to have offered 'Satyagraha' today were arrested this morning while returning from a Municipal meeting.

At Ahmednagar

Ahmednagar: Shrimati Makibal Apte, first woman 'Satyagrahi' who offered 'Satyagraha' by shouting anti-war slogans was arrested this morning. She was later tried in jail and sentenced to one day's simple imprisonment and to pay a fine of Rs 200, in default to three months' further imprisonment.

In Gujarat

Gajaraben Desai Arrested

Mrs Gajaraben Desai organizer of the Ladies' Section of the Congress Seva Dal was arrested to-day under the Defence of India Rules at Modasa village in Ahmedabad District, while offering Satyagraha by shouting anti-war slogans.—AP

Dohad Congressman Arrested

Mr Sukhadeo Trivedi, President of the Dohad Taluqua Congress Committee, was arrested to-day at Dohad for shouting anti-war slogans.—UP

In Karnatak

Satyagraha Starts Tomorrow

Belgaum: The second phase of Satyagraha in Belgaum District begins from 9th instant Sri Murlidhar Ghate, Member; Karnatak PCC will offer Satyagraha on 9th morning by reciting only war slogans at Belgundi Taluka in Belgaum. Eighty-three names have been approved by Gandhiji to offer Satyagraha.

In Hyderabad (Dn)

Hyderabad: Syed Mohamed Dastagir, Special Magistrate, sentenced three youths including Godesi, Veerabhadram to two years' rigorous imprisonment under the Hyderabad Defence Rules.

In CP and Berar

At Nagpur

Nagpur: A Bhandara message says that Mr Jakatdar, MLA, was arrested, for offering Satyagraha.

Mr Ananda Rao Kedar, President of the Saoner Taluka Congress Committee, was also arrested for offering 'Satyagraha'.

Shrimati Shanti Devi offered 'Satyagraha' this morning but was not arrested.

Arrested at Durg

Nagpur: A Durg message says that Mr D. Dhalsingh, a member of the Provincial Congress, offered 'Satyagraha' at Pirid village, thirty miles from Durg. He was not arrested.

Arrests and Convictions

Nagpur: Mrs Saraswatibai Dandekar, Mrs Shantidevi Sharma, Mrs Vidyawati Devadia, and Bhayyaji Sahasrabudhey offered Satyagraha yesterday and continue their tour to-day. Mrs Sharayutai Dhotre offered Satyagraha to-day at Wardha and Syed Fazlul Rahim at Kamptee. None of these Satyagrahis have been arrested so far.

Following Satyagraha arrests are reported from the mofussil:

Mr Anandrao Kedar at Saoner; Mr Govindrao Thakre, Member, Amraoti District Council at Pathrot; Mr Abuj, President, Basim Municipal Committee at Basim; Mr Kanayalal Innani at Karanja; and Pandit G.P. Khamparia, President, Jubbulpore DCC at Jubbulpore.

Among those convicted are Thakur Hirasingh Chouhan, General Secretary Amraoti Town Congress Committee, fined Rs 25 and Pandit Kunjlal Dube, President, Mahakoshal PCC sentenced at Jubbulpore to six months rigorus imprisonment.

In CP and Berar

Pleaders Arrested

Jubbulpore: Two Congressmen, Mr Murlidhar Mishra and Mr Kushiram Tewari, pleaders were arrested today under the Defence of India Rules for offering 'Satyagraha' and were remanded to jail custody.

At Wardha

Wardha: Wamail Rao Dani, Secretary of the Wardha Taluk Congress Committee, and Gopal Rao Wagle of Arvi were sentenced to pay a fine by Rs 10 and Rs 50 respectively for offering 'Satyagraha'. Two other Satyagrahis who shouted anti-war slogans were not arrested.

At Yeotmal

Yeotmal: Parashram Gourkar who offered Satyagraha at Wun was sentenced to imprisonment till the rising of the court and fined Rs 100.

In Delhi

Two Arrested in Village

New Delhi: Messrs Hariram and Sohanlal who initiated Satyagraha in the rural areas of the Delhi province this afternoon were arrested under the Defence of India Rules in their respective villages of Mahrauli and Shahdara for shouting anti-war slogans.

MLA Comes for Treatment

New Delhi: Pandit Pyarelal Sharma, MLA (Central), who was recently released on grounds of health from Meerut Jail, has arrived here for treatment of trouble in abdomen.

Swami Swaroopanand, a Congress worker, was arrested to-day under the Defence of India Rules in Narela village about twelve miles from Delhi. He was to have offered Satyagraha in the village to-day.

Pandit Sriram Sharma, MLA (Punjab), was arrested at 11 p.m. last night under Rules 121 and 38 of the Defence of India Rules. Pandit Sharma gave intimation to the District Magistrate of Rohtak yesterday that he would be offering Satyagraha to-day.—UP

In NWFP

Satyagraha in Bannu

Khan Mohd Jan Khan, Barrister-at-Law, member of the AICC and Mr Hukamchand MLA of Kohat offered Satyagraha to-day at Kakki village and in Gandhi Chowk, Bannu City, respectively after delivering speeches.

Malik Akbar Ali Khan, MLA, of Bannu having been admitted into hospital on account of some heart trouble could not take part in Satyagraha.—AP

In Bihar

Two Years for Labour Leader

Dhanbad: Satya Sen, a Labour leader of the Jamadoba colliery area and a member of the Forward Bloc, has been sentenced by Mr A.W. Khan, Senior Deputy Magistrate, to two years' rigorous imprisonment under the Defence of India Rules. He was prosecuted on a charge of disobeying an Externment Order served on him in March last, directing him to leave Chota Nagpur Division.

Bihar Satyagrahis Await Approval
Dr Rajendra Prasad has sent to Mahatma Gandhi for his approval 1,453 names of Satyagrahis selected for the second phase of the Satyagraha movement.

In Orissa

Maulana Athahar Jailed

Cuttack: Maulana Mohammad Athahar, who was arrested yesterday afternoon for offering Satyagraha, was sentenced to-day by the Town Magistrate to four months' simple imprisonment and a fine of Rs 100, in default three months' imprisonment.

Mr Sachidananda Padhi, who was arrested this morning for offering Satyagraha at Khandnagar, was sentenced by the Sub-Divisional Magistrate of Cuttack to three months rigorous imprisonment and a fine of Rs 100, in default further one month's imprisonment. He was placed in 'C' class.

At Puri

Puri: Mr Bhagban Pratihari, a member of the Puri Town Congress Committee, was arrested yesterday evening under the Defence of India Rules for shouting anti-war slogans. He was the first Congressman to offer Satyagraha in Orissa after the Christmas recess.

In Bengal

Police Raid

Calcutta: The Special Branch of the Calcutta Police searched the office of the Bengal Provincial Students' Federation for two hours today under the Defence of India Rules. Nothing incriminating was seized, nor was anybody arrested.

Leave for Subhas

At its special meeting this evening, the Calcutta Corporation recorded a letter from Alderman Mr Subhas Chandra Bose, asking for leave of absence from the House for a period of six months from 2 July last when he was arrested under the Defence of India Rules and for such further period as the Corporation might consider fit.

The Corporation expressed the opinion that it considered the absence of Mr Bose justifiable under the Calcutta Municipal Act.

Suresh Banerjee for Wardha

Dr Suresh Chandra Banerjee, ex-president of the All-India Trade Union Congress, left this evening for Wardha to see Mahatma Gandhi in connection with the Satyagraha movement in Bengal.

Prior to his departure Dr Banerjee sent the following letter to the Commissioner of Police Calcutta:

'I have been selected by Gandhiji to offer Civil Disobedience. Accordingly I have uptill now offered Satyagraha six times in different parts of Calcutta and suburbs. But I have not as yet been arrested. So I shall offer Satyagraha again on 12 January 1941 at 5:30 p.m. at Basak Bagan Cossipore, in the north suburb of Calcutta.

From Basak Bagan I shall proceed along Cossipore Road, Gun Foundry Road, Barrackpore Trunk Road towards Cornwallis Street.'

Assam MLA Arrested

Tezpur, 7 January

Mr Omeokumar Das, MLA, President of the Tezpur District Congress Committee was arrested while initiating Satyagraha at Tezpur for crying anti-war slogans at Tumukibamari, ten miles off the town. He was sentenced to six months simple imprisonment and a fine of Rs 200 in default further three months.—UP

Assam MLA Jailed

Calcutta: Mr Karunasindhu Roy, a member of the Assam Assembly, who offered Satyagraha yesterday at Scachnabazar, an interior rural area in Sunamanganj, was sentenced to one year's imprisonment to-day.

In Andhra

The following further convictions in connection with Satyagraha are reported.

At Tenali

Tenali: Mr Satyanarayana Chowdary, Chairman, Tenali Municipality and Member Andhra Provincial Congress Committee, was given five months rigorous imprisonment and a fine of Rs 500, in default to a further three months rigorous imprisonment.

Mr P. Sriramulu, District Board Member and Mr Saranu Ramaswami Chowdary, Member, Andhra Provincial Congress Committee, was given four months' rigorous imprisonment and a fine of Rs 200 each in default to further two months' each.

At Chittoor

Chittoor: Mr D. Srinivasa Iyengar, Secretary, Chittoor District Congress Committee, was given six months' simple imprisonment and Mr D.R. Krisnnana, President, Palamaner Taluk Congress Committee, four months' rigorous imprisonment.

Chittoor: Mr Munuswami Naidu, District Board member, was sentenced to four months' rigorous imprisonment for offering Satyagraha. The accused was arrested when he shouted anti-war slogans at Puttur.

At Kurnool

Kurnool: Mr Shamseer Baig, Member Karnool District Congress Committee, was sentenced to six months' rigorous imprisonment and a fine of Rs 500, in default to three months additional imprisonment.

At Bhimavaram

Bhimavaram: Mr Bhupathiraju Subbaraju, a landlord, was given six months' rigorous imprisonment and a fine of Rs 200 in default to three months additional imprisonment.

At Ellore

Ellore: Srimathi Mulpuri Chukkamma (wife of Dr Rangayya, President District Board) was sentenced to three months' rigorous imprisonment.

Ellore Satyagrahi Jailed

Mr Sathirazu Ramamurthi, General Secretary west Godavary Congress Committee, was sentenced to six months' rigorous imprisonment and awarded 'B' class by Mr Sheikh Ahmed, Divisional Magistrate, Ellore.

The accused was arrested for shouting anti-war slogans this noon at Dendulur.—AP

Tadepalligudem: Mr P. Venkataraju, was given six months' rigorous imprisonment and a fine of Rs 100, in default to three months' additional imprisonment.

At Bezwada

Bezwada: Mr P. Ganapathi Rao Patrudu, Vice-Chairman, Bezwada Municipal Council, was given, six weeks' rigorous imprisonment and fine of Rs 700, in default three months' imprisonment.

Not Yet

Mr Kala Venkata Rao General Secretary, Andhra Provincial Congress Committee, wires from Rajahmundry under date 7 January. Under urgent instructions from Mahatma Gandhi, I appeal to all Congress members of District Boards and Municipal Councils, who were assigned dates to offer Satyagraha, to retrain for some time more, pending receipt of further directions. From to-day no such Satyagrahi should issue any notice to the District Magistrate.

AICC Member Arrested

Paganeri, 7 January

Mr R.V. Swaminathan, Paganeri, Member, All-India Congress Committee, was arrested this morning for offering Satyagraha by shouting anti-war slogans in front of Perumal Temple. He was taken to Devakottai for trial this evening.—AP

Cocanada Congressmen Arrested

Cocanada, 6 January

Mr P.R. Mohan Rao, Secretary, City Congress Committee, Cocanada, was arrested this morning for shouting anti-war slogans. He was tried before the Divisional Magistrate, who sentenced him to simple imprisonment for six months.—AP

At Bellary

Bellary: Mr C.S. Rami Reddi, Member, Andhra Provincial Executive Committee, and President Rayadurg Taluk Congress Committee, was given six months' rigorous imprisonment and fine of Rs 200, in default to two months' additional imprisonment.

In Tamil Nadu

Madras Satyagrahi Convicted

Madras, 6 January

Mrs Rajam Raghuraja Bharathi member of the Madras District Congress Committee was sentenced to-day to three months' simple imprisonment and a fine of Rs 250 in default to three months' further imprisonment by the Chief Presidency Magistrate. Mrs Bharathi was arrested this morning in front of a temple at Pursawalkum while shouting anti-war slogans before a crowd. The Magistrate has recommended 'A' class for the accused.

Lady Volunteer Jailed

Madras: Srimathi N.S. Rukmani, a Congress lady volunteer who was arrested for shouting anti-war slogans in Park Town, was convicted and sentenced by the Chief Presidency Magistrate to three months' simple imprisonment and a fine of Rs 250 in default to three months' additional imprisonment. She was placed in 'B' Class.

Businessman Sentenced

Mr Mohanalal Morarji Jairam Mehta, Vice-President of Gujarat Mandal and a businessman, was sentenced to three months' rigorous imprisonment and a fine of Rs 250 in default to three months' additional imprisonment by the Chief Presidency Magistrate today. He was arrested while shouting anti-war slogans before a crowd at the junction of China Bazar and Mint Street. The Magistrate placed Mr Mehta in 'B' Class provisionally.

Editor Fined

Salem: The Sub-Divisional Magistrate, Namakal, sentenced this afternoon, Mr T.S. Chockalingam, MLA former Editor of *Dhinamani* and now a political prisoner to pay a fine of Rs 250, in default to four months' simple imprisonment under Section 570 IPC If the fines were collected the Magistrate ordered that Rs 15 be paid to the complainant. Mr Chidambaram Pillai Tahsildar. Mr Chockalingam was brought here from Trichy Central Jail to-day in connection with a case filed by the Tahsildar stating that he (Mr Chockalingam) had in the issue of 26 July of *Dhinamani* (of which Mr Chockalingam was the Editor at the time) published an article containing statements alleged to have lowered the complainant's prestige.

Trichy Convictions

Trichinopoly: Mr R. Maruthai, MLA, who was arrested this morning under the Defence of India Rules while delivering an anti-war speech and was sentenced later to one year's rigorous imprisonment.

Mr Manikka Pathar and Srimathi Rajamani Devi, who were arrested this morning for anti-war propaganda, were sentenced to one year's rigorous and four months' simple imprisonment respectively. Mr Maruthai and Srimathi Rajmani Devi were placed in 'B' Class while Mr Pathar was awarded 'C' Class.

At Coimbatore

Coimbatore: Mr I.V. Kaveti Naidu, Treasurer, Coimbatore Taluk Congress Committee, was given six months' rigorous imprisonment.

In the UP

Allahabad Arrest

Allahabad: Shrimati Ramkeli a woman Congress worker of Allahabad has been arrested under the Defence of India Rules.

Mr Radhey Shyam Pathak, Secretary, District Congress Committee, was sentenced to-day by the City Magistrate Allahabad to fifteen months' simple imprisonment under the Defence of India Rules. Mr Pathak has been recommended 'B' class.

At Lucknow

Lucknow: Mr A.J. Zaidi, President of the Lucknow Student's Federation was sentenced to-day to six months simple imprisonment under the Defence of India Rules and was recommended 'B' Class.

Two lady workers of Lucknow, Mussamats Kasturi Devi and Jainti Devi, who had intimated the authorities of their intention to offer Satyagraha on 7 and 8 January, respectively and were subsequently arrested, were sentenced by the City Magistrate to three–six months' simple imprisonment under the Defence of India Rules.

Sat Kumar Roy, Congress worker, was sentenced under the Defence of India Rules to nine months' rigorous imprisonment and placed in 'C' class.

A report from Hamirpur says that Mr Ramgopal Gupta, President of the Hamirpur District Congress Committee, was arrested yesterday before he offered Satyagraha. Choudhry Shiva Swarup Singh, President of the District Congress Committee, Moradabad has also been arrested under the Defence of India Rules.

At Dehradun

Dehradun: Mr Khurshedlal, President of the Town Congress Committee was sentenced to one year's imprisonment under the Defence of India Rules to-day. The trial took place inside the jail. He has been recommended 'B' class.

Twenty Arrests Reported

Arrests of twenty Satyagrahis have so far been reported from the districts in the United Provinces to-day when the second phase of the Satyagraha Movement was launched to-day.

At Saharanpur

Saharanpur: Pandit Heera Ballabh Tripathi, a member of the Provincial Congress Committee and president of the City Congress Committee, was arrested to-day under the Defence of India Rules for offering Satyagraha in the village of Saidpur Tehsil.

Nakur, District Saharanpur

Immediately after his arrest Mr Tripathi was taken to the court of the City Magistrate to stand his trial in a case arising out of the Cigarette Factory Strike.

At Cawnpore

Cawnpore

Mr G.G. Jog, a local Congress leader who was to offer Satyagraha on 8 January, was arrested this afternoon under Rule 38 of the Defence of India Rules.

Mr Hamid Khan, General Secretary of the City Congress Committee, has been arrested under Rule 38 of the Defence of India Rules.

Gonda DCC President Jailed

Gonda, 7 January

Pandit Mahesh Dutt Pandey, President of the District Congress Committee, Gonda, who was arrested yesterday in Pirprapadum village for offerings Satyagraha, was convicted and sentenced today under the Defence of India Rules to one year's rigorous imprisonment and a fine of Rs 5 or in default one week's further rigorous imprisonment.

9. Mahatma Gandhi's Instructions to Satyagrahis on Payment of Fines

CWMG, Vol. LXXIII, pp. 276–7.

Sevagram
10 January 1941

A very serious question confronts me in connection with the struggle. In many places magistrates have been imposing heavy fines on civil resisters, in some cases, without option of imprisonment. Civil resisters must not and cannot complain of whatever penalty is imposed on them, and Government will always take advantage of weaknesses of human nature. Hitherto I have advised that fines should not be voluntarily paid but that authorities must be left to collect fines by distraint. The result during the last struggle was a great deal of heart-burning and bitterness. Those who bought movables or immovables for a song incurred popular ill will. I hope that if Government wish to touch immovable property, they will not sell but confiscate it. For whenever the struggle ends, immovable property is bound to be restored to the original owners—the resisters. The late Bombay Government knew how difficult it was for them to restore to the resisters the immovable properties that had changed hands. I have, however, discovered what may be termed a flaw in the reasoning that I had applied to the infliction of fines. I now feel that even as a resister courts imprisonment, he is expected to court any other form of punishment, that is, fines. Punishment courted has to be joyfully suffered. Therefore, when fines are imposed and the person fined is able to pay he must do so willingly. The result may naturally be that such a person will be fined again and again. If he persists in his resistance, he may have no property left. This is nothing to be wondered at. As a matter of fact it is the essence of civil disobedience that the resister becomes indifferent whether the authorities take away all his property or not. Therefore all propertied persons who wish to join the struggle should do so well knowing that the whole of their property may be taken up by the Government. This is a struggle which has no ending except in success. Therefore those who may be fined should pay cash if they have it. If they have no cash and the Government attaches their property, it should be open to their friends to buy the same. This will be an effective check on the cupidity of those who would profit by exploiting others' loss and there will be no bad blood. One corollary to this reasoning is that even as I had declared that every inch of immovable property sold or confiscated by the Government would have to be returned to the resisters, so will every rupee taken in fines have to be returned to them on the struggle ending. It follows of course that those who pay the fines will have to offer civil disobedience till they are safely lodged in jail. It follows also that those propertied persons who do not wish to run the risk of losing their property must not join this struggle. I hope however that patriotic people who believe in the efficacy of civil resistance will not fight shy of losing all their possessions. Let them remember the words of Sheth Jamnalal:

> I have long since come to realize that much too heavy a price has been and is being paid by the few for the enjoyment of wealth and for the apparent safety of life. The price paid is the blood of the famishing millions and the manliness of those who should be ready to shed their blood for the defence of themselves, their families and their country.

10. Independence through Freedom of Speech: Gandhi on Scope of Present Struggle

Bombay Chronicle, 10 January 1941.

'Whatever may be the expansion, the present struggle launched by the Congress will never develop into a mass movement and, so far as I can see, it will remain individual civil disobedience and be confined only to those who believe in and fulfill my conditions.'

Thus says Mahatma Gandhi in the course of a letter to a prominent member of the Working Committee of the All-India Forward Bloc.

Explaing the issue Mahatmaji adds:

'Individual civil disobedience has undoubtedly been started on the issue of freedom of speech, but at the end of every issue there was the issue of the Independence of India.'—UP

11. Satyagraha—The Second Phase: Gandhiji on Importance of Constructive Work, by Mahadev Desai

The Hindu, 10 January 1941.

When a few friends were here the other day with the list of Satyagrahis in their province, Gandhiji went into the minutest details about the pledge the Satyagrahis had signed. 'I cannot myself vouch for the fact that they are spinning', one of them said, 'we get reports from districts and we have to take them on trust'. 'That will not do', said Gandhiji, 'You must go to the districts and find out not only that they spin, but whether they spin with their heart in it. Then they will be able to tell you how much they spin per hour, what count of yarn they spin, how much cotton they waste and so on.' So they went back with the lists. As they were going,

Gandhiji asked one of the leaders how much he was spinning. 'I know spinning', he said. 'But how much do you spin?' 'Five or ten yards', he replied. 'Five or ten yards a day, or a week, or a month?' asked Gandhiji, laughing. 'Not every day', was the reply. Evidently the whole thing could not bear further scrutiny.

Non-violence Issue

Then there is the question of non-violence. So many questions have been asked. Is it enough to believe in it as a policy or should one believe in it as a creed? The creed of the Congress limits non-violence to the winning of Independence, does the Satyagraha pledge take it beyond it? They forget the language of the Bombay resolution, which said: 'This committee firmly believes in the policy and practice of non-violence not only in the struggle for Swaraj, but also in so far as this may be possible of application, in free India.' It is the crisis of the present war that compelled us to think in terms of the future, in terms not only of winning Swaraj but of retaining Swaraj, and the Bombay resolution was a logical advance on the original position. In fact, when one comes to think of it, the argument is unassailable that if we would resort to arms to repel a foreign invasion, when we are free, there is no reason why we should not resort to arms.

A friend seriously said that many people believe that faith in the constructive programme meant a belief in the cult of Khadi, but it did not imply actual spinning. And another friend went to the length of asking me whether one who satisfied other conditions but was given to drink or to other vices was eligible as a Satyagrahi. There was, of course, a certain amount of irony in the question inasmuch as he suggested that some people who had gone to jail answered to this description. I reminded him that Prohibition was a main plank in the constructive programme and that self-purification was the very foundation of the movement. One could not help people getting in, in defiance of these prime considerations, and after all is said and done; every one is answerable to himself and God.

Spinning in Jail

But Satyagraha now enters a second phase. Questions like those I have mentioned do not trouble unsophisticated people from whose ranks most of the future Satyagrahis will be drawn. They have a firmer grasp of the fundamentals than our learned legislators and sophisters. Their questions errs on the side of ultra-conscientiousness. 'Must one insist on Khadi clothes even in jail?', 'May we fast if we are not allowed a *takli* or a spinning wheel?', 'May I have a week's respite after a release or go on offering Satyagraha immediately I am released?', and so on.

But let no one think that the elders who have gone are all lax in the practice of their principles. The reports received are most heartening and they prove that the self-purification aspect of the movement is in no way neglected by our front-rank men and women. Thus Sardar Vallabhbhai says, in a letter, that he is running a charkha club of which the most active members are ex-Premier Kher and the President of the Bombay Council of State, Shri Pakwasa. As they are all detenus they may have their food from outside, but they prefer to run their own kitchen. Shrimati Sarojini Naidu, when she came here after her unexpected release, told me that every one of the sisters in the Yeravada prison was spinning and also Shrimati 'Hansa' Mehta, who has a flair for literature and can devote all her time to literary pursuits, devotes two hours every day to spinning and her yarn is the finest. They have also their regular prayer-hours and every one is making the best of her time. In Sabarmati, Shrimati

Maniben Patel with several other sisters devotes several hours each day to spinning and regular reading of the Gita, and Minister Morarji Desai's and Speaker Mavlankar's wheels are never idle. Ministers Shukla and Mishra, in their seclusion in Seoni Jail, have kept up their regular spinning after their transfer from Nagpur, where Shri Vinoba's twenty-four hours are a perpetual example to the rest of the Satyagrahis. He devotes four and a half hours to spinning on the *takli*, teaching scriptures during the morning spinning and teaching the principles of spinning and Khadi shastra during the afternoon spinning. Nearly all of them attend the silent half-hour for takli spinning and no one misses the evening prayers. Vinobaji occasionally gives a sermon on some text of the Gita or a hymn. He devotes considerable time everyday to perfecting his study of the Koran. While in Dhulia Jail in 1932, he had delivered a number of sermons on the Bhagwad Gita, which have since been printed serially. He took these to Nagpur Jail for revision. Asked if he had been able to revise them, he said: 'If I can do so much, constructive work here, why should I bother to revise my sermons on the Gita?' Shri Jamnalalji devotes most of his time to spinning and a study of Urdu. Pyarelal who is a good spinner himself has acquired there, after a few days practice, the speed of 80 yards of 50 counts of yarn in half an hour on the *takli*. The whole routine there seems to be so ideally regular and the self-imposed discipline seems to be so hard that, when I interviewed Pyarelal the other day, the Superintendent jocularly said: 'You may be coming in here for rest, but remember that you have another boss here—Vinoba!'

Pandit Jawaharlal, we know, from his letter to his sister, is spinning plenty of strong good yarn everyday and as is his wont accounting for every minute of his time. Though he in no way shares the ascetic view of life, his fine tastes and high sense of cleanliness make him do most of his jobs himself, and his high sense of purpose leaves him no alternative but 'to scorn delight and live laborious days.'

12. Mahatma Gandhi's Instructions to Satyagrahis

CWMG, Vol. LXXIII, pp. 281–3.

12 January 1941

Long before his unexpected arrest Maulana Saheb had announced that before offering civil disobedience he would visit Sevagram and discuss with me important matters affecting the communal questions as also such other matters. But it was not to be. Non-popular rulers do not disclose their intentions to the people. They allow them to be inferred from their acts. Perhaps it is a legitimate inference to draw from Maulana Saheb's premature (from the Congress standpoint) arrest that they did not want him to meet me. There can be no cause for complaint in this. They may not be expected to consult Congress convenience. But it is proper for Congressmen to realize that the rulers have no faith in Congress non-violence. Probably they do not consider me to be a knave, but they do consider me to be a fool. In so doing, they only follow many others who think that Congressmen fool me and that the latter's non-violence is but a cloak for hiding their violence, if it is not a preparation for it. Our struggle, therefore, consists in showing that our non-violence is neither a cloak to hide our violence or hatred, nor a preparation for violence in the near or distant future. Therefore our success depends not upon numbers going to jail but on the sum total of the purity and non-violence we are able to show in all our activities. Numbers can count only when they are of the right type. They will positively harm the movement, if they are of the wrong type.

For me there is no turning back, whether I have many or very few satyagrahis. I would far rather be regarded as a fool but strong, than as a knave and a coward. Though the whole world may repudiate my claim, I must repeat that the struggle is God-guided. I am but a humble instrument in His hand. Without His guidance, real or imaginary, I should feel utterly impotent to shoulder the burden I am supposed to be carrying.

Let me now say how I visualize the struggle. Maulana Saheb having gone, there is to be no successor appointed. Every acting President in a province must be approved by me. It is not necessary that there should be one. All representative Congressmen from members of village to provincial Committees are expected to be in jail if they are fit and approved by me. If they are not, by reason of health or otherwise, they cannot be expected to function except in rare cases and that too under my approval. No fresh elections are to take place to replace those who will have gone. The idea is ultimately for every Congressman to act on his own and be his own president but nobody else's. That is the conception of a completely non-violent institution or society. Not much direction is required by those who have learnt the art of suffering. Everybody knows the conditions he has to fulfil for acquiring fitness for offering civil disobedience. They can be easily complied with by any adult who is sound in body and mind. No difficulty as to action arises so long as I am left free. For nobody can resort to direct action without my consent. My intention not to court arrest abides, but the rulers may have a different plan. If it comes, it will be the real time of freedom from external control, be it ever so non-violent as also of true test for everyone. I am not to appoint a successor. Thus if I am arrested, everyone will be under the discipline of his or her own conscience. In theory, therefore, a time may come when millions will be judges of their own fitness to offer civil disobedience.

This is not a struggle which can be ended quickly. We are resisting an authority that is in itself struggling to fight for life against a stubborn foe. The authority is related to a nation which knows no defeat. Those whose life is in danger either readily yield on what they regard as non-essential, or fight to the end on what they regard as essential. Its refusal to concede our demand shows that they think that our struggle comes under the latter category. Therefore our struggle must be coterminous at least with the European. Hence everyone who offers civil disobedience and gets a short term should know that on every release he has to repeat civil disobedience till the end of the struggle.

There are two tactics demanding attention. I have already issued a note about fines without the option of imprisonment.

The other is that of not arresting civil resisters at all. In each case the resisters should march on foot in easy stages in the direction of Delhi. It may be even two or three miles per day. The resister will march taking such food as the villagers may provide.

13. Mahatma Gandhi on Observance of Independence Day Text of New Pledge

The Hindu, 13 January 1941.

Wardhaganj, 11 January.

Mahatma Gandhi has issued the following instructions for observing Independence Day:

'I hope that every man and woman in India, whether Congressmen or otherwise, will realize the gravity of the struggle and will resolve, on the forthcoming Independence Day, upon dedicating himself or herself to the service of the country in terms of the millions.

'Swaraj, based on non-violence, does not mean mere transfer of power. It should mean complete deliverance of the toiling, yet starving, millions from the dreadful evil of economic serfdom. This can only be attained by the propertied few identifying themselves with the millions and by their readiness to sacrifice their all for the latter's sake.

'It must be a day of fraternization, the abolition of untouchability from our hearts, the giving up of spirituous liquors, self-spinning, and the sale and spread of Khadi, and village industries.

'There is to be no Civil Disobedience that day. For, we must not invite disturbance of our meetings, processions, and Prabhat Pheries on that day.

'The day may begin with Prabhat Pheries, followed by flag-hoisting and flag-salutation. In the evening there may be processions, terminating in public meetings where the pledge may be explained, clause by clause and administered by the Chairmen and solemnly accepted by the audience.

'Where there are already restrictions, they must be obeyed. From such voluntary obedience comes the strength for, and the right of, Civil Resistance.'

The Pledge

'A new Independence Pledge, exhorting people to keep ready for struggle, sacrifice, and the Constructive Programme, has been issued to-day, to be taken on Independence Day (26 January).

'The following is the full text of the Pledge (the last paragraph of which is an addition to the text of last year's pledge):

'We believe that it is the inalienable right of the Indian people, as of any other people, to have freedom and enjoy the fruits of their toil and have the necessities of life so that they may have full opportunities of growth. We believe also that if any Government deprives a people of these rights and oppresses them, the people have a further right to alter it or to abolish it. The British Government in India has not only deprived the Indian people of their freedom but has based itself on exploitation of the masses and has ruined India economically, politically, culturally, and spiritually. We believe, therefore, that India must sever the British connection and attain Purna Swaraj or complete Independence.

'We recognize that the most effective way of gaining our freedom is not through violence. India has gained strength and self-reliance and marched a long way to Swaraj, following peaceful and legitimate methods, and it is by adhering to these methods that our country will attain independence.

'We pledge ourselves anew to the independence of India and solemnly resolve to carry out non-violently the struggle for freedom till Purna Swaraj is attained.

'We believe that non-violent action, in general and preparation for non-violent direct action, in particular require the successful working of the Constructive Programme of Khadi, communal harmony and the removal of untouchability. We shall seek every opportunity of spreading goodwill among fellow-men without distinction of caste or creed. We shall endeavour to raise from ignorance and poverty those who have been neglected and to advance in every way the interests of those who are considered to be backward and suppressed.

'We know that though we are out to destroy the imperialistic system, we have no quarrel with Englishmen, whether officials or non-officials. We know that distinctions between Caste Hindus and Harijans must be abolished and that Hindus have to forget these distinctions in their daily conduct. Such distinctions are a bar to non-violent conduct. Though our religious faith may be different in our mutual relations we will act as children of Mother India, bound by a common nationality and common political and economical interests.

'*Charka* and *Khadi* are an integral part of the Constructive Programme for the resuscitation of the 700,000 villages of India and for the removal of the grinding poverty of the masses. We shall, therefore, spin regularly,; use for our personal requirements nothing but Khadi and so far as possible, products of village, handicrafts only and endeavour to make others do likewise.

'We pledge ourselves to a disciplined observance of Congress principles and policies and to keep in readiness to respond to the call of the Congress whenever it may come for carrying on the struggle for the independence of India.

'In view of the fact that Individual Civil Disobedience has already commenced and that a large number of Congressmen have already been imprisoned all over India, it becomes the special duty of every Indian to concentrate with redoubled zeal, on the Constructive Programme, without the fulfilment of which no Civil Disobedience, mass or individual, can help us to win and retain Swaraj. Concretely expressed, the Constructive Programme means the universalization of hand-spinning and Khadi and the popularization of village industries and village products. We recognize that the effective spread of non-violence must bring about communal harmony and the complete eradication of untouchability in every shape and form.'

14. Independence Day Pledge

Editorial, *The Tribune*, 14 January 1941.

The Independence Day Pledge, the text of which was published in our yesterday's issue, is different neither in form nor in substance from the one that was issued last year. But, it is fundamentally different from the original pledge that was issued in 1930 since when the Independence Day has been regularly observed all over the country. That pledge contained an indictment against the British Government. Much water has since flowed under the bridges and the indictment clauses in the pledge have been dropped, the declaration confining itself to laying down independence as the goal of the Congress and seeking to achieve that goal by non-violence. Excepting for the addition of a new clause, the 1941 pledge is a faithful copy of the 1940 pledge. The new clause refers to the fact that individual civil disobedience has already been launched and says that 'in view of that it becomes the special duty of every Indian to concentrate on constructive work, without the fulfilment of which no civil disobedience, mass or individual, can help us to win and retain Swaraj.' That the constructive programme will go a long way to help the country in its struggle for freedom is undeniable. But the too great stress that has been constantly laid on spinning may very likely defeat than fulfil the purpose in view. The greatest value of spinning and use of khaddar lies in the fact that these are symbolical of politically-minded Indians identifying themselves with the interests of the masses. Beyond that these two items have only a limited utility. There is no gain to the nation if a rich man spins' or wears *khaddar*. In fact in the case of men who run the administration the time spent on spinning can easily be more usefully employed. Nor are we able to understand how the use of khaddar is essential for 'winning and retaining Swaraj.' Countries are free not because they are draped in handspun stuff but for other reasons. Whatever good spinning or the wearing of khaddar may do, it will be unwise to make a fetish of it. By merely wearing khaddar or spinning yarn India will not become free.

As regards non-violence, on which even greater stress is laid, than on the constructive programme, in the new pledge, there is no doubt that under the existing circumstances it is the only method by which India can expect to attain her freedom. It is also true that by following the path of non-violence India has gained strength and acquired prestige as the pledge claims. But for retaining her freedom, after she has acquired it, India may have to adopt methods that may not be far different from those that are followed by other countries. But if ever India is called upon to use violence, she will do so not for the purpose of forcing her will on another country but for defending herself against the violence of aggressors.

Mahatma Gandhi's instructions, which accompany the pledge, are even more interesting. Gandhiji, as expected, reiterates his faith in the constructive programme. He wants the Independence Day to be observed as a day of national purity. Beside the sale of khaddar, on that day there is to be fraternization, 'abolition of untouchability from our hearts, the giving up of spirituous liquor, and spread of khadi and village industries.' All these are acts of merit which can only do the greatest good to the country. But the mere observance of the Independence Day or turning patriot for twenty-four hours will not hasten the advent of Swaraj. It is also doubtful that the constructive programme will receive full stimulus, when most of those who command the obedience of the people, are behind prison bars. The constructive programme would have received a fillip if Gandhiji, instead of advising the leaders of the people to launch Satyagraha, had called upon them to remain outside and do constructive work. The Congress Ministries were doing the greatest amount of constructive work, if constructive work means that a little more sunshine should be introduced into the lives of the people. Did not the Ministries make attempts to spread education and improve the economic condition of the people? Yet they were asked to resign and wander in the wilderness. The resignation of the Ministries was a great blow to the constructive programme of the Congress.

Gandhiji has suspended Satyagraha for the Independence Day. He has also ordained that the Government orders that may be in force should be respected on that day. This once again proves that Mahatma Gandhi, though he has launched Satyagraha, is anxious to avoid causing, embarrassment to the Government. A wise Government will not alienate the goodwill of such a person, specially as he commands the homage of millions of people. The time for reconciling Gandhiji is not past. He can be won over if the authorities will have the good sense to promise to grant India what is India's due. While India is in chains Britain's claim that she is a champion of democracy and freedom will not be accepted by the world.

15. Instructions to Provincial Governments on Observance of Independence Day, 17 January 1941

File No. 3/7/41-Poll (I), Home (Political) Department, NAI.

Express Letter

From

Home, New Delhi,

To

The Chief Secretaries of All Provincial Governments and Chief Commissioners (except Andaman & Nicobar Islands)

No. 3/7/41-Political (I), New Delhi, the 17th January 1941[1]

Congress Pledge and Gandhi's instructions regarding Independence Day were passed for publication on ground that most of the pledge had already been published on previous occasions and that neither additions to it nor Gandhi's instructions contained incitement of present anti-war compaign such as would render them prejudicial reports. On the other hand, pledge contains seditious passage to which attention has been drawn before and it is probable that, owing to existence of Civil Disobedience movement, greater interest will be stimulated in celebrations on Independence Day than has been the case during last few years. In these circumstances Government of India have considered whether action should be taken to ban pledge and prohibit meetings and processions on 26th January Such action could not be taken throughout India without committing Government to open conflict with Congress and their whole political programme: and in opinion of Government of India it would be mistake to make present issue an occasion for such conflict. They therefore consider that no action should be taken unless local circumstances render it essential in order to preserve the peace. If however attempts are made to use the occasion for anti-war demonstrations or incitement to continuance of civil disobedience based on anti-war propaganda, they should be dealt with under the law.

Additional secretary to the Govt of India

---

[1] The Viceroy in his telegram to the Secretary of State had informed him on 16 January 1941 of the instructions that the Government of India was issuing to the Provincial governments regarding the policy to be adopted by them on the observance of Independence Day.

16. Congress General Secretary's Circular on the Conduct of Satyagraha Movement

File No. P–1/1941, AICC Papers, NMML.

All India Congress Committee,
Camp–Sevagram, Wardha,
21 January 1941

Circular No. 32
All Prov. Cong. Committees:

Dear Friend:

Certain questions arising out of the conduct of the Satyagraha movement have been referred to me for clarification. I shall try to deal with them in this circular for the guidance of Congressmen and Congress Committees.

It must be clearly understood that the present movement is likely to be a prolonged one. Gandhiji has declared: 'For me there is no turning back.'[1] It is therefore of the first importance that in selecting Satyagrahis attention should be paid more to quality than quantity. Also Gandhiji has declared that every Satyagrahi on being released 'has to repeat civil disobedience till the end of the struggle.' In that case we must make sure of our material, care should therefore be taken to see that every intending Satyagrahi fulfills the conditions laid down by Gandhiji. For the convenience of the Provincial authorities a copy of the pledge to be signed by every Congressman offering himself for Satyagraha is being sent herewith. If any of the conditions laid down therein is not fulfilled the applicant must be rejected.

If on offering Satyagraha in the prescribed form he is not arrested he should 'march on foot in easy stages in the direction of Delhi....' The resister during the march has either to rely upon his own private resources for his food and so on, or accept what villagers may provide him with.

The Working Committee had contemplated no successor to the President in case of his arrest. None was needed because the struggle is under Gandhiji's sole guidance. In the case of Provincial Presidents, it will not be possible henceforward to have any elections. Whoever is in charge of the province now may recommend to Gandhiji the name or names of those who would in his opinion be able to help him (Gandhiji) in continuing the struggle in the province. Nobody can be in charge of a province if his name is not approved by Gandhiji. If approval has not been obtained before hand, it must be obtained immediately after assumption of duties.

As all office-bearers, members of executives and members of elected Congress Committees, are expected to court jail, provided they fulfill the conditions laid down in the pledge, there can be no committees normally functioning. They can either function for satyagraha or for the constructive programme. In both cases they must function under Gandhiji's advice and directions. They can function in no other way. No vacancies caused by jail going or otherwise need therefore be filled. If Congressmen occupying a representative position in a Congress organization does not offer himself for satyagraha he should vacate his office, and in terms of Gandhiji's instructions such vacancy shall not be filled.

In the case of Congress Committee subordinate to the PCCs, the latter or its acting President may abolish them if by so doing, friction is avoided and business transacted more smoothly. The policy to be adopted must apply throughout the province.

As long as Gandhiji is in our midst he must be referred to in all important matters. All doubts must also be referred to him. As the AICC Camp Office is functioning at present from Sevagram, it would save him unnecessary trouble if all the references are made through that office. The office is in constant and daily touch with him.

After Gandhiji's arrest, if it comes, he has declared that he is to appoint no successor and every Congressman 'will be under the discipline of his or her own conscience.' If his instructions are carefully and meticulously carried out while he is yet free, he envisages a time 'when millions will be judges of their own fitness to offer civil disobedience.'

Gandhiji and the AICC Office have been receiving applications for permission to offer satyagraha, direct. You will please take necessary steps through the press or otherwise to inform Congressmen and others that no such application can be entertained except through the provincial authority so long as any is in existence. If any application for satyagraha is rejected the applicant must be immediately informed along with the reasons for rejection, if any.

You will please acknowledge receipt of this circular and of every other circular or letter that may be sent from this office, as recently there have been complaints about the non-receipt of some of our circulars and letters from several provinces.

Yours Sincerely,
J.B. Kripalani,
General Secretary

---

[1] For text of Mahatma Gandhi's instructions to Satyagrahis, see Document No. 12 in this Chapter.

17. Vinoba Bhave's Statement in the Court, 23 January 1941

File No. 3/9/41-Poll (I), Home (Political) Department, NAI.

Copy of Written Statement
In the court of Mr B.N. Kunte, Magistrate First Class, Wardha. In criminal case no.71 of 1941 under Rule 34(6) d and k/38 (1) a (5) of the Defence of India Act. King Emperor Versus Vinoba Bhave.

Decided on: 24.1.41.
Statement by Shri Vinoba Bhave before the court on 23.1.41

> When I had the honour and pleasure of appearing before this court. I was new to the task set before me by the Congress. After nearly three months brooding behind prison walls, in comparative solitude I am convinced of the correctness of the step then taken. After all is said and done the Congress cause is the cause of peace in the midst of strife such as the world has never seen. It has been suggested that all Congressmen are not actuated by the same motive. This charge need not be denied in order to sustain the Congress position. It is the consolidated action of Civil resisters, which determines the character of the Struggle and not the variety of motives of individuals. I suggest that if the whole of India followed the Congress lead, the strife would automatically end. If there will be no room for British Imperialism there will be still less for Nazism or Fascism, for the incredulous world will have understood the significance of active non-violence practiced by nearly one-fifth of the human race. Congressmen, however, know that such a miracle may not happen to arrest the progress of the strife. But the Congress cannot abandon its sacred mission for fear of failing to convert the whole of India. Since it has faith in its mission, this is the time when through Civil Disobedience it must proclaim it to India and the world. For in the pursuit of that mission is to be found the way to India's freedom in terms of the masses, and in India's freedom is involved the deliverance of the exploited races of the earth as also of the small European nationalities which are encircled in Nazi and Fascist coils. It is therefore a libel on the Congress to say that its resistance is an aid to the totalitarian powers. If the Congress resists, as it does British Imperialism, it resists still more forcibly the totalitarian powers.

18. Gandhiji's Statement for the Guidance of Congressmen and Congress Committees, 24 January 1941

File No. 1/1941–2, AICC Papers, NMML.

'The Working Committee and the All India Congress Committee members must not offer satyagraha nor should those interested in reversing the Bombay decision do so. Apart from these, civil disobedience should continue without interruption', observes Mahatma Gandhi in a lengthy Statement wherein he holds that 'Civil Disobedience without the constructive programme will not lead India to independence. Shorn of it, Civil Disobedience becomes a violent method which is bound to prove ineffective in the end.'

Replying to a question whether discharged satyagrahis should hold or attend meetings and deliver speeches, Gandhiji says that they should do so. 'I don't want them to offer civil disobedience again immediately. That should be in decent haste, but ordinary civil disobedience may go on.'

'Let it be known', he adds 'I have no authority to suspend civil disobedience on extraneous grounds. That is for the Congress to do. As a new sworn to peace, at this critical moment, to suspend anti-war activity would be to deny myself'.

The following is the full text of Mahatma Gandhi's statement: 'The jail delivery that is going on to appease satyagrahis must be taken as a challenge to convene a meeting of the All India Congress Committee, which, will reverse the Bombay decision whose working is reflected in my conduct of the Satyagraha campaign.

'I have, therefore, advised the Maulana Saheb to convene a meeting of the All India Congress Committee at an early date, but until that decision is reversed civil disobedience has to go on. I must admit, however, that the conduct of the campaign has been rendered difficult by the government action in discharging civil disobedience prisoners, but if we are to reach our goal, we have to act our way through every difficulty. This one is nothing compared to what we are likely to have to face before we come into our own. If the All India Congress Committee meeting is to come, as it must, pending the meeting members of the Working Committee and the All India Congress Committee must not offer civil disobedience, nor should those who are interested in reversing the Bombay decision. Apart from these, civil disobedience should continue without interruption. Of course it will stand suspended on X'mas day, Boxing Day, and the New Year day.

'The questions naturally invites whether civil disobedience is to be offered in the manner by reciting the prescribed formula or in some other manner. I like the formula method. It gives direction and symmetry to the movement. There is great power in the reciting of the same formula in the same names. It invites the attention of the masses. The formula is not a mean thing. It is a protest of the nation against war as an arbitrator. It is a message of peace on earth and goodwill towards mankind. What is individual formula to-day will become, in due time that of the masses, but the authorities having discharged symbolical satyagrahis may refuse to rearrest them for reciting slogans. There are then two ways open to us. If they do not rearrest, there need be no dismay, and demoralization; the jail is not our objective. If recitation is not objected to, it will be foolish to court imprisonment for the sake of it.

'Dismay and demoralization arises because Congressmen in general have not realized the inevitable connection between constructive programme and civil disobedience. Civil Disobedience without the backing of the constructive programme can never lead us to independence. Shorn of it, civil disobedience becomes a method of violence bound to prove ineffective in the end. Moreover, civil disobedience, even if when it is mass, will only be offered by those who are bodily fit. Whereas the constructive programme is for all and will never be suspended. If the whole nation took it up in honesty, it is enough to give us complete independence.

'The presentation of constructive programme means constructing a structure of Swaraj. The whole theme of corporate non-violence, as I have conceived it, falls to pieces if there is no living faith in the constructive programme. To my mind Swaraj, based on non-violence, is a fulfilment of the constructive programme. Hence, while the authority jail us or not we must perceive the constructive programme.

'I have been asked whether discharged satyagrahis should hold or attend meetings and deliver speeches. They should do so; I do not want or expect them to offer civil disobedience immediately. That would be indecent haste but ordinary civil disobedience may go on. For the discharged ones let there be breathing time. Let them address meetings in their constituencies and study things at the meetings. They will expound their views on the general situation and not hesitate to interpret anti-war Congress policy. Symbolic satyagraha has a definite meaning. But it is open to the authorities to arrest Congressman for their speeches, even if they do not intend thereby to offer civil disobedience. That was how they arrested the Maulana Saheb and Pandit Nehru, not to mention lesser lights.

'Let it be known that I have no authority to suspend civil disobedience on extraneous ground. This is for the Congress to do so. For me personally, I have no choice as to suspend my anti-war activity would be to deny myself. Therefore, for those who think like me, whether we are misunderstood or not, we must express our faith through our action, hoping thereby that ultimately our way will be accepted by all warring powers as the only escape from a blood bath which is pending now to its lowest depth'.

19. 'The Red Shirt' Movement: Ghaffar Khan on its Objective

The Hindu, 24 January 1941.

Peshawar, 23 January.

Khan Abdul Ghaffar Khan has finished his tour of the settled Wazir area of the Bannu district, after addressing nearly a score of meetings.

Speaking at Naizam bazaar, Khan Abdul Ghaffar Khan dwelt on the growth of the Khudai Khidmatgar organization and the part played by it on reforming Pathan society. He deplored that both the people and the Government had failed to understand the real significance of the movement and treated it indifferently. 'I have now once again endevaoured to set our affairs in order, and I am hopeful that my mission will succeed. I cannot however fulfill this task alone. In the work of reconstruction and reorganization, your help is needed'.

Referring to the European war, Khan Abdul Ghaffar Khan said: 'These mighty nations are fighting for the preservation of their honour and independence, and are risking everything for the safety of a civilization they have evolved through centuries. Let us learn a lesson from them, and be prepared to sacrifice all when the hour of trial comes.'

Referring to the Frontier satyagraha, he said, 'Only those selected and ordered shall offer civil disobedience, and others shall wait. Let no one get over zealous to join in the struggle of his own accord'.

Present System of Education Criticized

Bannu, 23 January.

Addressing a huge gathering of villagers at Manden, Khan Abdul Ghaffar Khan said that the Khudai-Khidmatgar movement was intended to remove their miseries. 'Without your support, however', he contined, 'I would not have succeeded in the past nor shall I succeed in the future. Our efforts should be united, and I assure you, of my intention to fight any outside power that intends to rule over my people'.

Criticizing the present system of education, Khan Abdul Gaffar Khan observed: 'Our education is defective and totally unsuited to our genius. It produces selfishness and makes us unfit for any enterprise'.

'Can this Government', he asked, 'possibly impart true education, and see us develop into a living force? It is impossible to evolve a suitable system without achieving independence, when we shall have real authority to set things right'.

20. Join Congress and Win Freedom: Ahrar Leader's Appeal Bond between Majlis-i-Ahrar and Congress

The Tribune, 25 January 1941.

Multan, 23 January.

Malik Abdul Ghaffor Anwari, leader of the Punjab Ahrar Party, has issued the following statement:

'I have read various statements in newspapers, issued from time to time by several Ahrar leaders concerning the attitude of the Majlis-i-Ahrar towards the Congress and what attitude the Majlis should adopt towards the emancipation of India. The past ten years' record of the Majlis-i-Ahrar would show that the popularity, which it has gained is due to its services to the Muslim community and its support of the Congress.

'After the Khilafat movement, the Muslims of independent views separated from the Khilafat as there was a general political awakening. As long as the Khilafat had the support of the Congress, it worked well politically, but soon a reactionary element entered the Khilafat. In the last Civil Disobedience movement, the Ahrar Party worked side by side with the Congress and made sacrifices. Later on the Majlis-i-Ahrar was organized and joined the Congress as a member. There is no difference between the Ahrar Party and the Congress, and the Congress lives to-day among the Muslims in the Punjab due to the untiring zeal of the Majlis-i-Ahrar. It is regrettable that the valuable services rendered by the Majlis to the Congress are being wasted owing to presence of people who are against the Congress and are, infact capitalists and communalists. But the time has ccme when we should join the Congress and make all sacrifices and put such people in the background who bring bad name to the Congress.

'I do not deny the political importance of the Majlis-i-Ahrar, but I do wish it should co-operate with all political parties in the country in their fight for freedom. There are several political parties in India which are in the field to check the political advancement of India. But I wish there should be no clash with such parties. I appeal to all Ahrar workers who are popular among masses by their services that they should jump into the field and work in the Congress for the liberation of India. I congratulate Maulana Sayed Mohammad Daud Ghaznavi and his followers for adopting the right course and I have issued the manifesto accordingly.'

21. Independence Day: A Suggestion to Gandhiji

Bombay Chronicle, 25 January 1941.

This year's Independence Day, which will be celebrated tomorrow all over the country, is for several reasons invested with unusual solemnity. Millions will solemnly declare tomorrow in the words of the Independence Pledge: 'We pledge ourselves anew the independence of India and solemnly resolve to carry out non-violently the struggle for freedom till Purna Swaraj is attained.' At times some may feel that the way is long and weary and stewn with dangers all around. We see with our own eyes how even people better circumstanced than we are, who already enjoy independence, are passing through unprecedented suffering in order to defend their freedom against those who seek to deprive them of it. We can learn a lesson from their suffering, from their uncompromising adherence to the cause of freedom and democracy. We can all summon courage and hope by reminding ourselves of the poet's lines:

Freedom's battle, once begun,
Though baffled oft, is ever won.

Constructive Programme

When so many Indians are making all kinds of sacrifices for their country's freedom, those who for one reason or other cannot make such sacrifices may ask if they can do anything really helpful. Gandhiji has anticipated this question and has added a paragraph to the last year's Independence Pledge in the course of which it is stated: 'Concretely expressed, constructive programme means universalization of hand-spinning and *khadi,* and popularization of village industries, and village products. We recognize that effective spread of non-violence must bring about communal harmony and complete eradication of untouchability in every shape and form.' It may be noted here that Gandhiji has not specified all the items of the constructive programme. A few months ago he suggested many more items of an amplified programme. That included prohibition work, spread of Hindustani, promotion of literacy, and such other nation-building activities. While communal unity and *khaddar* should be the concern of all Congressmen, they may also devote some time to other selected items of the programme according to their capacities and opportunities.

If those who take the Independence Pledge tomorrow ask themselves the question which is the biggest obstacle in the way of Independence, most, if not all will feel that Hindu–Muslim distrust is that obstacle. Yet while all readily admit this and say in general terms that Hindu–Muslim unity must be fostered by all possible means, few definite plans or programmes to this end have been systematically followed, in the sense that khaddar, for example, is being organized. We concede that khaddar itself indirectly promotes communal unity. But the degree of unity that we need demands a more elaborate programme which promotes Hindu–Muslim unity directly and at many points, whatever may be the difficulties in the way of political negotiations between the Congress and the Muslim League. There are wide possibilities of frequent social fraternization and conscious co-operation in common pursuits. And these should be explored by leaders of both the communities who sincerely wish to promote unity between them. As regards the continued absence of any definite move for political negotiations, a charitable explanation is that premature negotiations at an unpropitious time raise great hopes only to be frustrated and in the end add to the existing bitterness. But people are now-a-days very subdued in their hopes where hopes have not given place to fears, and there is danger in merely waiting for a wholly propitious hour. In any case informal friendly talks arranged now and then cannot do any harm, and may conceivably realize hitherto unnaturally suppressed impulses, and other tendencies which may at least hasten a propitious time for fruitful negotiations. Several responsible persons have suggested that Gandhiji and Mr Jinnah should no longer delay a friendly meeting. We feel that millions have been silently yearning for some such move. Leaders like Mr Fazlul Huq and Sir Sikandar Hayat Khan have repeatedly promised to do everything possible for a settlement, even if it must be of a limited or tentative character. Is it too much to hope that on this historic Independence Day Gandhiji may suggest to Mr Jinnah an informal friendly meeting to explore the possibilities of cooperation between the Congress and the League?

22. Congress General Secretary's Circular on Satyagraha and the Local Bodies, 27 January 1941

File No. P–1/1940, AICC Papers, NMML.

All India Congress Committee,
Camp–Sevagram, Wardha,
27 January 1941

Circular No. 35
P–1/207
All Prov. Cong. Committees:

Dear Friend:

The question of the local bodies and the policy to be adopted with regard to them in respect of satyagraha has been fully discussed by Gandhiji with Babu Rajendra Prasad. He has now issued the following instructions:

'Conditions differ so vastly from Province to Province and even from District to District within the same province that it is not possible to lay down a uniform policy to be pursued by Congress Members of Municipalities and local Boards. Some general principles which should guide the determination of policy may be indicated and should be followed by the Provincial Congress Committee.

'In Local bodies where Congress has a majority and that majority continues even after some of the members of the Congress Party have, on their application, been considered fit and selected for offering civil disobedience, the Congress Party should continue in office and carry on the administration of the Board, provided (1) that the local body is not required to do anything against the general policy and programme of the Congress and (2) that smooth and efficient running of the affairs of the Board is assured.

'In local bodies where as a result of some members' offering Satyagraha or for any other reason the Congress majority becomes a minority, and the local body concerned does anything contrary to the Congress policy and programme, the Congress members should resign'.

'Even though there may be a Congress majority, if the members differ among themselves or otherwise fail to attend to the affairs of their board, they should be withdrawn.

'A person offering Satyagraha—whether he is an ordinary member of local body or holds any executive office—should not be given leave of absence, if such granting of leave involves strained interpretation of the law on the point. In all such cases the ordinary law or bye-law governing absence should be allowed to take its course.

'In deciding whether resultant bye-election should be contested or not, regard should be had to the prevailing condition of the locality concerned and to the effect such contest would have on the general working of the Congress programme. In no case will the Provincial Office incur financial liability for conducting elections.

'It is expected that Congressmen elected to local bodies on Congress ticket will fulfill the conditions laid down for civil disobedience and be ready to offer civil disobedience themselves if required to do so. If it is decided to retain control of a local body in the hands of Congress members, it is open to a provincial Committee to withhold permission from individuals whose presence it considers necessary for the smooth and efficient administration of a local body, even though they may be considered fit for civil disobedience.'

Yours sincerely,
J.B. Kripalani,
General Secretary

23. Satyagraha in Punjab

The Tribune, 30 January 1941.

Lahore, 29 January.

Following an intimation given to the District Magistrate of her intention to offer satyagraha, Shrimati Vidya Kumari, (Mrs Malik Ram Bhija Mal, Advocate) was arrested this afternoon from her residence in Krishna Nagar under Sections 38 and 121 of the Defence of India Rules.

She had to offer stayagraha on the 30th January at 5 p.m. by raising anti-war slogans in Krishna Nagar, a new abadi of Lahore. Today she sent intimation to the District Magistrate about intention of offering satyagraha. Under orders of the District Magistrate a case under Sections 38 and 121 of the Defence of India Rules was registered by the old Anarkali police. A police party headed by Lala Chuni Lal, Inspector of Police, visited this afternoon her residence in Krishna Nagar and took her under custody. After arrest she was brought to the District Court in a prison van and produced before the Duty Magistrate, Lala Ganga Bishen, who remanded her for one day to be kept in the Female Jail. She will be tried tomorrow by a local Magistrate.

The following reports of the second phase of Satyagraha which was launched in the province yesterday have been received by the United Press from the various centres in the Punjab:

Choudhuri Mansingh Rai, President, District Congress Committee, Karnal, and Pandit Madhuram Sharma, President, Panipat Congress Committee, were arrested yesterday under Rule 38 of the Defence of India Rules for offering satyagraha by shouting antiwar slogans. A meeting was held at Panipat where Pandit Madhuram Sharma was congratulated and a hartal was observed to-day.

Khan Abdul Ghaffar Khan, President District Congress Committee, Campbellpur, was arrested in his village under Rule 38 of the Defence of India Rules for an alleged objectionable speech made by him on the Independence Day. The hearing of his case has been fixed for the 31st instant.

Sardar Chanan Singh a member of the Punjab Provincial Congress Committee who has declared his faith in non-violence, and intimated the District Magistrate of Lyallpur of his intention to offer satyagraha by raising anti-war slogans, was arrested.

Srimati Parbeti Devi of Kamalja member of the United Provinces Congress Committee, has sent intimation to the District Magistrate of Sialkot of her intention to offer satyagrah at Narowal on the 30 th instant by raising anti-war slogans.

Comrade Bakshi Ram is offering satyagraha on the 30th instant. Choudhri Mohd Hussain, General Secretary, District Congress Committee, Karnal, is offering on 4 February, and Comrade Pannalal of Kaithal on 1 February.

Information has been received that on the eve of Independence Day a notice was served on the President and Secretary of the Khanewal Congress Committee, under Section 30 of the Police Act, prohibiting the taking out of any procession or the holding of any meeting on the

Independence Day. Accordingly, as instructed by Gandhiji, no procession or meeting was held.

Information has also been received that the Independence Day was celebrated with zeal and enthusiasm in the States of Malenkoti, Loharu, Jaipur, Bikaner and Jind. Orders under Section 144 CrPC being already in force in Sangroor, the nationalist workers met in a private house and adopted the pledge.

Mrs Aruna Asaf Ali, who came here this morning, interviewed Srimati Vedkumari and Shrimati Memobai in the Lahore Female Jail and left for Gujrat to interview Mr Asaf Ali in the Special Jail. She is likely to address a public meeting in Lahore tomorrow evening.

24. Mahatma Gandhi's Letter to *The Times of India*

CWMG, Vol. LXXIII, pp. 321–4.

Sevagram, Wardha
10 February 1941

Sir,

Your word to me written so earnestly in your issue of 7 February, demands a reply.

In spite of your disbelief, I must adhere to my faith in the possibility of the most debased human nature to respond to non-violence. It is the essence of non-violence that it conquers all opposition. That I may not express myself that measure of non-violence and the rest may express less is highly probable. 'But I will not belittle the power of non-violence or distrust the Fuhrer's capacity to respond to true non-violence'.

The illustrations you have cited in support of your disbelief are all unhappy because wholly inapplicable. A man is not necessarily non-violent because he lays down his arms. The Czechs, the Danes, the Austrians, and the Poles may have all acted most wisely, but certainly not non-violently. If they could have put up successful armed resistance, they would have done so and would have deserved well of their countrymen. Nor is it for me to blame them for submission when resistance became vain. It was, however, in order to meet such contingencies and in order to enable even the physically weakest persons, not to feel powerless against physically strong persons fully armed with modern weapons of destruction that satyagraha was discovered and applied in South Africa in 1907. And it has since been successfully applied under varying and even baffling circumstances. You will please excuse me for refusing to draw a distinction in kind between the forces I have had to cope with hitherto and what I may have to cope with if the Fuhrer attacked India. The prospect of his killing every satyagrahi causes neither terror nor despair. If India has to go through such a purgatory and if a fair number of satyagrahis face the Fuhrer's army and die without malice in their breasts, it would be a new experience for him. Whether he responds or not, I am quite clear that these satyagrahis facing the army will go down in history as heroes and heroines at least equal to those of whom we learn in fables or cold history.

You are, however, on less weak ground when you doubt the honesty or non-violence of my companions. You are entitled to throw the Poona resolution in my face. I have already confessed that the Poona resolution would not have been passed but for my momentary weakness. As to the want of honesty or defective non-violence, I can only say that the future alone will show whether satyagrahis were only so-called or as honest and true as human beings can be. I can only assert that every care has been taken in making the selection to ensure a fair standard of non-violence. I admit, however, that hypocrites have undoubtedly crept in. But I entertain the belief that the vast majority will be found to be true. The Congress President has been frank enough to define the limitations of his non-violence. But so far as I know his mind—and nobody does if I do not—his non-violence will be proof against any temptation within the limits defined by him. I should undertake to engage in non-violent resistance to the Fuhrer if I had companions with the Maulana Saheb's circumscribed belief. Whether such non-violence can stand the test or not, is a moot question. I have achieved success till now with such material.

You are incorrect in attributing to me a demand for unfettered liberty of the Press or speech. What I have said is that there should be unfettered liberty provided that it is not inconsistent with non-violence. I am not aware that Congress Ministers' restrictive action went beyond the proviso. If it did, it was certainly against the declared Congress policy and can be no guide or criterion for me.

The unkindest cut is contained in the insinuation that my demand for free speech, subject to the proviso mentioned, was 'a device for squeezing political concessions from the British'. There would be nothing politically wrong if political concessions were demanded even at the point of civil disobedience. But it is a matter of public knowledge that the Poona resolution has lapsed. And in so far as I am concerned, it remains lapsed so long as the war lasts. Civil disobedience would certainly be withdrawn if free speech is genuinely recognized and the status quo restored. I have never stated during previous movements that they were likely to be long drawn out. But I have done so this time because I believe that there can be no settlement with the Congress, short of complete independence during the pendency of the war, for the simple reason that the Congress cannot commit itself to active help in war with men and money. That would mean a reversal of the policy of non-violence which the Congress has pursued for the last twenty years. And independence cannot come through any settlement while the war lasts. Therefore so far as I know, the Congress will be satisfied with the fullest freedom to grow in non-violence. The Congress demand concerns all persons and parties.

You ask me in the face of all these facts whether it is 'fair or morally right to pursue his (my) present campaign'. You have answered the question yourself in the negative. But I may not accept your answer. In the first place, as shown above, I do not subscribe to your facts. Secondly, to accept your answer will be to declare my utter insolvency. I would be untrue to the faith I have unwaveringly held now for nearly half a century in the efficacy of non-violence. I may seemingly fail, but even at the risk of being completely misunderstood I must live and act according to my faith and belief that I am serving India, Britain, and humanity. I do not wish well to India at the expense of Britain as I do not wish well to Britain at the expense of Germany. Hitlers will come and go. Those who believe that when the Fuhrer dies or is defeated his spirit will die, err grievously. What matters is how we react to such a spirit, violently or non-violently. If we react violently, we feed that evil spirit. If we act non-violently, we sterilize it.

You ask me to devote myself to internal unity. Well, my passion for it is as old as that for non-violence. Indeed, my first non-violent experiment outside the domestic circle was to promote that unity. And I had considerable success. I ask you, therefore, to believe me that my effort for unity is not suspended but intensified by the present movement. The great beauty of non-violent effort lies in the fact that its failure can only harm those who are in it, while its success is sure to promote all-round good.

M.K. Gandhi

25. 'Deterioration of Congress': Nariman on 'Impossibility of Achieving Independence'

Bombay Chronicle, 22 February 1941.

'With the latest clarification of Gandhian, that is, Congress position, the Indian political situation assumes an entirely different aspect. The problem is no more transitory such as attitude towards War or interim Government during its pendency. The question is, whether India should have cent per cent non-violence or complete independence', says Mr K.F. Nariman in the course of a press statement.

'Gandhiji has, by progressive steps, driven his followers and the Congress to the only logical and inevitable choice—political and economic independence or non-violence. Obviously under present conditions, political independence cannot be achieved or maintained, without the use of violence in external and even internal affairs. The result is, that Gandhiji would rather not strive for that independence at the cost and sacrifice of his cherished creed of non-violence', says Mr Nariman.

Continuing he says:

'His goal and ambition is not to develop the National Congress into a full fledged political institution—a nucleus for either Constituent Assembly or future national government', but according to him 'the Congress will be satisfied with the fullest freedom to grow in non-violence.'

This frank confession fully justifies the criticism levelled by the present writer and others years ago that Congress was deteriorating under Gandhian leadership, from a political, organization into a 'Laboratory' for ethical and spiritual experiments for Gandhian creed of non-violence and such other fads. Patriotic Satyagrahis are no more soldiers of 'Swaraj' but serve the purpose of mere living exhibits for test-trials in the said laboratory.

However painful, the tragic alternative is inevitable, prospect of Hobson's choice is before them; as it is obvious, that in view of this latest view on strict adherence to non-violence in all circumstances and at all costs, it is impossible to achieve or maintain political independence for India. The National Congress must therefore, either give up the present Gandhian leadership or bid good-bye to its hitherto long cherished political goal of complete independence.

The present generation being obsessed and blinded, may worship him, but the historian will never forgive him and his followers for allowing such a God-sent opportunity for India's progress and development to escape without deriving the fullest benefit from the present situation.

26. League Threat to Congress: Jinnah on Satyagraha Movement

Bombay Chronicle, 24 February 1941.

The Council of the All-India Muslim League began its session this morning, Mr M.A. Jinnah presiding.

The Council unanimously adopted following resolution moved by Syed Ali Mohamed H. Rashidi (Sind):

'The Council of the All-India Muslim League is of the opinion that the Civil Disobedience movement started by the Congress is designed to bring pressure on the British Government to resile from the position it has taken in regard to the future constitution of India relating to the Muslims and other minorities and to concede to the Congress demands, which are fundamentally opposed by Muslim India as they are detrimental to their vital interest.

'Mr Gandhi himself soon after the Viceroy's statement of 5 November 1939 wrote the following in the "Harijan":

"So long as there is no workable arrangement with the Muslim League, Civil Resistance must involve resistance against the League."

'The starting of Civil Resistance without an arrangement with the League under the cloak of fight for liberty of speech is only a crude method of getting over previous statements and confusing the issues.

'Only a few days back Mr Gandhi is reported to have addressed the Secretary, Hindu Mahasabha, in the following words:

"If the Hindu Mahasabha was so inclined, it could partake in the re-organization of the Central Government, but the question of the Congress doing so would not arise so long as the Congress demand remained un-conceded".

'From the above in is clear that the Congress is fighting the British Government for the acceptance of the demands.

'The Council of the All-India Muslim League therefore, have no doubt as to the real motive and object of Mr Gandhi in launching and pressing vigorously his movement of Satyagraha and draw the attention of the British Government that if any concession to the Congress is made which adversely affects or militates, against the Muslim demands, it will be resisted by the Muslim League with all the power it can command, and the Muslim League desire to place it on record that if the situation demands, it would not hesitate to intervene and play such part in the struggle as may be necessary for the protection of the rights and interests of the Musalmans of this country.'

Tirade Against Mahatma

Speaking on the resolution, Mr Jinnah said that Gandhiji could not fool all people for all time. The Congress demand was really for a Hindu Raj. Mussalmans could not accept Constituent Assembly formed on adult franchise or even a National Government at the Centre such as was demanded by the Poona resolution of the Congress. Gandhiji at one time declared that he would not start Satyagraha without an agreement with Muslim League. But when British Government did not accept Congress demands, put forward one after another by Gandhiji or his Lieutenants Gandhiji shifted his ground to liberty of speech, and while professing not to embarrass the British Government, actually started Satyagraha claiming liberty to preach to his people not to help in prosecution of war. No Government engaged in life and death struggle such as British Government was to-day could tolerate that. Real motive of Gandhiji was to coerce British Government to concede Congress demand. If British Government yielded to that demand it would mean betrayal of Muslims, who had maintained attitude of benevolent neutrality, in spite of all provocation.

27. League's Logic

Editorial, *National Herald*, 25 February 1941.

Life would have been dull for the chiefs of the All-India Muslim League Council and Mr Mohamed All Jinnah if they had kept quiet unduly long. Between the Congress and the Government the world had been forgetting the existence of such an august body as the League and its more august president. There are, moreover, forces at work, as notoriously they always are in this country, which want to use the League to test the Congress with. 'As in the case of 'Deliverance Day' they would appear to have pulled the strings from behind, and the puppets have, with alacrity begun to act.

The Council of the League passed a resolution at Delhi on Sunday expressing the opinion 'that the civil disobedience movement started by the Congress is designed to bring pressure on the British Government to resile from the position they have taken in regard to the future constitution of India relating to the Muslims and other minorities and to concede to the Congress demands which are fundamentally opposed to Muslim India, as they are detrimental to their vital interests.' The absolute incorrectness of the interpretation of the position of the Congress in this resolution is quite obvious. If the civil disobedience movement had been intended to coerce anybody, it would not have been confused between the two boundaries of non-embarrassment of the Government and non-extinction of the Congress. It would have broken bounds like a river in flood and would have swept everything before it. It is only a well regulated channel, symbolic on the waters of our life, which should be neither dried up nor polluted by stagnation.

At the moment the movement has no further political objective than the attainment of freedom of speech. It is not related to the constitutional problem directly and substantially. The question therefore, does not arise of the Congress putting any pressure on the Government to do this or that in the field of high politics. Again it is wrong to say that any demand which the Congress has made or will make will be fundamentally opposed by Muslim India. The Muslim India in the care of the League and Mr Jinnah is a satellite body, whose motion and magnitude are fixed by the larger planet in whose orbit it moves, which at one time is the Congress and at another time is the Government. It cannot, therefore, be taken seriously, so long as it chooses to play a role which does not inspire respect or reveal confidence.

Choudhry Khaliquzzaman, in the course of a speech he made at the Council flung the unmerited accusation at the Congress that, instead of effecting a Hindu–Muslim settlement, it had launched satyagraha, probably under the impression that when the Congress leaders came out of jail the League would have disappeared. The League, he asserted, had come to stay and would become stronger and stronger every day and even after Congressmen came out of jail, the main problem of a Hindu–Muslim settlement would remain. Why, for a wonder, we ask is the Muslim League infected with the inferiority complex? Of two things one can always be certain, immediately or remotely, an Indo-British settlement and a Hindu–Muslim settlement. But the second can only be subsidiary to the first. Whether it should precede or it should follow has been a moot question, however, among the Leaguers themselves. An Indo-British settlement, considered in this light, has been invested with considerable difficulty. The game of Mr Jinnah has been extremely simple. Proceeding on the basis that the two sides of a triangle are greater than the third, he has allied himself with the British Government.

28. Gandhi–Bose Correspondence

Editorial, *The Tribune*, 25 February 1941.

The Gandhi–Bose correspondence[1], which we published in our issue of Sunday, is a revealing document in more senses than one. It shows, in the first place, that so lately as 10 January Mr Bose was still thinking in terms of a non-violent struggle for winning the political freedom of the country in which he was a firm believer. So strongly was he convinced of the necessity and desirability of carrying on this struggle that in spite of his serious grievances against the present Congress High Command and in spite of his well-known differences with the Mahatma regarding the scope of the struggle, he expressed his readiness to place his own services and those of the party of which he was the acknowledged leader at the disposal of the Mahatma for all they were worth. He could not possibly have done so if he had that intention of evading the lawful consequences of his action to which his enemies and detractors ascribe his undoubtedly unaccountable disappearance from the field of his labours. It is hardly believable that his ideas and springs of action underwent a complete transformation within the brief space of a fortnight. The second noticeable thing about the correspondence, which is closely connected with the first, is the energetic exception Mr Bose took to Mahatma Gandhi's statement that the differences between him and the Mahatma were fundamental. The exact words of the Mahatma were: 'As for your bloc joining CD, I think with the fundamental differences between you and me, it is not possible till one of us is converted to the other's view. We must sail in different boats, though our destination may only appear to be the same.' Mr Bose pertinently asked if the words did not mean that in the Mahatma's opinion the political goal of the Forward Block was fundamentally different from that of the rest of the Congress of which Mahatmaji was the accredited leader. As both groups professedly believe in independence, it is quite clear that their goals can be fundamentally different only if they mean entirely different things while using the same word. This last seems indeed to be the position of the Mahatma, for in his letter to the Secretary, Forward Block, timed 16 February, he wrote: 'Independence secured through violence would have contents different from that secured through non-violent means. My notion of Independence is independence for the poorest and the lowliest in the land'.

'Subhas Babu is a Congressman and the Forward Blocists are Congressmen as well. As such Subhas Babu and his associates in the Forward Bloc had all along advocated the means of non-violent mass struggle as the only potential force to secure independence and therefore independence thus secured is surely independence through non-violent means.'

In reality the Mahatma's statement involves a number of fallacies. In the first place it is an entirely disputable point that independence secured through violence must necessarily have contents different from that secured through non-violence. Independence may mean either the freedom of country from foreign domination or complete political and social freedom for the poorest and the lowliest in the land. In neither case can it be said with absolute assurance that the nature and contents of independence secured by violence must necessarily he different from those of independence secured by non-violent means. There is absolutely nothing to prevent a party after securing the freedom of the country from foreign domination, from adopting a purely democratic constitution conferring on each man or woman the status and position at once of an equal subject and an equal participant in the political sovereignty of the State. Secondly, as the Secretary to the Forward Bloc pointed out, the question of attaining independence by violent means does not arise in this case at all. No responsible public man in India and no responsible political party has ever entertained the mad and utterly impracticable design of attaining India's independence by violent means, and so far as Mr Subhas Chandra Bose and his party are concerned, it is easy to quote a hundred public utterances in which they have emphatically repudiated any such design. Thirdly, there is not and there never has been the slightest difference of opinion between the Bose group and any other group of Congressmen regarding the meaning and implication of the goal of political independence, so far as the masses of the people are concerned. Both have always professed the utmost solicitude for the freedom and well-being of the poorest and the lowliest in the land.

What Mr Bose still differs radically and fundamentally from Mahatma Gandhi is as regards the scope and applicability of the principle of non-violence in politics: and it is worthy of note that on this point the difference of opinion between the Mahatma and the overwhelming majority of those Congressmen whom he still looks upon as his comrades and lieutenants and whose offer of co-operation he had accepted for the purpose of the present Satyagraha movement itself, are no less fundamental than his differences with Mr Bose. Men like Pandit Jawaharlal Nehru and Maulana Abul Kalam Azad, to say nothing about Mr Rajagopalachari, Mr Satyamurti and Pandit Govind Ballabh believe as little in the possibility of either preventing foreign aggression on India, or carrying on the government of the country after freedom has been won, by absolutely non-violent means, as Mr Bose and the Forward Bloc, and if in spite of their undeniable differences with him the Mahatma has not hesitated to accept their offer of co-operation in the Satyagraha movement, it is difficult to understand why the existence of the same differences between him and Mr Bose should have prevented him from accepting Mr Bose's offer of co-operation. The difficulty is all the greater because the Mahatma says in the same breath that he and the Bose brothers remain 'members of the same family.' If the political goal of the Mahatma and Mr Bose are fundamentally different in what sense are they members of the same family, unless all that is meant is that both are Indians and fellow human beings?

For our part, we are not in the least sorry that the Mahatma did not accept Mr Bose's offer of co-operation, for we do not want the scope and dimensions of the present Satyagraha movement, which we consider both ill-timed and undesireable to be extended. Our sole complaint with regard to the Mahatma's attitude, as disclosed in the correspondence, is that it is not only illogical and inconsistent in itself but calculated to render united action for the attainment of India's political freedom extremely difficult. The Mahatma, now as ever, frankly recognizes the influences and authority which Mr Subhas Chandra Bose wields both in the country generally and in his own province in particular, but in the false name of discipline he refuses to take any action to compose the present differences between him and the Congress High Command. He entirely fails to see that the present is not a question of discipline or indiscipline, but primarily and principally a question of adjusting differences between a supposed majority and a powerful minority. It is entirely opposed to the theory and practice of democracy to make a fetish of discipline in such a case.

---

[1] For the text of letters exchanged between Mahatma Gandhi and Subhas Chandra Bose, see Appendix

Appendix

Correspondence between Mahatma Gandhi and Subhas Chandra Bose Before Sj. Subhas Bose's Sudden Disappearance

Amrita Bazar Patrika, 23 Februray 1941.

The offer of his services by Sj. Subhas Chandra Bose entirely at the disposal of Mahatma Gandhi in connection with the Satyagraha movement, and its rejection by the latter on grounds of 'vital and fundamental differences', constitute the main points of a correspondence that had passed between the two before Sj. Bose's sudden disappearance from his home last month.

The entire correspondence which has now been released to the press by Mr Mukundalal Sarkar, Acting General Secretary of the All-India Forward Bloc, with Mahatma Gandhi's permission, consists of four letters, two from each side.

Full Text of Correspondence

Writing to Mahatma Gandhi from Calcutta on 23 December, last, Sj. Bose said:

'When Mahadevbhai saw me in Presidency Jail, I took the opportunity of conveying a message to you. I requested him to tell you that if you launched a movement, then our services would be entirely at your disposal for what they were worth. I also wanted him to request you to take the initiative in settling the dispute in Bengal, so that the province could throw its whole weight into the movement. Since you have been appointed Dictator, you could easily take up this matter on behalf of the Congress. So I thought.

At the time, my fond expectation was that you would launch a mass movement, as you had done in 1921, 1930, and 1932—though Mahadevbhai told me that you had been thinking of Individual Civil Disobedience. Today it is clear that the movement launched by you is not on the issue of our national demand for Independence. Nor is this movement a mass struggle. If the Government were to permit anti-war speeches, it appears to me that the movement would come to an end. Nevertheless, we would like to co-operate with such a movement, despite its restricted scope and form, so far as it lies in our power, consistently with our political stand. We would like to know if you would accept our co-operation for what it is worth—and if so, what you would like us to do in pursuance of this offer of co-operation. This preferred co-operation is unconditional in the sense that whatever grievances we may have against the Congress High Command will not stand in our way. If and when the High Command deals with us unfairly and unjustly, we shall have to react accordingly. We may have to fight the arbitrary and high-handed action of Maulana Abul Kalam Azad at the present time. But this can never blind us to the larger issues before the country and there you can have our fullest co-operation, consistently with our political stand. I beg you to accept our offer of co-operation.

Regarding the Bengal situation I had told Mahadevbhai that if you desired unity you could have it for the mere asking and all that was necessary was a talk between you and my brother—Sarat Babu. Since then the situation had deteriorated. You have chosen to remain silent and indifferent. The Maulana has been rushing headlong along the mad path of what he calls a disciplinary action. I am not bothered about it because if he wills it and seeks it—we are ready to meet him on his own ground. He cannot affect our public position in the least and he has only been making himself ridiculous before the public of this province and thereby dragging the name of the Congress to the dust. Since Maulana's action seems to have your tacit approval I am not seeking your intervention in this matter. All that I desire is that despite this unfortunate side-show which has been forced on us we should co-operate where larger issues are concerned and so far as we are concerned, we are anxious to co-operate. In all sincerity I am offering you our co-operation.

I am sending this letter through a relative who is going to Nagpur. I am asking him to wait for a reply.

How is your health? The papers again give disquieting news. I am progressing, but slowly.

With respectful pranams.

Yours affectionately,
Subhas'

Mahatma Gandhi's Reply to Subhas Chandra Bose

Sevagram, Wardha
29 December 1940

My Dear Subhas

You are irrepressible whether ill or well. Do get well before going in for fire-works.

I have not been in consultation with Maulana Saheb. But when I read in the papers about the decision I could not help approving of it. I am surprised that you won't distinguish between discipline and indiscipline.

But I quite agree with you that either of you is more than a match for the Maulana Saheb as far as popularity is concerned. But a man has to put conscience before popularity. I know that in Bengal it is difficult to function effectively without you two. I know too that you can carry on even without the Congress. But the Congress has to manage somehow under the severe handicap.

Suresh wrote to me that Sarat was coming. I have been waiting. He can come any time he chooses and so can you too. You know you will be well looked after here.

As for your Bloc joining CD I think with the fundamental differences between you and me, it is not possible. Till one of us is converted to the other's view we must sail in different boats, though their destination may appear, but only appear, to be the same.

Meanwhile let us love one another remaining members of the same family that we are.

Yours,
Bapu

Sj. Bose's Second Letter

Sj. Bose wrote the following letter from Calcutta on 10 January.

'My dear Mahatmaji

I am glad to receive your letter of the 29th December—not so much for the contents, as for the clarification of your views which it contained. On this side, it is not merely my personal desire to offer hearty and sincere co-operation, but it is the desire of many who stand with me. For doing this, it is neither necessary nor desirable to surrender or abandon our political principles and convictions. As you are aware, that in the previous struggle, many worked shoulder to shoulder with ardent Gandhites while differing from them on several important questions. Why should not this happen again? I beg you to reconsider your decision.

There is one sentence in your letter the full significance of which I am not sure that I have grasped correctly. You have said—"Till one of us is converted to the other's view, we must sail in different boats, though their destination *may appear, but only appear to be the same.*" Does this mean that in your view our political goals are different? How could that be? Kindly tell me what exactly you mean.

There are so many people who are anxious to know our views on the subject under correspondence and some among them expect an agreement between us. Have I your permission to show them the correspondence and if necessary to publish it? So far, I have shown it to a couple of friends only.

I hope you are keeping well. I am better on the whole—but some of the complaints are obstinate.

With respectful *pranams*,

Yours affectionately,
Subhas'

Mahatma Gandhi
Sevagram

Mahatma Gandhi's Letter to Mukundalal Sircar

CWMG, Vol. LXXIII, pp. 336–7.

Sevagram,
16 February 1941

Dear Mukundalal,

I have your letter. I had to delay replying to you because I got your copy of Subhas Babu's letter first and then his own letter.

The differences in our case are vital and fundamental. Subhas Babu knows them, and I expect you too know them. Independence secured through violence would have contents different from that secured through non-violent means. My notion of independence is independence of the poorest and the lowliest in the land. But in political language, all of us—Communists, Socialists, Kisan-Sabha-ites, Labourites and others must think of independence though all will have different meanings for the same word.

So far as I am concerned, I have no objection to the whole of the correspondence being published.

You will please let me know as soon as news about Subhas Babu's whereabouts is known.

The Hindu, 24.2.1941

29. The Satyagraha Movement: Arrests Total 4,749

The Hindu, 4 March 1941.

The total number of arrests in connection with the Satyagraha Movement is 4,749 and the total amount of the fines imposed on satyagrahis is Rs 2,09,663, according to information received in the AICC office from the various provinces. The totals do not include the arrests affected and fines imposed in the Punjab from where figures have not yet been received.

This information is contained in a statement issued by the General Secretary of the All-India Congress Committee.

The United Provinces heads the list of arrests, the total number of persons arrested in the UP up to the middle of February being 1,495. Andhra heads the fines list, the total amount of fines imposed on satyagrahis there being Rs 76,533.

The following figures show the position in the respect of the various provinces:

Province	Arrests	Fines Rs
Ajmer	10	565
Andhra	882	76,533
Assam	176	3,145
Bengal	39	3,625
Bihar	242	4,340
Bombay	47	Not read
Delhi	39	2,050
Gujarat	296	6,150
Karnatak	210	5,385
Kerala	70	5,700
Mahakoshal	137	10,302
Maharashtra	221	1,915
Nagpur	21	5,215
NWFP	2	(now re-Nil Leased)
Tamil Nadu	434	29,030
United Provinces	1,495	38,000
Utkal	315	9,532
Vidarbha	123	8,176
	4,749	2,09,663

Figures for Punjab

There hundred and fifty two persons have so far been arrested, and convicted, and fines aggregating to Rs 27,036,, that is, have been imposed in connection with the Congress Satyagraha in the Punjab according to the statistics collected by the Punjab Provincial Congress Committee.

Among those arrested are two lady members of the Punjab Assembly, an English lady, fifteen members of the Punjab Assembly, three members of the Central Assembly, and seventeen members of the AICC.

Since the outbreak of the war one twenty persons, including seven members of the Punjab Assembly, have been detained without trial.

Mr Hem Raj Sentenced

Mr Hem Raj, General Secretary of the Lahore District Congress Committee, and Mr Tej Ram have been sentenced to two years rigorous imprisonment each.

Lala Behari Shah, Financial Secretary, Lahore District Congress Committee, has been sentenced to two years rigorous imprisonment under the Defence of India Rules.

The following are the other convictions:

Messrs Sobha Ram and Amarnath sentenced at Jhang to one year and nine months rigorous imprisonment respectively, Mr Menghamal of Dinanagar (Gurdaspur District) one year rigorous imprisonment, Mr Paritam Chand sentenced at Rohtak to one year rigorous imprisonment and fined Rs 200.

Sentence on Multan Congresss Leader

Dr Parshotamlal, Vice-President of the Multan Congress Committee, was sentenced to-day under the Defence of India Rules by the additional District Magistrate to one year rigorous imprisonment and a fine of Rs 500, in default, to further three months rigorous imprisonment.

Assam

Sylhet Congress President Offers Satyagraha

Mrs Sarala Bai Devi, President of the Sylhet District Congress Committee, offered Satyagraha at Sylhet, but she was not arrested.

Lady Congress Worker Arrested

Miss Amolparava Das, a prominent Congress worker of Assam, who offered Satyagraha at Salmara a few days ago, was arrested here today and remanded in jail custody.

Miss Das will be placed on trial before the Deputy Commissioner of Gauhati on 7 April along with two other satyagrahis, Miss Puspalata Sakia and Dr Bhubaneswar Barua.

UP

Over Fifty Arrests During Week-end

Over fifty persons were arrested in the United Provinces during the weekend for offering Satyagraha.

At Lucknow, Mr Beijnath Prasad, a Congress worker, was arrested yesterday. Shrimati Rameshwar Devi (Orai) was released yesterday on the fine of Rs 25 imposed on her being remitted by a friend.

Arrests in Almora

Sixteen satyagrahis were arrested in connection with the Satyagraha Movement in the district of Almora on Friday and Saturday last.

Six persons were sentenced to various terms of imprisonment at Almora and Ranikhet under the Defence of India Rules.

Delhi

Satyagrahi Sentenced to Thirty-six Months

Mr Ismail, a Congressman, was sentenced in connection with Satyagraha to eighteen months rigorous imprisonment on two counts and a fine of Rs 500, in default, to two months further imprisonment, the sentences to run consecutively.

Seth Kedarnath Goenka Released

On the advice of Mahatma Gandhi, Seth Kedarnath Goenka who was undergoing imprisonment in connection with Satyagraha, furnished a personal bond of Rs 500 demanded by the Additional District Magistrate. Orders were passed for his release on grounds of ill-health.

Seth Goenka was removed to his residence in an ambulance car.

Gujarat

Two Satyagrahis Arrested

Two satyagrahis were arrested to-day from different villages of Ahmedabad district.

Maharashtra

Mr B.V. Shikhare, General Secretary, Deccan States Peoples Conference and member of the Maharashtra Provincial Congress Committee, was sentenced to-day at Karad to one year rigorous imprisonment and fined Rs 25, default, ordered to undergo three months further imprisonment for offering Satyagraha.

Mr Phadke to be Detained in Nasik jail

Mr K.N. Phadke, a local pleader, who was arrested yesterday under Rule 26 of the Defence of India Rules and sent to Arvada Jail, has it is understood, now been sent to Nasik Jail, where he will be detained.

Bengal

Calcutta Satyagrahis Not Arrested

Seven persons, namely, Srimati Govindi Devi, Messrs Raj Narain Lal, Satyadeo Sharma, Prayag Narain Misra, Munshi Lal Vaisya, Sheo Chand, and Uma Shanker Shastri, offered Satyagraha to-day in different parts of Calcutta, but none of them was arrested.

Balurghat Congress Secretary Arrested

At Balurghat (Bengal), Mr Saroj Ranjan Chatterjee, Secretary, Balurghat Congress Committee, was arrested this afternoon, while shouting anti-war slogans in the local bazaar.

At Dacca, Mr Aswini Kumar Das, who was sentenced by the Sadar Sub-Divisional Officer of Narainganj to three months rigorous imprisonment and a fine of Rs 50 for distributing communist literature, was acquitted, on appeal, by the Sessions Judge.

Bihar

At Daltongunj, Mr Kuldip Sahay, General Secretary of the Palamau District Congress Committee, Pandit Jagnarain Pathak and Mr Hari Singh have been sentenced to various terms of rigorous imprisonment, ranging from two to four months and small fines.

Orissa

At Puri, Mr Fakir Charan Swain and Mr Gunanidhi Sahoo offered Satyagraha at Nimapara and Kakotpur respectively, but they were not arrested.

Central Provinces

There were two hundred nine prisoners in the jails in the Central Provinces, sentenced for political offences, stated Mr C.M. Trivedi, Chief Secretary to the CP Government at a press conference this afternoon. Of these, two were security prisoners, seventeen 'A' class, ninety-eight 'B' class and ninety-two 'C' class. The total number of persons sentenced in the province under the Defence of India Rules was 334 satyagrahis and thirty-three non-satyagrahis.

30. Mahatma Gandhi's Instructions to Satyagrahis

CWMG, Vol. LXXIII, pp. 377–8.

[Before 17 March 1941]

'Don't bring persons from villages into towns for offering satyagraha. Satyagrahis, if not arrested, may do house-to-house propaganda but it should not take the form of picketing. Satyagrahis should not enter the houses where they are not welcome.

Persons serving in local bodies should resign from the services before offering satyagraha.

When a Congress Committee is suspended, its work should be entrusted to an approved satyagrahi.

Lady satyagrahis, if unable to march to Delhi, may tour in their own districts and province.

Satyagrahis marching to Delhi should obtain a working knowledge of Hindustani.

Satyagrahis charged under the Nuisance Act may not offer any defence.

They may make it clear that their sole intention was to carry on anti-war propaganda, and plead not guilty to the nuisance charge.

Harijan Congress workers should devote themselves to constructive work.

Satyagrahi prisoners may refuse food only if it is unwholesome and un-eatable.

Satyagrahis who are let off with fines should continue the satyagraha without giving a fresh notice.

Satyagrahis able to pay the fine may not evade payment, but are not bound to sell their property to pay it.

For the facility and convenience of village folk, non-arrested satyagrahis should be provided with a certificate or a badge on the authority of the Provincial Congress Committee, testifying to his being an approved satyagrahi. The badge may differ from province to province.

Satyagraha may not be offered in a place where Section 144 is in force.

Fetters and handcuffs, and other things, should be borne cheerfully when being transferred from one jail to another.

Non-arrested satyagrahis marching to Delhi should, besides raising anti-war slogans and otherwise carrying on anti-war propaganda, propagate the constructive programme of the Congress. It must be explained to the masses that the best and most effective as also the easiest way in which they can help forward the struggle is by carrying out the constructive programme laid before the country by our leader.'

31. Nariman on Bombay Conference[1]: Suggestion to Gandhiji

Bombay Chronicle, 17 March 1941.

Mr K.F. Nariman, MLA, has issued the following statement on the Bombay Conference and after:

'Although the Bombay Conference has not made any direct contribution, still it will be indirectly helpful towards the solution; it will afford an opportunity that many Congress leaders behind the prison bars would welcome, to re-consider the whole position.'

'It would neither be fair nor proper for Gandhiji to assume the serious responsibility to take a decision on the momentous issue on behalf of the Congress, as far as we are aware he was appointed sole Dictator only to control and conduct Individual Civil Disobedience. As he himself has recently declared, Congress is still free to decide independently and he would accept its verdict, though he, as a conscientious objector, may not be following it.

'Besides Gandhiji has also recently condemned the Poona resolution as unworthy of the Congress, passed in a moment of weakness; and in principle and policy there is not much difference between the Poona Congress and the Bombay Conference resolutions.'

Consult the Leaders

'We are certain that the authorities concerned would afford reasonable facilities, if the leaders showed an inclination to reconsider the matter. A copy of the Bombay resolution together with a brief summary of proceedings, should be furnished to all the prominent leaders in detention or jail, including provincial and Central MLAs, and they should be permitted to express their views and opinions confidentially direct to the President; and similarly Congress leaders outside should also be permitted to communicate with him; and if the President Maulana Azad feels, after perusing and considering their views and opinions, that there is sufficient ground for re-opening the subject, Government should release all the leaders and prominent Congressmen on Parole for about a fortnight or a month, to enable them to discuss freely and decide independently on the basis of the Bombay Conference resolution.

'As stated in my previous letter that decision one way or other should not be influenced by Mahatmic views, but should be a genuine, independent, democratic, and constitutional verdict of the Congress and Gandhiji should not impose his suggestions in the form of an advice; we all must confess to our shame that even when Gandhiji makes a bare suggestion or advice the tallest amongst the Congress leaders simply succumbs, and both his intellect and power of thinking become so paralysed that he becomes unfit for any independent serious thought or action. As a measure of safety and precaution, and to prevent such an intellectual and mental collapse, it would even be advisable for Gandhiji to have a self-imposed ban and restriction, so that he should not attend the said conferences and positively refuse to give any advice or suggestion on the subject. His views are well-known to all members, and they must finally decide, either to assume responsibility or abdicate; and further, the voting should be by strict ballot, as at Poona they will have to make a choice between Gandhian leadership or present political objective; and if after such precaution, the Congress does refuse to reconsider, and deliberately decided to pursuit the present path and is determined, in the words of Gandhiji, to grow into non-violence and at the same time to grow out of practical politics, then at least the position will be clarified. Let them have one more chance to decide this momentous issue, after duly weighing the consequences and realizing its implications; after that none can blame Gandhiji as his Dictatorship will not be imposed as at present, but would be recognized as a result of democratic and constitutional verdict.

'An arrangement on the lines suggested above, is very desirable, and may either lead to the solution of the deadlock if not, at least, will clarify the political atmosphere, so that the other parties may proceed on the proposed path, with better justification and support, because they will not be charged with ignoring the Congress, if the Congress chooses deliberately to isolate itself.

'The Muslim League, too, for fear of being isolated and weakened will also be constrained to reconsider its position and thus the Bombay Conference may ultimately pave the way for a representative All Parties Conference that can only give a national and then final authentic verdict on such a vital issue.'

---

[1] For Bombay Conference, see Chapter 1, Document Nos 6 and 7.

32. Observance of National Week: Mahatma Gandhi's Appeal to Congress Workers

CWMG, Vol. LXXIII, pp. 387–8.

21 March 1941

The National Week will be soon upon us. Its observance has a double purpose: (1) to achieve self-purification through fasting on the 6th and 13th April, and (2) to increase mass consciousness by greater concentration on constructive work. The sixth of April 1919 saw an exhibition of a sudden and unexpectedly high spirit of swadeshi and mass manifestation of communal unity and a determination on the part of Congress Hindus to get rid of the canker of untouchability from Hinduism. The spirit of swadeshi centred itself on khadi as it was the central village industry of a universal character. During the twenty years since 1919 the constructive programme has widened. The other village industries have found expression through the AIVIA. Education has been linked with the villagers through Hindustani Talimi Sangh. There has been greater concentration on impressing women in the national service and, therefore, regarding them as valued co-workers on a par with men. The widening and working of the constructive programme is the only way in which active non-violence can express itself. Civil disobedience comes, if it must, at the end of the constructive programme, never in the beginning. We saw through experience, that we had to retrace our steps in 1919 as civil resistance had been resorted to without preparation through constructive service. Disobedience of laws can never be civil unless the resisters have learnt the art of voluntary obedience. This is impossible without tangible co-operative work requiring exact discipline and voluntary and whole-hearted obedience to rules and regulations.

Civil resistance is merely lawful and obligatory only in some cases, whereas constructive work is obligatory on all who belong to a non-violent organization. And civil resistance can be effective only when it is backed by constructive effort on a mass scale. Success of civil resistance can be measured by the success of constructive effort. Therefore, I hope that all Congress workers will, during the National Week from 6th to 13th April, devote their time to the constructive programme. Khadi and other village industries have always played a prominent part in the programme. For, all young and old, men and women can take part in it and the work can be measured in arithmetical terms. It is to be hoped that the response will be much greater than ever before.

33. Congress General Secretary's Circular on 'National Week' Observance, 23 March 1941

File No. P–1/1940, AICC Papers, NMML.

Circular No. 42
P–1/210,

To All Provincial Congress Committees

Gandhiji has issued an appeal for the observance of the National Week, 6–13 April 1941. The appeal has been sent to you and the press. This may be translated in the provincial languages and widely distributed.

Ever since the Week was introduced in our national life, Gandhiji has meant it to be for self-purification and greater and renewed effort towards the achievement of our goal of a free, united, and healthy India. What does Gandhiji mean by self-purification? He wants us to carry out a rigorous political self-analysis. This will show that we lack the unity, solidarity, organization, and sacrifice necessary for the pursuit of our just and right cause. Today humanity is involved in the most cruel and destructive war known to History. Most of the combatants are fighting either to retain or extend iniquitous possessions. Few are fighting for higher aims or even national existence. Yet all of them bring to their respective struggles more determination and greater self-sacrifice than we, who are fighting for our very existence, do. As long as this is the case we cannot fully succeed. It is therefore necessary that we strengthen our national character by cultivating the political virtues we lack.

We have no doubt made considerable progress towards our goal by our non-violent struggles in the past. But unless the non-violent fighter brings to his task atleast as much devotion and sacrifice as the violent fighter usually does, he may not prevail. If therefore, there have been no more startling results in the past, the fault is not of the weapon but of the wielder thereof.

What Gandhiji wants from us in the National Week is this rigorous self-analysis and initiation of future effort in that light. He further feels that the public virtues we lack can best be cultivated by a faithful adherence to the constructive programme. During the Week therefore we must redouble our efforts in that direction.

Every day must be marked by one or the other nation-building activity. There must be spinning demonstration everywhere. In popularizing Khadi, it would be best not only to push the sales but also take pledges for the habitual wearing of certified Khadi. Certified because, that alone guarantees the worker the minimum fixed by the Spinners' Association. Products of village industries must be popularized. Efforts collective and individual shoud be made for the removal of untouchability. If we want justice for ourselves, we should be prepared to render the same to others. We may not copy Western Nationalism, which must have freedom, independence, democracy, and other things, so that it may have the power to deny these good things to others. We may not also neglect the education of the public in our ideals and methods of work. For this, wherever possible, Prabhat Pheries and public meetings should be organized throughout the Week. At public meetings less emphasis should be laid on the cruel humiliation we suffered in 1919 in the Punjab and more on the recent policy of the Congress. Congress resolutions on the present war and our stand must be fully explained by chosen speakers.

The student's organizations have recently shown a keen desire to help in some way the present struggle. The National Week should afford them a golden opportunity to translate their laudable intentions into fruitful action. I would make the same appeal to our sisters and their organizations....

J.B. Kripalani

34. Extracts from Fortnightly Reports on Satyagraha and Other Political Developments in Madras Province (January to March 1941)

Fortnightly Reports from Government of Madras to Conran Smith, Secretary to Government of India, Home Department, Public (General) Department, Tamil Nadu State Archives.

(i) Fortnightly Report Dated 31 January 1941 for the First Half of January 1941

My dear Conran Smith,

Anti War Activities: As I have reported in my weekly reports, the Civil Disobedience Movement is now getting into full swing again. During the latter part of the last fortnight there have been arrests and convictions of civil disobedience offenders in twelve districts and in most districts the District Magistrates have received notices from many more intimating the dates on which they will commit Satyagraha. The new lists of Mr Gandhi's nominees are large and contain some thousands of names of the whole Province. But of these very many are unimportant persons and by far the majority have practically no influence whatever outside the immediate locality in which they live. The question of the treatment to be meted out to offenders of this sort has been dealt with in a report to the Government of India whose instructions are now awaited. By no means are all of those selected by Mr Gandhi are willing to offer Satyagraha. Six members of the Vizagapatam Muncipal Council including the chairman have refused for the second time. The Chairman of the Anakapalle Municipal Council has also refused. It is now reported that Mr Gandhi has decided to delete from the list of selected persons, District Board Presidents and Municipal Chairmen, so as not to reduce the valuable influence wielded by these personages in the matter of spreading Congress propaganda. The methods of committing Satyagraha have remained much the same and the commonest form is that of shouting simple slogans such as 'it is wrong to assist the War effort'. The practice of committing Satyagraha by distributing copies of Pandit Nehru's Gorakhpur statement, particularly in Malabar, to which I referred in my last report has practically ceased, following the seizure of copies and equipments from the office of the Kerala Provincial Congress Committees. There have been a few unsuccessful attempts at hartal in one or two isolated places as a protest against the imprisonment of Abdul Kalam Azad.

The students of the Annamalai University are still in a state of unrest. Trouble is apparently being engineereded by Sultan Mohmmad who is a member of the Working Committee of the All-India Students' Federation. He was forbidden to hold meetings within the University precincts, but addressed a gathering of some two hundred students just outside when he urged the celebration of Annamalai Day on the 15th January. The efforts of the University authorities to dissuade the students from the celebration were not successful, and the Sub Divisional Magistrate has issued orders under Section 144 CrPC prohibiting certain outside agitators from entering Chidambaram on this occasion and adequate police measures have been taken to prevent any untoward happenings if 'Annamalai Day' is observed. Students' meetings have been held in other places mainly protesting about the incidents at the Annamalai University but the strikes at Cocanada and Pollachi do not appear to have any political significance.

Anti-war posters and leaflets have appeared in various places but they are usually found to be the work of irresponsibles. Mrs Ranga, wife of Professor N.G. Ranga, MLA (Central) who is now a prisoner at Trichinopoly, has been active addressing meetings in the Chittoor District. At most of these meetings the speakers inveighed not only against Government but also against the Congress party. The question of allowing Mrs Ranga to continue at large is being considered....

Report on the Press for the First Fortnight of January 1941
Attitude of the Press in Regard to the War

The general tone, especially in the Indian section, is one of continued dissatisfaction with the policy of the Government in refusing to accede to the Congress demands. The arrest and conviction of the President of the Congress have been widely commented upon and surprise has been expressed that the man, who had in his own way done so much for the Government by resolving the difficulty in Sind, by bringing about communal amity in the Punjab and the United Provinces and set such a high standard of discipline, should have been put out of action. The appeal to India by certain members of Parliament has left the India section of the Press cold. They point out that there is nothing in it which will excite the imagination of India. The viceroy's statement of 8th August has been repeated and no disposition has been shown to recognize the Congress point of view. The fact that the All-India Liberal Conference, the All-India Christian Conference and the Hindu Mahasabha Conference at Madura have all rejected the Viceroy's offer and demanded Dominion Status and its being implemented by a truly national Executive at the Centre, is emphasized for demonstrating that the political situation is being allowed to deteriorate by the authorities.

Appendix
Tabular Statement of Action Taken Against Newspapers

The number of newspapers against whom action was taken during the fortnight is eight as contained in the list.

Appendix II

(A) Statement of persons prosecuted for political or anti-war activities under the ordinary law or Defence of India Rules from the beginning of the war.

Indian Penal Code, Criminal Procedure, Defence of India Rules Code, or special laws.

IPC		**CrPC**		Total	**Defence of India Rules:**								
					123	26	38	39	56	58	81	90	Total
124-A	153-A	188	108	6	1	7	554	66	59	1	3	1	692

Note: The figures received from some of the Districts are not complete. Revised figures will be furnished on receipt of further information.

Statement showing the total number of persons undergoing imprisonment or detention on the first of the month for political or anti-war activities under the ordinary law or Defence of India Rules.

IMPRISONMENT:	a.	Indian Penal Code	...
	b.	Cr Procedure Code	1
	c.	Other laws	–
	d.	Defence of India Rules	444
		Total	445
DETENTION:	a.	Defence of India Rule 26 (By order of Provincial Govt)	75
	b.	Defence of India Rule 26 (By order of Provincial Govt)	1
	c.	Defence of India Rule 129	–
			76
		Grand total	521

(ii) Fortnightly Report Dated 3 February 1941 for the Second Half of January 1941

DO No. P. 4–3.

My dear Conran Smith,

War: The satyagraha campaign has continued throughout the province. Many of those offering satyagraha now are quite unimportant persons but at the same time there are many who, while unimportant from Provincial standpoint, are yet possessed of no small influence in their immediate localities and persons of this class are being prosecuted and imprisoned in accordance with the general policy. During the past fortnight only two MLAs (one being a woman) have been arrested and convicted. Really unimportant satyagrahis have in some cases been ignored and this attitude on the part of the authorities has caused considerable bewilderment in Congress circles....The interest evinced by the general public in the movement varies greatly from district to district. In some cases large crowds collected to witness the offence while in others the offenders have received little or no encouragement from the public. Only in one district did any incident occur necessitating a lathi charge by the police to disperse the crowd consisting mostly of undesirable elements of the particular town. In Malabar there was a recrudescence of the distribution of leaflets but smart work on the part of the local police resulted in four cases in the arrests of the persons actually sticking up pamphlets at night. Anti-war leaflets have been distributed and posters affixed to walls in South Arcot district also.

Allegations that officials are resorting to coercive methods to collect money for the War Fund are still being made and the various cases are being carefully investigated by the Government. In one or two cases where enquiry has revealed that officials have been injudicious or overzealous in the wording of their circulars, disciplinary action has been taken.

Political: In Malabar all Congress Committees have been disbanded under the orders of Mr Gandhi and the conduct of the satyagraha campaign has been entrusted to a committee of five.

Independence Day was celebrated throughout the Province. The attendance varied from medium to good with a few exceptions, where it was definitely poor.

These celebrations were carried out in an orderly and unobjectionable manner, although in Madras City there was a large demonstration by students, but at this the more fiery speeches were really directed more towards protesting against the action of Government in detaining a number of students for communistic activities than towards a celebration of Independence Day itself. These detentions were ordered in view of the evidence of considerable communistic activity both in the Madras Students' Organization and in the Medical College at Waltair. All except one of the students whose detention was ordered have been arrested and sent to Jail in Vellore. At the same time Government considered the representations which had been made on behalf of those students of the Annamalai University who had been detained for similar activities a few weeks ago and they have been ordered to be released from Jail on condition that they enter into a bond, with their parents or guardians as sureties, not to take part in any communistic activities in future. They are also not permitted to return to their colleges but are required to live with their parents or guardians at the places where the latter now reside. Efforts to celebrate 'Annamalai University Students Day' on 15th January ended in nothing happening at Chidamabram and very poorly attended meetings elsewhere.

Appendix I
Report on the Press for the Second Fortnight of January, 1941

The attitude of the Press in the Madras Province towards the War continued to be one of friendliness to the cause of the British Commonwealth of Nations. The important events of the fortnight were reviewed with insight and sympathy by the papers published in English and in Indian languages.

The manifesto of the Liberals where they have referred in critical terms to the Defence and the Industrial Policy of the Government of India, condemened the lack of sympathy of the British Government in regard to bringing about a political settlement and referred to the encouragement given to the minorities in India, received widespread attention. Likewise, Mr Amery's interview with Sir Alfred Watson and Mr J.A. Spender's view were referred to as making no approach to the political problem which remained as serious as ever.

(iii) Fortnightly Report Dated 25 February 1941 for the First Half of February 1941

DO No. P. 4-4.

My dear Conran Smith,

War: 1 (Anti-war propaganda is stated to be carried on through the medium of village schoolmasters who are under the control of Congress managed District Boards. Action is being taken to provide machinery to combat this 'Whispering' campaign).

Satyagraha has been continued in all parts of the province but on a decreased scale. The new policy of ignoring the case of less important persons is reported to be having a very salutary effect in many parts.

Public interest in the movement has certainly not increased. To keep up such interest, steps are being taken by local Congress Committee to arrange for Satyagraha to be offered at the conclusion of a public meeting. Organizers of such meetings will in future be prosecuted under the Defence of India rules as well as the persons who offer Satyagraha. Some District Magistrates consider that the reduction in the number of satyagraha in the last fortnight is due to Mohurrum and that the numbers will increase again now that the festival is over.

Apart from recognized satyagrahis there have been the usual numbers of persons, mostly irresponsible, making anti-War speeches and distributing anti-War leaflets or affixing posters to walls at night. These have been dealt with under the Defence of India Rules, but in cases where the persons concerned have been of little or no importance, they have been detained in the sub-jail pending investigation and subsequently released—a form of treatment which they appear to dislike intensely.

Complaints of coercion on the part of officials in making collections for the War Fund have been rather more prominent again, but the chief investigator of these, C.N. Muthuranga Mudaliar, has now offered satyagraha and been convicted and sent to jail. He even dragged the subject into his statement in court at the time of trial.

The District Magistrate of Malabar reports that several socialists have been arrested, one of these being apprehended by Moplahs and produced before the Police. Arrangements are being made to reward the Moplahs suitably and if possible to make the awards publicly.

Professor Ranga on completion of his sentence for violation of the restriction order under Rule 26 of the Defence of India Rules has been re-arrested and detained in jail under Rule 26 of the Defence of India Rules.

Madras City received a visit from Mr J.B. Kripalani. His Chief purpose was to deal with domestic trouble in the Congress ranks, but he has also insisted that the Congress Councillors of the Corporation should resign as they are in a minority. Many of them were unwilling to take this step and some have actually refused to obey his edict.

Political: Mr M.N. Roy is touring in this province in the cause of the Radical Party and held the meetings at Tenali and Cocanada. At the latter place be addressed a meeting of the district War Committee at which he severely criticized Congress's anti-War policy.

Communist activities amongst students are continuing but their efforts have been greatly hampered by the recent arrests and detentions. These arrests are reported to be having a salutary effect in the Andhra Medical College and many parents are wiring to their children there to avoid any connection with politics. Guarantees for good behaviour as in the case of the students of the Annamalai University have been offered on behalf of students more recently arrested, but the Government have decided not to release them at present. The matter will be further considered a few months hence. Arrangements are being considered to segregate students from older communist detenus in the Vellore Jail....

Appendix I
Report on the Press for the First Half of February

The general tone of the newspapers, so far as the political situation in India is concerned, was critical. Mr Amery's reply to a question in the House of Commons that he had no further statement to make on India was widely deplored. One paper stated that his outlook was becoming narrower every day while others wondered why he should be so oblivious to the growing discontent in India....

(iv) Fortnightly Report Dated 4 March 1941 for the Second Half of February 1941

DO No. P. 4–5

My dear Conran Smith,

War: Satyagraha continued in practically every district but the number of persons offering civil disobedience has varied enormously. In one district the Public Prosecutor resigned his office in order to offer satyagraha. In various districts a number of less important offenders have either been ignored or prosecuted under the Town Nuisance Act and in one case under the Madras Traffic Rules. This policy of treating satyagrahis as trivial offenders against the ordinary law is reported to be successful, in that it denies the offenders the crown of martyrdom and the sentence of imprisonment which they desire. It is also reported that this policy is making it increasingly difficult for the Congress organizers to obtain fresh recruits for the movement as Congress partisans of influence and respect are not willing to lay themselves open to conviction for such petty offences or to be ignored and thus be placed under the necessity of repeating their performance from village to village. The Andhra Provincial Congress Committee has issued fresh instructions to satyagrahis in view of this new method of dealing with them. When prosecuted under the Town Nuisance Act, the Satyagrahis are to plead 'not guilty' and to defend themselves but if convicted they are not to appeal, but after payments of the fine they should proceed in a leisurely manner to march to Delhi and to report to the Committee any excesses in the matter of making collections for the War Fund of which they hear during their march. The infliction of substantial fines on Satyagrahis who can afford to pay them has also done much to discourage persons of this stamp from taking part in the movement.

Political: Mr M.N. Roy continued his tour in various parts of the Province. At most of the places which he visited he delivered speeches, which were anti Congress and urged cooperation with Britain in the War effort, but the formation of the Democratic Union does not appear to have made much headway as yet in this Province. Congress meetings and agitation have been primarily directed against the system of classification of political prisoners and in particular to protesting against any political prisoner being placed in 'C' Class....

(v) Fortnightly Report Dated 18 March 1941 for the First Half of March 1941

My dear Conran Smith,

War: Throughout the fortnight satyagraha has continued in practically all districts but a very large number of those who have offered satyagraha have been persons of so little importance that they have been ignored.

Among those who committed civil disobedience were two women; one is a Muslim gosha woman and the other was the President of the Nandyal Mahila Samaj. The former created little interest but a crowd of three thousand gathered to witness the offence of the latter.

This policy of ignoring the less important or dealing with them under the various nuisance sections has definitely caused a reduction in the number of influential people coming forward to offer Satyagraha, and this effect has been enhanced by the infliction of heavy fines in a number of cases. On the other hand, there has been some criticism of this policy by non-Congress Indians who say that is exposes Government to the charge of inconsistency and weakness. Of the relatively large number of those who have been ignored, only a few have started on the march to Delhi. Public interest in the movement appears to be maintained as far as can be ascertained from the exiguous and factual reports appearing in the Press and the agitation conducted against the principle of classification for political prisoners.

The number of persons present when satyagraha is offered and at meetings in this connection varies from district to district. In some districts as will be seen from the incidents quoted above large crowds are still attracted to this performance. Prosecution is being launched against persons who organize meetings and occasions for the offering of Satyagraha, and who have hitherto tried to keep themselves in the background. The utilization of the teachers controlled by District Boards for the purpose of anti-war propaganda is exemplified by the transfer of some two hundred teachers in the Madura district on account of their cooperation with the District War Committee. These transfers were ordered without consulting the District Education Officer and when he protested he was told that he was not consulted because no notice would have been taken of any observations he might have made.

Political: In Madras and Salem, there were meetings in connection with the visit of Mr M.N. Roy but so far no real active support has been forthcoming for the National Democratic Union. Congress committees have been dissolved both in Madras and Kistna districts and the affairs have been placed in the charge of nominated agents. At most of the Congress Party meetings resolutions protesting against the classification of political prisoners were passed.

Communist literature continues to come to notice in some districts and communist activities amongst the students are being continued. Police raids in Malabar have resulted in the discovery of a considerable amount of communist literature which in turn has led to be arrest of a number of persons concerned in that party's activities. There has been less activity amongst the various student organizations except in Madura but even there the position in the American College has improved, largely owing to the fact that the Principal's patience has been exhausted and there is now proper co-operation between the College authorities and the local officials.

(vi) Fortnightly Report Dated 3 April 1941 for the Second Half of March 1941

DO No. P. 4–7

My dear Conran Smith,

War: Satyagraha has been continued throughout the whole Province on lines similar to that in recent fortnights. From one district only comes any report of increasing activity. During the last fortnight there have been more prominent persons taking part than in recent weeks. Among these were an ex-Public Prosecutor, the Secretary of the Andhra Provincial Congress Committee, the President of a District Board, and Mr K.S. Gupta, MLA (Central). In addition to these Dr Pattabhi Sitarammayya has been detained under Rule 26 of the Defence of India Rules and Mr Shanmugasundaram Mudaliar who took a leading part in persuading the Ariyalur Panchayat Board to present an address to His Excellency only a fortnight ago is also amongst those who offered Satyagraha. The less important cases have been dealt with as before, use being made wherever possible of the provisions of ordinary law such as Sec 283 IPC and the Town Nuisance Act. Many have simply been ignored altogether. The District Magistrate of Bellary reports that he found the satyagrahi prisoners in the Alipuram Jail in a dispirited frame of mind and many of the 'A' class prisoners stating openly that when released they have no intention of taking further part in the movement.

Public interest remains much the same so far as it is possible to judge, but the Congress Organizers are still endeavouring to circumvent the actions of Government by devising new forms of Satyagraha. It was one of these schemes which was intended to arrange for at least hundred persons to offer Satyagraha in the various villages in three particular taluks at the same time and to do it by holding meetings rather than by simply shouting slogans that led to the arrest and conviction of Kala Venkata Rao, Secretary of the Andhra Provincial Congress Committee and to the detention of the Dr Pattabhi Sitaramayya. In Chicacole taluk of the Vizagapatam District prominent Congressmen are taking insignificant persons out to neighbouring villages and introducing them to the villagers that it is the insignificant persons who actually commit the offence. The District Magistrate is taking action against the organizers for abetment.

Political: Students have been much quieter in recent weeks but there is still considerable amount of communist propaganda going on throughout underground organizations amongst them. Several leading communists are still at large and communist literature continues to come to light.

A report has just been received that two policemen sent to execute arrest warrants against socialists in South Kanara District have been attacked by a mob and one of the constables killed. No further details have so far been received.

Appendix II
Report on the Press for the Second Half of March 1941

Nationalist papers continued to impress upon Great Britain the necessity for resolving the impasse in India, the opportunity to do so having been provided by the Moderates' Conference at Bombay. A few extreme Congress papers were very critical of the Bombay Conference resolution, while 'The Mail', which represents the European Community, was not over critical except in regard to the demand for fixing a time limit for the grant of Dominion Status. The nationalist press was on the whole on the side of the Bombay Conference resolutions.

Tabular statement of action taken against newspapers

Tamil Jothi was warned on 10th March 1941.

35. League Resolution on Satyagraha: Attempts to Establish Hindu Raj Throughout the Country

National Herald, 16 April 1941.

The subjects committee of the All-India Muslim League adopted a number of resolutions yesterday afternoon, included in which are the resolutions relating to the Satyagraha movement and the change of the creed of the Muslim League. Mr M.A. Jinnah presided at the meeting for the first time.

The resolution on Satyagraha runs as follows:

'This session of the All-India Muslim League is definitely of the opinion that the civil disobedience movement started by Mahatma Gandhi on behalf of the Congress, ostensibly for freedom of speech, is really meant to coerce the British Government to concede the Congress demands regarding the future constitution of India, which are really and virtually for a transfer of sovereign power to the Hindus and thus relegate the Muslim nation of 100 million and the Indian minorities to the status of subjects of the Hindu Raj throughout the country. It therefore draws the attention of the British Government that if constitutional changes, either interim or final are made without the approval of the All-India Muslim League, it would be construced as flagrant breach of faith on the part of the British Government with the Mussalmans of India and would be contrary to the solemn declarations and promises that have already been made to the Mussalmans of India by the recent announcements of the Viceroy, Secretary of State for India and his Majesty's Government, ending with the declaration of 8 August 1940 and amplification of it by Mr Amery on 14 August, 1940; and warns the British Government that if any attempt is made to depart from or modify in any way the above-mentioned declarations and pledges, the Mussalmans of India would be forced to resist every measure and method and to resist it with all the power that they can command.'

36. Mahatma Gandhi's Statement to *The Times of India*[1]

CWMG, Vol. LXXIV, pp. 2–4.

Sevagram, Wardha
19 April 1941

I have very carefully listened to the advance Press notes of *The Times of India*'s leading article which must have appeared this morning in Bombay. I acknowledge the friendly tone of the article, and I wish I could have given an encouraging reply; but I cannot.

I adhere to all that I said at the initiation of the struggle. When I launched out, I had no foolish illusion about a sudden miracle happening. It was conceived to be, and it remains, a silent declaration of unquenchable faith in the power of non-violence even in the midst of circumstances so terrible and so baffling as face the world today.

I believe more in the efficacy of the incalculable force of inscrutable divinity than in the efficacy of the calculated and calculable forces that the combined powers of destruction can bring into play on this little planet. That incalculable force has somehow or the other to act through human agency. How and when I cannot say. Whether that agency is the Congress or not, I cannot say. I proceed upon the faith that today the Congress is the only organization, however imperfect, however wanting in faith as an organization, still the only organization that stands definitely for peaceful measures.

That being my position, so far as I am concerned, there is no drawing back. Whether civil disobedience is offered by one or many is of no moment. It must continue against all odds. Congressmen can certainly repudiate it in more ways than one. It will then cease to be an organizational movement, and therefore I will admit it will cease to be effective in any shape or form. But I would be content if I still retain the faith to be the solitary witness of the power of non-violence.

I must resolutely deny that this movement, whether in conception or in execution, is communal or anti-Muslim or anti-English. There is sufficient evidence for those who want to notice it to show that extraordinary precaution is being taken to keep the movement within limits and absolutely innocuous.

Many Government people have admitted that it is wholly effective according to their conception. The writer of the article has said as much from his standpoint. And both are right. It was never intended that it would create an appreciable impression upon the war effort, but it is a moral, and from that stand-point a grand protest against the conduct of the war in the name of a free people. It is a token of the yearning of a political organization to achieve the freedom of 350,000,000 people through purely non-violent effort and therefore to affect the future destiny of the world. Again an ambitious claim, but it is there.

If I can help it, the Congress will disdain freedom at the sacrifice of a single legitimate interest that is consistent with the interests of the dumb millions, whether they are Hindus, Muslims or others. I must deny that if the Congress had held on to office in the seven provinces the Pakistan cry would have been less loud than it is today; but the giving up of office had an infinitely more moral basis than the avoidance of a tussle with Muslim interests or any other interests. The fundamental basis was India's dissociation from the war effort to which it was never invited to be party. This is putting it in its lowest term and in bald political language. As you know, my own basis is still more abstract still more moral and still more universal, but on that account none the less real or less practical.

I make bold to say that when the clash of arms has ceased and we have settled down to peace, permanent or impermanent, history will record that the Congress fight in its totality was a supremely moral fight and free from any injury to man's dignity.

To conclude this very unsatisfactory reply, as it would appear, to a friendly gesture, I want to plead one thing. Would friends ask me at this supreme moment in the life of the world and my own life, to deny a faith that has sustained me for nearly half a century? And let me interpolate one thought, however unwelcome it may be: I am convinced that if Britain will only be true to India, then, whether the Congress withdraws the struggle or not, everything can be settled satisfactorily. But unfortunately British statesmen have chosen the wrong path and have put imaginary obstacles in the way of India's freedom. But that is a chapter on which I have no desire to dilate.

---

[1] The statement, published on 20 April 1941, was issued in response to the appeal by *The Times of India* to Mahatma Gandhi to withdraw the Civil Disobedience Movement.

37. Mahatma Gandhi's Statement[1] to the Press on House of Commons Debate Held on 22 April 1941

CWMG, Vol. LXXIV, pp. 13–16.

Wardha
25 April 1941

I have read painfully the long report of the debate in the House of Commons on India. Distress has been known to have softened people's hearts and made them mindful of facts. But Britain's distress has evidently left Mr Amery absolutely cold and untouched. This callousness makes me more than every confirmed in my opinion that the Congress must abide by its policy of non-violence in spite of the heavy odds facing it.

Mr Amery has rendered no service to Great Britain by his contemptuous disregard of the situation as it exists in India and the facts that stare one in the face. He talks glibly of British rule having given peace to India. Did he not know what was happening in Dacca and Ahmedabad? Who was responsible for keeping the peace in these two places? I hope he will not throw in my face the fact that Bengal, at any rate, has self-government. He knows what a mockery that self-government is. He knows what little power for such emergencies toy Ministers have, whether they wear the Congress label, the League label or any other.

I ask the very pertinent question: Why has this long spell of British rule left the people so emasculated as to disable them from standing up against a few hundred goondas? It is a humiliating spectacle, more for the British than for us, to see thousands of people running away from their homes through sheer fright, because a few hundred goondas have found a favourable atmosphere for resorting to arson, murder, and loot. The first act of any government worth the name would be to teach its people the art of self-defence, but the foreign British Government had no concern about this fundamental welfare of India's citizens and so it deprived the people of the use of arms.

All the handsome tribute that Mr Amery pays to Indian troop's falls flat on Indian soil, because, leaving aside Congress non-violence for the time being, if India had been equipped and trained for self-defence and if India had become a voluntary ally of Great Britain, I hold that all European Powers combined for destruction would not have touched Great Britain.

Mr Amery has insulted Indian intelligence by reiterating *ad nauseam* that Indian political parties have but to agree among themselves and Great Britain will register the will of a united India. I have repeatedly shown that it has been the traditional policy of Great Britain to prevent parties from uniting. 'Divide and rule' has been Great Britain's proud and ill-conceived motto. It is the British statesmen who are responsible for the divisions in India's ranks, and the divisions will continue so long as the British sword holds India under bondage.

I admit that there is unfortunately an unbridgeable gulf between the Congress and the Muslim League. Why do not British statesmen admit that it is after all a domestic quarrel? Let them withdraw from India and I promise that the Congress and the League and all other parties will find it to their interest to come together and devise a home-made solution for the Government of India. It may not be scientific; it may not be after any Western pattern; but it will be durable. It may be that before we come to that happy state of affairs, we may have to fight amongst ourselves. But if we agree not to invite the assistance of any outside power, the trouble will last perhaps a fortnight and it will not mean even one day's destruction of human heads such as goes on in Europe today, for the simple reason that thanks to the British rule we are wholly unarmed.

Mr Amery, in utter disregard of truth, misleads his ignorant audience that the Congress wants 'all or nothing'. Let me remind him that in order to placate British sentiment, the Congress descended to the Poona Resolution and when at Bombay it undid the Poona Resolution, I authoritatively stated that the British Government could not at the present moment grant or declare India's independence and that, therefore, for the time being, we should be satisfied with the complete freedom of speech and pen. Was that 'all or nothing'? With Mr Amery's state of mind, I suppose it is too much to expect him to have the elementary grace to acknowledge the studied moderation of the Congress in its desire not to embarrass the British Government whilst it is fighting for its very existence. Not having that grace, he turns the Congress moderation against it and claims that the Congress civil disobedience has fallen flat.

It took my breath away when I read his statement about India's prosperity. I say from experience that it is a legendary thing. India's millions are becoming progressively pauperized. They are miserably clothed and underfed. Because there is one man's rule, he is able to produce a budget of millions. But I make bold to say that it is not only no proof of the prosperity of the famishing millions, but it is proof positive that India is being ground down under the British heel. It is the duty of every Indian who knows anything about the distress of the peasantry, to rise in rebellion against this autocratic rule. Fortunately for humanity, India's rebellion is a peaceful revolt and I hope it will be through exclusively peaceful effort that India will realize her natural destiny.

But I must not carry any further the painful dissection of Mr Amery's performance. It hurts me to have to undertake even this very brief analysis of his speech. But it is so amazingly misleading that I felt I would be failing in my duty if I did not point out at least some of the most glaring discrepancies in that unfortunate utterance. Surely he could have rested content with the undisputed sway that he exercises over the destinies of over four hundred million people.

---

[1] The statement was published in *The Hindu* on 27 April 1941.

38. Report of Mahatma Gandhi's Discussion with D.K. Gosavi[1]

CWMG, Vol. LXXIV, pp. 61–5.

15 May 1941

Q: Very few names from the third list of satyagrahis from Maharashtra (193 out of 1,072) are approved and permitted to offer Satyagraha. This permission business seems to be unduly delayed, and the satyagrahis are thus put to much inconvenience.

A: I propose to introduce a change in the technique about the passing of these lists of satyagrahis.[2] From the date on which the name of a prospective satyagrahi is forwarded to me for sanction by the Provincial Congress Committee the satyagrahi concerned has to stop his private activities and has to devote himself wholly to the working out of one or more of the items of the thirteenfold constructive programme, which expression is to be understood in the widest sense as explained in my article headed 'Implications of Constructive Programme' in the issue of *Harijan* dated 18th of August 1940.

Every prospective satyagrahi is expected to keep a log-book (or diary) in which he will daily enter the work done during the course of the day and the log-book shall be submitted to me through the PCC concerned at stated intervals, say, fortnightly or monthly. After going through the diaries I shall grant permission for satyagraha to deserving persons. Others will have to follow the said course till they get permission.

The satyagrahi may not expect any financial help from the Congress.

I know that on this very strict basis the number of satyagrahis will be reduced to a very large extent but what I am keen on its quality and not quantity. I shall not feel sorry if the number is reduced to any extent. Moreover, whilst so many satyagrahis are wandering about, I am anxious not to add to the list of wanderers.

Q: Don't you feel that you are unfair to the prospective satyagrahis in prescribing such a severe preliminary test to them only, while you allowed their predecessors in on a comparatively simpler test?

A: I don't think I am unfair. One thing that you must remember is that the above movement is evolving. Exigencies of the situation may demand varying conditions.

Q: Has the President of the PCC any duty towards the satyagrahis when they come out of jail?
A: Yes, he certainly has. He has to ask them to repeat satyagraha and find themselves again in jail, say, within about a week from date of their release. The PCCs need only report to me demanding special treatment and the instructions that will be by me in these cases should be followed and executed by the PCCs.

Q: How long will this process go on?
A: Indefinitely; that is to say, till we achieve our goal. Deep down me there is a feeling that the struggle will become progressively fiercer and we must pass through all such trials.

In this respect we must take lesson from the British who, in spite of all the severe losses and heavy odds against them, have maintained fine morale and are determined to carry on. We may not do less.

Q: If any satyagrahi who has enrolled himself on the original basis feels unable to accept the new basis, which will be the honourable way out for him?
A: He is free to withdraw his name and there is no disgrace attaching to any such honest withdrawal. I must not be deceived. To receive me is to deceive oneself and the nation. Every honest person can and should withdraw his name. He may continue to render services he can to the country. He does remain and does continue a Congressman as before. Congress does require and does appreciate his services also. But he cannot remain on the satyagrahi list as it is now envisaged.

Q: Can we start and develop a volunteer organization under the present circumstances?
A: By all means; the only condition is that it shall be organized on the basis of non-violence—unadulterated non-violence.

No trifling with non-violence will do and therefore no laxity in that request can be tolerated. One more point. The said organization should be pro-Congress and yet independent of the Congress. It can be an allied institution like AISA, and others.

Q: Can decent violence in self-defence under emergencies by any member of such volunteer organization be tolerated as an exception?
A: No, it cannot be. No such exception can be contemplated or provided against in advance, in an organization which is started specifically on the sole basis of non-violence. Such a person will have to leave the organization.

Q: 'Non-violent resistance is the best method; failing that, even violent decent resistance is tolerable but cowardice is unthinkable and condemnable'. That is what you have been preaching in this respect. But what you now say does not square with your above dictum.
A: That dictum is meant for those millions that have not yet accepted the creed of the Congress. It cannot apply to those organizations that are founded on the basic creed of non-violence. Those who desire to effect a change in the basic creed of non-violence must either change their General or go out of the organization.

Q: The Congress being largely suspended as an organization, what should be our policy this year as regards the annual enrolment of membership?

A: Under the circumstances there can be no obligation to enrol membership in the usual manner. New applicants, if they so desire, must however be enrolled as members and there should be no objection to realizing annual subscriptions from old members wherever practicable.

Q: Do you desire the starting of peace-brigades?
A: Certainly I do. Some time ago (*vide Harijan* 18th June 1938) I made certain concrete suggestions in that respect. I know very few will be found, at least in the beginning, to enlist in such an organization. A beginning may however be made by any small number or even singly. Such an organization cannot be conducted on the lines of democracy. It can only be a body of persons with a definite purpose. If the pioneers are the right sort of people they may gather followers in due course.

Q: What should be our attitude towards elections to local bodies?
A: As a rule, elections to such bodies should not be run in the name of the Congress. There may be no objection to Congressmen fighting the same on their individual responsibility. But this is a question which can be authoritatively decided only by Rajendra Babu and Acharya Kripalani.

Q: Can enrolled satyagrahis fight such elections individually?
A: No. I am quite clear on this point.

Q: What should be done in the case of those satyagrahis who have already put in their candidature for such elections?
A: They have either to withdraw from the election or from the satyagraha pledge; they cannot retain both.

Q: What should be the Congress attitude towards the registration of voters to the Legislatures—both central and provincial?
A: The Congress must pay full attention to this work. Congress may not ignore it.

---

[1] D.K. Gosavi was President of Maharashtra Provincial Congress Committee at the time. The Report was published in *The Bombay Chronicle* on 17 June 1941.
[2] See Document No. 44 in this Chapter.

39. Satyagraha in South India

The Hindu, 20 May 1941.

Mr K.K. Subbana Gounder, President, District Board, Coimbatore, who was arrested yesterday under the Defence of India Rules, was produced before Mr C. Ramachandran, Sub-Divisional Magistrate, who remanded him in custody for ten days. He was ordered to be given special treatment.

Previous to offering satyagraha, Mr K.K. Subbana Gounder auctioned the pieces of Khadi, woven out of the satyagrahis yarn. An amount Rs 130 was realized. He then explained the circumstances which led to the present satyagraha movement and in the end uttered anti-war slogans.

Lady Satyagrahi Sentenced

The Joint Magistrate Tindivanam, convicted and sentenced Srimati V.T. Krishnaveni Ammal, Member, South Arcot District Board and an ex-Municipal Councilor of Villupuram, who offered Satyagraha this morning, to three months SI and ordered her to be placed in 'B' class. She was taken to Vellore in the night.

Mr Sundaram Chettiar of Cuddalore was released from the Madras jail yesterday. Mr Shanmugam, Secretary of the Tindivanam Town Congress Committee, was released yesterday from the Cuddalore jail. Messrs S. Vaidyanathan, C.N. Dandapani, and C.S. Jayaraman, who were arrested at Madras on their march to Delhi, and sentenced to one month simple imprisonment, were also released yesterday.

Satyagraha at Salem

Messrs, T.V. Rangaswami Chettiar of Rasipuram and R. Varadarajan of Namakkal who were both tried yesterday by Mr S.A. Subhan Sahib, Sub-Divisional First Class Magistrate, Namakkal, were found guilty under the Defence of India Rules and sentenced to one month's rigorous imprisonment each.

Messrs V. Shunmukham Pillai and T.S. Arumukham who offered satyagraha this morning at Salem were both taken to the Salem Town Police station.

Mr A. Natesan who offered satyagraha last evening at Namakkal by shouting anti-war slogans was not arrested.

No Arrest at Periyakulam

Messrs Echappa Gounder, A.M.K. Krishnaswami Gounder (Kamayagoundanpatti), R. Dhimmayya, M. Mohamed Nainar Rowther, S.P. Narayanan (Cumbum), T. Karuppayya, (Guzhanur), Ayyappa Naicker (Narayanapuram), and Muthukkalai Thevar (Valandur) offered Satyagraha on Thursday at Periyakulam by shouting anti-war slogans.

A public meeting was later held at the Gandhi Maidan. At the close of the meeting the satyagrahis shouted anti-war slogans. But they were not arrested.

Messrs S. Muthuswami, President of the Gandamanaickanur Circle Congress Committee, S. Raju, President of the Anaipatty ValSangham and M.M. Raju of Anaipatty, who had visited more than 130 villages covering about 220 miles during the satyagraha march, arrived at Periyakulam to-day. They went round the streets shouting anti-war slogans. They also addressed a public meeting held at the Gandhi Maidan.

Arrest at Tanjore

Eight satyagrahis, who were not arrested till now, including a lady, of the Madura District, arrived here yesterday, on their march to Delhi. Mr Venkasami, one of the party, was arrested at the Congress House, Tanjore, by the Dindigul Police under the Defence of India Rules and taken to Dindigul.

Akkur Satyagrahi Not Arrested

Mr A.S. Kulanthavadivelu Pillai, a native of Akkur, offered satyagraha the day before yesterday at Akkur before a large gathering. As he was not arrested by the police, he started on a march to Delhi.

Mr N. Krishnayyan, who was arrested by the Town police under the Defence of India Rules for carrying on anti-war propaganda, and who was kept in remand day before yesterday, since the Town Police did not file any charge-sheet against him.

A batch of nine satyagrahis arrived here this morning from Kumbakonam on their way to Delhi. They went round the town uttering anti-war slogans.

Sentences at Cuddalore

Mr Vittal Srinivasa Rao was convicted under the Defence of India Rules and sentenced to-day by the local Sub-Divisional Magistrate, Mr Muhammad Abdul Kadir Dulvi, to six months rigorous imprisonment and to pay a fine of Rs 100, in default to undergo six weeks further imprisonment for shouting anti-war slogans this morning in Tirupapuliyur. He was placed in 'C' class.

Mr M.V. Balakrishna Nayudu was convicted and sentenced to-day under the Town Nuisance Act by the local Sub Magistrate, Mr U. Panchapagesa Sastri to eight days simple imprisonment for causing obstruction to traffic this morning in Manjakuppam by gathering a crowd near him.

Messrs R.K. Ramaswami and P.K. Ananthan of Bhavani, who were sentenced to one year SI in January last by the Deputy Collector of Gobichettipalayam, were taken to Alipuram Jail yesterday.

The following satyagrahis from Negapatam taluk have come here in the course of their march towards Delhi:

Mr Sathivadivel, who offered satyagraha on 2 May visited one twenty villages and addressed 27 public meetings. Mr Krishnaswami, who offered satyagraha on 2 May, visited 106 villages, covering 126 miles and addressed a public meeting. Mr S. Natesa Padayachi visited 126 villages covering 130 miles and addressed 29 public meetings.

Satyagraha at Tiruvannamalai

A public meeting under the auspices of the Town Satyagraha Committee, was held last night at the Jawahar Maidan with Mr G. Varadarajulu in the chair. Messrs S. Venkatswami Naidu of Ponneri, K. Rangaswami Chettiar, N.P. Ramachandran, and N.K. Mannikam spoke on the present political condition of India and appealed to the gathering to support the constructive programme of the Congress. At the close of the meeting they offered satyagraha by shouting anti-war slogans. They were not arrested.

Mr S. Krishnamurti offered satyagraha on 9 May at his native place Padagam, Polur taluk, by shouting anti-war slogans. He was not arrested.

Mr Munuswami, who offered satyagraha on 13 May, at Pillukadai Maidan by shouting anti-war slogans, was not arrested.

Andhradesa

Politicals Brought from Nagpur

In addition to the six Bellary satyagrahis brought here from Nagpur on 15 May, Messrs A. Venkata Reddi of Peddakadubur, ex-President of the Andhra District Congress Committee, and M. Bhima Rao were brought here yesterday. All the eight persons are kept on the Cowl Bazaar Station, pending receipt of further orders from higher authorities regarding their cases.

Satyagrahis Released

Messrs G. Venkata Reddi, Ch. V. Ramaneedu, and N. Suryanarayanarazu of the West Godavari District who were arrested at Nagpur and brought here and remanded in custody in the local sub-jail by Mr P. Tirupathi, Stationary Sub Magistrate, were released yesterday.

40. Satyagraha in Andhradesa: Over Thousand Arrests so Far

The Hindu, 22 May 1941.

The President of Andhra Provincial Congress Committee, has issued the following statement regarding the progress of Satyagraha for the period of six months ending with the 5th May, 1941, from 26 November 1940.

During this period of six months the satyagraha movement was carried on with great vigour and enthusiasm in the fourteen districts of Andhra. Of the 2,161 approved satyagrahis who offered civil disobedience; 1,115 were arrested, prosecuted and convicted; 1,046 were either not arrested at all or were let off some time after arrest.

These 1,046 satyagrahis have been engaging themselves, according to Gandhiji's instructions, in propaganda for which a special programme has been chalked out and is in operation in all the districts. They have covered not less than 4,919 villages; thirteen of them, who were marching to Delhi were arrested, 12 at Nagpur and one at Cuttack.

Fines imposed on the satyagrahis amount to Rs 1,06,658-2-0.

Thirty-four Muslims, 37 Harijans, and 65 ladies are among the civil resisters.

During the month under review the District Agents of West Godavari, Cuddapah, and Anantapur were arrested and convicted. According to Districts, in North Vizag 29 offered satyagraha, 26 were convicted; in South Vizag 54 offered satyagraha, 38 were convicted; in East Godavari 243 offered satyagraha, 126 were convicted; in West Godavari 257 offered satyagraha, 128 were convicted; in East Kistna 71 offered satyagraha, 55 were convicted; in West Kistna 110 offered satyagraha, 89 were convicted; in Guntur 454 offered satyagraha, 160 were convicted, in Nellore 117 offered satyagraha, 66 were convicted; in Chittoor 105 offered satyagraha, 62 were convicted; in Cuddapah 243 offered satyagraha, 38 were convicted; in Anantapur 288offered satyagraha, 70 were convicted; in Bellary 22 offered satyagraha, 12 were convicted; in Madras 44 offered satyagraha, all were convicted; 70 Legislators and AICC members offered satyagraha and all of them were convicted.

41. Intelligence Bureau's Note on Primary Membership of Congress, Dated 24 May 1941

File No. 4/7/41-Poll (I), Intelligence Bureau, Home (Political) Department, Government of India, NAI.

Below is a statement showing figures of primary Congress membership in the various provinces during the past three years:

Province	**Figures for**		
	1938–9	**1939–40**	**1940–1**
Ajmer-Merwara	13,151	6,700	6,250
Assam	37,321	56,633	56,000
Bengal	4,83,158	4,40,729	2,18,878
Bihar	5,63,269	2,76,704	1,83,731

(*Contd*) ...

... (*Contd*)

Province	Figures for		
	1938–9	1939–40	1940–1
Bombay			
(a) Bombay City and Suburbs.	661,936	60,368	18,631
(b) Maharashtra	1,48,544	1,15,137	87,240
(c) Karnatak	1,72,113	75,426	28,312
(d) Gujerat	92,418	80,101	55,231
Central Provinces			
(a) Nagpur	44,854	42,418	22,638
(b) Mahakoshal	1,26,554	1,10,119	Not received
(c) Vidarbha	78,396	44,733	14,878
Delhi	19,423	11,956	7,974
Madras			
(a) Tamil Nadu	3,64,393	2,06,152	
(b) Andhra	3,35,205	2,05,771	
(c) Kerala	55,031	49,266	
Total	7,54,629	4,61,189	3,12,418
NWFP	34,397	23,815	15,985
Orissa (Utkal)	1,98,325	1,26,126	45,792
Punjab	1,88,791	1,89,289	1,10,289
Sind	22,303	18,179	12,667
United Provinces	14,72,456	8,33,830	2,58,826
Total	45,11,858	29,73,452	14,81,616

Primary membership of the Indian National Congress during 1940–1 shows a steep decline. Compared with the immediately preceding corresponding period, the fall in all-India membership exceeds 50 per cent, while in certain parts of the country such as Bombay City and Suburbs and the United Provinces, membership has fallen by as much as 70 per cent approximately. It is possible that owing to the general disorganization of Provincial Congress offices as a result of the civil disobedience movement, a certain amount of inexactitude has crept into the figures for this year, but there is no reason to suppose that the figures are fundamentally inaccurate. The sharp decrease of about 33 per cent in the figures for 1939–40, as compared with those for 1938–9, was attributable primarily to the enforcement of a strict enlistment system as part of measures adopted that year to stamp out corruption in the Congress organization, but the 1940–1 decrease by more than 50 per cent over the preceding year is not wholly traceable to the same cause—except to a minor extent in Delhi. There is no information whether permanent registers of Congress members, prescribed in the revised Congress constitution of 1939, have actually been started, but it is certain that the present decrease in membership is due not to any change in the mode of enumeration but directly to failure to renew membership. The defection of Leftists (for example, the Royist group) and the arrest of several important organizers during the period immediately preceding the last date of enrolment had an adverse effect on recruitment. Postponement this year of general elections to various

Congress Committees and Executives deprived potential contestants of important appointments in the Congress organization of the most powerful incentive to insist on their respective supporters enlisting in large numbers. For the same reason, bogus membership was probably less prevalent last year than formerly. The resignation of Congress ministries caused a slackening of interest in Congress affairs but it would be unsafe to assume that Congress has become unpopular or noticeably lost its influence over the masses in provinces where it previously held undisputed sway. Anti-Congress activities of the Muslim League, the Hindu Mahasabha, and other political parties increased appreciably during the past year and were to some extent responsible for detaching 'waverers' from active association with Congress.

In Assam a large number of members were enlisted without realization of the usual membership fees, and many of those who were entrusted with the work of enrolling members misappropriated whatever amounts were realized.

The remarkable decrease in membership in Bengal is attributed to the open split which took place in 1940 between Bose's followers and the 'official' Congress organization. Separate figures are given of members of the recognized Provincial Congress Committee and the suspended Congress Committee. The suspended Committee and its allied groups did not participate in the recruitment drive last year. Reports show that in thirteen districts, the suspended Committee on its own enlisted 25,186 members.

In Bihar, the fall is due chiefly to (1) the preoccupation of Congress controlled local bodies in 'parish pump' politics and the consequent failure of members to devote attention to enrolment, (2) inter-caste ill-feeling and (3) wide-spread corruption in Congress executives which led to loss of Congress influence. One report attributes the decrease in Congress membership to 'sympathy for the British owing to their straightforward conduct of the war'.

In Bombay, there was apparently a general lack of enthusiasm in Congress matters at any rate till the commencement of the civil disobedience movement, although Congress itself continues to be as powerful as ever in this Province and capable of regaining the confidence of the people. The decrease in Gujrat is attributed partly to the fact that Congress workers were engaged in plans for the launching of the civil disobedience movement and paid little attention to the routine enrolment of primary Congress members. In Maharashtra the activities of the Hindu Mahasabha, the Muslim League, and the Independent Labour Party had some effect in slowing down recruitment, while in the Karnatak the discord between the Brahmins and Lingayats over the Ramdurg affair resulted in considerably diminished support for Congress from the Lingayat community.

The decrease in the Central Provinces and Berar is due partly to the inability of the late Congress government to do anything substantial for its supporters, and partly to anti-Congress propaganda carried on by the Hindu Mahasabha and the Muslim League. In anticipation of early arrest in connexion with satyagraha, Congress workers took little interest in the enrolment of members. (Figures of membership in Mahakoshal are not so far available).

Bogus membership has decreased in Delhi and with the defection of Shankarlal Bansal, corruption is less rampant.

The fact that the Congress Ministry is out of office with no immediate prospect of returning to power is considered largely responsible for the slump in Congress stock in Madras. Executive action against the Leftists of Kerala, who control Congress work in Malabar, was directly responsible for the decrease in Congress enrolment in that part of the Province.

All districts in the North-West Frontier Province have contributed to the decrease in the number of primary members, but the falling off is more marked in the Bannu and Dera Ismail

Khan districts where the people, particularly Hindus, have been concerned more with the protection of their lives and property from tribal depredations than with politics. The general decrease is ascribed to the growing unpopularity of the Congress, which, when in office, failed to fulfil its election pledges and later resigned for reasons which the general public, who are anxious to assist in the war, could not appreciate.

In Orissa the decrease is regarded as the result of (1) more stringent checking of members enrolled consequent upon a demand made by the Provincial Congress Committee that 75 per cent of the fees realized from members should be remitted to District Congress Committees by primary Congress Committees, and (2) Congress popularity which has been on the wane in this Province for some time. In Puri, enrolment was deliberately continued for about ten days beyond the prescribed date to enhance the district figure, but not much success was obtained in increasing membership.

In the Punjab, the reasons for the decrease are (a) continued internal strife in the Provincial Congress organization, (b) decrease in the Akali support for Congress, (c) arrest of active members, (d) absence of assistance in recruitment work from the Congress Socialist Party and (e) a general decline in public sympathy.

The fall in Sind is mainly ascribed to the fact that the Provincial Congress concentrated on the enrolment of satyagraha volunteers for the civil disobedience movement, which was ultimately not permitted, and consequently Congress Committees in Sind took little interest in the enrolment of members.

The sensational decline in the United Provinces is explained principally to be the result of 'lack of interest in political affairs generally and Congress in particular, more especially in rural areas. It should also be noted that the enrolment of these primary members took place after the Congress Ministry resigned, when the influence of Congress in districts had declined very heavily.' Further, in this Province, there have been defections of a large number of pseudo Congressmen, who had joined in the hope of capturing positions of power and patronage, and the opposition of non-Congress organizations has been steadily developing.

Home Ministry's Comments

The facts and figures given in the Intelligence Bureau's note of the 20th May are very interesting and significant and I think that they might be of use to the Secretary of State. The decline of Congress membership between 1938–9 and 1939–40 may largely have been due to Gandhi's attempt to purge the Congress registers of bogus names. But the further decline between 1939–40 and 1940–1 has no such major explanation and must in the main be taken to represent a real loss of ground in the country. The enumeration of causes for this decline province by province is of considerable interest as revealing the various factors on which Congress influence has been based. I agree with the thinking that the most significant cause is that stated in brief with reference to the Province of Madras, namely 'the fact that the Congress Ministry is out of office with no immediate prospect of returning to power'. This cause, of course, covers the remark made in the case of the United Provinces that the defections represent a large number of pseudo-Congressmen who had joined in the hope of capturing positions of power and patronage. The latter remark is somewhat difficult to reconcile with the view expressed by the Governor of the United Provinces in his recent note on the Satyagraha movement that the expectation of a return to power of the Congress is responsible both for the number of persons coming forward to offer Satyagraha and for a certain lack of initiative on the part of the Police in taking anti-Congress measures. I think, however, that the general inference to be drawn is that while it is doubtless true that if any circumstances occurred to restore the prestige and, therefore, fear of Congress, membership and support would no doubt revive, apart from such circumstances there is little genuine enthusiasm lying behind the support which Congress received in its days of influence, and if it became clear that Congress had become a 'back number' in the political field interest, in its activities and programme would soon vanish altogether and be diverted to the parties in whose hands the real power lay.

2. Whether this inference is right or not, however, the figures of membership for 1940–1 once more demonstrate the hollowness of the Congress claim to represent the whole country. A membership of under 15,00,000 in a population of 400,000,000 gives it no such status, nor does it leave any justification for the idea which interested advocates have sedulously propagated at home that Congress is the only political party capable of representing the nationalist movement in this country and, therefore, entitled to be treated with exaggerated deference and forbearance. This fact, if recognized, may be of great importance at the present juncture.

Initials
(Home Member)
24.5.41

42. Rabindranath Tagore's Statement on Eleanor Rathbone's 'Open Letter'

CWMG, Vol. LXXIV, pp. 401–3.

Santiniketan
4 June 1941

I have been deeply pained at Miss Rathbone's[1] open letter to Indians. I do not know who Miss Rathbone is, but I take it that she represents the mentality of the average 'well-intentioned' Britisher. Her letter is mainly addressed to Jawaharlal and I have no doubt that if that noble fighter of freedom's battle had not been gagged behind prison bars by Miss Rathbone's countrymen, he would have made a fitting and spirited reply to her gratuitous sermon. His enforced silence makes it necessary for me to voice my protest even from my sick-bed.

The lady has ill served the cause of her people by addressing so indiscreet, indeed impertinent, a challenge to our conscience. She is scandalized at our ingratitude,—that having 'drunk deeply at the wells of English thought' we should still have some thought left for our poor country's interests. English thought, in so far as it is representative of the best traditions of Western enlightenment, has indeed taught us much, but let me add, those of our countrymen who have profited by it have done so despite the official British attempts to ill-educate us. We might have achieved introduction to Western learning through any other European language. Have all the other peoples in the world waited for the British to bring them enlightenment?

It is sheer insolent self-complacence on the part of our so-called English friends to assume that had they not 'taught' us we would still have remained in the dark ages. Through the official British channels of education in India have flowed to our children in schools not the best of English thought but its refuse, which has only deprived them of wholesome repast at the table of their own culture.

Assuming, however, that the English language is the only channel left to us for 'enlightenment', all that 'drinking deeply at its wells' has come to is that in 1931, even after a couple of centuries of British administration, only about one per cent of the population was found to be literate in English,—while in the USSR in 1932, after only fifteen years of Soviet administration, 98 per cent of the children were educated. (These figures are taken from *The Statesman's Year-Book*, an English publication, not likely to err on the Russian side.)

But even more necessary than the so-called culture are the bare elementary needs of existence, on which alone can any super-structure of enlightenment rest. And what have the British who have held tight the purse-strings of our nation for more than two centuries and exploited its resources done for our poor people?

I look around and see famished bodies crying for bread. I have seen women in villages dig up mud for a few drops of drinking water; for wells are even more scarce in Indian villages than schools. I know that the population of England itself is today in danger of starvation and I sympathize with them, but when I see how the whole might of the British navy is engaged in convoying food vessels to the English shores and when I recollect that I have seen our people perish of hunger and not even a cart-load of rice brought to their door from the neighbouring district, I cannot help contrasting the British at home with the British in India. Shall we then be grateful to the British, if not for keeping us fed, at least for preserving law and order? I look around and see riots raging all over the country. When scores of Indian lives are lost, our property looted, our women dishonoured, the mighty British arms stir in no action, only the British voice is raised from overseas, to chide us for our unfitness to put our house in order.

Examples are not wanting in history when even fully armed warriors have shrunk before superior might and contingencies have arisen in the present war when the bravest among the British, French, and Greek soldiers have had to evacuate the battle-field in Europe because they were overwhelmed by superior armaments—but when our poor, unarmed, and helpless peasants, encumbered with crying babes, flee from homes unable to protect them from armed goondas, the British officials perhaps smile in contempt at our cowardice.

Every British civilian in England is armed today for protecting his hearth and home against the enemy, but in India even lathi-training was forbidden by decree. Our people have been deliberately disarmed and emasculated, in order to keep them perpetually cowed, and at the mercy of their armed masters. The British hate the Nazis for merely challenging their world mastery and Miss Rathbone expects us to kiss the hand of her people in servility for having riveted chains on ours. A government must be judged not by pretensions of its spokesmen but by its actual and effective contribution to the well-being of the people.

It is not so much because the British are foreigners that they are unwelcome to us and have found no place in our hearts as because while pretending to be trustees of our welfare they have betrayed the great trust and have sacrificed the happiness of millions of India to bloat the pockets of a few capitalists at home. I should have thought that the decent Britisher would at least keep silent at these wrongs and be grateful to us for our inaction, but that he should add insult to injury and pour salt over our wounds passes all bounds of decency.

---

[1] Eleanor F. Rathbone, an independent member of British Parliament, wrote an *Open Letter to Indian Friends* on 28 May 1941. Jawaharlal Nehru, in the long reply he wrote on 22 June 1941 (*SWJN*, Vol. 11, pp. 610–36) referred to the statement which Rabindranath Tagore had issued on the 'Open Letter' on 4 June 1941. Mahatma Gandhi, when asked about the British MP's letter by *The Hindu* correspondent, said, 'After Tagore's reply, should I say anything? Nothing.' (*CWMG*, Vol. LXXIV, p. 107)

43. Satyagraha Movement: The Stock-taking, by Mahadev Desai

The Hindu, 11 and 12 June 1941.

The second phase of satyagraha is over and we may well take stock of the situation. The movement by its very nature precludes calculation of material result. For its immediate objective is vindication of an elementary right, which we achieve, either by a free exercise of it or by courting imprisonment in the process. In the North-West Frontier Province the liberty is said to have been won, though the Government have not declared freedom of speech and pen. They simply do not arrest the satyagrahis, therefore it pays them not to do so. But our taking stock must not mean examination of what Governments are doing or not doing. We have to examine whether we have been acquitting ourselves of our task. The movement is part of the fight for Independence and therefore one of steady growth in us of truth, non-violence, and self-purification.

Severe tests were imposed this time upon the satyagrahis unlike as in previous movements, and so we have voluntarily exposed ourselves to the criticism of opponents. It will be idle to pretend that all has been well. Several complaints against satyagrahis have been received, but while some of them have been well-founded, many have been unfounded. Satyagrahis, we were told had been having a merry time or it, ordering things and eatables from outside and whiling away the best part of their opportunity. These can be few, if only because many will not be allowed any such things. But there are authentic accounts from various jails of many of them making the best of their time.

Shri Vinoba's Work

Shri Vinoba and his work every one knows and so about Pandit Jawaharlalji and Ranjit Pandit. All are able to give a good account of every minute of their time which is divided between spinning and reading or writing. But they are living in isolation. Let us cast a glance at those who are living in company. On the day Vinoba was arrested for the second time he sent just two lines to Gandhiji to say: 'With your blessings I have been able to make a good deal of headway in non-violence and purification of thought.' On the day he was released from prison he was loaded by his fellow-prisoners with yarn of their own spinning. This he got woven into several yards of Khadi before he went back to his old home in two days. So many who had never handled a carding bow before are good carders now and every one has been vying with the other in speed tests. Shri Brahmadatta, now released, beat all in attaining the maximum speed of 150 rounds in half an hour on the takli and Pyarelal has beaten all his previous records in fine counts. The latter has taken a whole library of the Qurans with him and bids fair to return an Arabic and Quranic scholar. The daily ritual of a half hour's congregational prayer is observed by all with practically no exception.

And if Shri Vinoba has done excellent work in jail, Sardar Vallabhbhai has done still better. For when he was outside he had little time for constructive work. Inside he used all his time for it. Everyone of his companions spins, and it must not be forgotten that among them are ex-Ministers like Shris, Kher and Gilder and his colleague on the Congress Cabinet, Shri Bhulabhai, who by the way, tried to fill up his lapse in Sanskrit learning by reading *Yoga Sutra* with Shri Munshi (now released because of illness). How I wish I could translate Sardar Vallabhbhai's Gujarati letters reproducing his idiom and his homely direct style. He gets up at four o'clock, devotes three-quarters of an hour everyday to a reading of *The Gita*, and *Mangal Prabhat*, looks after the varying comforts of his companions, and keeps them merry; there is regular spinning, and there are regular congregntional prayers:' We begin with the Ashram prayer, the Mian Saheb Nuri recites the Quran, and then Dr Gilder reads something form his scriptures. After this we have a hymn and then Ramdhoon. We read until nine o'clock when every one goes to bed. We are as punctual as a clock and so one never knows how time files.' As Shri Munshi has said in an article written since his release, the little yard with the hallowed associations of Gandhiji's fast against the Premier's Award has been converted by these political leaders into something very like a monastery.

News from the Punjab is mixed. I have letters to say that some who have signed the Satyagrahi's pledge and apparently spun and worn Khadi when outside have in jail foresworn their belief in both and openly declare that that was part of their game. Such things could not possibly be prevented in a big organization, but let us remember that hypocrites and deceivers ultimately deceive themselves. But there are a good many trusted and true men who are making the best of their time, doing their daily spinning prayer and study. Some of the Delhi friends were slack in spinning in the beginning, but all are doing it now....

Constructive Work in India

Let us look at the South. Two gentlemen just released from Trichinopoly Jail said that in the beginning there was some difficulty about getting the wheels. It was only in March that every one was allowed to have his own wheel and keep his own yarn. Almost every one is spinning. Once every week, there is congregational spinning. Rajaji takes a class in *The Gita* every day, learns Sanskrit and Urdu himself. Rajaji's own letter, received before these friends came, is a sample of his vivid epigrammatic style. 'Tell Bapu my love', he writes. 'I got his sweet little note sent through Narasimham. Evergreens are precious and stand all the delays of prison correspondence, I am quite happy, tell him. I am spinning and reading and completely avoid thinking of politics. I read with a good company of scholars and others, everyday some Valmiki, some Kural, some Bhagwad Gita, and some Tamil holy Vaishnavite books. Eighty-two beautiful chapters of Valmiki are over, so also, thirty chapters of Kural and few hundred verses of the Alwars (Tamil Vaishnava saints). The Gita has been done once rapidly and again taken up for reading with Shankara and Ramanuja. What a lot of hard nuts one finds. The simple faith of good men found in the Alwars writings is like honey. But what avails it to a hard heart like what I have! I have re-read a few plays of Shakespeare with some young boys. What a great man this ancient giant was.'

'My late colleague, Harijan Minister, Muniswami Pillai is working hard spreading the practice of the Charkha among us. He is a propagandist saint and engineer combined. He is my next bed—and looks after me like a mother. So also some others, including Dr Rajan and Bapineedu, Satyamurti is well but does not get as much sleep as he should.'

'Shri Satyamurti, by the by is in the Hospital with an acute attack of diabetes and insomnia. May he recover soon!'

Progress in Bengal and UP

News from UP like the Punjab is mixed. I have received information from two sources, which I cannot disbelieve to the effect that the bulk of the Satyagrahis in two districts are neither khadi-wearers nor spinners. Indeed, Three Satyagrahis themselves that their names had been included in the list, though they were neither Khadi-wearers nor spinners. Senders of list should not be surprised if the lists are more strictly scanned. I was surprised the other day to have a telephone call from a District to say that Satyagrahis in the prison of that district would do no task, unless they were ordered by Gandhiji to do so!!

There are very few good workers left in UP. The Government there have imprisoned most good workers, although they had not offered civil disobedience. They have not even left out Shri Dhiren Majumdar who is no politician, and who has been a constructive worker all these many years and who was when arrested even doing Government rural work. He has not been charged. He is simply detained. He does not know why.

In Bengal Dr Prafulla Ghosh is having a very busy time with regular spinning (five hundred yards an hour), study of the Gita with a Sanskrit scholar, and writing text-books in science. Shri Nibaran Chandra Sarkar in Comilla Jail has an extra-ordinary amount of spinning to his credit—75,000 yards in February, 65,000 in March, 45,000 yards upto 26th April. He has spun less in March and April, as he is devoting plenty of time to teaching and introducing spinning among the ordinary convicts, in co-operation with the jail authorities. Dr Nirpendra Nath Bose in Dum Dum Jail spins 750 yards daily and devotes six hours to study. Shri Kshitish Chandra Roy Chaudhri spins fifty yards daily and studies the Quran for six hours.

News from Assam was scarce, but now there is a letter from Shri Gopinath Bardoloi which gives an eloquent account of the life in Gauhati Jail. He is writing a book in Assamese on the Prophets and Teachers of Mankind and has asked one or two questions arising from his studies. He then writes: 'I am quite at peace with the life that we are leading, there is nothing to disturb our tranquility or even equanimity. There are other friends of our Assembly, Mian Fakhruddin Ali Ahmed, Ex-President, Provincial Congress Committee, and Deweshwar Sharma, our Chief Whip, is staying in a high-walled compound which was meant for some detenus. But the place is good nevertheless and the ground spacious for four people. We have two MLAs in another ward far away from us. We are a small party of Congress MLAs supposed to be functioning even now, for all the proceedings and papers connected with the Assembly come to us. I feel we are all making good use of our time. I spin about four hours and the average output is never below 1,000 yards. Shankar Barua spins about 1,000 to 2,000 yards daily, possibly a good record for any Satyagrahi. In presenting the list of MLA Satyagrahis before you I noted indifferent spinners against names of some of us, and not a regular spinner against Shri Bishnu Ram Medhi. My joy knew no bounds when I found that all produced better yarn than I. I feel I am not less busy in important matters now than when outside.'

There are the Delhi marchers or those who are not arrested. These easily number a few thousands. Some of them have covered themselves with glory. I have in mind Shrimati Damyanti Dharmadhikari and Shrimati Sharayutai Dhotre who carried the message of satyagraha and constructive programme to over eighty villages. Street cleaning, visit to the Harijan quarters, Congregational spinning and an evening meeting—this used to be their daily programme. Their tour was so effective that three temples were thrown open to the Harijans and an atmosphere of spinning and khadi was created wherever they went. Shrimati Prabhawati Jakatdar, the daughter-in-law of the veteran Satyagrahi Jakatdar, who paid heavy fines six times and earned six months imprisonment at last, is following in these two sisters' footsteps. The two are now having their well-earned rest in Nagpur Jail.

The work before these Delhi marchers is as interesting as it is difficult. In the Bengal villages a Satyagrahi has to go without food for several days because the villagers were afraid of entertaining a Satyagrahi, but his patience and perseverance converted a zamindar who undertook to see that he did not have to go without food wherever he went. Hundreds of

Satyagrahis in Andhra and Tamilnadu are having an experience of their lives. Here is an extract from a Tamilnad report:

> This is the reception we get. Come to my street or my part of the village and give the slogan they say. The Government Tahsildar, Deputy Tahsildar, Revenue Inspector, the Circle Inspector of Police, the Sub Inspector of Police, the Deputy Inspector of Schools, even the doctor of the adjoining village rural hospital—all came there several times'....

44. Instruction to Satyagrahis Issued by Congress General Secretary in Consultation with Mahatma Gandhi

CWMG, Vol. LXXIV, pp. 398–9.

17 June 1941

1. A released satyagrahi must seek to offer satyagraha as soon as possible. If for any reason he is unable to do so he must apply through President or officer-in-charge of the Provincial Congress Committee for exemption from Mahatma Gandhi and he should state the reasons for such exemption being granted.

2. From the date on which the name of a prospective satyagrahi is forwarded to Mahatma Gandhi for sanction, he is to suspend his private activities and devote himself wholly to working out one or more items of following thirteenfold items of the constructive programme:

(a) Hindu–Muslim or communal unity.
(b) Removal of untouchability.
(c) Prohibition.
(d) Khadi.
(e) Other village industries.
(f) Village sanitation.
(g) New or Basic Education.
(h) Adult education.
(i) Uplift of women.
(j) Education in hygiene and health.
(k) The propagation of Rashtrabhasha.
(l) Cultivating love of one's own language.
(m) Working for economic equality.

3. Every prospective satyagrahi is expected to keep a diary in which he will enter the work done by him during the day and this diary will be submitted to the Provincial Congress Committee concerned at fortnightly intervals. Permission to offer satyagraha shall be granted only to such workers who have proved their worth by their everyday work.

4. The new restrictions in passing lists of satyagrahis are considered necessary in the interest of the struggle as it is likely to develop in future and will become progressively more arduous. New satyagrahis that come in should, therefore, be such as can stand the new test. Complaints have been received in the office of undue delay in passing names. Those who have given their names need not, however, feel impatient at the delay. They should devote the interval to carrying out the constructive programme.

If any satyagrahi who has enrolled himself on the original basis feels unable to accept the new terms, he is free to withdraw his name and there will be no disgrace attached to any such withdrawal. He may continue to render whatever other service he can to the country. He remains a Congressman as before.

5. Enrolled satyagrahis cannot contest elections to the local bodies. Those who have put in their candidature for such elections, before being enlisted as satyagrahis, have either to withdraw from election or from offering satyagraha. As satyagrahis they cannot be in both places.

6. No released satyagrahi who is a member of a local board, unless specially exempted by Mahatma Gandhi, can attend its meeting. If he does, his name will be expunged from the list of satyagrahis.

7. Unarrested satyagrahis who are touring in their districts and those whose names have been approved are not to attend meetings of local bodies.

8. During the monsoons a satyagrahi may, if necessary, establish himself in a village, not his own, or a group of villages, and carry on satyagraha and constructive activities.

9. Unarrested satyagrahis, either touring in their districts or marching in the direction of Delhi, should send fortnightly reports of their work to the provincial office. The Provincial Congress Committees in turn will send a consolidated report of their work to the All-India Congress Committee office at stated intervals, fortnightly or monthly.

10. Complaints have been received about the intemperance of language of certain satyagrahis. Satyagrahis should know that vituperation and abuse are against both the spirit and letter of satyagraha and must, therefore, be invariably avoided.

45. Extracts from Fortnightly Reports on Satyagraha and Other Political Developments in Madras Province (April to June 1941)

Fortnightly Reports from Government of Madras to Conran Smith, Secretary to the Government of India, Home Department, Public (General) Department, Tamil Nadu State Archives.

(i) Fortnightly Report Dated 19 April 1941 for the First Half of April 1941

DO No. B. 4–8

My dear Conran Smith,

War: In my last report I referred to rumours of disquiet in the Vizagapatam fortress area. It is now reported that there has been one incident between some British soldiers and some Indian women which led to a very minor disturbance resulting in slight injuries to one soldier. The military authorities have placed, the town out of bounds and no further trouble is anticipated.

Satyagraha has continued in all districts, and in Madras there have been a few cases of disorderly behaviour which have been dealt with under the City Police Act. In Anantapur, some of those who had given notice of offering Satyagraha failed to do so. The policy of dealing with offenders under the nuisance sections of ordinary law has been continued with success and a very large number of unimportant Satyagrahis have been ignored. But on the whole the persons coming forward were of little or no importance. Two districts report an increase in activity, while four other districts report a lull in the progress of the movement. In several districts more important Congressmen who have been working behind the scheme, organizing meetings and occasions for the performance of Satyagraha, have been prosecuted and convicted for the offence of abetment. The number of Satyagrahis undertaking the march to Delhi showed some increase, but many of them have found their way beset with unexpected difficulties and once they have left their own district they have discovered that it becomes increasingly difficult to obtain free food from the inhabitants of the villages through which they pass. Some of those affected, have reported the matter to Mr Gandhi, and he has directed to them to return to their own districts and content themselves with moving from village to village without the necessity of continuing their march to Delhi. These wanderers are taking to door-to-door propaganda, as well as the now normal shouting of slogans, but this new technique is reported to be having extremely little effect on the general public. A public meeting was held at Cuddalore on the occasion of the release of two women who had completed their sentence for the offence of Satyagraha. These women complained of the absence of enthusiasm among women generally for the movement and told the audience not to be afraid of jail life as though the food was bad, other conveniences were provided. Another woman who had been released after serving here sentence has refused to offer Satyagraha again because she found that her family had suffered during her absence, and there are indications that others of the more important persons who have gone to jail are not likely to be willing to court imprisonment again after their release.

Political: The recent arrests have considerably reduced the activities of the Communist Party, but there has been a serious disturbance in South Kanara district where the Karshaka Sangha organized an attack on a police constable (as stated in my last report) which has resulted in his death. After the crime has been committed all those who had taken part fled to the surrounding jungle and it has been necessary to call out the Reserve Police and three platoons of the Malabar Special Police to comb out the jungle in search of the culprits. So far 34 have been arrested.

Owing to the enforcement of the rules for the classification of detenus there is trouble in the Vellore Jail and 74 detenus are now on hunger strike. Arrangements have been made to reinforce the jail staff to enable them to deal with the hunger strikers. A number of the strikers have asked to be forcibly fed, and refusal to comply with this request has caused some of them to give up their fast. A detailed report on this subject is being sent to the Government of India separately. There has also been a hunger strike by 170 convicted prisoners in Alipuram Jail, partially the sympathy with the detenus and partly to protest against their own classification....

Appendix I
Report on the Press for the First Half of April 1941

The attitude of newspapers in regard to the War continued to be quite satisfactory. Mr Churchill's reference to the part played by the Indian troops in the campaign in East Africa and was also noticed by certain newspapers.

Pakistan has loomed large in comments in newspapers in Southern India during the fortnight. Muslim papers have strongly criticized the condemnation of Pakistan by Sir Launcelot Graham, ex-Governor of Sind. *The London Times*, which criticized the Scheme, also came in for some amount of criticism by the same section of the Press. But the Nationalist papers and also the Mail have strongly criticized that session of the All India Muslim League.

The Bombay Moderate Conference received a good Press. Barring a few newspapers who are out and out Congress minded, there was a general disposition to welcome the resolutions adopted at that Conference. Mr Amery's repeated statement that the August offer stands was sharply and strongly criticized by the Nationalist press. *The Hindu*, for instance, characterized that offer as eternal. *The Hindu*, on the other hand, has also demanded that the Congress should give up Satyagraha. It writes that it is vitally necessary that the Congress should function again as a Political organization and should, irrespective, of what Britain may or may not do or what reactionary groups in the country might threaten, take up the active leadership for the people as a whole, call off Satyagraha and mobilize their energies for positive practical purposes. It concludes its leading article on the subject which has received a good deal of attention as follows: 'The limited Satyagraha launched by Gandhiji cannot, by the very nature of the case, help very much so far as the dominant need of the country today is concerned.... That need is an active and robust political leadership which would weld the masses into a dynamic and irresistible power'.

(ii) Fortnightly Report Dated 3 May 1941 for the Second Half of April 1941

DO No. P. 4–9

My dear Conran Smith,

War: The Civil Disobedience Movement, has continued and Satyagraha has been offered, usually by quite unimportant persons, in most districts; but the number of new Satyagrahis coming forward has shown a marked decrease in several his sentences of imprisonment addressed a public meeting at which he laid great stress on the 'dreadful sufferings' which he had endured while in Jail, and was promptly asked by the friends (his) to refrain from making such speeches as they would be calculated to discourage others from coming forward to offer Satyagraha. Large numbers of unimportant offenders continue to be ignored and they are wandering about either in their own or in neighbouring districts, allegedly on the march to Delhi. One man from the North Arcot District has already reached Delhi. According to the newspaper report, he claims to have walked a distance of rather more than 1,500 miles in 29 days. It is reported that when he asked what he should do next, he was told by Mr Gandhi to return to his district and do constructive work. Many of the persons who have been ignored have gone to Madras and offered Satyagraha there which accounts for the relatively high number of convictions in the City. Others have been ordered to conduct house to house propaganda in specific areas, but it is reported that this form of propaganda is not having slightest effect and that the villagers are already becoming extremely tired of the demands made by these Satyagrahis for free food and lodging, with the result that the wanderers are tending to congregate in the towns where they can at least get some slight notice taken of them. In two districts there have been prosecutions of more important Congress workers for abetment and further prosecutions for this offence are under consideration. As usual several cases have been disposed of under the Town Nuisance Act.

Political: The 28th session of the All-India Muslim League was held in Madras from the 12th to the 15th April and was well attended. The principal resolution passed at the sessions was one which modified the constitution of the League to provide that 'Pakistan' should be the avowed aim of the League. Mr Jinnah in his main speech issued a warning to Government not to ignore the League when devising a constitution for India. At the same time a Conference of the Indian States' Muslim League was held under the Presidency of Nawab Yar Jung Bahadur but it was poorly attended.

Mr Amery's statement in the House of Commons on the constitutional question in India has caused considerable disappointment to Congressmen as it did not seem to them to provide a basis for the withdrawal of the Satyagraha movement without loss of prestige. Meetings were held in various areas by the Political party organizations, and National week was celebrated with a greater or less degree of enthusiasm, but on the whole these meetings were poorly attended and of little importance.

The Hindu Mahasabha proposes to held a Conference at Plani on 3rd May. This has been prohibited by the District Magistrate under Section 144 CrPC on account of the communal tension still prevalent in the Madura district while the trials of those responsible for the Moharrum disturbances are going on, and because it was understood that Mr Jinnah intended to visit the District at the same time. It is now understood that Mr Jinnah has cancelled this visit. The Government have decided not to interfere with the discretion of the District Magistrate in the matter.

Eighty of the persons detained under Rule 26 of the Defence of India Rules in the Central Jail, Vellore went on Hunger strike as a protest against the classification of detenus and especially against the diet given to those placed in Class II. Almost all the hunger strikers were communists. The strike lasted for 18 days during which time the number of strikers gradually diminished to fifty-four. The strike finally ended unconditionally and the question of punishing the offenders or the investigators is under consideration. The Government have, however, decided to improve the standard diet of class II detenus as on a reference to the Government of India it was found that the diet given to the Class II detenus here was markedly worse than that given to the Class II detenus in the Deoli Camp.

Appendix I
Report on the Press for the Second Half of April 1941

The session of the All India Muslim League held in Madras took up a good deal of newspaper space. While the Muslim papers and their friends in other sections of the press welcomed Pakistan, the whole of the nationalist press condemned the attitude of the Muslims and the change in the creed of the Muslim League declaring that Pakistan was the Muslim League's political objective. The Mail criticized the scheme, as born of distrust, and warned the Muslims that European experience was decidedly against the dividing up of India.

The speech of Mr Amery, Secretary of State for India, in the House of Commons, involving what is described as the rejection of the demand made by the Moderates in the Bombay Conference has been severely attacked by the Indian Press except the Muslim section and the 'Viduthalai' of Erode, the organ of Mr E.V. Ramaswami Naicker, now the leader of the Justice Party. Strong feelings have been expressed by the nationalist press and the Mail, the organ of the European community in Southern India, criticizes the 'do nothing' policy of Mr Amery, recommends that the Executive Council should be expanded and argues that if the Finance portfolio is given to an Indian he will soon get a following in the country.

(iii) Fortnightly Report Dated 18 May 1941 for the First Half of May 1941

My dear Conran Smith,

Though the Satyagraha movement has been continued in most of the districts of the Province during the fortnight, many of the District Magistrates report that the movement is steadily languishing. Fewer persons are coming forward to offer Satyagraha and less and less notice is taken by the general public of those who do. By far the larger number of Satyagrahis was ignored except in Madras City where all cases are prosecuted; this has had the effect of attracting to Madras many of those who have been ignored in other places. This was particularly noticeable in the figures reported in my last weekly telegram which showed that only six residents of the City offered Satyagraha while there were 55 who had come into the City from outside. Many of the earliest Satyagrhis who were awarded shorter sentences of imprisonment are now being released. The most prominent is the ex-Minister Dr Subbaroyan. Those who have been released are showing very little desire to repeat the offence and go back to Jail. At meetings held to welcome them on their release most of them have complained of the treatment netted out to political prisoners, but are very silent on question of going back to Jail again. That the movement is losing its momentum seems to be recognized by the Congress party leaders themselves and there are indications of a new turn being given to the form of Satyagraha in place of the shouting of anti-war slogans. Satyagrahis in some districts are being instructed to hold definite meetings at which anti-war speeches are delivered. In other parts the door to door propaganda method is being continued but neither of these meetings appears to be having the least effect upon the general public.

Political: The various parties held meetings in the districts but while of some of the Congress meetings a more definite anti-war attitude was apparent, the Muslim League and the Justice Party continued to favour Britain and the war effort in Madras City and in the North Arcot District the Khaskar movement seems to be gaining some ground. The Hindu Mahasabha did not hold their meeting at Palni in the Madura district in defiance of the ban imposed by the District Magistrate as they had threatened to do. In South Kanara District the rounding up of those members of the Karshaka Sangham concerned in the murder of a police constable continued and 58 out of the 61 accused against whom a charge sheet has been filed for the apprehended. The District Magistrate has asked hold the appointment of a Special First Class Magistrate to hold the preliminary enquiry. As I have previously reported, it was necessary to utilize the services of a contingent of the Malabar Special Police to assist in rounding up these culprits and as often is the case in such circumstances this has been followed by complaints of police excesses. The South Kanara District Board has appointed a Committee consisting of two right wing Congressmen, an English businessman, an influential Muslim leader and one other, to make an enquiry into these allegations.

In view of the character and importance of the persons comprising this Committee, the District Magistrate did not consider that there was any objection to its carrying out this enquiry and did not immediately report on this to the Government. The Government have ordered the District Magistrate to take up the enquiry himself and not to await the action of a Committee whose existence has no legal status or sanction....

(iv) Fortnightly Report Dated 3 June 1941 for the Second Half of May 1941

DO No. P. 4–11.

My dear Conran Smith,

War: Although the Satyagraha campaign has been continued, there is no doubt that it has lost much of its impetus. The policy of refusing to arrest any Satyagrahi who is not a person of real influence and importance continues to be effective and has possibly had not a little to do with the fact that many of the earlier Satyagrahis who were convicted and sentenced to terms of imprisonment and who are now being released in relatively large numbers are very unwilling to offer Satyagraha again. Many of them have definitely refused to do so. There does not appear to be any great increase in the numbers adopting the new technique of addressing Anti-War meetings instead of shouting slogans. There have been one or two Satyagrahis addressing meetings of this sort in which the speaker has openly professed pro-German sympathies. In all such cases prosecution has been launched. In a number of districts there is a definite lull in the movement and in some, interest, both on, the part of the protagonists and of the public, is steadily languishing. There are however still quite a large number of Satyagrahis who have been ignored, who are wandering from village to village and from district to district professedly on their way to Delhi. As a result of correspondence between the Government of Madras and the Government of the Central Provinces, this Government have issued orders that Satyagrahis marching to Delhi should be arrested, as far as possible, in the border districts of this province and sent back to the headquarters of their native districts where they are at once released. This has been done in order to prevent large numbers of these wanderers proceeding to other provinces to add to the difficulties of other Governments.

Mr Gandhi has permitted the Congress party in Madras City to contest the forthcoming bye-elections to the corporations on the issue of the Congress attitude to the War and particularly of contribution to the War fund. It is understood that the permission had been given on the definite understanding that if the Congress party still find itself in a minority in the corporation after the elections are over, the newly elected Congress candidates shall resign immediately.

Political: Meetings of the different political parties have been held in various parts of province. Congress propaganda meetings have increased very considerably in Madras City, partly due to the forthcoming Corporation elections and partly to the fact that a number of their leaders are now being released after completing their sentences of imprisonment. In Madras City also there appears to be a definite attempt to encourage the Khaksar movement and four branch offices have been established. Although the Khaksars profess allegiance to the Muslim League, few prominent members of the League have taken part in their activities. On the 25th May there was a Khaksar gathering attended by about 70, of whom rather more than 29 went out for a day's camp to a village just outside the city. Although this gathering did not actually break any rule with regard to the wearing of uniform, and other things, it was quite clear that they were only observing the law in the latter and not in the spirit and the Government have therefore prohibited absolutely the wearing of the Khaksar uniform and the carrying of Belchas. The Hindu Mahasabha has also been active in various parts of the province and their main contention is that the Hindus must organize to defend themselves against Muslim acts of aggression. To this end the Mahasabha is planning to enroll young Hindu men into some sort of a youth League. At many of the Congress meetings the chief subject of the speakers was a complaint of the harsh treatment meted out of political prisoners. There has been little communist activity but an important arrest has been effected in Malabar where K.P.R. Gopalan Nambiyar, a District board member and first accused in the rioting case relating to the murder of a Sub Inspector in the Protest Day riots last September, has at least been captured.

Law and Order: Four communist prisoners escaped from the Alipuram Jail in Bellary on the night of the 8th May. So far they have not been re-arrested despite vigorous action on the part of the police. It appears that the escape was effected with the connivance of the Jail guard a sin addition to breaking out of the building where they were supposed to be confined the prisoners had to get through two electrified fences. The guards concerned have been charged before the stationery Sub Magistrate. When a police party went to the Adi-Dravida quarters in a village in Chittoor district for the detection of offences against the Prohibition Act, the inhabitants of the Cheri was found in a very drunken state and in an attempt to prevent detection of the illicit distillation of arrack they attacked the police party in sufficient numbers to force them to withdraw until a party of Armed Reserve could be brought up. It was not, however, necessary to resort to force as by the time the Reserve Police arrived all the men in the Cheri had fled. The ringleaders have since been arrested. In East Godavari district a case has been registered under Rule 19(1) (a) and (c) of the Defence of India Rules against T. Ramalingayya for attempting to send a private code out of India in a letter addressed to a New York firm. The figures of crime for the month show an increase of 88. This increase is chiefly under the heads of murder and burglary.

Report on the Press for the Second Half of May 1941

Some nationalist newspapers deplore the fact that though the War has been brought nearer to India than ever before, Great Britain still refuses to conciliate India. They cannot understand the British Government's hesitation to accept the resolution of the Bombay Liberals.

(v) Fortnightly Report Dated 18 June 1941 for the First Half of June 1941

DO No. P. 4–12.

My dear Conran Smith,

War: The Sathyagraha movement continues with apparently ever diminishing momentum. Many of those who were convicted in the early stages of the movement are now being released after completing their sentence but relatively few of them have shown the least sign of wanting to do anything which will land them in Jail again. In fact in a number of districts there is such a lull in the movement that only old Satyagrahis who have been ignored continue to wander about from village to village and district to district. Quite a large number have been arrested after crossing the border in the Central Provinces and these have returned to their own districts but few of them have shown any inclination to start Satyagraha again. A new form of propaganda which has been adopted in one or two places by a very limited number of Satyagrahis has been that of making speeches which are not only anti-War but definitely pro-German. In all such cases prosecution has been launched.

Political: In my last report I referred to the fact that the Khaksar movement appeared to be gaining some ground in Madras. It became very clear that this organization while pretending to observe the strict letter of the law on the question of wearing of uniform, carrying of arms, and in the practice of military drill was not really keeping to the spirit of the law. This being the case the Government of Madras decided to prohibit entirely the wearing of any form of Khaksar uniform and the carrying of 'Belchas'. Almost, however, before this decision could be put into force, the Government of India decided to declare the whole Khaksar organization unlawful and those orders of the Government of India were put into immediate effect. About 25 Khaksars from Madras and North Arcot districts had left for Nagpur before the ban was imposed to take part in the 'Mosque Satyagraha' but were arrested at Nagpur itself and are being sent back to Madras where they will be released. This Government consider that the movement has no leaders of outstanding importance in this province and that at the present juncture it is not necessary to proceed against any person simply for being a Khaksar. If the ban is defied by any member of the association, action under the Criminal Law Amendment Act will be taken immediately.

The other political parties have held a number of meetings as usual; the Justice Party being chiefly concerned with its anti-Brahmin campaign and with wooing the Muslim League. The Congress party have been particularly concerned as usual with the hardships of political prisoners. Mr Jinnah has visited the Nilgiris and addressed meetings both in Ootacamund and Coonoor. The Hindu Mahasabha continues to try and organize itself on stronger lines but is definitely adopting at the moment a Pro-War attitude. Communist activity appears to have been confined to trying to foment trouble amongst various labour unions but without any marked success and a number of communist leaders have been arrested either with a view to detention under Rule 26 of the Defence of India Rules or where possible for prosecution for some specific offence.

Press

Nationalist newspapers continued to be very critical about the British Government's attitude towards the political impasse in India. British women's message to Indian women concerning war effort had as little influence as the one made previously by Miss Rathbons. Dr Rabindranath Tagore's strong indictment of the British rule in India in reply to Miss. Rathbone's statement was welcomed by the nationalist press as representing the views of the Indian intelligentsia on the political problem.

(vi) Fortnightly Report Dated 4 July 1941 for the Second Half of June 1941

DO No. P. 4–13.

My dear Conran Smith,

The Satyagraha movement appears to be distinctly moribund. There have been extremely few cases in any districts except in Madras City where the special conditions of city life make it impossible to carry out the policy of ignoring even unimportant Satyagrahis. Consequently, many who have been ignored in other districts, but who are determined to go to prison, make their way to Madras eventually and there achieve their ambition. This accounts for the fact that between 80 to 90 per cent of the convictions in Madras City are of persons who have come from outside. It is reported that the Andhra and Tamil Nadu Congress authorities are endeavouring to intensify the campaign once more, but partly due to the more stringent conditions now laid down by Mr Gandhi and partly because those who have already been to jail and have been released are very unwilling to return to Jail, it is doubtful whether this attempted intensification will materialize. A few of those who have been released from Jail have again offer Satyagraha and as a general rule have been given heavier sentences for the second offence. This Government have issued instructions to the District Magistrate to press for really deterrent sentences in every case of a repetition of the offence. There have been one or more cases where speakers at meetings have delivered themselves of pro-German and strongly anti-British sentiments and in all such cases the persons responsible are being prosecuted.

Political: the bye-elections for the Madras City Council have been held to fill the vacancies caused by the Congress resignations and resulted in the Congress candidates securing 12 out of the 12 seats. The other political parties held their annual meetings but only, some of the Justice Party meetings call for any particular mention and even these were mainly concerned with a general vilification of the Brahmin community. As a sort of counter last to the support given to the Muslim League's proposals for Pakistan and their own for Dravidasthan, an anti-separationists Conference was held at Kumbakonam which was rather poorly attended until the organizers threw open to the incidents between those taking part and the partisans of the Muslim League.

The Khaksars remained quiet and there does not appear to be any intention of disobeying the ban on the organization. The Government of the Central Provinces reported that Khaksars were going from Madras to Nagpur and requested that this might be stopped. Orders for the immediate arrest of any Khaksars going to Nagpur were issued to all police officers.

A considerable quantity of communist literature was seized from various students and others in a school in Chittoor district. The papers are at present undergoing scrutiny and after this is completed, the question of prosecution of other suitable action will be considered. The proscribed 'Swatanthra Bharat' continues to make its appearance from time to time particularly in the Andhra districts and communists in that area have been trying to make trouble by utilizing any dispute, however shall, between the workers and their employers. Three of these communists have recently been detained and the strikes which they were engineering have consequently not come off. In Malabar an important arrest has been made in the person of a Nambudri communist on whom were found papers giving details of the party's underground organization. It appears that under the guise of organizing summer schools or Adult Education Camps communists have been doing considerable propaganda. This Government have therefore placed a ban on all such schemes unless the organizers have first obtained the sanction of the District Magistrate of the District in which a school is to be held. This ban has given rise to a great deal of misinformed criticism both on the platform and in the press where Congressmen and others are trying to make out that the Government wish to prevent the spread of education.

Miscellaneous: the event of the fortnight in Vizagapatam was the laying of the foundation stone, by Babu Rajendra Prasad, of the new ship building yard for the Scindia stream Navigation Co. Both Rajendra Prasad and the Chairman of the Co made speeches which were anti-Government to the extent that they blamed the Government for not giving more assistance to ship-building in India and anti-British to the extent that they complained that the British shipping interests had always tried to stifle Indian shipping concerns, but there was no attempt to discuss general political questions. There also appears to have been a distinct muddle about the issue of invitations to the function which has caused considerable dissatisfaction in Vizagapatam, particularly to the Municipal Council and the Harbor authorities.

Press: Nationalist papers wrote strongly about the unfairness of the Ministry of Information in England having issued the Talking Points of India and were surprised at these Talking Points being issued at a time when every opportunity should be taken to placate India. They also condemned the policy of the British Government in regard to shipping. The Government of India had chosen a course which could not but be inimical to Indian interests.

46. Mahatma Gandhi's Statement to the Press

CWMG, Vol. LXXIV, pp. 149–51.

Sevagram
6 July 1941

When Mian Saheb Iftikhar-ud-Din, President of the Punjab Provincial Congress Committee, and Dr Gopichand were with me the other day, Mian Saheb told me that there was some misunderstanding among some Congressmen about certain things which required clearing. I should have dealt with them earlier. But pressure of work and my limited capacity for disposal are responsible for the delay. I take them up now.

When the Punjab Bar patriotically took up the honourable role of *amicus curiae* and decided to bring before their High Court for revision the cases of satyagrahis in which, in their opinion, obvious injustice was done, I was delighted, not for the sake of the relief such revision might bring, but for the sake of the Punjab Bar and of purity of justice. Whilst satyagrahis must be indifferent to the sentences pronounced against them, they must welcome exposure of injustice especially when it is brought about at the instance of disinterested parties. When, therefore, Ismet Begum wired and wrote to me that her husband was much displeased and disturbed over the prospect of revision, I urged her not to interfere and asked her to tell her husband that there was nothing wrong about the revision and that if he was discharged it would be open to him to offer civil disobedience again. Of course the matter wears a different and ugly aspect when satyagrahi prisoners request the amicus curiae that they should take up their (prisoners') cases. Such conduct would be quite contrary to the satyagraha code.

Complaints are being made in several parts as in the Punjab that the new lists of satyagrahis are not being passed as fast as they are sent. There is no lack of despatch in the Punjab or any other province as to the lists. But I am in no hurry to pass them. I repeat for the thousandth time that the present Civil Disobedience is not only not designed to embarrass authority but care is being taken as far as possible to avoid all embarrassment. The merit as also the strength of the struggle consists in reducing embarrassment to the minimum whilst the British are engaged in a deadly life-and-death war. Moreover, since our struggle is going to be indefinitely prolonged—I give no less than five years—there need be no hurry to fill the jails. Mere filling of jails can bring us no nearer our freedom than we are now. The virtue lies in the people learning through the restricted civil disobedience the necessity of discipline, suffering and self-sacrifice. Every true example of satyagraha acts as a leaven working itself in the mass mind. During the initial stages I was purposely lax in scanning the lists. The result was that many crept in who had done no constructive work. Some had even no faith in it. These are a burden on the organization and positively hinder the march to freedom. I have said repeatedly that constructive work is the foundation for civil disobedience. It promotes discipline and conduces to the growth of non-violence in the worker. As time advances Congressmen must therefore expect increasing stiffness on my part. The conditions will be the same. Strictness will be confined to the enforcement. This is but natural if we are to grow from strength to strength and if we are to make the struggle increasingly purer. I can conduct it on no other terms.

Then Mian Saheb mentioned to me that some Congressmen had adversely criticized his move for achieving among all parties in the Punjab agreement about eschewing goondaism in the pursuit of their respective programmes. When the Mian Saheb told me that there was just a possibility of such an effort succeeding, I at once told him to make it and suspend for the time being his own civil disobedience and of those whose assistance he might consider necessary for the arduous task. Some Congressmen seem to have taken exception that Mian Saheb had invited to his meeting non-Congressmen and even communal leaders. The objectors forget that it is the essence of Mian Saheb's move to bring together all the opposite elements and see whether they could agree to eschew goondaism for the achievement of their respective purposes. Nor could there be in such a meeting decisions by counting heads. The end contemplated could only be achieved by the willing consent of the parties. In any event Congressmen should know that Mian Saheb has undertaken this difficult mission in consultation with me and with my whole-hearted consent. I hope that he will receive the closest co-operation of all Congressmen.

He is impatient to offer civil disobedience. As the head of the Congress in the Punjab, he thinks that his primary duty is to offer civil disobedience. I have told him that there is no such universal rule. On the contrary it is his clear duty, and of those whom he may select, to refrain so long as he and they feel that they can contribute their mite to the attempt to eradicate goondaism.

There remains the question of those who were prematurely released owing to the Punjab High Court decision about the insufficiency for the purpose of conviction of mere notices to offer civil disobedience. When I learnt about the decision, I had informed Mian Saheb that he should not be in a hurry to send them to jail and that when he paid his contemplated visit to Sevagram I should discuss the question with him and decide. He came and I advised that those who were not wanted for the peace move should re-offer civil disobedience.

47. Predicament of a Congress Activist

File No. G 9/1941, AICC Papers, NMML.

Perambur, 9th July 1941.

From
S.A. Mahelingam,
31, Ballard Street,
Perambur Post

To
My Most Revered Leader,
Mahatma Gandhi

My Dear Babuji,

Having had confidence that the Indian National Congress is the one and only Political Organization in India which makes no difference between man and man and which works for the uplift of the down-trodden masses, I got enrolled myself as a member several years back and from that moment onwards I have been wearing *Khadder* only and observing very strictly all the rules and regulations of the Congress. I am also a committee member of the local sabha (Sembiam Urban Congress Sabha) for the last three years and I am serving the Congress to my utmost capacity. I am a Harijan and an employee in the M. & S.M. Railway Workshops, Perambur. The major part of the work done in the Workshops at present is in connection with the War. Under the present circumstances, I request you to advise me whether I am violating the fundamental principles of the Congress and indirectly helping the Government in their War efforts. Certain workers have pointed out to me that by my being an employee in the Workshops I am indirectly helping the Government in their War efforts.

I am quite conscious of the truth of their argument but I only regret my inability to lodge a protest and if unwilling to resign my job.

Under the circumstances I pray, Father, that you will kindly say whether by my continuing to work in the Workshops I have in any way transgressed the principles of Congress regarding its attitude towards the present war.

Your most dutiful,
S.A. Mahelingam

48. 'Resignation from Congress was Better Than Expulsion!' Dr Satyapal Blames Inertia and Says He has No Faith in Present Movement

Bombay Chronicle, 15 July 1941.

'I am extremely disappointed with the inactivity and inertia that dominates the Congress policy at the present moment. There are two things which vitally affect our interests, namely internal security and resisting the foreign invasion. Even the most superficial reader of events can't shut his eyes to both these dangers being real and immediate', observes Dr Satyapal, former President of the Punjab Provincial Congress Committee in a statement to the Press, explaining why he has resigned from the Congress and has offered his services to the British Government in the prosecution of the war.

What has Congress Done?

'There may be some,' he continues who pay no heed to these things but every right-minded Indian has to keep both these things before him. What steps Congress has taken to secure internal peace? Communal differences are on the increase. Maulana Mazhar Ali's speech at the Ahrar Conference is an instance in point. The riotous element marches onward and life and property, persons, and possessions are in grave danger. What has the Congress done in this connection? Pious wishes and sermons will not meet the exigencies of the situation. The Congress should do something very solid and substantial in this connection. The question of foreign invasion is of still greater importance. What is the lead given by the Congress in this connection? What attitude is the country to adopt when such an emergency arises? Will we welcome the invader or will we watch the development, as if we are not at all concerned with the fate of our country?

Why Help Britain

There is a third alternative that we will support the British Government to repel the invaders. Congress does not wish the defeat of the British, because if it does so wish, why does it not embarrass the Government? Why does it not make it difficult for it to continue in India? If we have to co-operate with the Government at that stage, what harm can accrue if we help the Government now to keep the enemy at a distance from our country? I, therefore, have done nothing wrong in offering my services as a token of our helping the British to win the war, so that we may be saved from the evil fate of a foreign invasion.'

No Alternative

As regards his decision to resign from the membership of the Congress, Dr Satyapal says: 'I have resigned the membership because I have no other alternative. Mahatmaji's formula is 'Get inside or get out.' If one cannot find himself in full agreement with the views of Mahatmaji, he cannot be allowed to remain in the fold of the Congress.

The treatment meted to Shriyut Subhas Chandra Bose and Mr M.N. Roy is conclusive evidence on this point. Personally, I do believe that such a procedure is a tyranny of majority and retards the healthy growth of a democratic institution. But it is not the time to argue or advance reasons. It is an era of edicts, bulls orders, instructions, and directions. Mahatmaji has ordered that whosoever differs from the policy and programme enunciated and promulgated by him must not be permitted to remain within the Congress. I have voluntarily done what I would have been made to do compulsorily. I, therefore, am not to blame for resigning the membership of the Congress. If I would not resign I would be expelled. Resignation is certainly better than expulsion. My loyalty to the Congress admits of not the slightest change. I am steadfast and devoted in my relations with the Congress.

Reply to Critics

Replying to the criticism of his offer to co-operate with the Government, Dr Satyapal says: 'My offer does not at all concern the day-to-day administration of the Government of India. As far as the issue of Swaraj is concerned, I am second to none in my desire of immediate Swaraj being established in India. But during war, to help the sick and wounded is not that sort of co-operation which can be found fault with. But is the Congress and are Congressmen really non-co-operating with the Government? Is it non-co-operation to present petitions before the High Court directly or indirectly?

Is it Non-Co-operation?

'Is it non-co-operation to scramble for classification? Is it non-co-operation to pester authorities with requests for release on paroles? Is it non-co-operation to ask the Government to allow facilities to carry on business, while confined in jails? Is it non-co-operation to secure heavy contracts for near relations to request Sir Sikander to help the Unity Committee with his co-operation and money and to receive his blessings? Where is the non-co-operation? It may be the leaders of Satyagraha movement in our province are more co-operating with the Ministry than even the maligned helpers of the Government.'

Referring to the Satyagraha movement, Dr Satyapal says he would appreciate mass movement to force the issue of 'Swaraj' and he would be the first to joint it, but he had no faith in the present movement. It had produced almost no effect either on Indians or on the

Government. In his opinion Satyagraha movement in Punjab had miserably failed and instead of adding glory to Congress had humiliated it in the eyes of the Government and public.

49. Mahatma Gandhi on Poona Resolution[1]: Interview to A.S.N. Murti[2]

CWMG, Vol. LXXIV, p. 183.

Sevagram
4 p.m. to 4.20 p.m., 23 July 1941.

After the usual salutation, I waited just a minute when Mahatma said that he was [all] attention to me. And I began referring to the Poona resolution of the Congress, and invited his opinion to the possibility of arriving at an understanding on the basis of that resolution, if a way could be found for reconciliation. To this, Mahatmaji replied that the Poona resolution would not be revived. The psychological time is gone. I mention to him the restlessness that is becoming evident in the country, and if the Congress were not to revise its stand, it may lose ground. To this he said that even if the Congress were to find itself in the desert, it would prefer to be there, to sacrificing the country's interest and humorously said that sometimes the desert air did good. I mentioned to him that by the withdrawal of the Congress ministry, the little good that was attempted to be done had to be given up. He replied that weighing matters in the proper way, it was not worth while to put much emphasis on the attempted progress, when considerations far weightier were at stake. When Congress was out to put down imperialism, all these things were insignificant. Even if the Congress gave up non-violence, it had been found that as a purely political measure, the Poona resolution could not be revived.

---

1. The reference is to the Poona AICC resolution, 27 July 1940.
2. A.S.N. Murti belonged to Sarvodaya Bhavan, Chatrapur.

50. Mahatma Gandhi's Letter to Iftikhar-ud-Din

CWMG, Vol. LXXIV, pp. 191–2.

Sevagram, Wardha
28 July 1941

My dear Iftikhar,

I have your letter of the 25th instant. You are doing good work. I hope the District Committees will work so that Punjab, may become proof against goondaism. If the effort succeeds, it will produce a tremendous impression on the whole of India. I regard this work of yours as most important—much more than jail-going.

If those who have been discharged as a result of appeals do not go again, you need not worry. Their names should be removed from the lists.

No member has asked me for permission to remain on. I should not think of giving such permission. Every case of this type or any other I have invariably referred to you.

I have read all about Dr Satyapal. You should accept his resignation and of others who have copied his example. You have done well to refer to Rajendra Babu about the Parliamentary resignation. But it follows that if [he] gives up the four-anna membership, he should resign all other offices.

I personally think that you should ignore his Press statements.

You are quite right in doing what you have about Brahma Datta. He has written to me saying that he has apologized for his conduct. He is very impulsive.

If I have kept a copy of my letter1 to Lala Dunichand, I shall send it to you.

I share your grief about Lala Shamlal. I shall not accept any resignation directly. I enclose a letter of a Bhiwani correspondent. He complains that you gave too short a time to Bhiwani when you went there during your tour. He is afraid that the atmosphere is tense there. You will see.

Farooqi is angry with me because I did not approve of his statement of his visit to me. I told him that his statement was in the nature of an advertisement and sent him a brief one. He retorts that mine is an advertisement (I suppose for myself!)

My love to you and Ismat.

Yours,
Bapu

51. *The Times of India*'s 'Leaderette' and Mahatma Gandhi's Reply

(i) *The Times of India* on 'Mr Gandhi's Admission', 29 July 1941

CWMG, Vol. LXXIV, p. 408.

Mr Gandhi, in an interview with an American news agency, makes a candid and significant admission. When asked how many of his followers who are now in jail sincerely subscribe to his own belief that violence can never be right, he replies: 'I do not mind it being said that the majority are non-violent only out of policy. That is the weakest part of my campaign...' Impartial observers of Mr Gandhi's civil disobedience campaign have suspected as much from the beginning, and their suspicion has been confirmed of late by the departure from Mr Gandhi's ranks of men like Mr Munshi and Dr Satyapal. Mr Gandhi himself has now publicly recognized, and for the first time, that the non-violent slogan is being exploited politically. He also admits by implication that such exploitation is distasteful to him and, indeed, weakens his campaign.

When the campaign was first launched, it was widely believed that only those who were in full agreement with Mr Gandhi's interpretation of non-violence should offer themselves for jail. And yet, as we now know, a majority submitted their names, not out of conviction, but 'only out of policy'—some of them through a sense of loyalty to the party organization, others from more questionable motives. Nor can Mr Gandhi escape the largest share of the blame for allowing this inconsistency to develop. He is personally responsible for sanctioning the names of satyagrahis, and it is reasonable to suppose that in some instances at least he accepted nominees who he knew did not fulfil the conditions which he himself had laid down. If the presence in jail of those who went 'only out of policy' has weakened Mr Gandhi's campaign, then Mr Gandhi has proved that he is among his own worst enemies. Either he has been lax in interpreting his own rules of satyagraha or he has been deceived by the majority of those whose names were submitted. Mr Gandhi can best say which of these alternatives the right one is.

(ii) Mahatma Gandhi's Letter to *The Times of India*

CWMG, Vol. LXXIV, p. 199.

Sevagram, Wardha
31 July 1941

This is the concluding portion of your leaderette in *The Times of India*, [of the] 29th instant:

Either he has been lax in interpreting his own rules of satyagraha or he has been deceived by the majority of those whose names were submitted. Mr Gandhi can best say which of these alternatives is the right one.

I suggest a third alternative. I have neither been lax in the interpretation of my rules of satyagraha nor have I been deceived by anybody. You have omitted to read one sentence in my admissions: 'It is inevitable.' From the very inception of the movement in 1920 non-violence has been a policy and not a creed. I said in Bombay speaking at the AICC meeting on the reversal of the Poona resolution that with the majority non-violence was a policy. The weakness was therefore inherent in the movement. It should not be forgotten that I am trying the great experiment of using non-violence for the political freedom of the country. With me no doubt non-violence is an end in itself, though it is also a means for the attainment of the freedom of the country. With the vast majority of Congressmen it is and must remain a means. The weakness is thus inherent though none the less regrettable. The marvel is that in spite of the weakness, twenty years' experience has not weaned Congressmen from the non-violent policy, though it is open to it to change it any time.

In the light of the information I have provided, you will perhaps admit that the case you have made up against the Congress and me falls to the ground.

I am,
Yours sincerely

52. Report of Mahatma Gandhi's Interview to H.V. Kamath[1]

CWMG, Vol. LXXIV, pp. 295–7.

Sevagarm
5 September 1941

Q: Has the entry of Russia into the war altered its complexion and India's attitude thereto?
A: The entry of Russia into the war has not materially altered the complexion of the war. Expression of oral sympathy with Russia as a victim of aggression is not wrong but no purpose will be served by so doing so long as we cannot translate it into action. Russia is not wholly free from blame inasmuch as she has allied herself with imperialist power though it may be for the purpose of self-existence only. Had Jawaharlalji, who is a close student of international politics, not been behind the bars and thus free to express his views, his opinion in the matter would have weighed with me.

Q: Can you, Mahatmaji, envisage the emergence of a non-violent new world order in the Atlantic Charter?
A: No. I am not able to envisage in the Atlantic Charter the emergence of a non-violent new world order of my conception.

Q: What is your attitude towards the acceptance of office in the Viceroy's Executive Council by Congressmen such as Sjt Aney and Mr Nalini Ranjan Sircar?
A: I do not approve of the acceptance of office by Congressmen such as Sri Aney and Nalini Babu. Such action on their part has undoubtedly given a handle to the British Government for carrying on propaganda in America to the effect that India should now be satisfied in that even well-known ex-Congressmen have joined the Viceroy's Council.

Q: Is the satyagraha movement proceeding to your satisfaction? In what way is it different from the 1930 movement? Has the policy of non-embarrassment any political value or significance? What will be your attitude in case the Government conceded the right of freedom of speech? Is there any likelihood of intensification of the struggle in the near future?
A: The satyagraha movement is proceeding to my entire satisfaction. Pressure on a scale comparable to that of the 1930 movement is not being put on the Government, it is true, but that movement was different in character from the present one. But the main fact that the struggle is going on constitutes sufficient moral pressure, so much so that the British Government's position in America does not appear to be quite comfortable. The policy of non-embarrassment is a logical consequence of non-violence and in that way a political necessity, but I do not expect the British Government to reciprocate my chivalrous stand. There is no possibility of the Government conceding the right of freedom of speech, but if they did so honestly, I am bound to call off the movement. Bona fide recognition of free non-violent speech would mean a large step towards independence. Intensification of the struggle is not likely during the pendency of the war. Intensification will come at the close of the war if it became necessary.

Q: What is your attitude to the local *kisan* and *mazdoor* struggles?
A: I extend my sympathy to all local kisan and mazdoor struggles for their legitimate demands and such struggles cannot amount to embarrassment of the Government. My attitude cannot be otherwise, considering that I myself have been the author of such struggles in the past.

Q: In view of the fact that the word 'non-violence' does not appear in the Congress Constitution, what is the duty of Congressmen as regards non-violent conduct?
A: Though the word 'non-violence' does not appear in the Congress Constitution, it does in resolutions. Though there be no resolution of a plenary session of the Congress on the subject of non-violence, I expect Congressmen to abide by the AICC resolution so long as it is not modified or altered by a plenary session.

Q: Acharya Kripalani recently, in reply to Sardar Sardul Singh Caveeshar, said that the Forward Bloc is not a part of the Congress organization. The statement on Kripalaniji's part has created not a little confusion and misunderstanding among several Congressmen. I personally hold that the position of the Forward Bloc in the Congress is quite similar to that of the Congress Socialist Party. Could you kindly enlighten me with your opinion on the subject?
A: Though the Congress Constitution does not recognize separate groups within the Congress organization, Congressmen who owe allegiance to such groups have every right to remain in the Congress in their individual capacity if the groups are not inconsistent with the Congress resolution and policy. I never insisted that Congressmen who do not subscribe to my interpretation of non-violence should leave the Congress. The Congress Socialist Party is just as much not a part of the Congress organization as the Forward Bloc. The Congress Constitution makes no mention of either as being component parts of the Congress organization. The

Forward Bloc and the Congress Socialist Party are on a par with each other so far as their being part of the Congress organization is concerned.

Q: Have you, Mahatmaji, full faith in a Divine Power moulding our destiny?
A: Yes, I have full faith in a Divine Power guiding the destinies of India and of the world. It is this living faith that sustains me in the present crisis.

---

[1] H.V. Kamath was Organizing Secretary of the All-India Forward Bloc. The report was revised by Mahatma Gandhi and published in *The Hindu* on 5 November 1941.

53. Statistical Data (All-India) on Persons Detained and Imprisoned, September 1941

File No. 18/16/41-Poll (I), Home (Political) Department, NAI.

Statement showing the number of persons undergoing detention or imprisonment on the 1st or each month in connection with the Civil Disobedience Movement

	January	February	March	April	May	June	July	August	September
Madras	176	812	983	1170	1163	926	815	765	
Bombay	135	490	858	1334	1559	1801	1708	1283	956
Bengal	21	34	44	40	44	37	47	34	
UP	22	790	1404	4672	9342	8799	7593	Not yet received	
Punjab	14	40	Not stated	509	1053	1118	1129	900	795
Bihar	48	139	356	467	583	668	634	557	
CP	83	119	156	202	238	380	457	420	354
Assam	13	71	63	88	70	69	71	74	
Orissa	25	Not stated	338	279	245	230	212	190	74
Coorg	5	6	9	10	14	9	10	10	6
Delhi	22	46	64	81	108	117	126	132	
?	–	5	6	–	–	–	–	–	
		564	2552	4281	8852	14419	14154	12802	9829

The total number of those undergoing imprisonment or detention in connection with the Satyagraha movement on the 1st May 1941 was 14,419. The figures for the succeeding months were as follows:

1st June	14,154
1st July	12,802
1st August	9,829

The figures on the 1st of August by Provinces were:

Madras	765
Bombay	1283

Bengal	34
UP	5464
Punjab	900
Bihar	557
CP	420
Assam	74
NWFP	Nil
Sind	Nil
Orissa	190
CC's Provinces	142

54. Extracts from Fortnightly Reports on Satyagraha and Other Political Developments in Madras Province (July to September 1941)

Fortnightly Reports from Government of Madras to Conran Smith, Secretary to Government of India, Public (General) Department, Home Department, Tamil Nadu State Archives.

(i) Fortnightly Report Dated 21 July 1941 for the First Half of July 1941

DO No. P. 4–14.

My dear Conran Smith,

War: the Satyagraha movement appears to be a moribund. In quite a large number of districts no new cases have occurred during the fortnight and of the few old Satyagrahis still carrying on, none have achieved either interest or success amongst the people in the areas in which they have been wandering. Although a few of those who have been convicted and released after serving their sentences have again offended, practically no one of real importance has as yet done anything to court imprisonment again. Of those who are wandering about, most are making their way to Madras City because, for the reasons explained in my last report, the peculiar conditions of city life make it impossible not to arrest and charge them.

In the last fortnight at least 80 such Satyagrahis have been convicted in the city, while the number of residents who have been convicted is not more than one-eigth of that number. That the authors of the movement realize that it has misfired is clear from the fact that members of the Andhra Provincial Congress Committee have decided to strike off the party list the names of Satyagrahis who fail to offer Satyagraha again, obviously with the intention to use the threat of expulsion from future party favors as the means to revive flagging interest.

Political: Of the various political parties the Hindu Mahasabha has been the most active during the last fortnight. It celebrated the anti-Pakistan day in Madras and held its Tamil Nadu Provincial Conference at Tiruvannamalai on the 5th and 6th July the attendance at which was distinctly less than the organizers had hoped. The general theme of the proceedings was anti-Muslim and speakers also exhorted Hindus to leave Congress and join the Sabha for the protection of Hinduism. The Khaksar movement appears to be of a stand-still but from the North Arcot district there comes a report of some further enlistment. It is not quite clear whether the District

Magistrate has already instituted proceedings for defiance of the ban and this aspect of the question will be taken up by Government.

Communist influence have been discovered at work in a school in the Chittoor district and further investigation suggest that there is a considerable organization in that district though as yet it is in an immature state. It appears that this district has been utilized as a hiding place for communists from the Andhra Districts. From West Godavari it is reported that the communists are quiet but confidently expect that now that Britain and Russia are allied and are fighting side, by, ban on communism in this country will shortly be lifted.

In Coimbatore district communist agitators are responsible for recent strikes. In the Malabar district an important prosecution has been initiated under the Criminal Law Amendment Act in respect of an article in the newspaper 'Kahalam' encouraging Kashaka Sangam activities which, as I have already reported have been banned.

Press: Newspapers in South India differ very much in respect of the exchange of places between Sir Archibald Wavell and Mr Sir Claude Auchinleck. Some claim that India has been honoured by the transfer, that she is becoming a great nerve centre and that she is destined to play a great part in the future progress of the War. Others are inclined to regret that Sir Claude Auchinleck, who has inaugurated certain reforms of far-reaching significance in the realm of defence of India, is not allowed to put through those reforms in the Indian Army. Still others suspect that General Wavell has been transferred because he was unsuccessful in Greece and Grete.

Reports about the expansion of the Executive Council in the central Government have elicited different comments, some say that such an expansion is only temporary and is not to be taken in consonance with the Viceroy's August offer. Others feel extremely doubtful whether this expansion will conciliate public opinion in India. what is required is the establishment of a really National Executive in the Central Government.

(ii) Fortnightly Report for the Second Half of July 1941

The Civil Disobedience movement is just keeping itself alive and no more. In several districts no new Satyagrahis has come forward during the last fortnight and in a majority only a very small handful of previously ignored Satyagrahis are still active. Among those who have been released after serving their sentences only a very small percentage have repeated the offence and those who have done so have been convicted again and awarded deterrent sentences. The majority of the released Satyagrahis however are very unwilling to repeat the offence and the efforts of the Andhra Provincial Congress committee, to which referred on page three of my last report last fortnight, to revive the movement are not meeting with any success. In my last report I also referred to the fact that wandering Satyagrahis were making their way to Madras city where they could be sure of securing conviction. It is now reported by the District Magistrate of Guntur that Mr Gandhi has forbidden this practice. Opposition to the war effort has come from Madura Municipal council which resolutely refuses to allow war technicians to be trained in the Municipal workshop or to allow recruiting officers to occupy the Municipal Travelers Bungalow free even for few hours. This matter is engaging the attention of the Government of Madras.

Political: The announcement of the re-organization on a wider basis of the Viceroy's council has not so far evoked any marked comment or interest in this province, but even moderate

Congressmen declare that it is not far reaching enough and does not transfer any real power to Indians.

The Congress party held meetings in a number of places and speaking at a meeting to celebrate the anniversary of the Victoria club in Mannargudi, Mr T.T. Krishnamachari MLA spoke of the ineffectiveness of the present Satyagraha movement and suggested that a special session of the Congress should be convened to review the situation and to consider the desirability of Congressmen resuming office. The Justice Party continued to advocate the policy of creating Pakistan and Dravidastan to inveigh against the Brahmin control of the Congress. I referred last fortnight to some Khaksar activity in North Arcot district. Three unimportant persons have been convicted under the Defence of India Rules read with the Criminal Law Amendment Act for breach of the ban by wearing Khaksar uniform.

During the fortnight a considerable quantity of communist literature has come to light in various places and a number of arrests have been made in this connection. The communist organization in the Chittoor district, which was recently revealed by the discovery of communist literature in the Rishi Valley school, appears to have been very considerable if all yet ill-organized, ramifications in the district, but the police have been successful in unraveling most of them. One of the offenders is a clerk of the Collector's office and the collector is taking steps to dismiss him. A communist from Jaffna in Ceylon was arrested in the room of a student of the American college, Madura, on the 23rd July, and it was discovered that he had come to Madura to organize the party and that the student in whose room he was arrested was being taught to play the part of a 'post office'. The communist Paramasivam, whom I have previously reported as having been elected President of the Golden Rock Branch of the South Indian Railway Labour Union, has resigned that office. The moderate party in the union has obtained the upper hand with the result that the new President and some of the other office bearers are from the moderate section.

Press: The expansion of the Viceroy's Executive council, however, has met with disapprobation from the nationalist, Muslim and non-Brahmin press. There has been no tendency to criticize individuals who have been selected but the retention of the more important portfolios among European members of the council has been taken as an illustration of the British Government's unwillingness to part with power. Even the Mail says that a Defence portfolio could have been created and given over to an Indian.

Naradar and Lokopakari were advised and warned respectively during the fortnight.

(iii) Fortnightly Report Dated 18 August 1941 for the First Half of August 1941

DO No. P. 4–16

My dear Sir Richard,

War: The Satyagraha movement continues in its moribund condition. During the fortnight there have been a small number of cases of Satyagraha but very few of them were committed by new men. Most of the cases are unimportant Satyagrahis who have so far been ignored, but there have been a few cases of persons who have already served one sentence committing a second offence and in all the cases of this sort which have been brought before the courts deterrent sentences have been awarded. Among the new offenders are the Vice-President of the Chittoor District Board and a member of the Ramnad district Board. In the majority of the districts a complete lull has continued; and there are indications that opinion in Districts is beginning to veer round to the view that political parties should co-operate with the Government both in their own interests and in the interests of the country.

As the public take so little interest now in the usual form of Satyagraha, organizers in the Kistna District are now adopting a change in technique. They first of all announce that a meeting will be held to do propaganda for Khaddar and for the constructive side of the Congress programme and only when they have gathered a reasonable number of people to start shouting the anti-war slogans. In my last report I stated that it was understood that Mr Gandhi had forbidden the movement of Satyagrahis towards Madras. It is now reported that they are to be permitted to go to Madras provided they go on foot and do propaganda on the way.

Political: Sanatanists held a two days' conference in Ramnad district at which the social and religious legislation of Congress was attacked, and people were advised not to support the Congress. Except in North Arcot there is no sign of Khaksar activity but in that district four youths have already been sentenced for breach of the ban and another, four have been arrested and are awaiting trial.

A considerable amount of communist literature has been seized during the fortnight. One interesting case occurred in Guntur where six students tried to burn communist literature including copies of Swatanthra Bharat when a police search party came to their rooms. The police were, however, able to put out the fire and secure the bulk of the papers in a reasonable state of preservation. The rounding up of the communist organization in the Chittoor District, to which I referred last fortnight, is continuing satisfactorily. The student community has on the whole remained quiet, although efforts are being made, instigated mainly by communists, to form further student unions and federations. Some excitement appears to have been caused amongst the students in Coconada where the Principal of one of the colleges has been 'forced' (according to current rumors) to take leave. It is said that he is suspected of having misappropriated college funds but the students demonstrated against his being ordered to go on leave.

Press: On questions relating to India, opinion is sharply divided among papers in South India. For instance, while 'The Mail' the Justicite and Mussalman papers have no fault to find with Mr Amery's speech in the recent debate in the house of commons on India, nationalist papers have condemned that utterance in strong terms and one of them has frankly stated that Mr Amery is not the proper man for the India office. Mr Amery, it is said, has done nothing to ease the political tension in India. The same sharp division of opinion is to be found in respect of the debate in the House of Lords on the extension of the life of the Legislature in India. Nationalist papers have condemned the extension of the life as constituting a fraud on the electorate. Some of the speeches made during the debate, those of Lord Hailey and Lord Cotto, have been strongly criticized. Anglo-Indian and Mussalman papers, however, do not find anything objectionable in the debate.

(iv) Fortnightly Report Dated 3 September 1941 for the Second Half of August 1941

DO No. P. 4–17.

My dear Conran Smith,

War: The most interesting development in the past fortnight is, of course, the Anglo-Russian action in Marching into Iran. Most District Magistrates report that they have not as yet heard of the reactions of the Muslim community and that Muslim newspapers appear to be awaiting a 'Lead'. This suggests that the prompt action in forbidding the publication of the resolutions passed by the working Committee of the Muslim League has had the desired effect and that the terms of those resolutions have not yet percolated through to the Muslim rank and file.

The Satyagraha movement is now almost completely at a standstill. Only one person of any importance offered Satyagraha in the past fortnight. In Vizagapatam district in accordance with a mandate of the Andhra Provincial Congress committee that fourteen members of the District Board should offer Satyagraha (which would still leave the Board with a Congress majority for all practical purposes) a resolution was moved that the President of the Board should lead the way; but he refused to do so and the meeting broke up in some confusion. In most districts there is a complete lull in the activities of Satyagrahis and those released from Jail show no desire whatever to offer Satyagraha again. Of the 1212 persons released up to 20th June 1941, only twenty-eight are reported to have been convicted again and in to be doing propaganda. Among those released during the fortnight is Mr Satyamurthi, MLA (central), and Ex-mayor of Madras, who wasted no time in urging publicly that Congress should resume office in the provinces. Public interest in the Satyagraha movement has completely died away.

Political: Meetings of the Muslim League have taken place at various centers and at most of them resolutions were passed signifying approval of Mr Jinnah's action in compelling the resignation of the Muslim premiers from the Defence council in Madras city, a large meeting was held on Sunday, 24th August, at which the release of Allama Mashriqui and the lifting of the ban on the Khaksar movement was advocated. The meeting was entirely orderly and the speeches in no way objectionable.

The Congress party also held meetings throughout the country but most of these were confined to resolutions and speeches about the constructive programme and the now time-honoured complaint of the ill-treatment awarded to political prisoners. Although the Muslim meeting in Madras to which I have referred above was held ostensibly under the auspices of the Muslim League, there is little doubt that it was instigated by Khaksar leaders. Reports from North Arcot say that there have been rumours of organized attempts on the part of local Khaksars to defy the ban, but so far no incident has occurred. Twenty six persons, including five from Madras, have been arrested for appearing in public wearing Khaksar badges. Fifteen of these have tendered an unconditional apology which is under the consideration of Government.

Communists do not appear to have been so active in the last fortnight. A certain amount of communist literature has been discovered particularly in the Andhra Districts and a number of students have been arrested but released on bail pending a scrutiny of the literature seized from them.

Press: The proceedings of the working committee of the All India Muslim League have received a good deal of attention. It is stated that Mr Amery's statement made some time ago in parliament that responsible leaders of principal communities have gradually responded to the Governments invitation to serve on the National Defence Council is, to some extent, falsified by the resignations of two out of the four Muslim premiers from that council as a result of the pressure brought to bear upon them by Mr Jinnah. While on the one hand it is realized that the resignations have strengthened the hands of Mr Jinnah, it is also stated that the truculent attitude of the working committee appears to justify the action of the Congress.

The Madras press advisory committee was consulted in regard to the following three cases:

'Mathurubhumi', a Malayalam Daily, published some misleading headlines in two of its issues. These headlines were German claims. The Editor justified his action. The committee resolved that the Editor should be written to that the position taken by him to feature news whatever might be its source, was unsound and that where enemy successes were claimed, featuring, unless qualified as unconfirmed claims, should not be attempted.

'Andhra Prabha', a Telugu Daily, published in its leader some objectionable sentiments. The committee resolved that the attention of the Editor should be drawn to the article and he cautioned against such infraction in future.

'Vehini' a Telugu weekly published an objectionable article actionable under the Defence of India Rules and the Indian Press (Emergency powers) Act. The committee resolved that the Editor should be warned against writings of such character.

(v) Fortnightly Report Dated 21 September 1941 for the First Half of September 1941

DO No. P. 4–18

My dear Conran Smith

War: The Satyagraha movement was continued in a few places but as usual by non-entities. Congress propaganda was mainly concerned with criticizing Mr Satyamurthi's suggestion to return to office. Mr C.R. Srinivasan, Editor of 'Swadesamitran' in a speech at Salem vigorously supported by Mr Satyamurthi's plea for revision of the Congress policy and urged that the Congress should come back to office. At a Congress meeting in Tiruvanamalai in the North Arcot district one MLA who was recently released from jail is reported to have said that it was time for the Congress leaders to reconsider the Satyagraha movement. Report from South Arcot says that at a secret meeting local Congress men have resolved to revive Satyagraha in the district. In Coimbatore there was increased anti-war propaganda by old Satyagrahais, the increase is reported to be due to instructions from the High command.

Political: Muslim League propaganda meetings were held in Vellore and other places in the North Arcot district and resolutions were passed expressing confidence in Mr Jinnah, congratulating the Premiers of the Punjab and Assam on their resignation from the Defence council, appealing to Mr Fazlul Hug to resign his office likewise and demanding the removal of the ban on the Khaksar organization and the release of its leader, Allama Inayatullah Khan Mushriqui. The speakers in these places are also reported to have referred to the occupation of Iran and Iraq by the European powers and the incident of handing over a mosque in Lahore to the Sihs. There were meetings at Trichinopoly and other places where the President of the

Madras Muslim League and others spoke about Pakistan and the League's aims and activities. It is understood that secret Khaksar propaganda is being carried on in North Arcot. A certain individual having some influence among local rowdies appears to have been chosen as the leader of Khaksars. Two more Khaksaras of Vellore have given apology and the question of accepting them is under consideration.

The Justice Party held a meeting at Trichinopoly under the Presidentship of E.V. Ramaswami Naicker. The professed purpose of the meeting was to inaugurate an unemployment Bureau and a Better Living Association to solve the unemployment problem among non-Brahmins but Sir Muthia Chettiar who was the Principal speaker spoke mainly on the Tamil Language and Tamil Music.

At a poorly attended meeting of the Hindu Mahasabha in Madras city, resolutions were passed criticizing the introduction of Urdu as the National Language of Hyderabad and his approving the action of the Madras Government in recognizing Urdu as one of the languages qualifying for employment in Government service.

Sadique Ali, office Secretary of the All India Congress Committee, visited a number of places but his visit had no marked effect. It is reported that in spite of the final warning issued after a meeting of the Satyagraha Advisory Board at Tenali in the Guntur district, presided over by him, to the effect that the names of those who do not offer Satyagraha before 15th September 1941 would be struck off, no one has yet come forward to offer Satyagraha. At another meeting in the same district it is reported that Sadique Ali was faced with embarrassing questions, demonstrating the growing spirit of criticism within the Congress ranks.

About 30 students of the ceded Districts colleges met and decided to revive the students Association. Their activities will be watched. The Students Federation at Tiruvannamalai was disbanded in spite of the efforts of a few Congress socialists to revive its activities. The Secretary of the Andhra Provincial Students Federation cabled to the Russian Ambassador in London wishes for the success of Russia and received an acknowledgement of thanks. At a Students' conference in the Guntur district resolutions were passed urging greater support to Russia and condemning the Government order regarding Adult Education as well as the arrest of Student leaders.

A leading and active member of the communist party believed to be incharge of the Provincial production centre where from all the unauthorized and objectionable newssheets of the party emanate was arrested during the fortnight along with press compositor believed to be a courier of the party. The Police raided a house in Tellicherry and caught red handed a communist study class of six persons. Arrangements had been made for a socialist meeting at Pappinisseri where a disturbance took place in connection with the 'Protest day' celebrations in Malabar—to protest against the re-arrest of the accused who were acquitted in the Moraga Protest Day case but it so happened that a policy party appeared at Pappinissemi on that date and no meeting was held....

Press: Mr Churchill's reference to India has elicited warm disapprobation and keen disappointment from the nationalist press. While Mr Churchill's frankness is recognized it is stated that the denial of freedom to India and of the Eight points Declaration to this country prove that the Allied powers are not since in their protestations regarding their fight for democracy. Indian hopes have been dashed to the ground and it is asked whether Indian soldiers are fighting for the restoration of the freedom of Czechoslovakia and Poland and not for their own country. One paper remarks that some imagination is required for making Indian participation in War effort enthusiastic.

The majority of Muslim papers welcome Mr Jinnah's more in taking disciplinary action against those who have refused to resign from the Executive Council of the Viceroy or National Defence council according to the behests of the working committee of the All India Muslim League. The nationalist press, on the other hand show up the glaring inconsistency, of Mr Jinnah, declaration that he was for war effort, while at the same time he asks the Muslim Members of the Muslim League to resign their seats from places of influence and authority.

In the last fortnightly report it was mentioned that the Government were unable to accept the recommendation of the press Advisory committee to give a warning to the 'Vahini' a Telugu weekly and that they proposed to take action under the Indian Press (Emergency powers) Act, 1931. In Connection with the above an emergent meeting of the provincial advisory committee was convened on 19th September 1941 to suggest a reconsideration of the decision of Government.

(vi) Fortnightly Report Dated 4 October 1941 for the Second Half of September 1941

DO No. P. 4–19

My dear Conran Smith

War: Eighteen Congress members of the Vellore Municipal council have resigned as a protest against the council contributing towards the war Fund. This is a council in which the Congress have had on absolute majority but in spite of that were unable to defeat the resolution for a contribution to the War Fund.

The Satyagraha movement continues in a very moribund condition. A few new cases of Satyagraha are reported as having taken place during the fortnight but most of the small number of cases relate to previously ignored Satyagrahis of no importance. Very few of the persons who have been released from jail—and their number is now considerable—have repeated the offence. In a number of districts there have been no fresh cases at all during the fortnight. The feeling seems to be gaining ground in many quarters that with the completion of the release of the leaders and particularly as soon as Mr C. Rajagopalachari comes out of jail there will be a change of policy, but the exact form which this change of policy will take does not seem to be at all definite but one or two speakers have referred to the probability of the introduction of mass Satyagraha. Pubic interest in the movement if anything less than ever, and latterly Congress workers have been concentrating far more on the constructive side of the party programme and in organizing recruitment drives in to increase the number of members of the Congress.

Political: The various political parties have held meetings throughout the province and Congress, the Muslim League, and the Hindu Mahasabha in particular have been endeavouring to recruit new members from those parts of the country where they have the best following. The Justice Party have been celebrating the 63rd Birthday of their leader E.V. Ramaswami Naicker and he in addressing a public meeting in Salem made a speech which was simply one long tirade of abuse against Brahmins. Mr Churchill's explanation of the Atlantic Charter has been a disappointment to practically all parties who complain that there was no specific reference to the Indian problem and of the attitude to be taken in regard to it.

As I have previously reported seventeen Khaksars arrested in Vellore for a breach of the ban on the movement, have tendered unconditional apologies and the Government have accepted the apologies from sixteen of them, but the seventh was not accepted as there was reason to believe that the man in question was not sincere and was simply tendering the apology in the hope of being lot off to continue his agitation. The case against him is proceeding.

Press: The extension of the term of His Excellency Lord Linlithgow, Viceroy of India, has not been welcomed in the nationalist press. One paper remarks that this is a fair indication of the policy of the British Government which is not to move towards the application of the Atlantic charter to India.

The discussion in parliament in regard to the postponement of Elections bill has also had a sharp rebuke from the nationalist press. The organ of the Non-Brahmin community, 'Viduthalai', however, appreciates the reason given by Government for the postponement of elections.

In the last fortnightly report it was mentioned that an emergent meeting of the Madras Press Advisory Committee was convened on the 19th September 1941 to suggest a reconsideration of the decision of Government in regard to the 'Vahini'. The Committee urged that as the publication of the objectionable article in the 'Vahini' was the first offence after its revival a warning would meet the needs of the case. The Government accepted the recommendation of the Committee and requested the Convenor to issue a warning to the editor.

This Government have established a convention under which the Madras Press Advisory Committee will be consulted on specific cases relating to anti-war movement before action is taken by them except in cases of emergency. The Committee at its meeting held on 10th September has requested government to enlarge the scope of the consultation so as to include all cases where any news-paper is involved before action is taken by them instead of restricting consultations merely to cases relating to anti-war movement. The matter is engaging the attention of Government.

55. How Long?

Editorial, *National Herald*, 7 October 1941.

Occasionally a lone voice rises from some corner of India suggesting some variation in the Congress programme. Sometimes Gandhiji is criticized, sometimes it is urged that Satyagraha should be stopped or modified. Those whose voices reach us in this way from afar are a curious medley. There are of course those outside the Congress whose thin blood has never warmed to action and who are always sad that others do not think as they do. There is Mr M.N. Roy who finds frequent refuge in the columns of the Anglo-Indian press and who declared, more than a year ago, that the Congress was dead and buried, and who valiantly offered to shoulder the burden of ministerships, and even (so whispers reach us) the still heavier burden of an executive councillorship at the Centre. But, unfortunately, in spite of Mr Roy's gallant stand besides the much harassed British Government, his brave proposals did not lead to anything—neither to a ministership, nor to an executive councillorship and the Congress is still very much alive. Then there are our flery friends of the Forward Bloc, with their redoubtable leader, Sardar Sardul Singh Caveesher, thinking hard and deep, while less brave Congressmen indulge in Satyagraha and go to prison. They have thought hard now for over a year and we were hoping for some tangible result from their powerful celebration. So far all we have noticed is a demand for a meeting of the AICC, a worthy and suitable demand when a majority of the members are in prison. It is curious how the functioning of Satyagraha gives us an insight into people.

Then there is Mr K.M. Munshi who felt impelled and compelled to resign from the Congress because he disagrees with Gandhiji's view in regard to self-defence. It was not clear to us why resignations should follow this disagreement, for the Congress has Assembly chamber in New Delhi. Mr Satyamurti is eloquent, often forcefully so. But does he still think that the walls of British imperialism will crumble because of his, or other peoples, eloquence?

So these lone voices reach us, rather sad in their loneliness, while the great voice of India is silent behind prison bars. And even Mahatma Gandhi, who is out of prison, writes nothing and says little because of the humiliating conditions that prevail. But from time to time the little he says comes like a trumpet blast, fresh, clear, and piercing. It is not a bad thing that the few who are weary or downhearted should seek reponse or indulge in other activities. That will but strengthens the others.

How long will Satyagraha last? We do not know for the future is hid from us. Yet we know enough not only because of what our leader has said but also because we know something of the temper of our people. Gandhiji has told us to prepare for at least five years of struggle. That according to him is the minimum. It may be more. Clearly that implies not only the duration of the war but possibly after. It may be more. It implies that there is going to be no compromise with imperialism. Satyagraha has always been with us in some form or other during the past twenty years, just as the struggle for freedom is with us till freedom itself comes. The present form of Satyagraha was in a sense the product of the war. But its real causes lie deeper and essentially it is the outcome of our struggle for freedom and by that alone can it be determined. That is the true perspective, for there is no end except in freedom—all else is struggle—struggle, whatever shape or form it may take.

It is not only that the honour of India demanded this, though it is that, and that surely is enough for men and women of honour and spirit. But practical, hard-headed politics demand it also. To compromise with imperialism on any basis except that of freedom is to sell our chance of real freedom at a great crisis in history for miserable mess of pottage. That would be betrayal.

56. Orissa MLA's Letter to AICC Regarding Satyagraha and Local Bodies' Politics, 20 October 1941

File No. P-5/1941, AICC Papers, NMML.

From
Lokenath Mishra, MA, BL, MLA, (Orissa),
Village: Sanarhanga, PO Kudanagari, Dt Cuttack.

To
The Secretary, AICC, Shegaon
Wardha (CP)

(Through the President, PCC Utkal).
Sanarhanga, 20 October 1941.

My dear friend,

I am a humble Congress worker in Utkal and I was elected on Congress ticket to the Local Legislative Assembly. Obeying the country's call, I offered Satyagraha and suffered punishment for six months RI. After my release from the gaol in the last May I could not offer Satyagraha again within the scheduled time owing to various difficulties and troubles—and with permission, I have remained so long outside. I am now ready to re-offer Satyagraha recently.

As a Congress man I feel the Satyagraha movement in this province has been greatly hampered by the existence of the local bodies under the auspices of the Congress. In Ganjam district, the Board is run by expelled Congress people and therefore the Congress has nothing to do with that. But in Puri the Board is mainly controlled by Congress people and under that Dt Board is the Sadar Sub Dvn Local Board has in the meantime passed a resolution in favour of supporting war efforts. The leader of the Congress party in that Dt Board is fully against the Congress policy and programme. He and his party practically support and sympathise with the attempt of forming the coalition Ministry in the province. Inspite of repeated warning and advice from the President of the PCC, they remained adamant and preached their view-points among the people freely.

The Cuttack Dt Board is almost wholly formed by the Congress workers. Some of these members obtained necessary permission to offer Satyagraha and only four of them offered the same. Three of these were released after serving their terms of imprisonment. One of these three, Sree Sudhir Chandra Ghose, has again offered satyagraha. But the other two, Dr Sree G.S. Mohanty, MB, and Sree Gopinath (a co-opted member of the Kendrapara Sub-Divisional Dt Board) has withdrawn their names from the Satyagraha list and joined again the Board.

This Dt Board is going on with its usual routine work with various internal wrangling among the members, although this fact has been carefully kept secret so long. But some of the members are so troublesome that they have been creating mischief from the very beginning of the Board's working. As a resident of the Kondrapara Sub Div in this District, I have some personal knowledge of the working of the Local Board here. Sree Adwaita Bhallava Roy and Sarat Chandra Das, two elected members on Congress ticket, and Sree Gopinath Mohanty, a co-opted member of the Local Board, have done much mischief to lower the prestige of the Congress. They have punished the poor teachers in various ways. They have done no constructive work in their respective areas; rather they have been working in the Board in a destructive manner. These members have appointed some contractors on recommendation from among their relatives and friends so that they can obtain something from the Board through them. As a resident of the constituency from which Sree Adwait Bhallava Roy has been returned, I know fully well he receives traveling allowances from the Board by submitting false bills from his Headquarters where he does not ordinarily reside.

The two satyagrahis, Sree Gopinatha Mohanty and Dr G.S. Mohanty, who have left the rank and come back to the Board have some reasons for their doing so. Gopinath is a great mischief-maker and upper class village tout. He was once criminally convicted under P/5379 U/S. 379 IPC, when he was serving as an agent under a local landlord and misappropriated the landlord's funds. When the landlord filed a suit against him for recovery of his dues he escaped successfully by producing a forged receipt in the Court. He is doing no Congress work now and is creating much trouble by taking lead in party fractions in his own village.

As regards the other Satyagrahi Dr G.S. Mohanty, I know he has no difficulty in offering Satyagraha repeatedly. He is a well-to-do man and has no other encumbrance. He has withdrawn his name Satyagraha only to re-enter the Local Board and to capture the post of Chairmanship by plotting against the present incumbent. He has already formed a party with the said troublesome members, Sree Adwait Ballahava Roy, Sarat Chandra Das, Gopinath Mohanty and others. These members do not understand the principles of democracy and work with a view to satisfy each other at the cost of general public. Under the temptation of getting power and position for which he tried his utmost in the beginning and failed, the said doctor is blind enough not to see the sacredness of the Satyagraha movement.

Although these two Satyagrahis have withdrawn their names from the list of active satyagrahis, I believe by joining the Board again without obtaining the necessary permission from Gandhiji, they have acted clearly against the circular of the AICC For these arbitrary action of these Satyagrahis the discipline of the movement has become loose in this district and therefore some necessary steps may be taken against them without delay.

These members, with their power in the Board, have been able to make the atmosphere poisonous in the *moffusil* area of this District. People have become much disgusted with these Congress workers for their mischievous deeds, both inside and outside the Board.

Almost all the members of the District Board who are also Congress workers do no Congress work as is expected from them. Excepting only Sree Gourang Charan Das, the President, DCC, all other members are not helping the Congress programme in any way. Some of them, who obtained permission for offering Satyagraha, have not offered the same for personal gain, and having been unable to resist the temptation of the Board two Satyagrahis have again joined the same to do all sorts of mischief and to earn some petty income through fair and foul means.

So it is quite evident that the existence of the Congress party in this Board, instead of helping the present movement in any way, creates an adverse atmosphere against the Congress and is the source of temptation for many Congress workers to remain fully aloof from the present movement. So I think the dissolution of the Congress party in these local Bodies is overdue.

Due to some wrangling among the members and the Chairman of the Kendrapara Local Board, some new arrangement in the executive is going to be made by the District Board Congress party. But I think by doing this patch-work and thereby further augmenting the present discord among the Congress workers no purpose can be served, and his procedure of changing Chairman in the middle of one term would produce adverse effect on the public mind and its repercussions would be harmfull to our organization as well as to the interest of the public. So our workers should be called off from these Boards without further delay, and should be asked to help the present movement in any capacity for which they are fit.

For example you may kindly enquire into the working of the Local Board at Kendrapara under Cuttack Dt Board if you like, and satisfy yourself regarding my allegations made above. Similarly the Sambalpur Dt Council does not work smoothly. There is much wrangling among the members, the majority of whom have returned on Congress ticket.

So I request you to advise the President of the PCC to direct the Congress party to withdraw from the existing Local Bodies in this Province and to pay their wholehearted attention to the present Congress program.

With my humble *Pranams*.

I remain,
Yours faithfully,
Lokenath Mishra

57. Newspaper Report on Mahatma Gandhi's Meeting with Congress Leaders

Amrita Bazar Patrika, 22 October 1941.

Congress Decision Not to be Reversed: Parliamentary Activities, Leader's Parley with Mahatmaji

The decision of the Congress in regard to parliamentary activities in the provinces will not be reversed in the near future or at least till such time as developments warrant any change, it is understood in well-informed quarters here.

Congress leaders who are in Wardha had a prolonged discussion with Mahatma Gandhi at Sewagram to-day. Those who participated in the discussions included Mr C. Rajagopalachari, Sardar Vallabhbhai Patel, Dr Rajendra Prasad, Mr Asaf Ali, Acharya Kripalani and Mr Mahadev Desai, who recently had interviews with the Congress President Maulana Azad and Pandit Jawaharlal Nehru in prison.

The Hon Khan Bahadur Allahbux, Premier of Sind, who also interviewed Maulana Azad a fortnight ago, saw Mahatma Gandhi to-day.

While no indication is available in regard to the subjects on which the leaders held discussions, it is understood that meeting after eleven months they took an opportunity to exchange views on the progress of the Satyagraha movement and the general political situation in the country. Most of the members of the Working Committee present at Wardha have planned for a week's stay and it is presumed that every aspect of the Congress movement since last November, with particular reference to political developments in the country since then, will be subjected to a close scrutiny.

Mr Asaf Ali left for Bombay to-day to see Mr Bhulabhai Desai.

It is considered not unlikely that Congress members in the Central Assembly may attend the house for one week instead of one day as was originally intended.

58. Congress Policy Revision Urged

Amrita Bazar Patrika, 28 October 1941.

'*The Hindu*'s Comment'
Need for Realistic Attitude Towards March of Events

The need for a reorientation of its policy by the Congress is stressed by *The Hindu* in a three-column editorial under the caption 'Call off Satyagraha.'

'The Congress', says the paper, 'has always taken up a robustly realistic attitude towards the march of events affecting the fortunes of the country. Such an organization can not at this moment afford to think that the policy that was considered necessary and adequate more than a year ago is either necessary or adequate now. Both the course of international developments and the political and administrative changes inside the country have been too considerable to allow us to think that there is no need for a fresh attempt to see whether a reorientation of policy is not called for.'

Moral Protest

Proceeding, the paper says: 'We do not for a moment overlook the tremendous value of a moral protest against Britain's action in dragging this country into war as if the opinions of four hundred million people were of no account. That protest has resounded in all four corners of the world by now. If Satyagraha is suspended now, no one can be misled into supposing that Britain has succeeded in living down the opposition to her having adopted a high-handed attitude both in regard to India's entry into the war and her national aspirations.'

Concluding, the paper says: 'We know that Gandhiji does not regard the Satyagraha campaign as a political move, that for him it is the symbol of a great spiritual effort which may have a profound influence on human endeavour and aspirations in the not distant future.

'But we would respectfully suggest that a great political organization is hardly the medium for the propagation of such views or for the testing of their worth. While it would be wrong to suggest that he and those who think like him should give up what is to them an article of faith, we would venture to say that, realizing the plight of the country and the direction in which the thoughts of all progressive elements are moving, he should advise the Congress to revise its policy if it should be convinced that a change is called for in the best interests of the country.

'Mahatmaji has, at crucial times in the past given a new impulse to Congress activities by such unconventional and great-hearted leadership and we trust he will see that the time is ripe for another such change'.

59. 'Our Struggle': Mahatma Gandhi's Statement to the Press, 28 October 1941

File No. G–18 (P–II), AICC Papers, NMML.

Sevagram,
28 October 1941

Time seems to have arrived for a brief review especially as several leaders who have been discharged have met me and there has been much speculation about the trend or the result of these talks. The public should know that those who were not whole-heartedly with the Bombay Resolution have come out with their doubts confirmed. Similarly those who never had any doubts have become firmer than ever before in their opinion. As for me I never had any doubt as to the correctness of the Bombay Resolution and have none about the correctness of the steps hitherto taken in pursuance thereof.

Complaints reach me (1) that there is marked deterioration in enthusiasm; (2) that fewer people are coming forward now than before; (3) that those who are discharged are not seeking imprisonment again; (4) that there is no discipline among many satyagrahi prisoners, some of whom have no notion of non-violence or truth; (5) that the treatment of C class prisoners is inhuman in that the food given is bad in quality and deficient in balance. The result is that the majority of prisoners have suffered in health, making it impossible for many on discharge to seek imprisonment again without adequate rest and repair. There are complaints too about want of newspapers, books, and proper sanitation; (6) that the policy of non-embarrassment is unintelligible, as the Rulers themselves do not appreciate it, and the fight therefore should be intensified without regard to embarrassment; (7) that there is no life left in the Congress—there are no meetings, there are no demonstrations, no other activity, and that there should be a change of policy and programme even resulting in the resumption of full parliamentary programme, including ministries, that is, reversion to the Poona offer with suitable modification.

(1 and 2) I shall consider the first two together. Enthusiasm that is froth is of no use in non-violent action. Showy demonstrations and the like have a value in the initial stages. Continuous

feverish activity can only promote violence and therefore retard the steady march of non-violent action, call it battle, if that word is preferred. That fewer are coming forward is but natural. For it must be recalled that civil disobedience is individual and restricted to representatives, be they even elected members of village or *firka* committee. The list of representatives being limited, it must one day be exhausted. I have no doubt that if I made a general call and relaxed the conditions of enrollment I should be overwhelmed by applications. I have no machinery to examine such applications. In reality it will be mass action which does not admit of individual examination and choice. That call will not come before the close of the war. There is neither warrant nor atmosphere for mass action. That would be naked embarrassment and a betrayal of non-violence. What is more it can never lead to independence. Mass action at this stage without communal unity is an invitation to civil war. If civil war is to be our lot, it will come, but if I know the Congress mind, it will never come at the wish or invitation of the Congress.

(3) This complaint is partially valid. It is true that some of those who have been discharged are reluctant to go back. This is a novel experience for India. I had to do it in South Africa. The struggle demanded it there as it now does here. Self-suffering has no limit. In the former civil disobedience the occasion had not come to send the same resisters to jail again and again. In the present one it is inevitable. Any other course would reduce the struggle to a farce. The alternative suggested is that substitutes should be found for those who would not go in again. Surely that is not the way of suffering. And how can we think of gaining independence without a full measure of suffering? The greater the cause, the richer the suffering, therefore in this struggle they only will count who will seek imprisonment again and again, come what will. They may be very few. That will not matter. Of course those who are ill will naturally not be required to go till they are restored. Some have interpreted literally my statement that the discharged satyagrahis may take about a week before they go. Each case has to be judged on merits. Shri Vinoba went in twice within 72 hours of his discharge. He had to come to me before re-offering civil disobedience. Hence even that little delay. Shri Pyarelal took nearly a month before going in for the third time. There were unavoidable causes which need not occupy the reader's time and attention. I have mentioned two cases which I was personally regulating. They exemplify the elasticity I refer to.... I can otherwise utilize the services, as true soldiers of truth, of men and women who will whole-heartedly carry out instructions. Thus those who cannot for some just reason court imprisonment, should engage themselves in corporate constructive activity. Difficulty arises because many Congressmen, though they profess or believe in CD, have no faith in the constructive programme. I must proclaim from the housetop for the thousandth time that constructive programme is an integral part of the national movement and therefore also of CD I was therefore delighted that there was a wide response from the prisoners and the other Congressmen this time in the matter of spinning during the spinning carnival. I dare to believe that if Congressmen were enthusiastic believers in communal unity and removal of untouchability and the like, there would be no communal discord and there would be no antagonism such as it is for Harijans. We are the makers of our own destiny. It has been somewhat justly said that if I am a good General, I must not grumble about my men. For I must choose them from the material at my disposal. I plead guilty. But I have qualified my admission by the adverb 'somewhat', for I laid down the conditions from the very inception of the programme of non-violence. My terms were accepted. If from experience it is found that the terms cannot be worked, I must either be dismissed or I must retire. I retired but to no purpose. The bond between Congressmen and me seems to be unbreakable. They

may quarrel with my conditions but they will not leave me or let me go. They know that however unskilled a servant I may be, I will neither desert them nor fail them in the hour of need. And so they try, thought often grumblingly, to fulfil my conditions. I must then on the one hand adhere to my conditions so long as I have a living faith in them and, on the other, take what I can get from Congressmen, expecting that if I am true, they will some day fulfil all my conditions and find themselves in the enjoyment of full independence such as has never before been seen on earth.

(4) There are two sides to the complaint about indiscipline. I must here confine myself to satyagrahi prisoners only. I would naturally like the other political prisoners to attend to what I say. It is wrong to say that there is universal indiscipline among Congressmen or that all are unfit to be called satyagrahis. Cases of grave indiscipline have been brought to my notice. I know that violent men have crept into the organization under the guise of non-violence. But I know also cases of exemplary discipline. Everybody knows that there are in the movement and among the prisoners faithful Congressmen. I am conducting the struggle in their name and for their sake. It is through them that we may expect to win. This should mean no reflection on those who are weak but true. Even a child of seven who performs its allotted task faithfully will be entitled to the same credit as those who may cheerfully mount the gallows, if thereto called....

(5) C class prisoners' is almost a baffling question. I have said more than once that classification is bad in itself. But the Congress has come to no decision on the question. Meanwhile we must do the best we can. There is no manner of doubt in my mind that the treatment of C class prisoners is unhuman. I do not wish to blame either the Government or the prison officials. I admit that theirs is a thankless task. For ages almost they have been used to only one tradition. Their mind refuses to grasp the distinction between criminals and political prisoners. They would make no distinction between prisoners guilty of crimes and those who rebel against constituted authority. For them the politicals are worse than the others. But pressure of public opinion has compelled distinction. The result is highly unsatisfactory. The will on the part of the officials is lacking. Satyagrahis who seek imprisonment cannot with any dignity quarrel with the treatment they get, except when their honour is attacked. An irresponsible government, which the British Government in India is, may, as it often does, defy public opinion. Satyagrahis have still to court imprisonment. It is one of the gateways to liberty. They cannot stipulate as to the conditions of jail life....

It is cruel to distinguish between the food of the different classes. The needs in the majority of cases of the political prisoners are identical. I suggest that the rations of all political prisoners should approach what is known as balanced diet with the permission to replenish it at the prisoner's expense. As to sanitation and other matters, a non-official medical committee should make recommendations which should be given effect to at once. There should be identity of treatment in all the provinces.

Having said this, I must warn satyagrahis against hunger-strikes or the like. It is their duty to conform to the jail regulations in so far as they do not come in conflict with known rules of honour, nor self-made ones by hyper-sensitive temperaments. These ought not to court imprisonment. I suggest that it is a satyagrahi's first code of honour that he will conscientiously carry out jail discipline with the reservation just mentioned. Satyagraha is a process of silent conversion. Indiscipline and nagging are wholly inconsistent with the ambition of conversion. I am repeating these views of mine not without fear and trembling, for I know that jail officials have often quoted them on wrong occasions against satyagrahi prisoners. Of course in all I have said, there is nothing against carrying out constitutional agitation for jail reforms even as to the socalled criminals. A satyagrahi is a universal reformer. For him there is no distinction between criminals and non-criminals. He is out to render service to the whole of humanity to the extent of his ability and opportunity.

There is the question of newspapers and books. These are as important as food. Some would do without food but not without newspapers and literature. I hold that deprivation of this amenity is additional punishment for a political prisoner.

(6) Although I have dealt with the question of non-embarrassment in my previous statements, I see that it still continues to agitate many Congressmen. For one thing, it is part of the Bombay Resolution and effect should be given to it. It is inherent in non-violence. But it is also expedient. By causing embarrassment at this stage, the authorities must resent it bitterly and are likely to act madly. Of course it would be different if we had resorted to armed rebellion. Then the saying 'their difficulty becomes our opportunity' would apply. It is obvious that exactly the opposite rule should apply when an opposite method is adopted. It is worse than suicide to resort to violence, that is, embarrassment under cover of non-violence. We may not be 'temperate and furious' at the same time.

'But then to be logical you must give up CD altogether', says the critic. To give up CD would be folly. CD in itself is completely non-violent action. It is a duty in the face of violence without parallel. CD in the present case means assertion of the right to speak against participation in this war or all wars. If we cannot do even this much when the occasion demands it, we might as well give up non-violence. CD is the assertion of a right which law should give but it denies. If performance of a duty causes embarrassment, it cannot be helped. It is my duty to give up drink. It would cause some loss to the tavern-keeper. I am helpless. The authority can easily avoid embarrassment by recognizing the elementary right of non-violent free speech. Consideration whether the policy of self-imposed restraint creates an immediate impression on the authority is irrelevant. Blief that it must ultimately is inherent in belief in non-violence itself. We may not bear ill-will against the bitterest opponent.

(7) I do not share the belief that there is no life left in the Congress. 'Still waters run deep.' Congressmen are too much attached to the Congress to let the institution die of inanity. There seems to be no life because we have no spectacular show in the shape parliamentary programme or mass CD Things are going according to plan. CD is restricted to select individuals. It will be further restricted to those who re-offer CD as often as necessary. It does not matter if the number is reduced to ten or two. The two will represent the whole Congress. Does not one ambassador represent his people? One can be multiplied infinitely. Parliamentary activity has been almost stopped also according to plan. It may be, in my opinion, should be stopped completely. But I do not wish to rush things. Members of local boards have in many cases been withdrawn according to plan.

Then what are the Congressmen to do if they cannot or will not be allowed to offer CD and there is no parliamentary programme? The answer is simple. There are only two things for Congressmen to do. All to carry on the thirteenfold constructive programme and some select few to offer CD in addition. CD is a mighty weapon to be wielded effectively by only a few in the first instance. Constructive programme is to be worked by all Congressmen and even non-Congressmen if they will. How can people shut their eyes to its paramount importance? Even parliamentary programme without it is a mere farce. We have had it till 1920. I do not deny its usefulness, even as a farce is useful. But there is no such thing as a farce without the backing of a play. In 1920 the nation came into its own. Constructive programme was described in so many words to be a preparation for CD Parliamentary programme was given up in toto. The nation lost nothing by it. Parliamentary programme will have its definite place when we have a parliament of our own. Let it not be forgotten that this is expected to be a fight to the finish. It is true that CD will be suspended if genuine free speech is granted. If we do not find ourselves free at the end of the war, resumption will be a certainty. But that is idle speculation. If we do our present duty, whatever the circumstances that face us at the end of the war we shall be found ready.

Let me glance at the constructive programme. There is communal unity. It is worth much more than the whole parliamentary programme. Without it, the latter is useless. It becomes a field for interminable wrangling. Complete heart-unity takes us almost straightway to independence. Let me not be told that there will be no unity at all—or not in our lifetime. I must refuse to believe the negation so long as there are some men working for unity. If the Congress cannot, I know that no other institution can. For every Congressman must equally represent in his own person every Indian, no matter what his faith is. In that sense he belongs to all religions.

Then take untouchability. I repeat that if untouchability lives, Hinduism—and with it India—dies. Is that not a programme worth living for, dying for? And the spinning wheel, whose every turn brings India nearer her destiny? Surely it can fully occupy every day of every Congressman. And the wheel being the centre of our solar system, it includes all the planets in the shape of village industries.

The wheel brings us at once to the emancipation of India's manhood, *kisans,* labourers, and all those who are weary and heavy-laden. If this all-inclusive and mighty programme is not understood and appreciated by Congressmen, they do not know the A B C of non-violence, nor do they know the elements of CD.

This programme gives ample scope for public meetings, demonstrations, exhibitions and the like. No official Congress Committees need function for coordinating these activities. Wherever five earnest Congressmen are found, they can group together and organize them.

Congress will now see why I contemplate no change in the programme as it is going and why I am full of hope for the future of the country.

60. Satyagraha

Editiorial, *National Herald*, 2 November 1941.

The first official comment on the statement of Mahatma Gandhi, refusing to withdraw or suspend the Satyagraha movement, has come from the Congress Socialist Party. It would have been out of tune with the spirit and temper of the party if it had not stated through its general secretary and president of the present session of the Bihar Provincial Congress Socialist Conference, that it was not at all satisfied with the movement in spite of Mahatma Gandhi's assurance to the contrary. The party wants it to be intensified into a mass struggle for freedom to which it would be open to every Indian to contribute his share. What should delight Mahatma Gandhi's heart more than that every Indian would, and does contribute, his share. When that happens a mass struggle would justify itself, at any rate would be on the way to justifying itself. It is because that every solider has not done his duty that the general does not feel sure that the situation is ripe for mass action, apart from other necessary and delicately chivalrous consideration which are so characteristic of his way of thinking.

When Mr Purshottam Das Tricumdas proceed to point out that if the Congress or rather Mahatma Gandhi cannot be persuaded to start a mass struggle, we will still support the present movement because the alternative of total inaction, and constitutional talk will be utterly disastrous.' He not only speaks with a lively sense of realism but at the same time stresses the great gap between the Gandhian and the Parliamentary stand, which British perversity has deepened and widened. Mr Satyamurthi easily the most obstinate parliamentarian in this country must have been considerably nettled to read the statement of his friend and colleague, Mr Sri Prakasa, in the course of which the latter observes that he does not think that, as things are, one can envisage either the desirability or the possibility of parliamentary activities in the provinces where the constitution is at present suspended. 'I find it difficult,' says Mr Sri Prakasa, 'from the stand point of practical politics to understand how parliamentary activity, on the part of Congress Ministers, and Satyagraha on the part of Congressmen in general can go on side by side. The situation will be too embarrassing for all concerned, to say the least. Fresh from Wardha, Pandit Govind Ballabh Pant has neatly summed up the situation before us in his remark at a meeting at that place that nothing has happened to justify a change of policy. If it is to be a change, it can only be a change that will mean a fuller and a more striking remobilization of our resources....

61. Debate in the Central Legislative Assembly on N.M. Joshi's Resolution Recommending Release of Political Prisoners, 18 November 1941

Indian Annual Register, 1941, Vol. II, pp. 133–5.

Release of Political Prisoners

18th November: Mr *N.M. Joshi,* moved this resolution recommending that steps should be taken in agreement with Provincial Governments for the immediate and unconditional release of prisoners detained in prison and for the removal of restrictions imposed on some persons regarding their movements or actions, where the detention or restriction was due to holding or expressing opinions which, in the opinion of the Government, were prejudicial to the conduct of the war, or on charges for the actions connected with industrial disputes, whether the detention or restriction was with or without trial under the Defence of India Act or under the ordinary law. Mr Joshi said his resolution was of great importance and full of potentialities, if properly responded to, for the good of the country. The three classes of persons, whose release his resolution sought, were firstly, political prisoners; secondly Communists or revolutionaries who were merely suspected to be such, and thirdly, prisoners who had taken part either in the Kisan or labour movement. He estimated the number of satyagrahis and Congressmen who expressed opposition to war and were detained after trial as between three thousand and five thousand The Home Member had stated in reply to his question that the number of people detained without trial was more than 1,300 and the number of those who were not imprisoned but on whom restrictions had been imposed was about two thousand. Thus the number of people coming within the scope of the resolution was very large. Mr Joshi observed that his reasons for asking for acceptance of the proposal made in his resolution were, firstly, the release of political prisoners was necessary in the interest of the fundamental right of civil liberty, justice, fairplay, and humanity, and secondly, it was necessary in the interest of political wisdom. Dwelling on the first set of reasons, Mr Joshi referred to the number of people dealt with under the Defence of the Realm Act in England and said that out of 1,500 thus dealt with, 600 had been given freedom on the advice of the Advisory Committee. The newspapers this morning reported that members of Parliament were working hard to secure the privilege of scrutiny by a judicial tribunal of those people who had been deprived of their liberty under the Defence of the Realm Act. In India, he said, there was no such safeguard. Mr Joshi also referred to the fact that the Government of the North West Frontier Province did not imprison satyagrahis and no harm had come to that province. Speaking on the second set of reasons, Mr Joshi said the greatest need of the country was peace, tranquility, freedom from bitterness and discontent. The effort made by the Government to secure peace and tranquility and contentment had failed in the past; but he asked the Government to make another effort and even if that failed they must make further efforts. The Government might feel that this discontent had not affected their war effort but if the political deadlock was resolved, India's war effort would be multiplied several times.

Referring to Mr Gandhi's statement, Mr Joshi said, 'I never sought Mahatma Gandhi's approval of my resolution. I did not expect Mahatma Gandhi to approve of my resolution. He has made it clear that is intended to achieve self-government and he will continue it until self-government is achieved. I do not take a tragic view of Mahatma Gandhi's statement. In my judgment Mahatma Gandhi is not opposed to the release of political prisoners. He holds they have been unjustly put in prison. How could he be opposed to their release? The very fact that he says the country will resent the release of only one section of prisoners shows that he expects the release not only of satyagrahis but others imprisoned without trial. It would not be enough, Mr Joshi declared, if the Government of India merely released satyagrahis. He valued the freedom of the detenus and the Communists as much as he valued the freedom of satyagrahis and he hoped that the Government would accept his proposal.

Mr *Lakshmi Kanta Moitra* moved an amendment to omit the words 'in agreement with Provincial Governments'. He was opposed to any resolution of the House which was qualified. With the proclamation issued by the Governor General immediately after the outbreak of the war, the Central Legislature was empowered to make legislation in respect of all measures. The position was that Section 102 read with Section 113 of the Government of India Act made it perfectly clear that the Executive of the Central Government could take any measure they liked for the purposes of administration. The view that the Government of India was not competent to release all political prisoners was not sound. The speaker's view was that concurrence of or agreement with Provincial Governments in this matter was not necessary. It was a peculiar misfortune of legislators in this House that day after day they had to come to the Central Executive asking either for release of political prisoners or for amelioration of their conditions in jails. Referring to the 'crimes' committed by the satyagrahis, Mr Maitra said that two High Courts had held that the uttering of slogans alone was not a crime. It was the Central Government which was mainly responsible for detention of persons without trial, which was serious challenge to justice. These men in his opinion were philosophical anarchists without being guilty of any overt act. In conclusion, Mr Maitra appealed to the Government to associate themselves with the people, shake off their prejudices and make a generous gesture. If this was done nothing would be lost.

Sir *Reginald Maxwell,* Home Member, intervening in the debate on Mr N.M. Joshi's resolution urging the release of political prisoners, said that the matter raised by the resolution was one in which provincial Governments were closely concerned and the resolution itself recognized this fact when it asked the Government to take steps in agreement with provincial Governments.

Conditions were not the same in all provinces. Very far from it, a general agreement which the resolution postulated must in the nature of things take account of local differences and must require some time if it was to be reached at all. In these circumstances, the Home Member added, the Government were not in a position, as an immediate result of this debate, to anticipate the outcome of these consultations or at this stage to commit themselves or the provinces to any particular course of action. The whole matter needed further careful consideration. He was able to assure the House on behalf of the Government that this consideration would be given without unnecessary delay and in a sympathetic spirit. He hoped that in the light of this assurance Mr Joshi would not think it necessary to press his resolution. Sir Reginald point out that whether in the case of persons convicted or detained, the Central Government would have direct authority to carry out the resolution only in areas under their control, namely, in Chief Commissioner's provinces. The number of persons affected in this respect by this resolution constituted a small minority indeed. It was wrong to assume that the Central Government had the sole responsibility for the administration of the Defence of India Rules or for action, judicial or otherwise, taken thereunder. The Defence of India Act did not alter the structure of the Government of India or the division of authority and responsibility between the Central and provincial Governments. That the Central Government had passed legislation dealing with provincial subjects made no difference as regards allocation of executive authority after powers had been lawfully conferred. The Home Member went on to give a series of figures of persons covered by the resolution. The number of convicted persons in jail on 1 October was 7,216 under all the various Rules including those dealing with non-political offences. The total number of persons detained under Rule 26 was 1,759. The House, he observed, would admit that these were not large figures after two years of war among a population of 400 millons and in a country in which not all persons see eye to eye with the Government. The resolution, he pointed out, would apply only to certain categories among the numbers he had mentioned. These consisted of 6,148 persons convicted or detained in connection with the Civil Disobedience movement, about 1,300 other convicted persons, 95 other persons detained; and 366 persons restricted for political activities. Of these about 200 persons were those whose release would have been within the executive authority of the Central Government if the resolution was accepted in full. The Home Member declared that no one had been or ever would be convicted or restricted merely on account of his holding certain opinions. In every case action had been taken for something more than the mere holding or expression of opinion. Liberty of speech was necessarily more limited in war than in peace. The State must claim the right to regulate individual liberty of speech in the interest of national survival. This principle applied to many activities other than speech. After quoting Mr *Churchill's* observations on the necessary curtailment of liberties during the war, the Home Member reiterated it had always been recognized that the limitation of individual liberty was an unwelcome but necessary concomitant of war.

Sir *Reginald* went on to quote passages from Communist literature which declared that the war was an opportunity for which Communists were waiting and incited people to strikes, refusal to recruit or co-operate in the war effort and to a militant campaign of resistance so as to cripple 'the war machine of imperialism.' The object of the Communists, the Home Member declared, was not to find means of setting industrial grievances but foment strikes and keep them alive as long as possible. Even after Russia became our ally, the Communists continued to declare that the only way in which the Indian people could help in the war was in fighting for emancipation from imperialist domination; and that their attitude remained what it was before. If there was any doubt, the revelation now made about Mr *Subhas Bose* should convince everyone that the Government had to take every precaution against Fifth Column activity in this country. No Government could permit activities intended to obstruct the war effort and promote conditions of disorder in these critical days. He was sure that the Provincial Governments had used their powers with discrimination. It would be altogether wrong to assume that either the Central or the Provincial Governments had less regard for the principle of individual liberty than individuals in the House (cries of Oh oh). No one would be kept under detention longer than was necessary. Some periodical examination of these cases was necessary, said the Home Member. Something must be left to the discretion of Provincial Governments which he was sure would give attention to this matter. The House might rest assured that the Government were concerned to see that the grounds for detention in every case should be adequate and should be re-examined by very high authorities at suitable intervals.

The Home Member then referred to the demand for liberty of speech by *Mahatma Gandhi* and the Viceroy's reply thereto and said that in the face of the demand supported by threat of civil disobedience the Government were bound to take the threat seriously and could not have allowed the movement to develop unchallenged up to a point at which the Congress would have gained complete liberty to interfere with the war effort. Political or any other motives could not be regarded as an extenuation of offences deliberately calculated to weaken the resistance of the country or impair or undermine its war effort. He was entitled to say that the policy pursued in dealing with these offences was not vindictive and the Government had not taken more action than was necessary to assert the vital principle involved. 'It was largely due to the steady pursuit of that policy that we had the calm atmosphere in which to consider this resolution to-day', observed Sir Reginald. After giving the assurance that the question of release of political prisoners would receive careful consideration in consultation with the Provinces, the Home Member concluded by saying that he believed the country on the whole was tired of unrealities and only wanted to get on with the war. Those who had not surrendered their judgment to others, did not want the country to be stripped by the invading army and did not sympathize with those who, for whatever object, were adopting courses of action which, if successful, could only help Hitler.

After the debate in which Messrs *Deshmukh* and *S. Sant Singh* joined, Mr *Joshi* withdrew his motion stating that he had no other course but to give more time for the Government to come to a decision as the Home Member had wanted. He hoped that the Government would come to the right decision. The Assembly then adjourned *sine die.*

62. Andhra Pradesh Congress Committee's Circular on Satyagraha and Congress Members in Local Bodies, 27 November 1941

File No. G–23/1941, AICC Papers, NMML.

Andhra Provincial Congress Committee,
Madras, Circular No. 106

I. During the continuous tour for over a month throughout our province I had discussed with the presidents and members of the local boards and also the chairmen and municipal councilors who were available in each District, all matters relating to Local Administration, particularly the position to which the said bodies have been reduced during the past one year. It is generally acknowledged that the said local bodies have ceased to be autonomous bodies and have become creatures of the present Government ever since the Local Boards Act was amended in April last and the Governor had taken power to supersede them at his will under sub sec (2A) of Sec 45 as of the Madras Local Boards Act.

This was exactly what was done with regard to Provincial Autonomy before the Congress ministers resigned in October 1939. Kistna, Malabar, and Anantapur District Boards have become the victims of this amending Act and have been superseded without any just or proper cause.

II. As a protest against this and the general treatment meted out to the Local Bodies since the date of the amending Act, the Congress Presidents and members of the District Boards and the Congress chairmen and members of the municipal councils are hereby called upon to resign and withdraw from these bodies by the 15th of December 1941. It was for such and other causes that Shri Kripalani the General Secretary of the AICC, suggested that members of Congress Committees should not contest the next general elections of District Boards and Municipalities.

III. Nellore district does not come under this rule just at present because of the Hindu–Muslim troubles that have been going on for some time in Nellore Town. The District Board President and Municipal Chairman are amongst the members of the Congress Special Relief Committee appointed by me on behalf of the Andhra Provincial Congress Committee for raising funds and providing relief to the sufferers of both Muslim and Hindu communities. A special date will be fixed for Nellore when the present tension is relaxed and normal conditions are restored.

IV. Procedure for Adoption

A. District Boards: Instructions

1. The Leaders of the Congress parties in the District Boards should collect the resignations of all the Congress Members in duplicate and send both of them immediately to the Provincial Congress Committee office No. 1, Gopaldass Road, Mount Road, PO Madras. Tel: Swarajya, Madras.

2. The Congress Members of the District Boards are requested to send in their individual resignations in duplicate to their concerned Presidents immediately as soon as this Circular is received so as to enable their Leaders to send them on to the PCC without any delay as suggested above. The forms for the necessary resignations are herewith enclosed in duplicate which should be signed by each member and sent by the return post to their party leaders.

3. As per Section 16 Madras Local Boards Act the President's resignation shall be placed before the Board for acceptance first. The Board shall accept the resignation immediately in the meeting convened for the purpose. Thereafter the President continues as a member with others.

4. Then the resignation of all the members, including the President, shall be placed in the hands of the Vice-President who assumes the functions of the President under Section 22 A (1) of the Local Boards Act.

5. The Vice-President should by way of caution accept the resignations of each member and endorse the same even though the resignation takes effect soon as it is received by him, under Section 16 (a) and 22 A of Local Boards Act. By this process of elimination the Vice-President alone remains together with his membership.

6. The Vice-President should then tender his resignation both for his membership and Vice-Presidentship to the Collector immediately on the very day of the meeting convened for the acceptance of the President's resignation.

NB: The Vice-President should also tender his resignation in duplicate along with the rest of the members and hand them over to the President to be sent to the President APCC.

7. Special instructions are being given to the Presidents of the various District Boards for convening the meetings of the Board for acceptance of the President's resignations.

Since all the resignation papers of the individual Congress members will be handed over to the Vice-President by the President, AICC only after the meeting which will be convened for the acceptance of the President's resignations. All the Congress members of the District Boards are requested to attend the meeting without fail.

B. Municipalities: Instructions

(Under Section 81 of Madras District Municipalities Act)

1. Chairman: In case of Municipalities the Chairman should receive the resignations of the members of the Congress party including himself in duplicate and the Vice-Chairman would accept them immediately and send copies of them to the President APCC.

2. Members: The members of the Municipal Congress party including the Vice-Chairman are requested to give their resignations in duplicate immediately in the forms enclosed to this to their party leader who in his turn will accept and send copies of them to the President APCC.

3. Special instructions are being given to the Chairman of the various Municipalities for convening a meeting for placing their resignations, both to their councillorship and Chairmanship before the Council (In most of the Municipalities, except that of Palacole, there will be quorum even after the resignation of all the Congress members).

4. In case of Palacole Municipality the Chairman after accepting all the resignations of the fifteen members should send his resignation to the Sub-Collector, Narasapur, and hand it over to the Commissioner.

5. Therefore every member should act according to the instructions given herein and avoid enforcement of any disciplinary action.

The District Agents are also requested to help the Leaders of the Congress Parties in this behalf in their local bodies.

The action taken in this connection by the Congress party leaders of the various Local bodies should be communicated at once to the Provincial Congress Committee Office, Madras.

All the above procedure should be completed before the 15th of December 1941.

T. Prakasam
President

No. 1 Gopaldass Road
Mount Road, PO 27th November 1941

63. Mahatma Gandhi's Press Statement on Release of Satyagrahis,[1] 4 December 1941

File No. Miscellaneous VII/4, Rajkumari Amrit Kaur Papers, NMML; *CWMG*, Vol. LXXV, pp. 131–2.

As I said before the event I must repeat after the event that so far as I am concerned it cannot evoke a single responsive or appreciative chord in me. From my student days onward I have been and I still claim to be a friend of the British people. But my friendship cannot blind me to the fact that British representatives hold India as a bond slave. All the freedom that India enjoys is the freedom of the slave, not the freedom of an equal which is otherwise known as complete independence. Mr Amery's pronouncements do not soothe the festering sore. But they are like sprinkling chillies on it. It is in that setting that I am called upon to examine this release. If the Government of India are confident in the determination of all responsible opinion in India to support the war effort, the logical conclusion would be to keep CD prisoners in their custody because they produced the jarring note. The only meaning I can attach to the release, therefore, is that they expect that the prisoners will have changed their opinion in their self-invited solitude. I am hoping that Government will be soon disillusioned. Civil Disobedience was not taken up without the most careful consideration. It was certainly not taken up out of any vindictiveness. It was taken up and I hope will be continued in order to make good the claim of the Congress to let the British people and the world know that there is at the very least a large body of public opinion represented by the Congress which is utterly opposed to participation in the war—not because it wishes any disaster to British arms or victory to the Nazi or Fascist arms, but because it sees no deliverance from blood spillings either for the victors or the vanquished and certainly no deliverance for India out of this war. The Congress which seeks and claims to represent the dumb millions has for the past twenty years accepted non-violence as its unbroken policy to achieve India's independence. To stop CD, symbolic though it may be for the time being will be to deny its policy at the crucial moment. The Government claim that in spite of the Congress effort they are able to get all the men and money they want from India. Therefore the Congress opposition, in their estimate, can only be a moral effort and a moral demonstration. I am entirely satisfied with it because I am convinced that from the moral demonstration will arise, when the moment comes, a demonstration which will result in the attainment of India's independence—not the ascendance of this party or that. The Congress struggle covers every single unit in India. And now that the Congress President is expected to be out, it will be for him to consider whether and when to call the Congress WC and the AICC. These two bodies will determine the future policy of the Congress. I am but a humble instrument of service in conducting civil resistance. I would say, however, one word about the detenus and other prisoners. It sounds strange that those who have sought imprisonment are to be discharged and not those who are either detained without trial or imprisoned because they hold the freedom of their country dearer than their personal liberty. There is surely something utterly wrong somewhere. I therefore cannot rejoice over the Government of India's decision.

The Government of India is confident in the determination of all responsible opinion in India to support the war effort until victory is secured, and has reached the conclusion that those Civil Disobedience prisoners who have committed an offence symbolic in character can be set free. Effect will be given to this as soon as possible. There are provinces in which the numbers and local conditions may mean delay but before the end of December the Government of India hopes that all such prisoners will have been released. The prisoners will include Maulana Abdul Kalam Azad and Pandit Jawaharlal Nehru.

[1] Published in *The Hindu* on 6 December 1941.

64. The Call of India: Pandit Nehru's Message, Need of Sacrifice and Iron Determination

Amrita Bazar Patrika, 6 December 1941.

Pandit Jawaharlal Nehru has issued the following statement:

'To all my comrades, to Congressmen, to the people of the United Provinces, greetings. It is good to meet old friends again, to see familiar faces, to feel the warmth of the welcoming smile and the embrace and grip of comradeship. It is good to see the wide fields and the crowded streets and the ever changing panorama of humanity.

'A Trivial Change'

'But it is not good to go in and out of prison at the bidding of alien authority. It is not good to come out of the narrow confines of jail into the larger prison that is India to-day. The time will come surely when we break through and demolish all the prison walls that encompass our bodies and minds, and function freely as a free nation. But the time is not yet, and we may not forget this or rejoice at a trivial change which has no meaning.

No Peace for Us

'In this world of infinite suffering where violence and hatred and the spirit of destruction seem to reign supreme there is no rest or avoidance of travail. In this India where foreign and authoritarian rule oppresses and strangles us, there is no peace for us and the call for action in the interest of a free India and a free world comes insistently to our ears.

Call of India

'The call of India is there for those who wish to hear, the call of suffering humanity becomes more agonizing from day to day. So there is no rest for us but to carry the burden of the day and hold fast to our anchor. We have watched the heroic courage and infinite sacrifice of other people struggling for their freedom, especially of the people of China after four and half years of terrible struggle and of the people of Suviet Russia pouring their hearts' blood and destroying their own mighty achievements that freedom may live. Our conditions are different; our ways of struggle are not the same. Yet there is the same call for sacrifice and discipline and iron determination.

'The call of India continues to resound in our ears and tingle the blood in our veins. So let us go, forward then along the path of our choice and take all trials and tribulations with serenity and confidence and with smiling countenance.'

65. Congress President Advised to Convene Meetings of Working Committee and AICC

Mahatma Gandhi's Statement to the Press

CWMG, Vol. LXXV, pp. 136–8.

Wardhaganj,
7 December 1941

The jail delivery that is going on to appease of Satyagrahis must be taken as a challenge to convene a meeting of the AICC which, the Government of India have been evidently induced to expect, will reverse the Bombay decision, whose working is reflected in my conduct of the Satyagraha campaign. I have, therefore, advised the Maulana Saheb to convene a meeting of the Working Committee and the AICC at an early date, but until that decision is reversed civil disobedience has to go on.

I must admit, however, that the conduct of the campaign has been rendered difficult by the Government action in discharging civil disobedience prisoners, but if we are to reach our goal, we have to cut our way through every difficulty. This one is nothing compared to what we are likely to have to face before we come into our own.

If the AICC meeting is to come, as it must, pending the meeting members of the Working Committee and the AICC must not offer civil disobedience, nor should those who are interested in reversing the Bombay decision.

Apart from these, civil disobedience should continue without interruption. Of course it will stand suspended on Xmas Day, Boxing Day, and New Year's Day.

The question naturally arises whether civil disobedience is to be offered in the usual manner by reciting the prescribed formula or in some other manner.

I like the formula method. It gives directness and symmetry to the movement. There is great power in the reciting of the same formula in the same manner. It rivets the attention of the masses and men on identical theme. The formula is not a mean thing. It is a protest of the nation against war as an arbitrator. It is a message of peace on earth and goodwill towards mankind. What is individual formula today will become, in due time, that of the masses, but the authorities having discharged symbolical satyagrahis may refuse to rearrest them for reciting slogans.

There are then two ways open to us: if they do not rearrest, there need be no dismay and demoralization, the jail is not our objective. Freedom of speech is the immediate objective. If recitation is not objected to, we have advanced somewhat towards our objective and it will be foolish to court imprisonment for the sake of it.

Dismay and demoralization arise because Congressmen in general have not realized the inevitable connection between constructive programme and civil disobedience. Civil disobedience without the backing of constructive programme can never lead us to independence. Shorn of it, civil disobedience becomes a method of violence bound to prove ineffective in the end.

Moreover, civil disobedience, even when it is mass, will only be offered by those who are bodily fit, whereas constructive programme is for all and will never be suspended. If the whole nation took it up in earnest it is enough to give us complete independence. The prosecution of the constructive programme means, constructing the structure of swaraj.

The whole theme of corporate non-violence, as I have conceived it, falls to pieces if there is no living faith in the constructive programme.

To my mind, swaraj based on non-violence is a fulfilment of the constructive programme; hence, whether the authorities jail us or not, we must pursue the constructive programme.

I have been asked whether discharged Satyagrahis should hold or attend meetings and deliver speeches. They should do so. I do not want or expect them to re-offer civil disobedience immediately. That would be indecent haste, but ordinary civil disobedience may go on. For the discharged ones let there be breathing time. Let them address meetings in their constituencies and study things. At the meetings they will expound their views on the general situation and not hesitate to interpret anti-war Congress policy.

Symbolic Satyagraha has a definite meaning but it is open to the authorities to arrest Congressmen for their speeches even if they do not intend thereby to offer CD That was how they had arrested the Maulana Sahib and Pandit Jawaharlal Nehru, not to mention lesser lights.

Let it be known that I have no authority to suspend CD on extraneous grounds. That is for the Congress to do. For me personally there is no choice.

As a man sworn to peace, at this critical moment to suspend my anti-war acativity would be to deny myself.

Therefore, for those who think like me, whether we are misunderstood or worse befalls, we must express our faith through our action hoping thereby that ultimately our way will be accepted by all warring powers as they only escape from a blood-bath which is reducing man to his lowest depth.

The Bombay Chronicle, 8.12.1941

66. Jawaharlal Nehru's Speech, Allahabad, 14 December 1941

SWJN, Vol. 12, pp. 16–28.

The Priority of Independence[1]

After a long time I am here again addressing you at this Purushottam Das Park. I have said 'after a long time' for indeed a period of about fourteen months has elapsed. But time is, nowadays, a bad measure of the progress of the world, for what really counts is not the temporal gap but the progress which has been made and the eventful happenings that have taken place. If many big events come to pass within a short space of time the period should be regarded as a long one. On the other hand if nothing eventful happens during a long period of time it is negligible. What is happening in the world today and what we see around us, is changing the world so swiftly that our minds can hardly keep pace with the changes and grasp them. So I am justified in saying that a long time has elapsed. During these fourteen months many important events have taken place in India in connection with our freedom struggle and the war. I am not sure whether you have fully grasped their implications for they are rather intricate. We are simply watching the events without explaining to the people what is going on in the world. People no doubt read the news in papers and hears them on the radio, discuss them among themselves but can see nothing with their eyes. It is one thing to look at the chessmen and watch their game, but quite a different thing to understand and appreciate the play.

The war has reached the borders of India. Whether, it is near or far off, it must have, and it is in fact having, its repercussions on India. I do not wish that the war should spread to India and that her cities be bombed. I would be grieved if enemy planes drop bombs on Indian cities. But from one point of view, I would like it because it will rouse up this old country from its obvious slumber and make it think of the world events. Anyway, it is not in our hands and is a thing of the future.

Our country is facing grave issues and it is the duty of each one of us to consult our comrades, co-workers and institutions and unitedly to follow a course of action which is justified for India. If we lack teamwork, there will be sectional party factions which are reprehensible. The first lesson we have to learn and translate into action is that we must work unitedly and firmly. Even if we mark time there should be absolute harmony and resoluteness in our ranks.

We can of course retrace a false step but if we lose the power of marching, all is lost. It is, therefore, necessary for us today to ponder over these problems from all points of view and to arrive at a definite decision collectively, even though some individuals might not entirely agree with the final decision of the majority. For this very reason I should have kept mum and spoken only after due consultations, but I have been a sinner in this respect. Only seven or eight days back I was released from jail and during this interval you have seen my several speeches in the press. Notwithstanding my earnest desire to hold my tongue, I find that it becomes very difficult for me to restrain myself when I meet my friends and the public. It is impossible to reply to their questions by silence and something has to be said. I have therefore, said something although I have still refrained from saying a lot and have kept back the thousands of ideas which are crowding my mind.

Before addressing you I had the occasion of meeting and holding consultations with many leaders at Lucknow and I was much benefited by it. Jail life affords ample opportunities for cool thinking. There we get an opportunity to think over many things and this we cannot do when we are out of jail. But in a way we are cut off from the world and however much we might read newspapers and think deeply over a problem, we can never keep abreast with the times when we are out of touch with the public. Therefore, it is advisable for a man who has just been released from jail, after a long spell, to acquaint himself with the march of events and to study his environment with a view to find out what is happening and what can be done. I have been trying to do this for the last seven or eight days since I came out of jail, and I shall continue the effort. After a few days I shall go to Bombay and then to Bardoli where the Working Committee is going to meet. Important decisions will be taken there.

I want to remind you of a few things which form the main theme of discussions in and out of jail and among Congress leaders and public alike. It appears that different men hold different views and this is by no means surprising. India is faced with a number of problems today but the primary issue before her is that of her freedom. If anybody loses sight of it, he is a worthless man. It is with this larger issue of national freedom that the problems of India's poverty, unemployment, and illiteracy are linked up.

It is a settled fact that in the present-day world we cannot separate the problems of one particular country from the rest of the world. If we think that we are concerned only with the freedom of India and have nothing to do with the world, we are labouring under a delusion. What happens in one country today must have its inevitable effect on other countries. While the thought of India's independence should be uppermost in the mind of every Indian, you cannot remain safe in your country if the world is engulfed in a conflagration. You cannot ignore the world and think only of India's safety. Neither should you be swayed by communal sentiments whether you are Hindu or Muslim. If you are a Hindu and think only of Hindu interests or if Muslims think in terms of their interests only, then such sectional interests are reprehensible. A number of our countrymen entertain such views and they regard the interests of one community as higher than those of others but they are in the wrong. There should be absolute equality of rights and privileges. This means that the whole world is closely bound together.

The war has now spread to almost every part of the world. It is raging in all the three continents—Europe, Asia, and Africa. If peace is restored after this war and a treaty is signed, it will relate to all the countries of the world and not to any particular part of the globe. But it is India's independence that we have particularly to keep in view. After all if we Indians do not get independence, we are worthless. We Indians want our freedom, which concerns forty crores of people. This is a serious problem before the world. It is possible that these forty crores of Indians might be drowned but the world has reached such a stage today that if these forty crores of Indians are drowned they will go down with a big portion of the world including the British and their country. Such is the relationship of the world and India today. China is even bigger than India and she has an ancient civilization. You may rest assured that when a decision affecting the whole world is taken, India and China whose population is forty to fifty crores—about half the total population of the world—cannot be ignored. Therefore, if any person talks of the world without taking notice of India and China, under the delusion that India can be ignored for she is a small country, he understands neither India nor China. So the question of India's independence is a vital issue not only for India but for the whole world. This is the primary issue. All other problems are secondary.

The next question which arises is how to win this freedom. This is not a separate question by itself but is linked up with the first one. I shall explain this to you. It relates to the war and has become, much complicated. When the war broke out a little over two years ago the Congress issued a long statement. What was the British reply to it? They attacked our nationalism and the Congress. Satyagraha was, therefore, started and Congressmen courted arrest. Recently I and some other people have been released by the Government but the Satyagraha movement launched by Mahatma Gandhi has not yet been suspended and is still continuing. Of course we have been set free and we shall hold consultations and put forward what is finally decided, but the movement will continue unless the Congress decides another course of action. Now the intricate question which arises is that on the one hand we cannot help in the prosecution of the war; we do not want to render any help, nor are we cooperating in the war effort; at the same time we do not want to press those who are voluntarily cooperating in the war effort to desist from rendering help. But the way in which the British Government has been flouting our demands for the last two years and the statements issued by high-placed British officials with regard to India and the Congress, are still fresh in our minds. What conclusions have you drawn from them? I have drawn several conclusions. The first is that the British Government which rules over us has not changed its attitude towards us in the least.

If the war has brought about any change in the attitude of the British Government it is the increase in its arrogance and misbehaviour towards Indians. Remember, I always refer to the system of government and bear no grudge against any individual. I harbour no ill will against the British public but I shall ever remain hostile to a government like the present British Government which always tries to practise oppression on India and keeps her enslaved. It will always continue its efforts to hold Indians under perpetual domination no matter how many revolutions might take place in the world. It is annoying to read Mr Amery's statement. I have reiterated here more than once my ideas in that connection. Whatever be the final results the only possible attitude towards such a government today or at any time can be one of rebellion.

Mr Amery's repeated utterances in regard to India are calculated to create the maximum of dissension among Indians by various means. The way in which he talks of India and humiliates Indians is well known to the present-day world. No one can cast aspersions on India and speak against her freedom. We cannot bend our knees and beg for Swaraj. I do not do this and I hope no Indian is so devoid of self-respect as to do so.

The second point is that the war is a big affair and it is not confined to the British people and their Government. It is an international affair and many nations are ranged in opposite camps. The British Government is fighting against Hitler who is in Germany. We have no sympathy with him. Nazism is but another form of an oppressive imperialism. I regard these nations as tyrannical which are striving to bring the world under their subjection. You know Germans are a martial race and they are well versed in the art of warfare. We must admit that they have not betrayed weakness on any battleground but their weakness consists in their lack of forethought. Do they not know the huge toll of lives that would be exacted by the war? I have deeply thought over these matters and have also read a lot about them. Do you know what opinion Germans hold about Indians? They think themselves to be at the highest rung of the international ladder while the lowest position is allotted to Indians by them. So it is impossible for us to sympathize with them. Indians might be full of emotions of anger against the Government and they might very likely be led to think that their enemy's enemies are their friends, but this is muddled thinking and if we think like this we can do nothing great in our great country. We have to think which country is inimical to us. We are not filled with cowardly fear of the strong and we cannot help our enemy's enemies with a view to seeing our enemy defeated. That would be wrong for us. We have to think over all these points and carve out our destinies. Our friends in this war are the Chinese with whom we are closely related and who have our full sympathies. I think that China will play an important part in the future world. I hope and wish that India and China took a big step unitedly in the reconstruction of the future world. I am glad that the bonds of our relations with the new China are strengthening. China is also involved in the war at this end and we wish her to triumph.

You must have heard about Russia and might have heard adverse reports about its internal affairs. We know that in India, Russia is discussed in and out of Congress circles. I have disliked many things in Russia and have frankly expressed my views about them. Twenty-four or twenty-five years ago a new order was introduced in Russia. They had to face great hardships and to resort to violence but they placed the proletariat on a high pedestal. They committed thousands of mistakes; still they presented a new picture before the world and established the rule of the masses.

So these are the two things you have to bear in mind. The path shown to Indians by the Satyagraha movement gave them much encouragement and made them capable and strong. But we cannot introduce in India the Soviet system of government. You might be able to introduce minor changes on the Russian model but you cannot copy Russia. Like India Russia was also illiterate but you can hardly find any illiterate there today. They have improved the condition of the peasantry enormously. They have developed their industries and hundreds of factories are working there. So, you see that they made great strides in advancing their civilization and have presented a new picture before the world. This gave tremendous strength to the masses.

The same problems are cropping up in India also. We generally take too long to do a thing in this country but in Russia big things are done with a lightning speed. It was for this reason that the latent powers of the public were unfolded. When the potential mental energy of forty crores of our countrymen will find a channel, it will flow like a big river and our nation can achieve big results by united efforts. Some of us try to acquire strength but we do not know how to utilize it properly. We have not yet acquired the requisite strength but I assure you it is already there in your hearts in a potential state; only it is struggling for an outlet and we do not know how to unfold the channels. What has taken place in Russia is not the achievement of a single individual. Lakhs of people in Russia have laboured hard to achieve big results. We might disapprove of certain things in Russia, still we Indians have heart-felt sympathies with the Russians in their distress. About six months ago Germany made an unprovoked attack on Russia. A huge offensive was launched during the night without notice. This was an innovation. Formerly an ultimatum preceded an attack but now the practice is to attack a country first and declare hostilities later. Many countries were invaded in the present war but the invasion of Russia was the most surprising one. A fierce attack was launched in which fifty lakhs of troops participated simultaneously over a long front of thousands of miles, and German armies marched ahead. In the annals of world history we do not read of such a big battle being waged anywhere as was waged by Germany against Russia. I do not want that the new order which Russia has evolved should crumble to pieces.

It is this which makes the matter complicated. On the one hand the attitude of the British Government fills us with indignation and our only reaction to such an attitude can be one of opposition and rebellion against their system of government, but on the other hand we are anxious to avoid anything that might inflict any harm on our friends, China and Russia. There are also certain parties in England which sponsor the cause of India's freedom and there are certain countries in the world which are anxious to see India free such as America and others. So the question arises in the hearts of Indians as to what policy should be adopted.

It was in view of this that Mahatmaji launched the Satyagraha agitation. It was individual satyagraha but twenty-five or thirty thousand persons courted arrest in the movement. I am happy and proud to say our province contributed more than half of the total number of satyagrahis. But we must not take into account their number. Had it been a question of numbers alone, we could have sent lakhs of people from our own province. As you know, Mahatma Gandhi imposed several restrictions and refused permission to many people to offer Satyagraha because conditions and pledges had to be fulfilled for it. He used to tear off lists and to strike out the names of prospective satyagrahis who did not fulfil the conditions because he did not wish to embarrass those nations with whom we had sympathy. At the same time he wanted to show to the world the sort of treatment that was meted out to Indians. The people of India constitutionally are opposed to cooperation in this war. Of course, if we are granted independence, we can think of doing something. A slave cannot think of anything. He is quite inert. I think Mahatma Gandhi acted on these considerations. He had to keep up the balance between the two sides. This is my personal view of his actions. It is quite inappropriate for me to say anything about Mahatmaji. However, if we ignore the unimportant things and keep the important ones before us, I can say that the principles he laid down, and the manner in which he conducted the movement for two years, will remain immortal in the hearts of Indians. There should not be any misunderstanding about his motives. A good cause should not be sabotaged. Hence his technique was quite complicated. He did it, so that non-Congressmen may not accuse him of inactivity. But we shall keep up the balance of both the scales.

These are the different viewpoints which I have presented to you and every person can have his own opinion. But the fundamental policies which have been pursued in India under the leadership of Mahatma Gandhi have done good to India and the world. Our strength has increased by it. But the British Government thinks that it has not benefited us in any way. It may be so. My reading of the British rule in India is that it is devoid of reason and commonsense. As far as their contact with the Indian masses is concerned, they never pay any attention to them. They imagine that they have brought the Indian masses under their thumb, though this is entirely wrong.

We have to prepare ourselves against any eventuality. You should forget that we have to help the British Government in this war, but we should know how to react if India is attacked. We have to prepare ourselves to answer this question. I do not know how to give a clear-cut reply at this stage but I can certainly do so after studying the situation. Had we been independent we would have taken every step to safeguard India. But power is not in our hands. Then why are we asked to help the British Government? Does it mean that we should obey their orders blindly however worthless these may be? A civic guard has been formed in Allahabad and much rot is talked. Can the British Government save India by these methods? If they proceed in this manner in their own country, they too would lose their country. It is impossible for us to follow them like courtiers. If we are to follow like that, why should we follow worthless persons?

What should we do under such circumstances? This is a knotty problem. I want you to be clear in your minds about this point. You know that the battle for freedom in our country has been going on for the last twenty or twenty-two years under the leadership of Mahatma Gandhi on the principle of non-violence. The Congress accepted this as its principle for our freedom struggle. Mahatmaji adheres to it as his creed. It is right for him to do so but for a political institution like the Congress it is difficult to stick to it' under all circumstances. Congress accepted the principle but did not think or decide that, in the event of an attack on India, it would not keep an army to defend her, or it would not use police and armies to check dacoities. Mahatmaji wishes that India should have a government without police and armies. This is to be considered.

Today the papers have published a statement of Rajagopalachari regarding this matter and I wish to make certain observations in this connection. A perusal of Rajaji's statement or any other thing should not lead us to think that the issue of non-violence is no more before the Congress or the country. This is a misunderstanding and we need not be misled by this. We shall not keep armies or put up armed resistance to defend India but we shall take other steps. Thus a question of principle crops up and this makes a vital difference between ourselves and the British. But the British have only to gain by this because they will propagate to the world that we are divided on this issue of non-violence. They will say that we are not concerned with our defence and that they are carrying on the administration in the way they like. I warn you against this, as these questions are sure to arise and they are being actually raised before you, before me, and before the whole world. But at the present moment this is not the primary question before the Congress and the country. The Congress would give a suitable reply when this question actually arises. As I have already told you, the Congress would not keep any army to defend India. Sometimes, however, it is bad to attempt to do all the good things at one time as its consequences may be bad. The principle of non-violence appears to be quite good, for no gentleman or lady would like violence. Then there is also the problem of Hindu–Muslim differences which is a sign of backwardness. Whenever differences exist in a country it can be called a backward nation.

Can we not call the belligerent nations now at war to be backward in view of the destruction and havoc they are doing to themselves without substantial result? If this war continues like this, the world is sure to perish. Many countries in Europe have perished. Cities have been lifeless. Cities have been rendered lifeless. Corpses are lying uncared for.

Allahabad is quiet these days. If somebody loots and stabs somebody in your *mohalla*, you are frightened and you are shocked. You read about it in papers which make you sad. Similar feelings are created you read that two lakhs of men have been killed in Russia. Hence this war has become inhuman. There was a time when soldiers used to fight and weaker men and women used to live indoors. But today the combatants and non-combatants both are on the field. If the war continues in this way, the world is doomed. I want that hostilities should cease but this cannot come about at the bidding of myself, Mahatma Gandhi or the Congressmen. If all of us sit idle, no result would come out. We have to think how fearful war is. If this war does not come to an end, there shall be wholesale destruction. I do not like violence on principle, and its use even in domestic issues.

Today there are only a few powers in the world like America, Germany, Russia, Japan, and England. Other nations have no real existence. Our neighbouring countries like Iran and Iraq are under British possession and Thailand is under Japan. If we have to keep armies, they should be fully equipped like those of Germany and Russia; otherwise they would be of no use to us. Remember that India is a big country; it has the necessary strength and capacity to become a big and strong power if it gets an opportunity like China. It is not the number of forty crores that counts but the bravery of the people. The Indian armies fighting these days on various fronts are not really Indian for they consist of mercenary soldiers. No doubt the Indian troops have won admiration wherever they have fought and even German generals have praised them. They are not only brave but efficient fighters. They know the technique of the present war. Our comrades would have been equally brave fighters and, given an opportunity, they would have won the whole world for us. Indians have the necessary stamina and brains, the latter being of vital importance in the present war. We are not weak but we should like the war to end. Our country suffers and so do the others. We will reach nearer towards our goal of freedom, after this war. There cannot be any peace so long as war and atrocities continue in the world. In case other countries keep armies and do anything they like, we too cannot afford to go without them. We shall exert our full strength. Our country shall strain its every nerve. But you should remember the decision of the AICC held at Bombay. It was clearly stated there as to how far we could follow the principle of non-violence. Today we have to see and study what is going on in the world. I have given you an idea as to how far I am in favour of non-violence. I have also told you that although I am in favour of non-violence yet there are many difficulties that have to be faced. Nevertheless it is clear from the statement of Rajagopalachari that people should not forget the goal, whether they talk of violence or non-violence. The same question of men and administrative difficulties comes before us in another form in connection with the war. We do not know how to dispose of the question of violence and non-violence. If it comes before us in the long run, what shall we do? We should not sidetrack our goal of freedom before this question.

I do not know what meaning you have attached to the recent release of Congressmen, but I am sure you know that they have not been released because of any love for them in the hearts of the British. They have been released because of pressure from several sides. The greatest pressure was exerted by the very presence of prisoners in the jails. The pictures of accredited leaders of India in jails were before the Indian masses. It was a blot on the British Government. It was not liked by some people of America as well. At the outbreak of war with Japan, an amnesty was ordered. British policy, however, remains unchanged. Mere release of certain prisoners does not mean any change of policy in regard to the freedom movement. Our old policy of resistance and opposition to the British Government shall continue. I do not know how it will be possible. This is to be thought over. We have many things to take into consideration.

What shall we do if India is attacked? For the time being there is no danger to India but of course Burma is in the danger zone. Calcutta can be bombed. It would be improper for me to indicate a solution at these problems because it is not a question of our individual opinions or principles. Times are hard. We are perplexed to see the situation of the world. This is not an opportunity for us to mock at any country. We are under the British Government. We may oppose the Government but the English people are beset with trouble. Their men, women, and children have lost their lives in thousands. Their cities have been destroyed. The English masses do not wish to rule over India but to save themselves. Similarly we have sympathy with the German masses also. We have heartfelt sympathies with the Russians and the Chinese. We sympathize with their principles also. Hence we should not mock at others. If we realize our condition we are sure to find ourselves fit to be a laughing-stock for others. We have to hang our heads. The primary question for us is to increase our strength and organization in the whole country. I do not know of any organization other than the Congress whose network is spread out throughout the country. British rule may continue here or go. Even if it wishes to remain here it cannot. Go it must, it is only a question of time. The question which everyone asks is, when is the poverty of this country going to be removed and how can we save ourselves from the different kinds of losses which are inflicted on us?

It is a policy of the present rulers to frighten us by bringing the war nearer to India, so that they may continue here and we might go over to them. But we shall not yield to it at any cost. We have to think and present a united front even if it might be a false step. But if we are overtaken by fright or lethargy, we shall not be able to do anything, when more revolutionary days arrive. Remember that Mahatma Gandhi has emphasized this fact only. He has said that the war is a prolonged one and he will continue with his Satyagraha.

So far I have spoken to you of India's struggle. This will continue even after the European war. If we have strength enough we shall achieve the goal. These revolutionary catchwords will not take us far. It is a fight of endurance. Today countries are faced with hard tests. You can take the longest strides. China has been fighting for about four years. Thirty to forty lakhs of people have perished and the country has been ruined. Only a small number of persons courted arrest in this country. The cable which was received from Chungking is known to the world. A large part of Chungking has been destroyed by Japanese bombs. It was stated in the cable that Chungking is not what it was previously, but still the Chinese will remain firm and will not be frightened. If we have strength enough we shall reach our goal, otherwise if our lungs are defective and we are asthmatic, we cannot reach our goal. These empty slogans will not lead us to freedom.

People go to jail by offering Satyagraha. Many persons were arrested under DIR and interned at different places like Deoli. They did not offer any Satyagraha nor were they convicted or tried for any offence. Many have been released prematurely like Purnima. Purnima Banerji and Lal Bahadur Shastri have been released today. People courted arrest in hundreds and have suffered considerably in jails. You cannot know it. When we offer Satyagraha and go to jails, it does not mean that the public which does not offer Satyagraha should take rest, for this will make you idle. If you are not selected as a satyagrahi, the responsibility for keeping the Congress flag high is yours. You have to continue the routine meetings and other activities.

Then this grand welcome to Congressmen who go to and come out of jail is a farce. Those who are ready to sacrifice everything for the sake of their country demand your help and sympathy. Everybody should do his duty here. Do not think it to be merely a duty with selfish motives as it weakens you and the other nations go ahead in the meantime.

I offer my thanks for the welcome you have accorded me today. I appreciate it because I got an opportunity to see familiar faces of Allahabad. It is true that I should attend meetings to see you and renew my old bond of love. Whether I see you or not, I hope that we reside in the hearts of each other. I do not wish that we should rest content with this thought alone but we should accomplish the task which is on our shoulders. The world is changing today, and this is no time to sit idle. We should do more work in these revolutionary times. We should not think that this is to be done by a particular person. It is the work of every Indian, man or woman. One should do as much as one can. If one cannot move a hundred steps, he should at least walk fifty steps. If one cannot do so or if any person gives up his efforts, he proves his worthlessness and is a dead weight for world freedom.

---

[1] Published in the *National Herald*, 17 December 1941.

67. Extracts from Fortnightly Reports on Satyagraha and Other Political Developments in Madras Province (October to December 1941)

Fortnightly Reports from Government of Madras to Conran Smith, Secretary to Government of India, Public (General) Department, Home Department, Government of Madras, Tamil Nadu State Archives.

(i) Fortnightly Report Dated 20 October 1941 for the First Half of October 1941

DO No. P. 4–20

My dear Conran Smith,

Political: The Congress party has been very active in holding meetings throughout the province. The Muslims League has been active in certain districts and particularly in Madras city where preparations are in progress for the annual elections for the District and Provincial executive committees. It is further reported that rules have been drafted for the formation of a Muslim National Guard for the province. The Hindu Mahasabha has also been active and Dr Varadarajulu Naidu has taken part in meetings in several places. It is reported that he is reviving the Tamil Newspaper 'Tamil Nadu' with its headquarters at Salem. The Khaksars have not come to notice again since the prosecutions to which I referred in my last two reports.

Press: The Nationalist press has commented very severely upon Col Amery's broadcast to America. The papers say that the statement is full of half-truths and crude propaganda. A European newspaper suggests that equal facilities should be given to Indian leaders to broadcast to America.

Sir Sikandar Hyat Khan's call for an explicit assurance to India regarding her status has received a good press. Newspapers representing the Muslim and European opinion do not think much of it, but the Nationalist of press is of the view that even if men in the position of

Sir Sikandar Hyat Khan should think that there should be a clarification of the issue, then it is high time that Great Britain did something in regard to the matter.

The release from jail of political prisoners imprisoned in connection with Satyagraha is being made the occasion for comment upon the constitutional issue. Muslim newspapers are of the view that Congress should not be allowed to take up office again, but the nationalist press is divided on this question. The Indian Express, which may taken to represent the orthodox Congress view, says that the primary purpose was to assert the right of nationhood and demonstrate to the world that even small and weak peoples cannot be hustled into ward to which their consent is not obtained. It leaves some hope even for the disarmed.

It will continue so log as there is no revision of policy at the other end and will have more than achieved its limited purpose as a continuous and continuing protest against the deprivation of the right of even so much as to be consulted in a serious issue like war. On the other hand, *The Hindu* calls upon the Congress to assume its responsibilities to the electorate. It definitely says that the Congress should function in the Central Legislature once again as a strong and resolute opposition. The Congress, it says, has very definite responsibilities towards the electorate which are in grave danger of being neglected if some of the present policies are persisted in.

During the fortnight under review one case was brought before the Press Advisory committee in which an Editor published posters displaying alarmist captions about the war in Russia. The Convener, Press Advisory Committee promptly issued a warning to the Editor about the undesirability of publishing such posters. The 'Vahini' a Telugu weekly published in Madras, published in its issue dated 27th July 1941 a Telugu rendering of chapter headed 'The 3rd International and its place in history' from 'Selected works of Lenin', Vol. K., a prohibited book. The Government requested the Press Advisory committed to issue a warning to the Editor if they agreed that course was adequate to meet the needs of the case.

(ii) Fortnightly Report Dated 4 November 1941 for the Second Half of October 1941

DO No. P. 4–21

My dear Conran Smith

War: During the fortnight the lull in the Satyagraha movement has continued. A few old cases, nearly all by unimportant persons, have been reported but hardly any of those men who have already been released from jail have made any attempt to offer Satyagraha again, although Mr Rajagopalachariar is reported to have said that he is considering offering Satyagraha again. The release from jail of practically all the Congress leaders has led, quite naturally to a considerable increase in the number of meetings held by the Congress organizations throughout the province and the presence of the leaders has also resulted in a larger attendance in a good many cases. A number of these meetings have been organized primarily to welcome those who have been released. Others were held in connection with the celebration of Mr Gandhi's birthday and at all of them stress was chiefly laid on the constructive programme of the Congress rather than on anti-war activities. The other parties have been less active than usual. The All India Kisan Sabha held meetings on the 17th, 18th, and 19th of the month in the Chittoor district. The resolutions passed call for little comment being chiefly concerned with agriculture and matters intimately affecting the ryots and particularly in their relations with the Zamindars.

All the Ex-Congress Ministers who were convicted of the offence of offering Satyagraha have, with the exception of Mr Giri, been now released. The Government have decided to release on the 1st November seven persons, who had been detained before they actually committed Satyagraha including the Hon'ble Mr B. Sambamurthy, the Speaker of the Madras Legislative Assembly, and Dr B. Pattabhi Sitaramayya as, if they had been prosecuted and convicted of Satyagraha they would have been released about this time. None of the five communist detenus who escaped from Vellore some weeks ago has yet been apprehended. There has been little activity amongst acknowledged communists but what there is has been amongst students; but even students are beginning to take a different view of the general situation. The District Magistrate, Madura, in particular reports that he has noticed that even since Russia was attacked there has been a very marked change in the attitude of the student classes to the war and activities in aid of the war effort.

Law and Order: Allama Inayatullah Khan Mashriqui, a state prisoner in the Vellore jail has continued the fast which he began at Ramzan. He maintains that this fast is not a branch of jail discipline as it is a holy fast to death enjoined by his religion. The position is being carefully watched and the Government of India are being kept informed of all developments. A released Satyagrahi who was arrested in the previous fortnight for delivering an objectionable speech applied for bail which was refused in view of the recent amendment to Rule 130A of the Defence of India Rules. The High Court has confirmed the order passed by the Lower Court refusing bail. This case is of some interest being the first of its kind.

Press: The release of many Congressmen from jail after the expiry of their period of imprisonment, the statement which has come over Indian politics and the recent utterances by British Statesman in regard to India have compelled the press in South India to devote attention to the future of Congress politics. There is a sharp division in the Nationalist Press. *The Hindu* pleads for the calling off of Satyagraha while the 'Swadesamitran' desires that a change of policy should be made. Other newspapers however, say that implicit confidence should be placed in the leadership of Mr Gandhi.

The Government have already established a convention that the Press Advisory committed will be consulted on specific cases relating to anti-war movement before action is taken by them except in cases of emergency. The press advisory committee at its meeting held on 10th September 1941 passed a resolution requesting government that consultation with the committee may well be extended to all cases of action against a newspaper. Government have decided that they will consult the press advisory committee on specific cases whether relating to anti-war movement or not before action is taken by them, except in cases of Emergency.

(iii) Fortnightly Report Dated 18 November 1941 for the First Half of November 1941

DO No. P. 4–22

My dear Conran Smith

War: There have been very few cases of Satyagraha during the fortnight. In none of these were the persons of much importance. In many districts, there has been a complete lull. The recent statement by Mr Gandhi, reviewing the Satyagraha movement, has created some disappointment in Congress circles. Very few of those who have been released from prison show an inclination to offer Satyagraha again. One important exception is Mr Madhava Menon, Chairman of the Calicut Municipal Council. With the release of practically all the Congress leaders activity in the past fortnight has taken the form of meetings and processions to welcome the released Satyagrahis. At these meetings almost all the leaders have made speeches, but only one by Dr Pattabhi Sitaramayya has been made speeches, but only one by Dr Pattabhi Sitaramayya has been reported to have been sufficiently objectionable to warrant consideration whether proceedings should be taken against him.

Political: As I have already stated the Congress ex-ministers and other leaders have been extremely active in addressing Congress meetings in various parts of the province. For the most part they have confined themselves to urging their listeners to have complete faith in Mr Gandhi and to follow his lead without question. They have also exhorted Congressmen to carry on the constructive programme of the Congress. But their references to reputation of Satyagraha have not been marked with much enthusiasm except for the part which it has played in Nellore trouble;, the Hindu Mahasabha has not been much to the fore. It is reported that Mrs N.G. Ranga has been instructed by her husband (who is detained in Vellore Jail) to meet Dr Sitaramayya and Hon'ble Mr B. Sambamurthi (Speaker of the Madras Legislative Assembly) to discuss how far the Kisan Sabha can co-operate with Congress.

The second annual conference of the Madras student's organization was held in Madras on 1st and 2nd November. The President, N.D. Varadachari, urged the students to take advantage of the war to train themselves as fighters and technicians. The conference passed resolutions criticizing Congress leadership, and policy.

Law and Order: The detenus in Vellore jail went on hunger strike for one day on the 8th of November, as a mark of respect to Paramasivam of whom I have already made mention.

The superintendent of the Jail is taking suitable disciplinary action against the strikers. The detenus are also threatening a strike unless certain demands are conceded, some of which the Government consider reasonable. Allama Mashriqui continues his fast and regular reports on his condition are being sent separately to the Government of India.

Press: On the question of the release of political prisoners, different views have been expressed. A few nationalist papers have argued that more release would not do. But there should be a gesture on the part of the Government of India in regard to the easing of the political situation. But the majority think that such a release of both detenus and political prisoners would have the effect of enabling the politicians to review the political situation and adopt measures that may be suitable.

Similarly, in regard to Mr Gandhi's statement on Satyagraha, opinions vary. Some nationalist papers hail it as a stateman like and farsigted one. Others plainly say that self-mortification is not the remedy.

It is pointed out that the Congress is neiberating indefinitely in the name of restricted Satyagraha and the constructive programme. There is need for a dynamic political opposition in the country. It requires on the part of the representative responsible action to suit the new and changed conditions which confront this country.

(iv) Fortnightly Report for the Second Half of November 1941

Srirangam is a strong Congress centre and there is a strong Congress element connected with the High School. All the same, His Excellency's speech, which dealt with the war effort was received with acclamation as the general atmosphere was very enthusiastic.

War: In most districts Satyagraha has been quiescent, but in Malabar there have been two cases of important men offering Satyagraha again after release, but neither of them has as yet created much stir and the district Magistrate has not taken action against them. In fact he suggests that the reason for their offering Satyagraha again is more because they consider themselves to be rival candidates for the post of Malayali minister in the next Congress Government. Mr Prakasam an ex-Congress Minister has been extremely active during the fortnight addressing meeting in a member of districts. At one of these, in Bellary, he again urged that Congress ought not to return to office at present and even want so far as to say that India had no enemity with Hitler and need not fear him because he had achieved his position by non-violence. A speaker at another meeting urged his hearers not to render any help to the British in the war efforts as this would be a provocation to Hitler which in course of time might result in his invasion of India.

Political: As already mentioned above, Mr Prakasam has been doing a good deal of Congress propaganda work and another Ex-Minister Mr Muniswami Pillai has also been active in this direction. Congress meetings have been held as usual in most districts but for the most part these meetings have been concerned with the constructive programme of the Congress and criticisms of the treatment of political prisoners. A number of these meetings have been held to celebrate Pandit Nehru's birthday. The Justice Party and the Muslim League have held a few meetings which he addressed Mr Prakasasm, speaking on the subject of the formation of the Andhra Province so far forgot himself as to reveal what he alleged had taken place during a cabinet meeting and admitted that he had obtained through unspecified source in England access to dispatches from the Governor to the Secretary of State. He more or less accused Lord Erskine of double dealing in that he had given the cabinet to understand that he agreed with their decision and had afterwards written to the Secretary of State in exactly the opposite sense.

There has been little overt activity on the part of communists but none of the five detenus who escaped from the Vellore jail has yet been traced. A certain amount of communist anti-war literature has come to light, particularly leaflets about the escape of Subash Chandra Bose. One of these states that Bose after escaping from Calcutta went twenty-eight miles down river to a waiting submarine in which he escaped to a foreign country.

There was a one day strike by about hundred students of the Annamalai University allegedly as a protest against the lathi charge by the police on the students in Cawnpore. It appears however, that a communist cell is definitely working again in this University and this strike was an attempt on its part to test its strength. The College authorities are reported to be taking disciplinary action against those responsible for organizing the strike.

Press: The attitude assumed by the Government of India in regard to the question of release of political prisoners has been strongly criticized by the nationalist press. Sir Reginald Maxwell's speech has been a great disappointment and this section of the press wonders why so much importance should be paid to the views of the Governments of those provinces which are now under the Adviser-Regime. In respect of these powers the Government of India are supreme and their word is law. The release of these prisoners, if gracefully done, would allow the nationalists to come together and confer as to the best means of solving the present political deadlock, especially when India is threatenend from the east as well as the west. The Home Members speech was very disappointing, but it is hoped that the Government would still reconsider the question and order a general amnesty.

Mr Amery's speech at Manchester, in the view of the nationalist press, is not conducive to pour oil over troubled waters. The Urdu and sectional newspapers wonder how Mr Amery could have made any declaration of policy other than that which he did, but Congress and pro-Congress newspapers condemn the utterance as one which is not calculated to smoothen matters.

The debate in the Central Assembly on the Indo-Ceylon Agreement has been universally welcomed. The Amendment adopted by the Assembly is a virtual condemnation of the Joint Indo-Ceylon Report, and it is hoped that the Government of India would, in view of the strong expression of public opinion, see that Indians in Ceylon are treated properly and their rights are respected.

The formation of the Orissay Ministry has been the subject of very strong criticism in the nationalist press. Some papers say that the Governor should have kept himself aloof from the intrigues which proceded the constitution of the Ministry. The fact that he took part in it would appear to imply that the Government are anxious to tell the world that there are parties in the country who are prepared to co-operate with the authorities whatever may be the humiliation to which the country may be subjected. These newspapers ask the Congress members who have promised their support to the new Ministry to resign their seats and seek re-election. That alone would show whether the voters approve of their betrayal.

(v) Fortnightly Report Dated 23 December 1941 for the First Half of December 1941

DO No. P. 4–24

My dear Conran Smith,

Isolated instances of Satyagraha have occurred and are continuing despite the orders for a general release of Satyagraha prisoners. In Malabar, Mr and Mrs Madhava Menon have been the chief Satyagrahis while Mr Kelappan, Ex-President of the district Board gave up after a few days. There has been no public response to their demonstrations. On the whole the order for a general release of Satyagrahis does not seem to have aroused any marked enthusiasm. The Government of Madras are scruitinizing the cases of those covered by the order and batches are being released almost every day. In some districts there are signs that the release order has done something to encourage the view that Congress should resume parliamentary activities. Other than the few cases of sporadic Satyagraha already referred to and one case of the appearance of anti-war posters and leaflets, very little anti-war propaganda has been apparent in the fortnight.

Political: Meetings of the Muslim League, Hindu Mahasabha, Justice Party, and Congress have been held in various places, but the number of them hasbeen less than in recent weeks. The Congress party held secret meetings in the North Arcot district from which press representatives were excluded. It appears that at one of thee meetings it was resolved that no useful purpose would be served by offering Satyagraha again and that parliamentary activity should be revived. The Ex-Ministers Messrs Prakasam, Giri, Gopala Reddi and Dr T.S. Rajan have been active in addressing meetings. At a number of these meetings the usual resolutions criticizing the classification of political prisoners and complaining of the conditions in jail were passed but otherwise nothing of particular interest occurred. In the two west coast district only has any communist activity been reported. In South Kanara certain amount of communist literature has been seized and leaflets are reported to be in secret circulation in parts of Malabar district.

Press: The recent action of the Government of India in regard to the Release of political prisoners has been considered to be lacking in administrative ability and breadth of outlook. Detenus have been left out of account and the release is confined to persons who have been found guilty of Symbolic Satyagraha. A generous gesture was what was required but the Government of India have failed to rise to the situation.

68. Individual Satyagraha, from August 1940 to December 1941 Confidential Note of the Congress Working Committee, 28 December 1941

File No. 1/1941–2, AICC Papers, NMML.

Fourteen months have elapsed since the Working Committee held their last meeting and during this period the world has fallen ever deeper into the abyss of war and rushed headlong towards self-destruction. The members of the Committee have met again from prison and given earnest thought to all the national and international developments during this fateful period of human history. The burden of leading the Congress and the nation of this critical stage when old problems assume a new significance and war approached the frontiers of India bringing new problems to its train, is a heavy one which the Committee can only shoulder worthily with the full co-operation of the people of India. The Committee have endeavoured to keep in view the principles and objectives for which the Congress has stood during these past many years and considered them in the larger context of world conditions and world freedom. The Committee was convinced that full freedom for the people of India is essential, especially in the present state of world turmoil not only for India's sake but for the sake of the world. The Committee also held that real peace and freedom can only be established and endured on the basis of world co-operation between free nations.

The Committee gave full expression to their attitude towards the War in their statement issued on 14 September 1939, wherein they condemned Nazi and Fascist aggression and expressed their willingness to help the cause of freedom and democracy, provided the objectives of the war were clearly stated and acted upon, in so far as was possible, in the present. If freedom and democracy were those objectives, then they must necessarily include the ending of imperialism and the recognition of the independence of India. Subsequent pronouncement made on behalf of the British Government and their reactionary and oppressive policy made it clear that this Government was determined to maintain and intensify their imperialist hold and exploitation of the Indian people. British policy was one of deliberate insult to Indian nationalism, of a reversion to unrestrained authoritarianism, and encouragement of disruptive and reactionary elements. Every offer made by the Congress for an honourable compromise was rejected.

The Congress was therefore compelled, in order to defend the honour and elementary rights of the Indian people and the integrity of the nationalist movement, to request Gandhiji to guide the Congress in the action that should be taken.

Mahatma Gandhi desirous of avoiding embarrassment to his opponent as far as possible, especially during the perils and dangers of war, limited the satyagraha movement, which he started with selected individuals who conformed to certain tasks he had laid down. That satyagraha has now proceeded for over 14 months and about 25,000 Congressmen have suffered imprisonment, when many thousands of others who had offered satyagraha in the Frontier Provinces and elsewhere were not arrested. The Committee desire to express their respectful appreciation of Gandhiji's leadership and of the response of the nation to it, and are of opinion that this has strengthened the people.

Throughout this period the attitude of the British Government has been progressively hostile to Indian Freedom and it has functioned in India as a completely authoritarian Government, insulting with its general policy and its arrogant demeanour the deeply cherished conventions and feeling of the people. Neither the profession of freedom and democracy nor the perils and catastrophies that have come in the wake of war have affected this attitude and policy and such changes as have taken place havebeen for the worse. To submit to this policy is to give up all that the Congress has stood for the past twenty years.

The recent release of a number of political prisoners has no significance or importance and the circumstances attending it and official pronouncements made, make it clear that it is not connected with any change of policy. Large number of detenu who are kept in prison under the Defence of India Act without trial, and whose only crime seems to be that they are ardent patriots, impatient of foreign rule and determined to achieve the Independence of the country, still remain in prison. Recent arrests of prominent persons and their treatment in prison also indicate that the old policy is being pursued as before.

While there has been no change in Britain's policy towards India the Working Committee must neverthless take into full consideration, the new world situation that has arisen by the development of War into a world conflict and its approach to India. The sympathies of the Congress must inevitably lie with the people who are the subjects of aggression and who are fighting for their freedom. The Committee would thus like to advise the nation to align itself with the larger causes that are emerging from the storm of the hour and to give support to them and help in their success in conformity with its principles, to the best of its ability. But only a free and independent India can be in a position to do so. The whole background in India is one of deep-rooted hostility and distress of the British Government and not even the most far-reaching promises can alter this background, nor can a subject India offer voluntarily or willing help to an arrogant imperialism which is indistinguishable from the fascist authoritarianism.

The Committee is therefore as of opinion that the resolution of the AICC passed in Bombay on 16 September 1940 holds today and defines Congress policy still. That policy may have to be varied in detail application as the circumstances may require.

69. Congress Cabinet Meeting: Deadlock Continues, No Agreed Formula Yet in Sight

Amrita Bazar Patrika, 29 December 1941.

The deadlock in the Congress Working Committee continues. For the sixth day today the Committee continued its deliberations but an agreed formula is not yet in sight. According to informed quarters there are three main points of view that are now before the Committee, namely,

(1) Revival of the Poona offer and favouring the formation of Coalition National Governments for the duration of the war.

(2) Co-operation in the war efforts for the overthrow of Nazism and Fascism, provided that the British Government recognizes India's Independence and

(3) Opposition to all wars as advocated by Mahatma Gandhi.

It is understood that the Committee had so far the benefit of discussing certain draft resolutions but the fact that no resolution has been released shows that those drafts had fallen through for lack of unanimity. The issue of violence versus non-violence and its applicability in all spheres at the moment appears to have again come to the forefront of discussion. The close proximity of the war, it is understood, is undoubtedly having its influence on the discussions.

It is reliably learnt that two draft resolutions supporting the two view-points mentioned above are now ready and they will be discussed when the Committee resumes its deliberations tomorrow.

Mahatma Gandhi commenced his silence this afternoon and is expected to participate in tomorrow's discussions.

Non-violence Issue

The much important issue of non-violence at the present critical moment in the history of this country came up for a heated discussion last night at Gandhiji's camp after the Working Committee sitting was over. Sardar Vallabhbhai Patel, Mr Rajagopalachari, Dr Rajendra Prasad and Pandit Jawaharlal Nehru, were present and though discussions continued for about two hours, it appears no clear-cut formula to accommodate the different viewpoints could be arrived.

The discussions were resumed this morning at the President's Camp, when Dr Rajendra Prasad, Mr Rajagopalachari and Pandit Nehru were closeted with the Congress President for more than two hours. It is believed all avenues for rapprochement among different schools of thought on the issue of non-violence and its effectiveness in national life are being explored. Though at one stage of the discussions, it appeared that certain differences on this issue disappeared to a great extent, it is premature to say even now if the members could come in a complete unanimity in view of the fresh problems facing the Committee everyday, with the developments in the Far Eastern situation.

Definite indications are expected tonight though the main resolution expected not earlier than tomorrow evening.

70. Parting of Ways at Bardoli? Proposal for Conditional Support to War: Mahatma Not to Compromise on Non-violence

Bombay Chronicle, 30 December 1941.

After seven days of discussion, the Congress Working Committee, it is understood, has arrived at a tentative conclusion regarding the present political situation and on the question of the future policy and programme of the Congress.

It is understood that draft resolutions on three subjects are now ready and they need only final touches before they are released to-morrow.

Mahatma May Abdicate

Though no indication is yet available as to the nature of these resolutions, it is gathered that the Congress position arising out of these resolutions will be materially different from the present one of complete non-co-operation and Satyagraha, and this may lead to Mahatma Gandhi's relinquishing his 'de facto' leadership of the Congress to which he was called at the Bombay meeting of the All-India Congress Committee in September 1940.

Mahatma Won't Compromise

It is stated that on the question of non-violence Mahatma Gandhi expressed his inability to compromise, but it is pointed out that his relinquishing the leadership of the Congress need not necessarily mean that he would sever all connections with the Congress. On the contrary his advice and guidance would always be available to the Congress.

Congress Demand and War

As regards the political issue, it is understood that the resolution will reiterate the Congress demand for India's Independence.

As regards co-operation in the war efforts, it is gathered the Congress attitude will finally depend upon the attitude of the British Government towards the Congress demand and the restatement of the Congress position vis-à-vis the war.

To Oppose All Wars

It is not yet known what is to happen to the Satyagraha movement, but it is suggested that Mahatma Gandhi on his own individual responsibility may exercise freedom of speech to oppose all wars.

One of the factors, which clinched the issue it is learnt was the sharp difference between Mahatma Gandhi and the other members of the Working Committee on the question of opposition to all wars and opposition to this particular war.

Mahatma to Submit Statement

The Congress Working Committee adjourned at 6.30 in the evening to meet again tomorrow.

The Committee today discussed the draft resolution on the present political situation, which, it is announced, will be released tomorrow afternoon. Gandhiji was present in the afternoon's sitting.'

Although the main resolution on the political situation is still on the anvil and is likely to be finally disposed of tomorrow afternoon, the 'United Press' learns that incompatible viewpoints on the question of non-violence and of revision of the present Congress policy have not come anywhere near being solved, though it was discussed threadbare for the seventh day in succession. Difference of opinion appears to be prevailing with the approach to the problem, and it is learnt from talks in inner circles of the Congress that there may be a parting of ways with Gandhiji and his present policy.

The 'United Press' special correspondent gathers that the main resolution seeks to relieve Mahatmaji of all responsibilities and asserts that the Congress would agree to co-operation in so far as it relates to the defence of India, only if complete independence is granted without undue delay.

It appears Gandhiji may be left free to continue his policy of symbolic protest against all wars and to propagate the cult of non-violence in conjunction with protagonists of out-and-out non-violence.

The 'United Press' further learns in this connection that Gandhiji has submitted a statement to the Working Committee, which is likely to be released together with the main resolution.

Other Resolutions

It is stated that other resolutions before the Committee relate to the ARP organizations and the general duty of Congressmen under the present altered Circumstances, which was drafted by Babu Rajendra Prasad. The Committee, it is also learnt, has before it a fourth resolution which deals with the heroic struggle of the Chinese and the Russians and extends its sympathy and moral support to them in their present predicament.

Leaders' Talks

After the termination of today's deliberations, several members of the Committee busted themselves with group talks in the leaders' camp. Mr C. Rajagopalachari, Dr B. Pattabhi Sitaramaya and Mr Bhulabhai Desai were among those present. Simultaneous discussions were also held in Gandhiji's camp when Babu Rajendra Prasad, Sardar Vallabhbhai Patel and Acharya Kripalani were closeted for an hour with Gandhiji.

The Working Committee is expected to conclude its sessions on Wednesday, if not tomorrow itself.

Need of Change of Heart

'It is understood that the main resolution of the Congress Working Committee will refer to internal situation in the country and to the statements and speeches made on behalf of Britain denying India her natural right to complete freedom whereas recent developments have confirmed the conviction of the committee that India cannot function within the orbit of any imperial power and must attaint her status of a free nation which does not prevent close association with other countries within the comity of free nations.

The resolution, it is stated, will further deal with the refusal of the British Government to the constitution of even a provisional real national Government composed of persons commanding the confidence of the Indian public.

It appears that the resolution may also stress that unless there is a change of heart on the part of Britain and transfer of real power to the people of the country, it would be impossible to secure their whole-hearted co-operation at this crucial moment.

71. (i) Mahatma Gandhi's Letter to Maulana Abul Kalam Azad

CWMG, Vol. LXXV, pp. 189–90.

The following is Mahatma Gandhi's letter to the Congress President:

Bardoli, 30 December.

Dear Maulana Sahib,

In the course of the discussion in the Working Committee, I discovered that I had committed a grave error in the interpretation of the Bombay resolution. I had interpreted it to mean that the Congress was to refuse participation in the present or all wars on the ground principally of non-violence. I found to my astonishment that most members differed from my interpretation and held that the opposition need not be on the ground of non-violence. On re-reading the Bombay resolution, I found that the differing members were right and that I had read into it a meaning which its letter could not bear. The discovery of the error makes it impossible for me to lead the Congress in the struggle for resistance to war efforts on the grounds of ill-will against Great Britain. The resolution contemplated material association with Britain in the war effort as a price for guaranteed independence of India. If such was my view, and I believed in the use of violence for gaining independence and yet refused participation in the war effort as the price of that independence, I would consider myself guilty of unpatriotic conduct. It is my certain belief that only non-violence can save India and the world from self-extinction. Such being the case, I must continue my mission whether I am alone or assisted by an organization or individuals. You will, therefore, please relieve me of the responsibility laid upon me by the Bombay resolution. I must continue civil disobedience for free speech against all wars, with such Congressmen and others whom I select and who believe in the non-violence I have contemplated and are willing to conform to prescribed conditions, I will not at this critical period select for Civil Disobedience those whose services are required to steady and help the people in their respective localities.

Yours sincerely,
M.K. Gandhi

(ii) Events Take New Turn at Bardoli: Working Committee Relieves Mahatmaji of Responsibility

The Tribune, 31 December 1941.

The Congress Working Committee has passed a resolution relieving Mahatma Gandhi of the leadership of the Congress.

The resolution follows a letter addressed by Gandhiji to the Congress President, Maulana Abul Kalam, in which the Mahatma says that he should be relieved of the responsibility laid upon him by the Bombay resolution.

The resolution of the Working Committee which relieves Mahatma Gandhi of the responsibility laid upon him by the Bombay resolution, quoted a letter which the Congress President received from Mahatma Gandhi. In that letter Gandhiji says that he had interpreted the Bombay resolution to mean that the Congress was to refuse participation in the present or all wars on grounds principally of non-violence. He adds, 'I found to my astonishment that most of the members differed from my interpretation and held that the opposition need not be on the ground of non-violence'.

After reiterating his faith in complete non-violence and his difference with the Committee, Mahatma Gandhi says, 'Please relieve me of the responsibility laid upon me by the Bombay resolution. I must continue Civil Disobedience movement for free speech against all wars, with such Congressmen and others whom I select and who believe in the non-violence I have contemplated and are willing to conform to prescribed conditions.'

The Congress Working Committee has passed the following resolution:

'The Working Committee have received the following letter from Gandhiji and recognize the validity of the point he has raised and therefore relieve him of the responsibility laid upon him by the Bombay resolution referred to by Gandhiji, but the Committee assure him that the policy of non-violence, adopted under his guidance for the attainment of Swaraj and which has proved so successful in leading to mass awakening otherwise, will be adhered to by the Congress. The Working Committee further assures him that it would like to extend its scope as far as possible even in a free India. The Committee hopes that Congressmen, will render him full assistance in the prosecution of his mission including the offering of Civil Disobedience.'

72. Text of the Congress Working Committee Resolution on 'Political Situation', Bardoli, 30 December 1941

SWJN, Vol. 12, pp. 45–8.

Fourteen months have elapsed since the Working Committee held their last meeting and during this period the world has fallen ever deeper into the abyss of war and rushed headlong towards self-destruction. The members of the Committee have met again on their release from prison and given earnest thought to all the national and international developments during this fateful period of human history. The burden of guiding the Congress and the nation at this critical stage when old problems assume a new significance and war approaches the frontiers of India bringing new problems in its train, is a heavy one which the Committee can only shoulder worthily with the full cooperation of the people of India. The Committee has endeavoured to keep in view the principles and objectives for which the Congress has stood during these past many years and considered them in the larger context of world conditions and world freedom. The Committee is convinced that full freedom is essential even, and more especially, in the present state of world turmoil, not only for India's sake but, for the sake of the world. The Committee also holds that real peace and freedom can only be established and endured on the basis of world cooperation between free nations.

The Committee gave full expression to their attitude towards the War in their statement issued on 14 September 1939, wherein they condemned Nazi and fascist aggression and expressed their willingness to help the cause of freedom and democracy, provided the objectives of the war were clearly stated and acted upon, in so far as was possible, in the present circumstances. If freedom and democracy were those objectives, then they must necessarily include the ending of imperialism and the recognition of the independence of India. Subsequent pronouncements made on behalf of the British Government and their reactionary and oppressive policy made it clear that this Government was determined to maintain and intensify their imperialist hold and exploitation of the Indian people. The British policy was one of deliberate insult to Indian nationalism, of a perpetuation of unrestrained authoritarianism, and the encouragement of disruptive and reactionary elements. Not only has every offer made by the Congress for an honourable compromise been rejected, but public opinion voiced by organizations regarded as moderate has also been flouted.

The Congress was, therefore, compelled, in order to defend the honour and the elementary rights of the Indian people and the integrity of the nationalist movement, to request Gandhiji to guide the Congress in the action that should be taken. Mahatma Gandhi, desirous of avoiding embarrassment to his opponent as far as possible, especially during the perils and dangers of war, limited the satyagraha movement which he started to selected individuals who conformed to certain tests he had laid down. That satyagraha has now proceeded for over fourteen months and about twenty-five thousand Congressmen have suffered imprisonment, while many thousands of others who offered satyagraha in the Frontier Province and elsewhere were not arrested. The Committee desire to express their respectful appreciation of Gandhiji's leadership and of the response of the nation to it, and are of opinion that this has strengthened the people.

Throughout this period the attitude of the British Government has been hostile to Indian freedom and it has functioned in India as a completely authoritarian government, insulting the deeply cherished convictions and feelings of the people. Neither the professions of freedom and democracy, nor the perils and catastrophes that have come in the wake of war, have affected this attitude and policy and such changes as have taken place have been for the worse.

The recent release of a number of political prisoners has no significance or importance, and the circumstances attending it, and official pronouncements made, make it clear that it is not connected with any change of policy. Large numbers of detenus, who are kept in prison under the Defence of India Act without trial, and whose only offence seems to be that they are ardent patriots impatient of foreign rule and determined to achieve the independence of the country, still remain in prison. Recent arrests of prominent persons and their treatment in prison also indicate that the old policy is being pursued as before.

While there has been no change in Britain's policy towards India, the Working Committee must nevertheless take into full consideration the new world situation that has arisen by the development of the war into a world conflict and its approach to India. The sympathies of the Congress must inevitably lie with the peoples who are the subject of aggression from any quarter and who are fighting for their freedom. But only a free and independent India can be in a position to undertake the defence of the country on a national basis and be of help in the furtherance of the large causes that are emerging from the storm of war. The whole background in India is one of hostility and of distrust of the British Government and not even the most far-reaching promise can alter this background, nor can a subject India offer voluntary or willing help to an arrogant imperialism which is indistinguishable from fascist authoritarianism.

The Committee is, therefore, of opinion that the resolution of the AICC passed in Bombay on 16 September 1940 holds today and defines Congress policy still.

73. Instructions Issued by the Congress Working Committee, 30 December 1941

SWJN, Vol. 12, pp. 56–7.

Recent developments in the world situation have brought war near to India's frontiers. This may lead to internal dislocation in certain parts of the country and there is a possibility of some cities being subjected to aerial attack. Whatever dangers and difficulties might arise, the real antidote to them is to remain cool and collected and on no account to give way to nervousness and excitement. Congressmen must remain at their posts and continue their service of the people; wherever necessity arises they should yield places of safety to those in greater need and be ready to render aid to those who may require it.

The Congress can help and serve the people in the difficult times ahead only if its organization is strong and disciplined and Congressmen individually and Congress committees are able to command confidence in their respective localities.

Congress committees and Congressmen should therefore address themselves immediately to the task of strengthening the organization and reviving and maintaining contacts in villages and towns. Even villages should, as far as possible, revive the message of the Congress and be prepared to face such difficulties as might arise.

The constructive programme adopted by the Congress and explained from time to time by Gandhiji, is of particular importance at this juncture. It is meant not only to bring about unity among various groups, to remove disabilities which keep sections of the community backward and depressed, to promote self-reliance and the cooperative spirit among the people, to increase production and have fairer distribution but also furnish the best opportunity and means of contacts with the people and service to them which are necessary for winning their confidence. The Working Committee, therefore, call upon Congress committees and workers to further this programme intensively and thus exercise a steadying and strengthening influence in times of dislocation and uneasiness.

During such times there is always a possibility of trouble being created by unsocial elements in the country. To avoid the emergence of such a situation and to meet it when it arises, volunteers should be organized in both the urban and rural areas. Such organizations should be formed on the basis of strict non-violence and it should always be remembered that the Congress adheres to this principle. These volunteers may cooperate with other organizations working for similar ends. This volunteer organization is meant for rendering service to the people both normally and in the event of possible internal commotion. It should, therefore, avoid conflict with the authorities.

The prices of commodities have already risen and are causing distress among the people and no adequate steps have so far been taken by the authorities to meet this situation. These tendencies are likely to be accentuated in the future, and dislocation of trade and transport, due to stress of war, may lead to scarcity of the necessaries of life as well as of many other things which are of everyday use.

Big-scale industries in other countries have suffered heavily on account of the war and transport of goods has become difficult on account of military requirements. China has largely overcome these difficulties by a widespread development of village industries. India may have to face similar problems, and village and cottage industries afford a solution, desirable in itself and more particularly suited to the needs of the moment. Such industries can escape to a large extent the effects of dislocation of trade and transport.

It is therefore, necessary that this item of the constructive programme should be widely taken up and worked up with vigour and earnestness so that the countryside may be rendered, as far as possible, self-sufficient in regard to the necessaries of life.

The Committee would especially recommend to the villages the growing of food crops at least to cover the needs of the village and appeal to the grain dealers not to hold up stores for profit but to release them for consumption at fair prices.

In case of emergency, when instructions are issued to the public by the authorities for the preservation of life and property and the maintenance of public order. Congressmen should avoid conflict with the authorities and they should carry out such instructions, unless they are contrary to Congress directions.

The Committee do not contemplate any invasion of India in the near future, but in the event of any such attempt, Congressmen can on no account submit to it or cooperate with it even if the consequences of such noncooperation be death.

74. Mahatma Gandhi's Statement to the Press, Bardoli, 30 December 1941

CWMG, Vol. LXXV, pp. 190–2.

Bardoli,
30 December 1941

If anyone had thought, as I had thought, that the door to Congress participation in the present war on the ground of Congress non-violence was closed for ever by the Bombay Resolution, then they may now know that the Bombay Resolution had not quite closed the door. Undoubtedly, as the resolution said, the Poona resolution had lapsed, therefore, the Poona offer had lapsed. But the Congress has now, through the Working Committee, made it clear that the door is not barred altogether against Congress participation, certainly not on the ground of non-violence.

The key for unlocking the door remains principally in the hands of the British Government. The Working Committee has very properly declined to state the terms on which that door can be opened. It will depend upon varying circumstances, but, in my opinion, the Chief circumstance is the Government. Having been insulted often enough, the Working Committee would not court any further insult by making any offer. After all, its position is absolutely clear. Everbody knows what the Congress stands for and what it wants. Everyone should, therefore, know that nothing will be accepted by the Congress short of what it stands for. Therefore, the burden of the next step is cast on the Government. This is the chief thing that is relevant at the present time.

I have a pressing cable from those English friends who are interested in India's freedom and who are lovers of their own people. I have not replied to that cable. They have reminded me of Mr Andrews' legacy. Whatever the meaning of their reminder, my meaning could only be one. The one indissoluble bond between Charlie Andrews and myself was that we would never compromise our conscience on any account whatsoever. And, in all that I have done, I can fearlessly claim that I have been guided by my conscience.

I have made it clear in my letter to the Maulana Sahib that I could not possibly identify myself with the door to participation being kept open in any shape or form, because that would mean, in my opinion, a recantation of all that the Congress has stood for the last twenty years or more. I would not be guilty of selling that heritage even for the independence of India because it would not be real independence.

I feel that if any country has a message for the world, which is groaning under violence unknown perhaps to history, it is India. When India, through the Indian National Congress, accepted the policy of non-violence, so far as I know, no Congressman had thought that another war—and such a bloody war—was to come so soon as it has. The testing time, however, has come for India and I, who have an unchangeable belief in the efficacy of non-violence for the present distemper from which mankind is suffering, could not possibly in any manner, directly or indirectly, associate myself with participation in the war; and so I have stood out.

But the Congress contains men and women holding varying shades of opinion and therefore, it should be no wonder that the Working Committee represents those varying shades of opinion. It has at least three bodies or, rather, it has at least three bodies representing three schools of thought: a minority party, believing in non-participation on the ground of non-violence, pure and simple; the other believing that the Congress should not carry non-violence to the point of refusing association in the war under any circumstances and there is the third, which has many reasons almost as strong as the decisive reason of non-violence guiding the minority. The resolution which has been just handed by the Secretary of the Working Committee to the Press is a resultant of the efforts of these three bodies. I would like the public and Congressmen to read that resolution in that light. I hope everybody will appreciate the fact that the Working Committee has not come to any hasty decision. It did not mind what time it took in order to produce a resolution worthy of the great national organization that it represents.

I would say one thing to Congressmen that those who are believers in non-violence in the same sense that I am, have nothing to fear, as I interpret the resolution of the Working Committee. It not only leaves them absolutely free to hold that opinion but to propagate it for the acceptance of anybody who chooses. Only they remain in the Congress is not called upon to participate in the war effort. It is open to them to convert all Congressmen to their view. I am quite sure that the Working Committee will welcome such a conversion but I would warn Congressmen against indecision at this critical period in the national life and I would warn them also against weakly following this party or that for the sake of gaining power in the Congress. Those who do so will miserably fail to gain power for the nation. Personally, I would like the Congress, as I would like the whole world, to accept non-violence as the law of life in every department, social, political, and domestic. But there is no room for cowardliness. I would far rather that we all became violent than cowards. Let me hope, therefore, that every Congress will have his own convictions and the courage to enforce them.

The Hindu, 31.12.1941.

B. LEFT PARTIES AND GROUPS

I. Communist Party of India

75. Report of a Convention Organized by British Communist Party

Communist, Vol. III, No. 1, February 1941, P.C. Joshi Archives on Contemporary History, JNU.

British Communists Speak for the People!

The Congress of the People's Convention was held in London in the first week of January 1941. The attendance was so large that three halls had to be engaged to contain the overflowing audience. The preparations to call this Congress were made by a Council elected from all Trade Unions on the initiative of the journal 'Labour Monthly'. Besides the workers the audience was sprinkled all over with Soldiers and Airmen.

Before the proceedings began, a Presidium consisting of Comrades Adams, Pritt, Krishna Menon, Gallacher, Pollitt, R. Palme Dutt, Walker, and Lawther was selected.

The Session opened with a Statement read out by Comrade Rajani Palme Dutt who was received with tremendous applause. Then spoke Adams, organizer of the London Branch of the Union of Workers in the Building Trades. He reviewed the situation since February 1940 and remarked that while the capitalists were reaping huge super profits, this Congress had assembled to guard the rights of workers at home and to fight the enemy at home and abroad. That is, to fight the reactionary Home Government as well as the aggressor Fascist Government. He then went on to say that while there was a lot of talk about democracy, the National Government had recognized the reactionary Governments of Czechoslovakia and Poland. And now, they were bleeding the Colonies. The Ministry for Information was desperately hiding the fact about unrest in the Empire, especially in Africa and India. Nevertheless, the workers could understand the true state of affairs. The Ministry for Information said that not a pie from India or Africa was going to the war but only towards the education and welfare of Indians and Africans. Even if that were so, what about the huge profits that they reaped from India and Africa? Further, Adams pointed out the solidarity of the British and German workers. He said that both British and German Governments were striving to get the aid of the USSR which with its might was in a position to tip the scales in favour of the party it joined. But the policy of the USSR was one of neutrality and peace. The USSR would come to the aid of only a Peoples' German or British Government. He then went on to remind the workers of the Chartists and their glorious role in British working class history. He said that today it was imperative for British workers to unite and struggle against the strangling of their Trade Union and strike rights, which are being severally suppressed. Collective agreements had also been broken. At such a juncture, the workers must rise like the British Shop Stewards who were at that very moment fighting against low wages.

After Adam's speech, D.N. Pritt read out the main points of the programme of the Peoples' Convention.

They were:

1. Fight for Trade Union Rights.
2. Fight for Strike rights.
3. Fight for adequate war protection for workers.
4. Fight for a peace without reparations or annexations.
5. Fight for Peoples' Government instead of the present one.
6. Fight for the Independence of India, self determination for Africa and unification of Ireland.
7. Fight for friendly relations with the Soviet Union.

Various delegates then spoke.

A delegate speaking on behalf of the 'Russia Today' Society said that the British Government were almost at war with the Soviet Union as they had sheltered the Polish Government which had declared war against the Soviet Union.

Selsman, a girl delegate speaking on behalf of 3,000 Students said that many active and politically conscious students had been and were being expelled from the Universities.

Speaking on behalf of the Durham Miners' Union, a delegate said that in these mines there were 30,000 unemployed men to-day. The largest mine owner of that district is Lord Londenderry, who was known until just before the war, to be a great friend of Hitler's.

Speaking on behalf of the Union of Glasgow Transport workers, a delegate said that the workers there had refused to work throughout the day unless air raid shelters were provided for them. They had struck work. Further he said that though after the war, their weekly wages had risen by 7 shillings, the cost of living had gone up by 17 shillings.

Speaking on behalf of the workers of Coventry, a delegate described how inestimable damage was done there during air attacks due to the Town's unpreparedness. The people were short of electricity, gas and water. Shortage of food was remedied only after numerous representations by workers.

Speaking on behalf of the Committee of Shelter in London undergrounds, the delegate described the utter absence of air raid shelters in London working class districts. Even simple 'Anderson' shelters were tacking. Even though this was the case, the Underground Management and Government were unwilling that workers should take shelter in the Underground Railway Stations. Only when workers took matters in their own hands was this allowed. Even now the Managers of the London Underground Railway Co., were hostile. Some members of the Committee of Shelter in the Underground had recently been driven away by the police from the stations.

A delegate from the workers from Wickers Armstrong remarked that the workers of that firm had collected £50 to send delegates to this Congress.

Speaking on behalf of the Leeds Women's Cooperative the delegate questioned why the rationing was so unjust. If, she said, bread and meat were rationed for the workers why were the refrigerators of the rich so well stocked?

Speaking on behalf of the people in the country, a delegate said that the country folk were very discontented as evacuees from the cities were stuffed on to already overcrowded working folks' houses while the richer farmers had comparatively less evacuees to shelter.

Speaking on behalf of the India League Krishna Menon ridiculed all talk of 'democracy'. He said that a 'democratic Imperialism' was just about as true as a vegetarian tiger!

Remarking on the statement by the Labour Minister after he had been hooted at a Factory he visited, a delegate said that the Minister had put all the blame on the 'Reds'. But he said this was quite untrue. Recently suspecting their Communist leanings, the Labour Ministry ordered that 200 workers of a London factory be transported to the north. This would have meant a cut in wages for them. At a meeting of the 600 workers of that factory 593 voted for a strike, 7 abstaining. And the Ministry had to give in. Hence it was the militancy of the workers itself that was refusing to take it lying down from the Ministry.

Finally spoke Harry Pollitt. He remarked on the fact that whereas in 1917 such a Congress of the Peoples' Convention had been looked at resentfully by the workers and its delegates pelted with stones, during this war the workers were keen on the Congress and eager to be represented there. Moreover soldiers and airmen were present this time. He summed up the home and international situation and paid a tribute to the Shop Stewards who were leading the strike movement for higher wages.

The Congress ended with the singing of the Internationale.

(Moscow Radio, 17.1.41)

76. 'Whither?' Communist View of the Satyagraha Movement

Communist, Vol. III, No. 1, February 1941, P.C. Joshi Archives on Contemporary History, JNU.

No Chances

Winter is being left behind and spring is coming, not the familiar one of the ages, but the unimaginably grim prospect of two mighty giants coming to grips and using the whole wide world as their battle arena, trampling the people underneath, hurling at each other the entire material resources of humanity. Nothing like it has happened before. Each side is brushing itself up, manoeuvring for positions, clearing up its own rear, Dazed, the world looks aghast.

We in India are being told to rest content in our servile state with the thought that this is a war for freedom. But patent lies cannot become popular slogans and imperialism knows this and is taking no chances with the political situation in India. It is rapidly carrying through its political offensive against the national movement, sealing up the cracks before the zero hour for the battle for Britain strikes.

No Tall Poppies

The age old oppressor's trick is employed to drive us to the position of demoralized helplessness, an object demonstration that not one of us was big enough to stand up to the Sarkar. Maulana Azad was the Rashtrapati, busy bringing the Ahrars into the Congress? He is arrested and sentenced. And what more did it mean? 'Political observers here find in Maulana Azad's arrest, the Government's determination to carry on without a political settlement. It is pointed out in this connection that MAULANA AZAD WAS THE REAL ORIGINATOR OF THE POONA OFFER and stated more than once that he does not agree with Mahatma Gandhi on the issue of India's defence and will CO-OPERATE in this matter to the fullest extent'. (*National Herald*, New Delhi special correspondent, 5 January)

Gandhiji is the tallest in the land? It is a familiar remark of the *Presswallas* that the one man in India who enjoys civil liberties in Mahatmaji. His statements are unceremoniously banned!

Mopping up Fighters

Anyone who goes near the workers, peasants and students even for ordinary agitation and organization is immediately picked up. Wherever there are Communists the Special Branch Head Quarters of the police have no other job except to hunt down the underground centres of our Party. It is as if against all the fighters from the front of struggle—final mopping up operations was being carried through. The Japs too thought that each one was the final campaign against the guerrillas.

Press Licked into Submission

The Press is being gagged tighter and tighter and made innocuous without making much noise. The servile policy of the national leadership needed no revolutionary lead from press. The penalties under the Ordinance did the rest of the trick. The Indian Nationalist press, ever since 1920, has hardly been more servile. Gandhiji's own very first statement on war had made support to war compatible with Indian nationalism! Not struggle but settlement was sought for and the Nationalist Press was mobilized to mould popular opinion. On the top of this, notices of warning from the Censors' office and some fines sufficed to make the Press more Right than the Right Wing. And a foreign government, engaged in the greatest predatory war, is grandiloquently grateful for the UNANIMOUS support of the Press to its war-efforts. A judicious mixture of cajolery and threats has made the Nationalist Press lick the imperialist jack-boot. A 'struggle' is on, we are told. But the Anglo-Indian and nationalist editors continue to sit at the same table and arrive at a unanimous decision to appeal to the Government to 'consider' the special position of Gandhiji and the censors to 'consult' them before passing orders.

Throwing Out Feelers!

Congress has been battered out of shape, Communal and reactionary forces have had a free run. Workers that mattered as mass mobilizers are out of way. Why not test out the PRESENT strength of the Congress? This is why a few Central Assembly seats have been declared vacant. But the Government does not want large-scale provincial elections, on a wider franchise. This is the secret of short sentences to MLAs.

Waiting for a Show Down

The Government does not even make the pretence of seeking a settlement with the Congress. Amery has declared ones again that the August offer is the limit and we would be fools not to see the boon. This is all he can do. 'It is from the Indian side—from Indians to Indians—that the only effective "new approach" can be made', he rattled off in an interview to the Great Britain and the East. This is nothing more new than the proverbial monkey with the scale busily ensuring that the cats do go at each other.

Why not a Good-will Mission to India?,—suggested a voice in the Imperial Parliament thinking that Amery and Co may go too far. But the Secretary of State really considered it unnecessary. The explanation of his answer is the very 'struggle' of the Congress High Command. This is how the Indian situation is grasped by an imperialist publicist of repute. J.A. Spender, writing particularly for the American public, 'There is no need for alarm. India-British India as well as the India of the princes-is making handsome contribution to the war, both in men and materials and she will yet give us more of them.'

One can read any morning any nationalist paper and find pulsating in its columns as much struggle as there is life in mutton. You can get all the imperialist dope on war splashed through it, and read for yourself how heroic and self-sacrificing are the British in their unselfish war to resist Nazi aggression and emancipate the world, only they are not kind and generous enough to us in India and this is just what your paper is pleading for.

But is not Gandhiji an out and out opponent of the war? Yes, the *Times of India* asked the same question to the *Chronicle* and how could the Congress Ministries be trusted to carry on the war-effort if the acknowledged head of the organization opposed it. The *Chronicle* quoted chapter and verse to prove that the High Command was not so stupidly Gandhian as all that if something like the Poona offer had to be cashed, and that Gandhiji as a good democrat never stood in the way!

As if to ditto this we have *The Hindu* correspondent writing from Bombay and from inside knowledge 'He (Gandhiji) is not prepared to take any interest in any kind of negotiations at present...he would go on with his campaign till either the objective is achieved OR THE CONGRESS WC REQUESTS HIM TO CALL OFF THE MOVEMENT'.

And the Poona offer has been left far behind, like the Constituent Assembly of yore. *The Hindu* in a lengthy editorial 'End the deadlock' wants the Premiers and Ex-Premiers of Provinces to be put together, charged with paving the way for the post-war framing of a Constitution for a free India by 'agreement', Popular Government 'restored in all provinces, and 'substantial' changes in the Government of India along the lines BROADLY indicated in the Poona offer of the Congress, and it should not be difficult for the VICEROY to find out what are these changes

New Delhi correspondents are busy sending messages after messages about new moves for settlement. The latest is about 'influential circles' being busy preparing a memorandum for Viceroy and that the proposals are already in the hands of the Secretary of State 'but so far there is nothing to show that the Secretary of State has at the moment any new approach in mind'. (*Bombay Chronicle* 10.2.41)

A child's heart melts at the story of a lonely deer running after mirage, but what of a whole nation whose course is being directed towards an abyss and through political mirage?

Peace efforts by a subject nation express nothing else than the cowardice and treachery of its leadership. They are welcome to imperialism because they help to cover up its own offensive. Tons of facts and millions of words go to show, for all except the deaf and the crooked, that the running thread through the imperialist policy in India is WAIT AND BE FIRM, THEY WILL COME ROUND AND ACCEPT OUR TERMS, GO ON POUNDING.

This political offensive is part of a larger offensive Britain is waging in Africa and the Near East to safeguard the Eastern Empire, that is, the real colonial Empire. Cleaning up of Africa is the military part; Eastern Group Conference is the economic part, while this political offensive in India is the political part of ONE WHOLE POLICY. Who will say this is not jolly good sense for the British ruling class BEFORE the final 'burst up' in the West comes, when it has to stand up to Hitler and stake Britain itself?

No Mass Movement!

Against this growing imperialist offensive where is the Gandhian leadership leading the nation? After the suppression of his statements, rumours ran wild that Bapuji is going to do something big. All this is wishful thinking, good enough for gossip but having nothing to do with reality. The Mahatma got no new wand to take out of his magician's bag. There is no way out in his policy. He may be the Mahatma all right but he got to take a blow from Imperialism lying down, he can deeply MEDITATE over it—that is not banned, and just because he is Mahatma, he wields the big stick over Congressmen, not let them stray into the masses and shepherd them single file inside the prison gates. Such is the inexorable logic of the situation; such is the ignominious end of Gandhism.

'Whatever may be the expansion, the present struggle launched by the Congress will never develop into a mass movement and so far as I can see it will remain individual civil disobedience and be confined only to those who believe in and fulfil my conditions' (Mahatma Gandhi to a Forward Bloc leader, UP message 3.1.41)

'No Indian should dream that the present Satyagraha movement will develop into a mass movement as long as the leadership is in his hands' (Gandhiji in a letter to Delhi PCC, *Times*, 10 February)

This is exactly what he had foretold a year earlier, at Ramgarh. But then it was a question of investing Gandhiji with full authority over the Congress and he declared in AICC and open Sessions that if he did not want a mass civil disobedience he would not have come to them. After a year of imperialist offensive against the whole national movement TO-DAY he asks the nation not even to DREAM of a mass struggle and is emphatic that his Satyagraha won't go that way.

Independence Day

This year's Independence Day was planned out in the Gandhian way. 'There is to be no civil disobedience on that day'. We are in the midst of a struggle? But it got to be suspended to celebrate our march to freedom! Dilemma? Not at all. Satyagraha is not the struggle of the people but on behalf of the people; when they assemble it is off; they can't be let indoors to soil Satyagraha, they read a sermon out in the open and dispersed.

And even on Independence Day they need not necessarily assemble. 'Where there are already restrictions (by the police) they must be obeyed'. The hallmark of Congress movements so far had been defiance of the police, breaking through its cordons, tearing up its gag orders.

Where they could meet on this great day, what were they to be told? The Gandhian pledge was made more squarely Gandhian this year and the 'special duty of every Indian', it laid down was nothing else than 'concentrate with redouble zeal on the constructive programme'. For twenty years Gandhiji has been saying this and even while a World War is on and the imperialist structure is shaking to its foundations, he has nothing MORE, nothing NEW to add except spin, spin yourself away.

But the people assembled everywhere and in thousands. All the enthusiasm ended in thin smoke. The militant character of last year's demonstrations was missing showing the gap left behind in our national ranks by the arrest of hundreds of fighters. Being Sunday strikes of students and workers were out of the question. Yet Gandhism did not have it quite its way. Madras students had suffered the most under repression. Six hundred of them organized as squads on cycles paraded the streets throughout the day and assembled 10 thousand strong in their evening meeting and demonstration. A reign of terror had been let loose against Malabar Complete hartal at Calicut, a demonstration of 10 thousand predominantly workers and Muslims and a meeting of 25 thousand in the evening, held under the auspices of the Town Congress Committee. True the Gandhists kept aloof and did not even come to the meeting but organided their own affair quietly. And so on, even from the meagre press reports.

Kripalani however asked the people to stick indoors if the police banned the day. The Government thought better and let the day pass by. Only Sir CP, the Dewan of Travancore, with whom Dr Pattabhi went to negotiate peace, ordered that it was just 'not possible' to take a pledge severing the British connection on the soil of a state bound by treaty to the British.

77. 'Whither?' Communist View of the Bombay Conference

Communist, Vol. III, No. 2, March 1941, P.C. Joshi Archives on Contemporary History, JNU.

Discarded Begums

The 'most important event' of March, if you went by Press reports alone, was the Bombay Conference at the Taj, on 14 March, of the old, decayed and therefore discarded Begums of the British. Three Viceroy's own Ex-Executive Councillors, many more Chota Lats' Ex-, and Ex-Ministers most of them, and THEY discover that the Government has never been more isolated from the people. All experienced hands at the game but their calling itself is such that 'Experience has made me a cynic' (Sir Tej, on the eve). They had eaten the salt, they can't sit still, they must speak out. 'The present interminable controversies are going to end in disaster and I feel we are near that disaster' (Sir Tej again)! And he yelled aloud to the Burra Saheb of all the Sahebs to come and have a look for himself. Some of them were even indecent enough to gossip about how things were different when they were in the harem of such and such a Viceroy!

Their logic was something like this: There is hardly any difference between us and the Congress. But they of the Congress always spoil a good case by using such empty demagogy as 'Independence', 'National Government', and other things. Look at our resolution. There is neither Independence nor National Government in it. Let us see how the Government refuses THAT!

Miserable imbeciles! They measure Indian politics in 1941 with the yardstick of Indian Liberalism, model 1890. They naturally don't see the simple issue that what imperialism requires, in the second year of the Second Imperialist World War is not a few tail-coated and top-hatted dummies to adorn Cabinet seats but leaders who would 'deliver the goods', that is, who are capable of cheating the people and thereby chaining them to the British war-chariot.

Road Clear!

Commenting on the Bombay Resolution Dr Pattabhi said, 'The demand of the Congress is much simpler. We want only acknowledgement of Independence. But once the Status in conceded function follows as a matter of course': (UP, 18 March). What the President of the Andhra PCC and member of the WC means is this: What really matters is not how MUCH power you give us now but HOW you give it. After all, the settlement should be such that the Congress leadership should find little difficulty in ramming it down the throat of Congress masses. It must be capable of being popularized as a victory, as a decisive step towards Independence and all that!

This sort of settlement, imperialism won't give during the war, not as things are, and for two reasons, firstly it is afraid it would strengthen the Congress and the bourgeoisie vis-à-vis imperialism and secondly, what is the guarantee that such a settlement would be a proof against the recrudescence of revolutionary forces and mass upheavals during the war?

Gandhiji knows this and has sensed his way to this very conclusion. It has taken him months and months of deep meditation, and he had to go in for trials and commit errors, but has at last got the bearings all right. It took so unconscionably long because he is the leader of a bankrupt class. A compromise in the period of war, he feels, is almost impossible. He bled for the Westminster Abbey but is it not too much to expect the British rulers to listen to reason when they are being bombed, they do not believe in non-violence. He will go on bleeding, he will let the Indian people be bled, in Europe there is blood all round. After the war the British will come to him humbled and in need of his message, and India's freedom will come as a voluntary gift at the shrine of the sage, from the penitent sinners—the present masters of Britain and India. He also realized that it would be dangerous and difficult to carry a compromise through. Even at Sewagram, away from the maddening crowd, darling Nehru's alternate tears and thunder, did leave a bad taste in the mouth, foretold what Rajaji and Sardarji are going to get from the Congress millions, if their real politik becomes real. He meditated his purest, listened his hardest to the inner voice and after all GOT IT, the whole line of symbolic Satyagraha. The very basis of the new policy (dictated by his cumulative experience of months of war, long journeys to Delhi and Simla, and backed by his twenty years as a Satyagrahi General) was that the leadership has somehow to mark time and WAIT through the entire period of war, neatly balancing itself between Imperialism and the Revolution. It was this feeling that found its clearest expression in his letter to the *Times of India* on 15/2 in which he almost said: There was no question of co-operation with the Government as long as war lasted. The *Times of India* turned round and said: There you are, Congress never wanted to co-operate in the war, Gandhiji is irrevocably committed to hindering the war effort and it is because of this intransigence that settlement is not possible. The nationalist press, especially the Chronicle returned to the charge and proved again for the nth time, that the national Government's offer was not dead, it was only kept in cold storage, could be warmed up any time, let the Government show its hand, Gandhiji is not the WC, and has never stood in its way.

There was 'CONSTERNATION' among the compromisers as reported to the arch-compromiser, Gandhiji himself. Had Gandhiji ruled out compromise, for the entire war period, what hell..? To set all false fears at rest, and on the eve of the Bombay Conference, the General gave line-clear to the compromisers, if they must try their hand and burn their fingers. 'The only authority I have is to conduct campaign of Civil Disobedience.... When the time for settlement comes it will be for the Working Committee to decide what the terms shall be.' (Statement, 6th March). But he knew it was not coming so easy or so cheap. If it is, he won't stand in the way.

Gandhiji has given line-clear, not only for settlement with the Congress if the Government so desires but also between the Government and non-Congress parties if ANY settlement is to be had. 'If the Hindu Mahasabha were so inclined it could partake reorganization of the Central Government', said Gandhiji to the general secretary of the Hindu Mahasabha, but 'the Congress will be satisfied with the fullest freedom to grow in non-violence'. Columnfuls in the Nationalist press and Gandhiji's own other statements make clear what this means. Satyagraha will be withdrawn, the Congress will not oppose but remain benevolently neutral towards a settlement between the Government and non-Congress parties if the Congress is granted freedom of speech to non-violently preach its anti-war message, that is, register its normal protest without hindering the war-effort, keep up its oppositional prestige with the people, and its organization (that is, its electoral basis) intact. Something rather than nothing, best of both the worlds, in a mad world going to pieces. Would imperialism oblige?

Bourgeoisie Behind Bapuji

It would be going off the track to regard the Bombay Non-Party leaders Conference as being anything more than an exhibitionist party of old hags who are seized with the irrepressible desire to tell the world what they could do if somebody married them again. They represented nobody and were too old themselves to count for anything.

Real bourgeoisie, big business as a whole, is behind Bapuji. The annual meeting of the Federation of Indian Merchants' Chamber, on 22–3 March at Delhi, vigorously condemned every aspect of the war-economic policy of British imperialism and roundly demanded 'National Government' as an immediate step. Here is the voice of the bourgeoisie (Textile, Steel, Cement, Sugar, Indian shipping, Insurance, Banking, Cotton, and Seeds trade, and others, all rolled into one organization) and it has stressed the main demand which the Congress has put. The Delhi meeting rather than the Bombay Taj show is a better indicator of compromise moves.

Big business knows the value of Gandhiji's leadership and of the sham Satyagraha as a unique instrument of compromise in these difficult days of second World War. Therefore with one hand it secretly supports Gandhian satyagraha and the other it stretches out before imperialism.

The position of the bourgeoisie at present is as follows. It is doing well in Steel, Engineering, Cement, Cotton (textile), Cotton (trade), Sugar (not bad), Shipping, and other things. It is earning fair margins of profit with the existing capital investment. This improvement has come during the last few months, but it is chafing at the hundred and one restrictions which completely bolt and bar the way to industrial expansion just at the time when the GREAT OPPORTUNITY is there. Before its own jealous eyes the Australian and South African bourgeoisie is expanding its industries while it is assigned the slave's place in the Eastern Group Council. That is why it fully supports the present Satyagraha in its present form and is upholding the Congress demand for National Government, and hails Bapuji.

But—

There is going to be no compromise, no room for it. This is the reality. But ghostly shadows flit across and make a ghastly sight of our national movement. Every move for a sell-out gets the Mahatma's blessings but he is Mahatmic enough not to soil his own hands. Old dames may be no-good but their very dotage makes them traditional go-betweens, Sapru and Co can't sleep in peace, the younger ladies may put the price too high. Have no fears, says the Mahatma. I see no business going, bad times, but I give line-clear if you think I am seized with a Puritanical fit. 'Minimum demand' and 'fair basis for negotiations' shrieks the Chronicle. 'The Bombay Conference has uttered a warning and suggested a way out. Let Britain take heed before it is too late'. The *The Hindu*, 17 March, is as heroic as this. You are delving in ancient history if you bother about Independence—Constituent Assembly. You would be impossible, funny, my dear, if you trot out the Bombay AICC Resolution. Even the Poona resolution can be tucked away, what is the cash on and going. They are all dressed up, ready to go; only HE does not come. How cruel is the War!

78. Organize the Militants

Editorial, *Communist*, Vol. III, No. 2, March 1941, P.C. Joshi Archives on Contemporary History, JNU.

An average decent Congressmen, even a Satyagrahi, who believes in individual Satyagraha is a rarity. He readily admits it can't lead to Swaraj and that it is no serious struggle at all. He, however, argues that it is better than stalemate. SOMETHING instead of NOTHING. He is thinking hard groping his way to political alternatives to Gandhism, for a real way out. For Bose he has contempt—has he not already damned himself as an unprincipled mountebank? Against Roy he is indignant, it was he who talked loud for an alternative leadership to Gandhism and has landed himself in the company of Rajas and Nawabs and beats the drum for Britain's Imperialist War. About the CSP he does not bother, for he knows that the CSP has lost its entire membership to the Communists and the leaders have merged themselves with Gandhism, and just as Gandhi liquidates the Congress so does the CSP leadership dare not function the CSP. He listens to the Communists attentively, he admits international events make any sense only on the basis of Communist analysis, he concedes that the national policy of the Communists is really national. But he seeks to turn tail with: Communists are a handful, what can they do? More often than not he runs away to jail as a Satyagrahi, his conscience at rest for the time being, to carry on thinking 'more at peace with himself'! Such is one tragedy.

BUT were not there hundreds of Congressmen, and student, kisan, and Trade Union workers, who did not have any illusions about Gandhism whose one ambition in life was to organize and participate in a national mass struggle for freedom? The axe of repression fell upon them first, the most ardent and active of them, headed by their foremost leaders, are behind the bars. Only the very young and quite new cadres from among them yet remain out of jail-walls, and more often than not they wring their hands in despair, look longingly towards the closed jail-gates and whisper: the game is up, Gandhiji has betrayed the whole nation, we have already lost our leaders and nothing much can be done! Such is another tragedy.

These are the thoughts and practice of a whole lot of national workers. But if this were the whole reality inside our nation we would have to write the Indian Revolution off the pages of history and conclude that the Indian people have no future, the problem has only to be posed in this manner to turn back and realize that this helplessness of national workers is a temporary demoralization created by the policy of Gandhism and by their own inability to work out an effective alternative path. They miss the real meaning of events they think about, they fail to see the reality right under their nose.

Gandhiji refuses to fight the final battle for our freedom, while the imperialist war is on. He seeks settlement and to have it, he resorts to Satyagraha.

He escapes mass movement. Why? Because the mass movement has already reached a stage that it can't be 'controlled'.

He disbands the national organization–the Congress. Why?, because it can't be trusted to carry out his policy.

THESE are not the signs of strength but weakness of Gandhism. A key-point, the national leadership, is yet in their hands, but they are on the run before their following—the masses, they are breaking the sword of the nation—organization. Such is the measure of their weakness and here itself is the departing point for the alternative policy that will yet save the national movement from Gandhian disruption and it is,—

INTO THE MASSES!

FOR THEIR ORGANIZATION!

AND these are eminently practical slogans. There are thousands of Congressmen who have adored and built the Congress as a mass organization, who have been inside it to fight through it a mass struggle for Independence. They are losing faith in Gandhism and looking out for a lead, ready to plunge into any activity that will be demonstratively a more effective alternative to Gandhian Satyagraha. The Trade Union movement is now about twenty years old, has passed through hundreds of strike battles and through them has steeled hundreds of militants who have always held the Red Flag high and become the impregnable political base of the Communists. The first strike wave after the war broke under repression and the second one has already begun to rise. The Kisan Sabha movement is younger and lost all its leaders in the first round of repression but a core of militant kisans has been formed wherever the Kisan Sabha existed and fought the kisans' battles. Students, the youth of our nation, have made history, they launched successful mass political strikes despite Gandhian bans and after his sham Satyagraha, they have maintained the mass character of their organization, despite the Gandhian attempts to split them. In every section of our fighting people we have thousands of militant fighters left though the dominant national leaders have betrayed and real fighting leaders are behind the bars. They are anxiously groping for a lead, they await to be educated, organized and led into action.

ORGANIZATION of these militants is the key-job of the immediate present, if Gandhism is not to triumph, that is, reduced our national movement to ashes, if every mass organization that the best sons of our people have built is not to collapse under repression, if mass struggles are not to become a memory of the past instead of dress-rehearsals for the final battle.

WE Communists approach every honest non-Party national fighter thus: You say our policy is sound. Well then you must fight for it, for nothing is going to happen spontaneously. Come together, let us apply it to our local conditions, together with our Party comrades you carry it out in the mass organization you are working. The bourgeois leadership teaches you disruption and disorganization. Our Communism leads us to organization and unity and therefore we come to you. Ours is the only Party that has the experience of both legal mass work and illegal activity and it is unified through and embodied in our Party Committee. Pre-war reality is dead and so must be its ways and methods inside the national movement. Leaders cannot be available for direct leadership from day-to-day; the rank and file has to be educated and experienced enough to be able to carry on. Unprepared and spontaneous mass actions would collapse under the first blow of imperialist repression. Therefore, let us politically educate ourselves; technically organize ourselves, to be able to successfully act through our own mass organization.

HELPLESSNESS among the political workers is undoubtedly growing in face of growing repression and the futility of Satyagraha. The only way to overcome it and lead the people as a whole towards a mass national struggle is to educate and organize the national fighters so that they may successfully launch

ALL-IN ANTI-REPRESSION CAMPAIGN!
'MAHAGAI' STRIKES OF WORKERS!
KISAN ACTIONS AGAINST WAR BURDENS.

DURING the decisive year of the imperialist world war, the fate of our nation will be decided through the efforts of the Indian people to fight back the political and economic offensive of imperialism and transform the situation of imperialist war into a national war against imperialism.

WHAT Communists everywhere have to realize is that organizing the militants is tall talk if our own Party Units are not organized tip-top, if they are politically not educated enough to convince the non-Party fighters, if they are organizationally not active enough to win the confidence of militants as being the best and most self-sacrificing fighters themselves.

THE only ray of hope in present day national politics is that the national fighters, in growing numbers, are coming to realize that the policy of the proletariat is a real alternative to the policy of the bourgeoisie. The next step on which depends the future of our national movement is whether the Party of the proletariat is able to demonstrate to them that the way to make the alternative policy effective is a particular method of organization, that the CP advances not only a truly national policy but puts forward a method of organization that is at once really revolutionary and most democratic and it is their national duty to whole-heartedly co-operate in it as the only way out.

Thousands of national fighters, new and old, are looking to our Party for lead and guidance. To them all we say:

HELP OUR PARTY
TO EDUCATE AND ORGANIZE THE MILITANTS
FOR ORGANIZED MASS ACTIONS.

79. 'Whither?' Communist View of the War Situation, Amery's Speech of 22 April and Communal Riots

Communist, Vol. III, No. 3, April–May 1941, P.C. Joshi Archives on Contemporary History, JNU.

The British Lion At Bay Holds Closer To Its Prey. This sums the position, as it exists to-day.

Hitler opened his Spring-Krieg simultaneously on four fronts and on all Britain being badly badgered and the position of its rulers is admittedly very serious. In Atlantic, 'the arsenal of democracy' building 'a lane of warships' is yet a dream. The reality is the mounting shipping losses, which have been so heavy that the Admiralty has stopped publishing the weekly returns. The Luftwaffe has again asumed its terrific destructive work not only over London but over a series of coastal and industrial towns. The scare of invasion which the rulers had themselves stopped as worn-out is again being revived. In the Balkans the British at least succeeded in creating a new front for Germany. But the Nazi chiefs preceded an attack upon Yugoslavia by a powerful lightening blow in Libya. The neat British plan of sending masses of mechanized material, men and planes from Libya to the Balkans got seriously punctured. The Balkan venture ended in a fiasco. Yugoslavian Army surrendered in record-time. The retreat from Greece had to be as hasty and heroic as from France. The Suez once again menaced by a powerful pincer movement of German arms, one prong is closing upon it from Greece in the Aegean Sea while the other is thrusting its way through Libya. In the Far-Eastern theatre the clever designs of Anglo-American imperialism for strengthening and extending their Empires in South Pacific and their hold over China have suffered a severe set-back because of the Soviet-Japanese Pact. They would have very much liked continued friction between Japan and the USSR in the North Pacific while they went ahead in the South, but the Soviet did not oblige and chose security of its own Pacific frontier.

In short the British rulers are facing a situation which is strikingly similar to the one they faced last year about this time. There is growing impatience in a section of the ruling-circles with the present Cabinet. Not efficient in the Departments, no supreme leadership free to get things done. Labour Ministers are sabotaging Industrial Conscription. Such are the complaints of those who are demanding 'fresh blood' in the Cabinet. The demand is obviously for a more Fascist Government. On the other hand among the people and the workers specially there is growing impatience with war and the horrible conditions of life under it. The slogan, THROUGH A PEOPLES' GOVERNMENT TO A PEOPLES' PEACE, seems to be gaining ground.

Such is the situation in which the British ruling class finds itself. The prospect is more fascist measures in Britain, more ruthless and reactionary policy in India. Such is the blind and desperate logic of imperialism in crisis. It is necessary for us all to grasp here in India that there can be no other policy for the British rulers when it is a question of life and death struggle for world domination, and they are deep in quandary as they have never been before.

Not Only No But....

It is against this background that Amery's speech of 22nd April, in the House of Commons' debate, has to be viewed. It enunciated British imperialist policy in India in the present context of the war situation. What is important in Amery's latest is not the extension for one year more of the Advisers' regime in the seven provinces, nor the spurning of the Sapru's proposals, nor even the usual wail about lack of Indian unity and the juicy arguments against the Congress but the FORESHADOWING OF AN IMPERIALIST OFFENSIVE MORE SEVERE THAN EVER BEFORE, CLEAR-CUT PLAN TO UNLEASH THE FORCES OF RACTION AND DISRUPTION, DIRE THREAT TO DROWN INDIAN NATIONALISM IN BLOOD AND TEAR INDIA TO PIECES.

Amery's main fire was directed against the Congress and its leadership for it represents the great mass of the Indian people. To the national leadership he said:

You have been trying to twist the tail of the British lion, by resigning from the Ministries, by putting Premiers and ex-Ministers in jail, by keeping up a campaign of individual anti-war speeches and slogans which is not very but sufficiently annoying and embarrassing. These tactics will bring you nothing! We are determined to enforce the law ruthlessly against you.

While there is yet time, wind-up the regrettable show of Satyagraha, get back to your Provincial Ministries, and come to an agreement with other political parties to participate in the war-effort. Remember, we offer you no mean thing. We already recognize Dominion Status for India in advance—no ordinary status that, true not of the Westminster type but one eminently suited to India. It would be a glorious edifice supported by four historic pillars, namely the ICS, the British Financial Oligarchs, the British Army of Occupation, and the ancient order of the Princes. Under their spreading protection you will be free to frame any constitution you like provided you reach an agreement among various political parties. This is the glorious opportunity; seize it now, later you will repent.

With the advent of the Congress Ministries, under the new Constitution, we had thought you had after all taken to the sane path of Constitutionalism. But even then you failed to make-up with the minorities and the princes. And now, in these grim days, you have returned to your old mutton—political adventure and pressure-politics. You seem blind 'to the risk that no alternative constitution is now likely to emerge which could secure for the Congress as great a measure of influence and control over India as a whole as it would have exercised under the present Act'.

You wanted a price for your co-operation in the war. When we are in trouble and expected you to be loyal you let us down and used all the tricks you knew to have your way. You take us to be boobies or what, you think we have been sleeping all the while and have no other go except fall in your arms. There is Jinnah, go and face his Pakistan demand! You have to reckon with him now, a veritable Frankenstein. You shake in your boots? Now listen quietly, if you desire to preserve the unity of India and frame a constitution, under the conditions we provide, you will get even less power at the centre than under the 1935 Act. This is the only alternative before you now. Make up your mind. If you do not accept this, the only other alternative would be 'the dismal record of India's history in the eighteenth century', that is, open civil war and strife.

Amery's was a summary ultimatum to the Congress to surrender and the terms are: DIRE REPRESSION IF YOU PERSIST IN OPPOSITION, THAT IS, THIS SATYAGRAHA.

MORE REACTIONARY CONSTITUTION EVEN IF YOU SURRENDER. OPEN CIVIL WAR IF YOU REFUSE TO SUBMIT.

The Bubble Burst

During April Satyagraha ceased even being news, settlement rackets flew all over the sky. Everybody felt it was a matter of days, compromise was coming. Amery would make the gesture, in the House of Commons debate, and the rest will come as day follows the night.

It began with the Taj Conference, after Bapuji gave line-clear and Sapru his wisdom. The *Bombay Chronicle* ran a campaign, here is the minimum demand, grant it and everything would be OK. The *Hindustan Times* capped a series of editorials with its New Delhi special correspondent's message, on 3 April: Implement the August offer in the spirit of the Bombay Resolution by expanding the Viceroy's Council, have truce with the Congress, and it would be easy sailing. Birla's class desired Sapru to have the 'affair'—with the British, while Gandhiji was to remain chaste—with the people, and it may have best of both the worlds—cash in war orders through an efficient agent and retain the leadership of the people through an angelic channel. *The Hindu* in its editorial of 15 April went a step further and said, 'irrespective of what Britain may or may not do' the Congress should call off Satyagraha, go back to Ministries, to 'take up the active leadership of the people'. *The Statesman* jumped with joy and sugar-coated the pill, 'the country as a whole wants something to rally behind and that something is a truly National Government.' *The Times* on 19 April rounded it off with 'Return to Realities', individual civil disobedience was not a lubricant but an irritant, Jinnah was only flattering the Congress by imitation, against independence he had pitted Pakistan, if you see sense he won't have a leg to stand upon, call off the movement and admit your mistake, co-operate in the provinces—have coalition, and thus ease the situation for reforms in the Centre. Finally an eloquent appeal to the Mahatma to deliver the goods.

But Gandhi Baba is no fool, having grown grey in the service of the bourgeoisie. In a Special interview with *The Times* on 19th April, he refused to budge; he would carry on, wait, and pray for better days to come. Twenty year old General of the bourgeoisie, he knew better than all the nationalist organs put together that compromise was not coming in 'circumstances so terrible and so baffling, as face the world to-day'. His was a 'silent declaration', 'a moral protest'. Material compromise could not be had, moral capital was all that he could save out of the fire of a world war, but it would pay in the end when elections come, the Congress would spring up as a vast electoral machine. Satyagraha was the only strategy and no other possible.

'It was never intended that it would create an appreciable impression on the war effort', and for those who have eyes 'there is sufficient evidence... to show that extraordinary precaution is being taken to keep the movement within limits and absolutely innocuous.'

But facing both ways is the essence of wisdom when the politics of compromise and opposition have to be combined, therefore, 'if Britain would only be true to India then everything could be settled satisfactorily.'

This was all before Amery spoke. He needed a bombshell to prick a bubble because he was talking to the leadership of a nation and had to put the fear of God into them. The lesson for us is that those who were all ready for a sell-out are at the head of the movement. Black treachery had not been enacted because the enemy demanded surrender hands down, while they were dreaming of honourable (that is, profitable) compromise. It is Amery's victory, not the peoples.

Impotent Rage

If Congressmen nurse the illusion that Amery has knocked sense into Gandhiji, the ghost of compromise is gone, and now Satyagraha would be transformed into a serious struggle they are being blind while led to the grave. It is true, even *The Times* (1st May) admits, 'Mr Amery's speeches in Parliament have provoked in India a depressing chorus of disapproval. It would be idle to deny that this disapproval is tinged with bitterness and a deep sense of frustration.' Gandhiji is 'almost Catonic in his denunciation', in a lengthy statement he has trounced Amery to pulp as cheeky, ungrateful, liar and all. But in the end, 'Distress has been known to have softened peoples' hearts and made them mindful of facts. But Britain's distress has evidently left Mr Amery absolutely cold.' Therefore, boys, sit tight in jails, spin and pray, that will melt Amery's heart. Arguments instead of action are the policy of the bourgeois leadership even when faced with the imperialist ultimatum, fiddling with words while the enemy has let loose an avalanche.

After this lead from the Leader all are becoming (wordy) heroes. 'Amery will get it' shouts the *Chronicle*. How? Let Sapru join Sewagram and Bapuji bring off the miracle of a pact with Jinnah! How will Amery not come down! *The Hindu* joins issue 'Mr Amery like the bourbons learns nothing and forgets nothing.... It cannot be good for Britain either, to inspire in India that feeling of futility.' Sapru and Co, have not thrown up the sponge either, they are going to hold a more representative Conference in July.

The analysis of them all is Amery's 'no' cannot be permanent, he thinks he can do without us—the fool! Let him face Hitler's hell and he will come round. WAIT, the word will come.

Jinnah's Duet

Amery, Gandhi, Sapru do not by themselves fill the Indian political stage. Do not forget Jinnah Saheb! He combines the Deshgaurab's flair with the Mahatma's faith in himself and claims to decide the destiny of the Muslim millions. The Madras Session of the Muslim League was a replica of the Congress Session. There the Quaide Azam played the counter tune to the Mahatma's but in the same duet.

Pakistan is his individual Satyagraha. Ganhdiji has twenty year old Congress to pull down, while he is yet building his League. Gandhiji has headed the national storm for twenty years; he must ride something even if imperialism is to be allowed to ride rough-shod over the rest. Gandhiji needs some sort of 'struggle', Jinnah does not, thank imperialism, his 'Muslim masses' are more backward. A whirlwind campaign to popularize Pakistan serves his purpose as well. Noisy demagogy is his satyagraha.

He has to be his own Gandhi plus Sapru. He has been at the settlement game since the war began. He had tried all the alternatives, to close-up with the British, first as Gandhiji's equal, then as a leader of a grand non-communal combine of the Rest vs Congress, and also all by himself, but none of these came off. So at Madras the Quaide Azam talked of Pakistan, INDEPENDENT OF THE BRITISH. That's how he waits and watches. Why? Muslim masses—their fear! One needs at least this much to divert the anti-war and anti-imperialist sentiments of the Muslim masses in disruptive channels.

This is not all about Pakistan. As Gandhiji's Satyagraha is at once the cover for and the lever to achieve Rajaji's National Government, the Quaide Azam's Pakistan is the fig-leaf over terms of compromise, in the interest of the Muslim vested interests. During the duration of the war they can be categorized as:

1. Equality of the League with the Congress in the provinces—Coalition.
2. Equality of the League with the Congress and superiority over others at the Centre.
3. No stealing a march over us. Stop Satyagraha or we denounce it as a move against the Muslim masses.

Such is the Quaide Azam's strategy, true to the Hindustani proverb TUM DAL DAL TO HAM PAT PAT (you can come up the twigs! I can walk over the leaves, Catch me!) People say he is insanely anti-Gandhi. His psychology does not matter, in politics he has learnt the most from Gandhi Baba, and by faithfully imitating the Mahatma he has risen to be his peer, one bourgeois family after all!

Riot—Racket

Amery gave no empty threat. Mere words don't cut much ice in the days of war; everything has to be cashed on the spot. Communal riots were the background music to his Commons' Speech. They were properly timed, some preceding it and the rest followed to make his threat real and grim.

They were police-tricks put across through the Goondas' underworld. No more evidence is necessary than a few facts about the origin and course of the riots. At Dacca, a quarrel broke out between a few Hindu and Muslim goondas over a prostitute, and in the night some Hindu goondas stabbed six Muslims. The Holi was on and one should think a spontaneous riot could have easily spread; it may be easy but it was not left to chance. Huq took the plane to Dacca, he is the Premier you would say. Dr Shyamaprasad, the Hindu Mahasabha leader, too could afford to fly and was allowed to harangue his hardest while the Students' Goodwill Delegation was not allowed to open their mouths even inside college Halls. The Hindu and Muslim student youth of Bengal had upset before bureaucratic apple-carts. Planes were used for rushing the Police force? No, for aerial reconnaisance to witness the destruction caused. In the villages, the riot was worked up by strangers, that is, 'outside agitators'. The police looked while houses were set on fire and in some cases arrested those who tried to prevent arson.

At AHMEDABAD, the story was spread: the Sikhs are going to take out a procession with music before the Mosque. But nothing of the sort was the matter, the Sikhs themselves did not know about it! The scare did not spread. Next day it began with stabbing incidents, respectable local Editors have signed a statement to say that the affair was engineered and premeditated.

At BOMBAY, while the Muslims were assembled for Namaz at the Juma Masjid, the story was spread that Muslims had been stabbed in Abdur Rahman Street, quite near. When the crowd was coming out of the Mosque, stones were obligingly thrown at it. The rest followed, and even then it took three days to warm up.

The flames had to be spread North, what could be a more suitable occasion than the Anti-Pakistan Day of the Hindu Mahasabha. CAWNPUR was made to witness the fireworks and also BIHAR SHARIF.

With indecent hurry, giving the whole game away, *The Times* wrote editorially on 22nd April

> In the disintegrating political atmosphere of the country, with communal relations progressively deteriorating. Mr Gandhi carries a heavy responsibility in deciding to persist with his movement. Twenty years ago, following Chauri Chaura outrage, the Congress leader, despite opposition from his followers, courageously called off the Satyagraha Campaign and thus saved the country from a further spate of bloodshed and rioting. To day the position is not dissimilar. The political sky is dark with foreboding, and Dacca, Ahmedabad, and Bombay carry an ominous warning.... We ask Mr Gandhi again, in all sincerity and earnestness to reconsider his decision (to carry on with Satyagraha) before it is too late!

THE COMMUNAL RIOT IS THE IMPERIALIST ANTI-DOTE TO SATYAGRAHA. Age-old trick being put to new use, to demoralize the Congress opposition, scare it out of wits, force it to submit, and get quietly yoked on to the war-chariot of John Bull. We have only seen the first round. Gandhiji alone does not know pressure-politics!

New Stage

We are witnessing the passing over of our national movement, during the Second Imperialist War, to a NEW STAGE. We began with stalemate; from stalemate to surrender was the aim of imperialism, from stalemate to settlement of the bourgeoisie, from stalemate to struggle the ardent desire of the people. At the beginning of the war, the Congress dominated the scene; John Bull shook in his boots with the spectre of a united India rising in revolt while he was engaged with Hitler. He lined up with the national leadership, dangled the hope of settlement for months and months, got Gandhiji to sit tight upon the Congress while he rapidly flattened out all the forces of struggle and mopped up every national fighter within and without the Congress. He faced Gandhiji and after polite discussions it was found the gulf was unbridgeable.

Gandhiji wringing his hands went into the wilderness of Satyagraha while John Bull made sure that the every remaining or potential fighter was safely in as a Satyagrahi or otherwise. Face each other again? What nonsense, shouts John Bull hands down! Or face the communal blood bath instead. What is your strength? National unity! I will see it go up in smoke. Now not even thanks for letting me climb up your back to get on top of the Indian people. No time for such formalities. I am busy with Hitler. But here in India I am on top and not you. Speak up or I let loose war realities, the reign of blood and iron, brother set against brother. Such is the present phase we have entered.

Final Say Whose?

The entire bourgeois leadership is aghast. This is not what they had bargained for! They are screaming at their own creation. But the neck is of the people as a whole and the front is of the entire nation that is so seriously is danger.

The blood of our own people is not coagulated with fright, the front is being reformed. Our kisan pages would show that the kisan masses are bestirring themselves. The entire Reception Committee of the UP Kisan Conference was rounded up. The Malabar Kisan Sabha has been banned and armed police during April has been combing out not only villages but whole Talukas. The second wave of workers' strikes has not yet burst the bonds in any major industry except Textiles (Poona, Nagpur, Indore, and Bangalore this month) but things sizzling below the surface. Backward section of the workers are coming forward, for example, gharrywallas in Bombay, Lahore sweepers had to be arrested en masse, and other things. Indore States people, led by the workers, attacked police thanas and rescued their comrades. Students are silent because the examinations are on or holidays have begun. The blood of our people, all over the country is warm; their hands can and are striking. Prisons are becoming political schools. 12,000 satyagrahi lads in UP jails alone are thinking hard, under the Warders' danda, getting news of Satyagraha being in danger of going under the riots.

Blue funk and black treachery mark out the bourgeoisie, but the heart of the people beats true, some have began to sit up and think, a small section is hitting out. This alone is the bright spot in a picture of unrelieved gloom. A hero's courage to forge our fighting front and a Prophet's determination to see it win is demanded of every fighter today for the final word yet lies with the people, not Amery, not Gandhi, not Jinnah. Make the people see, speak, and act, they alone can make the riots and Satyagraha events of the past and a growing struggle for freedom the reality instead. (1 May 1941)

80. Four Bolsheviks Escape!

Communist, Vol. III, No. 4, June 1941, P.C. Joshi Archives on Contemporary History, JNU.

On 8th May, four political prisoners, Comrades P. Sivayya, T.R. Subrahmanyam, P. Sekharan, and O. Joseph successfully escaped from Allipuram Camp Jail. Newspapers featured the news on 10th. We give below the story of this Madras Dachau, what the politicals have to suffer, why they are struggling, how these heroic four fought inside the prison walls and successfully got out of them to be free to participate in the freedom struggle of us all.

Allipuram Camp Jail is on the outskirts of Bellary Town, 300 miles from Madras. It was once military barracks. During the First Imperialist War it was proposed to be used as a camp for war-prisoners, but before reconstruction was complete that war ended. But another war began. The Moplah peasantry rose in rebellion against the unbearable exploitation of Jenmi landlords. How they fought, how they were crushed is a well-known story of Indian people's heroism and British imperialism's barbarity. Hundreds of Moplahs were sentenced to transportation for life and lodged here. Later in 1930, during the CD days, the Camp Jail was re-opened to accomodate the fighters for freedom. During the last ten years it was lying idle. Buildings had become ruins. Grass and shrubs grew in abundance. Snakes found their safe abodes. When the Second Imperialist War broke out imperialism thought of Allipuram once again, this time to hold our prisoners. A hasty clean-up, barbed wire fixed all round and electrified and 700 'C' class and 100 'A' class politicals were bundled into it.

Released Satyagrahi prisoners give harrowing tales of life inside. Food? 'Boiled' rice is supposed to be the staple food, with pebbles, nails, and worms forming no inconsiderable part. Butter-milk ½ pints is recorded in the Jail Manual? It is euphemism for only an ounce of something like white-water.

Prisoners naturally fall ill. Medical Aid? But the compounder believes in medical research! The doctor prescribes one medicine, the compounder tries another to see if it won't do the same trick and be able to sell what is thus saved to the Chemists outside. His latest victim was N. Narayana Rao who got boils all over his face for a week.

What else? There are only six razors for 700 'C' class-wallas and you can imagine the ordeal of the weekly shave. No oil is supplied. No books allowed—except on religion. Lights are off at 9 p.m. and prisoners are left in pitch darkness. The Snakes want to find out all about these intruders who have come to be their co-dwellers. So they come out on their nightly rounds. On 24 April, at 2 a.m. it was no ordinary one but a king Cobra, 5 feet in length, and 7 inches in circumference, but the politicals did not want his company, shouted for help, woke up the Warder on duty, who killed it.

'Shut up!' is the greeting the prisoners get after an angry grunt, if they dare put up a complaint to the visiting Superintendent on the weekly 'File-Day'.

Does all this barbarism mean that the prisoners of our war are COWED DOWN? The rest of our story is the answer—NO!

On 5th April Vellore detenus went on hunger-strike. The news penetrated Allipuram Camp Jail, despite barbed wire fencing. Communist prisoners took the initiative to express solidarity, through a sympathetic hunger-strike, on 11 April one seventy-nine joined the hunger-strike, 45 of these were satyagrahis.

On 12th April, weakened by hunger-strike, they pleaded inability to do the allotted jail-task, carrying the food-pots from the kitchen. The jail officers were already off their heads, because of the hunger-strike, and seeing that the politicals had not yet been broken in. They decided to teach them a lesson.

On 13th April, the hunger-strikers were paraded before the Superintendent who ordered them to go to the kitchen and get out the food-pots. They held their ground and refused, trotted out an argument too—it was not a job prescribed in the Jail Manual! It was a not a game of wits, however. Here stood face to face, the worst and the best, that is in our country, and there followed the inevitable clash. The Superintendent put them on to water-carrying and cleaning up the barracks. While they were doing this they were suddenly lathi-charged and severely manhandled.

Comrades Sankaran Nambiar fell unconscious. Sivayya M. Jagan Mohan Rao, Kalyana Sundaram, and T.R. Subrahmanyam were singled out and received the due share of

'Ring-Leaders'. Still they refused to bend. They were locked up in the Quarantine' roof unbelievably low, of corrugated iron sheets, in this hot summer.

For two days neither food nor water was brought to them. Still they refused. Food at last was brought and by the jail staff itself! They won the first round.

Bad food or lathi-charge can't break Bolshevik spirit. This they had already demonstrated. But the leaders of this resistance to imperialist barbarity decided to have another and a final fling at their Jailors. On 8th night, the four made good their escape.

Next morning the wire-netting of the Quarantine Bloc was found cut and open. The Government thinks it was only a ruse to put the authorities on a false scent. It says that anyone trying to escape that way would have met a certain death at the electric barbed wires. It has arrested four Warders, including the Head Warder Jacob, as accomplices in their escape. Does this mean that the Communists, on the basis of their Communism, and by their brave conduct during the lathi-charge won over the stone-hearted Warders as well?

The *Bombay Chronicle* displayed the news of escape in a manner as to make it clear that they were not satyagrahis, thus guilty of the breach of Gandhian jail etiquette, but Communists. The Government inspired Press messages also try to drive home the same lesson, so that the people may look down upon such deeds. We Communists are proud of such glorious action. We are not rule-abiding Gandhian jail-birds. We are and will be fighters, whether inside or outside the prison-walls. Despite the emasculating Gandhian percepts the people hail such actions and welcome with open arms as heroes those who can bring them off.

And what a record these four fighters have! Their life has been the common story of the best sons of our people, who think and think till they find in COMMUNISM the answer to all their problems and own it up as their ideology, who fight and fight till their own experience leads them to our PARTY as the Party to which every national fighter must belong if he is serious about his job.

Sivayya was jailed in the 1932 CD movement, went for his BSc to Benares, got into Study-Circles and came to Communism. Back home in Andhra not to settle down in life but stir his people. He worked in Guntur District among students and workers and became one of our Andhra leaders. Second World War came and internment in his village. Escaped and became under-ground organizer. Towards the end of December the police hounds captured him, got 21 months of 'C' class. He is back again at his post and reports ready for duty.

T.R. Subrahmanyam went to jail in 1930–2 CD movement as a Gandhite. Got fed up with Gandhism and tried terrorism, got 3 years in the Madras Conspiracy Case. Saw that terrorism was futile and not revolutionary and joined up the Communists, began working heart and soul in the labour movement of Madras city. Won the love of all his comrades by his hard work and became the Manager of the Socialist Office in Broadway. Towards the end of 1939 he was given 3 months for selling legal Socialist literature. While on bail he was arrested again, charged with publishing the Tamil *Communist* and bundled off for 18 months.

We have not yet got the details of two Malayali Comrades Joseph and Sekharan. They were leading the strike struggle of Seamen in Calicut Port, given 18 months last June and sent to serve it in Allipuram.

A Bolshevik from Andhra, two from Malabar, one from Tamilnad, like Nandakishore and Kali Shankar before them from Red Cawnpur, decided that prison was not the place for them if they could rejoin the national struggle for freedom. Who would not be proud of them and say: HAIL COMRADES!

81. Nazi Aggression on Soviet Russia: Reactions of Communist and Congress Socialist Prisoners in Deoli Camp

File No. 7/5/41-Poll (I), Home (Political) Department, Government of India, Intelligence Report of Inspector Bapa Singh, Deoli, 5.7.41, NAI.

The declaration of war between Germany and Soviet Russia came as a rude shock to the Communists interned in this Camp. The Punjabis, as a whole, barring, few exceptions may be taken as Communists due to the compromise recently effected. They think that Hess[1] now in England has concluded a secret pact with the Britishers by virtue of which Germany is given free hand to invade Russia for the annihilation of Communism, a menace to all the capitalist countries including England, Germany and America, and others. They consider this pact to be a piece of supreme diplomatic victory for the Britishers as (according to them) behind it lies their evil intention to honour or dishonour it as it suits their purpose.

The Britishers are expected to have told Germany that it was difficult for them to make a *volte face* and turn on their side immediately but after some lip sympathy with Russia they will make open allies with Germany. They believe that England will see her own advantage and cannot remain true to either to Germany or Russia. They explain the present inaction of the Britishers due to the understanding with Germany, otherwise they ought to have planned a vigorous onslaught on Germany and improve the opportunity afforded to them. They consider that Germany will be helped by Britishers only if Russians gain remarkable victories so as to stem the tide of Communism. They think it a possibility that Britishers may sit on the fence till Russia is sufficiently weakened and help her at last to check exhausted Germany from her victorious path. This way they will crush Nazism and Communism with proverbial 'one stone'. They are very much sorry for the premature war with Russia as they expected Russia to bolster up both Germany and England to continue the war for their mutual destruction and ultimate victory of communism.

The reverses of Russia are very much felt by the Communists here and any good news from Russian side is cried up.

The Communists here do not consider Britain to be the allies of Russia at present and believe that their true identity is yet to be seen. They add that British policy in India as regards the arrests of Communists is symptomatic of their intentions and no abatement towards this side is noticeable. Under the circumstances they do not consider their release to be an immediate issue before the Government.

In their discussions they say that if Russia is defeated, international communism will receive a severe set-back but not a crushing defeat.

They believe that in the event of Russian defeat Communists all over the world including themselves will be butchered on idle pretexts, but they will be mistaken to think that they were finished.

The Congress Socialists and their camp followers who are in a minority do not make much comment on the war situation. They think all Imperialists to be equally bad. They think that Mr Gandhi may end the Satyagraha movement to concentrate on communal unity. They say that he is not so much keen on national independence as on international non-violence attended with truth.

From the above statement it would appear that they are very much fickle and tottering in their view and cannot come to any definite conclusion. The above may be considered a gist what the advanced Communists think and discuss. Generally they are perturbed by the development in war situation.

The members of the CC (Central Committee) prepare a review of war situation from time to time and consider their position. Their views may change in consonance with circumstances. It any specific information is required please send queries so that they may be answered properly.

---

[1] Rudolf Hess, one of the top leaders of the Nazi Party, had landed in Scotland with the objective of negotiating an agreement with Britain. He was interned by the British authorities. He was convicted as a war criminal at Nuremburg and sentenced to life imprisonment.

82. Soviet Day in Delhi and Malabar

Communist, Vol. III, No. 8, October 1941, P.C.Joshi Archives on Contemporary History, JNU.

The Delhi working class stirred to action at the news of the treacherous attack of Germany on the Soviets. The shop assistants took the lead in organizing the pro-Soviet propaganda in Delhi. Even before the AIKS decision to observe the Soviet Day was known, the Shop Assistants' Federation called a meeting to chalk out a programme of action for supporting the struggle of the Soviet people. We joined the meeting. Some Royists too, came in. A Committee for organizing the Soviet Day on 24 July was set up the date was chosen because it was a holiday for the shop assistants.

FB for Nazis!

The Committee invited the co-operation of all other political organizations in the city. The Forward Bloc refused co-operation—they said they were for the fascists (was not Bose supposed to be the guest of Hitler now!). Nevertheless, many Congressmen gladly helped us, so did the Provincial Students' Federation. We collected from the sympathizers Rs 60 to meet the expenses of the meeting.

The Royists did nothing. They wanted to be in the Committee to eulogize 'Churchill's fight against fascism' and to disrupt the work as we found later to our cost.

Public Reaction

The reaction was not very encouraging in the beginning. The ordinary petty-bourgeois who walks the streets was pro-German! Why? He wanted to lick his oppressive British rulers—but his Congress leaders didn't let him. In his demoralization, he adored the Germans who were giving his bosses a good kicking. It was an impotent slave's happiness and helplessness. The public were, therefore, confused. They looked at us and said to themselves: 'These follows, we know they are the darlings of our city, the best fighters against the British dogs—but how is it that they are denouncing Hitler who is such an enemy of the British?'

But we turned the tables with our propaganda all right, 'Down with Imperialism, Down with Fascism, Long Live that Soviet Union, Soviet is fighting for you. You must fight for the Soviet', thus blared forth our loud speakers and in the end, the people began to respond saying: 'Yes, we were not mistaken, these people remain the bitterest enemies of the Sarkar, and if they ask us to support the Soviot, there is good reason for it!' With such tremendous faith, the worker comrades spoke about the invincibility of the Red Army, its inevitable victory that the people could not but believe it. Some were puzzled and asked. 'Tab phir Angrez ka kya Hoga?

The Deceivers

We addressed more than 15,000 people and brought out several wall-posters. It was pity the loudspeakers could not work in the mill area due to difference in the electric current system, but we made it up with posters, hand bills and house-to-house propaganda. There was some dislocation in a workers propaganda meeting, as two hours before the time of the meeting, Chandoo Bibi came up, began a meeting with her followers and a few Royists and spoke in support of Churchill under cover of support to the Soviets. We came at the appointed time, and held another meeting which continued till after their meeting had dispersed. We hammered our line home. The workers saw the difference. Many of them were heard to say: 'Soviet must win and we must win too against the British'.

It was also a mistake to take the Royists in the Committee. They not only did nothing but sabotaged the only job given to them, that of getting the red-flag cards printed. That spoiled our chance of collecting money. In the Committee they objected to approve that part of the resolution for the Soviet Day's meeting which stressed the need of our fighting for independence against British imperialism. When we insisted on retaining it, the swinish brood left in a huff. Good riddance we said.

The Soviet Day

In the night before the Soviet Day, the streets were painted with our slogans in Hindi and Urdu. The students had made huge placards and also special posters for the schools. But the shop assistants beat all. The whole of Chandni Chowk was a blaze of red—not a lamp post but with its pair of Red flags!

The Day arrived. First, the Red Flag was unfurled at the Gandhi Grounds by Com. Farooqui. The mills were working; still many workers had absented themselves to attend the function. The University was closed and the students have gone home—the school students made up the lag. And we marched about a thousand strong, all carrying Red banners and festoons with slogans, from the Gandhi Ground to the place of meeting. In spite of the fact that the Arya Samajists had already started another meeting there just to spite us, our meeting drew a gathering of more than 5,000. Brilliant speeches were made and the people were so moved that the FB-wallas who had come to oppose us slunk away. Shrimati Satyavati of the CSP spoke in support of our main resolution. Com. K.M. Ahmed from Bengal and others also spoke. It was also resolved there to form a Friends of the Soviet Union Society at Delhi.

The agitation has made one thing clear. That the Friends of the Soviet in India Cannot be Bootlickers of Imperialism Asking Support for the Churchill's Government of War and Terror.

Malabar: Solidarity with the Soviet

Workers and nationalist Muslims of Tellichery announced meetings and demonstrations on 21st July to express solidarity with the Soviet Union. The local authorities promptly banned these meetings. Reason? The All-India Kisan Sabha had fixed 21st July as Soviet Day. Kisan Sabhas are banned in Malbar. Therefore, the Soviet Day meetings on 21st July are illegal. This piece of bureaucratic syllogism is unbeatable! Brute repression needs no logic.

In Calicut, a meeting of workers and citizens under the auspices of the Central Trade Union Council condemned the attack of Nazi Germany on the Soviet Union and expressed support to the Soviet people in the brave fight against fascist aggression. The resolution also criticized the indifferent attitude of the National leadership towards the Soviet Union's just war.

The Managing Committee of the Travancore Coir Factory Worker's Union in its meeting on 30 July expressed sympathy with the Soviet Union in its war against fascism.

83. Soviet Aid Campaign in Bombay

Communist, Vol. III, No. 8, October 1941, P.C. Joshi Archives on Contemporary History, JNU.

Bombay's Soviet Aid Campaign was remarkable for two reasons. First, it was organized and run entirely by the working class comrades. Secondly it was the first successful Paisa-Fund collection for the Soviet in India.

When the representatives of several Trade Unions met on 3 August to form the Soviet Aid Committee, they said: Mere meetings and demonstrations are not enough. If we cannot give substantial material aid to the brave people of the Soviet Union, because of our slave state, we must at least make a token collection. We must call upon every citizen, worker, student, every friend of the Soviet Aid Fund to express his or her support with the brave people of the Soviet Union and the heroic Red Army by paying a token copper to the Soviet Aid Fund.

The Committee invited the co-operation of all Trade Unions in the city and of student organizations. The response was good. The preliminary finance for running the campaign was raised from the quotas paid by the Unions and through special contributions of sympathizers.

On every evening during the Soviet Aid Weeks, there were street-corner meetings, chawl meetings and house-to-house collection. The Committee issued three handbills in Marathi, Urdu and English. They also brought out beautiful little cards printed in Red bearing the emblem of hammer and sickle and the appeal:

Pay one pice as a symbol of your love and support for the Soviet Union; To show your burning hatred against the vile Nazi hordes who are attacking the land of Socialism: To express your determination to defend the first workers' Raj.... Victory to the Red Army; Long Live the Unity of the Workers of all Lands!

These cards were exchanged for the paisa contributions.

On the two Sundays, there were cycle demonstrations which wheeled round the whole city of Bombay shouting a lusty chorus of the slogans of the campaign. In the evening there were big rallies in the Kamgar Maidan.

The campaign evoked remarkable enthusiasm and response among the workers. This was all the more remarkable in view of the fact that Bombay had no skilled agitators and propagandists left. All their stalwarts are behind the prison bars. All the same 20,000 workers signed the pledge of solidarity and the message of fraternal love and admiration to the Soviet people which is being sent to Comrade Maisky in London to be forwarded to the proper quarters.

The Mill bosses and their contemptible agents were annoyed at the huge success of the Soviet Aid Compaign. For two years they had tried every device—crooked and straight—to screw out money from the workers for the imperialist war fund. They had miserably failed.

Now they burned with spite and envy to see this welling up of voluntary enthusiasm for the Soviet Union's just and glorious war against the fascist murderers. Paid evil tongues whispered poisoned anti-Soviet lies, and tried to spread panic among the workers.

Did it affect the Bombay worker? Not him. He has his 13 years of bitter and dogged fight for the Red flag behind him, And does he not remember how the Soviet Trade Unions helped him with Rs 20,000 when 13 years back he was just making his first entry into the arena of working class organization? Did they not realize what was at stake? The only country in the world where the workers rule, where the Red Flag of Hammer and Sickle waves proudly over 24 years of gigantic Socialist achievements, has been attacked. The unique workers' and peasants' Red Army, the liberator of the oppressed peoples, the hope of the toilers is being assailed.

When they listened to the impassioned speeches about what marvels of heroism and sacrifice the Soviet men and women were performing, when they heard of the crushing losses that were being inflicted on the Nazi marauders, their heart leapt up, and their eyes were moist. 'Why don't you take more money? The Soviet Union must be victorious. What can we do to help in that victory? Tell us,' they asked.

'You can begin fighting for the victory of the Soviet Union here and now' came the reply. 'Strengthen your respective Red flag Union a hundred-fold. Strengthen the Party of the Red flag. Prepare for such great Mahagai struggles as Bombay has never seen before. Let your struggle light the torch of our country's long-delayed war for liberation. That is how we shall fight for the Soviet victory. For it will only come through people's victory in many countries and it will bring people's victory in every country'. In every meeting the workers showed their approval with the resounding chorus of:

Victory to the Soviet Union!
Victory to the Red Army!
Long Live the United Front
Of the Working Class
Of the world!

84. November Days Celebration: BPTUC Move Meetings in Support of Russia to be Held

Amrita Bazar Patrika, 4 November 1941.

At a meeting of the Working Committee of the Bengal Provincial Trade Union Congress, held on Sunday at its office, the following resolutions were adopted:

'On the occasion of annual celebration of the historic November Days this meeting of the Working Committee of the BPTUC, appeals to the Indian working class to realize the extreme gravity of the international situation and the seriousness of the dangers faced by the workers of the world owing to the menacing advance of the Fascists hordes in Russia and to rally round the Red Flag in defence of the Soviet Union, the first workers' and peasants' Republic and the unfailing torch-bearer of the freedom of all people of the world.

'The meeting pledges its full support to the Soviet Union on its heroic fight against the barbarous menace of Fascism and expects that the Indian working class would make the November days celebration a success.

'The meeting urges upon all Trade Unions to celebrate the November days from 7th to 17th November by holding meetings and demonstrations in support of the Soviet Union wherever possible, jointly with the BPTUC and joining the Central rally of workers to be held on 16th November at the foot of Octorlony Monument at 4 p.m. and on 17 November at Shraddhananda Park at 5 p.m.

'Every Union is hereby directed to pay one rupee as its contribution for the November days rally by the 7th of November.

It was decided to hold a meeting of the General Council, Union representatives, on 7th November (Friday) at 6 p.m. at the BPTUC office.'

85. India's Sympathy for Soviet Fight Against Nazism Mian Iftikharuddin's Address at Calcutta Conference

Amrita Bazar Patrika, 17 November 1941.

The anniversary day of the Russian Revolution was celebrated yesterday (Sunday) in Calcutta in a very impressive manner. There was a conference of workers representing about four lakhs of factory workers who pledged unqualified support to the Soviet Russia in men and money in their fight against Nazism.

Greetings to Soviet Russia

In another conference under the auspices of the Friends of the Soviet Union representing writers, artists, scientists, and intellectuals as well as workers, peasants, students, and other progressive elements from different parts of India over which Mian Iftikharuddin, the Punjab leader presided, fraternal greetings were sent to Soviet Russia wishing for the success of the Soviet arms.

A workers rally at the foot of the Octorlony (Monument) under the presidency of Sj. Mrinal Kanti Bose, President of the BPTUC passed resolutions in similar terms.

Their undying friendship for the Soviet Union and determination to uphold the ideal which the Union stands for was expressed by the All-India Conference of the Friends of the Soviet Union which met at the hall of the University Institute on Sunday afternoon.

The Conference resolved to set up an All-India organization to enlighten the general public about the condition of life and the work of reconstruction in the USSR Arrangement is also to be made for the dispatch to Russia a delegation of representative Indians with a view to strengthen the tie that exists between the two countries.

'The cause of the Soviet Union is the cause of humanity', observed Mian Iftikhar uddin, President of the Punjab Provincial Congress Committee, who occupied the chair.

Messages

Messages from Mrs Sarojini Naidu, Sir Sarvepalli Radhakrishnan, Prof. D.D. Kosambi of Poona, Dr Dhyanchand of the Patna University, Prof. K.T. Shah of Bombay and Prof. Ramkrishna Rao of the Andhra University were read out at the meeting:

'Success of all efforts on behalf of the valiant Soviet People' wired Mrs Naidhu.

'It they (the Soviet) fall', Sir Sarvepalli said in the course of his message, 'the future of civilization is indeed gloomy.'

In the course of a letter addressed to M. Molotov, Soviet Commissar or Foreign Affairs, through M.M. Maisky, Russian Ambassador in England, the Conference proclaimed their undying friendship for the Soviet people and determination to fight for Soviet victory which alone meant freedom for humanity, and...the Soviet Union had proved that so far as the social structure was concerned there should be as far as humanly possible, complete equality in the distribution of human wealth.

That was her greatest mission in the world, and the speaker thought that speaking coolly and conscientiously even the most ardent imperialist, even the most enthusiastic defender of capitalism, could not argue against this.

The Real Culture

There were people who contended that the Soviet had brought the question of material comfort to the forefront and therefore, had no cultural mission for the world. But, in the opinion of the speaker, it was for the sake of cultural values, literary values that the Soviet Union had come with the slogan, let the material needs fall into the background, let the material needs of humanity be common as air and water, and let not humanity fight like animals for food. By bringing the question of material need to the forefront the Soviet Union had told the world that unless the elementary problems were solved there was no possibility for real progress, real culture or any other intellectual pursuit.

So far as the economic ills of the world were concerned there was but only one solution for humanity, only one method of solving these difficulties—that is of central control of all means of production and distribution, in other words, Socialism. It could be safely said that every country in the world, in fact the entire humanity—ninety-nine per cent of the people of the world who called themselves poor and needy—did owe a heavy debt to the Soviet Union. And the cause of the Soviet Union was the cause of humanity.

If people were allowed to express their thoughts then ninety per cent of mankind would declare, no matter to which class or clime they belonged, that they supported the cause for which the Soviet Union was fighting so nobly and fearlessly.

Mian Iftlkhanruddin was sure that the conference started by Friends of the Soviet Union in Calcutta and other parts of India was the beginning of something great that would spread not only to all the provinces but to all cities and villages in the remotest corners of the country....

Ideal Exists

Speaking on behalf of journalists Sj. Satyendranath Majumder thought that Russia might suffer eclipse for the moment, but the ideal which she had stood for was indestructible. Long before the advent of Hitler, conquerors in all ages and climes had swept away empires and institutions but the ideal for which men had sacrificed their lives had continued to exist and inspire humanity. Hitler's armed might would one day be relegated in the pages of History but the ideal of Socialism would live for ever to imbue the down-trodden with hope and aspiration.

For giving unqualified support to the Soviet people in men, money and medical aid, the convention decided to set up a committee on all-India basis and appointed an organizing committee from the delegates to take steps in that direction.

The convention was impressive for more than one reason. It was organized and its business conducted by factory workers themselves without any outside help. The presidents—a presidium of four—were elected from among the worker-delegates and the gathering was addressed by the workers themselves.

The spacious hall of the University Institute and approaches to it were decorated with the workers' red flags and posters and portraits of Russian peasants and workers were hung.

The Eventful Revolution

The convention was declared open by Mr Mrinal Kanti Bose. President, BPTUC He gave a short account of the uprise of the workers and peasants of Russia against the Czarist Russia and made a reference to their present struggle with the Fascist and Nazi forces. He said that the convention had been called to voice the rejoicings of the peasants and labourers of this country at the victory of their classes in Russia over the Czarist Government in 1917. The peasants and workers of Russia had no education, no arms or ammunition; yet they succeeded in overthrowing the powerful imperialist government. That eventful revolution of the peasants and workers of the world happened in November on this day, and millions of workers and labourers all over the world had been celebrating that revolution on this day each year.

This year the celebration of November Revolution Day, Mr Bose continued, had an added significance. This year the same Russian peasants and workers who fought the Czarist Government were now fighting the Fascist and Nazi hordes. The ordeal through which the brave Russian people were now passing were immensely arduous than that of 1917. In that year they had to fight the Czarist Government alone, but this time they were fighting the capitalists of all the world over.

Fate of Workers

The fate of the workers and peasants of the rest of the world, particularly of India, was inseparably bound up with the outcome of the present Russo-German war. The workers of India wanted to see Russia coming out victorious and they would say to the Russian people: 'We the Indian workers and peasants are solidly behind you in your struggle for freedom—freedom not for you alone but for the working class of the world. We want to see you victorious and we pledge our whole-hearted support to you'. The Indian workers and peasants also wanted to address the other nations who are now fighting Nazism and Fascism that if they wanted to bring about a new world order at the conclusion of the war, that new order must be an order where the toiling masses would have the supreme voice....

Rally of Workers

A rally of the workers of Calcutta and suburbs was held this afternoon at the foot of the Octerloney Monument under the auspices of the Bengal Provincial Trade Union Congress. Mr Mrinal Kant Basu presided. Among others Messers A.M.A. Zaman, Sudhir Pramanik, Mrs Sakina Begum, Satish Ch. Sen were present.

The following resolutions were adopted:

> This rally of workers of Calcutta and suburbs sends its fraternal greetings to the Soviet Union on the occasion of the historic anniversary of the October Revolution and pledges its full support to the Soviet Union, the unfailing champion of freedom of all peoples of the world, and the first workers and peasants Republic on its heroic fight against Fascism, the spearhead of world reaction and counter-revolution.
>
> This meeting further decides to help Soviet Union directly by men and money and urges upon the Indian people to collect money for the people's Fund and give names for volunteers to help the Red Army so that thereby we can strengthen our fight for freedom.
>
> This meeting enters its emphatic protest against the unwarranted and unjustifiable interference with the workers' elementary democratic right in refusing the carters' procession at the eleventh hour.

This meeting is of opinion that this is a clear misuse of the power conferred on the Police Commissioner under the Defence of India Act, in view of the fact that the said interference was made against the mobilization of support to the Soviet Union, the ally of British in their fight against Fascist gangsters.

86. Soviet Aid Campaign in India

Communist, Vol. III, No. 8, October–November 1941, P.C. Joshi Archives on Contemporary History, JNU.

(The Council of the All-India Kisan Sabha which met on 8 July in Calcutta fixed 21 July as the Soviet Day and called for meetings and demonstrations of solidarity with the Soviet on the day. In appealed to all the progressive forces to unite and mobilize themselves for organizing aid to the Soviet.)

Bengal

The successful campaign in Calcutta, the Town hall meeting and the appeal of the intellectuals was already reported in our last issue. As a result, preparations are now afoot to set up a permanent organization: 'Friends of the Soviet Union.' Calcutta is taking the initiative in calling an All-India Conference of the Friends of the Soviet Union to be held in October. Bengal Provincial Trade Union Congress is organizing a workers' delegates' Convention for the support of Soviet peoples' war against fascism. Preliminary campaign of workers' meeting began on 20th September.

Bihar

21st July was celebrated with meetings in Patna, Chapra, Bankipore, Muzaffarpur, Fatehpur, and in Jemshedpur. Most of the meetings were held under the auspices of the Kisan Sabha. Bihar Forward Bloc also co-operated.

In August the Bihar Socialist Party celebrated the Soviet Week from 26th August to 7 September. The Programme consisted of meetings, processions, selling of Red Flag badges, with hammer and sickle, to raise aid for the Soviet.

Central Provinces and Berar

Kisan Sabhas of C P and Berar celebrated the Soviet Day on 21st July in Nagpur, Amraoti and in several other places with mass meetings which proclaimed solidarity with the Soviet and determination to aid the Soviet people in their noble fight against fascism.

Maharashtra

21 July was celebrated with meetings and processions in Poona, Amalner, Dhulia, and other places in Khandesh.

Orissa and Andhra

Soviet Day (21 July) meetings were also held in Puri (Orissa) as well as in several places in Andhra.

Punjab

Punjab Kisan Sabhas celebrated 5 September as the Soviet Day when kisans and workers held meetings in Lahore and other towns to express their solidarity with the Soviet people and their heroic Red Army in their war against Nazism. 'Paisa Fund' collections were also made on the Bombay model.

Bombay

Bombay and Suburban Marathi Literary Conference which met on the 19th August adopted a resolution of sympathy and admiration for the Soviet Union. The resolution embodied and endorsed the whole of the manifesto issued by the Calcutta intellectuals. This is significant in as much as the Conference is the representative organization of all Marathi writers of Bombay and the suburbs.

As a sequel to the successful Soviet Aid Week organized by the Bombay working class organization, a 'Friends of The Soviet Union' Association is being organized in Bombay.

29 September 1941.

87. The All Peoples' War Against Fascism and Our Policy and Tasks: Resolution of the Polit-Bureau, CPI, 13 December 1941

Party Letter, No. 56, 15 December 1941, CPI Library, Ajoy Bhavan, New Delhi.

1. With Hitler's attack upon the Soviet Union, the character of the war is fundamentally transformed. With that act Hitlerite Germany becomes the main aggressor and enemy not only of the Soviet Union, not only of the workers and oppressed peoples of Nazi-occupied countries of Europe and of Germany itself, but of the proletarians and peoples in every country. In this context, the war conducted by Britain and her allies against the fascist powers now assumes a new significance for the proletarians and peoples of all countries. Being a war aimed at the enemy of the international proletariat, against the enemy of the Soviet Union, it now becomes for the proletarians of all countries, an all-peoples' war against Hitler-fascism, and for the defence of the Soviet Union, the fortress of Socialism.

Not an Imperialist War but a Peoples' War

2. It is necessary to clearly understand how this turn in the international situation and the war came about. The Second Imperialist War arose really on the basis of two main conflicts: the old conflict between two imperialist blocs which was at the root of the last war and the new conflict between the Socialist Soviet Union and the capitalist world. The imperialist ruling class of Britain and America was trying to provoke the rival imperialist powers especially Germany and Japan against the USSR and thus getting their imperialist conflict solved at the expense of the USSR. The Soviet Union and the Communist Parties of the world, realizing the acute and imminent danger of the outbreak of an imperialist war and of an attack upon the Soviet Union, were seeking to create a powerful world front of democratic countries against the fascist aggressor countries, namely, Germany, Italy, and Japan. This front did not materialize because of the treachery of Social-Democracy which refused to fight against the reactionary intrigues of the pro-fascists in Britain and France. But all the same, the reactionary game of the reactionary rulers of Britain against the USSR was also foiled, thanks to the might of the Socialist Power. Hitler preferred to seal a non-aggression pact with the USSR. Defeated in its reactionary diplomacy, British imperialism launched a war against Germany. It was the reactionary policy of the British imperialists of nourishing the fascists to make them attack the USSR that led to the sharpening of the imperialist conflict which burst into the Second World

War. During the course of the twenty-two months of the war, that conflict was further sharpened due to the easy and decisive victories which Hitler won in Europe. Hitler's attack upon the Soviet Union sharpened that conflict still further and to such a pitch that it was qualitatively transformed for the working class all over the world. British imperialists suffered another defeat in their reactionary policy and had to throw overboard their anti-Soviet policy of the last twenty-four years and had to join the USSR as an ally, on terms of reciprocal aid, in their own interests. The camp of world imperialism was split sharply into two opposing camps in relation to the Soviet Union, in a manner as it had never happened before. Hitler-fascism with its allies stood isolated as the main enemy of the entire progressive mankind.

A basis was laid for the creation of powerful anti-fascist peoples' front extending over the whole world and to its victory in the alliance of USSR, Britain, and America. The war now becomes an all-peoples' war against the worst form of imperialism—fascism, which it becomes the supreme duty of the proletarians and peoples in every country to win.

What Proletarian Internationalism Demands

3. The attitude to the Communist parties towards any war is determined by the Leninist principle of proletarian internationalism, by the class character and the class aims of the governments conducting the war. Communists support all just wars, that is wars that are not wars of conquest but wars of liberation waged to defend the people from foreign attack and from attempts to enslave them or to liberate the people from capitalist slavery or lastly to liberate colonies and dependent countries from the yoke of imperialism. They oppose all unjust wars, that is imperialist wars, wars of conquest, waged to conquer and enslave foreign countries and nations. There is one single principle which determines the attitude of the Communist parties towards war and that is—proletarian internationalism, united struggle of the workers of the world against imperialism. It is imperative for all Communist Parties to rush to the defence of the USSR when it is attacked or when it has to defend itself against capitalist intervention, by every possible means. It is imperative for all Communist Parties to conduct a resolute struggle against imperialist wars to the point of revolution and the overthrow of their 'own' bourgeois government. The policy of all the Communist Parties towards the present war in its imperialist phase was guided by their internationalism, by their duty to further the cause of world revolution and of the defence of the USSR, its base, and not by any local or national considerations. Every Communist Party sought to mobilize the workers and the people under the slogan 'End The War!' and to overthrow the government in its own county and replace it by a peoples' government which would renounce imperialist aims and join up with the USSR in fighting for peace and for isolating the remaining imperialist aggressors. Similarly as soon as the Soviet Union was attacked by Hitlerite Germany in the midst of the imperialist war, the Communist Parties were required to recognize that the war waged by Britain against Germany become at once a part of the defence of the USSR. They therefore have to support it and strive to wage it in such a way that it ensures Soviet victory and the defeat of Hitler-fascism, The Communist Parties in all countries were required to recognize that Hitler fascism was the main enemy, and the war waged by the USSR in alliance with Britain and America, was a war which had to be won by all the peoples in the interests of defending the base of world revolution. This duty and attitude was imposed by the internationalism of our Party. No national or local conditions could render it invalid.

World Peoples' Front Against Fascism

4. In the six months which have followed Hitler's attack upon USSR, a mighty peoples' upsurge has grown up in every country which is growing stronger, broader and more unified on a world plane every day. It embodies the growing will of the workers and people in every country to destroy fascism—this vile curse of mankind,—and to make an end of polices and systems which nourished it to light this conflagration. It expresses itself in the extensive and heroic actions of the guerilla armies and the peoples of the Nazi occupied countries of Europe, which are assuming the form of a veritable peoples' war in Hitler's rear. It expresses itself in the growing discontent of the German people against the Hitler-regime. It expresses itself in the powerful initiative and activity with which the British and American workers and people are forcing their governments to carry on unfalteringly the war against Hitler and render full aid to the USSR. It expresses itself in the new offensive which the united forces of the Chinese people are launching against the new aggression of Japan in the Pacific. This world upsurge which is the flesh and blood of the growing international unity and action of the workers and the people of of all countries against fascism is taking place under the influence of two dominant factors. The first is the split and the crisis in the camp of world imperialism which has resulted in the isolation of the three fascist powers as the main international enemy, while grouping against it is a powerful anti-fascist front, headed by the USSR and joined by Britain and America. The second factor is the gigantic test which the Soviet people and the Soviet organization—the product of twenty-four years of Socialism and workers' rule—has stood as no other people or State in the world had ever done in victoriously fighting back the brute might of Hitler-fascism. The Soviet people and the Red Army by their unparalleled heroism, by the invincible unity, by their indestructible Socialist organization, are leading and inspiring the people in every country to conduct a resolute struggle against the fascist aggressors, to take their destiny in their own hands. In short, we are living in a new period when the anti-Hitler alliance which came into existence because of the might of the USSR and the quandary of the imperialist ruling class of Britain and America, is being transformed into a world front of the peoples against fascism. Under the stress of war and under the influence of Soviet leadership, this common front against fascism in every country is being strengthened, the balance shifting more and more in favour of the people and against imperialism. The anti-fascist front in every country, under the stress of the initiative and actions of the people, is becoming more and more a peoples' front. The people in Britain and America are counteracting the vacillations and sabotage of the imperialist governments in the vigorous prosecution of the war against fascism. They are fighting against their perpetuation of the repressive and autocratic rule in the colonies. It is this awakening and activity of the broad masses of the workers in all countries that strengthens the bond of unity between the peoples of the capitalist countries, with the Soviet people and with the colonial peoples. It is these actions of the people which strengthen the international unity of the world anti-fascist front into a world peoples' unity, and is making the world anti-fascist war into An All-Peoples' War For World Liberation. Peoples Of The World Are Moving Into Action, With Common Will, Not Only For The Victory Over Hitler, But Also For The Victory Of All The Peoples In Unity With The Soviet People And For A New And Higher World Order, Based Not On A New Imperialist Re-Division But On The Independence And Democratic Liberties Of All The Peoples. Such Is The Revolutionary Import Of The New period.

Where and Why we went Wrong

5. The present Polit-Bureau adopted a completely wrong policy to the war in the present phase because it forsook the standpoint of proletarian internationalism and adopted unconsciously that of bourgeois-nationalism. It failed to see that the character of the war waged by Britain jointly with the USSR and the duty of the Indian proletariat toward it, could not be determined by the relation in which the Indian people stood to Britain but by her relation to the fortress of Socialism and to the main enemy of the world proletariat. We looked at the war from the point of view of narrow bourgeois-nationalism and theorized that Britain was still conducting an imperialist war and that real aid to the Soviet people could be rendered by the British and the Indian people only when a peoples' government was established in Britain and freedom was won by the Indians. We repeated parrot-like phrases like 'Hitler is the main enemy', and said that the imperialist war has to be Completely transformed into a peoples' war but stuck fast to the bourgeois nationalist slogan that India could help the Soviet Union only as a free country. We lapsed into speculations and refuse to see the blunt fact that the war was already a people's war because we did not look at the war from the standpoint of internationalism and from the standpoint of the defence of the Soviet Union. For us who stuck fast to the standpoint of the narrow bourgeois-nationalism, the idea that the British imperialist government—the national oppressor in India—was no more conducting a war that was unjust and was now in the camp of progress which was at war with the camp of world reaction, was difficult to swallow.

Looking at the world situation according to our wishes and not as it actually exists, we failed to see that that very apparently unpleasant fact was the biggest defeat for British imperialism and its reactionary policy of twenty four years, and that it had placed the British and the Indian working class and people in an immensely strategic position, which it was their duty to utilize in the interest of world liberation and thus serve their own interests as well. Proletarian internationalism always and at every time, defines the tasks and policies for the working class of the people of each country in terms of the needs of the general struggle of the workers of the world against their common enemy—world imperialism. That is why it alone is the true guide for the Communist parties to evolve correct policies which at any given time correspond to the best interests of the people of its country while at the same time advancing the international struggle against imperialism as a whole. That is why by forsaking that standpoint, we betrayed not only our duty to the Socialist Fatherland and to the world proletariat in the all-peoples' war against Hitler fascism but also our duty to our own people. Failure to see that it was now a people' war led us to put forward the slogan: our freedom first and then we will fight for the Soviet, which was in practice the policy of Nehruism, which is subservience to Gandhian inactivity and sabotage of mass struggle and therefore, support to Rajaji's policy of surrender to imperialism and betrayal of the people. Refusal To Recognize The War As A peoples' War Led To A Virtual Refusal To Evolve A Practical Policy To Mobllize The People For Their Free, Voluntary And Effective Participation In The World Struggle, A Policy Which In The Given Situation Was The Key To Breaking The Stakmate In India, To Putting The People On Their Legs To Enabling Them To Play Their Part In The War Of World Liberation.

Guiding Lines of the General Policy

6. What are the main considerations which must determine the practical policies of all Communist Parties, which are everywhere striving for the defeat and annihilation of Hitler-fascism and the victory of the Soviet Union? In Germany and in the Nazi-occupied countries

of Europe, the main consideration is to do every possible thing to overthrow the Hitler-sponsored regimes, to sabotage its unjust war by every possible means. This requires in every country that the Communist Parties pursue the policy of building the united national front of all those who stand for the defeat of Hitler. In this connection it must be noted that the USSR has signed treaties of joint action with the former bourgeois governments of these occupied countries, which form the basis of such a united national front in countries like France, Yugoslavia, Norway, Greece, Czechoslovakia, Poland.

The main consideration which determines the policy of the Communist parties of the capitalist countries allied with the USSR is: Everything for the full and practical co-operation with the USSR; everything for a quick and decisive victory over Hitler-fascism. They have to take note of the fact that their governments allied with the USSR are yet a bourgeois and imperialist governments, which enslave the proletariat at home and the people in India and the colonies and which, therefore, cannot be relied to pursue the policy of 100 per cent aid to the Soviet Union, of ensuring peoples' victory over Hitler-fascism.

The policy of the Communist Parties in these countries is governed by the consideration: strengthen the anti-fascist front in their own countries and extend it to the colonies. The policy is not one of overthrowing the Churchill or Roosevelt Government but of supporting it while developing popular pressure to shake off its vacillation to fight its sabotage. The policy is one of peoples' initiative and activity, of building a united national front of all those who stand for the defeat of Hitler, for the consistent and vigorous prosecution of the war in the interests of the people, for the 100 per cent aid to the USSR. A ceaseless struggle of vigilance and exposure is carried on for the demands of the workers, soldiers and the people, for opening the new front in Europe to relieve pressure on the Soviet, for the freedom of India and the colonies so as to ensure their voluntary and free participation in the war. But the struggle is conducted in such a way that the main fire is concentrated upon the pro-fascists behind the government, the fifth-column of the main enemy of the people. It is conducted in unity with the people's struggle for winning the war, for raising production, for rendering 100 per cent aid to the Soviet. The policy of the Communists in these countries is governed by one slogan: win the war against Hitler-fascism and its allies, for the peoples, for the Soviet. They concentrate their main fire against one enemy—Hitler-fascism abroad and his friends in their own country. They strive to strengthen one front—the world front of the peoples against fascism, demanding and fighting for the liberation of colonies by their bourgeois governments.

Basis for Practical Policy in India

7. The basis of the general policy which the Indian working class and the Indian people have to adopt is determined by the same general considerations that obtain for the British workers. The fact that it is an all-peoples' war against Hitler-fascism—the main enemy of the USSR and of the world proletariat and the people—and that it has to be won in the interest of every people in the world, holds good for the Indian people as much as it does for the British people. The fact that we are enslaved, that war is enforced upon us, that war effort is indissolubly connected with imperialist slavery does not affect a jot the obligation that rests upon us to strike together in common with the other peoples of the world against the main enemy of mankind and for the defence of the USSR. This duty which our internationalism imposes upon our Party, namely, to mobilize the people, to develop such popular activity and initiative which will render the effective participation of the Indian people in the war in order to win victory for the USSR and for the other peoples, is to-day the main consideration which must

determine our practical policy. Our acceptance of the war as a peoples' war, our obligation to win it, is unconditional and is not determined by the dictates or desires of the imperialist government. It is enjoined by the common discipline of the international proletarian movement which has now to concentrate all efforts on the defeat of Hitler-fascism and its allies, for the victory of the USSR and of all the peoples.

This supreme task and the fact that Hitler-fascism and its allies are now the main enemies of the Indian people, and that the British Government, our national oppressor, is an ally, though a vacillating one, in the world anti-fascist front—these now must determine the Immediate Slogans and tasks for our struggle for liberation against British Imperialism. This is the second consideration. The plan of action put forward in the 'Proletarian Path' which was correct for the imperialist phase of the war, can no longer form our immediate task. Developing mass struggle against war in order to achieve the immediate overthrow of the British Government cannot be our slogan for the present situation. For that would mean splitting the world front of struggle against fascism and its sabotage. We would be betraying the world cause which dominates over all issues and therefore, we would be betraying the cause of our people as well. But this does not mean that our struggle against the imperialist autocratic government is suspended. On the other hand, it is waged in the new situation but in such a manner as to further and not hinder the one cause before us to-day—namely, to win the peoples' war against the fascist powers, and strengthen the front of the peoples against fascism.

In fact, the Indian people by swinging into action unitedly to achieve their free and voluntary participation in the peoples' war against fascism, will not only weaken the reactionary hold of British imperialism over India but will strengthen the cause of the British workers and the British people. By adopting this positive line of action, we would be defeating imperialism's reactionary policy to keep the Indian People out of the war. We would thus be defeating on a world scale the hindrances which the reactionary bourgeois circles in Britain are placing in the way of the anti-fascist front developing into a real peoples' front. By seizing the initiative to rouse the 400 millions of India to the consciousness of the supreme significance of the all-peoples war, to the will and to actions for battering down the obstacles which imperialism places in the way of people's participation in the war, we will be advancing the cause of our own liberation and sealing a firm bond between the national front and the front of the peoples of the world. By this policy, we weaken British imperialism and strengthen the Indian people as a unit of the world peoples' front against fascism.

Thirdly, therefore, our immediate task becomes to organize a 'Peoples' War Movement' and rouse the people to the understanding of the supreme significance of this peoples' war against fascism, as a war of world liberation headed by the Soviet Union, to develop their initiative and activity, to participate in the war so as to throw the full weight of India and her resources on the side of the progressive forces. And in as much as the conduct of the war is in the hands of the imperialist autocracy and the war effort and civil defence is entirely in the hands of irresponsible bureaucracy, this peoples' movement of winning the war has to be developed as series of struggles and skirmishes on every front, to smash the fetters which to-day chain the peoples' initiative and activity.

Fourthly, a series of political and economic demands of every section of the people will be raised from the very start of the 'Peoples' War' movement and fought for. But it must be clearly understood that they are Not a sort of a charter, the winning of which is to be made a condition precedent for the participation or co-operation in the war. Neither is our 'Peoples' War' movement a cover or screen just to develop mass struggle for winning such partial demands as

National Government, democratic right, release of prisoners, and other things. The crux of the matter is that we have to rouse among all sections of the people the consciousness and the will to play their part in the titanic battle that is being waged by the Soviet people and the other peoples of the world against the most brutal form of imperialism, and to inspire them to act and participate in that war, fighting at every step with the imperialist government and its bureaucratic administration, and forcing it to concede such demands and rights as will make that participation really popular and free and, therefore, effective. This is the main general consideration which should govern our general policy.

Royism is Subservience to Imperialist Government

8. The difference between our policy and that of Roy is as much as between the people and imperialism, revolution and counter-revolution. Roy has always been Zubatov-like agent of British imperialism whose job it was to spread disruption in the ranks of labour and left-nationalists by making deceptive use of radical slogans. That he too, to-day raises the slogan of 'a peoples' war' and parades himself as a supporter of the Soviet ought to deceive nobody. One has only to look at his attitude to war and actions when it was yet an imperialist war and to his practice to-day to see that he is a contemptible lackey of the imperialst bureaucracy. In the imperialist phase of the war, he shouted at first that it was an accidental war and then, an 'anti-fascist war', in order to confuse the nationalist ranks and to sabotage anti-war movement. When he failed in that task, he split away from the Congress to join hands with all sorts of anti-national and anti-labour reactionaries to form the National Democratic bloc, with the purpose of forming anti-national ministries. In the present phase of the war, he is mouthing slogans of peoples' war, solidarity with the Soviet and with the international proletariat, but in actual practice, he is attempting to split the trade union movement with the help of other Government agents like himself. Roy's 'Win -The War' Campaign is Nothing More Than Participating Together With His Handful Of Followers In The War Effort Organized By The Government. His Aim Is To Keep It In The Bureaucratic Framework. The Aim Of His Policy Is To Disrupt The Peoples' Movement And To Seek To Consolidate The Hegemony Of The Imperialist Bureaucracy In The War And In The War Effort.

Logic of Conditional Support: Policy of National–Bourgeois Parties

9. For the colonial bourgeoisie the war of their imperialist master is ALWAYS an opportunity for profit-making and extorting concessions from imperialism. This is the key to the understanding of the policies of the various groups in the Congress from Gandhi to the Congress Socialists. In the imperialist phase of the war, the policy of the leadership of the Congress was one of conditional co-operation and support to war. It was implicit in the 'September 1939' decision, and it was cashed in rupees, annas and pies in the Poona Resolution (July 1940). The counterpart of this conditional offer to imperialism was non-cooperation in the legislatures and ministries and a threat of satyagraha. The aim of this policy was to sabotage the anti-war struggle of the masses. When imperialism refused to make any concessions, they started the sham individual satyagraha with the purpose of waiting for a suitable opportunity for compromise while continuing the sabotage and disruption of the mass movement. The policies of the Congress Socialists and the Forward Bloc-ists which are only variants of the policy of the bourgeois leadership were directed to serve the purpose of keeping the radical nationalist elements under the influence of Gandhism. The Congress Socialists did it by playing the rebel opposition in Bengal. Such was bourgeois-nationalism in the imperialist phase of the war.

The policies of these groups in the National Congress in the present phase of the war are again directed towards the same end—surrender to imperialism and betrayal of the struggle of the masses. They are louder than ever in their opposition to war, and in their wordy demand for freedom. Gandhiji says, he will oppose all war because it is violence and wants to continue his symbolic satyagraha for repeating the pacifist formula, and the boycott of Legislatures. Nehru weaves a wreath of international slogans and lyrical tributes to Soviet and Chinese heroism and puts them round Gandhiji's neck: only when we get our freedom will we come forward to play our part in the world struggle, till then, 'long live Gandhi'. Rajaji sees the value of all this as a background against which to pursue negotiations for a surrender. The CSP now seizes the opportunity 'to expose the Communists' by saying that the war remains an imperialist war as long as India has not got her freedom. They shout for 'mass struggle', but will end by supporting Gandhi. The policy of all these froups amounts to one and the same thing. They Turn their Back Upon The People And Look To Imperialism For A Settlement. When a titanic battle is being waged by all the progressive people of the world, headed by the USSR, against fascism, when the fate of every people hangs upon the outcome of this battle, when people everywhere, not only in the Soviet Union, are acting in this war and changing the correlation of forces in their own favour and against imperialism, at such a time our national leadership does not lead our people along the path of initiative and activity in this war, towards the participation in the world struggle for liberation, but waits in futile passivity and stalemate hoping that imperialism would give them a hand. The policy which they are following is born of narrow nationalism and petty class motives which betray not only the world struggle but also the best interests of the people. Such is bourgeois-nationalism in the phase of the peoples' war.

Lead for Unity and Action

10. Our Policy in the present phase differs from the policy of the national bourgeois leadership in the same way as our policy in the imperialist phase of the war differed from their corresponding policy in that phase. Then they did not frankly and openly declare it to be an imperialist war which required an unconditional opposition. They dodged and prevaricated, put up constitutional opposition, made gestures of mass opposition to war, and ultimately settled down with the individual satyagraha to wait for compromise at the next favourable opportunity. One thing they did not want was to rely upon the people to put up real resistance against war. To-day again they refuse to recognie frankly the changed character of the war and refuse to rouse the people to the consciousness that they have to win it in common with the other peoples of the world in order to ensure their own freedom. They refuse to rely upon the people, to rouse them to such activity and initiative that will smash the obstacles which prevent India from playing her part in the struggle for world liberation and thus paving the way for her own liberation.

It is not enough for us to demarcate our policy from the policy of bourgeois nationalism and to expose it. We have to take the lead in achieving the broadest possible unity of all the progressive forces in the country, in order to develop a countrywide activity and initiative of the masses for realizing free and voluntary participation of the people in the war, for winning the minimum demands, such as responsible government and democratic rights, and other things, which are essential for making India's part in the war really effective while at the same time protecting the vital interests of the people. We have to make practical proposals to achieve such a unity and such mass action. The basis of such proposals to be made by us to the Congress, to the Muslim League and to the all-India workers' and peasants' organizations, for achieving a joint front, could be briefly outlined thus:

1. The Indian people must recognize that the war waged jointly by the USSR, Great Britain, and the USA and China against the fascist powers is a peoples war against fascism. The Indian people must strive to win it in common with the other progressive peoples in order to secure the victory of the USSR and of all other peoples, the annihilation of fascism and a peace and new order ensuring the independence and democratic liberties of all the peoples, and involving no annexations.

2. The Indian National Congress recognizing the changed character of the war, withdraws the individual Satyagraha and declares that it no longer opposes the war effort of the present government just because it is war effort.

3. A countywide united front campaign for rousing the people to the consciousness of the significance of the present war as an all-peoples' war of liberation, and awakening in them the will to win it should be started by the Congress jointly with other organizations. The campaign should lay the greatest stress on the crucial difference the entry of the USSR has made to the war, and on the heroic actions of the peoples of the Soviet Union, of China, of the occupied countries and of Britain and America in the struggle against fascism. The following demands are raised in this campaign as essential for winning the war:

1. Recognition of India's right to complete independence
2. Release of all political prisoners, detenus
3. Establishment of democratic liberties, the withdrawal of all war-time legislations restricting freedom of speech, press, organization, movement, and the right to strike
4. Power at the centre to be in hands of a National Government of popular representatives commanding the confidence of the people and having full power over all spheres of the government administration and the conduct of the war
5. Removal of all restrictions to the immediate development of industries to supply the demands of war and the needs of the people
6. Workers' demands ensuring that their conditions of living and work are improved and their right to organize and to strike is not curtailed
7. Kisans' demands including price control in their interest and generous remission to flood and famine-stricken areas
8. No enforced war levies of any kind
9. Distribution of war burden so that it falls on the rich and not on the poor.

4. The National Congress should call off the boycott of Legislatures and local bodies. It should seek to achieve a united front agreement with the Muslim League on the basis of the above three points, and should take the initiative in uniting the people for developing parliamentary and extra-parliamentary activity to win the war and protect the people by winning the above-mentioned demands. For the purpose of achieving this unity and action, the Indian National Congress should agree to form joint ministries with the League in the provinces, with the express understanding that the ministries pledge themselves to carry out the demands as far as lies in their power and to support the extra-parliamentary mass movement for their full realization.

We have to put forward these proposals in the coming AICC Session as well as to popularize them among the people and Congressmen.

Our Plan of Action

11. The activity of our own Party is, however, not determined by what the Congress and the other organizations decide. We strive hard to achieve such a unity which alone will make mass action and initiative possible on such a countrywide scale as to put the people on their feet for participating in the war as well as for winning their vital demands. But at the same time, we must chalk out our own independent programme and plan of action and carry it out. The fact that for six months we have given a wrong lead will now become a considerable obstacle in our way. That is why we have to develop our campaign in a series of steps which we have to take rapidly and one after another.

(a) To begin with, we must start immediately an explanatory campaign, firstly among our own Party Members, then among our militant sympathizers and supporters, among workers, students, kisans and Congressmen, and then among the people. We have to explain why the war now as a whole is a peoples' war against fascism, how it is the dominating issue before the whole world before which everything else dwarfs into insignificance. Explain how it is the entry of the USSR which has transformed the situation. Explain how the tremendous upsurge of the peoples' activity in the occupied countries, in England and in America is a direct result of the heroic deeds of the Soviet Union. Explain that the new turn in the war is not only the greatest defeat to the dark forces of fascism but is also unprecedented crisis of imperialism as a whole. In participating in this war, we are not reahly allying with imperialism but with the Soviet people, with the awakened people everywhere. Explain what fascist victory would mean, show how Soviet and peoples' victory is certain. Explain why through peoples' efforts alone can a victory be secured which guarantees world liberation and our own

(b) Soviet Aid Campaigns must be run again, not as before, isolated from the main issue of the war but in a manner as to bring out the leading role of the USSR in the all-peoples' war of liberation. Raise contributions, demand more and effective aid, raise the slogan: Open A New Front In Europe! strengthen the Friends of the Soviet Union Societies and popularize the achievements of the Soviet Union and the Red Army.

(c) Start a campaign of mass meetings of workers and kisans, students, Congressmen, wherein you popularize the following slogans:

All Aid to the USSR and China!

Support the War of the Peoples of the World Against Fascism!

To win the war, we must have democratic rights and civil liberties, release of political prisoners, responsible popular government at the centre, industrialization, granting of workers' demands.

(d) Thereafter, our 'Peoples' War' campaign is carried on as a campaign of vigilance and fight, exposing where the government's bureaucratic war effort oppresses or coerces the people and thus hinders the development of people's initiative and activity.

- *In the factories and workshops*, where production for war is carried on, we stand for workers' voluntary co-operation in increasing production. For this we demand proper dearness allowance, 25 per cent increase in the basic wage, recognition of unions and shop and mill committees, elected by workers for securing collective bargaining and quick solution of production difficulties on the spot, no curtailment of right of strike, repeal of all oppressive labour legislations, and release of all trade unionists and workers arrested for political or labour activity;

- *In the villages and rural areas*, we explain the significance of the war, create sympathy for the USSR, rally the people to support the war but resist all forcible levies, demand remissions for flood and famine-stricken areas, control of prices of necessaries, and other things.
- *In the recruiting areas*, we must get into touch with prospective recruits and explain to them the significance of the war as a peoples' war, the role of the USSR, the Red Army. Further political work among recruits, sending in of politically-conscious workers and kisans into the army will have to be undertaken as recruitment expands. Agitation for the betterment of the pay of Indian soliders, removal of racial discriminations, and other things, will have to be set up.
- *In the cities*, as the danger of air bombardment increases, we will have to expose the existing ARP and demand that it be handed over to popular bodies like the Municipalities so that popular initiative becomes really effective in their ensuring voluntary discipline and effective protection.
- *Throughout our campaign*, we persistently keep the demand for democratic liberties, release of prisoners, responsible government at the centre, industrialization, check on profiteering and equitable distribution of war burdens in the forefront as the essential pre-requisites for making India's war effort really effective.

13th December 1941.

88. On the New Line
Communist Party Polit-Bureau to All Party Members

Party Letter, No. 56, 15 December 1941, CPI Library, Ajoy Bhavan, New Delhi.

Dear Comrades,

New Situation

When did the imperialist war become a peoples' war? When Hitler attacked our Socialist Fatherland! This was the big and decisive event which produced a New Situation, in which the world, as we knew it before, was turned upside down. World imperialism began staggering to its doom, right under our own eyes, not as a remote prospect but in actual reality.

What are the main features of this historic phase?

1. One Imperialist rival, Hitler-fascism, got isolated before the entire progressive mankind as the main aggressor, the chief enemy of humanity. And Hitler-fascism sealed its own doom when it threw its murderous hordes into the Sovietland. For the first time, the peoples of all countries saw that Hitler's armies are not invincible. For the first time, Hitlerites are made to realize that victory over Sovietland is not easy, and now more impossible. The epic resistance by the Red Army has convinced the peoples of the world that not Nazi victory over the USSR but the end of Hitlerite regime will be the fate of Hitler-fascism at the hands of the glorious Red Army and the Soviet peoples, led by the great Stalin.

2. A split in the imperialist camp takes place when the other imperialist rival, British imperialism is forced to join the anti-fascist front and the alliance of the USSR, USA, and Great Britain is forged. Here was a decisive shift, after a series of big defeats of British imperialism.

British imperialism had nursed Hitler-fascism as the spear-head of the capitalist attack on the USSR. When Hitler, at the eleventh hour, quailed before the might of the USSR and signed a pact of non-aggression and on the contrary attacked British imperialism itself, it was an unimagined fiasco for British imperialism, such a defeat as led to an imperialist war instead of an anti-Soviet war for which British diplomacy had planned and worked through all the pre-war years.

When British imperialism tried to check Hitler's advance by spreading the war from one country to another in Europe, it only succeeded in handing over Europe to Hitler. British imperialist conduct of the imperialist war only resulted in strengthening its imperialist rival, who was now in a more advantageous position to challenge its own mastery over the world. This was another big defeat for British imperialism.

When Hitler attacked the Soviet Union, to clean up his socialist rear, to destroy the fortress of World Revolution, before he took the final plunge to settle accounts with British imperialism for the mastery of the world, and British imperialism in its own interests was forced to enter into an alliance with the USSR—that was its Biggest defeat in its career of unrelieved defeats throughout the world war, such a historic defeat as opened up the prospect of many more defeats at the hands of its own people and the peoples of the world. The fundamental class aim of British imperialism, an imperialist redivision of the world to its own greater advantage, could no more be realized; the USSR stood athwart it. Before the war, it had conspired and intrigued to smash the Peace Front against Nazism and isolated the USSR: during the war it is forced not only to enter itself the Anti-Nazi Front of Government but see the allied governments doing the same and sign pacts of agreement with the USSR. The traditional enemy of Socialism, the actual father of Nazism, has to declare war to death against Nazism, join the anti-Nazi front of governments and become the instrument to pave the way for a peoples' movement behind the front of governments. Such has been the cruel revenge of history on British imperialism, and the last word is not yet spoken.

3. After the imperialist war becomes a peoples' war, inside each country the most broad-based national unity behind their existing governments to win the war can be built. The balance decisively shifts in favour of the people. A modern war is a total war; it cannot be conducted victoriously without the active co-operation of the working people and the entire population mobilized in the armed forces, or civil defence, or production. In democratic countries, enjoying democratic rights, the people come into action to see that the war is not conducted at the cost of the people but to ensure Peoples' Victory and not profits for the capitalists and imperialist gains. The independent national existence of each country, the welfare of every people is at stake in the war against Hitler. This the entire people know, they sit across the reactionary plans to sell out to Hitler, to go back to the old order.

The war has already knit the peoples and states together in one Anti-Nazi Front. The war keeps the whole people mobilized for one common aim, victory over Nazi fascism. The people of every country come face to face with the actual obstacles on the road to victory, and it is a matter of life or death not to hurl them out of the way. The people are led to realize that they must take their fate in their own hands, to ensure that it will be a peoples' victory and their sufferings and sacrifices are not made in vain. Armed struggle and widespread sabotage in Nazi-occupied countries and in democratic countries, a growing peoples' movement to win the All-Peoples' War against Nazi-fascism is the beginning of the process that guarantees Peoples' Victory. They are being moulded into a mass movement by the events of the war, by mighty historic forces which are more powerful than the will of the rulers, and through the living instrument which alone can finally count—the People.

4. The USSR Enters The World Arena As The Leader Of The Anti-Nazi Front And As The World liberator.

In the pre-war period the policy of the Peace Front was the call of the USSR to the peoples of the world to preserve peace for the world. The reactionary rulers of most democratic countries smashed the building of the Peace Front.

In the period of imperialist war, the policy of Socialist neutrality enabled the USSR to show the peoples of the world how to preserve and safeguard peace for each country despite the flames of war around.

In the period of the peoples' war, the USSR actually demonstrates to the peoples of each country how to conduct the peoples' war, every day the contrast between the bourgeois way and the peoples' way becomes more and more glaring: one ensures peoples' victory and the other untold suffering or helpless panic (e.g., compare the life in London with life in Moscow, compare the Rostov offensive with the latest Libyan offensive and so on). The peoples of every land see on the Soviet Front living, model examples of a practical and effective leadership of the peoples' war. The very stress of war makes them take the next step: turn round to their own government and ask it to follow suit or answer to them. The USSR acts not only as the inspirer and teacher to the other peoples from within its own front but through the alliance of Anti-Nazi Governments, is able to shape the policy for the conduct of the war, and is a direct participant in the peoples' war.

As yet the imperialist rulers alone have shaped future history at the Peace Conferences. The whole of Europe stands enslaved, the rest of mankind is threatened with the worst slavery that humanity has ever known. Participation of USSR in the war means not only that Hitler-fascism will be defeated but during and after the war, peoples' revolutions in Europe and throughout the world will not be crushed in blood by any imperialist ruling class. The awakened peoples who fought for peoples' victory will find in the USSR their protector and liberator, the USSR is the greatest guarantee that the old order and status quo, another Versailles, will remain old history, and the new order which the all-peoples' victory will bring about, there will be all-peoples' peace, all-peoples' democracy and all-peoples' liberation. The USSR from being the leader of the Anti-Nazi Front will become the liberators of the peoples of the world, the leader of people's new world order of peace, prosperity and freedom for all the peoples of the world.

In a Nutshell

The turn from the imperialist war to the peoples' war means:

The world is split into two camps—of Progress and Reaction, Freedom, and Slavery.

Anti-Fascism is the basis of one common worldwide front.

This happening in the period of the world war makes it directly revolutionary, as it has never been before.

Victory depends as it never has before, upon actions of the people and they will change and act faster than history has yet recorded. For the first time in human history, a worldwide all-peoples' war against the main enemy of all is being fought.

British imperialism is a prisoner in the hands of the peoples of the world.

The USSR is acting as the leader of the rising world peoples' front.

Such is the New Situation. The imperialist war has become transformed into a peoples' war; it can be won only as a peoples' war and that means peoples' victory and its consummation is peoples' liberation.

It will be idle speculation to theorize about what will happen when, to get 'Clarified'. It will be empty scheme-making if we sat down to 'Discuss' when we will do what.

We have got a worldwide anti-fascist front which the peoples of the world were too powerless to achieve and to come to which, humanity had to undergo great sufferings; we have got it through the working of historical forces which are more powerful than ourselves—the insoluble contradictions of world imperialism and the might of the Red Army. The USSR is acting as the defender and liberator of humanity. The Battle For World Revolution Has Begun, And Victory Depends Upon The Actions Of The Peoples Of Every Land. Our Task Is To Line Up And Do Our Part Of The Job Among Our Own People. Before we can successfully understand our new line, effectively do our new jobs, we must realize how and why we remained blind to the biggest change in the fortunes of the war and of the world. Unless we re-educate ourselves, get away from all pre-conceived notions, liquidàte the remnants of the old line, we will not understand the character of the new period; we will not be inspired for our tasks, we will remain blind, defeatist, and passive. We have to assimilate the new situation in its entirety; we have to realize the strength of the new forces behind us; we have to grasp the revolutionary significance of the new period before we can really understand the new line and get on with our job.

New for Us

When the imperialist war becomes a peoples' war, it becomes a peoples' war for us no less than for the other peoples of the world. It is commonplace to say that India is a part of the world, what is necessary is to See that the world war has knit our fate with the rest of the world as nothing else could. The war envelops the globe, including India. The fascist claw covers the world, it is our immediate task no less than that of the rest of mankind to crush the life out of the beast of fascism, the vilest form of imperialism. Our immediate place is inside the common front, in our own interest. The Immediate Call Of History Upon The Indian People Is To Fight For World Liberation Though They Are Themselves Slaves To begin With. Should we be more afraid of Churchill than he is of Stalin? That will be nursing an old world prejudice and not see what is actually on—the battle of India's liberation gets merged with the battle of world liberation through the anti-fascist front, outside which, only Hitler and his gang stand.

What Is New For Us Is That Our National Front Has To Be Linked Up With The Worldwide Anti-Fascist Front. Our national movement has always stood for such a Policy, to-day this has to be made the policy of our Practice. What the pre-war remote perspective nursed on our fondest hopes was, has to be transformed into an immediate reality.

Our Freedom First? This is the slogan that suits Hitler most to-day!

Our freedom first? This is the slogan of those who expect freedom to come as gift or who look for a bargain with imperialism and talk of freedom only to keep the people behind themselves!

Our freedom first? This is the slogan of those who lack faith in our people, who do not want our people to act!

Just as in the phase of the imperialist war, we fought the battle of our liberation with anti-war struggles, similarly in the phase of the peoples' war we have to fight the battle of our own liberation by strengthening the cause of peoples' victory in the peoples' war.

How Can Our National Enemy Be Our International Ally? Just because it is so! It is his defeat, not our climb-down. The imperialist war turning into the peoples' war is a political windfall for the Indian people. The day of our liberation gets nearer, the cause of our liberation through the world war actually merges with the all-peoples' war against fascism, and we get the powerful and actual support of the peoples of Britain and of the world, and the backing of the USSR which has always stood for national freedom and self-determination. Our national enemy is in the same front with us, his very change of front puts us in an advantageous position; we advance and make him retreat a few steps in the interests of the common front! Right away, as also ultimately, the Indian people and Not British imperialism will gain out of India's participation in the all-peoples' war. Even the present forces ranged behind the anti-Nazi front are strong enough to defeat fascism. The foremost concern of all freedom loving peoples is to see that the common front is not disrupted, for the evethrow of fascism by itself means a terrible blow for world imperialism as a whole, and the stranglehold of British and American imperialisms would not be what it was. Whether British and American imperialism would exist at all depends upon the Actions of British and American peoples and of the peoples of the world. It will be idle speculation to make theories about it, our job is not to hug on to the past, not to dream about a rosy future but shape the actual present to make our great people play a people's part in the all-peoples' war against fascism, for that and no other, is the path of the Indian peoples' liberation too.

Why Not Start Immediate Nationwide Mass CD? Just because it can't be started! What was a real slogan of action in the period of the imperialist war becomes unreal and disruptive in the phase of the peoples war. Such is already the logic of life, despite the tyranny of phrases. Mass CD is the slogan of the CSP, left-bourgeois disruptors of the national movement, whose job is to keep in step with the Mahatma, just one step more to the left. These wordy heroes fight imperialism with their tongues and inside their heads.

What all Party Members have to realize is that the New Situation for our country as for all countries is that imperialist war has become a peoples' war and we can ignore it only at our peril, while it is our task to get linked with it. We have to recognize that the peoples' war is also our war, an all peoples' war and that it is in our interest as in the interests of all progressive humanity to win it, for an all-peoples' victory, in the interests of world liberation including our own. This means that We Make A Right-About Turn From The Slogans, Phrases, Outlook Of The Period Of The Imperialist War For The Simple Reason That It Is No More There!

We are a responsible political party. It is our task in a new situation to create New Forms for our national struggle and in the period of the peoples' war, with us enslaved, it means that we keep our national front intact and link it up directly with the anti-Nazi front on whose victory depends, not only our fate but the fate of whole humanity, behind which is rising the common world peoples' front for world liberation.

We are a practical party and in a new situation, it is our task not only to evolve a new form of struggle for it, but also to advance new slogans appropriate to the new stage, suiting the new form of our national movement. The key slogan of our party which guides all our practical political activity is: Make The Indian People Play A Peoples' Role In The Peoples' War.

We are a revolutionary party. We fight for our policy, now as always, through Peoples' Actions.

Every Party and class has been and is readjusting its policy to the new situation in order to cash it in its own interest.

Imperialist Policy

In the imperialist phase of the war, the policy of British imperialism was to keep India crushed, to mouth patriotic slogans about national unity and national defence, to make the bourgeois-national leadership surrender to itself, and batter down its opposition by encouraging disruptive forces within the national movement and by inciting communal riots.

In the phase of the peoples' war, whipped by the progressive opinion of its own country and of all its allies, driven by the very logic of the growing needs of the war, it [the British imperialism] sets out to bargain with the national bourgeoisie to get it to surrender for as low a price as possible so that the Indian people may be kept crushed by its own national leaders, so that India's men and resources may be available to it to conduct the peoples' war the imperialist way.

It will do the Indian people well to remember that imperialism does not want Indian Peoples' co-operation, Free And Voluntary, but seeks to settle up with the national bourgeoisie to be able to carry on its own way.

The Indian People Have to Transform Their Present Enforced Participation As Imperial Slaves Into A Free And Voluntary Participation As a People. This Means A Series Of Mass Actions Against The Imperialist Bureaucratic Autocracy To Be Able To Play A Peoples' Role In The Peoples' War, Effective, Unhindered And Free Ensuring With All The Might Of The Indian People, Peoples' Victory.

Bourgeois Policy

In the period of the imperialist war the bourgeoisie sabotaged the peoples' struggle through sham satyagraha and left the people at the mercy of imperialism. In the period of the imperialist war a united mass struggle of the Indian people would have ended the imperialist war, led to India's own liberation and a peoples' government in Britain, and the isolation and weakening of Hitler as the main aggressor if not his own overthrow, and no attack on the USSR would have taken place. The bourgeois disruption of the national movement prevented the Indian people achieving this and resulted in producing stalemate instead which bred demoralization and further disruption.

In the peoples phase of the war, the bourgeois leadership seeks to cash stalemate into a settlement to advance its own interests and seeks to palm it off as national settlement. The people once again come nowhere into the bourgeois scene. Not peoples' victory but its own gains, with the people as pawns, these are the guides to the national-bourgeois policy in the present phase.

The Transformation Of The Imperialist War Into The Peoples' War Means For The Indian People Under Bourgeois Leadership, That The Rot Of Continued Stalemate Has Become The Menace Of An Immediate Sell-Out To Imperialism.

The Policy of imperialism is to keep the people down, as they are, through a settlement with the national bourgeoisie.

For the bourgeoisie, this is the golden opportunity it was waiting for, all these war years, and its policy is to leave the people as they are and sell out to imperialism on what terms it can get for itself.

Our Policy

The policy of our Party is to make the Indian people play a people's role in the peoples' war Independently of the will of imperialism, independently of all bourgeois plans. Its Planks are:

- rescue the national movement from the mire of satyagraha
- restore national unity
- make the people act
- register a national advance by winning civil liberties and a responsible national government.

Our Policy Is In The Interests Of Our Entire Nation and it enables us to

- swing our people into action
- snatch the initiative from imperialism
- smash imperialist hegemony over the war

and to change the equation between imperialism and the Indian people in favour of our nation so that our people may do their part of the job to ensure peoples' victory in the peoples' war.

Our Policy is Based on

- faith in our people
- alliance of the peoples of the world, backed by the strength of the USSR.

Just because we are in a critical phase of world history and the biggest job of our lives faces our people, we advocate National Unity even broader than that represented by the Congress. We seek a Congress-League agreement as the broadest front for our own national unity. A joint declaration by the Congress and the League on the character of the war would radically change the situation, revive nationwide confidence and be a political defeat of the first magnitude for British imperialism, its utter isolation not only within our own country but it would unlink the Indian people from the imperialist aims and designs of the present British Government and hearten the struggling peoples of the world, strengthen the cause of freedom and progress.

The United Front Campaign is our lever to forge anew the unity of our nation, cement its bonds, and get our people into united action.

The leeway that we are now able to make with the U.F. campaign for the new period and new tasks, the speed with which we succeed in permeating the national movement with a consciousness of our new role as a nation, will be the decisive factors before and after the formation of responsible ministries, which is imminent. That will decide whether we are able to prevent surrender to imperialism or not, whether we are able to get out of the period of stalemate or not. The pre-Ministry mass campaign will then become the extra-parliamentary campaign to keep the compromisers in check and popular ministers on the straight path so that they protect and do not attack the people, ensure peoples' victory in the peoples' war and do not play the imperialist game. In the new period we now enter The unity of the parliamentary and extra-parliamentary fronts will acquire a new revolutionary significance in strengthening the people, loosening the imperialist stranglehold over our people, by effectively playing a real peoples' role, worthy of our great nation in the all-peoples' world war and finally for ensuring our own liberation when the day of reckoning arrives.

We and Imperialism

If our new policy is understood in old terms, in terms of the Party policy during the phase of the imperialist war, that will be not understanding it but misunderstanding it. If any comrade went on the old rails, he will find that we have suspended the struggle for national liberation and are allying ourselves with imperialism for the time being because Sovietland is in danger!

Our Alliance Is Not With British Imperialism But The Peoples Of Britain And Of The Whole World. Our policy is independent of the wishes of British imperialism. It is bourgeois-nationalism that seeks an alliance with British imperialism and falsely assures us that the concessions it will now get for us, will carry us to our freedom. Our policy is based on Peoples' Action now and always. Our movement for national liberation is on and will be on till victory is ours, only it is being waged with new slogans, under new forms just because the whole situation has changed.

Our policy is based upon winning from British imperialism, rights and liberties whose non-existence make us its colonial slaves, whose possession puts us on equal terms with the citizens of the rest of democratic countries and only by winning which we can really play a peoples' role in the peoples' war. Our policy is based on resisting the bureaucratic octopus which keeps our people down and winning for our people such democratic liberties that not imperialism but peoples' representatives and our peoples' strength will guide our future destiny, our participation in the peoples' war. Through peoples' action, through a Concrete struggle for our rights and liberties we undermine the hold of imperialism over our country and strengthen the might of our people; by dissociating ourselves from imperialist war aims and declaring the nation's war aims, we weaken imperialism internationally and do our bit to ensure that the all-peoples' war will ensure all-peoples' victory and not imperialist victory; by establishing a responsible National Government, we ensure that India's men and resources will be used in defeating fascism and not in advancing imperialist interests, for liberation of peoples and not for annexation of countries.

With the war in the Near East and Far East and India in a very strategic position, the Indian people occupy a key position. They, more than any other peoples, can thwart imperialist designs, defeat the realization of imperialist war aims and through their participation in the peoples' war do their best to ensure that it will be peoples' victory and peoples' liberation and nothing else.

Imperialism too wants our participation in the war but only As Imperial Slaves. This we resist. We enforce our participation as People, Free And Effective. This is how we enter the world war to ensure peoples' victory and our own liberation—not as a gift from imperialism but through the strength of the people, as a result of their victory. Our immediate job is to mobilize our own people and for victory, and we will have the peoples of the world behind India's cause.

By participating in the peoples' war we are not sacrificing our national cause, but strengthening it, not accepting imperialist hegemony but destroying it, it is not the USSR that needs our aid, it is we who get its powerful backing, our people cease to fight a lone battle but get allies in the peoples of all the countries. Such an opportunity was never ours. We have only to Act.

The bourgeoisie too wants to participate in the war but its policy is 'settlement with imperialism minus the people', and if it does not get its bargain, it turns round to the people with: 'nothing has changed, imperialism remains imperialism, spin [*Charka*] and organize, but do not act'. If it can get its profits and bargain out of the war, it is willing to help imperialism carry on the war the imperialist way. If it fails it leaves the people at the mercy of imperialism and pursues the policy of 'wait and watch'. It lies to the people when it says 'nothing has changed'. It knows that the world has changed and is changing, it hopes and prays that imperialism will get into a worse quandary and then come to it for 'settlement'. This is the policy of the cold-blooded Baniya who bothers only about his share, this makes the gambler and not the fighter. That is how from the camp of the national bourgeoisie, at the most critical time in our national and world history, emerge polices of negation, passivity, submission and no other. A positive policy of action, based on the people, is just what cannot come out of the bourgeois camp when the whole bourgeois world order is going topsy-turvy.

Such a policy can only come from our Party, the party of the international proletariat, of Marx, Engels, Lenin and Stalin. Imperialism in crisis functions blind, somehow carry on, and hopes to stick on to what exists. The national bourgeoisie waits on the imperialist pleasure, ready to be called in when Imperialism can't carry on its own. The fate of our people and of all peoples hangs in the balance. Peoples' Action alone can turn the scale, our policy is based on peoples' action now and hereafter, for they will make history, they alone are real, and ultimately count.

Sudden Turns and Twists

The period of the Second World War was described by Com. Dimitrov in its very beginning as ushering in a period of sudden turns and twists.

The biggest turn of the war took place when it got transformed from the imperialist war into the peoples' war, though we remained blind to it. When the whole situation changed we have changed our entire policy. This must be Cleary grasped.

The turns and twists in the new period of the peoples' war will be not less but more and also sudden. Our Party will have to react to them quickly and suddenly change its slogans of action. We hope we will be able to do it promptly and not belatedly. The guiding lines for the new period are already clear enough: In The All-Peoples' War

— All For Peoples' Victory!
— To Ensure All-Peoples' Liberation And Our Own!

But nothing will happen of itself, neither in our land nor in the world. This is elementary Marxism. The living core of our policy is:

— Everything Depends Upon Peoples' Action
— Now And Hereafter,

Our job is to make the people act and keep them in action all the while. Remember no other party in our country is going to stick to the people, none will make the people act. The national movement is on the eve of being divided into two camps, the compromisers will re-appear as ministerialists and as a part of the bargain with imperialism, keep the people down. Gandhi–Nehru–CSP will reappear with seemingly left slogans, they will mouth phrases to keep the people out of action. All Party Members must realize the supreme gravity of the situation. Imperialist war has become the peoples' war and Comrade Stalin will do our job for us!—such day-dreaming is not Bolshevism and is unworthy of any party Member. Our job in the new period becomes not less but more different, not simpler but more complicated. When you begin to discuss and implement the new policy you will find this out for yourself!

Right Away

Study all Party documents seriously and soberly and get an inspired understanding of the new line.

Unify your own unit behind the new line, secure a common understanding. Don't sneer at comrades who are slow, but convince them.

Defeat sham satyagrahis before the people.

Scotch the Gandhian Socialism of the CSP, their only capital is left phrasemongerng. Remember that among the non-Party fighters, after three years of political frustration under the bourgeois leadership, there is bound to be a left-nationalist swing-over. The CSP with 'Left' slogans hopes to capitalize it. That was the meaning of J.P.'s letter. Boldly face the CSP or the non-party Left. Frankly admit our mistake and give our reasons. Plainly tell him that we have changed our line just because the world has changed and we want to do our part in changing it. If he has a smattering of Socialism, show how our policy is based on internationalism. If he is a left-nationalist, show how our policy is based on peoples' action and not on left phrases. Draw him into our mass campaigns and you will see that all honest elements will swing over to us.

Campaign among the people for new slogans and policy: After unifying the Party ranks and sympathizers on the basis of Party documents, approach the recently released Congressmen and hold explanatory meetings with them as you did at the time of 'Unmasked' and 'Proletarian Path'. You will shortly get a pamphlet on the new situation which will be a simple and popular exposition of the new line, but a smaller pamphlet and not as big as 'Unmasked'. Only by 'discussing' with others we won't win the people for our policy. In the P.B. Resolution, we have given you our Party's programme for National Unity and Peoples' Action. Pick out the item on which you can campaign in your locality most effectively and vigorously—Civil Liberties, Soviet Aid or any other. Try to mobilize All the national fighters, militant workers and sympathetic students for the campaign you take up. Party agitators must popularize our peoples' war policy vigorously and boldly, in and through these campaigns, and more, as our resolution says, these campaigns must be Related to our political policy for the new period. The war is now a peoples' war, it must be won for peoples' liberation, it is imperialism that keeps the People out of the war. Explain the Character of the war. Explain how our policy is in our National Interest. Explain how it is based on Peoples' Action.

Comrades! Go Into Action!
Victory Will Be Ours!
Comrade Stalin Himself Leads The Battle That We Are Now Entering!
With Party greetings,

The Polit-Bureau.

89. CPI Draft Resolution for the Wardha AICC[1], 1942

Communist, Vol. III, No. 9, December 1941, P.C. Joshi Archives on Contemporary History, JNU.

1. The world shaking developments in the war which have taken place in rapid succession in the last seven months, beginning with Hitler's attack on the Soviet Union and ending with Japan's aggression in the Pacific and the entry of the USA in the world war, have fundamentally

changed the world situation. Not only is the peril of war already knocking at the eastern doors of India, but the character of the war itself has basically changed. After the German attack against the Soviet Union, the AICC recognizes that the grave situation requires a re-definition of the Congress policy in the present phase of the war and the chalking out of the plan of action which will not only protect the immediate interests of the Indian people, but further the struggle for independence and enable them to play their role in the battle for world liberation.

New Alignment

2. The events of the last seven months have brought about a new alignment of powers which completely alters the character of the war. The war now being jointly waged by the Socialist Soviet Union, Nationalist China, and the peoples of America and Great Britain against the brutal and deliberate aggression of the fascist powers can no longer be regarded as an imperialist war on the part of the former. It is now a single indivisible world-wide conflict in which a powerful and growing combination of progressive peoples standing for freedom, democracy, and peace, are ranged against Fascism and Nazism, the worst form of imperialism which stand for brutal violence, racial arrogance, enslavement and for the destruction of all cultural values of men.

Congress Policy Towards War and Fascism

3. The Congress has always expressed its 'entire disapproval of the ideology and practice of Fascism and Nazism and their glorification of war, violence and the suppression of the human spirit'. The Congress has always looked with apprehension at the growth of fascism and fascist aggression against Manchuria and China, Italy's attack against Abyssinia and Germany's annexation of Austria and Czechoslovakia, as events preparing for a new world war. The Congress has especially condemned the reactionary foreign policy of the British Government which had 'consistently aided the fascist powers and helped destruction of democratic countries'. The Congress always sympathized with the progressive forces of Britain, America, and France, which in collaboration with the USSR and China sought to create a world-wide front standing for peace through collective security and for the preservation of democracy and extension of freedom in order to prevent fascist aggression and to prevent the impending war.

Policy in the Imperialist Phase of the War

4. The policy of the fascist aggressors and their reactionary imperialist abettors, however, were stronger than the unity of the progressive forces. The war which Chamberlain declared against Hitler in September, 1939, was not a war against fascism or for the defence of democracy. It was but a culmination of the same reactionary policy of Chamberlain of 'aiding' and 'appeasing' the fascist aggressors so that they may attack the progressive forces of Spain, China, and finally, the USSR It was this policy which the Congress had condemned. It was the same age-old policy of British imperialism of aiding reactionary forces against revolutionary ones in order to preserve 'the balance of power' in Europe in its own favour and thus protect its mastery over the world. Chamberlain, pursuing an anti-Soviet policy, had aided and strengthened Hitler at the cost of destroying and weakening the democratic countries like Czechoslovakia and France in the hope that he may attack the USSR But Hitler impressed by the might of the USSR and deeming that the situation was not favouable enough for such a venture, signed a non-aggression pact with Soviet Union. It was against the betrayal by a fellow-imperialist that the Chamberlain Government declared war against Hitler. That is why Britain's war against

Hitler in its first phase, which lasted till the latter's attack upon the USSR, was not a war against fascism or for democracy, but one conducted in pursuance of imperialist aims. That is why the Congress rightly regarded the war in its first phase as one fought for fundamentally imperialist aims and pursued a policy of opposition towards it.

How it Became a Peoples' War

5. The turn in the war came when the reactionary policy of the British Government suffered a series of reverses and collapsed giving place to a new alignment of Britain and America with the USSR It was this policy which was responsible for the speedy collapse of the western front when Hitler's armies overran Norway, Denmark, Holland, Belgium, and finally France. It was this reactionary British policy of continued hostility to the Soviet Union and of weakening the democratic countries which enabled Hitler to enslave the western countries of Europe, to hold the threat of invasion over the head of Britain, to trample over the liberties of Yugoslavia and Greece and to reduce Hungary and Rumania into mere vassals. The result was that Hitler was immensely strengthened. With the resources of the entire Europe at his hand and having nothing to fear in the western front, he flung his entire military machine against the Soviet Union. He hoped that the reactionary section of the British ruling class, being chastened by Hitler's victory and pleased at the attack against the Soviet Union, the base of the world revolution, would come to a settlement with him over the division of the world. Hitler reckoned with reaction but left out of account the power of the progressive peoples and the bond that linked them with the USSR Instead of an anti-Bolshevik front of western European countries which Hitler expected to materialize, what came into existence was a united front of the British and American peoples with the USSR headed by their respective governments. The reactionary anti-Soviet policy of Chamberlain which was at the root of the second Imperialist War, was smashed to bits. The new alignment which came into existence was an alliance of the progressive peoples of Great Britain and America with the USSR against Hitler fascism and its allies. The war conducted by it became a just war, a peoples' war against fascist aggression. This is so firstly because the new alignment means a complete reversal of the reactionary anti-Soviet policy which the British Government pursued for the last twenty-three years for the furtherance of its imperialist domination over the world. Secondly, because the joint victory of this alliance would no longer result in an imperialist redivision of the world, thanks to the presence of the USSR in it, but into all-round peoples' victory and a just peace without annexations. Thirdly, because the new alliance is in essence a mighty united front of the peoples of Europe and America against fascism, which is developing into a powerful peoples' upsurge and transforming the war against Hitler and his allies into a war of world liberation, ensuring not only the crushing of fascism but the disintegration of world imperialism itself.

Support to the Peoples' War

6. The Indian National Congress recognizes the changed character of the war and realizes that the supreme issue before all mankind to-day is to achieve the final and complete victory of the world front of peoples against Hitler and his allies. The grave situation created by the Japanese aggression in the Pacific and the menace to the eastern borders of India only underlines the urgency of the all-in-struggle for the victory of the progressive forces. This is no longer a battle of rival imperialisms to which the Congress and the Indian people could afford to remain neutral or which they could oppose. It is a titanic conflict between the forces of progress and reaction on the outcome of which depends the fate and future of mankind. Imperialism in its

most brutal form will have won on a world scale if Hitler and his allies were to succeed. But the victory of the Soviet Union, China, and of the progressive peoples of Britain and America on the other hand will not only achieve the final annihilation of fascism but also the crippling of world imperialism and the liberation of the peoples all round.

7. Therefore, in view of the changed character of the war and in accordance with the policy which the Congress has always adopted towards the progressive forces against fascism and fascist aggression, the AICC declares that it records its full and whole-hearted support to the cause which the peoples of the Soviet Union, of China, of America, of Great Britain, and of the Nazi-occupied countries of Europe are defending so heroically against the armies of Hitler-fascism and its allies. The victory of this cause demands the free and voluntary co-operation of all the peoples of the world on the side of the anti-fascist front. It requires, particularly at the present juncture, the free and voluntary co-operation of the 500 millions of the peoples of India and Burma in the effort to stem the tide of Japan's aggression in the East. This is necessary not only in the interests of defence of the peoples of India and Burma from aggression but also in the interests of making an effective contribution to the achievement of victory in the all people's war against fascism.

British Policy Towards India: An Obstacle

8. It is the policy of the British Government of perpetuating the enslavement of India which comes up as a major obstacle in the path of achieving victory of the progressive forces over fascism. The British Government has persistently refused to apply its protestations about freedom and democracy (such as those in the Atlantic Charter) in India and has continued a regime of autocratic repression. It has pursued an economic and political war policy in total disregard of the well-being of the people. In the industrial and economic field, the British, guided solely by the interests of foreign capital, have refused to take measures to increase the defensive potential of the country as urgently required by the exigency of the war and by the needs of the people. It has used and still continues to use the provisions of the Defence of India Act for the wholesale repression of the patriotic and popular movements and for the complete suppression of civil liberties and democratic rights under the demonstrably false plea of suppressing activities prejudicial to the conduct of war. It has conducted and continues to conduct its war efforts by methods of coercion of the people and not by their voluntary co-operation, the measures it so far adopted for the military, air and naval defence of the country, are not only ridiculously inadequate but often accompanied by such revolting acts of bureaucratic and racial arrogances as to make them thoroughly hateful to the people. In short, the policies the British imperialist rulers of India have adopted in the conduct of war and defence have resulted in a situation in which the Indian people are left not only defenceless in the face of dangers and disasters which the new development of war may bring, but left shackled in a manner which makes it next to impossible for them either to organize their own defence or to play their own part in the world struggle against fascism.

Independent Policy of Unity and Action

9. The Congress condemns unequivocally this reactionary policy and declares that it will not prevent the Indian people from adopting a correct attitude towards the present war and from mobilizing the power of the people in order to smash the obstacle which prevents them from participating in it and from winning it for our own freedom and the freedom of the world. The recognition of the independence of India and the establishment of the National Government

enjoying the confidence of the people and the realization of democratic liberties are essential to transform our general support to the war into an active and effective material co-operation with the same. The Indian National Congress, however, recognizes that those demands cannot come as a gift from the British Government but will have to be won through struggle. In the present critical situation of the war, the issue of India's freedom has become one of urgent and vital importance not only to the Indian people, but also to all peoples who are conducting the war against fascism and its allies. The Indian National Congress recognizes gratefully that the advanced sections of the British and American peoples are raising the question of India's freedom as a part of their struggle to strengthen the anti-fascist front and to win the war. The Congress assures them that it is determined to adopt a positive policy towards the war and to mobilize the people for achieving their free and voluntary participation in the war. This policy of the general support to the war and withdrawal of individual satyagraha is not determined either by the recent releases of satyagrahis, nor will it be influenced by the vagaries of the autocratic repressive regime which the Government continues. It is determined solely by the interests of the Indian people, by their desire to further their struggle for independence and by their determination to play their part in the world struggle against fascism. In carrying out its policy it will rely on the unity and strength of its own people and upon the support it gets from the progressive forces of Britain and America and elsewhere.

10. In this situation, therefore, the only correct policy the Congress can adopt is one of forging positive mass sanction, by achieving the unity of the popular organizations and forces in the country, which stands for independence of the country, for communal amity and understanding and for effective participation of the Indian people in the world struggle against fascism. The urgent need of the moment is the formation of the broadest possible joint front, united on the basis of a positive attitude towards the war, determined to mobilize the people through parliamentary and extra-parliamentary actions, aimed at securing the recognition of India's right to independence, of the establishment of a National Government at the Centre, commanding the confidence of the people. For this purpose, the AICC hereby decides to call off the individual satyagraha and cancels the restrictions and bans imposed on the participation of Congressmen in the Legislatures and the local bodies.

Plan of Action

11. The AICC therefore, calls upon the Working Committee to get into touch with the Muslim League and other major popular organizations in order to achieve joint action and joint front on the following basis:

(a) The contracting parties agree that the war waged jointly by USSR, China, America, and Great Britain, and the other allies against the fascist powers is, in its present phase, a just war, which the Indian people must strive to win in common with the progressive forces, such as the Soviet Union, Nationalist China, and the peoples of Britain and America. They fully agree with the war and peace aims as they have been set forth by the leaders of the Soviet Union, namely the annihilation of Hitler fascism and its allies, securing of a durable and just peace not involving any annexations, and a new world order based on the independence and democratic liberties of all peoples, and their mutual co-operation.

(b) The recognition of the changed character of the war naturally implies that the attitude of the contracting parties towards the war effort even of the present government can no longer be of hostility or even of neutrality but such as will protect the interests and the democratic rights of the people and further the creating of mass sanctions for winning the major political demands detailed in para C.

(c) The contracting parties recognize that the main obstacle in the way of realizing the free, voluntary and therefore effective participation of the Indian people in this war for the proper defence of the country and ensuring the protection of the people's interests and liberties, is the autocratic and repressive policy of the British Government.

In order to eliminate this obstacle, the contracting parties must take joint action to forge parliamentary and extra-parliamentary sanctions to win the following demands: Recognition of India's right to Complete Independence;

(i) Formation of a National Government at the Centre responsible to the legislature and commanding the confidence of the people, and having full power over all spheres of government and administration and of the conduct of war;

(ii) Release of all political prisoners, detenus, establishment of democratic liberties, the withdrawal of all emergency legislation restricting freedom of speech, press, organization, movement and right to strike;

(iii) Policy of rapid industrialization and forcing the pace of industrial production to supply the demands of war and defence and the needs of the people;

(iv) Granting of workers' demands, the amelioration of the burden of debts, rents, and taxes, price control in their interest and the generous remission to flood and famine-stricken areas, special aid to increase food-grain production, to promote such handicraft production as required to replace shortage of goods due to war (e.g., handloom industry);

(v) No coercion of any type of war effort;

(vi) Equitable distribution of war burden.

(d) The contracting parties agree to run an all-India mass campaign of meetings and demonstrations, bringing home to the people the significance of the peoples' stage of the war, showing how the issue of India's liberation now becomes a part of the struggle for world liberation fought in common by the progressive forces of the world. The purpose of the campaign is to rouse the people to support the demands set forth above, the realization of which is essential for the people's effective participation in the war.

(e) The contracting parties agree to form stable joint ministries in the provinces pledged to support and implement as far as lies in their power the demands set forth above and to support the extra-parliamentary mass movement for their full realization.

Task of Congress Committee

12. The AICC calls upon the Congress Committees to resume normal activities of organization and of participation in the local bodies. The Congress Committees must in their respective areas undertake explanatory campaigns to bring home to the people the changed character of the war and the significance of the new policy adopted by the Congress. The Congress Committees must call upon the people and move them to support the main demand that the conduct of the war and of the Government must be entirely in the hands of the people's representatives, so that the country and the people's interests are effectively defended and the war conducted and won in a manner that furthers the cause of India's freedom. The attitude of the Congress Committees towards the war effort will be one of vigilance and co-operation so as to strengthen the hands of the popular ministries in their effort to make it more and more

popular and controlled and in the interest of the people. They must expose every case of bureaucratic coercion and fight for its elimination.

Conclusion

The AICC realizes that the policy which Congressmen and the Indian people have to follow in the grave and serious situation is an extremely difficult one. We have to realize that the struggle for our own liberation is to-day closely bound up with the war of world liberation which the USSR, China and the progressive peoples of Britain and America are waging in five continents and which is now knocking at our door. The reactionary policy of the British Government binds us down hand and foot and seeks to prevent us from participating in the war, from defending our own homes and interests effectively. The cause of the progressive peoples of the world, the cause of our own liberation, demands that we exert ourselves to smash this obstacle which prevents us from playing our rightful role. It would be unworthy of us as a great people unworthy of the traditions of our national struggle if we sat with folded hands and relied upon imperialism, upon the change of heart of imperialist rulers to unshackle us. We have to get up on our own legs and relying upon the inexhaustible strength of our people, put up a fight which cannot but gain for us the place of a free and equal combatant in the giant struggle which is shaping the destiny of mankind and our own. In this endeavour we will have the full support of the peoples of the USSR, of China, and of the advanced sections of the peoples of Britain and America.

---

[1] The AICC was scheduled to meet at Wardha on 15 January 1942 to consider the resolution passed by the Congress Working Committee at Bardoli on 30 December 1941. [For the text of the Congress Working Committee's resolution, see Document No. 72 in this Chapter.]

90. Conspiracy Cases Against Communists in Madras Province

(i) Madras Conspiracy Case [Extracts]

GOMs. No. 41 Public (General) Department, Dated 5.1.1942, Tamil Nadu State Archives.

In the Court of the Second Presidency Magistrate,
George Town, Madras
CC No. 2265/41 of George Town Court
CC No. 6/41 of Egmore Court

I, Sri V. Hanumantha Rao, BA, Second Presidency Magistrate, George Town, hereby charge you

1. Surendra Mohan Kumaramangalam
2. Subramania Sarma
3. Hanumantha Rao
4. Keraleeyan Alias Kunhappa Nambiar
5. P. Ramamurthy
6. C.S. Subramanyam
7. Umanatha Rao

as follows:

That you, between December 1939 and December 1940 (19.12.1940) at Madras and other places did agree with one another and with some persons known and with some other persons unknown, to do and cause to be done certain illegal acts to wit:

1. bringing into hatred or contempt, or to excite disaffection towards, His Majesty or the Crown Representative or the Government established by law in British India or in any other part of His Majesty's dominions; (36 (6) (e)) of the Defence of India Rules, 1939),
2 promoting feelings of enmity and hatred between different classes of His Majesty's subjects; (34 (6) (f)) of the Defence of India Rules, 1939),
3. influencing the conduct or attitude of the public or of any section of the public in a manner likely to be prejudicial to the defence of British India or to the efficient prosecution of war; (34 (6) (k)) of the Defence of India Rules, 1939)
4. instigating directly or indirectly the use of criminal force against public servants generally or any class of public servants or any individual public servants; (34 (6) (l)) of the Defence of India Rules, 1939),
5. encouraging or inciting any person or class of persons, or the public generally, to refuse or defer payment of any land revenue, tax, or other dues or amount payable to Government; (34 (6) (jj)) of the Defence of India Rules, 1939),
6. uniting into one organization the extremist elements in India, revolutionaries, labour and other unions with the object of setting up a state which would be controlled by the workers and peasants and thereby inciting directly or indirectly the commission of an offence punishable under Section 121-A, IPC; (34 (6) (m) of the Defence of India Rules, 1939),
7. making, keeping for distribution, and possession of documents containing prejudicial reports of the nature described in sub-rule 7 of Rule of the Defence of India Rules, 1939; (38 (a) (c), and 39 (i) (b) of the Defence of India Rules, 1939),
8. prejudicing the recruiting of or the attendance of persons for service, in any of His Majesty's forces; 34 (6) (d) of the Defence of India Rules, 1939), and
9. advocating commission of acts to impair the efficiency or impeding the working of Railways; (35 (i) (b) of the Defence of India Rules, 1939),

all of which are offences punishable under the Defence of India Rules, 1939, in furtherance of the revolutionary principles of Communist Party of India, an unlawful association, as per Government Notification No. F/7/S/34 dated 23rd July 1934—published in Fort St. George Gazette Part I dated 14.8.1934, and to do such other acts which may serve to facilitate the commission of the said offences, to conceal them and to prevent their detection, and all of you thereby committed an offence punishable under Section 120 (B) IPC read with Rules 38 (5), 39 (6), and 35 (4) of the Defence of India Rules.

Secondly, that you A-1, A-2, A-3, and A-4, in pursuance of the aforesaid conspiracy and in furtherance of the objects stated above were found without lawful authority or excuse on 19.12.1940 in House No. 79/3, Ramachandraier Street, Perambur, Madras, in the occupation of you all, in possession of documents detailed in Schedule A,—documents constituting prejudicial reports of the nature described in Sub Rule 7 of Rule 34 of the Defence of India Rules 1939, and you thereby committed an offence punishable under Rule 39 (6) read with Rule 39 (i) (b) and Rule 121 of the Defence of India Rules, 1939.

Thirdly, that you A-5, A-6, and A-7, in pursuance of the above said conspiracy and in furtherance of the objects stated above, were found without lawful authority or excuse, on 19.12.1940 in House No. 3, Singara Mudaly Street, Theagaraya Nagar, Madras, in the occupation of all of you, in possession of documents detailed in Schedule B,—documents constituting prejudicial reports of the nature described in Sub Rule 7 of Rule 34 of the Defence of India Rules, and you thereby committed an offence punishable under Rule 39 (6) read with Rule 39 (l) (b) and Rule 121 of the Defence of India Rules, 1939.

Fourthly, that you A-1, on or about 13.12.1940 in pursuance of the above said conspiracy and in furtherance of the instructions of the Communist Party of India, sent 500 copies of proletarian path (Tamil) (which is a prejudicial report) to Coimbatore through A-7 and you thereby distributed prejudicial reports and committed an offence punishable under Rule 38 (5) read with Rule 38 (i) (c) of the Defence of India Rules, 1939.

Fifthly, that you A-7, on or about 13.12.1940 in pursuance of the above said conspiracy and in furtherance of its objects abetted the commission by A-1 of the offence under Rule 38 (5) of the Defence of India Rules, referred to in count No. 4, in respect of the distribution of the Proletarian Path (Tamil) which is prejudicial report, and you, thereby committed an offence punishable under Rule 38 (5) read with Rule 121 of the Defence of India Rules, 1939.

Sixthly, that you, A-5, A-6, and A-7, between 14.9.1940 and 19.12.1940, made and kept for distribution the undermentioned documents* in No. 13, Singara Mudali Street, Theagaraya Nagar, Madras (in which house all of you were found together on 19.12.1940) and you thereby committed an offence punishable under Rule 38 (5) read with 121 of the Defence of India Rules, 1939.

*PE 349—Proletarian Path (Tamil) 6 bundles.
*PE 378—Communist for December 1940 (Tamil) 12 bundles.

All the above offences within my cognizance.
And I hereby direct that you be tried before me on the charge aforesaid.
Dated this 25th day of June 1941.

V. Hanumantha Rao
25.6.1941
Second Presidency Magistrate,
George Town, Madras.

Extracts from pages 191 to 193 of GOMs No. 41, Public (General) Department dated 5.1.42

Now the sentence to be imposed on each of the accused remains to be considered. A-7 the youngest among the accused is about 20 years old, and the age of A-5, the oldest, is 31 years. In ordinary criminal cases if offenders are of tender age possessing not much experience of the world and if they commit offences not realizing the consequences fully, they are dealt with leniently. In this case though the accused are comparatively young in years they do not deserve to be treated leniently. A-5 is a well seasoned political worker of over 10 years standing. A-1 and A-6 are people who had the benefit of western education in Cambridge and Oxford Universities. A-5 has good knowledge of Criminal Law Procedure. A-1 is a barrister-at-law himself. All the accused have joined the conspiracy to commit and facilitate commission of acts with a view to overthrow the British Government at the present juncture taking advantage of the fact that the Empire is preoccupied with war against Germany. Accused make no secret of their hatred and contempt for Government established by law in India. Day in and day out as they came to Court and as they left it—except on very few occasions when some of them did not attend Court being sick or for some other reason—accused shouted Communist slogans, at the highest pitch they are capable of. The slogan I could hear clearly is 'Communist Party Zindabad' which means long live Communist Party. They proclaim as it were from house tops that the Communist Party which is an unlawful association should live long. What for! To put an end to the British Rule. I refer to the shouting of slogans not to justify the sentences I am about the pass on the accused but to show the mentality and views of the accused. Deterrent sentences are called for in this case in view of the dangerous, deep-rooted and widespread character of the conspiracy. I accordingly pass the following sentences on the accused:

A-1 S.M. Kumaramangalam:

Count I.	RI for two years
Count II	RI for 18 months and fine of Rs 500 in default RI for six months.
	The sentences relating to Counts I and II will run consecutively.
Count IV	Rigorous imprisonment for two years.
	The sentence relating to this count will run concurrently with the above sentences.

A-2 Subramania Sarma:

Count I	Rigorous imprisonment for two years.
Count II	Rigorous imprisonment for 18 months.
	The sentences will run consecutively.

A-3 Hanumantha Rao:

Count I	Rigorous imprisonment for 18 months.
Count II	Rigorous imprisonment for 18 months.
	The sentences will run consecutively.

A-4 Keraleeyan alias Kunhappa Nambiar:

Count I	RI for 18 months.
Count II	Rigorous imprisonment for 18 months.
	The sentences will run consecutively.

A-5 Ramamurthy P.:

Count I	Rigorous imprisonment for two years.
Count III	Rigorous imprisonment for two years.
	The sentences relating to Counts I and III will run consecutively.
Count VI	Rigorous imprisonment for two years.
	The sentence relating to this count will run concurrently with the above sentence.

A-6 Subramanyam C.S.:

Count I	Rigorous imprisonment for two years.
Count III	Rigorous imprisonment for 18 months.
	The sentence will run consecutively.

A-7 Umanantha Rao:

Count I	Rigorous imprisonment for one year and six months.
Count III	Rigorous imprisonment for one year.
	The sentences relating to counts I and III will run consecutively.
Count VI	Rigorous imprisonment for one year.
	The sentence relating to this count will run concurrently with the above sentence.

(ii) Communist Conspiracy Case, Tirunelvelly, 1941 [Extracts]

GOMs. No. 63, Public (General) Department, Dated 6.1.42, Tamil Nadu State Archives.

Copy of letter No. Cl. 196/41 dated 18.3.41 from the District Magistrate, Tirunelvelly addressed to the Chief Secretary to Government of Madras

Sub.: Criminal Justice—Communist Conspiracy case—report—submitted.
Ref.: My report Cl. 196/41 dated 7.2.41
Govt Memo. No. 4521/41-1 dated 12.2.41 and
DO No. 7469-41-1 dated 11.3.41

A charge sheet has been laid against eleven persons for offences under Rule 38 (5), 39 (6) of the Defence of India Rules, Section 17 (2) of the Criminal Law Amendment Act and Section 120B (1) of the Indian Penal Code. A copy of the charge sheet is enclosed. The accused are all members of the Communist Party in India and they engaged themselves with others in a criminal conspiracy to carry out the communist programme. The case is pending trial in the court of the Sub-Divisional Magistrate, Koilpatti.

Of the 11 accused four persons, A. Ramachandra Nedungadi, V. Meenatchinathan Pillai, R. Veeraraghava Iyer, and P. Srinivasagam Pillai are detained in the Central Jail, Vellore under the orders of Government noted below:

A. Ramachandra Nedungadi	GOMs. 38/40, public (Genl) Deptt. dated 24.6.40.
V. Meenakshinathan Pillai	GO No. 121/41, Public (Genl) Deptt. dated 20.1.41
R. Veeraraghava Iyer	GOMs. No. 104/41, Public (Genl) Deptt. dated 17.1.41.
P. Srinivasagam Pillai	GO No. Ms. 171/41, Public Gl. dated 27.1.41.

The Sub-Divisional Magistrate, Koilpatti has reported that the Superintendent, Central Jail, Vellor wants the sanction of the Govt to send these persons to the Court of the Sub-Divisional Magistrate, Koilpatti for trial. I, therefore request that orders may be issued urgently by telegram to the Superintendent, Central Jail, Vellore to cause the production of the detenus before the Sub-Divisional Magistrate, Koilpatti at Tinnevelly on 21.3.41. The case is posted to 21.3.41 at Tinnevelly. A copy of this letter is being sent to the Superintendent, Central Jail, Vellore.

The charge does not require the sanction of Government as it does not fall within the scope of Section 196A CrPC.

Copy of Charge sheet in Palamcottah Station Crime No. 7/41.

Charge under Sec 17(2) of the Criminal Law Amendment Act V of 1908 as amended by the Act of 1937, Section 120B of the Indian Penal Code and Rules 38 and 39 of the Defence of India Rules.

Accused

1. Ramachandra Nedungadi
   S/o T.M. Ramavarama Nedungadi
   of Kothakurichi, Malabar
   (Thomas)—(Raju)
2. Baliah alias Mayandi Pandithan
   S/o Manikkar Pandithan
   Palamcotta. (Moni)
3. V. Meenakshinathan
   S/o Vasudeva Pillai
   Vikramasingapuram (Vanu)
4. R. Veeraraghavan alias
   R.V. Raghavan
   S/o Ramanujam Subramoniapuram
   alias Suppalapuram Sattur Taluk,
   Ramnad District (Kannan)
5. P.C. Rathinavelu Pillai
   S/o Chinnathambiah Pillai
   Pichivana St., Palamcottah.
6. Alagiri Thevan
   S/o Koppala Thevan
   Kalugumalai (Rajasekaran)
7. Isaianandham Pillai
   S/o Sudalaimuthu Pillai
   Pappankulam,
   Ambasamudram Taluk (Annatchi)
8. V. Ponnuthurai Chettiar
   S/o Veerabadra Chettiar
   Kailasa Oorni,
   Aruppukottai, Ramnad District
   (Ganapathi)
9. M.T.M. Somasundaram Chettiar
   S/o Madurai Malli Chettiar
   Maileri Chettiar,
   Sivankoil Street Aruppukottai,
   Ramnad District
10. P. Srinivasan
    S/o Perianayagam Pillai,
    Vikramasingapuram (Nesan)
11. Rajagopalakrishnan
    S/o Ramakrishna Thevan,
    Vasudevanallur (Rajandram)

The Accused noted in the margin are members of the Communist Party of India, which has been declared an unlawful association. Between the end of May 1940 and February 1941 they engaged themselves with others in a Criminal Conspiracy to carry out the Communist Party Programme, as set out in the 'Proletarian Path' in the Tinnevelly District and part of Ramnad District. In pursuance of the above criminal conspiracy, they formed a number of committees in various places of the above said districts and did the following acts:

(a) Prejudicial acts as defined in clause (6) of Rule 34 of the Defence of India Rules.
(b) were in possession of prejudicial reports coming under the purview of clause (7) of Rule 34 of the Defence of India Rules.

They are thus liable for:

1. An offence under Section 17 (2) of the Criminal Law Amendment Act V of 1908 as amended by the Act of 1937.
2. Section 120-B Clause (1) of the Indian Penal Code.
3. Rules 38 Clause (5) and Rule 39 Clause (6) of Defence of India Rules.

Copy of D. Dis. 196–41 dated 12.8.41 from the District Magistrate Tirunelvelly.

* * * *

Copy of D. Dis. 196–41 dated 12.8.41 from the District Magistrate Tirunelvelly addressed to the Chief Secretary to Government, Public (General) Department, Madras.

Sub.: Political Agitation—Communist Conspiracy case—Result—Reported
Ref.: Govt Memorandum No. 4521/41–1 dated 12.2.41.

All the eleven accused concerned in the case have been sentenced on 11.8.41 to the various terms of imprisonment given below the sentences to run consecutively. They were placed in the C Class.

Accused	Period of Sentence	
	Years	Months
1. Ramachandra Nedungadi	3	6
2. Baliah alias Mayandi Pandithar	2	3
3. V. Meenakshinathan	2	3
4. R.V. Raghavan	2	3
5. P.C. Rathinavelu	1	9
6. Alagiri Thevar	1	9
7. Issayanandan Pillai	1	9
8. Ponnudurai Chettiar	1	9
9. M.T.M. Somasundaram Chettiar	1	9
10. P. Srinivasan	2	3
11. Rajagopalakrishnan	1	9

91. Monthly Surveys Outlining Activities of the Communist Party of India (January–December 1941)

File No. 7/1/41, Home (Political) Department, NAI.

Secret

(i) Summary of Information Relating to Communist Party Activity

January 1941

1. General The headquarters of the Communist Party in Bombay and with it the central printing press, are the only functioning part of the illegal communist apparatus not dislocated or extensively disorganized by recent police action.

The latest arrests includes the BENGAL, PUNJAB, and MADRAS 'Secretaries' and several more UP 'underground' leaders. In MADRAS a clean sweep of all eight leaders of the Madras Communist Party, including S.M. Kumaramangalam, has provided material for a case under the Defence Rules read with Sections 117 and 120B IPC (abetment and criminal conspiracy) in the recovery of a huge quantity of illegal publications in English and local translations in Tamil and Telegu, together with typewriters and cyclostyle machinery for reproducing editions of the 'COMMUNIST' and the usual incriminating party correspondence. The latter includes an old letter from an outside district suggesting demonstrations with 'explosives' during the Viceregal visit to Madras last August. Also proof that a local lawyer, since arrested, was acting as the 'link between Madras and the Bombay central leaders.

The latter have yet to pay the price for all the mischief they have been plotting and planning in the name of 'communism'. One will now do so in the UP, where R.D. Bharadwaj has shared the fate of A.K. Ghosh and H.K. Mazumdar and been arrested in Cawnpore. With him were found Santosh Chandra Kapur the Cawnpore Mazdur Sabha leader, and Shiv Singh alias Nihal Singh an important Moscow—trained 'kirti' communist who has been prominent in the affairs of the UP Communist Party since his return to India from Moscow in 1935.

It is readily understandable therefore, why there is plenty of internal evidence of increasing alarm on the part of the central leaders—Adhikari, P.C. Joshi, and P. Sundarama Reddi (plus their few trusted helpers whose identity has yet to be fixed)—coupled with the realization that they have overestimated the 'revolutionary urge' of the Indian situation. In their own words: 'Revolution is not round the corner. We have first to build a party capable of organizing the revolutionary forces. The way is to perfect our own organization. There are no short cuts. We must prepare for a long-term battle with Imperialism'. This echoes advice from their foreign advisers who continue to labour under the delusion that the Communist Party in India will sooner or later dominate the Indian National Congress, when the communists will lead a successful mass movement harnessing the 'freedom struggle' for Independence with the discontent, both real and imagined, arising out of economic distress aggravated by the war, in combination of no rent no—tax campaigns, political strikes, and mass demonstrations. This belief remains unshaken despite the obvious discrepancy between programme and performance and the Congress leader's equally obvious determination to hold firm on control and to prevent any mass movement not of their own making and manner. When this much of the large volume of communist anti-war and other propaganda, and the leaders' efforts to recruit impressionable young men to a communist outlook on life, [,] [t] the paragraph which follows on the Nagpur Students Conference shows that these efforts are by no means unsuccessful and that the All-India Students Federation is now virtually a communist body and the communists' open or 'legal' platform.

2. The Bombay CPI Headquarters The Central leaders have issued instructions suspending all further correspondence by post which is of an incriminating nature, as well as cancelling existing post-box addresses. They have at the same time asked for new post-boxes and dak-collectory orders as follows: 'The noose is tightening and we don't want to give additional weight by keeping links which may break down. Provinces have been misusing our addresses. We do not know how far the damage will go. Keep documents and reports ready for us but don't post them'.

The latter suggestion of an extended Courier System is confirmed in subsequent instructions brought by courier from Bombay towards the end of December, announcing a monthly courier contact will personally visit each communist centre once a month, bringing with him the latest supplies of literature and party instructions, and collecting dak-accounts and subscriptions. For ordinary messages, which need not gear censorship, each province has been given a different Bombay post-box to write to in the hopes of minimizing the risk of disclosures. All 'party work' will to entrusted to couriers. Censorship may not therefore, for the time being at any rate, provided the same indication of communist plans as it has done hitherto.

3. CPI Publications There has been a very marked increase in the number of 'central publications' issued from Bombay, most of which have been printed with good type and on good paper. They include a 15th sixteen-page printed issued of the 'Communist'. Two pamphlets 'Marx on India', and 'A Contrast of Two Worlds—20 Years under imperialism and Socialism' reproducing extracts from R.P. Dutt's book 'India Today' published by Gollancz which as was anticipated, is regarded as the Indian communists' *vide mecum* and is to be made much use of as such. 'A Solider Hero' being the life of the Garhwali mutineer Thakur Chandra Singh, published in the name of Ramesh Chandra Sinha the former Secretary of the UP Committee. 'World Communists in Action—Fight Against War' forty cyclostyled pages purporting to give accounts of anti-war struggles and revolutionary activities of communist Parties throughout world. 'On Second Imperialist War and Our Tasks' giving a new instructional course of six lectures for the training of new party members ('cadres') explaining the programme of the CPI and the tasks of the communist party in India. And a four-page printed pamphlet 'Lenin's Advice to Students'.

Local translations of the 'Communist' and other local communist publications too numerous to mention, mostly cyclostyled, have come to notice in the Punjab (Urdu), Madras (Telegu and Tamil), Bombay (Marathi), Bengal, and Assam (Bengalee), Delhi and UP (Hindi). The January edition of the 'Communist' is under preparation with a view to its depstach from Bombay before 20th January, probably by courier or else by railway-parcel.

Single-sheet copies of the 'editorial' and leading articles from the December 'Communist' were sent in advance for 'party education' purposes. This method of showing an increased output of literature in order to conceal the weakness inside the communist ranks is likely to be repeated. There is even better cause for it this month.

4. Communist Party Finances The number of CPI 'central publications' once again draws attention to the party's finances. The question of funds has been touched on in several letters from the Bombay headquarters. There is the usual demand for arrears to be paid up and for fresh subscribers at the rate of a rupee each per month in return for the monthly 'Communist' and other printed and cyclostyled pamphlets, which includes postage or other delivery costs. The central leaders have at the same time admitted 'the new courier contact is going to cost us a fortune but there is no other way out'. In a letter last month to Madras appealing for money from a source which had previously provided ready cash for the publication of the 'Communist', they make it clear that their normal expenditure is Rs 100 a month. Another communication suggests an expenditure rate of Rs 2,000 a month.

It can be stated for certain that none of the provincial communist centres, with the possible exception of Bengal and Calcutta, has money. The subscriptions which with difficulty they collect (mostly from students) and the payments they send in return for the 'central publications' seldom exceed double figures and are invariably several months behindhand. In addition each local communist group is anxious to produce its own edition of the 'Communist' wherever finances and other circumstances permit. It is clear therefore that the small circle of intellectuals centred in Bombay calling themselves the Central Committee of the CPI, neither can nor do rely on provincial and local branches of the party for their money, and there is nothing to indicate they have any wealthy Bombay subscriber.

Although communist Party finances thus remain something of a mystery, there are good grounds for believing that the central groups is in receipt of occasional subsidies from abroad which are sufficient to keep both the 'illegal' publications going and to meet the central leaders' living and other expenses. Documents recently recovered in the UK have established it as a definite fact that this has been the case up till the outbreak of war, and that various appeals sent in the name of the CPI to the British Communist headquarters in London stressed the shortage of funds in India, adding for the benefit of the British communists' masters in Moscow, that success well attend the communist effort in India as surely as night follows day, if only a regular and larger subsidy is guaranteed. It is not possible to be more definite for the present, except to add that there is no indication of any subvention reaching India direct from Moscow, and that such money as the British communist leaders have sent does not exceed a few hundred pounds or go beyond the Bombay leaders [at] the Indian end, except in the shape of this large volume of printed matter.

5. The Nagpur Students Conference Three hundred student 'leaders' assembled at Nagpur for the sixth Annual conference of the Students Federation. History repeated itself and the 'spilt' which threatened to disrupt the student movement at the Madras Conference in 1938 owing to the rivalry between the competing Communist and Congress Socialist groups, and which dominated the Delhi Student Convention in 1939 presided over by Subhas Bose, completely disorganized the proceedings leading to the formation of two rival bodies each claiming the title of All-India Students Federation. Separate Conferences took place each of which passed its own resolutions. The communist section which was in a marked majority, was led by Doctor K.M. Ashraf of the UP and Hiren Mukherjee of Calcutta University. The rival Congress Socialist group led by M.L. Shah and Arabind Bose son of Sarat Chandra Bose (whose hostility towards Congress his son evidently does not share) supported Congress Satyagraha and demanded full obedience to Gandhi who alone knows how to achieve India's freedom. Division between the rival groups arose nominally over the question of M.L. Shah's visits to Wardha, and his acceptance of Gandhi's restrictions without consulting the Students Federation and subsequent failure to publish the resolution denouncing Gandhi's condemnation of Student strikes. Party rivalry was what really brought matters to a head, and the systematic and undeniably successful efforts of the communists to capture the Students Federation which has been under Congress Socialist control since its inauguration by Nehru at Lucknow in 1936.

Communist 'penetration' in the student movement has been gathering in strength during recent months practically in all provinces, but especially in Madras, the UP, and Punjab. The Communist Party planned an extensive 'student campaign' during November and December which contributed to the various demonstrations and students' strikes and led to a general atmosphere of indiscipline and restiveness. This in turn served to provide the communists with a majority in the Federation, thereby offering them a much needed legal platform as well as a profitable recruiting-ground. The Socialist members were evidently unaware of the Communists' success until a late stage, when they retaliated by seeking to disaffiliate the Bengal, Punjab, and Madras branches—the principal communist strongholds. The communists came to Nagpur having decided to force a split which would leave the militant student movement entirely under their control and made little attempt to conceal their more violent communist beliefs or to maintain any further pretence at a 'united front' with the Congress Socialists who were joined by the Bengal contingent owing allegiance to Subhas Bose and the 'Forward Bloc'.

The communists have since replaced M.L. Shah as General Secretary of the Students Federation by Muqimuddin Farooqui, the Delhi student who earned notoriety in November last when he was rusticated from Delhi University. They are planning to organize 'cells' in Colleges and Universities and to arrange for a wide distribution of communist literature amongst the student community. They have also issued instructions for the holding of student demonstrations in as many centres as possible on 26th January 'Independence Day' and announced an ambitious series of Student Conferences with K.M. Ashraf and other popular heroes presiding. The 'Student' published monthly from Nagpur has been adopted as the communist students organ.

Gandhi's keen interest in these developments is shown in his summoning of M.L. Shah to Wardha immediately after the Nagpur Conference. To this the communists replied by writing to Gandhi saying that Shah no longer represents the students of India, and abruptly stating that the Congress Socialists had caused the split in the student front by 'sectarian politics' and their threat to stifle the very existence of the student movement with rigid (Gandhian) restrictions.

6. Miscellaneous Early in December the Bombay directorate announced a new Cyclostyled 'Party Letter' to be issued once a week, presumably to replace the previous typed 'party circulars. The purpose of this new 'party letter' was stated to be to 'educate' party members in the latest party line and 'to supply a political lead to the provincial leadership in between the publications of the organ ('Communist') so as to strengthen the party organization.'

So far two 'party letters' Nos 1 and 2 bearing the dates December 1st and 9th have come to notice. These are in four parts. International politics (explaining the Soviet role); national politics (elaborating the editorial in the 'Communist'); party news, and party education containing lessons for new party members. The 'national politics' portion is uncommonly well-written, laying great stress on profiting from past mistakes so as to concentrate on building up a really effective communist organization in India 'Which alone can transform the situation' in the future. The portion dealing with international politics and the role of the Soviet is also, allowing for the angle from which it is written, unusually competently written and confirms the impression that the Bombay communist centre has helpers and advisers not necessarily confined to Joshi and Adhikari, and quite possibly of non-Indian extraction. Suspicion in this connection attaches to ACKROYD and SCHIFF of the UP but there may be others actually in Bombay.

Secret

(ii) Summary of Information Relating to Communist Party Activities

February 1941

1. General Apart from some further temporary success in converting impressionable students to a communist outlook, communist circles show clear signs of dropping spirits. Nevertheless communist literature of an extremely objectionable and inflammatory nature is still being fairly widely circulated, principally in Bengal, the Punjab, and Madras. The main Bombay Headquarters directing the secret (underground) organization and the communist's central press are also still intact and dangerous.

Open activity, except among students where the movement is anything but United and the prospects of serious mischief comparatively limited, is more or less at a stand still. Recent attempts to exploit restlessness on the GIP and other Railways over the question of 'war allowances' have not met with success; and communist-inspired Kisan agitation in rural districts in the Punjab, UP, Madras, and Bengal, has not gathered strength in the way the communists were hoping.

The scattered and subdued state of the Communist Party organization has been admitted in a new printed periodical called the 'Party Organizer', which the central leaders have issued during the month by post and courier from Bombay, stressing the need of reorganizing the Communist Party. This pamphlet is worth further mention, as few copies have so far fallen into police hands. It begins by detailing the heavy blows sustained during recent months in the break-up of 'provincial' headquarters in the UP, Calcutta, Bombay City, Punjab, and Tamilnad, Madras together with the loss of 'party records' and the exposure of post-boxes and local comrades 'identities, all of which are attributed to the weakness of the 'underground' organization and the inability of party members to work really secretly or to appreciate fully the 'illegal' and purely revolutionary or 'Bolshevik' role of the Communist Party under War conditions. It professes at the same time to welcome these widespread indications of 'police terror' as proof that Imperialism has correctly realized 'from where to expect the real and final danger', but this ingenious attempt to turn to advantage as something new the suppression of communism in India which has been Government's declared policy since 1934, does not even convince the writer for the next paragraph concludes: 'If the policy of the party is proving correct why should an organization grow weaker when all political factors are in our favour'.

The rest of the pamphlet details instructions for safeguarding the Communist Party as a secret revolutionary organization. A postscript is added telling communists not to fritter their energies or waste time thinking in terms of transforming (exploiting) Congress Satyagraha which the communist leaders now openly dismiss as a 'sham struggle' but to concentrate on building up the Communist Party in order to develop a mass revolutionary movement at some future and unspecified date. Mass revolution in other words remains the only sheet-anchor of communist policy which the leaders cling to with a compete lack of initiative, even at the risk of jettisoning the Congress 'united front'.

The Communists' Foreign Advisers on the other hand, fondly imagine that the communists in India form the most successful and loyal section of Congress anti-Imperialist front. This is shown by a leading article in a recent number of the official Comintern publication 'World News and Views' (formerly Imprecor) headed 'The Underground Struggle in India'—written by a young British communist who was in India until early in 1938 and managed to keep hidden his leading part in reorganizing and directing the communist movements in this country until comparatively recently when his papers were searched—which is loud in its praise of the 'technique of underground activity' as shown by the communists in India since war gave them their opportunity and the police the Defence of India Rules. It goes on to claim that the communists have greatly extended their influence over the Indian masses, and pays tribute to the period of reorganization in 1937–9 under a centralized (Bombay) leadership during the period of Congress administration when 'taking full advantages of the legal possibilities thus afforded the communist party was able to expand its legal work and to combine legal with illegal activities'. It concludes by seeking to differentiate between Gandhi's creed and Congress policy, in order to show that the communists have been the only determined and consistently anti-war' supporters of Congress anti-Imperialism, quoting from various of the Indian communists' manifestos—but noticeably—omitting the more violent portions—in support of this contention.

In relation to the Indian Communists' present position as an isolated sect of the Congress, which their own propaganda unmistakably shows them to be, they would be wiser to admit that they are their own worst enemies. The basic conviction of all communism however, is that it only needs a truly 'Bolshevist' party applying the correct tactics, to succeed. Hence the repeated Attempts to Reorganize the Party and the Campaign to Recruit Students, in respect of which the further moves of the Bombay Central Leaders require watching. The latter are said in the meantime to have been advised by R. Palme Dutt of the Communist Party of Great Britain to stick to the Congress 'anti-war' platform and not to antagonize Gandhi.

2. The Communist Party Organization Organized remnants of the communist organization are functioning in Bombay, Madras, Bengal, and the Punjab. Scattered units, more or less individual efforts, are endeavouring to make their presence felt in the UP, Bihar, CP, Delhi, and Assam. Communist influence in the youth and student movements is apparent in varying degree, in most provinces.

In Bombay, detailed examination of the records recovered during the successful raid on the Maharashtra and Bombay City Office last November has shown that over a dozen 'cells' were active in the Bombay neighbourhood. To a certain extent these have now recovered from the shock of this raid and the arrests which followed, and a new Bombay Committee—separate from the 'polit' buro or central headquarters under P.C. Joshi and Adhikari—has been formed with Dinkar Mehta, R.B. More, D.S. Vaidhya, Bhayyaji Kulkarni, and M.N. Valanju; all wanted communists, in charge. In addition D.S. Vaidya and R.B. More have formed a 'railway cell', which is responsible for a number of mischievous leaflets intended to cause discontent over 'War allowances' among GIP and other railwaymen. The more powerful Girni Kamgar (Red Flag) Union however, for reasons of its own, is anxious to prevent non-union communists gaining any hold over labour in Bombay, and is openly against strike agitation at present.

In Madras, the Malabar branch despite a number of useful arrests has continued to produce the 'Malayalam' and other illegal literature. In Andhra Communist leaflets and further issues of the Telegu 'Swatantra Bharat' have been aimed at arousing the peasantry, but without apparent success. The Tamilnad branch is more or less crippled by arrests and searches; only in Madura is there any sign of movement. Close collaboration between the Malabar police and the Franch police at Mahe led to a series of searches in Malabar and Mahe. In the former communist literature was recovered and several arrests made. At Mahe the French police discovered an unlicensed revolver together with some cyclostyle accessories which suggest, although there is no direct evidence of this effect, that Mahe has been used a centre for the production of illegal communist literature. The searches also disclosed that three Malayalees with communist connections had been enlisted in the Army. Dr K.V. Krishna and [a] Guntur communist intellectual have been active in Tamilnad and Kerala, chiefly amongst students. Presiding at the South Kanara Students Conference he condemned Congress Satyagraha as a feeble and ineffective performance and advocated a mass struggle against Imperialism. An agent reports that Dr Krishna also held a secret meeting in Calicut in which he showed his close interest in the Communist Party organization in Kerala.

In Bengali, a scattered 'district organization' remains in Calcutta, Barisal, Dacca, Rangpur, Hugli, and Dinajpur, and the Bengal Committee is sending regular instructions to a number of other districts as well as literature to Assam and Orissa including the Bengal 'Bolshevik' which has taken on a new lease of life. Literature has been seized in large quantities in Calcutta and elsewhere, but the main publication centre has so far eluded detection. There has also been an expansion of communist activity among the peasantry through Krishak Samities, making use of local grievances.

In the Punjab, the CPI organization is left in the hands of Harbans Singh Basi alias 'Rank' who according to a recent report was intending visiting Bombay to seek inspiration and advice. The Urdu 'Communist' continues to appear irregularly, but cyclostyled and no longer printed. The 'Kirti' (Sikh Communist) group is stronger and more active, and besides regular publication of the 'Lal Jhanda' in Urdu and Gurmukhi, appears to have joined forces with the remnants of the Punjab socialist Group in Rawalpindi, Lahore, and Delhi leading to joint publication of a Hindi 'Bolshevik' from Delhi, the circulation of which may extend to adjoining UP districts. The dangerous feature of Kirti-inspired propaganda is its constant appeal to Indian Army soldiers to join the ranks of the revolutionaries in the struggle for 'freedom'.

In the UP and Bihar the communists' burden has fallen almost entirely on youthful student shoulders whose efforts at present are confined in the distribution of such leaflets and other publications as they can obtain from Bombay or elsewhere.

In Assam an increased distribution of leaflets has been reported, and communist workers in the Surma Valley claim to have arranged shelter for absconders from Bengal. Successful raids in Gauhati have led to the recovery of a quantity of illegal communist literature at a local printing press and the question of prosecution is under consideration.

3. The Central Directorate Central leaders are shown to be still operating in the Bombay neighbourhood, where they also have first-class printing facilities as well as an electrically-driven cyclostyle machine at their disposal.

There has been a noticeable falling-off in interception of their postal correspondence, only eight letters during the month coming to notice. The probable explanation is that they are relying almost exclusively on the Courier System. In this same connection it is of interest that P. Sundarama Reddi one of the 'wanted' central leaders was caught at the Customs barrier, crossing the Goa frontier in possession of the latest literature and various 'party circulars' but unfortunately he managed to escape before his identity was fixed and whilst his papers were still being examined. It is possible therefore that the central leaders, especially P.C. Joshi, may be acting as couriers.

Only two new 'Central Publications' have come to notice during the month. The printed periodical 'Party Organizer' referred to in para 1, and a cyclostyled pamphlet 'The Sixth AISF (All India Students Federation) Conference.' Locally-produced pamphlets and other publications in the language of the locality, have been reported from Bombay (Gujrati), Punjab (Urdu, Gurmukhi, and Hindi), Bihar, Bengal (Bengalee and English), Madras (Malayalam and Telegu). It is also know that copies of the January 'Communist' in English and of various of the other CPI pamphlets detailed fast month (sic) were fairly widely distributed among the student 'contacts' who attended the Nagpur and other Student Conferences which have followed in such profusion, and have been furtively passed from hand to hand since.

4. Students and Communism The majority or communist section of the Students Federation with M. Farooqui of Delhi as its leading spirit, is shrinking into simply another aspect of the Communist Party organization. At the same disillusionment amongst students over the constant squabbles between the communist and non-communist groups, is reported from the UP and elsewhere.

There is really little to choose between the two groups, which merely reflect the rivalry between the Congress Socialist and the Communist Parties in exploiting immature youth in their attempts to bring about their own particular brand of revolution. Both groups have organized numerous 'days' and staged a number of conferences but without arousing much general enthusiasm. The Socialist Group called an All-India Students Convention at Benares at the beginning of February, presided over by Rajkumari Amrit Kaur who was sent by Gandhi to try to compose the differences in the student ranks, which are leading to awkward allegations by both sides which are evidently being taken seriously by the Congress leaders. The communists did their best to ruin the proceedings and held their own meeting in the Benares Hindu University which, with Cawnpore, is one of their principal and most vocal centres. Later a meeting of representatives from both groups was held with Rajkumari as president, but his led to nothing but recriminatory speeches followed by the usual statements to the press, and the gap between the two groups has further widened as a result. M. Farooqi and Professor Kalelkar of the Benares Hindu University represented the communists. An All-India States Students Conference and a Woman Students Conference was held at the same time, but neither were of importance. The Communists are however making efforts to arouse interest among girl students, and to encourage the formation of branches of the Students Federation in States' territory.

A meeting of the Communist section of the Students Federation is meeting in Delhi early in March 'to attend by M. Farooqi include Mrs Nergis Batliwallah (Bombay); S.N. Sehgal (Punjab); H.K. Thakur (Bihar); Sultan H. Muhammad, and A Gangadhar Rao (Madras); Prasanta Sanyal (Bengal); Romesh Chandra Sharma (Assam); H.K. Vyas (CP). M. Farooqi has in the meantime complained of the slipshod methods of working by provincial branches of the Students Federation, to remedy which and to provide a Centralized and co-ordinated movement, he has issued a series of 'Student Circulars' which are an exact parallel to the 'party circulars' issued by the CPI leaders. Emphasis is on the 'Central Office' (Delhi); monthly reports are called for; and an all-India monthly report will be issued in return, Farooqi and the other student communist 'connects' such as those mentioned above together with B.N. Mukerji of Nagpur, Amiya Das Gupta of Bengal, Gauri Shankar Bhattacharji of Assam, and T.K. Chaturvedi of Cawnpore, are evidently intended to provide the 'illegal' or open platform of the Communist party. Their degree of contact with the 'underground' CPI leaders is not yet established, but it seems probable that Mrs Nergis Batliwalla is the 'link' between the two, and has succeeded Radhey Kishen Gupta of Cawnpore who filled this rule before his rest.

5. Miscellaneous Following the release by the Madras Government of six students from Annamlai University on their entering into a surety for five hundred rupees against their future good behaviour, and their agreeing to live in certain specified place and not to engage in communist or other subversive politics, some of the remaining communist students still under detention decided among themselves to give any undertaking which would secure their release, with no intention of honouring it. There reasons, which they recorded in writing for one another's benefit, were that by remaining in jail they could serve no useful purpose and that their release would encourage other students and without it 'all our efforts will be in vain'.

There have been several clear cases of letters being smuggled in and out of detention jails together with communist literature. For instance there is positive information that R.D. Bharadwaj, Shiv Singh, and R.K. Gupta following their recent arrest in Cawnpore have succeeded in smuggling out of Cawnpore jail letters intended for their successors. There have been similar reports implicating Allahabad, Nasik, and Vellore jails, as well as the Deoli detention camp. In the latter connection a UP report states that Ajmer is intended to be made use of as a central point by reason of its position between the UP, Punjab, Delhi, and Bombay, and the presence in Deoli of many of the communist leaders from these provinces.

Secret

(iii) Summary of Information Relating to Communist Party Activities

March—April 1941

1. General Apart from local manifestations of communist-inspired agitation among the peasantry in Malabar, the Central Provinces, and a section of the Bihar Kisan Sabha, and amongst labour in the Communists' old stronghold the Cawnpore Mazdur Sabha which is threatening strikes over 'dearness allowances', the communist effort is at present confined to the Central Leaders' Frantic Efforts from Bombay to save themselves and the party's remaining guilty secrets from the police and to a loosely-defined campaign to spread communist ideas among students and the youth movement in general so as to provide badly-needed recruits for the Communist Party.

The keynote is the safeguarding followed by the strengthening of the Party. At the same time the war situation is leading Communists and other extremists once again to plan on an ambitious scale for instance, plans are under discussion for a representative gathering during the forthcoming CSP Conference at Patna at the end of this month, to review possibilities of a 'united front' of Communists and other extremist groups rallied round the red flag of revolution. Labour areas also report that local communist agitators are using the scare of air-raids spreading to India to induce workers to desert from their factories. How this fits in with the Communists' other plans has not yet been made clear, but the problem is capable of developing into a major one if any raids on this country take place.

2. Communist Plans Attempts to rally students on 'Security Prisoners Day' and the recent 'CP and Berar Political Conferences' in Nagpur form part of the leaders policy to concentrate on strengthening the Communist Party. Instructions for holding 'Kisan and Labour Conferences' so as to popularize the communist case through the exploiting of local grievances are part of the same programme, the leaders' intention being 'to mobilize the masses and to inspire them with confidence—for instance and fight for war allowances, the fight against the effects of the fall in price of land commodities, and protests against repression.'

These instructions are emphatic at the same time that every precaution should be taken to avoid arrest, and that anti-war propaganda and other actionable behaviour must remain temporarily in the background on the grounds that Safety First is essential if the party is to survive. To quote their own words again 'There is no question of our being at the head of the masses, there is no question of our being able to develop partial struggles into a revolutionary mass movement, unless we are able to fulfil the elementary requirements of the revolutionary vanguard to organize the Party'. This decision seems due, in part at any rate, to the influence of the many communists now in Jail who have been spending their time discussing plans and passing their ideas, in many cases in written form, to their friends outside. The failure and restrictions of the Congress Civil Disobedience campaign are added reasons for a more distant policy.

Meanwhile further arrests of local organizers, notably in Tamilnad and elsewhere in the Madras Province accompanied by numerous successful searches of provincial and local 'party headquarters, have added to the Communists' confusion and have prevented their plans meeting with any marked success. Every second man is suspected of disclosing information to the police, either through treachery or incompetence, and the Central leaders have not attempted to conceal their exasperation even from their closest followers.

3. Communist Funds Shortage of funds is another decisive factor, both on the part of the closely-guarded and hitherto fairly affluent central nucleus in Bombay as well as amongst local groups. This has led to renewed attempts—so far without success—to obtain money from foreign sources, Malaya and Ceylon being specifically mentioned in a recent cryptic message from Bombay to a Madras contact with previous experience in both these countries, who was however arrested the day after its receipt. The Central press in Bombay, and subsidiary presses in Madras, Bengal the CP, and Punjab are shown from internal evidence to be hard put to it to finance their propaganda, but the non-stop stream of illegal communist leaflets and pamphlets continues, although on a diminished scale except in the case of the Central press.

A recent 'Polit Buro Circular' stated in relation to the finances of the latter: 'Please remember that we need 1500/- per month merely to keep going'. It goes on to emphasize the urgent need of collecting regular subscriptions from party-members to keep the Central Directorate functioning. Another circular issued during March details a stock of nearly 6,000 back numbers of CPI publications which are available where these instructions came from, namely Bombay, including 800 spare copies of the January 'Communist'. These figures accord with previous estimates of the Bombay centre's expenditure on propaganda costs—The March issue of the 'Party Organizer' is even more explicit in a leading article headed 'May Day Call for 10,000 rupees', appealing to all party-members to rally in support of the CPI by providing a party fund for immediate use of the Central Committee. 'Our immediate need is ten thousand rupees for the rest of 1941. If you can't mobilize this sum the All-India centre of our party may have to liquidate itself. For lack of cash must we sink or stop work'. Further attempts to raise money both internally in India and from the Communists' foreign contracts are therefore to be expected, if these appeals mean what they say.

4. Propaganda and Party Instructions As stated above the average monthly output of 'central publications' has been maintained from the Bombay headquarters—the exact whereabouts of which continues to remain a closely-guarded secret. The latest publications include two further issues of the centrally-edited 'Communist' dated February and March respectively; a second issue of new 'Party Organizer' series also dated March; a pamphlet 'March on India' reproducing extracts from R.P. Dutt's banned book 'India Today'; and a pamphlet intended for a students 'AISF Conference Nagpur'. All the above were apparently printed at the same press, but on noticeably cheaper paper than previous issues. Distribution has been very secretly done, mainly through Couriers, and in smaller quantities than formerly.

Recoveries made during searches in Madras have also shown that the series of cyclostyled and typewritten 'Polit buro circulars' and 'Party Letters' from Bombay, which for over two months have not come to notice in the course of postal censorship, have continued nevertheless to be sent to the various Provincial centres at approximately weekly intevals. An examination of these documents indicates P.C. Joshi's and Dr Adhikari's drafting, and also reveals several clear hints of irregular contact between the CPI and the British Communist Movement (in respect of Comintern instructions). As regards the former, it is beyond the capabilities of any two pairs of hands, even of such convinced and experienced Communists as Joshi and Adhikari that the drafting, printing, and dispatch of this unending stream of propaganda, in addition to the direction of the party, could all be done by them alone; the conclusion is therefore that they have several trusted and well qualified helpers in addition to two or three press-workers running the Communists' Central press and cyclostyling.

The identities of the latter are unfortunately not yet known and the secrets of the Bombay CPI 'Central Office' have so far been singularly well kept. Recent disclosures—notably in Calcutta and in relation to the unexpectedly extensive CPI organization in Malabar and other parts of Madras—have demonstrated the Communists ability to keep their secrets hidden. At the same time this secrecy is enforced on them largely against their will and deprives them of the 'mass' character which is essential for the success of their movement. With the present tendency for the party to re-establish itself on a firmer but more 'underground' basis, and to resort to a purely defensive role in open activities, the movement is nothing if not limited in scope, and to this extent is under control. So long as the All India Centre remains intact however, whether in Bombay or elsewhere, the danger of reorganization is present and anti-communist measures must clearly be reckoned as incomplete. It is at the brains of any organization that it is most necessary to strike.

5. Students and Communism Owing to examinations there has been less activity among students, but the quarrel between the 'communist' and 'Non-Communist' groups has continued each side blaming the other for 'disruption'.

The consensus of recent reports shows that Communist influence among students has spread beyond recognition compared with the pre-war period, and out of all proportion to the numerical strength of the Communist Party. This does not necessarily mean that all student sympathizers' are active members of the Communist Party, but the danger of their drifting into this at a later stage is obvious. The number of young Indians at Universities or still in their colleges from their parentage and circumstances should play a useful part in the country's future but are instead being converted into useless members of society, if nothing worse, is causing considerable anxiety in non-official as well as official quarters, although the former have so far shown themselves singularly helpless in contributing towards any remedy. At the same time it is not only the existence of the communist organization in India which is to blame; the number of Indian students from well to do homes who during the two to three years have returned to India from studies abroad, having failed to pass their examination but heavily infected with result of systematic coaching in foreign communist organizations—is perhaps the major cause of communist infection. This aspect is at present under consideration.

Mr Gandhi meanwhile has continued to intervene in the affairs of the ALL INDIA STUDENTS FEDERATION, in his efforts to extend his control over students. The Communist Section however has the whip-hand in all the more vocal centres (with the exception of Bengal where the non-Communist group is anything but pro Gandhi) and will not easily be persuaded to loosen its grip.

Proposals to reconcile the rival factions in the AIS Federation have been put forward by Professor S. Kalelkar of Benares Hindu University (who is a communist sympathizer in secret) and have been publicly approved of by Gandhi. These provide for the appointment of an 'impartial tribunal' of five members to consider the origins of the dispute, in accordance with a formula which neither side was prepared to accept at the Benares Students Conference. The tribunal has yet to be appointed. In the meantime the Communists have decided among themselves that they will not agree to the Nagpur 'political resolution' (condemning Satyagraha and asserting the students' right to strike and to act independently) being reversed, and have also stipulated that both groups should be treated on an equal footing pending negotiations. The M.L. Shah Group on the other hand persist in calling the Communists the 'minority group' which they are not, and have also demanded that they should dissolve their 'rival federation' before unity talks begin. Disputes have also arisen over the handling of the Federation funds and reconciliation seems very far from being achieved on present indications.

M. Farooqi the Delhi 'General Secretary' of the Communist Section has written a long letter explaining the history of the dispute to Gandhi, in which he accuses the latter's two nominees M.L. Shah and Ansar Harvani of having deliberately provoked the split for party purposes and condemns their whole attitude as 'political dishonesty'. Gandhi's reply records his 'painful interest' in these allegations, and reiterates his wish merely to see all dissensions amongst students removed.

6. External Direction from the Comintern Below are quoted certain secret instructions recently received by the Central Committee of the Malayan Communist Party from the Southern Bureau (Hong Kong) of the China Communist Party (the Comintern's intermediary for the Far East). Apart from the references to India (c.f. recent attempt to establish contact between Indian and Malayan Communists referred to in paragraph 3) these are of considerable interest in illustrating the manipulation of the Communist movement in Russian interests.

The background to the instructions is that towards the end of last year the Malayan Communist Party, whose strength largely depends on the local Chinese Community, decided to concentrate on an anti-Japanese 'national salvation' front and to drop its former anti-British agitation. This sudden change in policy was necessitated by such international events as Japan's adhesion to be Axis, American and British loans to Chungking, and the re-opening of the Burma Road. The Comintern's subsequent instructions reasserting in such unambiguous terms that the main plank of the Communists' programme is an anti-British one, provide a timely reminder that the Moscow leopard is not willing to lose its spots. The Communist Party is recognizable as the instrument in that particular country of the foreign policy of the Russian Government. Its actions are determined by Moscow, and they change only as Moscow orders. The clearest thing which emerged from the complex shifts and evasions passing for the current 'party line' of the Communist International, is that the Communists will make no contribution to the common effort to destroy the advance of tyranny, and that all communist plans—if allowed to develop—aim at sabotaging the British war effort, regardless of the consequences of Nazi victory.

'The Imperialists' War is fast developing and there is every indication that it will become protracted. The two opposing forces—Germany, Italy, and Japan on one side, Great Britain and United States on the other—are making feverish preparations for a decisive battle. The atmosphere in the Near East and the Balkans is daily growing more intense, while an outbreak of hostilities in the Far East is imminent. It appears that this war will spread to every corner of the world and that every nation will be involved. Soviet Russia, however, is exerting every ounce of her effort to stay out, but of course, without neglecting to be fully prepared for any eventuality. Since the signing of the Tripartite Pact, Japan has been anxious to close the 'China Incident' in order to advance south. Such a plan threatens Malaya and the Dutch East Indies, and is certain to invite armed intervention by Great Britain and United States. Thus the clash of arms in the Pacific is only a matter of time.

'At such a time the revolutionary movement of the anti-Imperialist and anti-Fascist peoples all over the worled and of the anti-Imperialist nations for independence has been making steady progress under the leadership of the Communist Parties. Malaya is one of the places where the revolutionary movement is progressing. In the present circumstances the attention of the Imperialists in the Pacific has been focused on Malaya. On the one hand the British Imperialists, in order to maintain necessary war supplies and to make all necessary preparations for war, have made frantic claims on the people politically as well as economically. On the other hand, the Japanese in their southerward drive, have made Malaya and Netherlands East Indies their objectives. The former has caused a storm of opposition from all faces [forces?] in Malaya because of the hardships imposed, while the latter has heightened the anti-Japanese feeling among the people, especially the Chinese. Thus the whole of Malaya is filled with a revolutionary atmosphere. But the time for action has not yet arrived.

'As the Imperialists' war drags on, the dominating strength of the British Imperialists is bound to weaken. All the oppressed races should seize the opportunity to extend the anti-Imperialist War Front, and the Overseas Chinese should strengthen their anti-Japanese Front so that in future both can use the same slogan—*'Drive the British and Japanese Imperialists out of Malaya'.* We must realize that it is going to be a long and bitter struggle. Therefore the principal task of the Malayan Revolutionary Party is to gather full strength, and to educate and train the Working Committees of the Party in order that they may lead the masses and identify themselves with the Chinese Revolution and Indian Revolution in their struggle for victory. First of all we must try to eliminate all obstacles in order to pave the way for final victory. It is obvious that the Overseas—Chinese besides constituting the largest population in Malaya form the biggest and the most progressive force in the Malayan United Front. This Front consists also of two other nations—the Malays, who form one-quarters of the population but are very backward, and the Indians who occupy a more important position than the Malays owing to the influence of the revolution in India. Therefore the Overseas-Chinese should fully consolidate their strength and be the leaders of the struggle for independence. It is necessary for us to devise a precise and clear policy applicable to practical conditions in Malaya, and to check our work with experience gained from revolutionary activities in China.

'Soon after the outbreak of war among the Imperialists, the Malayan Communist Party issued slogans such as 'Opposition to the Imperialist' War' 'Opposition to British Imperialism' and 'Drive the British Imperialists out of Malaya', and decided to lead the masses in strikes, in order to extend political mobilization. As far as these principles are concerned, the Malayan Communist Party has not introduced any wrong ideas. In fact, it has, within that period, succeeded in:

(a) Initiating extensive strikes of 120,000 workers (from November 1939, to the following May).
(b) exposing before the masses the sins of the British Imperialists;
(c) establishing the Malayan General Labour Union; and
(d) succouring the labourers, and other things.

On the other hand, the Malayan Communist Party has adopted a wrong policy in:

(a) assuming that the activities of the bourgeoisie of the labouring the peasant classes were the activities of all classes in Malaya;

(b) assuming that a certain disastifacation among the landed-proprietors against British Imperialism was a large scale revolt of landed—proprietors of all nations; and
(c) assuming that a united front of all races can be obtained by strikes alone. This is a serious mistake and the outcome has been the disorganization and isolation of the Party and the arrest of a great number of Working Committee members.

'The Malayan Communist Party has investigated these questions and has declared its willingness to change its working methods. We would point out that, unless all comrades study these questions carefully, no effective changes can be made. At present, the task of the Malayan Communist Party is to make itself a political party, representing the peoples' anti-war, anti-Imperialist and anti-Japanese viewpoint and to co-ordinate the anti-British Imperialist and anti-Japanese efforts. The United Front should only employ such concrete slogans as:'anti-Malayan Patriotic Fund', 'anti-taxation', and 'anti-economic penetration' and should demand freedom to stage anti-Japanese campaigns, with the sole object of uniting the masses. It is not yet the proper time openly to use such slogans as 'Drive the British out of Malaya' and 'Defend Malaya'. The extensive Malayan youth activities are peculiarly necessary and significant. A careful estimate should be made of the importance of the educated classes in relation to the Malayan National Emancipation Movement. Opposition should be shown to any tendency to neglect its importance. Therefore, it is of paramount importance to gain control over the activities of the Overseas-Chinese youths and students. It is no easy matter to tackle the student problem as students are being suppressed in every way and it is no longer safe to organize associations of students of the leftist clique. As far as youth activities are concerned, we should on the one hand, try to establish additional local or cultural organizations, and on the other, form cells to develop the education of the students. The Malayan Communist Party should realize the necessity for such organizations and do its best to organize and direct them.

'It is however impossible for our revolution to be victorious without a stable organization. In view of the approaching crisis in the war, it is essential that the organization should be further stabilized and made more secret. An organization to be reliable should be administered by two Working Committees, one for open one for secret activities. The lower stratum of the organization should be formed with factory workers, students, and troops. The defences of the factory citadels should be strengthened. The system of direction of this section should also be improved upon. A concentrated form of leadership appears to be the most appropriate. Work, instead of devolving on one person, should be equally divided among the responsible members; and it is essential to enforce strict discipline in activities. Efforts should be made to intensify activities among the minorities especially the Indians, but at the same time no pro-British traitors should be allowed to mix with them. Therefore, only those Committee members, who are allotted this task, should devote themselves to the promotion of these activities. It is also necessary to intensify theoretical education in Marxism and Leninism, to raise the Party's standard of theoretical knowledge, and to introduce political discussions and any other means that will place the Party on the road to health.'

(iv) Summary of Information Relating to Communist Party Activities

May 1941

1. General Little has come to light during the past month about immediate Communist plans. The energy of the CPI is still mainly expended on the reorganization of the 'underground' party, the recruitment of students and youths, and the collection of money to make good the recent losses caused by the seizures in the United Provinces, Madras, and Bombay. The exact sources of CPI funds and the total sum possessed still remain obscure and full details of the response to the Central Committee's May Day' appeal for the collection of Rs 10,000 is yet not available. One indication of the correctness of the contention that the Bombay central group is short of money is that No. 3 (Vol. III) of the 'Communist' is published as a joint issue for the months of April and May 1941. Furthermore there has recently been a noticeable decline in the volume of Communist literature issued both by the CC of the CPI and in the Provinces. Bombay Communists have, however, just been able to collect Rs 700 by subscription and another Rs 1,200 by staging a Marathi drama for—ostensibly—the Detenu Relief Fund.

2. Communist Policy and Plans Relating to Detenus Communists are now paying much attention to the reorganization of their groups within various jails and detection camps. Party Letter No. 27 issued from the CPI headquarters, Bombay, lays down the policy to be observed by Communists both in prison and outside and further describes the 'brutal and inhuman treatment' meted out to security prisoners in the detention camps at Deoli and Nasik and in Indian Jails. Prisoners are asked not to start hunger-strikes yet because mass opinion outside the jails has so far not been mobilized (for which of course Congress is blamed), and the party Committees are ordered to maintain contact with the incarcerated, and to raise through the good offices of the Civil Liberties Union or independently, a campaign against the maltreatment of all political prisoners.

These instructions imply the establishment of contact by party workers in jails with their associates outside. That contact has been effected and is being maintained has long been known and Communist intrigues have been assisted by the inadequate supervision imposed by some officials over the less trustworthy members of their staffs. Deoli detenus are reported to have been in communication with Punjab Communists to whom directions have recently been conveyed. However, with the exception of the collection of subscriptions for detenus in Bombay, there is—despite the fact that many 'Protest' meetings have been held—little evidence of widespread public sympathy for these political 'martyrs'.

The internment of about one hundred and ten Communist detenus in the Vellore Jail is viewed with some concern by Madras officials and, in order to counter the possibility of the sudden release of a compact and well-organized machine to spread communism after the war is over, arrangements are being made by the Madras Government to split up this dangerous concentration of agitators.

3. Local Communist Activity Local Communist activities have like wise been limited and confined to Bombay city, Bengal, Madras, the Punjab, and the United and Central Provinces.

Bombay Communists attempted to organize a strike of Victoria drivers in late April but this effort failed owing to the communal riots. Similarly their efforts to stage a one-day strike on 'May Day' were frustrated by the imposition of bans on all meetings. They also engineered the Tata Oil Mills strike which led to the arrest of two agents of the Central Committee.

In Bengal the externment of some active workers and lack of money have considerably reduced Communist party activities in the industrial areas, but the Bengal Committee is now considering new methods to extend their control over labour in addition to carrying on propaganda among the peasantry against the Jute Restriction Scheme.

The Madras Provincial Government have recently declared the Karshak Sangh (Kisan Sabha), the Peasants' Association and the Peasants' Union in Malabar and other affilitated bodies to be unlawful associations. The Sangh was being used by the Kerala Communist Party (which operated under the cover of the former Kerala Congress Committee) to spread Communist and anti-war propaganda and incitement to acts of violence. It was under this cover that the riotous demonstrations on 'Protest Day' (15.9.40) were organized in Malabar by the Kerala Communist Party.

In the Punjab efforts have been made by Harbans Singh Basi (recently appointed by the Central Committee as General Secretary of Punjab Communist Party) to form a new provincial Communist Party which, it is forlornly hoped by the Deolli detenus, will at last unite those left wing political groups that for years past have warred with one another. To their credit, however, it must be admitted that representatives of the Kisan Party, Students Federation, TUC, CSP, and Lahore Congress had prepared to work in unison for a mass security prisoner's agitation. Otherwise, dangerous as the plans of the Kirti Kisan Party and some District Kisan Committees are, to strengthen their subversive influence over members of the Indian army, there is no sign of any definite progress in the revolutionary world. Such recent instances of Sikh discontent in the Army as have come to notice do not give grounds for anexiety, and are based mainly on the desire of individuals to avoid service overseas. However, these instances do call for the most careful attention to the grievances of sepoys and to the possibility that the so-called injustices are being exploited by Communist acquaintances.

Some interest is being taken by Cawnpore Communists in the labour demands for dearness allowances and a new Nihalist Party composed mainly of students has been organized for the purpose of distributing Communist literature. One recent report shows that in accordance with a secret Communist circular the Cawnpore Mazdoor Sabha members have been discussing plans to be followed to bring about a general strike in July.

There has been a serious strike affecting two important Nagpur textile mills and this has been followed by some discontent among the textile workers of Badnera. The Nagpur strike was started off by local Communists but the leadership was quickly snatched by R.S. Ruikar who is still in control, and who has now threatened a province-wide mills strike from the 1st June. In Amraoti the Communist group has planned a two month programme for the organization of local labour and the students. Elsewhere isolated srikes have been fomented or exploited by Communist Party supporters but nowhere has there yet been clear proof that the increasing labour unrest is in any way the result of central Communist direction. In fact one present indication is that CPI influence in Bombay over the important Girni Kamgar Union in being undermined by R.S. Nimbakar and others.

'May Day' was observed as usual in many of the leading cities but nowhere were there any remarkable demonstrations.

4. Students and Communism M.L. Shah's opposition to the communists' compromise formula continues and his demand still is that the communist group must be disbanded before any negotiations can be commenced. In the Students' Unity Convention, convened at Calcutta late in April by the Forward Bloc Section of the Bengal Provincial Students Federation, attempts were made to take advantage of the present split in the ranks of the Students. The Convention was, however, a failure. Meanwhile Shah has hinted that this incessant squabbling is too much for him and has suggested that he takes a holiday.

Secret

Note on the Peoples' Convention and the Communist Party of Great Britain

Thanks to the Press Adviser and censorship little has been permitted to appear in the Indian Press about the Peoples Convention held in London in January last. In fact about all that the Indian Student of communism has been able to learn yet about this Convention, its proceedings and resolutions, has been obtained from the Moscow Radio and from a published account in the 'Communist' (Vol. III, No. 1) for February, 1940 [1941]. Many references to this Convention are, however, now filtering through to the Indian public in British and American newspapers and revival of interest in the Convention may therefore he expected. In the 'Communist' it is emphasized that the bans placed on the 'Daily Worker' and the 'Week' are proof that the policy of the Communist Party of Great Britain is meeting with success and that in Britain growing antipathy to the war is finding expression in organized mass resistance by the working classes. In Peoples' Convention, it is contended, clearly demonstrated that the struggle against war and for a Peoples' Government is gathering force in England. These comments and further details about the Peoples' Convention published in the 'Communist' are, of course, very far from being unbiassed and were culled from the Moscow broadcast which honoured the Conventions' proceedings with one of the fullest commentaries ever devoted by the Stalin regime to a foreign political movement. But available evidence does tead to show that the Soviet has agreed to launch an active campaign to undermine Britain's war effort and it is now evident that this campaign is being prosecuted.

Organized by Harry Pollitt, D.N. Pritt, Ben Bradley, Rajni Palme Dutt, and others the Peoples' Convention was run by the Peoples' Vigilance Committee (which is equivalent to saying the Communist Party of Great Britain) with the main object of testing popular support for the Vigilance Committee's aim of establishing a People's Government, and achieving a Peoples' Peace, through, of course, the co-operation of the workers of the Axis countries. Held in the first week of January, the delegates included, in addition to many of the better known British communists, Krishna Menon. The programme of the Convention (which is reproduced as an appendix) was duly endorsed and speakers emphatically discoursed upon the alleged grievances of their own trades, exaggerating the poverty among the miners, the dangerous working conditions within the factories, the chaos in the engineering branches of industry, and the inadequate wages paid to labour in view of the rise in living costs. The net result of the Convention seemed to be that delegates would return to their factories and there try to extend their influence by agitation for better wages and conditions until a majority of workers would elevate a new party to parliamentary power which would carry out the Convention's programme in full. Several references were, of course, made to India in view of that part of the programme which demanded 'Freedom for India and the right of all colonial peoples to determine their own destiny' but only Krishna Menon's speech deserves mention here. He declared that first of all he desired to register the complete solidarity of the Indian workers with the object of the Convention. He regretted that he had received no messages from his Indian supporters and for this blamed the British Government, 'Which claimed to be fighting to preserve democracy', for having imprisoned thousands who would have been glad to send fraternal greetings to the Convention delegates. After declaring that Indians realized 'that there is no such thing as democratic Imperialism, any more than there is such a thing as a vegetarian tiger', he concluded by advocating the alliance of British and Indian workers to destroy Imperialism and end tyranny.

Innumerable Press opinions on this Convention and on British communist activities have been published in the last few months from which it can be said that British public opinion is summed up in the phrase that 'Communists are attempting to cut Britain's life-line'. At a meeting of Scottish Trade Unionists Mr Bevin, Minister of Labour, was in December last stung into declaring to his communist interrupters: 'You have been instructed to try to create the impression that the working-class of this country is disunited. We know that in the next few months' enemy strategy is going to be two-fold—he is going to talk peace, and he is going to prepare while he is talking peace, as he did after Munich. While he tries to kid us about peace, while he gets his friends in this country to shout peace—the most deadly weapons are being prepared to cut the life-line of this country'. In the house of Commons on the 19th of December Mr Herbert Morrison, the Home Secretary, declared that the Peoples' Convention is being organized by the Communist Party, who probably hope by means of such a gathering to gain some support from loyal people who have no intention of impeding the war effort, and are unaware of the ulterior motives for which the conference has been organized.... I must hold myself free to exercise, whenever the need arises, the power conferred upon me by Defence Regulation 39E, and it would be wrong for me at this stage to fetter my discretion by announcing before hand whether use will or will not be made of that power....I will, therefore, confine myself to saying that one of the disadvantages of prohibiting the meeting is that such a course would not be likely to contribute the enlightenment of those whom the organizers hope to beguile.' Again Sir Patrick Dollan, Lord Provost of Glasgow, a leading Scottish Socialist, in a Press interview made the definite charge that 'The Communists are concentrating on the Clyde to impede the Empire's war effort by exaggerating factory disputes, causing confusion and discouragement by criticizing all social services, anything which detracts from concentration on the war efforts.'

The policy of the Communist Party of Great Britain, since the outbreak of war, has led to several defections and the loss of valuable personnel to the Party but encouraging as these signs of communist weakness are they give no grounds for the adoption of any complacent attitude. It is now well realized, particularly in England, that in securing the internal disruption of European countries Hitler had employed simultaneously the forces of the extreme right and the extreme left. This policy Hitler has attempted to apply also to England, but fortunately it seems doubtful whether there is now in England any right wing organization which could be used as the spear head of the 'fifth column: At any rate those obsecure British 'quislings', whose activities achieved them jail and momentary notoriety during the first winter of the war, have latterly ceased to attract attention. But the same is not true of the extreme left. The Communist Party in England, though small, has the disproportionate strength of an organized body of fanatics and the fact must therefore be faced that in this war even in England there is a disciplined body of malcontents, and wittingly or unwittingly (probably the latter) these communists are Hitler's agents. Even at this critical moment they are throwing doubt on the Government's honesty of purpose and accusing them of representing the interests of the rich and calling on the people to fight them. This is the tenor of the resolution passed at the Peoples' Convention and thus, whether the British communists know it or not, they are playing into Hitler's hands.

The recent action taken by His Majesty's Government against the Communist Party's 'Daily Worker' (necessitated by its flagrant attempts to foment opposition to the prosecution of the war and its pernicious propaganda to cause unrest in the fighting forces in England) and against other communist publications shows that it is not considered safe to leave this handful of zealots to be smothered by public ridicule and obloquy. Nevertheless though these precautions have had to be taken there seems to be little likelihood at present of this potential 'fifth column' developing in England into a serious menace. Furthermore, the English communists have suffered severely from the defection and criticism of some of their ablest supporters, e.g., Victor Gollancz, Harold Laski and John Stratchey. The last, one of the few English communists of first rate caliber, is a lucid and powerful writer whose pen is now being employed to demonstrate with the utmost clarity that the Communist Party's present policy is wholly mistaken and that it is destructive of all that the communists professedly hold dear. It will, therefore, be no surprise if English communists dwindle in numbers and enthusiasm.

But can the same be said about India?

In India in so far as communists constitute an organized body of trained revolutionaries they are, and will remain, a very real danger. What they say or write and what heir English friends may say or write is largely immaterial for provided it is anti-English it matters not how illogical, unreasonable or untrue it is, it will feed their passion to get even with the English by hearing ill of them. Therefore it is sure to meet with favourable and even enthusiastic reception. Moreover, capitalist Imperialism in India will remain in genuine target for abuse from the communists of this country. This point has, as ever, been recently emphasized in the labour unrest of today and any decrease in this form of the propaganda cannot be anticipated.

To those, therefore, who wish to lay in a stock of anti-communist ammunition Victor Gollancz's book—'Betrayal of the Left'—is recommended. The defection of Gollancz (a Jew) from the communist Party of Great Britain may be discounted by many honest communists but his arguments that the communist policy since October 1939, if successful, could bring nothing but slavery and ruin to the people of Britain—and that the communist Party leaders are guilty of 'revolutionary defeatism', that the proposal to turn the Imperialist war into a civil war, cannot be achieved, as Lenin realized, without desiring the defeat of one's own Government and without facilitating this defeat and that the result of turning this Imperialist war into a civil war will bring about not an internal socialist revolution and general socialist peace but a victory for Hitler—cannot be easily countered.

Appendix
Document of the Month
Resolution of the People's Convention, 12th January 1941

1. Policy and programme

We, the 2,234 delegates of organization representing 1,200,000 workers assembled in the first meeting of the People's Convention in London, on 12th January 1941, DECLARE OUR CONVICTION

that the present Government represents the interest of the rich;

That only the unity and active struggle of the working people in their own interests, and the establishment of a People's Government truly representative of the working people, can save them from the disasters and sufferings which the war is bringing upon them.

WE ACCUSE THE GOVERNMENT AND THE RULING CLASS OF THIS COUNTRY

of bearing a heavy responsibility for this war by their entire policy since 1918, carrying on the war for aims of reactionary class interests and world domination, contrary to the interest of the people, placing all the burdens of the war upon the people, and forcing down their standard of living, while piling up profits for their own class; destroying democratic and trade union rights; fostering racial hatred amongst peoples; opposing the just democratic demands of India and the peoples of the British Empire;

neglecting equate air-raid protection of the people; promoting hostility to the Soviet Union; and generally pursuing policies which are leading the people to catastrophe.

WE PROCLAIM THE RIGHT OF THE COMMON PEOPLE

To a full, free, and happy life, which can only be won if wars are brought to an end by uprooting their causes, and if our labour and skill are devoted to producing the things we need and distributing them among all.

WE THEREFORE RESOLVE TO FIGHT FOR THE FOLLOWING PROGRAMME:

1. To raise the living standards of the people, including wages, pensions, compensation, insurance and unemployment allowances, and the restoration and extension of educational facilities.
2. Adequate ARP, bomb-proof shelters, and prompt and effective provision for all the needs of air-raid victims including re-housing and full and immediate compensation.
3. Restoration, safeguarding and extention of all Trade Union rights, and democratic rights and civil liberties.
4. Emergency powers to be used to take over the banks, land, transport, armaments, and other large industries in order to organize our economic life in the interest of the people.
5. National Independence for India, the right of all Colonial peoples to determine their own destiny, and the ending of enforced partition of Ireland.
6. Friendship with the USSR.
7. A people's Government truly representative of the working people and able to command the confidence of working people throughout the world.
8. A People's Peace, won by the working people of all countries, and based on the right of all peoples to determine their own destiny.

WE CALL on all working men, women, and youth, on all professional workers, on all those interested in peace and progress, to unite to fight for this programme in order by their solidarity and action to impose their majority will on the rulling class and secure their own Government.

WE CALL on all Labour, Co-Operative, and Trade union organizations, and all mass organization of the working people, to unite their ranks and combine their endeavours to organize this common fight for the victory of this programme.

WE PLEDGE OURSELVES, the delegates of the People's convention here assembled, to spread the message of the People's Convention, and to organize and extend the mighty movement of the people for the realization of this programme.

AND WE APPOINT AND MANDATE our National Committee, the elected representatives of the people, to carry forward the campaign, build up the organization of the movement, promote mass demonstrations, and all other activities in accordance with the programme; recall the

People's Convention, and in all ways lead the struggle to the victory of a People's Government and a People's Peace.

LET THE PEOPLE HAVE CONFIDENCE IN THEIR OWN STRENGTH THE PEOPLE ALONE CAN SAVE THE PEOPLE.

On the Activities of Labour Leader Ruikar

Copy of DO No. 1290–870-A/Con. dated 31st/1st August 1941 from C.M. Trivedi, Esquire, Chief Secretary to the Government of CP to H.C. Prior, Esquire, Secretary to the Government of India, Department of Labour, Simla.

Will you kindly refer to your DO Letter No. L. 876 dated the 28th June 1941, on the subject of Mr Ruikar's activities in this province? I am desired to say that Mr Ruikar's present activities are not, in the opinion of this Government designed to prejudice the war effort, although it is possible that, in some cases, they may have that effect and that if they did, this would not deter him from his plan of action. He is a politician with local and even wider ambitions; by profession he is a pleader with a small practice. His primary concern as a labour union leader is to secure for himself the maximum share or publicity in connection with industrial disputes which arise in the province but he is not always able to control the strike he has orgnaized. The weakness of Mr Ruikar's position is due, in part, to his inability to control the extremist sections in his party, and, in part, difficulties arising out of the rather difficult attitude adopted generally by employers towards trade union activities. It is not in the opinion of the Provincial Government correct to say that Mr Ruikar was interested in preventing a settlement of the recent strike in the Nagpur Textile Mills. He is, no doubt, whatever his motives, intensely anxious to promote the cause of labour and does not mind the protraction of a strike or industrial unrest, if he finds that his unionists are not receiving what he regards as a fair deal. At the same time, he suffers from the opportunism of the trade union politician and hesitates to press his recommendations of a compromise if the workers show themselves reluctant to accept its terms justifying a resumption of work. His stand in the recent strike in the textile mills in Nagpur was rather on the side of moderation than of communism or class hatred. In fact, he appeared to be battling all along with the extreme communist elements in the textile union, and whenever he had to lend his support to the strike it appears to be less than whole-hearted and intended essentially to maintain his position of leadership in the textile-union and in the labour world generally, his politics are no doubt anti-capitalist and also, so far as he identifies British Imperialism with capitalism, anti-British (though he allowed his son to enlist as a Private in the Central Provinces Urban Infantry Territorial Force in November 1940). On the declaration of the Russo-German war he issued two statements to the press condemning Hitler's attack on Russia and urging all Socialists to stand by Soviet Russia in this crisis. The statements further welcomed England's abandonment of her former policy of hostility towards Russia and her determination to help Russia in her fight against Fascism. The statements went on to urge that England would find a free and independent India a tower of strength and help. Recent indications have been that he is using his influence in left-wing circles in the same direction.

(v) Summary of Information Relating to Communist Party Activities

June 1941

1. General The CPI has achieved nothing during June but party instructions have been wilder and more alarming than usual. P.C. Joshi is reported to have paid a clandestine visit to the Central Punjab (and to be there still) whilst Dr Adhikari is said to have gone into Tribal Territory with Abdulla Safdar in the hope of establishing direct touch with the Comintern and thereby repairing the damage done by loss of indirect contact through the CPGB.

An explanation of this apparent lull in communist activity may be found in the growing anxiety of the CPI to save its now reduced cadre with the ultimate object of utilizing its members as a 'Fifth Column' in the event of a Soviet invasion of India. This presumption finds support in a recent CPI circular (said to have been issued to all Provincial Committees) in which certain preliminary instructions (connected with the possible invasion of India by the Soviet) are laid down, and in which emphasis is placed upon the necessity of working in strict secrecy and of abstaining from participation in Satyagraha movement. Further the Provincial Committees have been promised for as long as possible continued direction from the Central Committee. Pending India's invasion Party members are advised to implement the main items in the CPI programme (to start no rent campaigns and strikes and to suborn the armed forces), and in addition, to collect such secret information (useful from the view point of the Soviet), as they can, about the location of the armed forces, ammunition depots, factories, forts arsenals and Government buildings (for eventual destruction), and details of coasts, harbours, aerodromes, radio station, and other things. Party members are also asked to control the masses and check any communal disturbances which may break out. The last mentioned instructions in keeping with the CPI's attitude towards the recent communal disturbances which have been denounced by communists as the outcome of a preconceived plan of the British Government vested interests. Further evidence in support of this view is to be found in a printed leaflet in English headed 'An Appeal' issued in Bombay in connection with the communal riots. Similarly another leaflet headed 'Appeal of the Communists to the Ahmadabad public' published in Gujarati which was distributed in the Ahmadabad mill area blames the Government, the Congress and other communal organizations for the riots.

Recently, however, and indication of communist interest in Iraq and of their wish to raise the Muslim world against the British Government, by conducting anti-British and pro-Rashid Ali propaganda, came to notice in Kerala (Madras). Though no other instance is yet forthcoming Communists may be expected to exploit any such opening to work up Muslim resentment against British war moves in the Near East. The Russo-German developments have of course shocked communists the world over and a fall in CPI intrigues whilst the leaders readjust their policy to current events may therefore be expected.

3. Local Communist Activity Since the break-up of the peace-time Provincial Communist organization, communist activity in the Provinces has been directed by almost independent local groups. Such groups, (whose actual strength it is difficult to gauge but which can be said to consist mainly of second-rate agitators with very little mass support) continue incessantly to make a nuisance of themselves in the following areas:

Labour field: Bombay City, Gujarat (Ahmadabad), Maharashtra (Poona, Saswad, Parinche, Klhapur, Barsi, Sholapur), Andhra (Guntur, Bezwada, Nellore, Anantapur, Kistna, and East Godavery Districts), Tamilnad (Madras City, Coimbatore, Tinnevelly, Tanjore, Madure, Salem, and Arcot Districts), UP (Cawnpore, Lucknow Agra, and Jhansi), Bihar (Hazaribagh, Shahbad, Jamshedpur, and Jharia), CP (Nagpur, Jubbulpore, Amraoti, Ajola, Badnera), Assam (Gauhati, Kamrup, Dibrugarh, and Lakhimpur), Also in Bengal.

Student field: Bombay City, Maharashtra (Poona, Amalner, Karnatak, and Satara), Andhra (to a small extent in Guntur, Bezwada, Nellore, Anantapur, Kistna, and West Godavery districts), Tamilnad (Madras City, Coimbatore, Tinnevelly, Tanjore, Madura, Salem, and Arcot Districts), Malabar (Palghat and Mangalore), UP (Cawnpore, Lucknow, Allahabad, Benares, Agra, Meerut, and Jhansi), Punjab (Lahore, Rawalpindi, and Amritsar) Orissa (Cuttack), Bihar, (Patna and Monghyr), CP (Nagpur and Amraoti), Assam (Sylhet, Gauhati, Kamrup, Dibrugarh, and Lakhimour). Also in Bengal.

Kisans: Maharashtra (Khandesh, Barsi, and Kaira Districts), Malabar (Calicut, Kottayyam, Chirakkal, Palghat, Nadapuram, Nilambur), Orissa (Cuttak), CP (Wardha and to some extent in Jubbulpore), Bihar (Gaya, Bhagalpur, and Monghyr), Assam (Gauhati, Kamrup, Dibrugarh, and Lakhmipur). Also in Bengal where the Kisans are largely under CPI influence. In the Punjab there has been some intensification of village propaganda and numerous meetings were held in several districts (Amritsar, Lahore, Ludhiana, Kangra, Gurdaspur, Rohtak, Multan, Montgomery, and Shahpur).

4. Labour Still no evidence is forthcoming to show that the Central Committee of the CPI contemplates calling a general strike in the near future and in its absence all talk recently heard about a proposed general strike in India and in the CP textile Industries may be regarded as being of purely local origin. The chances of widespread trouble further reduced by the recent arrests of sixteen labour leaders in Bombay. Nevertheless there has been much open communist activity in the labour world. In the Central Provinces the strike of the Empress and Model Mills, Nagpur, threatened to extend to other mills in Akola, Badneram, Burhanpur, Ellichpur, Phulgaon, and Hinganghat and to develop into a province-wide textile strike commencing from the 26th June under the direction of R.S. Ruikar, President of the Council of Action. However in view of the Provincial Government's agreement to appoint a Textile Enquiry Committee, the Textile Union has called off the strike in the Nagpur mills. In Madras City a threatened strike of motor drivers was averted. In Bombay Communists took an activist part in the Lever Brothers Ltd. Strike and they have also been conducting the strike, in the Swastike Oil Mills. Action against those responsible is contemplated but meanwhile the arrest of sixteen local labour leaders under the Defence of India Rules will, it is hoped, give labour a chance to settle down. In Bengal Communists appear to be concentrating more on the peasants and students than on labour.

5. Deoli Detenus A report from the Deoli Camp shows that at first here was the usual Party factionalism among the communist security Prisoners. However, unity has now been brought about among all those professing allegiance to the CPI—thanks to the efforts of S.V. Ghate, the Madras Communist. This agreement has resulted in a merger of nearly all the Kirtis, Communists, and Socialists of the Punjab, but UP and Bihar Socialists still stand aloof. The heterogeneous cliques comprising the 1st class prisoners had formed a 'corporate Committee' for the sole purpose of airing their day-to-day grievances but with the arrival of the Socialist leaders J.P. Narain and Mohan Lal Gautam a separate Socialist group (with a total strength of forty-two against the hundred and forty in the communist group) was formed with Gautam as the spokesman. The failure of the recent hunger-strike initiated by this group has weakened socialist prestige in Deoli.

(ii) On their own the Communist bloc has also been threatening a hunger-strike on the questions of classification, the ban on common association, the discriminatory diet rates, the appointment of a judicial enquiry, etc. For the time being however no such development is likely.

(iii) In Deoli there are two camps for the two classes of prisoners. Camp I (Class one prisoners) contains 104 detenus, mostly of the UP but including 18 Punjabis, Camp II (class two prisoners) holds 93 detenus; 70 Punjabis, 12 Biharis, 7 of NWFP, and other things.

The detenus have organized a Central Committee in each camp, with a representative in charge of sections of about 20 detenus.

Camp I Central Committee	**Camp II Central Committee**
*B.T. Ranadive.	Sher Jang.
*S.S. Batliwala	Dhanwantri.
*S.A. Dange.	S.V. Ghate
*Z.A. Ahmad.	A.S.K. Iyangar.
Mahmud-uz-Zaffar	Ram Singh Datta.
Sohan Singh Josh	

* are temporarily incarcerated in the Ajmer Jail.

A third camp is to be opened shortly for newcomers.

(iv) Outside the camp, the Punjab Civil Liberties Union has, in pursuance of CPI instructions, been espousing the cause of the Deoli Detenus and attempting to mobilize public support by holding meetings, demonstration, and processions during 'Detenu Week'—16th to 23rd June. The detenus demands of release or trial and the creation of a single class for all detenus have also found some support from the Punjab Provincial Congress Committee, the Punjab CSP, Lahore Students, the Punjab Kisan Committee, the All-India Forward Bloc, and now the General Secretary of the All-India Students' Federation is attempting to win the support of other nationalistic political organizations for this end.

6. Communist Literature The Central Committee has only published the 'Communist' No. 4 for June 1941 some local branches have continued to issue their pamphlets (that is, in Bombay, Ahmadabad, Punjab, Kerala and Delhi). In Kerala several Party Letters, in Malayalam, were secretly distributed. These Letters condemn 'Police repression' and call upon the public to support the demands of the Deoli detenus, and other things. In Delhi, the 'Communist' in Hindi, Vol. III No. 2 dated 26th March 1941, has recently made its appearance. In the Punjab the 'Lal Jhanda' was distributed in the Jullundur district and anti-war posters have been discovered in Dera Ghazi Khan.

7. Student There has been no unusual students political activity. The Karnatak Students' Conference was held at Bijapur on 12/13th June 1941 under the presidentship of Jamnadas M. Mehta MLA but this was organized by M.N. Roy's followers. It was a poor show, thinly attended, and the President, whose address was mainly a criticism of Congress policy, stressed

India's duty to support Great Britain in the War. Aid to Britain was the subject of the main resolution passed.

(vi) Summary of Communist Activities in India

July 1941

1. General There has been little open Communist agitation apart from the Cawnpore Textile Strikes, which quickly collapsed with considerable damage to the Mazdur Sabha leaders who instigated them.

Beneath the surface, however, there has been much suppressed excitement in the Communist underworld, as well as indications of divided opinions over the Anglo-Soviet alliance. Whilst the Communist Party regards the alliance with evident misgivings and has found increasing difficulty in formulating a policy to keep pace with Soviet developments, the Congress Socialists claim that neither Russia's entry into the war nor the alliance with Britain makes any difference to India's attitude. M.N. Roy and his followers on the other hand suffer from no such delusions or hestitations, and have redoubled their efforts to organize an anti-fascist 'popular front' campaign with a 'fight-the-war' programme. This appears to have met with more success than Roy's earliest attempts to win rank and file supporters, and Royist propaganda is at present undoubtedly a considerable thorn in the Communist flesh.

2. Indian Communists and the War So far as India is concerned the Communist Party's attitude has undergone no change whatever. The war is still regarded as an 'imperialist war' and the Communists' duty to obstruct and impede the war effort has been reaffirmed in a pamphlet dated July 1941, issued over the name of the Polit-Bureau of the Communist Party of India (Section of the Communist International), surreptitiously circulated throughout the party's various strongholds. From this it is only necessary to quote the following unambiguous declaration:

'Our attitude towards the British Government and its imperialist war remains what it was. We must continue, nay intensify our struggle against both. We can render really effective aid to the Soviet only as a free people.'

No Comintern instructions have yet reached India, nor has there been any indication (apart from the shedding of the theme of 'World Revolution' from Moscow broadcasts) that the Communist International itself has abandoned its basic policy of 'revolutionary defeatism'—convert imperialist war into civil war—to which all communist parties have been committed since the Soviet invasion of Poland. In any case the Communists in each country must be judged by their own words and deeds rather than by the frequently changing protestations of a distant and, so far as India is concerned, extremely shadowy parent organization. Moreover the indications have for some time past shown that decisions as to party policy have been left much more in the hands of each Party's Central Committee than was the case formerly. This is partly due to the obvious difficulties of communication, and also to the fact that a great amount of the Communist 'Classics' deals specifically with the party's conduct in relation to 'imperialist war'.

Beneath a tedious volume of revolutionary-sounding phrases and expressions of verbal sympathy with Soviet Russia, the Communist Party of India's true object stands clearly exposed—to exploit for partisan purposes and their own selfish and illegal ends the life-and-death struggle in which the British Empire is engaged against the background of India's demand for independence.

The demand voiced by certain Civil Liberties Unions and other near-Communist bodies for the release of Communists and to legalize the Communist Party of India, merely because of the Anglo-Soviet agreement, is the thin end of a wedge whose only purpose would be to set free unprincipled political adventurers obsessed with a blind hatred of every existing form of constitutional government. The Communists declared aim is a revolutionary anti-war movement. In simpler words this means violent civil war, as their own secret instructions make clear beyond all doubt. Communist interest in the war, and in those taking part in it, is solely in so far as it will assist in possibility of the collapse of Russia, is amongst the reasons the Communists have themselves given for intensifying subversive agitation with a view of furthering internal revolution in India. In the circumstances the case for detaining the leading Communists in jail hardly needs re-emphasis.

3. The Central Directorate Dr Adhikari, P.C. Joshi, and P. Sunderama Reddy continue to supply the party's central direction from their secret hiding places. Their main energies are still expended on attempts to reorganize the underground party, the recruitment of students to provide badly-needed recruits, the collection of party funds, and the safeguarding of their own security. They are also able with the aid of certain but at present unidentified outside helpers to produce the monthly 'Communist', edit Party pamphlets, laying down party policy, and to produce a regular series of 'Party Letters' and other detailed instructions for party members in the various provinces, with whom they manage to maintain irregular but nevertheless direct contact.

Indications continue to point to Bombay being the party's main centre as well as the location of the central press, secret records, and numerous other party secrets which the central leaders have so far managed to preserve intact with unusual skill. Reports during the month show that Joshi and Adhikari have been moving about between Bombay—UP (Allahabad, Cawnpore, Meerut)—Nagpur—Calcutta, and that P.S. Reddy is in close touch with S. Indian Communists from his home province Madras. Adhikari is said to be assisted in Bombay by M.N. Valanja a member of the reorganized Bombay Committee (BC) of the CPI, and his contact with outsiders is thought to be though an Indian nursing sister in Bombay who has filled the gap caused by Mrs Nargis Batliwalla's arrest. Another female supporter Mrs Suhasini Jhambekar is suspected of being in charge of secret printing arrangements in Bombay.

Bengal reports indicate that P.C. Joshi's arrival has been expected in Calcutta to consider the reorganization of the Bengal party, and also possibly in connection with certain maneuvers regarding a proposed 'united front' between the CPI and the Bolshevik Party of India (BPI or all-India title of the Bengal Labour Party of Neharendu Dutt Mazumdar) with the object of forming a joint Committee on the issue of help to the Soviet Union. It has also been reported that Joshi is contemplating shifting the Central Committee's office from Bombay to Calcutta, but no convincing reasons for this chance are given or is there any confirmation of it.

Of considerable interest is the fact that secret information reaching the UP Special Branch which successfully led to the arrest in Aligarh on 16th July of the important terrorist absconders Kesho Ram Pande and Muktinath Sahi (suspects in the recent Ghazipur train dacoity) also led to the recovery from their possession of a collection of recent communist literature along with HSRA membership forms as well as arms and ammunition. Other documents recovered in consequence of their arrest point to secret courier contact between Kesho Pande and Joshi and

Adhikari in Meerut. It seems clear that the Communist Party in the UP were hoping to win over Kesho Pande and his terrorist group, and that Kesho Pande was to work in the Congress Socialist Party so as to obtain full information of the CSP on behalf of the Communist Party.

4. Publications Two new editions of the 'Communist' dated June and July (Vol. III Nos 4 and 5) have come to notice during the month. In addition the following three pamphlets and one book have been distributed.

1. 'On Communal Riots'.
2. 'Red Strategy in the Finnish War 1940' (extracts from the Military Correspondent of Hopkinson's News).
3. Soviet-German War—Statement of the Polit Buro.
4. History of the Soviet Union (Bolsheviks).

(This latter is a reprint of the book published by the Communist Party of the Soviet Union in 1939 as a standard 'text book' for the education of all Communists. It is priced four rupees, and this indigenous edition shows that the CPI has access to at least one fully-equipped printing press. Its price is doubtless intended to swell the party funds.)

The chance arrest of a Madras courier also led to the recovery from him, in addition to the above publications, of PARTY LETTERS Nos 38, 39, and 40, marked 'for members only'.

The first of these included a detailed report on the recent Ford Motor Workers' Strike in Bombay, blaming the Communists for not having had any hand in this and criticizing the Congress Socialists' weak handling of it in the following unguarded manner.

'We cannot afford to stop with so-called non-violence and work within the orbit of legal persuasion. It becomes necessary to intimidate and even to do something more at times.'

Party Letter No. 39 dated 17.6.41 is of more than usual significance in that it reproduces in full the original 'PROVISIONAL STATUTES OF THE COMMUNIST PARTY OF INDIA (Section of the Communist International)' recalling the fact—vide Appendix III to 'India and Communism' 1935 Revised Edition—that this was drafted in 1934 and published in the Official comintern publication 'International Press Correspondence' (now 'World News and Views'); and explaining that a new edition has become necessary as the old one is out of print. A footnote cautions each provincial Committee to prepare translations of this 'basic document' in the language of its province for use by party members adding: 'It should be noted this is not a document for free circulation. (It is however, read with the 'Draft Platform of Action of the CPI, useful documentary proof of the violent aims and intentions of the Communist Party in India).

(vii) Summary of Communist Party Activities in India

August 1941

1. General There has been no change in the Communists' 'anti-war' attitude, but developments since the Anglo-Soviet alliance and the growing realization of the implications to India of Russian defeat in the Ukraine, have obliged them to adopt a modified twofold 'party line'. The energies of the party, and of the various Communist-controlled organizations, have accordingly been divided into two separate channels of action.

The new two-fold policy is governed by the ingenious theory of 'two-wars'—the war on the Eastern front which Soviet Russia is fighting and which must be supported; and the war between Britain and German in the West, which is an 'imperialist war' and must therefore be resisted and obstructed. It consists on the one hand of the Communists seeking to organize a 'solidarity campaign' through Soviet Aid Committees and the collection of funds aimed at creating popular agitation—voiced through Civil Liberties Unions, Kisan Committees, and Student organistions—for the release of Communist prisoners, and at providing an opportunity to spread Communist doctrines (and recoup party funds) without fear of the consequences. On the other hand, the Communists plan to continue their anti-imperialist campaign by exploiting workers' and peasants' discontent and encouraging strikes and other disturbances, working through their secret party organization. These two lines, the one open and the other secret, are parallel and simultaneous. The Communists' perverted intelligence is incapable of seeing anything contradictory in a policy aimed at helping the Soviet Union by harming its ally Britain.

Thus after the initial period of confusion and uncertainty, the Communist position has crystallized something as follows: Britain is fighting an 'imperialist war' and the Soviet Union a 'just war'. The Communists support the latter only and their own 'anti-fascist front' (which is distinct from M.N. Roy's 'fight-the war' front) in order to assist Soviet Russia, but not to help Britain to victory. They have pushed the anti-war campaign into the background, but are far from having renounced it, and regard the new turn of events as presenting a good opportunity to restore lost strength and rally fresh supporters.

In general the Communist view is coloured by the idealistic love of the 'land of Socialism' and a hatred of its antithesis, the British Empire. This mental attitude may be altered temporarily by a desire for assistance in the defence of the Soviet Union, but the hatred of the Communists for the British Empire is fundamental and is to be seen throughout their propaganda and in all such activities as they are capable of. Documents recently recovered betray the Indian Communists' bitter disappointment and surprise, that Russia has become Britain's ally and not Britain's enemy. In the Punjab they have even professed to see in Japan's threat to India a chance of anarchy leading to the overthrow of orderly government, and the realization of their own self-seeking ends. The Jugantar (terrorist) party in Bengal is more explicit in stating: 'If there was a fight between Germany and Russia India would have sided with Russia unreservedly, but when Britain is involved in a war we must aim at the defeat of Britain.' Communist policy is and must always remain subversive and anti-British, however the party propagandists may attempt to disguise the fact. The Anglo-Soviet alliance has merely deprived them of one of their best arguments, and forced the two-fold policy referred to above.

3. CPI Activities in Province Secret information from various provinces reveals further recent instructions from the central directorate (BOMBAY) for the reorganization of provincial branches of the CPI, and attempts by the latter to improve inter-communication, which in the UP and Bihar have broken down altogether.

In the PUNJAB the former 'provincial committee' has accordingly been dissolved and a new Committee formed consisting of MAHMUD ALI as General Secretary, RAMESH CHANDRA, GURMUKH SINGH, MIR DAD KHAN, and Miss PERIN BHARUCHA. The new committee claims to have reached common agreement with the KIRTI KISAN (Baba or Sikh Communist group). As a result the Punjab CPI will take over publication of the 'Lal-Jhanda' and the Urdu 'Communist' is to cease and in return the joint accounts will be handled by Punjab CPI This temporary alliance between two loosely-defined rival groups whose ceaseless squabbles have been the main distinguishing feature of Punjab left-wing politics for year past, has probably been influenced by the 'Communist consolidation' inside Deoli detention jail, where the 'Kirti' and CPI leaders detained as Security Prisoners claim to have formed a 'United Front'. Were this to last beyond the jail walls, which is unlikely, and were it to imply the requisition by the CPI of the extensive Ghadr funds from ex-India which the Kirti Sikh group have hitherto jealously kept in their own hands, which is even more unlikely, the alliance would give the CPI access to ready cash which the Central leaders have long coveted, and lack of which has long been their major weakness. In relation to contact between the Punjab and the CPI Centre, it is significant that RAMESH CHANDRA AND PERIN BHABUCHA, both prominent in the student movement left for Bombay a few days before the organized student disturbances at the Bombay University Convocation.

A report sent by the scattered remnants of the BIHAR CPI to Bombay (Via Calcutta), a copy of which fell into the hands of the Bihar CID, gives details of the strength (and weakness) of the local Communist organization, and of the Central leaders' efforts at reorganization. The party strength is shown not to exceed twenty, most of whom are students and several the sons of respectable middle-class families who have taken to communism at College. In the absence of a regular Provincial Committee, party matters are in the hands of two student leaders assisted by five Comrades working as couriers. With difficulty a secret party office has been arranged in Patna, and a separate underground 'dump' for storing party literature and other compromising documents. Training-schools (study circles) have been arranged in two outlying centres, and the Patna centre maintains irregular contact with six Districts, but elsewhere the party has ceased to function. 'Two Comrades can be spared for training' (presumably in Bombay), but the report emphasizes the absence of keen and efficient party members. It claims however that the party is functioning successfully inside jail, and that a 'Consolidation' has been formed in Hazaribagh Jail among Security Prisoners and convicted persons. Released convicts from Hazaribagh are known to have been bringing out letters and instructions with them.

In the UP, KALI SHANKAR SHUKLA and NAND KISHORE DIXIT, the two 'underground' leaders who escaped from CAWNPORE jail some time ago, have been successfully re-arrested. A search for DEO NARAIN AGNIHOTRI—one of several UP Vakils who have been secretly abetting communist activities—failed to find Agnihotri, but led to the recovery from his female assistant KESAR SHUKLA of a quantity of incriminating documents, including instructions for couriers in evading the police and a list of local 'party names'. Another useful success was the discovery of a cyclostyle machine in the house of a college student which is almost certainly the machine used by Shukla, and Dixit in Cawnpore, for subversive pamphlets aimed at stirring up discontent among the Cawnpore workers. The UP CID consider that only a few more Communists remain to be rounded up before Cawnpore is cleansed of the Communist poison which has infected local labour for so long and turned the Mazdoor Sabha into a Communist 'strike union'instead of a legitimate trade union. AGRA new appears to be the centre for Communist activity in the UP with BATESHWAR PRASAD SHUKLA the principal link.

In MADRAS successful counter-measures have prevented repeated and fairly widespread attempts to revive Communist activity.

In ANDHRA, K. PATTABHIRAMIAH an underground leader who was evading arrest (and is incidentally an ex-Sepoy, responsible for several articles aimed at tampering with the loyalty of Indian soldiers) was caught crossing a canal in East Godavari district, in possession of a sword-stick with which he attempted to attack the police. A bag containing a dagger, five crude country-made bombs, and some Communist literature was recovered from him. The 'Swatantra Bharat' and local editions of the 'Communist' continue to appear in Andhra and

Malabar. In latter E.M. SANKARAN NAMBUDIRIPAD and other underground leaders are conducting the Kerala CPI and in touch with the Bombay directorate. Their activities, since the Communist-controlled 'Karshak Sangham' was declared unlawful, are mainly confined to secret 'study circles' and attempts to train party members in accordance with instructions from Bombay. The Kerala branch has been issuing a regular 'party letter', and latterly a weekly 'Communist bulletin'. The purpose of the latter has been stated as follows:

'The object of publishing those bulletins is to approach those who are connected with the party but at the same time are not members of the party, and to give them political education. This will give better facilities to come in contact with the majority of the public and draw them more towards the party. The Soviet-German war is the best occasion of such publication'.

On 21st August, the anniversary of the Moplah rebellion, cyclostyled Malayalam posters headed 'Twenty Years Before' issued over the name of the Kerala CPI, appealed to the people to join the Communist Party which could lead them in a successful revolution instead of deserting them as the Moplah leaders had done before. Judgment has been delivered in the COIMBATORE and TINNEVELLY Madras COMMUNIST CONSPIRACY CASES, with sentences averaging two years rigorous imprisonment against nine of the twelve accused in the former under Sections 120-B IPC 17(1) Criminal Law Amendment Act, and Defence of India Rules 38(6); and varying between three and a half years and one and three quarter years against all eleven accused in the latter case.

4. The Central Directorate P. SUNDARMA REDDY the absconding 'central leader' is believed to be back in BOMBAY whence he has been sending the Central Committee's instructions and party literature (in English) to districts in Andhra. There had been no further indication of P.C. JOSHI and Dr ADHIKARI's presence any where outside Bombay. BHOGILA GANDHI a wanted underground Communist, has been arrested in Ahmadabad in possession of illegal literature, having come there the same day from Bombay. S.H. JHABVALLA the Communist leader in the GIP Railwaymen Union has been organizing a 'Soviet Aid' Committee in Bombay, with the assistance of the Bombay TUC and the Girni Kamgar (Red Flag) Union. In the latter, communist influence seems to be regaining its former strong-hold and making preparations for further labour trouble in Bombay. Another railway 'contact' D.B. KULKARNI of the GIP Railway Union DHOND junction is reported to have been arranging the printing of unlawful communist literature in Dhond, and to have been visited there by Adhikari and D.S. VAIDYA and Chief CPI contact in respect of railway labour. DINKAR MEHTA an absconding Communist from Ahmadabad is reported to be moving in Surat and BARODA, and responsible for the circulation of Communist leaflets issued in the name of the Surat CPI

5. Communist Codes Recent messages passing between local Communists in Madras have been employing the code-word COMINTERN for important messages. The cipher is arranged exactly as in the Civil Cipher System, and is likely to be in use elsewhere.

6. Central Publications No further issue of the 'COMMUNIST' (in English) has come to notice; but two new central publications have appeared, but intended for the 'Soviet Solidarity Campaign' referred in para 1:

1. A printed pamphlet 'Questions and Answers on the Anglo-Soviet Agreement.'
2. A cyclostyled pamphlet 'Soviet Land today.'

7. Student Politics Unrest in the student community, after some months of comparative calm, has again shown itself in the BOMBAY CONVOCATION DAY disturbances, and attack by

AMRAOTI (Berar) students on the Director of Public Instruction, and unproarious scenes between the rival groups at the conclusion of the BIHAR STUDENTS CONFERENCE.

Instigated by the PROVINCIAL STUDENTS FEDERATION, Bombay students (both Communist and the rival group) planned to boycott all functions connected with the visit of Sir Maurice Gwyer, who was invited by the Bombay University to deliver this year's convocation address. R.P. Masani the Vice-Chancellor did his best to prevent hostile demonstrations, and the Chief Justice himself had a talk with student representatives on his arrival, in an endeavour to explain his reasons for his withholding the degrees of Delhi students. Nevertheless about fifty students of both sexes staged a black-flag demonstrations near the University Hall. A dead crow, wrapped up in paper, was thrown at one of the cars bringing the Governor and the chief justice to the University buildings, and other rowdy behaviour led the police to arrest some of the student demonstrators and to clear the way. The students' leaders have since made this action an excuse to stage meetings throughout the Bombay province, to condemn the conduct of the police and to organize student hartals and demonstrations, some of which have been marked by exceedingly intemperate speaking. The DIG, CID Poona has commented that these events show conclusively that College and School authorities, as well as the students' parents, are either powerless to exercise control and discipline or also have no desire to do so.

The AMRAOTI hooliganism took the form of a large black-flag demonstration on the arrival on tour of the DPI, followed by the throwing of stones and brickbats damaging Mr Tostevin's car and injuring ten students. The student demonstrators' grievance is that Mr Tostevin when Principal of the King Edward College Amraoti last year, was responsible for the withholding of the examination results of five students who took part in what is called the 'Tale episode'—the suicide by a degree student of that name who had been reprimanded previously by Mr Tostevin and in consequence took an overdose of opium.

The BIHAR STUDENTS CONFERENCE, which was preceded by a separate 'Cultural Conference' addressed by Sir Radhakrishnan and other distinguished persons, was organized by the Communist section and attended by M. Farooqi of Delhi, Mazhar Ali Khan of the Punjab, B.N. Mukharji from the Central Provinces, Lalita Shankar editor of 'The Student', Satish Kalelkar of Benares, and K.M. Ahmad of Bengal, all prominent in the Communist All-India Students Federation. Members of the M.L. Shah (rival) group, joined by Forward Bloc supporters and Royists, interfered with the second days' proceedings, and attempted to move a resolution that 'Students should not participate in or organize any political demonstrations nor should they give verdicts on political issues' in opposition to the Communists' main resolution that the student movement in India has an independent existence as part of the World Students Movement. This led to the breaking up of proceedings and the meeting ended in confusion. It is of some interest to compare the opinions afterwards expressed by the rival groups. The Communists claim a 'good success' despite the efforts of 'a handful of hired disrupters', and that the Bihar students are solidly with the Communist All India Students Federation. The other side claim they were successful in making the 'reds conference' a failure, but admit that the majority of Bihar students are disinterested and unorganized.

A meeting of the All-India Students Council was due to take place in CALCUTTA following the Bihar Conference, but reports have not yet come in. Its main purpose is to declare the policy of the All-India Students Federation in support of the Soviet Union. This forms part of the Communist Party's 'Soviet Solidarity' Campaign referred to in para I and is intended to call upon Students to organize Soviet Aid 'Days'; send telegrams pledging Indian student support to M. Maisky (with copies to the local press); form 'Friends of the Soviet Socialists' (these have already been formed in Bombay, Calcutta, and Delhi); and to organize debates, lectures, and poster exhibitions, explaining and popularizing the Soviet system.

The All-India Students Federation centred in Delhi with M. Faruqi as General Secretary, has shown much increased activity of late. In conjunction with the CPI leaders' new two-fold policy, and serving as an important part of it, the student campaign is aimed at four separate objectives: (1) Enlisting sympathy in the Soviet Aid Campaign. (2) Creating a popular demand for the release of Security Prisoners. (3) Persuading students to join the Students Federation out of sympathy with these 'popular causes'. (4) Collecting funds for the publication of 'The Student', and for use in party interests. The Communist Party is, of course, not mentioned by name in any of these connections.

(viii) Summary of Communist Activities

September–October, 1941

1. General In spite of the Soviet reverses and the modification in Communist policy which has taken place in other countries, Indian Communists, both in and out of jail continue with their 'anti-war' attitude which they seek to spread and to justify by the 'two war' theory outlined in the previous summary.

The latest Communist publications show not the slightest change in their habitual anti-British bitterness, nor in the extremist counsels advocated, based on the Communists' fundamental belief in revolutionary violence. The 'Party correspondence' however, betrays numerous contradictions and much confusion underlying the bluff and bluster of the handful of leaders supplying the party's central directorate from their secret Bombay bolt-hole.

2. Communists and the War The following extract from 'Party Letter No. 44', issued over the name of the Central Committee and secretly circulated last month, explains the Communists' war policy for the benefit of party members, some of whom have evidently expressed their doubts.

'The war is still an imperialist war as far as imperialist Britain and Nazi Germany are concerned,. It is a defensive war, a revolutionary war for the Soviet Union alone. Remember supporting the British war effort is not supporting the Soviet Union. It will only strengthen British Imperialism. Remember we cannot effectively support the Soviet without achieving our own People's republic here (India). For support of the Soviet war of national defence we must deal a death-blow to British Imperialism; fight for a democratic republic and for a people's army; and intensify our struggle against imperialism thousandfold.'

Another pamphlet, intended for more open circulation amongst 'sympathizers', seeks to reconcile the attitude of Communists in Britain and other countries who now support the war-effort, with the 'anti-war' attitude and policy of 'intensification of the struggle' which the party leaders advocate in India.

> We would not be aiding the Soviet by joining hands with the imperialist rulers. We would be harming and not helping the great cause for which the Soviet Union is fighting. As far as India and the colonies are concerned, the Imperialist character of the war is not a whit changed. In its international aspect the British war-effort in India is not so much for the defeat of German fascism, or for the defence of the Soviet Union, as it is for colony-grabbing in Africa, for keeping the Indian people in permanent slavery. Therefore the Indian people will not be advancing but going away from the great united front of the peoples which is being built against fascist aggression and for aid to the Soviet, by joining the imperialist 'win the war' campaign. It is right for the

> British Communists to participate in the war-effort and to intensify it. This is the tactical line they have to follow to proceed from Anglo-Soviet agreement to a united front of the British and Soviet people, by which they will convert imperialist war into a revolutionary war. We in India, to reach the same objective, have to adopt a different tactical line. We do so by combining a popular 'Help the Soviet Campaign' with our intensified struggle against imposed war-efforts, with an intensified struggle for freedom and democratic liberties.

3. Communist Plans Plans for the organization of 'Help the Soviet Campaigns' through locally organized 'Soviet Committees' have been circulated in accordance with the above policy, along with secret parallel instructions to concentrate on labour agitation, the purpose of which is stated to be to 'transform the strike struggle against the effects of the war into a people's struggle against British Imperialism.' The intention underlying this two-fold party line is to exploit workers' and peasants' discontent, and to sponsor pro-Soviet sympathy on the one hand, and any kind of disturbance on the other, capable of being turned to Communist advantage. In other Communist documents, youth is urged to revolt and to resist enlistment; workers to stage strikes for higher wages; and peasants to make extravagant demands. One document marked 'For trusted comrades only' boastfully claims: 'We are the only party in active opposition to the war effort.' Another states that the Communists' immediate aim and objective is 'to acquaint the workers, peasants, and students with the anti-imperialist struggle, and to organize the party to lead the mass struggle.' Instances of revolt in occupied countries in Europe have been quoted in party directives as proof of the glorious Communist future which lies ahead, and the example Indian comrades should follow. A recent letter from one of the central leaders detained in Deoli begins with the statement 'the most encouraging news is about the sabotage activities all over Europe.'

The only clear impression left by the sum total of these tortuous arguments, malicious distortion, and incoherent revolutionary phrase-mongering which go to constitute the Communist movement in India—more especially since the Anglo-Soviet alliance robbed them of their best argument—is of a collection of frustrated and maladjusted invidumuals, dominated by hatred and a thirst for revenge, and corrupted by the doctrine that the end justifies the mens, that conspiracy and deception have become ends in themselves.

4. Soviet Aid Campaign Two printed pamphlets 'The Anglo-Soviet Agreement' and 'The Soviet Peoples War Against Fascism' have been distributed in the attempt to justify Communist 'anti-war' arguments as being pro-Soviet, both in intention and effect. The foreword explains the special purpose of these pamphlets is 'to provide a useful weapon in the campaign of clarification in connection with our Soviet Aid Campaign.'

'Friends of the Soviet Union' Societies have made their appearance in Bombay, Calcutta, Delhi, Assam, and Nagpur. In the Punjab a joint 'Detenus and Soviet Aid Committee' has been announced, and in Bengal a 'Soviet Aid Committee' has been formed under The aegis of Bengal Labour Party by Niharendu Dutt Mazumdar. A 'Students Soviet Aid Committee' is also claimed by All-Indian Students Federation, but, this, like the others, is at present nothing but a paper organization.

Both the 'Friends of the Soviet Union' (centred in Bombay with CPI backing), and the 'Soviet Aid Committees' (centred in Calcutta and organized by the Bengal Labour Party), claim to be non-party and non-political organizations. They are in fact propaganda stunts, designed to enlist the sympathetic interest of persons who would not join a professedly Communist organization. Their structure alone and the identity of those responsible for their organization render it hardly necessary to demonstrate the hollowness of the claim to have no

Communist of other political connections. Apart from propagandist motives, their purpose is to utilize Civil Liberties Unions, the Students Federation, and the signatures of as many well-meaning intellectuals as possible to agitate for the release of Communists under detention on the plea of being actively pro-Soviet. There has not been a single instance of any of these Soviet Aid Committees having made any positive attempt to increase the supply of materials or man-power or otherwise to assist in India's war-effort.

5. Deoli Detention Camp Communists under detention in Deoli Camp, Rajputana, have made plans to resort to a mass hunger-strike. This is timed to coincide with the session of the Central Assembly, and to be preceded by an ultimatum making certain 'humanitarian' demands.

The latter are briefly repatriation to home provinces (to be followed by agitation for release); grant of family allowances and payment of traveling expenses to relatives when coming for interviews; cancellation of solitary confinement as a punishment; and abolition of the present rules of classification for security prisoners. The drafting of the ultimatum has been left to the Central Committee members in Bombay, but this has not yet reached Deoli. An appeal has also been made by the Communists to Congress Socailists, terrorists, and other non-communists detained in Deoli, to join forces in hunger-striking on a 'united front' basis. So far no agreement has been reached. Meanwhile the publication of the Jai Prakash Narain documents relating to Deoli is not likely to lessen the discord between the Communists and their Socialist rivals, whether in jail or outside. Both however appear to be equally tired of jail-life, and anxious to secure their release.

6. Communist Literature In addition to the pamphlets referred to above, printed copies of the monthly 'Communist' in English dated August and September, have been published by the Central Committee and distributed from Bombay. Cyclostyled translations in Urdu, Hindi, and Marathi, and local editions in Madras, Bihar and Bengal, repeating the additional and other extracts, have also come to notice. Circulation appears to be mainly among students.

7. Disguise Biswanath Dubey, an absconding Bengal Communist of some importance was recently arrested in Fyzabad District, UP. He had grown a beard as disguise. Recent reports indicate that several of other wanted Communist leaders have done liewise in order to hide their identity, and so as to enable them to move about more freely.

8. Miscellaneous Considerable excitement has been caused in Madras Communist circles, with possible repercussions elsewhere, over the escape last month from Vellore Jail of five leading Madras Communists including A.K. Gopalan Nambiar, through a hole dug in the outer-wall of the jail. The other four who escaped were C.V. Krishna Rao, K. Pattabhiramayya, C. Kannan, and D. Suryanarayana Raja. They are believed to have joined up with P. Sunderama Reddi and E.M. Sankaran Nambudripad the two principal CPI leaders 'underground' in Madras, and the four convicted Communists who made their escape from another Madras jail in May last P.V. Sirayya, T.R. Subrahmanyam, P. Sekhanan, and O.J. Joseph.

A.K. Gopalan Nambiar is an important member of the Communist Party organization in S. India and in 1939 visited Burma, Ceylon, and Malaya, on what subsequently proved to be CPI interests, collection of subscriptions and establishing foreign contacts. K. Pattabhiramayya, another of the four who escaped, is an ex-Sepoy (Indian Signal Corps) who on his arrest last August was found in possession of five country-made bombs, a sword-stick, and a dagger. In his statement after his arrest, when questioned about these weapons, he stated; 'I do not believe in individual violence but I have faith in mass revolution. I dedicate my life in the cause of the country like Comrade Bhagat Singh and others, and want to die like them. I have no faith in Gandhi's non-violence.'

9. Communist Party Couriers Copies of the latest Communist Party publication have recently been sent from Bombay by secret courier to selected provincial centres, whence they are distributed locally. Reliable information reveals that one such courier is a well-dressed Gujarati youth who gave his own name as 'Girdhari Lal (probably a party-name), and said he had come from Parel, Bombay, and has visited Agra, Delhi, Meerut, Lucknow, and Nagpur, during the course of a month's tour. He appeared to have contacts with the Students Federation (CPI section) in each of the places where he left bundles of literature, and he indicated he expected to make another tour after a month's interval. He spoke fluent English, and was about twenty-five years of ago, tall and of thin build. He was anxious to obtain cash payments before parting with any literature, and said the party was very short of money.

(ix) Summary of Communist Activites in India

November–December 1941.

1. General A distinct lull in the Communist underworld, has followed the excitement over the Deoli hunger strike. The central leaders of the CPI have been correspondingly restrained in issuing fewer of their usual written party directives, and an unusual gap in publication of the central 'Communist' is also evident.

Uncertainty as to what 'line' to adopt is, with little doubt, the cause of this hesitation. Most of the party are in jail, and following the release of Satyagrahis, are faced with the fact that their 'anti-war' policy is the main obstacle to their own release, in addition to being utterly inconsistent with any pro-Soviet protestations. The embarrassment of the remainder outside jail, who are responsible for party policy and numerically and otherwise much disorganized, has been further added to by M. Stalin's recent appeal for wholehearted support to the armies of Britain, America, and the Soivet on the part of all honest people 'not only in Europe but in Asia'.

How to combine verbal support for the 'anti-fascist front' without at the same time abandoning 'anti-Imperialist' role, is the problem confronting the Communists in India. Meanwhile, attacks on M.N. Roy for 'supporting the Imperialist war', and on the Congress parliamentarians for their 'bogus talk of freedom' show that anti-Imperialism continues to be regarded as an end in itself. Communist leaflets aimed at encouraging strike agitation have continued as before. Resolutions passed at Student Conferences and 'Soviet Aid' demonstrations, emphasizing the 'double aspect' of the war and seeking to distinguish between the British and Russian war-efforts, are further proof of no change of heart, and that the 'anti-fascist front' is supported by Indian Communists only in so far it affords fresh facilities to agitate against British rule in India. A Party Letter issued by the Central Directorate from Bombay last month in commemoration of 'November Day', makes this clear in the following declaration:

'Our main slogan this November is: Victory of the Soviet Union is bound up with the victory of all oppressed peoples over their expoliters. We must help to make Soviet victory possible, not by helping Imperialist rulers in their war effort, but by fighting harder for our own freedom.'

2. Communist Plans Reports from the UP and Punjab, confirm rumours elsewhere that the Communist Party directorate have called a secret meeting in BOMBAY, to review the situation.

This meeting may already have taken place and authentic details are so far lacking, but various indications point to such a meeting having been called.

One informant has stated that the Communists in India have come to the sad conclusion that no help from Soviet Russia can be expected so long as the war lasts. Communist plans should therefore be recent in terms of the post-war world, when the main Communist effort will be launched. Full advantage is to be taken meanwhile of the Anglo-Soviet alliance and the call for an 'anti-fascist front' to prepare for a workers' and peasants' revolution. If the present situation is fully exploited, the party hopes to be in a much stronger position after the war.

The whole record of the communists in India can be summed up as a series of hopes and disappointments in endless rotation, of which this latest phase is typical. It is no less typical of M.N. Roy's record of striving and failure, and of the motives underlying Roy's present fight-the-war stand. Intense dislike of Roy, coupled with the fact that any change in policy renouncing the 'imperialist' classification of the war would be tentamount to a declaration in favour of 'Royism', is another complication facing the CPI leaders, and a factor contributing the present hiatus. Some such change may nevertheless be forced, and will not be the first time the 'official' Communist Party of India has followed in Roy's foot steps.

3. Communist Activities Open activity as distinct from the secret plotting and planning of the party leaders, apart from supporting the Deoli hunger-strike demands and propaganda among students, has been confined to labour agitation. This has not been on a wide scale but threatens trouble capable of becoming serious notably in Bombay, the Central Provinces, and Cawnpore. 'Dearness allowance' agitation is everywhere on the increase with the continued rise in prices, and local Communist agitators are exploiting this situation wherever they are given the chance. Bombay is the main centre of this unrest, and is also the centre of the subversive undercurrent which seeks to give it a political complexion. This latter is traceable to the Bombay Girni Kamgar (Red Flag) Union, which in turn is directly under communist control, although the party leaders remain carefully in the background. Typical of Communist efforts to exploit this unrest, is the following extract from a leaflet bearing the inscription of the Bombay Committee of the CPI issued during the recent strikes in the GIP Railway workshops, appealing to Textile and other workers to join in a general strike.

'Discontent among the workers will go on increasing. The responsibility for transferring the present strike into a political strike rests on the shoulders of the Bombay workers. This will be possible only if Party organization is strengthened, party funds in large amounts collected, groups of sympathizers formed and militant workers properly organized. As it is expected a general strike will result on the demand for increased dearness allowance, it will be necessary to make preparations for this by secret groups of workers and secret committees in all mills.'

A report from Cawnpore indicates that a representative of the Communist section of the Mazdur Sabha, which has been attempting to foment agitation for extra wages and against increases in working hours in close imitation of Bombay, has recently left for Bombay with a report of the Cawnpore workers' demands and their preparedness for strike, to obtain the Communist Party's instructions and help. Another UP report is to the effect that an Agra contact recently visited Cawnpore with a detailed report, doubtless intended for the Central Committee meeting at Bombay referred to in para 2.

4. The Soviet Aid Campaign Earlier appreciations have mentioned CPI plans for the organization of a SOVIET AID CAMPAIGN, and the setting up of local groups of sympathizers calling themselves FRIENDS OF THE SOVIET UNION for the purposes of open propaganda, alongside parallel secret revolutionary activity on the 'Anti-Imperialist' front'.

Instructions issued in a 'party letter' last month confirm that by exploiting the slogan AID TO THE SOVIET, the CPI has two purposes in view:

1. To reorganize the party's scattered strength especially among students and intellectuals.
2. To secure the release of Communists detained under the DIR and at the same time to spread Communist doctrines without fear of the consequences in the guise of pro-Sovietism.

These instructions give a detailed programme for 'utilizing every legal possibility' to explain that the Soviet Peoples' successful resistance is identical with India's struggle for freedom. Victory for Soviet Russia is to be interpreted as victory over fascism and imperialism alike. Therefore India should help towards Soviet victory 'not by helping Imperialist rulers in their war effort but by fighting harder for our own freedom.'

A central organizing Committee has been set up in Calcutta. This was responsible for an inaugural All-India conference of the 'Friends of the Soviet Union Society' in Calcutta on 16th November, presided over by Mian Iftikharuddin President of the Punjab Provincial Congress Committee, and himself an ardent Communist. Some 600 persons attended including delegates from other provinces, the conference being labeled for the purposes of press publicity a gathering of 'writers, artists, and intellectuals' although most of them are more familiar as Communists. Resolutions were passed pledging support for Russia and expressing India's determination to uphold the 'ideal which the Soviet Union stands for'; and appointing an Organizing Committee to form branches of the FSU in all provinces. A 'Workers Convention' held at the same time, called for volunteers to join the Red army 'So that thereby we can strengthen our fight for freedom'. The Organizing Committee consists of Iftikharuddin of the Punjab as Chairman; Jagjit singh acting President of the All-India Kisan Sabha and Professor Hiren Mukharji the Bengal Communist as Secretaries. Assam, Orissa, Bombay, Bihar, Madras the UP, Central Provinces, and Sind are also represented, but such activities as are at present apparent, are in the hands of Bengal Communists.

A booklet in English and Bengali 'The Land of the Soviets' has been published by the Calcutta Committee. This is said to be in considerable demand among students. Provincial branches of the Students Federation have identified themselves with local Soviet Aid Committees; passing identical resolutions which are obviously imported drafts supplied by the Communist Party. A detailed 'Course of Study of the USSR' has also been issued on behalf of the Bombay branches of the FSU by A.M. HUNT a British School Teacher in Bombay, whose Communist sympathies and leading role in the Soviet Aid Campaign, support previous suspicions that he may be connected with the central leaders of the CPI in Bombay. Contact between Bombay and Calcutta in respect of the Soviet Aid Campaign unquestionably exists, but has not been confirmed by censorship and probably relies, like other Communist communications, on a system of couriers traveling by railway.

5. CPI Kirti Links Bombay and the Punjab are the two main centres of 'underground' Communist activity. Recent authentic information which the Punjab CID have obtained, has thrown valuable fresh light on secret negotiations between the CPI and Punjab Kirti (Sikh Communist) leaders which have been taking place in Bombay, although unfortunately without any clue as to the whereabouts of the Bombay centre.

Throughout the past two years and more, attempts have been proceeding to bring about a settlement between the official Communist Party of India (CPI) and the Kirti–Ghadr group of the Punjab, with its subsidiary centre in the Meerut 'Kirti Lahr' office (now defunct). In June–July last, Partly as the outcome of an agreement reached between member of the CPI Central Committee detained in Deoli and the concentration of Sikh Communists from the Punjab under detention, and also as the result of secret negotiations in Bombay between leading members of both groups who have evaded arrest, a tentative agreement was reached whereby the Punjab branch of the Communist Party was to be reorganized so as to include the rival Kirti group. In return the new joint party was to have control over the long-coveted Kirti–Ghadr funds.

Reorganization of the Punjab CPI accordingly took place, following further visits by representatives of the rival groups to Bombay, but the Committee appointed consisted mainly of a collection of young upper-class Muslim students, controlled by Mian Iftikharuddin, President of the Punjab Congress and de-facto head of the Punjab CPI. This reorganization was not at all acceptable to the Kirti Sikh Communists, who expected not only to control the new combination, but whose inner plans aimed at absorbing the CPI so that the Sikh Communist group became the All-India Communist Party, and recognized by the Comintern as such. Dissensions have again broken out, and the CPI and Kirtis are now once more open rivals, both in the Punjab and on the All-India plane. Negotiations are likely to continue however, as the Kirti group carries with it considerable ready money from the Ghadr Party ex-India and the Desh Bhagat Parwar Sahaik Committee in the Punjab, in exchange for the Comintern mandate and 'All-India' status vested in the CPI Both parties are moreover united in their hatred of British 'Imperialism' and in their fundamental belief in revolutionary violence.

The three principal Kirti conspirators who have been carrying on these negotiations in Bombay are HARMINDAR SINGH SODHI (of the Meerut 'Kirti Lehr'), ACHHAR SINGH CHEEMA, and HARBANS SINGH BASI alias 'Rank'. Of these Achhar Singh is now in custody: so is Dulla Singh Jalaldiwal, the Kirti absconder arrested in the Punjab in September in possession of eight thousand rupees. This money is now definitely known to have been paid to Dulla Singh by Harmindar Singh Sodhi, who is turn obtained it by exchanging American dollar notes in Bombay, to a total of over eighteen thousand rupees. These dollar notes did not come from any Ghadr or Communist sources, but from enemy agencies, under circumstances which are outside the scope of a summary of Communist activities.

The Punjab CPI delegates who have been visiting Bombay are MIR DAD KHAN (subject of Punjab CID look-out notice No. 17 dated 8.3.41), NAWABZADA MAHMUD ALI (AICC member), DANIEL LATIFIE, and ROMESH CHANDRA. The three latter are not underground, and prominent in the student field, in which capacity Romesh Chandra recently presided over a Karachi Students Conference.

6. Deoli Inside information has shown that the reason underlying the Deoli prisoners' hunger-strike and their demand for repatriation, was isolation from their respective revolutionary parties. They hope that following repatriation to provincial jails they will have no such difficulties in resuming party work, and that they will also be in a better position to agitate for release. None of the prisoners had any real complaint over their treatment in Deoli, apart from their isolation. Some are apprehensive that they will be far less comfortable elsewhere. If this is so, their intention is to revert to further hunger-strikes. A recent letter smuggled out by Jai Prakash

Narain soon after the Socialists had stopped hunger-striking, declares that 'the struggle that has so happily ended might again be resumed in provinces on a much wider scale.'

Relations between the Communists and Congress Socialists in Deoli are very strained, and all talk of a 'Communist consolidation' and 'united front' has been abandoned. The socialists openly accuse the Communists with having 'betrayed' them in having stopped hunger striking before they did. Jai Prakash Narain in particular is described as being worried. He admits in private that the letters published by Government were written by him, but is determined to deny their authorship in public. He has also stated in confidence that by the 'old method', he was thinking of blackmail of Employers rather than political dacoities, although the latter interpretation is not to be ruled out. Communist–Socialist relations outside jail are equally strained, and stand almost as much in their way as do the police.

7. Students and Communism Annual conferences of both groups (Communist and Congress Socialist) in the All-India Students Federation are due to take place in PATNA over Christmas. These are likely to disclose respectively the latest party decisions in respect of policy towards the war and internal developments in the field of Congress politics, whatever else they may disclose.

K.M. Ahmed of the Bengal PSF has taken M. Farooqui's place as Secretary of the Communist section (which is in a distinct majority), and also as the anonymous 'AISF Fraction Secretary' issuing secret Student Circulars, in addition to these issued openly in the name of the AISF. Two such circulars last month make it clear that, so far as the Communists are concerned, the AISF is to be utilized as an open platform for agitation for the release of persons detained without trial, and for the formation of 'Student cells' to enlist student sympathies to the CPI. At Patna an ambitious programme has been planned accordingly, including a debate on 'British Colonial policy in India' and a political Essay Competition, as well as the usual speeches and processions.

The rival Socialist Group are hoping to have the support of Yusuf Mehar Ali, the CSP leader recently released from jail as president, as well as Purshottamdas Tricumdas, F.H. Ansari, and others from the meeting of the Congress Socialist Party executive at Benares on 21/22nd December. M.L. Shah's announcement of the CSP Students Conference refers to the Communists as disruptors who 'stand exposed before the students and the country and has been isolated from the wider national movement.' This taunt is apparently based on the mistaken assumption that, following M. Stalin's appeal on the Russian Revolution Anniversary quoted in para 1, the Communists in India, like those in America and Britain, have switched from 'anti-war' to being enthusiastically pro-war. No such similar tendency to race to extremes is yet apparent.

II. Congress Socialist Party

92. Police Raids at Rawalpindi: Houses of Students Union Workers and Socialists Searched

The Tribune, 25 January 1941.

Rawalpindi, 24 January.

Under instructions from the Punjab CID simultaneous searches of about ten places were carried out by different parties of the city police in the small hours of the morning. Batches of the police headed by Sub Inspectors under the charge of Sardar Mohd Khan, City Kotwal, raided the houses of prominent Students Union and Socialist workers of the town including Maharajkishen and Bansilal, ex-Conspiracy Case prisoners, Mohan Singh, Chamanlal, student workers, Rawel Singh, Alaf Din, Socialists, and others. The hostel of the local College was also raided and the rooms occupied by two professors were searched. The police are reported to have taken from all these places a lot of books on different subjects, a number of pamphlets and periodicals and some letters. The 'Independence Day' badges prepared by the Pindi Students Union were also taken away by the police from the residence of Mohan Singh, a prominent worker of the Students Union. No arrest has so far been effected.

93. Congress Socialists and Satyagraha UP Party Leader's Statement

Amrita Bazar Patrika, 3 April 1941.

Clarifying the attitude of the Congress Socialist Party towards the Individual Satyagraha movement Mr Gopinath Dikshit, Acting General Secretary of the UP Congress Socialist Party, says:

> It pains us to hear that all sorts of invented lies about our attitude vis-à-vis the Satyagraha movement. The interested circles are not deterred from these deliberate misrepresentations in spite of our attempt made from time to time to clear our stand. The party as the left wing of the Congress cannot keep aloof from the present movement, as the struggle after all represents the will of the nation in howsoever restricted sense it might be. The members of our party are taking part in Satyagraha everywhere actively. From members of the National Executive down to the humblest worker on the Congress front, Congress Socialist Party have not lagged behind in courting imrisonment in the present struggle.

He adds, 'But we cannot neglect the constructive work among the masses which we consider of no less importance, specially in the present circumstances when the autocracy and the bureaucracy are out to harass the poor workers and peasants. It is therefore natural that our workers are busy at both these fronts. Our Generalissimo Gandhiji has also asked Congressmen to work amongst kisans. His followers working in constructive activities like spinning, Harijan uplift and Hindu–Muslim unity have also been precluded from the Satyagraha struggle.'—UP

94. Jayaprakash Narayan's View of Left Unity

Extract from *Socialist Unity and Congress Socialist Party,* by Jayaprakash Narayan, General Secretary, 1941, pp. 34–6.

File No. Confidential 784 (539–657), Home Department (Special and Political), Government of Bombay, 1941, Maharashtra State Archives.

Conclusions

The above history makes clear the efforts made by our Party to bring about unity in the socialist movement and how they failed. Except for the earlier months, this problem of socialist unity was really a problem of the coming together of the Communist Party and the Congress Socialist Party. We have seen how the tactics of the Communist Party made that impossible. But it would be a mistake to blame the Communist Party for those tactics. They were inevitable. In the very nature of things the Communist Party could not have behaved otherwise. This was not clear to us before, otherwise our Party would have been much stronger today. But now that it is clear, every comrade must fully grasp its meaning.

The inevitability of which we have spoken is inherent in the nature of the international communist movement. The movement is not formed from the bottom upwards. The 3rd International is not an organization of genuine working class parties or socialist parties that have developed in various countries, but a central organization controlled entirely from above by the Communist Party of the USSR with branches in the various countries. The 3rd International must have a branch in every important country (except those, such as Turkey, the government of which has a pact with the Russian government prohibiting the formation of such a branch). The Communist Party of India is such a branch. It cannot therefore unite with any other party and cease to be a branch. It is possible for the Communist Party to 'unite' with another socialist party only when the united party itself becomes a branch of the 3rd International—in which case unity is a misnomer or, when the Communist Party secretly works as such a branch within the united party hoping to capture it eventually—in which case again unity is a misnomer. Therefore, it is desirable once for all to give up vague talk of unity with the Communist Party. It is possible to unite with such socialist parties as are not sub-feudatories like the Communist Party but unity with the latter has no meaning. Its only meaning is that the Congress Socialist Party too becomes a branch of the 3rd International, that is, it becomes a part of the Communist Party.

Here, the question arises: why does not the Congress Socialist Party affiliate with the Communist International, that is, become amalgamated with the Communist Party? Is the Congress Socialist Party anti-Communist International or anti-Russia? It is neither.

But the question of affiliation is beset with grave and insuperable difficulties. The Congress Socialist Party is not a party transplanted from outside. It is a growth of the Indian soil. It was not inspired by any outside force. It grew and developed out of the experiences of the Indian people struggling for freedom. Its very formation was a protest and revolt against the line the 3rd International pursued in India. That initial fact was enough to instill into the Congress Socialist Party entire lack of respect for the wisdom and guidance of the International. Subsequent events did not improve matters. Immediately after the formation of the Party, the Indian branch of the International viciously attacked it. Leaders of the latter, including members of its Central Committee, rushed to denounce it as 'social fascist'. All this was not exactly calculated to draw us nearer the International. However, on our own initiative, we did attempt to draw nearer to the Communist Party, but were sorely deceived.

The International claims to be a leader of the World Revolution (though many working class parties in the world refute this claim and charge that the International has indeed betrayed the Revolution). As such, it was its duty to encourage and draw together all the revolutionary forces, wherever found. Instead it has functioned as a narrow sectarian Church, supporting its own sect and calling curses upon the heads of all others. In the six years of the life of the Congress Socialist Party, in spite of its standing as a significant revolutionary force in the country, the International made no attempts to get into contact with it or help or encourage it in any way. On the other hand its Indian agents did everything possible to destroy it. Is it not more appropriate to ask the leader of the world revolution, why it failed to draw the Congress Socialist Party within its fold?

In this connection might also be urged the wide divergence between the policies of the Congress Socialist Party and of the International as applied to India. Past differences have been indicated above. Let us turn to the present position. The Communist Party, once again is ploughing its lonely furrow and has pitted itself against the Congress, the Congress Socialist Party, the Forward Bloc. It is condemning outright the satyagraha movement. In a recent publication it made fun of even such a serious thing as the disappearance of Subhas Babu. The Communist Party alone will create and lead the revolution. This is the policy of the International. The Congress Socialist Party is totally different. It stands still for cooperation between various groups; it does not oppose the satyagraha movement, nor the Congress. It criticizes the inadequacies of the movement, its background of compromise, its future dangers, but cooperates with it, arguing that isolation with the national struggle (limited though it be) would be disastrous for the revolutionary forces. It at the same time works to develop the labour and peasant movements, with a view to precipitate a mass revolutionary struggle when the occasion arises. Thus, once again the Communist Party and the Congress Socialist Party, and therefore the International and the Congress Socialist Party are widely separated in their policies.

We might urge a last consideration. There is a large body of opinion, claiming to be Marxist, in the international working class movement which alleges that the Communist International is no more than a bureau of the Soviet Foreign Office, and that its policies are solely dictated by the exigencies of Russian foreign policy. Even such a sympathetic author as Edgar Snow in his *Red Star Over China* echoes the same sentiments in his discussion of the relations between the Chinese Communist Party and the Communist International. The frequent and violent twists and turns in the policies of the communist parties throughout the world before and after the War lend colour to this view. Whatever be the truth, one fact is clear that every communist party must follow the dictates from Moscow because Moscow alone knows what is good or bad for Russia. Now, the Congress Socialist Party, while recognizing that the position and role of the USSR must enter into every socialist calculation, is not prepared to follow dictates from anywhere. Moreover, affiliation with the International not only means following its dictates, but also being obliged to uphold any and every action of the Russian Government. We are not prepared for such subservience.

The above consideration should make it clear why we cannot affiliate with the 3rd International. We should add that our attitude nevertheless remains one of utmost cordiality (in spite of the International's attitude of hostility) and however futile it may be the hand of cooperation will always be extended by us.

To return to the Communist Party. It might be asked why, if it did not believe in unity, did it agree to send its members into the Congress Socialist Party. For two obvious reasons, it might be recalled that for some time it refused to have anything to do with us. But when it was ordered by the International to change its policy and to enter the Congress it found itself faced with a serious problem. It had no contacts with the Congress, and, of course, it must become at once the leader of the national forces. It was here that it found in the Congress Socialist Party an ideal instrument. The Congress Socialist Party held a strategic position within the Congress. The communists were anxious to get into the Provincial Congress Committees, the Executive, the All India Congress Committee, possibly the Working Committee. With their own resources it was impossible for them to get anywhere near them. They were not four-anna members yet. Here was the Congress Socialist Party with its members even in the highest committees. 'Three cheers for the Congress Socialist Party. Let us join it.' They did, and the Congress Socialist Party votes sent them as high as the All India Congress Committee and the Provincial Executives. In addition, being an open party, the Congress Socialist Party afforded a splendid platform for self-advertisement to these, till then practically unknown communists: What was the other reason for their entering the Party? It has been pointed out that in their view no socialist Party apart from the Communist Party had any right to exist. The growth of the Congress Socialist Party into an independent party was a danger to their monopoly. Therefore, they took advantage of the opportunity to enter the Party so as either to capture or break it up. These were the two purposes that brought them into the Party. But, in order to gain admittance, they had to accept the slogan of socialist unity, for; otherwise there was no reason why the Congress Socialist Party should have let them come in. So, behind the smoke-screen of unity, they worked out their plans.

The foregoing has made it clear that the whole idea of unity with a party like the Communist Party was misconceived and the fundamental difficulties were not understood. But apart from that the manner in which unity was sought to be brought about was itself a grievous mistake. It was very wrong to have admitted members of other parties into our Party. This was against all sound principles of organization. The experiment should never be repeated. It cannot but lead to internal confusion and conflict. It should be kept in mind that nowhere in the world has an attempt to unite two parties been made by allowing the infiltration of members of one into the other. The Congress Socialist Party tried it and found it to be a disastrous experiment.

In this connection a point is often made in Party discussions. Why was the Communist Party alone able to do fraction work? Why could not we do the same? For two simple reasons; Communists had the opportunity of doing it, because we had given them a place in the Party. We had no such opportunity, because we had neither the desire nor the occasion to enter their party. Secondly, and this is the more important reason, fraction work is contradictory to unity. We believed sincerely in unity; therefore, the question of fraction work did not arise at all.

Since the decision to expel the Communists was taken, persistent propaganda has been carried on by the Communist Party to represent it as an anti-communist drive. It should be fully understood that there was nothing anti-communist in that decision. It was a measure of self-defence taken against the anti-Congress Socialist Party drive of the Communist Party. The communists had no place in our Party by right; they had been admitted for a specific purpose, namely, that of uniting the two parties. When the Communist Party turned into an open enemy of the Congress Socialist Party and started a vigorous campaign to destroy it, and when the communists within the Congress Socialist Party began to function openly as its enemies, trying to undermine its influence and solidarity, the least that the Party could do was to remove them from its membership. No party can afford to keep within its ranks members who are its open enemies. It should, however, be realized at the same time that the expulsion of the communists was in no manner an offensive against the Communist Party itself as an independent party.

With relation to the expulsion of the communists a question is often asked, sometimes inspired by communists, whether the National Executive was a competent body to take such a decision. Is not the Party Conference the proper authority to decide such questions? The answer is that the National Executive was fully competent to take the decision in question. Since the beginning of this matter, it has always been the Executive that took decisions regarding it. The decision to admit the communists into the Party was not a decision of any Party Conference, but of the Executive at Meerut. Had it been a Conference decision, only another Conference could have rescinded it. As it was, the Executive was fully competent to rescind it. There was a reason why this matter was kept strictly confined to the Executive. The Communist Party was and is an illegal party. Any question relating to it could not be taken to the Conference. It was only during the Congress Ministries when a measure of civil liberties was enjoyed that the matter was first discussed with any measure of freedom.

In raising the question just discussed, it is the purpose of Communists to paint the Executive as an anti-communist body, and to suggest that if the matter had been referred to a Party Conference, the result would have been different. The history of our relations with the Communists, given in Section 3, is enough to show to what lengths the Executive went to accommodate them. When the Executive at Meerut decided to admit them into the Party, it was under no pressure from the rank and file. Subsequently, when even after clear proof of their disruptive tactics, the Executive bore with them, it was again under no such pressure. When the Andhra Party was handed over to them, when even after the Bombay decision, eight communists were admitted into the Allahabad Committee, it was not in response to any clamour from the rank and file. When even today, in spite of the Communist Party crusade against the Party, the Executive offers it its hand of cooperation; it is not out of any fear of the rank and file. Nothing can be more ridiculous than this attempt of the Communist Party to try to put the members of the Party against the Executive.

Another common, and often inspired question, is: why should there be two socialist parties; is not Marxism one and indivisible? This whole pamphlet is an answer to this question. Yes, Marxism is one and indivisible. The important question, however, is, how is Marxism to be applied to a given social situation? In 1934 too Marxism was one. Yet the way the Communist Party and the third International applied it, and the way the Congress Socialist Party applied it, were poles apart. There you have the answer in a nutshell.

A Marxist never tries to understand a social fact by itself. He understands it historically and in relation with other facts. We all wish that there were only one Marxist party. But, if we wish to understand how in a concrete situation two Marxist parties came to exist, we must look at the matter historically. During the national struggle of 1930–4, there was a considerable radicalization of the younger cadres of the Congress. By 1934 a coherent socialist group crystallized. Between this group and the existing group, that is, the Communist Party, there was an impenetrable wall in the shape of the latter's attitude towards and isolation from the Congress. A new party was bound to be formed: the Congress Socialist Party thus came into being as a result of the mistaken policy of the Communist Party and the Communist International.

What happened after this second party was formed has already been described in detail. Since its birth this Party, that is, the Congress Socialist Party, made attempts to create a single Marxist party. It failed because the Communist Party did not want unity. As a result of this historical process, there are still two parties in existence. The present differences between the two parties have already been discussed, as also the difficulty arising from the question of international affiliation. As long as these differences and difficulties last, there will continue to be two parties.

To many, this would appear to be unfortunate as it does to me, but in the circumstances described in detail in this pamphlet it is equally clear to me that it is inevitable. I am glad about one thing that in spite of the misgivings of some friends we tried the experiment as was consistent with the attitude of a party which from its very birth endeavoured to bring about as close a cooperation as possible between all the Socialist groups in the country, if not actual unity. I can also say with confidence that if the other groups had also adopted a less sectarian attitude the result of our endeavours might have been different. Let us hope that some day, not in the distant future, it will be realized that the cause is greater than petty fractional or sectarian advantages.

Left Unity

Related to the problem of organization is the problem of Left unity. It appears to me that there is a great deal of confusion regarding this subject. The question of left unity is one of the most vexed questions in the world. It is my view that the question, in the form in which it is raised, is insoluble. Left unity in the sense of unity of all left parties and groups is an impossibility. Those who talk of such a unity should first ask themselves why is there Left disunity to begin with. In other words, the question should be asked, why do separate Left parties at all come into existence. I think if that question were examined properly, it would be found that the same causes that first gave birth to separatist and sectarian tendencies would also prevent subsequent unification.

The experience of Left movements throughout the world shows that Left groups have not found it possible to unite or even to work together except on specific occasions and for short periods. This historical evidence has surely a lesson for us.

In our own country our experience has been no different. We made serious attempts on two occasions for Left unity. These attempts not only failed to achieve their object, but also left a trail of bitterness that still hinders work. Our past experience showed that while the CSP sincerely opened its doors to Left and Socialist groups and extended its hand of friendship to them, they only sought in all that an opportunity to enlarge their respective influence, recruit members, and build cells, 'bore from within', and to play other tricks that have been played all over the world in the name of Left unity.

Therefore, as far as I am concerned, I have no faith in so-called Left unity, and do not wish to experiment with it, any more. I think the far better course is for all Leftists to forget their little denominational enthusiasms and doctrinal fanatic isms, and to come into one wide, roomy fold and build a single party of Left nationalism and Socialism. Such a party today is the CSP It is possible to find fault with it and pick holes in it, but it is far more fruitful to join hands, to rub off our ideological angularities and fit ourselves into one large pattern in which doctrinal differences might be subordinated to one broad and bold design of common objectives, common methods and a broad common ideology. If the Left and Socialist movement in India is to grow, it could do so not through the unsteady and uneasy combination of various groups, who even when combining must explain and justify their separate identities, who even while trying to work together must work to strengthen their respective organizations by fresh recruitment and partisan propaganda, but by the growth of one large single party. I cannot conceive that there is any other party in India that can fill this role except the CSP. I therefore appeal to all fighters [for Left unity] to make the CSP their own. They have already done so to a very large extent. I appeal to the others also to do the same.

Local difficulties, difficulties of personal equation and old prejudices might stand in the way of some friends, but I should like to assure every fighter that as far as it may lie in our power, we shall see that these difficulties are removed from their way and the path left clear for them to cooperate in building up a real powerful organization.

95. Congress Socialist Party Circular, Issued by its General Secretary, 1 July 1941

Bombay City Special Branch Intelligence, Copy of CSP Circular of 1 July 1941, File No. Confidential 784 (539–657), Home Department (Special and Political), Government of Bombay, 1941, Maharashtra State Archives.

Circular

Congress Socialist Party

Ever since the beginning of the war the Congress Socialist Party has characterized it as an imperialist war. The Congress also suspected that it was imperialist, but in view of the protestations of the British Government that they were fighting for the cause of democracy and freedom, the Congress gave an opportunity to Britain to prove that they were sincere by a declaration of Indian Independence. As no such declaration was forthcoming the Congress ultimately did come to the conclusion that the war was imperialist.

The fact that Britain was fighting a Nazi enemy created a certain amount of sympathy for the British cause and led men like Syt Roy, the liberals and some others to go a step further when they urged complete and unconditional co-operation on our part with the war effort. The Communists, after they had recovered from the confusion and shock of the Hitler-Stalin Pact, lined up to a man all the world over as in India against any aid to Britain.

Britain has been called upon to declare her war or peace aims on innumerable occasions and the fact that she has not done so is by no means accidental. That Britain is fighting with her back to the wall to preserve the freedom of her people from the Nazi yoke can well be conceded. The question still remains whether Britain is equally interested in a new order wherein she will relinquish her yoke over India and Africa. The answer is to my mind very plain and is in the negative, because without India and the exploitation of her African Colonies Britain would be automatically relegated to the position of an obscure island in the North Sea. This fundamental fact lies at the back of the British policy towards India. Comparison with the behaviour towards Canada, South Africa, and Australia will make the position amply clear. Australia is a country of 7 million people. Every able bodied man and woman is being trained there in the art of defence. Ten thousand pilots are being trained every year in Australia. Industries which would be essential to such defence are being rapidly built up. The same is true of South Africa and Canada even to a larger extent. The armies from these Dominions are exclusively officered and led by their own nationals. Let us now look at India. While another lakh of men are being recruited in the 'Indian' Army no attempt is being made to train the ordinary citizen in the art of defence—I am not forgetting the farcical ARP and such things. But apart from this Britain does not dare to recruit a large 'Indian' army although in this land of starvation it would not be difficult to do so. The officers with the exception of the sprinkling of Indians are British or even other Europeans. Soon after the war a very revealing advertisement appeared not only in India but all over the East stating that Europens were required as officers for the 'Indian' Army. Where thousand pilots could be found and trained annually they are training a meagre three hundred. As for industries even a solitary automobile factory could not be tolerated. The whole move is to take as much of our money as we are willing to part with and as many of our men as mercenary cannon fodder as is compatible with the future safety of British Rule in this country, because even a temporarily mercenary army, if it is too large might after the end of the war be inclined to side with those who are claiming freedom and democracy for their own country, the freedom and democracy they were called upon to defend. I would like to ask why one hardly sees any Indian soldier in the streets or cinema theatres of Bombay when you find British, Australian, and New Zealand troops freely roaming the streets and filling the cinemas. Is it that they cannot be trusted outside their barracks? We know that British, Australian, and New Zealand troops are allowed to be entertained in private homes. The Indians can only be entertained in their barracks and may not exchange any words with even their entertainers. Is this an accident?

There are some people who think that if the Congress had continued in office and had offered unstinted co-operation, the British Government in India could never have resisted its efforts to prepare the country for its defence. In my humble opinion the Congress Governments would have been tolerated so long as they acted as tax-raisers and recruiting agents of the ranks at the bidding of the War Office. At the first attempt at interference with the general defence policy or of changing the complexion of the leaders of the Army, they would have been bundled out no doubt under some other excuse. I might be told that I am speculating and allowing my bias to run away with my judgment. I am afraid the charge would be unfounded for the simple reason that with the resignation of Congress ministries, the Government had a splendid opportunity of demonstrating to the people their bona-fides by launching a large and genuine defensive programme. But why should we go further? I should like to ask Sir Sikander, who in and out of season talks of our army, and the other ministries that have continued in office how far they have been able to influence the defence policy of this country. Has Sir Sikander suggested the training of ten thousand pilots and if so with what result? Apart from incurable optimists like our Liberal friends and short-sighted opportunists like Syt M.N. Roy it is clear to everybody that the British Government does not want our co-operation unless we render it as unquestioning slaves. The National Government, about which these gentlemen are talking so glibly and about which even some of the Congress leaders succumbed for some time, would be a mockery without the complete political independence of this country.

We cannot forget that for years now this country has had laws, which have permitted the locking up of men and women without any trial in concentration camps, where at present they receive treatment and other amenities much worse than that accorded to German and Italian nationals and prisoners of war. Can we come to any other conclusion but this that its Imperialist strangle-hold has not been relaxed and will not be relaxed. The instructions issued by Mr Amery to his hireling lecturers about India in America are an indication of the British mentality and their policy.

This is the real situation of this country. Since the attack on the Soviet Union by Germany the Communists in Britain and America have performed one of their amazing *volte faces.* The war to them has ceased to be Imperialist. England has not even recognized the Soviet Union as her political ally, much less has she accepted the position that in the final settlement, in case the war is won, she will not accept the arbitrament of Russia regarding the British Colonial Empire, including India. The Soviet Government has also not asked Britain what her war or peace aims are, nor is it in a position to do so. How then has the war ceased to be Imperialist? The attitude of the British and American Communists can be understood because in fact they are no more and no less than citizens and agents of the Soviet Government. To them the alliance of Britain has become very valuable because without such alliance there might be no Western Front. If they however think that their attitude is going to materially affect the decisions of either the British or the USA Government they will be living in a fool's paradise, because if by any chance Hitler and Stalin make peace again, their interest in the war will cease, and if the Soviet Government so declares, the war will again become 'Imperialist'. Both in Britain and in America the Communists will be used and then cast aside, unless in the meantime they have cast aside the governments in those countries.

The Indian Communists it seems will also follow suit if the statement of Mr Gallacher, MP or the article appearing in the *Bombay Sentinel* is any indication. To them their erstwhile preaching of uncompromising opposition to the war efforts in India will not be in any way incompatible with their fervent pleas for full support to such efforts if the Indian Government obligingly lets them out. Such antics have always amused us but we have never taken them as good or sensible politics.

But all this was, of course, only to be expected. For quite a decade now, the Communist International has sunk to the level of an adjunct of the Russian Foreign Office and danced to its varying tunes. As far back as 1935, a few of the best thinkers among Socialists in India had foreseen precisely such a development as had now happened, and its influence on events in India.

When a representative of the Congress Socialist Party visiting Moscow in 1935 asked Comrade Voigtinsky, Editor of the *Pacific Affairs*, a leading Soviet journal on international politics, what Indian Socialists and Communists should do in the event of Britain and Russia being on the same side in the next war, the Soviet spokesman replied:

> I would still expect Indian Socialists and Communists to attempt to strike a mortal blow at British Imperialism and to turn the occasion to your advantage by securing independence for India. An attack on such a broad and vital sector of Imperialism as India would be of immeasurably greater value to the forces of Socialism than the military assistance which a subject India can give.

This was undoubtedly sound Marxism. But unfortunately very different answers were received from Communist leaders in England and in India. Today those of us who feared that once again the Communists would prove to have their primary loyalty, not to their British working class, not the Indian Nationalist movements, nor even to their professed principles so clearly propounded by Lenin in his striking work on Imperialists War, but to the national policies of the Soviet State—find our prophecies fulfilled.

This does not mean that Socialists do not sympathize with the people of the Soviet Union against the German attack. The Congress Socialist Party would undoubtedly desire the victory of the Soviet Union as much as any one else. We should also be prepared if it were possible to make what contribution we can towards that cause, as was done by us in the case of China and Spain.

The only question is—will sympathy and aid be permitted by the British Government? Let us wait and see the response from the Government to the suggestion of Comrade Narandas Bechar of Karachi that Indians desiring to volunteer for service in Russia should be allowed to do so.

Whatever direct help can be sent to the Soviet Union in their hour of trial we should send. But if we are asked to believe that we can effectively help the Soviet cause by offering full co-operation to the British Government it is another matter, because it is beyond doubt as already pointed out that Britain does not desire the cooperation of a free India, but it seeks the submission of a subject race.

The Congress and the Nationalist movement in this country have framed their attitude towards the War on the basis of their own experience in past wars and in the interests of the Indian freedom movement.

Any cry that may arise for changing our attitude towards the War, based on the latest military developments abroad, will not only not help people of the Soviet Union but would disrupt the Indian national movement and would also involve a betrayal of Socialist principles which the Congress Socialists Party would not for a moment countenance.

Let those who urge that the entry of Russia into this War has changed its character remember that no accident will make the leopard change its spots overnight, nor will in similar circumstances Imperilaism cease to be what it was.

Purshottam Trikamdas
General Secretary.

Mantri House,
Bombay, 1 July 1941.

96. Extract from Intercepted Letter of Professor N.G. Ranga, MLA (in Madras Jail) to his Wife, Bharati Devi, July 1941

File No. 32/10/41-Poll (I), Intelligence Branch, Home Department Report, 16th July 1941, Home (Political) Department, NAI.

Secret

...'Russia in this War'

I know CP [Communist Party] will be anxious to change the whole policy in its anxiety to help USSR How these CPI wallahs are worrying themselves like hell! Dr Krishna wants that Satyagraha must be stopped by INC and every possible active assistance must be rendered to USSR and Britain as they both will soon be in military alliances. But most of these people are opposed to it. They are having continuous discussions. I concede the situation has changed with this attack on Russia. Though England will be anxious in its heart of hearts for the ultimate defeat or fall of USSR for the time being, it will be keen on helping or not troubling USSR as it wants Germany to be defeated or weakened by a long and prolonged engagement in Russia. So there may be some kind of working agreement between Russia and Britain. But are we to help Britain in the hope of assisting Russia? I am not in favour of that. For our help may not reach Russia but may assist Britain. Moreover while our freedom is not conceded, we may be strengthening Britain, our enemy.

I recognize that by today helping Britain we may be indirectly helping USSR, and thus, if and when they both succeed England may have to hearken to Russia's voice and thus grant us freedom. But what about the INC [Indian National Congress]? It will not change its view and so we will be discredited if we adopt a policy of active help in the war.

Secondly Britain will not (may not) agree to communicate our help to USSR It may only be content to make use of our collections for its own use. Moreover, the British stronghold over our prices and so on over agricultural produce, our labour and their wages and their exploitation through taxation, war expenditure in USA and UK and their conscription of our dollar resources and thus the dwarfing or preventing the growth of our industries will still continue to the progressive pauperization of our masses. How can we hope to persuade our people to forget all this and collect funds and help this Govt? How can it be fair to ask our pauperized people to contribute any more to this Govt or its warfare?

Yet how can we keep quiet while Russia is being endangered? Shall we not address Govt and Viceroy to enquire if they will allow us in collecting funds from our masses and sending them to Russia for the provision of ambulance services, that is, Red Cross? Govt dare not disagree or dismiss our request for it will be getting into military alliance with USSR. If it refuses, it will be its fault, will be exposed and our task will be over, and both CP here and Comintern there will realize how we wanted to do our duty. If however Govt agrees then we shall begin to collect; the president will move about India, seek the cooperation of all, particularly students and merchants and collect Rs 50,000 or one lakh.

We need not be afraid that such a programme will be criticized or damaned by INC or public. For has not Mahatmaji replied to Nellore District Judge's question regarding help to Red Cross, that Congressmen may contribute to it, if they so desired? Thus Gandhiji has thought it consistent with our fight for civil liberties and also for independence to help the Red Cross of Britain. Then how can our effort be inconsistent, when especially we wish to help the sufferers in the homeland of Socialism, when we do not form a pact with war-mongers either of Britain or of any other country?

Of course some will criticize us, as joining Roy or CP or War committees. We must be able to answer them. We can. (1) We will continue to demand our independence and freedom. (2) We will as in the past go on fighting for economic demands of masses. (3) We shall go on with our present Kisan Sabha activites. (4) We will not be cooperating with Br. Govt on War Efforts. (5) We will not join Roy.

Thus to pave our way, we shall address first a letter to Gnadhiji and if need be interview him, requesting him for guidance in regard to our proposal to render ambulance assistance (that is, collection of funds for the purchase of ambulance equipment for USSR in Russia), saying that since Russia is the homeland of the only Govt of workers and peasants and she is fighting in self defence, we wish to help her sufferers. I think Gandhiji will agree;—will have to agree. We will also address Poet Tagore and get his support....

Intelligence Branch,
Home Dept Report,
16 July 1941.

97. 'Deoli Papers', 31 July 1941[1]

Papers seized from Prabhavati Devi, Jayaprakash Narayan's wife, which were handed over to her by Jayaprakash Narayan whom she met in Deoli Camp on 29 July 1941 and sent by the Superintendent of Deoli Detention Camp on 31 July 1941 to the Intelligence Bureau; File No. 43/96/41-Poll (I), Home (Political) Department, Government of India, NAI.

Translation of Hindi letter from Jayaprakash Narayan to his wife

I sent you two letters last time mentioning threrein that if you received those, you should reply me with the hints—'All are well at the house of Babuni both at Burar and Daltonganj'. When I received your letter from Khandwa without the above hint, I was a bit perplexed. On enquiry I found out that the fellow who promised to deliver the letter became afraid and could not deliver it but kept it with him. Afterwards he returned the letter when he was threatened by me, that is why I had to send for you again. You will have to proceed to Bombay with this letter. You should ask Purusottam that he should write letters to me according to the instruction

I mentioned in my letter. You should also grasp the method. Take a big old book with a thick binding, tear the binding off, place the letter there, get the book again and send it.

Basawanji and others can also do the same of they want to send any special news.

With two or three other books, a novel of Premchandji should be sent. The binding of this book should contain the letter or the letter may be sent inside the binding of any other book and a mark of plus '+' should be made on its page No. 100 with pencil. I will open the binding of the book which will be marked with plus sign.

Basawan should be informed to go underground. While underground, he should recruit men for the Secret Party. Financial help should be procured according to the old method. We can not do anything except this. Sukulji also agrees with the above proposal.

Secret Party will not be a separate body from CSP but its name will be a different one.

Inform Ganga Babu if the other programme (going outside) is not possible at this time, he should work as a joint Secretary for all India Party. He should tour in the provinces and carry on the office work.

We were on hunger strike for four days about which I mentioned something in my letter. Get it copied at Bombay and take it with you for Bapuji. There are three separate documents in this connection with this letter. Take the copies of all the three documents with you.

N.M. Joshi MLA (Central) visited this place. We gave him everything in writing. Ask Purusottam to see him and take a copy for Bapuji. If he is not willing to give a copy to Purusottam, Bapuji can write to him for the same.

I came with this letter to hand it over to you but could not do so. That is why I am sending it again through the same man, if you could get this letter, tell me tomorrow in the interview that 'You had headache last night'. This will be a hint for me of the delivery.

If you meet Ghaffar Khan Saheb at Wardha, tell him that Hakim Abdussalam Khan Saheb, President, District Congress Committee, Hazara, is here in Camp II. He is keeping good health but has got pain in his hand like suspected gout. Khan Saheb should send news of Salam Saheb to the latter's house that he is well here. He has got a special complaint. The letters which he writes to his home, from this place reach his home after two or three weeks. The letters in question are censored here as well as by the CID Frontier. This complaint should be looked into. Comments against this process should be published in the Frontier papers.

There is another complaint. No paper from Frontier is given to him for reading. If you do not meet Khan Saheb at Wardha, then get a chit sent to him by Bapuji.

For PT
(Old Report)

A. Situation Here

(1) Political.

This Detention Camp is mainly meant for Communists. Therefore, Communists are naturally in large number here than others.

There are two camps here: Camp I and Camp II. In Camp I, there are Security prisoners of class I and in Camp II are those of class II.

In Camp I there are 104 prisoners—mostly from the UP. Of those 66 are in the CP consolidation. Among the remaining 38 are 8 CSP, 11 RSP (Anushilan), 5 HSRA, and 14 unattached and miscellaneous, e.g., Royist, Tagorite, Labour Party, Forward Block.

Of the 66 of the CP consolidation, about 35 were members of the CP before they came here. The others joined the consolidation here (before my arrival). Among those who joined are B.P.L. Bedi, Tilakraj Chadha, Kulbir Singh, and Kultar Singh (the last two are Bhagat Singh's brothers, and all the four were in the CSP before. Re. Punjab comrades in both camps see below).

Among the leaders of the CP who are here are Bharadwaj, Ajoya, Mirajkar, Ahmad, (in the other camp is Ghate).

Among the CSPs are Gautam, Jetley, and myself. You would not know the others. (All the Bihar comrades excepting myself are in Camp II).

Among the RSP are Jogesh Babu, Keshava Sharma, and others.

The HSRA (Hindustan Socialist Republican Association) group is nothing much to speak of. Not good material.

In Camp II were are over 90 prisoners. Of these about 72 are in the CP consolidation. About 6 or 7 are non-political. There are CSPs (Jogendra Shukla, Suraj Narayan, Shyamacharan Bharathwai). The others are independent or belong to other groups (Forward Block, Congress, Babar–Akali, etc.). Just as Camp I is predominantly UP, so Camp II is predominantly Punjab.

Now, about CP consolidation; there two important factors in it. One is that the (Punjab) Kirti-Kisan Party here has merged itself with the CP (all the Kirti leaders are here). This is not the first time that the Kirtis have joined with the CP, and one cannot be sure that this unity will survive the Camp. However, at least at present, they are together.

The second factor is that our Punjab comrades have joined with them. Saghar, Mangeram Vatsa, Richpal Singh, Thakur Govind Singh, Ram Kishen, and three others (who are not known to you) are in Camp II. Saghar has played the leading role in this affair. Our friend Kishori also did his bit by leading them to understand that at Hazaribagh I was also thinking along the same lines: (By the way, Kishori has also joined the consolidation. About him more later.)

It is a pity that I could not reach Deoli a couple of months earlier. However, there is nothing in this picture that I have drawn that need alarm or depress you. Since I came I have been discussing things with the Punjab comrades. Only one of them, Thakur Govind Singh, is irrevocably lost. All the rest agree that their decision is not at all final and that only after their release would they decide after consulting their All-India and Punjab friends. Tilakraj, Richpal, Vatsa (all very important members) are disgusted with the CP and have already decided that after going out they would advocate total separation from the CP and oppose those of their comrades who might advocate merging with it. Kulbir, Kultar, and at least two other comrades of Camp II are practically of the same view. I forgot to state Bedi's position. He has been much impressed with Dange and Ranadive (who were transferred to Ajmer before I arrived here) and has made close personal friendships with the Communists. Politically, his position is something like that of Saghar's. But whereas Saghar is deep, he is shallow, and seems to lack convictions. Saghar himself, while not wishing to make any definite commitment, does not seem to be very keen on what he has done. In any case, the majority of the Punjab comrades are definitely for leaving the CP consolidation after release. We have discussed the advisability of breaking away here, but have decided against it, at least till Munshiji comes here (We have been expecting him daily). Those Punjab comrades who are definitely with me are anxious not to create a split in their group here, as, they think, that would prejudice their cause outside. Anyway we are waiting for Munshiji.

Now, I do not want this news to get round among Party members in the Punjab or elsewhere. I have given you this information so that you may use it to good advantage with the utmost discretion. How you will do it, I do not know. But you must be very careful.

A word about Kishori. He has proved himself to be entirely lacking in self-confidence. He joined the consolidation before the Punjab comrades. His sole explanation to me was that he did not like to be isolated! He also has assured me that his decision is not final. But, I do not trust him. He tells me one thing and the others another. He carries on propaganda on such lines as J.P. is holding on to the CSP and is keeping it going only for the sake of leadership. He has tried hard to persuade Shukulji to join the consolidation. But Shukulji has been firm like a rock. I have come to maintain the highest respect for his integrity and robust political sense. Comrades in Bihar should be informed of Kishori's betrayal. But here also care should be taken that breaking of the news does not do more harm than good.

Before leaving the CP, I should mention that their attitude and behavior both are extremely hostile and extremely childish. When I came here they received me very cordially and Ajoy Ghosh proposed to me that I should also join the CP! You can well imagine the talk that took place between him and me. However, the interesting point in the talk was Ajoy's statement that since the declaration of war the CP has held that outside the ranks there were no leftists and no socialists. Therefore 'left unity' or 'socialist unity' has lost all its meaning now. He said that their present slogan was 'mass CP' (One thing I was forgetting. Among the CP fellows in our Camp most of them are young boys who do not count at all outside. In Camp II most are old Sikhs of the Kirti).

Coming now to the RSP. Their attitude before I came here was not satisfactory. They were also trying to recruit and therefore they were criticizing the CSP. Only Dr Jetley stood his ground firmly (that is, in Camp. There are no RSP in Camp II). Since I came here, however, their attitude has changed. I proposed to them that we must consolidate here, as well as outside. You will remember that I had a talk on similar lines with Pratul Babu when I was out. In this connection, I am anxious to impress upon you that I believe it to be absolutely necessary to bring the RSP into our fold. There is every possibility of it. In Bengal we cannot make any progress without this. I am saying so notwithstanding our Bengal friends. By 'bringing into our fold' I mean the RSP merging with the CSP and disbanding their group. This is possible on the following basis—the CSP to be the legal name of the party, and there to be an underground wing functioning under an illegal name. I am now convinced that if we have to successfully stand up against the communists, we must have an illegal organization and illegal activities. I want to suggest that contact and friendliest relations should be maintained with the RSP in Bengal.

From the HSRA also, I have got the better elements (two of them) completely with us.

As far as camp life is concerned and classes, and other things, all the groups and individuals except the communists are with us.

In Camp II also some independents have joined us. I conduct a class in the play ground every morning for them and CSP comrades there. (Here I should say that the people in the two camps were not allowed to associate with one another. But since a month ago association has been allowed in the common play-ground—between 6 and 7 a.m. and 6 and 7.30 p.m. daily).

Pandit Dhanraj Sharma is very hostile to the communists and comes to my classes. He is friendly to us here, but has his grievances against Avadheshwar and other friends. He is, however, unhappy about the split in the Bihar Kisan Sabha and agrees that after release we must see that unity is again restored.

(2) Concerning life in the Camp.
Generally speaking there is nothing much to complain of here. We live in Barracks in which there are four or five big rooms (eight to ten seated). There are also a few smaller rooms (double and four-seated). (I am at present in one of the ten seated rooms).

When I came there was a tense situation here. There were preparations for hunger-strike. Our people (including the RSP, and others) were unanimous in their interpretation that the CP fellows are thinking of the strike entirely in terms of Party propaganda. They were feeling that they must do something to bring themselves before the public's eye. Because of this our people were insisting that they would join the strike only if they gave an understanding that unless the minimum demands (which must be agreed upon beforehand) were fulfilled, the strike would not be called off. The CP fellows merely wanted a demonstration and were not keen about the demands except some minor ones (which have been already conceded now). Therefore they would not agree to bind themselves to any serious fight. When I came I advised that before serving an ultimatum (for strike) negotiations must be carried on with the authorities. As a result of negotiations the ration allowance of -/6/- daily of Camp II was raised to -/9/-, the privilege of association between Camps I and II, extra clothing for summer, ceiling punkhas, and other things, were granted. This took the edge off the strike preparation. In the meanwhile instructions were received from the CP headquarters outside that hunger-strike should not be started till schools and colleges open and the Central Assembly meets. That is, till their AISF and Mr N.M. Joshi have their platforms ready at hand to tom tom their great 'struggle'. Suddenly the strike fever went down.

In the meanwhile certain events, explained in a separate note prepared for the press, forced us to go on hunger-strike. In this the communists did not join with us. They did intimate to the authorities that they too would resort to hunger-strike, but this was when we had already gone without food for a day. Their demands were also lower-pitched than ours, and they withdrew their ultimatum (without going on hunger-strike) before we broke our strike. In this way they betrayed us and deliberately tried to weaken us. However, the next day, that is, on the fifth day we broke our strike when our demands were conceded.

To the short story of the strike (which has already been sent yesterday) you should add the following. On the fourth day of the strike our representatives were called to the office by the Superintendent—to discuss our demands. (They were: Professor Mota Singh, Gautam, Jetley, and Jogesh Chatterji). When no settlement was reached, the four were taken to another camp (which is at present vacant) and segregated from us. This aroused great indignation. The next day they were sent back and the other demands were conceded.

If possible, I shall enclose herewith a copy of our ultimatum, as well as a copy of our reminder to Govt of India in connection with our memorandum sent long ago.

(B) Suggestions re. Party Policy.

(1) Russo-German War.
The suggestion made in a separate not is entirely mine. Other friends, including Jogesh Babu, agree. But I do not press it. I had a talk with Saghar this morning. He is afraid that the line I have suggested would create confusion in the public mind. He thinks the line of the Punjab CSP as published in *The Tribune* is better namely, that we sympathize fully with Russia, but are

helpless to do any thing about it owing the policy of the British Govt My suggestion is more in the nature of a political stunt. However, I leave it to you and the Executive to settle the line. I think you should call another meeting of the Executive. It at least helps to keep the Party together.

In this connection we must at least express publicly our sympathy with Russia. Can't you send an ambulance corps on behalf of the CSP to Russia.

(2) Central Organization of the Party
It appears that since you returned from Patna you have kept no touch with the Party there, nor sent them any money. If this is the case with Bihar, which today is the most active unit of the Party, contacts with other provinces must be worse. This is very bad. The Centre should function properly and you can make it function so. I suggest that Ganga Babu be made a joint secretary of the Party and be made to stay in Bombay. (I suppose the other scheme about him will have to be given up in the changed situation)

Financing of the provincial branches is essential. You must manage this somehow.

(3) Party Propaganda
The international situation and the shift in the position of the CP's should be fully taken advantage of to push our propaganda forward. This is a very fine opportunity and must not be missed. All of you must give your fullest attention to this task.

(4) General Political Policy.
I read news of your withdrawal of the Satyagraha pledge. I liked it. But you must do something to bring out the Party's independent political line in contrast with this farce of Satyagraha. I have begun to feel very strongly that we must do something spectacular at this moment. We cannot do anything big. But we must make a political investment at this moment. It does not matter if most of you are sent to prison. In this connection, I have been feeling about Bihar, that instead of just holding Kisan conferences, the comrades should launch a Kisan struggle in a selected area or do something in the nature of 'action' as distinct from agitation.

Apart from Bihar, even on an all-India basis, we must do something to attract public notice and arouse enthusiasm among the youth. Do think of something.

An underground wing of the Party must be organized under a separate name—Revolutionary workers' Party of India or anything else. The Punjab Party, as you know, is doing its illegal work under the name of Communist League and is publishing an underground organ called the Bolshevic. An underground all-India organ is necessary to attract the youth if for nothing else.

(C) Technical Matters

It is a pity that none of you has tried at all to establish contact with us here. This is not difficult if you attempt. Ganga Babu has already spent some time here. He should be sent here again to make arrangements. He may go to Ajmer and take the help of friends there to establish contact with local people in Deoli. Some money is necessary for this and a little organization. If some one in Deoli village agrees to act as liason, the thing will become simple. Tailors, dhobis, cobblers from the village come inside the Camp almost weekly. Then there are ward boys in Camp Hospital. All these are poor people (and some of them may even be sympathetic). A little persuasion and money may do the trick. The communists have their regular contacts.

Till regular contact is developed I am suggesting the following method. I would want a reply to this note. Take a book of fiction have its binding opened and your letter inserted inside the binding and have that book bound again. Send the book along with a couple of other books. Let not the other books be fiction, so that I would know which binding to open. I shall write to you in the same manner, if possible.

I have some serious suggestions to make, which I would do only when the contact becomes perfect.

In the meanwhile, I would anxiously await the arrival of the fiction.

(D) Miscellaneous

(1) Re. Sardar Kulbir Singh (brother of Sardar Bhagat Singh) Important.
I have written about Kulbir above politically. He is with us in reality. At present he is very ill and is in the Camp Hospital. He is suffering from acute gastritis with haemorrhage. He vomits several times a day and throws up blood every time. He has grown very week. The local hospital is wholly inadequate for his treatment. The Civil Surgeon, Ajmer, also saw him some time ago, but his treatment is also not doing him any good.

News of his illness should be published in the press. Particularly in the Punjab press. Immediately after receiving this letter, news should be given to the press. The news should be so given that it is assured publication.

You should also write to Sardar Kishen Singh, MLA, Bradlaugh Hall, Lahore, giving him this news. Don't make the letter alarming, but give him the facts.

(2) Re. Shukulji
Jogendrabhai was rather bitterly speaking of the manner in which all of us have neglected his family. You must make arrangements for the education of his son—Chakradhar. It would mean not more than Rs 10 per month.

(3) Re. Dhanraj Sharma
Dhanraj Sharma is suffering from fistula and operation is necessary. He has applied for transfer to the Patna General Hospital, so that his people might be present. The Civil Surgeon, Ajmer, has recommended his transfer. Sharmaji wants that there should be some press propaganda about it. He also wants that Mr Yunus should be informed about it and should be requested to do the needful. Ganga Babu should manage this. Sharmaji also wants Sir Ganesh Dutt Singh to be informed of this.

(4) Re. Classification of Bihar Comrades
The Bihar comrades when they were in Hazaribagh were all placed in Class I. Here they have all been put in Class II. There should be some press propaganda in Bihar about this.

New Report
For PT

The 'Old Report' was prepared when Prabhavati came here last time. It was sent out in two instalments for being delivered to her, but the fellow who had agreed to do it funked it at the last moment. He first gave us to understand that he delivered both the letters. We were very happy. But when in Prabhavati's letter there was no mention of the code I had suggested I grew suspicious. Then we got at the fellow who had deceived us. He finally brought both letters back in tact. We are sure that he had not given them to the authorities.

There is not much to add to the Old Report. There is, however, one good news, Munshiji has arrived. His attitude is perfect. He is attempting to get the Punjab comrades out of the consolidation. We cannot say for sure what will be the result. Some are sure to leave the CP here. Others may leave when they go out. I have consulted Munshiji about your telling the Punjab comrades this news. He says at present nothing absolutely should be known to them. Therefore keep all this information absolutely to yourself. Send books and things to Munshiji. Write to him also. You must also keep the closest possible contact with the Punjab comrades and take a special interest in them.

N.M. Joshi was here with the special permission of Government. He came to find out facts about the Camp. A written statement was given to him on behalf of the whole camp concerning the memorandum sent to Government. (By the way, Government have replied to our memorandum rejecting all our demands except those already granted. See our reminder for the facts). Those of us who were on hunger-strike gave Mr Joshi a supplementary statement concerning the strike. A copy is enclosed herewith for your information. There should be some publicity of the facts given.

Important

I am enclosing one note to Sardar Sardul Singh Caveeshar from Professor Mota Singh and three notes from Munshiji to comrades Mangaldas, Nisar, and others. These notes should be sent to their destination with a messenger. Professor Sahib has written to Sardar Sardul Singh about the relations between the Forward Bloc and the CSP. Professor Saheb is a very leading figure among the nationalist Sikhs and he was a member of the Forward Bloc outside. Here he is very sympathetic to us. His letter must reach Caveeshar. Munshiji's letters are also valuable.

In this connection I have a suggestion to make. The CP attacks both the Forward Block and the CSP Yet the CSP and the FB don't join hands together. We let the CP exploit the CSP against us. Why should we have allowed Mrs Ranga to join hands with the communists? Why can't you people get in touch with Caveeshar, Kamath, and others who may be well-disposed towards and persuade them to join hands with them. The Bihar Golmal should not be allowed to spread throughout the country. I suggest that you go to Lahore and see Caveeshar as well as others who may be helpful. My talks with Subhas Babu when I was out should be fully utilized for this purpose. The Anushilan or the RSP should also be asked to help us in this matter. I think properly tackled, they would be very helpful. They have influence with the FB

The Bihar Kisan Sabha split was bad enough; the All India split makes me very anxious. Do let me know what the positions. Please send a full report.

I understand you had been to Wardha. I am anxious to know what talks you had there. What are the general political prospects?

What about the War? What course is it expected to take.

Tell Caveesharji or send him word that he should reply to Professor Sahib in the same manner as I have suggested to you. Let it be an old book on Sikhism.

Very Important

Before replying please read my letter carefully and make notes of the points which need replying. Then please prepare your report.

(Old Report)
Translation of Hindi letter from Jaiprakash Narain to Ganga Saran Singh of Bihar

Dear Ganga babu,

You should try to take permission to see me.

The other programme will perhaps be useless at this juncture. Therefore you will have to work in all India concern. Central work is not efficient.

You all should pay great heed to the matter I have mentioned in this letter.

Basavan should work in Bihar Underground and he should do our work—recruitment for underground party and underground publicity. You are responsible for the financial help.

Whatever the method I mentioned in my letter, you should also follow the same and send your own letter with Purushottam's letter in the same book.

You must have a knowledge of many things of this place. You should try your level best to have regular contact from inside the Camp.

I take leave from you as I am tired, writing letters.

Please inform me about receiving both the envelops. Prabha should mention in her weekly letter the following line—'All are well in the house of Babuni both at Murar and Daltonganj'.

There is no Marxist book here. Please send one copy of each from the books of Marx, Engels, and Lenin. Those books may be found in Bombay after due search. These books are necessary for the Class work here. You will have to smuggle some books here which are not allowed here—keep this also in your mind. I sent a letter yesterday; you must have received it by now.

Copy of a press note that we had prepared but could not send out. It may be used.

Nearly fifty security prisoners in the Deoli Detendion Camp including S. Mota Singh, Messrs Jayaprakash Narayan, Mohan Lal Gautam, Jogesh Chatterji, Dr G.K. Jetley, and Jogendra Shukla, had been on hunger-strike from 30 May to 4 June. For a long time past the prisoners in this Camp have been agitating for the redress of their grievances and for certain demands. In this connection they have sent repeated memoranda to the Government of India. While it is true that some minor demands have been fulfilled, the important ones, such as the demand for repatriation, family allowance, for the abolition of classification, the demand that no book that is not proscribed should be disallowed, and several others remain still unfulfilled. In connection with the last demand it may be mentioned that even such books as Pandit Jawaharlal's autobiography, Dr Seetaramayya's History of the Congress, novels of Dostoievsky, Capital of Carl Marx have been disallowed. While these questions were deeply agitating the minds of the prisoners here, matters were brought to a head by the conduct of the authorities and their callous attitude towards patients seriously ill in the Camp Hospital. The Medical Officer of the Camp is not only an incompetent doctor but also extremely unsympathetic and hostile to the prisoners. The demand for his removal has also been a long standing one. Deoli climate is very unsuitable and fever and stomach troubles are common. Other diseases too are not uncommon. There were at least five very serious cases in the Hospital of prisoners who had been very ill for weeks, and some of them for months. Repeated requests to send them to the Ajmer Civil Hospital for treatment had been rejected. Recently one of them suddenly developed symptoms of delirium due to extreme pain in abdomen. The Medical Officer on the pretext that the patient was insane, advised the Camp authorities to have him removed from the Hospital and threatened even to have him chained to his cot. On the patient's refusal to leave the Hospital a posse of armed guards was brought in to have him removed by force. This was resisted by all the patients in the hospital. When the news of all this reached the Camp, the Hospital being some furlongs away, there was great indignation. Nearly fifty prisoners, as mentioned above, soon thereafter gave notice to the authorities that unless steps were urgently taken to remove the serious cases to Ajmer or any other suitable Civil hospital, to transfer the Medical Officer, to improve conditions in the Camp hospital, to arrange for the Civil Surgeon,

Ajmer, to visit the Camp Hospital at least once every week till a new Medical Officer arrives, they would refuse to take any food. The lives of their sick fellow prisoners were sufficiently precious to compel them to stake their own lives for their sake. On the fifth day of the hunger strike the authorities agreed to all the demands and the hunger strike was broken.

From this the public should not be led to believe that all is now well in Deoli. All the important demands for which the prisoners had been agitating for months and in connection with which they had made representations to Government remain still unfulfilled. There is no doubt that unless something is done about them in the near future a very serious situation, much more serious than the one recently created, would develop in the Deoli Camp. Even with regard to the last hunger strike, though the authorities definitely promised that the Medical Officer would be immediately transferred, this has not yet been done. Nor the medical department is working satisfactorily enough. One of the patients who had been transferred to Ajmer has returned, and he reports that he was very badly treated by the Civil Surgeon, Ajmer, and was kept in a locked room. It is necessary that the public should demand a non-official enquiry to be made into the affairs of the Deoli Detention Camp. Unless this is done and the grievances and demands are looked into and satisfactorily settled, a grim fight will soon have to be launched, the consequences of which will all be the responsibility of the Government.

Copy of Reminder[3]

To
The Home Secretary,
Government of India,
Simla.

Through the Superintendent, Deoli Detention Camp, Deoli.

Sir,

I desire to draw your attention to a memorandum that I submitted, along with my other Comrades here, to the Government of India in March 1941. Though a quarter of a year has elapsed since the Government have not found it possible or urgent, except for a few trifling things, to do anything about the grievances and demands that had been set forth in the memorandum. The only items out of fourteen that the memorandum contained, about which anything had been done, are: clothes, shoes, convict workers, and association with our friends in the B Camp. Even with regard to these the situation is not altogether satisfactory. While the number of convict hands has been increased, that number is still inadequate, and our demands for barrack attendants still remains unfulfilled. As for clothes, there is unnecessarily delay in giving us the clothing that has already been sanctioned. Finally we are able to meet our Comrades of the Camp only for fixed hours and that also in the play ground. We are not allowed to go to each other.

The other eleven items among which are included all our vital and important demands, remain entirely unsatisfied. Even such an urgent matter as conditions in the Camp Hospital has remained largely unattended to. We have made repeated representations in this behalf to the Camp authorities but hardly to any purpose. It is reasonable to assume that Government have been kept informed of all these representations. If so, Government must know that we have lost all confidence in the present Medical Officer and have been pressing insistently for his transfer. But, though for the last two months we have been given plenty of promises, nothing has already been done in this most urgent matter. Nothing, therefore, examplified better the indifference and callousness of the Government and Camp authority alike to our life and suffering here than this painful affair.

To take another rather simple question; the question of censorship of books and other literature. The British Government lose no opportunity to impress upon world opinion the fact that they are fighting for freedom and democracy. Yet, the Government of India, which is only an agent of the much advertised British Democracy, finds it necessary to deny us the freedom of reading even such a scientific work as Karl Marx's Capital. Such obscuranticism can be rivalled only by the banning of Darwin's *Origin of Species* by Dr Goeboals in Nazi Germany. It must be known even to the Government of India that Capital does not preach the overthrow of the British Government. It is merely a scientific critique of capitalist economy, which has even in England today a few defenders. Another simple question that I had raised in the memorandum was concerning our daily food allowance. I had pointed out that the allowance of -/12/- was, particularly in view of the prices obtaining here, too inadequate for any decent standard of living. I had also pointed out that in 1932, when prices were substantially lower, detenus in this very Camp were allowed a much higher allowances.

Coming now to the vital demands that I had put forth before Government. To imprison us without trial is fascistic enough. To create invidious distinction among us by introducing the hateful principle of classification, to put our dependents and families to trouble and suffering by not providing for an allowance for their maintenance; to remove us from the provinces of our birth and residence, and thus to cut us off more severely than to deny us without cause the opportunity of earning our livelihood and yet not to provide us with a personal so that we may fulfil our every day needs. All these and many other disabilities mentioned in my memorandum are cruel, unjust, and oppressive in the extreme. A person, whose offence has been established in a Court of law, even though the law may not be expression of people's will, is expected to be prepared for a certain amount of suffering. In our case, who have been thrown into prison without cause, Government have, if they are at all guided by the principles of civilized administration, certain obligations and responsibilities. In our opinion, the least that Government can do is to discharge these responsibilities to grant the very reasonable and moderate demands that I and my other friends have set forth in their memorandum.

Finally, I desire to impress upon Government, particularly in view of the fact that already there have been so much delay in the necessity of expediting their decision on our memorandum.

I remain,
Yours faithfully,

Regarding our Policy concerning the War (Old Report)[4]....

---

[1] The Superintendent of Deoli Detention Camp sent copies of these papers to the Assistant Director of the Intelligence Bureau on 31 July 1941. Some parts of these papers were released to the press in October 1941.

[2] Purshottam Trikamdas, General Secretary of Congress Socialist Party.

[3] Some parts of the original typescipt reproduced here are not clear.

[4] The last section of the 'Deoli Papers' dealing with CSP's policy concerning the war has been reproduced in Document No. 90, Chapter 1.

98. CSP General Secretary's Statement on Government's Communiqué on 'Deoli Papers'[1]

Amrita Bazar Patrika, 18 October 1941.

Bombay, 17 October.

Mr Purshottam Trikamdas, General Secretary, Congress Socialist Party, has issued the following statement on the Government of India communiqué:

The publication by the Government of India of the letters alleged to be written by Sjt Jaiprakash who was the General Secretary of the Congress Socialist Party till his arrest is perhaps intended to create a misunderstanding, if not a scare among the public mind, regarding the party's activities and a word of explanation thereof becomes necessary.

Not the Party's View

The Government suggest that Sj. Jaiprakash is advocating the method of political dacoities for the purpose of raising funds for the party. The words used in the letter are 'old method' and the interpretation put by the Governments lacks neither ingenuity nor imagination. Assuming, however that Jaiprakash is suggesting such methods, I must make it clear that the suggestion can represent the views of Jaiprakash alone and not of the party. I have been a member or have been in continuous touch with the proceedings of the national executive ever since the inception of the Party, and I can state categorically that the party has never contemplated such methods. I can also state with confidence that such a suggestion were it to come even from a highly valued and esteemed comrade like Jaiprakash would not be acceptable to the party.

Insinuation Repudiated

The other insinuation that by the absorption of ex-terrorists in the party it would turn to their (ex-terrorists') discarded method require also a clear repudiation. The absorption of ex-terrorists in the party as in other political parties including the Congress is no new thing, but it has never meant nor can it mean that the party accepts or adopts the method of political terrorism. The fact that the party insists on everyone of its members being a member of the Congers leaves no doubt on the question. The party's programme also is quite clear when it contemplates mass political action to bring about a socialist society.

The party has all these years functioned openly and ever since the commencement of the war has never hesitated in expressing its opposition to the war in conformity with methods and policy of the Indian National Congress'—AP

---

[1] The communiqué, including selected passages from the 'Deoli Papers', was released on 16 October 1941.

99. Mahatma Gandhi's Statement on the Publication of 'Deoli Papers', 21 October 1941

CWMG, Vol. LXXV, pp. 34–6.

Wardhaganj,
21 October 1941

The publication of the statement attributed to Shri Jayaprakash Narayan, which he is stated to have attempted to smuggle from his place of detention, does not, so far as I can see, lead us anywhere. If the motive was to discredit the organization of which Jayaprakash Narayan is a distinguished member, it must fail.

Assuming the correctness of the charge against Jayaprakash Narayan, the method advocated by him is against the policy of truth and non-violence adopted by the Congress, and he deserves the severest condemnation. But it ill becomes the Government to condemn or discredit it. Frankly, all nationalist forces, no matter by what name they are described, are at war with the Government. And, according to the accepted canons of war, the method adopted by Jayaprakash Narayan is perfectly legitimate. He has had his training in America for seven long years and is a student of the methods adopted by Western nations in their fight for freedom. To practise deception, to resort to secret methods and even to plot murder, are all honourable and turn the perpetrators into national heroes. Are not Clive and Warren Hastings British heroes? If Jayaprakash Narayan was in the British Diplomatic Service and by secret diplomacy achieved something of importance, he would be covered with distinction.

The sensation with which the event has been disclosed to the Indian world is ill-conceived. The annotations in the communiqué are probably wholly unwarranted. When it is borne in mind that Jayaprakash Narayan is an untried detenu, the annotations look very like hitting below the belt. The Government should have shown Jayaprakash the document or documents seized, and published his answer if he had any to give.

The way in which his poor wife has been dragged in is unfortunate. She knew nothing of the attempt, for it was frustrated before anything could reach her. I may inform the public that Prabhavati does not share Jayaprakash Narayan's views. She was put under my charge by her parents when she was not yet fifteen and while, her husband Jayaprakash was still in America. She has wholly accepted my view of Indian politics and is one of my most faithful co-workers. As husband and wife, Jayaprakash Narayan and Prabhavati Devi are an ideal couple. Jayaprakash has never sought to impose his views on Prabhavati. He has never prevented her from freely coming to me. Indeed, he has encouraged her to come to me whenever she has been ill. She has never been taken into the secrets of the Socialist Party. The alleged communication has completely upset her, for she never thought that her husband would advocate the method attributed to him.

The suggestion made in some newspapers that the restrictions on prisoners should be tightened is wholly irrelevant to Jayaprakash Narayan's attempt. That it was frustrated is enough proof of the efficiency of the CID. Even if there is laxity, it can be no warrant for giving them bad or insufficient food, or keeping them in places far away from their homes, making it difficult or expensive for relatives to visit detenus. I have read Shri N.M. Joshi's very careful and over-moderate recommendations about the Deoli Camp. I have learnt enough about it to enable me to say, in the name of humanity, that the Camp should be disbanded and the prisoners should be sent nearer their homes. It is wrong, from every point of view, to bring prisoners from their provinces and concentrate them in a place where there is no facility either of provisions or medical assistance or other amenities of life. Prisoners of war are treated like princes compared to political prisoners, whose status would be any day superior to that of prisoners of war.

One word to Congressmen, while Jayaprakash Narayan remains the patriot we have known him, they must realize that his method is harmful in the extreme while a non-violent struggle is going on. I have said, repeatedly, that secrecy has no place in a non-violent organization. No underhand or underground movement can ever become a mass movement or stir millions to mass action. I am glad, therefore, that Shri Purshottam Tricumdas, Secretary of the Socialist

Party, has repudiated the method said to be advocated by Jayaprakash Narayan. Indeed, I would appeal to Jayaprakash Narayan to reconsider his philosophy and, if his reason can approve, to repudiate the method as a lapse from sound reason and the loyalty he owes to the Congress. What he has stigmatized as a farce of satyagraha is not a farce. It is the fine fruit of mature experience of thirty-three years' experimenting in truth and non-violence; and, if God wills it, I hope to demonstrate that from this farce will rise a reality which will compel admission even by Jayaprakash Narayan and those who think with him. Jayaprakash did not indeed go to prison as a satyagrahi, but he has not ceased to be a member of the Congress, and so it is not proper for him and others who think with him to retard the movement by their action, which is admittedly disloyal to the Congress.

The Hindu, 23.10.1941.

100. Report on CSP General Secretary's Speech at Bihar Provincial Congress Socialist Conference

Amrita Bazar Patrika, 1 November 1941.

Establishment of World Order: Socialists Aim

Our aim is the establishment of a world order necessarily to be based on non-violence and freedom. In view of this, the Congress Socialist Party can never be against the principle of non-violence which nevertheless is not a creed with us; but situated as we are—an unarmed people—and with the mechanized armies at the disposal of our rulers, a violent struggle has to be ruled out. Thus observed Mr Purshottam Tricumdas, General Secretary of the All India Congress Socialist Party, while presiding at the Bihar Provincial Congress Socialist Conference which commenced here to-day.

Explaining the attitude of the Socialist party towards the Satyagraha movement, Mr Tricumdas pointed out that they were not at all satisfied with it in spite of Gandhiji's assurance to the contrary. They wanted it to be intensified into a mass struggle for freedom to which it would be open to every Indian to contribute his share. 'But if the Congress or rather Gandhiji cannot be persuaded to do so, we still support it because it is an alternative to total inaction, and constitutional talks so dear to Rajaji and Satyamurti will be utterly disastrous' he said. Of late there had been a recrudescence of such talks in spite of the Atlantic Charter. The speaker emphasized that the Socialist party would fight this tendency with every ounce of its energy.

War and India's Position

Referring to the position of India with regard to the present international conflict, Mr Tricumdas remarked that the British Government had seen to it that they (Indians) were kept utterly unprepared and defenceless so that they should cling to them as their protectors. This policy had been continued even after the declaration of the war.

This helplessness of theirs led the more timid and unthinking among them to talk of unconditional co-operation. But luckily they were in a minority, and the majority in the country did not succumb to the specious plea and knew and hoped that a great opportunity for freedom was at hand. That this opportunity had not been availed of was no fault of their people.

Mr Tricumdas stressed the need of the presence abroad of a few Indian representatives like Mrs Kamaladevi Chattopadhyaya, whose duty would be to present the case of India to people 'who usually got the British tablets of misinformation of the type of talking points of Mr Amery.' Such a need had become imperative and he hoped that the Congress would lose no time in making good this deficiency.

Communal Problem

As regards the communal problem, the speaker remarked that this had been accentuated by the middle class politicians who visualized independence as jobs and more jobs and not food for the hungry masses, and who were really not concerned with the problem itself. Their duty with regard to this problem, he urged, was to bring home to the masses of their people that they had nothing to fear from one another and that their interests were much more common with themselves than with their co-religionist landlords or capitalists or Indian Princes. 'You as Socialists have no caste and can have non-caste [no caste] and that by your word and deed you will set an example to the masses which they will not be slow in following. If you do so you will have made a great contribution to the solution of the communal problem and to the achievement of real democracy in this country'.

Soviet Union

Criticizing the tendency, noticeable among a certain section of political leaders after the entry of the Soviet Union, of co-operating with the Government in their war efforts, Mr Tricumdas said that to talk of co-operation with Britain in such a situation as prevailed at present was 'senseless beyond measure and should be left to quick-change artists'. He however hoped that the Soviet Union would come out safe of the danger which confronted it and regretted that they could do nothing to help it.

Mr Tricumdas, in conclusion, referred to the spilt in the All-India Kisan Sabha, which he thought had left the party stronger in the field. He paid a tribute to the work done by the Bihar Provincial Socialist Party in the Kisan field and remarked that this was a country of Kisans and so long as the Kisans remained disorganized freedom would be far away.—AP

101. Mahatma Gandhi's Letter to Purshottam Tricumdas, 5 November 1941

CWMG, Vol. LXXV, p. 78.

5 November 1941

Brother Purshottam,

I was dissatisfied with your speech in Bihar to the same extent as I was satisfied with your comments on the statement regarding Jayaprakash. It amounts to this that the teeth for show and for chewing are different. And what a poisonous criticism of the Congress of which you are a member? If the Congress is as you believe it to be, what is the good of your continuing to be a member of the same? Your justification of the Congress policy at present appears to be a favour on it from a high position. I am writing this much as a friend of yours. This is not for discussion in the Press. No institution can advance by adverse criticism of any other institution. It progresses by its own strength.

Blessings from
BAPU

102. Punjab Socialist Conference: Mr Farid-ul-Haq Ansari's Presidential Address

The Tribune, 1 December 1941.

Gujranwala, 29 November

In the course of his presidential address to the fourth Punjab Congress Socialist Conference, which opened at Gujranwala to-day, Mr Farid-ul-Huq Ansari said that they had assembled at a very critical time, not only in the world history, but also Indian history. Hitler, having overrun, particularly the whole of Europe, had hurled his deadly war-machine against the Soviet Russia. The Red Army is defending its hearth and home most heroically. The whole world admired its (Red Army's) indomitable courage and resistance.

Capitalistic System Must Go

Proceeding Mr Ansari said that the present crisis had grown out of the inherent weaknesses and defects of our existing social order. A handful of people controlled and guided the destiny of tens of millions. It was curious that in our society people who produced wealth were deprived of that wealth by devices which were regarded as a virtue to-day. The goal of human society could never be that majority of people should lead a life of perpetual misery.

'If peace, tranquility, security, and decent living,' he said, 'are meant for all, then our duty is to create a social order in which there is absolute social justice and equality. Humanity can only lead its peaceful, existence by the abolition of the capitalistic system, which is the root cause of all the troubles.'

Mr Ansari said the 1914 World War was fought to end war for all time to come. But within a very short time the world had been enveloped into another gigantic war that was more bloody, more ferocious and more destructive than the last one.

Congress Attitude

Proceeding Mr Ansari said when the war broke out in 1939 and India was declared a belligerant, without her consent, the Working Committee of the Indian. National Congress invited the British Government to declare its war aims and wanted to know if Britain was fighting Imperialism and for the establishment of a new world order and how far their aims were going to be applied to India. The Working Committee gave an assurance that a free India with her energies released would gladly play her part for a world order based on freedom. But the British Government declined to declare its war aims.

'In spite of it the Congress offered to form a National Government with limited powers and to help in the prosecution of the war. This offer was formally ratified at Poona. You will remember that the Congress Socialist Party opposed the Poona resolution, as it was against the fundamental policy of the Indian National Congress. But Britain rejected the Poona offer. It was at this moment that the AICC at Bombay authorized Gandhiji to launch an individual civil disobedience on the issue of civil liberty—the freedom of speech. The Congress Socialist Party supported the Bombay resolution. We hoped that the Individual Satyagraha would develop into a mass struggle leading to India's freedom. We are disappointed, but we still feel that the present movement should continue. As an alternative the parliamentary programme, as advocated by some Congressmen, is neither feasable nor opportune'.

Concluding Mr Ansari Said

'Comrades, if you have the urge of freedom in you and if you want to lead India to its goal, you should develop the necessary sanction for achieving that end. We shall have to develop mass organization. Thus alone you can bring in the masses to fight the battle of freedom. Without the help, support, and active participation of the masses of India no struggle for freedom could succeed. Therefore, take courage and go ahead. Victory shall be yours. All the suppressed and oppressed nations of the world are watching you. You have to be the torch-bearer to free humanity from the domination'.

103. What India Wants: Transfer of Power Socialist Party Secretary on Release of Politicals

Amrita Bazar Patrika, 7 December 1941.

What was wanted was not the release of prisoners but the transfer of power to the representatives of the people, says Mr Purushottam Trikamdas, General Secretary, Congress Socialist Party in a statement to the press on the recent release of the political prisoners.

Mr Purushottamdas says: 'The release of the satyagrahi prisoners is one of those acts of irrelevancy with which the Government of India wants to delude us into believing that their outlook has substantially changed. I hope none of us will be taken in by it. While one feels glad to see and meet friends, nobody had ever asked the Government to release them. What we want is not the release of prisoners but the transfer of power to the representatives of the people. If the release of prisoners had been a prelude to this we would have certainly welcomed it, but of such a consummation there is not even a suggestion. Some of those Indians who have chosen to co-operate with the Government by joining the Viceroy's Council have even suggested that release would facilitate and help India's war effort. If so, they will find themselves sadly mistaken. Our opposition to the war is based on the fact that in spite of the Soviet alliance with Britain we think that Britain was and is fighting, apart for the purpose of safe guarding the freedom of her people at home, for the preservation of her empire. In the absence of the grant of freedom to India and the other colonies, the war must remain imperialist and we can have no truck with it.

'I do not want to discuss what the Working Committee or the All-India Congress Committee will do when they meet. Of one thing I feel sure that they will refuse to permit themselves and the Congress to be dragged on to the path of co-operation or constitutionalism. There is one suggestion which I want to put forward for their consideration. The British Government has of late been telling us that our political progress is barred by the lack of agreement among ourselves. Such an agreement I am sure will never be reached by discussions from the top. If the people however are left to themselves, such an agreement will not be difficult. Why not convene a constituent assembly to give the people's response to the British Government? Such an assembly will also be the sanction behind whatever demands it puts forward.'—AP

III. Radical Democratic Party

104. M.N. Roy on Congress Attitude to War

The Tribune, 1 January 1941.

Congress Popularity has Become Artificial
A New Party Should be Formed

Explaining the aims and objects of the leader's conference, Mr M.N. Roy dwelt on the danger of fascism to India and said that in the present situation non co-operation with the war effort of the Government could not be the standard of Indian patriotism. Now that the Congress had definitely chosen to go into the wilderness in order to avoid the responsibility of facing a complicated situation, it was a moral as well as public obligation of others to shoulder the responsibility. 'We believe that the Congress attitude towards the war does not truly reflect the welfare and aspirations of the Indian people. Therefore the Congress majority in the provincial legislative assemblies has become an empty formality. That formality can no longer terrify us or bind our hands'....

105. Radical Party Rally
Mr M.N. Roy's Criticism of Congress Attitude to War

Amrita Bazar Patrika, 3 January 1941.

Before a full house of the University Institute Hall on Thursday afternoon, Mr M.N. Roy analysed the scheme of political events which led them to break with the Indian National Congress on the issue of India's participation in the war, and form the Radical Democratic Party—the immediate objective of which was to mobilize the Indian masses in the struggle against Fascist menace.

The occasion was a public rally held in connexion with the conference for the inauguration of the Calcutta organization of the Radical Democratic Party. Mr Jamnadas Mehta presided.

Mr Roy said:

The world is experiencing the severest crisis of modern times. Either the crisis will be overcome by the world entering upon a new period of human progress on the basis of the splendid achievements of modern civilization, or the latter will break down, and the world will relapse into mediaeval barbarism. This grave menace to the future of mankind is represented by triumphant Fascism. India cannot claim immunity from that menace. The world crisis affects her as vitally as any other country. Yet the gravity of the situation is not fully realized by many among those who are regarded as the makers of her destiny. Particularly, the premier political organization of the country has failed signally to measure up to the occasion, and has itself become the first casualty of the crisis. Instead of joining the struggle against the menace of Fascism, the Congress has adopted a policy which virtually amounts to helping the victory of Fascism. This fatal blunder has been committed on the pretext of anti-imperialism which, as it is, represents nothing more revolutionary or progressive than impotent race animosity. Spitefulness is a characteristic feature of slave mentality which is a poor asset for the grim struggle for freedom. Having for years condemned acts of Fascist aggression, the Congress today refuses to resist it when the danger is knocking at our own door....

Change of Outlook

The Congress has succumbed to the crisis. But India must survive. Her future is linked up with the future of the world. The path to Indian freedom lies through a victorious struggle against Fascism.... Fascism or Fascist sympathy to-day provides a common platform to all the reactionary forces throughout the world including India. Therefore, the destruction of Fascism has become the immediate task of all the opposing forces. The failure to measure up to this momentous task, on any pretext, amounts to a betrayal of the ideal of freedom, whether national or social.

These considerations must determine further developments of the struggle for Indian freedom. The Radical Democratic Party rises on the ruins of the Congress to blaze a new trail, to lead the Indian masses towards the goal of national freedom and social liberation, which cannot be reached before the world is freed from the menace of Fascism. By mobilizing the people in the struggle against Fascism, our party will further the cause of Indian freedom.

New Inspiration

The movements for Indian freedom must discard false ideals and come out of the rut of conservative ideas hidden behind misleading slogans. It must be inspired with the spirit of our time, which calls for a ruthless revaluation of traditional values, as the basis for a new era of human progress. The entire world is in the throes of a re-birth. An order based on the power and privileges of a few thriving at the cost of the rest is breaking down under the impact of a terrific clash. India cannot remain unaffected. She must sink or swim together with the rest of the world. The Fascists and their sympathizers are the defenders of that passing order. They are endeavouring to prevent the inevitable collapse of a worn out and antiquated system through the violent suppression of the forces of progress which have opened before mankind the perspetive of a higher civilization and greater freedom. The fight against Fascism, therefore, is the paramount task of the moment. India must participate in that fight, simply because she is a part of the world, and her future is linked up with the future of the world. In course of that immediate struggle, the Indian people will acquire the power, and develop the will necessary for enforcing the programme of national freedom and social emancipation....

Congress Policy

The Congress policy as regards war is a logical consequence of Gandhism. Superficially, it appears to be determined by the Gandhist faith in non-violence or conscientious objection to war. Essentially, that is not the case. Gandhism is not only a conservative idealogy: it is a doctrine of social and cultural reaction. Admittedly, it is revivalism. Its spiritual affinity with Fascism is therefore palpable. I have not made this discovery to-day. In my book on Fascism written in 1934 I characterized Gandhism as the shadow of Fascism cast ahead.

The fomation of the Radical Democratic Party means a spilt of the Congress. Many Congressmen may not as yet leave the sinking ship. But our action is meant to rescue the spirit of the Congress from the wreckage. It is a split between the dead body and the immortal soul of the Congress, so to say. The few who still stand loyal to the professed political and social ideals of the Congress, as against Gandhism, are bound to join us sooner or later. The influence of Gandhism having prevented the Congress from acting according to the necessities of political freedom and social reconstruction, the task of implementing that historically necessary programme must be undertaken by some other organization. As a matter of fact, the Congress never adopted such a programme explicitly. But it was implied in its very existence. That programme, representing the urge of the popular masses, therefore, can be regarded as the soul of the Congress. The Gandhist Congress has lost that soul. The Radical Democratic Party rises to inherit it.

The content of the political ideal of national independence is determined by the necessity of social reconstruction, Indispensable for the progress of the Indian people. Under the influence of Gandhist revivalism, the Congress was misled by an entirely wrong idea of that historically necessary reconstruction of the Indian society. Consequently, Swaraj becomes a meaningless term. Economically, national reconstruction is visualized by the present leaders of the Congress as a reactionary, revivalist, process. This confusion about the ultimate object of the nationalist movement has persuaded the Congress to depart from its political programme and degenerate into a closed association for propagating and practicing doubtful moral ideals.

Party Programme

Politically the Radical Democratic Party will strive for the establishment of a genuinely democratic state under which effective political power will be vested in the masses of the people. The party will advocate a comprehensive programme of social reconstruction to promote the progress and prosperity of the nation as a whole. It stands for a rapid industrialization of the country with state aid, and under the control of the democratic state. The historically necessary radical reconstruction of the Indian society is conditional upon the removal of all antiquated institutions and the rejection of all reactionary ideas, which together obstruct the free economic development of the country, and impede the progress of the nation towards a high level of modern civilization. This programme of economic reconstruction puts a concrete content into the concept of national freedom which until now has been nothing more than an empty term, shrouded in all sorts of mystery.

While that remains our main task to-day we find ourselves in a great emergency. Before we could come anywhere near the goal of freedom, we are faced with the danger of losing even the relative freedom to carry on the struggle for political liberation and social emancipation of the Indias masses. The task of all the fighters for Indian freedom in the above sense is evident in the given situation. Under the reactionary influence of Gandhism the Congress has signally failed to measure up to that task. It has adopted a policy which will prejudice the chances of the Indian people ever becoming free. Therefore we had to break with the Congress on the issue of India's participation in the war. For the moment, the entire energy of the Radical Democratic Party will be applied for mobilizing the Indian masses in the struggle against the Fascist menace, because that nenace casts an ominous shadow on the entire future of our country. No country can be free in the midst of an enslaved world. Therefore, for guaranteeing her future freedom India must participate in the struggle for the freedom of the world.

Let the progressive forces come forward to shoulder the responsibility of shaping India's destiny. Let them build up the political party of the Indian people engaged in the historic struggle for the freedom of the world as well as its own freedom. I appeal to all the far seeing fighters for Indian freedom to take their rightful place in the ranks of the Radical Democratic Party which holds high the banner of freedom, and determined to carry it forward through the vicissitudes of the immediate struggle to ultimate victory.

106. M.N. Roy's Criticism of Congress Party

The Hindu, 4 January 1941.

Calcutta, 2 January.

Mr M.N. Roy inaugurated the Calcutta Organization of Radical Democratic Party at the University Institute Hall, this evening. Over 800 attended, mostly students.

Criticizing it for its 'unwillingness to fight Fascism effectively' while verbally opposing it, Mr Roy contended that the Congress was as an 'Association of Conservatives reactionary in outlook on social and cultural matters'.

Beyond the immediate programme of combating, Fascism Mr Roy's plan was to work for the 'establishment of a genuinely democratic State, where power will be vested with the masses through forward social and industrial reconstruction of the country'.

Mr Roy urged that the British working classes and Labour were in control at present in British politics and that 'betraying them by not participating in the war' would amount to helping Fascism. Mr Roy failed to explain, however, why 'democratic and Labour controlled' Britain has so far consistently refused to part with power and turned down India's demand for a National Government....

The Associated Press adds:

'Anti-imperialism loses all significance, if it goes to the extent of preferring Fascism' declared Mr Roy speaking at a rally held in the University Institute Hall this evening. The present world crisis, said Mr Roy, affected India vitally as any other country. Yet the gravity of the situation was not fully realized by many of those who were regarded as the makers of her destiny.

Referring to the Congress, the speaker contended that it had committed a fatal blunder on the pretext of anti-imperialism which represented nothing more revolutionary or progressive than 'Impotent race animosity'. 'Having for years condemned acts of Fascist aggression, the Congress to-day' he declared 'refuses to resist it when the danger is knocking at our own door. That is political bankruptcy, caused inevitably by the reactionary ideas and ideals of Gandhism which have persuaded the premier nationalist organization to reject nationalism for a set of fads and pseudo-moral dogmas'.

Mr Roy continuing said that 'while the Fascist hordes were nearing the Indian borders from both sides', Fascism was 'raising its head in our very midst'. The democratic and progressive forces must therefore fight simultaneously on two fronts. In this critical situation, old slogans lost their meaning. The hatred for Englishmen could no longer be the token of patriotism. It was positively reactionary and harmful for the welfare of the Indian people in so far as the 'sentiment coincided with willingness to welcome the Fascists as liberators'.

The Radical Democratic Party, he said, would further the cause of Indian freedom. It would strive for the establishment of a genuinely democratic State, under which effective, political power would be vested in the masses of the people. The party would advocate a comprehensive programme of sòcial reconstruction to promote the progress and prosperity of the nation as a whole. It stood for rapid industrialization of the country with State aid and under the control of the democratic State.

Mr Roy said that 'since the Congress had adopted a policy which could prejudice the chances of the Indian people ever becoming free, they had to break with the Congress on the issue of India's participation in the war'. He appealed to the 'progressive forces to come forward to shoulder the responsibility of shaping India's destiny'.

107. Mr Roy Organizes Anti-Fascist Rally

The Tribune, 14 January 1941.

Jamshedpur, 12 January.

A largely attended anti-Fascist labour rally was held here this afternoon under the auspices of the Radical Democratic Party. The gathering included many workers coming from outstations as far as Ranchi. The various oganizations participating in the rally included the Jamshedpur Labour Federation, controlling eighteen Unions in metal and mining industries with a total membership of 72,000, the Adibashi Sabha, the Metal Workers Union, the local Muslim League, and the Bihar Sikh Association. Mr Jaipal Singh, the Adibashi leader presided. Mr M.N. Roy was the main speaker at the rally, which was addressed also by Mr Manek Homi, President of the Labour Federation, Mr Jatin Mitra of the Tin Plate Workers Union, Mr P. Bahtasali, MLA and Mr Rajani Mukherji of Calcutta.

After the rally Mr and Mrs Roy were entertained at a public dinner by the Adibashi Sabha. During his one-day stay here, Mr Roy saw many local leaders who assured him of their co-operation. A conference will be held here shortly to organize the Chotanagpur Democratic Union.—AP

108. Report of Intelligence Branch on M.N. Roy, 27 January 1941

File No.128/41-Poll (I), Home (Political) Department, NAI.

Roy has been using Caucutta as his temporary headquarters this month so as to concentrate on labour and the Muslim League with Bengal as the most hopeful base. (Previously he said this of the UP) He has been endeavouring to cultivate the good offices of the Chief Minister and the Labour Minister, Mr Suhrawardy, and has received a certain amount of cautious encouragement, more especially from the latter who welcomes Roy's 'labour rallies' and propaganda as an antidote to Communist propaganda aimed against his own 'White Unions'.

The general attitude of the Bengal Cabinet over Roy is non-committal. Such accommodating spirit as they have displayed is confined to their sympathy with Roy's pro-war propaganda, and his obvious usefulness as a stick with which to beat their political rivals in the Congress High Command. The Chief Minister has pointedly asked Roy what numerical strength he has in the Congress provinces. Jinnah has advised him and his colleagues not to commit themselves in any way.

Roy has now left Bengal on a tour via Orissa down the east coast to Madras. The scheduled castes and labour are thought to be his objectives, but he will welcome supporters from whatever direction. He has made little headway in the formation of his National Democratic Union in Bengal. The plans for his 'All India Convention' in Delhi in early March (probably timed to follow the Muslim League meeting) now include an 'All-India Anti-Fascist Labour Conference'. Aftab Ali of Bengal is behind this deliberate attempt to split the TUC.

Secret reports continue to echo Roy's revolutionary and essentially Communist motives in seeking an 'anti-fascist' popular front. Two reports—one being by an old close confidant—emphasize Roy's admiration for Stalin's tactics, and his typically conceited belief that his anti-Fascist line is the policy Stalin would surely approve and is in fact the policy the Communist International will be forced to recognize as the correct policy for the whole of the Colonial Peoples 'nationalist' struggle. In one of his less-guarded moments, he has expressed his belief that the war will bring Communist revolutions in Europe and the UK. Hence his wish to have the forces of labour behind him in India so as to capture power 'on the crest of the general wave'.

There is other secret information clearly indicating Roy's wish to rehabilitate himself with the Soviet leaders, and proof that he has been in contact with at least one important Soviet contact in Europe, probably through his wife Ellen (a very ardent Communist and the driving force behind Roy's present move). Outwardly however, he is anxious to exclude all Communist appearances which accounts for his dropping of the title 'Peoples Party' for his National Democratic Union.

Roy does not consider his negotiations with Jinnah or other big leaders will produce much in the shape of concrete results. He attaches importance to the 'Committee' of his National Democratic Union merely as a cover for work in the labour and other fields, his main thoughts being (as always) the development of his 'party'. For this he is thinking in terms of working through War Committees, Civic Guards, Rural Developments, and others, and hoping for official recognition.

Dr Khare seems to be an ardent supporter. Others said to be enthusiastic are Jamnadas Metha of the Railwaymen's Federation, S.C. Mitra (Spraker Upper House Bengal) and Sir Henry Gidney. Homi in Jamshedpur is also said to have agreed to join forces with Roy as regards Jamshedpur labour. Like others who see in Roy's 'forward move' the best chance for themselves, Khare is going about saying the obstacle in the way of forming Coalition Cabinets is the Govt of India. The main purpose of the Calcutta Conference, according to an UP observer in fairly close touch, was to put pressure on the Central Govt and HE the Viceroy. Sir Sultan Ahmad has stated in Bihar in relation to Roy's movement that the only hope for pro-war bloc in coalition is through the formation of popular ministries. The key to this, he says, is in Mr Jinnah's hands. Roy appears reluctant to admit this.

He is said to be anxious to establish contact with the British Labour Party. This report is coupled with mention of Roy's lengthy interview with Mr Arthur Moore[1] in Calcutta on 30th December. The latter's interest in Roy's movement has not yet been explained.

In his latest written propaganda, Roy has been stressing what he calls 'the complacent attitude of the Government' and the 'sense of heplessness, apathy, and resignation spreading over the whole country killing the desire and the will for effective political action'. He has struck the same note in announcing his reactions to Mr Amery's latest pronouncement: 'We claim to represent the real interest of the Indian people. The complacency of officialdom is delaying the solution of the problem.' (These quotations, which might be thought to be from a 'Statesman' leader, are from the latest issue of Roy's paper 'Independent India'.)

---

[1] Editor of the Calcutta daily *The Statesman*.

109. Congress and the War: Mr M.N. Roy's Criticism

The Hindu, 9 February 1941.

Cocanada, 7 February.

Mr and Mrs M.N. Roy arrived here last evening by mail from Waltair. Mr Roy addressed a public meeting in the Town Hall, convened by Messrs M.V. Sastri, P. Bapu Rao, and S. Ramayy.

Dewan Bahadur K. Suryanarayanamurthi Naidu presided. The majority among audience were students.

Before Mr Roy arrived at the meeting place, Mr M.V. Sastri, Mr Munshi Ahmad Sheriff and the President appealed to the gathering to maintain silence and to hear Mr Roy.

Mr Roy during his address was jeered by some people in the audience several times whenever the word Fascism was mentioned. A section of the audience staged a walk-out when Mr Roy said that in the beginning of the war the Congress had declared its readiness to co-operate in the war effort on certain conditions. Those who left the meeting gathered on the road-side and the police asked them to go away without creating a disturbance. A rumour became current that some students were arrested by the police and the whole audience rose up to know what it was. Mr Roy had to stop his speech for a while and after it was known that no arrests were made, the audience gathered again. Mr Roy in the course of his speech criticized the present satyagraha campaign of the Congress and characterized it as 'Fascist regime'. He said that he was in jail for twelve years and would be prepared to suffer imprisonment for another twelve years if he was convinced that such a course would bring freedom to India any the nearer.

Mr Roy stated that the conscientious objection of the Congress to war had only come as an after thought after the Congress had offered its active co-operation in the prosecution of the war for a whole year although only on certain conditions. If the war was bad, a National Government at the Centre would not have made it any better, nor would it have given any mere substantial power to Indians.

The other argument with which Congressmen justified their anti-war attitude, Mr Roy said, was that India and not been consulted before she was declared a belligerent party. If they came to the conclusion that it was necessary to fight this war for a certain object, the mere fact that it had first been declared by England and England had dragged us into it did not alter that conclusion, did not remove the necessity of fighting this war. And if it was true that Fascism was the greatest menace of our time then it was necessary to fight it.

After describing the Congress attitude to Fascism and its sympathies with its victims like Spain, China, Austria, and Czechoslovakia, Mr Roy asked whether we should not sympathies also with the English people now faced with Fascist aggression. Within a short time he added the main theatre of war might he shifted very near to the frontiers of India. Communications between England and the East might be interrupted or altogether broken. The Fascist armies would sweep through the Balkans and the Near Eastern countries. In this part of the world they could be stopped only if India threw in her whole might her manpower, her resources, her fighter's spirit and her fervent determination to defeat Fascism and win freedom.

Proceeding, Mr Roy said apart from the fact that for the snake of the very opportunity of carrying on our fight for freedom we must contribute to the defeat of Fascism the prosecution of the war itself did in no way interfere with our fight for freedom. On the contrary, in the course of the war efforts India would have to be increasingly industrialized and militarized. The Congress had failed to recognize it. Going to jail at this moment was only an escape, it had neither the negative value of preventing India's participation in the war, nor the positive wake of bringing her anywhere nearer the goal of freedom. Therefore, he appealed to all the rational, intelligent, far sighted patriots to get together to rid themselves of the stupor of the deadlock, and give a new, determined and organized lead to the country, so that India, in the process of contributing to the liberation of the world from the menace of Fascism, might come to her own and take her rightful place in the future commonwealth of the free nations of the world.

With a vote of thanks to Mr Roy, the meeting ended.

IV. V.K. Krishna Menon and India League, UK

110. Intelligence Branch Reports on V.K. Krishna Menon and India League, UK

File No. 1/5/41-Poll (I), Home (Poll I) Department, Government of India, NAI

(i) On V.K. Krishna Menon's Activities, 3 April 1941

Under dated 16.1.41, V.K. Krishna Menon sent in, by letter, his resignation from Labour Party membership to the secretary of the party to forestall the termination of his membership by the Party on account of the role played by him at the People's Convention, and to make it appear that he had resigned on what he is pleased to term 'the larger issue'—which is to say the interpretation he has read, or professes to read, into the Labour Party's termination of his Parliamentary candidature. It is understood that in accepting his resignation and acknowledging receipt of his earlier (published) letters of 23rd December, the National Executive of the Party contented itself with the colourless comment that the NEC did not accept the interpretation which Menon had placed on the Party's letter dated 29th November and that the Party's attitude towards India was something clear and distinct from the position it had taken up in connection with the cancellation of his Parliamentary candidature by the Dundee Trades Council and the Labour Party.

2. On 19.1.41, Menon is understood to have spoken at the second day's Session of the London District Congress of the Communist Party of Great Britain, which met to implement the decisions taken at the People's Convention. (Menon was elected to the 'Committee of Twenty-Six' chosen to replace the Convention Committee; of these twenty-six, fifteen members (including D.N. Pritt, K.C., MP, of whose communist allegiance there is apparently now no doubt), are well-known Communists, and others, including Menon, if not actually Party members are definitely sympathetic towards the Communist cause. Menon has now offered to help the party in any direction in which use can be found for him and has informed at least one provincial organizer that he will accept an invitation to speak subject to Politt's approval. He has in fact burned his boats and professes to be indifferent to the consequences of his open association with the CPGB, but there are nevertheless signs that he is somewhat apprehensive that, owing to the suppression of the 'Daily Worker', the Party will no longer be able to give him the 'publicity service' which constituted its chief merit in his eyes. He is on exceedingly good terms with Harry Pollitt but on the other hand, R.P. Dutt is said to be anything but happy about the Party's new acquisition and is disposed to regard him as nothing more than 'on appro'.

Incidentally, Miss Agatha Harrison, who seems unperturbed over Menon's virtual secession to the CPGB, is reported to have shown copies of his correspondence with the Labour Party to H.S.L. Polak, the Privy Council solicitor: Polak is understood to have commented that if the reasons given for the termination of Menon's Parliamentary candidature were valid, they would have precluded the election to Parliament of Dadabhoy Naoroji. Polak would thus seem to have accepted Menon's interpretation of the Labour Party's case against him, and since that case has never been truthfully (that is, his communist connection) stated by the Labour Party they have only themselves to blame for Menon's capitalization of the situation

3. On 24.1.41 Menon attended a meeting of Communist leaders at which the preparation by him of certain document on India was to be discussed. The result of these discussions appears to have been a statement which materialized at Indian Independence Day meetings on 26th January, but was originally intended to have been distributed to delegates to the People's Convention. It is also quite probable that the Bulletin No.3 of the Colonial Information Bureau, which deals entirely with India and appeared on 26th January, was the result of Menon's discussions with his Communist associates, notably Michael Carritt: this bulletin bears hallmarks of his style and it is known that he has been taking credit for some pronouncement on India which appeared on 26th January.

4. The Indian Independence Day meeting at the Conway Hall, London, on 26th January, of which Menon had high hopes, seems to have fallen somewhat flat, partly owing to the suppression of the 'Daily Worker', the CPGB's 'Chief Whip' for such occasions, and partly no doubt, owing to a natural relaxation on the part of sympathizers after the climax of the People's Convention. Three speakers disappointed at the last moment, namely, Reginald Sorensen, MP, Mrs Rebecca Sieff and Michael Foot (*Evening Standard*). Those who did take part were D.N.Pritt, F.J. Horrabin, Ted Bramley, Professor Levy (London University) and R.F.O. Bridgeman, who deputized, as he so often does for a defaulting Chairman—in this case, Sorensen. Only about 150 were present and their reception of the speeches, particularly Pritt's was apathetic. A collection of £13. odd was taken and a song entitled *'Unite and be Free'* specially composed for this meeting by Alan Bush (Communist), was sung by Martin Lawrence and accompanied by the composer. (This lyric appears to have been a bowdlerized version of the already unlovely English text of the 'Internationale')

The speeches were as might have been expected. Bridgeman regretted the absence of the usual 'goodwill' messages from India, explaining that those who would normally have sent them were in jail. Ted Bramley made the stock Communist diatribe against British rule in India and said that it had been demonstrated by the USSR, that religious and political differences, where and when and if these existed, could be adjusted for the common good under Communist rule. Pritt—who seems to have bored the audience exceedingly—said that suppressions of newspapers and political imprisonments were the marks of a weak Government: he added that the 'Left must always play on the fears of the 'Right' and that from his recent campaigning he was aware that India's legitimate bid for freedom was a cause of considerable worry and concern to opponents of the working class. Horrabin said that the British working classes by sheer lack of interest were acquiescing in British domination of India: he nevertheless firmly believed that the War was being fought for democracy and that Indian Independence would presage ultimate victory. Levy stated that the test of a country's a policy was its social application: here Britain fell down because she professed democracy and countenanced its opposite in India. Menon himself explained how Individual Civil Disobedience has been substituted for mass civil disobedience and related how the arrest of Nehru had been the occasion of a two-day strike in the highly industralized city of Bombay: indicative of misrule in India was, he said, the continued application there of the sadistic Indian Whipping Act—the counterpart of what was to be found in Nazi Germany. He stressed the drive of the Government of India against any section of the Press which printed matter likely to foment opposition to the successful prosecution of the war, and concluded with an appeal for support for the India League and his campaign for the release of Nehru and for Indian Independence. To sum up, the speeches of Menon and Bramley were exceedingly vicious and the others comparatively colourless.

5. Independence Day meetings were also held on 26th January in Manchester, Birmingham and in Cambridge, the latter two under India League auspices. (No report is as yet available for the Manchester gathering). At Birmingham the audience numbered about 150, 80 of them being Indians. The Chairman announced that there would be a meeting of the Birmingham National Council for Civil Liberties of special interest to Indians on 15.2.41 (that is, to synchronize with the London Conference of the NCCL on 15th/16th February). The Birmingham conference was addressed by Leonard Barnes, his subject being 'Civil Liberty in the Empire'. Ahmed Hoosen Sader, Kr Diwan Singh, and four other Indians: the last five spoke in the vernacular: the Chair was taken by Alderman Harrison Barrow.

Both Miss Harrison (who brought with her a large quantity of the Indian League's latest literature) and Horace Alexander appeared to have confined themselves to speeches belabouring the point that if Britain is fighting for democracy she must logically grant Indian independence: Miss Harrison thought that the declaration of India's belligerency without her consent would go down as one of the blunders of history. She quoted Gandhi's remark at the time of the death of C.F. Andrews, 'It is possible for the best Indians and the best Englishmen to meet and never separate until a formula acceptable to both has been found', and suggested that this means of ending the deadlock might now be tried.

Sader made an impassioned speech in support of the demand for complete independence for India. 'India', he said, 'has not lived through the ages to go down before a proud and arrogant Empire' 'it does not matter what happens to many of us—to Nehru and the others, but it does matter to India: she must be free and independent if life is to be worth living'. Dealing with the point that a German victory would leave India in worse case than under British domination, he quoted (without acknowledgment) Menon's *bon mot* at the People's Convention, that a fish is not to be asked whether it prefers to be fried in butter or margarine—it does not wish to be fried at all. This was received with rapturous applause and so was his misquotation of the words addressed to the Viceroy ('and to the financiers who shape the policy of India'): 'You have sat too long in India; let us be done with you for God's sake'. He added that when the break came as it surely would, it might be a violent one, but 'we would rather the parting were in friendship and in that spirit the India League in Birmingham is arranging meetings and distributing literature to make for better understanding among Indian and British people.' He then announced the inauguration of a campaign for the release of Nehru and for Indian Independence and said that it was proposed to hold a Midlands Conference about April in Birmingham; this was to be one of a number of regional conferences, culminating in a National Campaign Conference to be held in London about July.

In moving the resolution calling for Indian freedom and the release of political prisoners, Mr Alexander said that the giving of independence to India whilst the war was in progress, would be a magnificent gesture which would have favourable repercussions throughout the whole world. The resolution was seconded by an Indian student (name unknown) and carried unanimously.

6. The Cambridge Indian Independence Day meeting was attended by some two hundred people and was addressed by Dr K.S. Shelvankar and four other speakers who represented

the Socialist, Labour, and Liberal Clubs of the University and also the Chinese Club. It was held under the auspices of the Cambridge Indian Majlis and the India Society of the London School of Economics. Shelvankar's main point was that repression and political arrests had been going on in India for years and the imprisonment of Nehru was only a culminating event in a series, not a new thing. Nor was the crisis new, it had been growing for decades: India had no sympathy or friendship for Nazidom nor had she any particular dislike for the British and no desire to embarrass Britain in her war against Germany, but for at least two years before war was declared she had made it clear that if India were drawn into another war, the Congress would not use its influence to further the prosecution of such a war. Public opinion in England appeared to regard it as a threat against the British middle class.... He also drew attention to the general and industrial backwardness of India and said that this state of affairs remained because it was to Britain's interest that it did. Dealing with the Hindu-Moslem question he was at pains to prove that none existed except in the eyes of the British Raj, but then made the somewhat surprising remark that 'The general belief is that the Moslems are an aggressive and ferocious people. He concluded with an attack on the Princes and an assurance to his audience that Britain's 'Divide and Rule' policy would work no longer.

7. On Friday 24th January, Cambridge students held a 'poster parade' protesting against the suppression of the 'Daily Worker'; one Indian, M.A. Latif, took part in the procession, others distributed leaflets advertising Indian Independence Day and sold literature. On 27th January a mass meeting of protest was held, it is understood, in the teeth of opposition from Conservative elements. Some 600 persons were present.

8. At all Indian Independence Day meetings this year there was a plentiful display of literature. As has been recounted in an earlier note, Menon had prepared a pamphlet entitled 'Britain's Prisoner' (that is, Nehru) specifically for this occasion. It is of interest to note that he consulted the Communist Party in regard to the references to the USSR it contains: it is also noteworthy that one firm of printers declined to set up the type to help out the Farleigh Press (Communist), because they considered the document 'too political'. An examination of the text explains the firm's scruples: the pamphlet is quite the most vindictive that Menon has yet written.

At Birmingham copies of 'Britain's Prisoner' and 'Why Must India Fight' (the latter appeared early on in the war) on sale and copies of leaflets, 'The (Congress) Declaration of Independence', 'Birmingham Branch (India League) Indian Independence Day 1941' and 'Indian Independence Day 1941' were distributed. The last quoted was written by Menon for this year's Independence Day celebrations to explain and compensate for the lack of messages from India: the other two were provided by the Birmingham Branch of the India League.

Cambridge seems to have rejoiced in two quite new ones not so far seen elsewhere, via No. 6 in the Communist Policy Series, 'India' (not yet seen), by Michael Carritt and 'Truth About India' (Can We Get It)? By Dorothy Hewitt, printed by the Marston Press (Communist) and published on Independence Day, 26th January, 1941. The Carritt pamphlet reiterates the usual grievances against British rule in India and is plentifully interspersed with what purport to be facts and figures: it concludes with the statement that the People's Government—when it is established—will immediately give complete independence to India. (It has not so far been possible to identify the writer of the second pamphlet. Inquiries are proceeding).

9. Menon is full of plans for conducting meetings in the Provinces in support of his 'Nehru Release' Campaign. On 29th January he held an Executive Committee meeting of the India

League to discuss future activities. On 30th January he was due in Manchester to attend an invitation meeting arranged by Mrs Winfred Horrocks, (Manchester Council for Democratic Aid) to prepare people for a Campaign. The following day he was to have addressed a meeting in Lancaster. On 1st February he was to have spoken in Newcastle.... On Sunday 2nd, he was due to speak in the St. Andrew's Hall, Glasgow, and thereafter at a meeting at Douglas Water, near Edinburgh.

10. He has selected Miss [Bhicoo] Batlivala to deputize for him as the Congress representative and guest of honour at the Annual Dinner of the Manchester Indian Association on 16th February when owing to his commitments to the Conference of the National Council for Civil Liberties in London, he cannot attend in person. This seems to cause him little regret as he feels it will be easier for Miss Batlivala to be effectively 'rude' to the Lord Mayor of Manchester to whose speech she will have to reply. (The guest of honour at this function is normally the High Commissioner for India, but it was resolved this year to invite the Congress representative instead, considering that the High Commissioner 'did not speak of India but only for his masters').

11. Arrangements are being made by B.F. Bradley for Menon to address a meeting in Dundee, probably on 2nd March. Provisional arrangement for such a meeting of 16th February fell through owing to Menon's prior engagement to address the Conference of the National Council for Civil Liberties in London on the 15th and 16th of February. He is understood to be taking considerable pains over the preparation of his 'report' for this Conference; (it will deal with the Colonies generally and not with India specifically) and to be supervising the efforts of Arthur Clegg (well known as a leading light of an Communist 'stooge' in the China Campaign Committee) and S. Subasingh a Ceylonese, who are contributing reports on Malaya and Ceylon respectively. Menon is also due to speak at a NCCL Conference in Cardiff on 15th March.

12. D.J. Vaidya (also known as 'Suresh' Vaidya), now employed in the '*March of Time*' and '*Time* and *Life*', London Offices, has recently established close liaison with Menon. The latter has given him a selection of articles by Nehru which, he understands, have not already been sent to the USA by the writer himself: these include one on 'Eastern Federation' and 'On the Verge', which Menon has used for a recent issue of 'Newsindia'. Vaidya apparently wants these for the magazine '*Life*': as he believes that this periodical 'wants to make a show of being neutral' he considers that Nehru's statement before the Magistrate would be unsuitable. He has also discussed with Menon the possibility of persuading Miss Indira Nehru to put her name to an article on Gandhi which would be written by Menon and himself. Menon cold-watered this idea, partly because he presumes that the USA would want a 'Pro-Gandhi' article and that Miss Nehru, thanks to the influence of her alleged finance, Feroze Gandhy, was likely to be anti-Mahatma in her views, and partly because he thinks it would be definitely preferable for him to write an unsigned article himself and thus be unfettered in his choice of comment. Vaidya is further understood to have offered to find American publishers for 'Unity Of India' (Nehru's forthcoming book) and for '*Glimpses Of World History*' (which appeared in this country some time ago). (In fact, he is willing to find facilities for anything that Menon would like to be published in the USA) It is also reported that he has put forward certain tentative suggestions to Allan Michie, (who is due to leave for New York in about three weeks' time,) presumably for pro-Congress propaganda in the USA. Michie is a journalist connected with the '*Time* and *Life*' American magazine combine, and Vaidya has presumably been associated with him in the London office.

(ii) Extract from the Overseas Security Bulletin for April 1941 (No. 6). Received from London

Secret

Indians in the United Kingdom: The India League

In Note 13 of the Bulletin (No. 2) reference was made to the activities of V.K. Krishna Menon, and a brief sketch of his career was included. This can now be supplemented as follows:

As the result of the termination of his prospective Parliamentary candidature for Dundee, which was confirmed by the National Executive of the Labour Party on 29th November 1940 Menon has resigned from the Labour Party and thrown in his lot openly with the Communist Party of Great Britain. His serious association with that party was the real reason for the termination of his candidature, though—very unfortunately for themselves—the Labour Party fought shy of saying so, and merely stated in general terms that it was felt that his allegiance to India made it impossible for him to give absolute loyalty to Labour Party. Menon has made much capital out of this statement which he has twisted to imply that a belief in the cause of Indian independence is incompatible with Labour Party membership and alleges that racial and colour discrimination have been made against him personally. There is no evidence to show he has become a member of the Communist Party or that he has wish to do so. His present activities are dictated by his desire for a platform and a large audience to address on the subject of Indian independence. Fomerly he used both the Labour Party and the CPGB to this end, but now his repudiation by the Labour Party throws him back entirely on whatever support he can get from the latter, and although the Communist leaders neither like him nor trust him, they are quite willing to use him up to a point. His first public appearance in the Communist camp, since his break with the Labour Party, was at the People's Convention 12 January 1941: he has since been appointed to the 'Committee of 26' and is speaking round the country as and when the CPGB sees an opening for him. With this work for the party he is combining a 'Campaign' for the release of Nehru and other Indian political prisoners and for the complete independence of India. It may be stated categorically that he is bitterly anti-British and entirely opposed to the War Effort; furthermore, that he will do anything he possibly can to vitiate the latter while keeping within the letter of the law. He is a member of the Overseas Sub Committee of the National Council for Civil Liberties and took a leading role in the conference of that body which was held in London on 15/16 February 1941; and, when this was functioning, represented India on the International Peace Campaign. His organization, the India League, maintains friendly relations with the Peace Pledge Union, but only for what can be got out of the latter in the way of advertisement for the cause of Indian independence.

Fairly active branches of the India League exist in Birmingham and Manchester. Attempts have been made to form tranches in Edinburgh and Liverpool, but nothing much has come of them. Menon has, however, active contacts in these places, as also Dundee, Swansea, Newcastle-on-Tyne, Sheffield, Cambridge, and others. His present objective is to form Campaign Committees wherever possible; these will then hold regional conferences to report eventually to a 'National Conference' which he hopes to hold in London about July.

(iii) On V.K. Krishna Menon's Activities, 5 August 1941

Menon's Position

Up to the date of the German attack on Russia, Menon's partnership with the People's Convention and the Communist Party of Great Britain was resulting in a good deal of help and publicity for the Indian Independence Campaign. From the end of June onwards, Menon's situation has undoubtedly deteriorated and is causing him anxiety which is affecting his health. There is no evidence of any actual rift, but each side of the alliance is finding the other some thing of an embarrassment in the changed situation and is compelled to exercise much forbearance and tact to avoid creating one. The state of affairs is a reflection of the difference of opinion which exists within the Communist Party itself—a difference which the Party is desperately anxious to conceal. Their agreed majority line now appears to be that in order to give maximum support to Russia, nationalist, or what might be called 'Home Front', objectives are not to be stressed. This does not mean the abandonment of such demands as freedom for India or, for that matter, for the British working class, but it does mean that the main emphasis is to be kept on unity of effort and that the fight for such objectives is parallel and subordinate to the main issue and is not to be used as a bargaining counter in relation to it. It therefore follows that the support which can now be given by the Party to Menon's Campaign is indeterminate, half-hearted and may dwindle still more, since Menon adopts the attitude that the fight for Indian Independence must go on at all costs, and the freedom of India is a perquisite [prerequisite] for India's support of the British–Soviet Pact—in spite of her admittedly anti-Nazi and pro-Soviet sympathies. Some of the Party leaders, having now got to the stage of pledging support on a broad basis for the Churchill Government, see no reason why the Indian National Congress and the Moslem League need be so squeamish in regard to the Government of India and think that in neglecting to support the war effort—now that half of it can no longer be called 'Imperialist'—these organizations are failing in their duty to the cause: moreover they consider that in consequence of this negative attitude, the Viceroy has been given a pretty opportunity to pack his Council with nondescript and reactionary elements. Menon's very different views are more of less shared by R.P. Dutt, but the latter is not on too good a wicket and is therefore careful not to encourage Menon too far in opposition: the same anxious demeanour is noticeable in the behaviour of B.F. Bradley. For once in a way the Indian students are in agreement with Menon and, in this case, Dutt, a fact which has not escaped the Central Committee of the Party. It is understood that the latter's reaction has been to arrange for a discussion to take place between the students, William Gallacher and Emile Burns as to the correct line for them to adopt, both here and on their return to India.

2. Menon addressed the London Convention Rally in connection with the Empire Day. He said that the British people in the United Kingdom had no idea of the misrule in India, where to think intelligently and to act for Indian freedom, were sure ways to imprisonment. The tyranny which had enslaved Indians these many years had to be ended, and the British must be made to realize that the time was fast approaching when India would be independent and free to determine her own destiny. He declared it was the inalienable right of the Indian people to have freedom to enjoy the fruits of their own toil and to have the necessities of life in order that they might have full opportunities of growth. If any Government deprives a people of these rights and oppresses it, the people have a further right to alter or abolish that Government. The British Government in India has not only deprived the Indian people of

freedom but has based itself on the exploitation of the masses and has ruined India economically, politically, culturally, and spiritually. The Revenue derived from India is out of all proportion to the people's income. The political status of India has never been so reduced as it is under the British regime and no reforms have given real political power to end repression in India, and inaugurate a new era of friendliness on a basis of mutual friendship and freedom.

Speaking at a People's Convention meeting in Sheffield on 16 June (afterwards going on to Doncaster), Menon delivered a particularly nasty speech. He said that the effects of the war were world-wide, but, as in the case of previous wars, the present one was supposed to be for somebody's good, yet that somebody never seemed to benefit by the efforts of the belligerent and 'this time, the people, as always, will lose'. He went on to say that there were three types of denizens of the globe, the free people of the USSR, the subject peoples of Empire, who are always exploited, and the exploiters. War was invariably conducted by the members of the last category: the ideals of war might change, but the sacrifices of the people were constant and the only solution lay in giving the people, who produce the goods, the control of their own industries, and thus in destroying the profit motive, destroy the incentive to war. Thus British armament manufacturers supplied the German Government with materials of war merely because they wanted a market. To retain their possessions, the 'haves' of the world would betray any part; for instance the Czech Government surrendered without a fight not because of Chamberlain, but because they feared their own people and the same sort of thing was still more patent in the case of France. He said that 'the present House of Commons was no safeguard against parallel happenings in this country, where the Home Secretary had greater power than any Stuart King; yet when a truly nationalistic movement...arises, it is mercilessly crushed'. Imperialism is more than Fascism in the bud. The Soviet Union is the subject of much speculation: the answer to the question 'What will it do now' is 'Mind the interest of its own people'. It is an example to the people of this country, who must realize the necessity of overthrowing the enemies of the people at home before tackling those abroad. Such an act would speak loudly to the German people and would encourage resistance on the part of the oppressed peoples. He then gave some 'facts and figures' regarding wage rates, and other things, in India and in the same way as were the people in this country, but the Indians knew they were being exploited.

Menon addressed People's Convention meeting in Scotland on 21st and 22nd June.

A special Executive meeting of the People's Convention was held in London on 26th July. As was not altogether unnatural in the case of an organization which had been brought into being for the purpose of agitating for the setting up of a People's Government, there has been a considerable amount of dissatisfaction amongst the leaders of the People's Convention over the latest developments in the Communist Party's policy. The Party has, of course, always had a considerable majority in the councils of the Convention, and there is little doubt that eventually the Convention will have to swing into line. Meanwhile, as an example of its hesitation, the Executive on the 26th July adopted a resolution condemning the Secretary of State for India's recent announcement as insufficient to 'release' India to take her part in the battle against Nazism. The resolution went on to say that if that Government were to recognize India as an independent nation and were to release Nehru and the 'thousands of Indian political prisoners' the Indian people would respond generously and magnificently. This resolution, it may be added, was drafted by Menon, who is himself a member of the Executive of the Peoples' Convention.

3. Although not previously a member of this Society, since the German attack on the USSR Menon has addressed several meetings under its auspices and maintains close contact with Pat Sloan, its leader. Incidentally, he is anxious to give the Russian Embassy assurances of Indian solidarity with the USSR, and been trying to secure a message to that effect from the Indian National Congress.

4. Press Contacts

Propaganda for the USA

Menon maintains close touch with D.J. Vaidya, who is employed in the London office of '*Life*' and '*Time*' (connected with the March of Time film concern). Vaidya, about the middle of July, informed him that he had a query from the USA as to whether the Civil Disobedience Movement was not slackening. He thought British propaganda must be at work, as reports were being circulated to the effect that people in India were abandoning the Civil Disobedience campaign to take on the new jobs which were being created by the war. He also intimated that it was being said that Hindu propaganda in the USA was being financed by the Nazis. Apparently Menon's first reaction to this was to cable Mrs Pandit telling her that there was a complete dearth of news in regard to India and asking her to keep him informed of developments and decisions.

Press Conference, London, 6th August.

Another reaction to Vaidya'a query would appear to be Menon's decision to hold a press conference in the St James Court Restaurant on 6th August. He hopes with this to achieve several objects, namely, (1) to contact American and Canadian pressmen: Miss Batlivala has been specially endeavouring to get in touch with Miss Helen Kirkpatrick (Chicago Daily News), Quentin Reynolds—who recently made the celebrated Sunday broadcast 'An open letter to Dr Goebbels', and Miss Dorothy Thompson, the famous New York Times columnist, who is now visiting this country; (2) to secure advance publicity for his forthcoming National Conference of the India League Campaign, and (3) to ventilate his views regarding the enlarging of the Viceroy's Councils. (These views are what might be expected—no advance has been made and the 'stooges' appointed are not even second rate; the proposed arrangement is an intensification of the situation and does amount to a constitutional issue: the British Government were putting into effect the settlement of 8th August 1940, which had been rejected; they were trying to find Indians who would play Quisling roles and were anxious to show America they had Indians in their 'cabinet').

There is some reason to believe that Menon is genuinely rather disappointed with the new demarche in India. He had certainly gathered from some of his contacts (Sorensen, and Michael Foot of the *Evening Standard*—and possibly others) that there was at least one member of the Cabinet who felt strongly that something comprehensive should be done to end the Indian deadlock and that a Labour Party Deputation would make representations to this effect. He evidently reached the conclusion that Mr Bevin was the Cabinet Minister in question and has been, or was in the early days of July, angling to secure an interview with him (through Sorensen)—not as a Minister, but as a member of the Labour movement. Mr Bevin is reported to have said to Mr Sorensen that if Indian Nationalists generally speaking could be more positive and less negative, something startling could be achieved within six months.

Menon maintains the closest contact with J.B. Appaswami who tells him what occurs at press conferences, and even passes on information which is given to the press 'in confidence'.

Menon has been writing an article on India and developments in regard to the USSR for the 'Labour Monthly'. He has had many discussions with R.P. Dutt and R. Page Arnot about this article which, of course, presents difficulties, as anything which appears in the 'Labour Monthly' has to have the cachet of the Central Committee of the Party and, as mentioned in the introduction paragraph of this note, Menon and R.P. Dutt do not entirely see eye to eye with the Central Committee on the subject of India.

(iv) On the Present Position of the India League, 5 November 1941

During the past two years there has been a progressive but decided change in the character of the India League. Though its objective remains the securing of independence for India, it can no longer be described as an Indian organization. Very few Indians belong to it and of these only some three or four, such as K.S. Shelvankar and Miss Bhicoo Batlivala have any influence on its policy and Menon continues to occupy the role of a Dictator. His past and recent attempts to coordinate the activities of Indians in the United Kingdom and to spur them on to concerted and forceful demands for independence have failed, largely because of his domineering methods and personal unpopularity with his compatriots, and he has been forced to work through other channels. Since the imprisonment of Nehru last year (November), up to some three months ago he has endeavoued by means of his 'India Campaign' to persuade the British public, but particularly the working classes, that freedom for India is *a sine qua non*, not only for the mobilization of her vast resources for the war effort, but also for the establishment of sound economic conditions for workers in the United Kingdom.

2. Relations with the Communist Party: This period coincides with a period of close assocition with the Communist Party of Great Britain and with the People's Convention. Menon's connection with the latter very largely offset the disadvantages he sustained through his break with the Labour Party and enabled him to secure an appreciable amount of support in Trade Union Circles, Cooperative Guilds, and from Pacifist organizations. With the Russian entry into the War, however, the Communist Party executed a new *volte face* which he has been unable to imitate in its entirety. Evidence accumulated during September and October indicates that there has been a decided falling off in the use made of him by the Party for the reason that the latter find him and the whole Indian question—exceedingly embarrassing. They have, in fact, shown themselves to be most reluctant to pronounce *ex cathedra* on the situation and have been driven to adopt a 'fluid' policy which is roughly (1) that Indian policy must be dictated by Indians: (2) that though the CPGB is supporting the British Government for the sake of Russia, it is not in a position to demand that the Indian movement shall similarly support the Government of India, or to urge it to abandon the struggle for independence. They therefore attempt to compromise by recommending a 'dual objective' course, suggesting that Indians should give the maximum aid to the war effort in order to help the Soviet while simultaneously pursuing a parallel drive for Indian independence. The contradictions in this recommendation have escaped nobody and Menon persists in upholding what the CPGB describe as the 'dangerous fallacy'—that India cannot render effective aid to Russia until she is herself free.

Such divergences among the leaders have naturally added to the existing confusion in the minds of Indians in the UK; this confusion has been further augmented by the declaration that the Atlantic Charter does not apply to India and by the characterization of the Indian nationalist movement as a 'fifth column' organization. As a consequence, P.B. Seal's so called 'Indian National Committee'—with its declared objective of setting up a purely Indian organization, has received the unexpected support of Surat Ali, Dr Sasadhar Sinha, and a few of the Indian students and propter hoc. a good deal of surreptitious support from the CPGB. This does not mean that the Party has revised its opinion of Seal, but merely that it proposes to use his organization over his head through Ali and the students. In short, the Party has once again been forced to the conclusion that Menon is not sufficiently opportunist for Communist purposes. His attitude that no India question can be tackled except through the India League and his persisting obsession with the cause of Indian independence while the USSR is in jeopardy, render him unadaptable. In the past he was useful to them as a purveyor of news from Nehru, but now, as merely exerting some influence in certain British circles, he fails to fill the role the Party cast him for, namely the contacting and coordination of Indians. They quite realize that he is disliked and distrusted by his compatriots, that his ideology is not suited to working class organizations and that the very name of the India League is anathema in the Labour movement as a whole. There has, however, been no open breach between him and the Party: each makes a certain show of consulting the other, but intrigues progress apace and there is now little, if any sincere cooperation. Menon, as a consequence of his break with the Labour Party, cannot afford a quarrel with the CPGB (which can still make or mar his meetings by granting or withholding the services of the Party whips) and is forced to consume substantial slices of something resembling humble pie and has once more been compelled to devise new tactics. These consist in direct approaches to prominent persons in every walk of life who are known to be sympathetic to Indian aspirations or, at least, desirous of ending the Indian deadlock. Illustrations of this new phase are to be found in his efforts to cultivate Mr Bevin, Mr H.G. Wells, Mr Winant, and leading press men and clerics.

3. India League meetings and activities of Branches: It must be admitted that Menon is still much in request as a speaker on India, but from the diversity of organizations applying, it may be taken that this is not so much a tribute to him or to the India League as a manifestation of a desire for information on the subject of India born of growing uneasiness and exasperation in regard to the Indian situation. This is evidenced by the somewhat startling fact that the India League has on several occasions: Menon is in the habit of deputing K.S. Shelvankar and some of the Indian students such as L.L. Haravu and R.C. Gautam to act as India League speakers at meetings which he cannot or does not wish to attend himself. He is unreasonable enough to show some jealousy at the growing demand for K.S. Shelvankar from organizations with which he himself originally put the latter in contact.

It is obvious too, that all though Menon has many individual supporters in different circles and is able to whip up a certain amount of enthusiasm for 'inaugural' India Campaign meetings in various districts, the seed more often than not falls on sterile or already over-occupied ground and the hoped for India League Branch either fails to germinate or develops into a sickly plant. Two cases in point are supplied by the Birmingham and Leeds Branches. Menon was exceedingly annoyed a short time ago to receive a letter from a Birmingham enthusiast who had attended the National Conference in London on 10th August, enquiring whether the India League had any representative in Birmingham—which is about the doyen of India League sub-establishments; and was doubtless little better pleased to be informed that the Leeds Branch was making little headway and that the Secretary's other commitments compelled her to ask to be relieved from her post. Norwich also, after a promising inaugural meeting has failed to carry out plans for the formation of a Branch and the same is the case with Lancaster. Even Welwyn Garden City, which embarked on India League activities with a tremendous flourish, now sees the greater need for concentration on aid to Russia and an India League recall conference which was to have been held there in October has had to be postponed to an indefinite date in November. Further illustrations of the fact that Indian intransigence disconcerts, it does not actually alienate proletarians now engaged on active help to Russia, are to be fund in the Welsh Conference held in Cardiff on 4th October which was very badly attended and in the case of an 'India' meeting held in Liverpool on 12th October, which is also to be regarded as a failure for the same reason. It must, on the other hand, be admitted that the Glasgow Conference on 6th/7th September, which Menon ran over the heads of Surat Ali and its Indian student and worker promoters (The Hindustan Majlis), represented a considerable initial success; but there are signs that Menon will not be able to follow this up by implementing the resolutions, particularly those affecting Indian seamen (whom he has no means of contacting) and that if anything is done, it will be done by Ali and the students, K.A. Said and Dayanand Naidoo of Glasgow.

4. Indian Committee for Aid to the Soviet People.

In order to counter the efforts of Surat Ali and the latter's colleagues in the Indian National Committee (whose Indian Political Conference on 12th October he did his utmost to sabotage), but still more, to dispel the impression that he is apathetic on the Russian question, Menon at the end of September formed under India League auspices an 'Indian Committee For Aid To The Soviet People'. This he describes as 'non-political' and though it functions from 165, Strand, the name of the India League is not shown on its circulars. Efforts are being made to collect money (with a target of £5000), and a certain amount of activity in connection with the project has been displayed by Indian students both in London and in Cambridge. On 24th October a public meeting was held by the Committee at Finchley Road, London N.W., which was addressed by Menon and by Herbert Marshall, an additional attraction being the presentation of Soviet films: only 50 persons attended however and the collection came to no more than £7. 0. 0. odd, leaving some £2–£3 for the objective after expenses had been cleared.

5. Menon and the Indian Students

Since Michael Carritt left London to take over the Party organization in Bradford, his duties have been undertaken by Arthur Clegg in regard to the Colonial Information Bureau, 'World New And Views' and also as the party link with Surat Ali and the Indian students. He is very decidedly encouraging his charges to oppose Menon and has assured them of party backing if they can build up a really representative Indian organization and/or bring out an 'Indian Front Bulletin' once more. He is reported to have commented that the Party supported Menon only because, in the absence of any organization with a united Indian platform, it was compelled to do so. He is reported to have suggested that Sinha's bookshop (which has been run at a heavy loss since the war: Sinha's debts are said to be in the region of £200) might be taken over as headquarters: it is, however, doubtful whether funds could ever be secured for this purpose. Though Ali's resentment against Menon becomes daily more bitter and he has accused him of being pro-Fascist and anti-Russian, he is not satisfied with the Party attitude either, and complains that their present non-committal stand in regard to Indian matters is positively semi-Fascist and is driving the Indian students into playing Menon's game for him.

6. India League Publications.

Menon is at present engaged on a pamphlet dealing with the Atlantic Charter which will be used for campaign purposes and is intended to stress the non-application of the Charter to India and the different situation which would eventuate if it were so applied. He is furthermore considering the publication of a small pamphlet on 'The Indian Worker' to deal rather more with conditions than with political questions, and also one on special Industries, such as Indian miners' conditions. He feels that for a pamphlet of that type a sale of 5,000 copies could be assured for Wales alone. He has discussed these projects with Clemens Plame Dutt, the CPGB publishing expert, and the latter has made the suggestion that in addition, Menon should produce later on, a more ambitious brochure dealing with the Trade Union questions and the growth of the movement in India. Menon is not anxious to embark on this as he feels that in the present confused state of the Indian Trade Union question, it would be bad strategy to pronounce upon it. It is not clear how any of these publishing ventures are to be financed, for at least £200 is at present owing by the India League to the Farleigh (Communist), Press and no clue as to how further funds are to be procured.

7. Anand's scheme for collective publication of books dealing with India.

It is more than probable that Menon's intention of issuing the above mentioned pamphlets is dictated by the desire to forestall the efforts of Mulk Raj Anand, who, in association with Sasadhar Sinha, Islam-Ul-Haque, and Dr K.S. Shelvankar, is sponsoring a scheme for the collective publication of books dealing with India. The two first pamphlets to be issued by Anand's group will be entitled 'The Defence of India' and 'Hindus And Muslims: The Communal Myth'. It is believed that Anand has funds in hand for the first but not as yet for the second. He is recently reported to have stated that as he has contracts for two more books, he will have to remain another year at least in England. He is now regarded as an established novelist and has been fairly prominent in the activities of the literary sub section of the People's Convention. Menon may also have learnt that the Communist Party has engaged Shelvankar to produce, if possible by Christmas, a book on India dealing more particularly with the economic question and the holding up of the War effort there.

8. Conclusions

To sum up, Menon has undoubtedly lost face with the CPGB owing to his lukewarm acceptance of the Party 'line' in regard to India and Indian aid for Russia while his India Campaign has lost effect owing to the preoccupation of the working classes with the Russian struggle. On the other hand, he is getting a hearing in intelligentsia circles and has succeeded in approaching some definitely prominent people, who, because of their increasing disquietude over the Indian situation in general and over the imprisonment of Nehru and other leaders in particular, may be described as being in the right objective condition to listen to him. Moreover, since there is no effective Muslim speaker in the field to put the other side of the Indian question and to dispute his superficially plausible arguments, he is still in a position to capitalize the little short of abysmal ignorance which prevails in this country on the subject of the Muslim Minority and the vast numbers which that Minority represents.

V. Forward Bloc

111. Sj. Subhas Bose Missing: Mysterious Disappearance from Home Detected on Sunday

Amrita Bazar Patrika, 28 January 1941.

Under circumstances of great mystery and dramatic import Sj. Subhas Chandra Bose has disappeared from his Elgin Road residence, which, according to the members of his house, was discovered on Sunday afternoon.

Since his release from jail Sj. Bose had been confined in his bed room. According to the medical certificates produced in the court, he was in a very bad state of health and on the ground that he would be unable to stand the strain of trial, repeated adjournments had been taken in the cases pending against him. It is now gathered from the inmates of his house that for the last few days he had not been seeing anybody. Shut up in his room away from the view of anybody he had been performing religious practices. On Sunday afternoon it was noticed that he was not in the room. According to the inmates of the house, Sj. Bose in all probability left the house in the course of the previous night.

Enquiries have since been made at various places, but the whereabouts of Sj. Bose have not yet been ascertained.

When the case pending against Sj. Bose came up before the Additional Chief Presidency Magistrate on Monday, the Advocate of Sj. Bose informed the court that he was missing from the house and his relatives did not know his whereabouts. The Magistrate thereupon issued a warrant for the production of Sj. Bose.

Later in the day the Special Branch police searched the house of Sj. Bose for three hours, the room occupied by Sj. Bose being subjected to minute search.

112. Mr Subhas Bose: No Clue as to Whereabouts Gandhiji Expresses Concern

The Hindu, 30 January 1941.

A further period of waiting and watching has failed to throw fresh light on the whereabouts of Mr Subhas Bose. Till the time of wiring this afternoon, no news has been received either from the police or Mr Bose's home regarding his mysterious and dramatic disappearance. Equally mysterious seems the way the news of Mr Bose's disappearance was known. Until yesterday's *Hindustan Standard* announced the news which came as a surprise to the public, newsmen, and news agencies and even the police authorities did not know of it. It is well-known Mr Bose's residence was being watched by the Special Branch, Police, but even they learnt of Mr Bose's disappearance only after seeing the newspaper report.

This morning, when your correspondent met Mr Bose's nephew, Mr Arabindo Bose, he was told none could tell when exactly Mr Subhas left his residence and where he could have gone. 'The last time I saw Subhas was Friday night and I talked with Subhas till the early hours of Saturday morning, when at 1 a.m. he retired. Subhas's Saturday mid-day meal was found untouched on Sunday noon, whereupon going behind the curtain, I found, Subhas was gone. Since his vow of silence was taken on 16th January, none except myself was permitted to see him. I know he was engaged these days in reading the Gita and other religious works.'

When your correspondent questioned Mr Arabindo Bose, as to whether Mr Subhas's mental and physical health was quite normal, Mr Arabindo Bose answered: 'Mr Subhas's mental condition was quite sound, though physically he was suffering from sciatica. I don't think Mr Subhas would come to physical harm since his tremendous will power used to sustain him during greater physical crises.'

It is stated by those who know Mr Subhas that he had a strong religious grain in his character and that he might have turned a *sanyasi*, and the latest suggestion made is that he might have gone to Tiruvannamalai to join the Ramanashram.

The *Amrita Bazar Patrika* speculating editorially on the reasons for Mr Bose's disappearance wonders whether Mr Subhas took the baffling and mysterious step because he found every political work he undertook lay about him in ruins. It asks how Mr Subhas in such a weak state of health could have gone unobserved. Even the question whether he is in India has been raised.

To all these questions, no clear answer has been forthcoming from any quarter. In the meantime, Mr Subhas who has caused a first class sensation by his secret and dramatic disappearance is causing an anxiety which deepens because the mystery still remains unsolved, in spite of the entire police force in the country being on the look-out.

Gandhiji Makes Enquiry

(Associated Press of India)
Calcutta, 29 January.

Ceaseless efforts to trace Mr Subhas Chandra Bose for the last three days, both by his own people and the police, have failed to yield any clue as regards his whereabouts and intentions. The anxiety grows more and more as time passes on. Enquiries from all quarters in and outside the province continue pouring in.

The latest to inquire about Mr Bose is Mahatma Gandhi, who in a telegram here this morning says: 'Startling news about Subhas. Please wire truth. Anxious. Hope all well—Bapu.'

Replying to Mahatma Gandhi's enquiry, Mr Sarat Chandra Bose in a telegram says: 'We are as much in the dark as the public about Subhas's whereabouts and intentions and even the exact time of his leaving. No news in spite of the best efforts for the last three days. Circumstances indicate renunciation.'

While different theories are being propounded in different quarters, Mr Sarat Bose and Mr Subhas Chandra Bose's close associates give greater credence to the theory of his having taken the step under some religious impulse.

113. Bose's Disappearance

The Hindu, 30 January 1941.

Calcutta, 28 January.

Mr Bose's sudden and mysterious disappearance not only concerns his relatives, friends and admirers, but the man in the street also, who is evincing keen interest in the matter. Many a theory is being propounded by all and sundry and the city is full of rumours and speculations.

While newspaper and news agency offices are receiving innumerable calls from the public, the two telephones at Mr Bose's Elgin Road residence have been continuously buzzing for the past two days, calls coming not only from the city and suburbs, but from far-off places connected by the Trunk Telephone with Calcutta.

The field of enquiry by Mr Bose's own people has now been extended to the whole country. They have drawn up a list of temples, ashrams, and institutions specially known for training in the practice of *yoga* and have sent telegrams to each of these places inquiring about Mr Bose. Messengers have also been sent to some of these *ashrams* and institutes, particularly those in Southern India, where it is felt there is a greater likelihood of his being found.

Mr Mukunda Lal Sarkar, Acting Secretary of the All-India Forward Bloc, has returned from Chandernagore only to report that Mr Bose could not be traced there.

In support of the theory of Mr Bose having disappeared under some religious impulse, it is recalled that in 1914, when he was a student of the Intermediate Class in Calcutta, Mr Bose suddenly left his hostel one morning unnoticed and was not to be traced for over six months. During this period, it is stated he visited almost all the important places of pilgrimage in northern India, as also several *sanyasis' ashrams* in the Himalayas in search of a 'Guru'. Having failed in his object, Mr Bose returned to Calcutta to resume his studies.

The most worried person in Calcutta today is the seventy-five year old mother of Mr Bose, who has been fasting since Sunday and could be persuaded to take a little food only this evening. She has directed that the doors of Mr Bose's room are to remain open day and night lest he finds them closed when he comes back.

Karachi Forward Bloc's Resolution

A resolution recording grave concern at the news of the mysterious disappearance of Mr Subhas Bose and praying for his safety and long life was adopted at a public meeting held under the auspices of the Karachi Forward Bloc tonight. Mr Govindanand presided.

114. Non-violence of Mahatma Gandhi: 'We Don't Believe in it' Forward Bloc Working Committee's Resolution

The Tribune, 23 July 1941.

The Working Committee of the All-India Forward Bloc concluded its two-day session after passing a series of resolutions touching the Satyagraha movement, non-violence as enunciated by Mahatma Gandhi, the war situation and political prisoners.

While strongly condemning the policy of the Government in dealing with Satyagrahis, the Committee declares that it has no faith in the utility of the Satyagraha movement as at present conducted by Mahatma Gandhi. The Forward Bloc strictly adheres to the Congress's creed which aims at achieving 'Swaraj' by all legitimate and peaceful means, but its members do not believe in non-violence as preached by Mahatma Gandhi. The Committee advises Congressmen who differ from Mahatma Gandhi in this respect not to resign from the Congress but remain within it and by fearless agitating to purify it.

The Committee also favours formation of National Defence Brigades all over the country with two-fold object of quelling internal disorder and defending the country against external aggression. The Committee pleads for removal of restrictions placed on the use of arms by Indians under the Arms Act.

Dealing with the question of politicals, the Committee strongly objects to the treatment meted out to political prisoners in various jails all over the country, sympathizes with the grievances of detenus and politicals including those lodged in Agra Jail, and protests against the Government's action in turning down reasonable demands made by them.—API

C. OTHER ORGANIZATIONS

115. The Liberal Federation's Demand

Editorial, *The Tribune*, 1 January 1941.

If after all that has been said in the press and on the platform anything was still needed to show that non-Congress political opinion in India was virtually at one with Congress opinion, both in its demand for complete national freedom and in its rejection of the Viceroy's August statement as inadequate and unsatisfactory, it has been furnished by the substantially identical resolutions on this subject passed by the annual sessions of the Hindu Mahasabha and the National Liberal Federation.[1] To the resolution of the Hindu Mahasabha we have referred already. With one important and some minor differences, the Liberal Federation took up the same position in its resolution. 'The National Liberal Federation of India', said the resolution, 'while desirous to satisfy the reasonable claims of minorities, is of opinion that the Viceroy's declaration of August last virtually gives them a veto on constitutional progress and protests strongly against the distinction drawn by Mr Amery between the status and the functions of a Dominion, which has created a grave apprehension in the minds of the people that what are called British obligations in India may permanently stand in the way of India's achieving the same freedom as the other Dominions enjoy.' The Federation further recorded its strong dissent from the recent statement of the Viceroy that the British Government could do nothing more than they had done already to enable India to enjoy Dominion status, and urged that it should be immediately announced that India would be accorded the status and functions of a Dominion as defined in the Statute of Westminster within a period not exceeding two years after the conclusion of the war. As regards the intervening period, the Federation was of opinion that the Central Government should be so reconstituted as to have by convention a fully national character.

The reconstruction of the Central Government, so that it may have a fully national character is exactly what the Congress demanded by the famous Delhi resolution of its Working Committee, and if the National Federation wants the same thing there is no difference in substance between its position in this matter and that of the Congress. We are not oblivious of the words 'by convention' in the Federation's resolution, but to our mind they make no difference to the position. After all the Congress itself can not have contemplated anything else by its resolution than the establishment of a National Government by convention first because the national government was to be provisional and secondly because it had expressly postponed the question of drawing up a new constitution for India till after the war. In the circumstances the only way open to the British Government to establish a National Government in India enjoying the confidence of all elected elements in the Central Legislature was by convention. What was clearly intended was that the present members of the Viceroy's Executive Council should resign and the Viceroy should after consulting leaders of the various elected elements in the legislature constitute a new Cabinet enjoying the confidence of those elements, it being understood that the cabinet as a whole should resign if and when it ceased to command the confidence of the elected elements. A short Act of Parliament would, of course, be needed in order to make this change possible, because the constitution of the present Central Government is governed by the Montague Act, and that Act provides that a proportion of members of the Executive Council should be members of the Civil Service. But this should be a simple affair once the British Government made up their mind to part with the reality of power in India. It certainly involves no issue of a fundamental character, for the British Government have already by the Act of 1935 definitely decided to abandon the rule of the Civil Service in India in the Central as in the Provincial spheres. But even if for one reason or another this cannot be done immediately, it should not be difficult to have the Service members of the Executive Council as a sort of ornamental figureheads, all important portfolios being entrusted to non-official India members enjoying the confidence of the Legislature.

In moving the resolution the Hon'ble Mr P.N. Sapru made a speech the greater part of which might easily have been delivered from the Congress platform. 'What we want', he said, 'is the reality of power, full control over our destiny, the control that the United Kingdom,

Canada, Australia, and South Africa have. Nothing else will satisfy the aspirations of the people of this country. Nothing else is worth looking at. What we are offered is not Dominion Status of the Statute of Westminster variety. What we are offered is controlled self-government within the imperialist structure, and if the truth is to be told there is a political deadlock in this country, because England is not clear in her mind what she means to do with India after the war. That feeling will not be removed by an equivocal declaration of policy with mental reservations.' What else have Congress leaders like Mr Rajagopalachariar been saying? Mr Sapru had no doubt in his mind that the Viceroy and the Secretary of State had been following a blundering policy all this time. Referring to the distinction drawn by Mr Amery between the status and the functions of a Dominion, Mr Sapru said that he did not care for status. What he cared for was power, freedom, and independence. 'If we have the reality of political power,' he added, 'the status will follow.' As might have been expected Mr Sapru had no patience with the *Pakistan* idea and the two-nation theory. 'How can you,' he said, 'negotiate in a reasonable atmosphere with people who talk not of Indian nationalism but two nations?'

The Federation itself recorded the same view by another resolution in which it emphatically 'opposed the suggested division of India into *Pakistan* and Hindustan as being against the best interests of the country.' 'The aim of India's political evolution' the resolution added, 'should be a democracy not qualified by considerations of race or creed and, therefore the Federation is definitely opposed to the permanent existence of communal electorates and the present Communal Award. At the same time, as it would not be practicable to effect this reform immediately owing to existing conditions, it considers that gradual steps should be taken to eliminate separate communal electorates by having joint electorates with reserved seats for a definite period.' Dr Paranjape, who moved the resolution, said that it was a great mistake to introduce religion in the political sphere, and to-day they were witnessing its dire results. As regards the Communal Award the distinguished Liberal leader described it as a standing obstacle in the path of India's progress as a real democracy. 'It was time,' he added, 'that they put their foot down on the communal virus and enunciate once for all their opposition to separate communal electorates.' In all this we have the pure milk of the Nationalist variety, and we congratulate the National Liberal Federation for its unequivocal pronouncement in these vital matters. On the main issue, the only difference between the Federation and the Congress is the difference between political opinion and action based on that opinion.

---

[1] The 22nd session of the National Liberal Federation was held at Calcutta from 28 to 30 December 1940.

116. All India Christian Conference Resolutions

The Tribune, 2 January 1941.

Need for All-parties Conference: Appeal to Gandhi and Jinnah

Five resolutions were passed by the All-India Christian Conference which is being held here[1].

The first resolution expressed grief over the imprisonment of several men and women in the country, specially the heavy sentence passed on Pandit Jawaharlal Nehru.

Responsible Government

A second resolution stressed the need on the part of the British Government of fixing a definite date after the conclusion of the war for establishment of full responsible Government in India.

As a preliminary to the establishment of responsible Government, a national Government responsible to the legislature should be formed at the Centre without delay.

The next resolution appealed to the leaders of different political parties, in particular to Mahatma Gandhi and Mr Jinnah, to agree to the convening of a conference of various important parties and interests in the country for the purpose of framing a constitution on a national basis. It directed the president of the All-India Conference of Indian Christians to take steps to implement the resolution.

By another resolution the conference recommended that the Indian Christian Association and missionary societies in the country should take steps to ensure correct recording of members during the ensuing census.

Share in Govt Services

'So long as the principle of communal representation is observed by Government in making appointments in the Government and railway service,' runs another resolution, 'it is both equitable and necessary that a separate percentage should be definitely allocated to the Indian Christian community in India.'

The Conference by another resolution deplored the action of foreign Christian missions in India in disregarding the opinion and sentiments of the Indian Christian community with regard to allienation of church and mission property now held by them in India and resolved that the mission bodies be urged to stop all such sales. An All-India Chruch and Mission Property Committee consisting of one member from each province were also constituted to evolve ways of stopping alienation of mission properties.

The Conference also regretted that the Viceroy had not consulted leaders of Indian Christians about the political situation.

---

[1] The annual session of the All India Christian Conference was held at Lucknow on 30 December 1940.

117. Begum Iftikhar-ud-Din's Speech at Azad Christian Conference

The Tribune, 6 January 1941.

Lahore, 5 January.

Present Struggle for Freedom: 'It is for All'

'It is not the Hindus, Muslims, Christians or the Sikhs who are fighting each other in India for their so called separate rights. It is the supporters of imperalism and the poor and ignorant masses who are engaged in a conflict. The struggle for rights is not between any communities but between the Haves and Have-nots', thus observed Begum Mian Iftikhar ud-Din, while unfurling the flag of the Azad Christian Youth League this afternoon at the Pandal of the Azad Christian Conference which opened here today.

The flag of the youth, she said, was the flag of freedom, peace, and progress and she felt sure that the Indian Christian youth would do their duty to the country and stand by what the flag represented.

Proceeding Begum Sahiba said: 'I belong to the Congress and bring to you felicitations on behalf of the National organization which is engaged at present in the unique struggle for freedom. I want to assure you that the freedom which the Congress is fighting for is meant not for any particular class of people but for the whole of India'.

Referring to the claim of the 'Qaid-Azam Jinnah Sahib' that democracy was ill suited to the Musalmans in India and was being insisted upon to crush the Muslims, Begum Sahiba pointed out that by chance the very day this view of Mr Jinnah was made public in the newspapers, the statement of Veer Savarkar who had suggested that democracy was bound to jeopardize the best interests of the Hindus was also published. 'Was that not interesting', asked Begum Sahiba. One could have certainly thought better of these communal gods' but for such utterances. 'It is a matter of shame', she said, 'for us all that a few top leaders are making any agreement in India impossible. The pity of it is that they are doing it not because the rights or privileges of any people are involved in any way, but they are doing so because their own leadership is endangered. I have no doubt, and I am sure, every lover of the freedom of India, which is the common Motherland of all of us, feels that neither Islam nor Hinduism is in danger'....

118. Azad Christian Conference: Report on Presidential Address

The Tribune, 6 January 1941.

Lahore, 5 January.

Let us Realize Our Duties more Than Our Rights

Dr Ram Chandra Rao, in the course of his presidential address said: I am really grateful to you for the opportunity given to me for approaching you and sharing with you some of the thoughts and ideas that have been uppermost in my mind for some time. I offer no apology for attempting to think aloud. It is only by removing the barrier between oneself and others that truth could be found and mental and moral values of things truly appraised. I am really glad that the Azad Christian Conference has been attempting to look at things from the national point of view. No doubt the country is sick of the communalistic view of things. Communalism has overreached its bounds and defeated its purpose landing us in a hopeless mess. Time has now come to take a wider view of things. You must see that our aspirations are in tune with national culture and ideas. We may not be able to do anything very spectacular, but we shall be on safe-ground so long as we are in tune with national culture and ideas. Modern science believes in averages. Decimal theory indicates that an attempt is constantly made by nature to return to the normal form. The extreme Science believes in continuous progress though there may be occasional lapses.

'In the world of nature the creative impulse is the strongest. Man is mortal, but mankind is immortal. Destruction is easier than creation. I take it that the Azad Conference is out to create. Destruction is sometimes necessary, but like the surgeon's cut remove, and prune judicially. Let us beware of the wholesale importation of foreign ideas: We should consider seriously whether foreign ideas suit the genius of our country. I think we should develop something indigenous to suit our needs. Of course, we should not be blind to international repercussions. We are a part of humanity and, as such, our national problems cannot but be a contribution to the progress of the world. I rejoice that the Azad Conference has come to take a national view of Indian problems. The time has come to get out of purely communal grooves. Discarding the spirit of isolation, we should fraternize with other communities in a friendly-manner. *Life* becomes full and more interesting when one gets into touch with those who think and feel differently. I take it that the Azad Christian Conference is anxious or is determined to face national issues in our country. The nation is made of village communities, which number about 200 lakhs. To this day the village community has been on the brink of starvation and has been steepped in indescribable misery. Again ignorance is simply colossal, illiteracy being the common factor all over the country. Nonetheless important is the task of purity. Nor is the question of communal harmony less important in the villages.

'Poverty of the grinding sort is the problem in the ancient country of ours. People in villages have plenty of time but no opportunities to make use of their leisure. Village industry, when properly planned and managed, should provide part-time work for villagers. A new order of village economy would be necessary. Every attempt should be made to maintain village organization.

Problem of Poverty

'The problem of Indian poverty could be solved, to a considerable extent, by the introduction of cottage industry in the villages of India. I trust the Azad Group would extend its support to village products and do every thing to popularize them. Of course, it should not be forgotten that man lives by food, and if India does not produce food for her millions, no country in the world could do it for her. Therefore, most up-to-date methods of agriculture should be introduced and village life should be organized on a co-operative basis. Fruit culture has not received consideration. it should. In spite of its faults, the attempt at prohibition has been a success and every effort should be made to prepare the ground for its introduction all over the country. Systematic propaganda should be carried on in each and every village, bringing home to the people the evils that are attendant upon liquor consumption. The Azad Group may have many opportunities of doing national work at this time. They could render valuable service by winning over the patrons of pubs to the attractive humanizing sphere of usefullness and service.

119. Azad Christian Conference Inaugurated

The Tribune, 6 January 1941.

No Time to Remain Aloof
Join Struggle for Freedom: Mahatma Gandhi's Method is Christ's Method

'Let the Indian Christians realize that it is no time to remain aloof from the Hindus and Musalmans. I ask them to make the voice of India stronger by joining their Hindu and Muslim brethren in their demand for self-Government and freedom,' thus observed Mrs K.L. Rallia Ram, in the course of her short address—while inaugurating the Azad Christian Conference this afternoon. The Conference was held under big Shamiana and was attended by a large number of Indian Christians.

Among those present at the Conference were Begum Mian Iftikhar-ud-Din, Begum Satnam Mahmood Ali, Mrs K.L. Rallia Ram, and Mr K.L. Rallia Ram.

The President-elect Mr Ramchandra Rao was given an ovation when he reached the pandal. He sat on a raised platform, every one else squatted on the floor.

Mr K.L. Rallia Ram, General Secretary of the Conference, read out messages received from different leaders. Mahatma Gandhi and the Congress President, in their messages wished the Conference success. Rajkumari Amrit Kaur in the course of her message (which was read out) expressed the hope that the Indian Christrians would come into the Congress-fold. She had written that a time had come when they could no longer remain out.

Mrs K.L. Rallia Ram, while inaugurating the Conference, appealed to the Indian Christians to join the Indian freedom movement which was now being conducted by Mahatma Gandhi.

Gandhiji's method, said Mrs K.L. Rallia Ram, was the method of Christ. She wished some Christians should have given the lead to the country to prove the efficacy of the method of Christ. But, as it happened, the leader of the Indian people who was a Hindu by birth had adopted the method of Christ to achieve the freedom of India.

Mrs Rallia Ram criticized the dreams of Hindu Raj and Pakistan as preposterous and pleaded for a united India where everyone who claimed India to be his or her home, would have a place. She asked Indian Christians to play their part in bringing about unity between Hindus and Mussalmans. The Indian Christians could do that work because they came from both the communities.

Proceeding Mrs Rallia Ram condemned the bane of communalism. Peace was being denied to the people and too much emphasis was being laid on religion. If religion resulted in creating conflicts between man and man, then that religion, she maintained, should be shelved.

The present day order, she concluded was a challenge to Christianity and she wished Indian Christians would rise to the occasion and see that justice and love prevailed. She had no doubt that a new world order would arise from the present conflict.

120. Giani Kartar Singh's Presidential Address at Akali Conference

The Tribune, 13 January 1941.

'Sikhs Must Make Sacrifice to Attain Freedom'

'How can we admit that the methods employed by Sri Hargobindji, Guru Gobind Singh, Lord Krishna, Lord Ram Chandra, and Prophet Mohammed were not sublime? In my opinion with the change of times, the sublime methods also undergo a change. For ending wars, sometimes violence, and sometimes non-violence can become a sublime method. I am also of the opinion that Individual Satyagraha may not perhaps be so useful and the British may well endure its pressure'. These views were expressed by Giani Kartar Singh, MLA, General Secretary of the SPGC in his presidential address at a very largely attended Akali Political Conference held this evening at Muktsar, the seat of a historic Sikh Gurdwara in the Ferozepur district on the occasion of the well-known *Magh Mela*. The huge Pandal was fitted with loud speakers and several Akali leaders attended the conference. Earlier the President was taken out in a dignified procession.

In his voluminous presidential address, Giani Kartar Singh discussed at length several important problems confronting the Sikh community, including the Congress attitude vis-à-vis non-violence, the Pakistan scheme, the effect of Socialism on the Sikh community and the census.

Giani Kartar Singh deplored the existing dissensions in the ranks of the community and appealed to all sections to unite in order to face the common foe, who was growing outside the ranks of the community as well as inside. He criticized the attitude of the Khalsa Nationalist Party, which by co-operating with the Unionist Ministry was undermining the Panthic solidarity.

He then criticized those young men, who propagated the Russian brand of Socialism, who were causing great harm to the community. These so-called Socialists wanted to fight for bread only, but the Akalis wanted to fight for religion, bread, freedom and self-respect.

Alluding to the outside enemies of the community, he said that the greatest opposition was from the Muslim League and its Pakistan scheme. Its object was to establish Muslim rule in the Punjab, NWF Province and Sind. If this scheme was ever given a practical shape, it would mean the revival of a rule of bigotry, and it would naturally weaken the Sikh faith and undermine the political entity of the Sikhs. For this reason, he appealed to the Sikhs to unite in order to oppose this dangerous scheme.

Continuing Giani Kartar Singh observed that as a very big minority, it was the duty of the Mohammedans to carry the Sikhs with them, so that there could be a joint solution of the minority problems. But the Muslims adopted a different course, though both the Sikhs and the Muslims had several common problems, as for instance the position of the two communities in the Army. To increase the strength and prestige of the province this could be useful to both. Both the communities were monotheists, and in any constitution of the country, protection of both was essential. It was a pity that not a single Muslim State had come forward to realize the significance of these matters. On the contrary owing to the injustice and intolerance of the Muslims towards the Sikhs, the gulf of their differences was being widened. It was the duty of every Sikh to oppose the Pakistan scheme without allowing these dissensions among the Muslims and the Sikhs to grow.

Referring to the coming census, he said that every Sikh having faith in the Gurus should get himself or herself registered as a Sikh, even if he or she, were a Sehajdhari (without the long hair).

Sikhs to Fight for Freedom

Discussing the constitutional problem of the country, Giani Kartar Singh said that the present constitution of the country was a hindrance in the path of their progress. The teachings of Guru Gobind Singh could not be propagated adequately under any foreign rule, and for this reason freedom was essential and the Sikhs must make sacrifices to attain that.

He said that the Congress had started its Satyagraha movement. Gandhiji's Satyagraha at present was not undertaken either for freedom or for a National Government through a Constituent Assembly, but only for the right of free speech.

If the struggle was undertaken for the establishment of a National Government, it would have been different. Gandhiji had become an enigma to him, and he failed to understand his mentality.

Continuing Giani Kartar Singh alluded to happenings at Kot Bhai Than Singh, Sargodha, restrictions on 'Jhatka' meat, Gurdwara Act Amendment Bill, and regretted that the grievances of the Sikhs were not being removed. He then criticized the Compulsory Primary Education Bill, which had overlooked the claims of Hindi and Gurmukhi.

He referred to the boast of Mr Jinnah that the rights of the minorities would be adequately protected in Pakistan. He asked if that was the protection that was now being given to the Sikhs by the Unionist Ministry. The Primary Education Bill dealt a severe blow to the culture of the Hindus and the Sikhs. He deplored the attitude of the Khalsa Nationalist Party in this matter. He said that the Punjab Government realized the futility of such agitations as had been launched hitherto.

He wanted the Sikhs to realize that the Congress would not help them in this matter. The Congress could help the Muslims in the matter of the Khilafat, Palestine, and Arabia and also the Pathans, who kidnapped the Hindus and Sikhs, but the Congress had not the courage to oppose the Muslim Government where injustice was being done on academics and students. The desire of students to protest against repression, their demand for freedom of speech and their demands for recourse to strike and picket were in accordance with actualities. The students not only reflected the political and social trends of the day according to the social class to which they belonged, but also consciously expressed opinion in accordance with their interests.

121. Congress Responsible for Deadlock: Sir Sikander's View

The Tribune, 15 January 1941.

That he was not in a position to appeal to the British Government to do anything to help in the task of putting an end to the present deadlock in India because the responsibility for the creation of the present situation lay entirely with the Congress, was the view expressed by Sir Sikander Hyat Khan, Premier Punjab, in the course of a talk with *The Tribune* Representative, before his departure tonight for Delhi where he has gone for a day to meet the Commander-in-Chief of India.

Mr J.D. Anderson, Joint Chief Secretary, Punjab Government, accompanied the Premier.

The Tribune Representative asked the Punjab Premier if he would use his influence with the British Government and his friendly relations with those in authority in the Congress, to bring about some sort of compromise between the British Government and the Congress and help in ending the present deadlock. The Punjab Premier replying said that he was too humble a person for playing that role for that gigantic task. He felt, however, that if he would get some response to his appeal which he made at the Nedous Hotel last night, then alone he could make an appeal to the British Government to make a move. His complaint was that the Congress, after its Delhi resolution, did not go to the logical end. It was his definite opinion that had the Congress, after its Delhi resolution, approached the Viceroy and asked for a clear elucidation of the Government's position and demanded that important 'portfolios' be handed over to the popular representatives, and if the Congress would have got no response from the Viceroy, then it might have been justified in following its present course of action. He was sorry to say that nothing of the kind had been done by the Congress before taking the step which has now resulted in the present situation. He felt, therefore, that the responsibility for the present impasse was entirely that of the Congress.

There were other difficulties now also because some other parties were pressing their demands.

122. Tej Bahadur Sapru's Appeal

Bombay Chronicle, 17 January 1941.

In a lengthy article in the Twentieth Century Sir Tej Bahadur has made one more appeal to all concerned to bring about at least a tentative political settlement. It may be remembered that he made a similar appeal last month offering certain specific suggestions for consideration by Government. There was, however, no response from Government. Sir Tej, therefore, now addresses himself primarily to the principal parties in the country but does not suggest any definite proposals as a basis for settlement. The time for such proposals, he says, will come when a serious attempt is made by party leaders to hammer out a constitution in a spirit of compromise. For the present he only suggests that we ourselves must settle the communal problem and that immediately, even if it be that the authorities hinder instead of helping its solution. More specifically he repeats his former suggestion that Gandhiji and Mr Jinnah should meet with a determination not to part till they have achieved at least a tentative settlement.

'Once', he says, 'they can go to the Viceroy and tell him 'this is our united demand for the temporary period of war', I doubt very much whether they can come back empty-handed.' And he hopes that this temporary settlement and the co-operation in working it out is bound to pave the way for a permanent settlement.

Need for Hindu–Muslim Settlement

We agree that we must ourselves solve the communal problem even if Government continue to hinder it and that attempts in this direction should be resumed immediately. They should also be kept up ceaselessly in spite of apparent failures. The Congress has made several attempts before and neither pessimism nor considerations of prestige will prevent it from resuming them. Sir Tej himself can render notable service in this matter and as a first step may well interview both Gandhiji and Mr Jinnah with a view to arranging a small representative conference to consider the whole communal problem. No conditions should be attached to the convening of the conference itself. At the conference every proposal will be considered on its merits.

Crux of the Situation

The question now arises as to what is to be done if for some reason or other a communal settlement is not reached soon enough. In such a contingency, Sir Tej rightly insists that Government should demonstrate to the people at large that England has made up her mind not only to raise the status of India but also to give her equal powers with the other constituent members of the Commonwealth. 'If India', he asks, 'is to be a full-fledged Dominion after the war, why hesitate to say so in words that admit of no doubt, and why also not do something now as an earnest of the things to come, even though it may not be perfect in every respect'? This is, indeed, the crux of the situation. If Britain makes a definite unequivocal declaration granting full freedom to India very soon after the war, and if a satisfactory beginning is made at once as an earnest, it will both transform the attitude of the Congress towards the war and will itself go a long way in helping a communal settlement. If on the other hand, Britain still refuses to take the steps suggested, the present campaign of non co-operation will certainly spread as is clear from among other things the proceedings of the Madura session of the Hindu Mahasabha.[1]

---

[1] The session was held from 28 December to 30 December 1940.

123. Liberal Leaders' Statement

Editorial, *The Tribune*, 20 January 1941.

The reply, which the eleven frontrank Indian Liberal leaders, including the President of the Liberal Federation, have given to the message of nine members of Parliament is comprehensive and cogent.[1] Not only the nine members of Parliament, but also the millions of Britishers, closely or remotely interested in the affairs of India, should read it carefully and digest it well. Its authors are neither visionaries nor hotheads. They are realists and moderates. On some of them highest honours have been conferred by the British Government. And all of them are unfailing friends of Britain. When they draw a picture, that is alarming, or sound a note of warning that is serious, it will be extremely foolish on the part of the British Government and the British people to continue to maintain their unimaginative and inflexible attitude towards India.

As the Liberal leaders have pointed out, if the British Government had acted wisely and courageously, not only the communal aberrations that prevent the evolution of Indian national unity would have disappeared, but the gulf that separates India from Britain, would have been bridged and the world would have witnessed the splendid spectacle of India voluntarily and heartily throwing the full weight of her vast resources on the side of Britain in her struggle against Nazism. To Hitler this spectacle would have been confounding, for in the face of it he would not have been able to declare that Britain had a skeleton in her cupboard and that she was not fighting to protect democracy but to protect her own interests. To Roosevelt, extremely sensitive to things indicative of the shrinking of the frontiers of democracy, this spectacle would have been the most convincing argument that America should give the fullest aid to Britain. The claim of Britain on the United States for help, which is entirely based on her contention that she is fighting for the preservation of human liberties, is weakened when it is pointed out by her critics that 'there is slavery in her own house hold'.

---

[1] The reference is to the statement which Indian Liberal leaders sent on 17 January 1941 in response to a better which nine members of British Parliament had address to the people of India on 23 December 1940.

124. End Constitutional Deadlock: Madras Democratic Union's Demand

The Tribune, 24 February 1941.

'The development of the international situation and its repercussions in India make it imperative that the constitutional deadlock, brought about by the anti-war policy of the Congress, be ended without any further delay so that the Indian people may avail of the present opportunity to grow up to the fullest stature of freedom and power', states a resolution adopted at the inaugural meeting of the Madras Provincial Democratic Union.

The resolution adds that enthusiastic voluntary and popular support is indispensable for India's making a decisive contribution to the defeat of Fascism. To secure that support, genuinely anti-Fascist non-official elements should be associated with the Government of the country without any further delay.

The resolution refers to the National Democratic Union formed at a conference in Calcutta in December last and supports the movement for the formation of a national democratic union, endorses its declaration and the programme contained there in.

The resolution adds: Realizing that far-sighted Indian patriots who are prepared to shoulder the responsibility of mobilizing the striking and defensive power of India in the fight against Fascism, however, cannot play their part effectively, with honour and credit, unless the Government of the country comes under popular influence, as far as possible, in the given situation, and the responsibility for the defence of India passes on the Indians themselves. 'Therefore, we urge the necessity of an early termination of the present deadlock by the establishment of emergency ministries in the provinces without any responsible government today, and the inclusion of independent popular representatives in the Viceroy's Council.'

The resolution also appeals to all the different political organizations which do not approve of the policy of the Congress, to come together on this common platform with the object of utilizing the great possibilities of the present situation for promoting the political advancement of the Indian people.

125. Report of Tej Bahadur Sapru's Speech at the Bombay Conference of Non-party Leaders' Conference, 14 March 1941

The Hindu, 15 March 1941.

Reconstruct the Centre: Non-party Leaders Call to Government, Immediate Settlement Urged

Bombay, 14 March.

The Proceedings

An earnest appeal to the Government of India to take the initiative in getting together leaders of the Congress and the Muslim League in an effort to resolve the present deadlock and if that attempt failed to mobilize the large mass of unattached opinion in the country was made today by the Rt Hon Sir Tej Bahadur Sapru, opening the Conference of Non-Party Leaders.

The Conference concluded at six p.m. after unanimously adopting the resolution moved by Sir N.N. Sircar.[1]

Sir Tej Bahadur Sapru, winding up the proceedings of the Conference, said that it was absurd for anyone to believe that the fortunes of four hundred million people could be settled by Radio broadcasts and statements to the press. Sir Tej Bahadur invited the Secretary of State for India and half a dozen British members of Parliament to visit India and see things for themselves, so that they could come to definite decisions regarding the future of India. The President deeply deplored 'the lack of imagination and big-heartedness on the part of British statesmen in dealing with the complicated problem of India.'

In opening the proceedings, Sir Tej Bahadur Sapru, stressed the importance of the Conference at this juncture and said that it was under a compelling sense of duty that he had agreed to attend it. Those who were present at the Conference were entitled to have their own views in regard to the political situation. It was no use for anybody challenging their capacity or their solution. It was enough for them that as men interested in the politics and future of the country and as men who had been watching the trend of events during the last twelve months or more, they were making an earnest effort to bring about a solution of the present deadlock at this critical juncture.

This Conference, Sir Tej said, was a conference of men who were approaching the Indian question as it had tended to become, not from the point of view of any particular party but from the point of view of the whole country. There were some at the Conference who were identified with strong party organizations; there were others who were not identified with any party organization. But he had reasons to believe that even men, who were identified with strong party organizations, realizing the supreme importance of the occasion, had put in the background their party views and had brought themselves into line with the general feeling that everything should be done in the interests of the country which may tend to ease the situation (cheers).

Congress Ministries Resignation

Proceeding to examine the position in the country, Sir Tej Bahadur remarked that out of the eleven Provinces, seven were at present being administered by Governors with the help of official advisers. He did not wish to shut his eyes to the realities of the situation. The situation of the Provinces arose in November, 1939, because the Congress Ministries in seven Provinces decided to tender their resignations. It was not, Sir T.B. Sapru said, his intention to attack any political party any more than to defend any political party, but he could not help feeling that it was a very shortsighted decision for the Congress to call out the Ministers. If the Ministers had been in their places to-day, much of the trouble that had arisen in the Provinces would not have arisen (hear, hear).

Similarly, Sir Tej Bahadur continued, the situation had been aggravated during recent months by the starting of the Satyagraha movement. He did nto want to hide the fact from any one that he was a confirmed unbeliever in that movement. He had not concealed it even from the great originator of the movement, Mahatma Gandhi. But whatever might be the convictions of Mahatma Gandhi on this point, he was fully prepared to grant that they were as deep as they were sincere. It was unfortunate that at a juncture like the present, the movement should have been started, and should have given rise to a great misapprehension as regards the Indian attitude towards the war.

Referring next to the war, Sir Tej Bahadur said that there was no one present here who did not realize the gravity of the international situation. They were beginning to realize that the war was coming nearer and nearer to the shores of India. He said that he had always maintained that the fruition of their aims and aspirations depended upon the success of England. Although he knew that in the bitterness of their hearts, some people compared Fascism and Nazism with British Imperialism, yet upon reflection they would find that there was a world of difference between the two. But he did not want to enter into a theoretical discussion. From a practical point of view and from the point of view of the country, it was very necessary that Britain should come out successfully from this gigantic war effort (cheers).

'Take the public into confidence'

Sir Tej Bahadur pointed out that the country had been helping in the war effort, if they were to believe all those broadcasts and statements issued by the Government of India, and that was about all the Government of India told them. Money was forthcoming in abundance from the different parts of the country and there had been no trouble about recruitment. Still many believed that there was a great deal more which might be done with the willing co-operation of educated Indians. It was with a view to helping in the successful prosecution of the war that they had assembled to take stock of the situation and to make suggestions as to how that end might be achieved.

'Frankly speaking', he said, 'I maintain, and maintain very strongly, that there has never been a Government of India more isolated from public opinion and from the main current of thought in the country than the present Government of India. The members of the Government of India should appear before the public, take the public into confidence and they must not assume that the Indian Legislatures, respectable bodies as they are, or one or two important political bodies, constitute the whole of India. I should like to see members of the Government of India appearing on the public platform and telling us what really is happening.'

They all knew, Sir Tej Bahadur went on, that on 8 August, the Viceroy had made an offer and that the Congress and the Muslim League had turned it down. Whether the reasons for the refusal were just or unjust, wise or unwise, was a matter of the past. What he would like to know was what had been done since. They had moved from August to March, repeated statements had been made in Parliament and outside by Mr Amery and they had been told time after time that there were unfortunate differences existing between the two organized bodies, the Congress and the Muslim League. The natural inference from these repeated references to these two organized bodies and the quarrels existing between them was that unless those differences were composed they need not expect any advance. That was an unfortunate position.

Appeal to Congress and Muslim League

'No one will be more pleased than myself', Sir Tej Bahadur Sapru continued, 'and I can speak on behalf of every one here, if these organized bodies compose their differences even at this stage. In your names and on behalf of those interested in true progress, I make an earnest appeal to leaders of these two organizations to review the situation, to see facts as they are, to indulge less in theoretical discussions and to grapple with the realities of the situation and to come to some settlement.

'I believe we have already exposed ourselves to a great deal of ridicule in this country and outside for our inability to compose our differences even at this critical juncture. It is, therefore, that I make an earnest appeal, to these two bodies and their distinguished leaders, to meet, to discuss things among themselves and devise some formula for a settlement of the outstanding disputes, because it is imperative that some day or other these disputes should be settled. If it seems necessary for either of these two bodies or to both of them to requisition the services of any one of us as common friends, I am sure none of us will stint our services.'

But if those bodies were not prepared to compose their differences, then the Conference should be prepared for some alternative, Sir Tej suggested. If the two bodies did not compose their differences, then surely it did not lie in the mouth of the British Government to say that because those two organizations could not compose their differences the rest of the country should be penalized and must wait until it pleased the leaders of those parties to be sensible and to be in a mood to compose their differences. That to his mind was an intolerable situation. It was not enough for the British Government repeatedly to refer to the existence of unfortunate differences. It was also necessary for the Government to say that they had done their best and that they were ready to do their best to bring about reconciliation between the two bodies. In that respect the British Government had done practically nothing. It was not enough for the Viceroy to call men to see them individually or in groups.

Government's Duty

Why could not the Government of India, Sir Tej Bahadur asked, muster courage and get together leaders of the two parties and call a conference? They should have done that long ago. When a critical situation of the same character arose in 1917 the then Viceroy, Lord Chelmsford, called a War Conference at which Princes were represented, the Congress, as it was in those days, was represented and even Mahatma Gandhi was present. It gave a great stimulus to activity in the country in support of the war at that time. It was, therefore, impossible to understand the present policy of the Government of India. They argued that, however good and estimable other people might be, they had no large followings and the Congress and the Muslim League were the only two bodies which had followings and as the latter were not prepared to compose their differences, the Government need not look at others. Sir Tej Bahadur's answer to that was that there was a vast mass of unattached opinion in the country which could have been mobilized by the Government. That they had not done. It was true that large following were behind great leaders, but it was equally true that if any leaders were worth their salt, they could create a following of their own. Things like that had happened in the country in the past as well as in other countries and he did not, therefore, understand the non-possumus attitude of the Government. Sir Tej Bahadur had reason to believe that if the Government of India moved in the matter or if the Secretary of State moved in the matter, those might be called upon to shoulder the burden who were willing, not permanently but only as a temporary measure during the period of the war. They would be prepared to vacate the places if and when the Congress or the Muslim League or both were willing to take up the burden. It all depended on who the men were who were selected. He refused to believe that a country of 400 millions was so devoid of men of experience and character that it would be impossible for the Government of India to find ten or twelve men who would command public support and confidence.

An attempt should seriously be made, Sir Tej Bahadur suggested, to bring the two parties, together and to persuade them to assume responsibility, but if that attempt failed there was no reason why an attempt should not be made to bring into seats of power other men who were ready to offer their services to serve the best interests of the country, not in a spirit of careerists or office-seekers but in a spirit of true servants of the country, who would not hesitate to make room for others if there should be a settlement between the major parties afterwards. It was in that spirit that he wanted the Conference to approach the resolution.

Sir Tej Bahadur emphasized that a united India would be a far greater asset to the British Government at the present critical juncture than a disunited India, and said that it was for the Government to take the necessary steps to bring about a united India. Let them make their contribution in that behalf. He hoped that there would be adequate response, at the same time, to their demands....

---

[1] The text of the Resolution is reproduced in Document No. 67, Chapter 1.

126. Depressed Class Uplift: Provision in New Constitution Dr B.R. Ambedkar's Suggestions

The Hindu, 17 March 1941.

Ahmedabad, 16 March.

The creation of settlements to be exclusively occupied by Depressed Classes, in uncultivated waste and forest lands, and a constitutional provision for an annual subvention of not less than Rs 20 lakhs in each province for the purpose, were advocated by Dr B.R. Ambedkar, presiding over the First Depressed Class Political Conference of Gujarat. He added that the harassment of the Depressed Classes by caste Hindus continued as before, and it would not stop till the Depressed Classes were removed to new settlements which should be placed in charge of a special board of commissioners.

Proceeding, he said that Mahatma Gandhi advocated the uplift of the Depressed Classes but opposed their gaining political power without which there could be no real uplift of the Depressed Classes. At the last Round Table Conference the speaker had demanded the same rights for the Depressed Classes as were given to the Muslims. But Mahatma Gandhi had resisted them and gone on a fast unto death.

Dr Ambedkar suggested the following provisions in the new constitution that might be framed: (1) representatives of Depressed Classes should be elected by separate electorates; (2) all Cabinets should include at least two representatives of Depressed Classes chosen by the members of the Depressed Classes in the legislatures. Once they were chosen, they should be irremovable during the life of the legislature; (3) Depressed Classes should be represented in the services, particularly revenue, police, and judicial departments in the proportion of fifteen per cent in the higher grades to be attained within ten years subject to the rule of minimum qualification; (4) Depressed Classes should have representation on the public services commission in each province; (5) a fixed sum should be allotted in the budget or expenditure on the education of Depressed Classes in each province.

Demand for Separate Electorates

The Conference concluded to-day after passing a string of resolutions the principal of which demanded separate electorates for the Depressed Classes instead of the joint electorates in all public bodies such as legislatures, municipalities, local boards, village panchayats, and others.

In the course of his concluding remarks, Dr Ambedkar, President, said that the Conference was a success in spite of the boycott by the Congressites.

127. 'Mahars are Unsteady in Public Work': Communal Panchayats are Squandering Public Funds on Frivolous Activity

Bombay Chronicle, 29 March 1941.

A stringent attack on the working of the Panchayats of the Mahar community in the city was directed by Dr B.R. Ambedkar in the presence of many of the prominent members of the Panchayats at a public meeting of the Depressed Classes held in the Bhatt High School Hall last night to consider the financial position of the Depressed Class Students' Hostel at Thana.

The Panchayats had been levying taxes of all sorts and under various pretexts on the community, he said. Most of that money used formerly to be spent on drinking bouts. But now that prohibition was introduced in the city the money was being spent on eating 'batasas' and distributing sweets.

'What has come over you, the elders and senior members of the community', asked Dr Ambedkar, 'that you should behave like children and want to indulge in sweets purchased out of public funds while the community has to face increasing competition with other communities in the struggle for life. Unless we discard these childish activities and take to the serious work of the social and educational advancement, our position might get even worse than it is to-day.'

Example of Others

Dr Ambedkar held before the Depressed Classes the example of the advanced Indian communities. Among the advanced communities, he said there were always a number of men who devoted themselves exclusively and life-long to educational and other social institutions in their communities without any hope of reward or even appreciation.

Among educated youths of the Depressed Classes however, the speaker witnessed the tendency to look-out for seats on local boards, municipalities, and similar other positions, and if they did not get these—and all of them could not possibly get these—then they gave up all interest in public work and sunk into total indifference to the fate of the community.

'Nibbling'

There were others who were so unsteady in their public work that they nibbled at one type of work for some time, then turned on to another, then shifted to third one leaving every institution they handle in a chaotic condition.

128. Congress and Satyagraha: 'Limited' Movement Sir N.N. Sircar's Suggestion

Amrita Bazar Patrika, 18 April 1941.

In support of the suggestion by *The Hindu* of Madras to the effect that Congress should call off Satyagraha and once again assume power and lead the country politically, Sir Nripendra Nath Sircar in a statement says:

'I am in general agreement with the leading article in *The Hindu* of the 15th instant except that unduly euphemistic language has been used in stating the conclusion—the limited Satyagraha launched by Gandhiji cannot help very much so far as the dominant need of the country to-day is concerned.

'Far from being of much help it cannot help at all, a fact which has been abundantly proved by the experiment which has lasted a pretty long time.

'Indeed it is not only of no help but it is a disastrous hindrance to the cause of India. It will require far greater courage in retracing footsteps and in trying to undo the almost irreparable mischief already done in courting imprisonment.

'The alleged spiritual technique is not understood by ordinary persons like myself, for whom resignation of Ministries can only mean shirking of duty when India is passing through fateful days owing to War and the grave international situation.

'It is not for me to give advice to the Congress press of the undue importance given to the Muslim League in certain quarters; I blame them much less than those whose voluntary exile is responsible for that situation.

'I have no grounds for believing that the salutary advice given to in the article, will be accepted by those to whom it is addressed, but I shall not be so rash as to make any forecast where politics are involved.'

129. 'Congress Must be Back': Need for Resumption of Office Rt Hon Sastri's Call

The Hindu, 27 April 1941.

Madras, 27 April.

'The times are very very critical. Not a moment is to be lost in finding out who are the most competent by spirit, by experience, and by courage, to help us. Judging all things, there is at present no body of people who have our trust in the same measure and who have therefore, laid upon them the supreme duty of coming back and resuming power and defending the people, as the Congress', observed the Rt Hon V.S. Srinivasa Sastri speaking last evening on the political situation in India with reference to Mr Amery's latest utterance. It was essential, he added, that 'the chosen leaders of the Congress' should be at the helm if the new situation that would arise every day and complications not to be foreseen now were to be successfully tackled. Mr T.T. Krishnamachari, who was the other speaker, wanted 'all people to combine to make an appeal to Mahatma Gandhi, who was always responsive to public opinion, to make it possible for Congress leaders to come back to their posts.'

The meeting was held under the auspices of the Saturday Club at the Ranade Hall. A large gathering of citizens and students was present on the occasion.

The Rt Hon Srinivasa Sastri, at the outset, referred to the statement made by Mahatma Gandhi on Mr Amery's recent pronouncement, and said that 'every line and every word of it breathes indignation—indignation of a type somewhat unusual with the Mahatma.' The speaker said that he had not had the time to revolve the statement in his mind and he dared not trust himself to make any observation on it. But he would recommend it to them [the audience] for profound study. He would also venture a comment on Mr Amery's speech, though he wondered whether they would agree with his interpretation of it.

'While standing by the famous August declaration and repeating all his old ideas', the speaker continued, 'Mr Amery has, upon this occasion, apparently with sincerity, regretted as much as most of us do, that the Congress should have retired, as it were, from the seats of power and chosen to support a campaign of civil disobedience. He does not say, as he might, and as he would have done if he had felt it, that the British Government feels relieved that there is no Congress Government sitting in any of the seven provinces. He says he and the Government of England are profoundly sorry that they have not got the assistance of the Congress Governments. If that is so, and if our appeal to the Congress leaders finds favourable reception and the Congress decides to come back to its positive duties in the country, may we hope that Mr Amery and the Viceroy will not have any difficulty but will welcome them with open arms?'

'Our Leaders Must be Back at the Helm'

Proceeding, Mr Sastri said, 'Our move in this province under the leadership of *The Hindu*, in calling on the Congress leaders to come back to their seats of authority in the various provinces, is supplementary to the Bombay Conference. The Bombay Conference, you will remember, dealt exclusively with the proposals for the reorganization of the Centre in India. The provinces were left alone, possibly under the feeling that if the Centre were reconstructed according to our wishes, the provinces would follow suit. We are here concerned with the provinces. But supposing Mr Amery's 'NO' were final and nothing would shake the determination of the Government of Great Britain to introduce changes in the desired direction—we should all very much regret it no doubt, but we need not for that reason give up this idea in reference to the provinces—if that unfortunate event happens, and Mr Amery digs his toes into the ground, the necessity for our having our chosen leaders in the seats of power is only rendered the more pressing. Remember, the present phase of the war is of the most alarming nature. It is a nameless terror that seizes our hearts to-day. All things look black and sinister. Maybe, as the Mahatma emphatically says, India would be thrown upon her own resources and Great Britain be unable to defend us any longer. Internal troubles of a very acute kind, inflamed by the communal animosities of which most disconcerting evidences are cropping up every day all over the country, disturbances stirred up by these and similar causes are likely to make us sleepless. Whom then should we have at the helm, supposing the British arm weakened—God forbid it—and we had to defend ourselves, shall we be a kind of unorganized assemblage of people or shall we have at the helm the leaders chosen by us? Maybe, they may not be able to do much for us, but still they are our leaders. New situations will arise every day. Complications not to be foreseen now may cloud the skies and cause nightmares to everyone amongst us. Should we or should we not have our chosen leaders at the helm? That is my point now and that has been my point for a long time.'

Advisers Rule Cannot be Countenanced

'Where are the people', asked Mr Srinivasa Sastri, 'whom with such acclaim, we elected to be our leaders in the various provincial cabinets? They are all in jail to-day. Who are occupying their places?, a Government by advisers, not our people and their paid employees.' Was that a state of things that a body of sensible electors could countenance? He did not mean to throw the blame on anyone. But he wished they should all express their view in the matter as sensible men, as householders with a stake in the country, with children to protect, with women whose honour was to them more sacred than anything else. What could they do, unorganized as they were?

Changing the picture, let them for a moment visualize it with the Congress leaders, as before, established in the various provincial Governments. Maybe they had only three—fourths of the authority that should belong to provincial Governments; but, still, they were armed with something with which they could stand forward, talk to outsiders and put down trouble-makers. 'Supposing we had leaders of that kind established in the various provinces, should we not be a little more emboldened than we are now? I tell you, whatever your feelings may be, I am full of alarm, I am full of concern. I feel abandoned—abandoned is the word—by those who ought to be here to protect me. That is the line that we take. We ask the Congress people to come back, lead us and protect us in this time of great trouble. Their place to-day as people, who hold our confidence and suffrage, is beside us and not in prison cells. They may be very usefully occupied there, spinning or carding or whatever else it might be; but that would not avail us when the enemy is at the door, when the robber and the dacoit are disturbing the peace of our homes. We want a Volunteer Force, organized, and held under tight control, doing policemen's duty but not doing policemen's oppression. We want a force animated wholly by the patriotic desire to be servants and defenders of the public. Now tell me, are the paid police the people whom we should trust to be so? Should we not ask for and should we not desire that a force directed and inspired by the patriotism and ideals of the Congress, and officered, controlled, and governed under Congress auspices should be at our disposal? Do not think that that time is far off. It looked far a few months ago; but to-day, it is quite near. To-morrow, before we wake up, trouble might come, and you will wring your hands and call aloud for someone whom you could trust. Men whom we trusted, whom we clothed with authority, to whom we assigned the special task of preparing the country for defending itself—those men are nowhere to be found. They must be brought back from jail and installed again in the places that they occupied before this wrong method was adopted.'

'Not a Moment Should be Lost'

As to how the Congress leaders are to be brought back, Mr Sastri said this could not be achieved by merely wishing it. The process and the *modus operandi* should be left to wiser heads acting together. 'Maybe, we might ask the Government to release them, so that they might consult together and devise measurers for the protection of the country which the Government might not be able, in spite of their obvious duty, to do. May be, we should ask the Congress leaders themselves to agree to come back and do their duty, if they are allowed to.

May be, two moves would have to be arranged together'. He had no clear notion of these just then. The times were very very critical, and not a moment should be lost in finding out who are 'the most competent by spirit, by experience, and by courage, to help us'. Judging all things, it seemed to him—he was not a Congressman—that outside the Congress, 'there was at present no body of people who had our trust in the same measure and who, therefore, had laid upon themselves, the supreme duty of coming back and resuming power and defending the people who so pathetically trust them.'

130. Madras Provincial Scheduled Castes' Federation Report of the Meeting

The Hindu, 6 May 1941.

Madras, 5 May.

To consider the present political situation in India, a special meeting of the Madras Provincial Scheduled Castes Federation was held yesterday, Dewan Bahadur R. Srinivasan presiding.

A resolution was adopted viewing with anxiety the march of the aggressors in the present war towards the East and regarding as most fortunate that at the present juncture the British Government was guided by an able Cabinet in which Mr Winston Churchill was the leader, who was supported by the United States of America.

The resolution further expressed the Federation's appreciation of the splendid efforts of HE the Governor of Madras, in marshalling the people of this Presidency on the side and in support of those who were carrying on the war against aggression, and regretted that in these circumstances some of the political leaders of India should try to embarrass the Government by putting forward demands for constitutional changes which, on account of their far-reaching consequences affecting the welfare of the various classes and communities, could not be granted without full discussion, and without the consent of the various elements of the population.

The Federation further expressed its appreciation of the recent statement of the Secretary of State for India in the House of Commons based as it was upon a full realization of the difficulties of the political situation in India and of the injustice which would be involved in the handing over of full power to any particular section of the people without regard to the views and wants of the other sections, and thus enabling the domination of certain sections over other sections, of the population. The resolution finally urged HE the Viceroy and the Secretary of State for India to persevere in their endeavour to secure a larger association of influential and representative Indians in the administration, both at the centre and in the provinces and thereby secure a more visible demonstration of the undoubted co-operation which the people were offering to the Government in their war efforts by way of financial contribution, and an increasing enlistment in the different departments of defence.

Rao Bahadur M.C. Rajah moved the resolution and Rao Saheb V. Dharmalingam Pillai seconded the same.

131. Complete Indianization of Viceroy's Executive Council Sikh Political Conference's Demand

The Tribune, 31 May 1941.

Lahore, 30 May.

'With all our strength in manpower and plentiful resources, we could have been formed into a first class world power for smashing Hitler and his associates at their very first rising, if the Government had been wise and sagacious enough to repose full confidence in India and made it an equal partner in the British Commonwealth of nations', said Sardar Gurbux Singh, advocate, while presiding over the Sikh Political Conference convened by the All-India Sikh League in the Minto Park on the occasion of the *Jor Ka Mela*. The conference was largely attended.

Maharani Gurcharan Kaur hoisted the Sikh flag.

Sardar Gurbux Singh began by paying a tribute to the late Sardar Sir Sunder Singh Majithia and referring to incarceration of Baba Kharak Singh. He also referred to the ex-Maharaja of Nabha.

Referring to the international situation the President expressed his regret over India's helplessness. He expressed the hope that the British Government would even now rise to the occasion and come to terms with Indian leaders.

Alluding to the Pakistan scheme of the Muslim League, the President said that the Muslim League was the creation of reactionary forces and the Pakistan scheme had been condemned by all right thinking persons. He demanded a clear and unequivocal declaration by the Secretary of State on behalf of the Government rejecting the possibilities of the Pakistan scheme ever being put into operation.

Proceeding, he said, 'I will be falling in my duty if I do not avail of this opportunity to say, that the policy of allowing preferential treatment to one community over the other and the mistake committed previously in allowing undue advantage to Muslim minorities in various provinces not allowed to other minorities in their provinces; and of providing special privileges to the Muslims even in their majority provinces, should be abandoned once and for all.'

He demanded due share for the Sikhs and said they did not want to remain slaves of any community.

While appealing for unity among the Sikhs, Sardar Gurbux Singh said, 'The Unionist Government which, as we fully well know, has always been treating us and our concerns with doubtful considerations has, through its 'Propaganda Minister' the Hon'ble Sir Chhotu Ram, started a scheme of splitting us asunder, in two camps—the Jats and the Non-Jats. He has for some time past been active in this direction and has, with his active assistance, been holding Jat conferences and meetings in Sikh *ilaqas*. This move is a highly dangerous one and we should keenly and promptly begin to counteract it.

'Sikhism and Sikhs as such know no castes, no creeds, and no distinctions amongst them. Politically, Sikhs have to rise and fall as Sikhs and not as Jats or Non-Jats.'

The President then pleaded for recruitment and said that the Sikhs should see that no encroachments are allowed on their hard-earned and well-deserved special privileges and rights in the army.

Chairman's Address

Earlier Sardar Harbans Singh Sistani, Chairman of the Reception Committee, in the course of his address demanded the establishment of the National Government in India and he maintained that if that was done Indians would give more willing co-operation in war effort. He condemned the new move of the Unionist Government to divide Sikhs into Jats and non-Jats. Sikhism, he maintained, knew no such distinctions. He also condemned restrictions on 'Jhatka' in the province.

Resolutions

Complete Indianization of the Viceroy's Executive Council and inclusion of a Sikh among the members was urged in a resolution adopted. The resolution stressed that in order to strengthen the defences of India it was essential that all members of the Viceroy's Executive Council should be selected from among Indian public leaders.

The conference passed a series of other resolutions, demanding, *inter alia*, that the position of the Sikhs in the Indian army should not be allowed to be impaired, and that they should be given at least one-third share in the administration of the Punjab owing to their historical importance.

By another resolution the conference condemned the Pakistan scheme, characterizing it as wholly anti-national and greatly detrimental to the best interests of the country. The conference expressed its firm belief that the present communal tension in the country was largely due to the propaganda that was being carried on in support of this scheme and that it would be impossible to achieve communal unity unless the Pakistan scheme was given up.

The conference deprecated the communal disturbances that have recently occurred in Bombay, Bihar, Bengal, and the UP and appealed to the leaders of the various communities in the country that they should all try their best to maintain complete concord between the different communities.

132. Governor General's Telegram to Secretary of State on Non-party Leaders' Conference, Poona, 29 July 1941

File No. 242/1941-Poll (I), Home (Political) Department, Government of India, NAI.

1. 1810-G. Non-Party Leaders Conference met at Poona 26th and 27th July. Reuters have cabled summary of two resolutions in message of 26th and points from certain speeches in message of 27th. This telegram is in amplification of those messages. Attendance at Conference not yet known but Mirza Ismail only Muslim mentioned in press reports.

2. In Subjects Committee on 26th morning draft resolution was considered advocating termination of 'one man rule' in provinces. Majority opinion was against this proposal as Conference should not be responsible for asking for non-official advisers, who would relieve Governors to some extent of odium of non-existence of responsible Government in seven provinces. Proposal was dropped and did not come before Conference.

3. Following are points from Sapru's opening presidential address on 26th afternoon. Dealing with allocation of portfolios on expanded Council Sapru strongly criticized withholding from Indians of Defence, Home, and Finance portfolios with which power and initiation of policy are associated; he maintained that all the new Indian Councillors were competent to hold these three portfolios. He also criticized division of departments at present held by Indians

and suggested that departmental work of Defence, Finance, and Communications Departments must also have increased. Discussing new Executive Councillors' work he said their primary task would be rendering every assistance in prosecution of war but they could not forget internal situation in country; they must advocate policy of conciliation. Despite his own opposition to satyagraha movement, he held strongly that as long as thousands remained in jail so long, Indian mind would be diverted from constructive channels to fruitless channels. Greatest service which new Councillors could render to country would be bringing about harmony between India's warring communities. Discussing Amery's speech in Commons last April, Sapru saw in it signs of surrender, and considered that if Conference continued pressing their demand even Amery would find suitable formula for taking another step forward. Considering that India was represented in League of Nations and that Wedgewood Benn in 1929 had said that Dominion Status was already in action in India, there was nothing constitutionally improper or revolutionary in the demand for equality of status for India's representatives at international and Imperial conferences; demand was that India's representatives should be appointed and instructed by Government of India and not led by the nose by the Secretary of State.

4. Following are additional points from speeches made on 27th. Jayakar considered that Government were not earnest about preparing defence of India; Amery had referred to untapped reservoir of Indian patriotism and ability, but nothing could be achieved unless defence portfolio was transferred to Indians. He however advocated axiom of Gokhale and Tilak, 'take what you get and fight for the rest'; for first time they had got non-official majority in Council, whose Indian members would be constantly in touch with Viceroy and able to influence him. Sir S. Radhakrishnan hoped that new Councillors would press for transfer of other portfolios and also work for release of satyagrahis and restoration of democratic government in provinces. Mirza Ismail regretted that when fate of nations was hanging in balance India should present to world picture of divided counsel. Hindu–Muslim problem was fundamental and until communal differences were composed, it was futile to expect lasting progress in India. Leaders of two major communities must be brought together by appointing constituent committee would help rather than hamper war effort. Pandit Kunzru considered expansion of Executive Council was denial of Amery's slogan 'India first'; he hoped new Councillors would combine and present Government with policy which had country's support, and also see that Council worked as collective body.

5. Moving second resolution regarding examination of main lines of future constitutional changes, Venkatarama Sastri was confident that Britain which had contributed so much to India's unity would not be party to division of country; he regretted country's sectional politics and warmly supported Mirza Ismail's suggestions. Moonje seconding resolution deprecated any idea of appeasement in dealing with communal problem.

6. Following is summary of Jinnah's comments on Poona Conference issued on 28th July.

Conference had misunderstood position in claiming credit for 'progress' despite continued lack of agreement between major political parties. Departure from Government's original intention that Executive should have representatives of major political parties with real share in authority of Government is really regrettable. Amery had emphasized that change was administrative not constitutional or political; nevertheless decision will block any scheme of associating representatives of political parties with real power and authority even within framework of present constitution. Real object of Sapru Conference is to put pressure on Government to modify declaration of last August and get Government to denounce Muslim

League proposal for Pakistan. I am confident that Government will not budge from their solemn declaration because that will involve grossest breach of faith with Muslim India and will be strenuously resisted by Muslims. Muslim League is not anti-Hindu movement, but there is large section of Hindu leaders who openly stood for keeping Muslims under domination of Hindu raj; leaders of this school of thought and leading members of Hindu Mahasabha are prominent stars of so-called Non-Party Conference.

133 (i) Mr Jayakar Urges Government to Resolve Political Deadlock

The Tribune, 4 August 1941.

Poona, 3 August.

'Muslim Leaders Keeping Pistol at Head of Government'
'We Can Only Turn to Congress for Search for Relief'

A plea that in the interest of all the present political deadlock in India should be resolved and that Congress and Mahatma Gandhi be persuaded to call off the Satyagraha movement and restore popular Governments, was made by Dr M.R. Jayakar, speaking at the Tilak anniversary.

'If, however for any reason this is not possible' Dr Jayakar said, 'the next best thing for the Congressmen to do is to resign from the Legislatures creating thereby vacancies which would compel Government to have a new election. If the present dog-in-the-manger policy of the Congress continued there will be no popular Governments in the eight provinces and the popular interests will suffer materially.' Dr Jayakar added: 'We have all reasons to hope that Mr Gandhi will have his attention invited to this side of the question and to the great harm that is being done to popular Governments in the provinces.'

Dr Jayakar continued: 'If, however, even this is not possible, the only thing left for us to try is to support demands of the Sapru Conference limited as they are to war time. Some of these have been partially granted leading to the hope that if effort is continued it may succeed in creating a wider charm in the stronghold of bureaurucratic power.'

Pakistan Movement

Referring to the Pakistan movement Dr Jayakar observed: 'Its technique is very skilful and astute and is primarily intended to create panic amongst the Hindu community in the hope that in this panicky condition the Hindus would surrender more and more rights in order to avoid the advent of Pakistan.

'It is, therefore, wise for the Hindus not to get panicky over this but deal with it in the way it deserved. The exponents of Pakistan astutely refrain from defining what is meant by Pakistan. Does it mean the creation of a corridor or belt from the Brahmputra to the Bosphorus so that a whisper in Assam may be heard in Istanbul, as the late Maulana Mohamed Ali once said? If not, all I can say is that it spells greater harm to the British Government than to Hindustan, especially after their experience in the present war of the Muslim countries included in this belt'.

Jinnah's Vain Mind

Referring to Mr Jinnah, Dr Jayakar said: 'Mr Jinnah has accused me of having changed my political views. He also said, 'little minds are satisfied with little things.' I wonder if he knows that 'vain minds are satisfied with nothing except themselves.' As for the change of political views, the change from fourteen points to Pakistan is a bigger change than any I have seen or espoused. I had seen many changes in my life but a minority, however important, calling itself a distinct 'nation'—distinct ethnologically, sociologically, politically and in all vital departments of life which can live with its sister community only in perpetual discord and isolation—this is the biggest change we have seen in our lives effected in the short period of a few months. Pakistan looks suspiciously like a smoke-screen behind which efforts are perhaps being made both in England and in India to drown completely the principle of majority rule and devise a constitution far removed from democratic principles by the inclusion of irremovable Executive and functional representation, and other things.

Notorious Fact

'The parties who can relieve the people of this country from this frustration and the consequent deadlock are: finally the Government who can transfer power to Indian hands and declare that India would be a free country in brief limit of time after the war. This would create a sense of realism which may prove attractive to the Congress and a large section of the Muslim community. The excuse of Government that there is no agreement among the parties is regarded as a plausible plea for not parting with power. No such agreement can be said to have been the basis of the Government of India Act 1935 and it is a notorious fact that the joint memorandum of the Indian delegates working with the Round Table Parliamentary Committee was completely ignored notwithstanding the fact that all Indians had joined in making the recommendations. It is material to remember in connection with the disappearances of the principle of majority rule to which I have referred the recent remarks of Mr Amery. In commenting on the disappearance of the Congress Governments from the provinces he deplored that Congress Governments did not realize when they voluntarily surrendered their power and authority in the provinces that they were deserting a form of constitution under which they enjoyed a large share of power and authority than they can ever expect to get in future. These are significant words emanating as they do from the supreme head of the British administration in India. They clearly indicate that the prospects of a constitution based on the British democratic principle of majority rules are seriously threatened and we need not be surprised if the British Government takes the fullest advantages of the Muslim opposition to majority rule and of the fact that the Congress Party in the Central Legislature joined the Muslim League Party in downing the Federal Constitution embodied in the Government of India Act on the basis of majority rule. We may take a warning from these words of Mr Amery which he has since confirmed in skilful terms in his late speeches.

Muslim Leaders' Clever Pose

'It is a clever pose of the Muslim leadership that it holds a pistol at the head of the Government of India and refuses to allow any constitutional progress in India even during the period of war without its sanction. That leadership simultaneously makes impossible all negotiations with the Congress leadership by insisting on impossible conditions which it must know can never be satisfied.

'The nature of these conditions is such that even 'negotiations are impossible on any national basis with the result very skillfully achieved that the present deadlock must continue' to complete the ruin of provincial administration in the Hindu majority provinces.

'It is therefore, in the interest of the Pakistani Muslims by all devices to continue the present deadlock as long as they can manage. It does them very little harm and they are not concerned with what is happening to the majority community in the eight provinces where the Congress Governments foolishly deserted their seats.

'It is, therefore, in the interest of all of us who are not Pakistani Muslims to stop this deadlock from continuing by all means in our power. Any relief in this direction being without hope at the hands of the Government or the Muslim League for reasons just stated we can only turn to the Congress for search for relief.'—API

(ii) Jayakar's Speech

Editorial, *National Herald*, 10 August 1941.

False Notions

More with amusement than with any serious anxiety, Congressman are watching the offensive which non-Congress elements are slowly developing against the Congress. These elements' concern is to allow their friends who have accepted places on the Executive Council to make a job of their work and then to facilitate the restoration of popular government in the provinces as a logical sequel thereof. In their mind burns the hope that if the Congress will not come back to office in the provinces, other Indian groups owning allegiance to the Poona Conference might be happily allowed to come in as the next best choice. Part of their propaganda consists in 'friendly' if direct attacks on Congress policy.

Returning to his recent charge at Poona, Mr Jayakar stated in a Bombay speech on Friday that the majority party in the provincial legislatures had only to return and the present vacuum would disappear—the vacuum into which the adviser regime had stepped. 'How can they come back?' asked Mr Jayakar. 'I am sure they can come back if the obstacle of satyagraha is removed'.

... When Mr Jayakar tells us that the deadlock can be summarily solved by the calling off of the Satyagraha and the return of the Congress to office, he is showing an indifference to the political events of the recent past and indulging in a misappreciation of the political possibilities of the immediate future which is utterly inexcusable in a senior politician of his status and standing. Why should the majority party return to office, when the conditions under which it resigned continue to be the same, if they have not grown definitely worse? By refusing to participate in a war into which India had been dragged, the Congress has not only vindicated its faith as an anti-imperialist body but has rekindled its soul. Every major act done, every major policy pursued by the British Government, since September 1939 has, constituted a grave affront to the intelligence and self-respect of our people. We may not have the ready strength to avenge the insults, but we have courage enough to forge the sanctions for the purpose. Satyagraha might in form be only a symbolic protest, but in effect it is far more than a symbol. It is a battle-standard, around which we are waging a controlled skirmish, preparatory to the greater battles to come. If it is a protest against the war in relation to India, it must, as per logic, continue as long as the war lasts. It would be wrong for men like Mr Jayakar to interpret it as a mere spectacular protest which might now be dropped somehow on the pretext that its symbolic meaning has been understood sufficiently well. Again, we are to learn that there is any logical connection between the calling off of satyagraha and the Congress returning to office. Even if the one is off, the second possibility need not occur. Let us remember that the

Congress resigned office in November 1939, and launched satyagraha after more than a year. It would not be right to interlink these positions in a reverse order. If the Congress comes back to office, it will not be while the war lasts or while the war continues to have its original complexion. By the logic Mr Amery is pursuing in his speeches, we are driven to the conclusion that the last thing the British Government care for would be to see the Congress back in office. We for our part are willing to reciprocate the compliment. The last thing the Congress care for is to work a British-made constitution.

134. 'Kick Both Congress and Muslim League' Sir Chhotu Ram's Outburst

The Tribune, 19 August 1941.

Lyallpur, 17 August.

'Your salvation lies in neither following the Muslim League nor the Congress. Mr Jinnah, though a big man and Mahatma Gandhi, even though regarded as a *Devta* by many people, do not, rather cannot, understand, and appreciate your miseries and woes. Both Mr Jinnah and Mahatma Gandhi are in the hands of the capitalists. They are their servants because the capitalists give them cheques worth lakhs of rupees to be spent by them in any manner in which they please. Your salvation lies in having trust in me and accepting the leadership of Sir Sikander Hyat Khan, because nobody else understands and knows your woes as I and Sir Sikander Hyat do', declared Chaudhri Sir Chhotu Ram, Revenue Minister, Punjab, in the course of a speech which he made today before a big gathering of Zamindars—generally known as junglis—in the interior of Lyallpur district at a Chunianwala Rest House in the Pir Mahal colony.

Officials, police, and civic guards remained busy in making arrangements for the meeting, which was addressed through the loud speakers provided by the Punjab Government.

Sir Chhotu Ram, accompanied by Sheikh Nur Mohd, Deputy Commissioner, Mr Mulkh Raj, SDO, and the Assistant Colonization Officer came to the meeting place amidst shouts of 'Chhotu Ram Zindabad', 'Deputy Commissioner Zindabad', and 'Sir Sikander Hyat Zindabad'. Nawab Saadat Ali Khan, MLA, read out a poem in which Sir Chhotu Ram was praised for all that he had done 'to save the poor peasants from the clutches of capitalists'. Pir Nasar-ud-Din, MLA who read out welcome address on behalf of the Zamindars, referred to their local grievances.

Sir Chhotu Ram's Reply

Replying to the address, Sir Chhotu Ram expressed his helplessness to do anything in the matter of removing the grievances, excepting one. His reason for his inability to fulfil their wishes was partly due to his ignorance of their grievances and partly because he confessed the permanent dues charged as revenue could not be reduced except at the time of *bandobast*. He, however, promised to look into the matter.

Sir Chhotu Ram continuing said that he had come to fulfil a promise made by the Premier sometimes back regarding the grant of land of local residents called the Tirni Guzars. The Government had now decided to give land to the local population in the area and the same would be given in another two or three months' time after arrangements for its distribution and watering it had been made. But on previous occasions when land was distributed among the local residents, there used to be certain conditions, for example, a land was given according to the members of a family or the animals like bulls, cows, and so on, one possessed.

'No Land to Agitators'

Sir Chhotu Ram declared that this time land would be given on an additional condition, that is, no one who agitates or joins any absurd agitation demanding the grant of land to Tirni Guzars and makes any representation again and again to the officers for that purpose, would be given any land. He laid special emphasis on this point and declared a number of times that no local agitators or those who joined agitation would be given any land. He also asked them not to be misled by any outsiders. The 'Salamdars'—those whose occupation it is to salam every officer, said Sir Chhotu Ram, would not get any land.

'Going to Stop this Loot'

Referring to what he called tyranny of the capitalists over the peasants and supporting his claim by quoting an instance of the stark poverty of the peasants, Sir Chhotu Ram declared: 'The capitalists have fleeced you now for a sufficiently long time. While the peasant worked, the capitalist had been looting him. I am going to stop this loot and see that no capitalist sucks your blood and fattens himself on that. I am making arrangements by which that blood would be returned to you.'

The Revenue Minister further declared that henceforth the poor would get the major share of lands. Lands which were leased out and which the peasants have been tilling for 10 to 15 years past would be taken away from those capitalists to whom these were leased out and given over to the toiling peasants, who have been working on these lands. The Government had decided that no one should hold on lease more than 5 squares of land. Those who had fattened on the blood of the poor would have now to meet the same fate.

Continuing Sir Chhotu Ram said that while distributing lands claims of the soldiers on active service would have prior consideration and they would be the first to get when Government distributed any land. Times had changed. Gone are the times, he said, when cunning capitalists used to buy land at cost of 'Kauris'. If, however, anyone, may be a non-Zamindar even, wanted to buy land, he could offer his bid at the time of auction of first grade land reserved for the purpose.

Appeal for Unity

Sir Chhotu Ram, then made an appeal for unity and asked people not to drink the poison of communalism. He however, asked them to do whatever their religion enjoined upon them in the discharge of their religious ceremonies. But they should not let religion interfere in their economic affairs. He warned the Zamindars not to fall in the clutches of the capitalists and unite just as capitalists united when their common interests required unity.

At this stage Chaudhri Sir Chhotu Ram brought in the issue of the Congress, the Muslim League, and criticized their leaders. He asked the Zamindars not to be led away into the belief that their salvation lay in the hands of the Muslim League or the Congress or Gandhiji or Mr Jinnah or Master Tara Singh. He declared that Mr Jinnah and Mahatma Gandhi were in the hands of the capitalists and 'they are their servants because capitalists give them cheques worth lakhs of rupees to be used in any manner in which they please.' Their salvation did not lie in the hands of the Muslim League or the Congress. It lay in their allegiance to the Zamindara League. Both he and Sir Sikander Hyat Khan knew their troubles and miseries.

Sir Chottu Ram Concluded

'Don't trust the Muslim League. Don't trust the Congress, Kick them both. There is no Congress in the Punjab. Rally round the flag of the Zamindara Government. Accept Sir Sikander Hyat Khan as your leader. It is your 'Raj' in the Punjab which our opponents want to end. If you unite, your 'Raj' will continue and I am sure to live to see the day when the Punjab Zamindars will live in happiness and prosperity.'

135. Text of Sikandar Hayat Khan's Statement, Simla, 1 October 1941

Governor General's Telegram to Secretary of State, 2 October 1941, File No. 242/1941-Poll (I), 1941, Home (Political) Department, Government of India, NAI.

2516-G. Following is practically full text of statement made to press at Simla on 1st October by Sir Sikander Hayat Khan.

When war broke out two obvious courses were open to British Government, either declaration that all political controversies must be hushed for duration of war because it was not possible to give adequate attention to intricate political problems when both countries were engaged in life and death struggle, or unqualified undertaking that India's political aspirations would be met immediately after war. They decided to adopt second alternative with certain reservations made to allay misgivings of Muslim India and Indian States. Important statements bearing on constitutional issue were made from time to time by Secretary of State and Viceroy. Churchill's recent statement is latest addition to these pronouncements. I wish it had never been made. It has evoked considerable criticism and resentment throughout the country. I do not propose to discuss its merits or demerits but I frankly confess, I cannot appreciate its necessity or object. It is unfortunate that Prime Minister should have broken his silence about India with a statement which has created feeling of despondency and dismay throughout country. His statement is a source of embarrassment to friends of British, and convenient and powerful argument to those who are always looking out for any pretext to question bonafides of British Government to stir up hostility and bitterness. I do not believe that Atlantic Charter even if it had been applicable to India would have brought us nearer to political goal any more than futile satyagraha movement. I believe that valour and sacrifices of our fighting men alone can win India's freedom just as they won 1921 Reforms by their sacrifices during last war, but even their sacrifices may prove ineffective if we fail to reestablish mutual confidence and intercommunal harmony.

2. One unfortunate result of Churchill's statement has been creation of possibly erroneous impression that earlier announcements of Viceroy and Secretary of State no longer hold field. It is urged that since Prime Minister's declaration transcends in importance and authority, pronouncements by other Cabinet Ministers' all previous statements are cancelled, including Amery's historic announcement undertaking to grant India same status and freedom within British Commonwealth which is enjoyed by any other unit not excluding Great Britain. I trust steps will be taken to remove this impression at earliest opportunity. Vast majority of my countrymen certainly share my belief that future destiny and safety of India lie in securing status of free and equal partnership in British Commonwealth. I am equally confident that if Prime Minister could see his way to make fresh declaration that India shall attain that status within reasonable time after war, say two or three years, all patriotic elements in country will welcome it with enthusiasm. If my proposal is acceptable I venture to suggest that announcement

should be made in simple unambiguous terms without being hedged in by avoidable qualifications. All that is needed is to declare future status of India in clear terms, and to add that select body consisting of representatives of all important interests in country including British will be set up to hammer out agreed constitution, and that if this committee fail to produce agreed solution within prescribed time British Government shall in collaboration with those elements who come forward to help in defence of India, devise suitable constitution conferring full dominion status on India. It is time both friends and foes were told where they stand. In fairness to both India and Great Britain it should be made crystal clear that those who are not with us in this war are against us. But this warning should follow declaration about future status of India, so that those who may be holding back on account of genuine doubts created by language of previous statements may have opportunity to reconsider position.

136. Need for Changed Programme: Dr Arundale's Appeal

Amrita Bazar Patrika, 16 November 1941.

'British are to be blamed because they foolishly rejected the Poona offer of the Congress and created a situation which is neither useful to India nor to themselves', said Dr G.S. Arundale, in an interview with the representative of the *Amrita Bazar Patrika* before the Doctor left for Gaya to-night.

When questioned as to why he had said that if Britain was deaf to India's demands, it was her own affair, Dr Arundale said that exactly it was her own affair and her indifference did not influence Indian attitude to her freedom movement.

Dr Arundale wanted Indians to unite as a strong nation, rise above begging mentality and settle up her own problems including that of communalism which he considered was but a trifling matter based on mere sentimentality. He wanted India to draft her own constitution as that would be a tough answer to Britishers' indifference to India's demand.

The Doctor could not reconcile himself to the present situation at home and thought that Gandhiji's passive resistance was much to be blamed. If Britain happened to err at a time in international crisis as regards India, why should India non-co-operate at a time which demanded her utmost service and sacrifice to release herself from the shackles of slavery? It was with this end in view that he wanted Indians to lend their support to the war efforts which were decidedly scanty for her defence and for the maintenance of her internal freedom and security.

Dr Arundale thought that Gandhiji's non-cooperation and non-violent struggle could not derive a better result. The Doctor said that he would, time permitting, meet Mahatmaji and request him to bring change in the plan of action and get the constructive aspect of the struggle more concentrated and useful.

Dr Arundale condemned the move of Pakistan and was convinced of its dangers, which would cripple India's dream of a nation, bidding for liberty. He thought that India would do well not to advertise Mr Jinnah, who is out to rob of India's great hopes with his own ambition to live in history as a one-time Dictator of Indians.

Call to Youths

Claiming himself as good an Indian with forty years' stay in the country as any other, Dr G.S. Arundale, the celebrated theosophist, delivered a lecture on 'India and War' at a crowded meeting held last evening at the Radhika Sinha Institute Hall, His Excellency the Governor presiding.

As a patriot, though not belonging to any particular brand of patriots, Dr Arundale held that the present war was India's war and as such India's youth—the hope of the world's liberation from the carnage—must stand as one and fight out the evil. He could not tolerate the colossal indifference of Indians who declared that the war had nothing to do with India or India had nothing to do with the war. It was a cataclysm and a catastrophe of the greatest magnitude, and in this world war, India would come out victorious. He regarded the V [Victory?] campaign as having a useful psychology at its back and should enthral every young heart who crave for protection of culture and civilization.

Analysis of War

Dr Arundale's analysis of war showed that until ignorance, greed and lust for ruling on man by man went extinct, violence must continue to strike and there would be no place for Gandhiji's much praised non-violence and its philosophy. Struggle for existence was the result of fears and selfishness and cruelty. Till every nation understood that it was in its own interest it left but taking recourse to violence, there could come no peace. The war spirit would endure long and out of this evil, will be born a new world where love and peace would prevail.

Dr Arundale recommended building up of character as a panacea of all ills. He wanted nations and creeds to educate themselves. It was lack of confidence in discipline and reverance of ideals that savagery and cruelty prevailed with full fury. War was not the result of bad economics, wrong laws and wrong government, but due to wrong characters.

India having been the pioneer of chivalry and freedom, it being the land of Aryans and the land of Kurukshetra, Dr Arundale hoped that India's full resources should be harnessed to assist Britain and India in peril. On the side of Godliness and goodness stood Britain and on the side of the devil was Germany with her cruel allies. It was therefore the duty of India to shake off the sentimentality and all her complaints to join the army of the goodness and help the world coming out of conflagration. He was sure that ill fate would befall India like that of Poland if she did not realize her duty and moved with the time and space to win war to secure her freedom.

India's Demand

He wanted Britain to widen her perspective and treat India with the hospitality she had received from her. But this was not the occasion for bargaining or haggling and hence keeping India's demand in suspense. India must give up her begging spirit and join the forces of God.

People of the Kurukshetra must no longer ask for charity and freedom from Britain and fight the greater Kurukshetra battle with more responsiveness. He hoped that Hindus and Muslims and Christians would stand in a line and create a history by defeating the black forces of devastation.

137. UP Non-party Conference Demands Transfer of All Portfolios in Viceroy's Council to Non-official Indians

Bombay Chronicle, 15 December 1941.

Lucknow, 14 December.

Resolutions demanding of the termination of the suspension of the constitution in the provinces, urging His Majesty's Government to make an unequivocal declaration that at the end of the war India would have the same freedom and equality of status as Great Britain and the Dominions; opining that all portfolios in the Governor-General's Executive Council including those of defence, finance, home, and communications should be entrusted to non-official Indians who would, for the interim period be responsible to the Crown; and that in the meanwhile the Government should deal with important matters on basis of joint and collective responsibility, were adopted by the first Non-Party Provincial Conference held here under the presidency of Raja Sir Maharaj Singh.

The Subjects Committee of the Conference met today under the presidentship of Sir Maharaj Singh at the residence of Kunwar Sir Jagdish Prasad. It was attended by Sir Jagdish Prasad, Raja Mahesawar Dayal Seth, and Lala Hariram. Mr Hirdayanath Kunzru who arrived in the evening joined the deliberations later.

The following three draft resolutions were adopted by the Subjects Committee:

1. This Conference is strongly of the opinion that in the provinces the rule of Governors with the aid of Advisers under Section 93 of the Government of India Act of 1935 should cease.
2. This Conference urges His Majesty's Government to make an unequivocal declaration that at the end of the war India will have the same freedom and equality of status as Great Britain and the Dominions.
3. This Conference supports the resolutions of the Bombay and Poona non-Party Conferences that all portfolios in the Governor-General's Executive Council, including those of Defence, Finance, Home and Communications, should be entrusted to non-official Indians who would in the interim period be responsible to the Crown. The reconstructed Government should deal with important matters of policy on the basis of joint and collective responsibility....

138. Liberal Federation on British Pledge Demand for Definite Time-limit for Dominion Status

Bombay Chronicle, 27 December 1941.

Madras, 26 December.

The 23rd annual session of the National Liberal Federation of India commenced this afternoon at the Rasika Ranjana Sabha Hall, Mylapore, Sir Bijoy Prasad Singh Roy, ex-Minister of Bengal presiding.

There was a large gathering of delegates and visitors from all over India including a number of ladies. Prominent among those present were Sir V.N. Chandavarkar, Right Hon V.S. Srinivasa Sastri, Sir Chimanlal Setalwad, Sir Cowasjee Jehangir, Pandit Hridaynath Kunzru, Dr R.P. Paranjpye, Dr G.S. Mahajani, Sir A.P. Patro, Mr P.N. Sapru, Mr T.R. Venkatarama Sastri, Sir Vepa Ramesam, Mr T.B. Gadre, and Miss Sherin Kesawala.

The proceedings commenced with the singing of 'Vandemataram' by a choir of girls from the National High School, Mylapore.

Sir P.S. Sivaswami Iyer, Chairman of the Reception Committee, then welcomed the delegates' whereafter Sir Bijoy Prasad Singh Roy, delivered his presidential address.

President's Speech

> In view of the chaos of political thought and undisciplined action, the need for a united front for the achievement of our political advancement is great. The group spirit, the partisan bias, class conflict, competing self-interest—all this is obstructing the path of our progress. It is unfortunate that in the absence of cohesion amongst the different political parties, communal, and sectional movements are gaining strength.

Thus observed, Sir Bijoy Prasad Singh Roy in the course of his presidential address.

Continuing Sir Bijoy Prasad said:

> The energy of the nation is being dissipated over a host of sectional causes. In normal times, we could wait, for the slow progress whereby movements gain in strength gradually and make for effective united action. But the present situation is likely to deteriorate beyond redemption if it is left to take its own course. Signs are visible which make it clear that the cause of Democracy is in jeopardy.
>
> The Congress definitely invokes the name of Democracy in all its moves, but its method and manner of execution have not the liberal contents of democracy.
>
> The Muslim League, in its basic deal, is very far from democracy as it stands for the vindication of particular community. The Hindu Mahasabha, in its present strength, is largely the result of reaction from communal bickerings.
>
> To make the political struggle effective, we must come together and present a united front. It is imperative that all of us should feel for the country and act as a united force. The factional fight which is going on may ultimately lead to the building of a strong party seeking to disavow democracy for its own purposes. We shall, in the event, stand defeated in the course of our struggle and in attaining the objective.
>
> The necessary consequence of such a struggle is the growth of a tyrannous party, intolerant of criticisms and authoritarian in issuing decrees. That will be the grave of our fight for the cause of democracy.
>
> I would, therefore, plead for national unity on democratic lines for the pursuit of our political struggle. If democracy is to be made a living force amongst us, we shall know how to feel for and act in cooperation with all.

Referring to the promise of the British Government to grant Dominion Status, the President said: 'the mere pledge of Dominion Status does not inspire enthusiasm amongst our countrymen because it is fastened round with three vague conditions:

1. there is no definite time-limit at the end of which the pledge will be redeemed;
2. the transfer of political powers should be consistent with certain historic and other obligations which the British Government have towards India;
3. the right of self-determination will be conceded only in the event of agreement amongst Indians themselves. This threefold brake emphasized in the recent declarations of the Viceroy and the Secretary of State for India, has rendered the pledge illusory and incapable of being redeemed. The history of British rule in India is strewn with many a broken pledge and they honoured such pledges only when the Indian national demand proved inexorable. It is a sad comment on British Statesmanship.

Referring to the present world war Sir Bijoy Prasad said that it was a mighty conflict between two systems of thought. The intensification of nationalism and the glorification of power-politics had given birth to Hitlerism. It was a challenge of the armed force to the human spirit of freedom. The present war, could only end when Hitlerism was destroyed.

Referring to the Pakistan Scheme of the Muslim League, the President stated:

> It is very unfortunate that in a land marked by comprehensive synthesis at every turn of historical process the theory of a hostile and dual attitude is gaining ground.
>
> The Pakistan movement as propagated is a challenge to the fundamental unity running through the whole continent of India; it is a repudiation of the unity of purpose which underlies the external multitudinous ramifications of society. Such a scheme leaves society open to the assaults of chaos and anarchy.

In conclusion Sir Bijoy Prasad observed:

> In the sphere of politics the transfer of power to Indians is necessary; in the field of economics, primary efforts should be the augmentation of national wealth with equitable distribution amongst all dynamic factors of production; in social matters, we should rise from the slough of listlessness and make our society more vigorous and responsive.

139. Present Deadlock: Sir P.S. Sivaswami Aiyer's Address at National Liberal Federation

The Tribune, 28 December 1941.

Madras, 26 December.

The 23rd annual session of the National Liberal Federation of Indian commuenced this afternoon at the Rusika Ranjana Sabha Hall Mylapore, Sir Bijoy Prasad Singh Roy, ex-Minister of Bengal presiding....

Sir P.S. Sivaswami Iyer, Chairman of the Reception Committee welcomed the delegates and presented his presidential address.

Chairman's Speech

The present deadlock in the country was far more largely due to the issue between Britain and India in regard to the unwillingness of the former to transfer real power to the people of India than merely the result of domestic problem arising from the failure and the two major communities to come together, observed Sir P.S. Sivaswami Aiyer.

'The deadlock', he said, 'is mainly due to the feelings of suspicion and distrust which have pervaded the relations between the people and the Government and between the different communities. These feelings have been encouraged by the attitude and policy of the British Government and the unreasonable intransigence of any particular party must be overcome by the authorities responsible for the situation. One of the devices which have been adopted for creating and keeping alive feelings of hostility is the separate electorate for the Hindus and Muslims, which was brought into existence by Lord Minto.'

'The refusal of Mr Winston Churchill to extend the Atlantic Charter even at this time of the gravest world crisis and the refusal to fix a date for the attainment of Dominion status betray a deplorable lack of statesmanship, and have contributed to deepen the suspicion of the people in the sincerity of British promises qualified by conditions, which cannot possibly be fulfilled in any near future.'

Incidentally, the speaker referred to the action of the Bihar Government and said:

'The arrest of Mr V.D. Savarkar, the president of the Hindu Mahasabha, and other members of the Sabha is an amazing act of folly, in keeping with the attitude of Mr Winston Churchill and other diehard Tories, who control the Cabinet.'

He added:

> The least that they can do, at the present moment to convince the people of the sincerity of their promises, is to accept and carry out the recommendations of the Non-Party Leaders' Conference, held under the wise guidance of our illustrious countryman the Rt Hon'ble Sir Tej Bahadur Sapru, and our distinguished elder statesman like Sir Jagdish Prasad, Sir N.N. Sarkar, and the Rt Hon'ble Mr Jayakar, and to restore responsible Government in the provinces, where it has been suspended.

No One Will Agree to Pakistan

Adverting to the Muslim League's demand for Pakistan, Sir Sivaswamy said: 'The demand of the Muslim community for the division of India into Pakistan and Hindustan is one which no Hindu, or for that matter anyone, sincerely interested in the national integrity and welfare of India, can possibly agree to'.

The speaker at the outset, referring to the war, said:

> However prolonged it may be, the resources of the Allied powers, and the justice of the cause for which they are fighting, justify a feeling of confidence that, in spite of the temporary setbacks and reverses the war will end in the victory of the Allied powers. It is however, bound to lead to an upheaval in the present order of things, political, economic, and social. New international and domestic problems will arise for solution and we in India cannot hope to escape the impact of the new forces and problems, more especially as the menace of war is approaching our own shores. The political parties in India will have to re-examine their position in regard to the political goal of India, their ideals, and policies; internal and foreign, and the methods, by whom they can achieve these ideals for the India of the future.

He emphasized the need for retaining British connection and said:

> The maintenance of the British connection has been part of the creed of the Liberal Party from the very beginning. While membership of the British Commonwealth of Nations is a source of strength, it is attended by no disadvantages. The tie which binds the members of the Commonwealth is not the result of coercion. Nevertheless, it has ensured mutual co-operation and assistance in times of danger, and has been able to withstand the strains and stresses of the world war and has tended to draw the members together more closely than ever.

Guiding Principles of India's External Policy

Proceeding, Sir Sivaswamy deprecated the Congress demand for complete independence and said:

> In the changing circumstances of the world, no country can afford to follow a policy of isolation. The fate of the nations which have adopted a policy of neutrality during this war must be a warning. Closer union with the British Commonwealth and alliance and co-operation with the powers that have combined to overcome the totalitarian powers of darkness and evil should be the guiding principles of India's external policy.

The speaker also criticized the policy of non-co-operation advocated by the Congress, and said:

> While it cannot be denied that, like hunger-strikes in jails, the policy of non-co-operation has had the effect of bringing prominently before the British public the feelings of resentment and distrust, and in some quarters, even a feeling of hostility, towards Britain, which have been engendered by Britain's treatment of our legitimate aspirations and by her fatuous failure to develop the military power and defensive strength of India with the object of keeping the country in a state of perpetual dependence and abject and humiliating helplessness. The Liberal Party is alive to the risks of non-co-operation and believes that the wisest course under the present circumstances is to rally to the support of Britain and help to inflict a crushing defeat upon the Axis Powers.

Concluding, he said:

> Whatever trouble and ordeals the war may entail upon us, there is no reason to despair of the future. Public opinion in England is gradually setting in favour of a fresh orientation of the policy of the British Government towards India. We are greatful to the members of the Labour Party and other members of Parliament, who have espoused our cause and to journals like the '*Daily Herald*,' the '*Manchester Guardian*' and the '*New Statesman*,' who have been supporting us. Public opinion in America is also in sympathy with our aspirations and efforts for the attainment of an honourable position in the British Commonwealth and of an equal and free partnership with Britain and the other members. We may therefore look forward to the fulfilment of our aspirations for Dominion status very shortly after the conclusion of the war.—API

D. Condition of Political Prisoners

140. British Women's Appeal Release Politicals to End Deadlock

Bombay Chronicle, 1 January 1941.

London, 31 December.

Twenty-three well-known women in a letter to '*Times*' appeal for 'a new approach to the Indian situation' and urge the British Government to 'co-operate' in finding a solution by releasing political prisoners.

The letter says:

'The present situation in India has been brought home forcibly to us by reason of the imprisonment of some leading members of the All-India Women's Conference—Mrs Vijaya Lakshmi Pandit for example. With this conference during past years many of us have had close and vital connection. We are fully aware of India's generous help to the war effort in terms of men, material, and money. But alongside this comes the disturbing news of the imprisonment of outstanding national leaders. We feel that this is not the time to go into the rights and wrongs that brought about the impasse. A new approach must be made. A new atmosphere must be operated.

Release Politicals

'In this connection we welcome the news from India that an effort is being made by Indians themselves to end this disastrous situation. Cannot the British Government on their side make it possible by releasing political prisoners, for men and women to meet together with a determination never to separate until an acceptable formula is found? We believe a solution can be found and we urge the British Government to co-operate in this effort to solve the constitutional deadlock'.

The signatories are Margery Bondfield, Vera Brittain, Elizabeth Cadbury, Hilda Clark, Kathleen Courtney, Margery Fry, Isabel Fry, Katharine Furse, Agnes Hardie, Barbara Duncan Harris, Agatha Harrison, Grace Lankester, Emmeline Pethick-Lawrence, Dorothea Layton, Frances Neville, Alison Nellans, H.N. Proctor, Edith M. Pye, Maude Royden, Mary Sheepshanks, Daisy Solomon, Frances Stewart, Edith Summerskill, and Sybil Thorndike.—Reuter.

141. Newspaper Report on Treatment of Satyagrahis in Madura

Indian Express, 21 January 1941.

Trial of Satyagrahis in Madras

Mr B.S. Sankaran, Secretary, Tamil Nad Congress Committee, has issued the following statement:

The trial of Satyagrahis in Madura District seems to have taken a peculiar course. Arrested persons are brought to the Additional District Magistrate who has taken it as a routine to try them only within the jail precincts. Even the press correspondents, lawyers and relatives of the accused are not allowed to be present during the trial. As late as 18th December 1940 I referred to the District Magistrate about this, who after twenty days informed me that he is not prepared to enter into correspondence with me on this subject.

On the 15th instant, two Satyagrahis, Messrs C.S. Chellappa and G.N. Muthusami Naidu were tried within the precincts of the Central Jail at Madura. Mr Chellappa's relatives including his sister, who came all the way from Madras for this purpose, were refused permission to see the accused or be present during the trial.

I understand that the Additional District Magistrate has refused permission to those accused to file their statements.

Under these circumstances, I am today writing to Mahatmaji to give permission to file an appeal on this ground. A correct version of what happened during the trial cannot be had, since that was held in camera.

The same Additional District Magistrate seems to have discharged one Srimathi Rengammal and has passed remarks that she is illiterate and unable to answer questions to her relating to the war. There was no lawyer, press reporter or anybody also present during the trial, and we have to take what the Additional District Magistrate says as correct.

In Madura Jail

I happened to meet five political prisoners who were transferred from Madura to Vellore on Wednesday night (15th instant). They were hand-cuffed and were detained in the Railway station platform from 6 p.m. to 10.55 p.m. On enquiry about their treatment in the Madura Jail, the prisoners complained that the buttermilk supplied to them was a mixture of rice 'vadi-kanji' and butter-milk. Even this stuff (it was stated) was not clean. There were (it was gathered) cockroaches in the morning kanji supplied to the prisoners. Evening and morning meals supplied to the 'C' class prisoners were of a low quality rice and had a rotten smell.

142. Deoli Prisoners Complaints to the *National Herald* and the Camp Superintendent's Reply

File No. 43/17/41-Poll (I), Home (Political) Department, NAI.

(i) The Hell that is Deoli
Lurid Light on Conditions of Security Prisoners

National Herald, 11 February 1941.

The following description of the conditions in the Deoli detention camp has been sent to us for publication:

Security prisoners are virtually treated as 'C' class prisoners. They are kept in congested barracks, in batches of ten or twelve in each room. The charpoys are close together, very little space being kept in between them.

No furniture is given, no table, no chair is supplied, not even at private cost.

The camp is surrounded by armed military guards. It is surrounded by barbed wire, each barrack is separated from the other by barbed wire. The staff is that of CID, even the compounders in the hospital are CID men.

The place is very malaria-stricken. Almost all have suffered from the disease since their arrival here. There is no proper medical treatment. There have been repeated attacks of malaria of a virulent type. No arrangement exists for surgical operations or for dangerous and serious cases, of which there are some. Baba Wasakha Singh is suffering from tuberculosis, Comrade Ghate from heart disease, Sirut Mukherji (Bihar) from renal-colic, Iyenger from Madras from colic, Hukam Singh from obstruction and colic, several have enlarged spleen and chronic malaria. Baba Bhagwan Singh has been in hospital ever since his arrest. No one is in good health. No mosquito nets are given—even private ones are not allowed to us. It is a necessity here. It is strange that even sick are not given special diet. They are allowed diet costing twelve annas to class one and six annas to class two. They can get diet of their own class. No medical diet is given.

Two Classes

There are two classes of prisoners, class one getting twelve annas per day and class two getting six annas per day for diet. Class one is given clothing on the scale of 'B' class prisoners in the Punjab jails; they get furniture also on the same scale. Class two prisoners are according to rules allowed no furniture, they are allowed 'C' class convict clothing. No plain clothes are given. Convict clothing is of the same type as that of 'C' class prisoners. It is quite inferior stuff. Clothing is quite insufficient. Warm clothing has not been supplied to all. Class two prisoners are not given shoes or footwears and socks. Repair of shoes is not done at Government cost, as is the case in all Punjab jails. Shoes here are a necessity. There is no good arrangement for attending on the sick in hospital. Friends are not allowed to visit or attend on them in hospital. When this concession was demanded the authorities refused. They called armed guards into the camp and threatened to take stern action.

Letters

There is an absurd rule that only one letter a week is allowed to be received. If more than one letter comes in the week they are withheld.

The censor is very strict in respect of books and papers. Even newspapers like the *Statesman* and the *C. & M. Gazette* are badly cut and mutilated. There are no good libraries near the place. The camp has no library of its own. Private books are censored.

Maps if any are taken out of them; blank sheets in the binding are torn away. Only fiction and very ordinary books are allowed. Hardly any book to the taste of prisoners is permitted. Even such books as on science by J.B.S. Haldane, a professor of science in Oxford, are withheld. 'Liberty in the Modern State' by Laski, 'Must War Spread' by Pritt is among the books withheld. No Magazines are given at Government cost.

Regarding interviews, the rules are very strict. One hour for relations and half an hour for friends. Both the interviewer and the interviewed are to be searched. It is a great humiliation. There is no arrangement for the stay of relations.

Utensils are quite insufficient, only one plate and one 'katori' is given; no spoon, no glass, is given for drinking water.

Water supply is very limited. If it is so in this season what will happen in summer. There is no arrangement for heating water in this season for bathing. There is no privacy in the bathroom.

One can receive money only from authorized persons, not even from friends. Prisoners have to give the names of those with whom they like to communicate and from whom they expect money. Sher Gul Khan received money from his mother which was returned.

Class one prisoners are allowed to spend Rs 10 a month, while class two prisoners are allowed to spend only Rs 5 a month within which to supplement. Security prisoners are allowed to supplement at their own cost but the limit of Rs 5 is so small that hardly anything can be bought, especially when the prices are so high. One can hardly buy clothes or books or fruits.

Humiliation

Punishments are given on every pretext. Some prisoners refused to carry their luggage on their heads to their barracks. Their bedding was withheld and is still lying in the office. They gave an application about it to the Chief Commissioner for which they were punished. There may be trouble any day. The humiliating treatment meted to the prisoners, the punishments that are given, may lead to trouble, unless the public, the press and the Government take steps to correct the present harsh attitude.

An insufficient number of convicts are allowed for kitchen work. Much of the work has to be done by the detenus themselves.

Regarding diet one has to remember that the Government give six annas a head to class two prisoners, but in fact this amount is equal to only three annas which is given to 'c' class convicts in the Punjab jails. Prices are so exorbitantly high that three annas can hardly buy anything. 'Atta' is Rs 5/10 per maund; ghee is Rs 2 per seer and Rs 80 per maund. Prices of vegetables are very high. Potatoes cost three annas per seer, raddish, turnips, carrots (muli, salgum, gajar) with leaves cost two annas per seer, Gur costs seven rupees and a half per maund. This list is enough to show that six annas do not go far. It is hardly possible to buy good quality stuff. Fruits are impossible to buy because of the very high price. At least twelve annas a day a prisoner will be needed to obtain healthy and wholesome diet.

Dependants

There are prisoners who have no one to look after their families and dependants. The condition of the families of some of them is such that it is difficult to say how they actually make both ends meet. Some have had their families virtually thrown on the streets. Government have refused to give allowance for their families. This question is very urgent and needs solution. Individual representations have been made to the Punjab Government. Without public pressure nothing will be done.

The rules do not permit association between class one and class two prisoners. It is absurd but they are not allowed even to avail themselves of the opportunity of monthly interviews. One can interview persons from outside but not from the other class. Another example of the absurdity of the rules is that the prisoners cannot change their seats. They are fixed like natural laws and cannot be shifted from one seat to another and from one room to another.

Having no contact with the outside world, it is difficult for the prisoners to move the public and, therefore, the Government, about this hell. If nothing is done there is every possibility that there may be sad occurrences. Mr N.M. Joshi moved a resolution in the Central Assembly about the conditions of the detenus now called security prisoners. He should be given a copy of the above facts and should be asked to move in the matter. The question is very important. Something must be done to ventilate the grievances of the detenus in this concentration camp, as well as about the allowance being given to all the detenus or their families.

There are prisoners from the Punjab, UP, Bihar, NWFP, Bombay, and Madras. There are seventy-six detenus in camp one of class first, and ninety in camp two of class two.

(ii) Camp Superintendent's Reply

From: Major R.F. Crarter, Superintendent, Deoli Detention Camp, Deoli, Rajputana

To: The Commissioner,
Ajmer–Merwara, Ajmer
Dated Deoli, the 13 March 1941.
No. X–411 of 1941

Memorandum:
Reference: Your endorsement No.B–65/1941 dated the 27th February 1941.

The account of conditions in the Deoli Camp as given in the article which appeared in the 'National Herald' dated the 11th February 1941 (returned herewith) appeared also in the 'Vir Bharat' (an Urdu daily of Lahore) dated the 27th January 1941.

The Deputy Inspector-General of Police, CID, Punjab, Lahore, informed me vide his letter No. 653-ADSB dated the 4th February 1941 (copy attached) that Security Prisoner Ram Chandra BA of Punjab managed to smuggle out a document which contained complaints against the living conditions in the Deoli Camp. I attach herewith a copy of my reply (No. X–190 dated the 7th February 1941).

I am of opinion that the information was smuggled out through Security Prisoner Om Parkash when he went to Lahore on the 8th January 1941 to attend the High Court or through one of my guards.

The same account of conditions in the Deoli Camp as appeared in the National Herald on the 11th February 1941 was published in the *'Search Light'* of Patna dated the 13th February 1941.

The article is more or less a copy of the petition signed by fifty-seven Class II Security Prisoners forwarded to you with my memorandum No. X–99 dated the 16th November 1940 in which I gave my criticism in detail. This petition was rejected by the Government of India vide your endorsement No. D.54/F.19 (14) dated the 29th January 1941.

It is not a true description of Deoli Detention camp as a whole but an exaggerated description of the conditions in Camp II of the Camp, that is, of Class II Security Prisoners, treatment of whom should generally correspond to that of 'C' Class convicted prisoners in jails. However, for ready reference, I give below my remarks brought up-to-date, as such articles as mosquito nets on recommendation of the medical authorities and smoking at their own cost have since been sanctioned.

	Statement as given in the article	My remarks
1.	Security prisoners are Virtually treated as 'C' class prisoners.	The treatment of Class II Security prisoners corresponds approximately to that of Class 'C' convicted prisoners vide 'Memorandum on Treatment of Security Prisoners' received with DO No. 43/12/40-Political (I) dated the 7th September 1940 from Government of India, Home Department, to Hon'ble the Chief Commissioner, Ajmer–Merwara.
2.	They are kept in congested barracks, in batches of ten or twelve in each room. The charpoys are close together, very little space being kept in between them.	The barracks they occupy are those which were occupied by the late Mina Corps and are far better accommodation than provided for 'C' Class convicted prisoners in jails and also better than the accommodation provided for the guards of this Camp. They are not kept in congested barracks, and the space between the charpoys is sufficient.
3.	No furniture is given, no table, no chair, is supplied, not even at private cost.	Furniture has been provided in accordance with the Hon'ble the Chief Commissioner's Notification which includes beds and mattresses which are not provided in ordinary jails. Class II Security Prisoners are not allowed individual tables and chairs but they have a 'common room' in which there are tables and benches where they can read and write letters, and do other things. Easy and deck chairs have been withheld as space does not allow for each prisoner to have his own deck chair and also for reasons of security. (One easy chair has been allowed on medical ground).
4.	The camp is surrounded by armed military guards. It is surrounded by barbed wire; each barrack is separated from the other by barbed wire.	The camp is surrounded by barbed wire and armed guards.
5.	The staff is that of CID even the compounders in the hospital are CID men.	The only member of the staff, who has any experience of CID work, is the one Inspector who has come from the Punjab. The compounders are not CID men nor is there any other CID staff on the staff of the Detention Camp.

Statement as given in the article	My remarks
6. The place is very malaria-stricken. Almost all have suffered from the disease since their arrival here. There is no proper medical treatment. There have been repeated attacks of malaria of a virulent type. No arrangement exists for surgical operations or for dangerous and serious cases, of which there are some. Baba Wasakha Singh is suffering from tuberculosis, Comrade Ghate from heart disease, Sirut Mukherji (Bihar) from renal-colic, Hukam Singh from obstruction and colic, several have enlarged spleen, and chronic malaria. Baba Bhagwan Singh has been in Hospital ever since his arrest. Iyenger from Madras from colic.	There have been a certain number of cases of malaria vide the figures given below: October 1940–11 out of 73 S.Prs. = 15 per cent November 1940–7 out of 132 S.Prs. = 5 per cent December 1940–20 out of 166 S.Prs. = 12 per cent January 1941–9 out of 166 S.Prs. = 5 1/2 per cent Provision is being made for supply of mosquito nets for Class II Security Prisoners vide your endorsement No. D–54/F.19(14) dated the 29th January 1941. The hospital arrangements are adequate. There have been no serious or dangerously ill cases up-to-date. Arrangements exist for surgical operations. Should any prisoner require any special treatment such as X-Ray or a major operation which cannot be carried out here, arrangements have been made for his transfer to the Victoria Hospital, Ajmer vide Paragraph 20 of the Deoli Detention Camp Order, 1940. The Civil Surgeon, Ajmer–Merwara, Ajmer, visited the Camp on the 6th November 1940 and 26th February 1941 and examined the sick Security Prisoners. I attach herewith a copy of my Medical Officer's report on each of the cases of Security Prisoners mentioned in the article.
7. No one is in good health.	Out of the eighty-nine Class II Security Prisoners eighty (twenty-six by five Lbs. and fifty-four by ten Lbs.) have gained in weight, six are stationary and three have lost weight.
8. No mosquito nets are given, even private ones are not allowed to us. It is a necessity here.	Please see my remarks at sub-paragraph (6) above. No request was made by a Prisoner to use his private mosquito net, nor have I withheld any.
9. It is strange that even sick are not given special diet.	I do not allow unnecessary luxuries. I have passed the attached special Diet scale for patients in the hospital. The Medical Officer has full description as to which diet the patient should be put on.

(Contd) ...

... (*Contd*)

Statement as given in the article	My remarks
10. They are allowed diet costing twelve annas to class one and six annas to class two.	The scales are quite adequate. Allowance in fixing the scales in question has been made for these prisoners being not convicted prisoners—otherwise the dietary of 'C' Class convicted prisoners prevailing in Ajmer, Punjab or UP jails is less than three annas. Reference is invited to your endorsement No. C–40/Conf. 19(14) dated the 27th November 1940.
11. No medical diet is given.	It is not a fact. Medical diet is given.
TWO CLASSES	
12. There are two classes of Prisoners, class one getting twelve annas per day and class two getting six annas per day for diet.	No remarks.
13. Class one is given clothing on the scale of 'B' class prisoners in the Punjab jails; they get furniture also on the same scale.	No remarks.
14. Class two prisoners are according to rules allowed no furniture, they are allowed 'C' class convict clothing. No plain clothes are given. Convict clothing is of the same type as that of 'C' class prisoners. It is quite inferior stuff. Clothing is quite insufficient.	Class II prisoners are allowed plain clothing as per scale sanctioned. No 'C' class convicted prisoners received special clothing in accordance with the Hon'ble the Chief Commissioner's Notification. The Hon'ble the Home Member, Government of India, saw this clothing and approved of it.
15. Warm clothing has not been supplied to all.	All Class II prisoners have been supplied with warm coats, quilts, and blankets.
16. Class two prisoners are not given shoes or footwear and socks. Repair of shoes is not done at government cost, as is the case in all Punjab jails.	Shoes, or footwear and sock are not supplied to Class II prisoners. They are not supplied to 'C' class convicted prisoners in jails. However, prisoners are allowed to wear shoes, brought by themselves or sent by relatives.
17. Shoes here are a necessity.	I agree that shoes are a necessity, but that they should be provided to only those prisoners who have not got shoes, and that they should be the ordinary country shoes costing not more than Rs 1/8/ per pair.

	Statement as given in the article	My remarks
18.	There is no good arrangement for attending on the sick in hospital. Friends are not allowed to visit or attend on them in hospital.	There exists adequate arrangement for attending on the sick in hospital. There are Compounders and Ward-boys for the purpose. In the late Jail, detenu companions were allowed to attend detenu patients in the Hospital. Owing to limited hospital accommodation and the attendants interfering with the medical arrangements and diagnosis of the cases and not carrying out instructions given to them by the Medical Officer, the practice has not been allowed this time.
19.	When this concession was demanded the authorities refused. They called armed guards into the camp and threatened to take stern action.	This relates to the particular case of Class I Security Prisoner Shatrughan Kumar. This affair took place on 11th December 1940. A brief history of the case is given below—The Security Prisoner was ordered by the Medical Officer to be taken to Hospital. He, encouraged by other Security Prisoners (including one Kesho Prashad Sharma who was formerly a detenu in the late jail), refused to obey the order. I then sent the Camp Officer into the Camp to persuade the Security Prisoners to allow the patient to be taken to Hospital. They refused. I then sent my Deputy Superintendent with orders that he would see that the patient was taken to the hospital by force, if necessary. The Deputy Superintendent returned after about half an hour and informed me that trouble was anticipated. I then went in myself and tried to persuade the Security Prisoners to allow the patient to be taken to Hospital but they refused. As trouble was expected I gave orders for the guard to 'stand to' outside the camp enclosure. I took in four guards armed with the usual 'lathis' and I was armed with a walking stick. No lethal weapons were or have been so far been taken inside the Camp compound. Persuation having failed I informed the Prisoners that they had fifteen minutes to make up their minds to let the patient be taken to Hospital. They gave way, so no force was used, and the patient was taken to Hospital.

(*Contd*) ...

... (*Contd*)

Statement as given in the article	My remarks
	A reference is invited to your Memorandum No. C-79/F. 19(14) dated the 20th December 1940 in which you asked me to inform the prisoner that no action was being taken on his telegram. 'He had no right to refuse to go to Hospital unless a companion was sent with him.'
LETTERS	
20. There is an absurd rule that only one letter a week is allowed to be received. If more than one letter comes in the week they are withheld.	Class II Security Prisoners are ordinarily permitted to receive one and write one letter per week vide paragraph 13(1) of the Deoli Detention Camp Order, 1940. If more than one letter arrives in a week the prisoner is informed of its arrival and he is allowed to choose which letter he wants. Extra letters received in the week are actually not withheld. He can take them in later weeks at the rate of one letter per week.
21. The censor is very strict in respect of books and papers. Even newspapers like the '*Statesman*' and the '*Civil and Military Gazette*' are badly cut and mutilated. There are no good libraries near the place. The Camp has no library of its own. Private books are censored. Maps if any are taken out of them; blank sheets in the binding are torn away. Only fiction and very ordinary books are allowed. Hardly any book to the taste of prisoners is permitted. Even such books as on Science by J.D.S. Haldane, a professor of Science in Oxford, are withheld. 'Liberty in the Modern State' by Laski, 'Must War Spread 'by Pritt are among the books withheld.	The censor staff is at presents grossly over-worked. The censoring of papers and books is carefully controlled by me. The Security Prisoners taste for books is well known. All they want are books on revolution, communism, and other things, which are withheld by me. I give below a list of some of the books withheld by me: 1. 'Seven Red Sundays' by Ramon J. Sender. 2. 'Bourgeois—Democratic Revolution and India' by Saumyendranath Tagore. 3. 'United front or Betrayal' by—Do—(encouraging strikes, and other things, in India). 4. 'Communism' by Ralph Fox. 5. 'Alexei, the Gangester' translated from the Russian by Stephen Garry. 6. 'Liberty in the Modern State' by Laski.—(Communism). This book has been notified as inadmissible to the Security Prisoners by the Punjab CID. 7. 'The Marxist philosophy and the Sciences' by J.B.S. Haldane. It is not a book on Science but deals with the philosophy of Karl Marx. 8. 'Must War Spread' by Pritt.

Statement as given in the article	My remarks
	Security Prisoners are beginning to understand that they will not be allowed this type of books and a better class of books is being sent by their relations and friends, hence fewer books are now being withheld. Both camps have small libraries—Hundred books a month are obtained from the Public Library, Ajmer at the selection of the Camp Librarians (Security Prisoners). There is no shortage of reading material in camps as there are hundreds of privately owned books in the camps. Some individual prisoners brought as many as 200 books. Only maps of Rajputana are disallowed in the interest of security. Prisoners were using blank sheets from books for illegal communication between camps. Blank sheets are now not Detached from the books, but each blank page is stamped with the censor stamp.
22. No magazines are given at government cost.	This is true, but prisoners receive numerous magazines from their friends.
23. Regarding interviews the rules are very strict. One hour for relations and half an hour for friends.	Interviews are ordinarily allowed to continue for an hour with a relative or half an hour with a person other than a relative in accordance with paragraph 11(8) of the Deoli Detention Camp Order, 1940.
24. Both the interviewer and the interviewed are to be searched. It is a great humiliation.	This is in accordance with paragraph 11(6) of the Deoli Detention Camp Order, 1940. It is no humiliation. The procedure of searching is very normal.
25. There is no arrangement for the stay of relations.	Deoli is a very small place and there are no hotels or Dak bungalows where visitors can stay and the visitors are informed accordingly. I regret that I am unable to make any arrangements for their stay here.
26. Utensils are quite insufficient, only one plate and one 'katori' is given; no spoon, no glass, is given for drinking water.	Complete cooking utensils are provided, also a cup and plate per prisoner in accordance with the rules. In addition mugs are provided at the common bathing places and separate mugs at the latrines. However, I recommend that a glass should be allowed at a cost of about 8–10 annas.

(*Contd*) ...

... (*Contd*)

	Statement as given in the article	My remarks
27.	Water supply is very limited. If it is so in this season what will happen in summer.	Twenty Gallons per day per head is the unit at which drinking and bathing water is supplied. This was the scale also in the late jail, and compares very favourably with the scale allowed to British and Indian troops in a standing camp vide extracts attached herewith.
28.	There is no arrangement for heating water in this season for bathing.	Prisoners are not supplied with hot water for bathing, but in any case in which it is considered essential by the medical authorities, water can be heated in the kitchens and as far as I know hot water is not provided in jails for bathing. It would not be possible without great expense in a Detention Camp.
29.	There is no privacy in the bath-room.	There exists a communal bathing shed for the purpose as was the case in the late jail. No more privacy seems necessary.
30.	One can receive money only from authorized persons, not even from friends. Prisoners have to give the names of those with whom they like to communicate and from whom they expect money.	Specified relatives and friends are allowed to send money vide paragraph 10 (1) of the Deoli Detention Camp Order, 1941. To check Security Prisoners communication and receipt of funds from undesirable persons the relatives and friends have to be specified. A number of friends of prisoners who have sent money have been Classified by the CID of their respective provinces as undesirable.
31.	Sher Gul Khan received money from his mother which was returned.	This is incorrect. A money order for Rs 20 was received on 24th December 1940 sent by his mother through one Baghmal broker of Jaranwali market.
32	Class one prisoners are allowed to spend Rs 10 a month while class two prisoners are allowed to spend only Rs 5 a month within which to supplement. Security Prisoners are allowed to supplement at their own cost but the limit of Rs 5 is so small that hardly anything can be bought especially when the prices are so high. One can hardly buy clothes or book or fruit.	This is in accordance with paragraph 10 (1) of the Deoli Detention Camp Order, 1940. Security Prisoners are permitted by me to exceed the limit of Rs 10 and Rs 5 to purchase essential clothing within reason. The requisitions are personally passed or refused by me. Moreover the prisoners receive clothing and other articles from their relatives and friends.

Statement as given in the article	My remarks
HUMILIATION	
33. Punishments are given on every pretext.	This statement is entirely false. There have been only the following occasions for awarding punishment: 1. To seven Class II Security Prisoners for not obeying my orders to carry their own luggage from the stores to the Camp. 2. To one Class I Security Prisoner (1) for writing a petition to superintendent in insulting language, and (2) continually refusing to attend roll call. 3. To one Class I Security Prisoner, and two Class II Security Prisoners, for disobedience of orders contained in paragraph 5(i) of the Deoli Detention Camp Order and paragraph 2(d) of Camp Order No. 6 dated the 25th October 1940 (issued by Superintendent)—communicating in unauthorized manner. 4. To one Class II Security Prisoner (Ram Chandra BA) for communicating with a person outside the camp in an unauthorized manner. These four punishments have had a very salutary effect.
34. Some prisoners refused to carry their luggage on their heads to their barracks. Their bedding was withheld and is still lying in the office.	This relates to the particular case of 7 Security Prisoners mentioned at sub-paragraph 33(1) above. The prisoners were never asked to take their luggage on their 'heads'. Arrangements were made for the carrying of the kits of the prisoners who were medically unfit to do so. Other prisoners were required to carry their own. All prisoners of Class I carried their own kit. Those of Class II (7 out of 90) who refused on the ground that they were political prisoners were told that their kit would be returned to them when they were willing to carry it. They have since carried their luggage to the Camp.

(*Contd*) ...

... (*Contd*)

	Statement as given in the article	My remarks
35.	They gave an application about it to the Chief Commissioner for which they were punished. There may be trouble any day. The humiliating treatment meted to the prisoners, the punishments that are given, may lead to trouble, unless the public, the press, and the Government take steps to correct the present harsh attitude.	Their petition dated the 13th November 1940 on the subject addressed to the Home Secretary to Government of India, New Delhi, was forwarded to you with my Memorandum No. X–110 dated the 19th November 1940. They were punished not for submitting the petition to the Hon'ble the Chief Commissioner but for disobedience of my orders. All prisoners who have since arrived have moved their own kit and there is no apprehension of trouble on this account. Regarding punishment I have given my remarks above.
36.	An insufficient number of convicts are allowed for kitchen work. Much of the work has to be done by detenus themselves.	There are at present 35 convicts serving as cooks, 'bhishtis', barbers, and sweepers. Since the arrival of 6 convict cooks from the UP the number of cooks is sufficient. One more is expected from UP and I am submitting proposals for convicts required for punkha pulling and extra barbers. Prisoners are not required to do their own cooking, but some prisoners take an interest in their meals and cook 'fancy dishes' for themselves and other prisoners.
37.	Regarding diet one has to remember that the Government give six annas a head to class II prisoners but in fact this amount is equal to only three annas which is given to 'C' Class Convicts in the Punjab jails. Jail prices are so exhorbitantly high that three annas can hardly buy anything.	Convicted prisoners' diet allowance is-/3/-per day per head. In this allowance of -/3/- they get the same quantity of rations as is allowed to convicts in the Punjab jails, -/6/- dietary scale in the case of Security Prisoners (Class II) is sufficient, as they are doing no labour. As will be seen from the articles of dietary requisitioned by Security Prisoners (Class II) on 1st, 2nd, 3rd, and 4th November, 1940 detailed vide paragraph 4(v) (a) of my Memorandum NO.X–99 dated the 16th November 1940, the food supplied is ample. Due to transport charges of commodities brought to Deoli and consequently high prices and to the fact that they are not convicted prisoners, the diet scale of class II prisoners has been fixed at -/6/-

	Statement as given in the article	My remarks
38.	Atta is Rs 5/10 maund. Ghee is Rs 2 per seer and Rs 80 per maund. Prices of vegetables are very high. Potatoes cost -/3/- per seer, raddishes, turnips, carrots (Mulli, Salgum, gajar) with leaves cost -/2/- per seer. Gur costs seven rupees and a half per maund. This list is enough to show that six annas do not go far. It is hardly possible to buy good quality stuff. Fruits are impossible to buy because of the very high price	The Contractor's prices are checked with those prevailing in Deoli, Nasirabad, and Ajmer. The rates of ghee, gur, and other things, have since been greatly reduced in accordance with market fluctuations. Radishes, turnips, and carrots were out of season and hardly procurable at the time at which the rates are given. In season they are supplied at cheaper rates. I would point out that it is quite unnecessary for prisoners to buy expensive English vegetables. There are many Indian vegetables which they can obtain far cheaper at local 'bazar' rates.
39.	At least twelve annas a day a prisoner will be needed to obtain healthy and wholesome diet.	For the reason that 1. the treatment of Class II Security prisoners corresponds to that of'C' class convicted prisoners, 2. they are not doing any labour, and 3. they are dyspeptic, I do not suggest that they require more food nor that their diet allowance be increased. Certain prisoners have asked if they may buy cigarettes, cups, and saucers from their dietary allowance, which proves that the dietary allowance, if anything, is excessive.
	DEPENDENTS	
40.	There are prisoners who have no one to look after their families and dependents. The condition of the families of some of them is such that it is difficult to say how they actually make both ends meet. Some have had their families virtually thrown on the streets.	I have no information regarding the conditions of the families of Security Prisoners.

(*Contd*) ...

... (*Contd*)

	Statement as given in the article	My remarks
41.	Government have refused to give allowance for their families. This question is very urgent and needs solution. Individual representations have been made to the Punjab Government. Without public pressure nothing will be done.	The Government of India (Home Department) in their letter No. 43/25/40-Political (I) dated the 28th November 1940 received Vide your endorsement No. C–72/Conf. 19(14) dated the 16th December 1940, have ruled that allowance for dependants cannot be granted as a general rule, applications from individuals in exceptional cases if supported by facts which would bring them within that category of may be forwarded to the Government which ordered their detention, for consideration on their merits. Accordingly those prisoners who have submitted petitions for grant of family allowance have been forwarded through you to provincial governments.
42.	The rules do not permit association between class I and class II prisoners. It is absurd. But they are not allowed even to avail themselves of opportunity of monthly interviews. One can interview persons from outside but not from the other class.	This is in accordance with paragraph 5 (i) of the Deoil Detention Camp Order, 1940. I am in entire agreement with this rule. It keeps the 'leaders' from the 'mass'.
43.	Another example of the absurdity of the rules is that the prisoners cannot change their seats. They are fixed like natural laws and cannot be shifted from one seat to another and from one room to another.	Seats in barracks are allotted to every Security Prisoner. Allotment of seats for the purpose of roll call and order in camp is necessary, as it would be an impossible situation for the roll call officer if prisoners were allowed to change their seats and rooms from day-to-day. Prisoners' requests for changes are considered and permission is granted when considered necessary.
44.	Having no contact with the outside world, it is difficult for the prisoners to move the public and, therefore, the Government about this hell. If nothing is done there is every possibility that there may be sad occurrences.	Prisoners take every opportunity to represent their grievances however petty they may be. Applications and representations to Government are made on every pretext, which are forwarded.

	Statement as given in the article	My remarks
45.	Mr N.M. Joshi moved a resolution in the Central Assembly about the conditions of the detenus now called Security Prisoners. He should be given a copy of the above facts and should be asked to move in the matter. The question is very important. Something must be done to ventilate the grievances of the detenus in this concentration camp as well as about allowances being given to all the detenus on their families	A reference is invited to my DO No. X–317 dated the 28th February 1941 regarding Mr N.M. Joshi.
46.	There are prisoners from the Punjab, UP, Bihar, NWFP, Bombay, and Madras. There are seventy-six detenus in Camp one of class first, and ninety in camp two of class two.	No remarks. On the 4th January 1941, the number of Security Prisoners was 77 class I and 90 Class II.

8. In my opinion the individuals detained here are as contented as can be expected when detained in any jail or Camp.

One Camp had an atheletic meeting last Saturday (8th March 1941) which they all seemed to enjoy. I attended the sports for half an hour. At the moment I do not consider that the prisoners here have any serious grievance, they have a number of minor grievances which are settled, if possible, as soon as they arise, keeping in mind security discipline of the Camp and the carrying out of Government's orders.

An official visitor is paying a visit here on the 18th of March when all prisoners will be at liberty to put forward their grievances which will be forwarded to you with my remarks. Security Prisoners will be given twenty-four hours notice of his arrival.

R.F. Craster
Major
Superintendent, Deoli
Detention Camp, Deoli, Rajputana.

143. N.M. Joshi's Resolution on Conditions of Detenus

The Legislative Assembly Debates, Official Report, Vol. 1, Government of India Press, New Delhi, 1941, pp. 107–43.

Debate in Central Legislative Assembly, 12 February 1941 (Extracts)

RESOLUTIONS *RE.* APPOINTMENT OF A COMMITTEE TO EXAMINE THE CONDITIONS OF DETENUS UNDER THE DEFENCE OF INDIA ACT—contd.

Mr President (The Honourable Sir Abdur Rahim): The House will now resume consideration of the following Resolution moved by Mr Joshi on the 15th November 1940.

'That this Assembly recommends to the Governor General in Council that he should take immediate steps to appoint a committee to examine and report without delay:

(a) Whether conditions under which the detenus under the Defence of India Act have to live in prisons are suitable and adequate; and sufficient privileges are granted to them for communication outside by way of letters and interviews; and if not, what improvements should be made therein;
(b) Whether their families are provided with suitable maintenance or not; and, if not, what assistance Government should give them;
(c) Whether those who are interned or externed under the Defence of India Act have difficulty in maintaining themselves or their families, and whether it is necessary to give them any assistance from Government; and in case, it is necessary, what should be the amount of such assistance.'

Sardar Sant Singh (West Punjab: Sikh): Sir, this Resolution of the Honourable Mr Joshi on the working of the Defence of India Act is a milk and water Resolution—so modest; he calls it a modest one, I call it something like the mildest one which could come from a Member who wants to keep his constituency in good humour as well as do the public service which he is called upon to do as a Member of this House. As a matter of fact, the working of the Defence of India Act the last two years in India shows that the Act is being used not with a view to the successful prosecution of the war alone, as was given out at the time when the Defence of India Act was introduced and carried through in this House, but for purposes other than those for which it was intended. I need hardly point out that under the pretence of the use of the Act, people have been detained who were engaged in lawful activities....

The Honourable Sir Reginald Maxwell (Home Member): On a point of order, Sir. Is the argument of the Honourable Member relevant to the Resolution which relates to the conditions under which detenus are confined?...

Sardar Sant Singh: I will proceed with this particular issue. The particular issue involved is that people have been detained and without trial who ought to be treated in a manner which may be called humane and the reason for this is obvious. First of all, these people have been detained without any specific charge having been brought against them. They do not know for what activities of theirs they are suffering detention under the Defence of India Act. And, secondly, their families are deprived of their services and of the livelihood which the detained people earned for their maintenance. Therefore, it is essential that the Government of India should work this Act in a spirit which should win the confidence of the public that it is being worked on humane and just lines. Now, taking certain instances in which this Act has been used against persons holding particular political views and of which instances have been quoted in the two speeches given by Maulana Zafar Ali Khan and Mr Joshi the other day, is it not fair that they should be provided with all the amenities of life during the period of their detention?...

... The conditions which the Committee will have to examine and report are contained in three parts of this Resolution. First of all, they will have to find out whether they are being detained in a place suitable for their health and whether sufficient privileges are being granted to them during the period of detention....The second point is about providing adequate allowances to the families of those who have been detained. So far as I remember, a question was asked in this House on this point and the Government reply was that they were not prepared to sanction allowances in such cases. May I know why a family should be deprived of the means of livelihood which an earning member of the family was providing them on account of that earning member being detained? Why should it not be the duty of the Government to provide the family with the same means of living in which the family was living before this person was detained? The justice and fair-play demand that in such cases the family should be granted adequate allowance. Under the circumstances, my submission is that the Government should take a sympathetic attitude towards this modest Resolution and accept it so that the confidence of the public may be restored in the Government's action in such matters. After all, detention without trial is not a normal course of giving punishment to a subject. It is an abnormal matter and as such it should be met with abnormal measure and that abnormal measure is that a humane treatment should extend in the working of this particular provision of the Defence of Indian Act rather than the strict technical procedure of a jail life. With these words, I support the Resolution....

Mr Lalchand Navalrai (Sind: Non-Muhammadan Rural): ...[H]aving heard the Honourable Mr Joshi who gave instances and who also pointed out the difficulties of these detenus, Government must have done something by this time. I would, therefore, like the Honourable the Home Member to tell us how far he has proceeded to remedy the wrong and to what extent further amenities have been afforded to these detenus. Now, Sir, it is a modest Resolution. I would say that it contains only one item. When we passed the Defence of India Act, we did not discuss it at any great length and passed it in the interests of the prosecution of the war. Some of its provisions were very extensive and in some respects they were harsh. In some other respects we merely gave a blank cheque to the Executive to administer that law in the interests of the exigencies of the war. But it was expected that when they were proceeding against persons who were to be confined as detenus either in jails or within certain areas or who were being externed, the treatment to be given to them would not be the same that is given to an ordinary criminal or a man who has gone into the detention on account of a crime involving moral turpitude. It was expected that the Government itself would do certain things so that no complaint may be made against it. But what has been the result? The result has been, as was mentioned by Mr Joshi and other speakers, that they are not given even ordinary comforts and ordinary amenities. Now, the point is, who are these people who have been detained and how they have been detained? They were not given any trial. The allegations against them were not proved in any court of law and they were not even proved to show that there was any substance in them beyond mere suspicions. We know how the CID reports come and in the cases under the Defence of India Act the CID must be very active to get even those men locked up against whom they even had an unfounded suspicion. And a word from the CID is more or less a death-warrant to the man against whom the report is made. It is very necessary, therefore, that the Government should go into these complaints and the grievances that have been made.

Now, Sir, the Honourable Mr Joshi has taken pains to collect facts. He has got facts and he has got proof of them. He told us that there are two categories of these detenus. Now, I will take up the grievance of those detenus who have been detained in jails. Now, so far as these men are concerned they had good station in life, they had good home comforts, and they could also take care of their families. Having been detained they were given a life which was absolutely different from that which they enjoyed before their detention. There ought to be certain considerations for them to see that, though they may not be given the same comforts as they used to enjoy in their private life, some concessions are given to them. If such concessions have not been given to them so far, they must be given to them at once. The first difficulty which has been mentioned is with regard to small matters of convenience. They are not being supplied soap or oil or materials for shaving.

An Honourable Member: They can grow hair.

Mr Lalchand Navalrai: That would also harm them. Now-a-days everybody is clean shaven. Apart from that, if a man has been accustomed all his life to get himself clean shaven, if all of a sudden he is forced to grow his hair, he would become sick. The other complaint is they are not being given newspapers. I know one or two newspapers are being given, but they are not worth reading. It has become almost the fashion now-a-days with everybody to read newspapers the first thing in the morning.

The other complaint was they are not given facilities for smoking. Here I must say plainly that I have no sympathy with this complaint. I am myself not a smoker and, therefore, I do not know what comfort they derive from smoking. But all the same I do not want to grudge them this comfort if they had been accustomed to smoking all their lives. I see that smoking has become a habit which has come from fashion only through contamination. If these people cannot do without smoking, then why should they not be given cigarettes.

The next complaint was with regard to food. Food should not be supplied to them as if they are criminals, but should be supplied to them as gentlemen. This complaint against food also should be removed. With regard to facilities for recreation, I should like to know from the Honourable the Home Member if any steps are taken to make them keep good health. I was simply astounded to hear from Mr Joshi with regard to the conditions for medical treatment. He quoted the instance of a man who was suffering from toothache and owing to acute pain when he approached the Officer in charge of jail to arrange for the extraction of his tooth, the poor fellow was told that he should pay the doctor's fees. Wherefrom could that detenu get the money for meeting the medical charges?...

...The other complaint is that people are kept apart from one another. Even two detenus are not kept together in some cases. I do not know why even those some cases should happen. It is for the Government to explain. Are they to be kept in solitary confinement? When they are in detention nothing should be done of a retaliatory nature. Such things are not right....

...With regard to daily allowances, I heard from my Honourable friend, Dr Banerjea, that previous to the enactment of the Defence of India Act, the detenus were being given certain allowances, and in some cases their families also were given some allowances. I do not know why it should be said that their families should not get any allowances. Where Government has good grounds to believe that the families are such that they can maintain themselves in spite of the absence of the detenu, in those cases, the families need not be given allowances;

but in cases where the detenu is the only breadwinner, then in fairness, Government should give the family some allowances for having deprived it of its breadwinner. The acuteness of the grievance is all the greater with regard to the detenus who have been externed and those who are asked to remain within a certain area and not to go out. It is something like double surveillance. In such a case, how can the poor externee make both ends meet?...

Mr Akhil Chandra Datta (Chittagong and Rajshahi Divisions: Non-Muhammadan Rural): ...Mr Joshi has also pointed out that as a matter of fact more comforts are given to the German prisoners and the Italian prisoners. It is very difficult to understand why more comforts are given to those with whom you are fighting and who are fighting you and why you do not care for the comforts of those whom you suspect of having some sort of sympathy with those people or who do not like to prosecute the war effort as much as you wish them to do. In any case, this is a matter which I do hope the Honourable the Home Member will throw some light upon. It is really extremely irritating to find that more comforts are given to German and Italian prisoners than to our own people....

Mr M.S. Aney (Berar: Non-Muhammadan): You want light or you want comfort?

Mr Akhil Chandra Datta: I want both and comfort. I do not wish to detain the House longer. My contention is that the rules on the subject should be given effect to loyally and properly; and with regard to family allowances there should be some provision made; we should like to know the policy of the Government on the question. Sir, I support the Resolution.

The Honourable Sir Reginald Maxwell: Sir, the speeches made in support of this Resolution have been very reasonable in tone and I am perfectly ready to give the House such information as I possess in answer to it. The latest available figures about the number of security prisoners detained under Rule 26 show that the number under detention at the end of last month was about 700. Of these, some 102 persons had been detained in connection with the *satyagraha* movement and I shall refer to these later. Leaving them aside, the number of prisoners with whom this Resolution is concerned is about 600 up to date. I think it will be admitted that a figure of this order, after eighteen months of war, and in a population such as that of India, does not indicate any excessive readiness on the part of the authorities to use their powers of detention. The majority of the prisoners detained come from the provinces of Madras, Bombay, Bengal, United Provinces, Bihar, and the Punjab; and the numbers from other provinces are insignificant or none....

Mr M.S. Aney: How many from the Punjab?

The Honourable Sir Reginald Maxwell: 115 from the Punjab.

Mr M.S. Aney: And Bengal?

The Honourable Sir Reginald Maxwell: 141.

Mr N.M. Joshi: May I ask whether the number of interned or externed persons is included or they are separate?

The Honourable Sir Reginald Maxwell: I am speaking of persons detained, not persons restricted. I will refer to persons against whom restriction orders have been passed, later on. I am speaking now of persons detained under Rule 26....

Maulana Zafar Ali Khan: Any one from the Indian States?

The Honourable Sir Reginald Maxwell: No. Excluding certain ex-military prisoners, the number detained by orders of the Central Government is 29 and the rest of the persons I have mentioned have been detained by orders of the Provincial Governments. Of the prisoners mentioned, 166 are detained at present at Deoli, including eleven of the Central Government prisoners, and the rest at Deoli come from the United Provinces, the Punjab, Bihar, and the North-West Frontier Province. The general conditions of confinement are laid down in the Deoli Detention Camp Order, a copy of which has been placed in the Library of the House. This applies in full only to the Deoli Detention Camp, but it has been supplied to all Provincial Government as a model for the treatment of their own security prisoners. It is being followed in general by the provinces with certain variations in detail. I should wish the House to understand that I can speak with authority only of prisoners detained at Deoli, that is, in the Central Government's custody. However, since the last debate I have written to all provinces asking them to clear up some points that were raised and they have supplied me with information about their own prisoners on some of the specific points about which anxiety was expressed.

Now, as regards the conditions of confinement, security prisoners are divided into two classes according to their state of health, education, status, and mode of living before arrest. The treatment of class I prisoners corresponds generally as regards diet and accommodation to that of B class convicts, and that of Class II prisoners corresponds to that of C class convicts,—in regard to diet and accommodation, I say. In other respects the privileges allowed to them correspond more nearly to those of A and B class convicted prisoners. For instance, security prisoners of both classes are allowed to wear their own clothes. They are not compelled to work, but they are encouraged to do so, and they will be paid for any remunerative work which they may do.

Of the 166 prisoners detained at Deoli, 77 have been placed in class I and 89 in class II. Exact figures are not available of each class in the provinces, and in some cases the classification is still under revision. It may, however, be taken as certain that a very large proportion of all the prisoners are in the higher class.

Maulana Zafar Ali Khan: You mean in the provinces?

The Honourable Sir Reginald Maxwell: Yes.

As regards the other privileges and conditions, firstly as regards letters, class I security prisoners are allowed to write two and receive four letters a week; class II prisoners may write and receive one letter a week. They are supplied with writing materials by Government. The House will remember that A class convicts are allowed only one letter a fortnight, and B class convicts only one letter a month so that these conditions compare favourably with those of convicts....

...As regards newspapers and books, all provinces, where there are any considerable number of prisoners, have made arrangements to supply them with a selection of daily or weekly newspapers from an approved list. Prisoners of course are allowed also to obtain papers from an approved list at their own expense front outside. At Deoli thirteen daily newspapers in various languages, two weekly papers, and one monthly are supplied to the prisoners at Government cost, and books are provided from the public library, Ajmer, and the Ajmer Jail library. Similarly in all provinces books are available to prisoners from the jail libraries.

As regards recreation, this is provided in various forms in most provinces, and where it is not provided free, games are also available at prisoners' expense. It must be understood that Government cannot afford to provide expensive facilities for recreation, and the prisoners have to take what is available, but at the same time at Deoli the facilities for recreation are very extensive both for indoor and outdoor games.

As regards the minor requirements commented upon in the debate, first, considerable concern was expressed about soap. I find on inquiry that this is provided everywhere at Government expense and the complaint is totally untrue. Government cannot, of course, provide soaps at the fancy of the prisoners, and I think that where there have been complaints; it is because the prisoners wanted scented soaps. Similarly, shaving is everywhere done by convict barbers if the prisoners do not possess their own shaving material; nobody goes without a shave. I think generally Honourable Members should beware of listening to complaints of this kind which they may get by letter or otherwise from security prisoners, who are not, in general, persons of good character. I myself visited the Deoli detention camp on the 28th December and saw everything. The result of my inspection was such that it rather surprised me. I had expected to find rather a bleak and barren place and the prisoners having a rather miserable time of it, but I found that the place was most excellently organized. It is true that the prisoners are behind barbed wire, but they have ample space within it. They have large recreation grounds provided for them and games are regularly organized. Their accommodation is ample and spacious and airy. I found them engaged, and apparently comfortably engaged, some playing chess, others reading, and so forth. They are provided with reading rooms where I found prisoners reading what they wanted. Their messing arrangements are excellent. I saw some of them having their meals. They appeared to be quite good, and at any rate the prisoners appeared to have no lack of appetite. All the standard equipment of the prisoners was shown to me, their clothing, bedding, and such things, which are supplied to them. I certainly thought that no prisoner could complain of the class of articles with which he was issued free by Government....

Sardar Sant Singh: Was it a paradise?

The Honourable Sir Reginald Maxwell: I am telling the Honourable Member what I saw. He may go himself if he likes.

Sardar Sant Singh: Just like the Andamans it was a paradise!

The Honourable Sir Reginald Maxwell: The medical facilities in particular I examined. Hospital accommodation within the detention camp is really excellent and is as good as I have seen anywhere. There are qualified doctors.

An Honourable Member: Have they medicines in stock?

The Honourable Sir Reginald Maxwell: I saw the health chart and found that the general health of the prisoners was remarkably good, including the records of their weights. Some of them have been gaining weight more rapidly than is good for their health.

An Honourable Member: Then why shirk an enquiry?

The Honourable Sir Reginald Maxwell: I certainly do not mind showing Deoli to any Honourable Member of this House. There is absolutely nothing to be concealed at Deoli as regards the treatment of these prisoners. At the time of my visit they did not know who I was. I went round with the Superintendent and the prisoners I believe were told by somebody when he was asked, 'This is some PWD man'. They had no idea who I was and I was able to listen to their ordinary complaints and remarks as we went round and I found scarcely anybody who had anything to complain of and on the whole they were on very good terms with the Superintendent....

Then I come to the next question of family allowances. The principle followed in respect of family allowances is that Provincial Governments may in exceptional cases grant allowances to the dependants of security prisoners when it is necessary on the ground that the detention has deprived the family of its income and left it in such destitute circumstances as to make assistance necessary. That is the principle agreed upon with the Provincial Governments. The number of applications received is comparatively small and all the cases are very carefully investigated. So far as information is available to me from what I have received from the provinces, allowances have been given in about a dozen cases, the amounts varying from Rs 35 a month to Rs 10 a month. However, not all these applications are such as require serious consideration. For instance, one province reports that in one case the brother of a prisoner asked for an allowance for himself and his family on the ground that the prisoner had been maintaining them, that is, family of the brother of the prisoner. In fact, no doubt a good many extravagant claims are made. While on this point, however, the House must remember that, if a person engages in revolutionary activities, it is he who lets his family down and not the general taxpayer who is expected to pay these allowances. The argument used by my Honourable friend Mr Aney, and I think, by Mr Akhil Chandra Datta, that the detention of the family breadwinner places an obligation on Government to provide for the maintenance of his family, would, if carried to its logical conclusion, apply also to convicts. What happens to the family of a person convicted of a crime who is detained in prison? It is an unfortunate thing that, when anybody renders himself liable to be deprived of his liberty, his family suffers. The only thing I can say about it is that we feel and sympathize with the family, but the person responsible for it is the offender.

An Honourable Member: But he has not been proved to be an offender.

The Honourable Sir Reginald Maxwell: In most cases, the persons whom we are now considering did not earn anything much by honest work of which they are now deprived. They were paid agitators.

Mr N.M. Joshi: That is also honest work!

The Honourable Sir Reginald Maxwell: Let them go to their masters, the persons who paid them for carrying on their subversive activities and ask them for the relief which their family needs.

Mr M.S. Aney: Can you prove who their masters are? If you prove that, your obligation is at an end.

The Honourable Sir Reginald Maxwell: I know some of their masters. Now, I will come to the question of persons not detained but restricted by orders under Rule 26. The question of allowance to persons restricted does not, of course, arise unless restriction to a particular area or exclusion from a particular area has involved loss of employment. It is chiefly in Bengal that restriction orders have been passed, and there most particular instructions have been given by the Provincial Government to employ these powers so as to interfere as little as possible with the normal life of the person affected. In some cases where it was found that hardship had been caused by these orders, the orders were modified in accordance with this policy in order to give the persons an opportunity to continue to earn their own livelihood. Fiftysix applicants in Bengal have applied for personal allowances and in two cases an allowance of Rs 10 a month has been granted. In the North-West Frontier Province an allowance of Rs 30 a month has been granted to one restricted person. Elsewhere no applications appear to have been received and the number of restriction orders is very small.

I would refer again to the persons detained for satyagraha. The usual practice has been not to take action against persons giving notice of their intention to commit an offence but to prosecute them after the offence has been committed. Where, however, the satyagraha demonstration was likely to create excitement or disturbance or to attract crowds, especially in large cities, the expedient has sometimes been adopted of arresting such persons in advance and detaining them under the Defence of India rules. This is chiefly being done in Bombay and it should not be repugnant to the promoters of the movement since they have expressed their wish to avoid disturbances connected with satyagraha. It must be remembered, however, that the persons so dealt with would in every case have been convicted of a substantive offence if they had not been arrested in advance. Their treatment as security prisoners does not compare at all unfavourably with that which they would have received as convicts and they should rather be regarded as self-ordained convicts and not really within the scope of this Resolution.

However, a great majority of the persons detained are not of the class which commits symbolic offences. Excluding Satyagrahis, almost all the persons detained are either communists or revolutionaries. About 94 were revolutionaries or terrorists arrested in Bengal. There are also, as I have said a certain number of ex-military prisoners and a few suspects detained for miscellaneous reasons connected usually with enemy activities. But the remaining number, about 480 persons, were, almost without exception, either acknowledged communists or else active supporters of the communist programme of violent mass revolution. Some of these, including especially those whose detention was ordered by the Central Government, formed the central directorate of the communist organization in India and their detention was necessary to cripple the communist machinery. In the case of all these persons, whether terrorists or communists, it is incorrect to say, as several speakers have asserted, that they were detained only on suspicion. Government have enough dangerous people on their hands not to wish to add to their number by mere arrests on suspicion. In every case where action of this kind has been taken, it has been based on definite knowledge of the activities of the persons concerned.

In many cases, no doubt, had the facts been known to the courts, a conviction would have been possible but this would have involved the disclosure of secret information and the institution of a series of trials which would certainly have been prolonged like the Meerut Conspiracy Case and is not a thing which can be contemplated in time of war. But it is sufficient justification for the action taken that it was known that these persons were plotting action which was definitely intended to help the enemy in this war or to prejudice the peaceful government in the country in ways which could not be tolerated in war. In war, we cannot take risks to the same extent as in peace. It is therefore irrelevant to argue that the persons should receive specially favourable treatment because they were not convicted. I can give the House an illustration of the kind of persons we are dealing with, out of their own mouth. I will read one or two passages from a publication called the 'Proletarian Path' which was published by the Communist Party at the Ramagarh session of the Congress. This document urges that 'India has to make revolutionary use of the war crisis' and it goes on to expound this revolutionary use. The first step is taken as follows:

'Political general strike in the major industries together with country wide no rent and no tax action constitutes the first step towards this objective'.

After developing that point, it goes on to say that when that stage has been reached 'the national movement will enter into a new and higher phase—the phase of armed insurrection' and it goes on to expound that further again. It says:

'In order, however, to smash the State machinery and not merely to paralyse it, in order to win over the rank and file of the army and not merely shake it up, the movement will have to develop into nation-wide armed insurrection'.

Now, listen to this:

'Storming of military and police stations by armed bands of national militia in rural as well as urban areas, destruction of Government institutions, actual offensive against the armed forces of the Government on the most extensive scale—these will increasingly become the chief features of the struggle.'

A programme of this kind is not the programme of any legitimate political party in this country and the action taken against the organizers is not taken for political reasons but solely as a matter affecting the security of the country in war. Under the arrangements described, the persons concerned are given privileges far more than they deserve or than would be given by other belligerent countries to their traitors. These persons are receiving all the consideration which humanity demands. They will not be tortured or ill-treated. We are not monsters....

Mr M.S. Aney: Thank God.

The Honourable Sir Reginald Maxwell: ...but, at the same time, so long as I am here they will not be pampered while their own action compels us to put them out of the way for reasons of safety during the time the country is engaged in a life and death struggle.

Now, a comparison has been made of enemy internees. Mr Joshi has compared the treatment of security prisoners with that of German and Italian detenus and said that he cannot understand why greater comforts and facilities should be allowed to the latter. The comparison is not a valid one because although civilian internees are not prisoners of war, they are, by international agreement, being treated in accordance with the principles of the Geneva Convention of 1929. It must be remembered that the treatment of British subjects, including Indians, similarly interned in enemy countries is on a reciprocal basis. We are, therefore, not free to do anything else but in any case I would not say on the merits that the distinction between enemy internees and security prisoners is not justified. I myself would in any case give the preference to enemy internees, who have nothing against them except that they owe allegiance to enemy countries, rather than to persons who have been deprived of their liberty for plotting their own country and against those who are fighting for it.

Now, Sir, some comparison has been made regarding the previous practice in regard to detenus.... The answer is that even if we assume that the previous treatment was not too lenient, the presence of war conditions does make a difference in what is appropriate or inappropriate. In times of peace, these people were at best a pest or a disease but not a fatal one. In war, they are traitors and so far as they do not meet the fate that traitors deserve, they may think themselves lucky.

Now, I come finally to the question of a committee. There is no useful function which a committee could perform. It is not a question of obtaining information, since Government have all the information which they need and are perfectly ready to place it at the disposal of the House. There is no question whether these prisoners have vital necessaries or are well looked after. Beyond that, the question of what further privileges or concessions should be allowed to them is a question of policy, not of fact. The Mover's intention is clearly only to set up a committee for the purpose of recommending concessions over and above what is really necessary. Where Government have the tremendous responsibility of maintaining the security of the country in a time of grave emergency such as this, they cannot divest themselves of it but must deal with the matter solely from the point of view of what is needed to win the war. Several speakers have spoken as though these prisoners were deserving of special sympathy, as though Government had almost to apologize to them for depriving them of liberty to carry on their plots. It is suggested that the action of Government can only be justified if these persons are made so comfortable that they have nothing to lose from their detention. If we wished to encourage others to carry on such plots, there could be no better way. I am not in the least apologetic. Government have nothing to apologize for in taking action which was necessary in the urgent interests of the country. These prisoners are not decent honest persons deserving of sympathy. The great majority of them are utterly worthless persons whose life is spent in plotting the downfall of society. They may perhaps be the Honourable the Mover's friends: I hope not: but other Honourable Members, I am convinced, will think differently of them and would join me in feeling that persons capable of the worst kinds of treachery do not deserve the sympathy of this House. Sir, I oppose the Resolution.

Sir Syed Raza Ali (Cities of the United Provinces: Muhammadan Urban): May I ask what the number of restricted persons is. I do not think the Home Member gave us that information.

The Honourable Sir Reginald Maxwell: I have not exact information about that but the best information I have shows that some 700 persons have had restriction orders of one kind or other passed against them: Of these, 561 are in Bengal, that is to say, the numbers in other provinces are comparatively small. The greatest number in any other provinces is 47 in Assam.

Qazi Muhammad Ahmad Kazmi (Meerut Division: Muhammadan Rural): Has the Honourable Member got the number in Delhi?

The Honourable Sir Reginald Maxwell: No, Sir, I am afraid I have not got the number in Delhi. I think there are none or only one or two orders passed in Delhi.

Sir Syed Raza Ali: Sir, the political creed of the Mover of this Resolution, my Honourable friend, Mr Joshi, is a sufficient indication that there is no desire on desire on his part to embarrass the Government in the present critical situation. The same, I am sure, is the feeling of this House. The feeling, so far as I am able to judge, of this House is that it does not want to do anything which would either embarrass the Government or have a prejudicial effect on the Government's efforts for the successful prosecution of the war....

...What he (N.M. Joshi) does ask is that a Committee should be appointed to go more or less into two questions. Broadly speaking, there are only two questions and no more. He wants the Committee to see whether the conditions under which these detenus are living are suitable. That really raises more or less questions of health and environment. Secondly, he pleads that in fit and proper cases allowances should be granted either to the detenus themselves or, in case where such detenus have left families without provision, to their families. I think both points, on the face of it, are reasonable. Let me make it quite clear that I have no sympathy with those who want to bring about a radical disturbance in our society either by violent or non-violent means.

An Honourable Member: Non-violent means also?

Sir Syed Raza Ali: Yes, non-violent means also. I have no sympathy with these people. After all, there is not much difference between the sort non-violence that is being practised in India today and the violence in some other countries. It is a case of six of one and half a dozen of the other. At present the non-violence that is being practised is really a farce. But I do not think I should say harsh words about those who through their own action have absented themselves from this House. Therefore, I will say no further. Anyway, the point is this that I do want to maintain the present structure of society and if there are any communists or Fascists or Nazis who want to bring about a revolution. I would certainly support the Government of India in such action as it takes against such persons. All the same, having said that much let me make it quite clear that there is no reason why every man should not be given a reasonable chance when he can have no recourse to a court of law....

Mr Muhammad Azar Ali (Lucknow and Fyzabad Divisions: Muhammadan Rural): Sir, there are only a few questions which I would like to ask the Honourable the Home Member and through him the Government on this Resolution. As the Honourable the Home Member himself has been to the Deoli jail and has inspected the conditions there, I was surprised to hear the arguments which he advanced in his favour. His argument was that he went to the Deoli jail and in that jail he went *incognito* to give an impression to the Deoli jail people, to the prisoners, and to the detenus as if he was a PWD officer. At the same time, his argument was that he did not receive any kind of complaints against the jail authorities or the conditions in the jail. I fail to understand the sequence of these two arguments which he has advanced. If a person goes there *incognito* how is it possible for the prisoners to go to him and to explain to him the conditions prevailing in the Deoli jail? I appeal to this Honourable House whether it stands to reason that when a person goes there *incognito*, how is he to be approached? How are the prisoners and detenus to represent to him the conditions prevailing there and is it possible that a detenu would dare to approach the Honourable the Home Member under those conditions? I submit it is absolutely impossible and, therefore, the argument that has been advanced by the Honourable the Home Member on this point falls flat....

The next point is this. How does the Honourable Member expect an old relative or an old mother or an old father of a detenu to go all the way to Deoli to interview the detenu. I understand Deoli jail is about 60 miles from the nearest railway station.

Mr N.M. Joshi: It is 75 miles from Kota which is the nearest railway Station for people from the Bombay side.

Mr Muhammad Azhar Ali: Sir, I was on the point of the functions of the Committee as proposed in the Resolution. One of their functions, it is reasonable to suggest, should be to see whether the rules framed for these detenus are fit for them and whether they are or are not properly observed. When the Honourable the Home member was in Deoli he could not possibly see to every detail in connection with these rules. Therefore, the committee should be formed to examine the defects of these rules and see how they are working. The Honourable the Home Member was good enough to dub these people, whether detenus or satyagrahis, as men of bad character, and that, I submit is very strong and unjustifiable language. Many of them are people educated in English universities, as much as any Englishman in this House, and also graduates of Indian universities. According to Government's present ideas they may not be good people today, but many of these people, including our Congress friends in this House, were even running the Governments in the provinces; and it is quite possible that when the new constitution comes these very friends of ours on the Treasury Benches will work under them and call them men of high character. It may suit Government now to call them men of bad character, but tomorrow, if it suits purpose, they will call them gentlemen of the first water.

Mr N.M. Joshi: What do they call Mr M.N. Roy now?....

Mr Amarendra Nath Chattopadhyaya (Burdwan Division: Non-Muhammadan Rural): Sir, I am surprised to see that there is an opposition even to this very modest Resolution which simply recommends to the Governor General to appoint a committee to examine and report on the conditions under which detenus under the Defence of India Act have to live in prisons. A man who has not been to prison as a detenu can hardly realize and appreciate the agonies of a detenu. The Honourable the Home Member goes *incognita* as a PWD officer and sees in Deoli Camp a happy family living there from day-to-day and perhaps he wished to exchange places with them. Why does he not change places with them? Their only crime is that they love their country and that they are anxious to have their own government. They cherish the philosophy of the communists or the socialists or the nationalists, and it is crime to cherish them or any of these political philosophies. If it is not a crime for the British Government to send somebody as an ambassador to Russia, the fountain-head of communism, why should it be a crime to study the history and philosophy of communism here in India? I may tell, Sir, that there is no communism or communists here, there may be students of communism. And those who study and appreciate communism are taken to be the greatest enemies of the British Government. These are men of education, culture, and social status who all of a sudden are taken from their homes and deprived of the liberty to work for themselves and their families and kept in confinement, depriving even their families of their means of livelihood and sustenance; and the British Government shamelessly say they are justified because these are traitors and men of worthless character. Sir, I never heard a more unworthy speech on the floor of this House than the one delivered by the Honourable the Home Member this day. To abuse persons behind their backs, while they are kept in prison form an advantageous position is not worthy of the Honourable the Home Member. We know who these men are and what character they bear and education they have, and it really hurts us when a responsible official on those Benches speaks in this strain and in such language and I wish that he should withdraw those remarks that fell from his lips. The Resolution says 'to report on the conditions'. What are the conditions? Free people doing their daily duties, carrying on their day to day routine work, doing some political work for the country, are all of a sudden taken into custody: and while they were expecting to have some sort, of even a mockery of a trial they are deprived of that privilege. Even the worst criminal, a proved criminal has a right to have a trial; but these political people, these political workers in a slave country like India, are deprived of that privilege; and still this civilized government shamefacedly says that there is justification for this. The Honourable Member says the conditions in these jails are fine and that he keeps them comfortable within the jail precincts. They have been given a long space to walk and a badminton ground and some kind of sports too and that is enough. Sir, it is not enough for any man it cannot be enough for any one deprived of liberty, I say, this government ought to be more humance and more human. No doubt this government is passing through very bad times and it is not for us now to embarrass them further; but if they continue like this, I am sure they will have to repent for it....

...Clause (c) of the Resolution says 'whether those who are interned or externed under the Defence of India Act have difficulty in maintaining themselves or their families and whether it is necessary to give them any assistance....' It requires no argument. The Honourable the Home Member asked what we intend to do with convicts. Are Government to give them family subsistence? Sir, convicts are generally those who have been proved to have committed some immoral act, who have been charged with some acts of moral turpitude. None of these things is applicable in the case of political workers. They have neither been proved to have committed any immoral act, nor to have committed anything treasonable or anything like it. Nothing has been proved against them. Unless you prove that they are guilty of something, you cannot punish them. This is bad in principle and in practice it cannot be better. Therefore I support the Resolution with the following words. The unworthy remarks made by the Honourable the Home Member should be withdrawn with regard to persons who have been incarcerated without any proof and without any trial. It is indeed a matter of pity that we should find the Honourable the Home Member saying here that these men are of worthless character and are traitors. Traitors to whom? Why should the Honourable the Home Member be allowed to use these words which are not worthy of him? Sir I do not wish to use stronger terms. With these remarks I support the Resolution.

Major Nawab Sir Ahmad Nawaz Khan (Nominated Non-Official): Sir I oppose this Resolution, because I think it is against the Defence of India Act....

Qazi Muhammad Ahmad Kazmi: Mr Deputy President, the time at my disposal being short, I will take up the question of restrictions first. The Honourable the Home Member was pleased to remark that restriction orders are being very carefully used in Bengal, but I would like to draw his attention to the way in which these orders are being put into effect, in a province which lies directly under the nose of the Central Government itself. I shall just read out for his information one of the notices that are usually served on alleged political workers some of whom had never acted as political workers, and even when they say that they have nothing to do with politics at present. Some of these people are of course political workers, but I do not think that any such orders as the one I am going to read out are justified in the case of either people who are actual political workers or who are believed to be political workers they having taken at some time of their life a part in political affairs. This is what this notification says:

'Whereas the Chief Commissioner of Delhi is satisfied that it is necessary to make an order under sub rule (1) of Rule 26 of the Defence of India Rules in respect of Sami Ullah, son of Nasir Ullah, by origin a resident of the Hardoi district in the United Provinces but more recently living in Kucha Chelan in the Faiz Bazar Police station area of the Delhi City with a view to preventing him from acting in a manner prejudicial to the defence of British India and the maintenance of public order:

Now, therefore, in exercise of the power conferred by the sub rule cited the Chief Commissioner is pleased to direct that the said Sami Ullah

(i) shall reside and remain within the limits of Delhi Municipal Ward No. 11 and shall not go outside those limits except in so far as it may be necessary for him to do so in order to fulfil the requirements of the next direction, and
(ii) shall attend the Faiz Bazar Police station every day at 8 a.m., 12 noon, 4 p.m. and 8 p.m., and report his presence to the officer in charge of that police station or such other police officer as the officer in charge may appoint for this purpose, and
(iii) shall not without the previous permission in writing of the District Magistrate of Delhi join or continue in any meeting or procession of more than twelve persons other than a meeting or precession of a purely domestic or religious character.

This order shall remain in force until revoked or modified by the Chief Commissioner.'

Now, Sir, this is a notification which cannot be justified. To call upon a person to remain within a particular limit in the city of Delhi is totally unjustified without assigning adequate reasons. And what is that particular limit? You will be astonished to know that it does not cover even 1/12th part of the area of Delhi. The person who has been served with this notice happens to live near the Juma Mosque, and that mosque happens to be outside the limits specified in the order, he cannot go there to say his prayers; as he is allowed to move about only in Ward No. 11. Again a person is asked to attend the police station so many times, and sometimes the police station happens to be a mile away, and so if a man has to attend the police station four times, it would mean he would have to walk eight miles day. The result is that he cannot go and attend prayers in the mosque which is just across the road from his shop. It is such a connection that one person has probably been convicted or action taken against him by the authorities because, according to the prosecution the offence was, not that he went to the graveyard, but only attended the *'fatiha'* (prayers) ceremony of his sister. I can tell the Honourable Member if he wants to make enquires as to what sort of persons have been served with such orders....

Mr Govind V. Deshmukh (Nagpur Division: Non-Muhammadan): Sir, Mr Joshi in urging for better treatment for detenus put his case like this: He said 'give the detenus the same treatment that you are giving to the Germans and Italians who are fighting against Britain' and we incidentally happen to go to war with Britain. He put his case very strongly. The Honourable the Home Member drew a distinction between these two cases. I am sorry be is not here at the moment. He said that the Italians and the Germans are loyal to their Government and their country. Indians are loyal to their country, but they are not loyal to the Government of this country as established by law today, whatever that law is.

An Honourable Member: Lawless law....

Mr N.M. Joshi: Mr Deputy President, I would like at the outset to thank the Muslim League Party and the Nationalist Party for the wholehearted support they have given to my Resolution and the proposals contained in that Resolution. Sir, some of my Honourable colleagues have blamed me for making my Resolution a very modest one. Unfortunately Sir, that is my fault. I am always a moderate and a practical man and I have no need to apologize for making my proposal a very modest one. Sir, the Honourable the Home Member in his speech I thought rather irrelevantly made some remarks about the character of the detenus. I feel, Sir, the Honourable Member was carried away by his enthusiasm in opposing my very modest proposal. Otherwise such an experienced man like the Honourable the Home Member would have seen that the remarks about the character of the detenus were not called for. I feel that his remarks were not only uncalled-for but unjust and unfair, undignified, and, if I may say so about a very prominent Member of this Assembly, very irresponsible. The Honourable Member said that these detenus were men of bad character.

An Honourable Member: Worthless.

Mr N.M. Joshi: He said they were worthless. He said he hoped I had no friends amongst them. Mr Deputy President, I have a number of friends amongst them, and not only that....

A Honourable Member: You must then be of a bad character.

Mr N.M. Joshi: I am proud of having their friendship as much as I would be proud of having the Honourable the Home Member as my friend. Mr Deputy President, I know some of the detenus very well. I know there are young men amongst them of whom every father would be proud. I do not know whether the Honourable the Home Member has a son or not, but let me tell him that amongst the young men whom he has detained in jail, there are young boys who will not be found to be less worthy than his own sons if he has any. I know of a young man who has been recently detained; he has passed the BSc in first class, he has won a prize, he has been given a fellowship in a Bombay college and he is no paid agitator. Let me assure the Honourable Member that his father is as wealthy as the Honourable the Home Member. I am sorry that the Honourable Member should have called these people also 'traitors'. They may be mistaken about the methods which they are following. But a Britisher who engages himself for the sake of pay in holding a foreign country in bondage should call an Indian who fights for the freedom of his country—it may be in a wrong way—to be a traitor is thoroughly unjustified. Sir, I am not a communist, I am too much of a democrat to be a communist. But to call the communists traitors is unjustified. Sir, the Honourable the Home Member said that he gives better treatment to the Germans and the Italians because he is forced to do so on account of the International Convention. Not only that—if he had stopped there, I wouldn't have said much—but he went further and said that, he did not see much fault in them except that there is a war between Great Britain and Germany and Italy. He should have known that amongst them there are Nazis and Fascists. It is not a fault to be a Nazi or a Fascist in the eyes of the Honourable the Home Member, but it is a fault to be a communist and to be a revolutionary. Well, Sir, I cannot accept his doctrine that a Nazi or a Fascist is a man who does his work by constitutional methods and he is a revolutionary. He objects to a man being a communist and a revolutionary. So, in the opinion of the Honourable the Home Member the Fascists and the Nazis who are in the Concentration camp in Ahmednagar have no other fault. But it is a fault, a great sin, to be a communist and a revolutionary. I hope the Honourable the Home Member will re-examine his views ad regards the comparative merits of a communist and a revolutionary on the one hand and a Fascist and a Nazi on the other. His Government has been telling the whole world that they are fighting the Nazism and Fascism and he, from his place in this House, sees no fault in being a Nazi and a Fascist. Well, Sir, I shall not deal with that question any further.

The Honourable the Home Member told us in the first place that there were only 700 people in the jails. He did not give us the number of people who were interned or externed. He did not know their number perhaps.

The Honourable Sir Reginald Maxwell: I did give the figure to the Honourable Member.

Mr N.M. Joshi: I am sorry I did not hear the figure which he gave.

The Honourable Sir Reginald Maxwell: I said that the number was about 700.

Mr N.M. Joshi: He told us that those people who were detained in jails were 700.

The Honourable Sir Reginald Maxwell: I said that the number of restricted was also about 700. I was asked after my speech and I gave the figure.

Mr N.M. Joshi: So, the number of the people who were detained was 700. Then, he said it is not a very large number. It all depends upon what standard we place before ourselves. A man who does not like to imprison people or detain people and who believes in freedom as I do will consider the number of 700 to be a very large one. The Honourable Member who sees no fault in being a Fascist and a Nazi considers the number 700 to be a very modest and a small one. It all depends upon the view which we take and the respect that we pay to freedom. To me it is a very large number. Then, he gave a description about the paradise that exists at Deoli. I would like the Honourable Member to go there and live there for a year. Then he will know what a hell mere detention in jail makes of a life. You may give all the facilities to a man and a palace to live in, but if he is in a jail in that condition he would prefer to be free and be even a poor man. Unfortunately, the Honourable the Home Member is not going to be in a prison nor even externed or interned.

Sir, I do not wish to go into the details of the question. The Honourable Member said that his Government do not want to pamper the detenus. Well, Sir, I am not asking the detenus to be pampered. I want the detenus to be treated justly and fairly. My first demand was that they should be given all the facilities in the jail and he said Government are doing for them all they could. Unfortunately, there is a difference of opinion. I and the other Members of the House feel that the Government are not dong what they ought to do. Moreover, we differ in facts. He told me that in all the jails soaps are being provided. My information is that they are not provided everywhere. He said that a man can get his tooth extracted without paying. He said that the toothache could be removed at Government expense. My information is that he is not right in making that statement. I also suggested that the families of the detenus should be given some allowances. Then, he said that these detenus are making very extravagant demands. He told us that somebody's brother writes that on account of the detention of his brother, he is deprived of his means of subsistence. Well, Sir, it is true that in India we consider the younger brother to be a responsibility of the elder brother. Perhaps in his own country that may not be so; but I know something of Great Britain and I know that even in Great Britain an elder brother will consider it to be his responsibility to maintain his younger brother if he has no parents. Sir, the Honourable Home Member told us that there are twelve people out of 700 who are getting family allowances. I would like this question to be examined as to how many of these 700 people deserve an allowance for maintaining their families and for their own small needs. If after the examination it is found that it is only twelve people who need this assistance, then the Legislature will have no complaint. I know something about the needs of these detenus. I make it my business to inquire whether there are any of them who need some help. I have a small fund at my disposal. We have a Committee and we use it quite properly. I sometimes inquire into the needs of the detenus and I am quite sure in my own mind that if I begin to help all the deserving cases, my fund would be exhausted in a short time. I am not therefore talking of the needs of the detenus without having some knowledge of their needs. The Honourable Member said that the number of applicants for assistance for their families is not very large. That fact shows that the detenus are not people who will write to Government for assistance to their families unless they have a real need. I have knowledge that some of the detenus in Nasik have already applied to the Government—I do not know whether they have applied to the Central Government or to the Provincial Government of Bombay. I do not yet know whether the Central Government or the Provincial Government of Bombay, to whomsoever they have written, have sanctioned those applications. I do not know their number exactly. I have copies of some of the applications which they have sent. The Honourable the Home Member himself admits that at least in some cases it is the duty of the Government to help the detenus by giving allowances to their families.

Then, Sir, the Honourable Member has not realized that although you give the detenus the privilege of interviews, they cannot avail of this for want of money. I know it costs about Rs 75 for a family to go to Deoli. I have some friends in Deoli and it is not easy for the wives of these people to go to Deoli every fortnight even though the Government have given them the privilege of having two interviews a month. I would, therefore, suggest, that the Honourable the Home Member should consider not only the question of the maintenance of the families of the detenus but to give railway fares to the relatives of the detenus who want to have interviews with them.

Sir, I do not wish to go into further details. But I would say one word about the argument which the Honourable the Home Member used in opposing my demand for the appointment of a committee. The Honourable the Home Member asked me what would be the function of this Committee. Well, Sir, the first function of this committee will be to examine, after looking into the condition of the detenus, whether the rules made by the Central Government and by the Provincial Governments are just and fair and meet adequately the needs of the situation, they should also see whether the rules made by the Government of India are being actually followed in all jails and prisons not only in provinces, but even in the Central jail at Deoli. I do not know what the rules are about the prisoners associating with each other, but I know that in Deoli, as the Honourable the Home Member described, there are two divisions of prisoners, the first and second division. These divisions are arbitrarily made. A man of the second division may have friends in the first division, with whom alone he has friendship, but some people have the misfortune of being put in the second division and they cannot mix with other people.

The Honourable Sir Reginald Maxwell: Snobbery.

Mr N.M. Joshi: It is not a question of snobbery, but it is a question of friendship. To my Honourable friend, it is snobbery but these people are not snobs. You have to choose your friends on account of similarity of temperament and of interest. The Honourable Member talks of snobbery. Let me assure him that if he would abolish all the classes in jails and prisons and in the concentration camps, he will always have my vote. I have always considered this division among the prisoners to be a wrong thing, to be an obstacle for jail and prison reform.

Mr Deputy President (Mr Akhil Chandra Datta) The Honourable Member's time is up.

Mr N.M. Joshi: It is the Government of India who have introduced this snobbery if anybody has done it.

I do not wish to say anything more except this that this committee, if appointed, has got enough work to do in examining the rules, in seeing that the rules are enforced or not and also in examining whether the Government of India have made sufficient provision for the destitute families, and for the needs of the detenus themselves.

The, Sir, I should like to make one suggestion before I sit down. It is true that a temporary committee will not meet the needs of the situation. There would be necessity for a permanent advisory committee to the Government of India and to the Provincial Governments in advising them whether assistance to the families is necessary or not, in particular cases. I hope, Sir, that the Honourable the Home Member will reconsider the view which he has taken about my Resolution and that he will bow to the public opinion of this House and accept the Resolution. If he does not do so, I hope the House will know how to do its duty and they will vote for my Resolution.[1]

---

[1] The Resolution was defeated with 23 voting in favour and 40 against.

144. Bengal Politicals: Proposal for Placing them in One Class Voted Down Demand for Revision of Jail Rules

Amrita Bazar Patrika, 8 March 1941.

An opposition proposal for the placing of all political prisoners in Bengal jails in one class and providing them with amenities not inferior to those allowed to the prisoners of Division I, was opposed by Government and eventually voted down, forty-two for and seventy-six against it, in the Bengal Legislative Assembly yesterday (Friday).

Complaint of Non-fulfilment of Agreement

The opposition complained that Government as yet had not given effect to the agreement entered between the Home Minister, Sir Nazimuddin and representatives of the opposition as a result of which the last hunger-strike resorted to by the security and other political prisoners in the Dum Dum and Alipore jails were called off. Sir Nazimuddin, it was stated gave them to understand that jail rules would be modified to provide amenities to the prisoners as soon as the strike would be called off.

Sir Bijoy Prasad Singh Roy, who is temporarily in charge of the Home Department owing to illness of Sir Nazimuddin, assured the House that Government stood by the assurance, if any, given by Sir Nazimuddin.

The question of securing attendance of any member of the House, and allowing him to take part in the proceedings who is arrested, detained, convicted or imprisoned on any criminal charge or otherwise, came up for consideration before the House yesterday on the report of the Privilege Committee.

The Committee had unanimously recommended in favour of such facilities being given to members of the legislature. The question was under discussion, when the Assembly rose for the day.

Yesterday was the non-official day. The House took up the partly discussed resolution on political prisoners and the amendment to it.

Classification of Politicals

The resolution was moved by Mr Atul Sen and read as under: 'This Assembly is of opinion that all the persons convicted in Bengal under the Defence of India Rules and the Indian Penal Code for offences against the state be placed in division I in jails.'

To this Mr Surendra Nath Biswas moved the following amendment: 'This Assembly is of opinion that all prisoners in Bengal jails, whether detained or convicted under the Defence of India Rules or kept under trial or convicted for offences against the state under the India Penal Code be placed in Division I or that a new special division be created similar to Division I and special rules framed in respect of their ration, interviews, letter-writing, supply of books and newspapers, and other reasonable amenities.'

The amendment was accepted by Mr Sen.

Resuming the discussion Mr Charu Chandra Roy said that the Government before the introduction of the present constitution used to classify the political prisoners separately and gave them special facilities. He referred to the last hunger-strike and said that the strike was called off on the definite assurance given by Government that their grievances would be looked into and remedied, as soon as possible. But up till now no arrangement had been made to allow the prisoners to read and appear at the examinations; they were only supplied with '*Azad*' and '*Statesman*' newspapers. Mr Roy stressed the necessity of remedying the grievances.

Politicals' Complaint

Mr Atul Krishna Ghose read a statement of the political prisoners in jails and said that it was stated that they were kept with the ordinary persons and they had complained of want of proper reading facilities. Mr Ghose said that the British Government accorded better treatment to the prisoner of wars. Why should they not extend facilities to the political prisoners of the country?

Mr Mozzamel Huq (Coalition Party) delivered a speech tauntingly referring to the grievances of the prisoners regarding the diet supplied to them....

Mr Santosh Kumar Basu referred to the agreement entered between the Home Minister, Sir Nazimuddin, and Mr Sarat Chandra Bose, Mr Santosh Kumar Basu and Mr Charu Chandra Roy, as a result of which the last hunger strike resorted to by the prisoners in Alipur and Dum Dum jails were called off. The basis of that agreement was that as soon as the hunger-strike would be called off Government would seriously take up the questions of revising the jail rules in regard to the amenities to be provided for the security and other political prisoners. They were expecting, Mr Basu said, that some definite result would be ensured in consequence of this agreement but unfortunately nothing had yet been done for the purpose of promulgating any rules which might have been amended. Their interest in the matter, Mr Basu said, was to protect their position as public men at whose assurance the hunger-strike were called off by the security prisoners. They gave them certain assurance on the basis of agreement with the Home Minister but those assurances yet remained un-fulfilled. Nothing had yet reached to them, Mr Basu said, that the rules had been amended and published and given effect to. But he had received information that the condition of the prisoners were the same as they used to be. He hoped that Sir Bijoy would look into the matter.

Sir B.P. Singh Roy's Assurance

The Hon Sir Bijoy Prasad Singh Roy said that Government stood by the assurance, if any, given by Sir Nazimuddin to Mr Santosh Kumar Basu and his colleagues. In fact Sir Nazimuddin in pursuance of the terms of agreement had examined the question in details and in respect of certain points draft rules had been framed. The rules relating to the questions of affording better treatment, diet facilities to read and sit for examination and communication with members of the legislature, had already been published. The other questions were still under examination, which involved serious financial questions. Sir Bijoy however assured the House that Government stood committed to the promises, if any, given by Sir Nazimuddin and the matter would be treated in a sympathetic spirit.

Continuing Sir Bijoy said that he understood that there was no undertaking given by Government at the time of the calling off the hunger strike that Government would give effect to these rules. Any assurance that might have been given, Sir Bijoy said, was quite independent of the calling off the hunger strike by the political prisoners.

Resolution and Amendment

Referring to the resolution and the amendment Sir Bijoy said that they were no new proposals. Government in this country had never accepted the motive of crime as the criterion of the classification of the prisoners. In fact the Jail Code defined that the classifications should be done according to the status, education and standard of living of the prisoners. That principle had been followed. Sir Bijoy knew that there was considerable volume or public opinion in the country that Government should accept the motive of crime as the criterion for classification of the prisoners.

Another ground on which this suggestion of placing the political prisoners in one class had been urged was that the so-called political prisoners were accustomed to a higher standard of living, were persons of education and culture. Sir Bijoy said that Government found it extremely difficult to change their policy and accept the suggestion that classification should be made on the basis of the motive of crime. Because, if once they decided motive to be the criterion, it was difficult to put a limit anywhere. Sir Bijoy cited the instance to show that motive of the crime as criterion of classification could not be accepted.

Certain grievances, Sir Bijoy continued, had been ventilated by the opposition members of the political prisoners. Sir Bijoy thought that they should not have been mentioned in connection with this debate, because they were merely individual cases. Government, however were prepared to look into them, if specific case was submitted to them. He hoped that opposition would appreciate the difficulty that Government faced in accepting the original resolution or the amendment.

The amendment of Mr Suren Biswas when put to vote was lost by 42 to 76. The original motion was lost without division....

145. Jawaharlal Nehru's Description of Conditions in Camp Jail, Lucknow From Jawaharlal Nehru's 'Prison Diary with Letters'

[Presumably end of March 1941]
SWJN, Vol. 12, pp. 568–70.

Camp Jail, Lucknow

This is a temporary jail, newly constructed for accommodating the overflow number of C class political convicts from the various jails in the United Provinces. The number of prisoners in it on the 2nd February, 1941 is said to have been about 1500.

The walls and roofs of the barracks are made of corrugated iron sheets. Just now the roofs have been ordered to be tiled. No berths have been constructed for sleeping purposes as we find in every other jail. The convicts have to sleep on undressed and uneven ground which hitherto was under cultivation. White ants, at times, not only eat up the clothes of the prisoners but also bite them during the night. There are no lights inside the barracks. In days of bitter cold the prisoners who had only two blankets and one piece of mat each for bedding and covering, passed the night sometimes shivering with cold. In barracks, meant for 25 convicts, often 35 are kept. Latrining arrangements for the night inside the barracks are both insufficient and indecent.

Fetters put on prisoners during transfers are removed as soon as the prisoners reach their destination. But in the camp jail, Lucknow, prisoners have often to remain in fetters for ten days or even more after their arrival, there being no arrangement for their immediate removal.

On the night of 30th January last, about 40 prisoners were transferred to this jail from Bareilly. It is said that none of them had blankets. Only a few had blanket coats and they had all to pass the night shivering with cold in the train.

The latrines outside the barracks consist of 20 seats for 160 prisoners and all the 160 it is alleged are allowed about 15 minutes for answering the call of nature.

Hospital arrangements are also said to be very insufficient and unsatisfactory. As regards food, even invalids are given gram in place of sago or *dalia* in the morning.

It is alleged that on the 20th of January when the prisoners were asked to parade, 4 or 5 of them out of 1200 refused to do so. At this the Deputy Superintendent, one Mr Lang, began personally to beat the five prisoners with a stick. They were then dragged into the barrack. On this the other prisoners got excited and began to shout national slogans. Mr Lang ordered all of them to be locked up. For 36 hours after this all these prisoners numbering about 1200, about 200 of whom were juveniles, were kept constantly locked in their barracks without food. They were not permitted to come out even for answering the call of nature.

It is said that as a protest against this behaviour of Mr Lang, one Syt Hulas Varma of Dehra Dun and a few others hunger struck on the 21st of January. They had taken no food up to the 2nd of February. During this hunger strike on the 29th of January water was refused to Syt Hulas Varma who was confined in a solitary cell. He asked his fellow prisoners in the adjoining cells for water, who being themselves locked up could not help him and so got excited and began to shout national cries which spread from barrack to barrack. This shouting lasted for about fifteen minutes, but no water was supplied. Instead alarm was sounded. Mr Lang with his men entered into the cells and the juvenile barracks and belaboured the prisoners causing serious injuries.

On the 30th of January one boy was removed to the district jail and there given 30 stripes for refusing parade. Juveniles are said to have been beaten for singing the flag song.

Some very young boys are alleged to have been put on hard tasks like flour-grinding and oil-pressing. As these prisoners could not complete their task on the 31st of January and on the 1st and 2nd of February about 1,400 prisoners were given practically no food. On the 1st they were given only a little *dal* boiled in water once in the day and on the 2nd only a little vegetable similarly boiled in water again once in the day and absolutely no *chapaties* on either of the two days. Some of them were even beaten for demanding food. One Syt Gopi Krishna Arora seriously injured his arm and skull.

On the 2nd of February some juvenile convicts had to be removed to the hospital on account of weakness due to semi-starvation.

It is said that all these 1400 convicts or so are kept locked inside their barracks for over 22 hours out of 24 every day. Some have been punished with crossbars and standing handcuffs in weak condition of health. All this, it is alleged, is being done to secure apologies.

Interviews have been stopped so that news of their condition may not leak out.

146. Deoli Camp Detenus Not to be Permitted to Sit for University Examinations

(i) Letter from Government of Madras to the Additional Secretary, Government of India, Home Department, New Delhi

Letter Ms. No. 768, Dated 18 April 1941, Public (General) Department, Madras to the Additional Secretary to the Home Department, Government of India, Tamil Nadu State Archives.

Sub: Political agitation—Security Prisoners—Permission to sit for University Examinations. Ref. Home Department letter No. 43/19/41-Political (I), dated 25.3.1941.

In reply to the Government of India's letter cited above, I am directed to say that neither of the two Security Prisoners belonging to this Province now detained at Deoli, namely, S.V. Ghate and A.S.K. Ayyangar, is likely to apply for admission to any examination. On general grounds, this Government consider it undesirable to allow Security or other Prisoners to take examinations while confined in jail.

9.4.1941

(ii) Reply from the Under Secretary of Government of India to the Chief Secretary, Government of Madras

Confidential letter No. 43/19/41-Political (I), Dated 9 July 1941, Home Department, Government of Madras, Tamil Nadu State Archives.

Sub: Question of permitting security prisoners to sit for University and other examinations

With reference to your reply to the Home Department letter No. 43/19/41-Political (I), dated 25th March/5th June 1941, I am directed to say that the Government of India have decided that no security prisoner detained in the Deoli Detention Camp will be permitted to appear for University or other examinations.

I have the honour to be,
Sir,

Your most obedient servant
For Under Secretary to the Government of India

147. 'Comrade Ajoy!' Demand for Transfer of Ajoy Ghosh from Deoli

Communist, Vol. III, No. 3, April–May 1941, P.C. Joshi Archives on Contemporary History, JNU.

Comrade Ajoy Kumar Ghosh is down with TB, both lungs affected. Comrade Ajoy was the very picture of good health all his life despite the arduous strain of a revolutionary life. He was hale and hearty at the time of his arrest in August 1940. In less than a year, as a detenu under the DOIA, first at Lucknow jail and now at Deoli, this is what imperialism has done to one of the foremost Communist leaders.

The unbearable heat of Deoli and lack of any decent medical attendance will kill Comrade Ajoy unless from every platform throughout the country the people raise their powerful fist and demand with one voice:

Decent and Human Treatment to All Detenus!
Transfer Comrade Ajoy To A Sanatorium!
Don't Kill Comrade Ajoy!

148. Hunger Strike in Vellore and Alipuram

Bombay Chronicle, 16 January, 17 April and 24 April 1941.

Vellore, 15 January.

A. Twelve 'C' class Satyagrahi prisoners have been ordered to be prosecuted before the Deputy Magistrate of Vellore under the Prisons Act.

It is alleged that seven prisoners went on hunger-strike in December because they were refused rice diet which they had asked, but were given ragi diet.

It is said that the five remaining prisoners who were given rice diet went on a sympathetic strike.

Madras, 17 April.

B. Alipuram Jail
Sympathy with fellow prisoners in Vellore jail

In sympathy with the hunger-strikers in the Vellore Central Jail, one hundred and seventy political prisoners in Alipuram jail are reported to be fasting since Friday last according to a report in '*The* Hindu'.

Mr B. Bhima Rao, MLC, the Report adds, has sent a telegram to the Government of Madras urging them to take prompt action and set up an independent enquiry in this connection.

Vellore, 24 April.

Sequel to Joint Appeal to Governor by Prominent Madras Citizens

Following the joint appeal by leading citizens of Madras, the detenus in Vellore Central Jail who went on hunger-strike on 5 April broke the fast yesterday. The condition of their health is reported to be improving now.

Leaders Appeal to Governor

An earlier Madras message states:

A joint appeal has been addressed to the Governor by leading citizens of Madras belonging to different schools of thought requesting him to intervene in the matter of the Vellore hunger-strike and remedy the situation.

The signatories have also appealed to the hunger-strikers to suspend the strike, thus strengthening their hands to carry on negotiations with the Government, to get their grievances redressed.

The signatories include Mr V. Ramdas Pantulu, Member, Council of State, Dewan Bahadur V. Bashyam Iyengar, Mrs Ammu Swaminathan, Diwan Bahadur K.S. Ramaswami Sastri, Mr S.M. Fassil Sahib, Mr D.S. Ramachandra Rao, President, All-India Christian Conference, Captain V.D. Nimbakar, and Mr K. Punniah, Editor, '*Sind Observer.*'

Text of Joint Appeal

The joint appeal to His Excellency the Governor says: 'We are greatly concerned to hear the reports of the serious condition of the detenus numbering about ninety in central jail, Vellore, who are reported to have gone on hunger-strike since the 5th April, the condition of some is reported to be precarious.

Whether the grievances of the detenus are such as will justify the strike or not, we have not at present sufficient information on the subject in the absence of a detailed communiqué from the authorities concerned. But it appears to us that the position has greatly deteriorated, due to the inaction of the authorities, and that if nothing is done immediately the position of the detenus may become grave and cause needless hardship.

Ease the Situation

We, therefore, request your Excellency to interfere in the matter and issue necessary instructions to jail authorities to look into the grievances of the detenus concerned and thus ease the situation.

We are also appealing to the hunger-strikers to suspend their hunger-strike in the meantime.'

The appeal to the detenus on hunger-strike says: 'We are greatly perturbed to hear disquieting reports of the serious condition of you all who have gone on hunger strike since fifth instant, the condition of some of you is reported to be precarious.

We have this day sent a requisition to His Excellency the Governor informing him of our grave concern in the matter and requesting His Excellency to immediately interfere in the matter, and thus ease the situation. We will do our best to ease the situation.

In the meantime you will be strengthening our hands if you will call off the hunger-strike for the present, pending further negotiations with the Government.

Please do suspend the hunger-strike.'

Detenus Give up Hunger-strike

The Government have received telegraphic intimation from Vellore Jail authorities that the detenus who were on hunger-strike have given up the fast to-day.

It is reliably learnt that the number of detenus on hunger-strike in Vellore Central Jail is sixty.

149. Behind the Bars!

Editorial, *Communist,* Vol. III, No. 3, April–May 1941, P.C. Joshi Archives on Contemporary History, JNU.

TWENTY THOUSAND would soon be the number of political prisoners, if it is not already so. Exact figures are not to hand. The AICC Communiqué for April put the UPfigure alone as 12,000 and at the beginning of March the AICC figure for the whole country was 5,000. All through the round of arrests is not slowing down but mounting up. There are more political prisoners in India than in any other land where the Union Jack flies. They are our best and from all sections of the people—Congress, Labour, Kisan, Student.

IMPERIALISM is wreaking its vengeance upon them, truth unbarred. 'The vast number of political prisoners ranging up to 80 per cent were consigned to C class and to a quality of food wholly abominable.' (Dr Pattabhi in the Indian Express, 10, February) News of mass beating inside prison-walls is becoming more and more frequent, from UPreleased prisoners, from

Nagpur Central Prison, report of meningitis and sun-stroke proving fatal and no adequate medical aid. Prisons are becoming hell and our country once again a vast prison house.

THE WORST IS THE PLIGHT of the detenus, victims of DOIA, locked up for an indefinite period, and chief among them are the Security prisoners, under Rule 26. The bulk of them are our own comrades but they include all. Maxwell put their number up to the end of February as seven hundred, of these hundred and two were Satyagrahis bagged before they could offer themselves for arrest, they include WC members, ex-Premiers and ex-Ministers of Congress Cabinets. Of the rest Maxwell classed four hundred eighty as Communists. The bulk of them are concentrated in jails and camps at Deoli, Nasik, Vellore, Alipur, Hijli.

OUR COMRADES are not only being kept isolated from the rest of the politicals but selected for specially bad treatment. Maxwell not only became Hitler's double when he barked at them in approved fascist bloodhound fashion. He has also learnt to behave and bite as well in the right Hitler way. The best and most experienced of the Communist leaders, in whom he sees 'the Central Directorium' of our Party, he has put in the Concentration Camp at Deoli, complete with barbed-wire, watch-tower, armed guards and all. Deoli can put Dachau in the shade, the same paraphernalia and the same reality within of a living death for the physically alive. The heat is unbearable and living conditions such as to guarantee the slow death of the victims without the odium of murdering them. Chronic ailments are becoming common among the comrades. Their pride in Ghate sinks into anxiety when they daily witness his heroic struggle to survive despite repeated heart-attacks, going unattended. Ajoy is down with T.B., both lungs gone. The Bombay comrades are collapsing under heat-strokes. Some of them would not come out alive; most of them would be so seriously damaged in health that they will no more be able to take active part in our Freedom's battle IF we let imperialism have its way with its victims, our own beloved Comrades.

THERE is no mistaking the cunning but brutal policy of the Government. It is:

1. Discriminate between the top Congress leaders and the mass of satyagrahis and thus sow seeds of demoralization.
2. Terrorize the mass of the prisoners, especially of the C class, by tightening up jail discipline and drilling their lives in a manner that their hands itch no more for 'struggle'.
3. Quarantine the Communists and squeeze the life out of them.

IMPERIALISM discriminates between prisoners and prisoners, that is for differing political reasons, but it makes its presence felt by all. If Communists are denied medical treatment, and the C class lads decent food, the foremost of the Congress leaders are being insulted and taught their place under the British Raj.

CONDITIONS OF TERROR inside jails, as they existed in 1930–2, are not only reappearing but have already become worse. What is distressing is not the growing terror itself but our seeming acquiescence in it. The Press on the whole is maintaining a cowardly silence. The people appear apathetic to the fate of their best sons and daughters. This was never so before in national movement. The Press had taken a leading part in exposure of conditions within the jail-walls and the people through meetings and demonstrations, had accorded magnificient support to every protest against terror and thus held imperialism in check. The Congress organization, whether legal or illegal, mobilized the people. To-day, relying on the policy of the national leaders and the sweeping provisions of the DOIA, imperialism is going full steam ahead. The Censor and threat of fines and confiscation guarantees a Press black-out, Gandhiji has disbanded the Congress, asked Congressmen to forget the masses, and all about meetings and demonstrations, but just sit, spin, and pray. Where there is the hindrance? This is how Gandhian Satyagraha encourages imperialism to sharpen its claws under our very eyes and dig them deeper into the bodies of our comrades and leaders, which it has taken at pleasure, as prey. Not one word has the Mahatma spoken or written about the political prisoners since his 'struggle' began. Humanity, chivalry, courage, even democratic virtue is being knocked out of the national soldiers under the Satyagrahi General. The people are left to their fate, that is, at the mercy of imperialism if they would stir. This is how the people have been made apathetic to the sufferings and tortures of those that served, organized and led them in numerous battles. Struggle encourages self-confidence in a people but Satyagraha is breeding demoralization. This is where Gandhism has brought our national movement—helpless, prostrate, and unable to stir.

BUT neither are the national fighters behind the bars are bloodless nor are we a nation of cowards. Hunger strikes of prisoners began in Bengal during December and the citizens of Calcutta, led by the students, organized by our Party, through mass mobilization, made their voice felt and forced Huq to hold back and improve the lot of the detenus. Our Vellore Comrades through a mass hunger-strike have made the Madras Government sit up. There is no trace of the Malabar Communist leader, Krishna Pillai, since his arrest, a mass campaign is set afoot throughout Malabar 'Where is Comrade Pillai? Hands off him!' Even the Gandhian daily Mathrubhumi is forced to ask the Government editorially to place before the people information about Pillai 'or else there is danger of the situation getting worse.' Hunger Strikes are becoming more and more common, in every province.

THERE IS NO TIME TO LOSE. Do we want the true sons of our people, drawn from all parties and Communities to fight alone against sufferings which are being heaped upon them because they served our country their best? Do we want more Jatin Dases? It would be our indelible shame if they become martyrs through hunger-strikes while it lies in our hands to organize such a powerful movement outside supporting their demands that they do not get hell at the hands of the enemy but when they rejoin the national ranks they come hale and hearty.

THE JOB is to make the people shake their fist, raise their united voice:

THE DECENT AND HUMAN TREATMENT TO ALL PRISONERS.

COMMUNISTS have to be at the forefront of this campaign, our comrades are suffering the most, but it is no Party issue. We would seek the co-operation of every decent Indian, of the parties, and all communities, for a really broad-based campaign in defence of detenus' and prisoners' demands.

FLOOD THE PRESS WITH EXPOSURE OF CONDITIONS INSIDE THE JAIL-WALLS. TAKE THE NEWS TO THE PEOPLE. RALLY THEM THROUGH MEETINGS AND DEMONSTRATIONS.

TO THE RESCUE OF IMPERIALIST VICTIMS!

KEEP THE ENEMY AT BAY!

HANDS OFF OUR NATIONAL HEROES!

150. Madras Government's Order on Conditions of Detention of Security Prisoners, 9 May 1941

Government of Madras, Public (General) Department, GO No. 962, 9th May 1941, Tamil Nadu State Archives.

POLITICAL AGITATION—Persons detained under Defence of India Rule 26—Conditions of detention—Revised rules—Issued

READ—the following papers:

GO No. 930, Public (General), dated 7th May 1940.
GO No. 1580, Public (General), dated 10th August 1940.
GO No. 2294, Public (General), dated 19th November 1940.
ORDER—No. 962, Public (General), dated 9th May 1941.

In exercise of the powers conferred by or delegated by the Central Government under sub rules (5) and (5-A) of Rule 26 of the Defence of India Rules, the Provincial Government are pleased to direct that the rules appended to this order shall be conditions detention applicable to persons ordered under Rule 26 to be detained in jails within the Madras Province (referred to in the Appendix as security prisoners). These rules supersede all previous orders prescribing conditions of detention for security prisoners.

2. The Inspector-General of Prisons is requested to admit to Government half-yearly reports on persons detained under the Defence of India Rules, similar to the reports prescribed in the State Prisoners Regulations on 10th January and 10th July or at more frequent intervals if it is advisable in any particular case.

3. With reference to Rule 25, the Inspector-General of Prisons is requested to submit for the approval of the Government proposals relating to matters not covered by the rules or the instructions already issued.

(By order of His Excellency the Governor)

S.V. RAMAMURTY,
Chief Secretary.

To

The Inspector-General of Prisons.
Copy to the Inspector-General of Police.
Copy to the Commissioner of Police.
Copy to the Superintendent of Police, Special Branch, CID
Copy to the Superintendent, Central Jail, Vellore.
Copy to the District Magistrate of North Arcot.
Copy to the District Superintendent of Police, North Arcot.
Copy to the Home Department.
Copy to the Government of India, Home Department (with CL)
Copy to the all Provincial Governments (with CL)
Copy to the Superintendent, Deoli Detention Camp, Deoli, Rajpatana (with copy of the GO No. 3735, home, dated 11th September 1940).

Appendix
The Security Prisoners Rules, 1941

1. Classification.—(1) Security prisoners shall be divided into two classes I and II according to state of their health and their education, status, and mode of living before arrest.

(2) The classification of each security prisoner shall be made by Government.

2. Accommodation.—Security prisoners shall not be locked up in their rooms except at night and if they so desire they may be in the same room. The lock-up may be between 8 and 9 p.m. Force may be used if any prisoner refuses to be locked up. A security prisoner may be allowed to mix freely with the other security prisoners of the same class. The Superintendent of the Jail may, however, confine any particular prisoner separately if he considers it desirable on grounds of health or for any other reason. Prisoners in class I will be supplied with articles of furniture which are allowed 'A' class prisoners and such other articles as are sanctioned by the Government. Prisoners in class II will be supplied with one table, one chair and one commode with pan and chamberpot. They will be allowed lights for reading up to 10 p.m.

3. Diet.—(a) Security prisoners in class I shall be supplied with the diet prescribed for 'A' and 'B' class convicted prisoners and those in class II with that prescribed for 'C' class convicted prisoners. This may be modified or increased on medical grounds on the recommendation of the medical officer of the jail.

(b) Security prisoners shall be allowed to bring their own feeding utensils but if for any reason they are unable to do so, the Superintendent of the Jail shall issue such utensils as he can conveniently issue.

4. Colthing.—Each security prisoner may wear his own clothes, and friends, if permitted to do so by the Superintendent, may send in extra clothes and bedding. Security prisoners who are unable to provide themselves with sufficient clothing and bedding shall be supplied by the Superintendent of the Jail with 'B' or 'C' class convicted prisoners' clothing and bedding according as they are placed in class I or II.

5. They will be supplied with toilet soap, oil, toothpaste, and tooth brush at the cost of Government. The scale of supply of these articles shall be at the discretion of the Superintendent of the Jail.

6. Labour.—Security prisoners may be assigned tasks by the Superintendent with due regard to their state of health, physical and mental capacity, character, and antecedents and may receive remuneration for their labour at such rates as may be prescribed by the Superintendent.

7. Discipline and searches.—Security prisoners shall for purposes of discipline be subject to such of the rules relating to civil prisoners as are not inconsistent with these orders or any other special orders passed by the Government in this behalf.

8. Every security prisoner and his cell or ward shall be searched not less than once a week, and after if the Superintendent of the Jail considers it necessary, by the Jailor, or Deputy Jailor, or Reserve Deputy Jailor, as detailed by the Superintendent. Special precautions shall be taken to make the searches thorough and the fact of the search shall be noted in the Jailor's report book.

9. (1) Private funds.—A security prisoner may receive, at intervals of not less than a month, funds not exceeding Rs 10 per month in the case of class I security prisoner, and Rs 5 per month in the case of class II security prisoner, and may spend those funds or a similar sum from his own private funds to supplement the amenities of life in the jail; provided that money

spent on the purchase of clothes and bedding and sports articles shall not count against the limit of Rs 10 and Rs 5.

(2) All funds so received shall be kept by the Superintendent and spent by him on behalf of the security prisoner.

10. Interviews.—(1) The Superintendent shall fix the days in the week on which interviews with persons other than a police officer may take place.

(2) No security prisoner shall be permitted to have an interview with any person (other than a police officer) except on the written order of the Government or of such officer as may be authorized by them in this behalf.

(3) Applications for interviews shall be made to the Government or to the officer authorized by the Government under sub-paragraph (2), in the form annexed to these rules and the permit, if granted, shall be communicated both to the applicant and the Superintendent.

(4) Notwithstanding the receipt of such a permit, the Superintendent may for special reasons refuse to allow an interview to take place on any particular day or for such period as he considers fit:

Provided that if his refusal extends to a period exceeding one month from the date on which he receives the permit he shall report his refusal and the reasons therefore to the Government or officer granting the permit.

(5) Interviews shall take place in the presence of an officer deputed by the Superintendent and such officer may terminate an interview at any time, if in his opinion the conversation is detrimental to the public interest or safety. The Superintendent of the Jail shall permit any police officer of not lower rank than a Sub-Inspector of Police, belonging either to the district or Central Special Branch to enter the jail to overhear conversations between security prisoners and outsiders on production of a request in writing from a police officer not below the rank of a District Superintendent of Police or Deputy Commissioner of Police.

(6) Every person permitted to interview a security prisoner and the security prisoner himself may be searched before and after the interview at the discretion of the Superintendent.

(7) The number of interviews shall not ordinarily exceed—
One per fortnight for a class 'I' security prisoner.
One per month for a class 'II' security prisoner.
And there shall not ordinarily be more than three visitors present (excluding children under twelve years) simultaneously at any one interview.

(8) The Superintendent shall appoint the time, place, and duration of each interview, and shall not ordinarily allow an interview to continue for more than one hour with a relative or half an hour with a person other than a relative.

(9) After the interview is over, the jail official present at the interview shall warn both the security prisoner and the visitor that future interviews are liable to be prohibited if the visitor indulges in any publicity on behalf of the security prisoner.

(10) The Superintendent may allow additional interviews by authorized persons for special reasons if he is satisfied that the circumstances make it necessary to do so.

11. Police interviews.—(1) Subject to the directions of the Government, the Inspector-General of Police or the Commissioner of Police may, by general or special order, authorize

any police officer either singly or with another police officer, and accompanied or unaccompanied by subordinate police officers, to interview any security prisoner.

(2) The police officers so authorized may, with the permission of the Superintendent, interview security prisoners in their cells or wards.

(3) In visiting the cells or wards every police officer shall be accompanied by such escort as the Superintendent considers necessary for his safety; but the escort shall, if the police officer so requires, stand out of earshot, but within sight, while he is speaking to any of the security prisoners.

(4) The police officers so authorized may, with the permission of the Superintendent, interview security prisoners in the ordinary interview room, without a Jail official being present.

(5) Any police officer authorized by the Government in this behalf may take photographs, register the finger-prints, and take specimens of the signature and handwriting of a security prisoner in the jail.

12. Correspondence and censorship.—(1) Security prisoners in class I shall ordinarily be permitted to write two and receive four letters per week and those in class II to write one and receive one letter per week, for which purpose they may be supplied at the cost of the Government with writing materials strictly necessary for this purpose. Telegrams will count as letters.

(2) No security prisoner shall write a letter to another security prisoner and not more than one letter shall be enclosed in one envelope except with the special permission of the Superintendent.

(3) Any letters or communications received for prisoners which are clearly franked to indicate that they come from a Government Office (that is, excluding any local fund office) should be delivered to the prisoners and should not be counted against the admissible number of letters received by prisoners. All other letters to and from security prisoners shall be perused by the Superintendent of the Jail and subject to any special orders of the Government shall be submitted by the Superintendent of the Jail direct to the Superintendent of Police of the district or the Assistant or Deputy Superintendent of Police in his absence, or other officer nominated by the Superintendent of Police, Special Branch, CID, who may, at his discretion, either forward the letters without delay or withhold them if they are in his opinion likely to be detrimental to the public interest or safety. The contents of all letters shall be limited to private matters. In case of doubt, the Police official referred to above shall refer the matter to the Superintendent of Police, Special Branch, CID, or other officer designated by the Government in this behalf.

(4) Every letter forwarded to or from a security prisoner shall be initialled and dated by the officer censoring the letter under sub-paragraph (3).

(5) All letters the dispatch or delivery of which is withheld under sub-paragraph (3) shall be sent to the Superintendent of Police, Special Branch, CID or other officer designated by the Government in this behalf for retention or destruction at his discretion, and the fact of such withholding shall be intimated to the security prisoner concerned through the Superintendent of the Jail.

(6) If in any communication made by, or intended to be delivered to, a security prisoner, anything objectionable from the point of view of jail discipline is found by the Superintendent of the Jail, he may delete the same or mark it for deletion and mention

what had been done when forwarding such communication to the Superintendent of Police of the district or the Assistant or Deputy Superintendent of Police in his absence or other officer nominated in this behalf. That authority may, notwithstanding anything hereinbefore contained, instead of withholding the delivery or dispatch of a letter, dispatch or deliver it after deleting any portion which in its opinion may be detrimental to the public interest or safety or the discipline of the jail.

(7) The receipt of and dispatch of telegrams by prisoners shall be subject to the same control as is hereinbefore provided for letters except that the number of telegrams which may be dispatched by a prisoner shall be within the discretion of the Superintendent of the Jail. The cost of telegrams should ordinarily be borne by the prisoners concerned.

(8) When the telegrams is to or from the Government, it shall be forwarded direct, provided that the Provincial Government will always be the intermediary in correspondence with the Central or another Provincial Government and that the Superintendent of the Jail has discretion to forward a petition submitted in telegraphic form by post instead of by telegram.

(9) Security prisoners shall attach to all their outgoing letters and telegrams a slip containing the full name and address and relationship of the addressee and of each person mentioned in the letter or telegram. These slips shall be sent to the Superintendent of Police, Special Branch, CID, Madras or other officer designated by the Government in this behalf, who, if he considers that the writer should not be allowed to correspond with the addressee, shall inform the Superintendent of the Jail for his future guidance.

(10) In addition to the paper supplied under sub-paragraph (1) a security prisoner who receives funds from outside may be allowed to purchase ordinary school exercise books for other writing purposes, but the pages of such books shall be numbered and the security prisoner shall not destroy any such book or remove the pages thereof.

13. Books and newspapers.—(1) Security prisoners may receive through the post any of the newspapers and periodicals allowed to 'A' and 'B' class convicted prisoners subject to the following conditions, namely:

(a) any postal article containing the newspaper or periodical shall first be opened by the Superintendent of the Jail or a person appointed by him for the purpose;

(b) where in the opinion of the Superintendent any other matter in such newspaper or periodical is unsuitable on grounds of public interest and safety such matter shall be deleted before the Newspaper or the periodical is delivered to the security prisoner.

(2) Security prisoners may purchase any book available in lists published by Messrs Higginbothams, Taraporevala & Co, G.A. Natesan & Co, or Thacker & Co, Bombay, without hindrance or censorship. As regards other books received through the post, the postal article containing the book shall first be opened by the Superintendent or any person appointed by him for the purpose and the delivery of such book to the prisoner may be refused by the Superintendent if in his opinion it is not suitable.

(3) In addition to newspapers, periodicals, and books which may be received through the post, any security prisoner who receives funds from outside may be allowed to purchase from such funds newspapers, periodicals, and books subject to the conditions laid down in sub-paragraph (1) and (2).

14. The Superintendent of the Jail shall forward with such observations as he may think fit, any representation which a security prisoner may submit to the Government.

15. A security prisoner—

(i) shall reside in the accommodation allotted to him by the Superintendent whether in an association ward or a cell;

(ii) shall not proceed beyond the limits of the jail area, that is, of the jail gardens and precincts save with the permission of the Superintendent given by general or special order in this behalf;

(iii) shall obey the orders of the Superintendent issued from time to time for the comfort, safety, and health, or for the discipline, orderly conduct and control, of security prisoners;

(iv) shall attend roll-call and answer to his name in person at such times and places within the jail as may be appointed by the Superintendent;

(v) shall conform to the standards of cleanliness and dress laid down by the Superintendent;

(vi) shall not do anything willfully with the object of affecting his own bodily welfare;

(vii) shall not have in his possession any coin, currency notes or negotiable instruments, any weapons, sticks, razors other than safety razors, pieces of iron or any other article which may be used as a weapon;

(viii) shall not exchange or sell any of his kit, equipment, clothes, furniture or other possessions supplied by or belonging to the Government.

(ix) shall not refuse to take the prescribed diet;

(x) shall perform such tasks as may be allotted to him by the Superintendent.

16. Any security prisoner who contravenes any of the provisions of Rule 12 (1) or Rule (15) or refuses to obey any order issued thereunder, or does any of the following acts, namely,

(i) assaults, insults, threatens or obstructs any fellow prisoner or any officer of the jail or any other Government servant, or any person employed in or visiting the jail, or,

(ii) quarrels with any person in the jail, or

(iii) is guilty of indecent, immoral or disorderly conduct, or

(iv) communicates or attempts to communicate with any person outside the jail in an unauthorized manner, or

(v) bribes or attempts to bribe any Government servant or any person employed in or visiting the jail, or

(vi) commits any nuisance or willfully befouls any well, latrine, washing or bathing place, or

(vii) disobeys the orders of, or shows disrespect to, any officer of the jail, or

(viii) willfully damages any property belonging to the Government or tamper with any locks, lamps or lights in the jail, or

(ix) receives, possesses or transfers any article in contravention of an order of the Superintendent, or

(x) feigns illness, or

(xi) willfully brings false accusation against any officer of the jail or fellow prisoner, or

(xii) omits or refuses to report as soon as it comes to his knowledge, the occurrence of any fire, any plot or conspiracy, any escape, attempt or preparation to escape, and any attack or preparation for attack upon any officer of the jail, or

(xiii) abets the commission by a fellow prisoner of any of the foregoing acts, or

(xiv) omits or refuses to help any officer of the jail in case of an attempted escape on the part of any of his fellow prisoners or of any attack upon such officer or upon any of his fellow prisoners,

shall be deemed to have committed a jail offence.

17. (1) Where upon such enquiry as he thinks fit to make, the Superintendent is satisfied that a security prisoner is guilty of a jail offence, he may award the security prisoner one or more of the following punishments:

(a) confinement in cells for a period not exceeding fourteen days;
(b) reduction or alteration of diet for a period not exceeding fourteen days;
(c) cancellation or reduction for a period not exceeding two months of the concession of receiving funds from outside;
(d) cancellation or reduction for a period not exceeding two months of the privilege of writing and receiving letters or of receiving newspapers and books;
(e) cancellation or reduction for a period not exceeding two months of the privilege of having interviews;
(f) cancellation of the privilege of wearing of his own clothes;
(g) reduction from Class I to Class II for a period not exceeding one month.

(2) If any security prisoner is guilty of a jail offence, which by reason of his having frequently committed such offence or otherwise is in the opinion of the Superintendent not adequately punishable by him under the provisions of sub-paragraph (1), he may with the approval of the Government forward such prisoner to the Court of a Magistrate of the first class having jurisdiction, and such Magistrate shall thereupon inquire into and try the charge so brought against the security prisoner, and upon conviction shall sometime sentence him to imprisonment for a term not exceeding one year;

Provided that where the act constituting the offence constitutes an offence punishable under the Indian Penal Code with imprisonment for a term exceeding one year nothing in this paragraph shall preclude the security prisoner from being tried and sentenced for such offence in accordance with the provisions of the Indian Penal Code.

18. The Superintendent may use or require to be used such force as may in his opinion be necessary to compel obedience on the part of any security prisoner to any lawful order issued by him.

19. When the Superintendent is of opinion that security prisoner should be given special medical treatment in any hospital outside the Jail, the security prisoner may, notwithstanding anything contained in the order of detention, be taken to such hospital or to the jail nearest to such hospital and detained there in custody until in the opinion of the Superintendent of the hospital he is fit to return to jail. In the matter of hospital accommodation, security prisoners shall be treated in the same way as prisoners convicted of offences connected with political movements as ordered in GO No. 3891, Home, dated 23rd September 1940.

20. When the presence of a security prisoner is necessary in a court of law either to stand his trial as an accused person or to give evidence in a case, the Superintendent shall, on receipt of a written requisition from the court countersigned by the District Magistrate concerned, arrange for the removal of the prisoner to such court notwithstanding anything contained in the order of detention.

21. Exercise and games.—Exercise should be within the jail area, that is, the jail garden and precincts as the Superintendent may decide.

Games, such as chess, carom, draughts, cards, and tennis may be allowed at the expense of the prisoners. Friends if permitted to do so by the Superintendent may supply them with tennis racquets or other sports articles.

22. Security prisoners may be allowed to smoke at their own cost.

23. Visits.—The District Magistrate shall visit the security prisoners in jail within his district at least once a month and submit a report to Government on the prisoners' health, general bearing and comfort, if he considers this necessary. The ordinary jail visitors shall not have access to security prisoners.

24. Miscellaneous.—All particulars relating to security prisoners shall be entered (without serial number) in the register of civil prisoners and all statistics of security prisoners shall be shown separately in jail returns.

25. Such other local instructions as may be necessary for the guidance of jail officers may be issued by the Inspector-General of Prisons with the approval of Government.

Annexure
Form of Application for Interview

All persons desiring to interview a prisoner are requested to furnish the following particulars:

Name of prisoner to be interviewed
Name of applicant
Relationship to prisoner of applicant
Full address of applicant
Purpose for which interview is desired

Dated
8.6.1941

Signature of applicant.
S.V.R.

To
The Public (General) Department.

151. Hunger Strike in Nagpur Central Jail:

(i) Demand to Government
Early Redress of Grievances Urged

Amrita Bazar Patrika, 14 May 1941.

Jubbulpore, 13 May.

The political prisoners confined in the Nagpur Central Jail who went on a day's hunger-strike on Friday last, it is learnt, have sent a representation to the Provincial Government for early redress of their grievances.

Among the demands formulated and submitted to the Provincial Government by the 'C' class prisoners are that the interview should be held in a room and that they should be allowed to supplement articles of food and other necessities from outside at their expense. They have further asked the Government that the prisoners who are brought to jail late in the evening by the police should not be kept without food the whole night and that all the correspondence and communications addressed to and by the 'C' class prisoners should be delivered promptly.

(ii) Hunger Strike in Nagpur Jail: 'C' Class Political Prisoners Grievances

Amrita Bazar Patrika, 3 June 1941.

This morning the 'C' class political prisoners in the Nagpur Central Jail went on one-day hunger-strike as a protest against indecision regarding purchase of ghee, fruits, cots at the prisoners' own cost. It is reported that 'A' and 'B' class politicals have also gone on fast in sympathy with the 'C' class prisoners.

It may be recalled that the 'C' class political prisoners went on hunger-strike on 9 May, demanding redress of their certain grievances.

At the Press Conference at Pachmarhi held on 19 May, the Chief Secretary to Government announced that Government had sanctioned supply of milk, sherbet, dahi (curd), and interview of 'C' class prisoners in a room, instead of from behind the bars, and also less restrictions in correspondence.

The present hunger-strike was undertaken, as no reply so far been received from the Government regarding other demands made by the 'C' class prisoners.

152. In Deoli-Hell

Communist, Vol. III, No. 4, June 1941, P.C. Joshi Archives on Contemporary History, JNU.

On 11th April the Deoli Detenus, after long suffering, submitted a Memorandum to the Government, the chief demands of which we have given in another column. In Bombay the drama staged by the Detenu Aid Committee had packed houses; the city's middle class youth had not forgotten its best. The campaign among the workers was a tremendous success. Hundred and fifty chawl meetings in the last month evoked an enthusiastic response. It came in hard-won annas and coppers. Tears of grief glistened in the eyes of men and women when they heard how Ghate was slowly dying and Mirajkar suffering. But they became tears of pride when they heard Dange and Ranadive were separated from the rest because they fought doggedly with the prison authorities. Deoli Day was observed in the North on 11th May. Even *The Bombay Chronicle* which listens to the Censor and swears by Gandhism wrote editorials supporting the detenus' demands. The echo of peoples' agitation has reached even the heights of Simla to inspire a lying AP message that things are not so bad. We give below an authentic account of what the detenus are suffering under. All quotations are from their own appeal to the people of which we have secured a true copy.

Editor

They are from all corners of our vast country—Madras, Bombay, Bengal, Behar, UP, Delhi, the Punjab, and NWF. About hundred of them are in camp No. 1 and 93 in Camp No. 2. Most of them are Communists, our experienced leaders, every one whom imperialism could bag to carry through its war against our democracy. Whatever their origin, they left everything to become professional revolutionaries, lived together like comrades, fought shoulder to shoulder. The enemy now turns round and artificially divides them on the basis of social status. Even inside the prison-walls imperialism seeks to rule by creating division! And detenus from one Camp are not allowed to meet those from the other.

Camp I detenus get a diet allowance of 12 annas and Camp II 6 annas only. All rations must be bought through the contractor whose prices are so high that they get only 50 per cent worth. Whenever anyone from Camp I is punished by the Superintendent the penal diet prescribed for him is the same that is given to Camp II detenus. This means that half the detenus are permanently living on penal diet, which is about the same grade given to ordinary criminals in other jails. It is mid-summer heat. There is great scarcity of water. The Superintendent promises to look into the matter but does nothing. For months and months bad food and insufficient water is what imperialism has been keeping them on, so that the 'Defence of India' may not be hindered.

'Since the Camp was opened almost every one of us has been suffering from malaria for which this place is notorius. Many of us have gone down in weight. The Camp Hospital is merely a mockery. There are two doctors whose ignorance of medicine is insignificant as compared to their callousness. Many serious cases are wholly neglected. Ajoy Ghose was declared by the Senior Medical Officer as being perfectly healthy but two days afterwards the X-Ray photo taken in the Ajmer Hospital showed that both his lungs are affected with T.B.

'The heat here is terrible. The hot winds of the desert blow throughout the day. In the night it is impossible to sleep.'

STARVE THE LIFE OUT OF THEM THROUGH UNDER-FEEDING AND THEN LEAVE THEM TO DIE, in the desert swamp, surrounded by barbed-wire. This is the fate of our national heroes in the British Imperialist Concentration Camp and they speak of ridding of Nazi menace!

The clothing is nothing more than two shirts and two pyjamas made of thick coarse cloth, 'which are impossible to wear either during the day or night, in a place like Deoli.' No warm clothing is given in winter, nor any foot-wear. The jailors of our Comrades are fighting a war for civilization!

'IT IS ALL MARTIAL LAW HERE.' They are punished arbitrarily, even the right of defence is denied. Letters are withheld for several months or solitary confinement with penal diet given on the mere report of convict Warders whose job is to spy on the detenus. Appeals to the Government against punishments imposed are not forwarded and instead the detenus concerned are further punished.

'Newspapers are censored so badly that even Anglo-Indian papers like *The Times of India*, *Madras Mail* and *Statesman* sometimes come to us as so many pieces of paper. Even Assembly discussions are scissored off. No book worth reading is permitted. We often hear from our relatives that our letters are mutilated to such an extent that they cannot make head or tail of the letters.'

The right of interview is nominal, for Deoli is hundreds of miles away from their homes and railway fare alone is prohibitive. Once a while when their relatives turn up they find Deoli is a place where they have nowhere to stay. They are shown scant courtesy by the Camp staff, who however shout 'Times is up' after fifteen minutes with their dear ones.

'Here we are completely in the hands of the CID who hold all posts in the Camp. Even the compounders in the Hospital are CID constables. The Camp is always surrounded by an armed military guard. Every week they practice false alarms leveling their rifles at us in a threatening manner.

'DEOLI IS HELL. THE CONDITIONS OF LIFE HERE ARE UNBEARABLE AND TO LIVE IN THIS HELL INDEFINITELY IS MADDENING.'

Let the people remember that it was in this very Deoli Camp that the Bengal State prisoners and detenus were kept last, that two of them committed suicide and seven went mad under conditions that were far better then than now. Let them also remember that the demands of present-day detenus are nothing more than what this very Government had conceded the Bengal detenus only a few years back.

A vindictive Government has condemned our heroes to slow death and daily tortures. Mass hunger-strike of the detenus is imminent. They have spent their young life fighting for better life for our people. Must they now risk it fighting for a human and decent life for themselves? The Simla Sahebs can be made to totter on their legs and treat these young leaders of our national movement humanely if we can rally people, for whem they suffered and struggled, under the Cry:

Hands Off Our Heroes!
Face Us First!!

153. Brief Diary of the Hunger-strike in the Deoli Detention Camp, from 30 May 1941 (10 a.m.) to 3rd June 1941 (11 a.m.)

File No. 43/65/1941 and KW—Poll (I), Home (Political) Department, Government of India, NAI.

26.5.41

On the 26th May 1941 Security Prisoner, Class I, Shatrughan Kumar (UP) was awarded seven days' cells for assaulting a Ward-boy in the Hospital.

Shatrughan Kumar was in attendance on another Class I Security Prisoner Beni Madho Rai who was a patient in the Hospital at the time.

At the investigation of other Security Prisoners, B.M. Rai began to feign lunacy and started calling for Shatrughan Kumar and eventually became violent during the night of 26th/27th May 1941.

27.5.41

On the 27th May, the Civil Surgeon, Ajmer, was summoned.

28.5.41

On the 28th May, the Civil Surgeon arrived at Deoli and recommended that B.M. Rai should be transferred to Ajmer for observation.

29.5.41

On the 29th May, B.M. Rai was sent to Ajmer.

On the same day 23 Class I Security Prisoners of Camp I wrote in saying they were going on hunger-strike from 10 a.m. on 30th May, unless

(1) all serious cases in the Hospital were transferred to Ajmer,
(2) the Medical Officer was transferred at once,
(3) the Civil Surgeon, Ajmer, visits the Camp twice a week until the new Medical Officer comes, and
(4) Shatrughan Kumar was released from the cells immediately and sent to Ajmer to attend on B.M. Rai.

30.5.41

On the 30th May, the Assistant Superintendent saw the Committee of Camp I but failed to persuade the 23 Security Prisoners from striking.

Petitions were received from 61 class I and 67 Class II Security Prisoners (Communists) saying they would go on hunger-strike from the 1st June if their two demands, namely, (1) serious cases to be sent to Ajmer and (2) Medical Officer to go at once, were not attended to. This second lot of Security Prisoners wished to be treated and dealt with separately from the first lot of 23 Security Prisoners.

The Hon'ble the Chief Commissioner, Ajmer–Merwara, Abu, and the Commissioner, Ajmer–Merwara, Ajmer, were informed by cipher telegrams of the strike, (vide No. X–925, dated 30th May 1941).

6 other Security Prisoners of Class I and 10 of Class II identified themselves with the first party of 23, and went on hunger-strike.

(Total hunger strikers = 39)

31.5.41

The 39 Security Prisoners remained on hunger strike on the 31st May 1941.

Commissioner arrived at Deoli and returned to Ajmer the same day.

Written report of the hunger-strike was sent to the Commissioner, Ajmer, vide this office No. X–1006, dated 31st May 1941.

1.6.41

On the 1st June, Civil Surgeon, Ajmer, arrived at Deoli and recommended the transfer of four cases to Ajmer.

B.M. Rai was returned to Deoli by the Civil Surgoen with the report that he was malingering.

The representatives of the hunger strikers were told that B.M. Rai was malingering and would be punished and that four cases would be transferred in the normal course to the Victoria Hospital as the medical authorities had advised. They were prepared to call off the hunger-strike, but B.M. Rai was segregated and this caused the hunger-strikers to continue the strike as they were not allowed to see him.

One more Class I Security Prisoner joined the strikers.

(Total No. of hunger strikers = 40).

2.6.41

On the 2nd June, B.M. Rai was awarded seven days' cells with reduction of his diet from annas/12/- to -/9/- per diem and the loss of the privilege of wearing his own clothes, for malingering. His punishment order was posted in Camp in the normal manner.

He went on hunger strike.

(Total No. of hunger-strikers = 41).

As Shatrughan Kumar's period of seven days' cells had come to an end, he was released.

The Superintendent met the Security Prisoners Z.A. Ahmad and S.S. Mirajker, the leaders of the Communist (the majority) party (not yet on hunger-strike) and explained the situation to them. They threatened that if the authorities attempted to segregate prisoners on hunger-strike from those not on hunger-strike the action would be opposed by them and an 'ugly situation' would arise. They were informed that those on hunger-strike would certainly be segregated and interference by them would be met by force. They were also informed that any interference by them would be considered as mutiny and action to prosecute those who would take part in it would be taken. They would on conviction be turned into 'C' Class convicts. This had the desired effect and the second lot of 51 class I and 67 class II Security Prisoners did not go on hunger-strike.

The Superintendent later sent for the four leaders of hunger-strikers. They at first said that they were too weak and refused to come to the office. An Inspector was sent in to explain to them that it was Superintendent's order to attend office immediately and advised them that it would be to their detriment if they did not come to office at once. They obeyed the order.

On arrival they were asked if they were still on hunger-strike. They replied in the affirmative.

Camp Order (copy attached) was read over to them and fully explained that they would be segregated and prosecuted and on conviction by summary trials would be turned into ordinary 'C' class convicts, thus losing all status of a Security Prisoner, if they did not call off their hunger-strike unconditionally, and that all arrangements had been made to deal with them. They were further told that no grievances would be listened to so long as they remained on hunger-strike. They maintained that they would continue the strike. They laid down the condition that B.M. Rai should be released from cells immediately and they would call off their hunger-strike. This was refused and they were again told that before any grievance could be looked into they must call off the hunger-strike unconditionally, but the question of release of B.M. Rai from the cells would not arise as his case was a matter of jail discipline and had nothing to do with them. They were then informed that they would be segregated in cells. They demanded they should be allowed to return to Camp to hand over Government property (such as cooking utensils, and other things). This was refused. They were informed that the District Magistrate had been wired for and he would be arriving next morning. They would be summarily tried and if found guilty would be sentenced to any term up to one year's rigorous imprisonment. They still continued to put up a very bold front. Consequently they were segregated. While in segregation food was kept by their side but they did not take it.

They were once again given (while in segregation) an opportunity that before prosecution and conviction they could still call off the strike unconditionally.

3.6.41

On the 3rd June, the Superintendent received information that they were willing to call off strike unconditionally. (They probably felt the pangs of hunger and feared their prosecution and conviction).

They were sent for to come to the office. They arrived in the office in a very different frame of mind from which they were on the previous day, and said they were willing to unconditionally call off the strike. They requested that they might be allowed to return to their Camp and take their first meal with their co-strikers and order them to call off the hunger-strike unconditionally.

They were put on their honour not to continue the strike once they had got back amongst their friends. It was fully explained to them that if they broke their word they would never be trusted again. They kept their word.

About an hour later a note, signed by leaders of hunger-strikers of both the Camps, was received that they had all broken their fast and taken a meal.

Medical officers were then sent to Camps to advise the late hunger-strikers as to what food they should take (that is, light diet).

B.M. Rai (in the cells) was informed that all Security Prisoners had taken their food and he called off his hunger-strike.

A telegram was sent to the Hon'ble the Chief Commissioner, Ajmer–Merwara, Abu, and Commissioner, Ajmer–Merwara, Ajmer, informing them that the strike had been called off.

154. Deoli Security Prisoners

Amrita Bazar Patrika, 14 June 1941.

Redress of Grievances
Immediate Impartial Enquiry Demanded

Lahore, 12 June.

Mian Iftikhar-ud-Din, President Punjab Provincial Congress Committee has issued the following statement:

'The attention of the Punjab public has recently been drawn through press and platform to the condition of political workers detained under the Defence of India Act in the Deoli Camp. In this connection news has also come that the detenus have submitted a memorandum to the Government of India for the redress of their grievances. As a result of the press news the Government too has issued a communiqué. The communiqué presents a picture of the Deoli Camp which is entirely different from the one the public has hitherto had in mind. After this, doubts have naturally arisen in the mind of every reasonable person as to the actual facts. The only method of setting at rest these doubts is that of an inquiry by an independent committee. The demand for an independent inquiry will be deemed necessary, not only by those who desire to see the detenus in a reasonably comfortable condition, to which their political position entitles them, but also by those who have the reputation of the Government of heart. And since the Government has shown a measure of sensitiveness on this question by issuing the communiqué mentioned above. I do not see why, if the facts contained in the communiqué are correct, the Government should feel shy of an impartial inquiry.

When this demand is put forward by the politically minded persons of this province, let it be made clear that the fact that those prisoners have been denied all justice and legal trial, has not been forgotten. Nor can any independent person vindicate the position of the Punjab Government, which whilst claiming itself to be a popular Government, has sent over a hundred of its citizens away from their homes and their province for political reason. It will not be out of place to mention that more than half of the detenus in Deoli are from this province. They include five MLAs and other political workers, whose reputation as brave and selfless public servants is not confined to the limits of the Punjab alone. All this, as I said, cannot be overlooked. The question of their trial and repatriation is extremely important. The point that needs to be emphasized in this statement, however, is that of the demand for an impartial inquiry into the conditions prevalent at the Deoli Camp and it is difficult for one to imagine one simple argument against the reasonableness of this demand.'—UP

155. Agra Jail Detenus' Grievances

Amrita Bazar Patrika, 15 June 1941.

Redress Demanded
Memorandum Submitted to UP Government

Lucknow, 14 June.

A lengthy memorandum setting forth their grievances and demanding their redress by the 20th of this month has been submitted by detenus confined in the Central Jail, Agra, to the UP Government. The memorandum is signed among others by Acharya Narendra Dev, Mr Gopal Narain Saxena (Fyzabad), Malkhan Singh, MLA, (Aligarh), and Mr S.S. Yusuf (Cawnpore).

The signatories state 'inter alia' that the present rules regarding the privileges of a detenu bear no resemblance to similar rules in the past and for all practical purposes the provisions of the UP Jail Manual have been made applicable to them. Arrangements for housing, furniture, provision for sickness, clothing, and other things, are not adequate. Permission has not been given for sleeping in the open during the night. The recent order discriminating between detenus is an innovation and is against the century-old practice. The daily allowance to division II detenus is insufficient.

It is pointed out further that the families of detenus who were earning members have to suffer great privations. It is urged that their premium on insurance policies must be paid by government, and facilities should be provided at Government cost for private study of detained students. Detenus from the UP transferred to Deoli should be repatriated.

Concluding the signatories state that unless their grievances are redressed this state of affairs could not be tolerated any longer and in case no satisfactory response is received by the 20th of this month, they reserve the right to resort to such methods including hunger-strike as they deem proper for the fulfilment of their demands after that date.—AP

156. The Security Prisoners Their Condition Enquiry Demand by Punjab Civil Liberties Union

Amrita Bazar Patrika, 21 June 1941.

A campaign to secure the signatures of prominent citizens on a memorial to be submitted to the Viceroy demanding an impartial enquiry into the conditions of security prisoners marked the commencement in Lahore of the 'C Class and Security Prisoners' Week' by the Punjab Civil Liberties Union.

The memorial, in addition, recommends better treatment for the detenus.

'We understand', the Memorial says, 'that nearly two hundred of His Majesty's subjects in British India are being detained in Deoli Camp without any trial according to the ordinary law of the land. The orders for their detention appear to have been passed, 'inter alia', under Rule 26 of the Defence of India Rules of 1939, framed under the Defence of India Act 1939, which Act is to remain in force during the continuance of the present war and for a period of six months thereafter.

'While in no way minimizing the gravity of the situation created by the present deadly struggle in which British Democracy is pitched against the brute forces of Fascism and while being perfectly alive to the importance of safeguarding the security of India in their grave emergency, we do most humbly submit that the rule of the law—for which British Democracy stands—demands that no subject of His Majesty should be deprived of his liberty by executive government without being found guilty by the King's Court under the ordinary law of the land beyond the possibility of reasonable doubt. The aforesaid detenus do not appear to have been given any opportunity of proving their innocence which normally speaking is to be presumed in their favour.'

The memorial makes the following suggestions:

1. That the detenus should be tried according to the ordinary law of the land, or
2. In the alternative at least a judicial enquiry by a retired high judicial officer or officers be held into the allegations by the executive government against these detenus.
3. An impartial enquiry be held into the conditions under which these detenus are being detained including the consideration of the grievances incorporated in the memorandum said to have been submitted by these detenus, and
4. The rules framed by Government for the extention of the detenus be made available to the public.

Pending a judicial enquiry, the memorandum requests the Government to remove the grievances of detenus regarding repatriation, classification, diet allowances, clothing, prisoners' and family allowances, writing of letters, censorship of newspapers, medical arrangements, parole and non-official visitors, and other things.—AP

157. Government of Madras for Deterrent Sentences

Copy of Confidential Memorandum No. 19451-1, Public (General) Department, Dated 25.6.1941, Tamil Nadu State Archives.

Sub.: Political Agitation: Persons convicted for second and subsequent offences—Instructions.

The Government observes that certain persons who have been convicted for a second time have been awarded very light sentences. While the Government have no desire to fetter the discretion of the courts in the matter, they do not consider that imprisonment for ten weeks, three months or even six months is an adequate sentence for a second conviction. The police should accordingly be instructed to press for deterrent sentences in all cases of second or subsequent convictions.

Deputy Secretary to Government

To

All District Magistrates
The Inspector General of Police
The Commissioner of Police, Madras
Copy to the Chief Presidency Magistrate, Madras
Copy to Home Department.

158. Dentenus in Agra Jail Their Representation Concession by the Government

Amrita Bazar Patrika, 30 June 1941.

The action taken by the UP Government on the representation made by detenus in the Agra Central Jail is set forth in an announcement which says:' Government received two representations from security prisoners in the Agra Central Prison dated 22 May and 4 June, 1941. The first of these reached the Government on 14 June and the second on 17 June. Government have issued orders to secure that any important representations made by prisoners may in future reach them more promptly.

Representations dealt with a large number of matters of very different degrees of importance. With regard to a considerable number of matters which were within his power the Inspector-General of Prisons has himself issued orders to the Superintendent of the Prison. Such matters included lack of privacy in latrines, provision of sheds for bathing, bathing platforms, supply of furniture, and clothing, delay in dispatch and receipt of letters and the supply of books. Government have supplemented these orders by authorizing the Inspector-General to incur without further reference to Government such expenditure as may be necessary to remove any substantial complaint of prisoners in regard to these matters.

Complaint that the prisoners were not allowed to sleep outside has been met by issue of orders granting such permission before the prisoners' representation reached Government.

Government have also increased the diet allowance of Class II prisoners from As. four to As. six per day pending further consideration of this matter.

Government have found themselves unable to agree to the prisoners' demand that the classification of prisoners into two classes which is common to all provinces should be cancelled, that monthly allowances should be given to all prisoners and their dependents, that student prisoners should be allowed to sit for University examinations, and that no prisoners should be transferred to Deoli and those prisoners who have been already transferred should be brought back from detention in jails in the province.

159. Madras Government's Approval of Segregation of Detenus, 21 July 1941

DO No. S/766-4/41, Home Department, Government of Madras, Tamil Nadu State Archives.

My dear Major Gill,

Segregation of various classes of detenus—Your SCDOs. No. nil dated 26.6.1941 and No. 1886/S1/40 dated 3.7.1941.

I am to say that for the present the Government approve of your proposals for the segregation of the various classes of detenus and leftist Defence of India convicts as detailed below.

(1) Student detenus to be accommodated in the quarantine of the Civil Debtors Yard, Central Jail, Rajamundry.

(2) Leftist detenus of greater importance and Rightist detenus, both of greater and lesser importance, to be accommodated in the old female enclosure of the Central Jail, Vellore. Classes I and II need not be separated.

(3) The Leftist detenus of lesser importance to be accommodated in that portion of the close prison at Vellore which has cellular accommodation for 180. Classes I and II need not be separated.

(4) Leftist Defence of India convicts to be accommodated in the quarantine in the Central Jail, Bellary.

2. I am to request you to give effect to such of these proposals as you have not carried out in anticipation of Government's Orders, as soon as possible.

3. The Government sanction the construction of a shed in the close prison of the Central Jail, Vellore for use as a common mess, and the electrification of the cells to be occupied by the detenus. They presume the expenditure on the construction of the shed can be met from the allotment under 'Petty Construction and Repairs', and that your estimate of the cost of electrification will not be exceeded. The Government agree as a special case, to the electrification being done by the jail electrician.

4. As you make no mention of A or B class leftists in Alipuram jail, it is presumed there are none at present. But if there are, I am to ask you to consider whether they might not, with advantage, be transferred to the Trichinopoly enclosure, where they can do no harm among the rightists at present confined there.

5. Apart from the suggestion in paragraph 4 above, as the enclosures at Trichinopoly gradually empty, Government would prefer to keep them available for future eventualities.

Yours sincerely,

Major G.S. Gill, IMS,
Inspector-General of Prisons.

160. Copy of Letter Given by Jayaprakash Narayan and Others to N.M. Joshi [before 31 July 1941][1]

File No. 43/96/41, Home (Political) Department, Government of India, NAI.

Dear Sir,

We take this opportunity of informing you of a serious situation that had developed in this Camp some time ago. We do not know if any news of it appeared in the press, or if it did how far did it represent things correctly.

Some time ago, to be exact from 30 May to [4] June 41 over forty of us security prisoners in both the camps here (over thirty in Camp I and about 12 in Camp II) were on hunger strike. We state briefly the circumstances that led to the strike and the sequence of it.

As you will come to know from the Camp representatives who will acquaint you with the general position, we have been agitating here for certain demands and for the removal of certain grievances. In the midst of this agitation matters were brought to a head by the conduct of the camp authorities and particularly by their callous attitude towards patients seriously ill in the Camp Hospital. As you will have come to know one of our most serious grievances has been in connection with the medical department of the camp. The Medical officer who has now been removed, was not only an incompetent doctor but also extremely unsympathetic and hostile to us.

For some time prior to our hunger strike there were a number of serious cases in the Camp Hospital. Repeated requests to send them to the Ajmer Civil Hospital for better treatment were rejected on various grounds. Suddenly one of the serious patients developed symptoms of delirium due to extreme pain in the abdomen. The Medical Officer, on the pretext that the patient had gone insane, advised the Camp authorities to have him removed from the Hospital, and threatened to even have him chained to his cot. On the patient's refusal to leave the Hospital a posse of armed guards was brought in to remove him by force! This was naturally opposed by all the patients in the Hospital.

When the news of all this reached the Camp, there was great indignation. Over forty of us, as mentioned above, soon thereafter gave notice to the authorities that unless steps were urgently taken (1) to remove the serious cases to Ajmer or to any other suitable Civil Hospital, (2) to transfer the Medical Officer, (3) to arrange for the civil surgeon, Ajmer, to visit the Camp at least once every week till a new M.O. arrives, we would refuse to take any food. There was also a fourth demand which would require a little explanation. Our friend, Mr Beni Madho Rai, who has been mentioned as having developed delirium, was being attended upon by a friend of his. This latter Comrade one day slapped a ward-boy in the hospital for his refusal to do something which it was his duty to do. For this the Camp authorities gave our Comrade solitary cell punishment and convict diet for a week. Since this happened, Mr Rai, though he was not informed of the punishment, kept demanding for his friend to be brought back. Considering the mental condition of this patient we had demanded simply on medical grounds, that the punished Comrade should be sent back to the hospital or to Ajmer if Mr Rai is sent there. We were forced to take recourse to this grave step on account both of the provocation caused by the calling of military guards to use force on a patient and of the realization of our helplessness to effect any improvement in the Hospital through any other means we felt that the lives of our sick friends were sufficiently precious to justify our staking our own for their sake.

Our strike ended on 4 June, all our demands having been conceded. But prior to this, an ugly incident occurred which we wish to bring to your notice so that you may realize better the attitude of the Camp authorities towards us. A day prior to our ending the strike the Superintendent who had been on leave took over charge and he called our representatives to discuss the issues of the strike. There was some difficulty in reaching an agreement on which the Superintendent ordered our representatives to be segregated from us and to be confined in Camp III, which was unoccupied. To call representatives of hunger-strikers for negotiation and then to punish them in this manner is a species of conduct which we better leave it to yourself to describe.

In this connection there are two other incidents which need to be mentioned. Mr Rai whose case has been mentioned was finally sent to Ajmer as a result of our pressure. There he was treated very badly by the Civil Surgeon who personally participated in having him dragged from the Hospital verandah to his room in which he was kept locked up day and night. Being treated in this manner, the patient asked to be sent back to Deoli and said that unless he was sent, then he would not take any food or medicine. There upon he was brought back, but the Civil Surgeon, Ajmer, sent along a report that he was malingering and was not ill at all! We demanded that a Medical enquiry be made into his case and the truth or otherwise of the report be established. But nothing has been done so far about this. On the report of the CS, the Supdt immediately put Mr Rai in solitary confinement for the offence of malingering! Fortunately at this very time the Chief Medical Officer, Ajmer–Merwara, a European gentleman visited the Camp. At our request he examined Mr Rai and on his recommendation he was taken out of the cell and his punishment was remitted.

Such is the manner in which the Medical Officer, the Supdt, and the CS have been behaving and such is the extraordinary manner in which this Camp is being run.

Among the hunger-strikers were the following:

Professor Mota Singh
Mohanlal Gautam
Jogesh Chatterji
Dr G.K. Jetley
Jogendra Shukul
Dhanraj Sharma
Keshav Prasad Sharma
Jayaprakash Narayan

---

1. Jayaprakash Narayan in his 'Deoli Papers' mentions N.M. Joshi's visit to Deoli Detention Camp and the statement that was given to him. A copy of this statement was enclosed with the 'Deoli Papers'. See Document No. 101 in this Chapter.

161. A Jail-view of Satyagraha, 7 August 1941

File No. 43/80/41-Poll (I), Home (Political) Department, Government of India, NAI. Translation of interesting portion from a letter written in Marathi by K.N. Joglekar dated 7 August 1941 to Mrs Ambutai Joglekar.

Nasik Jail,
7 August 1941.

My dear Ambutai,

It is my birth day to-day and is it not natural that I should be reminded of you! Several thoughts are occupying my mind. I feel inclined to take a stock of the life in general and pondering over the same, I am led to believe that a major portion of the life has been spent without much achievement. If I were to think for myself, I find no reason to be sorry. I have served the people honestly and selflessly. But the reason why I feel sorry is the attitude and sentiments in general of the people round about here. How narrow I find the general atmosphere here? The name of the Congress is exploited in the cause of the country and the public. But if the attitude of individuals here is seen, one gets disappointed. What mean, narrow and individualistic view is seen here! Hardly any one can be said to have faith in Satyagraha. How longingly all are waiting for the release from jail. But the formation of the Viceroy's New Executive Council has frustrated hopes of negotiations with Congress and as such all are found cursing Aney and others for the frustration of the hopes of release. Beside the recent announcement of Gandhi of intensifying the movement has disheartened many of them. I have never come across such a disappointing and filthy atmosphere. We witnessed two CD movements while our case was going on at Meerut. Both were failures, one after the other. That there was no public enthusiasm was never felt then. Though they could witness the failure of the movement, they had satisfaction of having done their duty. They felt proud of themselves that they were the soldiers in the struggle of independence. But now there is no trace of these sentiments. One cannot but feel that the Satyagraha was futile and that it was a deception of the public. So many have courted arrest and have come in this jail but honestly speaking no one seems to have any faith in the movement. They have come here because they want to have the right to get elected either in the Assembly in the new elections or in the Corporation. Seeing all this one is led to believe whether Gandhi is deceiving himself, the country, the people, the Government? One gets dejected at all this and the spirit gets suffocated to see how people are deceived by this dramatic performance. When the unlimited ignorance is seen, one feels the extent of the work to be done yet. One realizes the smallness of the efforts, thinking how difficult it was to lead the people step by step. The recent Tilak anniversary celebrations also go to impress the same idea, that one should do his duty without expecting the fruits of it. How futile it is that the work taken up seriously should die out in a day or two. Instead of this it is certainly beneficial in the end, that people should be taught to stand on their own legs, assisting them in the simple and small matters and how enormous is the work before us yet is felt by me while taking a review of the past life. Well?

The war seems to be in full swing. From the present tactics of Russia, she appears to be confident of facing the German attacks for long, which means that we will have to remain in jail for years together. I am keeping myself ready from that point of view and reminded of the jail life at Meerut. I spent 5 years there but the atmosphere was found to be very enthusiastic there. Only a month here but the crowding of people in the round about has disgusted me. Time used to fly away there in talking but here even mixing with people is found to be difficult and hence I feel lonely. Really speaking, this is a time to enjoy freely the field of literature but I am forced to restrict myself to reading singly and hence I am reminded of you the more.

162. Movements of 1,214 Restricted: 1,211 Persons Convicted Action Under Defence of India Act in Bengal

Amrita Bazar Patrika, 12 August 1941.

Replying to a question put by Mr Lalit Chandra Das about orders of restrictions under the Defence of India Act, Hon Khwaja Sir Nazimuddin, Home Member, said at yesterday's meeting of Bengal Legislative Council that the total number of persons whose movements have been restricted in Bengal up to the end of June 1941 are 1,214; persons taken into custody are 281, persons convicted and sentenced number 1,211. The total figure of those arrested is not available. The total numbers of persons called terrorist prisoners in jail are 69. There is no Khaksar restrained, convicted, detained or imprisoned. The Home Minister is not prepared on account of time and labours involved to point out how many of them are Hindus and how many Muslims.

Persons externed so far from Bengal are 18. Government are not aware that there is a widespread apprehension that the Defence of India Act is being misapplied to the consternation of a particular community. The circumstances do not warrant, said Home Minister, the institution of an Enquiry Committee to go into the cases of all sufferers under the Defence of India Act.

163. Jawaharlal Nehru's Letter to Inspector-general of Prisons, United Provinces, 23 August 1941 From 'Prison Diary with Letters'

SWJN, Vol. 11, pp. 683–4.

Sir,

For some time past various complaints have appeared in the public press in regard to the bad treatment accorded to the satyagrahi prisoners in the Camp Jail in Lucknow. Recently some very amazing charges have so appeared, which state that on at least two occasions lathi charges were made on the prisoners by orders of the jail staff and a large number were badly injured; that the conditions prevailing in the jail are abominable in the extreme; that food is frequently not given and when given is utterly unfit for human consumption; that about 200 of the prisoners were put in fetters and a large number in solitary cells; that prisoners are deliberately starved and kept in such a manner that they grow faint and utterly weak; that threats are continually being held out to them and are sometimes translated into attacks upon them; that sanitary conditions are non-existent; that there is no proper medical arrangement; that no newspapers or books are provided or allowed; that letters are seldom, if ever, received or dispatched; that two deaths recently took place among the prisoners, who were removed to King George's Medical Hospital on the point of death, where they expired within a few hours; that even when the Inspector General inspected the jail, the prisoners were locked up in their barracks and were thus unable to approach him. These are some of the charges made. I am not aware of any official denial of these charges, and, in any event, such official denials seldom err on the side of veracity and little faith is attached to them.

I have refrained from addressing you on this subject, in spite of repeated complaints appearing publicly about the Lucknow Camp Jail and other jails in the province, as I had no desire to interfere in any way with the jail administration of the province. That administration, and the Provincial Government behind it, is notoriously backward and incompetent, and the ideas that govern them in regard to the treatment of prisoners are reminiscent of the middle ages. But when gross, deliberate, and inhuman ill-treatment is added to the general incompetence, it becomes difficult to tolerate this state of affairs and to submit to it with quiet resignation. You have been good enough to accord me various conveniences and privileges which ordinarily are denied to the average prisoner. But these very conveniences and privileges become hateful to me when I realize that my friends and colleagues are being subjected to a treatment which can only be called barbarous. As you are no doubt aware, it has been our general policy to submit to jail discipline, unless this is considered humiliating. On the whole, we have all done this, and we have even put up with conditions which were deliberately meant to harass and annoy, but there is a limit to this and I fear, that if the conditions in the Lucknow Camp Jail are any indication of the policy of the Government functioning at present, it may become necessary for us to revise our policy and to refuse to submit to jail discipline, and invite the consequences of such disobedience.

I have ventured to write to you on this subject as it is of considerable importance and likely to have far-reaching consequences. I cannot remain a silent spectator of the insults to and the sufferings of my colleagues.

Yours faithfully,
Jawaharlal Nehru

164. Jawaharlal Nehru's Note in his Prison Diary on Lucknow Camp Jail, 25 August 1941

SWJN, Vol. 11, pp. 685–6.

25 August, Tuesday.

My letter to the IG was sent on to him yesterday, so I was informed. This has naturally ruffled the Supt. and Jailer somewhat. They are worried not because of the occurrences in Lucknow Camp Jail or because I have written to the IG, though the strong language of my letter is disturbing to them. Their main concern is where they come into the picture! They might be asked how I managed to get news of these occurrences, why were the newspapers delivered to me not censored. Why the particular items not blacked out or cut out?

So, the Suptd sent Shanti Prapanna Sharma on to me yesterday morning to say that he would send on my letter to the IG, but that in future particular passages in the newspapers relating to other jails would be removed. I was angry as it was full of indignation, and Shanti's message did not improve matters. I burst out at him and cursed the jail administration and all its works, and of course the Provincial Govt and the British Govt I told him that if any newspapers, with parts cut out of them, were delivered to me, I would hurl them out of my barrack. I was going to put up with no insults. Did they think that they could buy my silence or acquiescence in this evil deed by giving me a few so-called privileges? To hell with all these privileges. Did they think that they could separate us from our comrades and treat the latter as they wanted to? Every insult to the latter was an insult to me; every lathi blow to them was a blow to me. I was at war with the British Govt and all its underlings and I wanted no consideration and would give none—and so on. Poor Shanti was paralysed, and standing behind him the Deputy Jailer, in all his official glory of parade-day uniform, was also somewhat unnerved.

So Shanti went back, apologizing profusely, as if he had been in error or was in any way responsible! Later the Supt., Dr Srivastava, came round on his parade day inspection. He referred briefly to having sent on my letter to the IG and to the fact that newspapers were already censored by the Press Department of Govt and so no further censoring was necessary! And then he went on to speak to Ranjit about his health and c.

The National Herald came with a lurid tale of Jungle Law in Lucknow Camp Jail giving details of the number of persons injured during the lathi charges—over three hundred casualties, quite a large number of them serious. Other particulars. Anger blazed up within me and for the rest of the day kept smouldering. What should I do? What could I do? Just writing to the IG was ridiculously little. Yet what more could I do?

Towards evening a new idea formed itself in my mind—I should send out a statement for publication in the *Herald,* without the knowledge or approval of the jail authorities. That is, I should smuggle out a statement and thus deliberately commit a breach of jail discipline and an offence under the Prisons Act. The statement to be published under my name of course, and therein I would invite the jail authorities and the Prov. Govt to take action against me, to deprive me of my so-called privileges, in fact to do their damnedest. In that statement I would unburden myself on the Lucknow Camp Jail occurrences, other happenings in jails, the behaviour and incompetence of the Govt, and my contempt generally for the breed of quislings in this country!

How was I to send this out? Nan might come to visit Ranjit on the 30th or thereabouts and she could be made the messenger. Yet I did not like the idea of involving her directly. But whatever step I took, others would be involved—Ranjit of course.

And then my mind went on to consider choice phrases for this statement. The Battle of Lucknow Camp Jail! It was an angry and slashing draft that framed itself in my mind. Later it began to tone itself down—when the action was in a way strong, why use strong and undignified language—I would be making a public statement after ten months. It should be dignified.

Having thought of this method of taking action, I felt more at ease. And then it struck me that my days of writing and receiving letters were numbered. All this would be stopped soon enough. Therefore I hastened to write a few letters last evening and by tomorrow or the day after I shall finish off all that are necessary. Interviews also will stop....

165. N.M. Joshi's Report on Deoli Detention Camp, September 1941

The Bombay Civil Liberties Union Publication, File No. 24/14/41-Poll (I), Home (Political) Department, Government of India, NAI.

With the permission of the Government of India I visited the Deoli Detention Camp for Detenues or Security Prisoners in the month of July 1941. I arrived at Deoli on Sunday, 20th July and left it on Tuesday 22nd July. Major Craster, the Superintendent, gave me the necessary facilities and opportunities to see the various parts of the Camp and to come into contact with the Detenues for which my sincere thanks are due to him.

I visited barracks where the detenues live, the kitchens, and the dining rooms, the bathing places, and the sanitary arrangements, the library rooms, the playing field, and the hospital and heard what the detenues had to say about these arrangements. I also interviewed the representative committees of the two Divisions of the Camp and also interviewed those of the individual detenues who expressed their desire to talk to me.

When I visited the Camp, there were 215 detenues there, of whom, 107 belonged to Division I and 108 to Division II. Out of the total number, 103 belonged to the Punjab, 81 to UP and the remaining 31 to other Provinces taken together.

Two Fundamental Complaints

Apart from the fact that the detenues were detained without trial, the most fundamental complaints of the detenues were, first, demanding repatriation to their respective home provinces and second, asking for the abolition of the system of classifying the detenues into Division I and Division II giving unequal treatment; detenues in Division I being given somewhat better conditions in almost all respects than the detenues in Division II.

Repatriation

The demand for repatriation is based on two grounds. Firstly, the detenues complain that the place is malarious. Not being a medical man, I hesitate to express an opinion on this point. The Superintendent gave me figures regarding the incidence of malaria showing that the average number of cases of malaria is going down and that the average percentage of malaria cases for the months of April, May, and June of this year was 4.4 per cent.

The second ground on which the demand for repatriation is based is that the place being distant from the home provinces, on account of cost of travelling the detenues finds it extremely difficult to keep into touch with their families. The detenues are allowed two interviews in a month with the relatives or friends but only a very small percentage of detenues get the benefit of this concession. The grievance is well founded and ought to be removed by repatriating those detenues who want to be removed to their home provinces or by Government undertaking to bear the cost of travelling to Deoli by the relatives of the detenues for the interviews. I would suggest that the least the Government ought to do is to pay to the relatives of the detenues the travelling cost for a certain number of interviews in a year.

Abolition of Classification

The second fundamental demand of the detenues for the abolition of their classification into Divisions I and II with unequal privileges goes against the policy adopted by the Government of India recently regarding treatment of political and other prisoners. Without going into the question of the justification or otherwise for the policy, it has to be admitted that the policy does cause bitterness and heart-burning. The detenues, generally speaking, belong to certain well-defined political groups and do their work outside as equal comrades and their objection to being classified into unequal classes in prisons ought to be respected.

The classification being done by the Provinces applying different tests and by different officers, the result is patently irrational. When we find that out of the 103 detenues from Punjab, 17 are given Division I and the rest Division II and all the 81 detenues from UP are given Division I, the unfairness in actual classification becomes apparent. The injustice is felt more bitterly when detenues classified on different tests are brought together in one place like Deoli. Under these circumstances, the demand for the abolition of Divisions at Deoli is justified whatever may be the general policy of the Government as regards the treatment of political prisoners.

The detenues complained that persons in the two Divisions are not permitted to associate with each other. The Superintendent holds that as the detenues in the two Divisions are allowed to associate with each other freely on the playing field for two hours and a half daily, enough scope is given to the persons in the two Divisions to associate with each other. One hesitates to make suggestions for partially meeting this demand. But even if the abolition of the classification is not accepted, I would suggest, firstly, that there should be at least no discrimination between the two Divisions in the most primary needs of the detenues, namely, food and clothing, and secondly, there should be an enquiry by a competent person into individual cases of wrong classification. The difficulty due to the fact that the classification is done by Provinces has to be got over by securing the consent of the Provincial Governments to accept the decision of a competent person appointed by the Government of India for this purpose.

Food, Personal and Family Allowances

Food Allowances

Complaints regarding allowances for food are of two kinds: First that the allowance is insufficient and secondly that there is inequality between the allowance sanctioned for Division I and that for Division II. At present detenues in Division I are paid 12 *annas* dailyand those in Division II are paid 9 annas daily. When Government of India maintained a Camp for detenues from Bengal from 1932–8, the allowance was larger. The Superintendent confirmed that in 1932 the detenues were paid Re. one daily plus 3 annas for fish twice a week. But in 1935, the allowance was reduced to 15 annas daily and the fish allowance was cancelled. It is natural that the detenues should ask for the same amount on this occasion as the detenues were given on the last occasion and the claim is fortified by the fact that the present price level of food is very much higher than before. As regards the discrimination between the food allowance given to Division I and Division II, I have already suggested that the discrimination should be removed on other than economic grounds. But I support the claim of Division II for increase in the allowance even from the point of view of its adequacy for providing enough food of good quality. There is also a complaint that the contractors, having a monopoly, prices higher than the market rates are charged. The Superintendent should make an effort by some method such as by securing an authorized price list from Ajmer to convince the detenues that the contractors do not charge unreasonable prices or why a competitive system is impracticable.

Personal Allowance

The detenues demand an adequate personal allowance for purchasing certain articles of necessity and comfort such as tooth brush, tooth paste, shaving materials, and others. The Superintendent informs me that in 1932–8 a personal allowance of Rs 11 per month was paid for clothing, stationery, toilet, cigarettes, and other things. At present the detenues in Division I are permitted to spend up to Rs 10 per month and detenues in Division II Rs 5 per month, out of their private resources and the detenues are expected to secure some of the necessary articles out of this amount. But the figures of amounts received by detenues from their private resources show that only a small percentage of detenues can draw upon their private resources to spend Rs 10 or Rs 5 per month and the case for providing some personal allowance can be clearly established. The Superintendent informed me that on the former occasion articles of clothing and some other necessary footwear, soap, stationery, and other things, were purchased out of the personal allowance but at present clothing is provided free. But besides clothing, there are several necessaries of life which the detenues ought to have and Government should either provide them or give a personal allowance out of which they can purchase them. There is a complaint that detenues are not even permitted to receive money except from authorized persons. In my view there is no justification for this restriction. In the case of some detenues private money may not be available from relatives and personal friends. In such cases some organization interested in their welfare may be permitted to send them money.

Family Allowance

The detenues claim that as they have been deprived of their freedom for political reasons without any charge being established against them after a fair trial, Government ought to take the responsibility for maintaining their families. Governnient have on other occasions accepted the principle underlying this claim and even on the present occasion Government have agreed to pay family allowances in necessitous cases. A large number of detenues have sent applications to Provincial Governments for family allowances but, so far as detenues in Deoli are concerned, not more than two or three detenues receive such allowance. It cannot be easily believed that out of 215 detenues, family allowance is deserved only by such a small number. Moreover, there is good justification for not restricting the payment of family allowance only to necessitous cases when persons with responsibilities for maintaining a family have been deprived of their freedom without any charge of their having done any wrong being established against them in a fair trial.

Clothing, Medical Arrangements, Books, Newspapers, Furniture

I do not propose to deal in detail with the complaints regarding all the necessary articles and facilities. I shall content myself by making brief observations about some of them. As regards clothing, I have already suggested that there should be no inequality between Division I and Division II. I would also suggest that choice should be left to the detenues regarding the kind of cloth they should have and that when some article is found to be unserviceable, for which the detenue is not responsible, it should be replaced although such replacement may be in excess of the sanctioned schedule. One pair of *chappels* or shoes, in my opinion, will be found to be insufficient. In any case unserviceable shoes should be replaced by new ones before such replacement is due. Reasonable quantity of stationery should be provided at Government expense. There is good deal of discontent regarding medical arrangements which, is in my view, is due to the fact that a first class hospital with first class experts cannot be provided in an isolated camp for a total population of about four hundred, and the detenues being mostly city dwellers feel this need. To a layman's eye, the small hospital at the Camp appeared to be what a place like Deoli can expect to have and the staff possess the necessary university or other qualifications. But I shall refrain from expressing more definite opinion for fear of doing injustice either to the Superintendent or the medical staff on the one hand or the suffering detenues on the other. There are complaints regarding furniture being insufficient and I would suggest that the Division II detenues should be given a table and a chair each or at least some more chairs and tables for common use. Apart from the complaint regarding unjustified censoring of books and newspapers, there is also a complaint that there are not enough books to read and secondly some of the newspapers which the detenues would like to have are not available. At present an arrangement is made to get a stock of 100 books from the Ajmer Public Library, which is replaced from time to time by a fresh set of 100 books. To have more books involves only a question of cost. Regular supply of about 300 books every month may remove the complaint to a reasonable extent. The detenues are also asking for a radio set as a source of recreation and Government should not grudge expenditure of the necessary amount.

Committees

I was glad to find that two representative committees of the two Divisions in the Camp are recognized for discussing the complaints of the detenues with the Superintendent. I have no doubt that such discussions regularly and frequently held in a spirit of mutual understanding will help in the removal of at least smaller complaints.

Barracks

Most of the detenues have to live in big halls in the barracks devoid of all privacy. Although I do not know the feeling of the detenues in this matter, I would prefer smaller halls in which not more than three or four detenues should be expected to live. The detenues complain about over-crowding and to my eyes the complaint seemed to be real. But the Superintendent informs me that there is a barrack for the Division II detenues which is almost empty.

Censorship

Books: The detenues have a serious complaint that they are not permitted to have certain kind of books, specially books on Communism. One easily understands that Government should not permit books which they have legally banned, to be taken in the Camp. But I fail to understand why other books on Communism written in a scientific spirit should not be permitted to be used in the Camp. To serious students of economics and writers on the subject this is a great hardship and there are a number of such students in the Camp. I would urge upon Government the necessity to reconsider this matter.

Letters: There are also complaints that private letters sent and received by the detenues are unreasonably censored. One can understand in-coming letters to the detenues being censored only if they contain information which the detenues are not to be allowed to have on the ground that the information is likely to affect the life in the Camp, or the letters from detenues to their relatives being censored on the ground that they send out false information regarding their life in the Camp. But censoring of letters for any other purpose is in my judgment unjustified. I am unable to express any opinion on the actual censoring of letters in the Superintendent's office. Rules for the Deoli Camp prohibit correspondence between persons confined in different jails. This rule has no justification and this prohibition does not exist in the rules of some of the Provinces and as each such letter is subjected to censoring twice, there is no fear of any evil arising out of such correspondence.

Newspapers: Censoring of newspapers also can be defended only on the ground that a newspaper contains news which will affect the life in the Camp. To go beyond this is unjustified.

Breaches of Discipline

The Rules empower the Superintendent to impose several penalties for breaches of discipline, temporary confinement in a solitary cell being one of them. The Superintendent has assured me that this form of punishment has been used very rarely, only three times in the past nine months. I, however, feel that in these modern times this form of penalty may be altogether removed from the Rules.

Parole

Several cases of applications for parole to enable detenues to go to see their relatives in their serious illness, having been refused or even being replied to too late, were brought to my notice. Provincial Governments have to recognize the urgency of taking prompt decisions on such applications and also to recognize the claims of human feelings in their decisions.

Non-official Visitors

A suggestion has been made that non-official visitors should be appointed to visit the Camp from time to time. At present some official visitors pay occasional visits. But non-official visitors will give greater satisfaction to the detenues and it should not be difficult for the Government of India to secure for this purpose some responsible non-officials of recognized position in public life, members of the Provincial Legislature from UP or some members of the Central Legislature, and arrange their visits in such a way that some one of the non-official visitors may pay a visit every fortnight. Denial of regular inspection by responsible non-officials unnecessarily creates a feeling of mystery in the public mind. Regular visits by non-official visitors will also give a feeling to the detenues that their conditions of life are being examined and watched by responsible public men. It may also be suggested that the rules regulating the life of the Deoli Camp may be published and made available to any one who cares to read them.

166. Camp Superintendent's Report on Number of Security Prisoners in Deoli Detention Camp on 19 September 1941

File No. 43/1/41-Poll. (I), Home (Political) Department, NAI.

Statement showing vacancies available in Deoli Detention Camp, Deoli, on 19th September 1941.

	Accommodation available	**No. of Security Prisoners present**	**No. of Security Prisoners arrived on 19.9.1941 from Central Jail, Lahore**	**Total No. of Security Prisoners to date**	**Vacancies available**
Class I (Camp I)	127	108	–	108	19
Class II (Camp II)	96	94	–	94	2
Class II (Camp III)	100	41	1	42	58
Camp 'A' (Isolation Barracks)	12	3	–	3	9

167. Deoli Detenus' Letter to Chief Secretary, Government of India, on Resorting to Hunger Strike

Bimal Prasad (ed.), *Jayaprakash Narayan Selected Works,* Vol. 3, 2003, pp. 325–6.

To
The Chief Secretary,
Govt of India,
New Delhi

Sir,

We, the undersigned, find ourselves constrained to intimate Govt that in view of their attitude of continued indifference to our very fair and reasonable demands communicated to them nearly seven months ago, we are compelled to take recourse to the last weapon that is at the disposal of prisoners anywhere in the world namely that of hunger-strike.

We shall briefly refer to the circumstances that have led to this decision. On and about 31 March 1941, a memorandum was sent to Govt incorporating a number of our demands, the chief among which were: (i) granting to us the status of State prisoner, (ii) abolition of classification of detenus, (iii) payment of an adequate family allowance to all those who have got dependents or such liabilities to meet as insurance premiums, (iv) a daily diet allowance of Rs 16 [Re. 1-6] and a pocket allowance of Rs 32 per month, (v) repatriation to our respective provinces, and (vi) payment of traveling expenses to those who come to interview us.

A few months later we wrote to Govt again for permission to correspond with friends and relations who may be in other camps or prisons.

We had several occasions to remind Govt of these demands through official visitors who happened to visit the camp.

After considerable delay Govt granted a few of our minor demands. But all the major demands remain unfulfilled to this day. Besides, such ever-present grievances as lack of proper medical treatment, particularly of such serious cases as are beyond the competence of the local medical officers, the case of Sardar Kulbir Singh is an instance in point—the irksome treatment of the Camp authorities, censoring of letters, newspapers, books, and others, continue to remain unredressed. Lately the system of cell punishment has become intolerably common and the authorities seem to think that they are free to do with us as they please. Furthermore, even in the gravest circumstances such as the death of a near relation, parole, for which provision is made in the rules has been persistently denied to us. There has been only one such [*sic*] instance in all these many months which goes rather to support than deny our case.

Taking all these facts and circumstances into consideration, we have come to the conclusion that there is no other self-respecting course open to us but to stake our lives for what we consider our just rights and privileges.

Accordingly we hereby intimate Govt that unless we are satisfied before 22 October, 1941 regarding the questions stated above and in our memoranda of previous dates as also those that were mentioned by us from time to time, we shall resort to hunger-strike beginning from 22 October, 1941.

We remain
Yours faithfully,

1. Jayaprakash Narayan, General Secretary, AI Congress Socialist Party, Ex-member Congress Working Committee.
2. Damodar Swarup Seth, formerly General Secretary UP Congress Committee.
3. Mohanlal Gautam, MLA, President All India Kisan Sabha.
4. Dr G.K. Jetley, MBBS, Kisan leader of UP
5. Benimadho Roy, Revolutionary leader of UP
6. Kabul Singh, MLA (Punjab).
7. Harjap Singh, MLA (Punjab).
8. Munshi Ahmed Din, Leader, Punjab Congress Socialist Party.
9. Kulbir Singh and Kultar Singh, Brothers of Sardar Bhagat Singh.
10. Professor Tilak Raj Chaddha, Rawalpindi College.
11. Balwant Singh Dukhia, President District Congress Committee Hoshiapur.
12. Jogendra Shukla, Andaman returned Revolutionary leader of Bihar.
13. Shyama Charan Bhartwar-do-.
14. Shaukat Usmani, Member Communist International.
15. Jogesh Chatterji, Ex-Kakori prisoner.
16. Mota Singh Anandpuri, Sikh leader of Punjab.
17. Ramchandra, President, District Urban Congress Committee Lahore, and 191 others in all 208 Security prisoners in Deoli Detention Camp.

168. Amenities for Detenus

Amrita Bazar Patrika, 25 October 1941.

Conditions in the Deoli Detention Camp: Mr N.M. Joshi's Suggestions being Considered by Government of India

New Delhi, 24 October.

The Government of India, says a press note, are giving their careful consideration to Mr N.M. Joshi's suggestions in regard to the rules, amenities and conditions in the Deoli Detention Camp. Some time is bound to elapse before a decision can be taken owing to the fact that several Provincial Governments are also concerned and have to be consulted.

Mr Joshi visited Deoli in July and recently issued a pamphlet entitled 'Deoli Detention Camp—Impressions and Suggestions'. Two accounts of Mr Joshi's visit to Deoli based on its pamphlet have been published in the press, but both omit the general background of the visit together with certain passages which show that Mr Joshi was accorded every facility to ascertain for himself the manner in which the camp is being run and the detenus' views thereon. They also show that Mr Joshi was by no means dissatisfied with all that he saw. As these passages are relevant to a dispassionate consideration of Mr Joshi's suggestions, they are reproduced here.

Arrangements in Camp

At the outset Mr Joshi says:

> I visited barracks, where the detenus live, the kitchens, and the dining rooms, the bathing places, and the sanitary arrangements, the library rooms, the playing field, and the hospital and heard what the detenus had to say about these arrangements. I also interviewed the representative committees of the two divisions of the camp and also interviewed those of the individual detenus who expressed their desire to talk to me.

Dealing with the complaint that Deoli is malarious Mr Joshi says, 'Not being a medical man, I hesitate to express an opinion on this point.'

Dealing with the complaint that prisoners in the two divisions are not permitted to associate with one another Mr Joshi says:

> The Superintendent holds that as the detenus in the two divisions are allowed to associate with each other freely on the playing field for two hours and a half daily, enough scope is given to the persons in the two divisions to associate with each other. One hesitates to make suggestions for partially meeting this demand.

Medical Arrangements

On the question of medical arrangements Mr Joshi says:

> To a layman'eye, the small hospital at the camp appeared to be what a place like Deoli can expect to have and the staff possesses the necessary university or other qualifications. But I shall refrain from expressing more definite opinion for fear of doing injustice either to the Superintendent or the medical staff on the one hand or the suffering detenus on the other.

Censoring of Letters

As regards family allowances Mr Joshi noted that 'even on the present occasion Government have agreed to pay family allowances in necessitous cases.' In connection with the censorship of letters Mr Joshi says:

> One can understand incoming letters to the detenus being censored only if they contain information which the detenus are not to be allowed to have on the ground that the information is likely to affect the life in the camp, or the letters from detenus to their relatives being censored on the ground that they send out false information regarding their life in the camp. But censoring of letters for any other purpose is in my judgment unjustified. I am unable to express any opinion on the actual censoring of letters in the Superintendent's office.

The practice which Mr Joshi recommends is that actually followed in the camp; and it is a fact that the number of letters withheld was greatly decreased lately since the security prisoners have realized that they will not be allowed to send out false statements regarding camp conditions.

Breaches of Discipline

In referring to breaches of discipline and the punishment of confinement in a solitary cell, which he deprecates, Mr Joshi adds in his report that 'the Superintendent has assured me that this form of punishment had only been used three times in nine months.'

Personal Allowances

In dealing with the question of personal allowances Mr Joshi has noted that among the articles which the former allowance of Rs 11 per month was intended to cover only clothing is now provided free and that in the absence of such an allowance the prisoners are now short of various necessaries of life. In this respect Mr Joshi has not correctly understood the information given to him by the Superintendent. The facts are as follows: In view of the personal allowance of Rs 11 per mensem allowed to detenus in the late jail, security prisoners receive the following articles at Government expense instead:

Clothing and shoes and their replacement or repair, cooking untensils, plates, glasses, spoons, cups, and other things. Toilet articles such as soap, hair oil for sikhs, neemsticks or tooth-brushes, and powder, for those who are not accustomed to using neemsticks.

Razors, brushes, soap, hair-cutting machines, and nail clippers are supplied to convict-barbers who attend on the security prisoners.

The following articles of stationery are also provided free: writing papers, envelopes, pen, inkpot, ink, and stamps.

Exercise books are provided free to those prisoners who cannot afford to buy them and require them for genuine educational purposes.

Newspapers, which were also purchased from the previous Rs 11 allowance, are provided free.

From studying the prisoners' private cash accounts it appears that security prisoners mostly spend their private cash on articles such as cigarettes, biris, matches, face creams, greeting telegrams, and other things.—AP

169. Central Legislative Assembly: Debate on Deoli Hunger Strike, 29 October 1941

Indian Annual Register, 1941, Vol. II, pp. 113–15.

Mr Joshi, moving adjournment of the House, said that he was doing so in order that attention might be drawn to the grievances of the detenus and that the discussion in the House might result in a satisfactory settlement of the hunger-strike and the people of India might be free from the anxiety caused by it. He recalled the resolution on the grievances of the detenus and the debate on it in the Assembly last November and said that if Government had done something to meet those grievances at that time, this hunger-strike would perhaps have been avoided. The detenus made a representation on their grievances to the Government in April or May. Having heard about these grievances he himself visited Deoli with the Government of India's permission in July and published his impressions and suggestions. When the detenus made their representation to the Government of India, they expected prompt attention to those grievances. Unfortunately a good deal of time had been allowed to elapse. The grievances, Mr Joshi said, were that they were kept in Deoli which was far away from their homes, Deoli was no health resort, and when it was remembered that Italian and German prisoners were detained in cool Himalayan hills, the complaint of the Indian detenus was not difficult to understand. Further, it was difficult for their relatives to see them in Deoli because of the distance. Their other grievances were against their classification into A and B classes, absence of provision for their families and dependents, and inadequate allowances in jail, namely twelve annas for A class and nine annas for the B class.

It might be said that there was no justification for the hunger-strike but the detenus had waited for four or five months. He was not suggesting that they should not have waited longer but there was a limit, Government had stated they could not consider grievances unless the hunger-strike was given up. As one associated with labour, he knew that grievances were not considered until a strike was actually called and then the authorities said that they could not consider grievances until the strike was called off. He asked Government not to stand on prestige but only to consider whether the grievances were real or not and if they were real to remove them.

Mr *A.N. Chattopadhya* said what was asked for was pure and simple justice and added that these men belonged to the intelligentsia and were used to better amenities of life than those given them now. He urged the formation of a committee of the House to see the real conditions in Deoli so that they might testify if necessary from time to time as to the conditions of the detenus and on grievances which needed redress.

Mr *Govind Deshmukh* commented on Sir *Henry Gidney's* failure to see that it was now more than a month and a half since Government received Mr Joshi's report. If Government delayed equally long their consideration of some grievance relating to the IMS or to the Anglo-Indian community, Sir Henry Gidney would have been more impatient than the detenus had been. Mr *Deshmukh* asked, would the provision of a few amenities like repatriation to their Provinces and more opportunities to relatives to see them, increase the danger that the detenus were said to constitute to the State?

Sir *Reginald Maxwell,* Home Member, before replying to the debate gave the latest information about the hunger-strike and said that there were now 204 prisoners involved: their general health was satisfactory and none of them was seriously ill. He had no doubt, proceeded the Home Member, of Mr Joshi's sincerity but the House must remember that its reception of the motion would inevitably have its effect on the prisoners' action. He pointed out that their demands bearing on their physical well-being had been considered and a large number of them granted from time to time, such as, an increase in their diet allowance, clothing, mosquito nets and extra cooking utensils. But their demand was that they should be repatriated to their home provinces and he submitted that that was not a demand for which any prisoner was entitled to go on hunger strike. It had to be assumed that there were reasons for keeping these persons in Government custody and if their physical well-being was well looked after; he maintained it did not greatly matter where they were kept. The division into two classes, the speaker explained, was adopted after consultation with representatives of the Home Departments of the Provinces and it was not possible for the Central Government to alter that arrangement without consulting the Provincial Governments. The reason for the division was that, among the persons detained, some were definitely of high status; some had University Degrees, while others were cheap agitators. How, he asked, could both these classes be kept together? As regards daily allowance, the speaker said, the demand was that it should be increased to Re. 16. Their physical well-being, he declared, did not require the increase. As regards the demand for adequate family allowance to the dependents of the Security prisoners, he pointed out that in necessitous cases family allowances were being granted. Similarly, facilities to relatives to visit them and to enable the prisoners themselves to visit sick relatives had been granted.

Demands about their place of confinement, Sir Reginald continued, were political demands, and he maintained that they were demands which suited their own fancy but were in no way necessary for them. Mr Joshi's report, the Home Member went on, was seen by the prisoners themselves and before the strike started, they were warned that the consideration of the report would be prejudiced by any headstrong action on their part. He was himself taking up some of the suggestions made by Mr Joshi but the hunger-strike started and the whole thing fell to the ground. He explained that the present daily allowance was sufficient to provide the prisoners with many luxuries. For instance, in September alone these luxuries supplied to them included thirty-six tins of preserved pine apple, nineteen bottles of Australian honey (Sir *Cowasji Jahangir:* Why Australian?) 403 apples, 827 bananas, fourteen seers of almonds. (Mr *Jamnadas Mehta:* What is the number of the prisoners and over what period? You are misleading the House). The real reason, proceeded the Home Member, was political, and he quoted from Mr Jai Prakash Narain's letter which, he said, made it clear that the writer was thinking of strikes entirely in terms of party propaganda and was asking that strikes should be undertaken when schools and colleges were open and the Central Assembly was meeting. These prisoners, concluded the Home Member, were endangering their own lives and were not furthering their own cause. The House could definitely discourage such attempts; but give way to strikes of this kind he would not.

Mr *Jamnadas Mehta* said that even if 1,500 bananas were supplied to them in a month, it would come to fifty bananas a day. Divided among 200 prisoners it meant one-fourth of a banana each. Did the Home Member call it a luxury? Those nineteen tins of honey for a month divided among two hundred prisoners would be enough to wet their teeth and there would be nothing to go down their throat. 'I think', he added, 'it is a cruel joke to describe these as luxuries (cheers). To say that to people of high status accustomed to a better standard of living one-fourth of a banana is a luxury is to practise a joke on their susceptibilities. I would rather be out than eat your one-fourth of a banana in jail.' It was no consolation, even, that their physical well-being was looked after. They were not prisoners found guilty of any crime but were merely detained on suspicion. Hunger-strike was an extreme form of protest. It might be designed to synchronize with the opening of the Assembly. If the detenus wanted their grievances to be heard what was wrong in going on strike at the time the Assembly sat? That only showed their faith in this House. It was the most appropriate thing to do. If the House was not sitting there would be no one to listen to their grievances. To have his grievances ventilated in the best forum available to him was the right of the citizen. If Government were satisfied that the conditions in Deoli were so good, they should give members of the House an opportunity to visit that place. He asked the Home Member not to insist on withdrawal of hunger-strike before taking action.

Mr *N.M. Joshi* reiterated his intention that discussion in the House should expedite the ending of the unfortunate situation and that Government should, out of fairness and justice, be prompt in giving attention to the grievances of the detenus. In normal circumstances, the people who were in the Deoli jail would not themselves advocate a hunger-strike; but the detenus were not in normal circumstances. It was wrong to treat their hunger-strike as a threat. It was undertaken by people who were helpless and desperate. He would beg of the Home Member not to entertain false ideas of prestige or of what was subversive of discipline. Let him not wait till the strike was over. If the removal of the grievances would end the strike, Government's prestige would not suffer. Statements of Mr Jai Prakash Narain, which had been quoted in the House, he said, were those of a man living an abnormal and unnatural life under detention. Those statements could not be given much weight. He concluded by expressing the hope that the debate would induce the Government to take up a reasonable and generous attitude over this matter and remove the grievances. He also hoped that members of the Legislature would watch over this situation.

The motion was rejected without a division and the House adjourned.

170. Disband Deoli

Editorial, *Bombay Chronicle*, 1 November 1941.

Mr N.M. Joshi's adjournment motion in the Central Legislative Assembly on the Deoli hunger-strike was foredoomed to failure in the House as at present constituted. But for that very reason Government's spokesman might have been at least fair and dignified in his reference to prisoners who were starving and unable to defend themselves against his petty gibes and accusations. These men are not criminals. They may be, in the absence of judicial trial as innocent as their critics in the Assembly. Their grievances are many and long-standing. When they were not redressed and the prisoners went on a hunger-strike some months ago, they were persuaded to suspend it on the understanding that their grievances were being considered by Government. To help both Government and the prisoners in bringing about a settlement Mr N.M. Joshi visited the camp in July and published his impressions and suggestions shortly after. That his findings were reasonable is clear from the fact that Government approvingly published the other day lengthy extracts from his report. Gandhiji, who never approves of clamour for unnecessary amenities by prisoners, described Mr Joshi's recommendations as 'over-moderate.' The main recommendations were repatriation of the prisoners to their provinces, abolition of class distinctions, provision for families, and adequate allowances for themselves. Though the recommendations were 'over-moderate' the prisoners adopted them in the hope of a speedy settlement.

Callous Delay

Government, however, are still delaying their decisions, and when in their desperation the prisoners go on a hunger-strike, Government make that an excuse for further delay. The Home Member said in effect: 'Even if the demands are reasonable, we refuse even to consider them so long as the hunger-strike lasts, whatever the consequences.' Callousness can hardly go further. The Home Member also made an unworthy attempt to show that the prisoners were practically rolling in luxury as in one month they could purchase from their allowances quantities of honey, apples, almonds, and 827 bananas. But as Mr Jamnadas Mehta pertinently pointed out even if 1,600 bananas were supplied in a month to the 200 prisoners, it meant only one fourth of a banana each, and those nineteen tins of honey for a month divided among two hundred prisoners 'would be enough to wet their teeth and there would be nothing to go down their throat.' It is, indeed, a cruel and unworthy joke to suggest that the detenus live a life of luxury. The Home Member utterly failed to show that the detenus' demands were unreasonable. His plea that they were not genuine as being necessary for physical well-being but were only political propaganda is no argument but is only attributing motives. Two hundred men are not likely to invite pangs of hunger unless they are conscious of a grave wrong.

Expedite Justice

If Government have a sense of fairness and justice, they must stop indulging in irrelevant arguments. They must impartially and impersonally consider the justice of the demands, and as Gandhiji suggests, 'justice should be expedited in order to alleviate avoidable suffering.' As regards food the public will readily support Gandhiji's view expressed in the following words in his latest statement: 'It is cruel to distinguish between the food of the different classes. The needs in the majority of cases of the political prisoners are identical. I suggest that the rations of all political prisoners should approach what is known as balanced diet with the permission to replenish it at the prisoner's expense.' This is for all politicals in all prisons. So far as the Deoli Camp is concerned, the universal demand is that it should be disbanded at once and the prisoners should be sent to their own respective provinces. As Gandhiji remarks, 'it is wrong from every point of view to bring prisoners from their provinces and concentrate them in a place where there is no facility either for provision of medical assistance or other amenities of life.'

171. Jayaprakash Narayan's Letter to Mahatma Gandhi on Situation in Deoli Camp, 1 November 1941

Bimal Prasad (ed.), *Jayaprakash Narayan Selected Works,* Vol. 3, 2003, pp. 100–1.

Deoli Detention Camp
Deoli, Rajputana
1 November 1941

Dear Bapuji,

Love Pranam.

I hope you must have received my first letter. The situation here is becoming very grave. Maxwell's stubborn attitude shows the Government view. Under such grave conditions I request you to do one thing, that you should send Rajendra Babu or Pantji. I would prefer Rajendra Babu. They should seek permission of the Government of India for an interview with me. The interview should be without interception of the Camp authorities. After understanding the situation of this place and also statement of Maxwell in the light of our demand, Rajendra Babu should go to Delhi and try to bring about the settlement.

If his efforts fail then we are determined to die.

I am rather interested in this matter simply because the Government is making a wrong use by publication of the recent letters and that enhance our responsibility.

I hope you will be well.
Today is our eleventh day. I am OK.

Yours,
Jayaprakash

172. Deoli Prisoners' Hunger-strike: Calcutta Meeting

Amrita Bazar Patrika, 4 November 1941.

Goverment's Failure to Redress Grievances Condemned

Out of 204 hunger-striking prisoners in Deoli Jail about 50 are between 60 and 75 years of age according to a press report from Lucknow, quoted by Mr Santosh Kumar Basu while presiding over a meeting yesterday at Shraddhananda Park which declared that 'the prisoners had resorted to the extreme step as a result of the failure on the part of the Government of India to redress their grievances.'

Quoting the same press report Mr Basu stated that of the prisoners, 103 belonged to the Punjab and 81 to the United Provinces and the rest to other provinces. Of the 103 from the Punjab, 17 had been placed in Division I while 86 in Division II. But all the 81 prisoners from UP had been placed in Division I.

This distinction in the divisions was objected to by the detenus who demanded equal treatment and urged the abolition of the system of classification. Another demand of the detenus was the restoration of the cut in their daily allowances. The prices of necessary articles had already gone up and as a result of the cut, Mr Basu remarked, the detenus had been put to great difficulties.

The other demand, and the most important one, was for repatriation to their home provinces. Deoli was noted for its unhealthy climate and the prisoners who had been detained without trial had every right to remain in a healthy place. Further, it was a very expensive journey to Deoli and the relations could not go even once in a month to interview the prisoners.

The demands, Mr Basu said, were so modest and legitimate that any sensible man would have acceded to them without hesitation. Everyone expected a sympathetic statement from the Home Member in the Central Assembly. But Sir Reginald had not even said in his speech that he would consider the grievances.

Mr Basu said that it was now for the people to agitate in such a manner that Government would be forced to redress the grievances. He hoped that the people would not be found wanting in that.

Mr H.V. Kamath

Mr H.V. Kamath said that Sir Reginald Maxwell had told them that Italian and German prisoners of war were getting better treatment than the detenus because the Italians and Germans owed allegiance to their governments. By that Sir Reginald wanted to say that Indians should look upon the British Government as their own Government. But Mr Kamath said, he forgot that the present Government of India was not a people's Government. If that was so there would have been no occasion for them to court imprisonment.

Continuing Mr Kamath said that if the Government could not treat the detenus as prisoners of war it should at least accord them the facilities that were given to the detenus in England.

Sir Oswald Mosley, Mr Kamath said, was a detenu of the British Government in England. And he was allowed wine and beers which cost not less than two or three pounds. But here in India, the Government was reluctant to give the prisoners a rupee daily because it did not consider that was necessary for their physical requirements.

Concluding Mr Kamath said that he was satisfied that the detenus had gone on hunger-strike because it was their last weapon against the indifference of the authorities towards their conditions of living. There was no sign that the Government would redress their grievances. It was now for the people to make the Government accede to their demands.

173. Deoli

Editorial, *Amrita Bazar Patrika*, 6 November 1941.

The hunger-strike in the Deoli Detention Camp has given rise to an alarming situation. The total number of prisoners on strike has, according to a Press communiqué, risen to 225. One prisoner is reported to be lying seriously ill. Eight additional doctors and a number of additional compounders have been requisitioned. They have already arrived at the Camp or are on their way. The Indian members of the Viceroy's Executive Council who happen to constitute a majority of that body are on their trial. There in the Camp there are more than 200 security prisoners who have given up food for several days now as a protest against the treatment meted out to them. They had occasion more than once and repeatedly for months to put forth their grievances and place them before appropriate authorities. Mr N.M. Joshi, a nominated member of the Assembly, in no sense an irresponsible 'political agitator', paid a visit to the Camp with the permission of the Government and submitted a report. The full text of the report has not been published, but it is clear from the communiqué issued by the Government on the subject that the grievances generally are genuine and perfectly legitimate. For the Government have stated that Mr Joshi's report is under consideration and that some time will lapse before a final decision thereon may be taken by the authorities concerned. If Mr Joshi thinks that the Camp is perfectly in order and that the prisoners are being treated in the manner they should be, there was no occasion for the Government to make the announcement that the matter was being sympathetically looked into. Therefore, the conclusion is irresistible that the conditions in which the prisoners are permitted to live in the Camp are not what has been described by some spokesmen of the Government and their non-official agents. In this connection the comments made by an Anglo-Indian contemporary may be referred to as being evidence of a perverse mind that has inspired them. Our contemporary, for instance, writes:

'Mr Jai Prakash Narain writing from Deoli explained clearly the background of hunger-strikes in the camp. There are no grievances to speak of, he admitted, and when the authorities there are willing to remedy them if their attention is called to them.... The papers and the legislators who are dutifully 'tomtoming' the stunt take the public for complete fools, but they are not such fools as that.'

The suggestion contained in our contemporary's paragraph is mischievous. We do not take it for a fool, but does it suggest that if one is not a fool one must be a knave? We have never denied that the document ascribed to Mr Jai Prakash Narain is an astounding document. We have never denied that some of the sentiments therein expressed are repugnant to the creed of the Congress. As such they are disapproved by all sections of Congressmen, including the Congress Socialist Party of which Mr Jai Prakash Narain is such a distinguished leader. But have the Government of India, who have got the document published in this country and broadcast elsewhere, taken any satisfactory step to prove beyond doubt that the letter is Mr Narain's? Mr Narain is a prisoner and is not permitted by the rules of jail discipline to speak out. Even if the letter were a genuine document, Mr Narain might have something to say not only on its contents but also on the commentary that the Government have chosen to add to it. To exploit this letter, as members of the Government and the pro-Government newspaper Press are doing amounts to stabbing Mr Narain in the back and injuring a public cause. The whole thing is suspicious and positively unfair. We ask the Government of India if they have any case against Mr Narain, to give the latter an opportunity of defending himself before the bar of public opinion. Until that is done, it is nothing short of a public scandal that the Government and their henchmen should utilize a document for discrediting more than 200 security prisoners and confusing the public mind. Not a word has been said by Mr Joshi lending support to or in any way endorsing the alleged statements of fact regarding the conditions in the Camp as contained in the letter ascribed to Mr Narain. Evidently Mr Joshi stands by his own report and that report makes no secret of the fact that the treatment accorded to the prisoners leaves much to be desired.

Even apart from the bearing that Mr Narain's alleged letter may have on the situation in the Deoli Camp, it is against nature and the law of self-preservation that more than 200 prisoners should give up food for the mere fun of it. In certain conceivable circumstances a political strike may be a 'stunt', but who has ever heard that men starve themselves to death for keeping up a 'stunt' and persuade others to 'tomtom' it? And the Government themselves admit that in one case at least the condition is very serious and that additional medical arrangements have been deemed necessary to cope with the situation. Those who call it a 'stunt' must be either fools or knaves or both. It must be noted that these are prisoners who have not been convicted of an ordinary criminal offence involving moral turpitude or of any offence whatsoever. They are in the Camp because certain policemen have suspected them of being engaged in 'subversive' or 'prejudicial' activities. In the eye of the ordinary law of the land they are all innocent men. And these innocent men kept in detention without trial are being subjected to a sort of treatment which on the face of it is something which they are not prepared to put up with, hence the hunger-strike, privation of food, and water, the necessary hardship consequent on it, and the injury to body and mind. We say again that the Indian members of the Viceroy's Executive Council have a clear duty by these their countrymen. They would prove themselves unworthy of the positions they happen to hold if they be so short-sighted and thoughtless as not to yield to the prisoners' reasonable demands immediately on Sir Reginald Maxwell's bureaucratic thesis that there was nothing doing so long as the strike continued.

174. Deoli Detenus Break Fast: Forty-six Still on Hunger-strike Condition of Two Serious

Amrita Bazar Patrika, 9 November 1941.

New Delhi, 8 November.

The Government of India have received information that 184 of the security prisoners who were on hunger-strike at Deoli have called off their strike unconditionally and have broken their fast, says a press communiqué.

Forty-six security prisoners still remain on hunger-strike. Their general health is reported to be satisfactory.

Two are seriously ill

One security prisoner who had been placed on the seriously ill list has been taken off the list, and his relatives have been informed. One more is still on the seriously ill list, but his condition has slightly improved.

Mr Joshi's Statement

Mr N.M. Joshi MLA (Central) has issued the following statement to the press from Deoli:

> I came to Deoli with the permission of the Government of India to discuss the situation regarding the hunger-strike with the detenus concerned. I met representative committees of all sections and told them that several members of the Legislative Assembly and the general public have now fully understood their grievances and are watching their interests, and that we are anxious to see justice and fair treatment given.
>
> I also told them that I had met the Home Member and some other members of the Government of India and that I am convinced that the Government of India are seriously and sympathetically considering their grievances, and that they will come to a decision without undue delay.
>
> I therefore, appealed to them to call off the hunger-strike immediately. I also told them that it was necessary that my resolution for the release of political prisoners which is to be discussed in the Assembly on 12 November, should be discussed in a calmer atmosphere.
>
> I am glad to state that my appeal received a favourable response from a great majority of the hunger-strikes. I regret, however, that a group of hunger-strikers did not conscientiously feel justified in giving up the hunger-strike under the present conditions.

175. All India Detenus Day: Government Urged to Redress Grievances Public Meeting in Calcutta

Amrita Bazar Patrika, 10 November 1941.

The depth to which feelings in the country have been stirred over the hunger-strike of Deoli politicals was unmistakably indicated when on Sunday Calcutta along with the rest of India observed the All-India Detenus Day.

Congressmen, Trade Unionists, Kisan workers and students combined to organize meetings, processions and demonstrations all over the city.

Relief and release of the detenus were demanded at a crowded public meeting held in the evening at the Shraddhananda Park under the auspices of the Bengal Provincial Congress Committee.

Processions organized among others by the North Calcutta District Congress Committee, Bengal Provincial Students' Federation and peasant and labour organizations paraded the streets with placards supporting the demands of the Deoli prisoners.

Repatriation of the detenus to their respective provinces, abolition of class distinction in detention camps, provision of adequate allowance for the families of the politicals and granting of personal allowance to the detenus—these are some of the demands made by the meeting held on Sunday evening at the Shraddhananda Park under the auspices of the BPCC.

Sja. Labanyaprova Dutt, President of the Bengal Provincial Congress Committee, was in the chair.

Legitimate Demands

Sj. Bankim Mukherjee, MLA moved the resolution which, while expressing sympathy and concern for the hunger-striking detenus of Deoli and requesting the Government to fulfill their just and legitimate demands, condemned the action of the authorities in keeping them in detention without charge or trial. The resolution further demanded that the prisoners should be repatriated to their respective provinces, the class distinction exiting in detention camps should be abolished, detenus' families should be given adequate allowance, and food allowances should be increased and the politicals should be granted a personal allowance which would be such as would enable them to meet their personal needs.

The demands embodied in the resolution, said Sj. Bankim Mukherjee, had been reduced to irreducible minimum so that they might prove acceptable to the Government. The demands had been framed in such a manner as would leave the Government no valid excuse for their rejection. If in spite of this the Government refused to accept them, the public would see in that attitude nothing but an undue 'zid' on their part.

The people did not want that these patriots should sacrifice their precious lives on a comparatively trivial issue, if they were to embrace death that should be for a greater objective. It was to prevent the catastrophe, which would mean an irreparable loss to the country, that the demands had been made so modest as might be acceptable to the authorities.

Country Stirred to Depths

The hunger-strike, Sj. Mukherjee proceeded had stirred the country to its depths: over and above that had come the news of the lathi charge on the students at Cawnpore. That incident would intensify discontent not only among the students but among the general public as well.

Utilizing the letter alleged to have been written by Mr Jaiprakash Narain the Government attempted to dismiss the hunger strike as a piece of political stunt. The letter of Mr Narain, according to the speaker, did not prove that the detenus had no grievances. It was extremely regrettable that Sir Reginald Maxwell had sought to convince the members of the Central Assembly that the prisoners were living in luxury, but his speech itself had proved that the case was otherwise.

Sj. Bepin Behari Ganguly said that the hunger-strike had given rise to serious anxiety and concern in the country regarding the condition of the prisoners. Some precious lives, it was apprehended, might be lost in consequence of the strike.

Youth To take the Lead

It seemed, Sj. Ganguly proceeded; there was no other alternative before them but to start a serious agitation for the removal of the grievances of the detenus and for their eventual release. The Andamans political prisoners, he reminded the audience, had been repatriated only after the youths and students of Bengal had launched a tremendous movement for the same. This time too it was for the youth of this province to take the lead and force the Government to redress the grievances of the politicals and ultimately set them at liberty.

Mr Rezaul Karim wondered, while the British Government were loudest in justly condemning Hitlerian methods, they should be completely indifferent to the treatment that were being meted out to these men under indefinite detention—men whose only crime was their love of the motherland.

Even a murderer was given opportunity to defend himself but the detenus were deprived of even that elementary right and were accorded worse treatment than what was provided to ordinary convicts. Deoli was the Bastille of India and Indians waited for the day when that hated place would be razed to the ground.

Pundit Jeewanlal thought, that the hunger strike was a result of genuine grievances suffered from day to day by the prisoners and not a piece of political stunt as Sir Reginald Maxwell would have the country to believe. It had been the practice of the authorities to turn a deaf ear to the demands of political prisoners unless a Jatin Das or Haren Munshi by his sacrifice of life roused for the time being the conscience of the Government.

The Government could provide every amenity to the Italian prisoners of war confined in this country to those men who were their deadly enemies, but they did not find their way to meet the modest demands of those against whom they had no charge to bring.

Sj. Ranendra Nath Goswami moved a resolution demanding the release of all political prisoners. The resolution condemned the lathi charge made by the police on the student demonstrators at Cawnpore.

Others who addressed the gathering included Sj. Krishna Kumar Chatterjee, Mr Mansur Ali, Sj. Monoranjan Majumder and Sreemati Nirmala Roy.

Goaded to Desperation

No one, Sja. Labanyaprova Dutt observed, unless goaded to desperation would seek to put an end to one's existence. The enormity of the grievances the detenus were suffering from could readily be realized in the fact that it had left for them no other alternative but to adopt the drastic course. It was against human nature to court death for the sake of fun. Even a maniac would hesitate to take such an extreme step.

Gandhiji had refused to embarrass the British Government at the critical stage by launching a mass civil disobedience movement. Could it not be expected from the Government that they too should retrain from embarrassing the Indians at this hour of crisis?

Congress, Sja. Dutt went on, was pledged to strict non-violence. The only thing which the countrymen might do as a protest was to fill the jails again. The realization of this fact had emboldened the Government to treat the Deoli Politicals in such a manner and thus hurt the feelings of the entire country.

The demands of the Deoli prisoners were today not confined to the prisoners alone but they had become the demands of India as a whole. The Government should do well to take note of the fact. If on this rather trivial issue the authorities chose to trample upon the feelings of the people the reaction that their attitude would in the near future produce might be very serious, although non-violent in character.

Both the resolutions were adopted unanimously.

176. Release of Political Prisoners

Editiorial, *Amrita Bazar Patrika*, 11 November 1941.

The hunger-strike of the political prisoners at Deoli had deeply stirred the whole country, and the agitation among all classes of the people for their repatriation and release had been fast gaining in intensity and volume. The news that most of them had been induced by Mr Joshi to give up the strike was, therefore, hailed with a sigh of relief. Mr Joshi's resolution on the release of the political prisoners will shortly come up before the Central Assembly for discussion and it was to create the necessary calm atmosphere in which such resolutions might be properly discussed that many of the detenus were induced to give up the strike. We need not anticipate what the fate of that resolution is likely to be. It is now realized that the grievances of the detenus are quite legitimate, and the picture that Sir Reginald Maxwell had painted of the actual state of things in the Detention Camp had no existence except in his own imagination. Moreover, the reasons which he had set forth, in the old bureaucratic fashion, for refusing to consider the grievances of the detenus so long as the hunger-strike lasted, hold good no longer.

The only solution of the detenu problem that is likely to satisfy all political parties is the unconditional release of all political prisoners. Detention for an indefinite period of persons simply on the strength of police reports is certainly not a practice that can easily be reconciled with the profession of freedom and democracy; and whatever may be its justification in self-governed countries in moments of emergency, in a country like India, which is governed in accordance with the interests and whims of an alien governing class, the practice of detention without trial can scarcely be indulged in without further widening the breach that exists already between the rulers and the ruled. The interpretation that was put on the Atlantic Charter by the British Premier and the statements made thereon by the Secretary of State for India have not certainly tended to improve matters. The time, we think, has surely come when Britain might make a beginning by proving to the satisfaction of the Indian people that detention without trial is not one of the methods which she means to follow in the further administration of this country.

But whatever may be India's grievances against the British ruling class, there can be no doubt, as we have already pointed out, that there is genuine sympathy for Russia among the thinking sections of the Indian people, and that there is both among the Satyagrahi prisoners and the detenus, a considerable section which is prepared for Russia's sake to support by every means in its power the anti-Fascist front created by Russia, America, and Britain. Is it wisdom on the part of the British administrators in this country to neglect what help may be available from this quarter? Do they seriously believe that the addition to the Viceroy's Council of a few Indian Members who cannot give effect to the popular demand will help them to any appreciable extent in winning the sympathy of the people whom the imprisonment of Satyagrahis and detenus has already alienated?

It is rumoured that to allay popular discontent the authorities have decided to release many of the Satyagrahi prisoners, leaving the question of the detenus to be decided leisurely by some tribunal which may be set up in future for the purpose. It is further rumoured that the Viceroy is prepared to reduce the sentence passed on Pandit Jawaharlal Nehru to two years instead of four. Such a step may be quite in keeping with the British tradition, but we are afraid such half-measures will be absolutely out of place in an emergency like the present, and as Mr Satyamurti has pointed out in a recent speech at Bombay, 'the release will lose all its grace and value if Maulana Azad and Pandit Nehru are not also released simultaneously.' While this is certainly true, we believe Mr Satyamurti would have voiced public feeling more faithfully still if he had pointed out that the time had gone by when the release of prisoners belonging merely to the Congress-fold might have allayed public discontent. Statesmanship today requires greater imagination and broader sympathy; and the mere setting up of a tribunal which will go through police reports and adjudicate on dead records to decide the fate of the detenus will scarcely help to bridge the ever-widening gulf between the rulers and the ruled.

Speculation there has been in certain quarters as to whether the unconditional release of all political prisoners, including detenus, may not be expected to influence the attitude of the Indian National Congress towards co-operation with the British Government in their war efforts. We have no desire to count the chickens before they are hatched; but we believe no useful purpose will be served by forgetting the fact that, it was not to procure the release of the Satyagrahis and the detenus that Mahatmaji started his Satyagraha campaign. The question, therefore, whether the release of the detenus and political prisoners will justify the Congress in resuming Parliamentary activities is not, we are afraid, quite relevant to the point at issue. The detenu question is, after all, only a side-issue of the bigger problem of India's status; and we have not the least doubt that when the wider problem is satisfactorily solved, there will be no hesitation on the part of the Congress authorities to throw every ounce of India's moral and material strength on the side of Britain, America, and Russia to overcome the forces of tyranny and oppression and stand shoulder to shoulder with all honest people 'as champions of liberation not only in Europe, but in Asia.'

177. Bengal Students Federation Leaders' Statement on Deoli Hunger Strike

Amrita Bazar Partika, 12 November 1941.

The following statement has been issued by Coms. Sadhan Gupta, President, BPSF, Prasanta Sannyal, General Secretary, BPSF, Ajit Bhattacharjee, Secretary, CCDSF, Suresh Bose, Secretary, South Calcutta DSF, Sudhir Bhattacharjee, Office Secretary, BPSF and Jyotsna Roy, President NCDSF:

After two weeks of hunger-strike 184 Security Prisoners of Deoli have given up their fast, but forty-six others are still continuing it. We rejoice to think that so many brave fighters of our country will live to carry on our struggle for freedom. But let us not forget the forty-six others who are still in the gravest danger of their lives. Nor should we be lulled into inactivity by the cessation of hunger-strike by the others. Rather should it spire us to further efforts to see that the demands of the prisoners are speedily recognized by the Government. Now that the hunger-strike has partially stopped, only public agitation can compel the Government to do so.

That Government is adamant in its attitude is evident from the lathi charge on Cawnpore students who were observing the Deoli Day, in which several were injured, and the banning of Deoli Day observance in several districts of Bengal. We, therefore, propose the following programmes:

(1) In every school, college, hostel, and students mess through posters and meetings; we must counteract the Government propaganda and emphasize the real state of affairs in Deoli.

(2) To join demonstrations and public meetings with publicmen to demand the redress of the Deoli Prisoners grievances.

(3) Set up committees to collect books from students, professors, college unions, and the public for Security Prisoners.

We have behind us the traditions of a student movement which was effective in inducing Government to repatriate the Andamans prisoners and we hope we would meet with success this time also.

178. Detenus Continue Hunger Strike

The Tribune, 12 November 1941.

Why forty-six detenus are still persisting in hunger-strike: They want allowances for their families

Provincial Governments are being consulted telegraphically to arrive at a formula

New Delhi, 10 November.

Since his return from Deoli, Mr N.M. Joshi, MLA has had talks with the Home Member, Sir Reginald Maxwell, and relations of several detenus. He told me that forty-six detenus, who are still persisting in their hunger-strike, do so mainly on the question of allowances for their families, which on an average is estimated at Rs 75 per month if agreed to. At present no family allowance is given as a matter of right, but only in a few stray cases where provincial Governments concerned have thought it necessary.

The question largely rests with the provincial Governments and so these are being consulted telegraphically in order to arrive at a formula which would assure reasonable rates of allowance to the detenus. But the demand of the forty-six hunger-strikers is for more liberal allowances than what the authorities might be prepared to concede.

Most of these forty-six detenus are from the Punjab and include Sardar Kabul Singh, MLA, Sardar Harjap Singh, MLA, and Sardar Mota Singh. Prominent among those from the United Provinces are Mr Damodar and Mr Mohan Lal Gautam and from Bihar Mr Jaiprakash Narain.

The immediate problem is how to bring about the end of the hunger-strike of these forty-six detenus whom Mr Joshi could not succeed in converting. Mian Iftikhar-ud-Din, MLA, President of the Punjab Provincial Congress Committee, joined in conversations with Mr Joshi and Sardar Mangal Singh, MLA (Central). The latter had conversations this afternoon with Sir Reginald Maxwell and it is considered probable that he may go to Deoli to try to induce the detenus to suspend the hunger-strike on the assurance of a fair consideration of all their legitimate demands within a reasonable time. Meanwhile Sir Reginald himself is in telegraphic communication with provincial Governments concerned.

179. Mahatma Gandhi's Statement to the Press, 12 November 1941

CWMG, Vol. LXXV, pp. 92–3.

Wardhaganj,
12 November 1941.

I observe that there is a move to press the Government to release satyagrahi prisoners.

It is, perhaps, appropriate to mention that so far as I know there will be on the part of the Congress neither appreciation of nor response to any such gesture by the Government.

Those who may be discharged will have to be invited to re-offer civil disobedience if they are physically fit. Moreover, there will be great resentment if distinction is made between satyagrahis and those who are detained without trial. The Government should not be judges of what is reasonable.

What the public demand is this:

Let the Government keep the prisioners, but give decent treatment to the prisoners whether they hunger-strike or not. They need not take notice of such strikes when there is no reasonable cause for that.

The Deoli prisoners' demands as far as they are known are just. Let them end the terrible suspense by granting the demands and ending the hunger-strike.

Let them also examine the recently published weightly mainifesto by representative and prominent medical men from all India on the dietary of C class prisoners and make the necessary changes and redress such other disabilities which have no just basis.

I, therefore, suggest to those who are urging the Government to discharge satyagrahi prisoners that they will do well if they will concentrate on the relief herein suggested. It can be granted quickly without any political or other embarrassment.

Bombay Chronicle, 13.11.1941

180. Mahatma Gandhi's Telegram to Jayaprakash Narayan, 12 November 1941

CWMG, Vol. LXXV, p. 93.

STRONGLY ADVISE DISCONTINUANCE OF THE HUNGER-STRIKE BY YOU AND OTHERS. PUBLIC OPINION BEING CREATED FOR SECURING RELIEF. DR RAJENDRA PRASAD AND MIAN IFTIKHARUDDIN JOIN ME IN THE APPEAL. PRABHAVATI ANXIOUS TO MEET YOU. RESTRAINING HER PENDING DEVELOPMENTS.

The Hindu, 16.11.1941.

181. Mahatma Gandhi's Statement to the Press on Deoli Hunger Strike

CWMG, Vol. LXXV, pp. 96–7.

Wardhaganj,
14 November 1941.

I sent the following telegram to Shri Jayaprakash Narayan on the 12th instant.

To this, have just received the following reply:

Thanks for the telegram. Have explained the whole position to Sardar Mangal Singh. Our demands are reasonable. Please excuse inability to discontinue the hunger-strike. May do what you can outside. Do not send Prabhavati.

I have heard nothing as yet from Sardar Mangal Singh. I shall, no doubt, do so in due course. But the matter is too urgent to brook delay. I have heard that Shri Jayaprakash has lost heavily in weight. Forcible feeding can only be a temporary makeshift. Shri Jayaprakash is one of the most determined of workers. I flatter myself with the belief that if anything could have melted him our joint telegram should have. His preventing his wife from going to him is ominous. He wants no interference, emotional or other, with his decision.

So far as I can see, there is no political motive behind this hunger-strike. The refusal to consider the case until the hunger-strike is given up is a cruel joke. It would be an act of inhumanity if Shri Jayaprakash and his fellow-detenus are detained till their lives are in danger. I appeal to the Government, in the name of humanity, forthwith to grant the request of the detenus. The plea of ascertaining and carrying out the wishes of the Provincial Governments is irrelevant and untenable. The Central Government is in no way bound to oblige the Provincial Governments in matters where the life and liberty of the citizen is involved. There must be something radically wrong if the Provincial Governments are afraid to keep their own detenus within their borders.

This continuing hunger-strike shows the futility of discharging civil resistance prisoners who have themselves sought imprisonment. With what face can they come out when those who have not sought imprisonment are detained without trial and are hunger-striking for the minimum of conveniences to which every human being is entitled?

The Hindu, 16.11.1941.

182. Mahatma Gandhi's Telegram to Jayaprakash Narayan, 17 November 1941

CWMG, Vol. LXXV, p. 102.

KAMLADEVI HERE. SHE AND I CONSIDER YOUR DEMAND FOR SAME TREATMENT AS DEOLI INCAPABLE LITERAL EXECUTION. PUTS YOU WRONG BOX. YOU SHOULD BE SATISFIED WITH REPATRIATION AND END STRIKE AND AGAIN YOU WILL ESTRANGE PUBLIC FEELINGS BY PERSISTING IF REPATRIATION ASSURED. SARDAR RAJENBABU KRIPALANI JOIN.

Gandhi

183. Jayaprakash Narayan's Telegram to Mahatma Gandhi, 18 November 1941

Bimal Prasad (ed.), *Jayaprakash Narayan Selected Works*, Vol. 3, 2003, p. 102; *CWMG*, Vol. LXXV, p. 102 fn.

MUCH PAINED AT TELEGRAM. AFRAID YOU HAVE NOT UNDERSTOOD SITUATION CORRECTLY. REPATRIATION NOT OUR ONLY DEMAND. CANNOT FIGHT AFRESH FOR REMAINING AFTER REPATRIATION. THEREFORE ASKING FOR TWO SMALL ASSURANCES. FIRST PROVINCIAL GOVERNMENTS SHALL CONSIDER SYMPATHETICALLY DEMANDS ALREADY BEFORE INDIA GOVERNMENT. SECOND PENDING DECISION AT LEAST DEOLI STANDARD SHALL BE APPLIED NEVER INSISTED ON LITERAL APPLICATION. DEOLI STANDARD IN PUNJAB DETENUS ARE GIVEN C CLASS TREATMENT. FAIL TO UNDERSTAND HOW OUR POSITION UNREASONABLE. BOTH JOSHI MANGAL SINGH CONSIDERED IT REASONABLE. IF YOU SEND SOMEONE SHALL CONVINCE HIM COMPLETELY.

Jayaprakash

184. Madras Province—'Keep Detenus Locked Up at Night'

(i) Letter from the Inspector-general of Prisons to the Chief Secretary to the Government of Madras

Copy of letter No. 1061/S–1/40, dated 9.10.1941; GO No. 2615, Public (General) Department, dated 18.11.41, Tamil Nadu State Archives.

I forward herewith for favour of disposal petitions preferred by the marginally noted security prisoners consequent on stoppage of the privileges.

(1) M. Annapurniah (2) V. Subbiah (3) P.S. Veluswamy Gounder (4) T. Karuppiah Pillai (5) P. Ganapathi Row (6) A.C. Kannan Nair	2. I may state in this connection that the number of leftists is becoming too large for them to be permitted to sleep outside their cells at night. If there are 100 to 120 cots scattered all over the enclosure at night, guarding is absolutely impossible. It is therefore most dangerous to allow the leftists to be kept unlocked at nights. Besides this, all the objectionable propaganda meetings among them are held at night time when the officials leave the jail. This should be avoided at all costs.

Inspector-General of Prisons.

(ii) Confidential Letter from the Inspector-general of Prisons, to the Chief Secretary to the Government of Madras

Confidential letter No. 1061/S–1/40(1), dated 23.10.1941, Public (General) Department, Madras Govt, Tamil Nadu State Archives.

With reference to the Government Memorandum cited above I have to state as far as department is concerned I have made the position clear in my letter No. 1061/S1/40, dated 11.10.1941 wherein it has been stated that the Detenus should either be considered as prisoners or as gentlemen on a sort of modified parole. If it is the former, they must be locked up at night and not be allowed to go out of the jail for walks. If it is the latter, then we must expect escapes and these should not be considered as escapes but merely breaking parole.

The concessions were granted in the beginning when the number of Detenus was small. The persons detained early were men of substance and status. This is not the position now. Concessions were given because it was considered that their behavior in jails would be different from the ordinary jail population. This theory has been vitiated by the recent escape. If it was possible to guard prisoners effectively and still permit them to be unlocked at night, we would then have allowed ordinary jail population to be treated in the same way. Theoretically it may seem a simple matter to prevent escapes by effective guarding but in practice the case is quite different. If one visualizes about 150 prisoners scattered on dark nights in an area of 200 yards by 120 yards in small groups, some having their cots in one corner, others in a different place perhaps 150 yards away, all talking and chattering, others in groups having walks, and other things, the position becomes much more serious. After all there is only one man on duty at any particular time. Even if we increase the number to two, things are not much better. What chances have one or two men against 150 or more prisoners. Making a hole in the wall is only one of the methods they can adopt for escaping. If these prisoners get hold of one or both of these night guards, they have the whole enclosure to themselves. They have cots, almirahs, and other furniture which put against the main wall gives them all the facilities to climb over. They can let themselves down on the other side with the help of their sheets and blankets, etc. These kinds of instances can be multiplied indefinitely. I am therefore of opinion that the only effective way of guarding the Detenus properly is to keep them locked up at night, otherwise the jail and this department is at their mercy. I may be permitted to add that the withdrawal of these privileges is not to be considered as a temporary and a punitive measure but it is elementary precaution with a view to effective guarding. I personally have no objection if the Detenu Ranga is given the privileges of the rightists but if these privileges are restored to others it will merely be a thin edge of the wedge. I am returning the eight petitions sent with Confidential Government Memorandum No. 33937–1., public (General) dated 17.10.1941 with a request that privileges withdrawn should not be restored to the leftists now or at some future time—except Ranga—as the behavior of Detenus has shown that they are unworthy of preferential treatment of this kind. If the Government are pleased to order otherwise, we will naturally do our best but request that our disabilities and difficulties may be kept in view.

Inspector-general of Prisons

185. Mahatma Gandhi's Telegram to Home Member, Government of India, 19 November 1941

CWMG, Vol. LXXV, p. 106.

Wardha,
19 November 1941

HOME MEMBER
NEW DELHI

AM COMMUNICATION WITH JAYAPRAKASH NARAYAN VIEW ENDING HUNGER-STRIKE. HE AND HIS COMPANIONS REFUSE ABANDON STRIKE WITHOUT KNOWING NATURE FUTURE CONDITION ASSUMING REPATRIATION WILL BE GRANTED. HE WANTS ME SEND REPRESENTATIVE REMOVE POSSIBLE MISUNDERSTANDING. COULD YOU PLEASE WIRE AUTHORITY MAHADEV DESAI PROCEED DEOLI?[1]

Gandhi

[1] The authorization was given on 20 November 1941.

186. Madras Government's Memorandum on Categorization of Agitators

Copy of Memorandum No. 33634–3 dated 30.10.1941 of Public (General) Department GOMs No. 2663, Public (General) Dept, Dated 21.11.41, Tamil Nadu State Archives.

Sub: Political agitation—Detention under Rule 26 of D and I Rules—Principle regarding.
Ref: DM's letter dated 6.10.41.

In continuation of the instructions in GO No. 873, Public (General) dated 30.4.1941, the District Magistrate of Madura is informed that in the dealing with subversive and anti-war agitators and workers it has been the policy of Government to divide these persons into three categories. The categories and the action which Government considers suitable in respect of each are set out below:

(1) persons who are known to be revolutionaries and communists and are likely to go out of view and continue their activities while undergrounds—these are detained under Rule 26 (1) (b) of the Defence of India Rules:

(2) persons who are communists or revolutionaries but from their position and status in life, etc. are not likely to go out of view if left at liberty—these are normally restricted to their villages or some specified area under Rule 26 (1) (d) of the Defence of India Rules; and

(3) those who, like ordinary right wing Congressmen, do anti-war propaganda either openly or surreptitiously but are not likely, if left at liberty, to go underground—these are to be prosecuted whenever they commit any definite offence for which adequate evidence is forthcoming.

It appears to the Government that the District Magistrate regards surreptitious anti-war propaganda as 'Underground' activity. The Government cannot accept this interpretation of the word 'underground'.

Mr Shesha Ayyar cannot be regarded as falling in any but class (3) of the categories mentioned above and the Government consequently are not prepared to order his detention under Rule 26 (1) (b) of the Defence of India Rules.

The District Magistrate's attention is also drawn to the instructions issued in Memo. No. 26035/40-2, public (General) dated 18.10.1940 in which it was laid down that agitation and propaganda against contributing to or helping HE the Governor's War Fund should not, by itself, be regarded as a justification for launching a prosecution under the Defence of India Rules. In this connection the Government would observe that the proper answer to anti-war propaganda is a systematic and sustained campaign of counter propaganda wherever disaffected persons are openly or surreptitiously working to prevent or to hinder collections to the War Fund.

To
The District Magistrate of Madura.

187. Deoli and Montgomery Detenus Give Up Hunger-strike

Bombay Chronicle, 24 November 1941.

New Delhi, 23 November.

The Associated Press is officially informed that the hunger-strikers at Deoli have given up hunger-strike unconditionally.

The number of prisoners on hunger-strike was about fifty who had declined to give up the strike although a large number of others agreed to terminate it as a result of Mr N.M. Joshi's intervention earlier this month.

Lala Deshbandhu Gupta, MLA (Punjab) informs the Associated Press that he has received a telegram from Sardar Mangal Singh. MLA (Central), Secretary of the All-India Detenus Aid Committee saying that the Deoli hunger-strikers gave up the hunger-strike last evening.

Hunger-strike in Montgomery Jail Given up

Thirteen detenus in Montgomery jail who have been on hunger strike since November 5, in sympathy with the security prisoners at Deoli, have given up the strike. They broke the fast this afternoon as a result of the efforts of Dr Gopichand Bhargava, former leader of the Congress Party in the Punjab Assembly, who visited Montgomery today.

Dr Bhargava, who returned to Lahore in the evening, is expected to issue a detailed statement tomorrow.

188. Mahatma Gandhi's Statement to the Press after Discontinuance of Hunger Strike, 27 November 1941

CWMG, Vol. LXXV, pp. 115–17.

Wardhaganj,
27 November 1941

The discontinuance of the hunger-strike by the Deoli detenus relieves the terrible tension under which the public was labouring. It was not possible to contemplate with unconcern the starvation, even self-inflicted, of patriots, whether one agreed with their method or not. Let us hope that repatriation will be hastened and their treatment will not be worsened for their removal to their respective provinces.

I have read the Government communiqué describing the bewitching life in Deoli. I recall a similar description of life in the Andamans. It read like a fairy tale and yet most of the inmates preferred to return home. These descriptions, however truthful they may be in the estimation of the writers not themselves detenus, do not answer the reality as the detenus see it. The object of the communiqué, on the face of it, is to show that the condition in Deoli was superior to what it was in the respective provinces. If such was the case, it shows how correct and proper was the demand of the hunger-strikers that their condition on repatriation should be no worse than in Deoli. I should translate the demand thus:

(1) Repatriation should not be to a remote godforsaken place in the detenu's province. The object of repatriation would be wholly frustrated if the detenus are transferred to a place far away from their homes.
(2) The conveniences and food should be as near to Deoli's latest standard as possible.

That is so far as the prisoners' demands are concerned. But something more is needed. Seeing that the detenus have not been tried, the burden is on the Government to give them as decent a treatment as possible. War economy has no place in this connection, for detention is itself a war measure and could not be justified on any other ground. Therefore, they are entitled to family allowance and traveling expenses for their families when necessary. It should be remembered that most of the detenus are poor people. So much as to Deoli.

But I feel that the question of food, sanitation, and classification is and should be treated as an all-India question. I confine myself just now only to political prisoners, whether detenus detained on suspicion or satyagrahis who have courted imprisonment. If I had the authority, I would treat all prisoners alike, making a distinction only on the ground of health and habit. But I must not complicate the main issue by raising others [that] do not demand immediate solution. I think that classifications should be scrapped. At best they are arbitrary.

The scale prescribed in the very weighty and reasoned manifesto recently issued by eminent medical men representing the whole of India should be accepted forthwith as the minimum scale for all India, with such variations as staples grown in various provinces may demand. All political prisoners should have the right to supplement their food and other requirements from their own pockets.

All should be supplied with a selection of newspapers and magazines of known standing without any censoring. There should be no restrictions as to choice of books. What is not generally prohibited in India should be allowed to prisoners. They should be allowed to write letters and receive visitors on the same scale as in B class.

It should be common cause that no recognition should be given to hunger-strikes for wringing illegitimate concessions nor need they be penalized by refusal to consider legitimate demands on merits. For a prisoner under stress, hunger-strike is the last non-violent remedy. He seeks to end imposed suffering by self-imposed suffering. He thereby hopes to melt the heart of authority or at least enlist the sympathy of the public. Experience shows that the method is not to be despised. It has succeeded in several cases. But it is not easy to know always whether the cause for which a strike is undertaken is valid. We know, too, that Governments do not always come to a right decision in such cases. I have before me the case of a prisoner, who has given up his strike at my instance. The cause, as transpires in the record of the case before me, seems to have been more than valid. The vegetables served contained a dead scorpion. The men who had resorted to hunger-strike are now being tried for breach of jail regulations in that they refused the food served. There is the Chunar hunger-strike now going on for a fortnight. It is respect of the treatment of C class prisoners. I have wired pleading for its suspension.

I think that hunger-strikes should not be regarded as a crime, but whenever such a strike takes place it should be referred to a judicial tribunal with the right to the prisoner to be represented by a lawyer of his choice. If the cause is found to be valid, the grievance should be removed. If the hunger-strike is persisted in, although the finding is against the prisoner, the fast should be ignored. If the procedure recommended by me is adopted the probability is that strikes will automatically decrease. Where the cause is valid, the authorities will grant redress on a mere notice of hunger-strike and where the strike is found to be unjustified there will be no public sympathy. It follows that there would be no forcible feeding if the procedure I am recommending is adopted. In rare and obstinate cases a life may have to be lost. It is impossible always to prevent suicide, even by fasting.

Fasting has come to stay as a remedy for redress of grievances. It has its uses. An honest fast draws attention to a felt grievance and compels redress. What I have suggested is regularization of the humanitarian instinct and the rescuing of a useful institution from ridicule of contempt.

The Hindu, 29.11.1941.

189. Deoli is a Sort of 'Kala Pani', by Sardar Mangal Singh, MLA

The Tribune, 4 December 1941.

Deoli has been very much in the news owing to the hunger-strike by the detenus there. The place has acquired a great political importance all over India.

Deoli is a small village right in the heart of Rajputana. It is a God-forsaken place about 60 miles from the nearest Railway station. It is a sort of Kala Pani. It is reached by two pacca road one from Kotah via Bundi (57 miles) and the other from Ajmere via Nasirabad (71 miles). The only conveyance available is a bus from both places which leaves for Deoli in the morning and returns in the evening. In case you happen to miss this bus you are stranded for 24 hours. From Lahore to Deoli via Kotah is a 28 hour journey by express trains cum bus and costs Rs 12-9 (third class).

This, a small island of British territory in the midst of Rajputana States, is under the administrative control of the Chief Commissioner of Ajmere Merwar. It was acquired by the Central Government after 1857 for the purpose of establishing a cantonment and offices of the Agent, Rajputana States. Thus there grew up, besides the cantonment, a small Saddar Bazar and a number of Kothis around the spacious residence of the Agent. There is now neither the cantonment nor the office of the Agent. The Agent's house is now occupied by the Superintendent of the Deoli Detention Camp and the building which was formerly the office and mess is now used as the offices of the Detention Camp. It is said that Maharaja of Bharatpur was once detained here as a State prisoner for some time. The place was also used as a Concentration Camp for 500 Bengali detenus in 1936. The old camp was demolished in 1939. The present camp was built in 1940 with an accommodation of over 300 prisoners.

Owing to its unaccessibility and a long distance from the home districts of the detenus, very few of them could have had interviews with their relatives. The actual number is less than 10 per cent. Several years ago when the question of the Andamans was under consideration, Sir Henry Craik, the then Home Member of the Government of India, described the Andamans, as a 'Prisoners' Paradise.' It is no wonder that the present Home Member, the Hon'ble Sir Reginald Maxwell, gave a rosy picture of life in the Deoli Detention Camp. He only maintained the bureaucratic tradition in his outlook on jail administration. Deoli is certainly anything but a paradise and should forthwith go as a detention camp and the detenus should be brought back to their home provinces.

Chapter 3. Students' and Women's Movements

A. Students

1. Students' Role in National Struggle

Report on Dr K.M. Ashraf's Presidential Address to Bombay Provincial Students' Conference, 31 December 1940

Bombay Chronicle, 1 January 1941.

Doctor Ashraf's Address at Bombay Conference: 'Compromise Politics' Criticized

That students too could develop a national struggle and should build it up by co-ordinated local struggles on a mass basis was the exhortation of Dr Ashraf while presiding over the Bombay Provincial Students' Conference which met at Nappoo Hall, Matunga, on Tuesday afternoon.

Messages to the Conference wishing it success were received, among others from Mrs Sarojini Naidu, Mr N.M. Joshi, Mr Mathuradas Tricumji, the Mayor of Bombay, Dr K.B. Menon, Secretary of the Indian Civil Liberties Union, and Prof. Hiren Mukherjee, President of the All-India Students' Federation, besides several provincial student organizations.

In her message, Mrs Sarojini Naidu hoped that the 'young generation is unanimous in its ideals for a brave new world'. The Mayor of Bombay wished that students would 'get rid of a doubters attitude and think in a constructive and positive manner' as negation was a lifeless thing.

Communalism Deprecated

Mr Anand Kanekar, inaugurating the Conference, said that the younger generation should see that the world is made safe for democracy. It was to maintain that ideal that millions of young men had sacrificed their lives in the last war. He deprecated that communalism should influence young minds while there were national interests which were supreme. It was the privilege of youth to revel in idealism and great tasks awaited them. To ask Indian students not to participate in politics would be like asking the Oxford students not to participate in war.

Mr Nikhil Maitra, conveying fraternal greetings from Bengal students, said that at Nagpur the student organizations had achieved a unity in action when several critical issues faced them. It was a wrong outlook to look at it from a split-angle. Mr Vaswami from Sind also spoke.

Mr G.S. Patke, Chairman of the Reception Committee welcomed the delegates.

Dr Ashraf in the course of his presidential address said that the world was facing the close of a whole epoch of capitalism and imperialism. Critical times were before them. The situation was pregnant with disturbing factors as it was the case at the time of the Industrial revolution, when Feudalism gave way to Capitalism.

'Adventuring in Metaphysics'

In India compromise politics held sway. As Gandhiji said when offices were accepted, Constitutionalism had come to stay. The clock had been set back to the days of liberalism and compromise. Though in the 20 years of National struggle they had morally advanced, the present phase was one of a confession of political bankruptcy. They were then adventuring in metaphysics. The constructive programme of the Congress was an illusion while the problem of the anti-imperialist fight was still there. The struggle had then been concentrated in Gandhiji's hands. Gandhiji was honest in his outlook, but it should be understood that he was essentially 'an incorrigible reformer' and not a revolutionist, though earlier, he had started a grim fight. Then a talk of struggle was being kept up along with a continuous undercurrent of compromise.

Students' Role

The present struggle was so circumscribed that even Hindu Mahasabha was thinking of starting a similar one. He was of the opinion that mere filling of jails was of no avail unless the character of the struggle changed into a dynamic one. The compromise that was aimed at was between Imperialism and the vested interests in the country.

Proceeding he said that students could also make a contribution on a national scale if only they developed a sense of confidence. They could build up a Nation-wide struggle if they developed local struggles based on local day-to-day grievances on a mass basis.

In conclusion he appealed for unity in student ranks and opined that any differences among them should be on an ideological footing and not on personal issues.

---

[1] The Conference was held from 31 December 1940 to 2 January 1941.

2. S.A. Brelvi's Address at Khalsa College, Bombay

Bombay Chronicle, 13 January 1941.

Tasks in Wake of Freedom: How Students Can Promote Inter-communal Harmony

Whether India become a free and united great nation, wielding a great influence in moulding the new world order, which would come into being at the end of the war, or whether she would continue to remain a house divided against itself would be dependent on how the communal problem was solved, was the view expressed by Mr S.A. Brelvi, presiding over the fourth annual social gathering of the Khalsa College, Bombay, on Sunday evening.

Methods of Unity

Mr Brelvi suggested that the promotion of inter-communal marriages and the acquisition of a knowledge of Hindustani in both the Urdu and Nagari scripts, were two very good solvents of the communal problem.

Progress of College

Mr J.B. Raju, Principal of the College, said that the College was endowed, founded, financed and run by the Sikh Gurudwaras in the Punjab. During the last year the Gurudwaras had earmarked their surplus income for the college. This had enabled them to complete the building and adequately to fulfil every condition laid down by the Bombay University. The college, which had begun in June 1937, with but a 100 students, had at present 400 students on its rolls. He envisaged a great future for the college, although it was the youngest and smallest college in Bombay, without any long tradition behind it. He thought it would be the privilege of the college to build up a great and original tradition, not the least part of which was inter-provincial comradeship. It was not merely their object to get good examination results and produce ineffective, useless graduates, but to give the students opportunities to train themselves in the art of national leadership.

Mr S. Daljit Singh in a brief address on the 'Eternal message of Sri Guru Gobind Singh' said that the special and central message of Guru Gobind's thoughts was that it was the imperative duty of everyone to fight the forces of evil, even at the cost of their lives.

Mr S.A. Brelvi in the course of his speech congratulated the college and the students on the record of the year. Mr Brelvi expressed gratification at the fact that the small number of students in the college made it possible for them to get personal attention from the staff. It would be a wholesome principle to restrict the number of students that could be admitted to any college in order to secure such attention.

Tribute to Sikhs

Mr Brelvi, paid a tribute to the Sikh community for establishing and running the college. They had shown a true understanding of their religion by not making the college a purely denominational one. He hoped the college would grow from strength to strength.

Turning to the many problems that confronted the students, Mr Brelvi said that students the world over shared the common burden of helping all those that were striving to save freedom and democracy for the world. Britain was fighting very hard, indeed, but the true test of her professions was with regard to India. Whether Britain made the correct choice or not, it remained certain that India, like the rest of the world, was on the brink of an all-round revolution and if only Indians were true to themselves, they would be free at the end of the war. It was therefore, necessary for the students to understand how this revolution was being brought about and to equip themselves to play a worthy part in the changing world of today. A student who did not keep himself abreast of the currents of national and international events, did not deserve to be called a student, and would certainly not be a worthy citizen.

Split Deplored

In this connection Mr Brelvi deplored the differences that had arisen in the students' organization. There were so many points of unity and so few of differences between the students. They all loved their country, desired its independence and eager to serve her. They should, therefore, evolve an agreed programme which would obtain the maximum co-operation of the largest number of students.

Why We Want Freedom

Turning to the political problem, Mr Brelvi said that the freedom was not an end in itself but only a means to higher ends. They wanted, for instance, to fight the triple evil of poverty, illiteracy and unemployment. They could not do so as they had no political power. India was one of the richest countries in its resources and yet her people were one of the poorest. But they could not exploit her resources to advantage without political freedom. Therefore it was necessary that they should join the Congress, which was fighting for freedom for the last 50 years.

Continuing Mr Brelvi pointed out that although they could not progress far without political power, there was no guarantee that with political power they would be able to do all they desired. It was possible, as it had happened in most Western countries, for a few rich people to monopolize political power so that although wealth might accumulate, the vast majority of the people might still suffer from poverty, unemployment and insecurity. It was their duty to see that such a thing did not happen by making sure that political power was enjoyed evenly by the poorest as well as the richest person and it was exercised in such a way as to secure the fruits of intensive industrialization by all sections of the people.

Communal Problem

Adverting to the communal problem Mr Brelvi regretted that the problem was being aggravated. If students could do nothing more than promote inter-communal harmony, they would be rendering an incalculable service. Inter-communal differences were largely due to the fact that many Hindus and Muslims had enough religion to hate one another but not enough to make them love one another.

3. Student Movement in Bengal: Disruptive Tendencies Mr Faruqi Deprecates Division Among Students

Amrita Bazar Patrika, 20 January 1941.

The fourth session of the All-Bengal Students' Conference was held yesterday at the Asutosh Memorial Hall under the auspices of the Bengal Provincial Students' Federation. Mr M. Farooqui[1] of Delhi, against whom Sir Maurice Gwyer, Vice-Chancellor of Delhi University recently took disciplinary action, presided.

An account of systematic attempts to create division among the students was given by the President in the course of his address. He said that at the instigation of political bosses certain student–workers made efforts to capture the platform of the Students' Federation but failed. Some of them, he said, started parallel student organization in Bengal, Delhi, Punjab, Madras, Bombay, and other places styling them as Forward Bloc Students' Bureaus and their programme was to bring about disruption in and liquidation of the All-India Students' Federation. The President asked the student–leaders of the province to guard against this menace.

The Conference was addressed among others by Sj. Satyendra Nath Majumdar and Prof. M.D. Grey of the Scottish Church College, both of whom deprecated the tendencies of disruption in the student movement.

Pakistan Scheme Condemned

The Conference passed a number of resolutions on various subjects, important among them being a resolution on the Bengal Secondary Education Bill and the Pakistan Scheme of Mr Jinnah. The Conference condemned the Pakistan Scheme of Mr Jinnah and described it as anti-national. The Bengal Secondary Education Bill was characterized by the Conference as a retrograde measure calculated to hamper the progress of education in the province. As such it requested the Government of Bengal to drop the Bill.

Unity Appeal to Students

At the outset Mr K. Ahmed, who had been President of the BPSF for the last four years announced that he was addressing them as President for the last time as he was retiring. He warned the students community against the activities of disrupters who wanted to weaken the students movement which had been built up with so much labour. He appealed to students to stand united and not allow their movement to be shattered and disrupted by outside intervention.

Organizational Strength

Sj. Satyendranath Mazumdar, who opened the conference received a great ovation as he stood up to speak, said that as a journalist he had been observing the students movement grow up in the province during the last four years and he personally knew many of those who by devoted work had built up the organization to its present position. Every movement found its expression through some organization. So in order to maintain the vitality of movement and to carry it to greater success it was essential that the organizational strength of the movement should be zealously guarded.

It was a matter of great shame and sorrow, he said, that the students movement which had attained such strength should be sought to be disrupted by outside interference. As a nation they were weak and subject to many ills which were the lot of a dependent people. They could not enjoy many of the rights which as human beings they were entitled to. Their lives were ordered through a narrow routine. There was now a stir all over the world for the establishment of a new order of things. Before their eyes institutions and practices on which society had been built up on which the old world had so long clung tenaciously were collapsing. The students and youths all over the world were restive and were anxious to play their part in building up the new order of things. If the students of Bengal failed to contribute their due share in shaping the new order of things to come, before the bar of history they would be charged with grave dereliction of duty at the most critical hour. In the march for new order of things the students community had to keep pace with the forces of progress and play their due share in building up the new social order which would be created out of the ruins of the old order.

Students and Employment

When the students after the completion of their education knocked at the doors of business houses in search of employment, they found the doors barred and bolted to their face. The young men were told that their education, intelligence and character were of no use for employers as their hands were full. There could be no greater insult to humanity. This order of society in which the youths had no scope for their talents was bound to breed discontent. Students must play their due share in bringing this state of society to an end.

Proceeding Mr Mazumdar said that Bengalees on account of their weaknesses now took a back seat in the political field of India. Dissensions and disruptive spirit weakened their ranks. Bengalees very often destroyed big institutions through jealousy. They very often embarked upon a new venture with a great deal of drum beating but ultimately failed to stick to their ideal.

Their ideal, Sj. Mazumdar concluded, was attainment of independence without which they could not get rid of their misery. Let the students be the advance guard of the Indian army of independence, and let them march to their goal joining hands with the workers and peasants. Let not petty jealousy, mean intrigue disrupt their ranks. The enemies, he said, who made frontal attacks were very often easy to deal, but when they came in the garb of friends they succeeded in doing greater mischief.

'Sloganistic' Disease

Professor M.D. Grey of the Scottish Church College, addressing the students said that he had recently been observing the spread of a terrible disease in Bengal and that he might describe as 'sloganistic'. By that he referred to the wild and uncertain movement of those who suffered from excesses of slogan. It was a form of intoxication and he wished the students to guard against it. The cure for it, he suggested was solid thinking about the meanings of the slogans they used. Professor Grey took up the slogan of the Students' Federation to explain to them the meaning of it. The slogan was 'freedom, peace and progress'. What was meant by freedom, he asked. He said that freedom was not an end in itself. Freedom must always be freedom from something and freedom for something. He would discuss the meaning of freedom in its educational application. In that respect freedom meant freedom from interference.

Continuing he said that there were three kinds of interferences against which students must guard. It had already been stated, he said, that students of Bengal were in the danger of being politically exploited. It was a real danger and he hoped they would guard against it.

Communal Interference

Then there was the danger, which he said was the most important of all, of communal interference in education. It was a thing so serious that Professor Grey had no words to 'speak about' it. Because, it was not true that truth differed according to community or according to religions of the persons who spoke about it; truth was one and indivisible and it was not subjective to modification according to communities either of the persons who had given it or of the people who received it.

Professor Grey would regard it as a disease of the first order if there came to be in Bengal in a very considerable degree communal interference in education.

Then there was the interference from persons who were neither teachers nor students. He regarded such interference in education as highly regrettable. He believed that students and teachers could together work out a system of education suited to their needs. But that attempt was being hampered at every turn by people who were neither students nor teachers. Against this interference too he warned the students.

Destructive Tendencies

Addressing the students Mr M. Farooqi said that they had met immediately after the annual session of the AISF at Nagpur where they witnessed certain disruptive and destructive tendencies on the part of some student workers. That had been a set back for the Students' Federation. Those responsible for the incident did it consciously and deliberately in order to confuse the public mind. Facts had been distorted, misrepresented and coloured in ugly fashion in the statements issued by these disruptive workers.

It might be remembered, he went on, at the Delhi Convention of the AISF attempts were made by certain interested political parties to capture the platform of the AISF and to exploit the students for the furtherance of sectarian ends. Certain resolutions were brought forward there accusing this group or that inside the Congress. These attempts were regarded as thoroughly dangerous for the growth of a popular and mass students movement. If those resolutions would have been passed the Students' Federation would have become a party platform and so they opposed the resolution and defeated them.

Having been defeated on the All-India open platform the disruptors followed up their tactics in the provinces. They systematically sabotaged the policy of the Delhi Convention. Being in a privileged position at the top it was comparatively easier for them to pursue their disruptive policy effectively. Mr M.L. Shah, the ex-General Secretary of the AISF became the main spokesman of this group. He misused his position and tried to liquidate the AISF as the effective organization of the Indian students. His task of disruption was facilitated by the fact that many of the student-leaders who had fought for the unity and integrity of the AISF were thrown behind the prison bars.

Story of Sabotage

The actual story of the systematic sabotage was a long one. They all know what were happening in Bengal. The BPSF was being challenged as the only platform of the students of Bengal. Almost a parallel student organization known as the Forward Bloc Student Bureaus was springing up everywhere. What was being done in Bengal was also being rehearsed in other provinces, though in somewhat different manner. In the UP the disruptors were trying to tag the UPSF on to a certain struggle with which the students had nothing to do. In direct contravention of the basic policy of the AISF, a resolution was passed by the Executive of the UPSF supporting a certain political party with which the mass of students had not the remotest connection.

'In my own province Delhi' he continued, 'something very sinister and dangerous was being done. A certain student worker who had been turned out of the DPSF because of gross misconduct formed a parallel student organization known as the Delhi Students' Federation. He was joined by certain adventurers who had nothing to do with the students movements as such. This new organization of students brought out a manifesto accusing not only the DPSF but the AISF as well. The AISF was charged of having failed to satisfy the aspirations of the Indian students. It was suggested that like the Delhi Students' Association, there should also be an All-Indian Students Association. Strangely enough the Delhi Students' Association was being surreptitiously supported by the student leader of the Forward Bloc, Mr Ansar Havani, though he was a member of the Working Committee of the AISF. Even Mr M.L. Shah who was supposed to be the custodian of the honour and name of the AISF was telling his friends in Delhi that he would not mind the growth of a parallel student organization in Delhi if it could succeed in throwing out the present office bearers of the DPSF. Mind you, comrades, Nagpur was still far off. And the General Secretary of the AISF in spite of the nasty manifesto of the Delhi Students' Association was bolstering up this parallel students' organization.'

Sinister Move

Proceeding he said, 'When we assembled at Nagpur for the AISF conference these gentlemen realized that in the open conference their programme, the programme of disruption and liquidation of the AISF, would not be accepted. They knew that the majority of delegates was opposed to giving up the independent character of the AISF. So what to do? That was a big question for them and they solved it in the most dangerous manner. They thought they could do it by disaffiliating such potent units of the AISF as Bengal, Punjab, Madras and Bombay. We defeated their sinister moves. There was no way out for them except staging a walk out and denouncing their opponents as disruptors.'

Thus, he said, it would be crystal clear to everyone who could follow up these events that they, and not the Students' Federation were disruptors. 'We fought for an independent AISF. They fought for a sectarian AISF. They could not succeed.' In the Students' Federation, he observed the tactics of the political bosses should not find any opportunity of success. They would see to it that the students movement was kept free from the dirty jugglery of the political bosses of their country. They should see to it that the Students' Federation remained an independent students' organization under whose banner all students irrespective of their ideologies would gather together to fight in defence of their specific demands.

In conclusion he said that the Students' Federation was to-day faced with a crisis.[2] The disruptors had done their best to destroy the unity among the students. The slogan of the disruptors, in the words of the *Amrita Bazar Patrika*, was 'either you must rule or you must destroy.' Their attempts had been thwarted. But still they were up with their game. The students must guard against these disruptive elements. He stressed the need for more attention to organizational aspects of the movement than of agitation.

---

[1] On 22 November 1940, Muqimuddin Farooqui, who had passed his MA, had been informed by the Vice Chancellor of the University of Delhi that he was rusticated for one year and could not take his MA degree for not regretting his role in picketing on 16 November 1940 when the University had observed complete strike in response to the call given by the AISF to observe the day as Anti-Repression Day. He was elected General Secretary of the All India Students' Federation by its newly elected Working Committee at its meeting held on 28 December 1940 at Nagpur where the annual session of the AISF was held on 25–6 December 1940.

[2] The annual session of the All-India Students' Federation held at Nagpur (25–6 December 1940) marked a split in the organization, with one AISF led by M. Farooqui and the other by M.L. Shah.

4. Students in Action

Communist, Vol. III, No. 3, February 1941, P.C. Joshi Archives on Contemporary History, JNU.

Madras

First Round

The first round was fought what seems to be ages ago. The students of Madras Presidency have done so much since, that they scarcely have time to look back to the first round. But it was on Jawaharlal's arrest that the whole Presidency flared up. The strikes were by no means confined to Madras City. There were strikes in Annamalai University, and the people of Chidambaram marched with the students. 1,000 students came out of St Joseph's and other institutions at Trichy. At Madura, the workers gave the students their guidance and whole hearted support. After the strike on Jawaharlal's arrest, at Pollachi, the authorities punished the students. The students struck again and held out for 15 days. In the end the citizens intervened and settled the strike in favour of the students.

In Andhra, too, the college students of Nellore, Rajamundry, Cocanada, Vizag, Anantapur, Madanapalli went on strike. High school students in Cuddapah and throughout the Kistna and the West and East Godavari districts went into action. The peak was reached for Andhra at Chitoor where the High School students issued typed leaflets and pasted them in all the class-rooms and on the lamp-posts on the roads leading to the school. The Police placed a heavy watch, but the students had their strike, marched through the streets and had their meeting.

But the thunder-clap for the Police came in Malabar. The barbarities of 15th September had inflamed the youth of Malabar. They were like gun at full cock, ready to go off. They were thinking of a strike against repression, when news of Jawaharlal's arrest came. They went on strike and paraded the village streets. The strike was spontaneous. All the more remarkable, and magnificently instructive, were their slogans: 'Communist Party Zindabad' and 'Release Nehru'. This was the voice of the future, which spontaneously acclaimed the great party of the people. The parents of these children were filled with wonderment, and tears. The martyrs of September did not die in vain. The Police cursed, incredulous.

Second Round

The Madras Government decided to take drastic steps. They issued the notorious communiqué. They threatened the students that there would be no Government jobs open to them if they went on strike. The fools! Students are not mercenaries.

The counter-attack came promptly. In Madras City 2,500 students marched from Government House and held a meeting in darkness. There were speeches. Hundreds of shadowy figures listened intently. A voice rang out, pierced through the night: 'The Government did precious little to find employment for graduates. The threat of not getting jobs won't scare us.'

The DPI, however, miscalculated. He went to Anantapur to face the students. As soon as he entered the hall, there was a chorus: 'Withdraw communiqué'. The Principal scolded the students and declared the meeting open. The DPI was to be the last speaker. The students, in Gandhi caps, filed out of the room. The DPI was puzzled, he jumped up to deliver his speech. He attacked the Communists. But he is a fool. He threatens the students, he says: 'Higher education is not your right but a privilege conferred upon you by the Government, which can be withdrawn at a moment's notice'. This was the last straw. The handful left walk out in disgust.

But the DPI is an understudy, and a stupid one, too. The Governor himself thought he would have a go at overawing the students. He had the cheek to go to perform the opening ceremony of a new ward in Vizag Medical College. The students muster strong and decide to boycott the function. But the Gandhian students had received instructions from Gandhiji (who finds time for examining every detail concerning the health and the mood of the despots of our land) that they should make the function a cordial affair and take part in it, loyally. But the students met and decided that Gandhiji was not in possession of the facts, and his instructions need not be obeyed. So the reception to the Governor was attended by only a handful.

But the Governor experienced the biggest rebuff in Andhra University. When he came, the students gathered together in a certain college to receive him. The authorities very tactfully took him round everywhere except this particular place. But the students were determined not to be cheated like this. They surprised the Governor at a Garden Party and yelled out the appropriate slogans. Then they gathered together at the gate. The Governor lost his nerve and sneaked out by the back-door.

Annamalai Events

'Annamalai Day' has been celebrated all over Annamalai University. After the protest strikes on Jawaharlal's arrest, the Police came to conduct a search in the hostel. The students gave the Police a good thrashing. Then the Police lay low for a fortnight. On 2nd December, the District Magistrate camped at Chidambaram and sent word to the Vice-Chancellor that he wanted to see 5 students including a girl student. While they were talking to the Magistrate, they were cordoned off and arrested, to be detained in Vellore Jail.

The news spread like wild-fire. The students rushed to the scene to cheer their comrades. Then the Police made a lathi charge, wounding 37 and injuring more.

Even before the AISF conference had passed a resolution calling upon the students to observe 'Annamalai Day', there were strikes all over Madras Presidency. The Annamalai students struck for one day and also fasted for one day.

This was the third round. It is still being fought out.

Bengal

Governor in a Fix

On the morning of the 13th of December, the Governor of Bengal paid a visit to Bankura. On that very day Sushil Palit the local Congress leader, offered Satyagraha and was arrested. In the afternoon the Governor was holding a conference in a pandal erected for the purpose with local 'men of property' as to the ways and means of persuading the people to starve to pay for this war.

The students held a meeting 4 yards away from the pandal. Their slogans disturbed the Governor and the Police. 'Go back Governor', 'Down with Ordinance Raj' and 'Boycott War-fund'. The Police ordered them to disperse, but they refused point blank.

Then came a sudden lathi charge, and many were injured. After that the students took out a huge procession. People joined it in thousands. The procession swept past the pandal. Some of the puppets in the pandal can't stand the strain any longer. They shout 'Bande Mataram' and come out of the pandal. The procession paraded the main thoroughfares of the city, and terminated at the hostel.

The Police Superintendent was out to take his revenge. He pursued the procession into the hostel and made another lathi charge inside the college compound. The Principal then took a firm stand, and demanded of the Superintendent who had given him permission to make a lathi charge in his hostel. The Superintendent apologized, but made no secret of the fact that he would do it again if necessary.

Orissa

Against War

There has been a sensation in Cuttack. Four students of the local seminary school were ruthlessly caned and fined by the Head Master for refusing to pay the war levies. The Students' Federation took up the cause and has been successful. There was such a storm over the matter that the Government were forced to enquire into the matter and demand an explanation. The fine has been remitted. The students have won.

A Fancy Fair was organized in aid of the war fund. The Principal of Ravenshaw College tried to sell tickets among the students. The Professors were put on to the job. But the anti-war propaganda of the SF was so successful that out of 900 students, Not One bought a ticket.

Punjab

Militant Lahore

3,000 students from the Lahore Colleges came out on strike on the 11th of January as a protest against the arrest of V.D. Chopra, a student and a former Vice-President of the Punjab Students' Union, who was arrested under the DIAO [Defence of India Ordinance].

A Hunger-strike

On the 17th of December, 30 boarders of the Indraprastha Girls' College, Delhi, went on hunger strike. They were being forced to pay for the full board during the 15 days' Christmas holidays. The students made representations, but the Principal was adamant. Matters were taken before the Governing Body, but the Principal delayed matters. The girls lost their patience and started hunger strike. There were immediate results. In four hours the students had won. The hunger strike was called off.

UP

Still Hot

UP has become the centre of dissensions, the base of the disruptors of the student movement. But the mass of the UP students are continuing their long campaign, already two months old. Azad's arrest called forth a spate of strikes. 10,000 came out in Cawnpur, including the students of Christ Church College. The Principal and the Muslim Students' League attempted to break the strike, but there was complete solidarity between the Hindu and the Muslim students. There was a Complete Strike in the girls' institutions in the city. The students of the Balika Vidyalaya did not sit for their terminal examinations. In Lucknow, the students observed a two-minutes' silence at noon and held gate meeting after school hours. There were demonstrations in Fyzabad, Jhansi and Benares.

Meanwhile, our comrade R.K. Gupta, the famous Cawnpur student leader, was arrested. There was a market hartal in his home, Kalpi. In the Government Jubilee College at Lucknow, there was a two minutes' silence as a mark of protest against his arrest.

Bombay

VJTI Strike

The students of the Victoria Jubilee Technical Institute have gone on strike. The majority of the students have struck, under the leadership of the North Bombay Students' Union. What are the grievances of the students? Up to 1938 free medical attention was provided for the residents of the hostel. From 1939, the Principal began to charge Rs 7 per person for medical attention. The students protested vigorously, and the authorities promised to look into the matter and refund the fees already paid. But six months passed, and nothing was done.

The non-resident students have joined the hostel students. The strike is successful and continuing.

Tiny Thana Too!

Thana is a remote suburb of Bombay but not so remote from the path of struggle. The BPSF Circular on Anti-Repression Day was received only a day earlier, but the students made the demonstration a unique success. On the day of the Congress President's arrest the students came out on strike. Authorities have rewarded them by withdrawing free-ships and other things. Students' Executive has launched a campaign for their restoration and a strike would be called on the Inspection Day in case the authorities do not come to their senses in time.

On the day the first Satyagrahi of the town was to make his debut the students decided to do something. A students' procession of 200–300 (big one for Thana) marched to the village where Satyagraha was to be offered. They made all the streets echo with anti-imperialist slogans and it was the Right-wingers who reproached them for 'Down with Police Zoolum,' and when it was repeated still more aloud near the police-van, the Right-wing leader present openly rebuked the boys. All the boys saw without any argument, against whom 'Satyagraha Struggle' was directed.

The next day an anti-repression meeting, crowded by students—boy and girls alike—was held. The Right-wingers admit that it is the student workers who have infused life not only in the student masses but also made the City Congress a live and functioning body but...the Students' Executive is going ahead with a series of mass meetings, to popularize ONE resolution of the BPSF Conference in ONE meeting.

5. Women Students' Conference at Pindi

The Tribune, 11 February 1941.

'Take Part in Emancipation of Country'

(From Our Own Correspondent)
Rawalpindi, 9 February.

The Punjab Women Students' Conference opened its session this afternoon amidst scenes of great enthusiasm. Miss Lalli Bhagat performed the hoisting ceremony of the students' flag. Miss Sunder Kakkar delivered her inaugural address, in which she described briefly the aims and objects of the Women Students' Movement and brought home to all those present that the women students had a particular role to play in the civic life of the country and had to take a lion's share in the political upheaval of their Motherland.

After a song by Miss Hitt Kakkar, Miss Jasbir Bhagat, President of the Reception Committee, delivered her welcome address.

She said that this was the first time in the history of Rawalpindi, that a Women Students' Conference had been organized. She appealed to them to be united and reiterated her own determination to uphold the students' flag.

Presidential Address

Miss Gursaran Rai, the President-elect of the Conference then delivered her presidential address extempore. Miss Gursaran Rai reiterated her resolve that they would not rest till their destination was reached. Referring to the decisions of the All-India Women's Conference, she appealed to the women students of Rawalpindi to strive their every nerve in organizing the Students' Movement at 'Pindi', which had always been in the forefront of all movements. She pointed out the decisions arrived at the All-India Women's Conference held at Nagpur and added that women students should work side by side with male students to take the students' movement to its destined goal. It was in the fitness of the things, she proceeded further, that they should take the responsibility of organizing Women Students' Conference on their shoulders, adding that every woman, child and man had to take part in the battle for the emancipation of the country. Coming to the repression launched in this country, she referred to the prosecutions of student workers and protested against the arrests of Comrades Rajbans, Nawabzada Mazhar, Mr Chopra and Professor Chaddha. She also referred to the detention of about 360 students in Bengal and vehemently criticized the Circulars of the Madras and UP Governments regarding the activities of the students.

Resolutions

Miss Kushalya Kapoor of Lahore moved the first resolution which recorded its forceful condemnation of the repressive policy of the Government and considered recent communiqués of Madras and UP Governments as the measures designed to deny the very fundamental rights of the student community. The resolution further protested against the searches of student workers of Rawalpindi. It characterized the action of the Government as an attack on the civil liberties of the students' organization and expressed its resolve and determination to fight for the cause of Freedom, Peace and Progress. The resolution was seconded by Miss Sita Bakhshi and carried unanimously.

Miss Pushpa Sethi then moved a resolution on the adult education and stressed the need of spreading literacy amongst grown-up women. The resolution was passed.

Another resolution referred to the cultural activities of the women students and emphasized the necessity of starting women students' dramatic and other circles in their respective colleges and work side by side with the Union.

The demand for the inclusion of home nursing and handicrafts in the curriculum of their studies was incorporated in another resolution passed by the conference.

The last resolution of the session protested against the action of Gordon College authorities in imposing fines upon the students and asked the women students to 'be prepared.' The resolution further requested the Gordon College authorities to remit the fine in the interest of the institution itself.

6. 'The Soul (?) of an Imperialist'

The Student, Organ of AISF, February–March 1941.

It is time that British politicians paused to make sure whether their fight for the 'preservation of elements of civilization', is compatible with the irresponsible utterances of their paid agents here in India. Sir Maxwell, who holds the portfolio of Home Department, can well claim a successful comparison with his Nazi Replica, Dr Goebbels in so far as the use of abominable expression is concerned. He vented his spleen while speaking on the resolution regarding the detenues moved by Mr N.M. Joshi in the Central Assembly.[1] Normally the session of the Central Assembly is a tame affair, the general mass of our countrymen attaching little importance to this puppet parliament. But in the occasional utterance of those on the Treasury Benches one gets a glimpse of the soul of an imperialist.

Referring to the detenues, persons on whom history alone can pass its verdict, Sir Maxwell said, 'They are indecent, dishonest, utterly worthless persons.' This remark leaves us cold, knowing as we do the traditional hypocrisy in which the reactionary nurtured. But we cannot help remarking that not only does Sir Maxwell betray an unbalanced mind but also an unpardonable ignorance of history—unpardonable since he happens to be His Majesty's Minister. Does he know that the head of the Soviet Union was once a hounded revolutionary; does he so conveniently forget that the maker of modern Eire once used to be a 'wanted' man of the British Govt? Who can tell that this column of detenues, now behind the bars of Indian Bastilles, will not throw up Stalins and De Valeras—men who will rise to make a united nation out of the dust to which we have been condemned?

Sir Maxwell could not have descended lower when he said, 'the detenues are paid agitators'. We trust it is out of sheer spite which makes him utter such an ignoble expression; and since it is born out of malevolence its edges are blunt and do not deserve to be discussed. On the other hand may we appeal to Sir Maxwell to reflect with a calm mind whether the huge salary which officials like him enjoy is not a tremendous drain upon the poor resources of this country. Whether the detenues are paid agitators or not, the 'steel frame of bureaucracy' does stand like a dead-weight upon the nation's finances.

The art of Sir Maxwell lies in choosing vile words and fitting them in still viler contexts. He has used the epithet 'treachery' for the acts of the detenues. We very much wish he had in mind the lamentable story of broken pledges of Britain towards India which is the history of the British rule for a century and a half. Public memory is not too short to forget how the pre-war British policy led the fattening of Fascism at the expense of certain countries. We are at a loss for words to express the misdeeds of the Whitehall; but we are sure Sir Maxwell would have desisted from using 'treachery' for others if he was reminded of those acts.

We ungrudgingly give credit for knowing the signs of time to Sir Maxwell. He has made bold to say that the life of these detenues is spent in 'plotting the downfall of society.' A society which is based upon exploitation of man by man must fall; Sir Maxwell and his like would be poor props trying to support such a decaying system. The detenues have accepted sufferings and privations as their lot so that the greater humanity which lies submerged in dumb pangs of sorrow might emerge out as the true builder of a just social order. Sir Maxwell will agree, he is a complete stranger to any such idealism and that speaks for his bewildered outbursts when he senses the downfall of society of which he is supposed to be a pillar. And whatever Sir Maxwell may say, the underdog is determined to put an end to a hideous system of exploitation, and let us assure Sir Maxwell that his attempts to perpetuate it will prove abortive.

---

[1] See Document No. 143, Chapter 2.

7. 'Mr Jinnah and the Muslim Students'

The Student, Organ of AISF, February–March 1941.

We are constrained to read the advice given by Mr Jinnah to the Muslim students wherein he says, '—I hope that Muslims will not participate in any strikes directly or indirectly to support the Congress in this movement as their avowed objective is—'.

One can have serious political differences with Gandhiji and his individual Civil Disobedience or for matter of that, with any political creed. But in spite of these differences, one cannot ignore for a moment that our ultimate objective is Complete Independence and who has been more verbose in declaring it than Mr Jinnah himself? It would be sheer absurdity to imagine that a man who claims to be a champion of the cause of this country cannot visualize the necessity of a mass awakening amongst the youth of a country and their struggle against repression. The relation between political consciousness and the demand for civil liberties is that of cause and effect and it is nothing less than betrayal of gross ignorance to say that one can be separated from the other. The struggle of the students against repression is the expression of their solidarity and determination to achieve their objective. And the Muslim Students of this country have never lagged behind to show that they are united with all others in achieving this end. We are afraid Mr Jinnah has misunderstood the character of the student movement in India guided by the AISF which alone can claim to be above factionalism and that his disruptive advice is bound to fall flat.

8. All-Utkal Students' Federation Conference: Presidential Address

Amrita Bazar Patrika, 11 March 1941.

What Students Want
Rational Re-adjustment of Social Order
Sj. Satyendra Majumdar's Advice

Cuttack, 8 March.

Sj. Satyendra Nath Majumdar, President-elect of Seventeenth Session of the All-Utkal Students' Federation arrived here this morning by Puri Express. He was received at the station by students and garlanded amidst shouts of 'Inquilab Zindabad,' 'Students Unite' and other things.

The conference meets this evening at 6 p.m.

Youth's 'Revolt': Sj. Satyen Majumdar on Students' Future

Cuttack, 8 March.

A fervent appeal to the student community to awake betimes to the danger of mischievous attempts that are being made by some designing persons to create a split in the ranks of the students all over the country, and set their face sternly against such a nefarious move, was made by Mr Satyendra Nath Majumdar while presiding over the 17th session of the All-Utkal Students' Federation held here to-day.

Mr Majumdar observed that slowly and perhaps imperceptively, a new orientation was discernible in the outlook of the rank and file of the youth and student organizations in this country. The reasons for this were not far to seek. On the one hand the reins of the nationalist movement had passed out of the hands of the capitalists and the bourgeoisie to the poorer middle classes, vesting control of the supreme executive of the Congress to the real representatives of the masses: and on the other hand, the labour and peasant organizations which had grown up all over the country, began to agitate for a socialistic approach to the solution of the diverse economic problems affecting the interests of the masses. The youth and the students of India could not remain indifferent to these stirrings of a new life. They began to react to the new doctrines and dogmas which gained currency, according to their respective ideologies and temperament.

Present System of Education

Proceeding, the President pointed out how the present system of education and the social environment in which the youth of the country were moving, must inevitably tend towards narrowing their outlook and distorting their intellect. The present system of education, he maintained, had made of their youth, a race of service hunters, and their social atmosphere had done nothing except creating in them a feeling of overweening conceit about their intellectual superiority over the masses of their country. He sounded a note of warning that the time was not far distant when a mighty upheaval would sweep off this artificial growth in their social structure.

Mr Majumdar then stated that during the last 200 years of British rule over this country, the percentage of literacy had considerably deteriorated. A comprehensive scheme of primary education for the masses was prevalent in India till the 18th century. Not only that, even in the sphere of higher education, in literature, astrology, the healing art, philosophy and theology,

Indian scholars had in those days attained a world-wide reputation. To-day it was pure moonshine to expect even one primary school for a unit of three villages. There was to be found now-a-days, one middle-English school to minister to the needs of every 100 square miles, one high school for every 300 square miles and one college for every 4000 square miles. Except for a few Municipal towns and a limited area in the countryside, compulsory primary education had not yet been introduced. The appalling illiteracy of the masses was operating as a stumbling block to the all-round progress of the country.

'Revolt' Among Youth

Referring to signs of 'revolt' among the youth, the President said that an outlet must be found for ventilation of the deep discontent and grim despair which the youth had to labour under for no fault of theirs. Really speaking, what the student world had been agitating for was a more equitable and rational adjustment of the existing economic and social relations, and this was also the fundamental question at issue in their wider national movement. How long is the country to drag the dead-weight of a political constitution and a social order which have long outlived their utility? That is in essence the main question which had emerged out of the Indian freedom movement and that was also the problem which the student and youth organizations have sought to raise before the country for solution.

After briefly referring to genesis of the present war, the President in conclusion said, 'I beseech you, my young friends, to refuse to play the second fiddle to any political leader, however influential and eminent he may be. Resist all attempts that may be insidiously made to bring disunity among your rank and file. When our elders are busy in the dirty game of mud-slinging at one another, to the detriment of the best interests of the Motherland, may it be given to the younger generation to teach them a much needed lesson by showing unity and cohesion, and by their determination to put the sacred interests of the nation before self. Let this message of unity and good-will towards all section of the student fraternity go forth from this platform to-day.'—UP

9. 'Fill up the Breach on Student Front'

Communist, Vol. III, No. 3, March 1941, P.C. Joshi Archives on Contemporary History, JNU.

Two months ago, the enemies of the student movement were unmasked at the 6th Conference of the AISF at Nagpur. Unable to face the keen scrutiny of the fighter delegates, they made a tiny opening in the student fronts. For a full year of war, the disruptors of our national forces had not dared to disorganize the student ranks. But after the burst of strikes last winter, they took the plunge.

At Nagpur, the disruptors, known to the students as unprincipled adventurers, were not allowed to disrupt and paralyse the AISF from within. They fled in disorder. But was their fight the result of mere panic? Did it mean we had heard the last of them? No: those who think on these lines help the disruptors. THE WALK-OUT AT NAGPUR WAS A WELL-CALCULATED FIRST STEP IN THE POLICY OF DISRUPTION. THE BATTLE AGAINST THE DISRUPTORS HAS JUST BEGUN. Our student comrades need all their ingenuity, resourcefulness and, above all, A CORRECT UNDERSTANDING OF THE NEED FOR UNITY, if they are to wage this difficult battle. We have to see that the tiny breach is not allowed to widen; we have to see that the AISF does not become a detachment of leaders cut off from the base: the MASS of the student. To carry out these tasks, we have, first of all, to get the disruptors and their deeds up to the present in a correct perspective. We have, also, to understand how we Communists have baffled the disruptors up to date. Without such an understanding, we shall find ourselves HELPING the disruptors IN PRACTICE, while we fulminate against them.

Spear-head

Two months ago we wrote 'STUDENTS HEAD THE NATIONAL FORCE!' And we meant it! After a year of war, imperialism had cut a large portion of our anti-imperialist front to pieces. Both the leadership of the National Congress and the 'Left Opposition' had made the Congress into a battle-ground of factional claims instead of preserving and widening it as a battle-front against imperialism. Meanwhile, communal discord and regional separatism grew by leaps and bounds, resulting, finally in 'demands' on imperialism for Pakistan and Hindustan. But the AISF remained firm as a rock. On this sector of the front, the vicious attacks of the enemy and the capitulatory policy of the national leadership did not succeed in producing disunity and disorganization. Two months after the war, at the Delhi Convention, the efforts of the Forward Bloc to transform the AISF into an appendage of the Forward Bloc alone, was decisively defeated. But that was not all. Throughout the first year of war, the students not only preserved the pre-war unity of the students in the AISF, they forged unity with the communally-minded students who had hitherto been hostile to the AISF. (Holwell Monument agitation.)

Why United?

What was the cause of this remarkable unity? Was it the result of utter despair—a lifeless, despondent attitude? Or war it a unity based on the delusion that the national leadership was going to lead the people to independence and that a complete obedience to Gandhiji and his discipline was necessary? OR, finally, was it a FIGHTING ANTI-IMPERIALIST UNITY, a sign of the deliberate refusal of the students to allow the policy of disruption to find favour in their ranks?

The unity was certainly NOT the result of despair. But it was PARTLY based on the delusion that the national leadership would yet launch a campaign for the destruction of imperialism, and PARTLY based on A CONSCIOUS, DELIBERATE DESIRE NOT TO ALLOW THE COMPROMISING PATH OF THE BOURGEOISIE TO MISLEAD THE STUDENTS BUT TO STRIKE OUT ALONG THE PROLETARIAN PATH OF A UNITED STRUGGLE OF THE PEOPLE AGAINST IMPERIALISM. The great mass strikes which greeted the beginning of the satyagraha by Gandhiji, were partly launched with the hope (among some students) that the satyagraha would become a MASS SATYAGRAHA and was the BEGINNING of a real struggle; partly launched, under Communist leadership, with the determination to mobilize the students and thus show the entire people the proletarian technique of anti-imperialist struggle.

A Broader Basis

But the strike wave assumed unprecedented dimensions. It surged into new institutions, new towns, new districts, whole new provinces! It receded and burst back again and again in an angry flood. It was a prolonged conflict. Round upon round was fought out with imperialism and its ever-increasing agencies: the CID, the educational authorities, Gandhiji himself and the local Congress leaders.

The strikes were, in the main, SPONTANEOUS. This was at once a sign of the weakness of the AISF at the base AND a sign of the immense vitality of the youth of our land and its INSTINCTIVE, NATURAL acceptance of the weapon of MASS STRIKE, USED AS A POLITICAL DEMONSTRATION and for STUDENT RIGHTS. The youth had SPONTANEOUSLY accepted the proletarian weapons in the fight for liberation.

These strikes brought into ACTION hundreds of young people, belonging to all communities, provinces, of all parties and of no party. They learnt their own strength, they received a rich political education. The call had gone out to the most backward students and had received a response. THE BASIS WAS CREATED FOR A BROADER UNITY. The unity displayed in action had to be consolidated, made permanent. Here was a glorious opportunity to strengthen the base of the AISF to cement students' unity, to give an example to the whole country.

Alarm!

But we had to raise the alarm once! The national leaders had been marking time. They were seeking a favourable moment for their frontal assault on the student movement. The strikes inspired surprise and anger among them. MORE THE ENTHUSIASM WITH WHICH THE PEOPLE GREETED THE STRIKES MADE THEM LIVID. They could not wait any longer. Confident that the students would be cowed down by his threats, Gandhiji opened fire. The student strikes interfered with his satyagraha, they MUST STOP! Meanwhile, Jinnah called upon the Muslim students NOT to take part in mass strikes against repression—they were 'Congress-inspired'! Gandhiji and Jinnah, each in his own way, sought to drive the students out of the theatre of politics.

Mobilize!

The students are young. They have the courage of youth. They learn fast. But they DON'T discard their respected leaders overnight. They try again and again, they plead with them. They don't make up their minds in a flash. They test out their new leaders. The implications of Gandhiji's statements had to be explained to them PATIENTLY, frankly, honestly. They had to be told how Gandhiji had demanded a complete PARALYSIS OF THE AISF and the student movement. How he had declared that students either co-operate 'loyally' with the authorities, abide by ALL the rules and regulations of the institutions, or give up their studies and become satyagrahis.

The mobilization was good. Nagpur cried 'HALT' to the disruptors. The conspiracy to paralyse and disrupt the AISF from WITHIN, by stealth, was unearthed. This was the FIRST ROUND against the disruptors in the student ranks. It ended in the FIRST DEFEAT of the disruptors.

New Tactics

But the disruptors were well-advised. They did not act 'on their own'. They were cornered, but they did not give up. Guided by Gandhiji himself, they staged a 'split'. Their policy of paralysing and disrupting the students movement from WITHIN the AISF had failed. They changed their tactics. They staged the 'split' NOT in panic and despair, but as the WELL THOUGHT OUT FIRST STEP IN THEIR PATH OF DISRUPTION. Unable to take the AISF, the fortress of the students, by assault, they devised a new STRATEGY, that of surrounding the AISF and cutting it off from the source of all its strength; the mass of the students. They hoped to do this by spreading confusion, by raising false issues, by talking of a 'split' and by pretending that their pleas for unity had been turned down by the Communists who have 'captured the AISF.'

Why did they strike out so boldly and confidently on this path of disrupting the students' movement by driving a wedge between the AISF and the masses? Because, THE LINKS BETWEEN THE AISF AND THE MASS OF THE STUDENTS IS WEAK. The AISF has got enormous influence, but its BASE IS WEAK. The fighting front is magnificent, the rear is a tower of strength. But immediately behind the lines, the units of the AISF in the colleges, the schools and the institutions, which connect the base with the front and the leadership, the links are weak. The havoc wrought by naked imperialist attacks and the confusion spread by the disruptors CAN, together, achieve the purpose of PARALYSING THE STUDENT MOVEMENT. Hence, their NEW STRATEGY is to ATTACK THE AISF FROM WITHOUT and to lay a siege round the AISF and CUT IT OFF FROM THE MASS OF THE STUDENTS.

Battle Just Begun

When this is the position, it would be CRIMINAL FOLLY on the part of any sincere member of the AISF to think that THE LAST HAS BEEN HEARD OF THE DISRUPTORS. The DANGER OF DISRUPTION AND PARALYSIS IS NOT OVER, BUT IS GROWING, TAKING NEW FORMS, EXPRESSED IN NEW METHODS. In such a situation, the genuine stalwarts of the student movement MUST BEWARE of shutting their eyes to the danger and assuming that the great fight against the disruptors has been fought and won IN A SINGLE BATTLE AT NAGPUR.

Duped Fifth Column

The efforts of the disruptors to-day are directed towards two objectives. They hope, either to PLAY INTO THEIR HANDS BY JUSTIFYING THE 'SPLIT' AND THUS WIDENING THE BREACH IN OUR FRONT; OR, they hope to SCARE US into surrendering to them and having UNITY ON THEIR TERMS. Both lead to the same dead end for the student movement, its disappearance.

In the AISF itself, there are comrades who help them unwittingly to attain either of the above objectives. These are the DUPED FIFTH COLUMN of the disruptors in the AISF.

If we are to save the students movement in India from ruin, if we are to combat the disruptors skillfully and cleverly and foil their game, we have to make a beginning by rooting out the various trends in the AISF which objectively help the disruptors.

'Bad History'

We shall deal, first, with the pompous exponents of the 'theory' that the Nagpur 'split' was 'A HISTORIC NECESSITY'. These comrades make use of neat phrases to make absurd formulations which ASSIST DIRECTLY THE DISRUPTORS in their efforts to parade as the champions of 'unity', in their efforts to bring about a real split in the student movement.

The truth is that the disruptors have staged the fake 'split' (not a split at all) IN ORDER TO WORK UP A REAL SPLIT. This task becomes very much easier for them if their opponents declare that there was a real split at Nagpur, that they are proud of the split, that the 'split was a historic necessity'. The unorganized students hear the disruptors say, 'There you are, we told you the communists have captured the AISF and have driven out everyone else. The real fight was between the Communist clique and the rank-and-file of the AISF. Their 'AISF' is not the real AISF at all, but a Communist organization, which, they say, is a historic necessity. Come to our AISF. Leave them high and dry'.

INDIRECTLY, 'this theory' leads to complacency, a sad under-estimation of the strength of the disruptors, of their power of burrowing into the student base and sowing dissensions and spreading confusion. It leads to the neglect of the BASIC and URGENT tasks in the student movement to-day: the tasks of strengthening the base of the AISF.

Those who hold this view have failed to understand the BASIC TASK OF OUR PARTY IN THE PRESENT PERIOD. Our task in every sector of the front against imperialism is NOT to DESTROY UNITY and JUSTIFY SPLITS, BUT to preserve the unity built up through the last 20 years, to extend that unity for the final struggle against imperialism. Those who talk of splits that are 'historically necessary' submit to the tyranny of phrases and help the work of our enemies, the enemies of the people. Communists shall fight against this interpretation of the outrageous farce of a 'split' that has been forced on the students movement in order to force a real split in our ranks.

'Short Cuts?'

But these bad 'historians' have less sophisticated allies. These comrades say 'We got the AISF by all the rules of the AISF Constitution, all the rules of the game. Why waste time talking to the disruptors and trying to get unity? To let the disruptors into the AISF again is to create unnecessary difficulties'.

These comrades are against ALL attempts at unity that have been made under the initiative of the Communist students, at Nagpur and since Nagpur. They want short cuts to complete victory over the disruptors.

On the initiative of the Communist students, the AISF leadership has made repeated efforts to fill up the breach at the top. They have made repeated efforts to restore a formal unity in the AISF ON THE CONDITION that the POLICY OF DISRUPTION is not pursued: that strikes are not banned, that the provincial units of the AISF are not disaffiliated if they show signs of life.

But these efforts are A PART OF THE STRUGGLE AT THE BASE to bring about a real fighting unity of the students and to baffle the disruptors. These unity efforts are NOT concessions to the policy of disruption, they were not a desperate appeal 'to the hearts of the disruptors' in a fit of panic. They have been made, and will continue to be made, because Communists believe that no stone must be left unturned to cement the unity of the students and the people as a whole, on a democratic basis, and for the battle against the power that holds our country in chains.

This attitude is based on a desire to find short cuts to a final victory over the enemies of the people. It leads to complacency, an over-estimation of our own strength and of the AISF. It makes voting majorities the final and unalterable signs of strength and weakness. It fails to recognize that the student movement is a growing, developing movement, which is going through the twists and turns of a very difficult period and has to avoid the quicksand, feeling every step forward. It forgets the danger of the AISF running too far ahead of the masses.

A Magic Formula

Last come the veterans who are convinced that the remedies of the pre-war-period must apply to-day. They forget that we have entered a new period, in which our task is not merely to PREPARE for the coming final struggle IN THE FUTURE, but a period which has before it the IMMEDIATE TASK of mobilizing the entire people for the overthrow of imperialism. That is why they call for 'UNITY AT ANY PRICE'. They think the FORMAL UNITY of the AISF Working Committee is the magic unity which will solve most of the problems.

But this is a period in which the issue between the disruptors and ourselves is NOT one of FREEDOM TO PUT FORWARD OUR VIEWS MERELY, the issue is 'UNITY FOR ACTION OR UNITY

FOR LIQUIDATION'. There is no question that every student in the AISF has the right to put forward his own point of view. We Communists have always fought for that (at Madras in 1936 and Delhi in 1940) and we shall continue to do so. But we shall never submit to terms of unity which mean THE STOPPAGE OF ALL STRIKE-ACTION. To the conspiracy to kill the students' movement, we can be no party. To keep the student movement alive, to strengthen its base, to play our part in the people's struggle for liberation, we are prepared to unite with anybody.

A formal unity which helps us in the task of strengthening the movement is of immense help to us. But we shall NEVER gamble with an unconditional surrender and satisfy our conscience with a few unworkable 'constitutional safeguards'.

To Wind-up

To bring the 'duped fifth column' to its senses, however, it is not enough to make them realize how they aid the disruptors. It is necessary to tell them what has to be done PRACTICALLY to guard and strengthen the unity of the student movement by making the AISF a powerful organization, armour-plated at every point, without a single chink in its armour.

Such an organization would strike terror into the hearts of the disruptors who have sold their services to sworn enemies of the student movement. It would baffle the Police. It would survive the rapid fire of the imperialist forces in the coming months of spring. It would do more, it would once again, HEAD THE NATIONAL FORCES. Already, there are signs that Indian proletariat and peasantry is ready, with fists clenched, to go grimly into a life-and-death struggle in the coming months. Marching in step with the endless columns of the mazdurs and the kisans, the students would send a thrill through the whole nation and blaze a trail for the disappointed satyagrahis.

Immediate Tasks

1. Popularize the Nagpur resolution on unity.
2. Interpret the resolution, concretely, in the light of the offers of the disruptors.
3. Hold special meetings to ROOT OUT the THREE DEVIATIONS which assist the disruptors.
4. Reorganize the Students' Union in each city to have functioning units in every institution.
5. ACTIVIZE these units, make them function, by developing cultural campaigns.
6. Approach the healthy, athletic students by organizing athletic events under the auspices of the unit of the AISF.
7. Make special efforts to branch out among:
   (1) vaguely nationalist students torn with doubts over the 'split'—VERY PATIENT explanation and argument with them, NOT sharp polemics.
   (2) Communal students—armed with the Pakistan resolution.
   (3) Women students organized on the basis of their special rights and grievances.
   (4) High School students—again on the basis of their specific academic rights and grievances.

   We should ALWAYS remember that our efforts to branch out among these students would be doomed unless we have due regard to their political level when we are approaching them.
8. Make every effort to restore a formal unity at the top provided the right to strike and the INTEGRITY of the AISF is NOT in jeopardy.

10. Report on 'Students in Action'

The Student, Organ of AISF, April 1941.

Rawalpindi: Seven persons including the President, the General Secretary and other prominent members of the Pindi Students' Union have been arrested on a charge of rioting on 14 February when some policemen and members of the public were injured as the result of pelting of stones by a mob. All the arrested persons have been released on bail.

Sindh: Com. Hotu, Ex-General Secretary was arrested at Tando Adam on 26th January under DIR and later released.

Cawnpore: Mr Raghubans Ratan Gaur, a student of the Government Agriculture College, who commenced a 'fast unto death' on 25th January in the College premises, was arrested the same night.

The fast is stated to have been undertaken as a protest against his expulsion from the College.

Lucknow: Anand Singh, a student of Lucknow University has been arrested for an objectionable Speech.

S.K. Rai of Lucknow was sentenced to 9 months RI for an anti-war speech in a students' meeting.

Benares: Mr Balram Pande, President of the Sanskrit Students' Association, has been already under a warrant from Benares State.

Patna: About 20 university students residing in different Hostels, who it is reported, participated in the last Independence Day, have been penalized by imposition of fines on them by authorities.

Vizagapatnam: Comrades I.V.K. Vallabh Rao, General Secretary of the Vizagapatnam Students' Organisation and a member of Working Committee of APSF, B. Suryanarayan Maithy, student of Arts College, M. Rangayya and A. Ranganayakulu, students of Medical College were arrested in Vizagapatnam on the 22nd February and detained in Vellore jail.

Com. G. Ramkotiswar Rao MBBS Ex-General Secretary, APSF and a student of Christian College, R. Achutan, G. Secretary of Madras Students' Organization and a student of Law College, S.M. Akbari of Engineering College and K. Ganesan of Presidency College, all from Madras City, were arrested and detained on the 21st January.

Guntur: Orders have been passed by the Principal of the Engineering College, Guntur, expelling 7 students from the College, it is stated, on account of their activities in connection with the recent strikes. The offense committed by one student was distribution of legal handbills of the MSO about a meeting.

Madura: Mr N. Sankariah, a student of the American College and Secretary of the Madura Students' Organization was arrested under the DIR and remanded by Additional District Magistrate. The students of the college took out a procession and held a meeting at which a resolution was passed protesting against the arrest.

Coconada: In December 1940 nearly 12 students went on hunger strike before the Principal's room to persuade him to send up the 30 detained students in Intermediate for the University examination. After two days the Principal agreed before Dr V.V. Krishnayya whose services were requisitioned for negotiation, by the President of the DCC to send up all students except those who were short of percentage in attendance and whose conduct was questionable, and assured in public that there would be no victimization in any case. The hunger strike was given up, the Principal himself giving the first spoon of juice to the strikers. But later he issued a statement to the local press refuting the agreement and Dr V.V. Krishnayya gave an offensive reply to it. Then the Principal expelled eight Students and sent their T Certificates to their parents.

The 8 students later joined the Guntur College. The Principal thus grossly violated the agreement by his treacherous act.

G.S. Balaji Das

Bellary: Miss Meenakshi, a student of the Annamalai University who was recently detained in Vellore jail, has been brought to Bellary with a woman escort and entrusted to her father. She has been released on parole.

Under the conditions of the security bond she has to stay at Bellary and cannot therefore, continue her studies in the University.

Poona, 27 February: The Poona police searched today the room of Mr S.S. Narayane, a student of the Ferguson College on suspicion of being in possession of alleged Communist literature. The student, it is understood, has been arrested.

Strike in the Gujrat College, Ahmedabad: Two years back, Diwan Bahadur Kazi was appointed as Principal who slowly and slowly began to curtail the rights of the Students' Representative Council and even crossed the limits,

(1) by not allowing us to invite Dr Khan Sahib to address us.

(2) By taking away the minute book of the SRC.

(3) Prohibiting meetings

(4) Censoring on our news

(5) asking us to apologize for writing letter to M. Gandhi and threatened our president with disciplinary action. For this interference of the authorities in our legal rights we had to resolve to fight against the interference, on 7th January.

On the 21st January we went on a General Strike in Ahmedabad against the arrest of the two students workers J. Sutaria and D.N. Vashi. On this the Principal removed the names of our two main workers from College Rolls. With the help of the citizens we tried to negotiate but in vain. We held a meeting to decide further action in which out of 671 voters 512 voted for the strike and accordingly strike began on 28th January. Members of the Action Committee worked very hard. Lady students played their important part. Processions and meetings were taken. This strike lasted for only five days and by the intervention of some influential citizens a compromise was signed. Students were given their rights, victimized workers were admitted in college. Thus the glorious strike ended.

Moreina (Gwalior): Moreina High School students organized a procession to celebrate the Independence Day. At a students' meeting National Flag was unfurled and when the proceedings of meeting were about to follow the Head Master of the High School came to the place (a public place and the day was a General Holiday being Sunday) and interrupted the proceedings threatening the students with severe action for their activities.

On the 28th January he suspended Com. Ramgopal Bansal and his colleagues from the School. When despite every effort the Head Master did not withdraw his orders the students resorted to strike to establish their right and demand justice. A Police guard was posted at the school gates for two days. The strike however, ended in complete success and the students were re-admitted in the school.

Gauhati: Sixteen places mostly residences of students who are members of the Assam Students' Federation and the Radical Institute of Gauhati were searched on the morning of 10th February by the Gauhati Police. While no one was arrested the Police seized some allegedly communist literature.

Com. Bishnu Ram Bora, the Organizing Secretary, Assam Students' Federation, the General Secy, Jorhat District S.F. and a member of the All-India Students' Council, has been interned within the Jorhat Police Station of Sibsagar District.

Pushpalata Saikia, a student of Gauhati Law College was arrested on 1st March under DIR.

Sylhet: Six students of the M. College residing in the Hostel were asked by the Governing Body to leave hostel for taking a leading part in the celebration of the Independence Day within the hostel. They defied the order and the hostellers in a body supported them and demanded withdrawal of the said order. Principal in reply asked all to leave the hostel. A general hunger strike began on the 27th January 72 students, participating. Students from the College assembled in the hostel.

Sympathetic words came from all quarters. But, not merely words. Students from Pyari Mohan Public (now Rasamay Memorial) Academy, Madan Mohan College, Govt Madarsa marched in batches towards the hostel about 5 miles from the town and demanded withdrawal of the order. Sj. Baidyanath Mukherji, MLA a member of the Governing Body, called a requisition meeting of the GB and assured the hunger strikers that the previous decisions would come for reconsideration and the students will not have to leave hostel.

Hunger-strike was postponed pending the re-consideration of the whole affair.

Habiganj: On the 26th January students came out in a procession to celebrate the Independence Day inspite of the ban order under DI Act. Police tried to stop the procession but they could not. They arrested 10 and 6 more students, yet the procession continued. Just before the thana they blocked the path and kept back a section of the procession. There the students held a meeting in the thana compound. Another meeting was held in the Town Hall compound where the whole procession terminated.

The 16 students arrested were let off at 8 p.m. and then began another victorious rally of students round the whole town signifying victory.

Then came a back-door attack. The SDO sent a note to the Principal asking him to expel the students taking a leading part on the Day. The Governing Body sat and being naturally over-cautious took decisions according to SDO's note.

Students too learnt of the decision and demanded its withdrawal. In return the hostellers again were at the front of the attack; they were asked to leave hostel. They protested.

They began hunger-strike. Not only the hostellers but other students of the College also joined. The 'Camp' was overcrowded.

The students of the town were in a body stirred. Students from different institutions came in batches including lady students, to show sympathy, and demanded reversal of the decision.

Public sympathy was roused. In an informal gathering they supported students' cause.

But the timely interference on the third day of the hunger-strike, by Hon'ble Mr Moddabbir Hussain, Sj. Akhil Chandra Datta and others, the decision was rectified before it was too late.

Bhagalpur: Messrs Shiva Chandrika Prasad, Shyamal Kishore Jha, Bokhari and Rash Biharee, who have been convicted under DI Act, have been transferred to Hazaribagh. Some of them who appeared at the last Text Examination of the TNJ College, have been sent up for the University Examination.

Calcutta: Subodh Chandra Bose a student of Calcutta was arrested on 28th February under DIR.

Calcutta: The students of Bangabasi College organized a meeting on the 31st March in the College Common room protesting against the arrest of Com. Arun Kumar Bhattacharjee. Com. Bhabesh Banerjee took the chair and Comrades Sajal Roy Choudhury, Subodh Roy, Satya Dutt, Pradyut Mukherjee and Satyen Sarkar spoke.

The following resolution was adopted:

'This meeting of the students of Bangabasi College protests against the arrest of Comrade Arun Bhattacharjee, a student of this College and demands his immediate and unconditional release.'

Under the auspices of Forward Bloc Students' Bureau a protest meeting was held on 20 March in the College. Comrade Kashi Nath Seal presided over it. President addressed the meeting protesting against the arrest of student leader Panchanan Sinha, Secy of Vidyasagar College Forward Bloc Students' Bureau.

A resolution was passed at the meeting demanding the immediate release of Comrade Panchanan Sinha.

Midnapur: Com. Nandulal Sinha, a student of Midnapore was detained from continuing his studies in the College on account of a police report against him that he is a communist and an Ex-Andamanist. The students demanded intervention by the University authorities for his immediate readmission in the college. The Guardians, students and BPSF representative Comrade Barin Roy met the Principal and appealed to him for the readmission of Nandulal Sinha. But the Principal did not agree to reconsider the matter. As a result of this the students submitted an ultimatum and launched a strike on 24th February 1941. Propaganda was carried on by the Students' Federation throughout the city.

The Principal and other professors tried to frustrate the strike, and some of the students were threatened that their scholarships and half-freeships and freeships would be cancelled if they joined the strike. The hostellers were warned that they would be turned out of the College Hostel if they participate in the strike. The District Magistrate passed orders not to hold any meeting.

Still the movement was not suppressed. The strike continued. At last on the tenth day of the strike Com. Barin Roy came out from the Principal's quarters with smiling face and informed the general students that the Principal has requested the students to give up the strike and he will permit Nandulal Sinha to continue as student. He also informed that the Principal has assured the students that there will be no victimization. Students gladly suspended the strike.

Cuttack: The All Utkal Students' Federation, which met here on 16 March under the presidentship of Sj. Satyendra Nath Majumdar, adopted a number of resolutions criticizing the 'symbolic satyagraha' under the leadership of Mahatma Gandhi and emphasizing the necessity for a mass struggle. By another resolution reference was made to the rigours in Orissa schools placed on the students movement and appealed to the student community to start a countrywide propaganda.

Madhubani 27 February: The Working Committee of the Madhubani Students' Federation met on 27 February Mr Yakub presiding. It was decided to hold the Darbhanga District Students' Conference on the 8th and 9th March. A provisional Reception Committee with Sj. Siwanath Lal Karn as Chairman and Sj. Jogendra Jha as Secretary was formed. Prof. Abdul Bari will inaugurate the Conference and Mr Indradip will preside.

Madura: Mr Sankariah, a student of the American College and General Secretary of the Madura Students' Organization, who was arrested a few days ago, was ordered on March 13 to be removed to the Vellore Jail where he will be kept under detention under the Defence of India Rules.

Budaun, 16 March: A serious situation, it is alleged, is developing in the Government Girls' Normal School, Budaun, following a hunger-strike by inmates of the school hostel, as a protest against the treatment of the Hostel Matron.

Aligarh: A group of delegates of the Aligarh Nationalist Muslim students from the Aligarh Muslim University have decided to tour the provinces of Bengal, Bihar and Assam in order to combat the Pakistan Scheme of the League. The delegation will also lay stress on the students' role in the present crisis.

Bombay: Mrs Nergis Batliwala, wife of Mr S.S. Batliwala, Communist leader, now under detention, was arrested at her residence under the Defence of India Act on 22 March CID men carried out search in her place but it is reported nothing incriminating was found. She has been taken to the Yervada Jail. She was a prominent student worker and member of the AISF Executive.

The office of the Bombay Students' Federation was searched on the 7th April by the police and some papers were reported to have been seized. The search was carried under warrant issued by the Chief Presidency Magistrate, Bombay.

Benaras: Thomas Syriali, a student was arrested at the Examination Hall under DIR on 5th April.

11. 'Cat is Out of Bag' and 'Most Loyal'

The Student, Organ of AISF, May 1941.

'The question of launching direct action as contemplated in the Madura Resolution of the All India Hindu Mahasabha is to be decided by the All India Committee of Hindu Sabha.' This was a decision taken after the correspondence between Savarkar and Viceroy. Meanwhile, while expressing his opinion on Mr Amery's statement, Mr V. Naidu, the General Secretary, Hindu Sabha has expressed his complete satisfaction in the following words:

'Every patriotic Hindu will feel grateful to Mr Amery for his categorical statement disapproving of the agitation started by the Muslim League for a territorial division of India. I am sure if this sensible state of mind prevails in the British Cabinet and also in the other matters affecting India, Indo-British unity will very soon be accomplished.'

A poor consolation indeed! But not surprising.

Most Loyal

Precisely at a time when Hindu Mahasabha postponed its direct action, a voice of resentment and warning to Govt was raised from the Madras Session of the Muslim League. It was the voice of Quaide Azam. We were led to think that now it was the turn of Mr Jinnah to issue an ultimatum threatening direct action. But true to his 'tradition, heritage, and teaching of Islam' Jinnah does not believe in higgle-haggle, in bargaining. He believes in action, statesmanship and practical politics and thus his note of warning to British Govt runs as follows:

'Please stop this policy of appeasement towards those who are bent upon frustrating your war efforts and doing their best to oppose the prosecution of the war and the defence of India at this critical moment. Do you want at this moment to put them or place them in a superior and dominant position now and after the war. Change the corner stone of your (British) policy in this country.

'You are not loyal to those who are willing to stand by you and sincerely desire to support you....'

What an anxiety to get on with the Imperialist Masters? With his high claims about Pakistan, and protection of Islamic Culture and independent Muslim states, Mr Jinnah's conceptions do not take the Muslim masses an inch nearer their own emancipation.

12. Farooqui–Gandhi Correspondence on Split in the Student Movement, March 1941

The Student, Organ of AISF, May 1941.

(i) Farooqui's Letter to Mahatma Gandhi

Delhi, 9 March 1941.
Mahatma Gandhi
Sevagram (Wardha)

Dear Mahatmaji,

I am herewith sending you a long letter about the recent controversy in the students movement. The letter and the accompanying documents will, I hope, throw considerable light on the matter.

The need of sending you such a long letter has arisen because of your deep interest in the student movement in the country.

Sometime back you wrote a letter to Mr M.L. Shah, the Ex-General Secretary of the AISF, in which you unfortunately styled him as the General Secretary. Your letter has created considerable confusion in the mind of the public and many people think that Mr M.L. Shah's rival 'students organization' had your support and blessings. I am however, certain that Mr Shah has completely misrepresented the situation before you. As such I have been directed by the Working Committee of the AISF to lay all the facts before you. I hope you will kindly go through the whole communication and after judging the situation yourself, will please let me have your opinion in the matter.

Thanking you

Yours sincerely,
M. Farooqui
General Secretary, AISF
Delhi, 9 March 1941.

Mahatma Gandhi
Sevagram (Wardha)

Dear Mahatmaji,

On the 4th of January last a news appeared in the press that Mr M.L. Shah 'General Secretary of the AISF' would meet you the same evening to apprise you about the recent Nagpur Conference of the AISF. The same morning I sent you a telegram pointing out that Mr M.L. Shah was no more the General Secretary of the AISF and as such he could not authoritatively speak on behalf of the Indian Students. I further requested you to suspend your interview with him till my statement reached you by post. The next day I sent you the promised statement and also a copy of the statement of Prof. Hiren Mukherji of Calcutta University, who presided over the AISF Conference at Nagpur, with a covering letter. For a long time I did not know what happened to the said communication. I thought it was mislaid somewhere and did not reach you. My doubt has now been confirmed. The communication has come back to me after having passed through the DLO. It appears that my office did not stamp it adequately and you refused to pay an extra anna and accept it. I am sending the same once again along with this letter for your perusal.

Meanwhile, many more things have happened. Mr Shah and his friends have held a certain 'All-India Students' Convention' at Benares over which Rajkumari Amrit Kaur presided. I suppose she will convey to you all that happened at Benares. But placed as she was she could not have known much. After all she simply went there and presided and then went back. How could she know the reactions of an average student with regard to the show and also what was really the situation? I was personally present at Benares during the 'Convention' days. It is therefore, in the fitness of things that I conveyed to you what had really happened.

The Nagpur Conference of the AISF was a huge disaster from the point of view of Mr Shah and his associates. They had miserably failed to impress the assembled delegates from all over India. They and their pretensions had been thoroughly exposed. Prof. Hiren Mukherji's statement and my own will tell you that story. Mr Shah and his friends, however, would not admit their failure. But the announcement that they made soon after, falsified their own position. They claimed at Nagpur that their 'Convocation Hall Conference was the real conference of the AISF', while the Conference held under the presidentship of Prof. Hiren Mukherji was a Conference of 'disruptors', of 'Communists'. Well, if it was so, so much the better for them. But at the same time they announced a certain 'All India Students' Convention' to be held in the first week of February 'somewhere in UP'. (In other provinces they found their position precarious. But the UP students, they imagined, would back them up!) This announcement made the position clear. Mr M.L. Shah and his friends walked out of the AISF and would now set up a parallel organization after the Benares Convention. We all understood the game. But you seemed to be taking them rather too seriously. You blessed them by sending Rajkumari to preside over the so-called 'Students' Convention'. This naturally gave the impression that you had become a party to Mr M.L. Shah's game to set up a parallel AISF. Excuse my saying so, but this is the general impression.

However, inspite of your blessings and a plethora of conferences that they held simultaneously they failed to rally round the students under their banner. For instance when they started in a procession from the University gate not more than ten students joined them. This procession of 'University students' merged itself into the bigger procession of Rajkumari Amrit Kaur which was taken out in the city. The latter procession itself was a collection of the city people mostly. The students were few and far between. (It could not certainly be called the procession of a students' conference). In the open session there was a big crowd no doubt, but the students numbered hardly 200 and this figure included delegates from 'all over India'!

Now something about the composition of the delegates. There were about 50 of them. About two-third of them came from UP, and from only two or three centers of UP About half a dozen came from Bengal; one from Bombay (Mr Shah, a non-student); two from Punjab (one of them notorious for his disruptive activities in the students movement in the Punjab and now styling himself as the Organizing Secretary of the Punjab Forward Bloc—(He too is not a student.); and one from Delhi (non-student again!). No other province was represented. And this was their 'All-India Students' Convention'.

The other conferences—side-shows, ended in a bigger fiasco than the 'convention'. In the All-India States Students' Conference no delegate came from any state. The people who joined this conference were mostly those who had come for the convention. They were students reading in Allahabad and Lucknow Universities coming from some of the UP States. In the Women Students' conference only 3 delegates from outside were present. In the open session there were about 25 women students in all.

The resolutions that they passed were vague, more or less. They could not give any clear lead. In fact the convention was called to clarify the position of students with regard to the National struggle. They could not agree amongst themselves as to the precise nature of National struggle. They had to put up a show of unity—apparently, so they passed a vague resolution. This was a fiasco of their political line. The Forward Bloc students called it their victory. They declared that the convention though presided over by a lieutenant of Gandhiji justified the correctness of the political stand of their party (vide Hindustan Standard—9.2.41, Dak Edition). Mr Shah seemed to have swallowed this humiliation.

Nagpur was for Mr Shah and his friends the first disaster; Benares marked the second milestone on the same road.

Now I must say something about your statement (in the form of a letter to Mr Shah) [For the text of Mahatma Gandhi's letter to M.L. Shah, see Appendix-1 at the end of this document.] which was published in the press on the eve of the Benares convention. I am afraid your statement has given the impression to an average student that your interest in the recent controversy in the AISF is one-sided. You have pronounced your verdict without hearing the other side. And then you seem to be imposing Mr Shah upon the students by styling him as their Secretary. This was unfair when I had specifically stated in my telegram of the 4th January to you that he was no more the General Secretary of the AISF. Besides you do not seem to know the constitution of the AISF which clearly lays down that no one could be elected General Secretary for the third term (See page 10 (h) of the constitution, a copy of which I am sending herewith.) Mr Shah was elected General Secretary at the Calcutta Conference of the AISF in December 1938 and has already served two terms. How can he violate the constitution in his own favour? You may also be interested to know that Mr Shah is no more a student—like many of his associates. He has been practicing as a lawyer for the last 3 years.

The Conference of AISF at Nagpur unanimously elected me as the General Secretary for the forthcoming year. Therefore, as far as the AISF is concerned Mr Shah has nothing to do with it. He may have become the General Secretary of some self-styled students' organization; certainly not that of the AISF which has been functioning since 1936 and is a section of WSA (World Students' Association).

What you say about students and party politics in your statement I entirely agree. But who has been responsible for creating factions in the AISF and tagging it on to party politics? The history of the last one year, after the Delhi Convention of the AISF, has been a long series on the part of Mr Shah and his associates to exploit the platform of the AISF as the broad-based platform of the Indian students. They set up parallel students' organizations in several provinces—that was long before Nagpur. Forward Bloc Student Bureaus has been functioning in Bengal for a pretty long time. They challenged the duly constituted and elected Bengal Provincial Students' Federation, a branch of AISF. Mr M.L. Shah who was supposed to be the custodian of the honour and name of the AISF (when he was the General Secretary) did not even protest. He was surreptitiously supporting the FB Bureaus—potential seeds for future disruption in the students movement.

Mr M.L. Shah took advantage of his position as the General Secretary and also of the fact that a large number of the members of the Working Committee of AISF (who did not approve of his policy) were thrown behind the prison-bars. We call this political dishonesty.

The real controversy in the students' movement began in connection with the Anti-Repression Day of the 16th November last, when you issued a statement that you were against strikes. [For the text of Mahatma Gandhi's 'Message to Students', see Appendix 2 at the end of this document.] In that connection Mr Shah met you and gave you a certain assurance on behalf of the AISF. In your recent letter to Mr Shah you say he gave you none. But soon after his first interview with you he issued a statement to the press saying that he did give you an assurance. It was on the basis of this statement that we took him to task in the meeting of the Working Committee of the AISF held at Benares on the 8th December 1940. In that meeting we passed a resolution stating the position of the AISF vis-à-vis your own stand with regard to political strikes by students. We had asked Mr Shah to send this statement to the press immediately and a copy also to you. But the statement never appeared in the press, and as far as I know you were not sent a copy of the same. He did not apprise you of the resolution because it was a negation of his own policy. To put it frankly Mr Shah pitched himself against the AISF. Then came Nagpur. Before Nagpur he had made all possible attempts to send a majority of his own people to the Conference. He manipulated in connection with the presidential election, though he failed. When Mr Shah reached Nagpur he found that all his manipulations had been of no avail. The overwhelming majority of delegates were against him and his party policies.

Then he made the last desperate attempts to capture the AISF. It was through the Working Committee (old Working Committee, the majority of which was in jail) by dis-affiliating several strong units of the AISF that he wanted to play his dangerous game. When the Working Committee meeting started on the 23rd December Mr Shah found himself in a majority of one—5 to 4. But his fifth man was a substitute for Mr Amiya Das Gupta, the General Secretary of the Bengal Provincial Students' Federation and a member of the Committee who was interned in Bengal. Mr Amiya Das Gupta defied the police ban and came to attend the Working Committee meeting—to save the AISF from being disrupted through the tactics of Mr Shah and his friends. When he arrived in the middle of the meeting they were all non-plussed. This was the massacre of their hopes! Majority was converted into minority. They could not disaffiliate any of the provinces. There was no hope of their creating an artificial majority in the open session of the Conference. So they had no other choice left but to walk out of the Working Committee meeting. It was a face-saving device.

Now they took advantage of the fact that Mr Amiya Das Gupta could not appear in public. If he did he would be arrested. So they started saying that Mr Amiya Das Gupta was not present and that they (Mr Shah and his friends) were in a majority... Even today their main stand is that Mr Amiya was not present. Frankly speaking this is the height of political dishonesty. Mr Shah claims that he is one of your followers and that he is a satyagrahi. In other words he is a follower of non-violence and truth. But the sort of stand that he has taken up vis-à-vis Mr Amiya Das Gupta's presence is a clear and certain negation of Satya and Ahimsa. (In this connection kindly read a statement of Mr Ahmad Ali Alvi, a member of Mr Shah's new Working Committee. I am enclosing a copy.)

At Nagpur they could carry a very insignificant minority of delegates with them. The AISF Conference was held as previously arranged under the presidentship of Prof. Hiren Mukherji. The resolutions that we passed in this Conference gave a clear and definite lead to the students of India in the present period of international and national crises. I am arranging to send you a copy of *The Student*, the official organ of the AISF and all the resolutions of the Conference. They will throw some more light on the real situation vis-à-vis.

Before I close I may point out that ever since Nagpur all the Provincial Secretaries (duly elected before the Conference) recorded their confidence in the AISF with myself as the General Secretary. They have clearly stated that they have nothing to do with Mr Shah and his tactics, I wonder what Mr Shah will say to that. (I am sending a copy of the statement of Provincial Secretaries. See *The Student—Conference Supplement*).

In the face of these hard facts, may we expect that you will issue a press statement clarifying your position which is being so much misunderstood by students all over India?

You will excuse me the letter has become lengthy. It may bore you. But it was necessary in view of the importance that attaches to the matter discussed herein.

There is a lot of other material to show that Mr Shah is misrepresenting the whole thing.

With student greetings,

Yours sincerely
M. Farooqui
General Secretary, AISF

(ii) Gandhiji's Reply to M. Farooqui

Sevagram
Wardha CP
14 March 1941.

Dear friend,

I duly recd. your letter of 9th inst.

It is unfortunate that your letter which was under-stamped was not accepted. As many such letters are received, I have given instructions that as a rule all such letters should be refused.

As to the subject matter of your letter, whilst the contents are painfully interesting, I cannot express any opinion. But of one thing I am quite sure. There should be no dissentions among the students. I have therefore, accepted Prof. Satish Kalelkar's[1] formula that all disputes should be referred to an impartial tribunal accepted by the parties. Its findings should be accepted as final and binding by all the parties.

Yours sincerely
M.K. Gandhi

(iii) Second Letter of M. Farooqui to Gandhiji on 23 March 1941

Dear Mahatmaji,

Your letter of the 14th instant to hand. Thanks for the same.

It's heartening that you have accepted Prof. Satish Kalelkar's formula. I think we should now proceed to work in details and set up the tribunal. The sooner the work is done the better it is.

I endorse your appeal with regard to C.F. Andrews Fund. I am issuing a press appeal to students all over India to help in the collection work. We have been lately busy with collecting funds for the Security Prisoners and their families. We will therefore, find some difficulty in collecting money for a new fund. However, we will try.

Hope it finds you well.

Yours sincerely
M. Farooqui

---

[1] Professor Satish Kalelkar, son of Kaka Kalelkar, famous Gandhian, was then teaching at Banaras Hindu University. His efforts at bringing the two groups together did not succeed.

Appendix 1

The text of Mahatma Gandhi's letter to M.L. Shah [*CWMG*, Vol. LXXIII, pp. 299–300]:

Fragment of Letter to M.L. Shah

[Before 26 January 1941]

I am fighting the country's struggle. The country includes students as much as other parts of the body politic. I have, however, a special claim upon the students and they upon me, for I regard myself still a student and also because, from the very commencement of my return to India, I have been in close touch with them and many of them have served the cause of satyagraha. Therefore, even if the whole of the student world were to repudiate me for causes which in their very nature must be temporary, I am not going to be deterred from tendering my advice for fear of rejection. Students cannot afford to have party politics. They may hear all parties, as they read all sorts of books, but their business is to assimilate the truth of all and reject the balance. This is the only worthy attitude that they can take. Power politics should be unknown to the student world. Immediately they dabble in that class of work they cease to be students and will, therefore, fail to serve the country in its crisis. And you as General Secretary would be ill serving the cause of the students if you take part in power politics.

All communists are not bad as all Congressmen are not angels. I have therefore no prejudice against communists as such. Their philosophy, as they have declared it to me, I cannot subscribe to. I have great regard for Dr Ashraf's abilities. I have never questioned his love of his country but I am positive, he will one day be sorry for the wrong guidance he is giving to student world. But, inasmuch as he is enamoured of his views, as I am of mine, and we are equally obstinate, I despair of convincing him of his error and, therefore, never enter into argument with him. And he returns the compliment by avoiding me. But let the students remember that at the present moment I am fighting the country's cause. I am not an inexperienced general, but a seasoned solider of 50 years' standing. Let them, therefore, think 50 times before rejecting my advice which is that they must not dabble in strikes without reference to me. I have never said or suggested that they may never resort to strikes. They should not forget my recent advice to the Christ Church College students. I do not repent of that advice. Let them take full benefit of it.

In the first place you gave me one on behalf of the Federation. In the second place, even if you had given any, I would not have taken it from you because you had no authority to give me assurance in advance.

The Hitavada, 29.1.1941.

Appendix 2

Mahatma Gandhi's 'Message to Students' on students' desire to go on strike [*CWMG*, Vol. LXXIII, pp. 176–7].

Wardha
14 November 1940

I have received several letters from students in Madras and the United Provinces regarding their demonstration over Pandit Jawaharlal Nehru's arrest and imprisonment, and the threatened reprisals by the Government concerned. The students now desire to have a strike of protest and ask for my advice. When the whole world hangs its head in shame over the imprisonment of one of India's noblest and bravest sons, it is no wonder that the student world in India is shaken to its roots. Whilst, therefore, my sympathy is wholly with them, I must adhere to the view that the students were wrong in their walk-out as a mark of their resentment over Pandit Jawaharlal Nehru's imprisonment. The Governments of the provinces are more than wrong in their threats of reprisals. The students will, however, do well not to resort to the contemplated strike of protest. If they desire my advice, they should send an authorized representative who is in full possession of the facts, of which I have but a very superficial knowledge. I shall gladly give my guidance for what it may be worth. They know how much I would value their whole-hearted co-operation in the struggle I am endeavouring to lead. In any case they will spoil their own and damage the national cause by ill-conceived and hasty action.

The Hindustan Times, 15.11.1940.

13. Yashpal's Inaugural Address at CP and Berar Students' Conference, 10–13 April 1941

The Student, Organ of AISF, May 1941.

Politics is the privilege of the adults. Students must not meddle with it. They must make themselves ideal citizens of the future by abstaining from participation in civic life. All this task of reconstruction and reform which is being dinned into their ears, is taboo for them. They must not put their finger in it while they can help to mould the chaotic world to the new ideals. They must rely for all this reconstruction and reform on those who have allowed the chaos to increase and have their turn with the tangle when it has grown worse. This is the advice of the wise and old.

The Student is the citizen of tomorrow. Can he watch with indifference at this wastage of his inheritance? His responsibility to society and to his country is greater because he has right to expect more from it. Especially in a country where rank unconsciousness reigns student's responsibility to humanity, to his country-men and above all to himself becomes the more heavier. He must make his society adapt to new environments and developments and make it fit for himself and his kind.

What is politics? All social and collective life in contrast to self and so called spiritual indulgence is politics. How can students avoid or overlook it! To exclude the student from public and social responsibility would mean to make him individualistic and selfish. More so in this unfortunate country where individualism and lack of national feeling is the cause of our ruin. To advise students to concentrate on individual career building would deprive this country of the spirit of nationalism, of collective aspiration and effort.

Students know their place is on the front of national struggle. No persuasion of wiseacres will prevent them from going ahead and carrying the country further. At this critical juncture when the people of this country, deprived of all chance of life are looking for a new order, they are called upon to fight their battle. It is for the students—the dynamic and conscious part of the people—to see that people fight straight to their goal. The goal which definitely and decisively would be the government of the people, by the people for the people. The Government of people does not mean a government of the exploiters of the people in the name of the people. It is for the students to see that the Goal of Swarajya which has remained a hazy ideal before the people for over fifty years and a card in the hands of the shrewd politicians, serving their class interest, is clarified. This Swarajya would mean a real right of self determination by the toiling producers, the workers, the peasants and the petty employees. This Swarajya should categorically promise a minimum living wage to workers and employees, a living portion of agricultural produce to the peasant which would not be touched by land rent or any other tax. It should mean equal opportunities of education, physical development and employment to all classes and that nobody is born condemned to eternal starvation and ignorance.

This state of Swarajya will not be bestowed upon us by the power that survives on our exploitation. Neither will it come through the luxury of individual Satyagraha which aims at the so called moral satisfaction of protesting against the ruthless repression of foreign domination rather than at taking power of self-determination into the hands of people. Cause of the people can be fought only by the people. Individual action has no place in a people's fight. Resort to individual action to achieve the cause of people, belies lack of faith in the strength of the masses, for whom Swarajya is meant.

Our political leaders tell us that people of this country are not prepared to fight the battle of Swarajya. Don't the people of this country feel it difficult to maintain even their existence? Are they not starving? How is it possible, that the starving people should not fight for bread! If Swarajya had meant bread for the starving millions, they would have fought for it at the cost of everything, but Swarajya did never plainly mean this. It has always been high sounding and difficult puzzle to be understood by the starving millions of the country and the juggler's kerchief in the hands of shrewd politicians.

It is for the students to make this Swarajya a concern of the people. It is for the students to understand the intolerable exploitation which is making the life of the peoples of the country impossible in the present profit crushing machine of capitalism and its more intensive and extensive form, the imperialism. It is for the students to visualize an order in which the toiling producers of this land would attain the right of self-determination and the right to the produce of their labour. This Swarajya would not be achieved for the people by the Super Humans and great Sages, but by the people themselves, through their force of organized and determined numbers against whom no tyrant can stand.

Politics of this country is today yoked with spiritualism and religion which have always served a camouflage for the interests of exploiters. Politics in this country today means exploitation of the force of masses. Communalists whip-out the emotions of their communities and use this steam to further up the automation of their personal and class interests. The bourgeois nationalists use the patriotic emotions of the masses to whisk away from the imperial domination the political concessions in their class interest. And the suffering mass, the bulk of motherland, remains doubly exploited and down trodden. It is up to students, who have unbiased perception to realize that their interest, the interest of the nation and the interest of the humanity is identical with the interests of this toiling mass, caught in eternal starvation and stripped of the fruits of their labour.

Students must bring this mass to its proper place, on the front line of war to exterminate all exploitation and for all power to the vote of toilers. For this, students must weed out the superstition and dogmatism which cripple the mass and prevent it from its natural development. The forces which survive on rank ignorance of masses will not like the young and conscious generation to come forward to disillusion the people. But will the student remain a pawn in the hand of the wiseacres and betray the starving and trampled mass? If the students are true to ideal of 'Education' they must come forward and take the lead of war against the forces of darkness on which survives the vampire of human exploitation. Peace, Progress and Liberty can never be achieved without the right use of Politics and Students must come forward with courage and confidence to achieve it against whatever odds!

14. Students 'Pledged to Abolish Communalism'

Amrita Bazar Patrika, 14 May 1941.

The Working Committee of the All-India Students' Federation, which concluded its three-day session here on Tuesday, have issued instructions to the Provincial Students' Organizations to organize 'summer literacy camps' during the coming holidays.

Reviewing the communal situation in different parts of the country, the committee condemned the formation of relief committees on communal lines, observing that 'it is distressing to know that even in this humanitarian work, before rendering help to the victim, 'his religion is enquired into.'

A resolution adopted in this connection stated: 'We the students are pledged to abolish communalism and it is the youth of the country inspired by the idealism of serving the masses and of saving them from the exploitation by vested interests in the name of religion who are best fitted to undertake the work.'

The committee fixed 31 October as the last date for enrolment of primary members of the All-India Students' Federation. The committee recorded that during the last 3 months more than 400 student workers of the All-India Students' Federation have been gaoled, interned or externed and these include Mr Ansar Harvani, former General Secretary of the All-India Students' Federation, Mr Khagendra Nath Barbarua and Mr Arabindo Bose, members of the All-India Working Committee.

Mr M.L. Shah, General Secretary of the AISF, submitted a brief report of his tour of the Punjab, the North West Frontier Province, Sind, Delhi and the Central Provinces.

15. CID Report on Students' Federation Meeting, 28 May 1941, Srinagar

CID Diary for May 1941, File No. Nil, Political Department, 1941, J&K State Archives.

On the 28th May, the Students' Federation held a meeting at the New Uttam Talkies. About 500 persons attended the meeting. Omprakash, son of Mulak Raj Saraf, editor of the 'Ranbir' was in the chair. Abdul Haleem, student, moved a resolution to the effect that the attitude of the Principal of P.W. College was inimical towards the students and that he should announce the results of examinations before the date fixed for supplementary examinations, the students should be passed according to the conditions announced in the College weekly dated 29th February and that the fee for supplementary examinations should be reduced by at least rupee one, per student. Nazir Ahmed Bhalli supported the above resolution. The gathering passed it unanimously. Mohammed Basharat, shoe-dealer, read out poems in praise of freedom and usefulness of 'khaddar'. Ajodhya Nath Vaid congratulated students for their communal unity and said that they could not save themselves unless both Hindus and Muslims presented a united front. He added that a revolution was about to take place. At this the students raised shouts and forced the speaker to stop his speech. Abdul Haleem, student, read out a poem in praise of democracy. Beli Ram, student, observed that capitalists had robbed the poor. At this stage Mian Iftikhar-ud-Din, MLA, President of the Punjab Provincial Congress Committee, Nawabzada Mazhar Ali, Indar Kumar Gujral, Autar Narayan Gujral, a Congressite of the Punjab, entered the Hall. The gathering welcomed by shouting out 'Zindabad' for Hindu–Muslim unity. Omprakash read out an address of welcome to Mian Iftikhar-ud-Din and his companions. It was stated in the address that the students of Jammu welcome Iftikhar-ud-Din and others, as they were brave soldiers of India. Nawabzada Mazhar Ali thanked for the address and said that India has not progressed because there was no communal unity. Freedom, he added, was their birth right and the country which was not free was not worth living. Indians, he continued, should make similar sacrifices for their country as the English were making at present for theirs. It was the duty of the Students' Federation, he added, to combat those agencies which were placing obstacles in the way of their freedom. He concluded with an appeal to the students to realize their responsibility and act accordingly. Indar Kumar Gujral observed that in view of the world situation, Hindu–Muslim unity was very essential. The British Government, he added, had not kept its promise and their requests have not been considered. It was for this reason, he continued, that Jawaharlal and Maulana Azad and others, had courted imprisonment. The condition was such, he added, as required continued sacrifices, without which India could not be free. Autar Narayan Gujral told the gathering that he had recently been released from jail and that he had courted imprisonment for achievement of freedom for his mother country. He further said that they were not in favour of Hitlerism, but they wanted to free their country from the British. Iftikhar-ud-Din spoke next and said that he would address the students of the world among whom are the young men of Germany who were sacrificing their lives for a few selfish people and the young men of India who were sacrificing their lives at the bidding of Churchill for keeping India in bondage. He added that the situation in the world was very tense at present. Many free countries had lost their freedom and it was not known what will happen in another six months. Proceeding further, he expressed sorrow that Indians were fighting among themselves and did not listen to the voice of the Congress. They should, he continued, consider in their hearts how to get rid of their trouble. He had heard a Negro delivering a speech in America, in which he said that Negroes were barbarians once, but they were not beast-like as Indians were. Proceeding further, he appealed the young men to prepare themselves for sacrifices and said that he believed that this war will bring freedom to India. Hitler, he continued, was bound to lose. If Britain does not succeed in defeating him, America or Asia will bring about his ruin. Hitler was bound to fail, but the British would also have to restore freedom to these countries whom they have enslaved. They should strive for the creation of the new world, in which neither Hitler nor Mussolini nor Churchill would be successful. Omprakash thanked the above speakers....

16. AISF on Nazi Germany's Attack on USSR

The Student, Organ of AISF, July 1941.

With the unwarranted and treacherous attack on the USSR by Nazi Germany, the international situation has become more intriguing. The Nazi drive for world domination has become self-evident. This recent change in the international situation has made many intellectuals in India think to determine India's attitude towards this war. Intellectuals of Bengal, headed by Acharya Prafulla Chandra Roy, have issued a manifesto, showing the achievements of the USSR, unparalleled in human history, for the cause of humanity, thru its new socialist experiment, and calling forth India's sympathy and solidarity with the USSR. Various other statements have been issued, notable among them being the statement of Com. Gopal Halder, General Secretary, Kisan Sabha, in which he exhorts the Indian masses to render all help to the defence of the USSR. But at the same time, he makes it clear that only a free India can effectively help the Soviet people in their fight against the clique of Fascist war-mongers who dream of world domination.

We students also have to determine our attitude. Our General Secretary Com. Farooqui has already cabled to the Soviet Ambassador in Britain our sympathy and solidarity with the students of the USSR in their heroic fight against Fascism. Black reaction will spread over the whole world with the victory of Fascism over the USSR. Fascism is the enemy of the slogans on our banner—Freedom, Peace, Progress. Before the attack on the USSR by Germany, we had characterized the war as an inter-imperialist conflict and effectively carried agitation and mass action against it, as it entailed curtailment of our civil liberties. The USSR, the citadel of freedom and progress, the hope of humanity, was out of the conflict, amassing strength every day, guaranteeing the world the ultimate victory of Freedom, Peace and Progress.

Students of international affairs are aware that it was Soviet Russia which tried to create a Peace Front against fascism and war; it was Soviet Russia which championed the cause of 'collective security'. It was the Soviet Union which denounced the non-intervention policy of the League of Nations in the Civil War of Spain, adopted by it under inspiration of Britain and France and rendered all help to the Spanish Republic in its fight against rebel Franco. Coming nearer home, we find Soviet Russia's help to the Chinese people in their fight against Japanese imperialism, even though Britain sometime before closed the Burma Road to appease Japan. So this unprovoked attack on this citadel of freedom and progress by Nazi Germany has made us think. The intellectuals of Bengal have rightly expressed the sentiment of the down-trodden humanity and given a call for all help to the USSR.

All help to the USSR. How can that effectively be given? Should we help the war efforts of Imperialism and thereby strengthen imperialism, which strangles the life-breath of colonial peoples? Should help go to the USSR independent of imperialism? These are the various questions which arise in our attempt to help the USSR. We Indian youths are victims of imperialism and as such helping imperialism means tightening the bondage even more. Fascism is an evil which can effectively be fought by the peoples of the whole world. The war against Fascism must be made a people's war against Fascism. So, by raising the slogans of 'People's Army', 'Release of all political prisoners', 'Intensification of mass action', we must carry a new agitation for the liberation of our Motherland which is *essential for the effective* aid to the Soviet people in their fight against Fascism.

Independence of India is the Main Task in our Effort to Help the Soviet People. Therefore, we must gird up our loins and with redoubled vigour continue our struggle for national emancipation. But we can help the Soviet people indirectly by creating a pro-Soviet atmosphere in our own country. We must immediately take up the task of acquainting the people of the implications of this war by meetings, demonstrations, lectures and other means. Again, whatever little help we can send to the USSR, independent of Imperialism, we should try to organize as a gesture of our moral sympathy and solidarity in their struggle.

17. AISF General Secretary's Proposal for Observing Security Prisoners' Day, 12 June 1941

Copy of the letter sent to all political organizations.
The Student, Organ of AISF, July 1941.

Dear Friend,

During the last few weeks the attention of the public has been drawn to the conditions in which the security prisoners of the DIR are made to live. Of late some news have trickled down into the papers about the alarming condition of the detenues in Deoli Camp. From what we can make out of these news from that *Mystery Land* we feel that the authorities are making the condition of the detenues increasingly intolerable. The hunger-strike (which is reported to have been abandoned now) is a strong pointer in that direction.

I suppose you will agree that irrespective of the political affiliations of the detenues in Deoli and other Jails, it is our duty to see to it that they are treated as human beings. One may differ with their politics but still one cannot ignore their sacrifices to the cause of our country and our people.

It was with the above end in view that the All India Students' Federation took the initiative as early as February last—soon after Sir Reginald Maxwell's tirade against the detenues in the Central Assembly while speaking on Mr N.M. Joshi's resolution—and called the students all over the country to protest against the attitude of the authorities about the Security prisoners and also to demand better treatment for them. Accordingly all the Provincial and States' Students' Federations held protest demonstrations and meetings on the 19th March last. The All India Security Prisoners Day of the AISF brought thousands of students into the demonstration.

Later on the Forward Bloc and the Congress Socialist Party also gave a call for protest. At several places independent meetings were called for the same purpose.

But it seems the Govt is still adamant and is not ready to concede to the public demand. This sphinx-like attitude of the Govt can be changed by joint demand on behalf of all the Indian political organizations for humane treatment to our friends in jail. Such a joint demand will create the very atmosphere in the country which is essential for bringing about a concerted pressure on the Govt.

In this connection I venture to place the following suggestions before you:

1. A joint appeal may be issued on behalf of all such organizations as desire to participate for observing a certain day as the Security Prisoners' Day. On this Day we should have processions, meetings and other demonstrations. We should demand that a committee representing the public opinion in the country be appointed by the Govt and the said committee should visit Deoli and the jails where detenues are kept. The recommendations of the committee be generally accepted.
2. In view of the fact that the families of many of the detenues have been left in pitiable condition economically, it will be desirable if a Fund to help the families is opened under a joint appeal of all the organizations.

I should be really grateful to you if you could very kindly join with our organization for the above purpose.

Please let me know if you agree with the above suggestions and as to what day will be convenient to your organizations for the above purpose when we can have a joint protest.

Please also send us some suggestions as to how we can make our demand effective.

I should be anxiously waiting for your reply.

Thanking you very much.

Yours sincerely,
M. Farooqui
General Secretary,
AISF

The above letter has been sent to the following organizations:

Indian National Congress, All-India Congress Socialist Party, All-India Forward Bloc, All-India Majlis-i-Ahrar, All-India Majlis-i-Ittihad Millat, All-India Jamiat-ul-Ulema, All-India Azad Muslim Conference Board, All-India Trade Union Congress, All-India Kisan Sabha, All-India Muslim Students' Federation, All-India Muslim League, All-India Hindu Mahasabha, All-India States Peoples' Conference, All-India Shia Conference, All-India Hindu League, Servants of India Society, Anjuman-i-Watan (Baluchistan), National Liberal Federation, Hindustan Scouts' Association, All-India Civil Liberties Union, All-India Momin Conference, All-India Depressed Classes' League, Gandhi Seva Sangha.

18. Andhra Students 'Fighting Ignorance'

Communist, Vol. III, No. 5, July 1941, P.C. Joshi Archives on Contemporary History, JNU.

The Madras students leapt into fame through their political strikes last winter. The old Gandhian leaders may betray the nation but the youth fights on. Anti-police strikes while at school or college—but do what when vacations begin? This was their problem. Educate the people when at home? This was their decision. What could be more laudable?

Students offered themselves as volunteer teachers, they were trained for a week and got going. In the Yelamarru and Jemi–Golvepalli villages where they raised literacy by 15 per cent in six weeks—a better job than imperialism has done in its centuries over us! The technique was simple—trained teachers go and appeal to the villagers themselves to pay cash, grain and all, help to make the bondobast, they readily agree. Another round of meetings and adult men and women are asked to become students. The teachers sit with students older than themselves and bunch them up into classes. The teachers have the energy to run two and even three schools per day and more to spare. Open air lectures in the evening, on subjects of general interest, debates too to give a chance to all to speak and find out what is really the truth, mock parliaments for political discussions, sometimes music or a pantomime. The villagers were not just formally grateful to the youngsters for teaching the 'Three Rs' but found themselves becoming new men. At the end of the schools Agricultural Labourers' Association gave a dinner to the student–teachers and a number of villagers, 120 responded, bidding good-bye to the age-old caste humbug.

The boys got bucked up at seeing the old folk inspired, and organized 100 such village Adult Literacy Centres in Kistna district alone. East Godavari trained 30 student–teachers, organized 10 centres and educated 400 adults. Guntur ran 8 centres with 21 teachers and 355 students. Other reports are not to hand.

But the Government grew panicky and early June banned these schools as a 'Communist menace'. It had detained students leaders at Vellore, it had lathi-charged them *en masse* and now they were going to the people with the torch of knowledge! Stop even 'Three Rs' reaching the people, in such dire times as the twenty-first month of the Second Imperialist war, this was the basis of the imperialist fiat. Quite true, Communism is a menace to its existence, but **by the Ban Imperialism has Proclaimed Illiteracy to be its creed for the Indian People**! The villagers are asking what can ever be wrong with Communism if it can inspire our youngsters to teach us! We Communists get our strength for fight not only one or more such bans but imperialism itself, when we see that the best of the student workers, flowers of the youth, come to our Party as their leaders; when we see our Party boys mobilizing non-Party student workers to serve the people, and above all when we see that these young hopefuls, all together, manage to inspire their elders and get accepted by them as their 'teachers'.

19. 'Queer' Way of Communalists

The Student, Organ of AISF, August 1941.

Viceroy's Executive Council and the Defence Council

Crumbs of bounty have been thrown by Imperialism to lure Indians to lick imperialist jack boots. The Expansion hardly satisfies Indian aspirations. Even the Liberal leaders have expressed their disapproval of it. Indian aspirations can scarcely be met by doses of bounty from Imperialism/ it necessitated the revolutionary overthrow of Imperialism by the organized mass action of the youths, workers and peasants. Many leaders and political parties are dissatisfied because it failed to satisfy their expectation but it is curious to see the attitude of the two communal organizations namely the Hindu Maha Sabha and the Muslim League.

Swtantravir (?) Savarkar has expressed his gratification at the expansion and congratulated one of his partymen for getting a seat in it. The other great leader Mr Mohammad Ali Jinnah, is dissatisfied not because it hardly smells of Independence or even Dominion-status, but because Viceroy has chosen some of his partymen (Muslim League) in the Council without consulting him. Queer are the ways of Communalists!

20. Delhi Provincial Students' Conference, 25–26 May 1941

The Student, Organ of AISF, August 1941.

The Third Delhi Provincial Students' Conference was held from 24th to 26th of May under the Presidentship of Com. K. Ahmad, ex-President Bengal PSF. The Conference was inaugurated by Com. Randhir Singh Josh, a member of the WC of the Punjab PSF. Fraternal delegates from UP, CP and the Punjab also attended the Conference.

On the 24th of May before the actual proceedings of the Conference had commenced, police force under the orders of the District Magistrate forced its way into the Pandal, which was greatly resented by students and the organizers of the Conference. The organizers requested the police to withdraw but the latter having refused, Mr D. Sanghi, President of the Delhi PSF and Miss Saral Gupta, Chairwoman of the Reception Committee, waited upon the District Magistrate in a deputation to request him to cancel his order but the District Magistrate refused to meet the deputation. The Working Committee of the DPSF met immediately in the Pandal and decided to postpone the Conference for the day as a mark of protest against this high-handed and uncalled for action of the District Magistrate. The Resolution was moved before the Open Conference by Com. M. Farooqui which was later on withdrawn as a section of the students were opposed to the resolution, although they agreed that this attitude of the District Magistrate called for severest condemnation and so the regular Conference started after passing a resolution condemning this act of the District Magistrate.

Several messages from eminent personalities like Mian Iftikharuddin, President Punjab PCC, Dr Zakir Hussain, Vice-Chancellor, National Muslim University, Miss Indira Nehru, Kunwar Sir Maharaj Singh, Vice-Chancellor, Lucknow University Sir S. Radhakrishnan, Vice-Chancellor, Benares Hindu University, Com. Mazhar Ali, President Punjab PSF, Miss Perin Bharucha, member WC of the AISF and many others were received wishing success to the Conference.

Com. K.M. Ahmad in his presidential speech described the attitude of the students towards the melodrama that was being enacted in Europe. Referring to the 'split' at Nagpur he said that those who had assembled at Nagpur had made every effort to preserve the unity of the AISF and now it was for the students to see that the unity is not broken. Referring to the Pakistan and Hindustan schemes of the Muslim League and Hindu Mahasabha he characterized both of them as reactionary and clearly explained the stand of the AISF so far as the question of Hindu–Muslim Unity was concerned.

On the 25th when the Conference met and before the resolutions were taken up for discussion, Com. Ahmad announced that only delegates would be allowed to vote on the resolutions. This was opposed by a section of the audience (most of them were either hired goondas or non-students or those who were not members of the DSPF) who had come with the definite idea of breaking the Conference. Com. Ahmad stuck to his ruling. On this a motion for adjournment of the Conference was moved but Com. Ahmad insisted that even on this delegates would be allowed to give their verdict. The disrupters instead of trying to fight out the issue on a constitutional basis used violence and created a pandemonium in the Conference. Com. Ahmad therefore adjourned the Conference for the day.

The adjourned Conference again met on the 26th May and the various resolutions were discussed and adopted. By one resolution the Conference condemned the action of the Central Govt in banning the export of 'The Student'. Several resolutions relating to the demands of the local students such as Three Years' Degree Course, reduction of fees, women students and their demands, school students and their problems, literacy and students were passed. By another resolution the repressive policy of the Govt was strongly condemned, a resolution on National situation was adopted in which demand was made for starting mass struggle.

The Conference after adopting the secretary's report and the accounts of the DPSF and after a vote of thanks to Chair, came to a successful end.

21. Report of Students in Action

The Student, Organ of AISF, August 1941.

Calcutta: Com. Kamal Roy Choudhury, ex-Secretary of the All-Bengal Relief Committee, Secretary of the Bangabasi College Students' Federation, Vice-President of the Tipperah Students' Union, was served with an order on 12th July to leave Calcutta within 48 hours and reside in the District of Tipperah and inform of his actual place of residence and every change thereof.

The police raided the house of Com. Roy Choudhury, but did not find him in his house. He was, however, found afterwards and served with the order.

Com. Adhir Chakrabarty, ex-General Secretary, Vidyasagar College Union and President of the North Calcutta Students' Federation, was arrested on the 2nd July in Amherst Street while he was coming back from the Sraddhananda Park after addressing the Students' Siraj Day meeting.

Com. Pradyot Guha, General Secretary, Vidyasagar College Students' Federation, was arrested on 30th June last at his residence. He has been released on bail.

Sj. Sachin De, Convener, Bengal Provincial Forward Bloc Students' Bureau, was arrested on the 23rd June at 10 p.m. by the Special Branch of Police, Calcutta, under the Defence of India Act.

He was taken to the Lord Sinha Road, the office of the Special Branch, and detained there for the night. He was brought the following morning to the DIB office, Howrah for investigation and afterwards was brought under police escort to his residence at Belilios Lane, Howrah. The house was searched for over two hours but nothing objectionable, it is stated, was found.

The residence of Coms Kanak Kanjilal, Ranjit Guha and Madgil, three prominent student workers of Central Calcutta were thoroughly searched by the police early in the morning of 30th June. Later on Coms Kanjilal, Guha and Madgil were taken into police custody under the DIR.

Sj. Santi Sinha Roy, a student worker who was arrested on the 15th June by Special Branch Police under DIR was released on 2 July 1941 by Mr H.C. Gupta, ADM of 24 Parganas on bail of Rupees 250. During his arrest several houses in Calcutta were searched.

Dacca: Com. Subodh Roy, Secretary, Dacca District Students' Federation and a student of the 6th year class of the Dacca University, has been arrested and interned in his residence under the Defence of India Rules.

Bankura: Sj. Santabrata Chatterjee and Subodh Banerjee, who were connected with the last 'Bande Mataram' struggle, were refused admission into the third year class of the Bankura College.

The students are demanding their re-admission. A protest strike was a complete success.

The Tiluri strike has been settled. Students' demands were met after five days struggle.

Jalpaiguri: An order under the Defence of India Rules was served on Mr Nares Chandra Chakravarty BL, ex-President of the Jalpaiguri District Students' Federation, by the Deputy Commissioner of the District, restricting his movement within the Municipal area for a period of one year.

Sylhet: Sj. Kalika Proshad Bhattacharjee, a student worker, was arrested under Defence of India Rules for alleged find of Satyagraha bulletin in his house. He has been released on bail.

Jessore: The District Judge of Jessore reduced the sentence of imprisonment passed on M. Lutfar Rahman, a worker of the District Students' Federation, from six to three months' imprisonment.

Karachi: The repressive policy of Br. Imperialism is still going on. On 16th July Com. Shrikant Kanthi, ex-Joint Secretary of AISF was served with an externment order under Foreign Acts according to which he has not to reside in British India but to go to Mysore. Students were very much agitated over this act of the Govt. In a meeting they decided to go on strike. All the colleges of Karachi were closed. Thus the students replied befittingly to the repression of the Govt. It was later learned that the order has been relaxed for 10 days.

Lucknow: Mr Balaram Singh Srivastava, Students' Federation worker, was arrested on 3rd July at Lucknow under the DIR.

Agra: The first victim of police amongst the students was Com. Damodar Singh, Secy, Medical College Union and a member of the Executive of the ASF. The police searched his residence on 30th July early in the morning, but nothing objectionable was found. However, the police arrested him under Sec 129 DIR.

Two more searches were made at the residences of Coms Harnath and K.C. Nagar both of whom were members of the Executive of the Agra Students' Federation. The former was taken in custody under 129 DIR though nothing objectionable was found at both the places.

The Medical Students went on one day protest strike and held a meeting. Great sensation prevails amongst the students of Agra against these arrests.

Rawalpindi: Com. F.C. Mehta, ex-General Secretary, Rawalpindi Students' Union, who was arrested in January on account of three objectionable speeches under Sec 38 DIR, was sentenced to three years RI, one year for each speech. He has however been honourably acquitted by the Sessions Judge. In the course of the judgment, the Sessions Judge remarked that to speak against British Imperialism was no offence and it did not come under DIR and that there is difference between, British Imperialism and British Govt.

22. Bihar Students' Conference Attempt to Unite Different Groups

Amrita Bazar Patrika, 8 August 1941.

(From our Patna Office)

The Bihar Provincial Students' Conference will be held here on 23 and 24 August and under the presidentship of Mr Mazhar Ali of the Punjab Students' Federation.

District units have been asked to send their nominations by 17 August.

Mian Iftikharuddin will inaugurate the general conference. Sir Sarvepalli Radhakrishnan will inaugurate the cultural conference while some noted public men are also expected to attend the function.

In this connection attempts are being made, on behalf of the different students' associations in the province, to close up ranks and unite once again with a view to help in the progress of students movement. Informal talks among student–leaders belonging to different schools of thought are now proceeding with the object of leaving away their personal and political views and meeting together on a common platform to raise the students from inaction, political stalemate and rivalries.

They are trying to undo the mischief made at the Nagpur session of the All-India Students' Conference and particular stress is being given to bring the different students' organizations on one common platform, freed from group politics and party jealousies.

23. A Report on Mohan Kumaramangalam: An Ex-Cambridge Student Leader, 10 September 1941

File No. 7/2/41-Poll (I), Home (Political) Department, Government of India, 1941 NAI.

Intelligence Bureau

The following appears in the 'New Statesman and Nation' dated 14th June over the signatures of Raymond Williams, Chairman of Debates, and Maynard Smith, Ex-Chairman of Debates, Union Society, Cambridge:

'Indian Students'

'May we draw the attention of your readers to a recent occurrence in India which we believe to be of general as well as local interest? We refer to the trial of seven Indian students. One of whom is well remembered in British student circles.

'Mohan Kumaramangalam was a student in Cambridge until 1939, and was a respected member of the University. Among other distinctions he was President of the Union in the Lent Term, 1939, President of the Federation of Indian Students, and a member of the delegation of British students to Spain. He played a leading part in many democratic movements, and shared in the fight to prevent war and against Fascism.

He returned to India last year, and began work in the students movement there. In December he was Chairman of a Student Conference in Mangalore, Madras Province, when Police entered the room and fired on the meeting. Kumaramangalam and some others escaped, but were captured a few days later and put on trial, charged with being party to a criminal conspiracy and a member of an unlawful association. An unsuccessful attempt was made to hold the trial in private, the Police averring that witnesses would be reading documents 'containing Communistic ideas which might influence the public.' We do not yet know how the trial resulted.

'It seems from this instance that Indian student organizations are suffering at the hands of the authorities in the same way as the other political organizations. In registering our protest against this we cannot fail to relate this case to the general background of the political situation in India, where men working for the freedom and independence of their country are imprisoned by the British authorities. Individual examples give an indication of the real position in India which hardly correspond with the treatment or lack of treatment of the matter in the press of this country.'

Comment: Kumaramangalam was never shot at by the Police in Mangalore or anywhere else. He has moreover been prosecuted and convicted in the Madras Communist Conspiracy Case, in respect of attempting to impede and obstruct India's war-effort. This article in the N.S.& N. is but one example of several others forming a propaganda campaign organized by the University Labour Federation, a Communist-controlled organization in close touch with the All-India Students' Federation, which is capable of causing considerable mischief. It seems a pity that the India Office cannot give the lie direct to these misleading and ignorant statements relating to the Kumaramangalam case.

Home Dept (Mr Simms)
Copy to SGG (Public)—(Mr Saumarez Smith)
DIB u/o No. 69/Pol/37 II of 10 September 1941
(Director of Intelligence Bureau)

It seems rather late to put out a contradiction to this letter. I understand from Mr Bayley that the reference to police firing is a complete fabrication. The description of the charges prepared against Kumaramangalam is more or less correct except that it is not mentioned that the unlawful association is the Communist Party of India. The India Office was really not in a position to put out any statement in answer to this letter and probably did not attach much importance to it.

I understand that DIB's suggestion is that the India Office should keep a look-out for references to India in the English Press which are *prima facie* misleading, and either contradict them from its own knowledge or cable to us for the information. We have not found the India Office very forthcoming in regard to counter-propaganda and perhaps the best thing would be for PIO to find out Mr Joyce's attitude to the matter with, possibly, an indication that we were rather perturbed at the idea that our case so often went by default.

24. D.P. Dhar's Address at Kashmir Students' Conference, Srinagar, 31 October 1941

File No. B 24 75/1941, Political Department, Government of Jammu and Kashmir (General Records), Chief Secretariat, J&K State Archives.

Address of the Chairman of the Reception Committee, the Kashmir Students' Conference, 31 October 1941. (Durga Prasad Dhar)

Comrade President, Comrades,

I thank you for having asked me to accept the chairmanship of the Reception Committee. The fact that I have withdrawn since a year and a half from active students politics, stood in my way to accept this honour without hesitation. But your kind insistence left me no choice but to bow down to your will. However I cannot fail to express my gratitude to you for affording me this opportunity to participate in your deliberations, and reclaiming me from the tortures of self-imposed silence and inaction.

Let me begin by repeating what I have expressed *ad nauseum*, that I am not one of those who accept the role of natural leadership of the future generation allotted to youth by older men in their expansive moods of gratitude. I believe that the future does not belong to us as a matter of prescriptive right but has to be created by conscious effort. As consciousness is based on knowledge and future is built out of our present environments, the duty of analysing the social situation as it obtains today is primary. If we can turn our conclusion to release and intensify the forces implicit in society to which we belong, then and then alone will the right of leadership accrue.

The first fact that must be faced is the destruction of an illusion which has resulted in liquidating the independent magnitude of individual countries. No longer is splendour considered an attributive of isolation. The world of today does not believe that geographical exclusiveness is a firm basis of security. The sense of distance has vanished, yielding place to a closer interdependence of individual countries made stronger by manifold links. Apart from the fact that it has become a fashion to preface an address of this type by reference to the international situation, it is a historic necessity to try to understand the problem of our country in the perspective of the world scene.

It is obvious that the social situation today is critical. The first feature of the crisis is that it is 25 years old—just the age of youth. The war that began in 1939 was begot by the war that ended in 1918. The student community of today finds itself sandwiched between these two wars. The last Great War had completely shattered the old world with all its stable faiths and since then the mind of the world is split double. Everywhere the painful questioning cry is heard:

'My senses are icicles. Five points of importance: Why the pale Green light? Who scatters the leaves? How do we see?'

On the other hand there was that sense of frustration which at its best sought to cover its nostalgia by attributing to it the virtues of a positive attitude, and on the other hand there was a new faith in humanity recuperating the ancient laws. If defeatism had affected the soul and reduced it to the subconscious, the human spirit sought to integrate itself through various endeavours. Sur-realism in painting, stream of consciousness in novels, imagism in poetry, betrayed the urgent gropings, no less than the melancholy limitations of this attitude. Depths were explored if not with Dantesque clarity but at least with evident sincerity. The search for the primitive, the child-like and the exotic, was in reality a part of the search for the elemental. As such it expressed genuine dissatisfaction with the existing forms the lack of adequate recognition certain milestones in the path traversed by human beings in the course of their social evolution, which recognition alone could convert the negative quality of protest into a positive assertion of a creative faith. In short, the unconscious was treated as beyond the pale of historical process. By calling it basic, fundamental and universal it was given the status of an absolute. In this way one first rate contribution of the post-war world namely the application of psychoanalytical method to social phenomena came to nought: the mechanistic approach of the Freudian analysis acted as a serious impediment to social change.

The other aspect of human mind was represented by those who studied the objective social situation. In their opinion the capitalistic civilization had reached its doom and the nearness of its approach is registered by the perpetual strain to which the world has been put by war—declared and undeclared. Their analysis did not, however, stop there, it went further in envisaging the shape of things to come. Opinions differed from the Utopian Wellsian phantasy and Huxlian revival of intellectual aristocracy to the dictatorship of the proletariat.

The first feature of this crisis as I have pointed out in modest detail was a tremendous confusion that surrounded the objective as well as subjective analysis of the terrific social forces that shook the human mind. I would like to drag on this discussion a little further, describing the second feature of this as 'Crisis in Culture.'

The crisis in the bourgeois culture from my point of view is fundamental and therefore uncompromising. It is born out of a long historical process resulting in decay and stultification of culture. 'In art, science, religion, economics, and ethics,' says Caudwell, 'there is dissention and a thousand confessions of bewilderment and pessimism could be drawn from the writings of acknowledged leaders of contemporary culture from Einstein to Freud.' All the old easy confidence of a century ago has vanished. But who can deny the astounding achievements that characterize half a century of bourgeois culture. Genetics, quantum physics and relativity, the clever peeps of the psychologists into deeper recesses of our mind, the aeroplane, wireless, electric power and a thousand other inventions. 'Why then with this splendid record does it despair,' to quote Caudwell again. 'It departs because each discovery is like a Midas touch, which prepares a new disappointment. Quantum physics seems to have withdrawn reality from the domain of science by denying causality. The psychological discoveries have resulted in a hopeless muddle, in which each rival school is struggling for leadership. The increase in the productive powers has given rise not to plenty, peace and happiness, but famine, war and misery.' Anarchy is the key note of the crisis in all spheres. What is the explanation? For answer we must turn to the words of Herzen. 'We are not the doctors but the disease'. The bourgeois culture in its climax rests on an illusion. Having discarded the secondary illusions like God, morality, theology and metaphysics, in spite of what a Professor Jha here or a Dr Cousins there may say, it rests on a fundamental illusion. This illusion is based on Rousseauean conception of liberty. 'Man is born free but finds himself everywhere in chains.' A conception that was re-echoed by the Utilitarian Mill. In simpler words it means that man is free but for the intervention of social relations which circumscribe the field of his activity. The pursuit of this illusion would in its final analysis end in describing the beast of the jungle as the freest creature. But social relationship is a creation by which man attains fuller measure of freedom than the beast. Liberty does not mean absence of inhibitions but the presence of opportunities. 'Science,' says Sprigg, 'is the means by which man explores and is therefore social'. Art is the means by which man explores the essence of human heart and is therefore social. Yet tragically enough the bourgeois shutting its eyes to beauty, turning its back on science, only follows its stupidity to the end. It crucifies liberty on a cross of gold and if you ask in whose name it does this it replies 'in the name of personal freedom.'

In India our impact with the Britishers resulted in the growth of a hybrid cultural monstrosity. The stunted Indian culture fell into a state of coma, at a time when it was emerging into a new synthesis, transcending monarchist feudalism and acquiring the dynamics of an enterprising individualism and it put on the cast off garments of her masters. Culture ceased to be spontaneous and became a dustbin whose contents repelled all and attracted none. Under the shadow of essential bourgeois illusion described above, coupled with the banes of an unhealthy hybridization, Indian culture developed one more curious aspect. Indians discontented with the extant state of affairs without either necessary boldness to grasp or alter it, began wistfully to long for the days gone by. Instead of a logical and consistent evolution of culture and its social basis converging in a genuine sentiment of nationalism, the past was painted in terms of exquisite charm and attraction.

Rama Rajya became even a political slogan. India's past was glorified in rhyme and metre to make her people forget the present and ignore the future. I do not propose to discuss the Hindu and Muslim cultures, though these formed the subject of a good deal of discussion in the Educational Conference. Because I think that these slogans signify nothing but idiotic humbug. I do not want to drag myself and you my cultured audience to a level, where it becomes necessary to discuss humbug. But my advice to you would be, if I am at all in a position to advise, not to sink into muck and muddle of regrets about the vanished or vanishing ideals and doctrines. It is no use. They are gone or ought to be going. We should not be the mourners of a dying culture or the dead world, we should on the contrary, be its grave-diggers and see that it gets a quick and a secure burial. The Glory that was our past is an illusion, the tragedy that is our present, is a reality.

Besides this general decomposition of bourgeois life, a great economic disintegration was witnessed during the last quarter of a century which threatened the bourgeois purse. As a result the putrid elements of a class which was condemned to death by history organized themselves into a strong reactionary movement. This decaying capitalistic reaction assumed the form of Fascism. The most barbarous type of Fascism is the German Nazism. Born in an atmosphere of defeat and humiliation, it grew on the basis of its appeal to the lowest in man. The entire superstructure of the State was given a war basis. 'The Glory of the German Sword,' said Hitler, 'The Dagger is our best friend,' exclaimed Mussolini, 'Guns or butter' shouted Goering.' As a reply to these slogans our complacent tin gods of the White Hall went on harping the sickening tune of peace. But it was all ineffective, as the procession of our Municipal Saints against the epidemic which recently broke out in Kashmir. Essentially as a consequence of this policy of recoiling before threat, appeasement and surrender we are faced with a great catastrophe. To day titanic struggle is raging between Great Britain and Soviet Union on the one hand and the Fascist Militarists on the other. A conflict I am sure has set in the domain of your sympathies. Probably what I am about to submit here may surprise some of those who know that I was one of the earliest to advocate that students of India should declare complete indifference towards this war. But let me assure them that I still believe that the consequences of Imperialism are essentially similar—by devious ways they jeopardize all chances of constructive effort, damp all enthusiasm for a better living order, confound the will and darken the intellect. They live on war and destroy peace. But I find conditions different now. Today the whole of Europe lies bruised and humiliated under the Nazi heel of tyranny. On the one side the Nazis are already casting covetous looks at us not from far away and on the other side Japan is waiting like the bird of prey to swoop down and pounce upon us. In this hour of unparalleled danger to our country, is it not a crime to engage ourselves in intellectual jugglery, and meaningless doctrinal argument? Can we wait to see the military machine of the Nazis growing in strength and destroying the little freedom that is scattered over the world? Can we allow ourselves to be swept by the current of ideas, noisily proclaimed and basically false?

There are some people in India who go into ecstatic raptures over the exploits of Fascist warmongers. But let them remember that with every Fascist victory are mixed the wails of starving, miserable widows and torn children. 'The victory of Nazis', says Chatofin, 'will end in the resurrection of lower stage already passed by humanity, a retrogression to a period resuscitated in camouflage for the benefit of a few usurpers'. Will it not be tantamount to a reversal of history? Let us therefore solemnly promise to take intelligent interest in aiding the countries that have ranged against the Fascist barbarians. Let us also before concluding this conference send our warm greetings to the Youth of Soviet Union and Great Britain, who are so valiantly and heroically fighting for a cause that is as much ours as it is theirs.

I must crave your indulgence for dealing at unnecessary length with the world situation as it obtains today, and giving this short address the appearance of an essay, but I sincerely believe that even our small and petty looking problems cannot be explained—much less solved if we completely ignore the mighty background of world events and the basic elements of social processes. That students should not meddle in politics is an exploded myth and I am not one of those lovers of the 'Goody, Goody' talk about students confining themselves to text books and the play ground. They have to come into the field and it is no use consoling ourselves with the idle talk that things will shape themselves into an ideal scheme of their own accord. For the present I see that your immediate problems are covered by resolutions which will be the business of the conference to deliberate upon. I am sure these demands and resolutions will be 'sympathetically considered' as the courteous and cautious official language puts it, by the authorities particularly by your Prime Minister who has always evinced a kind and a sympathetic interest in the students community of Kashmir.

25. Mr Satyamurthi's Advice: 'Students and Politics No Active Part'

Amrita Bazar Patrika, 9 November 1941.

New Delhi, 7 November 1941.

'I am of the clear and emphatic opinion that it is neither good for politics nor for themselves, nor for the country, if students take active part in politics', declared Mr S. Satyamurthi, MLA (Central) addressing the students of the Hindu College, Delhi, this evening on 'students and politics.'

Mr C. Rajagopalachari, ex-Premier of Madras, presided.

Students, proceeded Mr Satyamurthi, were not qualified to play any useful part in politics. Politics in all countries of the world, except in totalitarian states where opposition was physically killed, functioned through parties and party leaders. And party leaders, in all democracies, had to make up their mind on any question. In order to go before the public and command the confidence of the voters, the leaders had to assert that their own views were right and those who differed from them were wrong. Hence it was not desirable that the future citizens of the country should even in the formative years of their life, start by being so categorical in their beliefs.

In these years of their life, they must learn to be able to see all sides of a question. They might have firm beliefs and opinions: but they must have the virtue of humility. Democracy, in which he firmly believed, could not work for a moment if the citizens of the state were incapable of understanding the other man's point of view and making allowances for it. He was very anxious that students should not become partisans from their early life.

The students, while they had the time and opportunity, should learn as much as they could about Indian and world politics. He was sorry to admit that in our country while there was no lack of patriots for sacrifice, there was not as much knowledge and information among the politicians as he would wish.

Advice to Students

Mr Satyamurthi exhorted the students to be actively patriotic and above all to be non-communal. He suggested that whenever the schools records asked for their caste and religion, they should first say they were Indians. Without taking active part in politics, they could develop an active sense of patriotism towards their great country and consider no sacrifice too great for the freedom of their country. At the same time, he warned the students that they should not run away with their emotions. While occasional spontaneous expressions of their patriotic feelings would no doubt meet with understanding and sympathy on the part of educational authorities, he strongly disapproved of student strikes becoming a regular phenomenon of college life.

26. 'Dangerous Pleading'

The Student, Organ of AISF, September–October 1941.

Mr Satyamurti, who many a time in the past has brought dishonor to the name of the Congress and the Nation by his pro-imperialist pronouncements, is once again on the scene. In his latest he has outdone his previous self. Speaking at a public meeting at Mylapore he said:

'While Mahatma Gandhi may be permitted to carry on Satyagraha in his own restricted way, the Congress could resume power in the provinces.'

We take it that Mr Satyamurti realizes the fullest implications of his statement and therefore we also take it that Mr Satyamurti would like the Congress Ministers to arrest congressmen and others who would then stand firm by the Ideals that the Congress has always held dear. He would like a rule of black terror to be instituted by the Congress Ministers to help the Imperialists to grow and win, and squeeze us all the more. In short Mr Satyamurti wants the Congress Ministers to act as smiths to make the chains binding India stronger, firmer and tighter.

But that is not all. Continuing the great parliamentarian says:

'If they (Sikander, Huq and others) could continue as Premiers he failed to see why Mr C. Rajagopalachari could not function as the Premier of Madras.'

Mr Satyamurti fails to see, but the World can see why it is not possible to function as Premiers *today without betraying the people, crushing them as under the Nazis and playing the tools of Simla*.

In his anxiety to assume office (shameful as it is) Mr Satyamurti is prepared to go even to this low depth. And the pity is that he draws his inspiration from the conduct of people like Sikandar—the agents of Imperialism.

Mr Satyamurti symbolizes the above tendency in our National ranks, and unfortunately this has had considerable backing from those who control the Congress today.

But such tendencies deserve detestation. They shall have to be fought and eradicated as dangerous trends in our National ranks, else it will devour us and destroy the rich heritage of the past struggle of the Nation.

27. Fight Against Imperialism and Support to Soviet Union

Editorial, *The Student*, Organ of AISF, November–December 1941.

On the 22nd June 1941, a detestable event took place which is bound to change the face of the world. It was the stabbing at the back of the Soviet Union, at the dead of night, by the enemies of mankind, the vilest in history, the German Fascists.

Ever since the rise of Fascism the Soviet Government warned the nations against its wiles. She fought skillfully against the conspiracy of the other great powers. She postponed the outbreak of a world imperialist war for years. In 1939, with the Soviet–German Pact she frustrated the efforts of the world imperialist to make a joint attack upon the Soviet Union. In the bitterness of defeat when the imperialist ruling class plunged the majority of human races into the present imperialist war, it was the USSR that strove to stamp it out, to restrict its arena.

For two years she grew in strength. She never suffered from illusions concerning the intentions of the German Fascists.

This growing strength of the USSR, the mounting anger of the enchained people of Europe stuck terror into the heart of Adolf Hitler. He did not wish to prolong the conflict against Britain and USA while the might of the Soviet increased by leaps and bounds. In mad description he appealed to the battle cry so dear to the hearts of the imperialist powers—a crusade against Communism. He hoped to buy the neutrality if not the active support of the terror-stricken foes of the USSR.

The unbending opposition of the people of Britain to a Fascist peace and their resolute support of the Soviet Union has determined the policy of the British and American Governments towards the Soviet–German War.

The Anglo–Soviet Pact of mutual assistance lays down the present policy of the British Government.

We regard this pact as the first great defeat of the forces in Britain in favour of a capitulation to Fascism and of the anti-Soviet war. It makes a retreat towards capitulation many times more difficult.

In this struggle against the imperialist capitulation we Indians have a DECISIVE role to play.

The Soviet victory and the fall of Hitler are ensured only through the full mobilization of peoples' forces against imperialism—the system which enslaves and not aids the Soviet Cause. It would serve only to strengthen the position of the anti-Soviet capitulators in Britain.

We also declare that we shall not merely be content with an extension of our moral sympathy to the Soviet people. We are not in a helpless position to-day because of our bondage as some make out. It lies within our power to render a more powerful, immediate and direct aid than almost any other nation in the world.

We declare that this can be done by fighting against the shameless illusions spread by the agents of Imperialism and by uniting as one man in the supreme effort to win our national independence. By smashing imperialism in India we shall undermine the strongest base of capitulators in Britain. By crippling and destroying Imperialism in India we shall make the Soviet Union and the world forces of Freedom, Peace and Progress safe for all times to come. We must aid the Soviet by fighting against the fascist and imperialist battle against Japan. India's successful struggle against Imperialism would make the whole continent of Asia—ancient, vast and civilized—going out of the imperialist stronghold.

We should declare on behalf of the world youth that we shall make it a matter of pride and honour for us to give no quarter to those who dared to strike at the frontiers of the Soviet Union. We shall fight with courage and vigilance against the open and secret enemies of the Soviet Union. We shall not rest until the last battle has been won against the despicable aggressors.

Whatever our politics, the youth has loved and admired the Soviet Union as the great land placed at the head of the forces of Freedom, Peace and Progress, the land where illiteracy, disease and unemployment have been banished, where knowledge is free and the mind without fear, where science, art and culture flourish and give unrestricted happiness to millions who freed from exploitation have built up a new civilization, the dream of the oppressed millions throughout the world. We have heard the voice of the Soviet youth calling out to the world in triumph: 'Ours is the land of Youth'.

We appeal to the students, the youth and the people of India to play a historic part in this great conflict. A campaign, limitless in its scope, swooping like a tide all over our great land is the order of the day. It must express our fighting solidarity with the Soviet people in their magnificent resistance.

28. Disturbance in Cawnpore and Student Demonstrators

File No. 5/21/41-Poll. (I), Home (Political) Department, Government of India, NAI.

(i) Report of the District Magistrate (Honcox), Cawnpore, 11 November 1941

On Sunday November the 9th which was celebrated by the local Congress as 'Deoli Detenus Day', a Congress meeting (3000) was held in which a resolution was passed condemning the authorities and the Police for the alleged lathi charge on the students and calling upon shopkeepers to hold a general hartal in sympathy with the students.

At 12 noon on November the 10th a large meeting of about 5000 students was held in the Tilak Hall. The meeting was a disorderly one and the shorthand reporter was assaulted and subjected to insult. After the meeting a large crowd of students streamed out of the Hall and went towards the jail in the Police Lines. The students arrested on Saturday were still in the jail and apparently the intention of the mob was to hold a demonstration outside the jail. Alexander the City Magistrate and Littlewart ASP who were on duty at the Kotwali went to the spot with a force of Police. They found that a large number of students had invaded the Police barrack lines premises and under their order constables cleared these lines. Also a large crowd of students had gathered on the road immediately opposite the Jail and the Police Lines. In the meantime Mr Gray, Managing Director, Begg Sutherland & Co. with his wife and another lady came in his car driven by his driver along this road. The rowdy mob of students attacked the car with brickbats. The car was damaged and a window broken whilst Mr Gray himself received slight injuries. This was at 1.25 p.m.

Also just about this time two other isolated European men in the vicinity were assaulted and knocked off their cycles by students.

Just after the attack on Mr Gray's car the City Magistrate and ASP arrived with their force of Police at the spot where the students had gathered on the road and began to disperse them. Brickbats were thrown by the students and at this moment a Military Staff car carrying Colonel A.F.F. Thomas, Deputy Controller-General of Inspector, Mr E.M. Souter, Controller of Supplies, UP and Major O'Connor and driven by an Indian driver came round the corner along the road where the crowd of students had assembled. The students threw bricks at the car and one brick hit Colonel Thomas on the shoulder. The crowd had attempted to stop the car and did not budge. The car knocked down two men in the crowd on the road and proceeded a few yards further on to the Police lines.

This incident was immediately followed by a heavy shower of brickbats thrown by the students at the Police and the magistrates. The Police were armed with Polo canes. They charged and cleared the crowd. All this had taken place within the space of a few minutes and immediately afterwards at 1.40 p.m. the SSP arrived at the spot and sent the two injured men in the SP's car to the hospital. The mob of students had in the meantime been dispersed.

Shortly after I issued an order under Section 144 CrPC prohibiting the carrying of arms, the gathering in groups of more than five and the taking out of processions.

I also informed the Officer Commanding the Station and arranged with him that the Military Civil Disturbance Column should stand by in the lines.

I then received information that two isolated constables, one on Traffic duty at the Kotwali crossing and the other patrolling with the City Magistrate at Gillis Bazar (also close to Kotwali) had been injured by brick bats. The City Magistrate also reported that a large crowd had assembled on the Meston Road at the Gillis Bazar crossing.

The SSP and I went down to the spot and found that the large crowd which had assembled was apparently not of students but consisted of the general public. Probably they had gathered because news had been received that one of the men knocked down by the car had died in the hospital.

Before our arrival one section of this crowd had thrown some brick bats at the City Magistrate with a very small force of Police, but the crowd dispersed when approached by the Police reinforcements led by the SP and myself. It was apparent that a bad Anti-European and Anti-Police atmosphere had been created and as a precautionary measure I issued a Curfew Order applying between 6.30 p.m. and 5.30 a.m. In the meantime I placed Magistrates on duty.

I omitted to mention that in the affair which occurred outside the Police Lines, one armed Police constable, apparently excited, had fired a shot into the air. I will hold the formal inquiry into this later. This morning everything was quiet and at about 9.30 a.m. the SSP and I went round the city and found all the shops including those on the Meston Road opened. Some of the students had also returned to their schools.

But later this morning things have deteriorated and most of the students have left their schools. Some of them have also been going round persuading shopkeepers to close their shops and some shops have been closed in consequence.

The SSP has arranged with the Inspector General of Police for reinforcement form outside the district and some of these have already arrived. The Inspector General told me on the telephone yesterday that he hoped to send 400 or 500 extra men.

The Military are still standing by.

I have informed the Chief Secretary of these events on the telephone yesterday evening. I am also sending him a copy of this letter direct.

I have also just got into touch with Powell Price and asked him to come over. He will be arriving tonight and I am calling a meeting of the heads of educational institutions so that he can speak to them tomorrow morning.

PS 5.30 p.m.

Since writing the above the situation has badly deteriorated this afternoon. At about 2.25 p.m. I and SSP received information that the Police on duty at Gillis Bazar cross roads will be stoned. We went to the spot and found a large crowd assembled pelting bricks at the Police. The crowd was dispersed by the use of tear gas which was followed up by some arrests. Other crowds then assembled further up the road and were also dispersed by tear gas which was in all used on four occasions, 14 rounds being fired.

Police patrols were then organized and sent out in the affected areas to make arrests of persons breaking the order forbidding crowds of more than 5 persons. In many cases they were stoned and had to make charges to clear crowds throwing bricks at them. Some Police constables received minor injuries from brick bats.

In all 52 arrests were made today mostly for breaches of the order forbidding crowds of more than 5 persons, although undoubtedly many of those arrested were amongst those who had been throwing bricks.

The previous orders under Section 144 CrPC including the curfew order remained in force and I have this afternoon issued another order prohibiting meetings of all kinds, whether within or outside buildings, except meetings of a purely social character.

The crowd which first assembled this afternoon and attacked the Police with brick bats appeared to be very largely composed of students, but the attacks on police afterwards were made apparently not only by students but also by some members of the general public.

All these disturbances which so far occurred were in a comparatively small area confined to Kotwali Police Circle.

The tear gas firing was extraordinarily accurate but my immediate impressions are that it is not sufficiently morally effective. The crowds dispersed at the time of firing but were quite ready to reassemble shortly afterwards.

We have so far obtained 200 extra Police (this includes the Cawnpore Contingent of Military Police) from outside district and the Inspector General of Police has promised the SP further assistance.

SP had a further consultation with Officer Commanding the Station this afternoon. We agreed that the time had not yet come to bring the Military into action.

I have also just been informed that Mr Littlewort ASP had to fire two shots with his revolver this afternoon when he was at the head of the Police patrol which was attacked. The formal enquiry will be held later.

L.P. Hancox,
District Magistrate.
11.11.1941.

(ii) The Cawnpore Incidents

With police excesses in this country we are familiar, indeed painfully familiar. Under the Defence of India Rules regime and the regime of the Advisers the police have become the most formidable single power in the land, almost an *imperium et imperio.* Power, like wine, corrupts. But is it necessary that it should go so far as it has gone in Cawnpore? The public of this province are seriously perturbed at the events which occurred there on Saturday and Monday last when the students were out to observe 'Detenus Day' in connection with the Deoli hunger-strike, and 'T.K. Chaturvedi Day' following the arrest, on Saturday of a popular leader of their community. On both days they were not allowed to take out their processions and on their refusal to disperse they were lathi charged. A number of people, running into a few hundreds, were injured on the two days, some of them seriously. A few dozen arrests were also made. At least two casualties of a fatal nature occurred in connection with the demonstrations. The citizens of Cawnpore have shown their sympathy spontaneously with the students and expressed their indignant protest against the high-handedness of the police by suspending business. And the officials have replied with a curfew order extending over nearly twelve hours and with prohibition of assembly of persons under the notorious Section 144.

The only crime of the students, besides refusal to obey an unjust order to disperse, would appear to be that they burnt the effigies of Mr Amery and Sir Reginald Maxwell, both of whom deserve, however, richly the honour. And they took out black flag processions, which did not by any means upset the delicate applecart of law and order. No one could describe their behaviour as unruly. They were disciplined, they were peaceful, they were non-violent

We have only to compare the unrestrained action of the Cawnpore police with that of their colleagues of Lucknow on Monday to present to the public the vivid contrast the two attitudes represent. Good sense prevailed in this city [Lucknow], with the result that the students procession of protest against the Cawnpore lathi charges was not only duly licensed, but when the demonstrators in their enthusiasm attempted to enter a forbidden zone, they were good-humoredly lead through it by the police officers themselves, who were by no means afraid that the crowds were going to crash the gates of the secretariat and disturb the peace of its denizens. Nothing untoward occurred. The Gomti was not set on fire. Could anything different have happened in Cawnpore if the police had behaved as they did not?

What was the justification for the extraordinary conduct of the Cawnpore police, except that they have come to regard themselves as a law unto themselves? They have played havoc with the labour class, and they are now turning their attention to the students. We can only tell them that in trying to suppress the youth of the country they are attempting a task which they will find to be going beyond the limits alike of discretion and of decency. Cawnpore is within an earshot of Lucknow, and the public would like to know how the local government propose to deal with the offending officers and put an end to their exuberance of misguided zeal. We must ask in particular what they propose to do in connection with the death that resulted from Mr Souter's car attempting to push through the crowd. Somebody will have to pay the penalty for this rash and negligent act, to say nothing further, which has cost the life of one person and resulted in serous injuries to two others.

Cawnpore is an important centre of war industry, and we would ask those who are interested in war effort whether they are not really impeding it by bringing about a serious dislocation of business by lathi charges, by curfew orders and by the hartals that inevitably ensue. If the empire is to be saved, it cannot be by the Cawnpore police, at the rate at which they are going about their business.

(iii) Full Translation of the Lithographed Leaflet in Urdu and Hindi Entitled 'Talibilm Kya Karen?' and 'Vidyarathi Kya Karen?' Issued on 11 November 1941, by the Secretary, District Communist Party, Cawnpore.

The Communist emblem—banner and the sickle—is conspicuous at the top right corner of the leaflet.

What Should the Student Do?

Fairs will be held annually at the mausoleums of the martyrs.

This will be a fitting commemoration of their patriotic fervour (Couplet).

Comrades!

The sanguinary rule of the police has commenced and 'lathi', batons, firing and gas are the order of the day. The dignity of the Govt has been humbled to the dust. The students of Cawnpore have assumed the role of torch-bearers of Indian revolution and the Communist Party of Cawnpore congratulates them on their exemplary work.

Youths! March on! Hundreds of your comrades have been clapped in prison. Many a comrade has been shot down while hundreds are groaning in hospitals. The corpses of martyrs are tossing before you. Blood for Blood. Come out with your heads wrapped in a shroud. Cast the laws of the Govt to the winds. Tear into pieces the police bayonets, the black laws, the Section 144 and the Curfew order. Snatch the reins of Government. Form Communist storm-troops, and start guerilla warfare. Give the CID dogs a taste of their misdeeds. Storm attacks are always successful. The Gandhites, Royists and Socialists will impart to you the lesson of peace and order; but bear in mind that you are going to change the history of India. The citizens of Cawnpore and lacs of workers are with you. The workers will launch a strike and join you. Do not go to attend colleges and schools so long as the arrested students are not released, Section 144 and the Curfew order are not withdrawn, the ban on processions is not lifted, an inquiry is not instituted into the police firing, unless the authorities do not apologize for their conduct and the detenus of Deoli are not released.

Form war councils in all schools and colleges for conducting the struggle. Make suitable arrangements to disseminate leaflets. Take out a procession of the martyred comrade.

Secretary,
District Communist Party,
Cawnpore.
11.11.41.

29. Police Use Tear Smoke on Mob Several Arrested Sequel to Students' Strike at Cawnpore

Amrita Bazar Patrika, 12 November 1941.

Cawnpore, 11 November.

Tear smoke had to be used by the police in four places to disperse the mob that had collected near the Kotwali and is reported to have thrown brickbats at the police. Students of almost all the colleges and schools had gone on strike to-day and the strikers marched through the markets in batches. The markets were later closed.

The situation deteriorated at about 2 p.m. when a mob gathered near the Kotwali and threw brickbats on the police who resorted to the use of tear smoke to disperse the crowd. The situation was soon brought under control.

The police patrolled the city and arrested several persons for defying an order promulgated under Section 144 CrPC prohibiting the assembly of more than five persons.

Seventeen persons were convicted and sentenced to pay a fine of Re 1 for breach of the curfew order.

Clash Between Police and Students

A serious clash took place yesterday between the police and the students near the police lines where a crowd of students had collected to go towards the jail to witness the case of the student leaders arrested on Saturday last for leading a procession which was banned under Section 144 CrPC.

The police charged the crowd with lathis resulting in injuries to several persons.

Early in the day the schools and colleges were closed to observe 'T.K. Chaturvedi Day' in accordance with the decision of the Students' Union. The students took out a procession and held a meeting in Tilak Hall where Mr Ranji Lal, a student leader was arrested. The students collected at the Kotwali gate and made anti-police demonstration.—AP

30. Students' Protest at Nagpur University Convocation, 29 November 1941

The Student, Organ of AISF, November–December 1941.

Lathis Deliver the Convocation Address

(Bravo Nagpur)

[The growing consciousness and unity amongst the student community of India under the banner of the AISF has become an eyesore to our Imperialist masters. In this growth, Imperialism sees the danger to its prolongation and stranglehold. It, therefore, seeks to crush it. 19th August was the turn of the students of Bombay. Then came Cawnpore. And now in quick succession follows the cowardice attack of the police on the peaceful and unarmed students of Nagpur and Gauhati. We need not add anything more to the reports that have already appeared in the press. But let us add that by these repressive acts the authorities are reaping just the opposite result. They are sowing the wind and shall reap the whirlwind. The voice and will of the students can hardly be suppressed by such methods. On the contrary, they shall give fillip to their determination and purpose to march ahead towards their goal—Freedom, Peace, Progress.

These and other acts by the police following in quick succession leave no doubts as to the anti-Imperialist character of the student movement in India. The students in their forward march have to contend with Imperialism itself. We congratulate the students of Nagpur on their bold fight. We have no doubt that the students of Nagpur, steeled through this struggle, will take their rightful place with their Comrades in other parts of India.—Eds]

The painful memories of the horrors perpetrated in the Jallianwalla Bagh were revived on the afternoon of 29th November 1941 when Mr Collins, the DSP, in true Dyerean tradition ordered the armed police to make a charge on the peaceful student demonstrators who had assembled in front of the University Square to register their protest against the high-handedness of the Vice-Chancellor and the Executive Council of the Nagpur University in refusing twenty students to receive their degrees in the Convocation.

The facts are as simple as they are few. The whole incident viewed in a proper perspective proves to be not the prologue but the epilogue to a grievous tale of wrong perpetrated by the Vice-Chancellor and the Executive Council. Stated briefly, the story is as follows:

The Tale Episode which culminated in the with-holding of the results of five unfortunate students who had taken up the cudgels on behalf of their late friend Tale was the starting point of the whole trouble. These five students were most unceremoniously rusticated from their college for their failure to tender an apology for their crime of demanding an impartial tribune to find out the facts of the case. The University took this extreme step of rustication solely on the evidence of the Principal, Mr Tostevin (an Englishman), without giving the victims the opportunity of putting their case before the Executive Council.

This was a grievous wrong. The student community felt it its supreme duty to get these wrongs redressed and save their five friends. And so they planned a protest march on the Convocation Day to show their disapproval of the University's high-handedness. The Vice-Chancellor got scent of this and in his anxiety to show an untarnished face to the assembly in the Convocation refused to allow about twenty students to receive their degrees in the Convocation ceremony. On the morning of the Convocation Mr B.N. Mukerji was arrested under the DIR. When at 1 p.m. in the afternoon students from all colleges began to assemble in the Regent Square to march in procession to the University square, the DSP along with the City Superintendent of Police dashed on the spot and took into custody our seven student organizers of the procession along with their flags and placards. This created a stir among the students whose number began to swell every minute till at 1.30 a procession marched from the Regent Square culminating in a meeting in the University Square. There students demanded the immediate release of their workers and grant of permission to attend the Convocation to the twenty students who were not allowed to attend the Convocation. The meeting continued till 2.30.

The Secretary of the Students' Federation was prepared to go even to the length of giving definite assurance to the DSP that no disturbance whatsoever would be created to mar the solemn proceedings inside the Convocation Pandal. But the DSP in the most flagrant and ungentlemanly manner retorted, 'I can't trust you'. After this without giving any warning to the students who had assembled in the University Square he ordered the police to make free with their lathis.

As a result of the first charge three students were seriously injured. The lathi charge, brutal and inhuman as it was, failed however, to crush the spirit of the students.

It served as a mortar to cement the students' unity and their resolve to consider no sacrifice too great for a cause which they held dear. They re-assembled and like a river in flood burst into the thick of the armed police rending the skies with their slogans: 'Democratize the University', 'Officialdom must go', 'We want elected Chancellor'. 'Reduce Examinations fees', 'Publish University Accounts,' and other things. For a moment even the DSP stood dumb at what he thought the childish audacity of these unthinking, unarmed, defenceless youngsters but his pride soon got the better of the amazement. 'Charge and disperse,' shouted the voice of authority and in a moment the police lathis began their work on the heads of the mammoth crowd of students. Again the students behaved in the same dignified and heroic manner. This time the number of students who were injured was even greater. After this the DSP gave his men full liberty to punish the 'mischief-mongers' as he called them and the police charged on them five times with their lathis between three and four O'clock. The climax was reached when a student crushed to jelly with the lathis of the police and panting for breath was gripped by the DSP, who with the cruelty and inhumanity as would have astounded Chengiz Khan asked him 'Haven't you had enough?' As a result of these lathi charges about 100 students were injured six of them seriously. In the Pandal itself two students were arrested and 26 students who were to receive their degree staged a walk-out.

On Monday the 1st December, as a mark of protest against the lathi charge a general strike was observed. All the local Schools, Colleges—even primary schools and girls institutions—were closed. A mammoth meeting of more than 8000 students was held in the Needham Park, which was also addressed by Prof. Humayun Kabir, MLC, Calcutta.

The students then marched in a procession to wait on Mr Kedar, the Vice-Chancellor, who in his turn refused to see them or any deputation from them.

Sympathetic strikes were observed by students at Wardha, Amraoti and other places.

31. Dr Hiren Mookerjee's Address at Punjab Students' Conference, 29 November 1941

The Tribune, 30 November 1941.

'Students' Impulses Must be Harnessed to National Service' 'India Belongs to Muslims as Much as to Hindus'

Lahore, 29 November.

'In the tumultuous world of ours the role of students is quite apparent. They are to mould the world after their heart's desire. Their generous impulses must be harnessed to national service. When in so many countries and above all in the Soviet Union, their brethren are shedding blood in freedom's battle, they in their servitude, can at least do all in their power to win freedom for the country. They are surely to think of no other brand of freedom than the one which permits our common people to build a new world and a new civilization. They are not by themselves a class capable of making history, and therefore, they must align themselves with workers' and peasants' movements. That our students realize this perfectly is seen in their slogan of 'Freedom, Peace and Progress' not indeed in the dead and formal sense of those oft abused words, but in their real dynamic connation.' These observations were made by Dr Hiren Mukerjee, in the course of his presidential address to the Punjab Students' Conference held this evening at the Bradlaugh Hall, which was packed to capacity. A large number of student delegates was present.

Dr Hiren Mukerjee called the Soviet solution of the problem of nationalities and minorities as a miracle. What used to be the Czarist prison of peoples, kept compulsorily in a position of 'planned backwardness', now breathes the air of happy freedom. 'Where in the world is such provision for the protection of linguistic and cultural minorities,' he asked? 'And why on earth cannot we adopt Soviet methods to deal with our minority problems which cannot just be washed away by empty slogans of Akhand Hindustan?'

No Believer in Pakistan

'I am no believer in Pakistan,' he added, 'I know that to the Muslim, India is his country perhaps even more so than in the case of a Hindu, for when a Hindu dies, his body is burnt to ashes but when a Muslim dies, he needs at least 6 feet by 3 of Indian soil'...'India belongs to the Muslim, at least as much as to the Hindu, in life as well as in death. But there are in the country undeniable regional peculiarities and cultural difference which must be protected. Political and economic salvation must come. That will not come by Hindu militancy nor by those who cry for Pakistan only to further their own electoral ambitions. Great problems need people of vision to give as a solution. Speeches from the Congress platform won't help us much.'

Concluding Dr Hiren Mukerjee said: 'Our national leadership has postponed our trials. Students are to awaken them from their slumber. They are to be reminded of the glory of India and the way as to how to keep that intact. I appeal to the students that they march on; their slogans must be shaped by their knowledge for knowledge of the forces operating in society will alone give them power to change the face of society... May it be the students' role to help to bring that world nearer' (cheers).

Com. Mahmood Ali's Speech

Comrade Mahmood Ali, inaugurating the Conference in the absence of Mian Iftikhar-ud-Din who suddenly fell ill, said: 'Attacks of British Imperialism will not weaken our forces. Students can never be terrified by oppression. They shall march on. They are to play a predominant role in the future so far as country's battle for freedom is concerned.' He also read Mian Iftikhar-ud-Din's letter to the Conference in which best wishes for its success were expressed.

Comrade Randhir Singh Josh, Chairman of the Reception Committee, in the course of his speech said: 'No disruptive forces can break our unity or create a split amongst us. We stand united. Ours is not a movement of individuals: it is the movement of the students of the whole province. We shall carry on the flag of 'Peace, Freedom and Progress.' He held that 'individual satyagraha had demoralized the masses and crushed the militant forces of the country. The students shall not surrender to British Imperialism. We are living in a country which is a slave country', he added, 'and for the students of a slave country, politics is the only recourse. We are not joining politics for the sake of fun.' Comrade Randhir Singh condemned the Indian system of education and compared it with that of China and hoped that Indian students would learn the lesson of resistance from their Chinese comrades. Russia, he held, was the expression of Indian students' aspirations.

Dr Kitchlew's Speech

Earlier Dr Kitchlew, performing the flag-hoisting ceremony, said: 'This war of imperialistic powers is for their own exploitation. We are sorry that Russia has joined the war. We have great sympathy for her in her titanic struggle.'

Referring to 'Peace, Progress, Freedom', he held that to have peace many sacrifices would have to be made. 'And in order to have real "progress", the country shall have to wait till the war is over. But we must be ready to have it.'

The session adjourned till tomorrow when it will meet at 2 p.m.

32. Punjab Students' Conference: Fight for Freedom Must Continue

The Tribune, 1 December 1941.

The Punjab Students' Conference met this afternoon for the second day at the Bradlaugh Hall under the Presidentship of Dr Hiren Mukerjee. Multi-coloured saris of the fair sex, a large number of delegates from all over the province and students of all communities were prominent.

Mrs Freda Bedi was pleased to find that the student community showed seriousness in their attitude towards life and had lively purpose to goad them on. She missed Miss Bharucha[1] whom she considered a real comrade with grand spirits who stood for the removal of disruptive forces which stood in their way.

Referring to the Russo–German war, she felt that nothing could kill the spirit of the USSR. 'If Russia dies', she opined, 'the spirit of communism would die and the labour voice will be hushed. But Russia will never die.'

She read a telegram from her husband expressing glowing greetings to the Punjab students and wishing them freedom and progress towards Soviets in the Province round which they all were to rally.'

Resolutions

Comrade Minto moved the first resolution on 'students demands.' It ran:

'This conference demands from the Punjab University that the application of the principle of two examinations a year be extended to the Intermediate students: a system of biannual examination for the Law classes be established, and extended to the PEL, and FEL classes; MA Economics course for BCom. Graduates be reduced to one year; the prices of text books which are rising rapidly due to the war be controlled: the college and hostel fees (particularly in the Government colleges) be reduced: fees charged for the various university examinations be reduced; post-graduate students who are taught by university professors only be not required to pay the college fees, nor be on the college rolls. That they be allowed to join the university directly and pay their fees which should be moderate; members of the Senate be elected: the ten years limit for registration of University graduates be completely removed. All graduates be automatically allowed to register themselves, all university classes should meet in the university: the priestly gowns worn on the Convocation Day be substituted by something national and more becoming for the convenience of students, their parents and hostel servants, all institutions be asked to allow a two hours mid-day break for lunch; the communal proportion for admission to the Government College and Government College hostels be abolished: merit and not recommendations from officials and men of influence be taken into account for admission to the Government College and University Hon's School classes: all sport committees be composed of persons unconnected with any of the colleges: entrance tickets for university sports be abolished, the sports functions be not used to collect funds for various purposes: the medium of instruction be changed to Hindustani; more stress be laid on technical and practical education; the right of freedom of discussion and organization which is essential for real university life, be guaranteed, and the Intermediate students of the Kinnaird College and students of the Khalsa College for Women be allowed to enroll themselves as members of the LSU[2] and to attend the meetings if they so like.'

Speaking on the resolution, Mr Minto condemned the system of education prevailing in the country and held that it 'produces continuous stream of clerks and perverts the minds of the youth, poisons their brains and leads them astray'.

Comrade Haim Raj, seconding the resolution, wanted a united front to force the Government, to get their demands accepted.

The second resolution passed by the conference related to Soviet–German war. It was moved by Comrade Usha Kohli and seconded by Comrade Dharam Pal. The resolution ran as follows:

'The war of Britain is still an imperialist war. Their collaboration with Soviet Union against their rival imperialist Germany, does not reflect any change in their war policy. Therefore the British people are charged with greater tasks. While their rulers will hesitate, the people must work for the complete implementing of the Anglo–Soviet Pact. They must strive for an all-out aid to the Soviet Union. But this pact cannot and will not become a reality until the war is purged of its imperialistic aims.'

Comrade Usha Kohli traced the history of the Russo–German relations and held that Imperialist war had entered its final phase. 'Russia's victory,' she held, 'will be peoples' victory all over the world'. British Government's aims were the same imperialistic though they were helping Russia. 'We in India, want mass action, moral support won't do. We must aid the Soviet by fighting against the Fascist and imperialist forces on the spot.'

Comrade Dharam Pal wanted the Punjab students to follow in the footsteps of their brethren in China and Russia and fight their battle for liberty.

At this stage Dr Hiren Mukerjee left the hall to catch his train for Calcutta. Comrade Mahmood Ali occupied the chair.

Before leaving the hall, Dr Hiren Mukerjee held that politics was an essential study for students as it equipped their minds with right glittering of knowledge to smash the miserable forces that stood in their way to the citadel of freedom. He advised solid activity by the rank and file of the student community.

Dr Kitchlew wanted that the future Government in India should not be after the Soviet model in toto but should be according to our own sentiments—an improvement on the USSR structure. 'My country' he added. 'should be free with our own efforts with our own power and not with the help of outsiders.' However he did not object if the students liked Russian ideologies as the Soviet system was still the best.

The Resolution was passed.

Mr Inder Gujral moved and Mr Randhir Singh Josh seconded the following resolution which was passed:

'As a mark of our determination to stand with the people of Soviet Union in their heroic struggle, we start one pice token fund. 4 pice from 4 people and not one anna from one man is our slogan. Let every student contribute to this fund and demonstrate his solidarity with the Soviet people.'

Mr Randhir Singh Josh moved the following resolution on 'National Situation.'

'We demand that the national leadership should knit up the various partial struggles of the Indian people, workers, peasants and the students, into one anti-imperialist fight.'

He held that India was betrayed by Indian leaders who have capitulated to imperialistic forces. The entire national front was going over to the enemies, he added. He did not like Individual Satyagraha but wanted mass action.

'Back to ministries' policy would be suicidal. He wanted the fight for freedom to be intensified.

Mr Sunder Lal seconding the resolution, opined that liberty would not come from Britain but was to be fought for.

The resolution was carried.

Mr Inder Mohan, moved the Resolution on 'C class and Security Prisoners.' The resolution ran:

'We demand better treatment for those who have been detained in the Deoli Camp and in the provincial jails. We call upon all the units of PSF to take up the lead given by the LSU and collect funds for C class and Security Prisoners.'

Miss Santosh Diwan appealed for funds to help the families of prisoners.

Mrs Hajra Ahmed criticized the Defence of India Rules and held it was sheer propaganda that the political prisoners in Deoli and in the Punjab were harmful people. It was sidetracking the issue to stand on the flimsy plea that those prisoners sought imprisonment because of their own actions, and now should not demand any rights as they were expected to do sacrifices.

The resolution was passed unanimously.

Messages from leaders all over India wishing the students conference a success were read.

Last night Mr Minto, the President of the Punjab Students' Federation, was at an 'at home' to the press, Dr Hiren Mukerjee and others.

The Conference concluded in the midst of cheers and slogans of 'Inqilab Zindobad.'

---

[1] Miss Perin Bharucha, later Perin Romesh Qandra, was a prominent leader of the All India Students' Federation in Punjab.

[2] Lahore Students' Union.

33. Agitations of Students in Assam

(i) About 30 Persons Injured, Lathi-charge by Police Students' Demonstration Sequel

Amrita Bazar Patrika, 7 December 1941.

About thirty persons received injuries as a result of a lathi charge by the police and a students' demonstration on the Gauhati–Shillong Road to-day, the injuries of two being rather serious. Following an incident this morning near the college premises in which a student was reported to have been assaulted, all the students of the local college and schools went on strike and staged the demonstration on the Gauhati–Shillong Road. The police made two lathi charges on the demonstrators, and dispersed them.

The Lawyers' Association of Gauhati adopted a resolution condemning the lathi charge by the police and sent a telegram to the Premier, the Education Minister and the Leader of the Opposition urging institution of an immediate non-official enquiry into the incident

(ii) Lathi-charge on Students, Gauhati Incident Protest Day to be Observed Today

Amrita Bazar Patrika, 11 December 1941.

In the course of a statement to the press Mr Sadhan Gupta, President, and Mr Arun Bhattacharya, General Secretary, Bengal Provincial Students' Federation, call upon the students of Bengal to observe to-day (Thursday) as a day of protest against the lathi charge made by the police on students at Gauhati. The District and Primary Committees are directed by the BPSF to observe the day.

In another statement Mr Sanat Rai Chowdhury, Joint Secretary, All India Students' Federation, says that more than 250 students including some girls received slight injuries. The injuries of about 60 were severe of whom 10 are still in hospital. Fourteen members of the All-India Students' Federation who took part in the demonstration were placed under arrest. The accused have been granted bail.

A meeting to protest against the lathi charge on Gauhati students and to consider the resolution adopted by the Senate of the Calcutta University empowering Principals of colleges to compel a student to take transfer certificate without adducing any reason will be held to-day (Thursday) at 1 p.m. in the common room of the Bangabasi College. A meeting will also be held at the Vidyasagar College.

(iii) Lathi-charge on Students Shillong Sympathy Girl Students' Committee's Resolution

Amrita Bazar Patrika, 21 December 1941.

(From Our Shillong office)

The Shillong Girl Students' Committee at a meeting held here under the presidency of Sreejukta Lila Barua passed the following resolution regarding the Gauhati incident:

That a Non-Official Enquiry Committee should be formed as soon as the new Ministry is formed.

That Mr Humphrey, Deputy Commissioner, should be transferred from Gauhati immediately.

That Mrs Rajbala Das, Principal of the R.K. Handique College should be removed from her post as soon as possible.

That the police authorities should refrain from using lathi and bayonets on the students in future.

34. Indira Nehru's Speech at UP Conference

Amrita Bazar Patrika, 8 December 1941.

Students' Role in Politics
Work in villages

Cawnpore, 6 December.

Inaugurating the fifth UP Students' Conference held to-day under the presidentship of Dr Hussain Zahir, Miss Indira Nehru said that she welcomed the idea when she heard that the UP Students' Federation was holding a cultural conference. She added that for the cultural advance of a people an atmosphere of political freedom is an absolute necessity. She continued, that the efforts of the students should be to raise the cultural and political level of their people to such heights where national culture would merge into the international. The student movement was a part of the general political movement in their Country. Those who endeavoured the change in basic organization of the society should not allow themselves the comforts of sectarianism. The students should not confine their activities to the students movement alone. They should go to the villages and establish contact with the peasantry. There was no reason why their dramatic clubs and music associations should not give performances in villages and why other students' societies should not reach out into the country and bring enlightenment to the people.

Dr Hussain Zahir, President of the conference, in his presidential address stressed the necessity of educating the illiterates and held that the students could take part in politics. He also dwelt at length on the international situation with special reference to India.

Mr S.S. Mehdi, Chairman of the Reception Committee, welcomed the delegates.—AP

35. Jawaharlal Nehru's Reply to Mian Iftikhar-ud-Din Regarding Schism in Students' Federation,[1] 8 December 1941

SWJN, Vol. 12, pp. 599–600.

... 2. As for the Students Federation, I am a little fed up with their quarrels and schisms. I have just been asked to give a message for the conference which is going to be presided over by Meherally. Possibly I might give a message but this is likely to consist of criticisms. Frankly speaking I am not interested in the new attitude of the students which chiefly consists in talking tall, criticizing the Congress, discussing fine points of ideology, and doing nothing. This of course is not a new development and I have watched something like this for the last two or three years. One must of course attach importance to students but I refuse to attach importance to people who do nothing and talk tall, whether they are students or others. I suppose the student world is going through some kind of inner crisis which will pain them a lot and out of which they will learn something. I should of course like you and Meherally to try to put an end to this schism. If you succeed, well and good. I do not think it is right or desirable for me to interfere. Partly I have no time for this kind of thing, partly I have no mood for it. They must gain my respect a little before they expect my time. Our students seem to me to be quite singularly rigid in mind and repeating set formulas and slogans without troubling to use their brains. Most of these formulas and slogans are dead and done with and have no application today. I suppose sometime or other they will realize this. It will be time enough then for me to try to help them. If anyone wants to see me in Allahabad, I shall gladly meet him. But it is neither good for me nor for them that I should go to Patna or anywhere else especially to smooth their ruffled hair and repeat platitudes.

You were of course quite right in writing about these matters to me because they are important. I hope, however, that you appreciate my viewpoint.

I am enclosing a copy of the message [*For the text of the message, see next document*] I am giving to the All India Students Conference to be presided over by Meherally. This is, as you will notice, an odd kind of message and if you care to use it at your conference, you can do so.

Yours sincerely,
Jawaharlal Nehru

---

[1] Mian Iftikhar-ud-Din in his letter of 16 December had requested Jawaharlal Nehru to become Chairman of the Friends of the Soviet Union proposed to be set up at the all-India level and to attend the AISF Conference scheduled to be held at Patna from 31 December 1941. The first part of his reply is reproduced in Chapter 1, Document No. 107.

36. Jawaharlal Nehru's Message to the All India Students Conference, 20 December 1941

SWJN, Vol. 12, pp. 601–2.

I understand that an All India Students Conference is going to be held at Patna soon and that this will be presided over by my friend Yusuf Meherally. I have been asked to give a message of good wishes for this conference. Students of course have my good wishes always. And yet I have hesitated to give this message as some news reached me, through the newspapers, in prison about squabbles and schisms in the student world. I did not try to follow what happened as such disputes did not interest me. But I gathered enough to be distressed. It seemed to me bad enough that students in India even in ordinary times should be behaving as political parties have been behaving. But it was infinitely worse that at a time of national and world crisis relatively trivial matters should create splits and rouse passions. It is always a test of a nation, a group and an individual, as to what it or he considers the first essentials. If secondary matters are given the first place, that nation, group or individual becomes secondary and counts for little. For students it is obvious that the bonds that should link them and the general national approach that should bind them together, are such that there can be hardly two opinions in regard to them. On it there could easily be unity and effective work, giving freedom for individual expression of opinion on other matters. If students forget their own job and consider themselves as the final judges of the nation's activities and split on that issue, they are perfectly welcome to do so, but they are not likely to advance their own interest or the national interest in this way. In this world of prejudices and horrors, none of us can afford to make catchphrases and slogans take the place of reasons and consecutive thoughts. Slogans are useful and desirable but they are dangerous companions for those who wish to use their minds and their intellects.

I do not know about the merits or demerits of the students' organizations that exist today and am quite unable to express my opinion on them. But I am well acquainted with the background and so I can presume to form an opinion based on general principles.

I am told that there is another students' organization called the All India Students Federation and that this organization is also holding some kind of a conference soon in Patna. Mian Iftikhar-ud-Din, a friend and a colleague, is, I understand, expected to preside over this conference. Thus both the prospective presidents of the two students' conferences are comrades of mine whom I respect. It seems odd to me that two such friends and comrades should be associated with rival organizations. It seems to me that it should be their first job, as well as that of the students, to put an end to this unseemly state of affairs. Possibly they may find it difficult today under the existing conditions. Possibly also it is better for the student world to learn through its own experience. Till they have so learnt, I am afraid they cannot expect much sympathy or help from outsiders who otherwise wish them well and would gladly cooperate with them.

I have ventured to express my opinion frankly to the students for there is little point in my repeating unmeaning platitudes. I am sure they will appreciate my frankness even though they may not agree with all what I have said. We dare not delude ourselves in these critical times by adopting any course or line of thought that evades the real issues.

Again I repeat that I wish well to the students, for after all the burden of the future rests with them. What they do today is of relatively little importance, except in so far as it prepares them and lays the foundation for future work. For them tomorrow is more important than today. If they wish to make tomorrow theirs, they will have to develop the methods of work and qualities which will bring them this heritage, or else others will pass them by, while they are in hue and dispute, and take the leadership of tomorrow.

37. Yusuf Meherally's Call at All-India Students' Conference at Patna

Bombay Chronicle, 29 December 1941.

Identify Yourselves with Struggle for Independence

Patna, 27 December.

A clarion call to take a deep interest in Students' Union and social problems and organize a trained and disciplined volunteer organization was made by Mr Yusuf Meherally in the course of his Presidential Address to the seventh session of the All-India Students' Conference (Shah Group) which commenced here this afternoon.

Mr Meherally at the outset referred to the Satyagraha movement of the Indian National Congress and its disassociation from the present war and said 'the resignation of the Congress Ministries a little earlier in eight out of the eleven Provinces of India and the subsequent imprisonment or detention without trial of representative Congressmen including hundreds of members of Legislatures and almost all the Ministers who had resigned served to dramatize Indian struggle before the world at large.'

Hindu–Muslim Problem

Proceeding Mr Meherally said:

'In fact the responsibility devolving on the student community in a country struggling for independence was far heavier than on their more fortunate brethren elsewhere.' Here the students have a two-fold duty to perform. The first was to identify themselves with the struggle for National liberation and secondly, to rebel against the deadweight of ancient customs and traditions that have long outlived their usefulness.

Referring to the Hindu–Muslim problem, Mr Meherally said the communal problem was essentially the result of three factors. The first of these was undoubtedly Government policy. The second was the fight for political power among the intelligentsia of the different communities and the third was the comparative failure of non-communal political organizations to approach the Muslim masses in substantially large numbers and bring them within their respective spheres of influence. While the economic approach was the most important, by itself alone it will not be able to achieve the needed results. A greater cultural fusion between the two communities was also very necessary.

Sympathy for Russia

Proceeding Mr Meherally referred to the war and said: 'With the coming in of Japan, the war has now spread to practically the whole world. It is not easy to foresee when it will end and how will it end. One question that is often being posed is whether the imperialist character of the war has changed after the entry of Soviet Russia. Our sympathies are naturally with the Russians in the great ordeal that they are facing so bravely; but situated as we are, the first task before the people of this country is to work for their freedom. The blunt declaration of the British Prime Minister that the provisions of the Atlantic Charter do not apply to India shows the direction the wind is blowing. It is clear that so far as India is concerned, the Imperialist character of the war remains unchanged.'

Split in Students' Movement

Concluding Mr Meherally referred to the split in the students' movement and said, 'I am strongly of opinion that the students' movement should not be made the tail-end of any political party. The need for a broad based movement was never so great as to-day—a movement such as this can only grow in an atmosphere of tolerance. You must avoid dogmatic formulae and be realistic to hear view-points other than your own. It is not rigid dogmas but beliefs tested by experience of life that contain seeds of inspiration.'—AP

38. Students Assert India is One and Indivisible

Bombay Chronicle, 30 December 1941.

All-India Conference Formulates Demands and Draws up Charter of Student Rights and Duties

Patna, 29 December.

The All-India Students' Conference concluded its deliberations last evening after adopting a number of resolutions.

The first of these resolutions on the national struggle stated: 'While maintaining their separate identity the students should identify themselves with the national struggle collectively as far as possible, resisting all attacks on their civic and academic rights, liberties and also co-operating within their own spheres with other organizations in the achievement of freedom.'

The resolution further viewed 'with alarm the intense repression that has been launched against the students and which has manifested itself in the shape of arrests, detention and searches under the cover of the Defence of India Rules'.

The resolution asserted that the student movement was an integral part of the national movement and as such they had to play an important role in the struggle for national liberation.

National Unity

Another resolution on national unity said that India was one and indivisible and that the political and administrative unity achieved in this ancient land was based upon a real cultural, social and economic unity produced by centuries of natural historical development. The resolution, while admitting that cultural freedom was necessary for the growth of this future common culture, warned the students of India against the misguided attempts to divide India into cultural zones with the right to separate on the ground that India was not one nation. The resolution deplored the communal differences and occasional communal outbursts in the country which were the product of the disastrous imperialist handling of an easily soluble social problem and domination of life in this country by vested interests.

A third resolution on unity among students' movement reiterated its desire for a united students' movement and noted with concern that the earnest efforts in this direction had not borne any fruit.

Students and War

The resolution on war maintained that its imperialist character had not changed and called upon the students to work for a new social order based on peacefulness and democracy wherein the recurrence of such war would be impossible in future and the exploitation of man by man and nation by nation would cease.

Students' Demands

A lengthy resolution on students' demands opined that it was only on the basis of students' demands that a real students' movement could be built up and therefore directed the Provincial Students' Federations, to intensify their struggle for the fulfilment of their demands. The resolution demand reduction in tuition, hostel and examination fees, complete freedom of thought, speech and association in and outside educational institutions, that the administration of educational institutions, particularly universities, should be democratized and that an exhaustive scheme should be drafted by the Government for the relief of unemployment among the educated classes and that it should be immediately put into practice.

Mr Yusuf Meherally the President, in his concluding remarks said: 'We are on the parting of ways. The international situation is fast developing day by day. No one can say what will happen tomorrow. It is at this time that the Congress should keep clear from all parliamentary activities and should greatly stiffen the struggle. To compromise is to obstruct the progress of the country'—AP

39. Conference of All-India Muslim Students' Federation, Nagpur, 26–27 December 1941

Indian Annual Register, 1941, Vol. II, pp. 403–5.

The Welcome Address

The Fifth Session of the All-India Muslim Students' Federation commenced at Nagpur on the 26th December 1941 under the presidency of Mr Mahomed Ali Jinnah.

Mr Abdul Qadir, Chairman of the Reception Committee, criticized the Congress rule in the Provinces and referred to the grievances of Muslim students, such as the singing of 'Bande Mataram'. Muslim students, who were League-minded, he stated, were made to suffer for their political views. The change-over in the administration under Section 93 of the Government of India Act had not, however, brought about any improvement. Mr Qadir assured Mr Jinnah that Muslim students wholeheartedly supported the League policy as regards Pakistan and the war.

Mr Nauman, Deputy President of the Federation, announced that the Chief Minister of Bengal had been removed from the life membership of the Federation. Their organization, he said, had become stronger in Bombay, Karachi and Lahore, and added that an All-India Muslim Girl Students' Federation would be formed at Delhi in March next. He expressed the hope that Mr Jinnah would live long to become the King of Pakistan.

Earlier, the Raja of Mahamudabad, hoisting the flag, said that the Pakistan movement had come to stay and even a thousand Savarkars could not check it.

The Presidential Address

Mr Mahomed Ali Jinnah began by reminding the students that, according to the constitution of their Federation, they were to fit themselves for taking their proper share in the struggle for the freedom of the country. They were not to participate in the political development taking place from day to day. Their primary duty was to concentrate on their studies.

Proceeding, Mr Jinnah said that the Muslim League had grown and was growing by leaps and bounds all over India. The Muslim League had made not only remarkable but miraculous progress (applause). The League had infused political consciousness among the Muslims, giving them a flag, a common platform and a goal.

'Government of India Act: A Dismal Failure'

Continuing, Mr Jinnah said that Muslims had no friends. They were surrounded by opponents in all directions and particularly in CP, where four per cent of the population was 'terrorized and cowed down.' But he had never felt prouder than when he heard and read of the magnificent stand taken by them in this Province. 'No nation has ever achieved its ambition without sacrifice. Therefore, it is obvious that the wretched Constitution which was enacted in 1935—even the Provincial part of it—has been a dismal failure in this country. We shall have to revise our notions and ideas as to the future. But I want the Muslims of this Province to be cheerful. Nothing will prevail which is unjust, unfair and dishonest'.

Mr Jinnah impressed on his audience that the key to the correct solution was in their own hands. They should not depend on anybody else. By that, he did not mean that they should become aggressive. Muslims had no designs on the Hindu or any other sister community, but Muslims would not submit to the domination of others in the sub-continent.

Referring to the Huq episode, Mr Jinnah said: 'I make Christmas present of Mr Fazlul Huq to Lord Linlinthgow. I make a New Year's gift of the Nawab of Dacca to the Governor of Bengal. I am glad that the Muslim League is rid of them. I am confident that the League will emerge stronger without these men who are guilty of gross breach of faith and betrayal of the Muslims in India. No man is indispensable in our organization'.

Turning to the political situation, Mr Jinnah said that he could not understand why Congress leaders did not honestly and frankly admit that they did not represent the Muslims; the League was the only authoritative representative body of the Muslims. Mr Jinnah analysed the Congress demands and declared that if those demands were accepted, the Muslims would be relegated to the position of a helpless minority. From the recent utterances of Congress leaders such as Mahatma Gandhi, Mr Nehru, Maulana Azad and Mr Rajagopalachari, he said, it was difficult to understand what the Congress wanted.

Analysing the Hindu Maha Sabha's demands, Mr Jinnah said that the Maha Sabha did not want to give the Muslims one iota beyond what they considered was the Muslims' due on a population basis. The motive behind the Maha Sabha's call to the Hindus to fill the ranks of the army, navy and air force, was to destroy the Pakistan scheme.

Continuing, Mr Jinnah argued that the demand for a declaration of Dominion Status one or two years after the end of the war was made so that the Constitution could no longer be framed with the consent of the minority party. In the first instance, the British were no such fools as to fall into this trap. And even if they did, a bad constitution would not last a fortnight (applause). Mr Jinnah read Mahatma Gandhi's Thirteen Point Constructive Programme and said that if Mahatma Gandhi added a fourteenth point namely, Pakistan, a settlement between the Hindus and Muslims would be very easy (applause).

Referring to individual satyagraha, Mr Jinnah quoted Mahatma Gandhi's own statement to show that the ultimate object of it was not to ensure freedom of speech, but 'the final goal of Purna Swaraj'.

Mr Jinnah reiterated the League view-point on war effort and said that Muslims could not give their all, 'unless they were placed in the position of having a real and genuine share in the responsibility and authority of the governments at the Centre and in the Provinces?.'

Concluding, Mr Jinnah urged the students to maintain unity and solidarity, and advised them not to resist or defy law and order. They must wait for the orders of the All-India Muslim League and then he (Mr Jinnah) would be the first to march with them.

Mr Jinnah in the course of his address, said that he found a family resemblance between the demands put forward by the Hindu Maha Sabha and the Liberal leaders and described Sir Tej Bahadur Sapru as subtle but dangerous.

Referring to the Congress resolution regarding the framing of the future constitution for India by a Constituent Assembly, he said his difficulty was in regard to the appointment of arbitrators for deciding the issues on which the minority differed from the majority. 'Who will appoint the personnel for arbitrator?' he asked. 'If I appoint arbitrators of my choice will the Congress accept it?'

'I ask you, is it not in the face of it futile and absurd to ask that the British Government should make a declaration that India should be granted Dominion Status one year or two years after the war? Can you imagine the British Government making such a declaration? In the first instance, they cannot do it and even if they do it, do you expect them to put Mr Savarkar on the gadi and do the policing of his Raj? As Mr Amery rightly points out, Dominion Status is not a medal or decoration I can put on your button-hole with a safety pin. This demand aims at eliminating Muslim consent to the future constitution. The British are not fools to fall into this trap, but even if they do it, that constitution will not last for a fortnight'.

Resolutions

The following resolutions were passed by the Federation:

The main resolution reads: 'This session, while deploring the failure of the Government to make satisfactory response to the offer made by the Muslim League for the active and whole-hearted association of the Muslims of India with the intensification of war efforts and the defence of India, appreciates the assurances given by Mr Amery and the Viceroy in their recent speeches regarding the framing of the future constitution of India. The Federation, however, wishes to sound a note of warning that any repetition of the so-called Gentleman's Agreement between the Congress and the Government and the return of single party Congress ministries without a previous settlement with the Muslim League would lead to a very grave crisis'.

By other resolutions, the Federation demanded the release of all political prisoners of all parties, including Allama Mashriqui, condemned the action of Mr Fazlul Huq and the Nawab Bahadur of Dacca and appreciated the stand taken by the League and Scheduled Caste members, and demanded the making of the Bombay University's syllabus acceptable to Muslims and the enactment of the Bengal Secondary Education Bill as it emerged out of the last session.

Mr Jinnah advised students to concentrate on education, economic and other aspects of national life and do constructive work during the holidays. They must not take an active part in politics.

At Mr Jinnah's suggestion, the Federation dropped its resolution regarding war effort and constitution-making and substituted the same by another resolution worded on the same lines as the one concerning Pakistan passed by the Muslim League. It also omitted from the resolution regarding the release of political prisoners all references to Deoli and Khaksar prisoners and also Siddiq Ali Khan.

40. Annual Session of All-India Students' Federation, Patna, 31 December 1941–1 January 1942

(i) Over 600 Delegates Arrive from Different Parts of India

Amrita Bazar Patrika, 1 January 1942.

War and Indian Students
Change in Federation's Programme Envisaged
Unprecedented Enthusiasm at Patna: Processions of Delegates Enliven City's Thoroughfares

Tuesday, 30 December.

Over six hundred students delegates from different parts of India have arrived in course of these three days to participate in the seventh annual session of the All-India Students' Conference which commenced here virtually since yesterday. Never before in the annals of Bihar students there has been such a great enthusiasm as is being noticed in this connexion. After a month's strenuous work, the Reception Committee has now justified that in hospitality and giving a new turn in students' politics, Bihar stands second to none.

Of all the provinces, Bengal has sent out the largest contingent of delegates including a large number of girl students. Bengal claims to have been thoroughly represented by her districts.

'Students unite' is the watchword, which is to guide the deliberations of the Patna session. Despite the attempts of student disrupters to bring in frustration in the present session, it seems that all such mischievous designs of the 'breakers' have been of no avail.

A series of processions of student delegates marched through important roads. For these days, Patna junction railway station wore a festive spectacle, when a number of members of the Reception Committee were found receiving the in-coming contingent of the delegates. Big banners and flags, carrying the insignia of the All-India Students' Federation are now decorating the house tops and buildings in which are housed the student delegates.

Mr K.M. Ahmed, Acting General Secretary, Mr M. Farooqui, Mr B.N. Mukerji of Nagpur, Miss Perin Bharucha, Miss Sarala Gupta, Mr G.M. Sadique of Kashmere, Mr Sadhan Gupta, Prof. Karwani of Sind, Mr Husain Zaheer, Mr Mahmud Ali are some of the student leaders, who have arrived here already.

The executive of the Federation met last night and this morning. The All-India Students' Council also met this morning.

From the trend of talks with some of the responsible student leaders, it is understood, the question of war will loom large at the session and the main controversy happens to centre round this important question.

It may be mentioned here that the All-India Students' Federation so long preferred to keep itself aloof from matters relating to war. Rather it ceaselessly carried a campaign and a very bitter one against any aid to war. But Soviets entry in the war has, it is gathered, brought a considerable change in their angle of vision. The Bihar Provincial Students' Conference, which met here about a couple of months back, made it sufficiently clear that India's student population ought to be totally indifferent to war efforts and the civil resistance ought to be made more wide and useful.

But Soviet's challenge to Fascism had encouraged the Indian students and they now think that until India regarded this war as the People's war, cause of students here would suffer. Along with activating war efforts, Students Federation will carry on struggle against inroads of Imperialism and Fascism and take up the cause of the exploited masses.

The bulk of the delegates here, it is reported, are in favour of bringing in this change and take a decision which would help students of the country to intensify war efforts. This opinion, however, makes it clear that this support to war does not commit the students to work for Imperialism which they feel will get liquidated in the process of war. This great change in one of the fundamentals of the Federation's programme is a result of Soviet's entry into war.

The section which means to oppose this proposed change in the programme is of the opinion that any participation in the war would be helping Imperialism. It thinks that Soviet's entry into war is no reason to change their attitude.

A peep in the different camps of student delegates gave one to realize that this historic change in students politics, is being discussed threadbare. It cannot be ascertained whether any official resolution to the effect that students ought to co-operate with the war would be adopted at the session. There is a likelihood of Federation's taking up this move unofficially and do necessary spade work amongst the students. As there is a sharp difference of opinion amongst the students, and as no further and fresh cleavage between the students are desirable, it is felt that no formal resolution be moved in the open session.

A resolution which seeks to bring unity amongst student would be officially moved and there is prospect of this being adopted. The executive of the Federation, it is learnt, does not accept the suggestion that other rival student organizations should be recognized. But when a common action was necessary, the Federation will ask its units to co-operate and keep up the prestige and dignity of the students unimpaired. The Federation believing it as a non-political organization thinks that any co-operation with political parties or student organizations, guided by political parties, would be suicidal to students and all attempts to check such a move would be made.

Another resolution asking different provincial organizations to take up full responsibility to conduct 'Student' an organ of student movement would be adopted.

Yet another resolution condemning the Government for wide repression of student politics and curbing students' prestige would also be officially placed at the session for adoption.

The following delegates with others are participating at the Patna session of the Students' Federation:

Punjab: R.S. Johri, S.P. Dang, Inder Kumar, Mahinder Sen, Santosh Singh, Sardul Singh, Kharait Lal, Miss G. Roy, Khursaid Minto, Partap Khapur, Daldar Raj, Girdhan Lal, Mohan Singh, Amara Singh, Manzar Lal, Dharam Pal, Miss Perin Bharucha, Miss Usha Khoble.

CP: A.B. Bardhan, S.C. Purehait, R.K. Kala, W.N. Despande, V.F. Sharma, D.M. Acharya, M. Manjari, S.K. Sahu, J.M. Chouban, V.N. Alekar, A. Singh, J.H. Kothari, T.C. Jain, Dapurkar, B.N. Mukerji, H.P. Gaur, L.N. Vash, K. Mukerji, N. Rajdarkar, M. Athmaley, Paradkar Khare, Kanetkar, Padke, Mangle, Ramawar, M.W. Kotakh, P.K. Thakur, S.D. Mukerji, S. Lazaraz, B.C. Khabra, S.K. Mukerji, D.L. Choube, G.C. Agarwal.

Delhi: D. Sanghi, M. Farooqui, Y.D. Sharma, K.N. Ahmed, M. Ishaque, Madan Mohan, Miss Sarala Gupta, Miss Sita Gupta, J. Sharma, Indar Singh and Mihir Roy.

Sind: S.G. Karwani, Moti Matwani, Santosh Darwani and eleven others.

Bengal: Prabhat Das Gupta, Kumaresh Chandra, Shanti Mukerji, Arun Bhattacharya, Shankar Roy Choudhury, Ananda Roy, Barin Roy, Debkumar Roy, Sadhan Gupta Sachin Sen, Sunil Sen, Robin Mitter, Mihir Bose, Santosh Bhattacharya, Subodh Roy, Sudhir Bhattacharya, Subrahanshu Mittra, Durga Roy, Sunil Bose, Tridib Ghose, Debkumar Bhattacharya, Miss Kalyani Mukerji, Ram Ranjan Moulik, Braja Dhar, Sajal Roy Choudhury, Ajit Bhattacharya, Sunil Moitra, Ashit Mukerji, Nirmal Chakravarti, Nirmal Gupta, Ajit Ghose, Ajit Neogi, Pravakar Sen, Gopal Sikrail, Biren Mitter, Prabhat Goswami and others.

Names of all the delegates could not be available but the following province have sent out their district delegates.

Bengal, Assam, Bihar, Orissa, Madras, Bombay, Hyderabad, Sind, Punjab, Kashmere, UP, CP, Delhi, Indore, Marwar, Malabar, Cochin, Kalikat, Mysore and some native states.

(ii) Mian Iftikhar-ud-Din's Presidential Address at All-India Students' Conference, 31 December 1941

Amrita Bazar Patrika, 2 January 1942.

India and the War
Peoples Debarred from Taking Part
Problem No More a National One
Punjab Congress Leader's Address to Indian Students

(From Our Patna Office)

Wednesday, 31 December.

'OUR greatest difficulty to-day is that we are not allowed by British Imperialism to play our historic role in the most critical juncture of human history—to fight for the freedom of liberation of the oppressed and enslaved peoples of the world. The national situation alone should not be the concern of Indian population. Our demand is not national independence but it is that Britain should fight fascism even at the cost of her empire, let her liberate the forces of people in the enslaved countries which are straining their leashes,'—thus observed Mian Iftikhar-ud-Din, President Punjab Provincial Congress Committee in his presidential address at the open session of the All India Students' Conference held here this evening.

Mian Iftikhar-ud-Din said in course of his speech:

Comrades, I suffer no misapprehension with regard to the reasons which led you to choose me as your president for this year. I know that in the first place I have to thank British Imperialism which by detention of important comrades have limited your choice to select me for this honour. But although I regarded this as a great honour I must confess that I was very hesitant to come to your conference even at the very last moment and the reason for my hesitancy was simply this that I was aware of the fact that it was impossible for me at this critical time to give you a correct lead, the proper lead, so far as the political situation of this country and the international political situation is concerned. But you were very kind to make it clear that what

I talk or what I say will not matter and will not affect you in any way (laughter). That assurance gave me the courage to come.

Hope for Students Unity

I come entirely unprepared before you. Till the last moment I could not make up my mind what to say to you. Let me tell you one word before I proceed further. Please take whatever I say as a loud thinking on my part. With this definite understanding between you and me I am going to do a bit of loud thinking. Before I proceed further I must tell you that the fact that I came to know that another students' conference was being held at Patna about the same time did not deter me in the slightest to discharge my obligations towards you. I hope that by coming here I may succeed in bringing about a complete unity. The first essential condition of any useful education, needless to say, was the growth of political consciousness among the students. No education could be possible without politics.

Present Situation

Regarding the present situation the president stated that the observation made by the African delegate, Dr Kalibella, to the world conference of students at New York in 1938 still rang in his ears. Dr Kalibella remarked that humanity in these days had nothing to fear from the savage population of Africa but from the savages who were at work in the laboratories of European countries inventing tools for speedy destruction of humanity. Mian Iftikhar-ud-Din said that Dr Kalibella spoke these words even before the commencement of the present war and his words have come to be true.

Internationalism First Concern

The President observed that in these days when the whole humanity was afflicted, it was not proper to think in terms of nationalism alone. The national situation alone should not be the concern of the Indian population. They must direct their attention to the international drama that was being staged in the continents of Asia and Europe. The centre of gravity had shifted from nationalism to internationalism. It should be internationalism which must be the concern of the day. Internationalism demanded that the resources of this country should be utilized for saving the world democracies from being destroyed by brute force. Why should not we then enter into the present drama in which 400 millions of people were in trouble? he queried.

Designs of British

The British, continued the president, had entered the war not with the aim of saving democracies of the world but with the purpose of maintaining the integrity of their empire. They had no sympathy either with socialism or any other 'isms' save and except imperialism. Before the declaration of the present war Britain did every thing in its power to divert the forces of Hitler to the country of freedom, namely, Russia of which it was a great friend to-day. So it was clear that Britain did not enter the war for the sake of the safety of democracy. Its primary consideration had always been to defend its imperialism.

Real Difficulty

It was very difficult for Britain, observed the president, to enthuse the Indian people to enter into war because they felt that its definite consideration was to defend feudal and imperial structures under which they were groaning even at the moment of present crisis. The British had made it very difficult for India to be enthused in the matter of 'all aids to war.' The difficulty was that Britain would not allow India or even capitalist India to help in this war.

Prerequisites for People's War

'We want to-day to mobilize ourselves, to have the control of our armies, to have the control of our foreign affairs, to have the power to continue the war against fascism, even after Britain has stopped its war against fascism. It is impossible to fully mobilize our resources to give peoples aid in this war inspite of the present attitude of British imperialism.

Exploitation to End

'Britain's attitude has put us in a most difficult position. Because we do not know of its actual intentions. Instead of making any positive use of the resources entrusted to them by the people of India, the British may use it at a later stage for some purpose entirely opposed to our interests and intentions. For I say this struggle will continue till fascism is destroyed, nay even imperialism is liquidated. Whatever the set backs the peoples' struggle might receive at different stages, the end of this mighty conflagration will leave only ashes of imperialism.

What Congress Stands for

'We should make it clear to the people of the world that our struggle is not national. There is of course the good old question of disunity in India and that is the answer that the imperialists put forth before the world. For a democrat person or for a democratic Government the Congress has given its final answer and the Congress answer is that we are prepared to admit the existence of various communities in this country, that we are prepared to have separate electorates for those communities who insist on it and who would send their representatives to a Constituent Assembly where they may sit together and decide the question of India's present and future. And if there is disagreement between the majority community and between the majority of the minority community on those questions, the Congress does not want the vote of the majority community to prevail and is prepared to refer to any tribunal, national or international, to decide. This is the most democratic offer that can be made.

'For the matter of that Mahatma Gandhi has committed himself that if the Muslims do insist on Pakistan they might as well have that too. So the plea of communal disunity does not arise as Congress has given a final and convincing answer to that.

India's Demand

'Our demand is not for national independence but it is that Britain should fight fascism even at the cost of her Empire. Let her liberate the forces of the people in the enslaved countries which are straining their leashes. We have found that Britain has been only half-hearted in this struggle. Even in England the voice of the people has not been sufficiently powerful to dissuade Churchill and his gang to continue to exploit the peoples of the Empire and concede their just demands. The same is the case with the capitalists in India who are but too eager to join in the war efforts for it will mean profits to them, but they are never prepared to make any sacrifices for it.

All Help to Soviet

'So in this complicated situation it is very difficult nay impossible to give a correct lead. But there is a common point for the people of the world, a complete unanimity in their resolve and which is to render all help to the Soviet Union, which is the greatest bulwark against the onslaught of fascist forces.

'If you want to make an investment of your moral and material support in perfect security, here is a gilt-edged security, even when British Imperialism has been liquidated, when Hitlerism has fallen, even then you will draw increasing dividends of human happiness in a world republic of socialism if you support Russia, if you support the Soviet in its life and death struggle'.

The first sitting adjourned till tomorrow afternoon.

Dr Zahir's Inaugural Address

Dr Hussain Zahir in his inaugural speech traced the revival of the students' movement in India from 1935, when people all over the world became increasingly aware of the menace of Fascism and Nazism. He deplored the factious tendency displayed by a section of students after the Nagpur session and recommended to the students the line advocated by Pandit Jawaharlal Nehru in his statement on the subject.

He thought participation by students in politics was not wrong and said that politics of the right type and healthy education are not contradictory but complementary. He, however, advised students to avoid being exploited by unscrupulous persons and parties. The students should not allow any interference with their right to study and education. Dr Zahir thought that the question whether students should resort to strikes if their right to study and to have knowledge was interfered with by educational bureaucrats was a thorny one. While strikes should not be used, any interruption of study would also be not advisable.

Student's Roles

He considered that students should concentrate on two roles that they have to play in the present-day world. Firstly, they had to aid in the spread of culture and knowledge. They should in this connection organize literary centres and other cultural activities to raise the intellectual level of the people.

Secondly, students should bring about a solution of the problem of communalism.

War and Education

The war was casting its deep shadows on the sphere of education, said Dr Zahir. He cited particularly the example of Bengal and the developments in that province following the declaration of that area as an emergency area.

During the last six months the nature and character of the war has been changed, declared Dr Zahir. He considered that the world was threatened by a brutal, vile and racial form of world domination. Nazism and Fascism were against all progressive ideals. Though he did not concede that the small ruling class in Britain had shed its imperialism still it could not be denied that Britain was now in the camp of progress.

Russia and China were not fighting for themselves only, but for Indians also. Their aim to Indian freedom was not indirect, but very direct. If Hitler overruns Russia and Japan defeats China nothing can prevent Germany and Japan from dominating the two continents of Europe and Asia. The national interests of India are identical with the interests of the peoples of the world. The defeat of Nazism and Fascism is a pre-condition to world progress.

India's War Efforts

Discussing how were Indians to throw in their weight in the present war, Dr Zahir said that the main stumbling block in the way of Indians fully helping the world democratic forces is the attitude of the Government of India. The latter were guilty of criminal delusion when they stated that India's people to-day were [with?] the Axis combination and not the British Government and therefore Indian opposition in the present war in any shape and form was invalid. It would be weakening the Soviet, the Chinese, the British and the Americans. 'We do not want the Indian war effort, however inadequate, to be hampered', declared Dr Zahir.

Only the people can win this war, a total war. The reactionary rulers and the fossilized generals must give way to people's representatives both in the civil and military spheres of defence. Only through winning this war and changing it into a people's war can the people come to their own. Only then would have the initiative passed into the people's hands.

Reception to President Elect

Magnificent reception was accorded to Mian Iftikhar-ud-Din, President, Punjab Provincial Congress Committee on his arrival from Lahore this morning by Reception Committee of the All-India Students' Conference early this morning.

The Presidential procession unique of its kind started from Patna Law College grounds and terminated at noon time. Mian Iftikhar-ud-Din and Dr Husain Zahir were seated in an open car and many girl delegates participated in the procession which swelled into thousands.

Every Provincial Students' Federation marched with its own Jatha and Federation flag. Bengal had the largest delegates who were found singing loud national anthem with Bihar delegates.

Mr Sadhan Gupta, President, Bengal Students' Federation was found escorted by his colleagues and leading Bengal contingent.

Mr Sadhan Gupta told the 'Patrika' representative that Bengal was overwhelmed with Bihar's hospitality and he felt that Patna stand of students would revolutionize India's politics. Students had to give their verdict on this war and all aid to Soviet and need of democratization of war efforts would help India to safeguard her frontiers against Fascist and Imperialist aggression.

Mr M. Faruqui and Mr K.M. Ahmed, General Secretaries of All-India Students' Federation told the 'Patrika' representative that the Patna session was going to marshal all youths and students to checkmate the Fascist greed for more power.

Different Provincial Federations of Students were shouting national anthems in their own vernaculars.

War and Students' Duty

Mian Iftikhar-ud-Din interviewed by 'Patrika' representative said 'Patna's enthusiasm and preparedness of representatives of Indian students speak of their progress and activity. I hope students at this hour of India's peril would fall in line all united and save India from internal and external Fascist and Imperialist menace. In India's fight for freedom students being vanguards needed more vigil and I think their national outlook of life would save India's honour and dignity.'

American students through cable to reception [committee] congratulates Indian students on their fight against Nazi menace and hope Indian students would achieve her freedom for which America stand pledged to-day.

At a specially decorated pandal Dr Hussain Zahir inaugurates conference and Mian Iftikhar-ud-Din Presides.

(iii) All-India Students' Conference Adopts Draft Statement of Policy on the Anti-Fascist Peoples' War, 1 January 1942

Amrita Bazar Patrika, 3 January 1942.

'Fascism must be Annihilated'
Indian Students' Resolve
Need for Change of Policy on
Soviet's Entry into War
Support to War-effort
Proceedings of Second Day's Conference: Federation's
Draft Statement of Policy

Thursday, 1 January.

Greater enthusiasm was in evidence among the delegates when they met for the second day amidst wild cries of Soviet and national slogans. Mian Iftikharuddin has left for the Punjab in view of his pressing engagements there. Mr Mohammad Sadique, President of the National Conference of Kashmere presided over the sitting.

The best of the features of the Conference was the great discipline which was maintained all through by the delegates drawn from different parts of the country. The student volunteers and delegates co-operated and throughout four hours' deliberations, harmony and peace prevailed.

Miss P. Barucha's Address

While moving the draft statement of policy of the All-India Students' Federation on the anti-Fascist Peoples' Front, Miss Perin Barucha (Punjab), member of the executive of the AISF explained at the outset the background in which the Imperialist war of 1939 broke out. She said that the world reaction was conspiring to build an anti-Soviet Front with the intention of destroying the base of world freedom. Fascism and Imperialism were hand and glove to encircle the USSR to smash the forces fighting for Freedom, Peace and Progress. This was a horrible spectacle for all of us in India and for all those who want human brotherhood. When Germany went in for a non-aggression pact with the USSR that was the beginning of rift in the camp of world reaction. But still British Imperialism was supported in India. The attitude of the AISF was that of uncompromising hostility to Imperialism.

Miss Barucha continuing said that it was then that Russia came into the war when the Fascist gangsters attacked the land of Socialism. The force of circumstances and the contradictions of Imperialistic capitalism drove British Imperialism into the camp of freedom, rather than into the camp of reaction. This was not in our seeking. If one of our enemies has been isolated from the camp to which he belonged that it was a thing which we should heartily welcome. This was the beginning of the people's way. The entry of America into the camp further added to our strength.

Miss Perin further said: 'It is in this context that we should look at things. We have not all of a sudden become friends of British Imperialism. We have not stopped our fight against Imperialism. The only thing is that the form of our struggle has changed and is now being fought on a higher plane. The cause of India's freedom has been taken up by the international front of Freedom, Peace and Progress'.

'Our job to-day', she said, 'is to annihilate Fascism that is those who are aligned against the front in which we ourselves have been placed by force of world circumstances. When the victory of our camp over our rival camp is completed, then we will go on with another struggle to annihilate Imperialism, which would have become weakened. Then our task will be easier. India's freedom is now nearer than it would have been otherwise'.

Concluding she said for all this change in the alignment of forces we should be grateful to the heroes of the Soviet Union, who had been fighting our war, the war of the peoples of the world. She appealed to the student delegates to stand by the international brotherhood.

Decay of Imperialism

Mr Sadhan Gupta, President of the Bengal Provincial Students' Federation while supporting the motion traced out the history of difference between Mr M.N. Roy and the Federation on war issue. He characterized Mr Roy as one who was not anti-Imperialistic as he did not believe that Imperialism was still going strong both in Britain and India. Mr Gupta held Mr Roy as undemocratic for his not tolerating other views with calmness and for his branding all forces barring his own as Fascist.

Mr Gupta further declared that cooperation with war efforts did not lead the students to adopt such a method but the entire plan was initiated because of the exigencies. He believed in the gradual decay of imperialism, now in death trap with Fascism. This new stand, moreover, would create a psychology among the masses and give them the real perspective to follow the correct lead to usher in a new era in India's political, social and economic history.

Mr R.N. Mehta (Lucknow) moving an amendment said that the statement being drastic ought to be referred to the provincial and district student units for consideration and pleaded for a special session to pass its judgment over this important issue. He said that there being no change in the war, it was not judicious to throw weight of Indian population to the war, which was entirely an Imperialist war.

Mr Rajendra Mishra (Patna) also lent his support to the amendment and said that as tone and tenor of the war remained unchanged up till now, it would be a gross mistake to support war efforts.

Mr Yagyadutt Sharma (Aligarh) supporting the motion said that no special session of the Federation was necessary and considerable time was allowed for consideration of the important issue. The policy which was placed before the House was, however, not going to be mandatory and students, who believed that it was not in the fitness of things, they could hold it up for themselves. But time had come when reality of the situation was properly appreciated. He acknowledged that without it being drastic, the stand to support war efforts and that unconditionally was a delayed decision. It ought to have been given in effect to much earlier in view of the war that had already crept in our land. Though students hereby gave unconditional support to the war efforts, they were requested to carry on the struggle to give more bread to workers and peasants and make them better thinkers and real builders of India's destiny. If even now students deferred back this issue which was a life and death struggle—it would be but stabbing back the Soviet.

Folly of Non-cooperation

Mr Sharma held that as students could no longer maintain an attitude of neutrality or non-co-operation, both of which would lead India to eternal disaster, it was the only course left for them was to activize and democratize war efforts, save the land and follow the victory of the Sovietland. This would alone give India the solution of immature deaths and diseases, starvation and nakedness, illiteracy and misfortunes. In the process of war, Imperialism would get liquidated and a new doctrine—a message of hope to live freely would be born. People's army would then be raised in India and Indian youths would line up against the Nazi or Japanese hordes now threatening Indian frontiers.

Mr Sharma said that mere idle speculation over the question of possible liquidation of Fascism and Imperialism would not help people of India. India's role of neutrality or non-co-operation would be a colossal betrayal to Soviet. He wanted students to understand the issue at hand with the fire and passion of youth. AISF did not believe in vilifying tactics or on force or compulsion. So long, he said, the Federation was on a wrong track and though it was a delayed decision, there was nothing to be sorry for. Federation being that of young people, it had to wait and watch and then decide and he hoped that now wisdom would dawn upon the student population to defend her country against foreign invasion and establish a Socialistic order in the land.

Mr Mohammad Sadique (Kashmere) who presided over the Conference then put the amendment to vote, when it was rejected by overwhelming majority.

The motion that the statement of policy to war be adopted was put to vote and was carried with nine delegates opposing it.

The President while declaring the motion adopted, amidst revolutionary slogans, congratulated for this logical and correct stand adopted by the representatives of the Indian students.

The Conference then adjourned till evening.

Statement of Policy

The following is the full text of the draft statement of the policy of the All-India Students' Federation on the anti-Fascist Peoples War, which was adopted at the open session of the AI Students' Conference held this afternoon:

From Hitler's treacherous attack on the USSR to Japan's unprovoked aggression in the Pacific, leading to America's entry into the world struggle, a series of events have taken place completely transforming the character of the war. The AISF must take note of this change and reformulate its policy towards the war. This policy must correspond to the historic duty of Indian students towards the progressive forces of the world headed by the USSR and towards our own national struggle for freedom.

A Peoples' War Against Fascism

Already with Hitler's attack upon Sovietland with Britain and America merging their war against Fascism with the war of the Soviet Union against the common enemy a fundamental change had taken place. The War has no longer the significance of an Imperialist War. It was now a just war, a peoples' war waged in defence of the Land of Socialism for the purpose of crushing Hitler–Fascism. It was now a war waged against the chief, the vilest, the most deadly foe of every nation in the world taken singly and together. It was a war waged for India's freedom by the most powerful allies, the strongest in numbers, that India ever had. This war was the greatest, the most effective struggle waged for India's freedom in her long history.

The aims and intentions of the British and American Governments did not matter one jot. What did matter, what was decisive was the big fact that these Governments had lined up with the USSR to conduct the joint war against the aggressor, the enemy of the USSR. The chief enemy had been singled out and was being crushed in isolation.

What did matter was the fact, the solemn fact that these Governments had given up the reactionary narrow class policy of hostilities to the USSR. They had stopped provoking war against the Land of Socialism, the Land of the Youth—the policy they had been pursuing for 23 years, the policy which in the last five years had brought disaster heaped upon disaster to the cause of progressive mankind. They had not only stopped provoking this war, they had lined up on the side of the USSR when at last that war did break out. What did matter now was the crucial fact that the camp of world imperialism was spilt and had taken sharply opposing sides in relation to the USSR. What mattered most was that this split was not a temporary diplomatic rupture but a deep a sharp split in war with the exchange of shot and shell and not words, with millions bitterly conscious of the issues.

In short, what mattered now to the workers and peoples of Britain and America who have no imperialist aims, who hate such aims, and for the Soviet peoples, the standard-bearers of the Socialist Revolution, was a single aim, a single purpose. This was that the joint war against Hitler–Fascism had to be won decisively counteracting all vacillation and sabotage by the allied imperialist Governments, ensuring a real victory for all the peoples with the final destruction of Fascism. That is why it was no longer an imperialist war but a peoples' war whose conduct the workers and peoples had to take in their own hands in alliance with the free peoples of the USSR. They had to fight this great common war for the victory of every nation.

Hitler–Fascism the Main Enemy

Hitler–Fascism had become the main enemy of all progressive mankind. With the 'Death to the Hitlerites' was ranged a formidable front of the progressive peoples headed by the millions of heroes of the USSR.

Was the brute forces of Fascism to batter down the fortress of Socialism, the base of the world revolution, the armed might of the emancipated workers which had consistently given unflinching support to the struggles of the oppressed peoples against Imperialism? But the issue of the war was not Fascism pitted against Socialism. The issue honestly and clearly put was much wider than that. Who was to win: the camp of black capitalist reaction headed by a contemptible gang of Fascist criminals or the far-flung camp of progress and liberation headed by the heroic Soviet people? That is how the issue in the war has to be viewed.

We announce our conviction with confidence, with pride, with joy. Let our call ring out! We never had a stronger, a prouder call to give. All honest decent folk today have to be partisans in this war: partisans in the camp of freedom and progress, partisans with the Soviet and Chinese people, partisans with the progressive workers and peoples of Britain and America. The attitude of us the students of India to this war is decided.

Two Camps: Reaction and Progress

With further developments taking place in the last few weeks, the war now becomes a war of the world front of the peoples against Fascism, against the aggression of the three Fascist States, Germany, Italy and Japan.

The aim on the side of the Fascists is world domination, the consolidation of black capitalist reaction on a world-wide scale, the annihilation of the noblest achievement of man—the Socialist civilization of the USSR, the destruction of the working-class and peasant movements all over the world, the destruction of our world youth movement and our use as cannon-fodder. It means the destruction of culture, progressive literature and the peoples' lore. It means the brutalization of man, it means the perpetuation of the enslavement of the colonial and backward peoples of the world by unbridled, proclaimed imperialism.

This aim is perfectly made clear to all by the Fascist butchers. It is visible in its ghastly agony in the unspeakably barbarous atrocities perpetrated by the Fascist hordes in Sovietland and in the occupied countries of Europe, in the regime of lawless brutality that has been established in the conquered countries.

The common purpose of the peoples of the USSR, of China and of the advanced sections of the peoples of Britain and America is not only defeat of the Fascist Powers but the annihilation of Fascism. The common aim is the liberation of the peoples enslaved by the Fascist brutes, is the defence and liberation of peoples living under the threat of Fascist enslavement. It is a final, peoples' victory and a peoples' peace, in which the destiny of each nation will be in its own hands, to gain democratic liberties and independence.

The Indian student movement demands that the Indian people and their great national organizations should now have a positive attitude towards this war. They must develop a popular initiative and activity in order to make sure that in its greatness and strength, unitedly, the Indian people play its rightful part in this world struggle for India's and the world's freedom.

The Peoples' Role in the Anti-Fascist Front

But let us recognize clearly that the imperialist Governments in the anti-Fascist front do not fully accept the peoples' aims in this peoples' war. They continue, still, to pursue their class aims sacrificing often the interests of the workers and the cause of winning the war to those of the capitalist profiteers. They continue the enslavement of India making the free, voluntary, and so the effective total participation of her people in the war impossible.

It is precisely this instability of the ally in the world front against Fascism that demands of the workers and the peoples of every country in this front the maximum of initiative, activity and vigilance—to see that the war is prosecuted vigorously and consistently with their aims and interests till victory is won. This shall have to be done in the most responsible fashion, never in a mood of carping criticism which can help the Fascists alone; never in a petty spirit of bargaining which helps the Japanese and the Germans and never the peoples. For, the urgent task before the advanced sections of the peoples everywhere is to forge the national unity of the peoples. With this, with earnest, sincere, fearless effort, to gain the peoples' initiative and leadership in the conduct of the war. Through hard work and bravery to stop the sabotage by the reactionary elements in the country, sometimes close to the Governments.

To transform the anti-Fascist front in every country in the world as a whole, already in existence, into a full peoples anti-Fascist front: such is the urgent task of the day.

War for World Liberation

The war for world liberation is already taking place today. A mighty peoples' upsurge is coming to fullness everywhere, with the impact of the unprecedented heroism, organization and staunch resistance the Soviet people are displaying. Into the occupied countries, the people are conducting a veritable peoples' war through large-scale, merciless sabotage and guerrilla actions.

In Britain and America, under the stress of war, the growing unity of the workers, the youth and the progressive sections of the people is becoming a powerful factor. It strives to force the Government to render full aid to the Soviet Union, to end the autocratic and repressive regime in India, to intensify the war while protecting the interests of the workers and the peoples.

A peoples' war demands that the peoples themselves unitedly act to strengthen the anti-Fascist front and to make it into a peoples' anti-Fascist front not only in every country but on a world scale: one war one front. This is being done by the peoples everywhere. That is why the British people demand of their Government to-day as an essential part of their resolute war against Hitler–Fascism and for victory the liberation of India.

This peoples' war against Fascism is not merely a war for the liberation of the peoples enslaved by Fascism. Under the stress of the peoples' untiring actions, under the influence of the Soviet Union, it is becoming a war of world liberation.

The Indian Peoples' Duty

Let us emphasize once and for all that it is precisely this aspect of this all-peoples' war—the aspect which shows sharply that the world mass struggle for freedom is on, that it has taken the most advanced form of all mass struggles, armed conflict—that demands of us, the Indian people, an urgent, drastic, revision of our policy and practice towards this war.

It is not enough to express sympathy or give our moral support to the war of the anti-Fascist front led by the Soviet Union. It would be wrong to say: 'we cannot do anything till we are free, till we are granted such and such demands'. The titanic struggle for world liberation raging in five continents which is now knocking at our very doors demands of us, the Indian people, that we 'Unite', hold up our heads and declare to the people of the world:

'We know this war is just. We are in it and we are determined to do everything to win it'

The cause of world liberation and Indian freedom demands that we give up our attitude of hostility, of non-co-operation or neutrality to this war. We have to step forth as the best, the most efficient and responsible champions of total war mobilization. By our united might we have to remove the impediments which the imperialist autocracy puts in our way, preventing our peoples' free voluntary and effective participation in our war.

We do not, therefore, suspend our national struggle for independence. It is through war mobilization and not through individual or mass satyagraha against the war that we shall guard the immediate interests of the people, that we shall take resolute strides on the road to independence. This is the most advanced form of struggle for liberation. We were unable to reach this stage through our own effort. The might of the Soviet people, of their Red Army, the stand of the Chinese people, the will of the British and American people who have become more revolutionary today in the mass than ever before—these forces have placed this weapon of peoples' war in our hands. This is what the unity of the world with India demands, this is what our own national interests demand, this is what the immediate need of every Indian demands, that we lift this weapon, that we use it for our liberation.

For Unity in Action

The Indian Students movement is emphatically of the opinion that the Indian National Congress and all other popular organizations in the country must reconsider their attitude towards the war. They must leave no stone upturned in order to chalk put an agreed policy in the immediate interests of the Indian people which will facilitate the participation, strong, whole-hearted and united, in the joint world struggle for freedom.

The supreme need today is national unity in the broadest possible front. This united front must wage a determined fight to win from the unwilling hands of the Government the acceptance of our minimum demands which will not only allow us to make our effective and honourable contribution to the world struggle against Fascism. It will accelerate our march to complete liberation. It will improve the lot of the people here and now. It will make us strong. It will give us a great national self-confidence. It will unite the entire nation as nothing else can.

The continuation of the symbolic individual satyagraha can neither make an effective contribution to humanity's war on Fascism, nor can it take us a single step forward to our liberation. It will please the Fascists and their lurking allies in the anti-Fascist countries. It will please no one else. What slight moral value it had in the epoch of imperialist war, vanishes today when the peoples march for world liberation?

Let it be very clearly understood, however, that neither our duty to humanity nor our duty to the nation is served by merging with the present Government, by sneering at our great national organizations. Mr M.N. Roy may repeat phrases about helping the peoples' war against Fascism, but he demands such help not because British Imperialism hinders the effective mobilization of the peoples in the war, not because peoples' action alone can win this war, but because, he thinks. British Imperialism has unaccountably disappeared from the face of the earth. No wonder, therefore, that Mr Roy, despite his strong abuse and brave words is not working to unite our nation for victory at this solemn hour, but is disrupting every great national organization, is splitting the unity of the people in the sacred name of peoples' war. Instead of patient explanation to a long-suffering people, Mr Roy showers abuse. Instead of making tireless and sincere efforts to build the united front of all our traditional peoples' organizations, he appeals to imperialism to have nothing to do with them. Our purpose is not to use the peoples' war as a stick with which to beat the best national, working-class, kisan and student fighters. Our purpose is to rouse the people to win their own war. Practice, no doubt, will show the correctness of our policy, as well as our differences with the policy of Mr M.N. Roy which are not of our seeking.

We believe that a united front of the National Congress, the Muslim League, of the national organisations of workers and kisan, of students must be built. This front must rouse the people to a complete understanding of the significance of the peoples' war, to support, to mobilize for it, to win it and to win independence through the struggle for victory. We put forward the following charter of minimum demands to be raised in the course of this campaign to secure the effective, free and voluntary participation of the Indian people to win the war:

(1) Recognition of India's right to complete independence.
(2) Release of all anti-Fascist political prisoners and detenus.[1]
(3) Establishment of democratic liberties. The withdrawal of all war-time legislation restricting freedom of speech, press, organization, movement and the right to strike.
(4) Power at the centre to be in the hands of a 'national government' consisting of popular representatives commanding the confidence of the peoples and having full authority over all spheres of Government, administration and conduct of the war.
(5) Removal of all restrictions on the immediate development of industries to supply the demands of the war and the needs of the people who shall do their utmost for the war.

(6) The just demands of the workers improving their conditions of living and of work be met and their right to strike must not be curtailed.
(7) Kisan demands must be met, including price control in their interests and generous and unstinted remission of rent and taxes in flood and famine-stricken areas.
(8) There must not be enforced war levies of any kind, on the poor. The peoples' war must be run in the peoples' way with their voluntary support.
(9) Redistribution of the war burden so that it is borne by the rich and not the poor.

It must be understood that this national Charter is not a threat but a practical programme of action. We do not put forward these demands and say that unless some of them or all of them are granted, we shall withdraw our support to this war. We do not put forward these demands so as to unmask the insane bureaucracy that rules India today, and say 'we have done our best, we can do nothing more. We cannot support the war'.[2] We have no illusions about him! Nor do we rely helplessly upon our comrades across the seas to understand this Government and win our battle for us. We do not wish to cheat history, we wish to make it. We do not say 'Grant these demands and we support your war. It is not their war, it is ours'.[3]

The Indian student movement appeals in all humility, seriousness and determination to the National Congress to call off the individual satyagraha and the boycott of the local boards and legislatures. It calls upon the National Congress and the Muslim League to reach a united front agreement to unite the people to fight jointly for the above demands, to form joint ministries in the Provinces forthwith to support that fight. This will create the conditions to bring about the broadest possible unity for developing mass actions to win the demands set forth in our charter of demands. This is the practical, positive course of action here and now to achieve India's full and effective participation in the war. Such a course will guarantee the quick and final victory of the forces of progress in the world. It will pave the way for India's complete liberation, put an end to demoralization, helplessness, despair.

Slogans for the Student Movement

This the 7th AISF Conference calls upon all members of the AISF, all members of our brother student organizations, all unorganized students not to wait until the Congress, the Muslim League and the Government have taken action. The students must take the initiative. They must popularize vigorously this policy. They must agitate for the adoption of the National Charter among all students and the people.

We appeal to all student comrades. We appeal to every one of our countrymen. We appeal to them to wake up to the colossal defeat which the Red Army and the British and other peoples have made our national oppressor, British Imperialism, suffer. Our brothers have won the greatest victory in history. They have won, they are winning today in the snow and the frost victories for us. Let us not be so blind in our hatred of our national oppressor as to draw back and refuse to fight the peoples' war merely because he is in the iron grip of our war. Let us fight this great fight with the passion and confidence with which we fought the three great national struggles that united us, made us conscious of our nationhood, won for us the admiration, the greetings of the world! Let our slogans ring out:

The war of the Soviet and British peoples is our war as well!
The Indian people have to win this war in their own interest!
Fight for demands of the national charter!
Unite the people to secure those demands!

Explain to the students and to all how this is humanity's war. We are not the enemies of humanity, the Fascist Beasts are.

This is the war for progress, for the freedom of all. Let us make our meaning clear by making known the achievements of the Soviet Union, the unparalleled heroism of the Soviet people in war. Let them know of the glorious fight for freedom of the peoples and the patriots in the prison that is Europe. Let them know of our friends and brothers, the workers and students in Britain and America and China. Let them know the facts of their marvelous initiative in carrying on this war of all the peoples against Fascism.

[The resolution was moved by Perin Bharucha
Seconded by Y.D. Sharma
Supported by Sadhan Gupta and Ali Sardar Jafri]

(iv) All-India Students' Conference Resolution on 'Communal Unity', 1 January 1942

Amrita Bazar Patrika, 3 January 1942.

Communal Unity
Need of the Hour
Indian Students on Nation's Duty

Patna, 1 January.

'The students of India firmly believe that immediate communal unity is the need of the hour and it would be a first step in a united struggle for freedom if the National Congress and the Muslim League were to unite to make a declaration of complete support to this war of people for freedom. They must not allow the insolence of the British Government to provoke them into continued dissensions at a time when the battle for India's freedom is being fought on a world scale'.

These observations are contained in a lengthy resolution on communal unity adopted by the seventh session of the All India Students Conference (Farooqui group) held here at its second day's sitting, Dr Husain Zahir presiding, owing to Mian Iftikharuddin's departure on important business.

The resolution attributes the riots to hirelings and recognizes that the riots thrived only because they found a suitable soil of mass demoralization created by the policies of the major political parties. As a method for removing the atmosphere of suspicion, the resolution demands the following declaration on behalf of students:

'Our national movement must declare that in a free India, statutory guarantees will prevent the oppression of any community or nationality however small, by any other, that its right to develop its language, culture and other things will be secured by law and infringements thereof punished. We want the national movement to guarantee, further the complete equality of all the nationalities comprising India. This must be done by recognizing as part of its demand for national independence; that every nationality which not only has its own language and culture but a compact territory to which it is bound by history and tradition, a community of economic life and psychological make-up will have the right to exist as an autonomous state in the voluntary federation of national democratic republics which free India will have the final right to secede at will from the federation if it so desires'.

Resolutions on students demands, greetings to world students, organizational programme, condemnation or repression on students, particularly at Cawnpore, Gauhati, Nagpur and Bombay, were also adopted.

By one resolution the conference demanded the immediate release of the political prisoners and detenus who were the best anti-Fascist fighters and hence the most fitted to lead the masses at this critical hour of the people's war.

The election of office bearers will be held tomorrow. Either Miss Baroocha or Miss Sarala Gupta is likely to be elected General Secretary.[4]—UP

---

[1] In the version published in *The Student*, February 1941, it reads, 'Release of all political prisoners and detenus'.

[2] The following words included in the text of the resolution published in *The Student* are missing in the *Amrita Bazar Patrika* report: 'Our people know their national oppressor well. They know that he is more insolvent, more of a disruptor today than ever before in our history.'

[3] The following words in the resolution are missing in the report: 'The British reactionaries fight as our prisoners, but cunning prisoners. They are mortally afraid of the peoples' initiative in this war. They do their best to divide us, to be insolent to us. They try to provoke us away from our war, keep us away from our battleground for freedom. Let them be provocative. We know that they are writhing in the iron grip of our war. The more they provoke us, more staunchly shall we support the war. We know them enough not to set them free when they are in our grip! We shall fight this war, we shall campaign for running it the peoples' way. We shall never withdraw our support to it until Fascism is finally killed. With the swift unfolding of events, we shall win each one of our demands and pass on to greater, bigger ones.'

[4] Perin Baroocha succeeded M. Farooqui as General Secretary of AISF.

B. Women

41. Only Women to Offer Satyagraha, No Males to Court Arrest that Day

The Tribune, 2 January 1941.

Bombay, 1 January.

The United Press understands that 26 January had been reserved by the Bombay Provincial Congress Committee for Satyagraha exclusively by women. On that day no males will be allowed to offer Satyagraha.

Although no instructions have been received from Wardha about the observance of 'Sabbath' day by the satyagrahis, the BPCC has decided not to allow anybody to offer satyagraha on Sundays henceforth.

42. Social Service Conference and Women

The Hindu, 3 January 1941.

Madras, 2 January.

The Social Service Conference organized under the auspices of the Madras Social Service Federation held its concluding session last evening at the P. Vijiaraghavalu Chetti Hall, Chintadripet, and adopted resolutions touching social problems in the city. Mrs V.T. Lakshmi Ammal presided.

... Mrs Lakshmi Ammal said that no social reform could be brought about in a day. But we could not be quiet in the meantime when there was so much of want, poverty, crime, injustice, ignorance and ill-health all around...

In her opinion, the President continued, education was the *sine qua non* of women's emancipation. In view of the peculiar conditions of our society, it was desirable that the economic independence of women was brought about before long, without impairing their place in the home. The purdah system, the dowry custom, child marriage, polygamy and the institution of Devadasis were despicable clogs on the wheel of social progress. It was high time to organize a united protest against the gross injustices underlying some of these social customs and habits. Every woman, she urged, should be judged by the same standard of morality as man. Our community, as it was, meted out entirely unequal and unjust treatment to women moral offenders for a mutual wrong. As a vigilance worker, she would appeal to them to take a more lenient and humane attitude towards those unfortunate girls and women who were mostly beguiled and betrayed into error. They should help them to be reclaimed, reformed and replaced in society.

43. British and Indian Women Meet: India's Demand, 'We Will Not Rest Till We Win Freedom'

The Tribune, 11 January 1941.

London, 9 January.

'India is the acid test of our claim that we are fighting for democracy. Britain, therefore, is morally bound to admit India's claim of freedom', declared Vera Brittain of the Peace Pledge Union at a meeting of British and Indian women in Conway Hall, London, this afternoon, supporting India's demand for self-determination and requesting the release of political prisoners.

Miss Batlivala, who is a practicing Barrister in London, declared that India was determined to fight for her freedom and would not rest till she won it.—Reuter

44. 'Freedom: Flowering of Human Spirit' Punjab Women Students' Conference at Lahore

The Tribune, 19 January 1941.

Lahore, 18 January.

In spite of the inclement weather and a chilly day, the Punjab women students with their usual enthusiasm held their conference this afternoon in the Lajpat Rai Hall.

A very large number of women students of local and mofussil colleges were present.

After 'Inquilab Zindabad' had been sung, Mrs Freda Bedi unfurled the Students' Flag. The flag, she said, represented Freedom, Peace and Progress. Without freedom, she explained, there could be no flowering of human spirit, no enjoyment, no satisfaction. By freedom they meant that there should be no restriction from without on their individual and national aspirations. It must be accompanied by peace which was necessary for war-stricken people and, more so, for women who stood to suffer. Women were the creators and preservers of peace. Progress was our objective so that there was freedom not for one class of persons or the other, but for the lowliest of the low.

Mrs Rameshwari Nehru who rose amidst loud cheers, while inaugurating the conference, said: 'I am a student, like you, engaged in studying the book of life in the university of the universe. I want to tell you, therefore, that your education does not end with your getting your degree. The real education begins afterwards and I want you to prepare yourselves for that, right from now onwards.'

Mrs Nehru regarded the young girls as nation's wealth. But she wanted them to be a 'useful' wealth.

She referred to the increasing feeling against the present education, especially education of the girls. The reason for that was their system of education which had a wrong basis and taught them a few things, but had created a gulf between those who claimed to be educated and the rest. A feeling had arisen that the educated were far above the ordinary human beings and they had nothing to do with those who really constituted the India of to-day. That was unfortunate. The result of that further division had been that society had taken quite another form, and the exploitation which was robbing the poor had increased.

Mrs Nehru regretted that selfishness had been on the increase in their country. Local Self Government had come to be a complete failure in India because people who were entrusted with the work generally did not discharge their responsibilities properly. Continuing, Mrs Nehru referred to the rights of women. She, however, maintained that they could not have their rights unless they proved that they deserved them. She wished to remind them that no one could have his or her rights unless he or she was prepared to discharge the responsibilities which always went with the rights.

Mrs Nehru pointed out how women in India were getting more and more rights without much struggle. Some of them had been in the Provincial Ministries. She advised the students to struggle for their rights but not for any personal gains or offices.

Referring to the motto inscribed on their flag, Mrs Nehru asked the girl students to remember that, while they wished to enjoy freedom, they must know that in freedom there were certain restrictions which they must always welcome. They must refuse to live sectarian lives.

Mrs Nehru was glad to find the girls shouting 'Inquilab Zindabad'. But she was not sure if they all understood the true significance of that slogan. She appealed to the girls not to raise false slogans.

They should not, she held, merely think of getting their degrees but of doing something real for their country. That was the way to bring about 'Inquilab.' If they did that, they would prove themselves to be the real wealth of India (cheers).

Miss G. Rai, Chairman of the Reception Committee, in her address of welcome referred to the growing strength of the women students movement in the Punjab.

Referring to the present situation Miss Rai criticized the leadership in India for having kept back the progressive forces. She regretted that their leaders had done their utmost, but in vain, to come to a compromise with British imperialism.

The students, she held, had already associated themselves with the freedom movement with the result that 360 students in Bengal were behind prison bars; and in their own province Rajbans, Mazhar and Chopra were detained in jails.

A group of students of the R.B. Sohanlal College then sang a song.

Begum Mian Iftikhar-ud-Din, who occupied the presidential chair amidst loud cheers, expressed her delight over the fact that women students in the Punjab were carrying on the national struggle, initiated by their brother students. She visualized a revolution in the very near future. It should be the mission of educated girls, she said, to spread the light of literacy. Women in India should not be down-trodden but should occupy the place they deserved.

Begum Sahiba felt sorry to say that in their unfortunate country where communalism was having its sway, no real constructive work was possible. She felt constrained to say that communalism gained in strength after the Congress Committee committed the mistake of accepting Ministries. That was the time when men like Mr Jinnah and Mr Savarkar grew jealous of the position of the Congress. Communalism, which was nothing but another name for selfishness must be put an end to, and organized effort should be made to see that the communal cries of communal leaders like Mr Jinnah and Mr Savarkar are not allowed to subdue the national voice of India which stood for freedom, peace and progress.

Miss Mahmuda Ahmed Ali, who offered felicitations to the conference on behalf of the students' movement in Kashmir congratulated the organizers of the women students movement on the success they had achieved.

Referring to the poverty of India and the state of helplessness from which the masses were suffering, she stressed the necessity of organizing the masses and especially the students, not on religious but on an economic basis.

Girl students, representing various women's colleges read the report of the Unions of their respective colleges which showed the progress of the movement in their respective colleges.

When these reports were being read out in English, Mrs Rameshwari Nehru suggested that the 'Comrades' would do well if they spoke their own language, that is, Hindustani. The President agreed with the suggestion but allowed the reports to be read in English as the translation would involve a waste of time.

Miss Victoria Singh (Forman College) moved the first resolution regarding 'National Struggle', which was seconded by Miss Suvira Mahar (Kinnaird College) and was adopted. The resolution stated that the antagonism between British imperialism and the people of India had been sharpened. The resolution criticized the attempt made by Indian leadership for a compromise and for being responsible for 'Symbolic Satyagraha', which prevented the masses from playing their part in the struggle for freedom. The resolution declared opposition to all repression as well as the illusion that the restricted Satyagraha is a serious struggle against imperialism.'

Miss Kitty Bharucha (Forman College) moved the second resolution which after being seconded by Miss N. Allah Buksh (Kinnaird College) was passed.

Academic Freedom

The resolution explained the attitude of the students vis-à-vis strikes in the colleges and while it condemned the attitude of the various college authorities, it declared that the students could not accept the advice of the leaders who said that there should be no political strikes. The resolution declared further that the students go on strike in order to fight for youth's right to education. 'We do not go on strike in order to give up our studies, we go on strike in order to carry on our studies and defend our academic freedom.' The resolution claimed that the students knew what discipline meant and their demonstrations, far from being thoughtless, were carefully planned and were no hindrance in the national cause.

The conference adopted the following resolution moved by Miss P. Bharucha and seconded by a number of girls:

'This conference strongly disapproves and condemns the shameful and irresponsible behaviour of certain Law College students towards a woman student and the journalists who intervened. This conference welcomes the decision taken by the Lahore Students' Union to investigate into what occurred on 11 January on the Rattigan Road and in take upon itself the responsibility of preventing the repetition of such behaviour on the part of students inside or outside the Students' Federation.'

'Students Charter'

Miss Maya Rallia Ram (FCC) moved the following resolution regarding students demands, which after being seconded by Kamla Sharma (Rawalpindi College), was passed:

This conference fully adopts and reiterates its determination to fight for the Students Charter of Immediate Demands placed before the Punjab University by the Punjab Students Federation:

1. To initiate a system of two examinations a year and to allow students to take their examinations in parts, if they so desire; 2. to change the medium of instruction to Hindustani; 3. to control prices of textbooks, which are rising rapidly due to the war, causing an increasing burden to the majority of students; 4. to remove completely the ten-year limit for registration of university graduates. All graduates should be automatically allowed to register themselves. Majority of the members of the Senate should be nominated; 5. to reduce the MA Economics course to one year for BCom graduates; 6. to establish a system of annual examinations for the Law classes, as is the case with other professional examinations such as Medicine; 7. to reduce the fees charged for various university examinations; 8. to see that all Sports Selection Committees are composed of persons unconnected with any of the colleges; 9. to remove the fine imposed on students who are unable to attend the Convocation to receive their degrees and 10. to allow us the right of freedom of discussion and organization, which is something essential for real university life.

Moving the resolution regarding 'Students and Repression', Miss Perin Bharucha, who was supported by a Kinnaird College student said that they were a part of the anti-imperialist force. They had joined the students movement not out of fun. They regarded the students movement and its ideal a necessity for the good of the students, who were part of a big world-wide movement. They were, therefore, determined to carry on the movement in spite of all the repression.

'Independence Day'

Several other resolutions were adopted by the conference. By one of these resolutions the conference called upon all women students to participate in the Independence Day celebrations; the conference expressed its solidarity with the Punjab Women Teachers' Union and welcomed the decisions of the All-India Students' Federation to form an All-India Coordinating Committee for Women to carry on work among women students.

A resolution deciding to form a Committee for the relief and comfort of political prisoners was passed. Steps taken by the students of the Kinnaird and R. Sohan Lal Colleges in this direction in having knitted pull-overs and socks, etc, for political prisoners, were welcomed.

A resolution protesting against the arrest of Mr V.D. Chopra and his detention in the Fort was passed.

It was also decided send a deputation to the Principals of the Khalsa College and the Kinnaird College to request them to remove the ban which had been imposed upon the women students against their becoming members of Punjab Students' Federation.

45. Harijan Women Court Arrest: Satyagraha in Kakori Village

National Herald, 21 February 1941.

Thursday, 20 February.

Three women satyagrahis were arrested by the Kakori police on Thursday. They were Shrimati Savitri Dwivedi, Rajrani Devi and Mohini Devi.

The village of Bharosa in the Kakori mandal presented a crowded appearance on Thursday. Hundreds of kisans, men and women, collected by 9 a.m. A crowd of 3,000 gathered at Mr Shiva Kumar Dwivedi's residence. Among them were Tulsi Ram Gupta, member of the DCC, Jagannath Prasad Saksena, member of the CCC and president of the Yahiaganj Ward Congress Committee, Drigpal Singh, Razzaq Ali, Iftikhar Ahmad and Ram Pratap Singh. A number of University students were also present.

A procession with hundreds of tri-colour flags and headed by 300 women and students of the local Kisan Vidyalaya started from the Kisan Pustakalaya. As it reached Moti Tola Mrs Rajrani Devi, a kisan woman satyagrahi aged 60 (Harijan) was seen standing near the well. She shouted anti-war slogans and distributed anti-war leaflets. She was arrested by the inspector of police and was profusely garlanded.

46. Indian Woman Awakened! Lady Rama Rau Explains Origin and Progress of Women's Movement

Bombay Chronicle, 26 February 1941.

The origin and the growth of the movement to 'raise the standard of the Indian womanhood' were explained by Lady Rama Rau in the course of a speech at a lunch given by the Rotary Club at the Taj [Bombay] on Tuesday.

It was described as a 'Ladies Day' and it was announced that 315 members and guests—a record attendance—were present.

The subject on which Lady Rama Rau spoke was 'Indian Women's Organizations'. Rotarian Sir Sultan Chinoy presided.

Origin of Movement

Twenty-five years ago, Lady Rama Rau observed, the first All-India Women's Organization was formed with a view to bringing the leading women together to enable them to think about the problems affecting Indian women. The incentive was derived from the fact that the Montague–Chelmsford Committee was about to begin its sittings in India. The speaker was connected with the Committee that was organizing this work and with the evidence placed before the Montague–Chelmsford Committee subsequently, they found that there was immense work for them to do in the sphere for emancipation of women, and thus the Women's Indian Association came into existence as an All-India body.

Education and Social Work

In 1919, Lady Rama Rau said the National Council of Women in India came to be first formed with a view to do social work among the Indian women. The speaker considered that the organization formed in 1927, namely, the All-India Women's Council to consider and discuss the question of women's education, was the most important one. A few representatives of five major provinces met, and so much enthusiasm there was and so much experience and knowledge were brought to bear in the discussions that next year representatives of the other provinces joined in the conference.

When Begum of Bhopal Discarded Purdah

Lady Rama Rau recalled the incident which took place in 1928 when the then Begum of Bhopal presided over the conference. They discussed the question of social reform and the Begum for the first time discarded her veil and boldly advocated the discarding of the purdah. Support to the Women's Conference grew more and more and during the last session at Bangalore, 160 delegates from 160 different centres attended.

The programme of work had grown gradually year after year, and thus they had passed through a great national movement in the country in which women had shouldered responsibility in social and political spheres. The consciousness of women had been roused and it was difficult to shove them out from the various activities. Indian women were alive to the work they had to do.

Legal Disabilities

The speaker, then, narrated a short account of the social reform work done by them. She stressed the need for the removal of women's legal disabilities and said that the laws of inheritance were so inadequate and wrong that it would take very many years for them to move the Government sufficiently to consider the position of Indian women, especially under the Hindu Law. The Royal Commission on Labour threw a flood of light on the conditions of women workers. The sub-committee of the Conference had collected a good deal of information on the conditions of women workers.

All the three women's organizations in India had extended their activities by participating constantly and with great interest in international questions relating to women. At a time when India was passing through a period of stress and bitterness and there were embittered feelings between the British and the Indians, Indian women invited the British women to attend their conferences as visitors and lend them their help, advice and co-operation. In her opinion, it was a bold step.

Concluding Lady Rama Rau appealed to the Rotarians to extend their help to the women's movement.

47. Bombay Presidency Social Reform Association's Views on Hindu Married Women's Right to Separate Maintenance

Bombay Chronicle, 6 March 1941.

... The [Bombay Presidency Social Reform] Association states:

Under the Hindu Law marriage is indissoluble, and the husband is entitled to require his wife to live in his house from the moment of his marriage. So long therefore as the Hindu law does not recognize divorce, a claim for separate residence and maintenance is the most effective remedy which the Hindu wife has against her husband's injustice or cruelty. During recent years Courts in India have held that the grounds which would be available to a wife to defeat a suit for restitution of conjugal rights would also entitle her to live apart from her husband and claim separate maintenance. The question, however, whether a particular ground is sufficient or justifiable, would, in the absence of a specific legislation on the point depend solely on the discretion of the judge. It is therefore desirable to have a legislation laying down specifically the grounds on which a Hindu wife should be entitled to claim separate residence and maintenance. For these reasons the Association is entirely in favour of the principle underlying Dr G.V. Deshmukh's Bill to give Hindu married women a right to separate residence and maintenance.

Amendments Needed

The Association however feels that if the law is to be really useful and effective the Bill would require considerable amendment. Firstly, the Bill does not contain any definition of 'Separate Residence.' It is no doubt true that a decree for separate residence in favour of the wife would not amount to a dissolution of the marital tie and consequently children born to the wife, who has obtained such a decree, would in law be legitimate unless it is proved that the husband had no access to the wife. The absence of a definition of 'Separate Residence' is however likely to serve an unscrupulous husband with a weapon to deprive the wife of her maintenance. On the birth of a child to her, he may be able to plead unchastity against the wife and thus deprive her of her maintenance. The Baroda Hindu Code has by Section 161 defined 'separate residence' as meaning 'separation of the husband and wife in board but not in bed, without dissolution of marriage'. The Association would suggest that a similar definition should find a place in the Bill under consideration.

Ground of Adultery

It is unfortunate that the draft Bill does not include adultery on the part of the husband among the grounds for separate residence and maintenance. The Association would suggest the inclusion of that ground. It is apprehended that the term adultery would not include the keeping of or visiting a prostitute by the husband. The definition of 'adultery' as given in the Indian Penal Code would not cover such cases. Keeping of a prostitute in the family house has been recognized by the Calcutta High Court as a sufficient justification for the wife to ask for a separate habitation and maintenance. The Association would therefore suggest that adultery and keeping a prostitute in the family house should be included among the grounds, for separate residence and maintenance.

Judicial Separation and Divorce

Though the word 'Judicial Separation' has been used in the title of the Bill, there is nothing in the Bill itself to indicate what the mover of the Bill wants to convey by that word. The draft Bill does not contain a definition of the word and a perusal of the provisions of the Bill leads one to believe that the mover of the Bill does not make any distinction between 'Separate Residence' and Judicial Separation. If this view be correct, it is difficult to understand the necessity of this Bill when a Bill for separate residence and maintenance has been introduced by the same Hon'ble Member.

48. Hindu Women's Property Rights

Editorial, *Bombay Chronicle*, 18 March 1941.

We would draw the attention of all interested in the reform of Hindu Law regarding women's property rights to the elaborate questionnaire issued by the Committee appointed by the

Government of India on this subject and published elsewhere in due columns. The questionnaire has arisen out of several Bills before the Central Legislative Bill sponsored by Dr Deshmukh and Messrs. N.V. Gadgil, A.C. Datta and A.N. Chattopadhyaya. The question of Hindu women's property rights has exercised the minds of Hindu jurists for several years past and agitation for reform in the matter led to the Hindu Women's Right to Property Act 1937. But as the Act was soon found to be defective—as piecemeal legislation often is—it had to be amended in 1938. Even the amended Act was not quite satisfactory and necessitated the Bills now before the Assembly. In the discussion on Mr Datta's Bill the view prevailed that legislation in respect of property rights should be comprehensive and such as would not lead to unnecessary legislation. It was also felt that public opinion should be built up in support of the desired reform so that Government might not block the reform on the plea of inadequate public support. Thus we have now the elaborate questionnaire designed to elicit informed public opinion, and it behoves all who desire reform in this social sphere seriously to consider the questionnaire and submit to the committee their replies to fit.

Constitutional Difficulty

The question of Hindu women's property rights bristles with difficulties. At the very outset one is confronted with a constitutional difficulty in the way of immediate legislation. As the questionnaire itself points out under the Government of India Act 1935 the Central Legislature can legislate with respect to succession to property other than agricultural land, but not with respect to succession to agricultural land. The result is that until Central legislation is supplemented by Provincial legislation there will be one law of succession in regard to agricultural land and another in regard to property other than agricultural land. And as most of the Provinces are now without their normal Legislatures, Provincial legislation on the subject can hardly be expected under present conditions. In these circumstances, there are two possible alternatives. One is that the Centre should legislate with respect to property other than agricultural land at once, but no legislation should come into force until some future date dependent in each Province on the date of the necessary supplementary provincial legislation. The other alternative is that the Centre should legislate (with respect to property other than agricultural land) at once and bring the law into force at once throughout British India leaving it to the Provinces to do whatever they think fit with respect to agricultural land. Neither alternative, however, is wholly satisfactory. In the first case there will be indefinite delay in the inauguration of complete reform, whereas in the second, reform will be only partial. But even under the existing Women's Rights to Property Act of 1938 there are different sets of rules for the two different kinds of property. And it will be a change for the better if the Act is really improved soon.

Need for Propaganda

It is not possible to consider here the specific rights of women suggested by the questionnaire. The best ways to safeguard the rights are best discussed by those reformers who have studied the law about the subject. It is necessary that in every city women's institutions and others interested in the reform should make concerted efforts to appoint competent committees to prepare suitable replies to the questionnaire, and later canvass public opinion in support of them. The All-India Women's Conference has actively interested itself in this cause and its various provincial branches should now take the initiative in eliciting public support for sound replies to the questionnaire. We shall be glad to publish brief well-reasoned letters or articles on the subject, provided they are written in a non-technical manner capable of appealing to the average reader. Experience has shown that reformers are often inactive and thereby enable Government to oppose reform on the plea that public opinion is not sufficiently favourable. Reformers owe it to themselves and to their cause to see that judgment does not go against them by default.

49. 'The Woman's Role'

Editorial, *The Hindu*, 21 March 1941.

There may be two opinions on the question whether women, particularly married women, should take to the professions. But there can be no question that a married woman's first duty is to the home. Nor is this duty one that can be discharged lightly, with little or no training for it. This point, among other things, was stressed by Mrs Rameshwari Nehru in her Convocation address at the Lahore College of Women last weekend. While stressing the need for women equipping themselves for a profession, thereby ensuring their economic independence, Mrs Nehru was even more insistent that the art of home-making should form a vital part of their education. 'Although I am strongly of opinion,' said Mrs Nehru 'that every woman should be trained to a profession so that she may be able to earn her living if need arises, I do not hold that every woman should necessarily take to work. Home-making is work of no mean order and those who choose to devote their full time to work in the home are as usefully employed as those working outside.' Marriage, in fact, is a vocation by itself and a new syllabus as comprehensive as life itself will have to be formulated for the purpose. Do the educational curricula followed by girls' institutions subserve this purpose? The answer is in the negative, for the simple reason that they are for the most part a replica of those prescribed for boys. In the words of Mrs Nehru, 'without any plan or forethought, our women have simply been thrown into a cast prepared for men and we all know how miserably that system has failed to satisfy the needs even of men.'

Indeed, Mrs Nehru's criticism of the present system of women's education takes the form of a severe indictment of modern 'educated girls'. She charges them with contracting expensive habits, a distaste for manual work, and the adoption of 'a standard of life not justified in a poor country like ours.' They lack that quality of give and take which the joint family system of former days, with all its drawbacks, taught to women, together with early training in habits of giving unselfish service to the family which were a great asset in later life. Nor does success in home-making consist merely in efficient house-keeping, in 'feeding the brute man,' to keep him in good humour. It is much more complicated than the 'dead picture' of a house well-furnished and cleanly kept. It is the woman's business to infuse life into the home. 'An understanding of human nature and the motive forces of human action, a knowledge of dealing with people, a habit of give and take are essential qualities for this purpose,' and, therefore, Mrs Nehru suggests that a study of human psychology, including child psychology, of sex life, of how to deal with fellow beings, should form part of a woman's education as a preparation for marriage. This might at first sight appear to be a tall order to women's educational institutions, but it may be worth making a trial by including these in the school and college curricula in the place of subjects which are assiduously studied by our girls but which are of no conceivable use to most of them in later life.

50. Better Status for Indian Women: Suggestions to Hindu Law Reform Committee

The Hindu, 9 April 1941.

Dr (Mrs) S. Muthulakshmi Reddi, in the course of a communication, suggests that the Hindu Law Reforms Committee, appointed by Government, should not merely confine itself to the questions arising out of the Bills before the Assembly, but should adopt the same procedure and make a comprehensive enquiry into the questions of marriage, divorce and property rights of Hindu women as a whole and take evidence from all representative women's organizations and well-known women social and public workers as well, and thus prove to the Hindu public the urgent need for such reforms.

Cases of deserted and destitute Hindu wives, she adds, are becoming increasingly common in Hindu Society. Also the existing Law of Hindu marriage is very cruel and unjust to them. Many and many young, healthy girls are deserted by their husbands for no fault of theirs. Hundreds and thousands of cases of ill-treatment, cruelty and mental agony caused by the immoral behaviour on the part of the husbands are happening daily in the Hindu homes. Hindu marriages, considered to be sacrosanct, are only binding upon the wife and not upon the husband. They must be made monogamous by legislation and concubinage that is now permitted by the Hindu Law, should be disallowed and penalized. Further, differential treatment is accorded by Hindu Law to illegitimate children born of a Brahmin father and those of a Sudra which is certainly neither fair nor just. The innocent child should never be punished for the fault and the sins of its parents. We have to undo all these wrongs and injustices perpetrated in the name of our religious laws, practices and customs. As inter-caste marriages are becoming very common, laws should be made uniform for all, and all differences based upon caste, such as in *Anuloma* and *Pratiloma* marriages, should be abolished by legislation in the interest of the strength and solidarity of the Hindu community. Unless the Hindu Laws are amended so as to give women, the mothers of the race a better legal and social status in Society the present and future generation cannot attain to the full dignity and nobility of the original Hindu race.

51. Women Satyagrahis Jailed in Nainital

National Herald, 17 May 1941.

The following women satyagrahis have been sentenced to various terms of imprisonment and fines in the Nainital district.

Shreematis Kunti Devi, Bhawani Devi, Saraswati Devi, Chandrawati Devi, Dhana Devi, Sarala Devi, Shaswati Devi, Devki Devi, Bhagwati Devi, Hansa Devi, Kunti Devi.

Several women satyagrahis, who were not arrested for offering satyagraha in villages were taken into custody by the Nainital police after they had shouted anti-war slogans before the UP Government secretariat....

52. Hansa Mehta on Hardships of Women Prisoners in Yeravada

Bombay Chronicle, 26 May 1941.

'Penal reformers all over the world are anxious to turn prisoners into reformatories where efforts are to be made to convert criminals into civilized human beings and as such respectable members of society.

Prisons in this country, unfortunately, work the other way.'

Thus concludes the article by Mrs Hansa Mehta, Former Parliamentary Secretary, the Government of Bombay, on the conditions of life of women prisoners in Yeravada Jail, from which she was recently released.

Queer Methods of Release

The following is the full text:

I have no personal axe to grind in this article. I had all the comforts that one can reasonably expect in jail. The one complaint that I have to make, however, is with regard to the method of releasing prisoners under detention. In trying perhaps to avoid unnecessary demonstrations Government does not realize to what inconvenience they put them—I am talking of women.

According to the latest Government orders, detenues are allowed to deposit not more than Rs 10 for 'A' class and not more than Rs 5 for 'B' class per month with the jail authorities. This amount hardly covers the extra expenditure one incurs during the month with the result that at the end of the month very little balance is left. The detenues are not told beforehand as to when they are to be released in order to enable them to make arrangements for conveyance and other things. Yeravada prison is far from any railway station so that the taxi hire would be expensive. If, therefore the released prisoners have to make their own arrangements at the last minute, they would naturally find it difficult to do so for lack of funds. Government, if they are unable to make suitable arrangements, and they should at least inform the detenues beforehand the date of their release in order to enable them to make their own arrangements for their departure....

Foul Latrines

The first and foremost question that requires immediate attention is that of sanitary arrangements. They are far from satisfactory. The number of latrines or privies may appear sufficient on paper but owing to a small number of tin pans being supplied—instead of baskets tin pans are used as there is no flush system—perhaps not more than half a dozen are actually used. Considering that the number of prisoners often is nearly over one hundred and fifty, half a dozen latrines can hardly be considered sufficient for the requirements of the prisoners. I wonder if the Municipal Rules would ever permit such meagre provision. Then, there is no proper drain; with the result that the atmosphere inside and in the vicinity of these latrines is very foul. The latrines are small uncomfortable cubicles with doors most of which have their bolts broken and therefore cannot be shut securely. Recently at the request of the political prisoners, some of the bolts were repaired, but so badly that most of them are again out of use.

Logic that Guides Jail Authorities

The sanitary arrangement for the night, that is within the barrack itself where prisoners are shut in for nearly twelve hours, that is from say 6 p.m. to 5.30 a.m. is again hopelessly inadequate. There is one small cubicle attached to the barrack with a small tin pan to be used for all purposes by, say, 28 prisoners—the maximum capacity of the barrack. The tin pan is perhaps meant to be used as a urinal only, but when prisoners are shut in for 12 hours it is not fair to expect them not to use it for other purpose as well. No separate arrangements are considered necessary for women during their monthly period. The edge of the pan is higher than the surface of the seat and therefore it is difficult to use the thing in a sitting posture. Standing posture is convenient for men and therefore, what is suitable for men is also suitable for women! That seems to be the logic that guides the jail authorities.

The same logic prevails with regard to bathing arrangements also. A shed is erected without any doors and women are expected to bathe together and wash together. There is no privacy and no separate arrangement is considered necessary for women, who do want privacy during their monthly period. At the request of political prisoners, some sort of temporary enclosure was erected for them, but the place selected is near the open drain of the latrines so that no one, with any sense of cleanliness, wishes to go near it, much less bathe and wash in it....

53. Complete Overhaul of Hindu Law: Women's Conference Executive's Demand

The Hindu, 1 June 1941.

The need for a radical change and a complete overhaul of the Hindu Law and a demand for the enactment of a universal equitable law to replace the different personal laws were made by the Standing Committee of the All-India Women's Conference in the course of a statement on the Hindu Law Committee's Questionnaire.

Protesting against the non-inclusion of any woman in the Hindu Law Committee and urging upon the immediate inclusion of some women representatives, the statement expresses regret that the Government had not seen their way to extend the terms of reference of the Hindu Law Committee so as to include the whole question of 'stridhan', its classification and inheritance, the guardianship of the children and their property and the question of divorce with its multifarious problems.

'In appraising the values of all personal laws, sex equality, consistent with social well-being is our guiding principle', adds the statement. Continuing, it says: 'We therefore hold that the laws of inheritance and succession concerning daughter and son, husband and wife, widow and widower, father and mother and others, should be determined on the principle of equality. Women in all estates should have equal rights with men in the matter of acquisition, holding and disposal of property. We realize that the most important of all economic rights for women is the right to work and to have facilities therefor. The main idea, however, behind this demand is not so much 'the economic relief' it will afford as the lost dignity for womanhood as well as an equal status with man, that will be regained by it.'

While the Committee did not want a lowering of the moral standard in regard to marriage, it pointed out, 'One-sided obligations have reduced our high ideals of marriage to a mockery. Desertion of wives is a common occurrence. We want polygamy abolished; we want the consent of both the parties made obligatory for marriage and we advocate that the dissolution of marriage be permitted on specific grounds.'

The Standing Committee warned against the futility of piecemeal legislation on the subject. Several of the bills which formed part of the subject matter before the Hindu Law Committee had in fact been promoted to rectify the mistakes of previous piecemeal legislation. There was a strong likelihood of the previous mistakes being repeated, and the Standing Committee appealed to the Hindu Law Committee to urge on the Government the imperative need for extension of the scope and time at its disposal in order to effect a thorough overhauling of the system.

54. Women's Conference

Editorial, *Bombay Chronicle*, 2 June 1941.

The Standing Committee of the All-India Women's Conference, which met in this city last week, was concerned mostly with the replies to the elaborate questionnaire issued by the Hindus Law Reform Committee. In the discussion of the replies the Committee felt convinced more than ever before that the Law Reform Committee's terms of reference were extremely narrow and needed to be much enlarged. That conviction is shared by many others who have discussed the questionnaire seriously. The Right Hon'able Mr M.R. Jayakar, who is both an eminent authority on Hindu Law and a champion of the rights of women, expressed the view at a public meeting organized by the Women's Conference that it would be best to drop the policy of piecemeal legislation in this matter, that Government should set up a Committee of experts to overhaul the whole system of law with reference to women and bring it in line with modern developments. It is also reported that revision of the whole body of Hindu Law, instead of piecemeal tinkering with it, is favoured by the bulk of the replies to the elaborate questionnaire issued by the Hindu Law Committee. It is even regarded as likely that the committee will take an early opportunity to approach Government for an enlargement of their terms of reference to enable them to carry out the full examination desired by the majority of legal opinion.

Extend the Scope

It is not surprising therefore that the Standing Committee of the Women's Conference has issued a statement appealing to the Hindu Law Committee to urge on Government the need for widening its terms of reference. The Women's Committee makes out a strong case for its appeal in the following terms: 'We deplore that in spite of our repeated requests the Government have not seen their way to extend the reference of the committee to cover the whole range of the Hindu laws. In spite of the Law Committee's interpretation of its terms of reference certain aspects of the Hindu law, such as the whole question of the *stridhan*, its classification and inheritance, the guardianship of the children and their property, the question of divorce with its multifarious problems have all been left outside the ambit of the questionnaire. Law after all is an organic whole and must be considered in its corporate character as such. Experience has shown that piecemeal legislation in the past has utterly failed and in some cases have defeated its own purpose for, all piecemeal legislation is, in principle, unsound.' We trust Government will grant the appeal made by so many interested in Hindu law reform. Government lose nothing by merely extending the scope of their inquiry. On the contrary their Committee's complete report will be a sounder document, the inter-related sections of which will have been more fully considered in all their bearings, each section in its relation to the whole. It is true that the amplified report will take much more time but that need not be regretted. Nor will the time be wasted, for it will be taken up with agitation among the public, a necessary condition for any reform. In any case whether the proposed reforms are narrow or wide in their scope, they do not seem possible in the next few months in the present circumstances. It will, therefore, be best to do the necessary spade-work in a wider field in the next few months.

Need for Propaganda

Whether the appeal of the Women's Conference and others is accepted by Government or not, the executive of the Conference will have to carry on active propaganda in support of its reform proposals. On account of their undue regard for ancient custom and shastras, many Hindus, men and women alike, oppose every kind of reform as being irreligious. To educate general public opinion in support of reform in spite of such hostility, the workers of the Conference, who are both specially interested in the reform in question and are fairly well-organized, should take the initiative in the necessary propaganda when they will surely get the active support of many others including legal experts. The Conference working in co-operation with bodies like the Bombay Presidency Social Reform Association, whose excellent memorandum, containing answers to the questionnaire of the Hindu Law Committee we published serially last month, will do well to publish popular literature on the subject in question through the Indian press, its own organ 'Roshni' and separate booklets. Work like this is invaluable. It helps not only the particular reforms now proposed but future social reforms also.

55. Insanitary Conditions in Yeravada Prison Must Go: All-India Women's Conference Executive Urges Jail Reforms for Women Prisoners

Bombay Chronicle, 24 June 1941.

The Standing Committee of the All-India Women's Conference has adopted a resolution drawing the attention of the Yeravada Prison authorities to the reported insanitary conditions in the prison for women prisoners, and hoping that the Prison authorities will look into the matter at once and carry out the necessary changes.

The Committee further hope that all necessary facilities will be given to women in Yeravada as well as in all other prisons in the Presidency, and not only women but prisoners in general.

By another resolution the Committee view with concern the 'appalling' conditions in several gaols and sub-gaols and lock-ups in India, particularly with regard to food and living and sanitary conditions, and urge the authorities concerned to look into the matter immediately and bring about the necessary reforms.

The Committee is of the opinion that political prisoners should in no case be treated like ordinary criminals, and all distinctions as between political prisoners should be abolished.

56. 'This 'Mahatma' is a Woman!' An Article by Freda Bedi, 'From My Village Window'

Bombay Chronicle, 7 August 1941.

There is a 'Mahatma' in the village. It is not quite clear how the title 'happened'; the probability is that she (for this Mahatma is a woman!) inherited it from her 'guru'.

If you saw her walking along the dusty, cactus-lined path that go from village to village, you might not know that was supposed to be holy. She is short, and on the plump side, say about fifty and she wears the simple dirty white homespun clothes that the villagers make for themselves. But you will notice that she does not wear the usual veil. There is a long piece of cloth wound round her head like a rough turban with a long tail behind. Underneath you might catch a glimpse of grey shaven hair. Behind her, the only visible sign of her, the only visible sign of her office, walks a small urchin of a boy bubbling with mischief, but wearing the classic saffron-coloured turban of the disciple.

Better that Way

She is rather reticent about her past. If you question her, she will tell you she was married and widowed as a child, and that she came, at the age of eighteen, with her woman 'guru', to this village and as she puts it, 'sat at her sacred feet.' 'It is good I did it, it is better that way' she says.

The child widow, in the orthodox Brahmin household, what life would she have had? You will agree, if you go with me to see her home that 'it is better that way'.

Enter a wide country doorway that has a small room inside it, cool and inviting after the roasting heat of the dry land outside.

Go a little further into the wide courtyard. A good half of its space is enclosed by a two-feet high brick wall, behind which loll the most delightful cows imaginable, mother cows and baby cows, and old cows, all having an indefinable air of well-looked after, even spoiled with affection.

At one side of the cows' enclosure is a small room with a verandah, which serves as a kitchen, and a room where her devoted servant and his family can live. Beyond that, behind the pomegranate tree, is a long room, with one side open to the sun and rain, a grand dump for huge 'degs', mud barrels to hold grain, sticks and broken chairs, and beds and rope. Two or three well-used string beds at one side show that it is used for visitors and as a general meeting place.

The 'Mahatma' is usually to be seen boiling the milk over the cow-dung fire, or hovering over the hearth or milking the cows. She is brusque and rather loud of voice speaking as a woman is allowed to speak who is independent of her neighbours for food. She is the 'Mother' of the villagers, knowing all their stories and their joys and their grief, concerned as any village housewife might be, with her kitchen and her cows.

Arrive at Any Hour

But hers is no exclusive home. Arrive at any hour of the day or night and there will be shelter for you. Come in for a minute on your burning journey to the village 'bazar', and you will get fresh cool buttermilk. Are you hungry? Then there is food for all who come freshly-cooked bread, and mango pickle, mango preserved in 'gur', a bowl of fresh milk, mangoes, too, when they are ripe on the trees.

There is a big garden and lands surrounding her home. The peacock cries in his human voice and flies like some great ship of the air, his long tail balanced behind him, to the nearest tree. It is the oasis of the village folk, growing like a great lake of trees, among the flat fields of rice and sugar-cane and maize, green among the patches of ploughed earth.

Bogus holy men, and 'Mahatmas' and the like, are something of a plague in the fair land of India. There are hundreds and thousands of cheap imitations, the real seeker is so rare as to be almost invisible. But what shall we say of our woman 'Mahatma'?

She Lives a Good Life

I don't know what her claims to holiness are except that she lives a good life. And that, after all, is real holiness and not the imitation variety. She has, to be sure, a little shrine in her upper rooms where the Holy Book lies and the picture of Guru Nanak and many rich cloths sprinkled with fresh roses and 'metia'. There, side by side, are two pairs of wooden shoes, carefully polished in the holy place itself. Perhaps they belong to her 'guru', the old woman, and to the 'guru' before that.

With an engaging simplicity, she will call out as the visitor enters 'Holy "Guru", see these people have come to see you' as though he were sitting in state in her little room.

Grain she gets from the villagers, even money from the richer ones and clothes. She has the produce from her own lands. But it all goes back again to the poor and the hungry and the thirsty, and that is why they give it to her. She is the Poor House since nobody else has seen fit to provide one, she is a sort of Municipal Kitchen and a Universal Provider.

In that Free India

In that Free India of the future we work for and dream of, when the poor will not cry in vain, and where there will be no room for the exploiters of men, there will be no place for the gangs of rogues and scoundrels who take the name of God and impoverish the peasants of India.

But there will still be room, I am sure, for this 'Mother of the Poor' and those who have taken from the richer to give to those who are in need. She who has walked along the village path with bare feet and fed those hungry ones who came to her will not be denied her right to live when the peasants give her back with free hands the food she has given them.

57. Baby Princess to Occupy Kolhapur Gadi? Maharashtra Mahila Mandal's Memorial to Viceroy Supports Women's Conference Resolution

Bombay Chronicle, 7 August 1941.

The Maharashtra Mahila Mandal, Poona centre, a branch of the Central Maharashtra Mahila Committee affiliated to the All-India Women's Conference, in supporting the resolution of the Standing Committee of the All-India Women's Conference regarding the 'succession of girls to gadis of ruling prince, when there happens to be no sons', have resolved that His Excellency the Viceroy be requested to give a favourable consideration to that resolution by giving effect to it in the case of the Kolhapur succession, by declaring the Kolhapur Princess, Baby Maharaj, as the successor to the Kolhapur Gadi.

The Memorial

The following is the text of the memorial which has been forwarded to the Viceroy:

The Standing Committee of the All-India Women's Conference in its meeting held in Bombay on 30th May 1941, discussed the question of Succession of Girls to Gadis of Ruling Princes where there happens to be no sons and passed the following resolution:

'Resolved that the Standing Committee of the All-India Women's Conference are of opinion that in the absence of a son, the daughter of a Ruling Prince should be allowed to succeed to the Gadi. They appeal to the Princes and the Government of India to accept this demand as a resolution of the equality of the sexes in the matter of inheritance and property right.'

The Maharashtra Mahila Mandal, Poona Centre, which is a branch of the Central Maharashtra Mahila Committee affiliated to All-India Women's Conference, in its meeting held in Poona on 14th July 1941, supported this resolution and resolved that His Excellency the Viceroy should be requested to give a favourable consideration to that resolution and that His Excellency might kindly give effect to it in the case of the Kolhapur Princess Baby Maharaj, by declaring her as the successor to the Kolhapur Gadi.

The Maharashtra Mahila Mandal further resolved 'that in case the resolution of the Standing Committee of the All-India Women's Conference does not meet with His Excellency's approval, His Excellency should be requested to allow Her Highness Maharani Tarabaisahiba of Kolhapur the same right of adoption of a son of her own free choice as other Hindu Widows of all classes in Maharashtra and in Western India have, under the Hindu Law.'

The above resolutions have been sent to HE the Viceroy.

58. Maharashtra Mahila Mandal—Resolutions Passed at the Constituent Conference, Malsiras, 15 October 1941

File No. 37, AIWC Papers, NMML.

... Educational

6. This conference is of opinion that women should keep on constantly endeavouring for the spread of adult education and for compulsory and primary education of small children.
7. This conference is of opinion that women's associations should endeavour to raise the pay of school teachers.
8. This conference expresses its appreciation of the Girl Scout Movement as sponsored, and women's associations should help in promoting the progress of this movement, and help in the work of providing education in good citizenship to our Girl-Children....

Labour

13. Women's associations should endeavour to see that no occupation or profession is closed to women by reason of their sex.
14. This conference request all employers to make arrangements for the organization of literacy classes within their establishments, so that no man, woman, or child connected with the establishment remains illiterate.
15. Women's Association should undertake the responsibility of organizing industrial homes to provide work for poor women, and to arrange for the sale of the goods therein.
16. This conference is of opinion that the Shops Act should be applied to domestic servants.
17. Women's Associations should endeavour to provide fresh uniforms twice in the year through Municipalities and local Boards for their menial employees who do the work of sweeping and latrine-cleaning
18. Preference should be given to women in need, when the question of employment in schools and other places is being considered, over married women who are comfortably settled.

59. Mrs Rameshwari Nehru's Call to Women of India

The Tribune, 7 November 1941.

Lahore, 6 November.

A call to the women of India to put forward the demand that the hunger strike at Deoli should be brought to an end is offered by Mrs Rameshwari Nehru, President of the All-India Women's Conference, in a statement to the press:

The hunger strike of the security prisoners at Deoli Camp, she says, is unfortunate. Its continuation is causing great anxiety to the public. It is particularly disconcerting to women. It is a great pity that matter should have been allowed to take this shape. The demands of the prisoners, as adumbrated by Shri N.M. Joshi are just and the Government should have conceded them long ago....

She urged that women and mothers... 'Should all, therefore come out of their homes to put forward the demand that the strike should be brought to an end and impending catastrophe stopped.'...

60. All-India Women's Conference: Madras Constituency Resolutions, 15 December 1941

File No. 37, AIWC Papers, NMML.

1. General

Peace:

a. While the conference is in whole-hearted sympathy for all victims of the War, it calls upon all women to work towards the establishment of a new world order, surmounting all barriers of race, creed, caste and nationality and thus bringing about a spirit of true patriotism and love of humanity, necessary for international fellowship, goodwill and lasting peace.

b. This conference believes that a change of heart in people and nations is the fundamental need of the world. This is the time for every woman and particularly each member of the conference—with God's aid—to begin to tackle the selfishness, apathy and pride, so common in us all, and to break down the social and racial barriers in everything that touches her life.

2. Communal Harmony

Realizing that women have a responsible part in bringing about communal harmony, this conference appeals to all women to work earnestly for such a unity, so that this communal problem would not continue to be an impediment to India's national progress.

61. All-India Women's Conference: Mrs Pandit's Appeal to Delegates

Bombay Chronicle, 24 December 1941.

Mrs Vijai Lakshmi Pandit, President-elect of the All-India Women's Conference to be held at Cocanada on 29 December 1941 in a press statement says:

'There appears to have been some misunderstanding in the minds of delegates that owing to the application of certain emergency measures in coastal towns, the Women's Conference at Cocanada was to be postponed. The Conference will take place as notified and the programme has not in any way been restricted.

'The world must go on in spite of wars and other difficulties. We must carry on our allotted tasks calmly and with such wisdom as we possess. It is only by this attitude that we can help those around us. The women of the warring countries are showing greatness in the face of grave danger. The women of India must not forget for a moment their responsibility at this hour.

'I am leaving Allahabad on 24th December and will arrive in Cocanada on the evening of 26th. I appeal to all delegates to attend the Conference'.

62. All-India Women's Conference, Cocanada Session

Amrita Bazar Patrika, 31 December 1941.

Cocanada, 29 December.

The sixteenth session of the All-India Women's Conference commenced sitting to-day in the Local Town Hall which was gaily decorated. The President-elect Vijaya Lakshmi Pandit was taken in procession to the Town Hall.

On the president's side of the dais were seated the Yuvarani of Pithapuram, Mrs Rameshwari Nehru, Mrs Kamala Devi, Mrs Urmila Mehta and Reception Committee Vice-Presidents and Secretaries.

The Maharaja of Pithapuram, the Yuvaraja of Pithapuram, Mr T. Prakasam, ex-Minister and Mr Anantanarayan, District Judge, were among the invitees.

The proceedings commenced with a national song and welcome verses. The retiring President, Mrs Rameshwari Nehru, proposed Mrs Vijayalakshmi Pandit to the chair and wished her a happy year of service and successful work. She was supported by Mrs Ammu Swaminathan and Mrs Cousins.

Messages Read

Mrs Urmila Mehta, the Conference Secretary, read her annual report and also a number of messages wishing success to the conference, including those from Mahatma Gandhi, Mrs Sarojini Naidu, Marshal Chiang-Kai-Shek, Miss Vera Brittain (England). Begum Hydarali, Maharani Lalita Devi of Vizianagram, Mrs Lancaster, the Rajkumari Amrit Kaur, Rani Lakshmi Rajwade the Maharani of Mayurbhanj, Mrs Subbarayan, Mrs Muthulakshmi Reddi, Dr Pattabhi Sitaramayya, Mrs Asaf Ali and Miss Harris (England).

Mrs Kamala Devi referred to Marshal Chiang Kai-Sheks' gift of a picture to Indian women, and while displaying the same explained, that it was a token of Marshal Chiang's good feeling and depicted China's struggle with Japan in the form of an eagle swooping down on the Rising Sun. The picture looked like a colour painting but was worked in thread in an air raid shelter when bombs were being dropped.

Ideals of Womanhood

After the presidential address the Maharaja of Pithapuram spoke on the ideals of womanhood and advocated social and legal reforms. Mr T. Prakasam in his speech appealed to women to carry on constructive work and to organize peace brigades of the type advocated by Mahatma Gandhi. Mrs Anne Guthris of America, who had just arrived from Calcutta, then conveyed the greetings of women's organizations of the United States, Philippines and other places.

Mrs Ray of Calcutta proposed the vote of thanks at 7.30 p.m. and with a national song the conference rose for the day.

63. Vijayalakshmi Pandit's Presidential Address at 16th Session of All-India Women's Conference

Bombay Chronicle, 30 December 1941.

Cocanada, 29 December.

Indian Women and New World Order: Call to Britain to Abandon Dual Role of Democrat at Home and Autocrat in India

That the establishment of world peace can be brought about only by rooting out the causes that lead to national wars and that among such causes the domination of one country by another and the exploitation of one people by another are the most potent and in the planning for a new world order women, including Indian women, should take their proper share, was stressed by Shrimati Vijaya Lakshmi Pandit in her presidential address to the 16th session of the All-India Women's Conference held at Cocanada on December 29.

Taking stock of the work of the Conference during the past 16 years Mrs Pandit pleaded for the co-ordination of all women's organizations in the country under some federal scheme, so as to avoid overloading in the work that is done.

I regret that it has not been possible for any visitors from overseas to attend this session of the Conference. You are perhaps aware that we had invited Miss Vera Brittain as one of our distinguished guests this year. She had accepted our invitation and we were looking forward to meeting one with whom we were already familiar through her writings. Her 'Letters to Peace Lovers' have struck a responsive chord in many Indian hearts. But permission for her to come to India was withheld in spite of every effort made by our Liaison Committee in England and by our retiring President here. Miss Brittain's views on war are well-known and the authorities felt that her presence in India might further embarrass an already tense situation. The decision of the authorities was unfortunate. At this critical period in the relationship between the people of India and those of England human contacts are important. Miss Vera Brittain's visit would have forged another link in that chain of friendship between our peoples which this organization has been slowly trying to create.

I should like to express my gratification at the presence of Shrimati Kamaladevi in our midst to-day after her long absence abroad where she has so ably represented India's cause in many countries. I am sure you will permit me to extend a welcome to her on behalf of the Conference.

War

For several years now our Conference has passed resolutions expressing its opinion against war as a method of solving international problems. At each session we have spoken in eloquent terms of the necessity for a united front by the women of India in condemning the forces of aggression. Unfortunately, however, our resolutions have not gone very far beyond the hall in which they were passed, nor has there been perhaps an adequate understanding on the part of the majority of our sisters of the implications of our anti-war resolutions. We have been far away from the horrors of war and it is not always easy to understand an issue, however vital, which does not concern one directly. The situation has, however, changed during the last year and to-day the possibility of war is nearer to India than ever before. From what angle are we going to approach the problem at this session of our Conference?

New World Order

In the West our sisters are thinking deeply over these problems. Progressive organizations are trying to find a better way of adjusting human and national relations in the post-war world. The great forces arising in the world to-day will ultimately help to shape the new world which will come into being after the war. It is in planning for a new world order that women should take their share, and for this it is necessary to know how we shall approach the problem. Unless we can define our attitude to-day it will not be possible to share in the task of building up to-morrow. The Women's International League for Peace and Freedom, in a statement issued a few months ago, has reaffirmed its belief as follows: 'War is a crime developing a vicious circle in which violence begets violence and reprisals.' It has declared itself in favour of a world-order based on a 'new attitude of man to man, and nation to nation, with a realization of interdependence and a renunciation of exploitation and profiteering.' But declarations to be effective must be implemented by action. The establishment of world peace by the ending of national wars depends on the removal of the causes of wars. They can only be rooted out by the ending of the domination of one country by another and the exploitation of one people by another. Women's organizations should throw all their weight in favour of world disarmament and peacefully labour for the establishment of a juster political and economic order.

Non-violence

I have been a member of the Women's League for Peace and Freedom for several years. I have also the honour to belong to the Indian National Congress whose official creed is non-violence. In spite of the criticism and ridicule which has been directed at the non-violent creed, there is an increasing number of thinking men and women all over the world who believe that if the world is not to destroy itself and revert to barbarism it must ultimately accept the principle of non-violence. As women we have a special responsibility cast on us. We must decide whether we shall ally ourselves to the forces of life or those of death. Are we going to join the group that by their acquiescence make wars possible? Shall we bear sons only that they may murder other women's sons and help to maintain a system which stands self-condemned? Or shall we raise our united voice in favour of a brave new world where human life and human liberty receive the respect which is their due, where progress and security are within the grasp of each individual? The choice is before us. The future, not for women only but for humanity as well, is what the women of today make of it. Let us not treat this matter lightly.

Freedom Denied to India

If you will bear with me, I would ask you to turn your attention for a moment to conditions in our own country. While Britain fights for democracy and the liberties of small nations, freedom is denied to India. The people of India have declared their opposition to the Fascist nations and their sympathy with the progressive forces of the world, but how can there be any real co-operation except on terms of equality? The authoritative nature of British rule in India contradicts Britain's announcements about her war aims. Unless the right of India to freedom is recognized, how can the people of India fight to preserve the freedom of other nations? Unless it is recognized that the new world must be built up on the co-operation of a free people in a free world order, what ultimate good can come of a victory even by the so-called progressive powers? These are the questions which face us.

Work of Women's Conference

Let us now look at the work we have been doing. The Conference during its 16 years has enlarged gradually and there has been a genuine effort to extend its scope and utility and to bring into its fold women in all walks of life. But if it is to be a living organization, one which carries weight and can claim to be truly representative of the womanhood of India, a much greater effort has to be made to widen our scope still further and to join forces with other progressive organizations which work for women. Our outlook too must become wider and though I do not wish the Conference to become involved in party politics, I do believe the days are gone when a group or organization can keep itself aloof from current political thought. Politics to-day have become part of our daily life, we cannot avoid their implication. We must therefore understand the difference between narrow party politics and those larger issues of nationalism which face us. We must not let ourselves be side-tracked by things which seem important but which are, after all, only a part of the bigger issue. Any piecemeal solutions can be nothing more than a patchwork, but a solution of the basic issues will automatically solve all our smaller problems. We should, I think, ally our Conference with all those progressive movements in India which work for liberty—the liberty of the individual as well as the liberty of the country. Today woman faces the world as an individual for the first time. Her problems are the problems of society, and while fighting for those legal, civic and economic rights, which are still denied to us, let us not forget that the whole question of rights for women is closely linked up with the social question which in its turn is part of the larger political question.

Need for Co-ordination

I believe in co-ordination. We have at present a number of organizations which are working for women in India. There is overlapping in the work that is done and sometimes leads to quite unnecessary opposition and jealousy. Our country is big enough for a number of organizations having similar aims to function side by side amicably and in the best interests of women. But unless there is some co-ordination of activity, progress must be delayed and slow. We have lost much time already; we cannot afford further delays without seriously risking our future. I would like to see a coordination of all women's organizations under some federal scheme.

In the past we have been in the habit of passing a number of resolutions. The report of our annual session would perhaps be a less imposing document minus the resolutions which add to its bulk, but I feel certain we could achieve more. We have in the past worked for the removal of illiteracy. This field is so vast that our results have been negligible. If we could concentrate for at least one year on this as the major item of our programme in every province we could achieve worthwhile results. A mass drive against illiteracy started by the Conference would instantly invoke a response from other progressive groups and would help us to establish closer contacts with the villages and with the workers in fields and factories. This would also be a means of educating women in the ideals of the Conference and developing in them a sense of their own responsibilities.

We have before us a scheme for a model village. The idea is good but there are many difficulties which will have to be faced. Such a project requires the undivided attention of those who take it up. For good work we require trained whole-time workers who will live in the village. I am not sure, however, if even then we can do anything of real value. The main problem of the village is one which the villager must solve himself, through a desire for better conditions. We can of course help to arouse consciousness. In the village project, besides literacy, medical aid and other things, which will naturally form part of any such scheme, I would like the question of cottage industries and co-operatives to receive the attention which is their due. Their importance cannot be stressed too strongly. For an agricultural country the cottage industry becomes a vital necessity—not as the rival of big industry but as a supplementary force which can help to solve the economic problem of the villager. The work done by co-operatives in China has shown how valuable their contribution can be to the national life of a country. We should therefore remember these two items when working out our village project.

This Conference has already expressed its views on the recommendations of the Hindu Law Committee. While we have appreciated the recommendations and are glad that the work of codifying the law of succession has been taken up, we must not forget that piecemeal legislation is of little value, and what is urgently required is the codification of the whole of Hindu Law based on the principles of equality of status between man and woman.

Remove Suspicion

And lastly may I appeal to you, my friends, to do your bit to remove the hatred and suspicion which have crept into our midst. We have been conscious of this unhappy state of affairs and our provincial branches have discussed the question from various points of view, but we have not done anything to create a better atmosphere. An organized effort on behalf of the Conference to restore harmony between the communities will I am sure have far-reaching results. India belongs to all of us. Her greatness is the result of that culture to which each sect and religion has contributed. Her past glory as well as her present fallen condition are the handiwork of her children. We cannot evade our responsibility by pleading other activities. Some of the work we have done may have value but if we can contribute even in a small measure to the unity of India we shall not have lived in vain.

64. Resolutions Passed by All-India Women's Conference, at its Cocanada Session on 30 and 31 December 1941

Indian Annual Register, 1941, Vol. II, pp. 278–9.

(i) Resolution on 'War and Peace' Passed on 30 December 1941

Resolutions of condolence touching the demise of Dr *Rabindranath Tagore*, and Mrs *Hirabai Tatu* were moved by the chair and passed to-day.

The following resolution proposed by the President and seconded by Mrs *Hannah Sen* on War and Peace was unanimously passed:

'This Conference is of the opinion that permanent peace cannot be achieved except on the principles of freedom and justice equally applicable to all nations and races, that an immediate and fundamental change in the present structure for a post-war world can be constructed only out of policies initiated and operated during the present war, and that Britain's statements regarding her war aims cannot make any moral appeal to the peoples of the world so long as she refuses to alter her present policy in regard to India.

'This conference reiterates its abhorrence of war and declares that if war is persisted in, it must inevitably lead not only to meaningless destruction but also to the deterioration of moral values. It, therefore, firmly believes that human progress is possible only in a world free from military domination and based on the acceptance of international disarmament.'

(ii) Resolution on 'Women's Volunteer Corps' Passed on 30 December 1941

Another resolution which runs as follows was also passed:

'In view of the critical times and the danger of air attacks, such as Rangoon has experienced recently, in all parts of India, this Conference resolves that instructions be issued to all its branches to concentrate in the immediate future on training their members for humanitarian work. This Conference is emphatically of the opinion that the duty of the Branches of All-India Women's Organization is to play their part in developing centres where their members will be trained to help the citizens in moments of crisis.

'Towards this end, it suggests that the following schemes be undertaken and that an AIWCs Voluntary Corps be formed independently of other organizations. Scheme of work—(a) allaying panic among the masses; (b) assisting in the evacuation of women and children from the threatened areas; (c) arranging for first-aid and emergency nursing courses; (d) facilitating the distribution of food and other necessities in the affected areas; (e) helping in protective measures and after-air attacks; and (f) tackling internal disruption.'

Another resolution urging that, in view of the abnormal rise in price of essential commodities and its consequent repercussion, the Governments, both Central and Provincial, should enforce the control of prices without delay, was also passed. The Conference then adjourned.

(iii) Resolution on Civil Liberties Passed on 31 December 1941

The Conference passed a resolution on civil liberties stating 'that in these times when encroachment on national freedom threatens to destroy those inherent individual rights which are so precious a heritage of civilization this Conference associates itself with such organizations all over the world as are striving to preserve the fundamental rights of all human beings, which, among others, are the rights of association, security of property, liberty of speech, freedom of the press, religious worship, street processions and demonstrations, and rights of personal security.' The Conference recorded its emphatic protest against attempts to curtail unnecessarily the civil liberties of Indian people and demanded immediate restoration of all such liberties.

C. CULTURE

65. 'Culture Through Illiterate Eyes': An Article by Professor Benoy Sarkar

The Student, Organ of AISF, December 1940.

In modern times the illiterate has hardly anywhere in East or West been treated by the cultured classes as of any worth whether as an intellectual person or as a moral agent. The present world-situation which is compelling the hyper-civilized peoples to march 'back to the caves' in which the palaeolithic races flourished furnished us with an occasion for re-examining the foundations of this traditional view of science and philosophy regarding the illiterates.

The psychological and ethical values of the human personality deserve to be transvalued in the light of objective realities about men and women based on statistical and comparative investigations. The students of science are called upon to realize that both in East and West, even in those regions which are used to universal, compulsory and free school systems, the railway coolies, plantation labourers, mine-workers, factory labourers, peasants, in other words, those occupational classes which constitute the majority of the 'gainfully employed' do not necessarily possess an intelligence and moral character inferior to those of the persons who academically, professionally and economically belong to the upper ten thousands.

We are speaking here of those men and women who happen to be 'unlettered'. It is to be noted that we are not using the word 'uneducated'. By the word 'unlettered' is to be understood a person who cannot read and write. The distinction that we make here is of profound significance in regard to the appraisal of human 'values'. A man who is unable to read and write is not necessarily uneducated or uncultured. Literacy is an essentially modern phenomenon, but culture and education have been going on in the human race for thousands of years. There were millions of cultured and educated men and women during the primitive, ancient and mediaeval epochs of history even in those regions and among those races where reading and writing were unknown. In other words, human intelligence is not as a rule dependent very much on book-learning and school going. The natural intelligence as well as practical experience of the teeming millions among the illiterates are, therefore, very valuable intellectual assets.

We may now institute a comparison of these illiterates with those who have acquired 'education' in schools and colleges. In other words, let us compare the peasants and mechanicians with school masters, lawyers, magistrates, doctors, journalists and political leaders. There is hardly anybody among the so-called educated classes who would venture to assert that as intelligent persons, that is, as men and women of common sense the cultivators and *mistris* do not understand the problems of their daily life, their family requirements, their village surroundings in the same way as do the school masters, lawyers, religious preachers and so on. Those who know the illiterates intimately admit, as a rule, that the fact of being ignorant in regard to reading and writing does not render them incapable of comprehending the interests of themselves, their families as well as their neighbours. On the other hand, it is also necessary to observe that a school-master, a lawyer or a doctor is after all an expert in one, two or three things of life. These alleged 'educated' persons can claim proficiency only in a very limited sphere of interests. The doctor is not an authority in problems connected with engineering, the engineer in questions involving a knowledge of botany, the chemist in questions of astronomy, and so on. The highest that one can possibly claim for these intellectual classes is that some one is a specialist in a particular line and a certain person in another.

Now, agriculture is also a profession of very great importance. The men and women, therefore, who are experts in agriculture, that is the illiterate cultivators, therefore, deserve the same consideration from the other members of the community as a lawyer does from the engineer and an astronomer from the chemist. Professions are to be respected as professions. The agricultural profession does not demand less intelligence, less dexterity, less shrewdness, less commonsense, less organizing ability than do the so-called learned professions. The same remarks hold good in regard to the profession of the blacksmith, weaver, potter and so on. The *mistri,* the cultivator and others in the so-called manual professions are as educated and cultured, although unable to read and write, as are the lawyers, doctors and the professors.

We are prepared to go a step beyond and assert that as a 'moral person,' that is, as one who as a free agent discharges the duty of his life in regard to himself, his family and his neighbours, the lawyer, doctor or the professor is not necessarily superior to the *chashi* coolie, *major, mistri* and all other manual workers. Let the members of the so-called 'educated class' place their hands on their breasts and compare their character as sons and daughters, as nephews and nieces, as uncles or aunts, as parents, as guardians, with those of the cultivators, factory workers, independent handicraftsmen. It is impossible to assert that the peasant as a class in his moral obligations and sense of duty towards relatives and kinsfolk as well as to the neighbours, lives on a lower plane than members of the so-called educated class. In regard to other functions of moral life also we can institute a comparison and we shall come to the conclusion that in regard to the activities involving money matters, the engineer, the contractor, the school-master, the landowner, the factory director and others do not, as a rule, enjoy an enviable position such as might give points to the members of the unlettered classes. We can take other items of private and public morality and we shall find that in criminal statistics, the cultivator, the artisan and the industrial worker do not figure oftener and in larger numbers, proportionally speaking, than do men and women of the so-called superior classes.

These discoveries, based on the experience of a very large number of public workers and scholars, lead us inevitably to the proposition that the illiterate is not a person who deserves to be differentiated from the so-called educated as an intellectual and moral being. And on the strength of this discovery we are prepared to formulate a doctrine which should counteract the superstition that has been propagated in Europe–America and later in Asia as well as, of course in India, to the effect that literacy should be the basis of political suffrage. Our observations entitle us to the creed that political suffrage should have nothing to do with literacy. The illiterate has a right to political life and privilege simply because of the sheer fact that as a normal human being he has factually demonstrated his intellectual strength and moral or civic sense. The rights of the illiterate ought to constitute in social psychology the foundation of a new democracy. A universal suffrage independent of all considerations as to school going, ability to read and write or other tests should be the very first postulate of social economics.

66. 'Crisis in Civilization' Text of Rabindranath Tagore's Lecture[1] on his 80th Birthday, Santiniketan, 14 April 1941

Indian Annual Register, 1941, Vol. I, pp. 334–7.

'With the advent of this year I have completed my eighty years of life. From the point I have now reached, I am enabled to see in clear perspective the vast stretch of time which I have already traversed. As I take a detached view of the beginning and development of my existence, I feel that in my own life as well as in the psychology of my country, a fundamental cleavage from the past has taken place. Believe me, this change has, within it, a profound cause of personal grief for myself.

'Our direct contact with the larger world of man was linked up with the contemporary history of the English people whom we came to know in those earlier days. It was mainly through their mighty literature that we formed our ideas with regard to these new-comers to our shores. In those days the type of learning that was served out to us was neither plentiful nor diverse, nor was the spirit of scientific enquiry very much in evidence. Thus, our scope being strictly limited, it was the prevailing fashion among the elite of those days to fall back upon the language and literature of the English. Their days and nights were eloquent with the stately declamations of Burke, with Macaulay's long-rolling sentences; discussions centred upon Shakespeare's drama and Byron's poetry and above all, upon the large-hearted Liberalism of the nineteenth century English politics.

'Though tentative attempts were being made for gaining our national independence, at heart, we had not lost faith in the philanthropy and generosity of the English race. This belief was so firmly rooted in the sentiments of our leaders that they hoped that the victor would of himself pave the path of freedom for the vanquished.

Influence of English Literature

'This belief was based upon the fact that English at the time provided the persecuted all over the world with a home and shelter in her hospitable land. Any one who had striven for the integrity of his nation was sure to receive the most warm-hearted welcome at the hands of the English. Thus, in their character I had seen the purest ideal of philanthropy and I was led to set them on the pedestal of my highest respect. The generosity of their nature had not yet been vitiated by Imperialist pride. Their noble nature was to us a source of perpetual admiration. About this time I had the opportunity of listening to the speeches of John Bright, both in and outside Parliament. Even as a boy I was struck with his largeness of heart which overflowed all narrow national bounds and spread its influence far afield. That is why even in these days when England had fallen from her former grace, I remember and cherish my recollections of those other days.

'Certainly that spirit of abject dependence upon the innate goodness of our rulers was no matter for pride. What was remarkable, however, was the wholehearted way in which we gave our recognition to human greatness even when it revealed itself in the foreigner.

'The best and the noblest gifts of humanity cannot be the monopoly of a particular race or country; its scope may not be limited nor may it be regarded as the miser's board, buried underground. That is why the English literature which nourished our minds in the past, even now conveys its deep resonance to the recesses of our heart.

Civilization East and West

'It is difficult to find a suitable Bengali equivalent for the English word 'civilization'. That phase of civilization with which we were familiar in this country was known as "good conduct", in other words, it was mainly a set of ethical codes. Narrow in themselves, these codes originated in a circumscribed geographical area. It was said that the rules of conduct which, for generations together, had held good in that strip of land, Brahmavarta by name, bound on either side by the rivers Saraswati and Drisadvati—were the rules to govern the society in general. In other words, conduct according to what our ancients said, was regulated by a number of traditions and conventions, however heartless or unjust they might have been. That is how a pharisaic formalism gradually got the upper hand of free thought and the ideal of "good conduct" which Manu found established in Brahmavarta steadily degenerated into socialized tyranny.

'During my boyhood days the attitude of the cultured and educated section of Bengal, nurtured on English learning, was permeated with a feeling of revolt against those formal laws of conduct. A perusal of what Rajnarain Bose has written, describing the ways of the educated gentry of those days, will amply bear out what I have said just now. In place of the codes of conduct we accepted the ideal of civilization as revealed in the character of the English people.

Parting of Ways

'In our own family this change of spirit was welcomed for the sake of its sheer rational force and its influence was felt in every sphere of our life. Born in that atmosphere and with my intuitive love of literature, I had naturally set the English on the throne of my heart. Such then was the state of affairs in the first chapters of my life. And then came the parting of ways, accompanied with a painful feeling of disillusion.

'I began increasingly to discover that those who accepted the best truths of civilization disowned them with impunity, whenever questions of selfishness and greed were involved. There came a time when perforce I had to snatch myself away from mere appreciation of literature and contemplation of the great world of civilization. As I emerged into the stark light of bare facts, the sight of dire poverty of the Indian masses rent my heart. Rudely shaken out of my dreams, I began to realize that perhaps in no other modern state had there been such hopeless dearth of the most elementary needs of existence.

'How could I help thinking that it was India that had kept replenishing the coffers of the British people? Such travesty of the human ideal, such aberration in the mentality of the so-called civilized races, such criminal and contemptuous indifference to the crores of helpless Indian people I could never have imagined. I had associated the character of the English race which I had come to respect through their literature.

Benefits of Industrialization Denied

'That mastery over machine through which the English had consolidated their sovereignty over their vast Empire, had been kept a sealed book away from the reach of this helpless country. And yet have we not seen with our own eyes what industrialization did to Japan and how within a short time she achieved wonders? I have also seen how Japan's civilized administration helped to distribute among her own people the fruits of her all-round progress. I have also been privileged to witness the unstinted energy with which Russia was trying to fight disease and illiteracy. Her industry and application has helped Russia in steadily liquidating ignorance and poverty and abject humiliation from the face of a vast continent. Her people have not observed distinction between one sect and another, one class and another. They have spread far and wide the influence of that human relationship which is above and beyond everything petty and selfish. Their astonishingly quick progress had made me happy and jealous at the same time.

'While in Moscow, I particularly liked one characteristic of Soviet administration and that was the pleasing fact that there was no conflict of interests on the score of Communal Award between Muslims and non-Muslims: a truly civilized administration impartially served their common interests.

'I have also seen Iran, newly awakened to a sense of national self-sufficiency, attempting to fulfil her own destiny, freed from the deadly grinding stones of the European Powers. It is significant that her good fortune dates from the day when she finally disentangled herself from the meshes of European diplomacy. With all my heart I wish well of Iran, may she deserve well at the hands of Fate.

'In the neighbouring kingdom of Afghanistan there is much to be desired so far as her education and society are concerned. But the fullest possibilities are there. And that is so, because up till now, she has not succumbed to the benumbing influence of any European Power, vaunting of its civilization. Thus, these countries are now well on their way towards real progress.

Helpless under Dead Weight of Administration

'Under the dead weight of British administration India remained at the very bottom—static in utter helplessness. So great and so ancient a civilization as China, came to be corroded with the fatal addiction to opium into which her people were coerced. This insidious move was doubtless a part of the policy of exploitation of the weak. When we were about to forget the shameful history of how the British had seized a portion of China, we were painfully surprised by another event.

'While Japan was quietly devouring North China, her act of savage aggression was considered a minor incident by the insolent veterans of British diplomacy.

'We have witnessed from this distance how slyly the British statesmen took away the bottom out of the Republic of Spain, and we have also seen how a band of courageous Englishmen chivalrously laid down their lives for Spain. Even though the English had not aroused themselves sufficiently to their sense of responsibility towards China in the Far East, in their own immediate neighbourhood they have not hesitated to sacrifice themselves to the cause of individual freedom. Such acts of heroism reminded me over and again of the true English spirit to which in those early days I had given my whole faith. I do not even want remotely to think of the feeling of amity that then existed between England and Germany. What puzzles me is how within so short a period its imperialist greed could bring about such tragic disintegration in the character of so great a race.

'One day I saw the English as a healthy nation, full of youthful vigour, ever ready to come to the help of those that needed it, and to-day I see them prematurely old, worn out by the plague of evil that has surreptitiously robbed the nation of its well-being.

Divide and Rule Policy

'I had to recount this tragic story of how gradually we came to lose faith in the civilization of the West. Coming back to India, we feel that the blackest of evils that has come in the wake of British administration was much more than the rulers' shameful neglect and apathy to provide the minimum amenities of civilized existence.

'Their failure is nowhere more apparent than in the cruel way in which they have contrived to divide the Indians amongst themselves. The pity of it all lies in the fact that now perhaps they want to lay the blame at the door of our own society. The ugly and savage culmination of Indian history would never have been possible, if communalism and provincialism and lack of mutual faith were not sedulously encouraged to grow to their present vicious form, by some secret conclave holding the highest responsibilities in the system of administration.

'I can never believe that Indians are in any way inferior to the Japanese, either in intellect or in capacity. The fundamental difference between the two lies in the fact whereas India is not only overcome, but is also overwhelmed by the British, Japan had never allowed her interests to be clouded over by the benevolent protectorate of some European Power. Our rulers have established what they call the government of "law and order"—or, in other words, a policeman's administration.

'It is now no longer possible for us to retain any respect for that mockery of civilization which believes in ruling by force and has no faith in freedom at all. By their miserly denial of all that is best in their civilization, by withholding true human relationship from the Indians, the English have effectively closed for us all paths to progress.

'And yet my good fortune has often brought me into close contact with really large-hearted Englishmen. Without the slightest hesitation I may say that the nobility of their character was without parallel—in no country or community have I come across such greatness of soul. Such examples would not allow me to loss faith in the race, which produced them. I had the rare blessing of having Andrews[2]—a Englishman, a real Christian and a true man—for a very close friend. To-day in the perspective of death his unselfish and courageous magnanimity shows all the brighter. The whole of India remains indebted to him for his various acts of charity which distinguished a life-time of dedicated service. But personally speaking, I am especially beholden to him because he helped me to retain in my old age that feeling of respect for the English race with which in the past I was inspired by their literature and which I was about to lose completely. Along with his memory the innate greatness of his people will abide with me for ever. I count such Englishmen as Andrews not only as my personal and intimate friends, but as friends of the whole human race. To have known them has been to me a treasured privilege. They made me believe that English prestige will be saved from every shipwreck if there were more of such Englishmen. Had I not met them, not even the faintest hope would mitigate my despair with regard to the Western nations.

'Meanwhile, the demon of barbarity has given up all pretence and has emerged with unconcealed fangs and teeth, ready to tear up the world and spread devastation. From one end to another the poisonous fumes of hatred defile the atmosphere. This plague of persecution, which lay dormant in the civilization of the West has, at least, roused itself to create havoc and desecrate the spirit of Man. In our present luckless, helpless poverty have we not already seen this world-wide destruction at work? A mortal combat has begun between one power and another, and no one knows what it will bring about in the end.

'The wheels of Fate will some day compel the English to give up Indian empire. But what kind of India will they leave behind, what stark misery? When the stream of their centuries' administration runs dry at last, what a waste of mud and filth will they leave behind them! I had at one time believed that the springs of civilization would issue out of the heart of Europe. And to-day when I am about to quit the world that stubborn faith has gone bankrupt altogether.

'To-day my one last hope is that the deliverer will be born in this poverty-stricken country and from the East his divine message will go forth to the world at large and fill the heart of man with boundless hope. As I proceed onward, I look behind to see the crumbling ruins of civilization, strewn like a vast dung-heap of futility. And yet I shall not commit the grievous sin of losing faith in man. I would rather look forward to the opening of a new chapter in his history after the cataclysm is over and the atmosphere rendered clean with the spirit of service and sacrifice. Perhaps that dawn will come from this horizon, from the East where the sun rises. Another day will come when the unvanquished Man will retrace his path of glory, despite all barriers, to win back his lost human heritage. To believe in the final and irrevocable doom of humanity is certainly a crime, but I shall not be guilty of hugging illusion for reality.

'Finally, I shall proclaim that the day has come when it will no longer be safe for the mightiest of powers to give vent to proud complacence. We must realize the truth of what our sages said:

'By iniquity a man may thrive, may see many a good in life, may conquer his enemies, but iniquity, at last, is sure to overwhelm and destroy him'.

---

[1] This is the authorized English version of Tagore's lecture in Bengali which was read out at Santiniketan on the occasion of the celebration of his 80th birthday by the Visva-Bharati. He passed away on 7 August 1941.

[2] C.F. Andrews.

67. 'The Public Servant'
A Short Story by Yashpal

The Student, Organ of AISF, April 1941.

What blessings did the Congress regime bestow upon the ignorant and helpless population living in remote villages has been hardly the concern of a middle class citizen. Reduction in land rent, postponement of escheats and peasants, debt were all Greek to him. He felt elated in Congress regime because he could walk dauntless into Secretariat buildings in *dhoti* and *chappals* and Sahib's orderly dared no longer snarl at him. Bureaucratic barriers seemed practically pulled down to decently clad persons. The mighty officials turned into docile servants and they could be assailed with a chit or a visiting card. The ministers could be bothered for the mere pleasure of it.

During that period, 'He' had the pleasure of doing this more then once. The Congress ministry vanished over-night through a constitutional process. But that flourish of His Excellency's pen which changed the Govt did not change suddenly the minds of millions of people whom the Congress regime had taught to think in the terms of 'Right'.

'He' had a grievance, which appeared to him legitimate and the result of a misunderstanding on the part of administration. He felt an urge to seek redress. A frank argument must result into right understanding, into a change of heart. And why should not the administration be trusted for reasonable attitude? It was the duty of the citizens to help the administration to arrive at right decisions. He, who shirked it, failed in his civic duty. And were not the Government officials, all of them public servants? And after all, Pantji had not reminded him and his like of the fact in vain!

The orderly, in flowing robes, is the first hurdle of Bureaucracy and its Herald as well, who assigns positions and offers salutations according to hierarchical status. Experience has taught him not to grudge a *salam* where he senses the slightest trace of respectability. For economy of a *salam* is likely to cause him greater embarrassment than the physical trouble of slight bow and a flourish of hand to forehead, before a person of decent appearance. 'He' accepted the *salam* as a matter of due courtesy. Shoved the visiting card into the coarse hand of the orderly and slipped his own hands into the pockets of his trousers to show that he was not uneasy. The orderly disappeared behind one of the chiks in the verandah. Reappeared with the card in hand and a little less courteously informed that the Sahib was just then a little bit too busy; would he mind waiting a few minutes.

'He' was shown to a chair in the side verandah, where he found some others on a similar mission. Visitors like him but with more solicitous looks, offering smiling *salams* to the orderly.

Ten, twenty, thirty minutes passed; a limit for a decent man to wait. 'He' began to fidget in the chair. Many a time the orderly made an appearance in the verandah and he thought it was his turn to enter. But the orderly passed without noticing his uneasiness, looking asquint at courteous smiles of other visitors and whispering brief replies.

It began to seem rather absurd and insulting for the respectable public to wait upon the pleasures of a public servant. How could he keep his aplomb? To counteract the insult of waiting long, 'He' lighted a cigarette, to show that he consented to wait. Not a bad idea to smoke a cigarette in the verandah of a District Magistrate. Not so bad a revenge for the slight of waiting long. Another fifteen minutes and insult began to weigh upon him intolerably.

'Is the Sahib still busy' He questioned the orderly. 'The Sahib! He has left for the Secretariat,' replied the now indifferent orderly.

Must be an urgent call—He consoled himself trying to excuse the Sahib. A public servant has so much to do!

On the second visit, the orderly recognized him and gave a rather cold *salam.*

'Is the Sahib in?'

'In the *gusul.*'

'He' himself moved to the waiting chair in the verandah. After a minute the orderly reappeared with a faded handwritten notice in three languages 'On Saturdays, interviews are granted to Government servants only'....

'What is the convenient day for the Sahib to grant interviews?' He asked to conceal his indignation.

'Any day.'

Monday is naturally a busy day with the accumulated work of Sunday. Therefore, 'He' presented himself at the Sahib's bungalow on the Tuesday following.

Again, a visiting card passed into the hands of the orderly. The orderly, after his manner, took the card in and coming out with a slow and leisurely gait, directed him to the side verandah. To pass the time in useful way, he began revising his case mentally. How to put it before the Sahib in the most effective and brief words. The quiet and spacious verandah facing beautiful beds of flowers was conductive to concentration. He decided anew how to open the conversation and how to conclude it. With a feeling of satisfaction, he looked at his watch—half an hour spent usefully. 'Today it will be over', He told himself shrugging his shoulders to shake off the lethargy that had begun to creep over him due to the cool and soothing breeze of the open space.

At the sound of footsteps at his right, he turned suddenly to ascertain if the orderly was not coming to call him. But the orderly passed by. Once more he went over his case and yawned looking at his watch—another fifteen minutes passed. Every minute passed pronounced his insignificance. Moments of expectation are long but 'He' wished them to be longer still, trying to believe that he has not waited too long.

Full one hour passed...another ten minutes over that. It was very humiliating to acknowledge that 'He' had waited so long unnoticed and may have to wait indefinitely. 'He' must enquire from the orderly, but the words died at his lips...may be the Sahib has forgotten that a visitor was waiting. He mustered up courage.

'Would the Sahib be busy too long yet?'

'The time for interviews is up to 12 noon only.'

He was smitten to the core. To complain of the ill-treatment before the orderly would have been to acknowledge his insignificance. It is his business to dispense *salams* and disappointments according to the disposition of the Sahib with equal indifference. The Deity of public service ensconced in his sanctum defies public approach. The tentacles of his orderlies hold it back. Public has no rights but to obey him.

Disgusted, 'He' threw himself in the tonga waiting out-side the premises. Contemptuous defiance of the public Servant gnawed at his heart. The humiliation, he was trying to swallow, suffocated him. His eyes glistened with red glare, he closed them and felt himself drowning in a bog of humiliation and impotent rage.

The tonga passed by the Assembly Chambers. It recalled to him the days when 'He' walked proudly under the august Dome feeling, '...here our representatives enact laws for us...our men work for our people....' In contrast was looming the contumacious affront of the public servant....

He was wronged...not 'He' alone... the whole of his people...every where in the country...public trampled by public servants...no rights... beseeching favours on bended knees at the alter of the Deity of public servant.

At home the people were satisfied to know that the Sahib was very amicable.

68. 'The Genius of Rabindranath Tagore' K.R. Kripalani's Tribute to Tagore on his 80th Birthday

The Student, Organ of AISF, May 1941.

When the child born 80 years ago, on the 7th day of May 1861, was christened Rabindranath, little could the parents have realized the prophetic significance of the name they chose. Rabi means the sun, and like the sun indeed was the child destined to shed light and warmth on his age, to vitalize the mental and moral soil of his land and to span the arch that divides the East from the West. The child was lucky to have been born in that part of India on which the dawn of renaissance had just broken and in perhaps the most gifted and versatile family in that part, a family bathed in the glow of the new radiance. A succession of remarkable Bengalis had already opened up new lines of vision before their countrymen in religious, social and literary fields. The Poet's father, Maharshi Devendranath Tagore, was himself one of the foremost religious thinkers and reformers of his age, and at least three of his elder brothers were gifted with uncommon sensibility and would have shone, each in his own light, had they not been eclipsed by the terrific blaze of their youngest brother's genius.

When one reviews the last eighty years of the Poet's life, one is struck by a diversity of powerful impressions and feelings. The very first is amazement at the incredible fecundity of his genius. From 1876 when the fifteen-year-old poet's compositions first appeared in print till 1941, there has not been a year in all this length of 65 years, when some new book, sometimes several, has not been written by him. It is calculated that no less than two hundred and fifty volumes, of varying size, have so far been published by him. His songs alone, quite apart from the main body of his poetry, which is not set to music, approximate to two thousand, and each a gem of melody set in exquisite verse. His paintings—a mere by-product of his late years—run to about fifteen hundred. During the current year, which ends with his 80th birthday, a year during the greater part of which he has been in bed, hovering between life and death, no less than eight volumes, five of verse, two of stories and one of boyhood's reminiscences, have been published, not to mention several speeches and addresses, dictated by him, the latest being the one on the Crisis in Civilization, which was read out to the members of Visva-Bharati, when his birthday was celebrated on 14th April at Santiniketan. It is a profoundly moving utterance, wrung out of the very depths of his disillusionment over the prospects of a civilization, on which his generation had built their hopes of a world harmony.

Amazing as such fertility of genius is, what makes it even more so is the endless variety of its creation. There is no field of literary activity in Bengal which has not been explored and enriched by his daring adventures, and many of these were virgin fields which his hands were the first to stir into fruitfulness. Poetry—lyric, narrative, dramatic; short story and novel—social, psychological; drama—tragedy, comedy, opera; essay, satire, allegory—nothing has escaped his hand, unless it be long epic, which the very versatility and the lyric intensity of his imagination has prevented him from undertaking. The critic who loves to label his subject as this or that is left confounded by the unbelievable range of such achievement. What to call him who is unsurpassed as a lyric poet, whose dramatic dialogue have caught in immortal words the profoundest poses of human conflict, the grandeur and subtlety of whose religious verse is like the voice of the Upanishads quivering in accents of human intimacy, whose short stories place him alongside of Chekhov, and who is unique as the author of an inexhaustible stream of songs as exquisite in their melody as in the words which embody it. 'He is a master, a master! cried Turgenev, at a loss for adequate words to describe the genius of Tolstoy. Even so one is dumb-founded with a mixed feeling of wonder and joy at magnificent outflow of Rabindranath's creative activity.

But this feeling in its fullness is possible only when one reads his works in the original language in which they were written. In all true poetry the relation between the thought and the embodying words is so subtle and intimate, that it is impossible to transpose the thought into some other medium without marring or mutilating it. The creative thought is charged with feeling which determines its form. And Rabindranath's poetry, in particular, is so intensely lyrical, so perfect a blend of the musical thought and the musical word, that it must baffle the most gifted translator.

Even the poet's own renderings into English, though they have achieved a new beauty and music of their own, do no more than partial justice to the original. The suggestiveness, atmosphere and the colour of the originals are lost in the process. Only the skeleton of the thought remains, which is responsible for the entirely erroneous impression among readers, familiar only with his English translations, that Tagore's poetry is monotonous and talks only of vague, mystic longings. That is the trouble—the translations can only 'talk', while the originals sing, their breath mingling with the reader's being, their motion transporting him into whatever mood the author was when he wrote them. The first, fine, careless rapture, which makes all the difference, is missing. If Tagore's poetry moves and is convincing even in translation, it only shows how substantial is the kernel of thought in it, how deep the voice of its spirit.

Versatility, vitality, unceasingly creating new modes of expression, 'as old and new at once as Nature's self'—this is the outstanding impression of Rabindranath's genius. These are qualities which by themselves are sufficient to place him alongside of the world's greatest masters of creative expression. But he is more than the mere maker of beautiful forms, more than the mere *saki* of the spirit's immortal wine. He is a great teacher as well, a great lover of humanity, a great crusader on the side of truth and justice. Like Plato he has brought heaven and earth nearer each other, but, unlike Plato, the earth he loves is the habitation of all mankind and not of one particular race or tribe to which he happens to belong. The religion he preaches is the religion of Man, the renunciation he extols is not of this world but of those baser passions of cupidity and hatred which distort man's life on this planet, the freedom he fights for is not the freedom of one people to exploit another, but the freedom of the human personality from all that stifles it, whether it be the tyranny of an external organization or the worse tyranny of man's own blind passion for power. All his life he has pleaded and striven for social justice, for the right of the poor to material well-being, of the citizen to self-government, of the ignorant to knowledge, of the child to natural development, of the woman to equal dignity with man. The world has reason to be grateful to a writer whose genius has been so consistently dedicated to the good of humanity. A great Gardener of the spirit's finest flowering, as great Fruit-gatherer of his people's culture, a great Sentinel of human rights and values, may many more birthdays find him still active and resplendent!

69. 'Cultural Unity in Pre-British India' An Article by Dr Nandalal Chatterji

The Student, Organ of AISF, June–July 1941.

Communal ill-feeling or rivalry as we see in the India of today is in many respects a new feature of Indian life. Even during the worst days of Muslim rule in Mediaeval times the relations between the Hindus and Muslims were decidedly much better than they are under British rule. At time some priest-ridden Sultan or Nawab may have allowed religious persecution or temple-breaking, but this was more an exhibition of royal puritanism and individual religious zeal than an organized civil war between the Hindu and Muslim communities. The communal problem in the sense in which the term is now used was practically unknown in the middle ages.

That there was no wide-spread communal antagonism in the mediaeval times was chiefly due to cultural interchange and fusion. Socially and religiously, the communities may have been isolated from each other, but there was no insurmountable gulf on the cultural plane. Living side by side in the same country, the communities could easily evolve a common platform in the sphere of their cultural life. Even in the religious sphere there was some interaction. Just as Islam wielded its potent influence on Hindu thought and religion, so did Hindu ideas and customs cast its invisible spell on the followers of Islam. Cultural assimilation continued throughout Muslim rule, and some liberal rulers purposely encouraged and even accelerated this process of cultural fusion. Cultural interchange which was responsible for communal harmony in those days was responsible for evolution of a national culture of which both the communities could be equally proud. In literature, fine arts and architecture mediaeval Indian culture underwent a remarkable transformation, and this new Indo–Muslim renaissance was entirely due to cultural unity of the Hindu and Muslim communities.

In Bengal, as in other parts of India, Hindu–Muslim relations were on the whole extremely cordial because of intimate and abiding cultural contacts between the two communities. Even during the reign of Aurangzeb when royal Puritanism was at its height, it was not unusual for a Bengalee Musalman poet to write *Vaishnava* lyrics on the eternal love of Radha and Krishna. Padmavat, the famous Hindi poetical work, was translated into Bengalee by a Musalman poet in the 17th century, and it will come as a surprise to people not conversant with the history of Bengalee literature that his work until its publication in 1893 was preserved and read almost exclusively by Muslims, although the poem containing as it does, long disquisitions on Hindu theology could apparently have no attraction for them. Bengalee Hindu poets likewise exhibited a similar regard for the religious books of the Muslims. A casual instance may be cited in illustration of this point. In the famous 17th Century Bengalee poetical work 'Manasamangala' there is a passage which indicates that a copy of the Quran was placed side by side with other sacred charms in the steel chamber constructed for the protection of the hero. From another old poem, 'Behula Sundari', it appears that the hero who is the son of a devout Hindu commenced his journey abroad on an auspicious day fixed by means of reference to the Quran, and he invoked *Allah* before departure. In a poem written in 1750 by a Musalman poet of Chittagong we read on the other hand that the Muslim hero went to the nether worlds to propitiate the *Saptarsis* or the Seven Sages of Hindu theology. Such instances could be easily multiplied to prove that there was mutual regard as well as tolerance among the Hindu and Muslim poets of Mediaeval Bengal.

The most remarkable example of cultural and religious rapprochement may be found in the emergence of a new inter-communal god, Satya Pir, whom both the communities jointly worshipped with equal veneration. The worship of Satya Pir is a unique contribution of Mediaeval Bengal to the cause of communal peace and understanding. That Hindus and Muslims could meet on a common platform even in the sphere of religion shows the extent to which cultural assimilation could go in this direction. In an old Bengalee work there is an interesting allusion to the propitiation of a Hindu goddess by a Muslim chief who summoned Brahmins to worship her on his behalf. It is worthy of note that Nawab Mir Jafar at the time of his death offered to drink the water of libation poured on the idol of the Goddess *Kiriteshwari*, and a few drops were actually poured down his throat by Maharaja Nanda Kumar. There is plenty of evidence in old Bengalee literature to show that Muslims frequently offered *puja* to Hindu gods and goddesses just as the Hindus often offered *Sirni* at the mosques. Hindus sometimes sought the advice and help of Muslim dignitaries in matters affecting their religion and society. An old document dated 1732 which records the triumph of the *Sahijiya* cult over orthodox Vaishnavism bears the signatures of a number of Muslim witnesses too.

That Hindu astrology was once held in high esteem by the Muslims of Bengal is now generally forgotten. The Muslim rulers did nothing without consulting the astrologers, and the chief astrologer was always present in the court. The 18th century English writer, Scrafton wrote in his 'Reflections on the Government of Indostan' that the Nawabs launched no new scheme without seeking the advice of the Hindu astrologer, and the latter's veto, in the words of this writer, was as effectual as that of a Tribune in the Roman Senate. Mir Qasim who was one of the greatest of the Bengal Nawabs was himself a keen student of astrology, and he is known to have passed his last days mostly in astrological calculations.

In the field of ordinary social life also the Hindu and Muslim communities lived in peace and some observed each other's social observances and festivals. The author of the 18th Century Persian chronicle of Bengal, *Muzaffarnama,* relates how in the time of Nawab Alivardi certain members of the ruling family enjoyed the Holi festival for several days at a stretch in the famous garden of Motijhil. On one occasion no less than 200 reservoirs were used for storing coloured water, and enormous quantities of *abir* (red powder) and saffron were kept ready for the gay revellers. Nawab Sirajuddaulah himself enjoyed the Holi festival in a similar style. Nawab Mir Jafar too took part in the Holi festival, and once when he was at Patna he is known to have celebrated the festival in the company of the entire gentry of the city on a sandy part of the river-bed screened all round with cotton curtains.

Communal harmony in social and cultural life reacted favourably on the relations between the two communities on the political plane as well. Although rivalry was not altogether absent in the political sphere, it was more a result of selfish considerations than of communal zeal or religious considerations. The Muslim Nawabs of Bengal were more often supported than opposed by Hindu nobles and officials. The Seths, the famous Hindu bankers of Bengal, were responsible for the success as also the ruin of more than one Nawab. In the conspiracy against Sirajuddaulah, which led to the rise of British power in Bengal Hindu and Muslim leaders joined alike regardless of communal considerations. In short, on no occasion do we find Hindu aristocrats or officials making a common cause against the Muslims as such. Treachery, intrigue and political maneuver were not uncommon, but in no way can they be ascribed to communal consciousness or communal grouping.

The communal problem of today is rooted in political rivalry, and it will baffle all attempts at solution if the remedy offered is purely of a political nature. That enduring communal harmony is possible only through cultural understanding is a lesson of Indian history which Modern India can ill afford to ignore.

70. Review of the Film *Naya Sansar*

The Student, Organ of AISF, June–July 1941

A Bombay Talkies' Production

Producer	Devika Rani
Director	N.R. Acharya
Story	K.A. Abbas
Songs	'Pradip'
Cast	Ashok Kumar, Renuka Devi, Shahnawaz, Mubarak, Desai, Pithawala, Suresh and others

No vocation perhaps commands as much respect of the student community as that a journalist. And the reason why a journalist or newspaper man is held in high esteem is that he is supposed to be in a position to impart to the people his noble ideals and uphold the great cause of 'Freedom and Truth'. Yet there seems to prevail considerable ignorance and misunderstanding about journalists whose life is considered to be full of gay romance and adventures. Thus, for instance, only a few people realize that a journalist has to contend against heavy odds while pursuing his noble mission; and still fewer people are aware of the fact that more often than not a journalist is forced to compromise his ideals to keep his body and soul together unless of course, he allows himself to be crushed completely under the heel of capitalist forces.

It is this struggle between capitalist forces on one hand and the idealist journalist on the other that lends drama to a journalist's life and social significance to his story. Naturally, in the first motion picture produced in this country on journalist's life we find that its screen-play has for its theme the battle that a conscientious newspaper editor or reporter with definite ideals has to wage against the reactionary forces which endeavour to curb his idealism. For selecting such a theme and depicting vividly the struggle, K. Ahmed Abbas, the author of the story of Bombay Talkies 'Naya Sansar' deserves high tributes.

And this is the outline of that battle. Puran, the hero of the story, is a chief reporter in a newspaper called 'Sansar'. He like the editor of 'Sansar' is imbued with the ideal of bringing to light true facts at all costs. And in pursuance of this ideal Puran is forced to encounter the capitalist clique of Dhaniram in the municipality when he exposes its money-grabbing schemes. In the battle that ensues, Dhaniram and his henchmen form one group against that to Puran and Premanand, the editor of 'Sansar'. And in the very first round Dhaniram succeeds by buying mortgage deed of 'Sansar' machinery and bringing pressure on Premanand to stop further exposures of his vile schemes; but in the second round Dhaniram gets a rebuff when he reads one morning in 'Sansar' a very damaging account of his activities. As a result of this in the third round Premanand compromises and Puran is sacked from 'Sansar' office; apparently Dhaniram is jubilant. But Dhaniram's smile soon fades when in the fourth round of the battle Puran scores many points by exposing Dhaniram and his gang one by one in his own paper 'Naya Sansar' for which he writes matter, composes, prints and even sells its copies. These scenes remind one of the civil disobedience days, when Congress bulletins were published. This exposure has a telling effect and the plutocrat who has agreed to finance Dhaniram's scheme of building a Zoo in the city withdraws his support; thus Dhaniram and his henchmen, thanks to Puran, lose a grand opportunity to earn 'easy' money, To avenge this defeat, in the fifth round of this battle, the unscrupulous Dhaniram plans to murder Puran by knocking him out under a truck belonging to 'Sansar'. The accident is duly staged and Puran is almost knocked out. So far the battle proceeds in the most realistic manner and its very development offers a scathing criticism of the way in which bourgeois money-machinery works to suppress truth for the aggrandizement of a few individuals. But, then the battle suddenly takes a turn. In the sixth round the same plutocrat who withdraws his support to Dhaniram comes on the scene and in quite a melodramatic fashion succeeds in handing Dhaniram and his henchmen over to the police for their plan to murder Puran; moreover, he saves Premanand from the clutches of Dhaniram by offering financial help; and thanks to the plutocrat, Puran who gets away with serious injuries, goes back to his former position as a chief reporter in Premanand's newspaper which is now called 'Naya Sansar' instead of 'Sansar'. And apart from the plutocrat, Puran is obliged to Asha, Premanand's ward and a reporter in 'Sansar' in love with Puran; for it is her helping hand that enables Puran to wage his fight. Incidentally side by side with the battle, develops the romantic triangle of Puran, Asha and Premanand; and as in battle, in this triangle also Puran wins in the end when Premanand himself offers Asha's hand to Puran.

The battle without romance would be as grim and sordid as it is in real life; and in the case 'Naya Sansar' would have resembled much to John Ford's creations and William Dieterle's film-biographies. But as it is, the bitter struggle has been embroidered with plenty of romance and comedy; and 'Naya Sansar' has that refreshingly humorous note that characterizes Capra pictures. This has been done obviously to cater for popular taste and has been done very successfully. But in conceding to the demands of box-office the author has deviated from his progressive stand-point. Here I must first admit that the scenarists Abbas and Mukerjee are to be congratulated for skillfully incorporating romance, and even the dances in the main pattern of the story. But even then the fact remains that the ending is not only hackneyed but inconsistent with the ideology of the author. For it must not be forgotten that while in the first five rounds the struggle between the idealist journalist and the money-machine of capitalists, notwithstanding the development of the romantic triangle, retains its social character, in the final round when the plutocrat takes things in hands, it strikes that individualistic note which more than anybody else Abbas himself has condemned vehemently. But for the plutocrat's intervention the story depicts the struggle not between merely certain individuals but between two forces of society. And hence while one acclaims Abbas for maintaining objective social spirit almost throughout the story, one is constrained to disapprove severely the subjective ending of the picture. Personally, I would have preferred to witness that in the end Puran's Paper is subsidized by people themselves in a co-operative spirit and in recognition of Puran's service to society rather than behold the spectacular way in which the plutocrat condescends to help Puran out of sheer subjective inclination.

Produced by S. Mukerjee, the production of 'Naya Sansar' does credit to all those connected with it. The best production so far from Bombay Talkies Studio 'Naya Sansar' is noteworthy for its realistic settings, for successful montage effects for departure from the 'orthodox' style of photography. The dialogue is spicy, sparkling with wit but at times too elaborate in details; the song–composition has the remarkable flair of poet 'Pradip', and the tunes maintain Bombay Talkies variety. Only 'Ek Naya Sansar' however is an inspiring song and it is bound to be a hit. Performances except that of Dhaniram by Jagannath are of very high standard; while Renuka and Mubarak act brilliantly, it is Ashok Kumar who carries the acting honours; that cigarette and felt-hat has undoubtedly given him a new personality which lends distinction to his performance. Incidentally, the background music leaves much room for comment; in fact, I might venture to suggest the Bombay Talkies executives should compel their music directors to see all Warner Bros films for which Max Steiner writes the music again and again.

The direction is just adequate, and there are no flashes of directorial effulgence to win applause from the critic. But the brilliant screen play more than compensates for the defect. In more than one way the screen-play of 'Naya Sansar' is a model worth emulation by other screen-play writers, but even then this screen-play has its minor flaws. The scenarists in order to explain everything have unnecessarily stressed even insignificant details with the result that the picture rather drags in the first half; then the time allotted to dances is also disproportionate and there are at least two songs which can be cut, without in the least undermining the entertainment value of the picture. Incidentally, somehow, Azurie's dances failed to appeal to me; I thought them just 'hocus-pocus', they too unnecessarily drag the story. Then, I could not understand why the scenarists resorted to hackneyed devices in the concluding sequences, I am of the opinion that both opening and concluding sequences demanded more trimming. And whatever the defects, 'Naya Sansar' like 'Bandhan' owes its success mainly to the brilliant scenario.

Before concluding this review I would take this opportunity to warn Abbas not to be carried away by the popular slogan that bitter truth must be presented with excessive sugar coating to make it palatable for popular taste. Let him not forget that if he sticks to happy endings and adopts Capraesque style he might land himself in the reactionary camp like Capra. Let him also not forget that if he administers sugar coated doses to the people, people might only consume the sugar and throw off the 'bitter' inside. If he keeps his eyes open to these pitfalls, there is no reason why we should not expect from him as progressive and thought-provoking pictures as 'Grapes of Wrath' and 'Emil Zola'.

71. 'All Must have Bread and Leisure': Artist Joins the Fight Poet Harindranath Chattopadhaya Interviewed

The Tribune, 6 October 1941.

'It was five years ago that I first visited the Punjab. Five years are a long time in the life of a nation—a change beyond recognition has taken place. Our mental and spiritual needs have altered and the goal which many of us have been seeking has become clearer and clearer to our ken. As a creative artist I have found with every year my art becoming more and more a part and parcel of a changing social structure for change is an inevitable necessity bearing the certainty of its own fulfilment in the womb of time,' said Harindranath Chattopadhaya when interviewed to-day by the 'Tribune' Representative.

The poet who has written millions of lines in poetry in English, Hindi and Bengali, who began writing poems when he was just eight, to whom waves of poetry come unceasingly on the typewriter, the dramatist par excellence, musician who sings the rapturing melodies at the asking without the excuses of an expert, actor who has few rivals in India, one and all bright with rare intelligence with the beam of youth mounting to a transparent glow as if in his veins ran lightning, gave his somber conclusions upon a large number of questions that were put to him. His judgment was comprehensively balanced and insight most penetrating.

Summoning grace and vivacity, versatility and cleverness to his side, gay, brilliant lovable Harindranath as the Bombay Press fondly calls him, continues, 'Life is rushing towards the goal of its own release through several channels and in several ways. Art is perhaps one of its most urgent methods of life's liberation, for Art is life itself. Viewed in its truest aspect, it bears a mission which is the mission of interpreting to humanity its own meaning hidden within and to itself.'

'But there is the smug and ivory tower attitude towards art and culture?' I asked.

'Yes! Five years back there was', the poet replied, 'but the soul, gradually yet swiftly realizing its oneness with the reality of life and human society has now begun to look upon the ivory tower as on a cramping prison cell. The need of an individual man for its own fulfilment widens into the need of an individual man to become the enchaining of men into the Man'.

'But how in these... struggles, combats and warfares?' I said.

With a smile escaping through the corners of his lips the poet answered: 'Yes! But they are the logical events of man striving to regain his true integrity. Man fights with many weapons, yet Art remains the sternest and the purest weapon, though even to-day there are many who do not realize it'.

'But in our country where even our social and political movements are still unripe. Art cannot take its honoured place as the weapon of the people', I blurted out.

'It will. It is destined to have this sooner or later', he answered, his stainless soul outshining the face, making his simplicity a grace.

'But revolutions are not made by Art', I queried.

'They are. They have been made by Art in other countries and they will be made in our country', he added warming up a little. 'In India', he continued, 'I am hoping that every sphere of Art which is still hopelessly commercialized will begin to master itself, unfetter itself from exploitation and become a world of joy and strength and inspiration to millions'.

'But men are fighting for bread and leisure,' I interrupted.

'They are. But some of us have won too much bread and too much leisure in the capitalistic structure which has given us opportunity for thinking cultural and artistic points. A few among them have come face to face with glory and wonder of life'.

'But it will always be difficult to find such Artists in India'. I said.

'No, though their number is few' the poet answered a little crossly. Otherwise most Artists in India I mean by Artists, writers, painters, musicians and actors—seem to be divorced the veered from all reality except the drab and vulgar reality of their talents as marketable wares, lack of study and contact with the tragedy not only around them but within themselves makes them the tools of the exploiting society and system. 'If any Artist', he warned, 'is to survive anywhere he must draw a daring and fiery radius from the small centre of his own individual living to the circumference, the immeasurable circumference of the life of man evolving rapidly into a new and immortal phenomenon'.

'Do you mean to say that the Artist must be progressive'. I asked.

'Yes the progressive Artist but not in a loose sense.' Harindranath replied as if breathing music. 'We are all talking of progressive poetry and progressive Art but nowhere as yet have they been clearly defined not even in the countries where these phrases were born. We shall be able to define them not from the intellect or by putting the words together from a dictionary but in time with the very evolution of progressive life unfolding its own terms and its own interpretations. In India I have come across a number of Artists and writers who have tried to impress the fact upon me that they were progressive but judging from the bulk of their creation it strikes me that decadence has been mistaken for progress; blatant outspokenness about sex and liquor verging almost on a state of dizzy insanity—a dare-devil use of words and subjects without any artistic or life value passed off for progressive Art and expression. To interpret decadence is to interpret death.'

'But that is because we are slaves'. I said.

'True. We have been enslaved not only by Governments but also by societies which are the reflections of the state of slavery —slaves of depression, slaves of inhibition, slaves of suppressed energies finding no healthy expression in life, for that would mean being outcaste of the very society upon which they are dependent. We must remove this slavery root and branch'.

Equipped with glittering treasures of the mind, Harindranath was driving forward when the clinking of glasses in the adjoining room gave an indication of the dinner hour and the distant jail bell rang monotonously to warn us that night was rapidly drawing closer 'Bread and leisure' I re-called the poet's words and got up to say 'Good Night'.

Biographical Notes

Abbas, Khwaja Ahmad (1914–1987) Born in Panipat, Punjab (now Haryana), grandson of Altaf Hussain Hali, an eminent scholar and Urdu poet; educated at Aligarh Muslim University; journalist, wrote the popular weekly column 'The Last Page' for over four decades; wrote screenplays, scripts and stories for numerous socially relevant popular films, many of them award winners (such as *Naya Sansar, Neecha Nagar, Dr. Kodnis ki Amar Kahani, Awara, Shree 420, Jagte Raho)*; was Director and in some cases producer of many outstanding films (such as *Dharti Ke Lal*, a film on Bengal famine of 1943, *Anhonee, Rahi, Shehar aur Sapna*); prolific writer, novelist, biographer, many of his books were translated into other Indian and foreign languages; awarded Padma Shri in 1969; received many literary awards.

Abdul Qadir, Shaikh (1874–1951) Born at Kasur, Punjab; studied at Foreman Christian College, Lahore; later went to Lincoln's Inn in England to study Law; practised law; Judge, Punjab High Court; Chief Justice of Bahawalpur state; made a mark in literature and journalism; Member, Punjab Legislative Council, 1923; Minister of education, Punjab Government, 1925–26; joined Muslim League and became its President in 1926; Member, Punjab Governor's Executive Council, 1927; Knighted, 1927; Member, Council of Secretary of State for India, 1934–37; Member, Viceroy's Executive Council for a short period in 1939.

Adhikari, Dr Gangadhar (1898–1981) Educated at Bombay; joined Berlin University in 1922 where he secured doctorate degree in Chemistry; came into contact with Indian revolutionaries in Berlin including M.N. Roy; returned to India in July 1928; arrested, tried and imprisoned with 29 other communist and trade union leaders in connection with the Meerut Conspiracy Case in 1929; released in 1933 and was active in trade union work in Bombay in the 1930s; became member of the Polit Bureau of CPI in 1939; was a member of the Central Committee from 1943 to 1950 and from 1953 until 1959, of National Council from 1959 until his death, and of the Central Executive Committee from 1959 to 1971; compiled and edited documents on the history of the CPI up to 1928.

Ahmad, Z.A. (1907–2000) Born in Omar Kot, Sindh; educated at Aligarh Muslim University; went to England in 1928 and studied at the London School of Economics and Cambridge University and got his Ph.D in 1935 for his work on Child and Female Labour in India; active member of a Communist group of Indian students which included K.M. Ashraf and Sajjad Zaheer; joined the Central office of AICC at Allahabad in 1936 in-charge of its economic wing and wrote his short book, considered very important, entitled *Agrarian Labour in India*; Secretary of UP Pradesh Congress Committee from 1933 to 1939; married to Hajira Begum who later became a prominent leader of the women's movement; member of the CPI which was then illegal since 1936; was arrested in August 1940 and after a few months in Agra Central Jail was transferred to Deoli Detention Camp where a large number of communists, socialists and other political prisoners were imprisoned; after release in 1942, involved in the peasant movement; Secretary of CPI in UP; was a member of the Polit Bureau of CPI from 1951 to 1964; CPI MLA in 1962 and MLC in 1978 in UP; CPI member of Rajya Sabha for four terms.

Ahmed, Fakhruddin Ali (1905–1977) Born in Delhi; his father belonged to Assam; after schooling, went to Cambridge, and was called to the Bar at London's Inner Temple; joined Congress, 1931; elected to Assam Legislative Assembly, 1935; Minister of Finance and Revenue in Assam, 1938–1939; jailed during Individual Satyagraha, 1940 and for over three years during Quit India Movement; held important portfolios in Assam Government and later in Union Government; President of India, 24 August 1974–11 February 1977.

Ahmed, Sir Sayyid Sultan (1880–1963) Born in Patna; educated at Gaya and Patna; left for England in 1902 to study Law and was called to the Bar in 1905; practised Law in the Calcutta High Court and later in Patna High Court; appointed judge of the Patna High Court, 1919–20; first Indian Vice-Chancellor of Patna University, 1923–30; Knighted in 1927; attended First and Second Round Table Conferences held in London, 1930–31; attended League of Nations as India's delegate, 1938; was a staunch advocate of support to British war effort; Law Member of the Viceroy's Executive Council, 1941–43; Advisor to the Chamber of Princes, 1945–47; resumed his practice in Patna High Court after independence.

Ajit Singh, Sardar (? –1947) Born at Khatkar Kalan village in the district of Jalandhar in Punjab; deported along with Lala Lajpat Rai to Mandalay in Burma (now Myanmar) for the agitation against increase in land assessment in Punjab, 1907; published revolutionary literature and set up a revolutionary society called Bharat Mata Society; escaped to Iran and went to Rome from there, 1908; shifted to Rio de Janeiro in Brazil during First World War and was in touch with Ghadar Party in San Francisco; went to Europe during Second World War and met Subhas Bose in Italy; after the defeat of Italy, was jailed in Italy and later, after Germany's surrender, in Germany; returned to India after release and died on 15 August 1947.

Ali, Asaf (1888–1953) Born at Delhi; studied at the Anglo-Arabic School and St. Stephen's College, Delhi; enrolled at Lincolns Inn, 1909 and called to the Barr, 1912; returned to India, 1914; began his legal career in Delhi; joined Mrs. Annie Besant's Home Rule League during First World War; participated in the Non-Cooperation Movement and was imprisoned; General Secretary of Congress, 1927; Member, Congress Working Committee, 1930; Member, Central Legislative Assembly, 1934–1946; arrested soon after the Bombay session of the AICC which adopted the Quit India resolution; released on health ground in May 1945; joined the Interim Government as Minister of Transport and Railways, 1946; Member of the Constituent Assembly; represented India at the UN, 1947–48; Governor of Orissa, 1948–52.

Ali, Sadiq (1910–2001) Born at Udaipur; educated at Udaipur and Allahabad University; participated in Civil Disobedience movement, 1930 and detained; took to Constructive Programme in the rural areas of UP and served as Office Secretary of the AICC from 1938 to 1948; took part in Individual Satyagraha and was jailed; associated with Kisan Mazdoor Praja Party which was formed in 1951; rejoined Congress; Member, Rajya Sabha, 1958–70; General Secretary, AICC, 1958–62; associated with Congress (O) after the split in Congress in 1969; Governor of Maharashtra, 1977–80, and of Tamil Nadu, 1980–82; connected with various Gandhian institutions.

Ali, Sir Syed Raza (1882–1949) Educated at Moradabad and MAO College, Aligarh; Member, UP Legislative Council, 1912, 1916 and 1920; took part in the Congress-League negotiations in 1916; Member, Council of State 1921–26; headed two deputations of Muslim members of Indian Legislature to Viceroy in 1922 and 1923 in connection with Turkish question; President, Bombay Session of Muslim League, December 1924; Member, Government of India's deputation to South Africa, 1925–26; Knighted, 1935; Member, Indian Legislative Assembly, 1939 from UP in a by-election caused by the death of Maulana Shukat Ali.

Allah Bakhsh Soomro (1900–1943) Born in Shikarpoor; Sindh; passed matriculation examination, 1918; Chairman, Sukkur District Local Board, 1928; Member, Bombay Legislative Council, 1926–36; formed the Ittehad United Party and elected to Sind Legislative Assembly in 1937; became Premier after the fall of Ghulam Hussain Hidayatullah's Ministry in 1938, from 23 March 1938 to 18 April 1940 and again from 7 March 1941 to 14 October 1942; presided over the Azad Muslim Conference held in Delhi from 27 to 30 April 1940 and condemned Muslim League's Lahore resolution on partition of the country; nominated by the Viceroy to National Defence Council, 1941; renounced Knighthood and the title of Khan Bahadur and resigned from the National Defence Council in September 1942 during Quit India Movement; removed from office by the Viceroy in October 1942; assassinated on 14 May 1943.

Alva, Violet (1908–1969) Educated at St. Xavier's College and Government Law College, Bombay; married to Joachim Alva, her classmate, and involved along with him in the freedom struggle; journalist; Advocate, Supreme Court; jailed with her five months' old child during the Quit India Movement, 1943; elected to Rajya Sabha in 1952 and again in 1960 (Joachim Alva was elected to Lok Sabha for three terms 1952–67 and to Rajya Sabha in 1969); appointed Deputy Minister for Home Affairs; connected with International Federation of Women Lawyers; participated in various international conferences and seminars; the partnership between Joachim and Violet Alva often compared to that between Sidney and Beatrice Webb, the British Fabian Socialists.

Amrit Kaur, Raj Kumari (1889–1964) Born at Lucknow, daughter of Raja Harnam Singh of Kapurthala who had become a Christian; educated in London; a close associate of Gandhiji; his Secretary for many years; arrested during Salt Satyagraha, 1930; imprisoned in 1937 on the charge of sedition; imprisoned again during Quit India Movement; actively involved in the Constructive Programme and various social reform activities; first Health Minister of India after independence.

Anand, Dr Mulk Raj (1905–2004) Born at Peshawar; was a victim of General Dyer's flogging order in India; after graduation from Punjab university went to England for higher education and secured his PhD in Philosophy; drawn to socialism; came into contact with some of the leading British poets, writers and literary critics; earned reputation as a major novelist in English with his novels *Untouchable* and *Coolie* which were first published in England in 1935 and 1936 respectively (and several others later) but banned in India because of the powerful projection of protest of the downtrodden against social and political oppression; returned to India, 1945; associated with the Progressive Writers' Association; was appointed Tagore Professor of Art and Literature at Punjab University, 1962–65; won the Sahitya Akademi Award, and the International Peace Prize of World Peace Council; was awarded the Padma Bhushan.

Andrews C.F. (1871–1940) Born at New Castle, England; priest of Church of England; came to India in 1904 and taught at St. Stephen's College, Delhi; India became his second home; a close friend of Rabindranath Tagore whom he first met in England in 1912; went to

South Africa in 1913 on the suggestion of Gopal Krishna Gokhale to support the struggle of the Indian community against discrimination; met Gandhiji in South Africa and the two became lifelong friends; became a supporter of Indian independence; accompanied Gandhiji to Second Round Table Conference, 1931; supported the cause of workers; associated with the campaign to end untouchability; participated in the temple entry movement; identified with the poor and laboured to end their suffering; Gandhiji gave him the title *Deenabandhu* (friend of the poor).

Arundale, George Sydney (1878–1945) Born in England; educated at Cambridge; came to India as Professor of English in the Central Hindu College, Benaras; married Rukmini Devi, 1920; drawn into Indian politics during First World War; Organizing Secretary of Home Rule League organized by Annie Besant; arrested and interned, 1917; devoted to the cause of promoting National Education; was President of Madras Labour Union; President of Theosophical Society, 1934–1945.

Asaf Ali, Aruna (1909–1996) Born Aruna Ganguli and educated at Lahore; married Asaf Ali, 1928; participated in the Civil Disobedience movement, 1930 and was imprisoned for a year; took part in the Individual Satyagraha, 1941; distinguished herself as an underground leader during the Quit India Movement; President, Delhi Provincial Congress Committee, 1947–48; joined Socialist Party, 1948; formed the left Socialist Group, 1950; joined CPI and became a member of its Central Committee, 1955–58; Mayor of Delhi, 1958–59; rejoined Congress, 1964; associated with Indo-Soviet Cultural Society, Afro-Asian Solidarity Movement and All India Peace Council; President, National Federation of Indian Women and All India Women's Conference; one of the founders of *Link,* a weekly newsmagazine, and *Patriot,* a daily; received the Lenin Peace Prize, 1965 and the Jawaharlal Nehru Award for International Understanding, 1991; was awarded Bharat Ratna posthumously.

Ashraf, Dr K.M. (1903–1962) Born in Daryapur village, Aligarh district; studied at MAO College (later Aligarh Muslim University); left to join Jamia Millia; rejoined Aligarh Muslim University and obtained his MA and Law degrees; went to England and obtained PhD for his thesis entitled *Life and Conditions of the People of Hindustaan, 1000 AD-1550 AD,* a pioneering work in the social history of Medieval India; became a Communist while in England; returned to India, 1932; joined Congress Socialist Party; made in-charge of Muslim Mass Contact Programme of Congress by Jawaharlal Nehru; Member of AICC and spokesman of the Communist group; presided over Calcutta session of AISF, 1939; attended Ramgarh session of Congress, 1940, detained in the Deoli Detention Camp, 1940; released in 1943; one of the leading mass campaigners of CPI; went to Pakistan in 1948 to organize Communist Party there; was arrested in Pakistan, was released and required to leave Pakistan immediately; went to England and resumed his researches in Medieval Indian History; returned to India in the mid-1950s and taught History at Kirori Mal College of Delhi University; went to Berlin as Guest-Professor, at Humboldt University, 1960; President of Medieval India section of Indian History Congress Session, Aligarh, 1960; died in Berlin.

Azhar, Mazhar Ali (1895–1974) Born in Batala, Punjab; educated at Government College and Law College, Lahore, joined Khilafat Movement, 1919 and jailed for a year and a half; one of the founders of Ahrar Party, 1929 and later its General Secretary and President; Member of AICC and General Secretary of Punjab Provincial Congress Committee; imprisoned for participating in Civil Disobedience Movement; Member, Punjab Legislative Assembly, 1924–1926 and 1934–45; opposed the demand for Pakistan; joined Forward Bloc, 1946; Migrated to Pakistan after independence and started his legal practice; poet and author of many books in Urdu.

Badruddoja, Syed (1900–1974) Studied, after schooling in Murshidabad, at Calcutta Madrasa, Presidency College, Calcutta and Calcutta University; practised law; associated with Krishak Praja Party and Muslim League; Councillor, Calcutta Corporation, 1940–43; Mayor, 1943–44; Member, Bengal Legislative Assembly, 1940–46; Member, Bengal Legislative Council, 1946–47; President, Independent Democratic Party; Member, West Bangal Legislative Assembly, 1948–52 and 1957–62; Independent Democratic Party Member, Lok Sabha, 1962–67 and 1967–70.

Bahadur Yar Jung, Nawab Mohammad Bahadur Khan (1905–1944) Born in Hyderabad in an influential family and educated at Madrasa, Darul-Uloom; founded Majlis-i-Tubligh-i-Islam, 1927 to counter Arya Samaj activities in Hyderabad; was associated with the Khaksar Movement for a few years; founded Majlis-i-Ittehad-ul-Muslimeen in Hyderabad State with the blessings of the Nizam; attended Muslim League sessions; founded the All India States Muslim League, the most powerful Muslim communal organization, in 1940 and was its President.

Bajaj, Seth Jamnalal (1889–1942) Born in a village in Jaipur State; met Gandhiji in 1915 and came to be known as his fifth son; Chairman, Reception Committee, Nagpur Session of the Congress, 1920; was imprisoned for 18 months for leading the Flag Satyagraha, Nagpur, 1923; active in Anti-untouchability work; gifted Segaon village (later renamed Sevagram) to Mahatma Gandhi, 1936; elected President, Jaipur State Praja Mandal, 1938, and played an important role in the Praja Mandal movement; was interned in Jaipur in 1939 for Praja Mandal activities; arrested during Individual Satyagraha, 1941.

Bajpai, Girija Shankar (1891–1954) Educated at Muir College, Allahabad, and Oxford; joined Indian Civil Service; was Knighted; Member, Viceroy's Executive Council for Education, Health and Lands, 1940; the first Indian Agent General of British Indian Government to the United States, 1941–1947; Foreign Secretary, 1947–1952; Governor of Bombay, 1952.

Bandyopadhyaya, Tara Shankar (1898–1971) Distinguished Bengali novelist; jailed during Non-Corporation Movement and Civil disobedience Movement; President, Anti-Fascist Writers' Association, 1941; author of 56 novels including *ganadevata* (1942) and 25 collections of short stories; Member, West Bengal Legislative Council, 1952–60; was awarded Padma Shree, 1962 and Padma Bhushan, 1968; received numerous literary honours, including Sahitya Akademi Award and Jnanpeeth Award; was President, Bangiya Sahitya Parishad.

Banerjee, Dr Suresh Chandra (1887–1961) Born in Chandpur, East Bengal, studied at Calcutta Medical College and became a doctor in 1914; active in the Home Rule Movement; joined War Commission, 1917 but resigned after the end of the War; joined the Non-Cooperation movement; imprisoned, 1930–32, during Civil Disobedience Movement; active in the trade union movement from 1933; President, All India Trade Union Congress, Nagpur session, 1938 and Bombay, 1940; participated in Quit India Movement and was imprisoned for three years; elected to Bengal Legislative Assembly, 1936 and 1946; associated with the formation of Indian National Trade Union Congress (INTUC), 1947; Labour Minister in Congress Government in West Bengal headed by Dr P.C. Ghosh; left Congress in 1951 to join Krishak Praja Mazdoor Party which later merged with Socialist Party; elected to West Bengal Legislative Assembly, 1957.

BANERJEE, PURNIMA (1911–1951) Active, like her sister Aruna Asaf Ali, in the freedom movement; imprisoned on several occasions including for offering Individual Satyagraha, 1941; joined Congress Socialist Party; took part in Quit India Movement; Member, UP Legislative Assembly; Member, Constituent Assembly.

BARDOLOI, GOPINATH (1890–1950) Born in Roha, Nowgong District, Assam; studied History and Law at Calcutta University; attended the special session of Congress at Calcutta, 1920; joined Non-Cooperation Movement, 1921 and gave up his legal practice; a front-rank leader of Congress in Assam; led the Congress in the Assam Assembly; Chief Minister of the Coalition ministry formed in October 1938; resigned when Congress decided to quit Ministries after the outbreak of the Second World War; arrested during the Individual Satyagraha Movement; imprisoned during Quit India Movement; Chief Minister of Assam when Congress formed the government after the War; Member, Constituent Assembly.

BARI, ABDUL (1889–1947) Born in Koilwar in Shahabad (now Bhojpur) district of Bihar; did his MA from Patna University; participated in Khilafat and Non-Cooperation Movement; served as a professor at Bihar Vidyapeeth; Secretary, Swarajya Party in Bihar, 1923; also member of Indian Independence League formed by Jawaharlal Nehru and Subhas Bose; elected to Bihar Legislative Council but resigned his seat and participated in the Civil Disobedience Movement; elected to Bihar Legislative Assembly, 1937 and became Deputy Speaker; Chairman of the Reception Committee of the Patna Conference, 1934 where Congress Socialist Party was formed; founded the Tata Workers' Union, Jamshedpur, 1936 and emerged as a leading figure in the trade union movement in Bihar; was critical of Congress ministry in Bihar for neglecting workers' interests; played an important role in the peasant agitations; elected President of Congress in Bihar in 1946 and accompanied Gandhi in the healing tours of riot-affected areas in Bihar; killed on 28 March 1947 due to, it is believed, mistaken identity.

BASU MRINALKANTI (1886–1957) Born at Fatehpur, Jessore (East Bengal); had his early education at Jessore, and collegiate and university education in Calcutta; actively participated in the anti-partition movement at Jessore, 1905; joined the Swarajya Party, 1923; Founder Secretary of the Indian Journalists' Association, 1922; played an important role in building up the Trade Union Movement.

BASU, JYOTI (1914– —) Born in Calcutta; educated at Presidency College, Calcutta; studied Law in England; practised at Calcutta High Court; joined CPI, 1940; Member of Central Committee, later National Council and Executive Committee of CPI; Member, Bengal Legislature, 1946–47; Member, West Bengal Legislative Assembly, 1947 onwards; leader of opposition in West Bengal Assembly with CPI(M) since its formation in 1964 following split in CPI; member of its Polit Bureau till 2008; Chief Minister of West Bengal, 1977–2000.

BEDI, B.P.L (1909–93) educated at Lahore, London and Berlin; President, Punjab Congress Socialist Party Conference, 1937; Joint Secretary, All India Kisan Sabha, 1938; President, Punjab Trade Union Conference, Rawalpindi; joined Communist Party of India while in detention at Deoli Camp; active in peasant movement; brought out with Freda Bedi and others *Monday Morning*, a weekly.

BEDI, FREDA (1911–1977) English by birth; married B.P.L Bedi; associated with *Monday Morning;* jointly edited with B.P.L. Bedi Karl Marx's *Letters on India,* Lahore, 1937; published, *Bengal*

Lamenting, 1944; converted to Buddhism; founder of Tilokpur, a Buddhist monastery in Himachal Pradesh.

Bhardwaj, R.D. (1908–48) Born in Boodhpur village in Meerut district, UP; started taking interest in freedom struggle from early school days; drawn to communist movement after meeting P.C Joshi when a student at Allahabad University, 1928; closely connected with the trade union activities in Bombay, Ahmadabad and Ajmer; imprisoned, 1934; became a member of the Polit Bureau of the Communist Party of India along with P.C. Joshi and Ajay Ghosh after his release in 1936; leading organizer of the Communist Party in Hindi region; joined Congress and was elected to AICC; took part in Ramgarh Congress while still underground; arrested and imprisoned in 1941; released in 1943 on health grounds having contacted tuberculosis; arrested on 4 April 1948 while convalescing at Delhi and died four days later.

Bhargava, Dr Gopi Chand (1889–1966) Born at Sirsa in Hissar district, Punjab (now in Haryana); educated at Hissar and DAV College, Lahore; MBBS from the Lahore Medical College; entered politics under the guidance of Lala Lajpat Rai; imprisoned during the Non-cooperation Movement, Salt Satyagraha and Quit India Movement; President, Lahore Congress Committee; Member, Punjab Legislative Council, 1927; resigned, 1929; gave up practice, 1935; Member, Punjab Legislative Assembly, 1937–40, 1946–51 and 1957–64; Premier, East Punjab, 1947–49; Chief Minister, Punjab, 1950–51; left Congress, in 1952 but returned in 1957; Minister, Punjab, 1959–64; President, Harijan Sevak Sangh and Gandhi Smarak Nidhi, Punjab, and Punjab Khadi and Gramodyog Sangh.

Bhave, Vinayak Narahari (1895–1982) Popularly known as Vinoba Bhave; born at Gagoda, Kolaba district, Maharashtra; gave up formal education after schooling; had knowledge of many Indian languages as well as Arabic, Persian and French; came into contact with Gandhiji; sent by Gandhiji to Wardha to set up an ashram, 1921; participated in the Nagpur Flag Satyagraha, 1923 and Salt Satyagraha, 1930 and was imprisoned; chosen by Gandhiji to be the first to court imprisonment during Individual Satyagraha, 1940; active in the temple entry movement and other anti-untouchability programmes; launched the Bhoodan movement for dealing with the problem of landlessness; set up the Paunar ashram; dedicated himself to the upliftment of people in the villages.

Bhopatkar, Laxman Balwant (1880–1960) Born in Poona (now Pune); an eminent lawyer; practised in Poona; MLA (on Swarajya Party nomination) in Bombay Presidency, 1923; took part in Civil Disobedience and underwent imprisonment; courted arrest, 1939 during Bhaganagar Satyagraha; worked for the abolition of caste and untouchability; veered towards Hindu Mahasabha in later years; author of numerous works, including on Law; popularly known as Annasaheb Bhopatkar.

Bose, Aurobindo (1921–1988) Son of Suresh Chandra Bose; politically active from student days; expelled from college for organizing a strike; associated with the Students' Federation; arrested in 1941 and detained for four years in Campbellpur, Punjab; passed BA (Hons.) examination while in prison and MA after his release; became a leading figure in the student movement after independence; joined Congress and was twice elected to West Bengal Legislative Assembly; associated with Indian National Trade Union Congress (INTUC).

Bose, Dwijendra Nath (1916–1989) Younger of the two sons of Satish Chandra Bose; educated at Calcutta; active in AISF as a student leader; helped in undercover liaison work between Subhas Bose and revolutionaries in other parts of India; involved in Subhas Bose's escape from Calcutta, January 1941; detained for five years thereafter in various jails, released in late 1945; associated with Forward Bloc after independence.

Bose, Sarat Chandra (1889–1950) Barrister and elder brother of Subhas Bose; a legal luminary of Calcutta High Court; a leading figure of the Congress in Bengal and member of Congress Working Committee, 1937–39; leader of Congress Party in Bengal Assembly; was privy to Subhas Bose's plans; kept as security prisoner outside Bengal till the end of the war; joined Interim Government but was dropped during the reshuffle when the Muslim League members joined; tried along with Suhrawardy the creation of independent united Bengal; left Congress, founded Socialist Republican Party; elected to West Bengal Legislature, 1949 in a bye-election defeating Congress candidate.

Brelvi, Syed Abdullah (1891–1949) Born in Bombay family belonged to Bareli in UP; studied at Elphinstone College, Bombay; joined *Bombay Chronicle*,1915; became and remained Editor of *Bombay Chronicle*, a leading nationalist newspaper from 1924 until 1949; was Chairman of Bombay Branch of All India Nationalist Muslim Party which was devoted to fighting against communalism; Member, Congress Working Committee, 1930; imprisoned twice during Civil Disobedience Movement; one of the founders of All India Newspaper Editors' Conference and its President during 1943–45; attended UN Conference on Press Freedom, 1948.

Caveeshar, Sardul Singh (1886–1963) Born at Amritsar; graduated from Punjab University; launched the *Sikh Review* in 1913; President of All-India Sikh League, 1921; actively associated with Congress in Punjab and was its Secretary; imprisoned for five years during Non-Cooperation Movement; Member, Congress Working Committee, 1928; imprisoned during Civil Disobedience Movement; resigned from Congress Working Committee when Congress decided to accept office in 1937; was a close associate of Subhas Bose and became President of Forward Bloc; was detained in Lahore Fort in 1942 where he was brutally tortured.

Chaddha, Tilak Raj (1914–1998) Prominent leader of Congress Socialist Party in Punjab; Lecturer in Economics, DAV Degree College, Rawalpindi, 1937; arrested in connection with anti-war activities, 1941 and kept in Deoli Detention Camp; elected to the Punjab Legislative Assembly while in jail, 1946; released later in 1946; resigned from Congress and Punjab Legislative Assembly, 1948; ceased participation in political activities and was Principal of a College in Yamunanagar in Haryana, 1958–79.

Chakravarti, Amiya (1901–1985) Born in Calcutta and educated at Calcutta, Hazaribagh, Patna and Oxford; taught at various places in India and abroad; a leading poet in Bengali language; was literary Secretary to Rabindranath Tagore; delegate to UNESCO in 1955–1957; won several awards including UNESCO Literary Award, Sahitya Akademi Award and Waturmull Award.

Chatterjee, Amarendra Nath (1880–1957) Born at Uttapara in the district of Hooghly of West Bengal; came into contact with revolutionaries during the anti-partition agitation in Bengal; established a Sramajibi Sangha (organisation of labourers), 1908 which was used as secret meeting place of revolutionaries; arrested in connection with the Howrah Conspiracy Case and went underground after his release; was arrested in 1923 and kept in detention till 1926; was elected to Bengal Legislative Assembly in 1929 but resigned in 1930 to participate in Civil Disobedience Movement and was arrested; joined the 'Congress Jatiya Dal' founded by

Pandit Malaviya, 1935; was a member of the Central Legislative Assembly, 1937–1945; joined Radical Democratic Party of M.N Roy.

Chattopadhyaya, Harindranath (1898–1990) Born in Hyderabad; brother of Sarojini Naidu; educated at Cambridge; distinguished poet, published several volumes of his poems; keenly interested in films, music and painting; acted in many films; married Kamaladevi Chattopadhyaya; socialist in his political outlook; Member, Rajya Sabha, 1952; awarded Padma Bhushan, 1973.

Chattopadhyaya, Kamaladevi (1903–1988) Born in 1903 at Mangalore; educated at Mangalore, Madras (now Chennai) and London (Bedford College and London School of Economics); married Harindranath Chattopadhyaya; actively participated in the freedom struggle; underwent several jail terms; one of the founders of Congress Socialist Party and presided over its session at Meerut in 1936; member of AICC and Congress Working Committee, 1946; a front-rank leader of the women's movement; President of All India Women's Conference, 1944; played an important role in reviving and promoting crafts; Vice-President, World Crafts Council; awarded Magasaysay for Community Leadership, 1966; Desikottama awarded by Viswa-Bharati University, 1970; Padma Vibhushan, 1987; Founder President, Indian Cooperative Union; Chairman, All India Designs Centre.

Chaudhuri, Rohini Kumar (1889– —) Born at Barpeta, district of Kamrup, Assam, received school education in various parts of Assam and higher education mainly in Calcutta; practiced as an Advocate; Member, Assam Legislative Assembly, 1927–45; Minister, Government of Assam, 1937–38, 1939–41 and 1945–46; Member, Central Legislative Assembly, 1946, Constituent Assembly, 1947–50 and Provisional Parliament, 1950–52; elected to Lok Sabha, 1952; worked for the rehabilitation and relief to the displaced persons after partition.

Chhatari, Nawab Muhammad Ahmad Said Khan (1888–1982) Born at Baghpat, Meerut, in a rich Zamindar family; educated in Mohammadan Anglo-Oriental Collegiate school, Aligarh; was granted the title of 'Nawab', 1915 and received various other titles from the British government; renounced these titles shortly before independence; elected to UP Legislative Assembly unopposed in 1920 and was a Minister in UP, 1923–25; Governor of UP for a few months in June-August 1928 and again in 1933; nominated to attend Round Table Conferences; Member of the Viceroy's Executive Council for a few weeks in 1932; was awarded the honorary Degree of Doctor of Laws by the Aligarh Muslim University, 1933; was a member of Muslim League for some years but did not play any active role in its activities; President, Executive Council of Nizam of Hyderabad, 1941–46; was associated with Aligarh Muslim University as Pro-Chancellor and Chancellor for several years.

Chhotu Ram (1881–1945) Born in small landowning family in Rohtak; educated at Lahore and Agra; founder President of All India Jat Mahasaba, 1906; Editor *Jat Gazette,* 1916–24; joined Congress in 1916 but resigned 1920 over the issue of Non-Cooperation Movement; elected to Punjab Legislative Assembly, 1923 and in all subsequent elections; Knighted by the British government and generally referred to as Sir Chhotu Ram; one of the founders of Unionist Party; served as a Minister in Punjab in Unionist Party Government, Minister for Agriculture, 1924–25, Education, 1925–27, Development, 1937–41 and Revenue, headed by Sikander Hayat Khan and after his death in 1942 in the government headed by Khizer Hayat Khan.

Das, Neelakantha (1884–1967) Born in village Sriramchandrapupre in Puri district of Orissa; studied at Ravenshaw College, Cuttack, and in Calcutta for his MA and Law; joined Calcutta University Post-Graduate Department as a Lecturer in Oriya and Comparative Philology; joined the Non-cooperation Movement in Orissa and was imprisoned, 1923; joined Swarajya Party, courted arrest, 1932 and 1933; Member, Central Legislative Assembly for two decades; President of Orissa Provincial Congress Committee after the death of Gopabandhu Das, 1928; left Congress in 1940 and was supporter of British war effort; formed a Coalition Government with the Muslim League in Orissa in 1941; leader of the Independent People's Party in Orissa Legislative Assembly after independence; Pro-Chancellor of Utkal University; awarded Padma Bhushan, 1960; author of many scholarly works in Oriya.

Datta, Bhupendranath (1880–1961) Born in Calcutta; joined the Bengal Revolutionary Society, 1902 and became editor of the *Yugantar*, an organ of revolutionaries in Bengal; arrested, 1907 on a charge of sedition and sentenced to one year's rigorous imprisonment; escaped to USA after his release and studied at University of New York and Brown University; obtained PhD degree from Hamburg University in Germany, 1923; Secretary, Indian Independence Committee, Berlin during First World War and was in close touch with the Ghadar Party in America; corresponded with Lenin; returned to India in 1925 and joined Indian National Congress; elected member of AICC, 1929; closely connected with peasant organizations and many trade unions; was twice President of All-India Trade Union Congress; an ardent critic of rituals and caste system; author of many books.

Desai, Bhulabhai (1877–1946) Studied at Elphinstone College, Bombay; taught English and History at a College in Ahmedabad and studied Law; started his legal practice in Bombay, 1905; associated with Liberal Party; joined Congress, 1930; Member, Congress Working Committee, 1934–35; imprisoned for one year, 1932; was elected to Central Legislative Assembly, 1934 and 1935; became leader of the Congress Party in the Assembly; imprisoned in December 1940 for offering the Individual Satyagraha; opposed the Quit India Resolution; evolved with Liaquat Ali Khan a formula for the formation of Interim Government, known as Desai-Liaquat Pact, 1945 (the Pact was denounced by Congress); the leading defence counsel for the INA prisoners at the Red Fort Trial towards the end of 1945.

Desai, Mahadev (1892–1942) Born in the village Saras, Surat district; graduated from Elphinstone College, Bombay, 1910; got Law degree, 1913; met Gandhiji in August 1917 and soon after became his Secretary and remained in that position till his death; participated in Champaran Satyagraha, 1917, Bardoli Satyagraha, 1928 and Salt Satyagraha, 1930, and suffered imprisonment; also arrested in 1921 when he was editor of *Independent* started by Motilal Nehru at Allahabad; returned to Ahmadabad after his release in 1923 and looked after the editorial work of *Navjivan;* 1924–1928; toured the country with Gandhiji and accompanied him to Round Table Conference in London in 1931; worked for the *Harijan* weekly and frequently wrote on major issues; arrested and sent to Aga Khan Palace, Poona, 1942 along with Gandhiji where he died on 15 August 1942; author of many books in English and Gujarati.

Desai, Morarji (1896–1995) Born in a village in Surat district; graduated from Wilson College, Bombay; joined Bombay Provincial Civil Service until 1930 when he resigned and joined Civil Disobedience Movement; imprisoned thrice during 1930–34; member, AICC, 1931; Member, Bombay Legislative Assembly, 1937; Minister in Bombay Government, 1937–39; offered Individual Satyagraha; imprisoned for three years during Quit India Movement;

Chief Minister, Bombay, 1952–56 and Commerce & Industries Minister, 1956–58; Finance Minister, Government of India, 1958–63; Finance Minister and Deputy Prime Minister, 1967–69; after the split in Congress, 1969, he was leader of Congress (O) in Parliament; after the defeat of Indira Gandhi, 1977 became Prime Minister.

DESHMUKH, DR G.V. (1883–1963) Born at Wadhona, Wardha district, Maharashtra; educated at Nagpur, Bombay and London; associated with Tilak, Savarkar and Dr Moonje; joined Swarajya Party; elected to Bombay Legislative Council, 1932, 1937 and 1946; Member, Indian Legislative Assembly, 1937–47 and played an important role in passing important legislation relating to women's rights; Professor of Operative Surgery, Grant Medical College, Bombay.

DEVI, PRABHAVATI (1906–1973) Born at Darbhanga, Bihar; daughter of Braj Kishore Prasad, one of the early associates of Gandhiji; married Jai Prakash Narain; stayed at Gandhiji's Ashram at Sabarmati when Jaya Prakash Narain was away in the United States for higher studies; took the vow of celibacy at the Ashram; jailed several times; shifted from Bhagalpur Jail in 1944 to serve Kasturba Gandhi in the Aga Khan Palace at Poona; founded Mahila Charkha Samiti, 1940 and Kamala Nehru Shishu Vihar, Patna, 1954.

DEVI, SARALA (1904–1986) Born in Cuttack; received early education in the village Pathasala and then up to middle school in Cuttack (family was not in favour of female education); greatly influenced by Rabindranath Tagore, to whom she was intimately known and by Gandhiji; one of the first women in Orissa to break the shackles of tradition and join the nationalist movement, along with her husband; was active in the freedom movement from 1920 till the achievement of independence; Member, Orissa Legislative Assembly, 1937–1944; contributed significantly to the welfare and emancipation of women; connected with Orissa Branch of All India Women's Conference; author of several books.

DEY, BISHNU (1909–1982) Studied at Calcutta University; Professor of English at Presidency College, Calcutta and Maulana Azad College, Calcutta; a leading Bengali poet; influenced by Marxism; associated with Progressive Writers' Association and Indian People's Theatre Association; winner of Sahitya Akademi Award, 1966, and Jnanpeeth Award, 1971.

DUNICHAND, LALA (1870–1945) Born in Lahore; educated at Lahore and, later in England where he studied law; practised Law at Lahore; presided over the Punjab Provincial Congress session held at Amritsar, 1918; prominent leader of the agitation against the Rowlatt Act, 1919; arrested and sentenced to transportation for life; released and attended the Amritsar session of the Congress, December 1919; participated in the Non-Cooperation Movement, 1921; arrested during Quit India Movement, 1942 but was released on health grounds on the condition that he would not leave Lahore and take part in political activities.

FAROOQUI, MUQIMUDDIN (1918–1997) Born at Amrehta in Saharanpur district, UP; joined St. Stephen's College, Delhi University, 1934; passed MA in History, 1940 and started studying Law; expelled from the University and his MA degree forfeited for organizing students' strike; MA degree was restored to him at a special convocation of Delhi University, 1989; President of Delhi Students' Federation, 1940; General Secretary, All India Students' Federation, 1941; arrested during Quit India Movement, 1942 and underwent one year's imprisonment in jails in Punjab; had joined Communist Party of India (CPI) as a student and also the Congress Socialist Party which was legal; Secretary, CPI in Delhi almost all through from 1945 to 1971; married Vimla Kapoor, a leading figure in the Women's Movement, 1954; from 1971, he worked at the headquarters of CPI and was a member of its Secretariat from 1981; Editor of *Party Life*.

Foot, Michael (1913– —) Born in Plymouth, England; educated at Oxford and was president of the Oxford Union; joined Labour Party, 1935; Member, the House of Commons, 1945–1955, 1960–1992; belonged to the left wing of the Labour Party; Minister in Labour Party Government, 1974; leader of the Labour Party, 1980–83; friend of India and supporter of India's independence; connected with many newspapers and editor of the left-wing *Tribune* for many years; supported the cause of freedom everywhere; condemned British-French-Israeli invasion of Egypt, 1956; advocate of nuclear disarmament and a leader of the Campaign for Nuclear Disarmament (CND) in Britain.

Gadgil, N.V. (1896–1966) Born in Ratlam, Madhya Pradesh; educated at Bombay, Baroda and Poona; practised Law in Poona; joined Congress, 1920; participated in all movements launched by Congress and was in jail for five years; President, Maharashtra Provincial Congress Committee, 1931; Member, Central Legislative Assembly from 1935; Member, Parliament after Independence; Cabinet Minister, Union Government, 1947–52; Governor of Punjab, 1958–62; Vice-Chancellor, Poona University, 1964.

Gandhi, Feroze (1912–1960) Born in Bombay, in a Parsi family; moved to Allahabad at a young age and completed his education there; came in contact with the Nehru family; joined the movement against Simon Commission, 1928 and was arrested and beaten by the police; met Gandhiji, 1931; went to London School of Economics for further studies; came in contact with V.K Krishna Menon at the India League and persons with Leftist views; influenced by socialist ideas; organized medical aid for China in war against Japanese aggression; imprisoned during Quit India Movement; Editor of *National Herald,* 1946–1950; one of the founders of Indo-Soviet Friendship Society, UP; elected to Lok Sabha from Rae Bareli, 1952 and 1957; exposed major scandals involving Ramkrishna Dalmia and Haridas Mundha and their collaborators in the government and bureaucracy.

Gandhi, Indira (1917–1984) Born at Allahabad; daughter of Jawaharlal Nehru and Kamala Nehru; educated at various places in India and Europe, including Viswa-Bharati and Oxford; while in England, joined the India League, 1938; came into contact with socialist intellectuals and leaders; also in touch with Indian students many of whom had been drawn to socialist ideology; returned to India, 1941; married to Feroze Gandhi, 1942; imprisoned for about eight months during Quit India Movement; associated with relief activities during communal riots at the time of partition; Member, Congress Working Committee, 1955; President, Congress, 1959; Minister, Information and Broadcasting, 1964 in Lal Bahadur Shastri's Cabinet; Prime Minister of India, 1966; adopted a radical socio-economic programme; nationalization of banks and abolition of princely privileges; challenged senior Congress leaders known as the Syndicate; won a massive majority in 1971 elections; war with Pakistan and emergence of independent state of Bangladesh (December 1971); declared Emergency on 26 June 1975; defeated in elections held in March 1977 and Congress rule replaced by rule of the Janata Party; became Prime Minister again in January 1980 after the Congress Victory in elections; Chairperson of the Non-Aligned Summit held in Delhi, 1983; made efforts to deal with the challenge of Khalistani terrorism, "Operation Blue Star", June 1984; assassinated by her security guards, 31 October 1984.

Ganguly, Bepin Behari (1887–1954) Born in village Baganda in Hooghly district of West Bengal; left his studies to participate in the anti-partition movement in Bengal, 1905; was arrested during First World War for plotting to get arms from Germany; joined Non-Cooperation Movement and was imprisoned; took part in the Salt Satyagraha; maintained contact with underground revolutionaries; arrested in 1930; detained at Deoli Detention Camp; imprisoned again in Quit India Movement; spent over 20 years in prison; involved in various social welfare activities after release in 1947; one of the founders of Indian National Trade Union Congress (INTUC); elected to West Bengal Legislative Assembly, 1952.

Gazdar, Muhammad Hashim (1898–1968) Born in a landlord family; studied engineering at Karnal and Poona; Member, Bombay Legislative Council, 1933–36; elected to Sind Legislative Assembly; founder of Sind United Party, 1937–46; Member, Sind Legislative Assembly, 1937–46; a leading figure in Sind Muslim League; Member, Council of All India Muslim League; Vice President, Sind Provincial Muslim League, 1941–43; Mayor, Karachi, 1941–42; re-elected, 1946; Member, Pakistan Constituent Assembly.

Ghate, S.V. (1896–1970) Born in Mangalore; came into contact with S.A. Dange and others in Bombay; took part in the conference in Kanpur, 1925; became Jt. General Secretary, later General Secretary of the Communist Party of India; one of the chief organizers of the famous textile workers' strike in Bombay, 1928, also one of the founders of the Girni Kamgar Union, Bombay; arrested in connection with Meerut Conspiracy Case, 1929 and released, 1933; brought out *New Age* monthly, 1936–1939; was arrested, 1940 and kept in Deoli Camp and Vellore and in other jails till 1944; Member, Central Committee, CPI, 1943 when still in prison; was arrested, 1948 and was released, 1950; Treasurer of CPI, 1953; remained with the CPI after the split in the Communist Party, 1964.

Ghaznavi, Abdul Halim (1876–1953) Born at Tangail in Mymensingh district in East Bengal; educated City College School and St. Xavier's College, Calcutta; a devout follower of Surendranath Banerjea; joined Congress, 1905 and was active in the Swadeshi Movement even suffering heavy losses; left Congress after the Surat split, 1907 and remained independent liberal; Member, Central Legislative Assembly, 1926–1945; delegate to the Round Table Conferences; was Knighted, 1935; industrialist and businessman; President, Muslim Chamber of Commerce, 1939–40 and Indian Chamber of Commerce, 1945–46; Chairman of India Steamship Company for several years.

Ghosh, Ajay (1909–62) Born in Mihijam (now Chittaranjan) in Bengal; after schooling in Kanpur where his father, a well-known physician, was settled joined University of Allahabad; joined Hindustan Socialist Republican Association (HSRA) and was closely associated with Bhagat Singh, Chandrashekhar Azad and other leaders of HSRA; was arrested, 1929 and was tried along with Bhagat Singh and others in the Second Lahore Conspiracy Case but released due to lack of evidence; involved in trade union movement in Kanpur, 1931 and was arrested; joined Communist Party of India, 1933 and became member of its Polit Bureau; played a prominent role in promoting the cause of National Front for the achievement of independence; detained in Deoli Camp, was released, 1941 on health grounds (had contacted tuberculosis); was imprisoned, 1948 after CPI adopted what is referred to as a 'sectarian line'; General Secretary of CPI, 1951 till his death and gave a new orientation to the policy and programme of CPI.

Ghosh, Benoy (1917–1982) Born at Calcutta; an eminent Bengali Marxist historian, journalist, sociologist and anthropologist; began his career as a journalist, associated with dailies like *Jugantar, Basumati* and *Swadhinata* and periodicals like *Bharat, Forward Block;* resumed his academic studies, moving away from CPI in 1948; well known for his historical writings.

Ghosh, Prafulla Chandra (1891–1983) Born in Malikanda village in the Dacca district; educated at Dacca College and Calcutta University; drawn into Anusilan Samiti, 1910 which he left, 1913; attended Calcutta Congress, 1917 and 1920; took up constructive work during Non-Cooperation Movement; was arrested during Salt Satyagraha campaign in Midnapore, 1930; supported Pattabhi Sitaramayya for Presidentship of Congress against Subhas Bose; was arrested during Quit India Movement; organized Krishak Mazdoor Party which merged with Socialist Party to form Praja Socialist Party, 1953; Member, West Bengal Legislative Assembly, 1956–1966; Chief Minister of West Bengal, 1947–48, and 1967–1969.

Ghosh, Sarat Chandra (1883–1958) Born at Kakardha village in Barisal district of East Bengal; involved in religious pursuits and preached Samanvayavad, religion of synthesis; taught in a school in Barisal for many years; participated in Non-Cooperation Movement; was arrested for sedition and sentenced to six months' imprisonment; underwent imprisonment again during Salt Satyagraha, 1930 and Quit India Movement, 1942.

Gidwani, Dr Choithram (1889–1957) Born in Hyderabad, Sind; drawn to the freedom struggle at an early age; met Gandhiji in 1915; one of the organizers of Congress in Sind; President of Sind Pradesh Congress Committee since 1920; imprisoned in 1922 for 18 months; imprisoned during Salt Satyagraha and Civil Disobedience Movement; elected to Sind Legislative Assembly when Sind became a separate province, 1937; jailed during Quit India Movement; opposed to partition; devoted himself to the task of rehabilitating refugees in India.

Guha, Biresh Chandra (1904–1962) Born at Banaripora in Barisal district of East Bengal (now in Bangladesh); made significant scientific contributions in the fields of Biochemistry and Nutritional Science; had been expelled from the Presidency College for joining Non-Cooperation Movement and for being sentenced to a month's imprisonment; after doing MSc at Calcutta University, went to London and obtained PhD and DSc degrees of London University; worked for Bengal Chemical and Pharmaceutical Works; Professor of Applied Chemistry in Calcutta University; adviser in the Union Government.

Gujral Inder, Kumar (1919– —) Born at Jhelum, now in Pakistan; educated at Lahore; involved in political activities from his student days; President of Lahore Students' Federation; participated in Quit India Movement and underwent imprisonment; moved to Delhi after independence; Vice-President, New Delhi Municipal Committee, 1950–1964; Member, Parliament, 1964–1976; Minister, Union Cabinet, 1972–76; Ambassador to USSR, 1976–1980; left Congress in the mid-1980s and joined Janata Dal; Minister, External Affairs in V.P. Singh's Ministry and again in the H.D. Devegowda-led United Front government; Prime Minister of India on 21 April, 1997 for eleven months.

Habibur Rahman Ludhianwi, Maulana (1892–1956) Born at Ludhiana, Punjab; educated at Madrasas of Punjab and Dar-al-Ulum, Deoband; one of the founders of the Jamiat-ul-Ulema, 1929 and of Ahrar Party; close to Congress; participated in nationalist activities; took part in the Azad Muslim Conference, Delhi, 29 April 1940; opposed Muslim League's demand for Pakistan; a leading theologian inclined towards socialist ideas.

Haldane, J.B.S. (1892–1964) Distinguished scientist; Fellow of Royal Society; academic career spanned Cambridge, London University, Indian Statistical Institute; was Member, Editorial Board of British Communist Party's daily, *The Daily Worker,* 1940–49; decided to settle in India later.

Haroon, Haji Abdoola (1872–1942) Born at Karachi; Joined Congress, 1917; President, Sind Provincial Khilafat Committee; joined Muslim League and was its President in Sind; was Knighted; elected to Bombay Legislative Assembly, 1923–26, and to Central Legislative Assembly, 1926–42.

Harvani, Ansar (1916– —) Born in Barabanki in UP; educated at Lucknow, Agra, Aligarh Muslim University; one of the founders of All India Students' Federation and its General Secretary in 1938; worked for *National Herald* and *Amrita Bazar Patrika*; follower of Subhas Bose; joined Forward Bloc and was member of its National Executive, 1939–48; was imprisoned in 1940 and again in 1942; released in 1946; President, All India Youth League, 1946–52; Member, AICC, 1946–52; elected to Lok Sabha, 1957 and 1962; resigned from Congress, 1977.

Hess, Rudolf Walter (1894–1987) Hitler's political Secretary, 1920; most important leader of the Nazi Party after Hitler and Goering; flew to Britain to negotiate peace shortly before Germany invaded Soviet Union; was arrested; tried at Nuremberg as war criminal and sentenced to life imprisonment; died in Spandau Prison in Berlin.

Hidayatullah, Sheikh Ghulam Hussain (1879–1948) Born at Shikarpur in Sind; educated at Karachi and Bombay; began political activities in 1904; Minister, Bombay Presidency, 1921–1928; Member, Bombay Governor's Executive Council, 1928–34; agitated for separation of Sind from Bombay; was Knighted in 1933; Member, Sind Legislative Assembly, 1937–47; first premier of Sind, 1937–38; joined Muslim League, 1936 and resigned soon after; rejoined, 1942 and headed Muslim League Ministry, 1942–47; not in favour of partition until 1946; Governor of Sind after partition, 1947–48.

Huq, A. K Fazlul (1873–1962) Born in Chakhar village in Barisal district of East Bengal; educated at Calcutta University; started legal practice in Barisal, moved to Calcutta to practise at the High Court there; joined Muslim League and was its Secretary in Bengal, 1913–1916; President, All India Muslim League, 1918; General Secretary, Indian National Congress, 1918–19; represented Indian Muslims at Round Table Conferences; Member, Central Legislative Assembly, 1934–36; broke with Muslim League and formed Krishak Praja Party, 1936; became Prime Minister of Bengal, 1937–43, first with a coalition Cabinet including the League, later the 'progressive coalition' without the League; moved the 'Pakistan' resolution at Lahor session of Muslim League, 1940; expelled from the League by Jinnah, 1941; dismissed by Governor, March 1943; replaced by Nazimuddin as the head of Muslim League government; rejoined Muslim League, 1946; Advocate General of East Pakistan, 1948–53; formed Krishak Sramik Party, 1954; Chief Minister of East Pakistan for a few weeks, 1954; Home Minister of Pakistan, 1955; Governor of East Pakistan, 1956–58.

Hydari, Akbar (1869–1942) Born in Bombay in a business family; graduated from Bombay University; served in Hyderabad State in various capacities from 1907; attended Round Table Conference, 1930 as leader of Hyderabad delegation; President of the Executive Council, Nizam's Dominion, 1939; President, South Indian Mahomedan Education Conference; President, All India Mahomedan Educational Conference; was Knighted and made Privy

Councilor, 1928; was awarded Degree of Doctor of Civil Law by Oxford University, 1930; Member, Viceroy's Executive Council, 1941 for Information and Broadcasting.

Ibrahim, Hafiz Muhammad (1889–1964) Born at Nagina in Bijnore district of UP; educated first at a madrasa and later at Aligarh Muslim University; elected to UP Legislative Assembly as a Muslim League member, 1937; joined Congress and became a Minister in Congress Government in UP; Minister in UP for a number of years after independence; Minister in the Union Government, 1958; Governor of Punjab after losing the Lok Sabha election in 1963.

Iftikharuddin, Mian (1907–1962) Born in Lahore; was educated in Aitchison College, Lahore and Balliol College, Oxford; returned to India in 1932; joined Congress, 1935; Member, Punjab Legislative Assembly, 1937–46; President, Punjab Congress, 1940–45; President, All India Students' Federation Conference, Patna, 31 December 1941–1 January 1942; attended All India Azad Muslim Conference, Delhi, February–March 1942; organized support for Soviet Union of the Nazi invasion; imprisoned for two years during Quit India Movement; joined Muslim League, September 1945; elected as Muslim League Member of Constituent Assembly, 1946; Minister for Rehabilitation in West Punjab (Pakistan), 1947; expelled from Muslim League, 1950; along with Shaukat Hayat Khan and others, formed Azad Pakistan Party, 1950; elected to Pakistan's National Assembly, 1955; Editor, English daily, *Pakistan Times,* and Urdu daily, *Imroz;* joined National Awami Party, 1957 with Khan Abdul Ghaffar Khan.

Ismail, Sir Mirza Muhammad (1883–1959) Born and educated in Bangalore; entered Mysore Government Service as an Assistant Superintendent of Police, 1905; Dewan of Mysore, 1926–41; implemented many developmental projects in the State; attended the Round Table Conferences held in London, 1930–32; was Knighted; Prime Minister of Jaipur, 1942–1946; was appointed Prime Minister, Hyderabad State, August 1946 at the request of the Nizam but resigned office, May 1947; acclaimed as an administrator; opposed to the partition of the country.

Ispahani, Mirza Abul Hassan (1902–1981) Educated at St. John's College, Cambridge; called to the Bar at the Inner Temple, 1924; joined family business of M.M Ispahani Ltd. at Calcutta, 1925; elected to Calcutta Corporation, 1933, Deputy Mayor, 1941–1942; Member, Bengal Legislative Assembly, 1937–1947; Member, Working Committee, All India Muslim League, 1941–1947; President, Muslim Chamber of Commerce, Calcutta, 1945–47; Member, Pakistan's Constituent Assembly, 1947; Pakistan's first Ambassador to U.S.A, 1947–1952; High Commissioner for Pakistan in the UK, 1952–1954; Pakistan's Ambassador to Kabul, 1973–1974.

Iyengar, S. Srinivasa (1871–1941) Born at Ramanathapuram; educated at Madras; set up his legal practice in 1898; appointed Advocate General of Madras, 1916, resigned, 1920; gave up his legal practice; President of Congress in Tamil Nadu; President of Gauhati session of Congress, 1926; elected to Central Legislative Assembly, 1926; Deputy Leader of the Swarajya Party in the Assembly; formed Independence League, 1928 and was its President with Jawaharlal Nehru and Subhas Bose as Secretaries; retired from active political life in 1930.

Jayakar, Dr M.R. (1873–1959) Born and educated at Bombay; studied Law in England; practised as barrister in Bombay High Court; Member, Bombay Legislative Council; Leader of Swarajya Party, 1923–26; Member, Central Legislative Assembly and Deputy Leader of the Nationalist Party, 1926–30; attended the three Round Table Conferences in London; Judge, Federal Court of India, October 1937–December 1938; played, on occasions, the mediator's role along with Tej Bahadur Sapru, between British Government and nationalist leaders; Vice-Chancellor, Poona University, 1948–56.

Josh, Sohan Singh (1896–1982) Born in Chetanpur village in Amritsar district of Punjab; joined the Akali Movement, 1921; imprisoned for three years; joined Bhagat Singh's Navjawan Bharat Sabha; founder of Workers' and Peasants' Party in Punjab, 1928; arrested in the Meerut Conspiracy Case in 1929; sentenced to seven years' imprisonment; joined Congress and was elected to Punjab Legislative Assembly, 1937; imprisoned during Quit India Movement; active in the CPI and in the Kisan movement; remained with CPI after the split; was one of the leading figures in CPI till his death.

Joshi, N.M. (1879–1955) Born at Goregaon in Kolaba district of Bombay province and studied at Deccan College, Poona for his graduation; taught in schools for many years; joined Servants of India Society, 1909; Secretary, Bombay Social Service League since 1911; studied problems of workers and started welfare centres for workers; attended the first conference of the International Labour Organization (ILO), 1919 and represented India at many ILO conferences later; one of the founders of All India Trades Union Congress and its Secretary till 1929; Member, Royal Commission on Indian Labour, 1929–32; attended as government nominee, Round Table Conferences; Member, Central Legislative Assembly, 1921–26; played a leading role in legislation regarding labour welfare; was a liberal in politics; effectively took up various national issues in the Assembly.

Joshi, P.C. (1907–1980) Born in Almora (then in UP); passed MA, Allahabad University, 1928; took Law degree, 1929 while in jail; came in contact with Marxists as well as nationalist revolutionaries during student days; involved in organizing secret underground Communist groups; arrested in connection with the famous Meerut Conspiracy Case, 1929 and the youngest of the 32 accused; released along with others, 1933; played an important role in bringing together Communist groups in different parts of the country with a functioning centre; became CPI's General Secretary; Communists under his leadership joined the Congress, and functioned as part of National Front; after German invasion of Soviet Union, CPI under P.C. Joshi's leadership adopted the slogan of People's War and opposed the Quit India Movement; played a central role in bringing writers, artists and theatre people close to the Communist movement and in mobilizing them in anti-imperialist, anti-fascist and pro-common people struggles; Joshi was replaced as General Secretary of CPI in 1948 when CPI's Calcutta Congress adopted what is generally referred to as 'ultra-Left' line; was expelled from the Party; was readmitted, 1951 and subsequently to various bodies of the Party; was editor of Party weekly, *New Age;* remained with CPI after the split in 1964; later, due to failing health, could not play an active political role; was engaged in writing the history of the Communist movement in India as a Fellow in Jawaharlal Nehru University; was married to Kalpana Dutt, the famous Chittagong revolutionary.

Kabir, Humayun (1906–1969) Born in Komarpur village, Faridpur district, East Bengal; educated at Calcutta and Exeter College, Oxford; President of the Oxford Majlis and Secretary of the Students' Union, 1930; taught Philosophy at Calcutta University and Andhra University; President, All India Muslim Students Conference, 1938 and All India Students Congress, 1944; also involved in trade union activities; Member, Bengal Legislative Council, 1936–45 and 1946–48; deputy leader of the Krishak Proja Party, 1937–45; associated with Abul Kalam Azad, acted as his Secretary at the Simla Conference, 1946; Joint Educational Adviser from

1948 and later Secretary, Ministry of Education, Government of India; Member, Rajya Sabha, 1956; was member of Lok Sabha, 1957–69; Minister of State first for Civil Aviation and then for Scientific Research and Cultural Affairs, 1957–62; Minister, Petrokum and Chemicals, 1963–1966; resigned from Congress and joined Bangla Congress in 1967; played an important role in the formation of United Front government in West Bengal, 1967; author of many books of poetry, fiction, biographies, philosophy and culture; drafted Maulana Azad's *India Wins Freedom* based on Maulana Azad's views narrated by Azad to Kabir.

Kamath, Hari Vishnu (1907–1982) Born at Mangalore; took his BSc.(Hons.) degree from Madras University; went to England and successfully competed for the Indian Civil Service examination; joined the Service in 1930, had occasional tiffs with his British bosses; chose Independence Day, 26 January 1938, to resign from the Service; met Congress President Subhas Chandra Bose in March 1938 and worked as his Personal Secretary; also joined the National Planning Committee as its Secretary, December 1938; left Congress, April 1939; Organizing Secretary of Forward Bloc formed by Subhas Bose; played a leading role in the first Left Consolidation meeting in Bombay, June 1939; played a leading role in the Anti-Compromise Conference at Ramgarh, March 1940; arrested for the first time, April 1940 in Bombay for his anti-war activities and sentenced to one year's imprisonment; detained from January 1942 to September 1945; elected to Constituent Assembly; Member, Provisional Parliament, March 1950–1952; lost in 1952 Lok Sabha election but won in 1955 and 1962 as a PSP member.

Kapoor, Malik Jeevan Lal (1897–1982) Born at Dera Ismail Khan (NFWP); educated at Lahore and Cambridge; President, Cambridge University India Majlis, 1920; Bar-at-Law, Inner Temple, 1922; Advocate, Lahore High Court, 1922–47; joined Congress, 1922; participated in Civil Disobedience Movement and was imprisoned for two months, 1930; President, District Congress Committee, Lahore, 1930–31; after independence, became Judge, Punjab High Court, 1949–57 and of Supreme Court, 1957–62; Chairman, Law Commission, 1961–68; Member, Minorities Commission, 1965–66.

Karim, Rezaul (1900–1993) Nationalist Muslim Congressman from Birbhum district, Bengal; author of many books in English and Bengali on the syncretic tradition in the sub-continent; against the 'Pakistan' proposal.

Karnik, Vasant Bhagvant (1903–1985) Educated at Bombay and Poona; participated in Non-Cooperation Movement; first General Secretary of Radical Democratic Party set up by M.N Roy; prominent leader of Indian Federation of Labour; Director, Labour Education Service, 1956; Editor, *Radical Humanist;* author of many books on trade union movement and biographies of M.N. Roy and N.M. Joshi.

Kartar Singh, Giani (1901–1974) Born in Lyallpur district, West Punjab; closely associated with Sikh religious leaders and Singh Sabha movement; General Secretary of Shiromani Akali Dal for many years; took part in the Non-Cooperation Movement and in the agitation against Simon Commission; prominent role in "Guru Ka Morcha" and in the agitation against Maharaja of Nabha State; Member, Punjab Legislative Assembly, 1937; broke away from Congress, 1941; put forward the demand for a sovereign Sikh State in case India's partition was agreed to.

Khaliquzzaman, Choudhry (1889–1973) Born at Chunar in Mirzapur district of UP; educated at MAO College, Aligarh, 1907–16; joined Congress, 1916; elected President of the Lucknow

Congress Committee, 1920; gave up legal practice during Khilafat and Non-Cooperation Movement; arrested, 1921; joined Swarajya Party, 1923; Secretary, Muslim Nationalist Party, 1929; Member, Central Legislative Assembly, 1930 and Congress Parliamentary Board, 1934; Member, UP Legislative Assembly, 1937; unhappy with Congress over Ministry formation in UP, 1937; joined Muslim League and revitalized it in UP; Member, Muslim League Working Committee, 1938–47; seconded the Lahore Resolution of Muslim League, 1940; Member, UP Legislative Assembly, 1946–47 and Constituted Assembly, 1946–47; migrated to Pakistan, 1948; Governor of East Pakistan, 1953–54, but played little significant role in Pakistan's politics.

Khan Bahadur Ahmed Bux (— —) The Raja Bahadur of Khallikote; attended the Conference of non-Congress members of the Orissa Legislative Assembly held in January 1941. In the same year he became member of the Orissa Provincial Democratic Union. He was also a member of the Provisional Committee, which was formed to discuss matters of the formation of the non-Congress Coalition Ministry in Orissa, 1941.

Khan Sahib, Dr (1883–1958) Born in a village Uttamanzai in Peshawar district, NWFP; brother of Khan Abdul Ghaffar Khan; studied medicine in Bombay and left for England, 1909 for higher medical studies and got his MRCP there; returned to India, 1920; joined Indian Medical Service; resigned, 1921 when his unit was ordered to proceed to Waziristan for action against the Waziris; got actively involved in the freedom struggle after the firing on in the Qissa Khwani Bazar, Peshawar, 1930; arrested and sentenced to three years' rigorous imprisonment in Hazaribagh Jail; released in 1934 but not allowed to enter his province or even Punjab; elected to the Central Legislative Assembly from his province in absentia as a Congress nominee; elected to the NWFP Legislative Assembly, 1937 and headed the first Congress Ministry in the Province, 1937–39; became Congress Chief Minister of NWFP again, 1945; dismissed a week after the partition and thrown into prison; after about six years in Pakistani jail, was released and joined Central Cabinet of Pakistan in 1954 as Minister of Communications; Chief Minister of West Pakistan, 1955; assassinated in Lahore, 9 May 1958.

Khan, Abdul Qaiyum (1901–1981) Born in Swat state; studied at Peshawar, Aligarh and London; started legal practise at Peshawar, 1926; Congress Member, Central Legislative Assembly, 1937–42; elected deputy leader of Congress Party in NWFP Assembly, 1942–45; joined Muslim League, 1946; staunch supporter of the demand for Pakistan; after partition, became Chief Minister of NWFP, 1947–53 by replacing Dr Khan Sahib's Ministry; President of Pakistan Muslim League, January 1970; following a split in the party, founded Pakistan Muslim League (Qayyum); Member, National Assembly, 1970 and was a Minister in Z.A. Bhutto's Government, April 1971-January 1977.

Khan, Hakim Abdus Salam (— —) Well-known freedom fighter of North-West Frontier Province; associated with the Indian National Congress; son of Khan Nur Muhammad Khan, a landlord and Chief of Achakzai tribune of Gulistan; an associate of Khan Abdul Ghaffar Khan; President, District Congress Committee, Hazara, 1939–40; arrested for anti-war activities and detained at Deoli Detention Camp, 1940–41.

Khan, Maulana Zafar Ali (1873–1956) Born in Sialkot district, Punjab; educated at Mission High School, Wazirabad, Mahindra Singh College, Patiala and MAO College, Aligarh; entered Nizam's service as translator in Urdu in Translation Bureau; Editor of *Zamindar,* an Urdu newspaper; was associated with both Muslim League and Congress; supporter of Khilafat

Movement, under house arrest, 1914–1919; was imprisoned, 1920–1925; joined Ahrar Party; sentenced to two years' rigorous imprisonment, 1930; left Congress, 1932 and later also the Ahrar Party; formed the Ittihad-i-Millat Party, 1935; active in Muslim League from 1937; Member, Central Legislative Assembly 1937–46; staunch supporter of the demand for Pakistan.

Khan, Maulvi Tamizuddin (1889–1963) Born at Khankhanpur in Faridpur district of East Bengal; educated at Presidency College and Calcutta Law College, Calcutta; joined Muslim League, 1915; took part in Non-Cooperation Movement, 1921 and was jailed for 14 months; elected to Bengal Legislative Council, 1926 and was re-elected, 1930; Secretary of Proja Party; Muslim League member in Bengal Assembly, 1937; Minister in Bengal Cabinet, 1938–41, and again during 1943–45; elected as Muslim League member of Central Legislative Assembly, 1946; staunch supporter of the idea of Pakistan; after partition, was member of Pakistan's Constituent Assembly, and its Deputy President and, after Jinnah's death, became its President; was unanimously elected Speaker of Pakistan's National Assembly, 1962.

Khan, Muhammad Zafrullah (1893–1985) Born at Sialkot, Punjab; educated at Lahore and Lincoln's Inn, London; practised Law at Lahore High Court; Member, Punjab Legislative Council, 1926–31; Delegate to the Round Table Conferences, 1930–32; President, Muslim League, 1931; Member, Viceroy's Executive Council, 1932 and 1935–41; was Knighted, 1937; Judge, Federal Court of India, 1941–47; Minister, Foreign Affairs, Government of Pakistan, 1947–54; Pakistan's Permanent Representative at the UN, 1961–64; President, UN General Assembly, 1962; Member, International Court of Justice, 1954–61, 1963–70 and its President, 1970–72.

Khan, Sikandar Hayat (1892–1942) Born in 1892 at Multan in western Punjab; educated at MAO High School, Aligarh and University College, London; was Honorary Recruiting Officer during World War I; Member, Punjab Legislative Council, 1921 and 1926; Member, Governor's Executive Council, 1929, and Revenue Member, 1930; Governor of Punjab, 1932–34; was Knighted in 1933; elected as Unionist member to Punjab Legislative Assembly, 1937; Premier of Unionist Party government, Punjab, April 1937-December 1942; favoured cooperation with the government in War effort; Member, National Defence Council; as Premier followed a non-communal policy and sought the cooperation of all sections of the population in his task; Member, Working Committee, Muslim League.

Kharak Singh, Baba (1868–1963) Born at Sialkot in Punjab; graduated from Punjab University, 1881; Chairman, All India Sikh Education Conference, 1912; came into contact with Gandhiji at Amritsar session of Congress, 1919; closely associated with Dr Saifuddin Kitchlew and other Congress leaders; leader, Gurudwara Reform Movement; presided over the Lahore session of the Sikh League, 1920 which was attended by Ali Brothers, Gandhiji and other nationalist leaders; gave a call to the Sikhs to support Congress and Non-Cooperation Movement; was imprisoned, 1921 and 1923; was arrested, 1935 for agitating against the Communal Award; was imprisoned, 1940–41 during Individual Satyagraha and again, 1944; Founder-President of Shiromani Akali Dal; formed Central Akali Dal due to differences with some Akali leaders on communal question; was opposed to the policy of some Akali leaders in supporting British war effort.

Khare, N.B. (1882–1969) Born at Nere village in Kolaba district, Bombay; studied at Lahore Medical College; joined Congress, 1919; Member, Central Legislative Assembly, 1935–37;

Chief Minister, CP & Berar, 1937–38; expelled from Congress, blamed Gandhiji for it; opposed to Congress attitude to the War; joined Viceroy's Executive Council, 1943–46; Prime Minister of Alwar State, 1947–48; joined Hindu Mahasabha, 1949 and became its President till 1951; Member, Lok Sabha, 1952–57; self-professed 'communalist', wanted the country to be named 'Hindu Rashtra'.

Khuhro, Muhammad Ayub (1901–1980) Born in Akil village in Larkana district, Sind; Member, Bombay Legislative Assembly, 1924–37; active in the movement for separation of Sind from Bombay; Member, Sind Legislative Assembly, 1937 onwards; Minister, 1942–44 and 1946–47; nominated as Member, Muslim League Working Committee, 1942; Chief Minister of Sind after partition, 1947–48, and again 1951–1953 and 1954; Defence Minister of Pakistan for a short period in 1955.

Kripalani, Acharya J.B. (1888–1982) Born at Hyderabad (Sind); studied at Karachi, Bombay and Poona; Professor at Muzaffarpur College, Bihar, 1912–17; associated with Gandhiji during Champaran Satyagraha, 1917, becoming his ardent follower; Professor, Benaras Hindu University, 1919–20; Principal, Gujarat Vidyapeeth founded by Gandhiji, 1922–27; took part in all movements started by Congress; General Secretary of Congress, 1934–46; jailed nine times, including during the Quit India Movement; became President of Congress, 1946–47; Member, Constituent Assembly; left Congress and founded Krishak Mazdoor Praja Party (KMPP) which in 1951 merged with Socialist Party to form Praja Socialist Party (PSP); Chairman of PSP till 1954 when he resigned; Member, Lok Sabha, 1952–62, 1963–71.

Krishnamachari, T.T. (1899–1974) Studied at Madras Christian College; built an extensive business in Madras; also worked for Lever Bros. as their Indian adviser; Member, Madras Legislative Assembly, 1937–42; elected to Central Legislative Assembly, 1942; joined Congress in the same year; Member, Constituent Assembly, 1946; Member of the Drafting Committee of the Constitution; Member, Parliament, 1952–67; joined Union Government as Minister for Commerce and Industry, 1952–56, Finance 1956–8, Minister without portfolio, 1962–63, Minister of Finance, 1963–65.

Kultar Singh (1918–2004) Younger brother of Bhagat Singh; associated along with his brother Kulbir Singh with Nawjawan Bharat Sabha and Hindustan Socialist Republican Army; joined the Congress Socialist Party, 1934; arrested for anti-war activities, 1940 and detained along with Kulbir Singh at Deoli Detention Camp; joined the hunger-strike led by Jayaprakash Narayan there; released, 1946; associated with the Kisan Movement, Punjab.

Kumaramangalam, Mohan (1916–1973) Son of Dr P. Subbarayan and Radhabai Subbarayan; studied at Cambridge, President, Cambridge Union and for some time Secretary, Federation of Indian Students' Societies in Europe; became a Communist while a student in Britain; went to Spain during Civil War, 1937; returned to India and enrolled himself as an advocate of Madras High Court, 1939; remained underground until December 1940 when he was arrested and sentenced to 3½ years' imprisonment; released, 1942; after independence, was underground again and was arrested, 1950 for his communist activities and imprisoned for nine months; was active in trade union movement; joined Congress in the 1960s; a leading Lawyer; was Advocate General of Madras for a short period; Member, Lok Sabha; Minister, Steel and Mines in the Union Cabinet, 1971; played an important role in strengthening Public Sector; killed in an air crash near Delhi, 1973.

Kunzru, Hirdayanath (1887–1978) Born at Agra; educated in Allahabad and London; joined Servants of India Society, 1909; resigned from the Congress in 1920 with other Liberals and was one of the founders of National Liberal Federation; Member, Legislative Council, UP, 1921–23, Central Legislative Assembly, 1927–30, Council of State, 1937–46; advocated Indianization of Civil Service and Armed Forces; critical of Britain during the war for not granting full self-government to India; President, National Liberal Federation, 1934; elected Life President, Servants of India Society in 1936; Member, Constituent Assembly, 1946–49 and Provisional Parliament, 1950–52; Council of States, 1952–56; Member, States Reorganisation Commission, 1953–55; Member, Rajya Sabha, 1952–62; President, Indian School of International Studies, 1955–70.

Lakshmibai Rajwade, Rani (1887–1984) Daughter of Moropant Joshi, a nationalist, social reformer and promoter of women's education; joined Grant Medical College, Bombay, and went to England for further medical studies; married to Maj. Gen. Raja C.R. Rajwade of Gwalior; practised medicine in Bombay; an active member of All India Women's Conference and was honorary Organizing Secretary, 1930–35; Chairperson of Sanding Committee of AIWC for two years and its President, 1939; headed the section of Women's Welfare, Education and Advancement under the National Planning Committee.

Madni, Maulana Husain Ahmad (1879–1957) A leading Islamic theologian and scholar; educated at Deoband Seminary; joined a group of young revolutionaries in Kabul to work for the overthrow of British rule, 1911–12; was arrested and jailed in Malta, 1914–1919; leader of Jamiat-ul-Ulema-i-Hind; joined hands with Congress in various movements; participated in Khilafat Movement and was imprisoned, 1922; took part in Civil Disobedience and Quit India Movements and imprisoned in 1930, 1932 and 1942; stood for united Indian nationhood; opposed the two-nation theory and the demand for Pakistan.

Mahmud, Dr Syed (1889–1971) Born at Ghazipur; educated at Aligarh, London, Cambridge and Germany; joined Home Rule League, 1917; took part in Non-Cooperation Movement; General Secretary, Central Khilafat Committee, 1921–26; was jailed, 1922; General Secretary, Indian National Congress, 1923 and 1929–1936; Member, Bihar Legislative Assembly, 1937–39 and 1946–52; Member, Congress Working Committee, 1940–45; imprisoned during Quit India Movement; Education and Development Minister, Bihar, 1937–39; staunch opponent of communalism and two-nation theory; Member, Lok Sabha, 1952–62; Minister of State for External Affairs, 1952–57.

Maitra, Pt. Lakshmi Kanta (1893–1953) Lawyer, with successful practice in Nadia district, Bengal; Member, Central Legislative Assembly, 1934 and leader of the Congress Nationalist group; Member, Constituent Assembly, July 1947; Member, Provisional Parliament, 1950–1952.

Majumdar, Hemaprabha (1888–1962) Born in Khilpara in Noakhali district, Bengal; married to Basanta Kumar Majumdar who belonged to the revolutionary group Jugantar; Basanta Kumar was detained in 1915 and after his release in 1920 had joined Non-Cooperation Movement; was arrested in 1921; Hemaprabha became active in Non-Cooperation Movement in 1921 and led the women's wing in Calcutta; took part in Civil Disobedience Movement and was jailed in 1932; Member, Bengal Legislative Assembly, 1937–46; Joined Forward Bloc, 1939; stayed on in East Pakistan after independence.

Majumdar, Niharendu Dutt (1903–1999) Born in Bijitpur, Mymensingh; educated in Santiniketan, Dacca, Calcutta and London; came in touch with Labour Party and trade union movement in London; on return, joined Bengal Labour Party, 1933; played a leading role in the famous Dockers' strike (involving 14,000 workers), 1934 and Jute Mills strike, 1937; joined CPI, 1936 and became Member of Legislative Assembly, 1937; left CPI, 1939 and organized Bolshevik Party; took part in Quit India Movement and was imprisoned, 1942–45; joined Congress, 1946 and was elected to the Assembly, 1946; Minister, West Bengal Government, 1948–52; gave up trade union and political activities and had a successful legal practice in Calcutta High Court.

Majumdar, Satyendranath (1899–1954) One of the most reputed Bengali journalists and writers of the pre-Independence period; joined *Ananda Bazar Patrika*, 1922 and was its Editor, 1926–1941; participated in freedom struggle and was arrested three times; closely associated with Progressive Writers' Association in Bengal; joined *Arani*, a pro-communist Bengali journal, as Editor, 1941; associated with Globe News Agency.

Mashriqi, Allama Inayatullah Khan (1888–1963) Born in Amritsar; had a brilliant academic record securing MA degree in Mathematics from Punjab University; later studied at Cambridge; active in the educational field after his return; joined Indian Education Service, 1919–32; staunch believer and advocate of Islamic way of life; popularly known as Allama Mashriqi; attended the Islamic Conference at Cairo, 1926; opposed the proposal of electing the Sultan of Egypt as the Khalifa-ul-Muslimeen on the ground that a vassal ruler could not be the spiritual leader of the Islamic world; communal in his approach to politics; opposed the Indian National Congress; also critical of Muslim League; launched Khaksar (Servants of God) Movement in 1931 to revive the great tradition of the Muslim conquest of the world; a strong advocate of workers and the poor and adopted *belcha* (spade) as his party's symbol; author of numerous books and pamphlets; was imprisoned, 1939 and 1940–43; advised Jinnah to make an honourable compromise with Congress; spent the last years of his life in Pakistan in relative obscurity.

Mavalankar, G.V. (1888–1956) Born at Baroda; educated at Law College, Bombay; started legal practice, 1913; took part in the Kaira movement led by Gandhiji, 1918; Secretary, Gujarat Provincial Congress Committee, 1920–22; President, Ahmedabad Municipality, 1930–33 and 1935–36; participated in all movements launched by Congress and underwent imprisonment several times; worked in promoting Constructive Programme activities such as Khaddar, National Education and removal of untouchability; Trustee, Sabarmati Ashram; Member, Bombay Legislative Assembly and its Speaker, 1937–45; Speaker of Constituent Assembly when, after independence, it functioned as Parliament; Speaker of the first Lok Sabha which came into being in 1952.

Medhi, Bishnu Ram (1890–1981) Born in Hajo village in Kamrup, Assam; educated at Presidency College, Calcutta; enrolled as Pleader in Gauhati Bar, 1914, and as Advocate in Calcutta High Court, 1931; active role in all movements launched by Congress beginning with Non-Cooperation Movement; suffered imprisonment, 1921, 1930, 1932, 1940 and 1942; came to known as the Iron Man of Assam; President, Assam PCC, 1930–39; Member, Assam Legislative Assembly, 1938 and 1946; Minister, Finance, Revenue and Legislation, 1946–50; Chief Minister of Assam, 1950–57; Governor of Madras, 1957–62.

MEHERALLY, YUSUF (1903–50) Born at Bombay, educated at Calcutta and Bombay; founded, when a college student, the Young India Society, 1925; played a leading role in the formation of Bombay Provincial Youth League in 1928; launched National Militia in 1929 with himself as its General Officer Commanding, to spread the message of the freedom struggle and to rouse the people; founded *Vanguard*, 1929; *Vanguard* was suppressed in 1930 and he was jailed; imprisoned again, 1934 for two years; founder-Member, Congress Socialist Party, 1934; General Secretary, CSP, 1940; Presided over All India Students Federation Conference (M.L. Shah group), Patna, 1941, and was arrested soon after; elected Mayor of Bombay, 1942, when in jail; was arrested again and released, 1943 on health grounds; connected with Socialist Party's monthly *Janata* during the last year of his life.

MEHTA, CHUNILAL (1888–1968) Industrialist, Managing Director of a large number of companies in Bombay and Director of others, including United Bank of India; President, Bombay Shroff Association for many years; Sheriff of Bombay, 1935–36; President, FICCI, 1941; was Knighted, 1942.

MEHTA, HANSA (1897–1995) Born at Surat and educated in Baroda, Bombay and London; took part in the anti-Simon Commission agitation and Civil Disobedience movement; was jailed in 1930 and 1932; founding-Member and Secretary of the Bombay Branch of All India Women's Conference (AIWC); President, AIWC, 1945–46; Member, Bombay Legislative Council, 1933–40 and 1940–50; founder-Member and Vice-Chancellor of Maharaja Sayaji Rao University, Baroda, 1949–58; represented India at international conferences; was awarded the Padma Bhushan, 1959.

MEHTA, JAMNADAS M. (1884–1955) Lawyer and trade union leader; Member, Bombay Municipal Corporation since 1922; Member, Central Legislative Assembly, 1929–30 and 1941–45; President, All India Railwaymen's Federation, 1931–44; President, Indian Federation of Labour, 1941–44; Member, AICC; Mayor of Bombay, 1926–27; Minister of Revenue (Finance), Government of Bombay, 1937; Indian workers' delegate to International Labour Conference, 1934–1944.

MENON, DR K.B. (1897–1967) Born at Talipparampa, Kannur district, Kerala; educated at Calicut, Madras and USA; joined Ghadar Party in USA, 1925; brought out a journal *Independent India, 1925–30;* returned to India, 1936; Secretary, Civil Liberties Union, 1936; Joint Secretary, All India States' People's Conference, 1937; after the arrest of Gandhi in 1942, formed a socialist group in Kerala and was involved in a sensational Bomb Case; was sentenced to ten years' rigorous imprisonment; after his release in 1946, joined Socialist Party and later Proja Socialist Party and Samyukta Socialist Party; Member, Madras Legislative Assembly, 1952–57, Lok Sabha, 1957–62 and Kerala Assembly, 1965; took part in the agitation against the first Communist Government in Kerala, 1959.

MISHRA, LOKENATH (1902–1966) Born in Sanadhanga village of Orissa; graduated in 1924 from Ravenshaw College, Cuttack, passed MA English in 1926 and B.L. in 1928 from Patna University; involved in various social activities and campaigned against untouchability; started a secret society in 1942 along with Surendranath Dwivedi and others; was imprisoned on a charge of conspiracy for five years; Secretary, Gandhi Smarak Nidhi, 1948; Secretary, Utkal Pradesh Congress Committee, 1949–1952.

Mody, Hormusji Peroshaw (1881–1969) Born in Bombay in a rich Parsee family; studied at Bombay and passed LLB examination, 1906; influenced by Pherozeshah Mehta, Gokhale, Ranade and Dadabhai Naoroji; began his career as an advocate, later took to business; was a liberal in his thinking; Chairman of Millowners' Association for many years as well as various other bodies of trade, industry and banking; Member, Central Legislative Assembly, 1929–43; Member, Viceroy's Executive Council for Supply, 1941–43; Acting Governor of Bombay, 1947; Governor of UP, 1949–52.

Mohamed Ali, Maulana (1878–1931) Born at Rampur and educated at Aligarh and Oxford; Chief Education Officer, Baroda State, 1904–10; started an English weekly, *Comrade,* 1911 and an Urdu daily, *Hamdard,* 1913; imprisoned along with his brother Maulana Shaukat Ali, 1915–1919; close to Gandhiji; leader of the Khilafat Movement and Non-Cooperation Movement; President, Indian National Congress, 1923; played a leading role in the setting up of Jamia Millia Islamia, 1920, and was its first 'Shaikhul-Jamia' (Vice-Chancellor); estrangement with Congress from mid–1920s; took part in the first Round Table Conference in London, died there soon after on 5 January 1931; buried in Jerusalem.

Mohanty, Gopinatha (1914–1991) Born in Koraput district; a celebrated novelist and short story writer; received Jnanpith award, 1964.

Mookerji, Radha Kumud (1884–1963) Educated at Berhampore and Calcutta; Professor of History, Mysore University, 1917–1921; Professor of Indian History at Lucknow University; Vice-President, All India Hindu Mahasabha; elected Member, Bengal Legislative Council; published many books which include *A History of Indian Shipping, The Fundamental Unity of India, Harsha, Men and Thought in Ancient India, Ashoka.*

Mukherjee, Dr Harendra Coomar (1877–1956) Born in a renowned Christian family; educated in Ripon School and College, passed MA English from Calcutta University; obtained PhD from Calcutta University, 1911 and joined English Department of the University, 1914; served the University as Head of the Department of English, 1937–1942—a period during which was a member of the Legislative Council of Bengal; Member of the Constituent Assembly; appointed Governor of West Bengal, 1951.

Munshi, K.M. (1887–1971) Born at Broach, Gujarat; educated at Broach, Baroda and Bombay; married Lilavati, 1926; elected to Bombay Legislative Council, 1927, but resigned during Bardoli Satyagraha; joined Congress, participated in Salt Satyagraha and was imprisoned, 1930; Member, Bombay Legislative Assembly, 1937; Home Minister, Bombay government, 1937–39; arrested during Individual Satyagraha; resigned from Congress after his release in 1941; Defence Counsel in cases relating to Quit India Movement; rejoined Congress, 1946; Member, Constituent Assembly, 1946–50, and Provisional Parliament, 1950–52; Agent-General of Government of India to Hyderabad, 1948; Minister of Food, Government of India, 1952; Governor, UP, 1953–58; left Congress, 1960 and joined Swatantra Party; author of several books in Gujarati and English; founded the Bharatiya Vidya Bhawan, 1938.

Nag, Dr Kalidas (1892–1966) Ideologist and educationist; General Secretary, Royal Asiatic Society of Bengal, 1942–46.

Naicker, E.V. Ramaswami (1879–1973) Born at Erode in Tamilnadu; led the Non-Brahmin Movement in Tamilnadu; was drawn into the freedom struggle under the influence of

P. Varadarajulu Naidu and V.O. Chaidambaram Pillai; joined Congress and was arrested in 1920 during Non-Cooperation Movement; led the Vaikom Satyagraha in Travancore, 1924–25; launched the Self-Respect Movement, 1925 to defend the interests of the downtrodden communities; visited Russia and Europe in 1931 and was influenced by socialist ideas; was imprisoned several times including in 1937 when he launched anti-Hindi agitation during the Congress government in Madras; joined Justice Party and became its President; reorganized the Justice Party in 1944 as Dravida Kazhagam which advocated the establishment of an independent Dravidanadu; strong advocate of the eradication of superstitions and religious practices and of social reform and abolition of caste system; popularly referred to as 'Periyar'.

Naidu, Dr P.V. Vardarajulu (1887–1957) Born at Rasipur in Salem district of Madras; participated in the movement against the partition of Bengal, 1905 and the Swadeshi movement; trained in indigenous system of medicine and became a medical practitioner; joined Congress and was President of Tamil Nadu Congress Committee and Member of Congress Working Committee, 1925–26; campaigned against untouchability as a crime against society and religion; also active in the trade union movement and was associated with AITUC; joined Hindu Mahasabha in later years and became President of its branch in Tamil Nadu; Member, Madras Legislative Assembly, 1952–57.

Naidu, Sarojini (1879–1949) Born Sarojini Chattopadhyaya at Hyderabad; educated at London and Cambridge Universities; became an accomplished poet at a young age; married Dr Govindarajulu Naidu, 1898; active in various political and social reform programmes; came into contact with Gokhale, Tagore, Jinnah, Annie Besant, Gandhiji and Jawaharlal Nehru; total involvement in the freedom struggle and emerged as a major nationalist leader; returned the Kaiser-i-Hind medal, 1919; President, Bombay Pradesh Congress Committee, 1920; President, Nagpur session, Congress, 1925; took a leading part in Civil Disobedience Movement and was imprisoned; attended Second Round Table Conference, 1931; imprisoned during Quit India Movement; presided over the Asian Relations Conference, 1947; Governor of UP after independence until her death on 2 March 1949.

Narang Gokul Chand (1878–1969) Born in Baddoke Gozain village in Gujranwala district, Punjab; studied at Lahore and Calcutta, and later in England and Switzerland; taught at DAV College at Lahore for a few years; connected with Arya Samaj and its social and educational activities; condemned the Jallianwala Bagh massacre as a 'slaughter'; was arrested during the Martial Law in Punjab; Member, Punjab Legislative Council, 1920–46; Minister, Local Self-Government and Industries, Punjab, 1930; was Knighted, 1934; was generally a supporter of the government and opposed to the Congress; Vice-President, All India Hindu Mahasabha; President, Punjab Hindu Mahasabha.

Nariman, K.F. (1888–1948) Born at Thana, near Bombay; gave up legal practice to participate in Non-Cooperation Movement; President, Bombay Youth League, 1928–29, and All India Youth Conference, Calcutta, 1929; was imprisoned for breaking the Salt Law, 1930 and for participating in Civil Disobedience movement; released, 1933; President, Bombay Pradesh Congress Committee from 1934; Chairman, Reception Committee, Bombay Congress, 1934; elected to Bombay Corporation, 1924–39; Mayor, Bombay, 1935–36; Member, Bombay Legislative Assembly, 1937, but was not included in the Congress Ministry led by B.G. Kher; critical of the functioning of Congress government in Bombay; took part in the legal defence of INA prisoners.

Nazimuddin Khwaja (1894–1964) Born at Dacca; educated at MAO College, Aligarh, and Cambridge; Chairman, Dacca Municipality, 1922–29; Member, Bengal Legislative Council, 1923; Education Minister, Bengal, 1929–34; joined Muslim League and elected as Muslim League candidate from Calcutta to Bengal Legislative Assembly, 1937; Member, Muslim League Working Committee, 1937–47; strong supporter of Pakistan scheme; Home Minister, Fazlul Haq's Coalition Ministry, Bengal, 1937–41; Prime Minister of Bengal in 1943 after the fall of Fazlul Haq's government, for two years; Member, Pakistan Constituent Assembly; first Chief Minister of East Pakistan; became Governor-General of Pakistan, September 1948, following M.A. Jinnah's death; Prime Minister of Pakistan after Liaquat Ali Khan's death, 1951; dismissed by Ghulam Mohammad, who had replaced him as Governor General on 17 April 1953.

Nehru Rameshwari (1886–1966) A prominent social worker; actively participated in freedom movement; was imprisoned, 1942; Honorary Adviser and President, Central Advisory Board for rehabilitation of displaced women; Editor of *Stri Darpern* from 1909; Founder-President, Delhi Women's League (Delhi Branch of AIWC), 1926; President, All India Women's Conference, 1940; President, London Committee of Women's Organization and Women's Committee of India League, 1931–32, President, All India Harijan Sewak Sangh; President, Afro-Asian Solidarity Committee; was awarded Padma Bhushan, 1955 and Lenin Peace Prize, 1961.

Nichlos-Roy, Rev James Joy Mohon (1884–1959) Born in Shella village in Khasi Hills, Meghalaya, then a part of Assam; passed BA from Scottish Church College, Calcutta; founder-leader of the Church of God in the United Khasi-Jaintia Hills, 1904; married Nora Evelyn Nicholas, an American; drawn into nationalist movement from early 1920s; joined Congress, 1926; Executive Committee Member of Assam Provincial Congress Committee till 1956; Member, Assam Legislative Council and Assembly from 1921 till his death; was Minister in Assam Government four times holding different portfolios, 1927–1956; Member, Constituent Assembly and its Advisory Committee; unhappy with the way Hills' State issue was dealt with; resigned from Assam Ministry, 1956.

Nimbkar, R.S. (1899–1948) played an important role in holding the first session of AITUC in October 1920 in Bombay; General Secretary, Bombay Municipal Workers' Union; joined textile workers' struggle in Bombay and became prominent in Girni Kamgar Union; was arrested in the Meerut Conspiracy Case, 1929 and was in jail along with other leaders; held various posts in AITUC from Treasurer to serving as a member in some of the important committees; represented AITUC in the attempts at forging unity among the divided central trade unions; arrested for leading textile workers' strike in Bombay, 1940. Throughout his life Nimbkar remained loyal to the cause of the working class.

Noon, Malik Muhammad Firoz Khan (1893–1970) Born in Hamoka village, West Punjab; educated at Aitchison College, Lahore, Wadham College, Oxford and Inner Temple; Member, Punjab Legislative Council, 1920–1936; Minister, Punjab, 1927–1930 and 1931–36; Indian High Commissioner in London, 1936–41; Member of Muslim League Council, 1927; Member, Viceroy's Executive Council, 1941–42, for Labour, and from July 1942 to August 1945 for Defence; renounced his Knighthood; Muslim League Member, Punjab Legislative Assembly, 1946; after Partition, became Member, Pakistan Constituent Assembly and Punjab Legislative Assembly, 1947–50; Governor of East Pakistan, 1950–53; Chief Minister, Punjab 1953–55; Prime Minister of Pakistan, 1957–58.

Obaidulla Sindhi, Maulana (1872–1944) Born in a village in Sialkot district,f Punjab; became a Muslim at the age of 15 and soon after joined Dar-ul-Ulloom, Deoband; after completing his education taught at a Madrasa and later at Deoband for some years; moved to Kabul in 1915 and planned to oust the British rule with the support of Russia and Turkey; later joined Congress and set up a branch of Congress in Kabul, 1922; visited Russia, 1923 and from there went to Turkey to work for India's freedom; returned to India, 1939 after the British government lifted the ban on his entry demanded by Congress and several provincial governments; presided over the Conference of Bengal *Ulema,* June 1939; addressed the open session of the Sind District Congress Committee, July 1940; established a new political party with a progressive social and economic outlook and set up its offices at Karachi, Lahore and Delhi; died in 1944 due to ill-health and old age.

Pandit, Vijayalakshmi (1900–1990) Born at Allahabad, younger sister of Jawaharlal Nehru; attended Amritsar session of Congress, 1919 and took part in Non-Cooperation Movement; arrested in 1932 during Civil Disobedience Movement; elected to UP Legislative Assembly and became Minister in the Congress Government, 1937–39; arrested in 1940 during the Individual Satyagraha and in 1942 during the Quit India Movement; President, All India Women's Conference, 1943–44; re-elected to UP Assembly, 1946; headed Indian delegation to UN after independence; President, UN General Assembly, 1953–54; India's Ambassador to USSR, USA and High Commissioner to UK; Governor of Maharashtra, 1962–1964; Member, Lok Sabha, 1952, 1964 and 1967; resigned from Lok Sabha, 1968; left Congress and joined Congress for Democracy after the Emergency, 1977.

Paranjpye, R.P. (1876–1966) Born at Murdi village, Ratnagiri district, Maharashtra; educated at Poona and Cambridge; Principal, Fergusson College, Poona, 1902–24; Member, Bombay Legislative Council, 1913–23 and 1927; Minister, Bombay Government, 1921–23 and 1927; Vice-Chancellor, Lucknow University, 1932–38 and Poona University, 1956–59; Indian High Commissioner in Australia, 1944–47; a social reformer and prominent leader of National Liberal Federation.

Patro, A.P. (1875–1946) Born at Barhampur, Ganjam district, Orissa; educated at Madras; Member, Madras Legislative Council, 1920–36; Minister in Madras Government, 1921–27; was Knighted, 1924; attended Round Table Conferences, 1930–32; Member, Council of State, 1937; one of the leading figures of Justice Party.

Polak, Henry Solomon Leon (1883–1959) Friend and co-worker of Gandhiji in South Africa; Assistant Editor, *The Transvaal Critic,* later joined *Indian Opinion* and became its Editor in 1906 during Gandhiji's absence in England; became full-fledged Attorney in 1908 after having served an apprenticeship with Gandhiji; visited India as a representative of the Transvaal British Indians in 1909; arrested after the Great March into the Transvaal in 1913.

Prakasam, Tanguturi (1872–1957) Born at Kanuparthi village in Ongole district of Andhra Pradesh; gave up legal practice and joined the freedom struggle; President, Andhra Pradesh Provincial Congress Committee, 1921; took part in the agitation against Simon Commission, 1928; started a nationalist English daily *Swarajya;* Revenue Minister in Madras Government headed by C. Rajagopalachari, 1937; Chief Minister of Madras State, 1946 for about an year; first Chief Minister of Andhra State, 1953; popularly referred to as Andhra Kesari (Lion of Andhra).

Radhakrishnan, Dr Sarvepalli (1888–1975) Born in Tirutani near Chennai; studied at Vellore and Madras; taught Philosophy at Presidency College, Madras, Mysore University and Calcutta University; Spaulding Professor of Eastern Religions and Ethics at Oxford University, 1932–52; was Knighted, 1931; Vice-Chancellor of Andhra University, 1931–1936, and of Banaras Hindu University, 1939–48; led Indian delegation to UNESCO, 1946–52; Indian Ambassador to USSR, 1949–52; Vice-President of India, 1952–62; President of India, 1962–67; conferred with numerous honours, including Bharat Ratna.

Raghavendra Rao, Dr E. (1889–1942) Born at Kamptee, Nagpur; educated at Bilaspur, Nagpur, Oxford, London and qualified for the Bar from the Middle Temple; joined the Home Rule Movement, 1917; elected President of the Central Provinces Provincial Congress Committee, 1921; played a notable part in Swarajya Party's victory in the 1923 elections; broke away from Congress and formed Nationalist Party, 1927; Minister in the Central Provinces twice; Governor of Central Provinces, 1936; elected to Provincial Legislature, 1937; formed an interim ministry when the Congress declined to accept office and was Chief Minister from April to July 1937; appointed Adviser to Secretary of State for India, 1939–41, Civil Defence Minister in the Viceroy's expanded Executive Council, 1941.

Rajah, M.C. (1883–1943) Born and educated in Madras; joined Teachers' College, Saidapet, as a Teacher in 1906; reorganized the Adi Dravida Mahajana Sabha, 1916; elected President of All India Deparessed Classes Association, 1926; favoured British rule for the protection of backward classes; given the title of Rao Behadur, 1922; first Adi Dravida Member of Madras Legislative Council; emerged as an active member of the Justice Party; resigned from Justice Party, 1923 in protest against its attitude to Dalits; Deputy Leader of the South Indian Liberal Federation Constitutional Party.

Ramamurti, P. (1908–1987) Born in a village near Kumbakonam in Thanjaam district of Tamilnadu; educated at Presidency College, Madras and BHU; took Part in Salt Satyagraha, 1930 and was jailed; imprisoned again, 1932; joined others in forming Congress Socialist Party in Tamilnadu and was Member of CSP's Executive Committee, 1935–39; joined CPI and active in trade union movement; was arrested, 1937 and 1940; one of the accused in Madras Communist Conspiracy Case, 1940–41; Member, AICC; arrested during mill-workers' strike in Madurai, 1946–47; released on 14 August 1947; was elected to Lok Sabha and made a mark as a parliamentarian.

Ranadive, B.T (1904–1990) Prominent Communist leader, joined the Communist Party of India, 1928, and was member of its Central Committee, 1934–35, 1943–48, and Polit Bureau, 1943–48, and its General Secretary, 1948–50; jailed several times; elected to the Central Committee and Polit Bureau of the C.P.I. (M), 1964; President, Centre of Indian Trade Union, 1970–90; Editor, *Marxist Miscellany*, 1982–89; author of many books.

Ranga, N.G. (1900–1995) Born in Nidubrolu village in Guntur district, Andhra Pradesh; came in contact with G.D.H. Cole and other socialist intellectuals in England; taught at Pachaiyappa's College at Madras for a few years; Member, Central Legislative Assembly, 1930 and 1935–45, organized many Kisan Satyagraha Campaigns since 1931 in Andhra region; one of the top ranking leaders of the peasant movement; Member of AICC from 1930 for 20 years; underwent imprisonment many times; Member, Constituent Assembly, 1946–50; Member of Parliament for many terms; joined Swatantra Party founded by C. Rajagopalachari in 1959 and returned to Congress in 1973.

Ray, Acharya Prafulla Chandra (1861–1944) Born in Raruli–Katipura village of Khulna district, East Bengal; studied at Calcutta and Edinburgh; started his teaching career as Lecturer in Chemistry in Presidency College, Calcutta, 1889; founded Bengal Chemical and Pharmaceutical Works in 1892, which pioneered India's Chemical Industry; first Palit Professor of Chemistry, Calcutta University, 1916–36; though not involved in active politics, played a leading role in promoting Swadeshi, social reform and education; popularly known as Acharya.

Ray, Nihar Ranjan (1903–1981) Educationist, historian and art critic; educated at Calcutta University and University of Leiden, Netherlands; Professor of History of Fine Art, Calcutta University; politically active from early days; associated with *Liberty* founded by Subhas Bose and later with *Kranti,* mouthpiece of the Revolutionary Socialist Party (RSP); was jailed during Quit India Movement; after retirement from Calcutta University, was Director of Indian Institute of Advanced Study, Simla till 1973; Chairman, Indian Council of Historical Research, 1980–81.

Reddi, Dr S. Muthulakshmi (1886–1968) Born in Pudukottah State; educated at Madras; obtained medical degree, 1912, the first girl student to take degree from Madras Medical College; went to England to specialize in gynaecology and paediatrics, 1925; Deputy President, Madras Legislative Council, 1926–30 and played an important role in the passage of important social legislation such as abolition of the Devadasi system; resigned from the Council, 1930 in protest against the arrest of Gandhiji and joined Congress; was involved in women's movement from early days; actively associated with Women's Indian Association and was its President, 1933; President of Fifth Session of All India Women's Conference, Lahore, 1930; founded the Avvai Home at Adyar, Madras, for destitute children; founded Cancer Institute, Madras, 1955; conferred with Padma Bhushan, 1956; one of the most distinguished women of modern India.

Reddy, B. Gopala (1907–1997) Educated at Visva-Bharati, Santiniketan; active Congress worker since 1931 and was jailed several times; Minister in Congress Government in Madras, 1937–39 and 1946–47; President, Andhra Pradesh Congress Committee, 1953; Chief Minister, Andhra Pradesh, 1955–6; Minister in the Union Cabinet till 1958.

Roy, Manabendra Nath (1983–1954) Born in Arbolia village in 24-Pargana district of Bengal; involved in revolutionary movement since the age of 14; left India, 1916 and involved in revolutionary movements in Mexico and Europe; founder of Communist Party of Mexico; Member, Executive Committee, Communist International (Comintern); was in China as Comintern representative, 1927; expelled from Comintern, 1929; returned to India, 1930 and attended Karachi session of the Congress, 1931; was arrested in the Kanpur Communist Conspiracy Case and served a 6-year prison sentence from 1931; founded Indian Federation of Labour and the Radical Democratic Party; supported the British war effort for its anti-fascist nature; dissolved Radical Democratic Party after independence and formulated the philosophy of Radical Humanism.

Saadullah, Syed Mohammad (1885–1955) Born in Gauhati (now Guwahati); educated at Guwahati and Calcutta; taught Chemistry in Cotton College, Guwahati, 1908; practised Law at Guwahati, 1909–19 and at Calcutta High Court, 1920–24; Member, Assam Legislative Council, 1913–20 and 1923; joined Muslim League; Minister for Education and Agriculture, Assam, 1924–29; Member, Executive Council, Assam Government, for Law and Order and PWD, 1929–30, for Finance, Law and Order, November 1930–April 1934; Member, Assam

Legislative Assembly, 1937; Prime Minister in the Coalition Ministry, May 1937–September 1938 when Congress formed the Ministry; again Muslim League Prime Minister, November 1939–January 1942; Muslim League Member, Assam Legislative Council, 1946; supported the demand for Pakistan; renounced Knighthood which had been conferred on him in 1928; Member, Indian Constituent Assembly and served on its Drafting Committee.

Sachar, Bhim Sen (1893–1978) Born at Peshawar in North West Frontier Province (NWFP); educated at Lahore; Secretary, Punjab Provincial Congress Committee, 1921; was arrested; Registrar, National University, Lahore; was arrested during Individual Satyagraha, 1940 and detained during Quit India Movement; Member, Punjab Legislative Assembly, 1936–45; Leader of Congress Party, Punjab Legislative Assembly, 1940; Finance Minister in Coalition Government formed with Unionist Party, 1946; after partition, Member, Constituent Assembly of Pakistan from West Punjab; migrated to India in September 1947; became Chief Minister of Punjab for a few months in 1949 and again from 1952 to 1956; Governor of Orissa, 1956–57, Andhra Pradesh, 1957–62; Indian High Commissioner in Ceylon (now Sri Lanka), 1966–67.

Saha, Meghnad (1893–1956) Born in Shaoratoli village near Dacca; educated at Dacca, Calcutta and London; Professor of Physics at Calcutta University and later at Allahabad University; Palit Professor of Physics, Calcutta University, 1938; Fellow of Royal Society, 1927; President of 21st session of the Indian Science Congress, 1934; founder of Saha Institute of Nuclear Physics, Calcutta; Member of the National Planning Committee set up by Subhas Bose under Jawaharlal Nehru's Chairmanship; elected to Lok Sabha in 1952 as an independent candidate.

Sambamurti, Bulusu (1886–1958) Born at Dulla village in Andhra; studied Law at Madras Law College; started his legal practice in Kakinada, 1911; joined Home Rule League of Dr Annie Besant; gave up his legal practice and took part in the Non-Cooperation Movement; Member of AICC; Member, Congress Working Committee, 1928; President, Andhra Congress Committee, 1927, and its Secretary, 1935–37; was imprisoned twice during Civil Disobedience Movement, 1930 and 1931; was elected to Madras Legislative Assembly, 1937 and was its Speaker; was imprisoned during Quit India Movement; played a leading role in the activities of Andhra Mahasabha; after independence, was active in the movement for the creation of separate Andhra State.

Sanyal, Dr Nalinaksha (1898–1987) Educated at Calcutta and London; student of Harold Laski at London School of Economics and obtained his PhD from there; Professor at Calcutta University; a leading figure in Bengal Provincial Congress Committee in 1930s; was imprisoned a number of times; Member, Bengal Legislative Assembly, 1939–47; left Congress in 1967 and elected MLA on Bangla Congress ticket; Minister for a brief period; Retired from politics after the fall of this ministry.

Sarkar, Nalini Ranjan (1882–1953) Born in Mymensingh district of East Bengal; studied at Dacca and Calcutta; joined the movement against partition of Bengal and Non-Cooperation Movement; became one of the leaders of the Congress and of the Swarajya Party in Bengal; Member, Bengal Legislative Council, 1923–28; Mayor of Calcutta, 1935; joined Krishak Praja Party; Finance Minister in Fazlul Huq's Ministry, 1937–39; Member, Viceroy's Executive Council, 1941–43; resigned when Gandhiji went on fast; rejoined Congress, 1947; Minister of Finance, West Bengal, 1948–51.

Sastri, V.S. Srinivasa (1869–1946) Born in Valangaiman village in Tanjore district of Tamilnadu; educated at Kumbakonam; joined Servants of India Society, 1907 and became its President, 1915–27; attended Congress session at Madras, 1908 and played a part in formulating Congress-Muslim Pact, 1916; Member, Madras Legislative Council, 1913–16, Imperial Legislative Council, 1916–20, Council of State, 1920–25, Privy Council, 1921, and Royal Commission on Labour, 1929; associated with National Liberal Federation from the early years of its formation; attended the First and Second Round Table Conferences, London, 1930–31; played a crucial role in defending and promoting interests of Indians in South Africa and other countries; Vice-Chancellor, Annamalai University, 1934–40.

Satyamurti, S. (1887–1943) Born in Thirumayam village in Pudukottai district of Tamil Nadu; educated at Madras; joined Congress, 1919; Leader of Swarajya Party in Madras and was elected to Madras Legislative Council, 1923–30; participated in the Civil Disobedience Movement and was imprisoned in 1931 and 1932; President, Tamil Nadu Pradesh Congress Committee, 1935–36; Member of Central Legislative Assembly and deputy leader of Congress Party, 1935–43; Mayor of Madras, 1939–40; was imprisoned during Individual Satyagraha, 1940–41, and again in 1942 during the Quit India Movement; was closely associated with the setting up of Annamalai University.

Satyapal, Dr (1885–1954) Born at Wazirabad, Gujranwalal district of Punjab; educated at Forman Christian College and Medical College, Lahore; medical practitioner; one of the prominent leaders of anti-Rowlatt Act agitation in Amritsar; his deportation along with Saifuddin Kitchlew from Amritsar on 10 April 1919 led to widespread protests with the British authorities perpetrating the massacre at Jallianwala Bagh to suppress them; participated in Non-Cooperation Movement and was imprisoned, 1921; took part in Civil Disobedience Movement, 1930, was imprisoned for three years, re-arrested and imprisoned in 1934 on charges of sedition for two years; Member, AICC; President, Punjab Provincial Congress Committee for many years; joined the army as a Doctor during the Second World War; returned to political life after the War; Speaker, Punjab Legislative Assembly, 1952–54.

Shah Nawaz, Begum Jahan Ara (1896–1979) educated at Queen Mary's College, Lahore; daughter of Muslim League leader Sri Muhammad Shafi; first woman member of Muslim League; Woman Member at the Round Table Conference, 1930–32; Member, Punjab Legislative Assembly, 1937 and Parliamentary Secretary till 1943; visited USA as part of Muslim League Mission, 1945; imprisoned for a brief period in 1947; Member, Pakistan Constituent Assembly.

Shah, M.L. (1914– —) Born in village Jeholi, Kaira district, Gujarat; studied at Ahemedabad and Bombay; participated in students' movement and was General Secretary, All India Students Federation, 1939–40 and of one group of that organisation after its split in 1941; Member, Congress Socialist Party; was arrested for participating in Quit India movement, 1942; was released, 1943; took to business, 1944; established a charitable Trust.

Shah, Prof. K.T. (1888–1953) Eminent economist; General Secretary, National Planning Committee set up by Subhas Bose when he was Congress President in 1938; Member, Constituent Assembly; Member, Fundamental Rights Sub-Committee of the Advisory Committee of Constituent Assembly.

Sharifa Hamid Ali Begum Grand-daughter of Badruddin Tyabji; got education against all odds of the time; disregarded purdah; well-versed in Urdu, Persian, Gujrati, English, Marathi and French; attended 1907 session of Indian National Congress; took part in the Swadeshi movement; worked for the emancipation of Harijans; made a campaign to make Sarda Act applicable to Muslim girls also; brought out 'nikah namah' for Muslim women which has since been in use; Chairwoman of Governing Body of All India Women's Education Association; took part in Round Table Conference, 1933; appointed to Muslim Sub-Committee of the National Planning Committee, 1939; active member of All India Women's Conference and served as its Honourary Treaurer; was President of its Allahabad session in January 1940.

Shastri, Lal Bahadur (1904–1966) Born at Mughal Sarai, UP; Studied at a school in Benaras and later at Kashi Vidyapith; General Secretary, Allahabad District Congress Committee, 1934 and later its President; General Secretary of UP Provincial Congress Committee, 1935–37; elected to UP Legislative Assembly, 1937; re-elected in 1946 and was Premier's Parliamentary Secretary and later a Minister; General Secretary, AICC, 1951; Union Railway Minister, 1951–1956; resigned after a railway accident; re-inducted in Union Cabinet in 1957; became Prime Minister following Jawaharlal Nehru's death in May 1964; concluded Indo-Pak agreement at Tashkent after the Indo-Pak War of 1965; died soon after signing the agreement at Tashkent.

Shukla, Pandit Ravi Shankar (1877–1956) Born in Sagar; studied at Raipur, Nagpur, Calcutta and Allahabad; joined and remained in the Congress from 1897; gave up his legal practice during Non-Cooperation Movement; was arrested in 1921; imprisoned again during the Civil Disobedience Movement, Individual Satyagraha and Quit India Movement; elected to Legislative Assembly of CP and Berar in 1937 and was first Minister for Education and later Prime Minister, 1938–39; re-elected to State Assembly, 1946 and was Premier, CP & Berar from 1946 and of Madhya Pradesh when the province was reorganized as Madhya Pradesh.

Shukla, Yogendra (1896–1966) Born at Jalalpur in Muzaffarpur district of Bihar; studied at Muzaffarpur; came into contact with the Anusilan Samiti revolutionaries and involved in revolutionary activities; closely connected with Bhagat Singh and Batukeshwar Datta and the Hindustan Socialist Republican Party; was involved in several conspiracy cases and served several terms in prison; joined Congress Socialist Party in 1938 and was soon rearrested; detained in Deoli Camp and, later in 1942, escaped along with Jayaprakash Narayan and others, from Hazaribagh jail; was arrested and imprisoned till 1946; Member, Bihar Legislative Council, 1958–59.

Singh, Baldev (1902–1961) Born in a leading family of Punjab; Member, Punjab Legislative Assembly, 1937–48; Minister for Development, Punjab, 1942–46; joined Interim Government, 1946–47; Member, Constituent Assembly; Minister of Defence, 1947–1952.

Singh, Mota (? –1960) Akali leader; founder-Member, Shiromani Gurudwara Prabhandhak Committee; associated with Ghadar Party; declared 'proclaimed offender' by the Government; was arrested in 1922 and sentenced to five years' rigorous imprisonment; associated with Kisan Sabha; arrested and detained at Deoli Detention Camp, 1941.

Singh, Sardar Mangah (1892–1987) Prominent Congress leader; jailed several times during the freedom struggle; took up the cause of Gurdwara Reform Movement; Member, Congress

Working Committee, 1923, 1925 and 1930; President, Central Sikh League and Shiromani Gurdwara Prabandhak Committee, 1926; Member, Indian Legislative Assembly, 1934–46; fought against communal forces.

Sinha, Sachchidananda (1871–1950) Born at Arrah in Shahabad district, Bihar; educated at Arrah, Patna and Calcutta; went to England in 1889 and was called to the Bar from the Middle Temple in 1893; on his return to India campaigned for the creation of a separate Province of Bihar; elected to the Imperial Legislative Council, 1910; played a crucial role in the creation of the new Province of Bihar and Orissa, 1912; President, Bihar Provincial Congress Committee, 1916–1920; started *The Searchlight* at Patna, 1918; elected to Bihar and Orissa Legislative Council, 1931; Leader of Opposition until 1937; was appointed the first non-official Vice-Chancellor of Patna University, 1936–44; represented Patna University Constituency in Bihar Legislative Council, 1937–1946; Member, Constituent Assembly.

Sitaramayya, Dr Pattabhi (1880–1959) Born at village Gundugolanu, West Godawari district, Andhra Pradesh; educated at Ellore and Madras; practised as a doctor, 1906–16; associated with Congress from very early days; Member, AICC, 1916–1952 and of Congress Working Committee for many years; was imprisoned during Civil Disobedience Movement; contested for Presidentship of Congress with Gandhiji's support in 1938 but was defeated by Subhas Bose; was imprisoned during Individual Satyagraha, 1941 and during Quit India Movement,1942–1945; President, Andhra Pradesh Congress Committee, 1937–38; President, All-India States' People's Conference, Karachi, 1936 and Navasari Convention, 1938; Working President, All India States' People's Conference, 1946–48; Member, Constituent Assembly; President, Jaipur session of Congress, 1948; Governor, Madhya Pradesh, 1952–57; author of many books including *History of the Indian National Congress* (2 vols.).

Srinivasan, Kasturi (1887–1959) Journalist; educated at Presidency College, Madras; joined his father's paper, *The Hindu,* and became its Managing Director, 1934; President, All India Newspaper Editors' Conference, 1940–44; received Padma Bhushan award, 1954; Set up Press Trust of India in partnership with Reuters and was its first Chairman; Vice-Chairman of International Press Institute, 1951.

Srivastava, Jwala Prasad (1889–1954) Born in a landowning family in UP; educated at Allahabad and Manchester College of Technology; a leading industrialist of UP; proprietor of *Pioneer* newspaper form 1932; was Knighted; Member, Viceroy's Executive Council, with charge of Civil Defence, 1942–43 and Food, 1943–46; Member, Constituent assembly, 1947–49; Member, Lok Sabha, 1950–52 and Rajya Sabha, 1952.

Subbarayan, Dr P. (1889–1962) Born in the family of Zamindar of Kumarapalayam in Salem district of Tamilnadu; educated at Oxford and Dublin; Member, AICC 1920 and again 1937; Member, Madras Legislative Council; associated with Justice Party for a few years; Chief Minister, Madras, 1926–30; elected unopposed to Madras Legislative Assembly, 1937–46; Minister for Law, Madras, 1937–39; Member of Constituent Assembly; Law Minister and later Home Minister, Madras, 1947–48; Ambassador to Indonesia, 1949; Member of Rajya Sabha, 1954–57, and then of Lok Sabha; was Cabinet Minister in the Union government, 1959–62; Governor of Maharashtra, 1962.

Suhrawardy, Hussain Shaheed (1893–1963) Born in Midnapore and educated at Calcutta, Oxford University and Gray's Inn; practised Law at Calcutta; Member, Bengal Legislative

Council, 1921; supported the Swarajya Party; Deputy Mayor, Calcutta Corporation for year years when C.R. Das was Mayor; Secretary, Bengal Provincial Muslim League; Muslim League member, Bengal Legislative Assembly, 1937; Minister, 1943–45 in the Khwaja Nazimuddin Ministry in Bengal; Chief Minister in the Muslim League Ministry in Bengal, 1946–47; worked for the creation of United Bengal; remained in India after partition and toured with Gandhiji to end communal riots in Bengal; migrated to Pakistan in December 1947; one of the organizers of Awani League; Prime Minister of Pakistan, September 1956–October 1957; launched the National Democratic Front and was arrested, 1962.

Swaminathan, Ammu (1896–1978) Married to Dr Swaminathan, a leading lawyer in Madras; one of the founder members of All India Women's Conference; joined Congress, 1934; imprisoned for two years during the Quit India Movement; Member, Central Legislative Assembly, 1945 and also of the Constituent Assembly; Member, Lok Sabha, 1950–57, and of Rajya Sabha, 1957–60; mother of Captain Lakshmi of the INA and of Mrinalini Sarabhai, the well-known dancer.

Syed, G.M. (1904–95) Born in Sann village, Dadu district, Sind; connected with Congress and Khilafat Movement; Vice-President of Karachi Local Board, 1929 and later its President; Member, Sindh United Party; President of Sind Provincial League, 1938; Member, Muslim League Working Committee, 1941; Member, Sind Legislative Assembly, 1937; Minister, Sind government, 1940; launched Progressive Muslim League, 1945; elected to Sind Legislative Assembly, 1946; brought about the downfall of League Ministry headed by Ghulam Husain Hidayatullah; founded Sind Awami Party; set up Jeay Sind Mahaz, 1972 to campaign for an independent Sind; was imprisoned or in solitary confinement for over 30 years in Pakistan.

Tara Singh, Master (1885–1967) Born in Haryal village of Rawalpindi district in West Punjab; educated at Rawalpindi, Amritsar and Lahore; helped to set up Khalsa High School at Lyalpur and was its Headmaster; one of the leaders of the Gurdwara reform movement; a leading figure in the Akali movement and also associated with the Congress; advocated creation of Azad Punjab during the War after Muslim League's demand for Pakistan was growing strong; founded Panthic Party in 1946, to fight Punjab Assembly elections and won 20 out of 23 Sikh seats; during talks with Cabinet Mission, stated that he stood for united India but demanded a separate Sikh State in case Pakistan was conceded; after independence, agitated for the creation of Punjabi Suba (Punjabi-speaking State); suffered a serious political setback in 1961 when he broke his fast-unto-death.

Thakurdas, Purshotamdas (1879–1961) Businessman; Spokesman for Indian business on numerous public occasions; was Knighted, 1923; Delegate to Round Table Conference, 1930–32; Member, Bombay Legislative Council; Member, Central Legislative Assembly; nominated Member, Council of State.

Tottenham, George Richard (1890–1977) Entered Indian Civil Service, 1914; Assistant to Resident, Travancore & Cochin, 1917; Secretary, Army Department, Government of India, 1932; Member, Council of State, 1936; was Knighted, 1937; Diwan, Bharatpur State, 1939; Additional Secretary, Home Department, Government of India, 1940–46.

Trikamdas, Purshottam (1897–1969) Born at Bombay; studied at Bombay and Cambridge; Member, Bombay Home Rule League; Joint Secretary, Bombay branch of the Swarajya Party, 1924; participated in the Salt Satyagraha, 1930; Founder-Member, Congress Socialist Party and member of its National Executive, 1934; Member, AICC, 1945; Chairman, Socialist Party, 1948.

UPADHYAYA, S.D. (1899–1984) Born at Brahmanpuri, Almora district of (then) UP; participated in the Non-Cooperation Movement, 1921; joined Motilal Nehru as his Private Secretary, 1923; associated with Jawaharlal Nehru since 1931; was imprisoned during Civil Disobedience Movement; held as security prisoner during Quit India Movement, 1942–45; Member, Lok Sabha, 1952–57, 1957–62, 1962–67 and of Rajya Sabha, 1967–70.

USMAN, MOHAMED (1884–1960) Educated at Madras Christian College; Member, Madras Legislative Council, 1921–23; Member, Executive Council of the Government of Madras, 1925–34; was Knighted, 1928; Acting Governor, Madras, 1934; Vice-Chancellor, University of Madras, 1940–42; Member, Viceroy's Executive Council, 1942–46.

VISVESVARAYA, M. (1861–1962) Engineer, scientist and administrator; Chief Engineer, Mysore State, 1909; Diwan of Mysore, 1912–18; Member of many committees on technical and economic affairs set up by Bombay Government and Government of India.

WALCHAND HIRACHAND (1882–1953) Born at Sholapur, Maharashtra; inspired by Dadabhai Naoroji; devoted to establishing industries in India; started several industries including a shipyard at Vizagapattanam (now Vishakhapatnam), an Aircraft factory at Bangalore and an Automobile factory at Kurla, Bombay; also associated with sugar, construction and several other industrial activities.

YAKUB, MAULVI MUHAMMAD (1879–1942) Educated at MAO College Aligarh; President, Muslim League session, Calcutta, December 1927–January 1928; Member, Central Legislative Assembly, 1924–38; Secretary, Muslim League 1930–35; was Knighted; Member, Council of State, 1938–42; Reforms Adviser to the Nizam Government, 1941.

ZAHEER, DR HUSAIN (1901–75) Born in one of the leading families of UP; son of Sir Wazir Hasan who had been judicial Commissioner and later Chief Judge of Oudh; educated at Lucknow, Oxford and Heidelberg; taught Chemistry at Lucknow University from 1930; closely associated with Congress and left-wing anti-imperialist bodies; attended the December 1941 session of AISF and spoke on the need for unity against fascist aggressions; Principal, Government City College, Hyderabad, 1946–48; Director, Regional Research Laboratory, Hyderabad, 1948–62; Director-General, Council for Scientific and Industrial Research (CSIR).

Index